The Children Act in Practice

The Children Act in Practice

Third edition

Richard White
LLB, Solicitor, White & Sherwin, Croydon

Paul Carr
MA, Barrister
Director of Legal Services and County Justices' Clerk,
Essex Magistrates' Courts

Nigel Lowe
LLB, Barrister
Professor of Law,
Cardiff Law School,
Cardiff University

Consulting editor
The Right Honourable Lady Justice Hale DBE, MA (Cantab)

Butterworths
LexisNexis™

Members of the LexisNexis Group worldwide

United Kingdom	LexisNexis Butterworths Tolley, a Division of Reed Elsevier (UK) Ltd, Halsbury House, 35 Chancery Lane, LONDON, WC2A 1EL, and 4 Hill Street, EDINBURGH EH2 3JZ
Argentina	LexisNexis Argentina, BUENOS AIRES
Australia	LexisNexis Butterworths, CHATSWOOD, New South Wales
Austria	LexisNexis Verlag ARD Orac GmbH & Co KG, VIENNA
Canada	LexisNexis Butterworths, MARKHAM, Ontario
Chile	LexisNexis Chile Ltda, SANTIAGO DE CHILE
Czech Republic	Nakladatelství Orac sro, PRAGUE
France	Editions du Juris-Classeur SA, PARIS
Hong Kong	LexisNexis Butterworths, HONG KONG
Hungary	HVG-Orac, BUDAPEST
India	LexisNexis Butterworths, NEW DELHI
Ireland	Butterworths (Ireland) Ltd, DUBLIN
Italy	Giuffrè Editore, MILAN
Malaysia	Malayan Law Journal Sdn Bhd, KUALA LUMPUR
New Zealand	LexisNexis Butterworths, WELLINGTON
Poland	Wydawnictwo Prawnicze LexisNexis, WARSAW
Singapore	LexisNexis Butterworths, SINGAPORE
South Africa	Butterworths SA, DURBAN
Switzerland	Stämpfli Verlag AG, BERNE
USA	LexisNexis, DAYTON, Ohio

© Reed Elsevier (UK) Ltd 2002

A CIP Catalogue record for this book is available from the British Library.

ISBN 0 406 94003 7

Typeset by M Rules, London
Printed and bound in Great Britain by Clays Ltd, St Ives Plc

Visit Butterworths LexisNexis *direct* at www.butterworths.com

Foreword

The Children Act 1989 has now been in force for more than ten years. It was so successful in what it set out to do that we have largely forgotten what life was like before it. We now have a uniform code of law governing the care and upbringing of children, with the same law and procedures in all courts and an integrated family justice system. We also have a uniform code of law governing the social services to be provided for children in need. Now that we no longer have to puzzle about the complexities and injustices of the old law, we can concentrate on the very real practical problems these cases are bound to bring. Two loom very large.

One is mainly administrative. Ensuring the regular delivery of quality services for children and their families is no easy matter. There is a constant battle between competing demands on diminishing resources, not only in money but more importantly in people who can do the difficult and demanding work of protecting children from harm and looking after them when harm has been done. The recruitment and retention crisis in social work is serious. But the public only takes notice when there is a tragedy like those of Maria Colwell, Jasmine Beckford or Victoria Climbie. The kind of notice the public then takes is not necessarily going to encourage more people to accept the challenge of working to protect children from harm.

The other problem is mainly legal. Article 6 of the European Convention on Human Rights requires that 'In the determination of his civil rights and obligations . . . everyone is entitled to a fair . . . hearing within a reasonable time by an independent and impartial tribunal . . .' But children's cases, and particularly care cases, regularly take so long these days that there is a real risk that the delay, rather than the merits, will decide the case. Why are they taking so long? What can be done about it?

These practical problems raise more fundamental questions about the purpose of children's cases and the role of the courts in deciding them. Put simply, is the role of the court to decide who should be responsible for bringing up a child and leave them to it? Or is it to decide how the child should be brought up? The Children Act took a middle course between the speed and simplicity of the old care proceedings in the juvenile courts and the protracted complexity of wardship proceedings in the High Court. In the former, the grounds were proved and an order made and that was the end of the matter. In the latter, theoretically the court took charge of the child's upbringing until he was adopted or grew up.

Ten years on, what has emerged is closer to wardship. The courts and the parties are reluctant to treat the proceedings as one short episode in the family story. The court proceedings tend to be used by everyone for the purpose of expert assessment, even if in some cases this could have been done before the proceedings started. The story is still developing as the case proceeds, making it very different from ordinary civil litigation, which has a clear-cut beginning, middle and end. In ordinary civil litigation, there are pleadings in which the issues are defined at the outset; the issues usually look backwards, righting a wrong which has already been done, rather than planning for the family's future; the issues do not change much as the case proceeds and the often chaotic lives of the principal parties move on; their subject matter does not involve a living human being with his or her own wishes and feelings which develop and influence events. Although the Civil Procedure Rules have borrowed ideas, such as timetabling and jointly instructed experts, from the family jurisdiction, case management in most civil cases is simplicity itself compared with case management in family cases.

Because the story is always continuing, and the aim is to promote the best possible future for the child, the courts have been reluctant to hand over control of the child's upbringing to the local authority. The temptation has been to hang on as long as they can because of the difficulty of getting the case back to court should things go wrong. But it was clearly the intention of the Act that they should hand over control as soon as it was clear that the local authority would have to have responsibility for looking after and bringing up the child for the foreseeable future. Courts cannot deliver quality care for children. Courts cannot choose between the competing demands upon social services resources. Money spent on lawyers is better spent on children and their families. But both courts and local authorities may breach the rights of either the child or the family under the European Convention of Human Rights if they get it wrong. While the parents may be able to get the case back to court, either under the Children Act or under the Human Rights Act, who is there to stand up for the child's rights? Both parents and child have the right to respect for their family life, but if a child has to be deprived of his birth family for his own good, does he not also have the right to the very best we can offer him in return?

Not surprisingly, therefore, the Court of Appeal in *Re W & B; Re W* [2001] EWCA Civ 757 held that the court should fill the gap through the mechanism of 'starring' crucial milestones in the care plan to be brought back to court if they were not met; not surprisingly, however, the House of Lords, in *Re S (Minors) (Care Order: Implementation of Care Plan)* [2002] UKHL 10; [2002] 2 WLR 720; [2002] 2 All ER 192 held that this was taking the Human Rights Act too far; both courts agreed that there was a serious problem to be addressed. Parliament may be expected to do something about it in the current Adoption and Children Bill.

The law is for children and their families and not for lawyers. This book, however, is mainly for the lawyers – a handy, practical but always thoughtful guide from the usual team, unchanged since the first edition way back in 1989.

Brenda Hale
21 March 2002

Preface to the third edition

The Children Act 1989 came into force on 14 October 1991. It provided a code and structure for much of the law relating to children. It could never provide simplicity for such a complex area of human relationships. A decade on there has been substantial development of policy and philosophy of core principles, volumes of statutory instruments, guidance and case law, and many treatises on the subject. It is difficult to know where to draw the boundaries when writing on a subject with so many borders.

Much of what we wrote in the preface to the second edition remains true and bears repetition.

> 'The effect of social legislation like the Children Act may not be fully appreciated for some years to come. As predicted, however, the Act has brought about fundamental changes in the law relating to children.
>
> It is easy to forget some of the problems of the old system, scattered legislation, confusing concepts of custody and care, conflicting court jurisdictions and uncertain criteria in public law cases. The progress made in providing a suitable legal framework should be recognised, although inevitably a book of this nature will pay considerable attention to problems which have arisen. Many of the difficulties highlighted by practice under the Act would have come to the surface in any event, perhaps in a worse form.
>
> Nonetheless we have to face the fact that the Act created expectations about welfare and legal services to be provided for children and their families. These expectations have not been fulfilled. Delays in legal proceedings are all too common, in spite of the acceptance of the principle that it is likely to prejudice the welfare of the child. Professional services and resources which could bring to fruition the good intentions of the legislation have simply not been sufficient.'

We have found in practice that it is most useful to have in one relatively small bound volume the Act, court rules and commentary. We have attempted to state the law as we believe it to be at 31 August 2002.

This book is not intended to be a comprehensive analysis of all the law relating to children or even the Children Act 1989. With some exceptions we have decided to maintain the structure of the second edition, seeking to lay out the core principles and the way in which they are implemented, while at the same time drawing attention to those areas where there are problems.

Constrained as ever by space, we have maintained the emphasis in the text on Parts I to V of the Act, though in the light of developments we have necessarily to take account of the Human Rights Act 1998 and the European Convention on Human Rights, parts of the Adoption and Children Bill 2002 and activities in the international field. We have not attempted to deal with the major changes in the Care Standards Act 2000 and the work of the National Care Standards Commission, nor can we begin to tackle the major changes in the field of adoption, education and youth justice.

Once again we have to thank Butterworths for their forbearance in waiting for the manuscript. We again owe an enormous debt to our consulting editor, Lady Justice Hale, for her extensive reading of the manuscript. We should also like to thank Stephen Pizzey for his observations on Chapters 6 and 7 and Sharon Willicombe for typing much of the manuscript. Finally as ever, we thank our families, who now provide us all with somewhat different insights into working with the Children Act, than when we wrote the first edition.

Richard White, Paul Carr, Nigel Lowe
September 2002

Preface to the second edition

The Children Act 1989 came into force on 14 October 1991. With it came numerous rules and regulations and extensive government guidance. A considerable body of case law has since been developed.

We have included the Act as it is in force at 1 September 1995. Constrained by space we have chosen to concentrate in the text on Parts I to V of the Act and related provisions. This involves the general principles, private law arrangements, and public law provisions relating to local authority responsibilities for the support of children and their families and the care and protection of children who may be suffering significant harm. We have also examined how the courts are operating. There have been few developments in relation to Parts VI to X concerning children's homes, private fostering and childminding and day care but substantial statutory annotation has been included. Adoption, possibly the subject of forthcoming legislation, education, another major area of new law, and financial provision, now much affected by the Child Support Act 1991, have all been excluded. The volume of material on what remains shows how extensive and complex the provisions have become in a short period.

The effect of social legislation like the Children Act may not be fully appreciated for some years to come. As predicted, however, the Act has brought about fundamental changes in the law relating to children. It is easy to forget some of the problems of the old system, scattered legislation, confusing concepts of custody and care, conflicting court jurisdictions and uncertain criteria in public law cases. The progress made in providing a suitable legal framework should be recognised, although inevitably a book of this nature will pay considerable attention to problems which have arisen. Many of the difficulties highlighted by practice under the Act would have come to the surface in any event, perhaps in a worse form.

Nonetheless we have to face the fact that the Act created expectations about welfare and legal services to be provided for children and their families. These expectations have not been fulfilled. Delays in legal proceedings are all too common, in spite of the acceptance of the principle that it is likely to prejudice the welfare of the child. Professional services and resources which could bring to fruition the good intentions of the legislation have simply not been sufficient.

The sheer volume of legal development since the first edition required extensive consideration and analysis. Accordingly the task of writing a second edition was more time consuming than expected. Some of the policy conflicts which continue to develop have made it difficult to construct a coherent analysis at times. By the time the book is published, some of the problem areas we have identified may have been resolved and others may have emerged.

We continue to owe a debt of gratitude to Butterworths, who have shown forbearance in waiting for the manuscript. We thank Mrs Justice Hale, again our consulting editor, for her insights, now from the Bench, into the operation of the Act. Thanks also to Kathryn Bates, Patricia Burns and Hilary Carr for typing much of the manuscript. Finally, we wish to thank our ever patient families, who continue to illuminate the realities of working with the Children Act.

Richard White, Paul Carr, Nigel Lowe
September 1995

Preface to the first edition

The Children Act 1989 received the Royal Assent on 16 November 1989. It will, when implemented, bring about the most fundamental change of child law this century. Much of it has been the subject of debate for six years, yet some of the most complex provisions only found final form shortly before their enactment and were, therefore, not adequately debated in Parliament.

At the time of going to press we believe that most of the Act is likely to be implemented in October 1991. Four provisions have been brought into force already. Rules of court in relation to the evidence of children and their upbringing are expected to resolve an urgent problem as to admissibility. The position of an unmarried father as regards his child in care has been improved. In paternity cases applicants have been made responsible for choosing a blood tester from an authorised list. With effect from 16 January 1990 funds can be made available for a child to be sent for treatment outside England and Wales, for example, at the Peto Institute in Hungary.

The remainder will come soon enough. There is much work still to be done on the rules and regulations, which will be so important to practice. However, we have endeavoured to produce the book as quickly as possible, because we believe it to be vital to have an early understanding of the principles of the legislation, so that the detail can be more easily placed in context as it is published over the next eighteen months.

The law is bound to reflect the complexity of the subject. It is impossible to put into the statute all the detail that one might wish to see in establishing principles of law for children. Nevertheless, we are concerned about the degree of power given to the Executive to amend statute and the volume of delegated legislation, both of which will control how practice develops.

We have had to write within constraints of time, space and ability to interpret amendments which have been tabled late in the day. We have attempted to examine all the important parts of the Act and to relate them to each other.

We owe a considerable debt of thanks to Butterworths, for their efficiency and patience and their determination to ensure that the book was published quickly. We thank Professor Brenda Hoggett, our consulting editor, who gave extensively of her wide experience and understanding of the principles underlying the legislation.

Legislation of this length inevitably generates its own complexity. The Children Act will be no exception. It would be wrong, however, to dwell on negatives, for the Act does much to improve child law and given a fair wind by Government, judiciary and practitioners will provide a sound basis for good practice for the 1990s and beyond.

Richard White, Paul Carr, Nigel Lowe
December 1989

Contents

Table of Statutes

References in this Table to *Statutes* are to Halsbury's Statutes of England (Fourth Edition) showing the volume number and page at which the annotated text of the Act will be found. References in **bold** type indicate where the sections of an Act are set out in full or in part.

Table of Statutory Instruments

Table of Cases

PARA

M

S

T

PARA

Chapter 1

Introduction

1.1 The Children Act 1989 brought about the most fundamental change in our child law and has fairly been described by Lord Mackay LC as: 'the most comprehensive and far reaching reform of child law which has come before Parliament in living memory'.[1] Apart from two minor provisions[2] the CA 1989 was fully implemented on 14 October 1991. Since then the Act has been amended on a number of occasions and further important changes will be made by the Adoption and Children Bill 2002. The Lord Chancellor's Department has also published a 'Scoping Study' examining the reasons for delay and assessing the consequential need for reform.[3]

1 502 HL Official Report (5th series) col 488.
2 Viz s 5(11) and (12) which came into force on 1 February 1992 (SI 1991/828), discussed at para 3.109. A few provisions had been implemented before 14 October 1991.
3 *Scoping Study on Delay in Children Act Cases* (March 2002). For a reference to the draft report see Finlay 'Delay and the Challenges of the Children Act' in *Delight and Dole* (Eds Thorpe and Cowton) 5 at 10 et seq. This study is discussed in ch 4.

1.2 In association with the new legislation, new rules (since modified in the light of practice) brought about important changes in procedure and rules of evidence. Fundamental changes were also made to the court structure creating in effect a specialist division at every level. Accompanying the unified jurisdiction provided for by the CA 1989 were new rules dealing with the allocation and transfer of cases. Even the very function and role of the courts when dealing with children was changed by the CA 1989 and its accompanying rules. In short the 1991 reform was not simply directed to substantive law change but radically affected all aspects of legal practice concerning children. What then prompted this wholesale change in this key area of law?

THE GENESIS OF THE ACT

1.3 The CA 1989 was the product of a long and thorough consultation process. That process began with the Review of Child Care Law set up in 1984[1] by the then Department of Health and Social Security and assisted by the Family Law team at the Law Commission. That review concerned the public law relating to children, and in particular the local authority services to be provided for children and their families and the procedures to protect children where families fail. It produced twelve informal consultation papers during 1984 and 1985 and a Report to Ministers in September 1985 which was published as a further consultation paper.[2] The Review's recommendations were essentially accepted by the government in their White Paper, 'The Law on Child Care and Family Services'.[3]

1 In response to a recommendation of the Second Report of the House of Commons Social Services Select Committee, 1983/84 on Children in Care HC 360–361 (the Short Report).
2 Review of Child Care Law (DHSS, 1985).
3 1987 Cm 62.

1.4 At the same time as the Review was investigating the public law relating to children, the Law Commission was undertaking a full-scale review of the private law on the allocation of responsibility between parents and other individuals. That review began with an examination of the law dealing with the consequences of birth outside marriage[1] and the resulting legislation, the Family Law Reform Act 1987, removed most of the remaining differences between children whose parents were married to each other, and those who were not. Against this background the Commission examined most of the remaining aspects of the private law, publishing Working Papers on Guardianship,[2] Custody,[3] Care, Supervision and Interim Orders in Custody Proceedings[4] and Wards of Court.[5] The first three of these working papers resulted in the Commission's Report on Guardianship and Custody, published in 1988.[6] Annexed to that Report was a Bill to give effect not only to the Law Commission's recommendations but also to show how an integrated scheme of court orders might look. That Bill was taken up by the government and expanded to cover virtually all the civil law relating to children, apart from adoption (to which, however, some modifications were made)[7] and education (although it does deal with children not being educated properly).[8] It was this Bill that eventually became the Children Act 1989.

1 Law Com No 118, Illegitimacy (1982) and Law Com No 157, Illegitimacy (1986).
2 1985, Working Paper No 91.
3 1985, Working Paper No 96.
4 1987, Working Paper No 100.
5 1987, Working Paper No 101.
6 Law Com No 172. It might also be mentioned that various procedural aspects of child law were examined in the Report of the Matrimonial Causes Procedure Committee (the 'Booth Committee') HMSO 1985 and further explored in the Lord Chancellor's Department's Consultative Paper: Improvements in the Arrangements for Care Proceedings, 1988.
7 Viz by Sch 10, but which is not discussed further in this work.
8 Viz by providing for education supervision orders under s 36, discussed at paras 8.180 et seq.

1.5 Important though the reviews of the public and private law were, it was the 'Cleveland crisis' that provided the final impetus for reform. As Lord Mackay LC said, it was a coincidence of the two reviews together with the Cleveland Report[1] which provided 'an historic opportunity to reform English law into a single rationalised system as it applies to the care and upbringing of children'.[2]

1 Report of the Inquiry into Child Abuse in Cleveland 1987 (the 'Butler-Sloss Report'), 1988 Cm 412.
2 'The Child: A View Across the Tweed' [1988] Denning LJ 89, 93.

1.6 The Cleveland Report was concerned with the removal of scores of children from their families because of alleged sexual abuse. In those cases the concern was that the authority had acted too precipitately but in a number of other inquiries, notably those investigating the deaths of Jasmine Beckford,[1]

Tyra Henry,[2] Kimberley Carlile[3] and Doreen Aston,[4] all of whom either were or had been in local authority care, the concern was that the local authority had not acted quickly enough. However, all these reports were influential in the final shaping of the CA 1989 and contributed much to a balanced view of the procedures needed to protect children, especially in the early stages where abuse is suspected.

1 A Child in Trust: Report of the Panel of Inquiry Investigating the Circumstances Surrounding the Death of Jasmine Beckford, London Borough of Brent, 1985.
2 Whose Child? The Report of the Public Inquiry into the Death of Tyra Henry, London Borough of Lambeth, 1987.
3 A Child in Mind: Protection of Children in a Responsible Society, Report of the Inquiry into the Circumstances Surrounding the Death of Kimberley Carlile, London Borough of Greenwich, 1989.
4 Report to the Area Review Committee for Lambeth, Lewisham and Southwark London Boroughs, 1989.

1.7   Another important influence on the final shape of the CA 1989 was the European Convention on Human Rights. Even before its direct incorporation into English domestic law by the Human Rights Act 1998,[1] there had been pressure from Europe for reform of English law to give effect to the fundamental rights of parents and children especially in relation to family life as protected by Article 8. In particular there had been concern about the then inability of parents to challenge local authority decisions restricting parental access to children in care.[2] As others have pointed out,[3] many of the reforms relating to care proceedings and in particular those giving parents and others the right to challenge contact decisions made by local authorities,[4] were inspired, if not positively mandated by the United Kingdom's obligations under the Convention.

1 For a discussion of the 1998 Act see paras 1.41 et seq.
2 See eg *R v United Kingdom* [1988] 2 FLR 445, E Ct HR, *O v United Kingdom* (1987) 10 EHRR 82, *H v United Kingdom* (1987) 10 EHRR 95, E Ct HR and *W v United Kingdom* (1987) 10 EHRR 29, *B v United Kingdom* (1987) 10 EHRR 87, E Ct HR.
3 Eg Bainham *Children: The New Law, The Children Act 1989*, p 5.
4 Under s 34, discussed at paras 8.145 et seq.

1.8   Coincidentally, at the same time that the CA 1989 was being debated the final touches to the United Nations Convention on the Rights of the Child 1989 were also being made, and no doubt the latter's provisions were borne in mind by those drafting the domestic Act.

1.9   Another influence on the CA 1989 was the House of Lords' decision in *Gillick v West Norfolk and Wisbeck Area Health Authority*[1] which was concerned with an older child's capacity to consent to medical treatment in cases where he has sufficient understanding to make up his own mind. The Act recognises[2] the importance of ascertaining and taking into account the child's own wishes to an extent commensurate with his age and understanding. The question of whether the preferences of a mature child should not only be taken into account but be determinative of the matter in question provoked considerable debate during the passage of the Bill.[3] In general, however, save in certain specified instances,[4] the Act does not give mature children the right to act independently of those with parental responsibility. On the other hand, the effect of its promotion of the child's own view, and in particular of provisions allowing the child himself to apply for leave to seek certain orders,[5] should not be underestimated.

1 [1986] AC 112, [1985] 3 All ER 402, HL.
2 Viz under s 1(3)(a), discussed at para 2.41.
3 See Bainham *Children, The New Law*, p 5.
4 Viz under ss 38(6), 43(8) and 44(7), discussed at paras 8.27, 7.23 and 7.55 respectively.
5 Viz under s 10(1)(a)(ii), (8) and (9), discussed at paras 5.115 et seq.

1.10 Although the Cleveland crisis undoubtedly prompted speedy reform, the Act did not endorse all of the Butler-Sloss recommendations. For example, the recommendation that there should be an 'Office of Child Protection' which was further explored by a Lord Chancellor's consultation paper,[1] was not taken up. Similarly, the recommendation to maintain the role of wardship in child care cases was not accepted. Indeed quite the contrary line is taken by the CA 1989 with the result that local authorities can no longer look to wardship at all as a means of obtaining a care order.[2]

1 Improvements in the Arrangements for Care Proceedings, 1988. But note the subsequent creation of CAFCASS, discussed at paras 10.5 et seq and the Children's Commissioner for Wales.
2 Discussed in detail in ch 12.

THE AMBIT OF THE CHILDREN ACT 1989

1.11 The CA 1989 has a wide ambit covering both the private and public law relating to the care and upbringing of children and the provision of services to them and their families. Under the Act there is a unified structure both of law and jurisdiction. In general all courts have the same powers when dealing with children.[1] There is now concurrent jurisdiction at all levels to hear care proceedings.[2] Similarly, proceedings can be transferred from a magistrates' court to a county court and vice versa, as well as between county courts and the High Court. One, perhaps unexpected, result of this new uniformity of jurisdiction is that it has been held that a magistrates' decision as well as that of a higher court, can create an estoppel per rem judicatam. As Ward J put it in *K v P (Children Act Proceedings: Estoppel)*:[3]

> 'one of the fundamental philosophies of [the Children Act] was that there should be a common jurisdiction exercised by magistrates' courts, county courts and High Court. It seems to me to be wholly invidious to say that if a matter is heard and determined by the justices the High Court should not take any account of their findings and should act dismissively towards them. That seems to me to undermine the important foundation of this new jurisdiction, namely that we all exercise it in the same way.'

1 An exception, however, is with respect to the powers to make financial provision for children under Sch 1 to the CA 1989, the magistrates' courts having more limited powers than the two higher courts. See further *Clarke Hall and Morrison*, Division 4.
2 However, under the Children (Allocation of Proceedings) Order 1991 proceedings must normally be commenced in the magistrates' court, see Family Proceedings Courts (Children Act 1989) Rules 1991, Sch 1.
3 [1995] 1 FLR 248 at 253, though note, courts are generally reluctant to allow issue estoppel to impede their ability to determine what is in the interests of a child. See further para 11.16.

1.12 In providing a uniform set of powers the Act replaced much of the previous legislation. For example, the Guardianship of Minors Acts 1971 and 1973, the Children Act 1975, the Child Care Act 1980 and the Children and Young Persons (Amendment) Act 1986 were repealed together with those provisions of the Children and Young Persons Act 1969 dealing with care and supervision orders in civil proceedings and those of the Family Law Reform Act 1969 conferring statutory powers in wardship proceedings. The Matrimonial Causes Act 1973 and the Domestic Proceedings and Magistrates' Courts Act 1978 were amended as to ensure that the powers to make orders relating to children in those proceedings are governed by the CA 1989.

1.13 Apart from providing for new orders in both the private and public law field, the Act rewrote the law relating to the provision of services for children and families by local authorities,[1] children's homes[2] and private fostering and child minding.[3] Furthermore both substantive and consequential amendments were made to adoption law[4] and a number of other statutes, notably those dealing with child abduction, were substantially amended to bring them into line with the CA 1989. The Act also affects other proceedings not otherwise primarily controlled by it, for example, in adoption proceedings, currently governed by the Adoption Act 1976,[5] and domestic violence proceedings under Pt IV of the Family Law Act 1996, courts can exercise their s 8 powers.[6]

1   Under Pt III and Sch 2, discussed in ch 6.
2   Under Pts VI–VIII, as revised by the Care Standards Act 2000, not discussed in this work.
3   Under Pt IX , X and XA (as revised by the Care Standards Act 2000) respectively, not discussed in this work.
4   By Sch 10, not discussed in this work.
5   Though this Act will prospectively be replaced by the Adoption and Children Act 2002.
6   See s 8(3), discussed at paras 5.101 et seq.

SOME KEY CHANGES UNDER THE ACT

1.   New concepts

1.14 In producing what the Department of Health's Introduction to the Children Act 1989[1] describes as a 'practical and consistent code', the CA 1989 embodied three fundamental changes of concept, namely, parenthood replacing guardianship as the primary concept, 'parental responsibility' replacing the concept of parental rights and duties, and new powers to make residence orders rather than custody orders.

1   HMSO, 1989, Foreword.

1.15 With regard to the first, as the Law Commission had observed,[1] before the Children Act the law had no coherent legal concept of parenthood as such. Instead rights and duties were based upon the concept of guardianship, rather than parenthood, and although its significance had diminished it was still the case immediately before the CA 1989 that the father was, during his lifetime, the sole guardian of his legitimate child. The CA 1989 abolished the concept of parental guardianship[2] and the term 'guardian' is now reserved for those formally appointed to take the place of parents upon their death.[3]

1   Law Com No 172, para 2.2.
2   S 2(4).
3   Guardianship is discussed at paras 3.97 et seq. Cf 'Children's Guardian' which is the term introduced by CAFCASS to replace what were formerly known as 'guardians ad litem' and who represent children either in public law proceedings (see paras 10.21 et seq) or adoption

proceedings and 'Special Guardianship' which is to be introduced by the Adoption and Children Bill 2002 to provide more secure residence orders for non parents, discussed at paras 5.161 et seq.

1.16 The introduction of the new concept of 'parental responsibility' is of particular importance under the Act. As Professor Hoggett (now Hale LJ) has said:[1]

'The [Act] assumes that bringing up children is the responsibility of their parents and that the State's principal role is to help rather than to interfere. To emphasise the practical reality that bringing up children is a serious responsibility, rather than a matter of legal rights, the conceptual building block used throughout the [Act] is 'parental responsibility'. This covers the whole bundle of duties towards the child, with their concomitant powers and authority over him, together with some procedural rights for protection, against interference . . . It therefore represents the fundamental status of parents.'

The meaning and scope of this vital concept is discussed in chapter 3.

1 'The Children Bill: The Aim' [1989] Fam Law 217.

1.17 The third change is the provision through s 8 of a fresh set of powers replacing the former powers to make custody and access orders. These powers are more flexible than the former and are intended to be less emotive. To this end they are drafted in clear and simple terms designed to settle practical questions (principally with whom the child is to live and whom the child can see) and not to confer abstract rights. In this way it was hoped that the symbolism of victory[1] that had come to be attached to custody and related orders would not be associated with these new s 8 orders.

1 See King: 'Playing the Symbols – Custody and the Law Commission' [1987] Fam Law 186.

1.18 Section 8 orders provide the 'basic menu' of the Act in that they can be made, either upon application or by the court acting on its own motion, in any 'family proceedings' including, therefore, proceedings brought by individuals or by local authorities. Another change relates to who can initiate or intervene in existing proceedings to seek a s 8 order. This is controlled by s 10[1] under which the Act adopts an 'open door' policy by allowing anyone (not otherwise entitled to seek an order) to seek the court's leave to apply for an order.

1 Discussed at paras 5.112 et seq.

2. Changes in Public Law

(a) Services for children and families[1]

1.19 The Act provides a comprehensive statement of the social services that must be provided by local authorities for families and children. For the first time services for handicapped and disabled children are brought under the same umbrella as those for other children in need. An important object of the Act is to promote these services as positive help for children in need. Emphasis is placed on the need for local authorities and families to work in partnership. Authorities are under a positive duty to consult the parents and children, and to promote contact between the child and his parents, family and friends. Even if compulsory measures are taken, the authorities remain under the positive duty to promote contact. The Act ended the local authorities' former powers to assume parental rights by administrative means. Instead, if compulsory measures are thought necessary, the authority must apply for a court order. Unless and until such an order is made, those with parental responsibility can remove the child from accommodation.[2]

1 Discussed in ch 6.
2 See s 20(8), discussed at paras 6.33 et seq.

(b)   A single threshold for state care and supervision[1]

1.20 Among other key changes in the public law field is the creation of a single statutory route into care: only if the statutory threshold in s 31 has been satisfied can the courts make a care or supervision order. Consistent with this philosophy of the courts' former powers in matrimonial and wardship proceedings to commit children into care of their own motion was ended.[2] The underlying philosophy of this threshold was explained by Lord Mackay LC in his Joseph Jackson Memorial Lecture:

'the integrity and independence of the family is the basic building block of a free and democratic society and the need to defend it should be clearly perceivable in the law. Accordingly, unless there is evidence that a child is being or is likely to be positively harmed because of a failure in the family, the state, whether in the guise of a local authority or a court, should not interfere.'[3]

1 Discussed in ch 6.
2 Though note the powers under s 37, discussed at paras 5.158 and 7.5.
3 (1989) 139 NLJ 505 at 508.

3.   General principles[1]

1.21 Section 1 of the CA 1989 sets out a number of basic principles intended to be of general application both in the private law and public law context. The basic controlling principle in all cases where a court is considering what order, if any, to make is, pursuant to s 1(1), to treat the child's welfare as the paramount consideration. Additionally, the Act provided[2] for the first time a statutory checklist to help the courts determine what is for the child's welfare. Similarly new to English law is the enjoinder to the courts under s 1(2) to have regard to the general principle that delay in determining questions about a child's upbringing is 'likely to prejudice the welfare of the child'. To avoid delay the court was given for the first time both the power and the duty to impose timetables for proceedings.[3]

1 Discussed in ch 2.
2 S 1(3).
3 Under ss 11(1) and 32(1), discussed in ch 4, paras 4.43 et seq. Similar powers will be introduced in adoption proceedings by the Adoption and Children Bill 2002.

1.22 Another innovation of the CA 1989 is the direction to the court by s 1(5) not to make an order 'unless it considers that doing so would be better for the child than making no order at all'. This provision requires justification in every case of why it is in the child's interests that any order be made. It is no longer sufficient that each party consents to an order being made, though the court is not prevented from making an order in such circumstances. The operation of this provision is discussed in chapter 2.[1]

1. See paras 2.62 et seq.

4. Procedural changes

1.23 The 1991 reforms radically affected all aspects of legal practice concerning children. These changes ranged from the introduction of entirely new rules governing procedure and evidence to changes in court structure and the creation of new Committees charged with overseeing the working of the Act.

(a) Procedure and evidence

1.24 Procedure under the CA 1989 is principally governed by two sets of rules, namely, the Family Proceedings Rules 1991 (FPR 1991) and the Family Proceedings Courts (Children Act 1989) Rules 1991 (FPC (CA 1989) R 1991), now both considerably amended. The former Rules replaced the Matrimonial Causes Rules 1977 and govern the procedure for all the higher courts' jurisdiction over children. Chapter 4 of these rules specifically governs applications under the CA 1989. The latter Rules, which govern procedure in the family proceedings courts, solely concern Children Act applications.[1]

1 Procedure under the Domestic Proceedings and Magistrates' Courts Act 1978 is governed by the Family Proceedings Courts (Matrimonial Proceedings etc) Rules 1991, SI 1991/1991. Note: the Civil Procedure Rules 1998 do not generally apply to family proceedings but see para 1.40 below.

1.25 The rules are a virtual mirror image of each other both in content and chronological order differing only where court structure dictates. For example, while the Family Proceedings Rules 1991 refer to the 'proper officer' the Family Proceedings Courts (Children Act 1989) Rules 1991 refer to the 'justices' chief executive' for procedure and 'justices' clerk' for quasi-judicial decisions. In line with the principle of unity of jurisdiction between the courts and of facilitating easy transfer from one level to another, applications and orders are made on a common set of forms, copies of which are set out at the end of each set of rules. Although the original forms were themselves the outcome of long deliberation, many felt there were too many of them and that they required too much and at times, repetitive, information. There was also widespread criticism of the requirement, outside the context of divorce, to have separate forms for each child. To meet these criticisms the Rules were amended, with effect, from the beginning of 1995,[1] of reducing the number of forms, simplifying their content and requiring only one application per family rather than per child.

1 Viz by the Family Proceedings (Amendment) (No 4) Rules 1994, SI 1994/3155 and the Family Proceedings Courts (Children Act 1989) (Amendment) (No 2) Rules 1994, SI 1994/3156.

(b) The creation of a comprehensive liaison network

1.26 Another important innovation of the 1991 reforms was the creation of a comprehensive liaison network to underpin the working of the Act. This network was intended to promote co-operation not only between the courts themselves but also among court users. In this way it was hoped to promote some of the key aims of the Act, namely, to avoid delay and ensure commonality of practice throughout the country and at each court level.[1] It was also intended to provide the means by which the major issues can be quickly identified and addressed, not just locally, but also nationwide.[2]

1 See the Children Act Advisory Committee's Annual Report (CAAC Report) 1992/93, p 4.
2 See the CAAC Report 1993/94, p 4.

(I) FAMILY DIVISION LIAISON JUDGE

1.27 An important part of the liaison network is the appointment of a High Court Judge of the Family Division as Liaison Judge for each of the seven circuits in England and Wales. The Liaison Judge has the following role, namely, to:

(a) identify which circuit judges should be appointed to hear Children Act cases;
(b) act as a channel between the Lord Chancellor and the judiciary;
(c) assist in bringing together others, including magistrates and those responsible for support agencies to discuss matters of concern;
(d) preside over the annual regional conference on family proceedings on their own circuit.

It is through this mechanism that there is a regular review on a circuit level of work at all court levels.

(II) THE CHILDREN ACT ADVISORY COMMITTEE, ADVISORY BOARD ON FAMILY LAW AND CHILDREN ACT SUB-COMMITTEE

1.28 The overall operation of the CA 1989 was initially monitored by the Children Act Advisory Committee. Established in 1991 and chaired by a High Court judge[1] with membership[2] comprising, inter alia, representatives of various government departments, and key personnel concerned with the everyday working of the courts, the Committee continued to function until July 1997.

1 Initially by Booth J and then, from July 1993 until its demise in 1997, by Bracewell J.
2 Current and immediate past membership is set out in the Committee's Annual Reports.

1.29 During its six years of work the Advisory Committee's terms of reference and consequent centre of focus changed. Originally, the terms were:[1]

'To advise the Lord Chancellor, the Home Secretary, the Secretary of State for Health and the President of the Family Division on whether the guiding principles of the Children Act 1989 are being achieved and whether the court procedures and the guardian ad litem system are operating satisfactorily.'

In 1993 these terms were broadened[2] to comprise both the giving of advice:

'On the progress of Children Act cases through the court system, with a view to identifying special difficulties and reducing avoidable delay; and

to promote through local Family Court Business Committees commonality of administrative practice and procedure in the family proceedings courts and the county courts and to advise on the impact on Children Act work of other family initiatives.'

These terms were reviewed again in 1995 but although they were not formally changed, in view of the continuing problems experienced in connection with the issue of delay, the Committee was asked to make that issue its focus of work during what turned out to be its last two years of office.[3]

1   CAAC Report 1991/92, p 5.
2   CAAC Report 1992/93, p 4.
3   CAAC Report 1994/1995, p 7.

1.30   The Advisory Committee did valuable work, producing a total of five Annual Reports. Its Final Report, published in 1997, contains a useful summary of the recommendations it made in its previous reports and of the action taken.[1] In addition to its Final Report, the Committee also produced a 'Handbook of Best Practice in Children Act cases' which was intended[2] as a 'comprehensive reference tool for use by all those involved in the preparation and conduct of public and private law Children Act proceedings'

1   CAAC Final Report, 1997, at p 8.
2   Reproduced in *Clarke Hall and Morrison* at 1 [20001].

1.31   As mentioned in its 1994/1995 report,[1] Lord Mackay had indicated that as the Committee was set up to monitor a new Act it should have a finite existence. The Committee was eventually wound up in 1997. However, some of the Committee's work was taken over by the Advisory Board on Family Law which was created in 1997 primarily to advise the Lord Chancellor on the implementation of the Family Law Act 1996. That Board's remit[2] included maintaining 'an overview of the working of the policy embodied in the Children Act within the family court system' and, to provide continuity with the work of the former Advisory Committee, it was decided that membership of the Board would include a Family Division judge or a Court of Appeal judge with Family Division experience.[3] The appointed member was Wall J. At the Board's first meeting it was agreed to establish a Children Act Sub-Committee, chaired by Wall J, and which would report to the Advisory Board. The Sub-Committee thus assumed some of the responsibilities of the former Advisory Committee though its remit was rather different, being 'to maintain a more strategic overview of the major policy issues and not to become involved in operational issues.'[4] Among the documents produced by his Sub-Committee were a Report on Parental Contact in cases where there is Domestic Violence and a Report on 'Making Contact Work'. However, following the Government's decision not to implement Pt II of the Family Law Act 1996, it was decided to wind up the Advisory Board at the end of 2001 and with it, the Children Act Sub-Committee. Consequently no body is currently concerned with monitoring the operation of the Children Act, which is surely a matter of some concern.[5] However, the Lord Chancellor's Department is currently consulting on the desirability of creating an overarching Family Justice Council which, inter alia, would have 'the challenging target of improving outcomes for those who came into contact with the family justice system, especially children.[6] One of the objectives the Government proposes for the Council is ... to reduce delay'.[7] It is suggested that the Council should be supported by specialist sub-committees on key subject areas, such as proceedings involving children.[8]

1   CAAC Report 1994/1995, at p 8.
2   See the Advisory Board on Family Law's Fourth Annual Report, para 1.9.
3   CAAC Final Report 1997, a p 7.

4 Advisory Board's Fourth Annual Report, at paras 1.10–1.12
5 See the criticism by Hale LJ in 'The Way Forward' in *Delight and Dole* op cit 149 at 152. Note also the comments about the lack of central direction made in the Lord Chancellor's Department's Consultation Paper 'Promoting inter-agency working in the family justice system' (CO 04/02).
6 Ie the LCD consultation paper, op cit at n 5.
7 See the *Scoping Study on Delay in Children Cases*, op cit, at paras 34 and 229.
8 See the Consultation Document, op cit, at paras 46 et seq.

(III)   THE FAMILY COURT BUSINESS COMMITTEES AND THE FAMILY COURT FORUMS[1]

1.32   In 1991, two new local committees were set up to provide local reviews of the working of the CA 1989. The first were the Family Court Business Committees which are concerned with the management of cases in terms of the availability of resources, priorities in relation to other litigation and sound practice in transferring cases between courts. The Committee is chaired by the designated family judge and serviced by the court administrator. The Business Committees at first reported to the Children Act Advisory Committee and then to the Children Act Sub-Committee and minutes of their meetings are disseminated among other Business Committees in the surrounding areas.

1 See the review in LCD Consultation Paper: 'Promoting inter-agency working in the family justice system'.

1.33   The Second Committee, originally known as the Family Court Services Committee, was intended to provide a forum for professional concerns about issues arising under the CA 1989 and the conduct of the various agencies and professions in safeguarding children's welfare. Like the Business Committee, the Services Committee was chaired by the designated family judge, but had a wider membership than the former.

1.34   The role of the two committees was reviewed by the Council for Family Proceedings which concluded, inter alia, that there was a need to distinguish more clearly between the committees' respective roles.[1] In particular it recommended that the Services Committees should be replaced by a more flexible style of meeting to be called the Family Court Forums. This change was implemented in August 1994. The amended terms of reference of the Forums are:

(i)   To promote discussion and encourage co-operation between all the professions, agencies and organisations involved in or concerned with family proceedings and to provide occasions for this to occur at each care centre;
(ii) To consider issues which arise locally in the conduct of family proceedings;
(iii) To recommend action which can be taken locally to improve the service provided to the parties to family proceedings; and
(iv) In addition to routine meetings FCFs will consider whether special events, seminars, study days or conferences are required locally to disseminate good practice, new arrangements and ideas or to examine problems.[2]

Although a designated judge will continue to have overall responsibility for the Forum the Children Act Advisory Committee recommended that an alternative chairman be nominated for a specified period or a particular meeting 'if this seems appropriate having regard to the expertise required for the topic in hand'.[3]

1 See the Children Act Advisory Committee's Annual Report 1993/94, p 5 and [1994] Fam Law 662.
2 See above.
3 CAAC Report 1993/94, p 6.

(IV) COURT USER COMMITTEES

1.35 The Advisory Committee regarded the role of the Business Committee as 'pivotal' to its own role. In fact both committees provide an important opportunity for local and national problems of administration to be discussed and remedied outside the context of particular litigation. They are not, however, the only committees. Even before the 1991 reforms some areas had developed court user committees comprising practitioners and representatives from agencies concerned in family proceedings. Some courts have retained this committee which again provides a forum for identifying and resolving any problems that they may have. The key difference, however, is that the Business Committee and Family Court Forum provide the opportunity of discussing local problems facing both the county court and family proceedings court.

(c) Role of the courts

1.36 An important result of the many procedural changes is that the courts' role changed. For example, all courts have a greater managerial role consequent upon the duty to impose timetables and to give directions to adhere to that timetable. Indeed, it is under the Act that for the first time that the courts themselves were placed under a duty to ensure the speedy disposal of cases. All courts are expected to take an active role in proceedings. As the Department of Health's Introduction to the Children Act 1989 puts it:[1]

> 'Under the Act the courts have an independent duty to do what is best for the child. If the courts are to discharge that duty often they will have to take an active part in the proceedings rather than simply acting as umpires between the contending parties.'

Further encouragement to take a proactive role is the general requirement of advance disclosure of evidence and the greater powers of the court to control what further evidence should be adduced. The impact of this proactive duty is discussed in chapter 4.

1 HMSO 1989, para 1.51.

SOME KEY CHANGES SINCE THE ACT

1.37 During the ten years since the CA 1989 first came into force there have been numerous decisions concerned with its interpretation and application. Similarly, there have been numerous amendments both to the Act and the Rules. These developments will be discussed throughout this work. There has also been a number of important new statutes, such as the Crime and Disorder Act 1998, Access to Justice Act 1999, the Protection of Children Act 1999, the Care Standards Act 2000 and the Children (Leaving Care) Act 2000. Mention should also be made of the Children and Family Court Advisory and Support

Service (CAFCASS) created by the Criminal Justice and Court Services Act 2000 which came into operation on 1 April 2001. This service replaces under a single umbrella, the former court welfare service and the guardian ad litem service. This new service is discussed further in chapter 10. Over and above these changes, there have been three major developments outside the Children Act 1989 but which nevertheless affect its operation, that should be adverted to more specifically in this introduction, namely, Welsh Devolution, the Civil Procedure Rules 1998, and the implementation of the Human Rights Act 1998.

1. Welsh devolution

1.38 Consequent upon Welsh devolution is the need for separate Welsh statutory instruments and regulations to govern devolved issues such as those relating to child care. This means that care now needs to be exercised when determining the application of regulatory law. It is noticeable that the Welsh regulations tend to be published some time after their English counterparts. Furthermore they may not be identically expressed.

2. The Civil Procedure Rules 1998

1.39 Following the so-called 'Woolf Reforms'[1] the civil litigation system was radically overhauled and the former Rules of the Supreme Court 1965 and the County Court Rules 1981 were replaced by a new set of rules known as the Civil Procedure Rules 1998 (CPR). These reforms were intended to: improve access to justice and reduce the cost of litigation; reduce complexity and modernise technology and improve unnecessary distinctions of practice and procedure.[2]

1 See *Access to Justice* (HMSO 1996).
2 See *Access to Justice* (Interim Report, HMSO, 1995), Introduction.

1.40 In some ways these reforms built upon ideas pioneered in the Family Division particularly following the CA 1989.[1] The CPR themselves, however, do not generally apply to family proceedings,[2] which instead continue to be governed by the Family Proceedings Rules 1991 (in the higher courts) and the Family Proceedings Courts (Children Act 1989) Rules 1991 (in the magistrates' courts). However, this does not mean that the family practitioner can ignore the CPR. The CPR provisions apply to the assessment of costs in the higher court proceedings,[3] and govern both appeals to the higher courts[4] and applications for judicial review.[5]

1 See eg Burrows 'Woolf and the Family Lawyer' [1999] Fam Law 223.
2 See CPR 1998, Pt 2, r 2.1.
3 Viz in accordance with Pts 43, 44, 47 and 48. See further paras 4.61 et seq.
4 CPR 1998, Pt 52. Note in this respect the important change that, even in family proceedings, leave to appeal to the Court of Appeal is generally required: r 52.3, discussed further at paras 13.11 et seq.
5 CPR 1998, Pt 54.

3. The Human Rights Act 1998

1.41 A most significant post-Children Act development has been the Human Rights Act 1998, which came into force in October 2000.[1] It is not intended here to provide a definitive discussion of the application of the 1998 Act[2] but rather to highlight some key points and to stress the underlying importance of the Convention when applying the CA 1989 and determining lawfulness of the acts of local authorities and the courts.[3]

1 SI 2000/1851.
2 For a fuller discussion of the Human Rights Act 1998 see eg Swindells, Neaves, Kushner and Skilbeck *Family Law and the Human Rights Act 1998,* Horowitz, Kingscote and Nicholls *The Human Rights Act 1998 – A Special Bulletin for Family Lawyers,* Supperstone, Goudie and Coppel *Local Authorities and the Human Rights Act 1998*, and *Butterworths Family Law Service,* Vol 5A, Ch 6.
3 Though note the warnings against making unnecessary and unhelpful references to the Convention, see *Daniels v Walker (Practice Note)* [2000] 1 WLR 1382 and *Re F (care proceedings: contact)* [2001] 1 FCR 481.

1.42 Although the United Kingdom was one of the original signatories to the Convention (having ratified it in 1951) and, since 1966, has allowed individuals to take their complaints to the European Court of Human Rights in Strasbourg, the Convention remained an international obligation and did not form part of domestic law. This meant that the UK courts were not obliged to take the Convention into account when applying domestic law.[1] What the Act does is:

- oblige all domestic courts at all levels to take Convention case law into account when deciding a question relating to a Convention right;
- provide that, so far as it is possible to do so, primary and subordinate legislation must be read and given effect to in a way that is compatible with Convention rights;
- empower the higher courts[2] to make declarations of incompatibility if satisfied that a statutory provision is incompatible with a Convention right;
- make it unlawful for public authorities to act in a way that is incompatible with a Convention right save where the authorities are obliged to do so by primary legislation;
- permit persons to bring proceedings against a public authority acting or proposing to act in a way made unlawful by the 1998 Act; and
- empower the courts to give an appropriate remedy, including damages in respect of any act (or proposed act) of a public authority which is (or would be) found to be unlawful.

1 Though this did not prevent courts from having regard to the Convention particularly when construing legislative ambiguities. For a discussion of the pre 1998 Act position see eg Duffy 'English law and the European Convention on Human Rights' (1980) 29 ICLQ 585.
2 Viz the High Court and the appellate courts, see s 4(5).

1.43 So far as child law is concerned the most relevant 'Convention rights' for the above mentioned purposes are those provided by Arts 8 and 6(1) of the Convention.[1] The former provides:

'Everyone has the right to respect for his private and family life, his home and his correspondence.'

However, this right is qualified by Art 8(2) which states:

'There shall be no interference by a public authority with the exercise of this right except such as in accordance with the law and is necessary in a democratic society in the interests of national security, public safety or the economic well-being of the country, for the prevention of disorder or crime, for the protection of health or morals, or for the protection of the rights and freedoms of others'.

Article 6(1) provides:

'In the determination of his civil rights and obligations or of any criminal charge against him, everyone is entitled to a fair and public hearing within a reasonable time by an independent and impartial tribunal established by law. Judgment shall be pronounced publicly but the press and public may be excluded from all or part of the trial in the interest of morals, public order or national security in a democratic society, where the interests of juveniles or the protection of the private life of the parties so require, or to the extent strictly necessary in the opinion of the court in special circumstances where publicity would prejudice the interests of justice'.

1   These and all other 'incorporated' Articles are contained in Sch 1 to the 1998 Act.

1.44   These, however, are not the only Convention rights of relevance to child law. For example, both Arts 3(1) and 5(1) have already been relied upon in certain crucial cases.[1] Article 3 provides:

'No one shall be subjected to torture or to inhuman or degrading treatment or punishment'.

Article 5(1) provides:

'Everyone has the right to liberty and security of person. No one shall be deprived of his liberty save in the following cases and in accordance with a procedure prescribed by law: . . . (d) the detention of a minor by lawful order for the purpose of educational supervision or his lawful detention for the purpose of bringing him before the competent legal authority; . . .'

Furthermore Art 14 also has to be taken into account.[2] This provides:

'The enjoyment of the rights and freedoms set forth in this Convention shall be secured without discrimination on any ground such as sex, race, colour, language, religion, political or other opinion, national or social origin, association with a national minority, property, birth or other status'.

1   Art 3 has obvious relevance to the issue of disciplining the child, see eg *A v United Kingdom (human rights: punishment of child)* [1998] 3 FCR 597, [1998] 2 FLR 959, (1999) 27 EHRR 611, E Ct HR, but its significance can go beyond this, see *Z and others v UK* [2001] 2 FCR 246, [2001] 2 FLR 612, E Ct HR, in which it was held that a local authority's failure to take adequate measures to protect children who were known to be ill-treated by their parents breached Art 3. See further para 13.70. Art 5 has obvious relevance to secure accommodation, see *Re K (A Child) (Secure Accommodation Order: Rights to Liberty)* [2001] Fam 377, [2001] 2 WLR 1141, [2001] 2 All ER 719, CA, discussed at paras 9.5 et seq.
2   *Note:* Art 14 can only be relied upon in conjunction with another Article. It does not provide an independent Convention right. Protocol No. 12 does make discrimination an independent right but the United Kingdom has not signed it.

1.45   The Convention does not specifically confer rights on children, rather it confers rights on everyone, including children. This, however, means that Art 8, for example, confers the right to respect for family life both on parents and children which therefore calls for a balancing exercise should those rights conflict.

1.46   The obligation to take Convention case law into account when deciding a question relating to a Convention right is provided for by s 2 of the 1998

Act. By 'case law' is meant not only the judgments of the European Court of Human Rights but also the opinions of the former Commission and includes decisions on the admissibility of claims.[1] The obligation, however, is only to take such case law into account. The jurisprudence is not binding in any strict sense of precedence and indeed it is open to the English courts to go further than the European Court.[2] It has been well said,[3] however, that a court that ignores Convention case law will clearly run the risk of an appeal.

1 See s 2(1)(a)–(d) of the 1998 Act. A useful chart of relevant Convention case law can be found in *Clarke Hall and Morrison* at 1[4001] et seq.
2 See eg *Fitzpatrick v Sterling Housing Association Ltd* [2001] AC 27, [1999] 3 WLR 113, 4 All ER 705, HL.
3 See *Family Law Service* at para 5A[4006].

1.47 A crucial provision in the 1998 Act is s 3 which provides that so far as possible primary and subordinate legislation must be read and given effect in a manner that is compatible with the Convention. Although this provision entitles the courts to depart from earlier domestic precedents insofar as they are thought to be incompatible with Convention rights, as Lord Nicholls stressed in *Re S (Minors) (Care Order: Implementation Of Care Plan), Re W (Minors) (Care Order: Adequacy Of Care Plan),*[1] it does not entitle the courts to legislate. As he put it: 'Interpretation of statutes is a matter for the courts, the enactment of statutes, and the amendment of statutes, are matters for Parliament'. As against this, however, it has also been stressed[2] that s 3 of the 1998 Act obliges courts to find an interpretation of a statute which is compatible with the Convention if at all possible. In other words, as Hale LJ has said[3] 'the 1998 Act was carefully designed to promote the search for compatibility, rather than incompatibility'.

1 [2002] UK HL10 at para [39], [2002] 2 WLR 720 at 731, [2002] 2 All ER 192 at 203, applying *Poplar Housing Regeneration Community Association Ltd v Donoghue* [2001] EWCA Civ 595 at para [75], [2001] 3 WLR 183, [2001] 4 All ER 604, per Lord Woolf CJ and *R v Lambert* [2001] UK HL 37 at paras [79]–[81], [2001] 3 WLR 206, [2001] 3 All ER 577, per Lord Hope.
2 *R v A (No 2)* [2002] 1 AC 45, [2001] 2 WLR 1546, [2001] 3 All ER 1, per Lord Steyn.
3 In *Re W and B (children) (care plan), Re W (children) (care plan)* [2001] EWCA Civ 757 at para [50], [2001] 2 FCR 450, [2001] 2 FLR 582, not directly commented upon by HL on appeal, reported as *Re S*, supra at n 1.

1.48 Notwithstanding the encouragement to find compatibility, s 4 of the 1998 Act specifically empowers the High Court and the appellate courts to make a formal declaration that a provision of primary legislation is incompatible with a Convention right. Although such declarations do not affect the validity of the legislation in question, which will continue to apply, the expectation nevertheless is that the offending provision(s) will consequently be amended.[1] Given the importance placed on finding compatibility it is not surprising that s 4 declarations are rare (there have so far been no such declarations in the field of Family Law). Furthermore, declarations can only be made in respect of specific provisions. It is not therefore sufficient to allege that the whole scheme of an Act is incompatible.[2]

1 See s 10.
2 See *Re W and B (children) (care plan), Re W (children) (care plan)* [2001] EWCA Civ 757 at para [50], [2001] 2 FCR 450, [2001] 2 FLR 582, per Hale LJ, impliedly upheld on this point by HL on appeal, see *Re S (Minors) (Care Order; Implementation of Care Plan), Re W (Minors) (Care Order: Adequacy of Care Plan)* [2002] UKHL 10 at para [41], [2002] 2 WLR 720, [2002] 2 All ER 192, per Lord Nicholls.

1.49 Another significant part of the Act is that enabling individuals to enforce their Convention rights against a public authority. A 'public authority' for these purposes is widely defined and includes local authorities and the courts.[1] The scheme of the Act in this respect was well described by Lord Nicholls in *Re S*.[2] As he put it:

> 'Sections 7 and 8 of the Human Rights Act 1998 have conferred extended powers on the courts. Section 6 makes it unlawful for a public authority to act in a way which is incompatible with a Convention right. Section 7 enables victims of conduct made unlawful by s 6 to bring court proceedings against the public authority in question. Section 8 spells out, in wide terms, the relief a court may grant in those proceedings. The court may grant such relief or remedy, or make such order, within its powers as it considers just and appropriate. Thus, if a local authority conducts itself in a manner which infringes the article 8 rights of a parent or child, the court may grant appropriate relief on the application of a victim of the unlawful act'.

Actions, which can only be brought by victims of the unlawful conduct,[3] must generally be brought within one year of the act complained of, or 'such longer period as the court or tribunal considers equitable in all the circumstances.'[4] Insofar as a complaint is sought in respect of a judicial act, it can only be by way of an appeal or judicial review.[5]

1 S 6(3) states that 'public authority' includes: (a) a court or tribunal, and (b) any person of whose functions are functions of a public nature . . .' on which see *Poplar Housing and Regeneration Community Association Ltd v Donoghue* [2001] EWCA Civ 595, [2001] 3 WLR 183, [2001] 4 All ER 604, CA. But note *R (Heather and Another) v Leonard Cheshire Foundation* [2002] EWCA Civ 366, [2002] 2 All ER 936, CA, voluntary sector home for the disabled funded by local authority held not to be exercising public functions.
2 *Re S (Minors) (Care Order: Implementation of Care Plan), Re W (Minors) (Care Order: Adequacy of Care Plan)* [2001] UK HL 10 at para [45], [2002] 2 WLR 720, [2002] 2 All ER 192.
3 S 7(7) defines such victims by reference to Art 34 of the Convention. It is confined to a person who is directly affected by the act or omission. In *A and B v United Kingdom* [1998] 1 EHRLR 82, for example, a father of a son who was beaten by his stepfather was not considered a 'victim'.
4 S 7(5).
5 S 9. Damages cannot be awarded for judicial acts committed in good faith except under Art 5(5) (for an arrest or detention contravening Art 5), when they are payable by the Crown, s 9(3), (4).

1.50 We discuss the impact of the Convention on specific aspects of the application of the Children Act throughout the book. Suffice to say here that at the time of the implementation of the 1998 Act while it was not anticipated that the Act would be vulnerable to many successful substantive law challenges (the Act after all had been drafted with the Convention very much in mind), there was speculation about the compatibility of the paramountcy principle, the status of unmarried fathers and the lawfulness of secure accommodation orders. There was concern too not so much as to the lawfulness of the power to make care orders (given the need to satisfy the threshold provisions) but rather whether the response to a finding that s 31 has been satisfied is proportionate to the needs of the situation. In particular it was questioned whether it could be justified to make a care order where the child will be living at home. Concern was also expressed as to whether the lack of power of the courts to oversee care plans was Human Rights compliant. Procedurally, the law and practice under the CA 1989 were anticipated to be more vulnerable. There was speculation, for instance, both as to whether requiring grandparents to have court leave to apply for a s 8 order and requiring local authority foster parents to have local authority consent to apply for court leave, was human rights compliant. There was concern too as to compatibility of s 91(14), (15) and (17), which impose respectively discretionary and automatic leave requirements. Further concerns had been expressed about the rules of hearsay and the right of cross examination as they applied in children's cases. There were worries about the ability to obtain ex parte orders, particularly emergency protection orders and speculation about the legality of hearing children's cases in private.

1.51 As will be seen, many of these concerns have already been addressed either domestically, as for example, regarding the compatibility of the paramountcy principle[1] and the lawfulness of secure accommodation orders,[2] or by the European Court, as in the case of not giving unmarried fathers automatic parental responsibility.[3] Other issues remain to be addressed while still others that were not speculated upon earlier, have since been brought before the courts. In this latter regard it seems that the remedies provided for by ss 7 and 8 may well prove rather more extensive than originally envisaged.[4] One important matter that does appear to have been resolved is whether or not the 1998 Act can have a so-called 'horizontal effect', that is, determining the rights as between individuals.[5] Contrary to earlier suggestions,[6] it now seems accepted that it can.[7] That is not to say that the Act directly allows individuals to sue one another under the Convention; rather it is because it is accepted that Convention jurisprudence[8] establishes that there are positive obligations upon the State to ensure that the individuals' rights are protected.[9] Furthermore, since courts, as public authorities, are obliged to act compatibly with Convention rights, they must, when deciding an application between individuals, apply domestic law in accordance with those rights.[10] Since so much of family law is concerned with private litigation, this conclusion is not without significance for the future development of child law.

1　See eg *Re L (A Child) (Contact: Domestic Violence)*, *Re V (A Child)*, *Re M (A Child)*, *Re H (children)* [2001] Fam 260, [2000] 4 All ER 609, discussed at para 2.5.
2　See *Re K (A Child) (Secure Accommodation Order: Right to Liberty)* [2001] Fam 377, [2001] 2 WLR 1141, [2001] 2 All ER 719, CA, discussed at paras 9.6 et seq.
3　See *B v UK* [2000] 1 FCR 289, [2000] 1 FLR 1 in which the European Court held that English law did not breach the Convention, see further 3.44.
4　See further paras 13.72 et seq.
5　For extensive discussion of this issue see Wade 'Human Rights and the Judiciary' [1998] EHRLR 520, Buxton 'The Human Rights Act and Private Law' (2000) 116 LQR 48 and Hunt 'The "Horizontal effect" of the Human Rights Act' [1998] Public Law 423.
6　See eg Buxton LJ in *Re G-A (permission to remove child from jurisdiction: human rights)* [2001] 1 FCR 43, sub nom *Re A (Permission to Remove Child From Jurisdiction)* [2000] 2 FLR 225.
7　See *Payne v Payne* [2001] EWCA, Civ 166, [2001] 1 FCR 425, [2001] 1 FLR 1052, per Thorpe LJ and Butler-Sloss P.
8　As established by *Marckx v Belgium* (1979) 2 EHRR 330, E Ct HR.
9　See eg *A v United Kingdom (human rights: punishment of a child)* [1998] 3 FCR 597, [1998] 2 FLR 959, E Ct HR.
10　See the discussion in *Family Law Service* at 5A[4044].

Chapter 2

General principles

2.1 Section 1 sets out the general principles that are to be applied in court proceedings, namely:

(1) the child's welfare is paramount in deciding all questions about his upbringing and the administration of his property;
(2) regard is to be had to the general principle that delay in deciding any question with respect to the child's upbringing is likely to prejudice the child's welfare;
(3) in contested applications for s 8 orders and in all care or supervision proceedings, the courts should, when applying the welfare principle, pay particular regard to certain specific matters contained in the statutory welfare checklist; and
(4) the court should not make any order under the CA 1989 unless to do so is considered better for the child than making no order.

THE WELFARE PRINCIPLE

2.2 Section 1(1) lays down the cardinal principle in child law that:

'When any court determines any question with respect to:
(a) the upbringing of the child; or
(b) the administration of the child's property or the application of any income arising from it,
the child's welfare shall be the court's paramount consideration.'

As Ward LJ observed in *Re A (Children) (Conjoined Twins: Surgical Separation)*:[1]

'The peremptory terms of this section should be noted. It places the court under a duty to do what is dictated by the child's welfare'.

Although modelled on the Guardianship of Minors Act 1971, s 1, which it replaced, this principle is not an exact replica. It also differs from that recommended by the Law Commission.

1 [2001] Fam 147 at 180, [2000] 4 All ER 961 at 993, CA.

1. 'Paramount' not 'first and paramount'

2.3 Unlike the 1971 Act, which directed the court to treat the child's welfare as its first and paramount consideration, s 1(1) of the CA 1989 simply directs the court to treat the child's welfare as its paramount consideration. However, it was neither contemplated nor intended that the omitted words 'first and', would lead to a change of practice.[1] Although in the past the word 'first' had, in the words of the Law Commission,[2] 'led some courts to balance other considerations against the child's welfare rather than to consider what light they shed upon it', that view had long ceased to be the law, and the CA 1989's paramountcy formulation reflects the previous well established position encapsulated by Lord MacDermott when he said in the leading case, *J v C*,[3] that the principle connotes:

> 'A process whereby, when all the relevant facts, relationships, claims and wishes of parents, risks, choices and other circumstances are taken into account and weighed, the course to be followed will be that which is most in the interests of the child's welfare as that term has now to be understood. That is the first consideration because of its first importance and the paramount consideration because it rules upon or determines the course to be followed.'

In the past it has been said[4] that in effect *J v C* established, and s 1(1) confirmed, that the child's welfare is the court's sole concern and other factors are relevant only to the extent that they can assist the court in ascertaining the best solution for children. However, it now seems clear, following the implementation of the Human Rights Act 1998, that such an approach cannot be correct since too little attention is paid to the need to respect the rights of parents. In other words in interpreting s 1(1) respect must be given to *each* person's rights, though where a child's interests conflict with other persons' interests, the former should prevail. Whether even this interpretation is compatible with the European Convention on Human Rights is discussed below.

1 See eg *C v C (A Minor) (Custody: Appeal)* [1991] 1 FLR 223 at 230, CA, in which Balcombe LJ commented that it seemed to him that the new wording would not make 'any material difference' to the law.
2 Report on Review of Child Law, Guardianship and Custody (Law Com No 172, 1988) para 3.13, citing *Re L (infants)* [1962] 3 All ER 1, [1962] 1 WLR 886, CA and *Re F (an Infant)* [1969] 2 Ch 238 at 241.
3 In *J v C* [1970] AC 668 at 710–711, [1969] 1 All ER 788 at 820–821, HL. See also *Re K D (a Minor) (Ward: Termination of Access)* [1988] AC 806, [1988] 1 All ER 577, HL. For a detailed discussion of the development and application of the welfare principle, see Lowe 'The House of Lords and the Welfare Principle' in Bridge (ed) *Family Law Towards the Millennium – Essays for P M Bromley* (Butterworths, 1997) at 125 et seq.
4 See eg para 2.4 of the previous edition of this work.

2.4 In choosing the paramountcy formulation, the government rejected the Law Commission's recommendations,[1] that 'when determining any question under the Act the welfare of any child likely to be affected shall be the court's only concern'. The Commission were unhappy with a pure paramountcy formulation, being concerned, inter alia,[2] that litigants might still be tempted to introduce evidence that had no relevance to the child in the hope of persuading the court to balance one against the other. Even if this fear had been justified (which was doubtful given that the paramountcy formulation had been well tested before the Act and seemed to produce the right balance both in terms of the evidence submitted and the weight put on it) the Law Commission's own formulation carried the equally undesirable risk of courts refusing to hear evidence unless it directly addressed the question of what was best for the child.

1 Clause 1(2) of the Draft Bill published in Law Com No 172.
2 See above, para 3.14.

2. Is the paramountcy principle Human Rights compliant?

2.5 In cases governed by s 1(1) it is clear that where the parents' and the child's interests conflict, as in *J v C*[1] itself, it is the child's interests that must prevail. In *Re L (A Child) (Contact: Domestic Violence)*[2] Butler-Sloss P commented that this prevailing preference for children's interests was entirely compatible with Art 8(2) of the European Convention on Human Rights. As her Ladyship pointed out, in *Hendricks v Netherlands*[3] it was held that where there was a serious conflict between the interests of a child and one of his or her parents which could only be resolved to the disadvantage of one of them, it was the child's interests that had to prevail under Art 8(2). Further, in *Johansen v Norway*[4] the European Court of Human Rights commented that a parent was not entitled under Art 8 to have such measures taken that would harm the child's health and development. Similarly, Thorpe LJ had no doubts as to the compatibility of the paramountcy principle with the Convention. As he observed in *Payne v Payne*:[5]

'whilst the advent of the 1998 Act requires revision of the judicial approach to conclusion, as a safeguard to an inadequate perception and application for a father's rights under Arts 6 and 8, it requires no re-evaluation of the judge's primary task to evaluate and uphold the welfare of the child as the paramount consideration, despite its inevitable conflict with adult rights.'

1 [1970] AC 688, [1969] 1 All ER 788, HL.
2 *Re L (A Child) (Contact: Domestic Violence), Re V (A Child) Re M (A Child), Re H (Children)* [2001] Fam 260 at 277, [2000] 4 All ER 609, at 620.
3 (1982) 5 EHRR 223. In fact this case was decided by the Commission and not the European Court of Human Rights as suggested by Butler-Sloss P.
4 (1996) 23 EHRR 33.
5 [2001] EWCA Civ 166 at [57], [2001] 1 FCR 425, [2001] 1 FLR 1051. But for a challenging discussion of this issue see J. Herring 'The Human Rights Act and the welfare principle in family law – conflicting or complementary?' [1999] CFLQ 223. See further Herring *Family Law* 346 et seq, H. Reece, 'The Paramountcy Principle: Consensus or Construct?' (1996) 49 *Current Legal Problems* 267 and A. Vine, 'Is the Paramountcy Principle Compatible with Article 8?' [2000] Fam Law 826.

3. Comparison with UN Convention

2.6 Section 1(1) might be compared with Art 3(1) of the UN Convention on the Rights of the Child 1989 (to which the UK is a party) which states:

'In all actions concerning children, whether undertaken by public or private social welfare institutions, courts of law, administrative authorities or legislative bodies, the best interests of the child shall be a primary consideration.'

2.7 This Article provides an international obligation[1] to apply the best interests of the child test and as such is clearly similar to the paramountcy test under s 1(1) of the CA 1989.[2] However, the enjoinder to regard the best interests as a *primary* consideration is not as strong (though possibly more Human Rights compliant) as to regard the child's welfare as the *paramount* consideration. On the other hand, by applying both to administrative authorities and legislative bodies, Art 3(1) is wider than s 1(1) which only applies in court proceedings.

1 As a matter of strict law, since the UN Convention has not been incorporated by statute into English domestic law, courts are not bound to apply it, see *British Airways v Laker*

Airways [1985] AC 58, [1984] 3 All ER 39, HL and more specifically *Re P (Children Act: Diplomatic Immunity)* [1998] 1 FLR 624 at 628, per Stuart-White J and *R v Central Criminal Court ex p S* [1999] 1 FLR 480 at 487, per Sullivan J. Nevertheless, as Ward LJ said in *Re P (a Minor) (Residence Order: Child's Welfare)* [2000] Fam 15 at 42, sub nom *Re P (a child) (residence order: restriction order)* [1999] 3 All ER 734 at 756, although the Convention may not have the force of law it commands and receives respect. It might be noted that under the Children's Commissioner for Wales Appointment Regulations 2001 (SI 2001/3121), the Children's Commissioner for Wales has to 'have regard' to the UN Convention in the discharge of his duties. This is the first reference to the UN Convention in UK legislation

2   Indeed in *Payne v Payne* [2001] EWCA Civ 166, [2001] 1 FCR 425, [2001] 1 FLR 1052, at para (38), Thorpe LJ went as far as to say that the paramountcy principle was 'enshrined' by Art 3(1).

4.   When the principle applies

2.8   As s 1(1) states, the paramountcy principle applies whenever a court is called upon to determine any question about the child's upbringing or the administration of his property. Section 1(1) is therefore of general application and is not restricted to Children Act proceedings. It is established, for example, that the provision is applicable to wardship proceedings,[1] including non-Convention[2] child abduction cases,[3] and to the exercise of the High Court's inherent jurisdiction.[4]

1   *J v C* [1970] AC 668, [1969] 1 All ER 788, HL (discussed further at para 2.9). The wardship jurisdiction is discussed in ch 12.
2   Ie cases not governed by either the European or Hague Conventions on international child abduction. For details see *Clarke Hall and Morrison* on Children, Division 2.
3   See *Re L (minors) (wardship: jurisdiction)* [1974] 1 All ER 913, [1974] 1 WLR 250, CA – the locus classicus before implementation of the Child Abduction and Custody Act 1985, and *Re F (A Minor) (Abduction: Custody Rights)* [1991] Fam 25, [1990] 3 All ER 97, CA and *Re JA (child abduction: non-convention country)* [1998] 2 FCR 159, [1998] 1 FLR 231, CA – post the 1985 Act. But note the conflict of view over the application of the principle of comity between *Re JA (Child Abduction: Non-Convention Country)* above, *Re M (Abduction: Non-Convention Country)* [1995] 1 FLR 89, CA and *Re M (Minors) (Abduction: Peremptory Return Order)* [1996] 478, CA, discussed *Clarke Hall and Morrison* at 2 [34].
4   *Re A (Children) (Conjoined Twins: Surgical Separation)* [2001] Fam 147, [2000] 4 All ER 961, CA. *Re T (a minor) (wardship: medical treatment)* [1997] 1 All ER 906, [1997] 1 WLR 242, CA and *Re W (a Minor) (Medical Treatment: Court's Jurisdiction)* [1993] Fam 64, [1992] 4 All ER 627, CA. The High Court's inherent jurisdiction is discussed in ch 12.

2.9   The paramountcy principle applies equally to disputes between parents and other individuals as well as to disputes between parents. In *J v C*[1] a child born in England to Spanish parents was fostered owing to the mother's illness. Later the boy was received into care and then made a ward of court. The parents' subsequent application for care and control was refused, the House of Lords holding that even assuming the parents to be 'unimpeachable' nevertheless their interests could be, and were in this case, outweighed by the child's welfare. Notwithstanding *J v C*, however, in disputes with other individuals over a child's upbringing, the parent's position is prima facie the stronger. As Balcombe LJ put it in *Re W (a Minor) (Residence Order)*:[2]

'It is the welfare of the child which is the test, but of course there is a strong presumption that, other things being equal, it is in the interests of the child that it shall remain with its natural parents, but that has to give way to particular needs in particular situations'.

Certain more recent decisions[3] have taken this to mean that in deciding disputes between parents and non-parents the court is not required to conduct a balancing exercise of deciding which home is better for the child, but should instead consider whether there are compelling reasons for deciding that the child should not live with the parent. Whether this is a correct application of the paramountcy test may be questioned since it arguably places the parent(s)' interests above those of the child and anyway comes perilously close to saying that there is presumption in favour of parents, which is questionable given that the application of presumptions in children cases is now generally frowned upon.[4]

1   [1970] AC 668, [1969] 1 All ER 788, HL. See also *Re P (a Minor) (Residence Order: Child's Welfare)* [2000] Fam 15, sub nom *Re P (a child) (residence order: restriction order)* [1999] 3 All ER 734, CA.
2   [1993] 2 FLR 625 at 633 expressly approving similar comments made by Lord Donaldson MR in *Re H (a Minor) (Custody: Interim Care and Control)* [1991] 2 FLR 109 at 113, CA, who in turn was explaining earlier dicta (per Fox LJ) in *Re K (a minor) (ward: care and control)* [1990] 3 All ER 795, [1990] 1 WLR 431, CA.
3   Viz *Re D (a minor) (natural parent: presumption of care)* [1999] 2 FCR 118 at 126, sub nom *Re D (Care: Natural Parent Presumption)* [1999] 1 FLR 134 at 141, per Sumner J sitting in the Court of Appeal. See also *Re D (Residence Order: Natural Parent)* [1999] 2 FLR 1023, per Johnson J. See also the discussion by Neill and Ward LJJ in *Re M (Child's Upbringing)* [1996] 2 FLR 411 at 452–453 and 455–456, CA – a striking example of preference being given to the birth parents. But note, Thorpe LJ's suggestion in *Re O (family appeals: management)* [2000] 2 FCR 404, [2000] 2 FLR 334, that the Court of Appeal had fallen into error in *Re M*.
4   See in particular *Payne v Payne* [2001] EWCA Civ 166, [2001] 1 FCR 425, [2001] 1 FLR 1052, CA discussed further at para 2.68.

2.10   As the Department of Health's Guidance to the CA 1989 states,[1] the paramountcy principle applies whenever a court is considering whether to make a s 8 order (ie regardless of who the parties are or in which proceedings the issue is raised or what the issue is).[2] Furthermore, it has been held that the amendments to what was then the Foster Placement (Children) Regulations 1991[3] by the Children (Protection from Offenders) (Miscellaneous Amendments) Regulations 1997[4] do not prevent the court from applying the paramountcy principle when considering whether to make a residence order or a care and control order in wardship.[5] It applies when considering whether to make a parental responsibility order under s 4[6] and to applications made under s 13 both for leave to change a child's surname[7] and to remove a child from the jurisdiction.[8]

1   Guidance and Regulations, Vol 1, Court Orders, para 2.57.
2   Including for example, a child's religious upbringing and determining whether a boy should be ritually circumcised: *Re J (child's religious upbringing and circumcision)* [1999] 2 FCR 345, sub nom *Re J (specific issue orders: muslim upbringing and circumcision)* [1999] 2 FCR 678 per Wall J – decision upheld by Court of Appeal see [2000] 1 FCR 307, [2000] 1 FLR 571. See also, *Re P (A Minor) (Residence Order: Child's Welfare)* [2000] Fam 15, sub nom *Re P (a child) (residence order: restriction order)* [1999] 3 All ER 734, CA.
3   SI 1991/910, now replaced in England by the Fostering Service Regulations 2002 (SI 2002/57).
4   SI 1997/2308, inserting reg 4 (4A) into the 1991 Regulations.
5   *Re J (fostering: person disqualified)* [1998] 3 FCR 579, [1999] 1 FLR 605, CA.
6   *Re RH (a minor) (parental responsibility)* [1998] 2 FCR 89, at 94, sub nom *Re H (Parental Responsibility)* [1998] 1 FLR 855 at 899, CA, per Butler-Sloss LJ. This issue, however, may not be beyond doubt: see *Re G (a Minor) (Parental Responsibility Order)* [1994] 1 FLR 504 at 507–508, CA and *Re E (a minor) (parental responsibility)* [1994] 2 FCR 209 at 715, [1995] 1 FLR 392 at 397, CA in which Balcombe LJ pointed out that it was at least arguable that such applications do not concern questions relating to a child's upbringing. But for convincing arguments to the contrary, see Hershman at [1994] Fam Law 650.
7   *Re B (Change of Surname)* [1996] 1 FLR 791 at 795, CA, per Wilson J. The paramountcy principle equally applies to applications to change names under s 33(7) (discussed at para 8.138),

see *Re S (change of surname)* [1999] 1 FCR 304 at 307, [1999] 1 FLR 672 at 674, CA, per Thorpe LJ.
8 *Payne v Payne* [2001] EWCA Civ 166, [2001] 1 FCR 425, [2001] 1 FLR 1052, per Thorpe LJ.

2.11 With regard to public law proceedings under the CA 1989, the paramountcy principle applies to the so-called welfare stage of care proceedings, that is deciding what, if any, order should be made *after* deciding whether or not the statutory threshold under s 31 has been satisfied.[1] It also applies to applications to discharge care orders under s 39[2] whether or not to make contact orders under s 34,[3] and both to the question of whether leave should be given to a local authority to withdraw their application for a care order[4] and to whether to grant a stay of order.[5]

1 *Humberside County Council v B* [1993] 1 FLR 257, per Booth J, cited with approval in *F v Leeds City Council* [1994] 2 FLR 60, CA. See also *Re T (A Minor) (Care Order: Conditions)* [1994] 2 FLR 423 at 429, CA, per Nourse LJ. The welfare stage of care proceedings is discussed at paras 8.81 et seq. Note also *Re D (Simultaneous Applications for Care Order and Freeing Order)* [1999] 2 FLR 49, CA, in which it was held that by hearing the freeing for adoption application first, in which the child's welfare was (pursuant to the Adoption Act 1976, s 6) the first consideration, the judge had compromised the application of the paramountcy principle in his subsequent consideration of the care order application.
2 See eg *Re T and E (Proceedings: Conflicting Interests)* [1995] 1 FLR 581.
3 *Re T (minors) (termination of contact: discharge of order)* [1997] 1 All ER 65, [1997] 1 WLR 393, CA and *Re B (Minors) (Termination of Contact: Paramount Consideration)* [1993] Fam 301, [1993] 3 All ER 524, CA.
4 *Southwark London Borough v B* [1993] 2 FLR 559, CA.
5 *Re M (application for stay of order)* [1996] 3 FCR 185, CA.

2.12 Although there is some authority for saying that the paramountcy principle applies to considering whether to make s 91(14) orders,[1] the matter is not free from doubt as there is also authority for saying that the paramountcy principle does not apply to s 91(15) and (17) applications,[2] which is in line with the ruling that it does not apply to deciding whether to give leave to a non-parent to make a s 8 order application[3]. Whether a sensible distinction can be made between imposing a leave requirement to make an application and granting leave may be doubted since in each case the issue is essentially the same, namely, having to weigh in the balance restricting freedom of access to the court and protecting the child. Accordingly, the better view seems to be that in none of these cases is the child's welfare paramount in the sense that it is the exclusive and automatic overriding concern[4] but rather to recognise, as Wilson J suggested when sitting in the Court of Appeal in *Re R (Residence: Contact: Restricting Applications)*,[5] that 'in the discretionary exercise under s 91(14) the best interests of the child must be weighed fully against the fundamental freedom of access to the courts without even an initial screening process.'

1 *Re P (A Minor) (Residence Order: Child's Welfare)* [2000] Fam 15 at 37, sub nom *Re P (a minor) (residence order: restriction order)* [1999] 3 All ER 734 at 752, CA, per Butler-Sloss LJ. S 91(14) orders are discussed at paras 5.154 et seq.
2 At any rate this seemed to be the implication of Simon Brown LJ's comment in *Re T (minors) (termination of contact: discharge of order)* [1997] 1 All ER 65 at 74, [1997] 1 WLR 393 at 402, that the court should consider a s 34(9) application for the discharge of a s 34(4) order 'with the child's welfare in mind as the paramount consideration – *save only in the limited circumstances provided for by s 91(7) when the court's leave is required*'. (Emphasis added). See also *F v Kent County Council and Others* [1993] 1 FLR 432, per Sir Stephen Brown P.
3 See *Re A (Minors) (Residence Orders: Leave to Apply)* [1992] Fam 182, [1992] 3 All ER 872, discussed at paras 2.17 and 2.25.

4 Though note such an interpretation is not in any event 'Human Rights Compliant', see para 2.5.
5 [1998] 1 FLR 749 at 757 applying Waite LJ's approach in *B v B (Residence Order: Restricting Applications)* [1997] 1 FLR 139, 146 namely that the courts should have s 1(1) in mind in applying s 91(14) and consider 'whether the best interests of the child require interference with the fundamental freedom of a parent to raise issues affecting the child's welfare before the court as and when such issues arise.'

5. When the principle does not apply

2.13 The paramountcy principle is not of unlimited application. It does not directly apply outside the context of court litigation and even where an issue is before a court it will only apply provided the child's upbringing or the administration of his property is directly in question and even then only if the principle has not been expressly or impliedly excluded either by the CA 1989 itself or by some other statute.

(a) *Paramountcy principle does not apply outside the context of litigation*

2.14 The paramountcy principle only applies, if at all, in the course of litigation. Unlike Art 3(1) of the UN Convention[1] it has no direct application to institutions, administrative authorities or legislative bodies. Furthermore it does not apply to parents or other individuals with respect to their day to day or even long-term decisions affecting the child. As one commentator has put it:[2]

'It can hardly be argued that parents, in taking family decisions affecting a child, are bound to ignore completely their own interests, the interests of other members of the family and, possibly, outsiders. This would be a wholly undesirable, as well as an unrealistic objective.'

Accordingly, parents are not bound to consider their children's welfare in deciding whether to make a career move, to move house or whether to separate or divorce.[3]

1 Set out in para 2.6.
2 Bainham: *Children: The Modern Law*, (2nd edn), p 38.
3 Cf Dickens: 'The Modern Function and Limits of Parental Rights' 97 LQR 462, 471, who asserts, correctly it is submitted, that parental responsibility is not to do positive good, but to avoid harm.

2.15 The paramountcy principle does not govern the application of Pt III of the CA 1989.[1] As Butler-Sloss LJ said in *Re M (Secure Accommodation Order)*:[2]

'The framework of Pt III of the Act is structured to cast upon the local authority duties and responsibilities for children in its area and being looked after. The general duty of a local authority to safeguard and promote the child's welfare[3] is not the same as that imposed upon the court in s 1(1) placing welfare as the paramount consideration.'

In Butler-Sloss LJ's view[4] 's 1 was not designed to be applied to Pt III of the Act'. Accordingly, in deciding, pursuant to s 17(1), what level of services to provide for children in need in their area, local authorities are not obliged to treat the welfare of individual children as their paramount consideration,[5] nor similarly, when deciding pursuant to s 22, on how best to discharge their duties in relation to children looked after by them[6] though in this latter instance the welfare of the child will remain an important consideration.[7]

1   Pt III is fully discussed in ch 6.
2   [1995] Fam 108 at 115, [1995] 3 All ER 407 at 412, CA, discussed further at para 9.26.
3   Ie pursuant to ss 17(1) and 22(3).
4   [1995] Fam 108 at 116, [1995] 3 All ER 407 at 413, expressly disagreeing with comments to the contrary in Vols 1 and 4 of the Department of Health's Guidance and Regulations on the CA 1989.
5   Indeed, s 17 is so phrased so as to avoid the duty being applied to individual children at all, see further para 6.4.
6   Indeed s 22(6) expressly states that the need to protect members of the public from serious injury overrides any duty even to promote and safeguard the interests of any individual child let alone treating that child's welfare as the paramount consideration.
7   Per Charles J in *Re P (Children Act 1989, ss 22 and 26: Local Authority Compliance)* [2000] 2 FLR 910 at 923.

(b)   Paramountcy principles do not apply unless child's upbringing etc is directly in issue

2.16   Even if an application relating to a child is before a court, that child's welfare will only be the paramount consideration provided the issue falls squarely within the terms of s 1(1), that is, it must directly concern the child's upbringing[1] or the administration of his property.

1   *Note*: s 105 excludes 'maintenance' from the definition of 'upbringing', see further para 2.24.

2.17   Pre-Children Act case law established that the paramountcy principle did not apply to applications that only indirectly concerned a child's upbringing and it is clear that the same approach applies to s 1(1) of the CA 1989. It was on the basis that it was held in *R (P) v Home Secretary*[1] that the paramountcy principle had no application to the lawfulness of prison policy to separate children once they reached 18 months from their imprisoned mothers and partly on this basis, that it was held in *Re A (Minors) (Residence Orders: Leave to Apply)*[2] that s 1(1) does not apply when determining whether to grant adults[3] leave to apply for a s 8 order, since, in Balcombe LJ's words:

'in granting or refusing an application for leave to apply for a s 8 order, the court is not determining a question with respect to the upbringing of the child concerned. That question only arises when the court hears the substantive application.'

Similarly, in *Re H (A Minor) (Blood Tests: Parental Rights)*[4] it was held that the child's welfare is not the paramount consideration when determining whether to give directions for what is now scientific testing (formerly blood testing)[5] in paternity cases.

1   *Regina (P) v Secretary of State for the Home Department and another, Regina (Q and Another) v Secretary of State for the Home Department and another* [2001] EWCA Civ 1151, [2001] 1 WLR 2002. See in particular para [89] per Lord Philips MR.
2   [1992] Fam 182 at 191G–H, [1992] 3 All ER 872 at 878 a–b.
3   For the position of children seeking leave see paras 5.115 et seq.
4   [1997] Fam 89, [1996] 4 All ER 28, CA, applying the earlier ruling in *S v S, W v Official Solicitor* [1972] AC 24, [1970] 3 All ER 107, HL. Note, however, that following the amendment of the Family Law Reform Act 1969 by the Child Support, Pensions and Social Security Act 2000, s 21(3) (b) now provides that in the absence of the consent of the person having care and control of a child under the age of 16, a bodily sample may nevertheless be taken from the child

'if the court considers that it would be *in his best interests* for the sample to be taken' [Emphasis added] for the application of which see *Re T (a child) (DNA tests: paternity)* [2001] 3 FCR 577, sub nom *Re T (Paternity: Ordering Blood Tests)* [2001] 2 FLR 1190, and *Re H and A (Children)* [2002] EWCA Civ 383, CA.
5 The power to make directions for the use of scientific tests rather than blood tests to determine paternity came into effect on 1 April 2001 when the amendment of s 20 of the Family Law Reform Act 1969 by s 23 of the Family Law Reform Act 1987 was implemented by the FLRA 1987 (Commencement No 3) Order 2001 (SI 2001/777).

2.18 Other cases in which it has been held that the paramountcy principle does not apply are:

- determining whether an unmarried father should be served with notice of care proceedings;[1]
- resolving a mother's application that the father cease to be a party to the discharge of care proceedings;[2]
- considering whether a parent be committed to prison for a flagrant breach of a court order concerning a child;[3]
- determining whether to issue a witness summons against a child;[4]
- deciding whether to make directions for interim assessments under s 38(6);[5]
- in resolving a dispute between a birth mother and an adoptive mother over the disposal of their deceased child's remains, the deceased's daughter's interests were not paramount;[6]
- preventing publication of a book alleged to be harmful to a ward of court;[7] and
- determining whether to grant permission to use evidence previously admitted in wardship proceedings in subsequent criminal proceedings.[8]

1 *Re X (Care: Notice of Proceedings)* [1996] 1 FLR 186, per Stuart-White J.
2 *Re W (Discharge of Party to Proceedings)* [1997] 1 FLR 128, per Hogg J.
3 *A v N (Committal: Refusal of Contact)* [1997] 1 FLR 533, CA.
4 *Re P (Witness Summons)* [1997] 2 FLR 447, CA on the basis, per Wilson J, 'that the question of whether to issue a witness summons against a child is not a question with respect to her or his upbringing [so] that s 1(1) does not apply . . .' See also *R v Highbury Corner Magistrates' Court, ex p Deering* [1997] 1 FLR 683, DC, per Schiemann LJ and the cases there cited.
5 Per Holman J in *Re M (Residential Assessment Directions)* [1998] 2 FLR 371 at 381–382 and per Charles J in *Re P (Children Act 1989, ss 22 and 26: Local Authority Compliance)* [2000] 2 FLR 910 at 923.
6 Per Hale J in *Buchanan v Milton* [1999] 2 FLR 844 at 857.
7 *Re X (A Minor) (Wardship: Jurisdiction)* [1975] Fam 47, [1975] 1 All ER 697, CA.
8 *Re S (Minors) (Wardship: Police Investigation)* [1987] Fam 199, [1987] 3 All ER 1076.

2.19 It can be a matter of fine judgment as to what matters directly concern a child's upbringing and what do not. There are two areas in particular in which the application of the paramountcy principle is problematic, namely, with regard to publicity and to procedural issues.

(I) PUBLICITY

2.20 In *R v Central Independent Television plc*[1] it was held that if the allegedly harmful publication does not relate to the care and upbringing of children over whose welfare the court is exercising a supervisory role then not only is the child's welfare not paramount it is not relevant at all. Even where publicity does directly concern the child and interferes with the court's supervisory jurisdiction, the child's welfare has not generally been held to be paramount but must instead be weighed in the balance with freedom of the press.[2]

Although this latter view was repeated by the majority in *Re W (wardship: discharge: publicity)*,[3] a different line was taken in *Re Z (A Minor) (Identification: Restrictions on Publication)*.[4] In that case, having held that a mother's waiver of the child's right of confidentiality concerning her treatment at a unit specialising in treating special educational needs was an aspect of parental responsibility, the court ruled that determining whether to make an order prohibiting publicity was governed by the paramountcy principle.[5] Ward LJ distinguished previous cases on the basis that the case before him uniquely involved a parent who wished to exercise her parental responsibility by wanting her child 'to perform for the making of the film' about her treatment.

1   [1994] Fam 192, [1994] 3 All ER 641. See also *Re R (Wardship: Restrictions on Publication)* [1994] Fam 254, [1994] 3 All ER 658, CA and, more recently, the detailed analysis in *Kelly v BBC* [2001] Fam 59, [2001] 2 WLR 253, [2001] 1 All ER 323, per Munby J (on which see Woods [2001] CFLQ 209) and *Medway Council v BBC* [2002] 1 FLR 104, per Wilson J.

2   *Re H-S (minors) (protection of identity)* [1994] 3 All ER 390, [1994] 1 WLR 1141, sub nom *Re H (Minors) (Injunction: Public Interest)* [1994] 1 FLR 519, CA.

3   [1996] 1 FCR 393, [1995] 2 FLR 466, CA. See also *Oxfordshire County Council v L and F* [1997] 1 FLR 235, per Stuart-White J.

4   [1997] Fam 1, sub nom *Re Z (a minor) (freedom of publication)* [1995] 4 All ER 961, CA.

5   But note Wilson J's query in *Medway v BBC*, supra at para [29], whether, bearing in mind Art 10 of the European Convention on Human Rights, a child's welfare should override freedom of expression even if the paramountcy principle is otherwise applicable.

(II)   PROCEDURAL ISSUES

2.21   Although, on one view it may be said that the paramountcy principle can also apply to procedural issues,[1] an alternative analysis[2] is that in certain instances the courts, motivated by their concern to protect children generally, will not rigidly apply all procedural rules designed to produce overall justice to parties to litigation but will nevertheless only refrain from applying them in a particular case where they are satisfied that to do so would be harmful to the individual child concerned. Such an analysis can be justified upon the basis that issues such as disclosure only indirectly concern the child's welfare and is arguably supported by the majority's reasoning in *Re L (A Minor) (Police Investigation: Privilege)*[3] in which leave was given to the police to see a medical report written by an expert engaged by the mother in the course of care proceedings.

1   It is certainly arguable that, in deciding that a parent did not have a right to see the Official Solicitor's report compiled in connection with an application to look after the child, and that the court had the power to withhold it from the parties, the House of Lords in *Official Solicitor v K* [1965] AC 201, [1963] 3 All ER 191 was applying the paramountcy principle. The headnote, for example, at [1965] AC 202, states 'that the paramount consideration of the Chancery Division in exercising its jurisdiction over wards of court was the welfare of the infants'. The headnote to the All England report is in similar terms: see [1963] 3 All ER 191.

2   See Lowe 'The House of Lords and the welfare principle' in *Family Law Towards the Millennium Essays for PM Bromley* (ed Caroline Bridge, 1997, Butterworths) ch 4, and Lowe and Douglas *Bromley's Family Law* (9th edn, 1998, Butterworths) 329–331.

3   [1997] AC 16, [1996] 2 All ER 78, HL. It may be noted that at first instance Bracewell J, whose judgment was upheld by the House of Lords, expressly said (see [1995] 1 FLR 999 at 1007]) 'The application before me does not relate to the upbringing of the child and, therefore, is not governed by s 1 of the Children Act 1989'. See also *Re D (Minors) (Adoption Reports: Confidentiality)* [1996] AC 593, [1995] 4 All ER 385, HL, which establishes that non-disclosure of reports should be ordered only when the case for doing so is compelling.

2.22 It is implicit in *Re L*[1] that not all procedural rules can be changed even to protect children – so for example, legal professional privilege attaching to solicitor-client communications is absolute[2]. The same is true for the rules of appeal, as was established in *G v G*,[3] in which the House of Lords rejected the argument based on the paramountcy principle that special rules of appeal apply in custody cases. Put in theoretical terms, the issue of when an appellate court should intervene does not directly concern a child's upbringing and hence the paramountcy principle does not apply. Furthermore, as the normal rules of appeal do not inhibit the courts from performing their proper role of safeguarding the child's interests, there is no need to provide special rules.

1 *Re L (A Minor) (Police Investigation: Privilege)* [1997] AC 16, [1996] 2 All ER 78, HL, discussed further in ch 11.
2 Following the House of Lords' ruling in *R v Derby Magistrates' Court, ex p B* [1996] AC 487, [1995] 4 All ER 526.
3 [1985] 2 All ER 225, HL.

(III) OTHER AREAS OF UNCERTAINTY

2.23 There is uncertainty as to whether the paramountcy principle applies to the question of whether to give leave to interview children involved in court proceedings with a view to preparing an adult's defence in criminal proceedings;[1] to the determination of forum conveniens[2] and, in the case of non-Convention abductions, to the application of the principle of comity.[3]

1 *Re F (Specific Issue: Child Interview)* [1995] 1 FLR 819, CA, in which Waite LJ was prepared to assume in that case that s 1(1) of the CA 1989 did apply and *Re M (Care: Leave to Interview Child)* [1995] 1 FLR 825, in which Hale J held that the child's welfare was not the overriding consideration. But in the light of the case law on the issue of witness summons, it is submitted that the child's welfare is *not* the paramount consideration.
2 Thorpe J in *Re S (Residence Order: Forum Conveniens)* [1995] 1 FLR 314 at 325 who thought s 1(1) did not apply and Waite J in *Hallam v Hallam* [1992] 2 FCR 197, sub nom *H v H (Minors) (Forum Conveniens) (Nos 1 and 2)* [1993] FLR 958, who thought it did apply. See also *H v H (A minor) (no 2) (forum conveniens)* [1997] 1 FCR 603, per Bracewell J.
3 *Re M (Abduction: Non-Convention Country)* [1985] 1 FLR 89, CA and *Re M (Minors) (Abduction: Peremptory Return Order)* [1996] 1 FLR 478, CA which held that it can be assumed that in the absence of evidence to the contrary the foreign court in question will apply principles acceptable to an English court, and *Re J A (Child Abduction – Non-Convention Country)* [1998] 1 FLR 231, [1998] 2 FCR 159, CA which held that because the child's welfare is paramount no assumption about the foreign law can be made so that evidence will be required in every case before a return order can be considered.

(c) Paramountcy principle does not apply if excluded by other statutory provisions

2.24 Even if the child's upbringing is directly in issue, the paramountcy principle might not always apply. It will not if statute expressly provides an alternative test or expressly excludes its operation. Adoption applications, for example, directly concern the child's upbringing, but in deciding these matters[1] the court is expressly bound by s 6 of the Adoption Act 1976 to treat the child's welfare as its first (but not paramount) consideration.[2] The child's welfare is similarly expressed to be the first consideration in proceedings relating to the adjustment of property and financial matters on divorce.[3] Section 105(1) of the CA 1989 expressly excludes maintenance from the definition of child's upbringing and so disapplies the paramountcy principle not just to maintenance applications but also to any other application for financial provision (ie a lump sum or property order) for a child under Sch 1 to the CA 1989. In this latter regard Sir Stephen Brown P observed in *K v H (Child Maintenance)*,[4] that the provisions of Sch 1 deal comprehensively with financial provision for children[5] and should not be confused with applications relating to upbringing or the administration of the child's own property to which s 1(1) does apply.

1 Aliter if, in those proceedings the court is considering whether to make a s 8 order.
2 *Re B (adoption: child's welfare)* [1995] 2 FCR 749, [1995] 1 FLR 895. But note this weighting will be changed to the paramountcy test by the Adoption and Children Bill 2002.
3 MCA 1973, s 25(1), see *N v N (consent orders: variation)* [1994] 2 FCR 275, [1994] 2 FLR 868, CA and *Suter v Suter and Jones* [1987] Fam 111, [1987] 2 All ER 336, CA.
4 [1993] 2 FLR 61 at 64. See also *B v B (Transfer of Tenancy)* [1994] Fam Law 250 (Salisbury County Court), on which see Douglas [1994] Fam Law at 251.
5 For a discussion of these powers see *Clarke Hall and Morrison*, 4[31] et seq.

2.25 Statute can impliedly exclude the application of s 1(1). It is established, for example, that the paramountcy principle is inconsistent with the duties of a local authority under s 25(1)(b)[1] and therefore has no application to the question of making secure accommodation orders.[2] Similarly, the criteria set out in s 10(9) for determining whether to grant adults leave to apply for s 8 orders have been held to be inconsistent with the application of the paramountcy principle.[3] Most importantly, although in general terms the paramountcy principle applies to proceedings under Pts IV and V of the CA 1989, it will only come into play provided the applicant can satisfy the court that the preconditions for a care order or for an emergency protection order have been made out.[4] It has also been said that the question of whether the future of children should be decided in one part of the UK rather than another is determined by statute and that their welfare is not the paramount consideration in reaching that decision.[5]

1 Viz 'that if he is kept in any other description of accommodation he is likely to injure himself or other persons'. See further para 9.10.
2 *Re M (A Minor) (Secure Accommodation Order)* [1995] Fam 108, [1995] 3 All ER 407, CA, discussed at para 9.25.
3 *Re A (Minors) (Residence Orders: Leave to Apply)* [1992] Fam 182, [1992] 3 All ER 972, CA.
4 See eg *Humberside County Council v B* [1993] 1 FLR 257 and *F v Leeds City Council* [1994] 2 FLR 60, CA, discussed further at paras 8.81-8.82.
5 Per Millett LJ in *M v M (Abduction: England and Wales)* [1997] 2 FLR 263 at 275 F, applying the Domicile and Matrimonial Proceedings Act 1973, Sch 1, para 8(1), which provides for mandatory stays if matrimonial proceedings have been instituted in a related jurisdiction in which the parties were habitually resident for one year when they last lived together. Cf para 9 which gives the court a discretion to stay if the parties were not so habitually resident.

2.26 In other cases it is the whole scheme of the legislation rather than a specific provision that impliedly excludes the paramountcy principle. The courts have refused, for example, to apply the paramountcy principle to interfere with discretionary powers clearly vested by Parliament in another body or court. Accordingly, the principle cannot be invoked to interfere with the discretionary powers vouchsafed to local authorities to look after and manage children in their care,[1] nor to interfere with the discretionary power vested in the immigration service.[2] It is clear that the child's welfare is not the paramount consideration when determining applications under the Hague Convention on the Civil Aspects of International Child Abduction 1980.[3] The paramountcy principle has also been held to be ousted by a successful claim to diplomatic immunity under the terms of the Diplomatic Privileges Act 1964.[4]

1   *A v Liverpool City Council* [1982] AC 363, [1981] 2 All ER 385, HL which remains good law. See also *Re B (Minors) (Termination of Contact: Paramount Consideration)* [1993] Fam 301 at 309, [1993] 3 All ER 524 at 529–530, per Butler-Sloss LJ.
2   *Re Mohamed Arif (an Infant)* [1968] Ch 643, [1968] 2 All ER 145, CA. It was held in *R v Secretary of State for the Home Department, ex p Gangadeen, R v Secretary of State for the Home Department, ex p Khan* [1998] 1 FLR 762, [1998] 2 FCR 96, CA that treating the child's welfare as an important but not paramount consideration is not contrary to art 8 of the European Convention on Human Rights, having regard to such decisions as *Abdulaziz v UK* (1985) 7 EHRR 471. Note also *R v Secretary of State for the Home Department, ex p Teame* [1994] 3 FCR 132, 1 [1995] 1 FLR 293, CA – residence order does not prevent deportation.
3   See eg *Re M (A Minor) (Child Abduction)* [1994] 1 FLR 390 at 392, CA, per Butler-Sloss LJ. A similar position applies to the European or Luxembourg Convention on the Recognition and Enforcement of Custody 1980. Both these Conventions are discussed in *Clarke Hall and Morrison*, Division 2.
4   See *Re P (children act: diplomatic immunity)* [1998] 2 FCR 480, [1998] 1 FLR 624.

6.   Balancing the welfare of more than one child

2.27   One of the inherent difficulties in applying the paramountcy principle is with respect to cases involving two or more children with conflicting interests. This issue can arise either where the applicant is a child or where the application concerns siblings.

(a)   Child-parents and babies

2.28   In *Birmingham City Council v H (a Minor)*[1] in which a 15-year-old mother sought contact with her baby[2] the question was raised as to whose welfare was paramount, the baby's or the mother's. At first instance Connell J held that the baby's welfare took priority over the mother's. The Court of Appeal disagreed. Taking the view that the question of contact with the baby related to the upbringing of the mother and that the question of contact with the mother related to the upbringing of the baby, they held that while the welfare of both taken together should be considered as paramount to the interests of any adults concerned in their lives, as between themselves the court should approach the question of their welfare without giving one priority over the other.

1   [1994] 2 AC 212, [1994] 1 All ER 12, HL.
2   Both mother and baby had been made the subjects of interim care orders.

2.29   The House of Lords rejected the Court of Appeal's reasoning and allowed the baby's appeal. Confining their observations to the application of s 34 in general and of s 34(4) in particular,[1] their Lordships ruled that it is the child in respect of whom the application is being made (ie the baby) whose interests are paramount. In reaching this decision their Lordships expressly left open the more general question[2] 'as to whether an application by a parent who is a child for contact with its own child could be a question with respect to the 'upbringing' of the child who is a parent or whether that question related only to the child's position as a parent and not to its 'upbringing'.' It is submitted that that approach would have provided a simpler test and would have been in line with the jurisprudence just discussed of confining the paramountcy principle to issues *directly* concerning the child's upbringing.

1   Section 34, which deals with the specific question of contact with a child in care, is discussed at paras 8.145 et seq. The narrowness of the House of Lords' approach has not escaped criticism, see Douglas: 'In Whose Best Interests?' (1994) 110 LQR 379.
2   [1994] 2 AC 212 at 223, [1994] 1 All ER 12 at 19, per Lord Slynn.

2.30 *Birmingham* was followed in *F v Leeds City Council*[1] which concerned a care order application in respect of a baby removed from a 17-year-old mother within hours of the birth. The mother appealed against the making of a care order arguing that the baby's welfare alone should not have been taken into account as the paramount consideration, since she herself was a child whose upbringing was in question. Rejecting her appeal, it was held that following the *Birmingham* decision the correct approach in determining whether the baby's welfare or that of the child-parent was paramount, was to identify which child was the subject of the application, and which child it was whose welfare was directly involved.[2] In the case before them the answer was clear since it was the baby and not the child's mother with respect to whom the application was being made and who was thus the subject of the application and the only child to be named in the order. It therefore followed that no question relating to the mother's upbringing arose and hence the court was not required by s 1(1) to treat the child-mother's welfare as the paramount consideration.

1   [1994] 2 FLR 60, CA.
2   [1994] 2 FLR 60 at 63, per Ward J.

(b)   Balancing the interests of siblings

2.31   The position where siblings are involved is complicated. In some instances the relative weighting of their respective welfare interests may simply be determined by the form of the litigation. In *Re F (Contact: Child in Care)*[1], where a child in care wanted contact with his four siblings who were not in care, Wilson J observed that where an application was properly made under s 34 of the CA 1989 (viz where the parents or siblings were content to have contact but which was opposed by the local authority) the welfare of the child in care would be the paramount consideration, since that child would be the 'named person'. On the other hand, if that child applied for a s 8 order with his siblings, it would be the latter's welfare that would be paramount since the siblings would be the 'named persons'. Another example is *Re T and E (proceedings: conflicting interests)*[2] in which it was held that the interests of a child who was the subject of an application to revoke a care order prevailed over the interests of her half-sister who in the same proceedings was the subject of an application to free for adoption, since it was only with regard to the former application that the paramountcy test applied.[3]

1   [1995] 1 FLR 510.
2   [1995] 3 FCR 260, [1995] 1 FLR 581. See also *Re S (Contact: Application by Sibling)* [1998] 2 FLR 897 at 908, per Charles J.
3   As noted in para 2.24 above, in adoption proceedings (including freeing for adoption) applications, the child's welfare is pursuant to s 6 of the Adoption Act 1976, only the first consideration. Note also *Re D (Simultaneous Applications for Care Order and Freeing Order)* [1999] 2 FLR 49, CA, referred to at para 2.11, n 1, above.

2.32   Where each child is the 'subject' of the same proceedings their welfare should be equally weighted which theoretically means that *each* child's welfare should be the court's paramount consideration. In practice, however, where the siblings' interests conflict, it may be impossible to accord paramountcy to each child. In such cases the approach applied in both the *Birmingham* and *Leeds* decisions is of no help and instead one is driven to the approach applied by the Court of Appeal in the *Birmingham* case, namely, to balance the children's interests and find a preponderance in favour of one or the other.[1] A similar approach also seems inevitable in resolving applications concerning sibling children where their interests conflict. This was Wall J's view in *Re T and E (proceedings: conflicting interests)* in which he commented, obiter:

> '. . .where a number of children are all the subject of an application or cross-application to the court in the same set of proceedings, and where it is impossible to achieve what was in the paramount interests of each child, the balancing exercise described in the Court of Appeal [in the *Birmingham* case] has to be undertaken and the situation of least detriment to all the children achieved.'

This approach has now been authoritatively endorsed by the Court of Appeal in *Re A (Children) (Conjoined Twins: Surgical Separation)*.[2]

1   [1995] 1 FLR 581 at 587.
2   [2001] Fam 147, [2000] 4 All ER 961.

2.33   *Re A* concerned the issue of whether conjoined twins should be separated when to do so would preserve the life of the one (Jodie) but inevitably kill the other (Mary). In reaching the decision to sanction the operation Ward LJ, applying the Court of Appeal approach taken in the *Birmingham* case, said:[1]

> 'If the duty of the court is to make a decision which puts Jodie's interests paramount and that decision would be contrary to the paramount interests of Mary, then, for my part, I do not see how the court can reconcile the impossibility of properly fulfilling each duty by simply declining to decide the very matter before it. That would be a total abdication of the duty which is imposed upon us. Given the conflict of duty, I can see no other way of dealing with it than by choosing the lesser of the two evils and so finding the least detrimental alternative. A balance has to be struck somehow and I cannot flinch from undertaking that evaluation, horrendously difficult though it is.'

A less dramatic example of the balancing approach is the pre-1989 decision in *Clarke-Hunt v Newcombe*[2] in which the Court of Appeal, having commented that there was not really a right solution but which of two 'bad solutions was the least dangerous' to the children's long term interests, upheld a decision not to separate two brothers but to place them together with their mother even though it was against the elder boy's wishes and possibly slightly detrimental to his interests.

1   [2001] Fam 147 at 192, [2000] 4 All ER 961 at 1006.
2   (1982) 4 FLR 482, CA.

7.   The meaning of welfare

2.34   The term 'welfare' as such is not defined in the CA 1989 but a good explanation of what the court is looking for was given in a New Zealand case by Hardie Boys J who said:[1]

> '"Welfare" is an all encompassing word. It includes material welfare, both in the sense of adequacy of resources to provide a pleasant home and a comfortable standard of living and in the sense of adequacy of care to ensure that good health and due personal pride are maintained. However, while material considerations have their place they are secondary matters. More important are the stability and the security, the loving and understanding care and guidance, the warm and compassionate relationships, that are essential for the full development of the child's own character, personality and talents.'

1   In *Walker v Walker and Harrison*, noted in [1981] NZ Recent Law 257 and cited by the Law Commission in its Working Paper No 96, Custody (1985), para 6.10. Note also Butler-Sloss P's comment in *Re A (medical treatment: male sterilisation)* [2001] 1 FCR 193 at 200, [2001] 1 FLR 549 at 555, CA that 'best interests encompasses medical, emotional and all other welfare issues', referred to by Ward LJ in *Re A (Children) (Conjoined Twins: Surgical Separation)* [2001] Fam 147 at 180, [2000] 4 All ER 961 at 994.

2.35   Ideally, the court should be concerned to promote the child's long-term future.[1] However, while there are cases where the court has clearly anticipated future contingencies such as parental acquisition of employment and remarriage,[2] or where regard has been had to furthering the child's education and general prospects,[3] inevitably the court will tend to concentrate on the immediate ties and environment of the child.

1   Unless perhaps where the short-term disadvantages are so overwhelming as to rule out the long-term option: see eg *Thompson v Thompson* (1986) 150 JP 625, [1987] Fam Law 89, CA.
2   See respectively, *Re DW (A Minor) (Custody)* [1984] Fam Law 17, CA and *S (BD) v S (DJ)* [1977] Fam 109, [1977] 1 All 65, CA.
3   See *May v May* [1986] 1 FLR 325, CA (order made in favour of father who was more academic than the mother) and cf *Re DW (A Minor) (Custody)* [1984] Fam Law 17, CA and *Re O (infants)* [1962] 2 All ER 10, CA (boy's long-term future better in Sudan, girls' in England).

2.36   Although the CA 1989 does not define 'welfare' it introduced a checklist of relevant factors to which in certain circumstances[1] the court must have regard when deciding what, if any, order to make. Such a checklist had been recommended by the Law Commission[2] both 'as a means of providing a greater consistency and clarity in the law' and 'as a major step towards a more systematic approach to decisions concerning children'. The advantage of the list is that it enables everyone from the judge to the litigant, the advocate to the CAFCASS officer, to focus on the same issues at the same time.

1   See para 2.39 below.
2   Law Com No 172, paras 3.17 et seq.

8.   The checklist

2.37   The checklist, which is contained in s 1(3), is as follows:
'(a) the ascertainable wishes and feelings of the child concerned (considered in the light of his age and understanding);
(b) his physical, emotional and educational needs;
(c) the likely effect on him of any change in his circumstances;
(d) his age, sex, background and any characteristics of his which the court considers relevant;
(e) any harm which he has suffered or is at risk of suffering;
(f) how capable each of his parents, and any other person in relation to whom the court considers the question to be relevant, is of meeting his needs; and
(g) the range of powers available to the court under this Act in the proceedings in question'.

This checklist is not exhaustive and indeed might properly be regarded as the minimum that will be considered by the court.[1] It is always open to the court to specify other matters which it would like to see included in a welfare report.[2]

1   In *Re R (a minor) (residence order: finance)* [1995] 3 FCR 334, [1995] 2 FLR 612, it was held that it was quite proper to take into account financial considerations.
2   Viz under s 7, see post paras 10.11 et seq. See also Law Com No 172, paras 3.18 and 3.21.

2.38 The content of the checklist follows that recommended by the Law Commission, save for that under s 1(3) (g), the purpose of which is to emphasise the court's duty to consider not only whether the order being sought is the best for the child but also to consider the alternatives that the Act makes available.[1] This duty also reflects the general policy of vesting in the courts at all levels greater responsibility for the management and conduct of children cases.

1 It will be noted that under s 10(1)(b), discussed at para 5.107, courts are empowered to make s 8 orders on their own motion.

(a) When the checklist applies

2.39 Section 1(4) directs the courts to have regard to the checklist in contested s 8 applications[1] and all proceedings under Pt IV of the CA 1989 (ie in all care and supervision applications).[2] There is, however, nothing to prevent the courts from considering the checklist in other applications if they so choose and indeed particularly in contested applications under ss 4, 5 and 13[3] it would seem prudent to do so. In *Re B (Change of Surname)*[4] Wilson J commented that, notwithstanding that he did not have to apply the checklist to determine an application for leave to change a child's surname, the list remained 'a most useful aide memoire of the factors that may impinge on the child's welfare.' In *Payne v Payne*,[5] in which an application for leave to remove a child from the jurisdiction was made under s 13, Thorpe LJ went further commenting 'Although technically an application brought under s 13(1) is not subject to the welfare checklist, it has been held that the trial judge should nevertheless take the precaution of regarding the checklist factors when carrying out his welfare appraisal'.

1 Restricting the application of the checklist to contested cases follows the recommendation of the Law Commission (see Law Com No. 172, para 3.19) who felt that if s 1(3) applied to all cases the court might have felt compelled to investigate even those cases where there was no choice as to where and with whom the child should live. In their view such an investigation would not only have been a waste of resources but also an unwarranted intrusion into family autonomy.
2 For discussion of the practice where it is mandatory to apply the checklist see para 4.60.
3 Discussed respectively at paras 3.55 et seq, 3.100 et seq and 5.27 et seq.
4 [1996] 2 FCR 304 at 306, [1996] 1 FLR 791 at 793, CA. But whether he was right to consider applications for leave to change names were properly made under s 13 rather than s 8 has been questioned by Hale J in *Re M (leave to remove child from jurisdiction)* [1999] 3 FCR 708 at 715, [1999] 2 FLR 334 at 340, discussed at para 5.38.
5 [2001] EWCA Civ 166, para [30], [2001] 1 FCR 425, [2001] 1 FLR 1052, CA.

2.40 Although s 1(3) specifically directs *the court* to have regard to the checklist, it will clearly be useful to legal advisers and their clients both in preparing and in arguing their case. The Law Commission envisaged[1] that the list would enable parties to prepare relevant evidence and, by focussing clients' minds on the real issues, might help to promote settlements. In this sense the list is perhaps best regarded as being applicable in the context of litigation rather than as being confined to actual court proceedings In any event, as Holman J pointed out in *Re K (care proceedings: joinder of father)*[2] the Rules[3] require the now named children's guardians[4] to have regard to the checklist when carrying out their duties.

1 Law Com No 172, para 3.18.
2 [1999] 2 FCR 391 at 398, sub nom *Re B (Care Proceedings: Notification of Father Without Parental Authority)* [1999] 2 FLR 408 at 415.

3   Viz FPR 1991, r 4.11(1), FP (Children Act 1989) R 1991, r 11(1).
4   Formerly known as guardians ad litem.

(b)   Applying the checklist

(I)   THE ASCERTAINABLE WISHES AND FEELINGS OF THE CHILD CONCERNED CONSIDERED IN THE LIGHT OF HIS AGE AND UNDERSTANDING

2.41   Although reflecting pre-CA 1989 practice,[1] s 1(3)(a) provides the first statutory enjoinder on the courts to consider the child's own views in the private law context other than in adoption.[2] Such an enjoinder was long overdue[3] and, in any event, is now reflective of an international obligation pursuant to Art 12(1) of the UN Convention of the Rights of the Child 1989 which provides:

'States Parties shall assure to the child who is capable of forming his or her own views the right to express those views freely in all matters affecting the child, the views of the child being given full weight in accordance with the age and maturity of the child.'

By referring to the child's 'wishes and feelings' s 1(3)(a) is wider than art 12, which is confined to 'views'. Very young children can have discernible 'feelings' even if they cannot yet express their 'views'.

1   See *Re P (A Minor) (Education)* [1992] 1 FLR 316 at 321, CA, per Butler Sloss LJ
2   See s 6 of the Adoption Act 1976.
3   Though whether it should have been part of the checklist can be debated. It could be argued that such wishes are independent of their welfare. Moreover, having a separate requirement to listen to children would have given greater recognition to children being treated as individuals in their own right. For the importance of listening to children and the impact of the CA 1989 in this respect see *The Children Act Now – Messages from Research* (Department of Health 2001), ch 5.

2.42   Despite being placed first in the welfare checklist, the child's view is not expressed to be determinative.[1] As Butler-Sloss LJ put it in *Re P (minors) (wardship: care and control)*:[2]

'How far the wishes of children should be a determinative factor in their future placement must of course vary on the particular facts of each case. Those views must be considered and may, but not necessarily must, carry more weight as the children grow older'.

On the other hand, it has also been said that where all other factors are evenly balanced it is appropriate to recognise the extra significance of an older child's views.[3] Nevertheless the court's *obligation* is to consider the child's wishes and feelings but not necessarily to give effect to them. It must be remembered that the child may have been coached or brainwashed[4] by one parent and that sometimes even an older child's wishes can be so contrary to their long-term welfare that the court may feel justified in overriding them. In *Re M (Family Proceedings: Affidavits)*,[5] for example, a father applied for a residence order based largely on his 12-year-old daughter's wishes. Although the welfare report indicated that either parent was suitable as a carer, since the child had hitherto lived with her mother and had not had the opportunity to have any clear idea of what living with her father would really be like (the contact visits to her father had always taken place at the paternal grandparents' home), the judge upheld the welfare officer's 'instinct' that her long-term welfare would be better governed by her remaining with her mother. The Court of Appeal agreed and rejected the argument that, given either parent was suitable, the child's view should have tipped the balance. It accepted that the judge had properly taken the child's wishes into account but was not obliged to follow them, if, as here, it was not felt to be in the child's interests to do so.

1   *Re W (minors) (residence order)* [1992] 2 FCR 461, CA; *Re W (A Minor) (Residence Order)* [1993] 2 FLR 625, CA.
2   [1992] 2 FCR 681 at 687. See also *M v M (Minor: Custody Appeal)* [1987] 1 WLR 404 at 411, CA, per May LJ.
3   *Re F (Minors) (Denial of Contact)* [1993] 2 FLR 677, CA. See also *Re P (minors) (wardship: care and control)* [1992] 2 FCR 681 at 689H per Butler-Sloss LJ, cited by Cazalet J in *Re H (a Minor) (Shared Residence)* [1994] 1 FLR 717 at 724E. Note Wilson J's comment in *Re B (Change of Surname)* [1996] 1 FLR 791, CA, that it was virtually unknown to make residence or contact orders that run contrary to the wishes of normal adolescent children. However, this comment should perhaps be treated with caution. It certainly should not be regarded as a statement of principle. For pre-CA 1989 cases where the child's wishes proved decisive see eg *Marsh v Marsh* (1977) 8 Fam Law 103; *Clarke Hunt v Newcombe* (1982) 4 FLR 482, CA; *Williamson v Williamson* [1986] 2 FLR 146, CA; and *Re P (a Minor) (Education)* [1992] 1 FLR 316, CA.
4   See eg *Re R (a Minor) (Residence: Religion)* [1993] 2 FLR 163, CA, in which the wishes of a nine-year-old boy to remain with a member of the Exclusive Brethren were overridden.
5   [1995] 2 FLR 100, CA. See also *Re DW (a Minor) (Custody)* [1984] Fam Law 17, CA; *Clarke-Hunt v Newcombe* (1982) 4 FLR 482, CA, cf *Re M (Child's Upbringing)* ('the Zulu boy case') [1996] 2 FLR 441, where the 10 year old's wishes seemed to be ignored – see the editorial at (1996) 146 NLJ 669. See also cases such as *Re W (a Minor) (Medical Treatment: Court's Jurisdiction)* [1993] Fam 64, [1992] 4 All ER 627, CA, *Re E (a Minor)* (1990) 9 BMLR 1 and *Re M (child' refusal of medical treatment)* [1999] 2 FCR 577, where a 16 and a 15-year-old childrens' refusal to have medical treatment was overridden.

(II)   THE CHILD'S PHYSICAL, EMOTIONAL AND EDUCATIONAL NEEDS

2.43   A wide variety of 'needs' can be relevant under s 1(3)(b) ranging from:

physical needs in the sense of adequate accommodation;[1]

emotional needs in the sense of attachment to a particular parent[2] or to a sibling or even to a family. It is also considered to be a fundamental emotional need of a child to have an enduring relationship with both parents. With regard to sibling support, as Purchas LJ said in *C v C (Minors: Custody)*:[3]

> 'It is really beyond argument that unless there are strong features indicating a contrary arrangement . . . brothers and sisters should wherever possible, be brought up together, so that they are an emotional support to each other in the stormy waters of the destruction of their family.'

Attachment to the family becomes important in disputes between parents and third parties and, as we have seen,[4] positive reasons are required before residence orders will be made in favour of non-parents.

medical needs so that provided it is for the child's benefit it is within the court's power to make an order for taking a bodily sample to ascertain whether the child is HIV positive,[5] and

educational needs either in the sense of parental commitment to the importance of schooling and completion of homework[6] or from the point of view of religious upbringing.[7]

In practice, the child's needs together with the parent's capabilities are the major concern in most cases.

1 Cf *Stephenson v Stephenson* [1985] FLR 1140, CA.
2 See the discussion at para 2.47.
3 [1998] 2 FLR 291 at 302, CA. Cf *Re B (T) (a minor) (residence order)* [1995] 2 FCR 240, CA in which it was held that on the facts maintaining the status quo was more important to the child than being with his siblings. See also *B v B (Residence Order: Restricting Applications)* [1997] 1 FLR 139, CA, in which on the facts a decision to split the siblings was upheld on appeal, and *Re D (Care: Natural Parent Presumption)* [1999] 1 FLR 134, CA, in which it was held that too much importance had been attached in that case to the need to keep the siblings together.
4 See para 2.9.
5 *Re C (HIV Test)* [1999] 2 FLR 1004, FD and CA, and *Re W (a minor) (HIV test)* [1995] 2 FCR 184.
6 *May v May* [1986] 1 FLR 325, CA.
7 See *Re J (child's religious upbringing and circumcision)* [1999] 2 FCR 345, sub nom *Re J (Specific Issue Orders: Muslim Upbringing and Circumcision)* [1999] 2 FLR 678 – decision upheld by Court of Appeal, see [2000] 1 FCR 307, [2000] 1 FLR 571.

(III) THE LIKELY EFFECT ON THE CHILD OF ANY CHANGE IN HIS CIRCUMSTANCES

2.44 Section 1(3)(c) is the statutory enactment of the 'status quo' or continuity factor which in practice is a particularly important factor in resolving private law disputes, the courts being well aware of the dangers of removing a child from a well-established home. As Ormrod LJ said in *D v M (Minor: Custody Appeal)*:[1]

'it is generally accepted by those who are professionally concerned with children that particularly in the early years, continuity of care is a most important part of a child's sense of security and that disruption of established bonds are to be avoided whenever it is possible to do so.'

1 [1983] Fam 33 at 41, [1982] 3 All ER 897 at 902–903, CA.

2.45 Good reasons will have to be adduced, to justify moving a child from a well-established home[1] even on an interim basis.[2] Nevertheless the status quo is only a factor and the court may well think that the child's welfare in any particular case might be better served by being moved. As Ormrod LJ pointed out in *S v W*:[3]

'the status quo argument depends for its strength wholly and entirely on whether the status quo is satisfactory or not. The more satisfactory the status quo, the stronger the argument for not interfering. The less satisfactory the status quo, the less one requires before deciding to change.'

1 See eg *Re B (residence order)* [1998] 1 FCR 549, [1998] 1 FLR 368, CA, in which the first instance judge was held wrong to have placed speculative improvements in contact over and above the consideration of continuity of care. See also *Re B (T) (a minor) (residence order)* [1995] 2 FCR 240, CA in which, on the facts, maintaining the status quo was thought to be more important to the child than being with her siblings, and *Re L (Residence: Justices' Reasons)* [1995] 2 FLR 445 – inadequate reasons given by magistrates for upsetting the status quo.
2 See eg *Re J (Children: Ex Parte Order)*[1997] 1 FLR 606 in which Hale J observed (at 609) that ex parte orders handing over a young child to a parent with whom she has not lived for 20 months should surely be exceptional. See also *Elder v Elder* [1986] 1 FLR 610, CA and *Re W; Re L (Minors) (Interim Custody)* [1987] 2 FLR 67, CA.
3 (1981) 11 Fam Law 81 at 82, CA.

2.46 The maintenance of the status quo becomes a stronger argument the longer the child has been with the party and is especially powerful if the other party has lost contact with the child. On the other hand, if, as in *Allington v Allington*,[1] the parties have only been separated for a few weeks and the absent parent has maintained regular contact with the child there can effectively be no status quo argument at all. In assessing what the status quo is the courts should examine the whole history of the case and not simply the position immediately before the hearing. Hence, where a parent has 'snatched' a child from the other, the court may properly regard the status quo as being the position prior to the snatch. There is, however, no *principle* where a child has been detained by the non-residential parent beyond the agreed period that the child be automatically returned to the residential parent pending the court decision as to the child's future.[2]

1   [1985] FLR 586, CA.
2   *Re J (a Minor) (Interim Custody)* [1989] 2 FLR 304, CA.

(IV)   THE CHILD'S AGE, SEX, BACKGROUND AND ANY CHARACTERISTICS OF HIS WHICH THE COURT CONSIDERS RELEVANT

2.47 Consideration of the child's age is obviously linked to other matters such as the child's wishes and when combined with sex can be relevant to the choice of parents. In *Re W (a Minor) (Residence Order)*,[1] Lord Donaldson MR considered that 'there is a rebuttable presumption of fact that the best interests of a baby are served by being with its mother'. However, apart from babies it is clear, as Butler-Sloss LJ said in *Re S (a Minor) (Custody)*,[2] that 'there is no presumption that one parent should be preferred to another parent at a particular age [of the child]'. However, within this approach the court is prepared to acknowledge that certain arrangements are more often consistent with good child raising than others. As Lord Jauncey put it in *Brixey v Lynas*:[3]

> 'the advantage to a very young child of being with its mother is a consideration which must be taken into account in deciding where lie its best interests in custody proceedings in which the mother is involved. It is neither a presumption nor a prin-ciple but rather recognition of a widely held belief based on practical experience and the workings of nature . . . However, where a very young child has been with its mother since birth and there is no criticism of her ability to care for the child only the strongest competing advantages are likely to prevail.'

1   [1992] 2 FLR 332 at 336, CA.
2   [1991] 2 FLR 388 at 390, CA.
3   1996 SLT 908, [1996] 2 FLR 499, HL (Scotland). See also *Re S (Children)* [2002] EWCA Civ 583 in which a residence order was granted to the mother notwithstanding that she was the 'bread winner' and the father had taken on a 'house husband' role and in which Thorpe LJ referred to the 'very different role and functions of men and women'. See also *Re W (a Minor) (Custody)* (1982) 4 FLR 492, CA, per Cumming Bruce LJ. But, for examples of residence orders being granted to fathers, see *Re K (a minor) (residence order)*[1999] 3 FCR 365, sub nom *Re K (Residence Order: Securing Contact)* [1999]1 FLR 583, CA, inter alia, because the mother was found to be untrustworthy; and *Re D (a child) (Residence: Ability to Parent)* [2001] EWCA Civ 742, [2001] 2 FCR 751, CA and *Re E (children) (residence order)* [2001] EWCA Civ 567, [2001] 2 FCR 662, CA in both of which adverse findings were made about the mother's ability to look after their children.

2.48 The child's 'background' can include his religious upbringing. In the case of very young children (and probably any child of no fixed religious beliefs) the question of religious upbringing will have little bearing on the outcome of the case.[1] In *Re J (child's religious upbringing and circumcision)*[2] where the child concerned (aged 5) was being brought up as a non-practising Christian in accordance with the convictions of his mother with whom he lived and as a non-practising Muslim when staying with his father, and who could therefore be said to have no settled religious faith, Wall J declined to make a specific issue order that the child be brought up in the Muslim religion.

1 See *Re C (MA) (an infant)* [1996] 1 All ER 883 at 856 and 864–865, CA.
2 [1999] 2 FCR 345, sub nom *Re J (Specific Issue Orders: Muslim Upbringing and Circumcision)* [1999] 2 FLR 678–decision upheld by Court of Appeal, see [2000] 1 FCR 307, [2000] 1 FLR 571.

2.49 On the other hand, where religious faith is clearly part of the child's upbringing, the court may well consider that continuation of religious observance is vital if the evidence suggests that otherwise the child could suffer emotional disturbance.[1] In this respect it is to be noted that as Scarman LJ once commented:[2]

'it is not for the court to pass any judgment on the beliefs of parents where they are socially acceptable and consistent with a decent respectable life . . .'

Being a Jehovah's Witness, for example, does not ipso facto mean that that parent should not be granted a residence order.[3] In *Re H (a Minor) (Custody: Religious Upbringing)*,[4] the court took the view that:

'mere indoctrination with the beliefs and tenets of this narrow faith is not of itself indicative of harm or that harm will occur to the child so indoctrinated, provided there is an understanding and level-headed parent in charge of the child.'

A similar latitude might not, however, be given in respect of membership of what the court considers to be an extreme sect. In *Re B and G (Minors) (Custody)*[5] the decisive factor in denying a father and stepmother of what would now be a residence order in respect of children they had been looking after for five years was that they were scientologists and so held views which were found to be 'immoral and obnoxious'.

1 This certainly influenced Willmer LJ in *Re M (infants)* [1967] 3 All ER 1071 at 1074, CA.
2 *Re T (Minors) (Custody Upbringing)* (1975) 2 FLR 239, CA and repeated in Purchas LJ in *Re R (A Minor) (Residence Religion)* [1993] 2 FLR 163, CA.
3 Although parties are sometimes asked to undertake not to involve their children, for example, in the house-to-house visiting conducted by Jehovah's Witnesses: see eg *Re C (Minors) (Wardship: Jurisdiction)* [1978] Fam 105, [1978] 2 All ER 230, CA.
4 (1980) 2 FLR 253.
5 [1985] FLR 493, CA. The court felt that it could not rely on the father's undertaking to remove the children from 'the evil forces of scientology'.

2.50 Notwithstanding the foregoing there is no rule or legal principle that it can never be right to force a child to abandon his religious beliefs, since ultimately such beliefs are subservient to what is perceived as being overall in a child's best interests.[1] This is well illustrated in *Re R (a Minor) (Residence: Religion)*[2] in which the court was faced with the stark choice of either granting a father a residence order in respect of his nine year old son, in which case the child would effectively be excluded from the Exclusive Brethren within which society he had hitherto grown up, or granting a residence order to members of the sect, in which case, because of the strict rules of the fellowship, his son would no longer even see his father. In upholding the first instance decision to grant the father a residence order, the Court of Appeal made it clear that their decision was not based on a value judgment as to the tenets of the particular religion, strict though they were, but rather on what was thought to be in the boy's long term interests, to continue to be brought up by his father.

1   See Balcombe LJ in *Re R (a Minor) (Residence: Religion)* [1993] 2 FLR 163 at 180, CA.
2   See above.

2.51   In appropriate cases, for example where the care giver has a different religion from that of the child, it is open to the court to make a residence order on condition that the child's upbringing will be continued.[1] On the other hand it could be a condition of a residence or contact order that the adult does not involve the child in his religion.[2]

1   For the power to impose conditions on s 8 orders see paras 5.84 et seq.
2   See eg *Re R (a Minor) (Residence: Religion)*, supra, where an aunt was granted contact upon her undertaking not to speak or communicate with the child in any way in relation to religious or spiritual matters or make any reference to the Exclusive Brethren as a religious group.

2.52   Racial origin, cultural and linguistic background[1] are issues that should be considered under this head and on occasion are likely to prove difficult in both private and public law proceedings.

1   Consideration to which local authorities must have specific regard under s 22(5)(c), see para 6.45.

2.53   The preservation of links with the child's culture and heritage are important issues that should not be overlooked. Such considerations were a key motivating force in *Re M (child's upbringing)*[1] in which the Court of Appeal ordered the return of a Zulu boy to his mother in South Africa, while in *Re M (a minor) (section 94 appeals)*[2] the failure to address the question of race when denying contact of a mixed race girl (who was confused about her racial origin) to her black father, was held to justify the Court of Appeal reversing the decision. Nevertheless, important though culture and heritage may be, the rule remains that it is the child's welfare that is the paramount consideration. Thus in *Re P (a Minor) (Residence Order: Child's Welfare)*,[3] in which Jewish Orthodox parents sought to have their child (born with Downs Syndrome) returned to them, notwithstanding that for the previous four years she was living with a non-practising Catholic couple under a residence order, the Court of Appeal upheld the first instance decision that on the evidence of the child's limited ability to understand and appreciate the Jewish religion, her religious and cultural heritage was *not* an overwhelming factor.

1   [1996] 2 FCR 473, [1996] 2 FLR 441, CA.
2   [1995] 2 FCR 435, [1995] 1 FLR 526. Cf *Re P (a minor) (transracial placement)* [1990] FCR 260, [1990] 1 FLR 96, CA, and *Re N (a Minor(Adoption)* [1990] 1 FLR 58.
3   [2000] Fam 15, sub nom *Re P (a child) (residence order: restriction order)* [1999] 3 All ER 734, CA.

(V)   ANY HARM WHICH THE CHILD HAS SUFFERED OR IS AT RISK OF SUFFERING

2.54   The 'harm' referred to in s 1(3)(e) has the same meaning as it does for the purposes of establishing the threshold conditions under s 31 and accordingly means both ill-treatment and the impairment of health or development.[1] It clearly covers both physical and psychological trauma. It also covers sexual abuse which, if proved, is likely to be a significant factor,[2] but even so may not inevitably mean that the abuser should not, for example, be allowed contact.[3]

1 S 105(1) provides that 'harm' has the same meaning as in s 31(9), discussed at para 8.41. Note that under the Adoption and Children Bill 2002, the definition harm will be extended to include 'impairment suffered from seeing or hearing the ill-treatment of another'. This is to emphasise the potential harm caused to a child for example by witnessing violence perpetrated by one parent on another.
2 See eg *Re B (a Minor) (Care Order: Criteria)* [1993] 1 FLR 815.
3 *H v H (Child Abuse: Access)* [1989] 1 FLR 212, CA; *L v L (Child Abuse: Access)* [1989] 2 FLR 16, CA; *C v C (a Minor) (Child Abuse: Evidence)* [1988] 1 FLR 462. Cf *Re R (a Minor) (Access)* [1988] 1 FLR 206, CA.

2.55 Apart from actual harm, s 1(3)(e) also encompasses 'risk' of harm. Such a risk could, for example, emanate from the parents' past alcoholism,[1] or sexual abuse. It is, however, established that s 1(3)(e) deals with actual harm or risk of harm and not with possibilities.[2]

1 See eg *Re L (residence: justices' reasons)* [1995] 2 FCR 445.
2 See *Re M and R (Child Abuse: Evidence)* [1996] 2 FLR 195 at 203, applying the same test as applies to s 31 following the House of Lords' ruling in *Re H (Minors) (Sexual Abuse: Standard of Proof)* [1996] AC 563, sub nom *Re H (minors) (child abuse: threshold conditions)* [1996] 1 All ER 1 discussed at paras 8.51 et seq. See also *Re P (Sexual Abuse: Standard of Proof)* [1996] 2 FLR 333, CA. See also *Re W (minors) (residence order)* [1998] 1 FCR 75, [1999] 1 FLR 869, a case concerning the mother and her partner's uninhibited approach to nudity – in which the first instance judge was held to: 'have allowed his instinctive reaction against the uninhibited behaviour of [the] couple – to override all other factors in the case . . . His decision was not based on a proper assessment of the case and was made on a false premise, that is to say that the behaviour and attitude of the mother and the partner created a serious risk of abuse to these children, a serious risk which has no substance in fact and with no evidence to support it'.

(VI) HOW CAPABLE EACH OF THE CHILD'S PARENTS, AND ANY OTHER PERSON IN RELATION TO WHOM THE COURT CONSIDERS THE QUESTION TO BE RELEVANT, IS OF MEETING HIS NEEDS

2.56 A wide variety of circumstances can be brought under this factor, ranging from the medical condition of the parents to their lifestyle. In the private law context, it is established that while lesbianism is a factor to be taken into account, it does not per se render a mother unfit to look after her child.[1] No doubt the same is true of homosexual fathers. It is to be noted that as well as parents the capability of any other persons in relation to whom the court considers the question to be relevant must also be examined. This will clearly include any new partner of a parent.[2]

1 *C v C (Custody of Child)* [1991] 1 FLR 223, CA; *B v B (custody of children)* [1991] FCR 1.
2 *Scott v Scott* [1986] 2 FLR 320, CA.

(VII) THE RANGE OF POWERS AVAILABLE TO THE COURT UNDER [THE 1989] ACT IN THE PROCEEDINGS IN QUESTION

2.57 Section 1(3)(g) directs the court to consider not only whether the order being sought is best for the child but also to consider the alternatives that the Act makes available. This is particularly important in the context of care proceedings, since it is therefore incumbent upon the court to consider not only whether or not to make the care order but whether a s 8 order, for example, a residence order, would better serve the child's interests.[1]

1 See further paras 8.18 et seq.

Delay prima facie prejudicial to the child's welfare[1]

2.58   Section 1(2) enjoins the court, in any proceedings in which any question with respect to a child's upbringing arises, 'to have regard to the general principle that any delay in determining the question is likely to prejudice the welfare of the child'.[2] Since this provision applies to any proceedings concerning any question concerning a child's upbringing,[3] it is not confined to proceedings under the CA 1989 but applies equally, for example, to adoption proceedings or to proceedings under the High Court's inherent jurisdiction. It will be noted, however, that the timetabling provisions do not apply to proceedings other than those under the CA 1989 (though in practice they are applied to proceedings under the inherent jurisdiction).[4]

1   A study, commissioned by the Lord Chancellor has reviewed the reasons for delay and assessed the need for reform, see *Scoping Study on Delay in Children Act Cases* (Lord Chancellor's Department, March 2002). For comments on the draft Report, see Finlay 'Delay and the Challenges of the Children Act' in *Delight and Dole* (eds Thorpe and Cowton) 5 at 10 et seq. See further the discussion in ch 4.
2   Attention to the need to avoid delay is specifically mentioned in para 15.1 of the *Practice Note: Devolution Issues and Crown Office Applications)* [1999] 3 All ER 466.
3   Note, however, the exclusion of maintenance from the definition of 'upbringing' under s 105(1).
4   Discussed further at para 4.43 et seq. Note that prospectively similar provisions will apply to adoption proceedings under the Adoption and Children Bill 2002. The inherent jurisdiction is discussed in ch 12.

2.59   The case for making provision about the harmful effect of delay was cogently argued by the Law Commission.[1] They pointed out that 'prolonged litigation about their future is deeply damaging to children, not only because of the uncertainty it brings for them, but also because of the harm it does to the relationship between the parents and their capacity to co-operate with one another in the future'. Despite its importance, however, neither the Law Commission's draft Bill nor the Bill originally presented to Parliament made the avoidance of delay a general principle. Indeed it was only at the final House of Lords' stages that this provision was 'promoted' to the opening section, Lord Mackay LC commenting:[2]

'After the welfare principle, the need to avoid delay is one of the most important policies underlying the Bill. It is therefore proper that it should appear in clause 1.'

1   Law Com No 172, para 4.55. The Commission's comments are echoed in the Department of Health's Guidance and Regulations Vol 1, Court Orders, para 1.8.
2   512 HL Official Report (5th Series) col 720.

2.60   Notwithstanding s 1(2), it should not be thought that delay[1] is always detrimental to a child's welfare. As Ward J observed in *C v Solihull Metropolitan Borough Council*,[2] while delay is ordinarily inimical to the welfare of a child, planned and purposeful delay may well be beneficial. Hence, the delay of a final decision in order to ascertain the result of an assessment is obviously for rather than against the child's interests. In *Re B (a Minor) (Contact) (Interim Order)*,[3] magistrates were held to be 'plainly wrong' in refusing to make an interim contact order during which arrangements for the reintroduction of contact were to be assessed because it infringed the principle of the avoidance of delay as set out in s 1(2). It may be similarly beneficial to a child to make a temporary order to allow 'a volatile family situation' involving children to settle down.[4] On the other hand, what s 1(2) aims to prevent is unnecessary and unplanned delay for reasons that have nothing to do with the child's welfare.[5] It would similarly be wrong to put off a difficult decision by making an interim order, or to subvert the policy of allowing local authorities to administer care orders in their own way.[6] As Ward LJ put it,[7] to delay a harsh decision is to delay for 'no purpose'. As the criterion to be applied is the welfare of the *child,* detriment to the *family* is not of itself a relevant factor. It was on this basis that *Re T-B (Care Proceedings: Criminal Trial)*[8] held that the fact there was a pending criminal trial was not enough to justify delaying the hearing of care proceedings.

1 In any event, as has been observed (Butler et al: 'Children Act and the Issue of Delay' [1993] Fam Law 412) delay is a relative phenomenon and needs to be distinguished from 'duration'. A complex case may, quite appropriately and expeditiously, remain in the courts for several weeks while a relatively simple matter that ought to be dealt with within days may take three weeks and hence be subject to significant delay, yet still be of moderate duration'.
2 [1993] 1 FLR 290 at 304.
3 [1994] 2 FLR 269.
4 As in the pre-Children Act decision, *Re S (minors) (custody)* [1992] 1 FCR 158, CA.
5 For recent examples in which delay was thought to have prejudiced the children's welfare, see *B v B (Minors) (Interviewers and Listing Arrangements)* [1994] 2 FLR 489, CA, and, most strikingly, *Re A and B (Minors) (No 2)* [1995] 1 FLR 351.
6 See further paras 8.89 et seq.
7 In *Re M (child's upbringing)* [1996] 2 FCR 473 at 492, [1996] 2 FLR 441 at 460, CA.
8 [1995] 2 FLR 801, CA.

2.61 Although the principal effect of s 1(2) is to place the onus upon the courts to ensure that all proceedings concerning children are conducted as expeditiously as possible, practitioners also have a duty to ensure that a case does not drift. As Wall J has said:[1]

'Solicitors for the parties, whatever their forensic stance and irrespective of whether or not delay may be tactically advantageous to their client, have a duty in children's cases to ensure that a case does not drift and is either brought to a hearing or resolved in some other way with the minimum of delay.'

According to the same judge in another case:[2]

'The courts have a duty to be positive in ensuring that applications once launched are not allowed to moulder'.

To this end, courts are directed[3] in applications for s 8 orders and orders under Pt IV of the CA to draw up a timetable and to give appropriate directions for adhering to that timetable. These powers are discussed in chapter 4. It has been held that in view of s 1(2), a court can, in appropriate cases, depart from the recommendations of a children and family reporter even though the reporter did not attend court to give oral evidence.[4]

1 In *B v B (Child Abuse: Contact)* [1994] 2 FLR 713, at 736.
2 *B v B (Minors) (Interviews and Listing Arrangements)* [1994] 2 FLR 489 at 492, CA. See also *Re A and B (Minors) (No 2)* [1995] 1 FLR 351.
3 Viz under ss 11(1) and 32(1).
4 Per Hale J in *Re C (Section 8 Order: Court Welfare Officer)* [1995] 1 FLR 617, CA (welfare officers are now known as children and family reporters). Note also, *H v Cambridgeshire County Council* [1996] 2 FLR 566, leave refused for a mother to show papers to a consultant child psychiatrist given her own delay in taking steps to identify a suitable expert under the terms of an earlier order for leave.

ORDERS TO BE MADE ONLY WHERE THE COURT IS SATISFIED THAT MAKING THE ORDER IS BETTER THAN MAKING NO ORDER

1. Introduction and background

2.62 An important and innovative principle is provided by s 1(5), namely, that whenever a court is considering whether to make one or more orders under the CA 1989 with respect to a child, it 'shall not make the order or any of the orders unless it considers that doing so would be better for the child than making no order at all'. This provision[1] is intended to focus attention as to whether any court order is necessary. It was part of an underlying philosophy of the CA 1989, namely, to respect the integrity and independence of the family save where court orders have some positive contribution to make towards the child's welfare. According to the Department of Health's Guidance and Regulations,[2] s 1(5) has two main aims:

'The first is to discourage unnecessary court orders being made, for example as part of a standard package of orders. If orders are restricted to those cases where they are necessary to resolve a specific problem this should reduce conflict and promote parental agreement and co-operation. The second aim is to ensure that the order is granted only where it will positively improve the child's welfare and not simply because the grounds for making the order are made out as, for example, in care proceedings where the court may decide that it would be better for a particular child not to be in local authority care.'

1   Which implements the Law Commission's recommendations with regard to private law proceedings, see Law Com No 172, paras 3.2 – 3.4, and those of the Child Care Review (DHSS, 1985) paras 15.24–15.25 and the government's White Paper, The Law on Child Care and Family Services Cm 62, 1987, para 59, with respect to public law proceedings.
2   Vol 1, Court Orders, para 1.12.

2.63 The Law Commission were concerned[1] that under the pre-CA 1989 law many orders relating to children were merely 'part of the divorce package'. The Commission accepted that, while sometimes orders might bring stability and certainty even in uncontested cases, there was a risk that in other cases orders would polarise the parents' role and perhaps alienate the child from one or other of the parents. In line with this policy the court's duty under s 41 of the Matrimonial Causes Act 1973 to investigate the child's circumstances in divorce proceedings was profoundly changed. Instead of having to be satisfied that the arrangements were satisfactory or the best that could be made in the circumstances or that it was impracticable for the party or parties to make any such arrangements, the court now only has to *consider* the proposed arrangements and then only in exceptional circumstances can it delay the granting of the decree absolute.[2] Accompanying this substantive change was the equally important procedural change that instead of conducting this inquiry by means of a formal hearing, the duty is now discharged essentially by reading the papers.[3] Section 1(5) undoubtedly applies to public law proceedings as well as to private proceedings, and was envisaged[4] as directing the courts to consider notwithstanding that the conditions for a care order were established,[5] whether it was in the particular child's interests to make any order.

1   Law Com No 172, para 3.2
2   MCA 1973, s 41, as amended by Sch 12, para 31 to the CA 1989.
3   Ie by the district judge reading the detailed Statements of Arrangements for children which must accompany the divorce petition: FPR 1991, r 2.2(2).

4   See Review of Child Care Law (DHSS, 1985) paras 15.24 – 15.25), The Law on Child Care and
    Family Services (Cm 62, 1987) para 59, and the Department of Health's Guidance and
    Regulations, Vol 1, Court Orders, para 1.12.
5   Viz under s 31, see para 8.38 et seq.

2.   When the section applies

2.64   As s 1(5) itself states, it applies where a court is considering whether or
not to make one or more orders under the CA 1989. Accordingly, it has no
direct application in proceedings in which courts are considering whether or
not to make orders relating to children outside the Act.[1] In this respect, s 1(5)
has a narrower ambit than either s 1(1) or s 1(2).

1   Eg orders under the Adoption Act 1976 or under the wardship or inherent jurisdiction.
    Presumably, however, there is nothing to prevent the court from taking a similar approach, if
    they so choose.

2.65   In *K v H (Child Maintenance)*[1] Sir Stephen Brown P held that s 1(5)
does not apply to applications for financial provision[2] for a child under Sch 1
to the Act since, like s 1(1), which his Lordship took to be the general controlling provision for the overall application of s 1, s 1(5) 'is principally directed
to orders relating to the upbringing of a child, the administration of a child's
property or the application of any income arising from it'. Accordingly, since
an application for financial provision neither concerns the child's upbringing
nor the administration of his property, s 1(5) does not apply. The alternative
reason for holding s 1(5) inapplicable was that, given that it is clearly in a
child's interests that proper provision be made for his financial needs, a court
order is preferable to relying on the parties' oral agreement[3] since that provides
a better means of safeguarding the future both in the sense of providing for
future variations and of being able to deal with any subsequent enforcement
issues.

1   [1993] 2 FLR 61.
2   Viz periodical payments, which was what *K v H* concerned, or lump sums or property orders.
3   Aliter for written agreements which can, subject to the Child Support Act 1991, be varied by
    the court eg under Sch 1, paras 10 and 11 to the CA 1989.

2.66   Whether his Lordship was right to say that s 1(1) provides overall control of the operation of s 1 may be debated but in practice it is likely to be the
case that s 1(5) will not apply if s 1(1) does not. For example, in *Re M (a
Minor) (Secure Accommodation Order)*,[1] which established that s 1(1) does
not apply to the question of whether to make a secure accommodation order
under s 25,[2] Butler-Sloss LJ expressly held that because of the need to protect
the public as well as the child, s 1(5) does not apply either. Again, in deciding
whether to grant leave to apply for a s 8 order where it is established that the
paramountcy principle does not apply[3] it seems right to say that s 1(5) is also
subsumed by the criteria set out in s 10(9).[4]

1   [1995] Fam 108, [1995] 3 All ER 407, CA.
2   Secure accommodation is discussed in ch 9.
3   See *Re A (Minors) (Residence Orders: Leave to Apply)* [1992] Fam 182, [1992] 3 All ER 872,
    CA, discussed at paras 2.25 and 5.118 et seq.
4   In particular s 10(9) (c) which directs the court to consider the risk of harm to the child that
    the proposed application might cause. See further paras 5.117 et seq.

3.   The application of s 1(5)

2.67   The application of s 1(5) has proved problematic. It quickly became referred to as establishing a 'non intervention principle' or 'no order principle'[1] but insofar as these epithets suggest that orders are presumed to be unnecessary, their use has been deprecated in some quarters. As one commentator has pointed out,[2] neither the Law Commission nor statute says that court orders are presumed to be unnecessary and 'most certainly' neither suggested that in public care proceedings there is a legal presumption against the making of care or supervision orders. In his view, if epithets are required, a more accurate one would be the 'no *unnecessary* order principle'.

1   It was memorably described as 'privatising the family' by Cretney 'Privatising the Family: The Reform of Child Law' (1989) Denning LJ 15. See also Bainham 'The Privatisation of The Public Interest in Children' (1990) 53 MLR 206. Other (eg Douglas 'Family Law under the Thatcher Government' (1990) 17 JLS 411 at 415, n 17) referred to it as establishing a policy of deregulation or non-intervention.
2   Bainham 'Changing families and changing concepts – reframing the language of family law' (1998) 10 CFLQ 1 at 2–4.

(a)   The substantive law

2.68   Although the clear import of s 1(5) is that orders should not be made under the CA 1989 unless they are considered to be for the *child's* welfare, the precise application of the sub-section remains uncertain. The most detailed analysis is that of Munby J in *Re X and Y (leave to remove from jurisdiction: no order principle)*[1] in which his Lordship emphasised[2] that the 'burden is on the party applying for an order to make out a positive case that on a balance of probabilities it is in the interests of the child that that order should be made'. However, this analysis was disapproved of by the Court of Appeal in *Re H (children) (residence order: condition)*[3] Thorpe LJ commenting, that he did not think that the dicta drawn from the House of Lords' cases bears 'the weight of the edifice that Munby J sought to build on them'. However, that comment was made in the context of whether any order should be made rather than the specific one sought, Thorpe LJ taking the view that where there is acute dissension among the parties 'No order is simply not an option. The court has to impose one order or the other in the application of the paramount principle of welfare'.[4] Perhaps more telling is Thorpe LJ's earlier comment in *Payne v Payne*[5] that he 'did not think that such concepts of presumption and burden of proof have any place in Children Act 1989 litigation where the judge exercises a function that is partly inquisitorial'. Even in *S v M (Access Order)*,[6] one of the House of Lords cases relied upon by Munby J, Lord Clyde observed that 'true questions of the burden of proof will almost invariably fade into insignificance after any inquiry'.

1   [2001] 2 FCR 398, [2001] 2 FLR 118. On which, see the comment by Douglas at [2001] Fam Law 345–346.
2   Applying principles said to be distilled from the House of Lords' decision in *Dawson v Wearmouth* [1999] 2 AC 308, [1999] 2 All ER 353, relying in particular on comments made by Lord Mackay (at 321A and 359(c)–(d)) and Lord Hobhouse (at 325H–326E, 363(g)–(364(d))). According to Munby J there is no difference in substance between what was said by the House of Lords in this case and what they said in the earlier Scots case, *S v M (Access Order)* [1997] 1 FLR 980, sub nom *Sanderson v McManus* 1997 SC (HL) 55.
3   [2001] EWCA Civ 1338, [2001] 3 FCR 182 [2001] 2 FLR 1277.

4   This comment might be drawn upon to support the position by Phillimore and Drane 'No More of the 'no order' Principle' [1999] Fam Law 40 that the 'no order' principle has no place in contested applications.
5   See above at para [25].
6   [1997] 1 FLR 980 at 989.

2.69 Notwithstanding that it is wrong to place weight on the burden of proof it remains the case that the court must be satisfied that an order is for the benefit of the child and that in carrying out this task the court must evaluate the evidence rather than applying any presumption. Convincing the court of the benefit to the particular child of the order sought will be easier to satisfy in contested applications. Indeed, it has been said that making 'no order' is inappropriate if the court is clearly charged with the responsibility for settling a dispute. In *Re W (a Minor) (Contact)*,[1] upon a father's application for defined contact following the mother's refusal to comply with a previous order for reasonable contact and her declared intention not to obey any further order, the first instance decision to make a 'no order' was held to be an abdication of responsibility. The point has also been made that there is a clear distinction between dismissing an application and making a 'no order'. If the making of the latter is tantamount to dismissing a parent's application for contact, as opposed to holding than an order was not necessary, then, according to Wall J in *D v D (application for contact)*,[2] the court should at least take a proactive role and consider whether any further application should be made and, if so, when and in what circumstances.

1   [1994] 2 FLR 441, CA. Note Thorpe LJ's comment in *Re H (children) (residence order: condition)* [2001] EWCA Civ 1338, para [19], [2001] 3 FCR 182, [2001] 2 FLR 1277, referred to above at para 2.68. See also *Re P (a Minor) (Parental Responsibility Order)* [1994] 1 FLR 578.
2   [1994] 1 FCR 694.

2.70 While it might be easier to persuade the court to make an order in contested cases it by no means follows that no order can be granted if the parties are agreed. In this respect reference can still usefully be made to the Department of Health's Guidance on the CA 1989:[1]

'There are several situations where the court is likely to consider it better for the child to make an order than not. If the court has had to resolve a dispute between the parents, it is likely to be better for the child to make an order about it. Even if there is no dispute, the child's need for stability and security may be better served by making an order. There may also be specific legal advantages in doing so. One example is where abduction of the child is a possibility, since a court order is necessary for enforcement proceedings in other parts of the United Kingdom under the Family Law Act 1986, and under the European Convention and under the Hague Convention an order will be necessary if the aggrieved party is, for example, an unmarried father or a relative who would not otherwise have 'rights of custody'. An advantage of having a residence order is that the child may be taken out of the country for periods of less than one month without the permission of other persons with parental authority or the court, whereas without an order this could amount to an offence under the Child Abduction Act 1984. Also if a person has a sole residence order in his favour and appoints a . . . guardian for the child, the appointment will take effect immediately on that person's death, even where there is a surviving parent. Depending on the circumstances of the case, the court might therefore be persuaded that an order would be in the child's interests.'

1   Vol 1, Court Orders, para 2.56.

2.71 Although it is easy to advance the argument that there is a need for stability and security, if s 1(5) is to have any meaning the court cannot, as a matter of routine, make orders for this reason. Indeed, in the past, the Children Act Advisory Committee expressed concern[1] that applications are still being made (and presumably granted) so as to provide the parent with care with the security of an order even though there is no dispute about the child's residence or contact. Similarly, since it can be argued in *every* case that the holder of a residence order can remove the child from the United Kingdom for periods of less than one month and that any guardianship appointment comes into force on the residence holder's death, the court will surely require some especial justification for making an order on that basis.

1   CAAC Report 1992/93, p 25.

2.72 One circumstance not mentioned in the *Guidance* but which could justify the making of a residence or contact order is where the applicant, for example an unmarried father or relative, has no parental responsibility, since it can always be argued that unless an order is made he or she will not otherwise have legal standing in relation to the child.[1] In *B v B (a Minor) (Residence Order)*[2] Johnson J accepted this argument when he granted in what he described as 'the unusual circumstances of the case' an unopposed application for a residence order by a grandparent with whom the child had been living for 10 years. The Court of Appeal have also warned of the dangers that might result from deciding to make no order simply because the parties appear to be in agreement. In *Re S (a minor) (contact: grandparents)*[3] a grandparent sought a contact order. By the time the matter came to court, the judge was persuaded that the mother would permit contact, and therefore, did not make a contact order, relying on s 1(5). On appeal it was felt that, having decided that it was in the child's welfare to have contact with the grandparent, and given the history of antagonism between the parties, the contact order should be made, even if the parties were in agreement at the time of the court hearing. The making of the order would ensure that contact did take place and avoid the need to return to court in the event of a disagreement.

1   See s 10(4) and (6).
2   [1992] 2 FLR 327. Another circumstance that might justify the making of a consent order is where it can be shown that without an order the person looking after the child will not be accorded priority on a local authority housing list. Although this practice was deprecated by the Children Act Advisory Committee (see CAAC Report 1992–93, p 25), if local authorities are still operating this policy (for the position when the Act was first implemented see Yell (1992) 89 Law Soc Gaz (August Issue), p 20), it would seem to be in the child's interests that a residence order be made.
3   [1996] 3 FCR 30, [1996] 1 FLR 158.

(b)   The application of s 1(5) in practice

2.73 A study by Bristol University found that 'no orders' were made in about 5% of cases[1]. National statistics point to a declining proportion of 'no orders'. Early indicators the early indicators were that about 9% of all private law orders were of 'no orders',[2] a proportion which was still reflected for example in 1996.[3] However, in 2000 this proportion dropped to about 4% of orders.[4] As against these figures it remains the case that the number of applications for residence orders (though rising) are still below that for custody orders made before the Act. In other words, the impact of s 1(5) might be greater than the number of 'no orders' suggests.[5]

1 See Bailey-Harris, Barron and Pearce: 'Settlement culture and the use of the 'no order' principle under The Children Act 1989' [1999] CFLQ 53. They also found that at county court level practitioners and district judges took a variety of approaches to s 1(5).
2 See the second edition of this work at para 2.49, based upon the analysis of the CAAC Reports 1991/92 and 1992/3.
3 See the analysis of Lowe and Douglas, Bromley's *Family Law* (9th edn) p 464 based on Table 5.3 of the Judicial Statistics Annual Report 1996.
4 Based on an analysis of the Judicial Statistics Annual Report 2000, Table 5.3 (2001, Cm 5223).
5 A point well made by Cretney and Masson *Principles of Family Law* (6th edn) at 659.

2.74 Although, as we discuss in chapter 8, s 1(5) at one time seemed to have led local authorities not to bring cases before the court, in fact relatively few 'no orders' were made in the public law context. In the first nine months after implementation 'no orders' accounted for 3% of the total number of disposals made in public law proceedings[1] and, based on the 2000 statistics, now accounts for about 2% of the disposals.[2] This should occasion little surprise since one would have expected fewer 'no orders' being made in the public law context, particularly in care proceedings under s 31 since if the statutory threshold is satisfied there is likely to be a good reason to make an order.[3] Conversely if s 31 is not satisfied a dismissal seems more likely than an order of 'no order'. In the former case there is likely to be a good reason for making an order whether or not proceedings are contested. In other words, in public law proceedings, the issue of consent is much less significant than in private law.[4]

1 See CAAC Report 1991/92 Table 2.
2 Based on Judicial Statistics Annual Report 2000, Table 5.2 (2001, Cm 5223).
3 In many cases not making an order would amount to a dereliction of the court's duty: see eg *Re B (a Minor) (Care Order: Criteria)* [1993] 1 FLR 815 at 821.
4 However, the fact that the parties are agreed does not absolve a court from investigating the facts for itself; see *Re G (a Minor) (Care Order: Threshold Condition)* [1995] Fam 16, sub nom *Re G (a Minor) (Care Proceedings)* [1994] 2 FLR 69.

3. Form of order

2.75 If the court decides to make no order then a formal order to that effect must be made.[1] A decision not to make an order still ranks as a 'decision' and reasons for making it should therefore be given.[2]

1. FPR 1991, r 4.21(4); FPC (CA 1989) R 1991, r 21(6).
2 *S v R (parental responsibility)* [1993] 1 FCR 331.

4. The inter-relationship of the welfare principle and the 'non-intervention' principle

2.76 Although s 1(5) can be seen as complementing the welfare principle since it cannot be in the best interests of a child to be the subject of unnecessary court orders, it has been argued[1] that in reality the welfare principle has been 'hijacked by non-interventionism' on the basis that the non interventionist stance taken in the CA 1989 means that parental wishes, especially where both are in agreement, will determine an increasing number of issues affecting children.

1 Bainham 'The Privatisation of the Public Interest in Children' (1990) 53 MLR 206, 221. See also Bainham 'The Children Act 1989, Welfare and Non-Interventionism' [1990] Fam Law 143, 145.

2.77 Although there is some tension between s 1(1) and 1(5) it is surely going too far to say that the welfare principle has been 'hijacked' by the operation of s 1(5). As we have seen,[1] even in the private law context, the proportion of 'no orders' made under s 1(5) is relatively small (though of course it is unknown how many applications are simply not being pursued).[2] Furthermore, most agreements are likely to provide the best arrangements that can be made for the children in the circumstances. In any case it may be questioned whether the pre-1989 Act law was so very different.[3] Under the former law the courts were generally reluctant to interfere with arrangements agreed between the parents. Under the CA 1989 the difference may simply be that the court may make no order at all rather than making an order reflecting the parents' agreement. Nevertheless there is a danger that by making no order in the light of parental agreement the court could overlook the child's wishes. If they do so in the case of older children there could be a breach of Art 12 of the UN Convention on the Rights of the Child.[4] Accordingly, courts should be alive to this possibility and seek some assurance that the child in question does not object to the arrangements agreed between the parents.

1 See para 2.43
2 Nor should the number of withdrawn applications be overlooked, since a proportion of these withdrawals may have been motivated by a desire to avoid a 'no order'. The number of withdrawals greatly exceeds that of 'no orders'. For example, in 2000, 459 care order applications were withdrawn compared with 177 'no orders'. 176 contact applications were withdrawn compared with 68 'no orders' while in private law proceedings 3078 applications for residence orders were withdrawn compared with 941 'no orders' and 5419 contact applications were withdrawn compared with 2067 ' no orders': Judicial Statistics, Annual Report 2000 (2001 Cm 5223), Tables 5.2 and 5.3.
3 In any event, it can be questioned whether the welfare principle itself is truly child-centred. See eg Maidment *Child Custody and Divorce*, p 149 who argues that decisions in the past were 'made by adults for adults about adults'.
4 Under which there is an international obligation for courts to give due weight to a child's views. See also para 2.41.

Chapter 3

Parental responsibility and guardianship

INTRODUCTION

3.1 The Law Commission[1] recommended that parenthood should become the primary concept, with that of 'guardian' being reserved for those formally appointed to take the place of parents upon their death. Further it pointed out that, scattered throughout the statute book were such terms as 'parental rights and duties', or 'powers and duties' or the 'rights and authority' of a parent. Not only were these terms inconsistent with one another but as the Commission had earlier commented:[2] 'it can be cogently argued that to talk of 'parental rights' is not only inaccurate as a matter of juristic analysis but also a misleading use of ordinary language'. Accordingly, the Commission recommended the introduction of the concept of 'parental responsibility' to replace all the ambiguous and misleading terms referred to above, arguing that although such a change 'would make little difference in substance . . . it would reflect the everyday reality of being a parent and emphasise the responsibility of all who are in that position'.[3]

1 Report on Guardianship and Custody, Law Com 1988, No 172, Pt III.
2 Law Com No 118, Illegitimacy, 1982, para 4.18.
3 Law Com No 172, para 2.4.

3.2 The government accepted the Commission's recommendations and 'parental responsibility' has now become a pivotal concept of the CA 1989. Guardianship, on the other hand, now exclusively refers to the status of those formally appointed to take the place of parents after their death.[1] The concept of parental guardianship has been abolished.[2]

1 Not to be confused with 'Children's Guardian' which is the term introduced by CAFCASS to replace what were formerly known as 'guardians ad litem' and who represent children either in public law proceedings (see paras 10.20 et seq) or adoption proceedings, nor with 'Special Guardians' to be introduced by the Adoption and Children Bill 2002 (see paras 5.161 et seq).
2 Section 2(4) of the CA 1989 expressly abolishes the rule of law that a father is the natural guardian of his legitimate children, while s 3 of the Guardianship of Minors Act 1971, which provided (in the case of legitimate children) that upon the death of one parent, the other became the guardian, has been repealed (see Sch 15).

PARENTAL RESPONSIBILITY

1. Contexts in which parental responsibility is relevant

3.3 Parental responsibility is concerned with a number of different relationships. It can embrace both the idea that parents must behave dutifully

53

towards their children and that responsibility for child care belongs to parents and not to the state.[1] Both these important ideas are embodied in the CA 1989. The former is well summed up by Lord Mackay LC, who said,[2] when introducing the Bill, the concept of 'parental responsibility':

'emphasises that the days when a child should be regarded as a possession of his parent – indeed when in the past they had a right to his services and to sue on their loss' are now buried forever. The overwhelming purpose of parenthood is the responsibility for caring for and raising the child to be a properly developed adult both physically and morally'.

This comment is echoed by the Department of Health's introductory guide to the Children Act[3] which states that parental responsibility:

'emphasises that the duty to care for the child and to raise him to moral, physical and emotional health is the fundamental task of parenthood and the only justification for the authority that it confers.'

Both these comments reflect in turn the earlier landmark decision of *Gillick v West Norfolk and Wisbech Area Health Authority*[4] in which, at any rate, Lords Fraser and Scarman emphasised that parental power to control a child exists not for the benefit of the parent but for the benefit of the child.

1 Eekelaar, 'Parental Responsibility: State of Nature or Nature of the State?' [1991] JSWFL 37.
2 502 HL Official Report (5th series), col 490.
3 'Introduction to the Children Act 1989', HMSO 1989, para 1.4.
4 [1986] AC 112, [1985] 3 All ER 402, HL. See further para 3.32.

3.4 It is the enduring nature of responsibility, particularly when allied with the need to justify intervention under s 1(5),[1] that encapsulates the idea that responsibility for child care belongs to parents rather than the state. By providing that responsibility should continue despite, for example, a court order that the child should live with one of them, parents 'are to understand that the state will not relieve them of their responsibilities'.[2] This is underscored by the fact that responsibility cannot be voluntarily surrendered to a public body[3] and that even where a care order is made compulsorily placing the child in local authority care parents still retain their responsibility.[4] In short the CA 1989 through the concept of parental responsibility emphasises the idea that 'once a parent, always a parent' and that prima facie responsibility for deciding what should happen to their children even upon their separation should rest with the parents themselves.[5]

1 Discussed at para 2.62 et seq.
2 Cretney 'Defining the Limits of State Intervention: The Child and Courts' *in Children and the Law'* (ed Freestone, 1990) 58 at p 67.
3 Ie where the child is 'accommodated' by a local authority under s 20 (discussed in ch 6) parental responsibility is not acquired by the authority, see the discussion by Eekelaar, op cit para 3.3 above at pp 40–42.
4 The effect of care orders is discussed at paras 8.132 et seq.
5 Cf the Matrimonial Causes Procedure Committee (the 'Booth Committee') 1985, para 3.2.

3.5 Apart from the parent-child and the parent-state relationships, there is another relationship in which the concept of parental responsibility is relevant, namely, as between parents and other individuals. It can be as important to parents that they can look after their children without interference by other individuals as by the state. On the other hand, de facto carers need some authority to take normal 'day-to-day' decisions whilst looking after the child. These potentially conflicting standpoints are resolved by the CA 1989 in that parents with parental responsibility, are nevertheless permitted to 'arrange for some or all [of their responsibility] will be met by one or more persons acting on his behalf.'[1] Furthermore, those without parental responsibility but who have care of the child can 'do what is reasonable in all the circumstances of the case for the purpose of safeguarding or promoting the child's welfare'.[2]

1   Section 2(9), discussed further at para 3.95.
2   Section 3(5), discussed further at para 3.96.

2.   The practical effects of the changed terminology

3.6   Although the change of terminology from rights and duties to responsibility was neither intended nor expected to make a change in substance to the law, its effect upon lay persons should not be underestimated, for saying a parent has responsibilities rather than rights in itself conveys a quite different message. In any event there is more to the notion of parental responsibility than just a change in terminology. As s 2 makes clear not only can more than one person have parental responsibility at the same time but perhaps more importantly a person does not cease to have responsibility because someone else acquires it.[1] Furthermore each holder of responsibility can in theory[2] continue to exercise it by himself or herself without having to consult any other holder subject only to the overriding condition that he or she must not act incompatibly with any existing court order.[3] These detailed provisions created a scheme which gave effect to a coherent general philosophy much more consistent with a 'responsibility' based framework than with 'rights' based notions'[4] Ironically, following the implementation of the Human Rights Act 1998, this framework now has to operate in a much more 'rights' orientated context, though whether this will make any practical difference remains to be seen.

1   Section 2(5) and (6), discussed at paras 3.89 et seq.
2   But note the case law discussed at para 3.92.
3   Section 2(7) and (8), discussed at para 3.89.
4   Cretney, op cit para 3.4 above.

3.   The meaning and scope of 'parental responsibility'

(a)   The need to define parental responsibility

3.7   Parental responsibility needs to be definable by one means or other so that parents can know what they can or cannot do in relation to their child and, equally importantly, so others can know what the parents' position is. It is also important because the court's powers can sometimes be dependent on its scope. A 'prohibited steps order' can only be made to prevent any 'step which could be taken by a parent in meeting his parental responsibility for a child'.[1] A 'specific issue order' can only be made to determine 'a specific question which has arisen, or which may arise in connection with any aspect of parental responsibility for a child'.[2] Jurisdiction can also be dependent upon its scope since 'in a matter relating to parental responsibility over a child of both spouses, where the child is habitually resident in that Member State,' Art 3(1) of the Brussels II Regulation[3] vests exclusive jurisdiction in courts having jurisdiction under Art 2 (ie to hear divorce, nullity or separation proceedings).[4]

1 Section 8(1), discussed at paras 5.70 et seq.
2 Section 8(1), discussed at paras 5.73 et seq.
3 Ie Council Regulation (EC) No 1347/2000 on the jurisdiction and recognition and enforcement of judgments in matrimonial matters and in matters of parental responsibility for children of both spouses.
4 For a discussion of this Regulation see Lowe 'New International Conventions Affecting the Law Relating to Children – A Cause for Concern?' [2001] IFL 171, Nicholls 'Children and Brussels II' [2001] Fam Law and Shannon with Kennedy 'Jurisdictional and Recognition and Enforcement Issues in Proceedings Concerning Parental Responsibility under the Brussels II Convention' [2000] IFL III. Note that for this purpose the final arbiter of the meaning of parental responsibility is the European Court of Justice at Luxembourg.

3.8 The question remains whether parental responsibility should be defined by means of a general statutory provision or simply left to case law and statutory provisions dealing with specific points. While the English Law Commission favoured the latter strategy, the Scottish Law Commission considered that there are advantages in having a general statutory definition, namely:[1]

(a) that it would make explicit what was already implicit in the law;
(b) that it would counteract any impression that a parent has rights but no responsibilities; and
(c) that it would enable the law to make it clear that parental rights are not absolute or unqualified, but are conferred in order to enable parents to meet their responsibilities'.

1 Scot Law Com. Discussion Paper No 88 Parental Responsibilities and Rights, Guardianship and the Administration of Children's Property (1990) para 2.3.

(b) Lack of a comprehensive statutory definition

3.9 The CA 1989 does not contain a comprehensive definition of what 'parental responsibility' comprises. Section 3(1) states that it means 'all the rights, duties, powers, responsibility and authority which by law a parent of a child has in relation to the child and his property'. Responsibility is also stated to include the rights, powers and duties which a guardian of the child's estate (appointed before the CA 1989 came into force) had, viz the right 'to receive or recover in his own name, for the benefit of the child, property of whatever description and wherever situated which the child is entitled to receive or recover'.[1] On the other hand, by s 3(4)(b), parental responsibility does not include rights of succession to the child's property. This implements the Law Commission's recommendation[2] and emphasises that the incidents of parenthood with which the parental responsibility concept is concerned are those which relate to the care and upbringing of a child until he grows up. While this must include some power to administer the child's property on his behalf it does not include the right of succession. The latter right is a feature of being related to the deceased in a particular way and operates irrespective of who has responsibility for his upbringing.

1 Section 3(2) and (3).
2 Law Com No 172, para 2.7.

3.10 The provision in s 3(1) seems a poor one.[1] It immediately refers one back to the rights and duties model which 'responsibility' was supposed to replace.[2] However, the Law Commission did not consider it practicable to include a list of what parental responsibility comprises, pointing out[3] that such a list would have to change from time to time to meet differing needs and circumstances and, in the light of *Gillick v West Norfolk and Wisbech Area Health Authority*,[4] would have to vary with the age and maturity of the child and circumstances of the case.

1 It was described as a 'non definition' by Lord Meston in the debate on the Bill: HL Debs Vol 502, col 1172.
2 Note Ward LJ's criticisms in *Re S (Parental Responsibility)* [1995] 2 FLR 648 at 657.
3 Law Com No 172, para 2.6.
4 [1986] AC 112, [1985] 3 All ER 402, HL.

3.11 In contrast, the Children (Scotland) Act 1995, implementing the recommendation of the Scottish Law Commission,[1] provides first by s 1(1):

'a parent has in relation to his child the responsibility
(a) to safeguard and promote the child's health, development and welfare;
(b) to provide, in a manner appropriate to the stage of development of the child;
   (i) direction
   (ii) guidance
to the child;
(c) if the child is not living with the parent to maintain personal relations and direct contact with the child on a regular basis; and
(d) to act as the child's legal representative, but only in so far as compliance with this section is practicable and in the interests of the child.'

To enable a parent to fulfil those parental responsibilities, s 2(1) provides that a parent: has the right:
'(a) to have the child living with him or otherwise to regulate the child's residence;
(b) to control, direct or guide, in a manner appropriate to the stage of development of the child, the child's upbringing;
(c) if the child is not living with him, to maintain personal relations and contact with the child on a regular basis; and
(d) to act as the child's legal representative.'

1 See para 3.8 above.

3.12 Although the Scottish legislation might be thought to provide helpful *general* guidance as to the meaning of parental responsibility, the absence of such guidance in English Law has not so far proved problematic and accordingly it seems unlikely that reform of the CA 1989 would be deemed worthwhile.[1]

1 But note the call for reform along the Scottish lines in People Like Us (Report of the Review of the Standards for Children Living Away From Home – the Utting Report) (Department of Health and Welsh Office, 1997) para 6.2 and recommendation 9.

(c) Some further preliminary observations

3.13 A distinction needs to be drawn between the responsibility of parents with parental responsibility or guardians and that of other persons.[1] It is only the former, for example, whose agreement is required for the child's adoption; who can appoint a guardian[2] and who (probably) have a right to bury or cremate the deceased child.[3] The responsibility of local authorities is narrower still in that they cannot cause a child in their care 'to be brought up in any religious persuasion other than that in which he would have been brought up if the order had not been made'.[4] Responsibility is narrowest for those in whose favour an emergency protection order has been made.[5]

1 Indeed, it may be that some responsibilities are properly regarded as incidents of parenthood rather than of parental responsibility. In this respect the Law Commission's comment (Law Com. 172 at para 2.7) that they were only concerned with incidents of parenthood relating to the care and upbringing of children and not specifically with incidents that attached to parents qua parents, is to be noted.
2 Sections 12(3) and 33(6)(b) expressly state that those with responsibility by virtue of a residence or care order made in their favour do not have the right to agree to refuse to agree or the making of an adoption order or to appointing a guardian for a child.
3 Cf *R v Gwynedd County Council, ex p B* [1991] 2 FLR 365, CA.
4 Section 33(6)(a).
5 Viz only to take 'such action in meeting his parental responsibility for the child as is reasonably required to safeguard or promote the welfare of the child, (having regard in particular to the duration of the order)': s 44(5)(b), discussed at para 7.42.

3.14 The exercise of parental responsibility may be qualified by agreement of the parties (for example, the father agreeing that the child is to live with the mother) or by order of the court. In the latter instance the extent to which responsibility can be asserted is effectively limited by the paramountcy of the child's welfare which principle the court is bound to apply in any proceedings concerning his upbringing or the administration of his property.[1]

1 Ie under s 1(1) discussed at paras 2.2 et seq.

3.15 The older the child the less extensive and important parental responsibility may become. As Lord Denning MR so eloquently put it in respect of custody:[1]

'. . . it is a dwindling right which the court will hesitate to enforce against the wishes of the child, the older he is. It starts with the right of control and ends with little more than advice.'

1 *Hewer v Bryant* [1970] 1 QB 357 at 369, [1969] 3 All ER 578 at 582, CA. Even so parents may not lose all their responsibility even where their child is 'Gillick competent' see post, para 3.32.

3.16 There is no known tort of interference with parental rights nor therefore with parental responsibility. This was established in *F v Wirral Metropolitan Borough Council*[1] in which the parents argued that what was originally understood by them to be a short-term placement with foster parents and to which arrangement they had agreed, and which ended by becoming a long-term arrangement to which they had not agreed, constituted a wrongful interference with their rights. The parents argued that Art 8 of the European Convention of Human Rights and the European Court's decision of *R v United Kingdom*[2] recognised a right of consortium between parent and child as one of the 'fundamental elements of family life'. After an exhaustive review of the cases the Court of Appeal unanimously concluded, in Purchas LJ's words:

'neither under the old common law, apart from the action per quod servitium amisit nor under modern authority is there a parental right necessary to found a cause of action against a stranger upon which the common law would grant a remedy in damages.'

1 [1991] Fam 69, [1991] 2 All ER 648, CA, on which see Bainham 'Interfering with Parental Responsibility. A New Challenge for the Law of Torts' (1990) 3 Jo. of Child Law 3. See also *Re S (a Minor) (Parental Rights)* [1993] Fam Law 572.
2 [1988] 2 FLR 445, E Ct HR.

3.17 The absence of responsibility does not necessarily mean that a person has no obligation towards the child. For example, unmarried fathers have a statutory duty to maintain their children regardless of whether they also have parental responsibility.[1] Conversely, as the Department of Health's *Introduction to the Children Act 1989* observes:[2]

'. . . the effect of having parental responsibility is to empower a person to take most decisions in the child's life.' It does not make him a parent or relative of the child in law, for example, to give him rights of inheritance, or to place him under a statutory duty to maintain a child.'

1 De facto carers also have a statutory duty to protect the child and to ensure that the child is properly educated, see respectively, paras 3.26 and 3.39.
2 See above at para 2.4.

(d) What parental responsibility comprises

3.18 While it may not be possible to state with certainty the precise ambit of responsibility, the following would seem to be the more important aspects:[1]

- Providing a home for the child;
- Having contact with the child;
- Protecting and maintaining the child;
- Disciplining the child;
- Determining and providing for the child's education;
- Determining the child's religion;
- Consenting to the child's medical treatment;
- Choosing the child's name and agreeing to its subsequent change;
- Consenting to the child's marriage;
- Agreeing or withholding agreement to the child's adoption;
- Applying for or vetoing the issue of a child's passport;
- Taking the child outside the United Kingdom and consenting to the child's emigration;
- Administering the child's property;
- Representing the child in legal proceedings;
- Appointing a guardian for the child; and
- Disposing of the child's corpse.

1 For detailed discussion see Lowe and Douglas, above at 350 et seq, and *Clarke Hall and Morrison*, above at 1 [97] et seq.

(I) HOUSING AND LOOKING AFTER THE CHILD

3.19 The key aspect of parental responsibility is that of looking after and bringing up the child. Based upon the common law right of a person to possession of his child, it now seems better to say that those with responsibility have a prima facie[1] responsibility to provide a home for the child and the power to determine where the child should live.[2] This responsibility is protected by the criminal law to the extent that persons without responsibility commit the crime of child abduction if they remove the child without lawful authority.[3] As between individuals with parental responsibility the right is qualified to the extent that removal of a child outside the United Kingdom without the consent of other individuals with parental responsibility can amount to a crime.[4] Associated with providing a home is the necessary accompanying power, inter alia, physically to control children at any rate until the years of discretion. As Lord Lane CJ once commented, restraint of a child's movement is usually well within the realms of reasonable parental discipline.[5] Responsibility also includes the power to control the child's movements whilst in someone else's care.[6] On the other hand a parent and, presumably therefore, any other person with parental responsibility, can commit the common law crime of kidnapping[7] or unlawful imprisonment[8] if a child (old enough to make up his own mind) is forcibly taken or detained against his will.

1 Ie unless a court order (viz a residence, care or emergency protection order) has been made giving someone else that prima facie right.
2 See *Re M (Minors) (Residence Order: Jurisdiction)* [1993] 1 FLR 495 at 499 per Balcombe LJ.
3 Child Abduction Act 1984, s 2.
4 Child Abduction Act 1984, s 1.
5 *R v Rahman* (1985) 81 Cr App Rep 349 at 353, CA. See also *Re K (A Child) (Secure Accommodation: Right to Liberty)* [2001] Fam 377, [2001] 2 WLR 1141, [2001] 2 All ER 719, CA (but cf Butler-Sloss P and Thorpe LJ applying *Nielsen v Denmark* (1989) 11 EHRR 175, E Ct HR, discussed at paras 9.4 and 9.5), *Hewer v Bryant* [1970] 1 QB 357 at 373, [1969] 3 All ER 578, at 585, CA, per Sachs LJ.
6 *Fleming v Pratt* (1823) 1 LJ OS KB 194.
7 *R v D* [1984] AC 778, [1984] 2 All ER 449, HL.
8 *R v Rahman*, supra.

(ii) Discipline

3.20 Associated with the power of physical control is the power to discipline the child. A person with parental responsibility may lawfully chastise and inflict reasonable corporal punishment upon the child.[1] What is reasonable is a question of fact and will depend upon the age and strength of the child and the nature and degree of punishment.[2]
If it goes beyond what is reasonable it is unlawful and renders the individual criminally liable for assault, or, depending on the gravity, for more serious offences.[3] If it amounts to degrading punishment,[4] or is inflicted without parental consent it is in breach of the European Convention on Human Rights.[5] The power to discipline a child may be delegated[6] but it seems it can only be exercised by those in loco parentis to the child.[7] However, corporal punishment is forbidden in all schools,[8] children's homes,[9] and foster placements.[10]

1 See the review by Elias J in *The Queen on the Application of Williamson v Secretary of State for Education and Employment* [2001] EWHC Admin 900, [2002] 1 FLR 493 at 498, paras [19] et seq. *R v Hopley* (1860) 2 F & F 202; *R v Woods* (1921) 85 JP 272, CYPA 1933, s 1(7).
2 Where reasonable chastisement is raised as a defence to criminal charges, a judge should direct the jury to consider the following: '(i) the nature and context of the defendant's behaviour; (ii) the duration of that behaviour; (iii) the physical and mental consequences in respect of the child; (iv) the age and personal characteristics of the child; (v) the reasons given by the defendant for administering the punishment.' *R v H (Assault of Child: Reasonable Chastisement)* [2001] EWCA Crim 1024, [2001] 3 FCR 144, [2001] 2 FLR 431, CA.
3 CYPA 1933, s 1 and *R v Derriviere* (1969) 53 Cr App Rep 637, CA. Note that an unreasonable restraint of a child's movement can render a parent guilty of unlawful imprisonment: *R v Rahman* (1985) 81 Cr App Rep 349, CA.
4 Cf *Costello-Roberts v UK* [1994] ELR 1 – slippering a seven-year-old held not to be 'degrading'.

5   See eg *A v United Kingdom (Human Rights: Punishment of Child)* [1988] 2 FLR 959, E Ct HR, and *Campbell and Cosans v UK* (1982) 4 EHRR 293, E Ct HR.
6   Either expressly as in *Sutton London Borough Council v Davis* [1994] 1 FLR 737, or impliedly, as in the case of schools.
7   See eg *R v Woods* (1921) 85 JP 272 – unlawful for an elder brother to administer corporal punishment on his sibling where both were living with their father.
8   Education Act 1996, s 548, as substituted by s 131 of the School Standards and Framework Act 1998, which as Elias J pointed out in *The Queen on the Application of Williamson*, supra, above at para [16], removes the defence of justification which is necessary if the intentional infliction of physical harm is not to be considered unlawful, rather than prohibits corporal punishment as such.
9   Children's Homes Regulations 2001 (SI 2001/3967) reg 17(5)(a), which simply prohibits the use of any form of corporal punishment.
10 Fostering Services Regulations 2002 (SI 2002/57), reg 28(5)(b), Sch 5, point 8, which requires foster parents in England to make a written agreement not to administer corporal punishment.

(III)   PROTECTION

3.21   The common law duty to protect, inter alia, a child[1] has largely been replaced by the Children and Young Persons Act 1933, Pt I, which makes certain forms of behaviour criminal offences.[2] The offences are dependent on the likelihood of the child being caused unnecessary suffering or injury.

1   In fact the common law duty is owed by anyone who willingly undertakes to look after another who is incapable of looking after himself. It can therefore continue after the child's majority, see *R v Chattaway* (1922) 17 Cr App Rep 7, CCA (starvation of a helpless daughter aged 25), and can extend to a step-child or foster child, see *R v Bubb* (1850) 4 Cox CC 455; *R v Gibbons and Proctor* (1918) 13 Cr App Rep 134, CCA.
2   See *Clarke Hall and Morrison* 7[1001] et seq for further details.

3.22   A parent has no duty parallel with the statutory duty placed on a local authority having the care of a child, to promote his or her welfare.[1] On the other hand it has been said that there is a 'natural and moral duty of a parent to show affection, care and interest'.[2]

1   CA 1989, Pt III, see ch 6.
2   *Re P (infants)* [1962] 3 All ER 789, [1962] 1 WLR 1296, an adoption case.

(IV)   CONTACT WITH THE CHILD

3.23   Prima facie parental responsibility encompasses seeing or otherwise having contact with the child. While not an absolute right since in any litigation it will be contingent upon the child's welfare, nevertheless as Lord Oliver said in *Re KD (a Minor) (Ward: Termination Of Access)*:[1] 'As a general proposition a natural parent has a claim to [contact with] his or her child to which the court will pay regard and it would not I think, be inappropriate to describe such a claim as a "right"'. This 'claim' is protected to the extent that there is a statutory presumption of reasonable contact between a child in local authority care or under emergency protection and, inter alia, those with parental responsibility.[2] These latter provisions were enacted following the European Court of Human Rights ruling[3] that the absence of any right to challenge a termination of contact by a local authority amounted to a breach of arts 8 and 13 of the Convention. Art 9(3) of the UN Convention on the Rights of the Child 1989 also provides:

'State Parties shall respect the right of the child who is separated from one or both parties to maintain personal relations and direct contact with both parents on a regular basis, except if it is contrary to the child's best interests.'

1 [1988] AC 806 at 827, [1988] 1 All ER 577 at 590.Cf *Sanderson v McManus* 1997 SLT 629, sub nom *S v M (Access Order)* [1997] 1 FLR 980, HL (Scotland) in which Lord Hope held that the onus was on the unmarried father to establish that continued contact was for the child's welfare.
2 Sections 34(1) and 44(13).
3 See *R v UK* [1988] 2 FLR 445. Note also the subsequent decisions: *Hokkanen v Finland* (1995) 19 EHRR 134, [1996] 1 FLR 289, E Ct HR – failure by the Sate to enforce a parent's right of access held to be in breach of Art 8; *Elsholz v Germany* [2000] 3 FCR 385, [2000] 2 FLR 486, E Ct HR – denial of continuing contact with his child by an unmarried father without obtaining expert psychological opinion together with a dismissal without a hearing of the father's appeal, held to be a breach of Art 8; *Ciliz v The Netherlands* [2000] 2 FLR 469, E Ct HR – deportation of divorced father before the conclusion of a contact hearing also held to be in breach of Art 8.

3.24 Given that it is a normal assumption that a child will benefit from continued contact with both parents[1] it may be that parental responsibility properly encompasses the prima facie duty to allow the child to have contact with either or both parents. Whether such responsibility extends to a parent having an obligation him or herself to maintain contact with the child can be debated.[2]

1 See eg Lord Oliver in *Re KD*, supra at 827 and 590 respectively and *M v M (child: access)* [1973] 2 All ER 81, per Wrangham J at 85 and per Latey J at p 88.
2 In Scotland the Children (Scotland) Act 1995, s 1(1)(d) (set out at para 3.11) clearly states that a parent has a responsibility to maintain personal relations and direct contact with the child. But even supposing that there is a theoretical duty to see the child, it would be difficult to enforce this order against an unwilling parent or even on an unwilling child.

3.25 If parental responsibility encompasses the power to control the child's movements it seems to follow that it includes the power to restrict those with whom the child may have contact. In *Nottingham County Council v P*,[1] in which it was sought to exclude the father from the matrimonial home and to restrict his contact with the children, Ward J saw 'the force of the submission' that steps taken by a parent in meeting his parental responsibility are necessarily wide steps and could extend to controlling contact with the other parent. In *Re M (Care: Leave to Interview Child)*[2] Hale J was more forthright, commenting: 'Until the child is old enough to decide for himself, a parent undoubtedly has some control over whom he may see and who may see him.'

1 [1994] Fam 18, [1993] 3 All ER 815.
2 [1995] 1 FLR 825, following *Re F (Specific Issue: Child Interview)* [1995] 1 FLR 819, CA.

(v) MEDICAL TREATMENT

3.26 Any person over the age of 16 who has responsibility (in the sense of having de facto control) for a child under the age of 16 has a duty to obtain essential medical assistance for that child.[1] However, in most cases,[2] before any treatment can be given, medical practitioners need a valid consent, for without it they may be open to a prosecution for battery upon the child or for one of the graver forms of assault, or be subject to a claim in tort for trespass for which the practitioner may be liable for loss regardless of fault.[3] Prima facie anyone with parental responsibility, including a local authority,[4] can give a valid consent to the child's surgical, medical or dental treatment. However, this power of consent does not necessarily extend to all forms of treatment. Furthermore this power is without prejudice to the ability of a 16 to 17-year-old or a 'Gillick competent' child under the age of 16 to give a valid consent, nor does it preclude the court from subsequently overriding an otherwise valid consent or from sanctioning treatment otherwise opposed. In any event no practitioner can be forced to give treatment contrary to their clinical judgment.[5] Hence, as Lord Donaldson MR observed in *Re W (A Minor) (Medical Treatment: Court's Jurisdiction)*,[6] no question of consenting or refusing consent arises unless and until a medical or dental practitioner advises such treatment and is willing to undertake it and:

> 'Regardless of whether the minor or anyone else with authority to do so consents to the treatment, that practitioner will be liable to the minor in negligence if he fails to advise with reasonable skill and care and to have due regard to the best interests of his patient'.

1 Children and Young Persons Act 1933, s 1.
2 Medical practitioners have long been advised that on the basis of the common law defence of necessity emergency treatment may be given if the well-being of the child could suffer by delay caused by obtaining consents. Ministry of Health Circular F/19/1/1967 and Home Office Circular 63/1968. See also *Re F (Mental Patient: Sterilisation)* [1990] 2 AC 1 at 52, sub nom *F v West Berkshire Health Authority (mental health act comr intervening)* [1989] 2 All ER 545 at 548, per Lord Bridge, and, in particular *Re A (Children) (Conjoined Twins: Surgical Separation)* [2001] Fam 147, [2000] 4 All ER 961, CA, per Brooke LJ.
3 See eg *Re R (A Minor) (Wardship: Medical Treatment)* [1992] Fam 11 at 22, [1991] 4 All ER 177 at 184, CA per Lord Donaldson MR.
4 *R v Kirklees Metropolitan Borough Council, ex p C* [1992] 2 FLR 117.
5 *Re J (A Minor) (Child In Care: Medical Treatment)* [1993] Fam 15, [1992] 4 All ER 614, CA.
6 [1993] Fam 64 at 83, [1992] 4 All ER 627 at 639, CA.

3.27 Although, as a general rule anyone with parental responsibility can give a valid consent to the child's medical treatment, the power is subject to a number of qualifications. First, not all those with parental responsibility are in the same position. In particular those having responsibility by virtue of an emergency protection order only have authority to take such action 'as is reasonably required to safeguard or promote the welfare of the child'.[1] Hence, while such persons can give a valid consent to day-to-day treatment they cannot agree to major elective surgery. In these cases, however, the applicant can seek a court direction.[2]

1 Section 44(5)(b).
2 Section 44(6)(b).

3.28 Secondly, although the power of consent vested in those with parental responsibility extends to most forms of surgical, medical or dental treatment including treatment of drugs or for drug abuse and, by analogy with s 8(2) of the Family Law Reform Act 1969, diagnostic procedures such as HIV testing and, by reason of s 21(3) of that Act, (as amended), the taking of bodily samples from the child to be used in tests to determine paternity, and ritual male circumcision,[1] even parents with parental responsibility are not empowered to consent to all forms of treatment.

1 *Re J (child's religious upbringing and circumcision)* [2001] 1 FCR 307, sub nom *Re J (Specific Issue Orders: Child's Religious Upbringing)* [2000] 1 FLR 571, CA.

3.29 According to Lord Templeman in *Re B (a Minor) (Wardship: Sterilisation)*,[1] sterilisation of a girl under 18 should only be carried out with the leave of a High Court judge. In other words, even parents, with parental responsibility cannot give a valid consent. Notwithstanding that Lord Templeman was the only Law Lord to suggest this, as Lord Donaldson MR has subsequently put it in *Re W (a Minor) (Medical Treatment)*[2] parties might be well advised to apply to the court for guidance. Whether a similar requirement extends to other forms of treatment has yet to be decided.[3] However, High Court leave is not required to perform an operation for therapeutic reasons even though a side effect (but not the main purpose) will be to sterilise the child.[4] Furthermore it has been held that notwithstanding that a decision as to sterilisation is a matter for the judge, parents (or others with parental responsibility) nevertheless retain the responsibility for bringing the issue before the High Court.[5]

1 [1988] AC 199 at 205 [1987] 2 All ER 206 at 214.
2 [1993] Fam 64, [1992] 4 All ER 627, CA. This is also the position in Australia: see *Department of Health and Community Services (NT) Secretary v JWB and SMB* (1982) 66 ALJR 300 (Australian High Court).
3   It might conceivably cover all irreversible treatment for non-therapeutic reasons.
4 *Re E (a minor) (medical treatment)* [1991] FCR 771 [1991] 2 FLR 585, per Sir Stephen Brown P. Note that in *Re B (A Minor) (Wardship: Sterilisation)* [1988] AC 199, [1987] 2 All ER 206, the Law Lords rejected the legal relevance of the notion of a non-therapeutic sterilisation.
5 *Re HG (specific issue order: sterilisation)*[1993] 1 FCR 553, [1993] 1 FLR 587, discussed further at para 5.124. See also *Practice Note* [1993] 3 All ER 222.

3.30 A third qualification on the power of consent of those with parental responsibility is the age of the child. Although according to, *Re W (A Minor) (Medical Treatment: Court's Jurisdiction)*,[1] those with parental responsibility retain their power to give a valid consent throughout the child's minority, it seems clear[2] that

(1) a child aged 16 or 17 or who is 'Gillick competent' if under the age of 16 can give a valid consent which cannot be countermanded by an adult;[3]
(2) although in theory a valid consent may be given by an adult with parental responsibility notwithstanding the opposition of the 'Gillick competent' or 16 or 17-year-old child, in practice no treatment should be given without prior court sanction;[4]and
(3) any decision by a parent can subsequently be overridden by the High Court.[5]

1 [1993] Fam 64, [1992] 4 All ER 627, CA.
2 This view was most clearly expressed by Lord Donaldson MR but seemed also to be accepted by Balcombe LJ, both of whom expressly rejected the contention that Lord Scarman should have been taken to be saying in *Gillick v West Norfolk and Wisbech Area Health Authority* [1986] AC 112, [1985] 3 All ER 402, HL that parents of a 'Gillick competent' child had no right at all to consent to medical treatment of the child.
3 See Lord Donaldson in *Re W*, above [1993] Fam at 83–84, [1992] 4 All ER at 639. The child's consent can, however, be overridden by the court: see para 3.35.
4 This, at any rate, was Nolan LJ's view in *Re W*, above [1993] Fam at 94, [1992] 4 All ER at 648–649. Lord Donaldson MR, at 84 and 640 respectively, thought that a child's refusal was a very important consideration for parents deciding whether themselves to give consent.
5 See para 3.35.

3.31 Section 8(1) of the Family Law Reform Act 1969 provides that the consent of a minor over the age of 16:

'to any surgical, medical or dental treatment which, in the absence of consent, would constitute a trespass to his person, shall be as effective as it would be if he were of full age; and where a minor has by virtue of this section given an effective consent to any treatment it shall not be necessary to obtain any consent for it from his parent or guardian.'

By s 8(2) the power to give a valid independent consent extends to 'any procedure undertaken for the purposes of diagnosis' (which would include HIV tests) and 'to any procedure (including, in particular, the administration of an anaesthetic) which is ancillary to any treatment . . .' However, this statutory right of consent does not extend to the donation of blood or organs.[1] It would also seem that the power of consent does not extend to the child's own sterilisation.[2]

1 *Re W (a Minor) (Medical Treatment: Court's Jurisdiction)* [1993] Fam 64, [1992] 4 All ER 627, per Lord Donaldson MR. Nevertheless there would seem to be a non-statutory power to consent to such treatment provided the child is 'Gillick competent'; see para 3.33.
2 See para 3.29.

3.32 Although it might have been inferred from s 8(1) that a child below the age of 16 cannot give a valid consent, relying in part on s 8(3) which provides that 'Nothing in this section shall be construed as making ineffective any consent which would have been effective if this section had not been enacted', it was established by *Gillick v West Norfolk and Wisbech Area Health Authority*[1] that provided they are of sufficient age and understanding, children under the age of 16 can give valid consent. In *Gillick* it was specifically held that a doctor may in certain circumstances lawfully prescribe contraception for a girl under 16 years of age without the consent of her parents. In so holding the majority of the House of Lords considered that a girl could have legal capacity to give a valid consent to contraceptive advice and treatment including medical examination. Whether she gave a valid consent in any particular case would depend on circumstances, including her intellectual capacity to understanding advice. There is no absolute parental right requiring the parents' consent to be sought. Speaking of medical treatment generally, Lord Scarman said:

'It will be a question of fact whether a child seeking advice has sufficient understanding of what is involved to give a consent valid in law. Until the child achieves the capacity to consent, the parental right to make the decision continues save only in exceptional circumstances. Emergency, parental neglect, abandonment of the child, or inability to find the parent are examples of exceptional situations justifying the doctor proceeding to treat the child without parental knowledge and consent, but there will arise, no doubt, other exceptional situations in which it will be reasonable for the doctor to proceed without the parent's consent.'

Applying this to contraceptive advice and treatment he said:

'. . . there is much that has to be understood by a girl under the age of 16 if she is to have legal capacity to consent to such treatment. It is not enough that she should understand the nature of the advice which is being given: she must also have a sufficient maturity to understand what is involved'.

Lord Fraser set out five preconditions before a doctor would be considered justified in prescribing contraceptive treatment:

(a) that the girl (although under 16 years of age) will understand his advice;
(b) that he cannot persuade her to inform her parents or to allow him to inform the parents that she is seeking contraceptive advice;
(c) that she is very likely to begin or to continue having sexual intercourse with or without contraceptive treatment;
(d) that unless she receives contraceptive advice or treatment her physical or mental health or both are likely to suffer; or

(e) that her best interests require him to give her contraceptive advice, treatment or both without the parental consent.

1   [1986] AC 112, [1985] 3 All ER 402, HL.

3.33   The test for determining what has become known as 'Gillick competence' seems particularly strict in the case of contraception and the courts seem similarly cautious when considering a child's competence to refuse life saving treatment.[1] In *Re R (a Minor) (Wardship: Medical Treatment)*[2] it was held that competence is not to be assessed at a particular moment in time but in conjunction with the child's whole medical history and background. 'Gillick competence' cannot therefore fluctuate on a day-to-day basis so that a child is one day regarded as competent but not on another. If the child is held competent then, unlike the statutory right conferred by s 8 of the Family Law Reform Act 1969, the power of consent extends to donating blood and organs.[3]

1   See, for example, *Re L (medical treatment: Gillick competency)* [1999] 2 FCR 524, [1998] 2 FLR 810 – 14-year-old girl who had had a 'sheltered life' and who was in a life threatening condition but who could not be told of the potentially 'horrible nature' of her death if she did not have a blood transfusion, held not be 'competent'; and *Re S (a Minor) (Consent to Medical Treatment)* [1994] 2 FLR 1065 – 15 and a half-year-old girl, who appeared not to understand of the inevitability of her death and of the pain and distress if her treatment was discontinued, held not to be 'competent'.
2   [1992] Fam 11 at 25–26 (per Lord Donaldson MR) and 31 (per Farquaharson LJ), [1991] 4 All ER 177 at 187 and 191 respectively.
3   *Re W (A Minor) (Medical Treatment: Court's Jurisdiction)* [1993] Fam 64 at 84, [1992] 4 All ER 627 at 639, per Lord Donaldson MR.

3.34   Although s 8 of the 1969 Act and *Gillick* establish that 16 or 17-year-olds and those who are 'Gillick competent' under the age of 16 can give valid consents to medical treatment, they are not to be taken to imply that such children have a right of veto. On the contrary it is established that the court can override such children's refusal and, at any rate according to Lord Donaldson MR in *Re W*, even parents can in theory give a valid consent.[1]

1   See para 3.30 above.

3.35   A court can override a decision by a parent to consent or refuse consent to the child's medical treatment. In *Re D (A Minor) (Wardship: Sterilisation)*,[1] Heilbron J declined to permit a sterilisation operation on a child after the mother had consented. Conversely, in *Re A (Children; Conjoined Twins: Surgical Separation)*[2] the Court of Appeal sanctioned, contrary to the parents' wishes, the separation of conjoined twins notwithstanding that the inevitable result would be to kill the weaker twin but preserve the life of the stronger twin. In *Re C (a minor) (HIV testing)*[3] the court ordered, contrary to the parents' wishes, an HIV test to be carried out on a baby. Other examples include *Re B (A Minor) (Wardship: Medical Treatment)*[4] in which an operation to save the life of a Down's syndrome baby was sanctioned notwithstanding the parents' opposition; *Re B (Wardship: Abortion)*,[5] in which the court, overruling the mother's objections, gave permission for a 12-year-old to have an abortion and *Re R (a minor) (blood transfusion)*,[6] in which the court overrode the opposition to a blood transfusion for their baby by parents who were Jehovah's witnesses. It is equally established that the court can override both a 16-year-old and a

'Gillick competent' child's refusal to consent to treatment. In *Re W (A Minor) (Medical Treatment: Court's Jurisdiction)*[7] the Court of Appeal held that a 16-year-old anorexic child's refusal of life saving treatment should be overruled, though it was also emphasised that such a refusal should not be overridden lightly since it 'is a very important consideration in making clinical judgments and for parents and the court in deciding whether themselves to give consent'.[8]

1 [1976] Fam 185, [1976] 1 All ER 326.
2 [2001] Fam 147; [2000] 4 All ER 961, CA.
3 [1999] 3 FCR 289, [1999] 2 FLR 1004, per Wilson J. But note the judge declined to order the mother to stop breast feeding her child. After detailed consideration the Court of Appeal refused permission to appeal against Wilson J's judgment, see [1999] 2 FLR at 1017.
4 (1981) 3 FLR 117.
5 [1991] 2 FLR 426.
6 [1993] 2 FCR 544, [1993] 2 FLR 757, discussed further at para 12.35.
7 [1993] Fam 64, [1992] 4 All ER 627, CA. See also *Re C (Detention: Medical Treatment)* [1997] 2 FLR 180, per Wall J, *Re L (medical treatment: Gillick competence)* [1999] 2 FCR 524 at 527, [1998] 2 FLR 810 at 813, per Sir Stephen Brown P, *Re M (child: refusal of medical treatment)* [1999] 2 FCR 577, [1999] 2 FLR 1097 (in which Johnson J overrode an intelligent 15-year-old girl's refusal to consent to have a heart transplant because she did not want someone else's heart) and *Re E (A Minor) (Wardship: Medical Treatment)* [1993] 1 FLR 386, in which a 15-year-old Jehovah's Witness' refusal to consent to lifesaving blood transfusions was overruled.
8 Per Lord Donaldson MR at [1993] Fam 84, [1992] 4 All ER 640.

3.36 The High Court's powers of consent are wider than those of a parent. They can extend to sanctioning a child's sterilisation,[1] and, in relation to a terminally ill child, to authorising treatment to relieve the child's suffering but not to achieve a short prolongation of life.[2] On the other hand it is established that the court has no power to order a medical practitioner to treat a child contrary to his clinical judgment.[3]

1 See *Re B (A Minor) (Wardship: Sterilisation)* [1988] AC 199 at 205, [1987] 2 All ER 206 at 214, per Lord Templeman. See also *Re R (A Minor) (Wardship: Consent to Medical Treatment)* [1992] Fam 11 at 25B and 28C–F, [1991] 4 All ER 177 at 186g and 189c–d, CA In that case the court said that it would accept opinions of medical staff looking after the child if they decided that the aim of nursing care should be to ease the ward's suffering rather than to achieve a short prolongation of life. See also *Re C (a minor) (medical treatment)* [1998] 1 FCR 1, [1998] 1 FLR 384, per Sir Stephen Brown P – the best interests of a 16 month-old child suffering from the fatal disease, spinal muscular atrophy, was, as the medical team recommended, to be taken off a ventilating machine; *A National Health Service Trust v D* [2001] 2 FCR 577, [2000] 2 FLR 677, in which Cazalet J observed that allowing a child to die with dignity fell within Art 3 of the European Convention on Human Rights (as established by *D v United Kingdom* (1997) 24 EHRR 423) and could not therefore be considered to be in breach of the right to life under Art 2. Note also *Royal Wolverhampton Hospitals NHS Trust v B* [2000] 2 FCR 76, [2000] 1 FLR 953, in which the court granted a declaration that a terminally ill child be treated in accordance with a paediatrician's advice'.
2 *Re C (A Minor) (Wardship: Medical Treatment)* [1990] Fam 26, [1989] 2 All ER 782, CA.
3 *Re J (A Minor) (Child in Care: Medical Treatment)* [1993] Fam 15, [1992] 4 All ER 614, CA.

3.37 In deciding what order to make the primary decision for the court is what is in the best interests of the child and not the reasonableness of the parents' refusal of consent.[1] It has been held[2] in a case of a 16-year-old anorexic child, that the court's inherent power includes the authorisation of her detention in the clinic for the purposes of treatment as well as the power to authorise the use of reasonable force, if necessary, for the purpose.

1   Per Butler-Sloss LJ in *Re T (a minor) (wardship: medical treatment)* [1997] 1 All ER 906, [1997] 1 WLR 242, 'on the most unusual facts of the case' it was held that the child's best interests required that his future treatment should be left in the hands of his devoted parents. Accordingly, the Court of Appeal declined to override a parental refusal (contrary to medical advice) to consent to their 18-month-old child having a liver transplant.
2   Per Wall J in *Re C (Detention: Medical Treatment)* [1997] 2 FLR 180. See also *A Metropolitan Borough Council v DB* [1997] 1 FLR 767.

(VI)   EDUCATION

3.38   As Ward LJ has observed[1] 'arranging for education commensurate with the child's intellectual needs and abilities is [an] . . . incident of the parental responsibility which arises from the duty of the parent to secure the child's education'. This responsibility derives from the common law right of a parent to determine what education the child should receive.[2] Parents' rights to determine their children's education are also protected by the European Convention on Human Rights to the extent of respecting their religious and philosophical convictions.[3]

1   *Re Z (A Minor) (Identification: Restrictions on Publication)* [1997] Fam 1 at 26, sub nom *Re Z (a minor) (freedom of publication)* [1995] 4 All ER 961 at 980, CA.
2   For a striking example, see *Tremain's Case* (1719) 1 Stra 167. See also *Andrews v Salt* (1873) 8 Ch App 622 – father's wishes to be respected after his death.
3   Protocol No 1, Art 2.

3.39   At common law, because the duty was unenforceable,[1] parents could formerly choose not to have their children educated. However, since the Education Act 1944 (now consolidated by the Education Act 1996) parents of every child between the ages of five and 16 have had to ensure that the child receives 'efficient full-time education suitable (a) to his age, ability, aptitude and (b) to any special education needs he may have, either by regular attendance at school other otherwise'.[2] 'Parent' for these purposes includes any person who is not a parent but who has parental responsibility for the child or who has care of the child.[3] Failure to perform this duty can result in a criminal prosecution[4] and the child may be subject to an education supervision order.[5]

1   *Hodges v Hodges* (1796) Peake Add Cas 79.
2   Education Act 1996, ss 7 and 8.
3   Education Act 1996 s 576(1). This definition can cover a local authority foster parent: *Fairpo v Humberside County Council* [1997] 1 FLR 339.
4   Education Act 1996, s 443. Formerly, parents could be fined but not imprisoned for a breach of a school attendance order for failure to secure regular attendance at school. However, under the Education Act 1996, s 444(8A), parents can now be imprisoned for up to three months where they know that their child is failing to attend regularly at the school and fail without reasonable justification to cause him to do so. See further *Clarke Hall and Morrison* 4[621].
5   CA 1989, s 36, see paras 8.180 et seq.

3.40   Those with parental responsibility or who have care of children can discharge their duty by ensuring that they attend independent rather than state schools or even by educating them at home, provided in this latter instance the local education authority is satisfied that the child is receiving efficient and full-time education suitable to his age etc. Disputes between individuals (usually divorcing parents) about appropriate schooling may be resolved by means of a specific issue or prohibited steps order under s 8 of the CA 1989.[1] Where state education is relied upon, except in the case of a child permanently excluded from two or more schools, education authorities are required to comply with 'parental' wishes as to choice of school save, importantly where compliance would 'prejudice the provision of efficient education or the efficient use of resources; if the preferred school is a foundation or voluntary aided school and compliance would be incompatible with any arrangements between the governing body and local education authority or if arrangements for admission to the preferred school are based on pupils with high ability or with aptitude and compliance would be incompatible with those criteria.[2] To enable a reasoned choice to be made 'parents' must be given information about the primary and secondary education available.[3]

1 See eg *Re A (children) (specific issue order: parental dispute)* [2001] 1 FCR 210, [2001] 1 FLR 121 and *Re P (a minor) (education)* [1992] 1 FCR 45, [1992] 1 FLR 316, CA.
2 Education Act 1996, s 9 and the School Standards Framework Act 1998, s 86 et seq. See further *Clarke Hall and Morrison* at 6 [522]. For the position of children with special educational needs, see *Clarke Hall and Morrison* 6[901] et seq.
3 School Standards and Framework Act 1998, s 92.

(VII) RELIGIOUS UPBRINGING

3.41 A person with parental responsibility has a right to determine the child's religious education, though there is no duty to give a child a religious upbringing. As Wall J said in *Re J (child's religious upbringing and circumcision)*[1] 'Parental responsibility . . . clearly includes the right to bring up children in a particular religious faith, or in none.' Based on the common law,[2] this right to determine the child's religious education is protected to the extent that a local authority cannot cause a child in their care 'to be brought up in any religious persuasion other than that in which he would have been brought up if the order had not been made.'[3] Adoption agencies must also, when placing a child for adoption have regard, so far as practicable, to any wishes of the child's parent or guardian as to the child's religious upbringing.[4]

1 [1999] 2 FCR 345 at 353, sub nom *Re J (Specific Issue Orders: Muslim Upbringing and Circumcision)* [1999] 2 FLR 678 at 685 – decision upheld by Court of Appeal, see [2000] 1 FCR 307, [2000] 1 FLR 571, CA.
2 *Andrews v Salt* (1873) 8 Ch App 622. The rule, see eg *Hawksworth v Hawksworth* (1871) LR Ch App 539, that unless there were exceptional circumstances, children had to be brought up in the religion of their father, was abolished by the Guardianship of Infants Act 1925, s 1.
3 CA 1989, s 33(6)(a).
4 Adoption Act 1976, s 7. But, note, under the Adoption and Children Bill 2002, there will be a more general requirement upon adoption agencies to have regard to the child's religious persuasion when placing the child for adoption, rather than specifically having to have regard to parental wishes.

3.42 Parents with parental responsibility and those caring for the child can require a child's exclusion from religious studies lessons and school assembly.[1] Although the courts will seek to pay 'serious heed to the religious wishes of a parent'[2] (and indeed to prevent a parent bringing up his child *simply* on the basis of his religious belief is contrary to the European Convention on Human Rights),[3] in the event of a dispute the court must treat the child's welfare as the paramount consideration.[4]

1 School Standards and Framework Act 1998, s 71, discussed in *Clarke Hall and Morrison* at 6 [607].
2 *J v C* [1969] 1 All 788 at 801, per Ungoed-Thomas J.

3 Art 9 on which see *Hoffman v Austria* (1993) 17 EHRR 293, [1994] 1 FCR 913, E Ct HR.
   Note the comment at [1994] Fam Law 673. But a parent's right to manifest his religion has to
   be balanced against the welfare of the child and the rights of the other parent – see Thorpe LJ
   in *Re J (child's religious upbringing and circumcision)* [2000] 1 FCR 307 at 311, [2000] 1 FLR
   571 at 575, CA.
4 See eg *Re S (Minors) (Access: Religious Upbringing)* [1992] 2 FLR 313, CA; *Re P (a Minor)
   (Residence Order: Child's Welfare)* [2000] Fam 15, [1999] 2 FCR 289, sub nom *Re P (a child)
   (residence order: restriction order)* [1999] 2 FCR 289, sub nom *Re P (a child) (residence order:
   restriction order)* [1999] 3 All ER 734, CA, discussed at para 2.53, and *Re J (child's religious
   upbringing and circumcision)* [1999] 2 FCR 345, sub nom *Re J (Specific Issue Orders: Muslim
   Upbringing and Circumcision)* [1999] 2 FLR 678 – decision upheld by Court of Appeal, see
   [2000] 1 FCR 307, [2000] 1 FLR 571, discussed at para 2.48.

WHO HAS PARENTAL RESPONSIBILITY?

1. The position at the child's birth

(a) Married parents

3.43 Section 2(1) of the CA 1989 provides that where the father and mother
of the child were married to each other at the time of the child's birth, they
each have parental responsibility. The reference to a child whose parents were
married to each other at the time of his birth must, as s 2(3) emphasises, be
interpreted in accordance with s 1 of the Family Law Reform Act 1987. Read
with s 1(2)–(4) of the 1987 Act, s 2(1) refers to a child whose parents were married to each other at any time during the period beginning with insemination
or (where there was no insemination) conception and ending with birth, but
also includes a child who:

(a) is treated as legitimate by virtue of the Legitimacy Act 1976, s 1;
(b) is a legitimate person within the meaning of s 10 of the 1976 Act;
(c) is an adopted child within the meaning of the Adoption Act 1976, Pt IV;
     or
(d) is otherwise treated in law as legitimate.

Stated simply s 2(1) means that both the father and the mother automatically
each have parental responsibility in respect of their 'legitimate children'.[1]

1 Which expression should be taken to include adopted children and children in respect of
   whom a parental order has been obtained under s 30 of the Human Fertilisation and
   Embryology Act 1990, discussed in *Clarke Hall and Morrison* at 1[378] et seq.

(b) Unmarried parents

3.44 Where the father[1] and mother of the child were not married to each
other at the time of the child's birth[2] s 2(2) provides that the mother but not the
father has parental responsibility for the child. In *B v UK*[3] an unmarried
father complained that by only according to married fathers automatic responsibility English law discriminated against unmarried fathers in the protection
given to their relationships with their children as compared with the protection
given to married fathers and was therefore in breach of art 14 taken in conjunction with art 8 of the European Convention of Human Rights. The
European Court of Human Rights ruled the complaint inadmissible since,
given the range of possible relationships between unmarried fathers and their

children, there exists 'an objective and reasonable justification for the difference in treatment between married and unmarried fathers with regard to the automatic acquisition of parental rights.' Notwithstanding this ruling it is proposed to change the law so that unmarried fathers will have parental responsibility if they are registered as fathers on the child's birth certificate.[4]

1   This includes a man deemed to be the legal father by reason of the HFEA 1990, s 28(3) (discussed in *Clarke Hall and Morrison* at 1 [370]) if he is not married to the mother: *Re D (a child) (IVF treatment)*[2001] EWCA Civ 230, [2001] 1 FCR 481, sub nom *Re D (Parental Responsibility: IVF Baby)* [2001] 1 FLR 972, CA.
2   For the meaning of which see para 3.43 above.
3   [2000] 1 FCR 289, [2000] 1 FLR 1, E Ct HR.
4   See the Adoption and Children Bill 2002, discussed further at para 3.67.

ACQUISITION OF PARENTAL RESPONSIBILITY AFTER THE CHILD'S BIRTH

3.45   Although parental responsibility is automatically assigned either to each of the married parents or to the unmarried mother at the time of the child's birth, the Act makes clear provision for others to acquire responsibility after the child's birth.

1.   Acquisition of parental responsibility by unmarried fathers

3.46   As s 2(2)(b) states, an unmarried father does not have parental responsibility for his child unless he acquires it in accordance with the provisions of the CA 1989. He can acquire responsibility in the following ways:

(1)   by subsequently marrying the child's mother;
(2)   upon taking office as a formally appointed guardian of the child;
(3)   by making a parental responsibility agreement with the mother;
(4)   by obtaining a parental responsibility order;
(5)   by obtaining a residence order in which case a separate parental responsibility order must be made;
(6)   (prospectively) by being formally registered as the child's father on the birth certificate.

(a)   Subsequent marriage

3.47   By subsequently marrying the mother, the father brings himself within s 2(1) of the CA 1989[1] and, provided the child is under the age of 18 at the time, will therefore automatically have parental responsibility. Although the Act does not expressly say so, because conferment of responsibility is an *automatic* consequence, the parents' subsequent marriage must be regarded as overriding any prior parental responsibility order or agreement, which means that responsibility cannot then be ended by a court order[2] other than adoption or a parental order under the Human Fertilisation and Embryology Act 1990.

1   Which, pursuant to s 2(3), must be interpreted in line with the Family Law Reform Act 1987, s 1(3)(b) of which, includes the parents' subsequent marriage.
2   Cf parental responsibility agreements and orders which can be ended by a court order see paras 3.75 – 3.76.

(b) Guardianship

3.48 To become a guardian, the father must formally have been appointed as such by the child's mother, or by the court in accordance with s 5 of the CA 1989.[1] Such an appointment can only take effect after the mother's death.

1 Discussed at paras 3.100 et seq.

(c) Parental responsibility agreements

3.49 Pursuant to s 4(1)(b) the father and mother may by a parental responsibility agreement provide for the father to have parental responsibility for the child. Such agreements, however, only have effect if they are made in prescribed form and recorded in the prescribed manner,[1] as provided for by the Parental Responsibility Agreement Regulations 1991.[2] Once made an agreement remains in effect notwithstanding that the couple live together or subsequently separate, though, it can be ended by a court order.[3]

1 Section 4(2).
2 SI 1991/1478, as amended, discussed at para 3.51.
3 See paras 3.75 and 3.76.

3.50 There are no prescribed age limits on those making agreements and there is no reason to suppose that valid agreements cannot be made by parents under the age of 18.[1] On the other hand, it seems unlikely that valid agreements can be made with respect to an unborn child.[2] A local authority holding children under a care order has no power to prevent the mother from making a parental responsibility agreement with the father.[3] By analogy with *Re S (A Minor) (Parental Responsibility Jurisdiction)*[4] it would appear that the child does not have to be habitually resident or present in England and Wales before an agreement can be made though, presumably, at least one of the parents must have some connection (viz habitual residence or domicile) with the jurisdiction. On the other hand, because the agreement must be signed and witnessed in a family proceedings court, county court or the Principal Registry,[5] it must be completed in England and Wales.

1 Ie an analogy should not be drawn with capacity to make contracts since parental responsibility agreements are probably best regarded as being agreements sui generis and not strict contracts since it is difficult to see what consideration is given by the father when making the agreement.
2 Agreements may only be made in respect of a 'child' as defined by s 105(1). There is a presumption against interpreting such definitions as including children en ventre sa mere, see *Elliot v Joicey* [1935] AC 209, HL See further para 3.86, n 3. Query whether an agreement can take effect after the mother's death?
3 *Re X (Minors) (Care Proceedings: Parental Responsibility)* [2000] Fam 156, [2000] 2 All ER 66 in which Wilson J held that the facility under s 4(1)(b) is self-contained and does not depend upon the exercise of parental responsibility. Cf *Re W (minors) (removal from jurisdiction)* [1994] 1 FCR 842 in which the High Court accepted an undertaking not to make a parental responsibility agreement.
4 [1998] 1 WLR 1701, [1993] 2 FLR 921, CA, discussed further at para 3.55.
5 See para 3.51 below

3.51 The power to make parental responsibility agreements implements the recommendation of the Law Commission, which pointed out[1] that although the father could apply for what was then a parental rights and duties order under s 4 of the Family Law Reform Act 1987, the need to resort to judicial proceedings to obtain parental responsibility seemed 'unduly elaborate, expensive and unnecessary unless the child's mother object[ed]'. Being aware of the dangers of undue pressure being exerted upon mothers to make such agreements,[2] the Commission recommended a relatively formal procedure by which to be binding, the agreement would have to be in a prescribed form and checked by the county court. However, this recommendation was not initially implemented. Instead, all that was originally required was that the agreement, in prescribed form,[3] be signed by both parents, witnessed and subsequently filed in the Principal Registry of the Family Division. However, as the Children Act Advisory Committee observed,[4] this informal scheme had not been without its difficulties. In some cases agreements had apparently been filed with the mother's signature forged. Accordingly, in January 1995 a new procedure was introduced whereby applicants must first complete the details set out in the form[6] (a separate form is required for each child) and then take it to a local family proceedings court or county court or to the Principal Registry, where a justice of the peace, a justices' clerk[7] or court officer authorised by a judge to administer oaths, will witness the parents' signature and sign the certificate of the witness. The duly completed form, together with two copies, should then be taken or posted to the Principal Registry.[8] Sealed copies will be returned to the mother and the father,[9] while the record is open to public inspection. No fee is charged to the parents for the formal recording of their agreement though a charge is payable by those wishing to inspect the record.[10]

1 Law Com No 172, para 2.18.
2 It was because of the potential pressure, that the Law Commission did not recommend the power to make binding agreements in their earlier report see Law Com No 118, Illegitimacy 1982, para 4.39.
3 Contained in the Schedule to the 1991 Regulations, as amended.
4 In their CAAC Report 1992/93, p 13.
5 See SI 1994/3157.
6 Viz the child's name, gender, date of birth and date of 18th birthday and name and address of both mother and father. A new form, issued by SI 1994/3157, was re-issued by SI 2000/2262 and now contains updated accompanying notes.
7 There would appear to be no power to delegate this function to Deputy Clerks or other authorised legal officers.
8 Article 3(1).
9 Article 3(2).
10 Article 3(3).

3.52 Notwithstanding the 1995 reforms the formalities for making binding parental responsibility agreements remain perfunctory. The Notes attached to the Agreement Form[1] warn mothers that as they will need to prove their maternity they should take to court the child's full birth certificate. There is, however, no comparable advice concerning the man's paternity. Both the mother and father are, however, required to prove their own identity and signature and are advised to bring a photocard, official pass or passport. There is no investigation of whether the agreement is in the child's best interests or of why the parents are entering into it.

1 Revised in 2001 by SI 2001/2262.

3.53 The notes explain that the agreement will not take effect until the form has been received and recorded at the Principal Registry but that once it has, it can only be brought to an end by a court order or upon the child reaching 18. It also warns: 'The making of this agreement will affect the legal position of mother and father. You should both seek legal advice before you make the Agreement.'

It explains that the name and address of a solicitor can be obtained from the Children Panel, local family proceedings court or county court, Citizens Advice Bureau, a Law Centre or a local library. It also mentions that the parents could be eligible for public funding.

3.54 Whether such warnings, coupled with the need to take the agreement to court for witnessing, are sufficient to allay the fears, expressed both by the Law Commission and during the passage of the Bill,[1] that mothers may be bullied into conferring rights upon the fathers at a time when they are particularly vulnerable to pressure,[2] is hard to say. Perhaps not surprisingly, following the introduction of the requirement of having to have agreements witnessed in court, after a steady rise between 1992 and 1994, the number of agreements fell substantially in 1995,[3] but since then they have been increasing.[4] However, it can be anticipated that the numbers will sharply fall once the proposal[5] that unmarried fathers should have parental responsibility if they are named as the father on the child's birth certificate comes into effect.

1 See particularly Lord Banks, 502 HL Official Reports (5th series) cols 1180–1182 and 503 HL Official Report col 1319, and Doggett, 'Unmarried fathers and s 4 before and after the Children Act 1989' (1992) 4 JCL 39, 40.
2 In *Re W (A Minor) (Residence Order)* [1992] 2 FLR 332, CA, a mother did assert that she had signed an agreement under pressure, though this was under the old procedure.
3 According to the CAAC Report 1993–94 (Appendix 1) 2941 agreements were registered in 1992, 4411 in 1993 and 'around' 5280 in 1994. In 1995, the numbers fell 36% to an estimated 3455 (CAAC Report 1994/1995, Appendix 1).
4 In 1996 the number of agreements rose 4% to an estimated 3590 (CAAC Final Report 1997, Appendix 2). Statistics of agreements are no longer published but Douglas: *An Introduction to Family Law* 52 and Cretney *Family Law* 10–025 comment that there are currently around 3000 per annum. Many have commented that, given the annual rate of around 20,000 births outside marriage, the number of agreements is relatively low. However, as Douglas comments (relying on research by Pickford 'Unmarried Fathers and the Law' in *What is a Parent?* (eds Bainham, Day Sclater and Richards) apart from ignorance of the procedure 'inertia and diffidence about raising the issue with the child's mother may also play a part. Some fathers may be concerned that asking the mother to make an agreement with them will suggest a lack of trust and a feeling of insecurity and impermanence in the relationship with the mother and that it may be best to let sleeping dogs lie.' To meet the problem of ignorance it might be helpful if a pamphlet explaining the legal position could be handed out at antenatal clinics
5 Viz under the Adoption and Children Bill 2002, see further para 3.67.

(d)   Parental responsibility orders

3.55 Under s 4(1)(a) the court may, upon an application by an unmarried father (ie not upon its own motion) order that he shall have parental responsibility for the child. Applications may be made to the High Court, county court or the family proceedings court.[1] If there is a doubt about the applicant's paternity, and a fortiori if paternity is disputed, it will have to be proved before the action may proceed.[2] It is implicit in every order made under s 4 that the man in question has been found or adjudged to be the father of the child in question.[3] An application may be made only in respect of a 'child', that is a person under the age of 18.[4]

According to the Court of Appeal in *Re S (a Minor) (Parental Responsibility: Jurisdiction)*[5] it is not necessary for the child to be habitually resident, present or even born in England and Wales to found jurisdiction to make a s 4 order. Presumably, though this is by no means clear from the judgment, the applicant (or mother) must have some connection (viz habitual residence or domicile) with England and Wales.

1   Section 92(7). In practice the majority of applications are made to the family proceedings courts; nearly 70% of the 3,332 orders made in 1992/93 were made by magistrates'CAAC Report 1992/93, Appendix 1, p 93.
2   See *Re F (a Minor) (Blood Tests: Parental Rights)* [1993] Fam 314, [1993] 3 All ER 596, CA.
3   Per Johnson J in *R v Secretary of State for Social Security, ex p W* [1999] 3 FCR 693, [1999] 2 FLR 604.
4   Section 105(1). For the reasons discussed at paras 3.53, n 2 and 3.89, n 3 it is not thought orders can be made in respect of unborn children.
5   [1998] 1 WLR 1701, [1998] 2 FLR 921, CA per Butler-Sloss LJ who pointed out that the jurisdictional rules set out by the Family Law Act 1986 (see *Clarke Hall and Morrison* at 1[577.3] et seq) do not expressly apply to s 4 orders and which should therefore be interpreted as not curbing jurisdiction to make such orders.

3.56   Section 4 applications are sometimes referred to as freestanding applications to distinguish them from residence order applications by unmarried fathers in which s 4 orders are made as an ancillary but automatic consequence of making the residence order.[1] As Waite J commented in *Re C B (a minor) (parental responsibility order)*.[2]

'there is an unusual duality in the character of a parental responsibility order: it is on the one hand sufficiently ancillary by nature to pass automatically to a natural father without inquiry of any kind when a residence order is made in his favour; and, on the other hand, sufficiently independent, when severed from the context of a residence order, to require detailed consideration upon its merits as a freestanding remedy in its own right.'

1   Discussed at para 3.65.
2   *Re CB (a minor) (parental responsibility order)* [1993] 1 FCR 440 at 450, [1993] 1 FLR 920 at 929.

(I)   Deciding whether to make a s 4 order

3.57   It seems to be accepted that that in deciding whether to make a parental responsibility order the court should treat the child's welfare as its paramount consideration,[1] and be satisfied that making the order 'would be better for the child than making no order at all'.[2] There is no enjoinder to have regard to the welfare checklist[3] though there is nothing to prevent the court from considering it if it so wishes. In theory this means that the court is not obliged to have regard to older children's wishes yet, as has been pointed out,[4] given that, if the father applies instead for a residence order which is opposed by the mother, the court must have regard to the child's wishes, it is difficult to see why the checklist should not apply to contested s 4 applications. Furthermore, since a child with sufficient understanding may, with leave, apply to have the order ended[5] it is logical to assume that such a child's view is relevant to deciding whether to make the order in the first place.[6] The restriction under s 9(6) which prevents the court from making s 8 orders in respect of a child aged 16 or over, save where the circumstances are 'exceptional', does not apply to s 4 orders.

1   Pursuant to s 1(1), see *Re RH (a minor) (parental responsibility)* [1998] 2 FCR 89 at 94, sub nom *Re H (Parental Responsibility)* [1998] 1 FLR 855 at 859, CA, per Butler-Sloss LJ, but note the arguments discussed at para 2.10, n 6.
2   Pursuant to s 1(5), discussed at paras 2.62 et seq. It could be argued that this provision does

not apply because a parental responsibility order relates to the parent and not the child. Although this argument seems stronger than that in relation to the inapplicability of s 1(1), it is still likely to be rejected since it can reasonably be said that as parental responsibility exists for the benefit of the child, parental responsibility orders also relate to the child.

3   Set out by s 1(3), discussed at para 2.37. Under s 1(4) a court is only required to consider s 1(3) when hearing contested s 8 applications or applications under Pt IV.
4   Doggett, op cit para 3.54, n 1 above, at p 41.
5   Section 4(3)(b) and (4) discussed at para 3.75 and 3.76.
6   In practice it is not unusual to ask for a welfare report when no doubt the child's view can be brought to the court's notice.

3.58   According to, *Re H (Minors) (Local Authority: Parental Rights) (No 3)*,[1] in deciding whether to make an order the following factors will undoubtedly be material namely:

• the degree of commitment which the father has shown towards the child;
• the degree of attachment which exists between the father and the child; or
• the father's reasons for applying for the order.[2]

1   [1991] Fam 151, sub nom *Re H (minors) (adoption: putative father's rights) (No 3)* [1991] 2 All ER 185, CA. See also *Re C (minors)* [1992] 2 All ER 86 at 93, CA in which Mustill LJ stated the basic test to be: '. . . was the association between the parties sufficiently enduring; and has the father by his conduct during and since the application shown sufficient commitment to the children, to justify giving the father a legal status equivalent to that which he would have enjoyed if the parties had married?'
2   The basic application form, CI, specifically asks the applicant to state his reasons for making the application.

3.59   It became established that the so-called '*Re H*'[1] considerations should be expressly considered in all freestanding s 4 applications,[2] and furthermore provided a concerned though absent father fulfilled the '*Re H* test' then 'prima facie it would be for the welfare of the child that such an order be made'[3]. However, in *Re RH (a minor) (parental responsibility)*.[4] Butler-Sloss LJ, in particular, disapproved of the notion that case law had created a presumption that a devoted father will ordinarily be granted an order. As she put it, the '*Re H*' requirements' are an important starting point when considering the making of a s 4 order but they are not the only factors and even if they are satisfied the court still has an overriding duty to apply the paramountcy test and to determine whether the making of an order is for the child's welfare. The point is well put in *Re M (handicapped child: parental responsibility)*:[5]

'parental responsibility is not a reward for the father for his commitment to and involvement with [the child] but an order which would only be made in [the child's] best interests.'

1   *Re H (Minors) (Local Authority: Parental Rights) (No3)* [1991] Fam 151 at 158, sub nom *Re H (minors) (adoption: putative father's rights) (No 3)* [1991] 2 All ER 185 at 18.
2   Per Thorpe J in *S v R (parental responsibility)* [1993] 1 FCR 331, [1993] Fam Law 339.
3   Per Leggatt LJ in *Re H (Parental Responsibility: Maintenance)* [1996] 1 FLR 867 at 872 and per Balcombe LJ in *Re G (a minor) (parental responsibility)* [1994] 2 FCR 1037, [1994] 1 FLR 504, CA. See also Balcombe LJ's similar comments in *Re E (a minor) (parental responsibility)* [1994] 2 FCR 709 at 716g.
4   [1998] 2 FCR 89 at 94–95, [1998] 1 FLR 855 at 859–860, sub nom *Re H (parental responsibility)* CA and repeated by Butler-Sloss LJ in *Re S (Parental Responsibility: Jurisdiction)* [1998] 2 FLR 921, CA. See also *M v M (Parental Responsibility)* [1999] 2 FLR 737, CA, referred to in para 3.63.
5   [2001] 3 FCR 454.

3.60 It is evident that the courts are generally disposed to grant orders to committed fathers. In *Re C and V (contact and parental responsibility)*,[1] Ward LJ commented that because a child needs for is self-esteem to grow up, wherever it can, to have a favourable positive image of an absent parent then, applying the paramountcy test, 'wherever possible, the law should confer on a concerned father that stamp of approval because he has shown himself willing and anxious to pick up the responsibility of fatherhood and not to deny or avoid it'. This is reminiscent of his earlier comment made in *Re S (Parental Responsibility)*:[2]

'It is wrong to place undue and therefore false emphasis on the rights and duties and the powers comprised in 'parental responsibility' and not to concentrate on the fact that what is at issue is conferring upon a committed father the status of parenthood for which nature has already ordained that he must bear responsibility'.

A similar point was also made in *Re S (a minor) (parental responsibility)*[3] in which Sir Stephen Brown P emphasised that a s 4 order does not affect the day to day care of children but does provide status for the father.

1 [1998] 1 FCR 52, [1998] 1 FLR 392, CA in which an order was made notwithstanding that the father had been convicted of possessing obscene literature (comprising indecent photographs of children) and was not paying maintenance to the children.
2 [1995] 2 FLR 648, CA.
3 [1995] 3 FCR 564. See also *Re A (a minor) (parental responsibility)* [1996] 1 FCR 562.

3.61 Consistent with the emphasis upon the consequent status conferred by a parental responsibility order it has been held that orders can be made notwithstanding that the child is in local authority care or is about to be freed for adoption, nor is the question of enforcement necessarily decisive.[1] In *Re H (a minor) (contact and parental responsibility)*,[2] an order was made even though the father had been denied a contact order. Indeed in *Re C and V (contact and parental responsibility)*[3] the Court of Appeal stressed that applications for contact and parental responsibility were to be treated as wholly separate applications so that the dismissal of the former did not necessarily mean that the latter should also be dismissed. On the other hand in *Re H (Parental Responsibility: Maintenance)*[4] it was held that the court should not use its power to make a parental responsibility order a weapon to force a father to make maintenance payments for the upkeep of his child. In all cases, however, the test remains whether it is for the child's welfare that an order be made. Lack of insight into a daughter's needs and an inability to get on with social workers is not reason in itself to refuse an order,[5] nor similarly is it justifiable to base a refusal solely on the acrimony between the parents,[6] nor because of transsexuality.[7]

1 See respectively *D v Hereford and Worcester County Council* [1991] Fam 14, [1991] 2 All ER 177, [1991] FCR 56; *Re H (Minors) (Local Authority: Parental Rights) (No3)* [1991] Fam 151, [1991] 2 All ER 185, CA; *Re C (minors) (parental rights)* [1992] 2 All ER 86, [1991] FCR 856, [1992] 1 FLR 1, CA.
2 [1993] 1 FCR 85, [1993] 1 FLR 484, CA.
3 [1998] 1 FCR 52, [1998] 1 FLR 392, CA. See also *Re M (Contact: Family Assistance: McKenzie Friend)* [1999] 1 FLR 75, CA, per Ward LJ.
4 [1996] 1 FLR 867, CA.
5 See *Re G (a minor) (parental responsibility order)* [1994] 2 FCR 1037, [1994] 1 FLR 504, CA.
6 *Re P (a Minor) (Parental Responsibility Order)* [1994] 1 FLR 578.
7 *L v C* [1995] 3 FCR 125, sub nom *Re L (Contact: Transsexual Application)* [1995] 2 FLR 438 – in which a 'father' who to outward appearances was a woman was granted a s 4 order.

3.62 Although failure to satisfy the so-called '*Re H*' criteria is likely to lead to a refusal to make a parental responsibility order it may be that where the commitment and attachment criteria cannot presently be met because, for example, the father has never seen the child, it will be appropriate to adjourn the application to see whether the criteria can be established in the future.[1]

1 See *Re D (a child) (IVF treatment)* [2001] EWCA Civ 230, [2001] 1 FCR 481, sub nom *Re D (Parental Responsibility)* [2001] 1 FLR 972, CA.

3.63 In practice, parental responsibility orders are usually granted, but not all applications succeed. Indeed, according to the statistics about 6% are refused.[1] For reported examples of where an order was refused see:

- *M v M (Parental Responsibility)*[2] in which it was held that because the father was mentally incapable of discharging the functions embraced within the concept of parental responsibility, it was not in the child's interests to make a s 4 order;
- *Re J (Parental Responsibility)*[3] the child, now aged 12 and who was born after the parents' separation, had infrequent contact with her father and between whom there was minimal attachment (the child herself not wanting to see her father). Moreover, the raison d'être for the father applying, namely his concern about the mother's involvement with drugs, no longer existed;
- *Re P (parental responsibility)*[4] in which the father was found likely to use the order inappropriately (viz he was deeply confused over sexual boundaries and had little appreciation of the difference between abusive and appropriate behaviour);
- *Re RH (a minor) (parental responsibility)*[5] in which the father had been violent towards the child;
- *Re T (a minor) (parental responsibility: contact)*[6] in which the father was violent towards the mother;
- *Re L (A Child) (Contact: Domestic Violence)*[7] – father's violence and desire to control the child;
- *Re P (Parental Responsibility)*[8], in which the Court of Appeal dismissed an appeal against a refusal to make an order based in part on the father's criminal conduct, holding that a court was entitled to take into account, as relevant but not conclusive, factors that the father was in prison and the circumstances of the criminal conduct for which the sentence was imposed;
- *Re D (a child) (IVF treatment)*[9] – case adjourned to see whether a man deemed to be a father under s 28(3) of the Human Fertilisation and Embryology Act 1991 could demonstrate the necessary commitment to the child following a period of indirect contact;
- *Re G (a child) (domestic violence: direct contact)*[10] – order refused because of the child's fear and anxiety about the father; and
- *Re M (handicapped child: parental responsibility)*[11] – order refused because the father was likely to misuse it to interfere with the mother's care thus causing her stress and potentially undermining her ability to care properly for the child.

1 In 2000, for example, out of 8524 court disposals 511 (6%) were refused: *Judicial Statistics 2000*, Table 5.3. In 1999 there were 686 (8%) refusals out of 8478 court disposals – see Table 5.3 of the *Judicial Statistics 1999*.
2 [1999] 2 FLR 737, per Wilson J.
3 [1999] 1 FLR 784.
4 [1998] 3 FCR 98, [1998] 2 FLR 96, CA – father found in possession of a number of photographs of pre-pubescent children.

5   [1998] 2 FCR 89, sub nom *Re H (Parental Responsibility)* [1998] 1 FLR 855, CA.
6   [1993] 1 FCR 973, [1993] 2 FLR 450, CA. See also *Re P (Terminating Parental Responsibility)* [1995] 1 FLR 1048, discussed below at para 3.76. But note that even where a mother has a genuine fear of the father, it might still nevertheless be appropriate in the child's interests to make a parental responsibility order, see *Re M (Contact: Family Assistance: McKenzie Friend)* [1999] 1 FLR 75, CA.
7   [2001] Fam 260, [2000] 4 All ER 609, CA.
8   [1997] 2 FLR 722, CA. See also *K v W* (11 March 1998, unreported), per Judge Anwyl QC, in which an order was refused because of the mother's vulnerability due to mental illness; this in turn made her vulnerable to stress with a resulting high risk of stress to the children.
9   [2001] EWCA Civ 230, [2001] 1 FCR 481, sub nom *Re D (Parental Responsibility: IVF Baby)* [2001] 972, CA.
10 [2001] 2 FCR 134, per Butler-Sloss P.
11 [2001] 3 FCR 454.

3.64   Once it is found to be in the child's interests that both parents should have parental responsibility it should be reflected by the making of a s 4 order and not by making 'no order' pursuant to s 1(5) of the CA 1989.[1]

1   Per Wilson J in *Re P (A Minor) (Parental Responsibility Order)* [1994] 1 FLR 578. For discussion of the effect of s 1(5), see paras 2.73 et seq. In view of this ruling the number of 'no orders' seems remarkably high, 227 (3%) out of 8524 court disposals in 2000 – see *Judicial Statistics 2000*, Table 5.3.

(e)   Residence orders

3.65   An unmarried father can apply for a s 8 order without also applying for a parental responsibility order. However, in such cases if a court grants the father a residence order then by s 12(1) it is also bound to make a separate s 4 order.[1] The importance of the s 4 order being made separately is that it will not automatically come to an end if the residence order is ended but will require an express order ending it, if the child is still a minor.

1   Where, on 14 October 1991, an unmarried father has an 'existing' statutory custody or care and control order in his favour, a s 4 order in his favour is deemed to have been made: CA 1989, Sch 14, para 6(4)(a).

3.66   The obligation under s 12(1) to make a separate s 4 order only applies where the court makes a residence order. It does not apply if the court only makes a contact order in his favour. Since the father will be in a stronger legal position if he has a parental responsibility order in his favour rather than simply a contact order[1], and a fortiori than if he has no order at all, it is generally sound advice to couple applications for s 8 orders with a s 4 order application.[2] Since contact and parental responsibility do not go hand in hand, each application should be considered separately.[3]

1   See para 3.72 below.
2   As *Re H (A Minor) (Contact and Parental Responsibility)* [1993] 1 FLR 484, CA shows, the court on occasion may grant a s 4 order even if it refuses to make a contact order.
3   Nevertheless it seems practice can vary as to whether courts consider it appropriate to make a s 4 order as well as a contact order'see eg the comments by Bennett and Walsh at [1994] Fam Law 91, 92 and the letter by Criswell at [1993] Fam Law 90.

(f)   Being registered as the father on the child's birth certificate

3.67   Based on a suggestion canvassed in a Lord Chancellor's Consultation Paper,[1] the Adoption and Children Bill 2002 will formally amend s 4 of the

CA 1989 to provide that the unmarried father will acquire parental responsibility if he becomes registered as the child's father.[2] Although this is an automatic consequence of registration it does not put unmarried fathers in exactly the same position as married fathers in that, as in the case of parental responsibility orders and agreements, the court can, upon application by any person with parental responsibility, or with court leave, the child himself, order that the father shall cease to have that responsibility.[3]

1 Ie (1) Court Proceedings for the Determination of Paternity; (2) The Law on Parental Responsibility for Unmarried Fathers (1998) paras 39 et seq.
2 Registration must be under UK legislation viz the Births and Deaths Registration Act 1953, ss 10(1) and 10A(1), Registration of Births, Deaths and Marriages (Scotland) Act 1965, s 18(1) or the Births and Deaths Registration (Northern Ireland) Order 1976. Consequently foreign registrations or registrations in the Isle of Man or Channel Islands will not be sufficient. But note the Secretary of State's powers to add to this list of enactments in the prospective s 4(1B). It is to be noted that for the purposes of entitlement to parental leave, unmarried fathers have for sometime been deemed to have parental responsibility if they are registered as the father, see the Maternity and Parental Leave etc, Regulations 1999, SI 1999/3312, reg 15.
3 See the proposed s 4(2A) and (3).

3.68 This provision is likely to have a significant impact. According to the Office of National Statistics[1] about 80% of births outside marriage are registered by both parents[2] and were this trend to continue[3] it would mean that the vast majority of unmarried fathers would have parental responsibility without the need to take any further action. In other words it would significantly reduce the use made of parental responsibility agreements or orders. Furthermore, although this new provision will *not* be retrospective it may in the future make it hard for the courts to refuse to make a s 4 order in favour of men registered as the father before implementation of the change.[4]

1 ONS 2001, Social Trends 31.
2 Of these about 75% of parents live at the same address.
3 One fear, canvassed by the Lord Chancellor's Consultation Paper is that such a change in the law might have the perverse effect of discouraging unmarried fathers from identifying themselves at registration or even lead to a general reduction of the rate of birth registrations.
4 But note Wilson J's comments on *M v M (Parental Responsibility)* [1999] 2 FLR 737 at 744.

(g) The effect of parental responsibility orders and agreements

3.69 The effect of a court order[1] or a properly recorded agreement is the same, namely, each confers parental responsibility upon the unmarried father. In most cases he will share responsibility with the mother or, if the mother is dead, with any formally appointed guardian. He could also share responsibility with some other person in whose favour a residence order has been made.

1 A parental rights and duties order made under the Family Law Reform Act 1987, s 4 and in force on 14 October 1991 is deemed to be a parental responsibility order under s 4 of the CA 1989: Sch 14, para 4.

3.70 In general terms an unmarried father with parental responsibility is in the same legal position with regard to the child as if he had married the mother.[1] However, without responsibility the father is regarded as a 'parent' for most purposes of the CA 1989.[2] He has, for example, the right to apply without leave to the court for a s 8 order[3] and a prima facie entitlement to reasonable contact with a child in local authority care.[4] He must be informed of an application for an emergency protection order[5] and has a right to apply for its discharge.[6] He also has rights of succession to his child's estate.[7] Furthermore, the lack of parental responsibility does not prevent him from being liable for child support.[8] On the other hand conferring parental responsibility upon unmarried fathers does not alter the status of the child. Hence, the child will still not take British citizenship through the father, nor will he be able to succeed to a title of honour through his parents. Furthermore, as the courts have stressed,[9] the granting of a s 4 order does not per se entitle the father to interfere with the day-to-day running of affairs affecting the child, at any rate whilst the child is living with another carer.

1   See eg Dept of Health's Guidance and Regulations, Vol 1, Court Orders, para 2.5.
2   The term 'parent' includes the unmarried father unless the provision indicates to the contrary: Family Law Reform Act 1987, s 1(1).
3   Ie under s 10(4). See *Re C (Minors) (Adoption: Residence Order)* [1994] Fam 1, sub nom *Re C (minors) (parent: residence order)* [1993] 3 All ER 313, CA.
4   Ie under s 34.
5   Section 44(13).
6   Section 45(8).
7   Administration of Estates Act 1925, s 46.
8   On the contrary unmarried fathers can be 'absent parents' or 'non resident parents' for the purposes of the Child Support Act 1991 and are 'liable relatives' under the Social Security Administration Act 1992, ss 78(6) and 105(3). For this reason Waite J must be regarded as being mistaken when he commented in *Re C (Minors) (Parental Rights)* [1992] 1 FLR 1 at 9 that upon being vested with parental responsibility the father assumes 'an immediately enforceable burden' to maintain the child. Nevertheless it is to be noted that it is implicit in the making of every s 4 order that the man in question has been found or adjudged to be the father and can be so relied upon by the Child Support Agency: *R v Secretary of State for Social Security, ex p W* [1999] 3 FCR 693, [1999] 2 FLR 604, per Johnson J.
9   See *Re S (a minor) (parental responsibility)* [1995] 3 FCR 564, *Re A (a minor) (parental responsibility)* [1996] 1 FCR 562 and *Re P (A minor) (Parental Responsibility Order)* [1994] 1 FLR 578.

3.71   Notwithstanding the courts' entreaties not to concentrate on the rights conferred by a s 4 order,[1] it is nevertheless instructive to enquire how the legal position of an unmarried father changes once he has parental responsibility. The principal effects are set out in the following chart.

1   See eg Ward LJ's comments in *Re S (a minor) (parental responsibility)* [1995] 3 FCR 225 at 234, [1995] 2 FLR 648 at 657, CA.

3.72

2.   Checklist: the effect of the unmarried father obtaining parental responsibility

Effect	Authority
1. He can give withhold his agreement to a proposed adoption or an order freeing the child for adoption.	Adoption Act 1976, s 72
2. He can to remove his child (under the age of 16) from local authority accommodation, and, if he is willing and able to provide accommodation or to arrange for accommodation to be provided for his child, may object to his child being accommodated in the first place.	Children Act 1989, s 20(7), (8).
3. He will automatically be a party to care	FPR 1991, Appendix 3

proceedings.	FPC (CA) R 1991, Sch 2.
4. He can appoint a guardian.	Children Act 1989, s 5(3).
5. He can give a valid consent to his child's medical treatment and require full medical details from the child's practitioner.	Access to Health Records Act 1990; Re H (A Minor)(Shared Residence) [1994] 1 FLR 717.
6. He can consent to his child's marriage.	Marriage Act 1949, s 3(1A)(a)(i).
7. He is empowered to express a preference as to the school at which he wishes his child's education to be provided; to withdraw his child from sex education in local authority or grant maintained schools and to receive full comprehensive reports from his child's school; and to be involved in the procedure for statementing of a child with special educational needs;.	School Standards and Framework Act 1998, ss 86, 71 and the Education Act 1996, Pt IV.
8. He may refuse to give consent for his child (under the age of 16) to be taken outside the United Kingdom.	Child Abduction Act 1984, s 1(3)(a)(ii).
9. He will be entitled to sign passport applications and to oppose the granting of a passport for his child.	UK Passport Agency Guidance.
10. He has 'rights of custody' for the purposes of the Hague Convention on International Child Abduction	Hague Convention on the Civil Aspects of International Child Abduction 1980, art 3

3.73 Although a s 4 order strengthens the unmarried father's legal position in relation to his child, the mother loses relatively little by the making of the order. She is under no general obligation (but see below) to consult with the father about the child's upbringing[1] and, so long as the child is living with her, the father has no right to interfere with the day-to-day management of the child's life, and indeed any attempt or threat to do so can be controlled by a s 8 order.[2] What the mother undoubtedly loses is the unilateral right to remove the child from the UK[3] and, more controversially, it may be that she needs to consult the father about a change of school[4] or surname.[5] She also loses the ability to appoint a guardian to take effect upon her death, unless she has a residence order in her favour.[6]

1 By reason of s 2(7), discussed further at paras 3.90 et seq.
2 See eg Ward LJ's comments in *Re S (Parental Responsibility)* [1995] 2 FLR 648 at 657.
3 Under s 1 of the Child Abduction Act 1984 she will require the father's consent (unless she is unable to communicate with him or he is unreasonably refusing to give it).
4 See *Re G (a minor) (parental responsibility: education)* [1995] 2 FCR 53, [1994] 2 FLR 964, CA, discussed at para 3.92.
5 See *Re PC (Change of Surname)* [1997] 2 FLR 730, discussed at para 3.92.
6 Section 5(7), discussed at para 3.114.

3.74 The fact that a s 4 order does not entitle an unmarried father to interfere in his child's day-to-day upbringing prompts the question as to why applications are made. The judiciary themselves have commented that the growing number of applications is based on a fundamental misunderstanding of the nature of the order.[1] For some, however, formal recognition of what has been described[2] as the exercise of their 'social parenthood' will undoubtedly be important. Whatever the reasons, the number of such orders has steadily increased from 2,762 in 1992, 5587 in 1996 to 7786 in 2000.[3]

1   See eg *Re S (a minor) (parental responsibility)* [1995] 3 FCR 225, [1995] 2 FLR 648, in which Ward LJ commented that s 4 applications 'have become one of those little growth areas born of misunderstanding. In *Re S (a minor) (parental responsibility)* [1995] 3 FCR 564, Sir Stephen Brown P similarly commented that there was 'a fundamental misunderstanding of the nature of a parental responsibility order.'
2   Eekelaar 'Parental Responsibility – A New Legal Status?' (1996) 112 LQR 233 at 235.
3   See Table of *Judicial Statistics* respectively for 1992, 1996, and 2000. Even so these numbers represent a small proportion of the overall total of unmarried fathers. See eg Butler, Douglas, Lowe, Noakes and Pithouse 'The Children Act and the unmarried father' (1993) 5 Journal of Child Law 157. As we point out at para 3.68, the number of orders will sharply decline once fathers acquire parental responsibility by being registered as the father.

3.   Ending parental responsibility orders or agreements

3.75   Parental responsibility orders and agreements remain effective notwithstanding that the couple live together or subsequently separate. They will, however, automatically end once the child attains his majority[1] and, as already discussed,[2] if the father subsequently marries the mother during the child's minority. Apart from these instances parental responsibility may be brought to an end only upon a court order to that effect. Such an order may be made upon the application (ie not of the court's own motion) of:

- any person who has parental responsibility for the child (this will include the father himself) or,
- with leave of the court, the child himself.[3]

In the latter case, the court may grant leave only if it is satisfied that the child has sufficient understanding to make the proposed application.[4] The court may not end a s 4 order while a residence order in favour of the unmarried father remains in force.[5]

1   Section 91(7) and (8).
2   At para 3.47.
3   Section 4(3).
4   Section 4(4). For a similar requirement when seeking leave to apply for a s 8 order, see s 10(8), discussed at para 5.122.
5   Section 11(4). Read literally, this would allow a court to end a s 4 agreement even though a residence order in favour of the father is still in force, but it seems inconceivable that a court would do so; see further para 3.76.

3.76   In deciding whether to end a s 4 order or agreement, the court must regard the child's welfare as its paramount consideration and be satisfied that discharging the order is better than making no order at all.[1] Nevertheless, the court should surely be slow to bring a s 4 *order*[2] to an end. It should not, for example, be thought that the ending of a residence order in the father's favour automatically means that parental responsibility should also come to an end. In any event, a separate order expressly ending the s 4 order will be required to end the father's parental responsibility.[3] In *Re P (terminating parental responsibility)*,[4] Singer J emphasised that the ability to apply to terminate parental responsibility should not be used as a weapon by the dissatisfied mother of a non-marital child. Nevertheless on the facts responsibility was terminated, the father having been responsible for inflicting appalling injuries on the child.

1   Section 1(1) and 1(5) and see *Re P (terminating parental responsibility)* [1995] 3 FCR 573,[1995] 1 FLR 1048.

2   There may be more reason to end an agreement. For example, if it could be shown that the mother had been subjected to undue pressure to sign, that might provide a good reason to make an order under s 4(3).
3   A separate order will also be necessary where, by virtue of Sch 14, para 6(4), a s 4 order is deemed to have been made, ie the ending of a custody or care and control order in the father's favour does not end his parental responsibility.
4   Supra. Cf *Re G (child care: parental involvement)* [1996] 2 FCR 1, [1996] 1 FLR 857, CA, in which an appeal against revocation of a parental responsibility agreement was successful.

4.   Acquisition of parental responsibility by step-parents

3.77   As originally enacted the Children Act made no special provision for step-parents to acquire parental responsibility. Instead they were treated like any other individual non-parent (see below). However, the Adoption and Children Bill 2002[1] will make provision for a step-parent who is married[2] to the child's parent who has parental responsibility[3] to obtain parental responsibility either by agreement or by court order.

1   Inserting s 4A to the CA 1989. This implements a long-standing proposal which was included in cl 85 of the Draft Bill attached to *Adoption – A Service for Children* (Department of Health and Welsh Office, 1996).
2   Ie cohabitation is insufficient.
3   Accordingly, the provisions will only apply to a step-mother if she is married to a father with parental responsibility. But presumably this provision can be triggered if the father acquires parental responsibility *after* his subsequent marriage to his step-mother.

3.78   So far as agreements are concerned, if both parents have parental responsibility (ie because they were married, the father was registered as the child's father, or because of a parental responsibility order or agreement) then the agreement must be made between the step-parent and *both* the child's mother and father.[1] Presumably, the formalities for making these agreements will be the same as for those between parents.[2]

1   Aliter where only the mother has parental responsibility, in which case the agreement should only be with her.
2   Discussed at paras 3.51 – 3.54.

3.79   The court's power to make a parental responsibility order will be exercisable only upon the application of the step-parent[1] which puts the step-parent in the same position as the unmarried father. However, unlike the unmarried father, no provision is made for the automatic making of a parental responsibility order, following the making of a residence order in a step-parent's favour.[2] Consequently, unless the step-parent has a separate parental responsibility order in his favour (or responsibility by way of agreement) responsibility will cease upon the ending of the residence order.[3]

1   See the prospective s 4A(1)(b).
2   Ie s 12(1) of the CA 1989 will continue to apply only to unmarried fathers.
3   For this reason, step-parents might well be advised when applying for a residence order to also seek a parental responsibility order.

3.80   As with agreements and orders as between parents, those with step-parents can be brought to an end by a subsequent court order,[1] either upon application by *any* person[2] with parental responsibility, *or* with leave of the court,[3] by the child himself.

1 See the prospective s 4A(3).
2 Ie the non-resident parent can apply.
3 The court must be satisfied that the child has sufficient understanding to make the application, see the prospective s 4A(4).

5. Acquisition of parental responsibility by other individuals

3.81 Individuals who are not parents of the child (including step-parents) can acquire parental responsibility by becoming that child's guardian, by being granted a residence order in respect of the child; or by being granted an emergency protection order in respect of the child.

(a) Guardianship

3.82 To become a guardian, an individual must formally have been appointed as such either by a parent with parental responsibility or a guardian, or by the court in accordance with s 5 of the CA 1989.[1] Such an appointment can only take effect after the death of the parent or parents with parental responsibility.[2]

1 Discussed at paras 3.100 et seq.
2 Or, if a residence order is in force, on the death of the appointing parent in whose favour the order had been made; see para 3.114.

(b) Residence orders

3.83 Any person, who is not a parent or guardian and, in whose favour a residence order is made, has parental responsibility while the order remains in force.[1] Such persons do not, however, thereby acquire the right to consent to, or refuse consent to, the making of an application to free a child for adoption, nor to agree or refuse to agree to the making of an adoption order nor to appoint a guardian.[2] It is only a residence order that gives parental responsibility. Consequently, other s 8 orders, for example, contact orders, do not have this effect. Furthermore, non parents with care and control under wardship[3] do not have parental responsibility since legal control of the child will remain vested with the court.[4]

1 Section 12(2). A similar rule applies to those who have a custody or care and control order in their favour made under the Domestic Proceedings and Magistrates' Courts Act 1978, the Children Act 1975, the Matrimonial Causes Act 1973, the Guardianship of Minors Acts 1971 and 1973, the Matrimonial Causes Act 1965 or the Matrimonial Proceedings (Magistrates' Courts) Act 1960: Sch 14, para 7. Because parental responsibility only lasts as long as the order it will come to an end when a care order or even an interim care order is made since that supersedes previous orders (including, custody orders): *Oxfordshire County Council v S (a Child) (Care Order)* [2000] Fam Law 20.
2 Section 12(3).
3 Wardship is discussed in ch 12.
4 See eg *Re RJ (minors) (fostering: wardship)* [1999] 3 FCR 646, sub nom *Re RK (Wardship)* [1999] 1 FLR 618.

(c) Emergency protection orders

3.84 Any individual who has an emergency protection order in their favour has limited parental responsibility for the duration of the order.[1]

1 Section 44(4) and (5), discussed at para 7.42.

6. Acquisition of parental responsibility by local authorities

3.85 Local authorities can acquire parental responsibility in one of two ways, namely, by having a care order[1] or an emergency protection order[2] made in their favour. We discuss this issue in chapters 8 and 7 respectively. Local authorities cannot acquire parental responsibility by any other means. They do not acquire responsibility, for example, when children are remanded to local authority accommodation under the Children and Young Persons Act 1969, s 23.[3]

1 Section 33(3)(a).
2 Section 44(4)(c).
3 *North Yorkshire County Council v Selby Youth Court Justices* [1994] 1 All ER 991, [1994] 2 FLR 169. For discussion of s 23 of the 1969 Act see *Clarke Hall and Morrison* 7 [157] et seq.

FOR WHOM RESPONSIBILITY EXISTS

3.86 Parental responsibility exists in respect of a 'child', that is, a person under the age of 18.[1] It is a moot point whether responsibility can exist for a married child.[2] In the absence of any indications to the contrary, references to 'child' in the CA 1989 must be taken to mean a live child.[3] Accordingly, no one can be considered to have parental responsibility until the child is born.[4]

1 Section 105(1).
2 Cf para 3.79.
3 Following the 'rule' in *Elliot v Joicey* [1935] AC 209, HL. For a similar interpretation of 'child' under the Children and Young Persons Act 1969, see *D (A Minor) v Berkshire County Council* [1987] AC 317, [1987] 1 All ER 20, HL. See also *R v Newham London Borough Council, ex p Dada* [1996] QB 507, [1995] 2 All ER 522, CA, interpreting s 75 of the Housing Act 1985.
4 It therefore remains the case that fathers have no right to prevent the mother having an abortion, see *Paton v British Pregnancy Advisory Service Trustees* [1979] QB 276, [1978] 2 All ER 987 and *C v S* [1988] QB 135, [1987] 1 All ER 1230, CA. They do, however, have a power of veto over the use, storage or disposal of an embryo in vitro: Human Fertilisation and Embryology Act 1990, Sch 3. See further Douglas, Law Fertility and Reproduction pp 82–83, 187–189 and ch 3 and Kennedy and Grubb *Medical Law: Text and Materials* (3rd edn) 1283 et seq.

DURATION OF PARENTAL RESPONSIBILITY

3.87 An important aspect of parental responsibility is its enduring nature, that is, it is not lost merely because someone else acquires it. Nevertheless responsibility does not have unlimited duration. As it can only exist in respect of a 'child', parental responsibility ends in all cases upon the child attaining his majority. It will clearly end upon the child's death.[1] Upon the making of a parental order[2] or an adoption order[3], parental responsibility is transferred to the person or persons in whose favour the order is made.[4] Non parents who have responsibility by reason of a residence order and local authorities that have responsibility by reason of a care order only have responsibility for the duration of the order.[5] Similarly, those who have responsibility by reason of an emergency protection order only do so for the duration of the order.[6]

1 Though note *R v Gwynedd County Council, ex p B* [1992] 3 All ER 317, CA, which establishes that a parent retains the right to bury (or, presumably, cremate) the child notwithstanding that the child had until his death been in care.
2 Viz an order made under the Human Fertilisation and Embryology Act 1990, s 30.

3   See s 12(3) of the Adoption Act 1976. Parental responsibility is transferred to the adoption agency upon the making of a freeing for adoption order. Under the Adoption and Children Bill 2002 the making of placement agreements or orders (which will replace the freeing provisions) will not extinguish the birth parents' parental responsibility.
4   Apart from these orders there is no other means of depriving parents of their *automatic* parental responsibility during the child's minority. However, if such power exists in a foreign jurisdiction then the courts in this jurisdiction may be forced to recognise it, see eg *Re A M R (adoption: procedure)* [1999] 3 FCR 734, [1999] 2 FLR 807 – in which an order made in Poland depriving Polish parents of their parental authority was held to deprive them of parental responsibility under English law. It was insufficient for the latter purposes that the parents retained a right to seek contact.
5   Sections 12(2) and 33(3).
6   Section 44(4)(c).

3.88   There is pre-CA 1989 authority for saying that the right of custody ended upon the child's marriage[1] and that it was suspended whilst the child was serving in the armed forces[2] but it remains to be seen whether a similar position will be taken with regard to parental responsibility. There is conflicting opinion as to whether responsibility ceases in respect of any aspect of a child's upbringing about which the child himself is sufficiently mature to make his own decisions.[3] Perhaps the better view in each of these situations is that parental responsibility does not end but that the scope for its exercise is limited.

1   *Hewer v Bryant* [1970] 1 QB 357 at 363, [1969] 3 All ER 578 at 585, CA, per Sachs LJ; *R v Wilmington Inhabitants* (1822) 5 B & Ald 525 at 526 and *Lough v Ward* [1945] 2 All ER 338 at 348.
2   *R v Rotherfield Greys Inhabitants* (1823) 1 B & C 345 at 349–50.
3   Cf Lord Scarman's comment in *Gillick v West Norfolk and Wisbech Area Health Authority* [1986] AC 112 at 186, [1985] 3 All ER 402 at 421–422, which suggests it does, but which was specifically rejected by Lord Donaldson MR in *Re R (A Minor) (Wardship: Medical Treatment)* [1992] Fam 11 at 23 [1991] 4 All ER 177 at 185. See also *Re W (A Minor) (Medical Treatment) (Court's Jurisdiction)* [1993] Fam 64, [1993] 4 All ER 627, CA.

SHARING PARENTAL RESPONSIBILITY FOR A CHILD AND THE RIGHT OF INDEPENDENT ACTION

3.89   As s 2(5) provides, more than one person may have parental responsibility for the same child at the same time, while s 2 (6) makes it clear that a person with parental responsibility does not cease to have it solely because some other person subsequently acquires it.

Where parental responsibility is shared then, by s 2(7), each person who has it 'may act alone and without the other (or others) in meeting that responsibility' except where a statute expressly requires the consent of more than one person in a matter affecting the child. This power to act independently, however, is subject to the important limitation under s 2(8), that a person with parental responsibility is not entitled to act in any way that would be incompatible with a court order.[1] Since ultimate responsibility for a ward of court vests with the court,[2] the warding of a child must operate at least to limit the freedom to exercise parental responsibility. Accordingly, notwithstanding s 2(8) the absence of a court order[3] does not necessarily mean that a parent may always exercise his responsibility without qualification.

1   But note also certain limitations placed upon the ambit of s 2(7), discussed at para 3.92 below.
2   See eg *Re E (SA) (a minor) (wardship)* [1984] 1 All ER 289 at 290, per Lord Scarman. Wardship is discussed in ch 12.
3   A child becomes a ward of court immediately the originating summons is issued, ie, without the need for any court order.

1. The position between married parents

3.90 Under s 2(1) each married parent has parental responsibility and by s 2(7) each may act independently and without the other, subject only to express statutory provisions to the contrary. This latter qualification preserves, for example, the embargo imposed by s 1 of the Child Abduction Act 1984, against one parent taking the child (under the age of 16) outside the United Kingdom without the other's consent[1] and maintains the need to obtain each parent's agreement to an adoption order as laid down by s 16 of the Adoption Act 1976. Where parents separate or divorce, each continues to have parental responsibility even if a residence order has been made in favour of one of them. A parent whose child does not live with him should still be regarded in law as a parent and should be treated as such by, for example, schools and therefore be given information and an opportunity to take part in his child's education. Furthermore it was envisaged that where that parent has the child with him then, subject to not acting in a way that is incompatible with any court order, he would be able to exercise his responsibilities to the full.

1 In this regard it will be noted that neither parent can unilaterally change the child's habitual residence: *Re S (Minors) (Child Abduction: Wrongful Retention)* [1994] 1 FLR 82, per Wall J. and *Re A (Wardship: Jurisdiction)* [1995] 1 FLR 767, per Hale J.

3.91 The ability to act independently was intended to mean not simply that neither parent has a right of veto but also that there is no legal duty upon parents to consult each other[1] since, in the Law Commission's view[2] such a duty was both unworkable and undesirable. It was expressly contemplated that even where a residence order had been granted in one parent's favour, subject to not acting incompatibly with a court order, each parent could still exercise that responsibility without having to consult the other and with neither having a right of veto over the other's action. Referring to the example of child living with one parent and going to a school nearby the Law Commission considered that while it would be incompatible for the other parent to arrange for the child to have his hair done in a way which would exclude him from the school, it would be permissible for that parent to take the child to a sporting occasion over the weekend, no matter how much the parent with whom the child lived might disapprove.[3] According to the Commission the intended independence of each parent was to be seen as part of the general aim of encouraging both parents to feel concerned and responsible for the welfare of the children.[4]

1 Thus resolving the uncertainty of the former law which seemed to impose no duty to consult but did confer a power of veto. See Law Com Working Paper No 96, Custody, para 2.34 et seq.
2 Law Com No 172, para 2.7.
3 See above at para 2.11.
4 See above at para 2.10. For a criticism of this position see Bainham [1990] Fam Law 192, 193 who argues that it is difficult to see how failing to provide for consultation could promote joint parenting following marital breakdown.

3.92 Despite the apparently clear wording of s 2(7), the Court of Appeal in *Re G (a minor) (parental responsibility: education)*[1] held that there remains a duty to consult at any rate over certain decisions. In that case a father who had custody, care and control under a court order, arranged for his son to attend a local education authority boarding school without informing the mother. In Glidewell LJ's view:

'... the mother, having parental responsibility, was entitled to and indeed ought to have been consulted about the important step of taking her child away from day school that he had been attending and sending him to boarding school. It is an important step in any child's life and she ought to have been consulted'.

It remains to be established whether the duty to consult extends to other 'important steps' and, if so, what constitute such steps. It has since been held that s 2(7) does not entitle one spouse to change the child's surname without the consent of the other,[2] while in *Re J (child's religious upbringing and circumcision)*[3] the Court of Appeal accepted the proposition that notwithstanding s 2(7) no one holder of parental responsibility should be able to have an incompetent child circumcised against the wishes of any of the others. Accordingly, where holders of parental responsibility disagree, circumcision should not be carried out without leave of the court. Although in one sense it makes no difference whether or not there is a duty to consult for in either case in the event of a disagreement the burden will be on the complaining parent to take the issue to court, the courts' approach to s 2(7) seems questionable.

1 [1995] 2 FCR 53, [1994] 2 FLR 964.
2 Per Holman J in *Re PC (Change of Surname)* [1997] 2 FLR 730 at 735–736, sub nom *Re C (minors) (change of surname)* [1997] 3 FCR 310 at 316–317.
3 [2000] 1 FCR 307, sub nom *Re J (Specific Issue Orders) (Muslim Upbringing and Circumcision)* [2000] 1 FLR 571.

2. The effect of a third party acquiring parental responsibility

3.93 By s 2(6) neither parent loses parental responsibility solely because someone else acquires it through a court order. This means, for example, that upon divorce a father does not lose parental responsibility for the child even if a step-parent acquires it under a residence order made in his favour. In this situation the mother, step-father and father all share responsibility and, subject to not acting in a way that is incompatible with a court order, and subject to the case law discussed above[1], each will be able to exercise their responsibilities independently of the others. Another effect of s 2(6) is that parents do not lose parental responsibility when a local authority obtains a care order, nor when an emergency protection order is made.[2]

1 See para 3.92.
2 See further paras 7.42 and 8.134.

3.94 Although by s 2(6) parental responsibility is not lost *solely* because someone else acquires it, that does not mean that a court order can never end a parent's responsibility. An adoption order will clearly do so. As Lord Mackay LC said during the debates on the Bill[1] the word 'solely' is used advisedly here. An adoption order deprives a parent of parental responsibility not solely because adoptive parents acquire it but because s 12(3) of the Adoption Act 1976[2] expressly extinguishes the previous parents' responsibility.

1 588 HL Official Report (5th Series) col 1175.
2 As amended by Sch 10, para 3 of the CA 1989 (a similar provision is made in the Adoption and Children Bill 2002). A similar position obtains on making a parental order under s 30 of the Human Fertilisation and Embryology Act 1990, see Parental Orders (Human Fertilisation and Embryology) Regulations 1994 (SI 1994/2767), Sch 1.

DELEGATION OF PARENTAL RESPONSIBILITY

3.95 Whilst preserving the previous position that a person with parental responsibility may not surrender or transfer that responsibility to another person save by a court order, s 2(9) permits those with parental responsibility to delegate some or all of their responsibility to one or more persons acting on their behalf. As the Department of Health's Guidance and Regulations states[1]:

> 'Informal arrangements for the delegation of parental responsibility are covered by s 2(9), which provides that a person with parental responsibility cannot surrender or transfer any part of their responsibility to another, but may arrange for some or all of it to be met by one or more persons acting on his behalf'.

Such delegation can be made to another person who already has parental responsibility[2] or to those who have not, such as schools[3] or holiday camps. This provision is primarily intended to encourage parents (regardless of whether or not they are separated) to agree among themselves on what they believe to be the best arrangements for their children. Section 2(9) does not, however, make such arrangements legally binding. Consequently, they can be revoked or changed at will. Furthermore, as s 2(11) provides, delegations will not absolve a person with parental responsibility from any liability for failure on his part to discharge his responsibilities to the child.[4]

1 At para 2.10.
2 Section 2(10).
3 But note the embargo on inflicting corporal punishment, discussed at para 3.20.
4 For example, not to neglect, abandon, expose or cause or procure a child under the age of 16 to be assaulted or ill-treated etc under ss 1 and 17 of the Children and Young Persons Act 1933.

THE POSITION OF THOSE CARING FOR A CHILD WHO DO NOT HAVE PARENTAL RESPONSIBILITY

3.96 Resolving the confusion of the pre-CA 1989 law,[1] s 3(5) provides that those who are caring for a child but who do not have parental responsibility, 'may (subject to the provisions of this Act) do what is reasonable in all the circumstances for the purpose of safeguarding or promoting the child's welfare'. As the Department of Health's Guidance and Regulations observes,[2] what is reasonable 'will depend upon the urgency and gravity of what is required and the extent to which it is practicable to consult a person with parental responsibility'. In other words all that s 3(5) does is to clothe de facto carers with the minimum power necessary to provide for the day-to-day care of the child. So, for example, while a carer may be able to consent to the child's medical treatment in the event of an accident, he will not be able to consent to major elective surgery. Indeed it may be difficult for the carer to convince a doctor that he has sufficient authority to consent to medical treatment which may be desirable but not essential.[3] Whether a significantly greater latitude for action should be given to those caring for orphans remains an interesting point. It is on the basis of s 3(5) that it is thought that a foster parent of a child being accommodated by a local authority could properly refuse immediately to hand over the child to a parent who is drunk or who turns up in the middle of the night. On the other hand, s 3(5) does not empower a de facto carer to change a child's habitual residence merely by taking him out of the jurisdiction[4] nor to obtain a passport for the child[5]. It has been held[6] that because they do not have parental responsibility local authorities have no power to transfer an 'accommodated' child from residential care to foster care without the parent's permission. Anyone who cares for a child is obliged not to assault, ill-treat, neglect, abandon or expose the child in a manner likely to cause unnecessary suffering or injury to health.[7]

1 See Law Com No 172, para 2.16.
2 Vol 1, Court Orders, para 2.11.
3 See eg, Johnson J, comments in *B v B (A Minor) (Residence Order)* [1992] 2 FLR 327 at 330 that notwithstanding s 3(5) a maternal grandmother who was the de facto carer, found in practice that the education authorities were reluctant to accept her authority to give consent, for example, to the child going on a school trip, and insisted upon having the mother's written authority.
4 Per Lord Slynn in *Re S (A Minor) (Custody: Habitual Residence)* [1998] AC 750, [1997] 3 WLR 597, [1997] 4 All ER 251, HL.
5 Per Butler-Sloss LJ in *Re S (Abduction: Hague and European Conventions)* [1997] 1 FLR 958 at 962.
6 *R v Tameside Metropolitan Borough Council, ex p J* [2000] 1 FCR 173, [2000] 1 FLR 942.
7 Children and Young Persons Act 1933, s 1.

GUARDIANSHIP

1. Introduction

3.97 The term 'guardian' has a variety of meanings[1] but the specific concern of the following discussion is the institution of legal guardianship over children during their minority. Formerly, the concept of guardianship was a complex one. However, following its reform by the CA 1989 guardianship can now be said to be the legal status under which a person has parental responsibility for a child following the death of one or both of the child's parents. In other words a 'guardian' is someone who has been formally appointed to take the place of the child's deceased parent.[2]

1 See, for example, the use of 'guardianship' under the Mental Health Act 1983, s 10(1) under which a guardian may be appointed for a person who has attained the age of 16 and who is, or appears to be suffering from a mental disorder. Note also the proposed creation of 'special guardians' by the Adoption and Children Bill 2002, discussed further at paras 5.161 et seq. The term 'guardian' is not to be confused with a 'children's guardian' who is a person appointed to represent a child in legal proceedings. See paras 10.21 et seq.
2 Cf 'special guardians', to be created by the Adoption and Children Bill 2002, whose appointment would take effect during the parent's lifetime, see post paras 5.161 et seq.

3.98 The law of guardianship is exclusively controlled by ss 5 and 6 of the CA 1989.[1] The concept of parental guardianship is abolished following the express abolition by s 2(4) of the rule of law that a father is the natural guardian of his legitimate children and the repeal (in Sch 15) of the Guardianship of Minors Act 1971, s 3 which provided that upon the death of one parent the other became the guardian of any legitimate child. Accordingly, save for where the unmarried father becomes a guardian[2] the status is now confined to non parents formally appointed to take the place of a deceased parent or parents.

1 This is not to say that an English court will not recognise a guardianship appointment made abroad, though in that context there has been a dispute over the meaning of 'guardian' for the purposes of the Adoption Act 1976. In *Re N (adoption: foreign guardianship)* [2000] 2 FCR 512, sub nom *Re AGN (Adoption: Foreign Adoption)* [2000] 2 FLR 431, Cazalet J, agreeing with HHJ David Gee in *Re AMR (adoption: procedure)* [1999] 3 FCR 734, [1999] 2 FLR 807,

considered that the definition of 'guardian' in s 72(1) of the 1976 Act (which states that 'unless the context otherwise requires' a guardian has the same meaning as in the CA 1989) did not prevent a court from recognising a foreign guardianship order. Cf Holman J in *Re D (adoption: foreign guardianship)* [1999] 3 FCR 418, [1999] 2 FLR 865, who considered that the term 'guardian' was confined to those appointed in accordance with s 5 of the CA 1989. It is submitted that the former view is to be preferred. The Adoption and Children Bill 2002 will not alter the definition of 'guardian' in this respect.

2   Eg upon the mother's death following an appointment by her or the court.

3.99   With one exception it is not possible to appoint different types of guardian.[1] The exception is the High Court's inherent power, preserved by s 5(11) and (12),[2] to appoint the Official Solicitor to be a guardian of a child's estate. Guardians of the estate apart, any person appointed a guardian under s 5 has parental responsibility.[3] This conferment of full parental responsibility was considered by the Law Commission to be central to the role of guardians. As they put it:[4]

'The power to control a child's upbringing should go hand in hand with the responsibility to look after him or at least to see that he is properly looked after. Consultation confirmed our impression that it is now generally expected that guardians will take over any responsibility for the care and upbringing of a child if the parents die. If so, it is right that full legal responsibility should also be placed upon them.'

One consequence of having parental responsibility is that guardians can themselves appoint guardians.[5] Appointments can also be made by the court or a parent with parental responsibility.

1   For a detailed discussion of the various types of guardian that existed before the CA 1989 see Guardianship (Law Com Working Paper No 91, 1985) pp 29–46.
2   Implemented 1 February 1992: SI 1991/828 and governed by CPR 1998, r 21.12, replacing, as from 26 April 1999, RSC Ord 80, r 13. See further para 3.108.
3   Section 5(6). However, those appointed as guardians of the child's estate, or for one specific purpose (eg to give or to withhold agreement to the child's marriage) before s 5 came into force, can only act within the terms of their appointment: Sch 14, para 12.
4   Law Com No 172, para 2.23.
5   This was new under the CA 1989.

2.   The court's power to appoint guardians

(a)   Appointing individuals

(I)   WHEN THE POWER MAY BE EXERCISED

3.100   Under s 5(1) the court[1] may appoint an 'individual' to be a child's guardian if:

(a)   the child has no parent with parental responsibility for him; or
(b)   a residence order has been made with respect to the child in favour of a parent or guardian of his who has died while the order was in force.

Under s 5(2) the above powers of appointment may be exercised in any 'family proceedings'[2] either upon application or 'if the court considers that the order should be made even though no application has been made for it'.

1   Ie the High Court, county court or magistrates court: s 92(7).
2   Defined by s 8(3), see para 5.101 et seq.

3.101   Applying s 6(c) of the Interpretation Act 1978 (which states that, unless there is a contrary intention in the statute, the singular includes the plural), the court may appoint more than one guardian. On the other hand, by confining the power to appoint an 'individual', it is clear that the court cannot appoint a body such as a local authority to be a guardian nor can it appoint what has been described as an 'artificial individual' such as a director of social services, who would in effect be the local authority.[1] This restriction is contrary to the recommendations made in the Government's White Paper *The Law on Child Care and Family Services*,[2] and has already proved inconvenient.[3]

1   Per Hollis J in *Re SH (Care Order: Orphan)* [1995] 1 FLR 746 at 749.
2   Cm 62 (1987).
3   See *Birmingham City Council v D, Birmingham City Council v M* [1994] 2 FLR 502, in which the local authority unsuccessfully sought care orders in respect of orphans accommodated by them, essentially to obtain parental responsibility. Cf *Re SH (Care Order: Orphan)*, supra, and *Re M (Care Order: Parental Responsibility)* [1996] 2 FLR 84, in which, in different circumstances, care orders *were* made in respect of orphans. See further para 8.68.

3.102   Section 5(1) provides in line with the general restriction against appointing guardians during the lifetime of a parent with parental responsibility that the court's power only arises (1) where the child has no parent with parental responsibility or, (2) upon the death of a parent or guardian in whose favour a residence order[1] was in force.[2] Although the former embargo is strict[3] it nevertheless only applies where the child has no parent with parental responsibility. The court can therefore appoint a guardian even though the child already has a guardian (other than the child's unmarried father[4]) and it can also make an appointment notwithstanding that the child's unmarried father is still alive[5] provided he has not obtained parental responsibility, for example, by agreement with the mother or under a court order (ie under s 4).[6]

1   Or an existing custody order see Sch 14, para 8(2).
2   Unless a residence order or an existing custody order was also made in favour of the surviving parent: s 5(9) and Sch 14, para 8(2).
3   See *Re A, J and J (Minors) (Residence and Guardianship Orders)* [1993] Fam Law 568 – no power to appoint an elder sibling to be a guardian because father was still alive notwithstanding that he was living out of the jurisdiction and was believed to be suffering from mental illness.
4   Since a guardian has parental responsibility (s 5(6)) presumably an unmarried father who is a guardian will for these purposes be regarded as a parent with parental responsibility.
5   As was the case under the previous law: *Re N (Minors) (Parental Rights)* [1974] Fam 40, [1974] 1 All ER 126.
6   Discussed at paras 3.49 et seq.

3.103   The court's power to appoint individuals to be guardians under the CA 1989 is narrower than that formerly provided by s 3 of the Guardianship of Minors Act 1971, since it no longer arises simply upon the death of one of the parents. This means that a case like *Re H (an infant)*[1] in which a father opposed the dead mother's sister's application to become the child's guardian, can no longer arise. Instead, in such cases application must be made for a s 8 order. This narrower power brought our law into line with the Recommendation of the Council of Europe.[2]

1 [1959] 3 All ER 746, [1959] 1 WLR 1163.
2 Parental Responsibilities, Principle 9. As the Law Commission pointed out (above, para 2.27), before the Children Act amendments, we were the only member country of the Council of Europe that permitted guardianship to operate during the lifetime of a surviving parent.

(II) WHO MAY APPLY?

3.104 The CA 1989 is silent as to who can apply to become a guardian but it is generally thought that any individual[1] (including, in theory, a child) may apply to be appointed. There is no requirement that leave of the court must first be obtained. On the other hand an application can only be made under s 5 by an individual himself wishing to be a guardian. However, since under s 5(2) the court has power in any family proceedings to make an appointment of its own motion, once proceedings are in train there would seem nothing to stop any other interested person, including the child himself, from applying to seek the appointment of another individual to be a guardian.[2]

1 But not a 'body' such as the local authority, see para 3.101.
2 Such a possibility was canvassed by the Law Commission in their Working Paper No 91, para 3.49.

(III) IN RESPECT OF WHOM MAY APPLICATIONS BE MADE?

3.105 An application may be made only in respect of a 'child', that is, a person under the age of 18.[1] There is no express embargo against making an appointment in respect of a married child, although it remains to be seen whether in practice the courts would be prepared to make an appointment in such a case.[2] On normal principles of construction there is no power to appoint a guardian of a child until it is born.[3]

1 Section 105(1).
2 A similar problem obtained in respect of the former law, but the Law Commission Paper (see Working Paper No 91, para 3.64) was inclined to leave the question open.
3 See the authorities cited at para 3.86, n 3.

(IV) EXERCISING THE POWER

3.106 In deciding whether to make an appointment, the court must regard the child's welfare as the paramount consideration and to be satisfied that making an order is better than making no order at all.[1] It is not however, obliged to have specific regard to the factors set out in s 1(3),[2] though the court is free to do so if it so wishes.[3] There is no restriction comparable to that under s 9(6) with respect to s 8 orders that appointments relating to 16 or 17-year-olds should only be made in 'exceptional circumstances'.

1 Section 1(1) and (5).
2 This is because the direction to do so under s 1(4) applies only to contested applicant for a s 8 order or to application for an order under Pt IV of the Act.
3 Cf *Southwark London Borough v B* [1993] 2 FLR 559, CA. In contested cases it would seem prudent to apply the checklist.

3.107 Since s 5 proceedings rank as 'family proceedings' the court can make either upon application or upon its own motion, any s 8 order in addition to or instead of appointing a guardian.[1] To help the court to decide what, if any, order to make, it may order a welfare report pursuant to its powers under s 7.[2]

1 Section 10(1) discussed at para 5.107 et seq.
2 Discussed at paras 10.11 et seq. This power, which was introduced for the first time by the CA 1989, implements one of the Law Commission's suggestions (Working Paper No 91, para 3.54) for improving the procedure and criteria for court appointments of guardians.

3.108 Although the court is empowered to appoint more than one guardian at one time or on different occasions, it seems unlikely that a court would appoint a subsequent guardian knowing that two or more guardians would be in conflict.[1] It has also been said[2] that it would be unusual, though not an absolute bar, to appoint persons as guardians who have never actually seen the child in question.

1 See Hershman and McFarlane *Children, Law and Practice* G [30] relying on *Re H (an infant)* [1959] 3 All ER 746, 1 WLR 1163 discussed at para 3.103.
2 Per Purchas LJ in *Re C (minors) (adoption by relatives)* [1989] 1 All ER 395, [1989] 1 WLR 61, CA.

3. Appointing the Official Solicitor as guardian of the estate

3.109 Contrary to the Law Commission's recommendation,[1] the High Court's inherent power to appoint a guardian of a child's estate is preserved.[2] However, only the Official Solicitor can be so appointed and even then only when the consent of the persons with parental responsibility has been signified to the court or when, in the court's opinion, such consent cannot be obtained or may be dispensed with.[3] Furthermore appointments may be made only in certain defined circumstances, namely, when the Criminal Injuries Compensation Board notifies the court that it has made or intends to make an award to the child; when payment to the child has been ordered by a foreign court or tribunal or when the child is absolutely entitled to the proceeds of a pension fund; or in any other case only where such an appointment seems desirable to the court.[4] In practice such appointments are likely to be confined to cases where the parents are dead or where it is unsuitable for them to be involved (for example, where they had caused the injuries to the child).

1 See Law Com No 172, para 2.24 in which the Commission recommended the abolition of the power arguing that trusteeship would adequately and more appropriately fill any gap.
2 By s 5(11) and (12).
3 CPR 1998, r 21.12(2), replacing Ord 80, r 13(1).
4 CPR 1999, r 21.12(1), replacing Ord 80, r 13(2).

4. Private appointment of guardians

(a) Making an appointment

3.110 Any parent with parental responsibility (ie not an unmarried father without such responsibility nor other individuals having parental responsibility by reason of a residence order being made in their favour) and any guardian may appoint an individual to be the child's guardian.[1] Although reference is made to 'an individual', it is clear that more than one person may be appointed as a guardian.[2] Furthermore an additional guardian or guardians can be appointed at a later date.[3] There is nothing to prevent an appointment being made by two or more persons jointly.[4]

1 Section 5(3) and (4). The power of a guardian to make appointments was new under the CA 1989. Note the consequential amendment of s 1 of the Wills Act 1837 in Sch 13, para 1. Note under the Adoption and Children Bill 2002, individuals appointed as 'special guardians' (discussed at paras 5.161 et seq) will also have power to appoint a guardian.
2 This is implicit in s 6(1) which refers to 'an additional guardian'. In any event under the Interpretation Act 1978, s 6(c) unless there is a contrary intention, words in the singular in a statute presumptively include the plural. But 'individual' does not include a 'body', see para 3.101.
3 Section 6(1).
4 Section 5(10).

3.111 There is no restriction or control on who may be appointed (even another child, it seems, could be appointed)[1] nor are there any means of scrutinising an appointment unless a dispute or issue is subsequently brought before the court.[2] Appointments can be made only in respect of children under the age of 18.[3]

1 Although it may seem questionable for one child to have parental responsibility over another, there are occasions when such a power could be useful, see *Re A, J and J (Minors) (Residence and Guardianship Orders)* [1993] Fam Law 568, referred to at para 3.102, n 3.
2 See para 3.123 for discussion of the court's power to remove a guardian.
3 Section 105(1). Query whether: (a) an appointment can take effect once the child is married; or (b) an appointment is valid if made before the child is born but where the child is alive at the time of the appointer's death? On this last point cf para 3.105.

3.112 Whereas before the CA 1989 the appointment had to be by deed or by will, under s 5(5), it is sufficient that the appointment 'is made in writing, is dated and is signed by the person making it'. This simpler method of appointment is intended to encourage parents (particularly young parents who are notoriously reluctant to make wills) to appoint guardians.[1] Section 5(5) does not preclude appointments being made in a will or deed, since clearly such means will satisfy the minimum prescribed requirements.[2] An appointment made by will but not signed by the testator, will be valid if it is signed at the direction of the testator in accordance with the Wills Act 1837, s 9.[3] An appointment will also be valid in any other case provided it is signed at the direction of the person making the appointment, in his presence and in the presence of two witnesses who each attest the signature.[4] These latter provisions cater for the blind or physically disabled persons who cannot write, but not for those who are absent or mentally incapacitated.[5]

1 See the Law Commission's comments at Law Com No 172, para 2.29.
2 See Lord Mackay LC's comments at 502 HL Official Report (5th Series), col 1199.
3 Section 5(5)(a).
4 Section 5(5)(b).
5 Cf Guidance and Regulations, Vol 1, Court Orders, para 2.18.

(b) Revoking an appointment

3.113 Section 6 deals with the formerly complex question of revocation of appointments. Under s 6(1), a later appointment revokes an earlier appointment (including one made in an unrevoked will or codicil) made by the same person in respect of the same child, unless it is clear that the purpose of the later appointment is to appoint an additional guardian.[1] It is also open to the person who made the appointment (including one made in an unrevoked will or codicil) expressly to revoke it in a signed written and dated instrument.[2] Under s 6(3A) a dissolution or annulment of marriage on or after 1 January 1996 revokes an appointment of the former spouse as a guardian unless a contrary intention appears from the appointment.[3] For the purposes of this provision the dissolution or annulment includes both those made by a court of civil jurisdiction in England and Wales and those recognised in England and Wales by virtue of Pt II of the Family Law Act 1986. Section 6(4) further provides that an appointment made in a will or codicil is revoked if the will or codicil is revoked. An appointment, other than one made by will or codicil, will also be revoked if the person making it destroys the document with the intention of revoking the appointment.[4]

1 This reverses the former position following s 20 of the Wills Act 1837 that an appointment under a will cannot be revoked by a subsequent appointment by deed and it ends the debate (on which, see Bromley and Lowe's Family Law 7th edn, p 531) as to whether an appointment by deed can be revoked by a later deed.
2 Section 6(2).
3 This provision was added by the Law Reform (Succession) Act 1995 and note the consequential changes made to Forms M5, M9 and M10 by the Family Proceedings (Amendment) Rules 1996, SI 1996/816, r 3. As Barton and Wells 'A Matter of Life and Death – The Law Reform (Succession) Act 1995 [1996] Fam Law 172, 174 point out, the appointment of a *cohabitant* would not be revoked by the couple's subsequent estrangement.
4 Section 6(3).

(c)   When the appointment takes effect

3.114   Under the CA 1989 an appointment no longer automatically takes effect upon the death of the appointing parent. Instead, under s 5(7) the appointment only takes effect immediately upon the death of the appointing person where:

(a)   following that death the child has no parent with parental responsibility[1] (but it will take effect where a non-parent has responsibility, for example, by having a residence order in their favour); or
(b)   there was a residence order (or existing custody order,[2]) in favour of the person making the appointment immediately before his death (unless a residence or 'existing custody order' was also made in favour of the surviving parent[3]).

In this latter instance, the surviving parent has no right to object but he can apply to the court for an order ending the appointment.[4] Where the child does have a parent with parental responsibility, the appointment will take effect only upon the death of that person.[5]

1 It will, therefore, take effect if the child's unmarried father is still alive, unless he has obtained parental responsibility in one of the ways discussed at paras 3.46 et seq.
2 Sch 14, para 8(2).
3 Section 5(9) and Sch 14, para 8(2).
4 Section 6 (7). See further para 3.123 below.
5 Section 5(8).

3.115   The rationale of delaying the operation of a guardianship appointment is to avoid unnecessary conflict between a surviving parent and a guardian appointed by the deceased parent. As the Law Commission said,[1] there seems little reason why the surviving parent should have to share parental responsibility with a guardian who almost invariably will not be sharing the household. In effect, the law protects the surviving parent from interference by an outsider though if that parent wishes informally to seek the help of the appointee he can also do so without jeopardising his parental status. In such circumstances, however, the surviving parent can no longer object to the appointment although he can, under s 6(7), seek a court order to end it. On the other hand if the appointee wishes to challenge this position he will need to seek the court's leave to obtain a s 8 order.

1   Law Com No 172, para 2.27.

3.116   While this basic standpoint seems right where the child was living with both parents in a united family before the death of one of them, different considerations apply where the parents are divorced or separated. Endorsing the Law Commission's view,[1] the law takes the position that if there was a court order that the child should live with the parent who had died, that parent should be able to provide for the child's upbringing in the event of his death. However, the rationale of this standpoint has been questioned by one commentator, who said:[2]

'The survivor will, of course, have joint parental responsibility with the guardian but will have the onus of bringing the child's position before the court in the event of a disagreement between them.[3] This is not very easy to reconcile with the ethos of continuing parental responsibility following divorce. It casts the non-residential parent in the role of an outsider who is liable to interfere with the child rather than that of a concerned parent who is anxious to step in to the breach left by the deceased'.

There has also been criticism of not making provision for cases where the spouses are separated, or even divorced but where there is no residence order.[4] The father, for example, may simply have abandoned his family. As the Scottish Law Commission said: 'In many of these cases it might well be desirable for an appointment of a guardian to be capable of coming into operation, even though there is a surviving parent somewhere'.[5]

1   Law Com No 172, para 2.28.
2   Bainham: Children: The New Law, para 2.40. See also Bainham: Children: The Modern Law (2nd edn, 1998) 185.
3   Eg under s 6(7) application can be made to the court to end the appointment.
4   Such a scenario is now more likely to arise since it will be by no means uncommon, because of the so-called non intervention principle under s 1(5), for no-residence orders to have been made.
5   Discussion Paper No 88, Parental Responsibilities and Rights, Guardianship and the Administration of Children's Property (1990) para 3.11.

(d)   Disclaiming the appointment

3.117   Section 6(5) provides, a formal right to disclaim an appointment. This right, which applies only to appointments made by a parent or guardian (ie not to court appointments), must be exercised 'within a reasonable time of his first knowing that the appointment has taken effect'.[1] Furthermore, it must be disclaimed by an instrument in writing, signed by the appointee, and recorded in accordance with any regulations that may be made by the Lord Chancellor.[2]

1   See by way of example, *Re SH (Care Order: Orphan)* [1995] 1 FLR 746, in which it was said that local authority foster parents intended to revoke a guardianship appointment by the mother.
2   Section 6(6). To date no regulations have been made.

3.118   Welcome as this power is, it does make it all the more important for parents to discuss their proposed appointment with the person concerned. It seems desirable for some official guidance to be published reminding parents of the desirability of prior consultation.

(e) Effect of being appointed a guardian

3.119 Except where the Official Solicitor is appointed guardian of a child's estate,[1] all persons appointed as guardians, whether privately or by the court, have parental responsibility for the child.[2] The effect of this is to place guardians in virtually the same legal position as parents with parental responsibility. The key difference is that, unlike a parent, a guardian is not a 'liable relative' under the Social Security Administration Act 1992,[3] nor a 'non resident parent' under the Child Support Act 1991,[4] and no court may order a guardian to make financial provision for or transfer property to the child.[5] This means that although guardians are under a duty to see that the child is provided with adequate food, clothing, medical aid and lodging[6] and to educate the child properly,[7] no financial orders can be made against them.[8] The absence of any legal liability on guardians to maintain their children might seem at odds with the general policy of awarding them full parental responsibility. The Law Commission, however, considered[9] that apart from representing a major change of policy, the imposition of financial liability upon guardians might 'act as a serious deterrent to appointments being made or accepted'. Guardians have no rights of succession upon the child's death, nor can a child take British citizenship from his guardian.

1 For an account of the legal position of a guardian of the estate see Law Com Working Paper No 91, para 2.23.
2 Section 5(6).
3 Sections 78(6) and 105(3).
4 Under s 3 of the 1991 Act (as amended by the Child Support, Pensions and Social Security Act 2000) only 'legal' parents can be 'absent or non resident parents' and hence liable for child support.
5 Viz under the powers conferred by the CA 1989 s 15 and Sch 1.
6 Under the Children and Young Persons Act 1933, s 1(2)(a).
7 Under the Education Act 1996, ss 7, 8 and 576(1).
8 This will be so even if the guardian has obtained a residence order' see *Clarke Hall and Morrison* 4[4].
9 Law Com No 172 at para 2.25.

3.120 A guardian is in a stronger legal position than a non-parent in whose favour a residence order has been made. Unlike the latter[1] a guardian has the right to consent or withhold consent to the making of an application to free a child for adoption, to agree or withhold agreement to the child's adoption and to appoint a guardian.

1 See s 12(3), discussed at para 3.83

5. Termination of guardianship

(a) Death, majority or marriage of the child

3.121 The guardian's duties cease if the child dies.[1] They automatically end when the child attains the age of 18.[2] Whether the guardian's powers cease upon the child's marriage is perhaps debatable for, while s 5 imposes no such express limitation, it may well be held that there is no scope for the operation of guardianship. In any event, it seems unlikely that a guardian would be permitted to interfere with the activities of a married child even if the guardianship continues.

1 Though query whether a guardian has a duty to bury or cremate a child? Cf *R v Gwynedd County Council, ex p B* [1992] 3 All ER 317, CA.
2 Section 91(7), (8).

(b) Death of the guardian

3.122 Guardianship ends upon the death of a sole guardian unless, pursuant to the powers vested by s 5(4), the guardian has appointed another individual to be the child's guardian in his place. If a guardian dies leaving others in office, the survivors continue to be guardians.

(c) Removal by the court

3.123 For the first time, county courts and magistrates' courts as well as the High Court can end any guardianship appointment made under s 5. Such an order can be made at any time upon the application of:

(1) any person who has parental responsibility; or
(2) the child himself, with leave of the court; or
(3) upon the court's own motion in any family proceedings, if the court considers that it should be brought to an end.[1]

In deciding whether to end the guardianship, the court must be guided by the welfare principle.[2] In reaching its decision the court is entitled to order a welfare report.[3] If it decides to end the guardianship, the court may appoint another individual to take the former guardian's place. It is also open to the court to make a s 8 order. Where the court orders a guardian's removal it may well have to consider appointing a new guardian (or alternatively making a residence order) to prevent a hiatus in parental responsibility for the child.[4]

1 Section 6(7).
2 Ie pursuant to s 1(1). If the guardian expresses his unwillingness to continue, it is unlikely that the court will hold it to be in the child's interests for the appointment to continue. For cases where the court has forcibly removed a guardian in the past, see the cases cited by Bromley and Lowe's *Family Law* (9th edn) p 409.
3 Ie under s 7, discussed at para 10.11.
4 See Bainham *Children – The Modern Law* (2nd edn) 187.

6. Impact of the CA 1989 upon existing appointments

3.124 Any guardianship appointment made under the Guardianship of Minors Act 1971, ss 3 to 5, the Sexual Offences Act 1956, s 38(3) or under the High Court's inherent jurisdiction and taken effect before 14 October 1991 is deemed to be an appointment under s 5 of the CA 1989.[1] This means that such guardians have, since 14 October 1991, had parental responsibility and are themselves able to appoint a guardian. In the case of appointments under the Sexual Offences Act 1956 the appointment shall not have effect for any longer period than that specified in the order.[2]

1 Sch 14, para 12(1).
2 Above, para 12(2).

3.125 Appointments made under the 1971 Act but which had not taken effect as at 14 October 1991, will not take effect during the lifetime of any surviving parent who has parental responsibility, unless the appointing parent had a residence order or existing custody order in their favour at the time of death.[1]

1   Sch 14, para 13.

Chapter 4

Work in the courts

INTRODUCTION

4.1   The principles in s 1 of the Act are not confined to substantive law but have affected family courts themselves. The requirement of s 1(1) that the welfare of the child is paramount[1] is reflected in procedures that are less confrontational and non-adversarial.[2] The avoidance of delay[3] is reflected most clearly in the obligation on courts to monitor the course of proceedings and work to a timetable, and to be proactive in the management of cases.[4] Since one means by which delay may be reduced is the more efficient use of resources, the structure of courts under the Act has more nearly aligned the jurisdiction of the courts dealing with family cases and facilitated the allocation of cases to the most suitable tribunal.

1   See paras 2.2 ff.
2   See *Oxfordshire County Council v M* [1994] 1 FLR 175, per Stephen Brown P and *Practice Note: Case Management* [1995] 1 All ER 586, [1995] 1 FLR 456 and see *Re R (Care: Disclosure: Nature of Proceedings)* [2002] 1 FLR 755 at p 771D.
3   CA 1989, s 1(2).
4   See, for example, *Re A and B (Minors) (No 2)* [1995] 1 FLR 351, per Wall J.

THE COURTS

4.2   The High Court, county courts and magistrates' courts are given jurisdiction over proceedings under the CA 1989.[1] Although this creates a largely concurrent jurisdiction there are express restrictions on the jurisdiction of magistrates' courts which may not entertain any application or make any order involving the administration or application of any property belonging to or held in trust for a child or the income of any such property.[2] In addition the Children (Allocation of Proceedings) Order 1991[3] specifies that particular proceedings must be commenced in specified courts.[4]

1   CA 1989, s 92(7).
2   CA 1989, s 92(4).
 SI 1998/2166, SI 1999/524, SI 2000/2670 and SI 2001/775 and 1656 made under Sch 11 to the CA 1989.
4   See para 4.15 ff.

1.   Jurisdiction

4.3   Jurisdiction to make 'Part I orders'[1] over children is governed by the Family Law Act 1986.[2] Accordingly, jurisdiction to make a section 8 order other than in circumstances where divorce, nullity or judicial separation proceedings are continuing, vests in the UK court of the jurisdiction where the child is habitually resident;[3] and failing that, in the UK court of the place where the child is physically present.[4]

1 Ie a s 8 order (but not an order varying or discharging such an order) and orders (other than a variation or a revocation) made by the High Court under its inherent jurisdiction so far as it gives care of a child to any person or provides for contact with, or the education of the child: Family Law Act 1986, s 1(1)(a), (d).
2 For a detailed discussion of which see Lowe 'The Family Law Act 1986-A Critique' [2002] Fam Law 39.
3 See eg *Re S (A Minor) (Custody Habitual Residence)* [1978] AC 750, [1997] 4 All ER 251, [1997] 1 FLR 1.
4 See eg *Re M (a minor) (immigration: residence order)* [1995] 2 FCR 793, [1993] 2 FLR 858.

4.4 Jurisdiction of the courts in England and Wales is amended by the European Communities (Matrimonial Jurisdiction and Judgments) Regulations 2001[1] so as to comply with Council Regulation (EC) No 1347/2000 of 29 May 2000[2] which has direct effect on domestic law. Legislation affected includes the Family Law Act 1986 with regard to the jurisdiction of the courts of England and Wales to make orders in, or in connection with, matrimonial proceedings with respect to children of both parties. The effect of Council Regulation (EC) No 1347/2000 is in essence to provide for jurisdiction based on habitual residence, or nationality or domicile, in proceedings for divorce, legal separation or marriage annulment.[3] Where a court is 'seized' of proceedings for matrimonial etc. relief in a jurisdiction of one of the European Union States (other than Denmark), that first court has exclusive jurisdiction, and any second court in which the same relief is applied for, must stay the proceedings, and usually decline jurisdiction[4] subject to limited exceptions.[5]

1 SI 2001/310.
2 Sometimes referred to as 'Brussels II', for discussion of which see *Clarke Hall and Morrison* 2[35.1] and Lowe 'New International Conventions Affecting the Law Relating to Children-A Cause for Concern?' [2001] IFL 171.
3 Article 1.
4 Article 11.
5 Article 15.

4.5 There is no specific provision establishing the jurisdiction for an application under Pt IV of the CA 1989. In relation to s 8 orders there is jurisdiction if the child was habitually resident in England or Wales or present in England and Wales at the relevant[1] time and not habitually resident in any other part of the United Kingdom.[2] In relation to public law proceedings it has been held that, as the child may be in need of care and protection, a non-restrictive interpretation of jurisdiction should be adopted. Accordingly, the jurisdiction under Pt IV is at least as extensive as that for s 8 orders under Pt II of the CA 1989.[3] Indeed it is more extensive in that it has been held that where a child was living in England at the time of the application but was habitually resident in Scotland, the child's presence at the time of the application gave the court jurisdiction throughout the duration of the proceedings, since any other interpretation would undermine the scheme of the Act to provide protection for children where appropriate.[4]

1 Relevant time, ie at the commencement of the proceedings or any continuous action preceding them: *Re M (a minor) (care order: significant harm)* [1994] 3 All ER 298. The relevant date is the same whether it is alleged that the child is suffering harm or is likely to suffer harm: *Southwark London Borough Council v B* [1998] 2 FLR 1095.

2   Family Law Act 1986, s 3(1).
3   *Re R (Care Orders: Jurisdiction)* [1995] 1 FLR 711.
4   *Re M (care orders: jurisdiction)* [1997] 1 FCR 109, [1997] 1 FLR 456. For jurisdiction in
    respect of parental responsibility orders or agreements, see paras 3.50, 3.55.

2.   The High Court

4.6   The substantive reform of the law effected by the CA 1989 was accompanied by changes to the procedure and jurisdiction of those courts dealing with family cases. Whilst the effect on county courts and magistrates' courts has been substantial, the jurisdiction of the High Court was affected so far as was necessary to take account of the CA 1989 and was subsequently modified to accommodate proceedings under the Human Fertilisation and Embryology Act 1990 and appeals under the Criminal Justice Act 1991 in respect of orders authorising the use of secure accommodation.

3.   County court

4.7   There are for the purposes of the Children (Allocation of Proceedings) Order 1991, the following classes of county court: divorce county courts, family hearing centres[1] and care centres.[2] In addition there are non-designated county courts which retain jurisdiction over domestic violence proceedings and also adoption centres.

Family hearing centres are competent to hear applications under Pts I and II of the CA 1989[3] The general scheme is that these centres hear all contested s 8 applications made under Pt II.[4] Family hearing centres are not competent to hear care and related proceedings transferred from the magistrates. Such applications have to be heard by the care centres.[5] Care centres and the Principal Registry of the Family Division have full jurisdiction in both public and private law cases. Designated care judges, who act as the chairman of the local Family Court Business Committee and the Family Court Forum[6] are based at care centres together with nominated care judges and nominated district judges. Special jurisdictional arrangements have been made for London in that the Principal Registry of the Family Division is designated for the purposes of the 1991 Order as being a divorce county court, a family hearing centre and a care centre.[7] District Judges of the Principal Registry have jurisdiction in care proceedings.[8]

1   Listed in Sch 2 to the Order.
2   Listed in Sch 3 to the Order.
3   Children (Allocation of Proceedings) Order 1991, arts 16 and 17.
4   Above, Art 16.
5   Above, Art 18.
6   See para 1.32.
7   Above, Art 19.
8   Family Proceedings (Allocation to Judiciary) Directions 1999 [1999] 2 FLR 799 Sch para (h)
    column (iii).

Judiciary

4.8   The President of the Family Division of the High Court is responsible for approving the various types of judge to whom family proceedings may be allocated.[1]Circuit judges may be appointed as either 'designated family judges' or 'nominated care judges'. Designated family judges are based at the care centres and have primary responsibility for hearing the care cases transferred from the magistrates' courts. Nominated care judges also sit at a care centre[2] and are able to hear substantive hearings and emergency protection orders arising in child care cases transferred from the magistrates' courts. They also have jurisdiction in 'family proceedings.'[3] Certain district judges ('the gate-keepers') have been nominated and they are responsible for the allocation of care cases[4] and are able to deal with emergency protection orders and inter-locutory matters within transferred cases.

1   Family Proceedings (Allocation to Judiciary) Directions [1999] 2 FLR 799 amended by the Family Proceedings (Allocation to Judiciary) (Amendment) Directions 2002 (30 August 2002).
2   But note that with the consent of the parties proceedings can be heard at a non-care centre court: County Courts Act 1984, s 3(3).
3   Defined by the CA 1989, s 8(3) and (4) and see para 5.101.
4   See para 4.15 ff.

4.9   The formal allocation of judges to cases is governed by the Family Proceedings (Allocation to Judiciary) Directions 1999 as amended[1] which in essence provide that:

1   [1999] 2 FLR 799 amended by the Family Proceedings (Allocation to Judiciary) (Amendment) Directions 2002 (30 August 2002).

PUBLIC LAW CASES

4.10   Circuit judges nominated for *public* family proceedings and district judges of the Principal Registry have jurisdiction to hear *any* application under Pts I, II, IV and V of the 1989 Act.

District judges nominated for public family proceedings have a more limited jurisdiction in relation, inter alia, to care and supervision and contact with children in care in that they only have jurisdiction to deal with:

(a)   interlocutory matters; or
(b)   unopposed hearing; or
(c)   opposed hearings where the application is for a contact order and the principle of contact is unopposed.

PRIVATE LAW CASES

4.11   Circuit judges nominated for *private or public* family proceedings, deputy circuit judges or recorders nominated for *private or public* family proceedings, district judges of the Principal Registry and district judges nominated for *private or public* family proceedings are competent to hear any private law applications.

District judges (other than those of the Principal Registry and those nominated for private or public family proceedings) have a more limited jurisdiction in that they have jurisdiction only in respect of interlocutory hearings and unopposed trials, but also have jurisdiction in applications under s 10 of the CA 1989 for a section 8 order in *opposed* trials limited to where:

(a) the application is for a contact order and the principle of contact with the applicant is unopposed; or

(b) the order is (or is one of a series of orders which is)
   (i) to be limited in time until the next hearing or order, and
   (ii) the substantive application is returnable before a judge . . . who has full jurisdiction in all circumstances.

A deputy district judge only has jurisdiction in interlocutory matters or unopposed hearings.

The effects of the 2002 amendments to the Family Proceedings (Allocation to Judiciary) Directions 1999[1] include the introduction of a private law ticket for district judges which provides them with jurisdiction to deal with a wide range of private law proceedings under Parts I and II of the 1989 Act. For adoption proceedings however, any judge is now required to have a distinct adoption ticket.

1   [1999] 2 FLR 799.

4.   Magistrates' courts

4.12   Jurisdiction in family proceedings in the magistrates' court is that of a District Judge (Magistrates' Court) or justices sitting in the family proceedings court. A District Judge (Magistrates' Court) must be nominated by the President of the Family Division of the High Court to sit in family proceedings courts[1] and must sit as chairman with one or two lay justices unless it is impracticable to do so.[2] Justices are appointed to the Family Panel at the October election meeting and serve for three years and may be reappointed.[3] After appointment but before commencing to sit, panel members are required to undertake induction training and a course of basic training after they have commenced sitting. They are subject to regular appraisal in accordance with the Magistrates' National Training Initiative. Additional training and appraisal must be undertaken by those who are to chair courts since these must generally be presided over by the chairman of the panel or an elected deputy. The general training has the aim of inculcating knowledge of the Act and its philosophy whilst chairmanship must also equip justices to be more proactive in conducting the court hearing and to be able to articulate reasons for their decisions. A bench which includes lay justices must include so far as is practicable both a man and a woman.[4] Provision is made for combined family panels comprising justices from more than one petty sessions area.[5] The Children Act Advisory Committee encouraged the forming of a combined panel for a Commission Area as this was perceived to have the advantage of flexibility and to make the best use of judicial resources.[6] Further studies have reinforced the view that family proceedings courts should be concentrated at fewer centres to maintain the expertise of the justices and the court staff.[7]

1   Magistrates' Courts Act 1980, s 67(2)(a).
2   Magistrates' Courts Act 1980, s 66(1).
3   Family Proceedings Courts (Constitution) Rules 1991, SI 1991/1405, r 4. The next triennium commences on 1 January 2003.
4   Magistrates' Courts Act 1980, s 66(2).
5   Magistrates' Courts Act 1980, s 68.
6   CAAC Report 1993/4, p 47. Low volume and range of caseload for some panels was identified as

an inhibition on the effective use of the resources of family proceedings panels in *MCSI A Review of Case Administration in Family Proceedings Courts* (May 2001) para 2.32.

7 See the *Scoping Study on Delay in Children Act Cases* (Lord Chancellor's Dept 2002) para 91ff and J Hunt *Professionalising Lay Justice – The Role of the Court Clerk in Family Proceedings* (Lord Chancellor's Dept 2002).

The justices' clerk

4.13   The function of the justices' clerk is to provide expert legal advice to the lay justices and to conduct the ordinary business of the court[1]. The clerk is required by the rules[2] in consultation with the justices to record the reasons for their decision in writing before[3] the decision is announced. This requires a greater presence in the retiring room than in other proceedings[4] and it is acknowledged that the clerk will frequently assist with the structure of the reasons.[5]

No transcript is taken of proceedings in the family proceedings court but the clerk is required to keep a note of the oral evidence that is given at the hearing[6] and the clerk must take notes which are as complete as possible and which must be sufficient to support the findings of the justices.[7]

The justices' clerk has some powers to make interlocutory orders in proceedings. However, these powers are limited as follows. A justices' clerk may not make any s 8 order and may only make an interim order in public law proceedings in the limited circumstances set out in r 28 of the Family Proceedings Courts (Children Act 1989) Rules 1991, ie not unless:

(a)   a written request for such an order has been made to which the parties and any children's guardian consent and which they or their representatives have signed;

(b)   a previous such order has been made in the same proceedings, and

(c)   the terms of the order sought are the same as those of the last such order made.

The role of the clerk may be performed by the Clerk to the Justices himself or may be delegated to one of his authorised legal advisers under the Family Proceedings Courts (Children Act 1989) Rules 1991[8], which also extend the clerk's powers in interlocutory matters. However the clerk's powers under these rules, whilst analogous to those of a district judge, are not as extensive.[9]

1   See *Practice Direction: (criminal: consolidated)* [2002] 3 All ER 904 55.
2   FPC (CA 1989) R 1991, r 21(5).
3   Above.
4   *Practice Direction: (criminal: consolidated)* [2002] 3 All ER 904 55.
5   CAAC Report 1991/2, p 10 and see *Re W (A Minor) (Contact)* [1994] 1 FLR 843. Also, J Hunt *Professionalising Lay Justice – The Role of the Court Clerk in Family Proceedings* (Lord Chancellor's Dept 2002).
6   FPR 1991, r 4.20; FPC (CA 1989) R, 1991 r 20.
7   See *C v Surrey County Council* [1994] 2 FCR 165, sub nom *Re C (A Minor) (Contribution Notice)* [1994] 1 FLR 111.
8   Rule 32 and see the Justices' Clerks Rules 1999, SI 1999/2784. Justices' Clerks' assistants who act as court clerks must be qualified in accordance with the Justices' Clerks (Qualification of Assistants) Rules 1979, SI 1979/570 (as amended).
9   See para 4.10–11.

5.   The legal profession

4.14   The need for a non-adversarial approach and for timeliness in the conduct of proceedings requires that advocates should have the necessary expertise.[1] In public law cases representation of children is usually undertaken by solicitors from the Law Society's Children Panel who are specially trained and assessed as having the necessary skills but this does not necessarily apply to representation of parents which may cause undue delay. Solicitors may also be members of the Law Society's Family Panel and many solicitors who practise in family cases are also members of the Solicitors Family Law Association and, if they have passed the necessary written examination, members of the SLFA's family panel. There is no equivalent Panel for barristers although they may become members of the Family Law Bar Association.

The Law Society has published a 'Family Law Protocol' with the support of the Solicitors' Family Law Association, the Legal Service Commission and the Lord Chancellor's Department which sets out best practice for practitioners in all aspects of private law family disputes and incorporates the Solicitors' Family Law Association Code of Practice for members.[2]

1   For the responsibility of solicitors and counsel to prevent delay, see *B v B (Child Abuse: Contact)* [1994] 2 FLR 713; and in pre-hearing reviews, see *Re G (children) (care proceedings: wasted costs)* [1999] 4 All ER 371, [1999] 3 FCR 303, [2000] 1 FLR 52 and to ensure proper preparation of the case, see *Re R (Care: Disclosure: Nature of Proceedings)* [2002] 1 FLR 755.
2   The Law Society 2002. See particularly, Pt III: Children (private law).

ALLOCATION OF PROCEEDINGS

4.15   The Act for practical purposes created a single jurisdiction in family matters exercisable by magistrates' courts, county courts and the High Court.[1] The allocation of proceedings is principally governed by the Children (Allocation of Proceedings) Order 1991.

1   See paras 4.2 et seq.

1.   Commencement of proceedings

4.16   By article 3 of the Order certain proceedings, namely those concerning local authorities (including, principally, care and related proceedings, those concerning the Child Support Act 1991 and applications for parental orders under the Human Fertilisation and Embryology Act, s 30) have to be commenced in a magistrates' court. Under Art 4, applications to extend, vary or discharge orders made under the CA 1989 must be made to the court that made the original order. Apart from these provisions the 1991 Order does not regulate the court level at which other proceedings must be started. However many other cases will be 'self regulating' in the sense that those concerning children in divorce cases must be made, in the first instance, to a divorce county court, while those concerning children in maintenance applications under the Domestic Proceedings and Magistrates' Court Act 1978 must be made to a magistrates' court. There is, however, no substantive restriction on the initial allocation of 'free standing' applications for section 8 orders or other Pt I orders under the CA 1989 but practice has determined the more suitable venue for certain applications.[1]

1   See paras 4.27 and 4.32.

4.17   Where an application under the CA 1989, Pts I, II and Sch 1 is made to a county court, it is to be commenced in a divorce county court.[1] If, however, an application is made for a s 8 order in a divorce county court which is not also a family hearing centre then if the court is notified that the application will be contested, it must be transferred to a family hearing centre[2]. Where applications under Pts III to V of the CA 1989 are to be commenced in a county court, they must be commenced in a care centre,[3] though, with the parties consent, the case can be heard at a non-care centre.[4]

1   Children (Allocation of Proceedings) Order 1991, art 14.
2   Above, art 16(1).
3   Above, art 18(1).
4   County Courts Act 1984, s 3(3).

2.   Transfer of proceedings

4.18   The rules for transferring proceedings under the CA 1989 are solely governed by the Children (Allocation of Proceedings) Order 1991.[1] Provision is made for the transfer of proceedings under the CA 1989 from one magistrates' court to another by Art 6; from one county court to another by Art 10 and for the transfer of proceedings from a magistrates' court to a county court by Arts 7 and 9 and vice versa by Art 11. Provision is also made for the transfer of cases from a county court to the High Court and vice versa under Arts 12 and 13.

1   Ie ss 38 and 39 of the Matrimonial and Family Proceedings Act 1984 do not apply: Art 5.

Contravention of order

4.19   Article 21 of the Children (Allocation of Proceedings) Order 1991,[1] specifically provides that proceedings commenced or transferred in contravention of the order are not invalid and no appeal lies against the determination of proceedings on the basis of such contravention alone.

1   SI 1991/1677, as amended.

PROCEDURE

1.   Rules

4.20   Proceedings under the Children Act are governed by two sets of rules: the Family Proceedings Rules 1991[1] in the case of High Court or county court applications, and the Family Proceedings Courts (Children Act 1989) Rules 1991[2] in the case of magistrates' courts. Although it was not possible to formulate one set of rules for all three courts, the rules are, so far as practicable, to the same effect.[3]

1 SI 1991/1247, amended by SI 1991/2113, SI 1992/456 and 2067, 1993/295, SI 1994/808, 2165, 2890 and 3155, SI 1996/816 and 1674, SI 1997/637, 1056 and 1893, SI 1998/1901, SI 1999/1012 and 3491, SI 2000/2267 and SI 2001/821.
2 SI 1991/1395, amended by SI 1991/1991, SI 1992/2068, SI 1993/627, SI 1994/809, 2166 and 3156, SI 1997/1895 and SI 2001/615 and 818.
3 At the time when the Act was implemented the Lord Chancellor was responsible for the High Court and county courts and the Home Secretary for the magistrates' courts. Responsibility for magistrates' courts was transferred to the Lord Chancellor by the Transfer of Functions (Magistrates' Courts and Family Law) Order 1992, SI 1992/709. As part of the implementation of the White Paper 'Justice for All' (Cm 5563) and the proposals for a unified court administration, further consideration is being given to formulating a single set of rules.

2. Forms

4.21 At all court levels proceedings are commenced by application either on a prescribed form or where there is no form, in writing. In certain applications such as those under s 8 where the applicant is not entitled to make application, he must obtain the leave of the court.[1] In the magistrates' court the applicant must obtain the leave of the justices' clerk[2] when making an ex parte application or an emergency protection order.[3] The Rules prescribe a number of forms which include a 'core' application form, which for certain applications is supplemented by an additional form. Application is made in respect of a family where appropriate instead of each child as formerly, although for statistical purposes the number of individual children is still recorded.

In accordance with the non adversarial, inquisitorial nature of proceedings, the object of the forms is to ensure disclosure of relevant information at any early stage. In addition to full details of the child and the applicants, forms may require a description of the child's circumstances, the family structure, the reasons for making the application and proposals for the child's upbringing if an order is made; full disclosure is expected.[4]

In public law proceedings witness statements setting out the evidence in support of the application must be filed in the court and served on the parties.[5] The applicant will be required to submit details of plans for the future care of the child and any requests for directions, including restrictions on contact. The level of details given will be determined to some extent by the stage reached in the investigation of the child's circumstances. Any plan should consider the welfare checklist of factors and why an order is necessary.[6] In private law proceedings for a s 8 order however, the emphasis is on avoiding the situation being inflamed by restricting the opportunity of the parties to make allegations and counter allegations so as to provide an opportunity for mediation to be explored. Accordingly, the information which may be supplied with the forms is limited and parties may not, for example, file statements until such time as the court directs.[7]

1 See paras 5.122ff.
2 Or authorised legal adviser, see para 4.13.
3 FPC (CA 1989) R 1991, r 4(4).
4 See para 4.36.
5 Family Proceedings Courts (Children Act 1989) Rules 1991, r 17.
6 Ie to comply with the principles in s 1, see the discussion in chapter 1. See *Re G (child case: parental involvement)* [1996] 2 FCR 1, [1996] 1 FLR 857, CA.
7 Family Proceedings Courts (Children Act 1989) Rules 1991, r 17(4)(5), Family Proceedings Rules 1991 r 4.17(4)(5).

3. Filing the application

4.22 The applicant must file his application together with sufficient copies to be served on each applicant.[1] A case number will then be applied to each application and a court file created. Files are in a standard format to facilitate transfer between the three levels of court.

1 Family Proceedings Rules 1991, r 4.4 (1)(a); Family Proceedings Courts (Children Act 1989) Rules 1991, r 4 (1)(a).

4. Service

4.23 On receipt of the filed documents the court must fix the date, time and place for a hearing or directions appointment, endorse the date so fixed on form C6 (and form C6A where appropriate – notice of hearing to parties and non-parties) and return them to the applicant.[1] The applicant must then serve the endorsed copy of the application within the number of days prescribed before the date fixed for the hearing or directions appointment on each respondent. The respondents and those on whom notice must be given are prescribed for each type of proceeding by the Schedule to the rules.[2] Detailed rules about service are contained in the Family Proceedings Rules 1991, r 4.8 and the Family Proceedings Courts (Children Act 1989) Rules 1991, r 8. Once an application has been made it may only be withdrawn with leave of the court.[3] In the case of applications for an order under s 8 of or Schedule 1 to the Act, the respondent must file and serve an acknowledgement in 14 days.[4] The court has power, inter alia, to abridge the times specified for sending documents.[5]

1 Family Proceedings Rules 1991, r 4.4(2); Family Proceedings Courts (Children Act 1989) Rules 1991, r 4(2).
2 Family Proceedings Rules 1991, App J; Family Proceedings Courts (Children Act 1989) Rules 1991, Sch 2.
3 Family Proceedings Rules 1991, r 4.5; Family Proceedings Courts (Children Act 1989) Rules 1991, r 5. See *Re N (Leave to Withdraw Care Proceedings)* [2000] 1 FLR 134.
4 Family Proceedings Rules 1991, r 4.9; Family Proceedings Courts (Children Act 1989) Rules 1991, r 9.
5 Family Proceedings Rules 1991, r 4.8(8), as amended; Family Proceedings Courts (Children Act 1989) Rules 1991, r 8(8) as amended.

5. Parties

4.24 In public law proceedings, the child and any person with parental responsibility for the child will automatically be given party status.[1] The court may also direct that others be joined to the proceedings. The court may direct that a father not having parental responsibility should not be served with notice[2] or that he be discharged from the proceedings.[3] If a father, without parental responsibility, wishes to participate in the proceedings, he should be permitted to do so, unless there was some justifiable reason for not joining him as a party.[4] A person against whom allegations have been made (but who is not a party) can be given leave to intervene and permitted to take part in the proceedings to the limited extent of his involvement, but has no right to be made a party.

1 Family Proceedings Courts (Children Act) R 1991, Sch 2.
2 *Re X (care: notice of proceedings)* [1996] 3 FCR 91, [1996] 1 FLR 186.

3   *Re W (Discharge of Party to Proceedings)* [1997] 1 FLR 128.
4   *Re B (Care Proceedings: Notification of Father Without Parental Responsibility)* [1999] 2 FLR
    408. See *Re P (care proceedings: father's application)* [2001] 3 FCR 279, [2001] 1 FLR 781
    where a very late application to be joined as a party was refused as to grant the application
    would disrupt and delay the proceedings which had already been listed for trial. The father's
    human rights had to be balanced against the child's need to obtain a resolution of proceedings.

4.25   In addition to the parties and others on whom notice must be served as
specified in the rules, in 'relevant'[1] proceedings, any person may file a request
in writing[2] that he or another be joined as a party (or cease to be a party).[3] The
court may of its own motion, join a person as a party. At or before the first
directions appointment in, or hearing of, relevant proceedings, the applicant
shall file a statement that service of a copy of the application has been made on
each respondent, and notice of the proceedings has been effected under the
FPR 1991 r 4.4(3), FPC (CA) R 1991 r 4(3); and the statement shall indicate:

(a)   the manner, date, time and place of service; or
(b)   where service was effected by post, the date, time and place of posting.[4]

Service on behalf of a child shall be effected by the solicitor acting for the
child, or where there is no such solicitor, the children's guardian, or justices'
chief executive. Service on a child shall be effected by service on the solicitor
acting for the child, or where there is no solicitor, the guardian, or where there
is neither a solicitor nor a guardian, with leave of the justices' clerk or the
court, the child.

1   Ie proceedings under the CA 1989, any statutory instrument made under the CA 1989 or any
    amendment made by the CA 1989 in any other enactment: Family Proceedings Courts
    (Children Act 1989) Rules, r 1, CA 1989, s 93(1) and see the Family Proceedings Rules 1991,
    r 4.1.
2   The absence of a written request does not automatically invalidate the order. The facts and cir-
    cumstances, including the urgency of the situation, must be considered: *Re O (Minor) (Leave
    to Seek Residence Order)* [1994] 1 FLR 162, per Ewbank J.
3   Family Proceedings Rules 1991, r 4.7(2); Family Proceedings Courts (Children Act 1989)
    Rules 1991, r 7(2).
4   Family Proceedings Rules 1991, r 4.8(7), Family Proceedings Courts (Children Act 1989)
    Rules 1991, r 4(7).

6.   Reviewing allocation

Public law

4.26   On receipt of the application, the clerk of the court will consider
whether the proceedings should be transferred to a higher court or consolidated with other proceedings. The Children (Allocation of Proceedings) Order
1991[1] provides that a magistrates' court may, on application by a party or of
its own motion, transfer a case to the county court, where it considers it in the
interests of the child having regard to delay, whether it would be appropriate
for the proceedings to be heard with other pending proceedings and whether
the proceedings are exceptionally grave, important or complex in particular
because of:

(a)   complicated or conflicting evidence about the risks involved to the child's
      physical or moral well-being or about other matters relating to the welfare
      of the child;

(b) the number of parties;
(c) a conflict with the law of another jurisdiction;
(d) some novel or difficult point of law; and
(e) some question of general public interest.

A case can be allocated to another court at any time, but should where possible be allocated sooner rather than later to avoid delay in fixing a hearing.[2] Average delay between application and decision to transfer is 10 weeks[3] but there appear to be wide variations in practice.[4]

1   SI 1991/1677, as amended.
2   See also *Handbook of Best Practice in Children Act Cases* (Children Act Advisory Committee, June 1997) on first appointment in the county court in *Clarke Hall and Morrison* at para 1[20010].
3   *Scoping Study on Delay in Children Act Cases* (Lord Chancellor's Dept 2002) para 103.
4   In a sample considered by MCSI the period varied between nil and 22 weeks: MCSI *A Review of Case Administration in Family Proceedings Courts* (May 2001) para 2.13.

4.27   Article 9 provides that, in the event of a refusal by a magistrates' court to transfer such proceedings, any party to the case may then apply to the appropriate care centre for a transfer. In that latter event the proceedings can be transferred to the care centre, the High Court or sent back to the magistrates' court. If a district judge orders the transfer of proceedings to a magistrates' court in accordance with art 11, an appeal against that decision may be made to a judge of the Family Division of the High Court or to a circuit judge (except where the order was made by a district judge or deputy district judge of the Principal Registry).[1]

1   Children (Allocation of Proceedings) (Appeals) Order 1991, SI 1991/1801.

4.28   The county court may transfer a case to the High Court, having regard to:[1]

(a) delay;
(b) whether the proceedings are appropriate for determination in the High Court; and
(c) whether such determination would be in the interests of the child.

1   The Children (Allocation of Proceedings) Order 1991, SI 1991/1677, art 12.

4.29   Transfers significantly to accelerate proceedings to the county court have not caused any apparent concern in so far as they do not appear to be common.[1] Lateral transfers are also not common, which suggests that there is scope for developing better practice.[2] They have generally been confined to the need to consolidate proceedings, or because one or more of the parties is resident within the receiving court's jurisdiction.[3] The 'complexity' provisions are the most common reason for transfer[4] and have been a source of judicial comment. The power to transfer public law cases down from the county court to the family proceedings court is rarely used.[5] The significance of proper use of the power to transfer cases would seem now to be greater because of the pressure on court resources created by a steady increase in the number of applications in care proceedings.[6]

1   From a peak of 14% of transfers in public law cases to a steady figure of 3% (CAAC Report 1993/94 Table B, p 70). In 1998 the number of transfers were: public law cases – 172; private law cases – 176.

2 Lateral transfers in 1994 were: 78 (High Court to High Court); 1365 (county court-county court); 473 (family proceedings court to family proceedings court). (Source: Lord Chancellor's Department.)

3 CAAC Report 1992/93, p 48; Dame Margaret Booth *Avoiding Delay in Children Act Cases* (Lord Chancellor's Dept) para 5.6.1; and see *W v Wakefield City Council* [1995] 1 FLR 170 (consolidation of proceedings in respect of members of same family).

4 75% of all transfers in public law cases: *Scoping Study on Delay in Children Act Cases* (Lord Chancellor's Dept 2002) para 99 (a figure remarkably consistent with the 74% in the CAAC Report 1993/94 Table 1B, p 70).

5 74 cases over the three year period 1996-1998: *Scoping Study on Delay in Children Act Cases* (Lord Chancellor's Dept 2002) para 100.

6 From 2657 care applications in 1992 to 6728 in 1998 (Judicial statistics) and see Beckett *The Great Care Proceedings Explosion* BJSW (2001) 31, 493-501.

COMPLEXITY

4.30 In *C v Solihull Metropolitan Borough Council*[1] Ward J said that a serious and unexplained injury to a baby was a grave and important case and should be transferred up from a magistrates' court. Where there is a conflict in the evidence of professionals of significant experience eg medical experts, the magistrates should consider whether the case should be transferred to a county court which could then consider whether to transfer the case to High Court.[2]

1 [1993] 1 FLR 290.
2 *Re S (A Minor)* (20 July 1992, unreported), FD (referred to in CAAC Report 1993/94, p 50).

4.31 Early estimates of the impact of the allocation provisions that between 15% to 25% of all cases would make their way to the higher courts.[1] Current data would suggest that family proceedings courts deal with about two thirds of public law cases[2] but there is some evidence that these proportions vary considerably in different areas. Variations between circa 6–7% and 50% of cases being transferred up to the county court from family proceedings courts have been identified[3] and in one case more than 50%.[4] Recommendations have been made that the criteria for transfer be reviewed.[5] Magistrates have, however, expressed some concern at the loss of 'quality work' to the higher courts and that guidance may have underestimated the ability of the family proceedings court to deal with longer cases.[6] The Children Act Advisory Committee expressed the view that family panel magistrates are capable of hearing straightforward cases lasting up to four to five days providing that the magistrates are able to sit on consecutive days and there are no complex issues involved.[7]

The *Scoping Study on Delay in Children Act Cases*[8] examined perceptions of the level of service provided by family proceedings courts. Local authorities and children's guardians considered family proceedings courts provided an efficient and effective service but legal professionals considered that they could be slow and sometimes lacked case management skills. The *Scoping Study* identified the following problems :

* case management in some family proceedings courts;
* waiting for magistrates written reasons;
* justices'clerks having insufficient sanctions to enforce directions.

A working group has submitted a report to the Lord Chancellor's Department suggesting ways of tackling these and other issues including recommendations for Rule changes to enable judgments with reasons to be given orally, with written reasons to follow within a specified time. The report will be published in the autumn of 2002 alongside the Lord Chancellor's Department response to the group's recommendations.[9]

1 CAAC Report 1992/93, p 46. The CAAC Report 1993/94 (Table 1A, p 70) suggested that approximately 80% of public law cases are dealt with by the magistrates' court.
2 *Scoping Study on Delay in Children Act Cases* (Lord Chancellor's Dept 2002) para 80.
3 (Beckett: Anglia Polytechnic University 2000).
4 The Magistrates' Court Service Inspectorate thematic review *A Review of Case Administration in Family Proceedings Courts* (May 2001) identified a Magistrates' Courts Committee where more than 50% of cases had been transferred (Table 1).
5 *A Review of Case Administration in Family Proceedings Courts* (HMMCSI May 2001) para 2.13. See also Dame Margaret Booth's Report on *Delay in Public Law Children Act Cases* (Lord Chancellor's Dept 1996) and *Scoping Study on Delay in Children Act Cases* (Lord Chancellor's Dept 2002) para 118.
6 CAAC Report 1992/93, p 57 and The Magistrate December 1994. However, in 1998 only 88 public law cases were transferred from family proceedings courts to the county court on the ground of length of hearing.
7 CAAC Report 1993/94, p 50. Now followed in practice, see MCSI *A Review of Case Administration in Family Proceedings Courts* (May 2001).
8 Lord Chancellor's Department 2002.
9 *Scoping Study on Delay in Children Act Cases* (Lord Chancellor's Dept 2002) para 115.

Private law

4.32   The rules governing the transfer of private law proceedings are less specific than those governing public law. In contrast to art 7, art 8 merely states that where a magistrates' court 'having regard to the principle set out in s 1(2) [ie the need to avoid unnecessary delay] . . . considers that in the interests of the child the proceedings can be dealt with more appropriately in [a] county court it may order the transfer accordingly'. *R v South East Hampshire Family Proceedings Court, ex p D*[1] however, establishes that when considering whether to transfer a case to a county court, a magistrates' court shall not limit consideration merely to the single issue of delay as provided for by art 8 but have regard to the overriding principle that the welfare of the child is the paramount consideration and consider other matters, such as complexity, before refusing an application. Applications can now be made under art 9(4) to the county court following a magistrates' clerk's refusal to transfer a private law case. Further, art 11(2) permits a county court to transfer a private law case back down to a magistrates' court.

1 [1994] 2 All ER 445, [1994] 1 FCR 620, [1994] 2 FLR 190.

4.33   Article 12 of the 1991 Order[1] empowers county courts to transfer proceedings to the High Court. In the private law context it is established that the following types of cases should be heard in the High Court:

* applications by children for leave to apply for section 8 orders;[2]
* applications for sterilisation of a child;[3]
* cases in which a blood test is being disputed;[4]
* cases in which HIV tests for children are being sought;[5]
* cases in which it is sought to impose a restraint upon the freedom of the press;[6]
* cases in which a party seeks leave of the court to withhold information from the parties;[7]

- claims for declarations of incompatibility under s 4 of the Human Rights Act 1998 or cases raising an issue which may lead to the court considering making such a declaration;[8]
- cases, particularly those involving litigants in person, in which there are unresolved allegations of possible breaches of the Hague or European conventions on International Child Abduction.[9]

Applications for leave to remove children from the jurisdiction should be made either to the High Court or county court depending upon the complexity or difficulty.[10]

1 The Children (Allocation of Proceedings) Order 1991, SI 1991/1677, art 12.
2 *Practice Direction (applications by children: leave)* [1993] 1 All ER 820 (but only the application for leave and not necessarily the substantive application).
3 *Re HG (Specific Issue Order: Procedure)* [1993] 1 FLR 587; *Practice Note (Official Solicitor: Sterilisation)* [1996] 2 FLR 111.
4 *Re F (A Minor) (Blood Tests: Parental Rights)* [1993] Fam 314, [1993] 3 All ER 596, CA.
5 *Re HIV Tests* [1994] 2 FLR 116n, sub nom *Re X (a minor)* [1994] 2 FCR 1110.
6 *Re H-S (minors) (protection of identity)* [1994] 3 All ER 390, sub nom *Re H (Minors) (Injunction: Public Interest)* [1994] 1 FLR 519, CA.
7 *Re C (Disclosure)* [1996] 1 FLR 797.
8 *Practice Direction (Human Rights Act 1998: citation of authorities)* [2000] 2 FCR 768, [2000] 2 FLR 429.
9 *Re D (Abduction: Acquiescence)* [1998] 2 FLR 335, see also *Re H (Abduction: Habitual Residence: Consent)* [2000] 2 FLR 294. (The same principle would suggest that Brussels II issues should also be moved to the High Court).
10 *MH v GP (Child Emigration)* [1995] 2 FLR 106.

7. Directions appointments

4.34 On receipt of an application in public or private law proceedings, the court administration must fix a date for a hearing or directions appointment (case management conference).[1] Directions may be given by the court or by a district judge (High Court and county court) or a single justice or justices' clerk (family proceedings court). A directions appointment at an early stage in the proceedings will serve as a 'case management conference' to make any necessary directions, including timetabling, to avoid drift in the proceedings. In proceedings in the Family Division of the High Court at the Royal Courts of Justice each case is allocated to a High Court judge and a date fixed for a management conference. This conference and all further hearings including directions hearings will where practicable, be conducted by the allocated judge who will manage the case to, and adjudicate at, the final hearing.[2] Prior to the final hearing, there may also be a pre-trial review to ensure that the case is trial ready.

1 Family Proceedings Rules 1991, r 4.4(2); Family Proceedings Courts (Children Act 1989) Rules 1991, r 4(2). The average period between a public law application and first listing is 10 days MCSI *A Review of Case Administration in Family Proceedings Courts* (May 2001).
2 *Practice Direction-Judicial Continuity* [2002] 3 All ER 603, [2002] 2 FCR 667, [2002] 2 FLR 367, FD.

Scope of directions

4.35 At a directions hearing, which may be held at any time during the course of the proceedings, directions may be issued under the Family Proceedings Rules 1991 r 4.14(2) or the Family Proceedings Courts (Children

Act 1989) Rules 1991, r 14(2). Guidance on the expectations of the court at directions has been given both by decided cases, Practice Directions and *The Handbook of Best Practice in Children Act Cases.*[1]

1 Reproduced in *Clarke Hall and Morrison* at 1[20001]ff.

Case management

4.36 General guidance on the management of proceedings has been given by the President in *Practice Note: Case management*[1] applying to family proceedings in the High Court and all care centres, family hearing centres and divorce county courts. The President has informed justices' clerks that the guidance is equally applicable to family proceedings courts:

'1 The importance of reducing the cost and delay of civil litigation makes it necessary for the court to assert greater control over the preparation for and conduct of hearings than has hitherto been customary.

Failure by practitioners to conduct cases economically will be visited by appropriate orders for costs, including wasted costs orders.

2 The court will accordingly exercise its discretion to limit:
(a) discovery;
(b) the length of opening and closing oral submissions;
(c) the time allowed for the examination and cross-examination of witnesses;
(d) the issues on which it wishes to be addressed;
(e) reading aloud from documents and authorities.

3 Unless otherwise ordered, every witness statement or affidavit shall stand as the evidence in chief of the witness concerned. The substance of the evidence which a party intends to adduce at the hearing must be sufficiently detailed but without prolixity; it must be confined to material matters of fact, not, (except in the case of the evidence of professional witnesses) of opinion; and if hearsay evidence is to be adduced, the source of the information has to be declared or good reason given for not doing so.

4 It is a duty owed to the court both by the parties and by their legal representatives to give full and frank disclosure in ancillary relief applications and also in all matters in respect of children.

The parties and their advisers must also use their best endeavours:
(a) to confine the issues and the evidence called to what is reasonably considered to be essential for the proper presentation of their case;
(b) to reduce or eliminate issues for expert evidence;
(c) in advance of the hearing to agree which are the issues or the main issues.

5 *Superseded by Practice Direction (Family Proceedings: Court Bundles).*[2]

6 In cases estimated to last for five days or more and in which no pre-trial review has been ordered, application should be made for a pre-trial review. It should, when practicable, be listed at least three weeks before the hearing and be conducted by the judge or district judge before whom the case is to be heard and should be attended by the advocates who are to represent the parties at the hearing. Whenever possible, all statements of evidence and all reports should be filed before the date of the review and in good time for them to have been considered by all parties.

7 Whenever practicable and in any matter estimated to last five days or more, each party should, not less than two clear days before the hearing, lodge with the court, or the Clerk of the Rules in matters in the Royal Courts of Justice in London, and deliver to other parties, a chronology and a skeleton argument concisely summarising the party's submissions in relation to each of the issues and citing the main authorities relied upon. It is important that skeleton arguments should be brief.

8 *Superseded by Practice Direction (Family Proceedings: Court Bundles).*

9 The opening speech should be succinct. At its conclusion other parties might be invited briefly to amplify their skeleton arguments. In a heavy case the court

might in conjunction with final speeches require written submissions including the findings of fact for which each party contends . . .'

1   [1995] 1 All ER 586, [1995] 1 WLR 332, [1995] 1 FLR 456, FD.
2   [2000] 1 WLR 737, [2000] 1 FCR 521, [2000] 1 FLR 536, FD.

4.37   This guidance is supplemented by the *Practice Direction (Family Proceedings: Court Bundles)*:[1]

'1   The following Practice Direction applies to all hearings in family proceedings in the High Court, to all hearings of family proceedings in the Royal Courts of Justice and to hearings with a time estimate of half a day or more in all care centres, family hearing centres and divorce county courts (including the Principal Registry of the Family Division when so treated), except as specified in paragraph 2.3 below, and subject to specific directions given in any particular case, 'Hearing' extends to all hearings before judges and district judges and includes the hearing of any application.

2.1   A bundle for the use of the court at the hearing shall be provided by the party in the position of applicant at the hearing or by any other party who agrees to do so. It shall contain copies of all documents relevant to the hearing in chronological order, paginated and indexed and divided into separate sections, as follows:

(a)   applications and orders;
(b)   statements and affidavits;
(c)   experts' reports and other reports including those of a guardian ad litem, and
(d)   other documents, divided into further sections as may be appropriate.

2.2   Where the nature of the hearing is such that a complete bundle of all documents is unnecessary, the bundle may comprise only those documents necessary for the hearing but the summary (paragraph 3.1(a) below) must commence with a statement that the bundle is limited or incomplete. The summary should be limited to those matters which the court needs to know for the purpose of the hearing and for management of the case.

2.3   The requirement to provide a bundle shall not apply to the hearing of any urgent application where the circumstances are such that it is not reasonably practicable for a bundle to be provided.

3.1   At the commencement of the bundle there shall be:

(a)   a summary of the background to the hearing limited, if practicable, to one A4 page;
(b)   a statement of the issue or issues to be determined;
(c)   a summary of the order or directions sought by each party;
(d)   a chronology if it is a final hearing or if the summary under (a) is insufficient;
(e)   skeleton arguments as may be appropriate, with copies of all authorities relied on.

3.2   If possible the bundle shall be agreed. In all cases, the party preparing the bundle shall paginate it and provide an index to all other parties prior to the hearing.

3.3   The bundle should normally be contained in a ring binder or lever arch file (limited to 350 pages in each file). Where there is more than one bundle, each should be clearly distinguishable. Bundles shall be lodged, if practicable, two clear days prior to the hearing. For hearings in the Royal Courts of Justice bundles shall be lodged with the Clerk of the Rules. All bundles shall have clearly marked on the outside, the title and number of the case, the hearing date and time and, if known, the name of the judge hearing the case.

4   After each hearing which is not a final hearing, the party responsible for the bundle shall retrieve it from the court. The bundle with any additional documents shall be relodged for further hearings in accordance with the above provisions . . .'

1   [2000] 1 WLR 737, [2000] 1 FCR 521, [2000] 1 FLR 536, FD.

8. Directions

4.38 Forms of standard directions for family courts were set out in the Children Act Advisory Committee Report[1] and many courts subsequently developed their own forms. Standard directions in the Family Division for public law proceedings under Part IV and, to a certain extent, private law proceedings under Part II of the 1989 Act are set out in a Practice Direction.[2] Much of the guidance in the Practice Direction is equally relevant to other family courts and the scope and nature of directions which a family court may give are set out in the Practice Direction which is reproduced at p 729. Directions given in one court can be carried forward until amended, if the case is allocated to another court,[3] although it would not normally be necessary to make directions (other than to appoint a children's guardian) when transferring a case to the High Court.[4]

1 Report 1993/4, pp 26 and 27.
2 *Practice Direction-Judicial Continuity* [2002] 3 All ER 603, [2002] 2 FCR 667, FD.
3 Family Proceedings Rules 1991, r 4.14(9); Family Proceedings Courts (Children Act 1989) R 1991, r 14(11).
4 *Practice Direction-Judicial Continuity* [2002] 3 All ER 603, [2002] 2 FCR 667, [2002] 2 FLR 367, FD.

General considerations

4.39 Directions may be given of the court's own motion, in which case the parties must have been given notice and the opportunity to make representations, or on the written request of one party either on notice to the other parties or with their written consent.[1] In difficult child cases it is bad practice for directions to be sought and given in writing without the attendance of the parties.[2] In practice, the most convenient course is for the court to arrange an oral hearing at which the parties are required to attend.[3] Counsel who have conduct of the substantive hearing should attend if possible.[4] In 'specified' (ie public law) proceedings the children's guardian (formerly the 'guardian ad litem') must attend unless excused by the court,[5] whereas in private law proceedings a children and family reporter (the former 'welfare officer') may be ordered to attend.[6] On receipt of an application, the court administration must fix a date for a hearing or a directions appointment.[7]

1 Family Proceedings Rules 1991, r 4.16; Family Proceedings Courts (Children Act 1989) Rules 1991, r 16.
2 *Re A and B (Minors) (No 2)* [1995] 1 FLR 351, per Wall J.
3 Family Proceedings Rules 1991 r 4.14(3); Family Proceedings Courts (Children Act 1989) Rules 1991, r 14(5).
4 *Re MD and TD (children's cases: time estimates)* [1994] 2 FCR 94.
5 Family Proceedings Rules 1991 r 4.11(4); Family Proceedings Courts (Children Act 1989) Rules 1991, r 11(4).
6 Family Proceedings Rules 1991 r 4.13(3) Family Proceedings Courts (Children Act 1989) Rules 1991, r 13(3).
7 Family Proceedings Rules 1991 r 4.4(2); Family Proceedings Courts (Children Act 1989) Rules 1991, r 4(2).

4.40 In a county court where a difficult case is likely to be heard by the judge, the district judge should direct that an appointment for directions should be listed before the judge who is to hear it or before the designated judge[1] who may then maintain control over the course of the case.[2] In a family proceedings court for practical reasons the majority of directions appointments are conducted by the justices' clerk. However, the justices' clerk does not have the same extensive powers to deal with interlocutory matters as that of a district judge. The justices' clerk may not grant leave for a person to become a party to proceedings and where he considers it inappropriate to make a direction on a particular matter he must refer it to a full court. The justices' clerk may not make any s 8 order and may only make an interim order in public law proceedings in the limited circumstances set out in r 28 of the Family Proceedings Courts (Children Act 1989) Rules.[3] Accordingly directions appointments may be conducted by the justices' clerk before the normal sitting of the court.[4] If, for example, the parties agree to an interim or final order the matter can then be referred to a full court sitting later that day although with the increase in business in some courts, directions appointments may be listed separately with time slots of sufficient length to permit full exploration of the issues while reducing waiting time for the parties.

In care proceedings in the family proceedings court, the justices' clerk should fix an early return date for a hearing before the court which may then determine whether any interim order is required although a children's guardian may be appointed in advance by the justices' clerk.[5] Otherwise an application under the Children Act should be listed for an early directions appointment. A directions appointment is more informal than a court hearing and in the county court will be in the district judges' chambers, in the magistrates' court in any available room or a court room whichever is most suitable. The court is expected to adopt a proactive and rigorous approach to the issues in the case with a view to ensuring that all the issues have been appropriately defined and addressed.[6]

Counsel and solicitors for the parties have a part to play in the proper preparation of case to avoid delay. They must ensure that a case does not drift and is either brought to a hearing or resolved in some way with the minimum of delay.[7] Advocates should use their best endeavours to attend the case management conference and any directions hearings.[8] Counsel and solicitors must talk to each other freely about case preparation and when advocates attend a pre-hearing review, it is their collective responsibility to ensure:

(1) that the issues in the case to be addressed at the final hearing are clearly identified;
(2) that the evidence to address those issues is either already available or that directions are sought from the court to ensure that it is available in good time for the hearing;
(3) that all the expert witnesses in the case have been sent – or will prior to giving evidence be sent – all relevant material which has emerged since their reports were written; or where the material required by an expert witness has not been seen by that witness, that the material will be sent and a further report, if necessary, commissioned;
(4) that the witnesses required to give evidence at the hearing have been identified;
(5) that the length of time required for the evidence of each witness has been appropriately estimated;
(6) that the witnesses have been time-tabled;
(7) that expert witnesses, in particular, have been allotted specific dates and times for their evidence; and that the length of time allotted for their evidence has been carefully assessed to ensure that it can be given without the

witnesses being inconvenienced by having to return to court on a second
occasion to complete their evidence;

(8) that the documents required for the case are in good order and bundled
appropriately; that there is a chronology and, where required, a short
statement of case from each party;

(9) that the guardian's report will be available in proper time for the hearing;
and

(10) that appropriate reading time and time for the recording of reasons has
been allowed to the justices.[9]

1 *B v B (Child Abuse: Contact)* [1994] 2 FLR 713 at 736, per Wall J.
2 *Re A and B (Minors) (No 2)* [1995] 1 FLR 351. For judicial continuity in the High Court, see
para 4.34.
3 See para 4.13.
4 CAAC Report 1992/93, p 50.
5 Justices' Clerks' Rules 1999 Sch para 39; Family Proceedings Courts (Children Act 1989)
Rules 1991, r 10.
6 *Re G (children) (care proceedings: wasted costs)* [1999] 4 All ER 371, [1999] 3 FCR 303,
[2000] 1 FLR 52.
7 *B v B (Child Abuse: Contact)* [1994] 2 FLR 713.
8 *Practice Direction-Judicial Continuity* [2002] 3 All ER 603, [2002] 2 FCR 667, [2002] 2 FLR
367, FD.
9 *Re G (children) (care proceedings: wasted costs)* [1999] 4 All ER 371, [1999] 3 FCR 303,
[2000] 1 FLR 52.

4.41 The court is required to make a note of any oral evidence that is given
although proceedings are normally conducted by representations.[1]
Directions must be recorded in writing and served on parties who were not
present[2] but this is in reality done in all cases.[3] Each direction should specify precise dates for compliance and should not be left open ended.[4] Good
practice would suggest that the court administration should record in a
diary the dates by which the various directions should be complied with.
Documents received by the court should be date stamped on receipt and the
listing officer can prompt the parties where necessary. At the conclusion of
a directions appointment the case must never be adjourned generally; a date
must be set for either a further directions appointment or a hearing before
the court.[5]

1 Family Proceedings Rules 1991, r 4.20; Family Proceedings Courts (Children Act 1989) Rules
1991, r 20. For considerations whether the court should limit oral evidence see paras 4.54.ff.
2 Family Proceedings Rules 1991, r 4.14(10); Family Proceedings Courts (Children Act 1989)
Rules 1991, r 14(12).
3 A form of directions was recommended by CAAC (Report 1993/94, pp 26-27).
4 See *Re A and B (Minors) (No 2)* [1995] 1 FLR 351.
5 See the *Handbook of Best Practice in Children Act Cases* (CAAC1997) reproduced in *Clarke
Hall and Morrison* at 1 [20001] ff.

9. Ordering welfare reports

4.42 The court is not bound to order welfare reports in every case.[1] If delay
would prejudice the child's welfare, the court might have to balance the advantages to be gained from a report against the disadvantage of the time it takes
to obtain it.[2] It has been held that the decision whether to ask for a welfare
report lies within the judge's discretion and cannot be appealed.[3] Reports can
be ordered at any stage of proceedings. In the case of magistrates' courts proceedings a single justice can order a report.[4]

If a report is ordered, a date for the hearing should be fixed and not listed for hearing 'on the first open date after the court welfare officer's report is available'. The desirable practice is to ascertain when the report can be expected and to fix a specific date in the light of that information.[5] Once appointed, the proper officer or justices' clerk must notify the welfare officer of any decisions made during the course of the proceedings and of the date for hearings, for example, in connection with applications to withdraw an application.[6] Best practice is now consolidated in a *Best practice note for the judiciary and family proceedings courts when ordering a court welfare officer's report* in the *Handbook of Best Practice in Children Act Cases* (CAAC June 1997).[7]

1 The appointment and duties of CAFCASS officers are considered in chapter 10.
2 Cf *Re H (Minors) (Welfare Reports)* [1990] 2 FLR 172, CA. FLR 142, CA.
3 *Re W (Welfare Reports)* [1995] 2 FLR 142, CA.
4 Family Proceedings Courts (Children Act 1989) Rules 1991, r 2(5)(c).
5 *B v B (Minors) (Interviews and Listing Arrangements)* [1994] 2 FLR 489, sub nom *B v B (minors: residence and care disputes)* [1994] 2 FCR 667, per Wall J. New National Standards will be issued by CAFCASS see para 10.8 and see *'Putting Children and Young Persons First: Principles and National Standards Draft Policy – A Consultation Paper.'* (CAFCASS May 2002) see para 10.8. The Draft Standards propose inter alia that cases will be allocated to CAFCASS officers within a specified time; an officer will inform his/her manager of any conflict of interest; and reports will be submitted within the timescale set by the court, see para 10.19.
6 Family Proceedings Rules 1991, r 4.5; Family Proceedings Courts (Children Act 1989) Rules 1991, r 5.
7 Reproduced in *Clarke Hall and Morrison* at 1[20001] and see para 10.11.

10.   Timetable for proceedings

4.43   In proceedings in which any question of making a s 8 order arises ie generally private law proceedings, and where the court is hearing an application under Pt IV (care and supervision proceedings), a court is required to draw up a timetable with a view to disposing of the application without delay and to give such directions as it considers appropriate for the purpose of ensuring, so far as is reasonably practicable, that the timetable is adhered to. The court may be robust in insisting that any timetable is met such as in *Re B and T (care proceedings: legal representation)*[1] where parents who had failed to comply with directions were effectively precluded from legal representation by the refusal of an application made by solicitors who had just been instructed for an adjournment on the first day of a five day hearing. Having regard overall to the fairness of the proceedings and the need to balance the rights of the parents against the rights of the children to an early determination of their future, the parents' rights under Art 6(1) of the European Convention on Human Rights were not breached.

1 [2001] 1 FCR 512.

11.   Length of hearings and listing

4.44   'There is compelling if only anecdotal evidence that Children Act cases are taking longer' per Butler-Sloss LJ in *Re M*[1]. Apart from the time taken from application to final hearing there is evidence that the length of court hearings has increased. For example in *Re M (a Minor) (Appeal: Interim Order) (No 1)*[2] the time estimate at first instance of 10 days overran to 25 days.

Dame Margaret Booth noted in her report on Avoiding Delay[3] that 'in some care centres cases overrun their estimates to a serious extent' but that many judges expressed disquiet about intervening during the hearing for fear that the parties, and in particular parents with a difficult case, might feel that they have not had the opportunity to be heard. However, members of the Solicitors Family Law Association and the Family Law Bar Association generally welcomed the judge intervening to control long-winded and sloppy advocates and to keep a grip on the case.

1 [1993] 1 FLR 822. 'There are . . . cases not infrequently taking 10 or 15 days to hear . . .' (CAAC Report 1992/93, p 24).
2 [1994] 1 FLR 54, CA.
3 *Avoiding Delay in Children Act Cases* (Lord Chancellor's Dept 1996) para 2.14.1.

4.45 Judicial concern at the accuracy of time estimates has resulted in two *Practice Directions* intended to improve the accuracy of time estimates[1] and a recommended form of Certificate of Time Estimate.[2] There is some uncertainty as to the stage in the proceedings at which a timetable should be set. Initially it was considered that a timetable should be set at an early stage.[3] However, this may, if judicial case management is not sufficiently robust, lead to repeated cancellations of the final hearing date with consequent delay and waste of court resources. On the other hand although there is some evidence that fixing the trial date at a later stage, even at the pre-final hearing review, may be of benefit, there may be drift in the earlier stages unless there is firm judicial control.[4]

1 *Practice Direction: Children Act 1989: Hearings Before High Court Judges: Time Estimates* [1994] 1 FLR 108; Note: *Re MD and TD (minors) (time estimates)* [1994] 2 FLR 336.
2 CAAC Report 1993/94, p 28. See now the *Handbook of Best Practice in Children Act Cases* reproduced in *Clarke Hall and Morrison* at [20001]ff.
3 This is implicit in *Practice Direction-Judicial Continuity* [2002] 3 All ER 603, [2002] 2 FCR 667, [2002] 2 FLR 367, FD (reproduced at p 729).
4 See MCSI *A Review of Case Administration in Family Proceedings Courts* (May 2001) paras 2.21–2.26.

4.46 Some additional initiatives have also been taken to reduce the length of hearings. Where possible parties are encouraged to agree a chronology and set out those facts not in dispute. This will enable the court to tailor its investigation to the facts of the individual case before it and the extent of the agreement.[1] In complex cases it is recommended that the court should be provided with an agreed statement of the issues and also skeleton arguments and a local authority should set out the findings it wants to satisfy the threshold criteria.[2] The court may in the light of the written evidence and the extent of any agreement, decide that an oral hearing is unnecessary, or limit the areas on which oral evidence is to be given.[3] The same judge is not precluded by bias from hearing subsequent applications in respect of children even where he has expressed firm views which may have been in favour of, or against a particular party. In fact it is more desirable that he should do so,[4] and justices have been commended by Wall J for having sat on all hearings of a particular case.[5] In *Re M (a Minor) (Appeal) (No 2)*[6] the Court of Appeal faced with the necessity of considering an appeal with an original time estimate of four days, imposed a tight timetable on the hearing which included a limitation on the length of oral submissions, and concluded the appeal in the two days that were available.

1 *Re G (A Minor) (Care Proceedings)* [1994] 2 FLR 69, distinguishing *Devon County Council v S* [1992] Fam 176, [1992] 3 All ER 793.

2 CAAC Report 1993/94, p 21 and see *Practice Note: Case Management* [1995] 1 All ER 586, [1995] 1 FLR 456.
3 See para 4.55 and *Re R (Care: Disclosure: Nature of Proceedings)* [2002] 1 FLR 755.
4 *Re M (Minors) (Judicial Continuity)* [1993] 1 FLR 903; and see *Re G (a child) (care order: threshold criteria)* [2001] 1 FCR 165, CA (same judge should preside at the disposal stage of a split hearing in care proceedings).
5 In *F v R (Contact: Justices' Reasons)* [1995] 1 FLR 227.
6 [1994] 1 FLR 54. [1994] 1 FCR 1.

12. Service of statements

4.47 Parties must file and serve on the parties and any officer of CAF-CASS:

(a) written statements of the substance of the oral evidence which the party intends to adduce at the hearing or directions appointment; and
(b) copies of any documents, including experts' reports upon which the party intends to rely, at or by such time as the court directs.[1]

In proceedings for a s 8 order no statement or copy may be filed until such time as the court directs,[2] and no file, document information or statement, other than those required or authorised by the Rules, should be served or made without leave of the court.[3] Subject to any direction of the court about the timing of statements, supplementary statements may be filed, as can, with leave, written amendments to the documents already served.[4]

Evidence or documents not filed in accordance with the Rules cannot be addressed or relied on at the subsequent directions appointment or hearing without leave of the court.[5] The principles of the law of evidence and their application to proceedings relating to children are discussed in detail in chapter 11.

1 Family Proceedings Rules 1991, r 4.17(1); Family Proceedings Courts (Children Act 1989) Rules 1991, r 17(1).
2 Family Proceedings Rules 1991, r 4.17(5); Family Proceedings Courts (Children Act 1989) Rules 1991, r 17(5). See para 4.22.
3 Family Proceedings Rules 1991, r 4.17(4); Family Proceedings Courts (Children Act 1989) Rules 1991, r 17(4).
4 Family Proceedings Rules 1991, rr 4.17(2) and 4.19; Family Proceedings Courts (Children Act 1989) Rules 1991, rr 17(2) and 19.
5 Family Proceedings Rules 1991, r 4.17(4); Family Proceedings Courts (Children Act 1989) Rules 1991, r 17(4).

13. Sanctions

4.48 There are no direct sanctions for breach of directions although some breaches might amount to professional misconduct[1] and, as the *Practice Note Case Management*[2] makes plain, the court does have power in appropriate circumstances to make an award of costs against a party or personally against his representative. In addition, where in the High Court and county court the direction is properly phrased in injunctive terms,[3] it is clear that a failure to comply would be punishable as a contempt. In the magistrates' court a similarly worded direction made by the court (but not by a single justice or the clerk) might be punishable under s 63(3) of the Magistrates' Courts Act 1980.[4]

1   Cf *Re M* (1989) Times, 29 December, CA.
2   [1995] 1 All ER 586, [1995] 1 FLR 456, see para 4.36.
3   See para 5.131.
4   See para 5.138.

14.   Reading time

4.49   Justices who are to deal with a case must read any documents before the hearing.[1] They should be able to do this at their leisure rather than under the pressure of knowing that the parties, their advocates and witnesses are waiting.[2] Justices' clerks are encouraged where practicable to deliver the papers to the justices at their homes.[3] There is no equivalent procedural rule for the higher courts but in complex cases the same judge should have conducted the final directions appointment and should be familiar with the case. If not, it would be difficult for proper control to be exercised over the course of the evidence.[4] Furthermore, in all issues of any substance, the directions hearings should always consider judicial reading time and the listing offices should be contacted to ensure that the required reading time is allocated.[5]

1   Family Proceedings Courts (Children Act 1989) Rules 1991, SI 1991/1395, r 20(1). This is mandatory: *S v Merton London Borough* [1994] 1 FCLR 186, even for an interim hearing: *Hampshire County Council v S* [1993] Fam 158, [1993] 1 All ER 944.
2   *M v C (Children Order: Reasons)* [1993] 2 FLR 584.
3   CAAC Report 1992/93, p 51.
4   See *Practice Note: Case Management* [1995] 1 All ER 586, [1995] 1 FLR 456.
5   *Re A Care Hearing* [2002] Fam Law 484, FD.

COURT HEARINGS

1.   Privacy and restrictions on reporting proceedings

4.50   There is a restriction on the persons who may be present at hearings of 'family proceedings' before family proceedings courts[1] and where it is considered expedient in the interests of the child, representatives of the press may be excluded.[2] Hearings and direction appointments in the High Court and county court concerning proceedings under the CA 1989, are, unless the court otherwise directs, heard in chambers.[3]

Although the general rule in art 6(1) of the European Convention on Human Rights requires civil proceedings to be held in public, a state may designate a class of proceedings as an exception to the general rule. Exclusion of press and public can be justified in order to protect the privacy of a child and parties and to avoid prejudicing the interests of justice. Furthermore, the publishing of such judgments is not required to be made available to the public.[4]

Publicity in proceedings before magistrates is restricted by statute.[5] In the higher courts limited protection is given by s 12 of the Administration of Justice Act 1960[6] but the High Court may impose specific restrictions under its inherent jurisdiction[7] or may, conversely, give leave for confidential information to be disclosed for other purposes.[8]

1   Magistrates' Court Act 1980, s 69
2   Family Proceedings Courts (Children Act 1989) Rules 1991, r 16(7).

3 Family Proceedings Rules 1991 r 4.16(7). For the appellate courts, see Domestic and Appellate Proceedings (Restrictions of Publicity) Act 1968, s 1 (appellate courts). See *Re P-B (a minor) (child cases: hearing in open court)* [1997] 1 All ER 58, [1996] 2 FLR 765, CA. See also *Re B (Hearings in Open Court)* [1997] Fam Law 508. For a review of privacy in family proceedings generally, see *Clibbery v Allen* [2002] EWCA Civ 45, [2002] 1 All ER 865, [2002] 1 FCR 385.

4 *B v UK* [2001] 2 FCR 221, [2001] 2 FLR 261, ECtHR.

5 See Children and Young Persons Act 1933, s 49, Magistrates' Courts Act 1980, s 71, CA 1989, s 97.

6 Section 12 does not prevent publication of the names and addresses or photograph of the child nor of details about the order: *Re L (a minor) (wardship: freedom of publication)* [1988] 1 All ER 418, *Re W (Wards) (Publication of Information* [1989] 1 FLR 246, sub nom *Re W (Minors) (Wardship: Contempt)* [1989] Fam Law 17.

7 See *Clarke Hall and Morrison* I[1215]ff.

8 For example in criminal proceedings, see eg *Re K (Minors) (Disclosure)* [1994] 1 FLR 377.

2. Order of speeches and evidence

4.51 Subject to any directions given by the court, evidence is adduced in the following order:

- the applicant;
- any party with parental responsibility for the child;
- other respondents;
- the children's guardian; and
- the child if he is a party to the proceedings and there is no children's guardian.[1]

There is no prescribed order for speeches. This is subject to the direction of the court whose power may extend for example, to declining to hear an advocate's closing speech, although this would be extremely rare.[2]

1 Family Proceedings Courts (Children Act 1989) Rules 1991, SI 1991/1395, r 21(2).
2 *F v Kent County Council* [1993] 1 FLR 432.

3. Attendance of child at hearings

(a) Specified proceedings

4.52 The child is a party to specified proceedings,[1] but the Rules provide[2] that they shall take place in the absence of the child if the court considers it in the interests of the child, having regard to the matters to be discussed or the evidence likely to be given, and the child is represented by a children's guardian or solicitor. The child therefore has no absolute right to attend the hearing. It should not be routine practice for children to be in the court throughout care proceedings. Children's guardians should think carefully about arrangements for children to be present and be prepared to explain them to the court.[3] If a child is likely to be unruly the court could refuse to allow him to attend.[4] The decision whether or not to see the child is a matter for the discretion of the judge.[5]

1 CA 1989, s 41(6), Family Proceedings Rules 1991, rr 4.1(1), 4.2(2), Family Proceedings Courts (Children Act 1989) Rules 1991, rr 1(2), 2(2) ie applications in public law proceedings under Pts IV and V of the CA 1989, for secure accommodation, to cause a child in care to be

known by a new surname or to be removed from the jurisdiction, to approve arrangements for a child in care to live outside England and Wales, to extend the duration of a supervision order.
2   Family Proceedings Rules 1991, r 4.16(2); Family Proceedings Courts (Children Act 1989) Rules 1991, r 16(2), (7).
3   *Re C (A Minor) (Care: Children's Wishes)* [1993] 1 FLR 832; *Re G (Minor: Care Order)* (1992) Times, 19 November.
4   *Re W (A Minor) (Secure Accommodation order: Attendance at Court)* [1994] 2 FLR 1092.
5   *Re C (Section 8 Order: Court Welfare Officer)* [1995] 1 FLR 617 and *Re CB (Access: Court Welfare Report)* [1995] 1 FLR 622. See para 11.30 ff.

(b)   Private law proceedings

4.53   In proceedings in the High Court and the county court, the child may begin and prosecute any family proceedings by a next friend and may defend such proceedings only by a guardian ad litem.[1] The practice formerly was for the views of the child to be conveyed to the court by means of the report of the court welfare officer (now children and family reporter). However, this may not always a sufficient mechanism by which the court could see and hear children and give effect of their rights under the European Convention in Human Rights. In *Re A (a Child) (Separate Representation in Contact Proceedings)*[2] there had been allegations that the father had sexually abused the child during supervised contact. The court was satisfied that as there was a possible conflict of interest with the mother, the child needed to be separately represented for the allegations of sexual abuse to be properly investigated for which a welfare report was insufficient. In any family proceedings where it appears to the court that the child should be made a party and be separately represented, the court will refer the matter to CAFCASS Legal.[3]

1   Family Proceedings Rules 1991, r 9.2.
2   [2001] 2 FCR 55, CA.
3   See *A (a Child) (Separate Representation in Contact Proceedings)* supra.

(c)   Oral evidence

4.54   The *Practice Direction*[1] recognises the increasing prominence of written statements. Originally perceived by the Rules as a form of written disclosure of oral evidence to be given at the hearing,[2] the statements have been accepted as a hybrid form of evidence between submissions which do not count as evidence at all, and oral evidence given in the witness box.[3] Judicial attention has increasingly been given to the extent to which written statements may supplant the right to give oral evidence.

The evidence to be relied on at the hearing is required to have been served on the parties and the court in advance, otherwise a party may not seek to adduce such evidence without the leave of the court. At the hearing therefore it is not necessary for a witness to recite his statement but he may confirm that it is true, amplifying and updating the contents where necessary and answer the questions of the other parties and of the court. 'The practice of inviting witnesses to give evidence in chief of matters contained in their statements is to be discouraged.'[4]
In some situations the parties do not have the right to insist on oral evidence being given.[5]

1   *Practice Note: Case Management* [1995] 1 All ER 586, [1995] 1 FLR 456
2   See para 4.22.
3   *S v London Borough of Merton* [1994] 1 FCR 186, [1994] Fam Law 321.
4   CAAC Report 1993/94, p 23 and see *Practice Note: Case Management* [1995] 1 All ER 586, [1995] 1 FLR 456.
5   Cf also where the court refuses to entertain the application at all, a power assumed to exist in *Re S (Contact: Prohibition of Applications)* [1994] 2 FLR 1057; see para 8.165 but not to be exercised unless the case is 'hopeless', see *Re M (Contact)* [1995] 1 FLR 1029.

4.55   In two wardship cases where the advent of the Children Act had provided a fortuitous opportunity for a parent to seek to undermine orders in wardship, the Court of Appeal upheld a principle enunciated in an earlier first instance decision[1] and rejected a contention that an applicant in all applications for which leave is not required is entitled to a full trial unless the respondent can satisfy the stringent test required to justify striking out proceedings in ordinary civil litigation, since a distinction is to be drawn in proceedings concerning children.[2] In proceedings for an interim order 'the circumstances prevailing will almost certainly not permit full evidence to be heard',[3] and it is not always necessary for oral evidence to be called.[4] In *Re B (Minors) (Contact)*[5] the Court extended the principle that a judge is not obliged to hold a full hearing, permitting the parties to call oral evidence and cross-examine any witnesses they choose:

> 'In my view a judge in family cases has a much broader discretion both under The Children Act 1989 and previously to conduct the case as is most appropriate for the issues involved and the evidence available . . .There is a spectrum of procedure for family cases from the ex parte application on minimal evidence to the full and detailed investigations on oral evidence which may be prolonged. Where on that spectrum a judge decides a particular application should be placed is a matter for his discretion. Applications for residence orders or for committal to the care of the local authority or revocation of a care order are likely to be decided on full oral evidence, but not invariably. Such is not the case on contact applications which may be and are heard sometimes with and sometimes without oral evidence or with a limited amount of oral evidence.'[6]

The considerations which should weigh with the court are:

(1) whether there is sufficient evidence upon which to make the relevant decision;
(2) whether the proposed evidence (which should be available at least in outline) which the applicant for a full trial wishes to adduce is likely to affect the outcome of the proceedings;
(3) whether the opportunity to cross-examine the witnesses for the local authority, in particular expert witnesses, is likely to affect the outcome of the proceedings;
(4) the welfare of the child and the effect of further litigation – whether the delay in itself will be so detrimental to the child's well-being that exceptionally there should not be a full hearing. This may be because of the urgent need to place the child, or the emotional stress suffered by the child;
(5) the prospects of success of the applicant for a full trial;
(6) does the justice of the case require a full investigation with oral evidence?[7]

1   *Cheshire County Council v M* [1993] 1 FLR 463.
2   *W v Ealing London Borough Council* [1993] 2 FLR 788.
3   Per Cazalet J in *Hampshire County Council v S* [1993] Fam 158, [1993] 1 All ER 944.

4 See *Re F (A Minor) (Care Order: Procedure)* [1994] 1 FLR 240 and *Re D (Contact: Interim Order)* [1995] 1 FLR 495 (where the principle of contact is not disputed).
5 [1994] 1 FLR 1.
6 Above at 5, per Butler-Sloss LJ.
7 See *Re B (Minors) (Contact)* [1994] 2 FLR 1 at 6.

4.56 The gravity of the potential outcome of the proceedings is an important factor in determining whether any of the criteria are met. Therefore, in determining an application for the grant of leave to place a child who was the subject of a care order in an adoptive placement in Scotland which was in accordance with the parents' previously expressed wishes, the court had little difficulty in refusing a full hearing especially where the delay caused by an adjournment would have been detrimental to the child.[1]
On the other hand where the relevant evidence does not point clearly in one direction, the court will normally require oral evidence. So, for example, in an application for leave to apply for a s 8 order, where two contentious views are put before the court in writing, the court will not normally form a view without some further evidence, usually from the witness box.[2] The more relaxed and flexible procedures of the family court must be handled with the greatest care and in such a way that, unless the interests of the child make it necessary, the rules of natural justice and the rights of the parents are fully and properly observed.[3]

1 *Re W (Care: Outside Jurisdiction)* [1994] 2 FLR 1087.
2 *Re R (minors)* [1995] 1 FCR 563, sub nom *Re F and R (Section 8 Order)* [1995] 1 FLR 524.
3 *Re G (a Minor) (Care: Evidence)* [1994] 2 FLR 785.

4.57 Where the parties are agreed that a care order is appropriate and on the facts supporting the fulfilment of the threshold criteria, the court's investigative duty can be limited to reading the documents and approving an agreed order. The process of agreement is facilitated where the statements of the local authority are objective and balanced.[1] Proceedings should not be prolonged to resolve differences as to expressions in admissions made which pass the 'threshold'; the terminology of those making them should be accepted.[2] Where the need for an order is agreed but the factual basis is disputed, the court should limit its investigation to those parts of the evidence which are directly relevant to the issue of significant harm and findings which are necessary for the proper disposal of the case.[3] However, if the concessions are not sufficient to give a full understanding of allegations of sexual abuse and the care plan depends on depends on the harm which has actually occurred, or where the credibility of the children has been impugned, further investigation may warranted.[4] Parental concessions need to be sufficient for the local authority to draw up a care plan for the court's approval.[5] CAAC advised that the court should invite parties in such cases to submit an agreed statement of facts so that the need for oral evidence will be unlikely and that where feelings are running high the court may adopt the statement without reading it aloud.[6]

1 *Re JC (Care Proceedings: Procedure)* [1995] 2 FLR 77.
2 *Stockport Metropolitan Borough Council v D* [1995] 1 FLR 873.
3 *Re G (A Minor) (Care Proceedings)* [1994] 2 FLR 69 and see *Devon County Council v S* [1992] Fam 176, [1992] 3 All ER 793.
4 *Re M (Threshold Criteria: Parental Concessions)* [1999] 2 FLR 728, CA.
5 *Re W (children) (threshold criteria: parental concessions)* [2001] 1 FCR 139, CA.
6 CAAC Report 1993/94, p 32.

4. Decision

4.58 All tiers of family court must give reasons for the court's decision and state any findings of fact when making an order or refusing an application.[1] This is particularly important where the decision is contrary to expert evidence and the general weight of evidence[2] or departing from advice from a professional witness in a s 7 report.[3] After the final hearing the court must deliver its judgment as soon as is practicable.[4] Where it is in the interests of the child, the higher courts can take the 'unusual' step of giving the court's decision at the conclusion of the argument with reasons to be given later.[5]

In the family proceedings court however there is an additional requirement that before the court makes an order or refuses an application, the court must state any findings of fact and complete Form 22 and state the reasons for the court's decision. The clerk must record in writing the names of the justices constituting the court and, in consultation with the justices, the reasons for the decision and any findings of fact.[6]

1 Family Proceedings Rules 1991, r 4.21; Family Proceedings Courts (Children Act 1989) Rules 1991, r 21(6).
2 See *Re A (a child) (mental health of mother)* [2001] 2 FCR 577, CA.
3 *Re J (children) (residence: expert evidence)* [2001] 2 FCR 44, CA.
4 Family Proceedings Rules 1991, r 4.21(3); Family Proceedings Courts (Children Act 1989) Rules 1991, r 21 (4).
5 See *Re B (Minors) (Contact)* [1994] 2 FLR 1, CA.
6 Family Proceedings Courts (Children Act 1989) Rules 1991, r 21(5).

5. Justices' reasons

4.59 The giving of reasons and announcing of any decision[1] may be adjourned and deputed to one of the justices constituting the court by which the decision was made[2]. But it is not permissible, even with the consent of the parties, for the justices to announce their decision immediately after the hearing but defer giving their reasons and findings of fact to a later date.[3] The requirements of r 21(5) of the Family Proceedings Courts (Children Act 1989) Rules 1991 are mandatory and a failure to record the reasons before announcing the decision will mean that the decision cannot stand.[4] These requirements apply on the hearing of an application for an interim order as they do for a substantive order[5] and for a decision on an interim application as to disclosure of a medical report;[6] also when hearing an application for leave[7] or to withdraw an application[8] or when refusing an application for an adjournment.[9] Reasons must also be given when considering an application for an education supervision order.[10] On appeal, the only findings of fact and reasons to support the justices' decision will be those announced at the time the decision is delivered and it is therefore not possible for the justices subsequently to elaborate on their original reasons.[11] The rationale of the rule is that it will be necessary for the bench of three justices to have a prior discussion before the decision is made and to have the opportunity to retire and, with the assistance of their clerk, to record their findings and reasons.[12] In this way the clerk can assist the justices where necessary to structure their reasons and distil them into written form.

Waiting around for justices to give their written reasons is cited as a procedure which makes the family proceedings court less attractive than the county court and it has been suggested that the rules should be amended to permit justices to fie their reasons orally and in the order, with full written reasons to follow as happens with reserved judgments in the higher courts.[13]

1 The decision to make 'no order' under s 1(5) is a 'decision' and requires the giving of reasons: *S v R (parental responsibility)* [1993] 1 FCR 331. See further paras 2.62ff.
2 Family Proceedings Courts (Children Act 1989) Rules 1991, r 21(6).
3 *Re K (minors) (justices' reasons)* [1994] 1 FCR 616.
4 *W v Hertfordshire County Council* [1993] 1 FLR 118, and *Re W (A Minor) (Contact)* [1994] 1 FLR 843.
5 *W v Hertfordshire County Council*, supra and *F v R (Contact: Justices' Reasons)* [1995] 1 FLR 227.
6 *Re NW (A Minor) (Medical Reports)* [1993] 2 FLR 591.
7 *Re M (Prohibited Steps Order: Application for Leave)* [1993] 1 FLR 275.
8 *Re F (a minor) (care proceedings: withdrawal)* [1993] 1 FCR 389.
9 *Essex County Council v F* [1993] 1 FLR 847.
10 *Essex County Council v B* [1993] 1 FLR 866.
11 See *Hillingdon London Borough Council v H* [1993] Fam 43, [1993] 1 All ER 198; *N v B (children: orders as to residence)* [1993] 1 FCR 231.
12 *Re W (A Minor) (Contact)*, n 4 supra, and see *Essex County Council v B*, n 10 supra.
13 Scoping Study on Delay in Children Act Cases (Lord Chancellor's Dept 2002) para 115.

4.60 Although the High Court is mindful that lay justices are not trained lawyers[1] nevertheless their reasons must attain a minimum standard which will, it is submitted, explain their decision not only to the appellate court but most importantly to the parties concerned.[2] Guidance on the structure of justices' reasons has been given in *R v Oxfordshire County Council (Secure Accommodation Order)*[3] and in *S v Oxfordshire County Council*[4]. In these cases justices' had used a proforma which was commended to magistrates[5] but nevertheless justices' should be careful that any proforma caters for the situation with which they are dealing.[6]

Justices' reasons should address the welfare checklist where this is applicable to the proceeding:[7]

> 'It is unacceptable for any court to make a bland statement that it has 'considered all aspects of the welfare checklist' without further particularisation unless, elsewhere in the course of its judgment or reasons, it has, in considering the evidence or in making findings, dealt in detail with the relevant aspects on the checklist, thereby demonstrating that it has applied its mind to the relevant factors'.[8]

The court should therefore address important issues in the case such as race[9] and record facts significant in the making of the decision and the court's assessment of the credibility and reliability of at least the more important witnesses.[10] Important issues of disputed fact must be resolved[11] or if, on the making of an interim order, the justices have deliberately refrained from making findings, the fact that they have so refrained, and the reasons why should be explained.[12] Reasons must also be given for departing from the recommendation of a children's guardian[13] or children and family reporter.[14]

1 *Re J (A Minor) (Residence)* [1994] 1 FLR 369 per Singer J, also *Re B (Procedure: Family Proceedings Court)* [1993] Fam Law 209 and *Re M (a Minor) (Contact: Conditions)* [1994] 1 FLR 272.
2 See *Re J (A Minor) (Residence)* supra.
3 [1992] Fam 150, sub nom *R(J) v Oxfordshire County Council* [1992] 3 All ER 660.

4   [1993] 1 FLR 452.
5   See also *Re B (Procedure: Family Proceedings Court)* [1993] Fam Law 209, CA.
6   See *Re R and G (Minors) (Interim Care or Supervision Orders)* [1994] 1 FLR 793.
7   *Re O (a minor)* [1992] 4 All ER 905, [1992] 1 WLR 912.
8   *Re D (Contact: Interim Order)* [1995] 1 FLR 495, per Wall J and see *D v R* [1995] 1 FCR 501.
     However, on appeal the court has been prepared to assume that judges approved to sit in
     family cases have had the welfare checklist in mind; *Re A (a minor)* [1994] 2 FCR 125, sub
     nom *Oldham Metropolitan Borough Council v E* [1994] 1 FLR 568, and see further for the
     checklist, para 2.37.
9   *Re M (Section 94 Appeals)* [1995] 1 FLR 546.
10 *H (a minor) (care proceedings)* [1992] 2 FCR 330 and see *Re M (A Minor) (Contact:
     Conditions)* [1994] 1 FLR 272.
11 See *F v R (Contact: Justices' Reasons)* [1995] 1 FLR 227.
12 *F v R (Contact: Justices' Reasons)* [1995] 1 FLR 227.
13 Formerly 'guardian ad litem'. *Re W (A Minor) (Secure Accommodation)* [1993] 1 FLR 692.
14 Formerly 'welfare officer'. *Re M (Section 94 Appeals)* [1995] 1 FLR 546 and *F v R (Contact:
     Justices' Reasons)* [1995] 1 FLR 227.

6.   Costs

4.61   Costs are generally in the discretion of the court.[1] In children cases it is unusual to order costs[2] but this is not a presumption.[3]

1   Supreme Court Act 1981, s 51; Family Proceedings Courts (Children Act 1989) Rules, r
     22(1).
2   *Re G (a minor) (wardship: costs)* [1982] 2 All ER 32, *Gojkovic v Gojkovic (No2)* [1992] Fam
     40, *Sutton London Borough Council v Davis (Costs) (No 2)* [1994] 2 FLR 569.
3   *Re M (Local Authority's Costs)* [1995] 1 FLR 533.

Personal liability of legal representative for costs

4.62   The court may disallow wasted costs or order a legal representative to meet such costs. 'Wasted costs' means any costs incurred by a party as a result of any improper, unreasonable or negligent act or omission on the part of any legal or other representative or any employee of such a representative; or which, in the light of any such act or omission occurring after they were incurred, the court considers it is unreasonable to expect the party to pay.[1]
Failure to comply with the *Practice Note: Case Management*, and delays caused by practitioners could be dealt with under these provisions.[2] Practitioners have been warned that liability for wasted costs might arise if adequate time estimates are not provided.[3] In *B v B (wasted costs order)*[4] a wasted costs order was made in respect of an 'unsustainable' appeal against a direction of a deputy district judge setting a trial date. The appeal was without merit and incapable of succeeding so as to an abuse of the appellate process. As the matter was discrete from the main issues in the case, the court felt able to make a wasted costs order before the final substantive hearing. A solicitor who has instructed counsel does not abdicate his professional responsibility although the more specialist the advice sought from counsel, the more reasonable it is likely to be for the solicitor to rely on it.[5] For guidance on the making of wasted costs orders see *Ridehalgh v Horsefield*[6].

1   Supreme Court Act 1981 s 51(6), (7) and (13). See *Medcalf v Mardell* [2002] UKHL 27,
     [2002] 3 All ER 721 for jurisdiction to make costs against the legal representative of any other
     party to the same proceedings including a barrister in respect of conduct other than when
     exercising a right of audience in court.

2 [1995] 1 All ER 586, [1995] 1 FLR 456, see para 4.36.
3 *Practice Direction* [1994] 1 FLR 108 and *Re D (Minors)* (1994) Times, 2 March.
4 [2001] 3 FCR 724, FD.
5 In *B v B (wasted costs order)* supra, responsibility was apportioned as 75% to counsel and 25% to the solicitor.
6 [1994] 2 FLR 194, CA.

Chapter 5

Private law orders

INTRODUCTION AND BACKGROUND

5.1 In this chapter consideration is given to the court's powers under Pt II of the CA 1989 to make orders, other than financial orders,[1] in what are termed 'family proceedings'.

1 The powers to make financial orders are governed by s 15 and Sch 1. For a discussion of these powers see *Clarke Hall and Morrison*, Division 4.

5.2 In its report on Guardianship and Custody the Law Commission commented[1] that while the main principles of the pre-1989 Act were reasonably clear and well accepted, the details, particularly concerning custody, were complicated and confusing.[2] The Commission was also concerned that the law made the stakes too high. As they pointed out[3] all the research evidence[4] shows that children who fare best after their parents' separation are those who are able to maintain a good relationship with both parents. While recognising the obvious limitation that law cannot make people co-operate, the Commission argued that at least it should not stand in their way. Hence, if the parties can co-operate with one another, the law should intervene as little as possible, but if they cannot the law should at least try to 'lower the stakes' and avoid the impression that the 'loser loses all'.

1 Law Com No 172, 1988, para 1.1.
2 See, for example, Priest and Whybrow Custody Law and Practice in Divorce and Domestic Courts (1986) (Supplement to Law Com Working Paper No 96).
3 Above, para 4.5.
4 Notably, that of J S Wallerstein and J B Kelly Surviving the Breakup (1980, Grant McIntyre). See also Wallerstein and Blakeslee Second Chances: Men, Women and Children A Decade After Divorce (1989, Bantam), Cockett and Tripp *The Exeter Study: Family Breakdown and its impact on Children* (1994); Richards and Dyson *Separation, Divorce and the Development of Children: A Review* (1982); and Rodgers and Pryor *The Development of Children from Separated Families: A Review of Research from the United Kingdom* (1998).

5.3 With the above considerations in mind, and with the general aim of making the law 'clear, simple and, we hope, fairer for families and children alike' the Law Commission recommended, inter alia, that: (a) orders should be made only where the court believes it is the most effective way of safeguarding or promoting the child's welfare; and (b) the differing powers of the various courts under the different jurisdictions to make custody and access orders should be replaced by a new set of powers designed to be less emotive and more flexible and which are common to all courts. The first of these recommendations has been implemented by s 1(5)[1] and the second by Pt II of the CA 1989.

1 Discussed ante at paras 2.62 et seq.

THE COURTS' POWERS UNDER PART II: THE GENERAL STRATEGY

5.4 Instead of the previous statutory powers to make custody, care and control, custodianship and access orders[1] the courts are empowered to make a range of orders, collectively known as 'section 8 orders', namely, 'residence orders', 'contact orders', 'prohibited steps orders' and 'specific issue orders'. While the first two roughly equated to (although they are not the same as) custody and access orders, the latter two orders were introduced for the first time by the Act. They were modelled on the wardship jurisdiction and implement the Law Commission's recommendation[2] to incorporate the most valuable features of the prerogative jurisdiction into the statutory jurisdiction. Overall, the s 8 powers are intended to concentrate both the court's and the parties' minds on the practical issues which generally arise with respect to children, rather than on the allocation of theoretical rights and duties.[3]

1 Viz under the Matrimonial Causes Act 1973, s 42(1) and (2); the Domestic Proceedings and Magistrates' Courts Act 1978, s 8(2) and 14; the Guardianship of Minors Act 1971, ss 9, 10, 11 and 14A; the Children Act 1975, ss 33(1) and 34(1); and the Adoption Act 1976, s 25, all of which were repealed by CA 1989, Sch 15.
2 Law Com No 172, para 1.4.
3 See Hoggett 'The Children Bill: The Aim' [1989] Fam Law 217 at 219. But for a classic example of not applying the CA 1989, see the first instance decision in *Re A (children) (shared residence)* [2001] EWCA Civ 1795, [2002] 1 FCR 1777, CA.

5.5 Although s 8 orders are closely associated with private law disputes they can be made in *any* family proceedings[1] including, therefore, in public law proceedings. In other words the s 8 powers provide, what has been described[2] as, a basic menu of orders available under the Act.

1 For the full meaning of which see paras 5.101–5.102.
2 See Cretney *Family Law* (4th edn) 242.

5.6 To put these powers into perspective it is of interest to note the number of orders made annually respectively in private and public proceedings in the years 1992–2000.

(see table opposite)

5.7 Part II also provides a clear plan governing who can apply for an order. The basic scheme (under s 10) is that some people, for example, parents (with or without parental responsibility) or guardians, are entitled to apply for any s 8 order, while others, for example, relatives, are able to seek the court's leave either to intervene in existing 'family proceedings' or to initiate their own proceedings to seek a s 8 order.

5.8 Another important change made by the CA 1989 was the removal of the court's power in matrimonial and other private law proceedings concerning children to make committal to care or supervision orders. Instead, under

Number of orders made annually 1992–2000[1]

Order	1992		1993		1994		1995		1996		1997		1998		1999		2000	
	Private Law	*Public Law*	*Private Law*	*Public Law*	*Private Law*	*Public Law*	*Private Law*	*Public Law*	*Private Law*	*Public Law*	*Private Law*	*Public Law*	*Private Law*	*Public Law*	*Private Law*	*Public Law*	*Private Law*	*Public Law*
Residence	16515	1234	22314	1470	2319	1502	25505	1081	27660	1075	25841	921	24204	761	21286	929	25809	1365
Contact	17589	n/a	27780	n/a	31486	n/a	35280	n/a	40330	n/a	40660	n/a	39500	n/a	41862	796	46070	1177
Prohibited Steps	6103	773	6631	542	5971	299	5799	243	5783	194	5190	55	4307	141	4770	213	5345	227
Specific Issues	1379	127	1563	93	1807	41	1741	40	2277	74	2108	74	1834	60	2034	57	2457	79

1 The 1992–1998 statistics are taken from the Children Act Report 1995–1999 (2000, Cm 4579) Tables 10.1 and 10.2 and the 1999–2000 statistics are taken from the Judicial Statistics Annual Reports 1999 and 2000 (respectively Cm 4786 and Cm 5223) Tables 5.2 and 5.3.

s 37[1] the courts can direct the local authority to investigate the circumstances but it is for the authority and not the court to decide whether an application for a care or supervision order should be made. However, in place of these former powers courts are now empowered under s 16, to make 'family assistance' orders, the object of which is to provide short-term help to the family.

1 Discussed at paras 5.158 and 7.5 et seq.

SECTION 8 ORDERS

5.9 The expression 'a section 8 order' means any of the orders mentioned in s 8(1), that is, a contact order, a prohibited steps order, a residence order and a specific issue order. It also includes any order varying or discharging such an order.[1] In making any of these orders the court has further supplemental powers under s 11(7)[2] which are designed to ensure maximum flexibility.

1 Section 8(2).
2 Discussed at paras 5.84 et seq.

1. Residence orders

5.10 A residence order 'means an order settling the arrangements to be made as to the person with whom the child is to live'.
Residence orders determine with whom the child is to live, and indeed, in their simplest form the order need do no more than name the person *with whom* the child is to live. Although determining with whom the child will live effectively determines *where* the child will live, in the absence of a prohibited steps order[1] or, unless the court adds a direction or a condition,[2] the person in whose favour the residence order has been made is free to live in or subsequently move to any location *within* the UK.[3]

1 See *Re H (children) (residence order: condition)* [2001] EWCA Civ 1338, [2001] 3 FCR 182, [2001] 2 FLR 1277, CA.
2 Viz under s 11(7) (discussed at paras 5.84 et seq). See in particular *Re S (a child) (residence order: condition)* [2001] EWCA Civ 847, [2001] 3 FCR 154, CA.
3 But not *outside* the UK without either court leave or the consent of everyone with parental responsibility: s 13(1)(b), discussed at paras 5.35 et seq.

5.11 Residence orders should be seen for what they are, namely, orders determining with whom the child is to live and nothing more. They should not normally be regarded as a means of reallocating parental responsibility. This is more obviously so as between married parents since, based on the fundamental principle that 'changes in the child's residence should interfere as little as possible in his relationship with both his parents',[1] each parent retains full parental responsibility and with it the power to act independently unless this is incompatible with a court order, regardless of who has a residence order.[2] But even where the making of a residence order does have the effect of conferring parental responsibility, as it does when made in favour of those who do not already have it,[3] it is inappropriate to make the order *solely* for that purpose. This is well illustrated by *N v B (children: order as to residence)*[4] in which a cohabitant, having discovered just before the hearing that he was not the father, failed in his attempt to obtain a shared residence order.[5] Although it was acknowledged that this was the only means by which he could acquire parental responsibility, Thorpe J nevertheless refused to interfere with the justices' decision, to grant a residence order to the mother and defined contact to the applicant, holding that it would be inappropriate and 'quite artificial' to make a shared residence order solely for that purpose. However, in *Re H (shared residence: parental responsibility)*,[6] the Court of Appeal upheld the making of a shared residence order so that the stepfather had parental responsibility for his step-son, since on the facts the child would otherwise be confused if he did not have the comfort and security of knowing not only that his stepfather (whom he had only just discovered was not his natural father) wished to treat him as his child but that the law would give some stamp of approval to that de facto position. In Ward LJ's view unlike *N v B* where, as he put it, a shared residence order would be likely to foment disputes which would ill serve the children's welfare, this was a case where a shared residence order was 'not artificial but of important practical therapeutic importance' and where its making reflected 'the reality of the father's involvement and . . . the need for him to be given some status with the school to continue to play his part as both parties wish to do.' In *G v F (shared residence: parental responsibility)*[7] Bracewell J considered that *Re H* had made it clear that a shared residence order may be appropriate for the purposes of conferring parental responsibility on a non-parent provided it was not simply a device or the sole reason for the application.

1   See Law Com No 172, para 4.16.
2   See paras 3.89 et seq.
3   Ie under s 12(2), (3); see para 5.26.
4   [1993] 1 FCR 231, sub nom *Re WB (Residence Orders)* [1995] 2 FLR 1023.
5   Shared residence orders are discussed at paras 5.13 et seq.
6   [1996] 3 FCR 321, [1995] 2 FLR 883, CA.
7   [1998] 3 FCR 1, sub nom *G v F (Contact and Shared Residence: Applications for Leave)* [1998] 2 FLR 799. Note also *Re AB (a minor) (adoption: parental consent)* [1996] 1 FCR 633, sub nom *Re AB (Adoption: Joint Residence)* [1996] 1 FLR 27 in which an adoption order was made in favour of one partner and a joint residence order was made in favour of the unmarried couple, in part to ensure that both had parental responsibility.

5.12   Under s 11(5) where as a result of a residence order 'the child lives, or is to live with one of two parents who each have parental responsibility for him', that order will cease to have effect if the parents live together for a continuous period of more than six months.[1]

1   For an example of where such an order did come to such an end see *Re P (Abduction: Declaration)* [1995] 1 FLR 831 at 834, CA.

(a)   Joint and shared residence orders

5.13   Although residence orders are said to settle the arrangements to be made as to *the person* with whom the child is to live,[1] they can, both because of the general presumption under the Interpretation Act 1978, s 6(c) that words appearing in a statute in the singular include the plural and the implication of s 11(4) (see below), also be made in favour of more than one person.[2] A court can therefore make an order in favour of a parent and step-parent,[3] a cohabiting couple,[4] grandparents,[5] or foster parents[6]. In these cases, what may be conveniently described[7] as 'joint residence orders' are made in favour of couples living together, but the power is not so restricted, for residence orders may also be made in favour of two or more persons who do not live together. These latter type of orders have become known as 'shared residence' orders. In theory it is within the court's powers to make both a joint and shared residence order in favour of both parents and their respective new partners, though as yet there is no reported example of such an order.

1   A residence order cannot, therefore, be made in favour of the child himself, see further para 5.126, n 1.
2   In theory there is nothing to stop the court making an order in favour of more than two people, although in practice it is rarely likely to do so.
3   See eg *Re H (shared residence: parental responsibility)* [1996] 3 FCR, [1995] 2 FLR 883, CA.
4   See eg *Re AB (a minor) (adoption: parental consent)* [1996] 1 FCR 633, sub nom *Re AB (Adoption: Joint Residence)* [1996] 1 FLR 27 (see above para 5.11, n 7), and *Re C (A Minor) (Residence Order: Lesbian Co-Parents)* [1994] Fam Law 468 (joint residence order made to the mother and her female cohabitant).
5   See eg *Re W (A Minor) (Residence Order)* [1993] 2 FLR 625, CA.
6   See eg *Re M (a minor) (adoption or residence order)* [1998] 1 FCR 165, [1998] 1 FLR 570, CA.
7   Ie it is not a legal term of art.

5.14   Shared care arrangements can take different forms, for example the child living during term-time with one parent and school holidays with the other or spending weekdays with one and weekends with the other parent. Rather than having to reflect these arrangements by making a residence order in favour of one parent and contact in favour of the other, the Law Commission believed[1] that it would be 'a far more realistic description of the responsibilities involved . . . to make a residence order covering both parents'. In so recommending the Commission were not suggesting that children *should* share their time more or less equally between their arrangements, which arrangement they thought would rarely be practicable or for the child's benefit. On the other hand, they were recommending the reversal of *Riley v Riley*[2] in which it had been held that courts could not as a matter of principle make what would be now a shared residence order.

1   Law Com No 172, para 4.12.
2   [1986] 2 FLR 429, CA. Cf *J v J (Joint Care and Control)* [1991] 2 FLR 385, CA in which the Court of Appeal sanctioned a joint caring arrangement even before the CA 1989.

5.15   Although it has long been accepted that in the light of the statutory framework of ss 8 and 11(4) the disapproval in principle of shared care and control in *Riley v Riley*[1] is no longer good law,[2] the courts' approach to the making of such orders has been an evolving one.

1   [1986] 2 FLR 429.
2   Per Butler-Sloss LJ in *A v A (minors) (shared residence order)* [1994] 1 FCR 91 at 99 [1994] 1 FLR 669 at 677 and *Re D (children) (shared residence orders)* [2001] 1 FCR 147,para (21) at 151, sub nom *D v D (Shared Residence Order)* [2001] 1 FLR 495 at 498–499, per Hale LJ.

5.16   Early post-CA 1989 authority[1] suggested that shared residence orders should only be made in exceptional circumstances but this was resiled from in *A v A (minors) (shared residence order)*[2]. In upholding an order dividing equally the time the children were to live with each parent outside school term time, Butler-Sloss LJ commented[3] that whilst it was a matter for individual discretion, in general terms it had to be demonstrated that there was a positive benefit in making in what she termed the unusual order of shared residence as opposed to making the more conventional one of residence to other and contact to other. But in what is now the leading case, *Re D (Children) (Shared Residence Orders)*,[4] the Court of Appeal distanced itself both from the requirement of exceptional circumstances and of the need to show positive benefit. Hale LJ said that she:[5]

'would not add any gloss on the legislative provisions, which are always subject to the paramount consideration of what is best for the children concerned.'

Butler-Sloss P agreed and, having pointed to the Court of Appeal's developing application of the new concept, said:[6]

'Now nine years later with far greater experience of the workings of the Act it is necessary to underline the importance of the flexibility of the Children Act 1989 in s 8 orders and, consequentially, that the Court of Appeal should not impose restrictions upon the working of the statute not actually found within the words of the section.'

1 *Re H (a minor) (residence order)* [1993] 1 FCR 671 at 682–683, [1994] 1 FLR 717 at 728, per Purchas LJ.
2 [1995] 1 FCR 91 at 101, [1994] 1 FLR 669 at 678, CA.
3 Above at 100 and 677 respectively. See also *Re H (shared residence: parental responsibility)* [1996] 3 FCR 321, [1995] 2 FLR 883, CA, in which Ward LJ referred to shared residence orders as being 'unusual'.
4 [2001] 1 FLR 147, sub nom *D v D (Shared Residence Order)* [2001] 1 FLR 495.
5 Above at para (32) at 154 and 501 respectively.
6 Above at para (39) at 155 and 502 respectively.

5.17 In *Re D* itself the Court of Appeal upheld a decision to make a shared residence order where the children were in effect living with both parents, had homes with each of them and appeared to be coping well with the arrangements, but where the parents themselves were at loggerheads over the arrangements and had frequently resorted to court proceedings. The hope was that the order would reduce the conflict between the parties.[1]

1 Cf *H v H (a minor) (No 2) (forum conveniens)* [1997] 1 FCR 603, in which Bracewell J refused to make a shared residence order because she thought that in that case it would be 'a recipe for conflict.'

5.18 Notwithstanding *Re D* it should not be assumed that such orders will readily be made. The argument that a child needs a single settled home will be a strong one in most cases and will generally militate against the making of a shared order, particularly if there is no history of the child living in the different households.[1] As the Department of Health's Guidance and Regulations, says:[2]

'... it is not expected that it will become a common form of order because most children will still need the stability of a single home, and partly because in the cases where shared care is appropriate there is less likely to be a need for the court to make any order at all. However, a shared care order has the advantage of being more realistic in those cases where the child is to spend considerable amounts of time with both parents, [and] brings with it certain other benefits (including the right to remove the child from accommodation provided by a local authority under s 20), and removes any impression that one parent is good and responsible whereas the other parent is not.'

1 See *Re A (children) (shared residence)* [2001] EWCA Civ 1795, [2002] 1 FCR 177, CA.
2 Vol 1 *Court Orders*, para 2.28, expressly approved by Butler-Sloss P in *Re D* above at para (40) at 155 and 502–503 respectively. Her Ladyship had previously approved this passage in *A v A (minors) (shared residence order)* [1995] 1 FCR 91 at 100 [1994] 1 FLR 669 at 674.

5.19 Where a residence order is made in favour of two persons who do not live together, then, under s 11(4), the order may specify the periods during which the child is to live in the different households concerned. Such directions may be general rather than specific and in some cases may not be needed at all. Since a residence order only settles the arrangements as to the person with whom the child is to live, any other conditions that are needed must be specified separately by the court acting under the powers vested by s 11(7).[1] Indeed, given that under a shared residence order neither carer is obliged to consult the other unless this is specified in the order, it is important that the order is clear on points which are fundamental to the success of the arrangement.[2]

1 Section 11(7) is discussed at paras 5.84 et seq.
2 See Cretney and Masson, *Principles of Family Law* (6th edn), p 676.

(b) 'Interim' residence orders

5.20 The combination of s 11(3), which permits a court to make a s 8 order 'even though it is not in a position to dispose finally of [the] proceedings', and s 11(7)(c), under which orders can be made for a specified period, enables courts to make interim provision by way of a residence order for a limited period.[1] The Act, however, makes no distinction between a final residence order and one made as an interim measure.[2] Hence *all* such orders, even those expressed to last for a matter of days, have the same effect, and will, for example, discharge any existing care order[3] confer, for the duration of the order, parental responsibility on those who do not already have it,[4] and empower the residence holder to remove the child from the UK for a period of less than one month.[5]

1 It is apparently possible to make an interim residence order to run alongside the main order; see *Re M (minors) (interim residence order)* [1997] 2 FCR 28, CA.
2 As Bracewell J observed in *S v S (Custody: Jurisdiction)* [1995] 1 FLR 155 at 157; 'it has become common parlance to speak of 'interim residence orders', but in fact there is no such creature within the Children Act 1989'.
3 Section 91(1) and note *Re R-J (fostering: disqualified person)* [1998] 3 FCR 579, [1999] 1 FLR 605, CA.
4 Section 12(2).
5 Section 13(2). Presumably this power of removal is subject to the length of the order – an order expressed to last only a few days cannot be taken to vest a power of removal in excess of that. 'Interim' orders are recognised and enforceable under the European Convention on Recognition and Enforcement of Decisions Concerning Children 1980: see *Re S (a Minor) (Custody: Habitual Residence)* [1998] AC 750, [1997] 4 All ER 251, HL, discussed in *Clarke Hall and Morrison*, Division 2. They also take effect as a 'superseding' order for the purpose of the Family Law Act 1986, see *Re S* supra and *T v T (Custody: Jurisdiction)* [1992] 1 FLR 43, on which see Lowe 'The Family Law Act 1986 – A Critique' [2002] Fam Law 39 at 46–47.

5.21 Where an 'interim' order is thought justified, careful thought needs to be given to its length, and mindful of the general enjoinder under s 1(2) to treat 'delay' as prima facie detrimental to the child's interest, courts should ensure that they are no longer than absolutely necessary.[1] It has been held[2] in relation to children in the interim care of a local authority that even a so-called 'interim residence order' should not be made as a temporary expedient.

1 See eg *Re O (Minors) (Leave to Seek Residence Order)* [1994] 1 FLR 172, where, on the facts, five weeks' duration was thought too long. See also *Re Y (a minor) (ex parte interim orders)* [1993] 2 FCR 422, discussed post, para 5.24.
2 *Re R-J (fostering: disqualified person)* [1998] 3 FCR 579, [1999] 1 FLR 605, CA.

(c) *Ex parte applications and orders*

5.22 Although applications for residence orders can be made ex parte,[1] they should only be granted exceptionally. In *Re G (minors) (ex parte interim residence order)*,[2] Butler-Sloss LJ commented:

'In my judgment, it is very rare indeed that it is necessary to have an ex parte interim residence order. The only situation that I can think of is where there is a "snatch" situation – child abduction. There obviously will from time to time be other exceptional circumstances in which it is necessary for the protection of children that there should be an ex parte order'.

Furthermore, as Hale J observed in *Re J (minors) (ex parte orders)*:[3]

'courts obviously have a special responsibility to ensure that ex parte orders which could cause harm to the interests of an adult or a child are not made without good reason. Orders requiring the handing over of a very young child to a parent with whom she has not lived for 20 months should surely be made only in exceptional circumstances.'

1 FPR 1991, r 4.4(4), as amended by SI 1992/2067 and FPC (Children Act 1989) R 1991, r 4(4), as amended by SI 1992/2068. Originally no such provision had been made.
2 [1992] 2 FCR 720 at 72, [1993] 1 FLR 910 at 912D.
3 [1997] 1 FCR 325 at 329, [1997] 1 FLR 606 at 609.

5.23 Ex parte orders are most likely to be justified in the context of abduction. In *Re B (Minors) (Residence Orders)*,[1] for example, in which a mother 'snatched' one of four children of the family from the father (from whom she had separated a few days earlier) it was held justifiable to make ex parte residence orders to secure the return of the child and to prevent further snatches of the remaining children. Ex parte orders are commonly sought and sometimes granted in the context of international child abduction, ironically not infrequently at the behest of the parent who has wrongfully brought the child to the UK.[2]

1 [1992] Fam 162, [1992] 3 All ER 867.
2 See eg *Re O (child abduction: undertakings)* [1995] 1 FCR 721 [1994] 2 FLR 349, *Re M (Child Abduction) (European Convention)* [1994] 1 FLR 551, and *Re AZ (A Minor) (Abduction: Acquiescence)* [1993] 1 FLR 682, in which ex parte orders were granted and *Re S (minors) (abduction)* [1993] 2 FCR 499, [1994] 1 FLR 297 where the application was refused.

5.24 Although ex parte residence orders can justifiably be made to protect a child from immediate physical or moral danger, the circumstances need to be compelling. In *Re G (minors) (ex parte interim residence order)*,[1] an allegation that the mother had been taking cannabis was not thought to justify making an ex parte order in favour of the father. Even where an ex parte order is justified, as in *Re Y (a minor) (ex parte residence orders)*[2] where a grandmother successfully applied after the mother, who had a history of mental instability, had phoned her, threatening to commit suicide, it was held wrong to make the order stand for 12 weeks. In Johnson J's view it was unacceptable to make an order ex parte with no prospect for an inter partes hearing within seven days save in exceptional circumstances.

1 [1992] 2 FCR 720, [1993] 1 FLR 910, CA. See also *Re P (a minor) (ex parte interim residence order)* [1993] 2 FCR 417, [1993] 1 FLR 915, CA, in which it was held wrong to have made an ex parte order because the child was in no immediate danger since she was already under the scrutiny of the local authority.
2 [1993] 2 FCR 422.

5.25 In most cases[1] those wishing to challenge an ex parte order should await the full hearing rather than appeal it,[2] though an absent party wishing to challenge an ex parte order can apply to the court that made it for a discharge or variation.[3] Such applications should be on notice and not ex parte but should normally be on short notice.[4]

1 An appeal might however be justified if the return hearing is fixed too far ahead as in *Re Y (a minor) (ex parte residence orders)*, supra.
2 See *Re G (minors)* [1992] 2 FCR 720, [1993] 1 FLR 910, CA.
3 Per Purchas LJ in *Re P (a minor) (ex parte interim residence order)* [1993] 2 FCR 417 at 420, [1993] 1 FLR 915 at 917–918. See also to similar effect, *Re H (a minor) (wardship: challenging ex parte order)* [1994] 1 FCR 673, [1994] 2 FLR 981, CA.
4 Per Purchas LJ in *Re P*, supra, at 420 and 918 respectively.

(d) Effect of residence orders

(i) PARENTAL RESPONSIBILITY

5.26 Whilst in force residence orders confer parental responsibility on those in whose favour they are made such as relatives or foster parents who would not otherwise have that responsibility.[1] In the case of unmarried fathers who do not already have parental responsibility, the court is bound, upon making a residence order in his favour, to make a separate parental responsibility order under s 4.[2]

1 Section 12(2), but note the restriction of that responsibility under s 12(3), discussed at para 3.83.
2 Section 12(1), discussed at paras 3.65–3.66.

(ii) CHANGE OF CHILD'S SURNAME

5.27 Under s 13(1)(a), it is an automatic condition of *all* residence orders[1] that no person may cause the child to be known by a new surname without either the written consent of every person who has parental responsibility or leave of the court.[2] Although it is not a *statutory* requirement to have the child's consent,[3] in *Re C (minors) (change of surname)*[4] Holman J left open whether the consent of an older child, particularly those aged 16 or over, was both necessary and sufficient. In any event if the child objects to the change of name he can seek leave to apply for a prohibited steps order to prevent the change.[5] Applications for formal changes of surname should be made to the Central Office (Filing Department), and must be supported by the production of the consent in writing of every person having parental responsibility. In the absence of such consent the application will be adjourned until court leave is given.[6]

1 For a similar rule where the child is subject to a care order, see s 33(7) and (8) discussed at paras 8.138 et seq.
2 Query whether leave is necessary to use a hyphenated name: see *P v N (child: surname)* [1997] 2 FCR 65 (Dorchester County Court) which suggested not. Sed quaere? Note in *Re R (a child)* [2001] EWCA Civ 1344, [2002] 1 FCR 170, sub nom *Re R (Surname: Using Both Parents)* [2001] 2 FLR 1358, in which the parents were urged to use both their names, there was no suggestion that in absence of the parties' agreement, court leave was not required to sanction the change. For the difficulties of enforcing an embargo against a name change see paras 5.133 et seq.
3 Though attempts had been made to amend s 13 so as to require the child's consent, see 502 HL Official Report (5th Series) col 1262 by Lord Meston and 503 HL Official Report (5th Series), col 1347 per Lord Elwyn Jones.
4 [1997] 3 FCR 310 at 320, sub nom *Re PC (Change of Surname)* [1997] 2 FLR 730 at 739.

Nonetheless the support of a 16 year-old for a name change did not inhibit the court from refusing the change in *Re B (a minor) (change of surname)* [1996] 2 FCR 304, [1996] 1 FLR 791.
5 See Lord Mackay LC 502 HL Official Report (5th Series) col 1264.
6 *Practice Direction (minor: change of surname: deed poll)* [1995] 1 All ER 832, [1995] 1 WLR 365.

5.28 Section 13(1)(a) implements the Law Commission's recommendation[1] which, like the Court of Appeal in the pre-CA 1989 decision, *W v A (Child: Surname)*,[2] considered a child's surname to be an important symbol of his identity and relationship with his parents and that while it may be in his interests for it to be changed, it was not a matter on which a parent with whom the child lives should be able to take unilateral action. Case law since the Act reflects this attitude. In *Dawson v Wearmouth*[3] the House of Lords held that a court should not sanction a change of a child's surname unless there is some evidence that it would lead to an improvement in his or her welfare. In any event s 13(1)(a) can only operate as an inhibition on the adult residence holder. As Wilson J observed in *Re B (minors) (change of surname)*:[4]

'It does not, because in effect it cannot, prescribe the surname which the children ask teachers, friends and relatives to attribute to them'.

1 Law Com No 172, para 4.14.
2 [1981] Fam 14, [1981] 1 All ER 100.
3 [1999] 2 AC 308, [1999] 2 All ER 353.
4 [1996] 2 FCR 304 at 308, [1996] 1 FLR 791 at 795, CA.

5.29 It has been held[1] that wherever there is a pre-existing residence order,[2] applications to change names are properly made under s 13(1)(a) rather than for a specific issue order under s 8[3] (conversely, where there is no pre-existing order application must be made for a s 8 order).[4] Although technically this means that there is no *obligation* to apply the welfare checklist,[5] it remains a useful aide mémoire.[6] A more serious consequence of requiring applications to be made under s 13 is that the consequential directions are probably not enforceable.[7] As with all applications directly concerning children's upbringing, in resolving disputes over children's names, whether under s 13 or s 8, the child's welfare is the court's paramount consideration.

1 By *Re B (minors) (change of surname)* [1996] 2 FCR 304, [1996] 1 FLR 791, CA. But note the query raised by Hale J in *Re M (leave to remove child from jurisdiction)* [1999] 3 FCR 708, [1999] 2 FLR 334, discussed at para 5.38.
2 Similarly if there is a pre-existing custody or care and control order made before the CA 1989, as in *Re B*, supra.
3 This in any event is implicit in r 4.1(2)(a) and (c) of the FPR 1991 and by the different form for the order under s 13, viz Form C 44 as opposed to C 43, which is required by r 4.21(5).
4 *Re C (minors) (change of surname)* [1998] 2 FCR 304 at 305, [1998] 1 FLR 549 at 550, CA, per Wilson J, *Dawson v Wearmouth* [1999] 2 AC 308 at 325 [1999] 2 All ER 353 at 363, per Lord Hobhouse and *Re W (A Child) (Illegitimate Child: Change of Surname)* [2001] Fam 1, [2000] 2 WLR 258, CA, per Butler Sloss LJ at para (9).
5 Viz that provided by s 1(3), discussed at paras 2.37 et seq.
6 Per Wilson J in *Re B*, supra. In *Re C*, supra, Ward LJ suggested the checklist would apply regardless of whether the application was under s 8 or s 13.
7 See *Re P (Minors) (Custody Order: Penal Notice)* [1990] 1 WLR 613, discussed at para 5.133.

5.30 The current legal position with regard to names has been summarised by Butler-Sloss LJ in *Re W (a Child) (Illegitimate Child: Change of Surname)*[1] as follows:

'(a) If parents are married they both have the power and the duty to register their child's names.[2] (b) If they are not married the mother has the sole duty and power to do so. (c) After registration of the child's names, the grant of a residence order obliges any person wishing to change the surname to obtain the leave of the court for the written consent of all those who have parental responsibility. (d) In the absence of a residence order, the person wishing to change the surname from the registered name ought to obtain the relevant written consent or the leave of the court by making an application for a specific issue order. (e) On any application the welfare of the child is paramount, and the judge must have regard to the s 1(3) criteria. (f) Among the factors to which the court should have regard is the registered surname of the child and the reasons for the registration, for instance recognition of the biological link with the child's father. Registration is always a relevant and an important consideration but it is not in itself decisive. The weight to be given to it by the court will depend upon the other relevant factors or valid countervailing reasons which may tip the balance the other way. (g) The relevant considerations should include factors which may arise in the future as well as the present situation. (h) Reasons given for changing or seeking to change a child's name based on the fact that the child's name is or is not the same as the parent making the application do not generally carry much weight. (i) The reasons for an earlier unilateral decision to change a child's name may be relevant. (j) Any changes of circumstances of the child since the original registration may be relevant. (k) In the case of a child whose parents were married to each other, the fact of the marriage is important and I would suggest that there would have to be strong reasons to change the name of the father's surname if the child was so registered. (l) Where the child's parents were not married to each other, the mother has control over registration. Consequently on an application to change the surname of the child, the degree of commitment of the father to the child, the quality of contact, if it occurs, between father and child, the existence or absence of parental responsibility are all relevant factors to take into account.'

1   [2001] Fam 1 at 7–8, [2000] 2 WLR 258 at 263–264 (para 9).
2   Where both register independently of one another, the first registration prevails, see *Re H (Child's Name: First Name)* [2002] EWCA Civ 190, [2002] 1 FLR 973, CA.

5.31   This summary is intended only as guidance with each case having to be decided upon its own facts upon the basis of the paramountcy principle. Nevertheless it is clear from the post CA 1989 case law that the burden of having to show that a change of name is for the child's benefit is a hard one to discharge. Ward LJ put it well in *Re C (a minor) (change of surname)*[1] when he said:

'... there is a heavy responsibility on those who seek to change a child's surname ... good and cogent reasons should be shown to allow a change.'

1   [1999] 1 FCR 318, [1998] 2 FLR 656, CA.

5.32   For examples of judicial refusals to sanction name-changes see:

- *Re F (minors) (change of name)*:[1] leave was refused since there was no reason to suppose that a young girl was going to be embarrassed or particularly unusual in being registered at a school under a different name from the current surname of her mother.
- *Re B (a minor) (change of surname)*,[2] in which the Court of Appeal upheld a refusal despite the children's wish for change. Whilst agreeing that 'orders which ran flatly contrary to the wishes of normal adolescent children were virtually unknown to family law', that principle did not extend to the formal change of surname from that of the father to the stepfather since[3] that would only serve to injure the link between the

father and the children, which was not in the latter's best interests. In so ruling Wilson J said 'there was no opprobrium nowadays for a child to have a different surname from that of adults in the household'.

- *A v Y (child's surname)*:[4] a specific issue order that a child be known by his father's name or a double surname was refused on the basis that he would be confused by a change of a name he had known for four years.
- *Dawson v Wearmouth*:[5] a father's application for a specific issue order to change his one month old child's name to his, (registered by the mother in her ex-husband's name) was refused because he could not demonstrate that such a change would be for the benefit of the child.
- *Re R (Change of Surname: Spanish Practice)*:[6] a mother was not permitted to change a child's surname on taking up residence in Spain since no benefit to the child could be shown. The parents, were, however, encouraged to consider the use of both surnames in line with Spanish practice.

1 [1994] 1 FCR 110, [1993] 2 FLR 837 n.
2 [1996] 2 FCR 304, [1996] 1 FLR, CA. See also *G v A (children: surname)* [1995] 2 FCR 223n. For a striking pre-Children Act example, see *W v A (Minor: Surname)* [1981] Fam 14, [1981] 1 All ER 100, application refused even though the child was emigrating to Australia with his mother and stepfather.
3 This was because the inhibition against a change of name lay against the mother rather than against the child. As Wilson J pointed out, above at 308 and 795 respectively, the child himself is free to ask others to address him in whatever name he chooses regardless of any s 13 directions.
4 [1999] 1 FCR 577, [1999] 2 FLR 5, per HH Judge Tyrer.
5 [1999] AC 308, [1999] 2 All ER 353, HL.
6 [2001] EWCA Civ 1344, [2001] 2 FLR 1358, CA.

5.33 For examples of permitted name-changes see:

- *Re S (Change of Names: Cultural Factors)*:[1] Muslim mother, divorced from the Sikh father and now living in a Muslim community, permitted to use Muslim names, including her current Muslim nickname for the child in daily life and at school but not formally to change the child's name since that would contribute to an undesirable elimination of his Sikh identity.
- *Re W (Child) (Illegitimate Child: Change of Surname)*[2] in which one mother[3] was permitted to change her son's name to avoid him having the same name as his father who was a notorious criminal and thus to protect him from what she genuinely feared was a real risk of harm if his identity was revealed in the new locality where they were living, and another mother[4] was similarly allowed to do so following the father's convictions for indecent assaults both upon a 17-year-old girl and his 11-year-old niece.
- *Re H (Child's Name: First Name)*[5], in which a mother, whose own registration of name was cancelled because it was made after the father's registration, was permitted to use her given name for the child, though no order to that effect was thought necessary.

1 [2001] 2 FLR 1005, per Wilson J.
2 [2001] Fam 1, [2000] 2 WLR 258, CA. This case comprised three separate appeals.
3 Viz in the *Re A* case.
4 Viz in the *Re B* case.
5 [2002] EWCA Civ 190, [2002] 1 FLR 973, CA.

5.34 Case law suggests that it might be easier to persuade the court to sanction a change of name that has already occurred than to permit a prospective change. In *Re P (minors) (parental responsibility: change of name)*[1] the court rejected an application by an unmarried father that his name be restored to his two children. The names had been changed some time ago, following the father's long term imprisonment, when the mother decided to make a fresh start both for herself and her children and it was not in their interests for the name to be changed back. In *Re C (a minor) (change of surname)*,[2] notwithstanding that the unmarried mother's original decision to change her child's surname following the breakdown of her relationship with the father was not initially justified, the Court of Appeal resolved nevertheless that a further change now was not in the child's interests.

1 [1997] 3 FCR 739, [1997] FLR 722, CA.
2 [1999] 1 FCR 318, [1998] 2 FLR 656, CA. See also *Re (minors) (change of surname)* [1998] 2 FCR 544, [1998] 1 FLR 549, CA.

(III) REMOVAL OF CHILD FROM THE UNITED KINGDOM

5.35   Under s 13(1)(b), where a residence order is in force, no person may remove the child from the United Kingdom (ie England and Wales, Scotland and Northern Ireland) without either the written consent of every person who has parental responsibility or leave of the court. In *Re H (children) (residence order: condition)*[1] the Court of Appeal rejected the argument[2] that s 13(1)(b) requires court leave to remove the child from the jurisdiction rather than from the United Kingdom. Accordingly, there is no obligation upon the person with a residence order to seek permission to relocate anywhere *within* the United Kingdom though it is open to someone else (normally the other parent) to seek to prevent that relocation either by means of a prohibited steps order[3] or, possibly, by the imposition of a s 11(7) condition.[4] However, to succeed in such an application the circumstances will need to be exceptional.[5]

1 [2001] EWCA Civ 1338, [2001] 3 FCR 182, [2001] 2 FLR 1277, CA.
2 Relying on inter alia the side note to s 13 which refers to 'removal from jurisdiction, s 108(12) which applies particular provisions of the CA 1989, but not s 13, to Northern Ireland and to the exercise of power under s 101 to make delegated legislation in making the Children (Prescribed Orders – Northern Ireland, Guernsey and Isle of Man) Regulations 1991 (SI 1991/2032).
3 Prohibited steps orders are discussed at paras 5.70 et seq.
4 Section 11(7) conditions are discussed at paras 5.84 et seq.
5 See *Re S (a child) (residence order: condition)* [2001] EWCA Civ 847, [2001] 3 FCR 154, CA and *Re H*, supra, in which a prohibited steps order was made preventing the father, in whose favour a residence order had been granted, from taking the children to Northern Ireland on a permanent basis.

5.36   Temporary removals for less than one month

Under s 13(2), a person in whose favour a residence order has been made can remove the child for a period of less than one month without anyone's permission. This latter provision places those with a residence order[1] in a special position since under the Child Abduction Act 1984[2] it is normally an offence to remove a child under the age of 16 outside the United Kingdom without the consent[3] of those having parental responsibility or leave of the court. Presumably, a shared residence order gives each parent the right to remove the child for less than one month.

1 But not those with a pre-Act custody or care and control order in their favour. Such persons therefore need leave of the court to take the child abroad even for a temporary period – sed quaere?

2   For a discussion of this Act, see *Clarke Hall and Morrison*, 2[11].
3   Though, unlike the requirement under the CA 1989, the consent does not have to be in writing. Note the qualifications to the consent requirement under s 1(5) of the 1984 Act.

5.37   Permitting unrestricted temporary removals, which was new under the CA 1989,[1] is intended to allow a person in whose favour a residence order has been made to make arrangements for holidays without having to seek the permission of the 'non-residential' parent(s) and without even having to give notice. There is no limit on the number of temporary removals permitted. In cases of dispute, however, a prohibited steps order can be made to curtail the right or a restriction of the right can be added to the residence order under s 11(7).[2]

1   The provision implements the Law Commission's (Law Com No 172, para 4.15) recommendations.
2   See eg Department of Health's Guidance and Regulations, Vol 1, Court Orders, para 2.27 and Lord Mackay LC 503 HL Official Report (5th Series), col 1354. S 11(7) is discussed at paras 5.84 et seq.

5.38   Removals for more than one month

Where permission is sought to take the child out of the United Kingdom for more than one month specific application for leave must be made to the court.[1] Where leave is sought under s 13 then under s 13(3) the court may grant leave either generally or for a specified purpose. However, it is not entirely settled whether leave should be sought under s 13 rather than by way of a specific issue order. Applying *Re B (minors) (change of surname)*[2] in relation to names, it seems that they should. However, this was queried by Hale J in *Re M (leave to remove child from jurisdiction)*.[3] As she pointed out, in the absence of a residence order an application must be made for a s 8 order, but 'if a person can apply [for a s 8 order] when there is no residence order in force, it is odd that they should have to use a different route when there is a residence order. The Family Proceedings Rules[4] may provide for a different route but it does not follow that it is the exclusive or only route'.

1   According to Thorpe J in *Harris v Pinnington* [1995] 3 FCR 35, sub nom, *MH v GP (Child Emigration)* [1995] 2 FLR 106 such applications should be heard either in the High Court or county court depending upon the complexity of the case. (Cf his earlier comment in *Re L (a minor) (removal from jurisdiction)* [1993] 1 FCR 325 that such applications should made to the High Court). But in *Re K (removal from jurisdiction: practice)* [1999] 3 FCR 673, 676, [1999] 2 FLR 1084, 1086–1087, Thorpe LJ has since said that where applications involve considerations of foreign legal systems and which may require the putting in place of mirror orders, they should normally be dealt with by a Family Division judge.
2   [1996] 2 FCR 304, [1996] 1 FLR 791, CA, discussed at para 5.29.
3   [1999] 3 FCR 708 at 715, [1999] 2 FLR 334 at 340.
4   Viz FPR 1991, rr 4.1(2)(a) and (c) and 4.21(5).

5.39   No matter by what route or by whom (it is equally open to the non residential parent, for example, to seek leave to remove a child) the matter is raised, the court's general approach should be the same,[1] namely, that in deciding whether to grant leave the court must apply the paramountcy of the child's welfare under s 1(1). However, in applying that principle a distinction is to be drawn between seeking leave to remove children outside the United Kingdom (the so-called 'external relocation cases') and applications to take children to another part of the United Kingdom (the so-called 'internal relocation cases').[2]

1   See *Re S (a child) (residence order: condition)* [2001] EWCA Civ 847, [2001] 3 FCR 154, CA. Technically, whereas it is mandatory to apply the welfare checklist in contested s 8 applications,

it is only discretionary to do so under s 13, though even then Thorpe LJ has said in *Payne v Payne* [2001] EWCA Civ 166, para 33, [2001] 1 FCR 425, 437, [2001] 1 FLR 1052 at 1063 that courts should nevertheless take the precaution of having regard to it.

2   See Thorpe LJ's summary in *Re H (children) (residence order: condition)* [2001] EWCA Civ 1338, paras 16 and 17, [2001] 3 FCR 182 at 187 [2001] 2 FLR 1277 at 1281–1282.

5.40   External relocation applications

The leading case, *Payne v Payne*,[1] affirmed both that the CA 1989 had not altered the underlying factors that should be taken into account in determining whether to give leave and that the 'internal application' of the European Convention on Human Rights following the implementation of the Human Rights Act 1998 did not 'necessitate a revision of the fundamental approach to relocation applications formulated by this court and consistently applied over so many years.'[2] Nevertheless to guard against a risk of 'too perfunctory an investigation resulting from too ready an assumption that the [primary carer]'s proposals are necessarily compatible with the child's welfare', Thorpe LJ suggested[3] that courts should adopt the following discipline, namely:

'(a)   Pose the question: is the mother's application genuine in the sense that it is not motivated by some selfish desire to exclude the father from the child's life? Then ask is the mother's application realistic, by which I mean founded on practical proposals both well researched and investigated? If the application fails either of these tests refusal will inevitably follow.

(b)   If however the application passes these tests then there must be a careful appraisal of the father's opposition: is it motivated by genuine concern for the future of the child's welfare or is it driven by some ulterior motive? What would be the extent of the detriment to him and his future relationship with the child were the application granted? To what extent would that be offset by extension of the child's relationships with the maternal family and homeland?

(c)   What would be the impact on the mother, either as the single parent or as a new wife, or a refusal of her realistic proposal?

(d)   The outcome of the second and third appraisals must then be brought into an overriding review of the child's welfare as the paramount consideration directed by the statutory checklist insofar as appropriate.'

1   [2001] EWCA Civ 166, [2001] 1 FCR 425, [2001] 1 FLR 1052, CA. Note that Munby J's application of a different test in *Re X and Y (leave to remove from jurisdiction: no order principle)* [2001] 2 FCR 398, [2001] 2 FLR 118, was expressly disapproved by the Court of Appeal in *Re H (children) (residence order: condition)* [2001] EWCA Civ 1338, [2001] 3 FCR 181, [2001] 2 FLR 1277.

2   Above at para 35, per Thorpe LJ agreeing with Ward LJ's earlier conclusions in *Re G-A (a child) (removal from jurisdiction: human rights)* [2001] 1 FCR 43, sub nom *Re (A Permission to Remove Child from Jurisdiction: Human Rights)* [2000] 2 FLR 225, CA, in which it was held that permission to remove a child permanently from the jurisdiction does not, per se, breach the other parent's 'right to family life' under art 8 of the European Convention on Human Rights.

3   Above at para 40.

5.41   In *Re H (application to remove from jurisdiction)*[1] Thorpe LJ commented that while applications for permanent removal require profound investigation and judgment, not at lot is to be gained by seeking support from past decisions. In general terms, however, the test applied by the courts is that, provided the request is reasonable and bona fide,[2] and the plans for the removal can be demonstrated to the court's satisfaction as being reasonably well prepared and thought out,[3] leave will be granted unless it can be shown to be against the child's interests.[4] In this latter regard factors such as education and the relationship with the 'non-residential' parent are likely to be of more weight in the case of older children.[5] Against this the courts are also prepared to give some weight to the unhappiness or bitterness that a refusal of leave might cause.[6]

1   [1999] 2 FCR 34, [1998] 1 FLR 848, CA.
2   See eg *Tyler v Tyler* [1989] 2 FLR 158, CA in which it was found that the mother's dominant motive for seeking leave to take the children to Australia, was bitterness towards her husband. Leave was refused.
3   See eg *K (a Minor) (Removal From Jurisdiction)* [1992] 2 FLR 98; *M v A (Wardship: Removal From Jurisdiction)* [1993] 2 FLR 715 and *Re T (Removal From Jurisdiction)* [1996] 2 FLR 352, sub nom *Re T (a minor) (order as to residence)* [1996] 3 FCR 97, CA in which leave was refused because the applicant's plans were ill-thought out and little researched. Cf *Re W (minors) (removal from jurisdiction)* [1994] 1 FCR 842 where the allegation of ill-thought out plans failed on the facts, Thorpe J holding that the applicant was not required to guarantee the precise details of the future life but merely had to establish the interest, capacity and capability to pursue the plans. In *Re M (Leave to Remove Child From Jurisdiction)* [1999] 2 FLR 334 it was held that leave would be given in advance of detailed plans on the facts.
4   See eg *Lonslow v Hennig* (formerly Lonslow) [1986] 2 FLR 378, CA, *M v M (Minors) (Removal From Jurisdiction)* [1992] 2 FLR 303, CA and *Harris v Pinnington* [1995] 3 FCR 35, sub nom *MH v GP (Child: Emigration)* [1995] 2 FLR 106. Cf *Re K (application to remove from jurisdiction)* [1999] 2 FCR 410, [1998] 2 FLR 1006 in which leave was granted notwithstanding the adverse conditions that then existed in Nigeria.
5   See eg *M v M (minors) (jurisdiction)* [1993] 1 FCR 5, CA in which leave was refused the trial judge having been held to have given insufficient weight to the children's (aged 12 and ten) own views. In *Harris v Pinnington MH v GP (Child: Emigration)*, supra, leave was refused because of the overriding importance of maintaining and developing the relationship between child and father. See also *Re C (leave to remove from jurisdiction)* [2000] 2 FCR 40, [2000] 2 FLR 457, CA in which leave was refused because of the adverse impact of the child's (aged 6) contact with the father. (Thorpe LJ dissenting).
6   See eg *Re B (minor) (removal from jurisdiction)* [1994] 2 FCR 309, CA.

5.42   When granting leave, the court should assess all risks (for example, enforcement of a contact order) and build in all practical safeguards (for example, notarised agreements and mirror orders),[1] not simply trusting the parent or accepting undertakings.[2] The court may, in granting leave, impose conditions, for example requiring the deposit of a sum of money until the parent with leave obtains 'authentication' of the contact order in the foreign court and complies with an order relating to the child's education; upon evidence of compliance, the deposit would be released,[3] or requiring the swearing of a solemn oath on the Quran.[4]

1   Ie an order made in the jurisdiction to which the child is being taken.
2   *Re K (removal from jurisdiction: practice)* [1999] 3 FCR 673, [1999] 2 FLR 1984, CA.
3   *Re S (Removal From Jurisdiction)* [1999] 1 FLR 850, CA. In *Re L (Removal From Jurisdiction: Holiday)* [2001] 1 FLR 241 the mother was required to deposit a bond which was to be released upon the child's return.
4   *Re A (security for return to jurisdiction) (note)* [1999] 1 FCR 284, [1999] 2 FLR 1n, *Re L (Removal From Jurisdiction: Holiday)* supra.

5.43   The question of whether a parent should be given leave to remove a child permanently from the jurisdiction is distinct from that of who should have residence of the child. Accordingly, it by no means follows that because an application for leave to remove has been refused the applicant should lose residence of the child.[1]

1   *Re T (a minor) (order as to residence)* [1996] 3 FCR 97, sub nom, *Re T (Removal From Jurisdiction)* [1996] 2 FLR 352, CA.

5.44 Internal relocation applications

Although, the person with residence does not require leave to relocate *within* the United Kingdom,[1] such a proposal can be challenged by the non resident parent. *Re S (a child) (residence order: condition)*[2] establishes that whereas a principal carer will ordinarily be granted leave to remove a child outside the United Kingdom unless the court concludes that it is incompatible with the child's welfare, no condition restricting the area of residence within the United Kingdom will be imposed on the principal carer save in exceptional circumstances. The rationale for this less stringent approach is that, in Thorpe LJ's words in *Re H (children) (residence order; condition)*[3] within 'the same sovereignty there will be the same system of laws, with the same rights of the citizen, rights for instance to education, health care and statutory benefits'.

1 Aliter outside the United Kingdom, including therefore to the Isle of Man or the Channel Isles.
2 [2001] EWCA Civ 847, [2001] 3 FCR 154.
3 [2001] EWCA Civ 1338 at para 20, [2001] 3 FCR 182 at 188, [2000] 2 FLR 1277 at 1283. Note also his Lordship's distinction between seeking to relocate within the European Union and further afield.

2. Contact orders[1]

5.45 A contact order 'means an order requiring the person with whom the child lives, or is to live, to allow the child to visit or stay with the person named in the order, or for that person and the child otherwise to have contact with each other'.

These s 8 contact orders should not be confused with 'care contact orders' under s 34. The former exclusively control contact between individuals and cannot be made in favour of a local authority nor while the child is in care.[2] The latter exclusively control contact with a child in local authority care.[3]

1 For an invaluable discussion of the practicalities of making contact work and for important recommendations to improve the current system, see *Making Contact Work* (A Report to the Lord Chancellor by the Advisory Board on Family Law; Children Act Sub-Committee, 2002).
2 Section 9(1) and (2), discussed at paras 5.97 and 5.98.
3 Discussed at paras 8.146 et seq.

(a) Indirect contact

5.46 In general terms contact orders provide for the child to visit or stay with the person named in the order the emphasis thus being on the child rather than parent.[1] Contact orders embrace both physical and non-physical contact and may therefore range from long or short visits to contact by letter or telephone.[2] Indirect contact can also be by email or even video recording.[3] For the purposes of s 10(6), under which applications may be made without leave to vary certain s 8 orders,[4] there is no rigid compartmentalisation between direct and indirect contact.[5]

1 This, as the Department of Health's Guidance and Regulations, Vol 1, Court Orders at para 2.29 points out, is in contrast to access orders, which contact orders replaced, which provided for the parent to have access to the child. It should also be noted that while the child is with

the parent, that parent may exercise all his parental responsibility subject to not doing anything incompatible with a court order.

2   For examples of contact by post see *Re P (minors) (contact: discretion)* [1999] 1 FCR 566, [1998] 2 FLR 696, *A v L (contact)* [1998] 2 FCR 204, [1998] 1 FLR 361 and *Re M (a minor) (contact: conditions)* [1994] 1 FCR 678, [1994] 1 FLR 272, each involving letter contact with a father in prison; *Re P (Contact: Indirect Contact)* [1999] 2 FLR 893 indirect contact with a father who had just been released from prison; *L v C* [1995] 3 FCR 125, sub nom *Re L (Contact: Transsexual Applicant)* [1995] 2 FLR 438 – indirect contact with transsexual father; *Re D (a child) (IVF treatment)* [2001] EWCA Civ 230, [2001] 1 FCR 289, sub nom *Re D (Parental Responsibility: IVF Baby)* [2001] 1 FLR 972, CA, indirect contact with a man deemed to be the father under the Human Fertilisation and Embryology Act 1990, ss 28(3) and 29(1B). For examples of indirect contact being ordered with violent or abusive parents, see *Re S (Violent Parent: Indirect Contact)* [2000] 1 FLR 481, *Re H (Contact: Domestic Violence)* [1998] 3 FCR 385, [1998] 2 FLR 42, CA and *Re M (Sexual Abuse Allegations: Interviewing Techniques)* [1999] 2 FLR 92.
3   See 'Indirect Contact via Video-tape' [1997] Fam Law 310, which might be a particularly useful way of re-establishing contact.
4   See para 5.111.
5   *Re W (application for leave: whether necessary)* [1996] 3 FCR 337n.

5.47   Whether a contact order is necessarily directed against the person with whom the child lives or is to live, as the opening part of the definition suggests, or whether the closing words 'or for the person and the child otherwise to have contact with each other' can properly be regarded as empowering a court to make an independent order simply providing for the child to have contact with a person named in the order, has not expressly been addressed by the courts. However, in *Re H (minors) (prohibited steps order)*[1] the underlying assumption was that such orders are directed against the person with whom the child is living etc. This distinction is relevant when determining the power to:

(a)   prohibit contact;[2]
(b)   to make provision for contact in a freeing for adoption order;[3] or
(c)   enforce the order.[4]

1   [1995] 4 All ER 110, [1995] 1 WLR 667, [1995] 2 FCR 547, [1995] CA, 1 FLR 638, discussed further at para 5.53.
2   See para 5.53.
3   See paras 5.69.
4   See para 5.135.

(b)   General considerations

5.48   Orders may provide for the child to have contact with any person (including, where appropriate, a sibling) and more than one contact order may be made in respect of a child. A contact order can be the sole order even between parents and may be appropriate where there is no dispute as to the person with whom the child is to live. Orders can provide for contact to take place at Contact Centres. The role of these Centres has been said[1] to be 'one of the most important developments of the last ten years'. They are useful as a means of providing a temporary venue for supported contacted in cases where the child's parents are unable to provide an alternative. They are not, however, intended to be places for contact over the long-term, nor are they ipso facto the equivalent of professionally supervised contact. Orders can also provide for contact to take place abroad.[2] However, since jurisdiction to make orders is based on the child's habitual residence or physical presence,[3] if the child is neither present or habitually resident here, jurisdiction is confined to amending existing orders.[4]

1 See *Making Contact Work*, supra at ch 8.
2 *Re F (a Minor) (Access out of Jurisdiction)* [1973] Fam 198, [1973] 3 All ER 493.
3 Family Law Act 1986, s 1, discussed in *Clarke Hall and Morrison* 1[577.3] et seq.
4 *Re S (a minor) (residence order: forum conveniens)* [1995] 2 FCR 162, [1995] 1 FLR 314, per Thorpe J.

5.49 Although courts can make orders for 'reasonable contact',[1] if that is the sole order between the parents then, having regard to the s 1(5),[2] one may question the need to make the order at all. Such an order might, however, be justifiable where the applicant is not a parent, for example a grandparent, since without an order that person has no locus standi in relation to the child[3] and it might be valuable if the person with whom the child lives is hostile to the absent parent having contact and who might therefore seek to prevent it. Where restricted or supervised contact is thought appropriate the court may attach directions or conditions under s 11(7).[4]

1 Before the CA 1989 orders for 'reasonable' access were very common and the Department of Health's Guidance and Regulations, Vol 1 Court Order at para 2.29 anticipated that orders for reasonable contact would be the 'usual order'.
2 Discussed at paras 2.62 et seq.
3 Cf the similar arguments, discussed at para 2.72, as to making s 8 orders generally.
4 Section 11(7) is discussed at paras 5.84 et seq. Note also *Leeds County Council v C* [1993] 1 FCR 585, [1993] 1 FLR 269 which establishes that there is no power under s 11(7) to order a local authority to supervise contact.

5.50 Contact orders requiring one parent to allow the child to visit the other parent[1] will automatically lapse if the parents subsequently live together for a continuous period of more than six months.[2] While the child is with a parent on a contact visit that parent may exercise parental responsibility, at any rate with respect to short term matters,[3] without consulting the other provided he does nothing which is incompatible with any existing court order.[4]

1 Note: if the order is directed against someone other than a parent or if the child is permitted contact with a third party it will not lapse because of the parents' cohabitation.
2 Section 11(6).
3 But, possibly, not to take important steps that have long term consequences for the child, see eg *Re G (a minor) (parental responsibility: education)* [1995] 2 FCR 53, [1994] 2 FLR 964, CA and the other cases discussed at paras 3.96–3.97.
4 See paras 3.94 et seq.

5.51 In *Re S (a minor) (contact: evidence)*[1] it was held that a subpoena duces tecum should be issued against the police to produce a video of an interview with a five-year-old child in which she made allegations of sexual abuse against her father so as to have the best evidence available to determine the contact application. Nevertheless Hale J observed that it was not always wrong to consider proportionality between the benefits to the welfare of the child and the resources to be expended on the inquiry. In *Re B (minors) (contact)*[2] it was held that a judge need not always hold a full hearing permitting the parties to call oral evidence and cross-examine any witnesses they may choose. A judge has a broad discretion to decide a contact application on the basis of written evidence provided at any rate there is sufficient evidence upon which to make the decision and having duly taken into account such factors as whether the evidence sought to be addressed at the full hearing was likely to effect the outcome, whether the delay that could be caused by the full hearing would be exceptionally detrimental to the child's welfare, the prospects of success of the applicant at the full trial and whether the justice of the case required a full investigation with oral evidence. *Re B,* however, represents the exceptional case and where oral evidence is heard, including evidence from a Children and Family Reporter, the parties, no matter how weak their case may be, ought to be allowed to cross-examine and be given the opportunity to give their own oral evidence.[3] Where expert evidence is adduced it is wrong for a judge to ignore it.[4]

1 [1998] 3 FCR 70, CA.
2 [1994] 2 FCR 812, [1994] 2 FLR 1, CA. See also *Re M (Contact)* [1995] 1 FLR 1029.
3 *Re I and H (Contact: Right to Give Evidence)* [1998] 1 FLR 876, CA.
4 *Re M (minors) (contact: evidence)* [1998] 2 FCR 538, CA, judge erred in following welfare officer's opinion rather than the expert opinion of a doctor.

(c) Interim contact orders

5.52 Section 11(3) permits a court to make an interim contact order where it is not in a position finally to dispose of the proceedings. However, courts should be cautious about making interim orders where the principle of contact is in dispute and substantial factual issues are unresolved.[1] Where sexual abuse is alleged against a parent and the child is showing behavioural problems then, even if on the available evidence abuse is not likely to be established but further investigation is necessary, while it might be appropriate to allow contact to continue, it is not appropriate to make an order for staying contact.[2]

1 Per Wall J in *D v R* [1995] 1 FCR 501, sub nom *Re D (Contact: Interim Order)* [1995] 1 FLR 495.
2 *Re W (a minor) (staying contact)* [1998] 2 FCR 453, [1998] 2 FLR 450. It may not, however, be possible, particularly in domestic violence cases, to make an interim order without hearing oral evidence or the advice of a Children and Family Reporter: see *Re M (Interim Contact: Domestic Violence)* [2000] 2 FLR 377, CA and *D v R* supra.

(d) Prohibiting contact

5.53 When the CA 1989 was first implemented it was thought that orders denying contact required a prohibited steps order. As the Department of Health's Guidance and Regulations stated:[1]

'a s 8 order is a positive order in the sense that it requires contact to be allowed between an individual and a child and cannot be used to deny contact'.

However, this reasoning was rejected by the Court of Appeal in *Nottingham County Council v P*,[2] Sir Stephen Brown P commenting:

'We agree with the judge that the sensible and appropriate construction of the term contact order includes a situation where a court is required to consider whether any contact should be provided for. An order that there shall be 'no contact' falls within the general concept and common sense requires that it should be considered to fall within the definition of 'contact order' in s 8(1).'

On this analysis prohibiting contact has to be considered as part of a s 8 contact order. However, in *Re H (minors) (prohibited steps order)*,[3] the Court of Appeal subsequently made a prohibited steps order against a mother's former cohabitant preventing him from having or seeking contact with the children to whom it was considered he posed a risk. It was held that it was only by this means that an order could be directed (and thus enforced) against the man. Butler-Sloss LJ commented that had a 'no contact' order been made it would have been directed against the mother who would thus have been obliged to prevent contact. That would have been inappropriate in this case since she neither wanted the children to have such contact nor, more importantly, had she the power to control it.[4] This ruling seems preferable to *Nottingham* and it is suggested that all prohibitions of contact are best achieved by a prohibited steps order.

1   Vol 1, Court Orders, para 2.30.
2   [1994] Fam 18 at 38 – 39 [1993] 3 All ER 815 at 824, CA, discussed further at para 5.81.
3   [1995]4 All ER 110, [1995] 1 WLR 667. Nottingham was not cited by the court.
4   The children were of school age and, as Butler-Sloss LJ said, 'With the best will in the world the mother could not protect her children going to or from school or at school or at play . . .'

(e)   Denying contact with a parent

5.54   As between parents it is rarely necessary to make formal orders prohibiting contact, it being normally sufficient simply to refuse an application thereby leaving the primary carer in sole control. Nevertheless by whatever order it is to be achieved denying contact between a child and a parent is a serious issue. As Butler-Sloss LJ pointed out in *Re R (a minor) (contact)*,[1] the principle of continued contact is underlined by Art 9(1) of the United Nations Convention on the Rights of the Child 1989 and endorsed in the CA 1989. Furthermore as the European Court of Human Rights held in *Glaser v UK*,[2] Art 8 of the Human Rights Convention 'includes a right for a parent to have measures taken with a view to his or her being reunited with the child and an obligation of national authorities to take measures' both in public and private law proceedings. However, the court also acknowledged that the obligation of national authorities to take measures to facilitate contact by a non-custodial parent after divorce was not absolute and that where it might appear to threaten the child's interests or interfere with his or her Art 8 rights, it was for those authorities 'to strike a fair balance between them'.

1   [1993] 1 FCR 954 at 961, [1993] 2 FLR 762 at 767.
2   [2000] 3 FCR 193 at 209, paras (65)–(66), [2001] 1 FLR 148 at 168.

5.55   The general approach, established by *Re H (minors) (access)*,[1] is for the judge to ask himself whether there are cogent reasons why the child should be denied contact with a parent. It has since been said to be helpful to cast the relevant principles into the framework of the welfare checklist, namely, to consider whether the fundamental need of every child to have an enduring relationship with both parents is outweighed by the depth of harm that, might thereby be caused.[2] In *Re P (minors) (contact: parental hostility)*,[3] Wall J summarised the principles as follows:

'(1)   Overriding all else, as provided by s 1(1) of the CA 1989, the welfare of the child is the paramount consideration, and the court is concerned with the interests of the mother and the father only insofar as they bear on the welfare of the child.

(2)   It is almost always in the interests of the child whose parents are separated that he or she should have contact with the parent with whom the child is not living.

(3)   The court has powers to enforce orders for contact, which it should not hesitate to exercise where it judges that it will overall promote the welfare of the child to do so.

(4)   Cases do, unhappily and infrequently but occasionally, arise, in which a court is compelled to conclude that in existing circumstances an order for immediate direct contact should not be ordered, because so to order would injure the welfare of the child: see *Re D (a Minor) (Contact: Mother's Hostility)* [1993] 2 FLR 1 at 7G, per Waite LJ.

(5) In cases, in which, for whatever reason, direct contact cannot for the time being be ordered, it is ordinarily highly desirable that there should be indirect contact so that the child grows up knowing of the love and interest of the absent parent with whom, in due course, direct contact should be established.'

1 [1992] 1 FCR 70 at 74F,[1992] 1 FLR 148 at 152C, per Balcombe LJ, CA.
2 *Re M (minors) (contact)* [1995] 1 FCR 753, [1995] 1 FLR 274, CA.
3 [1997] 1 FCR 458 at 473, sub nom *Re P (Contact: Supervision)* [1996] 2 FLR 314 at 328, CA, relying on *Re O (a minor) (contact: indirect contact)* [1996] 1 FCR 317 at 323–325, sub nom *Re O (Contact: Imposition of Conditions)* [1995] 2 FLR 124 at 128–130, CA. Cf *S v M (Access Order)* [1997] 1 FLR 980, sub nom *Sanderson v McManus* 1997 SLT 629 in which the House of Lords held, on an appeal from Scotland, that technically the onus of proof is on a parent (in this case an unmarried father) to show that continued contact is for the child's welfare, though as Lord Clyde observed 'true questions of the burden of proof will almost invariably fade into insignificance after any inquiry.'

5.56 In principle the same approach applies regardless of whether the parents are married to each other[1] but in practice it may be easier to persuade a court to deny contact to an unmarried father.[2] There is, however, said to be no presumption of contact with step-parents[3] or grandparents.[4]

1 There may, however, be a different approach with regard to *step-parents* in the sense that it will have to be shown to be in the child's interests to preserve continued contact: cf *Re H (a minor) (contact)* [1994] 2 FCR 419, [1994] 2 FLR 776, CA, where an order was made and *Re C (a minor) (access)* [1991] FCR 969, [1992] 1 FLR 309, CA, where an order was refused.
2 See eg the comment at [1994] Fam Law 484, referring to *Re D (a minor) (contact: mother's hostility)* [1993] 1 FCR 964, [1993] 2 FLR 1, CA and *Re H (a minor) (parental responsibility)* [1993] 1 FCR 85, [1993] 1 FLR 484, in which respectively the mother's and the step-father's hostility was held to justify prohibiting contact. But cf *Re M (Contact: Supervision)* [1998] 1 FLR 727, CA – in which an unmarried father was granted supervised contact notwithstanding his problems over drugs and alcohol abuse, occasional lack of control over his temper and the lack of a permanent home. Note also *Re C and V (minors) (contact and parental responsibility)* [1998] 1 FCR 52, [1998] 1 FLR 392, CA in which a man was denied contact with his own child but granted contact with a child who was not his blood relation.
3 *Re H (A Minor) (Contact)* [1994] 2 FLR 776. Cf *Re C (a minor) (access)* [1991] 1 FCR 969, [1992] 1 FLR 309, CA.
4 *Re A (section 8 order: grandparent application)* [1996] 1 FCR 467, [1995] 2 FLR 153, CA. See also *Re W (contact: application by grandparent)* [1997] 2 FCR 643, [1997] 1 FLR 793; *Re S (Contact: Appeal)* [2001] Fam Law 505.

5.57 Notwithstanding the predisposition to preserve contact with both parents, there are occasions when it is not in the child's interests to do so. Examples include:

- *Re C (Contact: No Order for Contact)*[1] in which indirect contact was refused with a father who had been absent over a three year period and against whom the child had an extreme adverse reaction;
- *Re F (minors) (denial of contact)*,[2] in which contact with a transsexual father was refused primarily because of the children's (boys aged 12 and 9) own wishes;
- *Re H (children) (contact order) (No 2)*[3] where, contrary to the children's wishes, no contact order was made with a father who was suffering from Huntingdon's disease and who had in the past threatened to kill himself (and unknown to them) the children, it being found that the mother was at risk of suffering a nervous breakdown if a contact order was made;
- *Re T (a minor) (parental responsibility: contact)*,[4] in which an unmarried father was denied contact because of his violence towards the mother and his blatant disregard for the child's welfare;

- *Re C and V (minors) (parental responsibility and contact),*[5] in which the child had severe medical problems requiring constant and informed medical attention which the mother, but not the father, was able to give, and

- *Re D (a minor) (contact: mother's hostility)*[6] and *Re H (a minor) (parental responsibility)*[7] in which respectively the mother's and the stepfather's implacable hostility towards contact with an unmarried father was held to justify prohibiting contact.

1 [2000] 2 FLR 723.
2 [1993] 1 FCR 945, [1993] 2 FLR 677, CA.
3 [2000] 3 FCR 385. This was the rehearing of the case remitted by the Court of Appeal reported as *Re H (children) (contact order)* [2001] 1 FCR 49. Cf *Re M (contact: parental responsibility: McKenzie friend)* [1999] 1 FCR 703, [1999] 1 FLR 75, CA, in which previously successful contact was overshadowed by the mother's fear of the father, though in this case, indirect contact was still granted.
4 [1993] 1 FCR 973, [1993] 2 FLR 450, CA.
5 [1998] 1 FCR 52, [1998] 1 FLR 392, CA.
6 [1993] 1 FCR 964, [1993] 2 FLR 1, CA.
7 [1993] 1 FCR 85, [1993] 1 FLR 484. See also *Re B (a minor) (contact: stepfather's opposition)* [1998] 3 FCR 289, [1997] 2 FLR 579, CA, in which the dismissal of the father's contact application was justified because of the child's stepfather's threat to reject the child and the mother.

5.58   Despite the foregoing cases concerning parental hostility, it has been said[1] that judges should be very reluctant to allow one parent's implacable hostility to deter them from making a contact order where they believe the child's welfare requires it. In *Re P (minors) (contact: discretion)*[2] Wilson J considered that hostility towards contact can arise in three different situations. The first is where there are no rational grounds for the parent's hostility, in which case the court should only refuse an order for contact if satisfied that it would create a serious risk of emotional harm to the child. The second is where the parent advances grounds for the hostility which the court regards as sufficiently potent as to displace the presumption that contact is in the child's best interests. In this case the hostility as such becomes largely irrelevant. The third is where the parent advances sound arguments for the displacement of the presumption of contact but where there are also sound arguments the other way (ie the arguments are rational but not decisive). In such a case the hostility 'can itself be of importance, occasionally of determinative importance, provided, as always, that what is measured is its effect upon the child'. Where one parent makes contact difficult or impossible for the other the court could transfer residence. However, this is a remedy of last resort and should not be adopted to solve a relatively straightforward contact problem.[3]

1 Per Balcombe LJ in *Re J (a minor) (contact)* [1994] 2 FCR 741 at 749, [1994] 1 FLR 729 at 736. See also *Re S (Contact: Grandparents)* [1996] 3 FLR 30, [1996] 1 FLR 158 and *Re P (minors) (contact: parental hostility)* [1997] 1 FCR 458, sub nom *Re P (Contact: Supervision)* [1996] 2 FLR 314, CA. But note *Re D (contact: reasons for refusal)* [1998] 1 FCR 321, [1997] 2 FLR 48, CA, in which Hale J observed that the term 'implacable hostility' usually refers to the type of case where no good reason could be discerned for a parent's opposition to contact.
2 [1999] 1 FCR 566 at 574–575, [1998] 2 FLR 696 at 703–704. On the facts the case was held to fall into the third category and Wilson J upheld the decision to refuse direct contact (despite the older child's (aged seven) wishes) with a father in prison but to allow limited contact.
3 Per Thorpe LJ in *Re B (residence order: status quo)* [1998] 1 FCR 549 [1998] 1 FLR 368, CA. Note *Re F (contact: enforcement: representation of child)* [1998] 3 FCR 216, [1998] 1 FLR 691, CA on whether it is appropriate to attach a penal notice to a contact order. See also paras 5.135 and 140 generally on the question of enforcement of contact orders.

5.59 In addition to refusing to make a contact order, the court can also make an order under s 91(14) restraining future applications without its leave.[1]

1   Section 91(14) orders are discussed below at paras 5.154 et seq.

(f)   Contact and domestic violence[1]

5.60 Violence does not per se justify a refusal of contact;[2] it is a matter of discretion, not principle. But in *Re M (minors) (contact: violent parent)*[3] Wall J commented that too little weight was sometimes given to the need of a violent parent to change behaviour so as to demonstrate fitness to have contact. In *Re H (minors) (contact: domestic violence)*[4] the Court of Appeal refused to interfere with a decision that despite the judge's misgivings about the father, including his violence, there was not enough to outweigh the normal principle that contact was in the children's interests.[5] In *Re A (minors) (domestic violence)*[6] resumption of contact with a previously violent father was denied. Interim contact orders in cases of domestic violence raise particularly difficult issues. The court may allow indirect contact in cases where direct contact is not considered appropriate.[7]

1   For a general discussion see [2000] Fam Law 630. See also Butler-Sloss P at [2001] Fam Law 355.
2   *Re F (a child) (contact order)* [2001] 1 FCR 422 and *Re H (minors) (contact: domestic violence)* [1998] 3 FCR 385, [1998] 2 FLR 42, CA.
3   [1999] 2 FCR 56, [1999] 2 FLR 321 – contact was refused.
4   [1998] 3 FCR 385, [1998] 2 FLR 42, CA.
5   Note also that non-molestation orders may be made under the FLA 1996, s 42(2)(b) in any family proceedings of the court's own motion.
6   [1999] 1 FCR 729; and see also *Re D (Contact: Reasons for Refusal)* [1997] 2 FLR 48; *Re P (Contact: Discretion)* [1998] 2 FLR 696; *Re M (contact: parental responsibility McKenzie friend)* [1999] 1 FCR 703, [1999] 1 FLR 75.
7   *Re S (Contact: Indirect Contact)* [2000] 1 FLR 481.

5.61 In the leading case, *Re L (a Child), Re V (a child), Re H (a Child) (Contact: Domestic Violence)*,[1] the Court of Appeal dismissed four appeals by fathers against orders allowing them indirect contact, but refusing them direct contact in cases of a background of domestic violence between the spouses and partners. Approving the approach taken in *Re H (minors) (contact: domestic violence)*[2] and *Re M (minors) (contact: violent parent)*,[3] it was held that there were no presumptions for or against contact with a violent parent, and the only principle applicable was the paramountcy of the child's welfare as set out in the CA 1989, s 1(1) and the checklist in s 1(3).[4] Drawing both on *A Report to the Lord Chancellor on the Question of Parental Contact in Cases Where There is Domestic Violence*[5] which was presented to the Lord Chancellor on 29 February 2000, and on an expert report (now published)[6] prepared by Dr Claire Sturge and Dr Danya Glaser on contact from a child and adolescent psychiatry perspective, Butler-Sloss LJ commented:[7]

'The family judges and magistrates need to have a heightened awareness of the existence of and consequences (some long-term) on children of exposure to domestic violence between their parents or other partners. There has, perhaps, been a tendency in the past for courts not to tackle allegations of violence and to leave them in the background on the premise that they were matters affecting the adults and not relevant to issues regarding the children. The general principle that contact with the non-residence parent is in the interests of the child may sometimes have discouraged sufficient attention being paid to the adverse effects on children living in the household where violence has occurred. It may not necessarily be widely appreciated that violence to a partner involves a significant failure in parenting – failure to protect the child's carer and failure to protect the child emotionally. In a contact or other s 8 application, where allegations of domestic violence are made which might have an effect on the outcome, those allegations must be adjudicated upon and found proved or not proved. It will be necessary to scrutinise such allegations which may not always be true or may be grossly exaggerated. If however there is a firm basis for finding that violence has occurred, the psychiatric advice becomes very important. There is not, however, nor should there be, any presumption that, on proof of domestic violence, the offending parent has to surmount a prima facie barrier of no contact. As a matter of principle, domestic violence of itself cannot constitute a bar to contact. It is one factor in the difficult and delicate balancing exercise of discretion. The court deals with the facts of a specific case in which the degree of violence and the seriousness of the impact on the child and on the resident parent have to be taken into account. In cases of proved domestic violence, as in cases of other proved harm or risk of harm to the child, the court has the task of weighing in the balance the seriousness of the domestic violence, the risks involved and the impact on the child against the positive factors, if any, of contact between the parent found to have been violent and the child. In this context, the ability of the offending parent to recognise his past conduct, be aware of the need to change and make genuine efforts to do so, will be likely to be an important consideration.'

1 [2001] Fam 260, [2000] 4 All ER 609, CA.
2 [1998] 3 FCR 385, [1998] 2 FLR, CA.
3 [1999] 2 FCR 56, [1999] 2 FLR 321 – contact refused.
4 But note that the definition of 'harm' is prospectively to be extended by the Adoption and Children Bill 2002 to include 'impairment suffered from seeing or hearing the ill-treatment of another'.
5 The Advisory Board on Family Law: Children Act Sub-Committee, Chairman Wall J. See http://www.open.gov.uk/lcd/family/abfla/dvconreport.pdf. See now its full report, *Making Contact Work*, supra.
6 [2000] Fam Law 615.
7 Above at 272–273 and 616 respectively.

5.62 In *Re L* Waller LJ set out the following propositions:[1]
'(1) That the effect of children being exposed to domestic violence of one parent as against the other might up until now have been underestimated by judges and adverse alike.
(2) That alleged domestic violence was a matter which should be investigated and findings of fact should be made because if it was established, its effect on the children exposed to it and the risk to the residential carer were highly relevant factors in considering orders for contact and their form.
(3) That in assessing the relevance of past domestic violence it was likely to be highly material whether the perpetrator had shown an ability to recognise the wrong, or less commonly she, had done and the steps taken to correct the deficiency in that perpetrator's character.
(4) That there should, however, be no presumption against contact simply because domestic violence was alleged or proved. It was one highly material factor among many which might offset the assumption in favour of contact when the difficult balancing exercise was carried out.'

1 Above at 301 and 643–644 respectively.

5.63 Subsequent to *Re L*, Butler-Sloss P refused direct contact to a violent father who had killed his wife.[1] All contact was also refused in a case,[2] where there had been 'unusually high levels of domestic violence', because of the harm to the living child with the mother suffering from psychological and emotional conditions induced by that contact. Refusal of contact in cases of domestic violence where there is a risk of emotional destabilisation to the child promotes the child's right to family life with its primary carer pursuant to Art 8 of the European Convention on Human Rights.[3]

1   *Re G (Direct Contact: Domestic Violence)* [2000] 2 FLR 865, FD.
2   *Re M and B (children) (contact: domestic violence)* [2001] 1 FCR 116, CA; and see also *Re K (Contact: Mother's Anxiety)* [1999] 2 FLR 703, CA.
3   *Re Q (Contact: Natural Father)* (2001, unreported).

(g)   Contact and adoption

5.64   As proceedings under the Adoption Act 1976 rank as 'family proceedings'[1] courts are empowered either upon application or their own motion both in adoption and freeing for adoption proceedings to make s 8 orders, including contact orders.[2]

1   See s 8(4)(d), see para 5.102. Proceedings under the Adoption and Children Bill 2002 will similarly rank as 'family proceedings'.
2   See eg the Department of Health's Guidance and Regulations, Vol l, Court Orders, para 2.64.

5.65   In adoption proceedings the issue of contact can arise in two contrasting ways, namely, as a competing application or for post adoption contact. With regard to the former, *G v G (Children: Concurrent Applications)*[1] establishes that the competing applications should be heard concurrently, though the principle of trying the issues together should not inhibit the court's discretion to deal with interlocutory or interim matters. When making an adoption order the court is empowered to make a condition of contact under s 12(6) of the Adoption Act 1976 or a contact order under s 8.[2] However, once the adoption order has been made the power to make any subsequent orders for contact is confined to s 8.

1   [1993] Fam 253, [1993] 2 WLR 837.
2   See *Clarke Hall and Morrison*, Division 3, paras [272] et seq. But note under the Adoption and Children Bill 2002 there will be no power to add conditions.

5.66   Although empowered to do so courts will not readily impose an order for contact against the wishes of the adopters,[1] and, where they are agreed that contact should continue it has been held[2] that there is no need for an order.[3] Once an adoption has been made the birth parents cease to be the legal parents and require court leave to apply for a contact order.[4] Leave will not readily be given; as Thorpe J said in *Re C (a Minor) (Adopted Child: Contact)*,[5] since an adoption order is intended to be final, a fundamental question such as contact should not be reopened unless there is a fundamental change of circumstances.[6]

1   Though in this regard a distinction might be drawn between providing for contact with siblings or other relatives and for contact with the parents, see *Re C (A Minor) (Adoption: Access)* [1989] AC 1, [1988] 1 All ER 705, HL.
2   *Re T (a minor) (contact order)* [1995] 2 FCR 537, [1995] 2 FLR 251, CA.
3   Though this is not to say that orders are never made: see eg *Re O (a minor) (adoption)* [1996] 1 FCR 540, sub nom *Re O (Transracial Adoption: Contact)* [1995] 2 FLR 597.
4   *Re C (A Minor) (Adopted Child: Contact)* [1993] Fam 210, [1993] 3 All ER 259.
5   Above at pp 216 and 264 respectively. It is submitted that a similar position obtains after the making of a freeing order. Birth parents, become 'former parents' and require court leave to

apply for a s 8 order: *Re C (Minors) (Adoption: Residence Order)* [1994] Fam 1, sub nom *Re C (minors) (parent: residence order)* [1993] 3 All ER 313, see para 5.110.
6 For the procedure see *Re T (Minors) (Adopted Children: Contact)* [1996] Fam 34, [1996] 1 All ER 215, CA, which established that in most cases it is sufficient to notify the local authority (if that was the adoption agency) of the application but that in some cases it might be necessary to transfer the case to the High Court and to bring in the Official Solicitor.

5.67 *Re R (a minor) (adoption: contact order)*[1] establishes that courts are empowered both to make an order freeing the child for adoption[2] and an order under s 8 to preserve contact between the child and the birth family pending the adoption.[3] However, in practice courts are reluctant to bind prospective adopters particularly where the child is already placed and so rarely make contact orders with freeing for adoption orders.[4]

1 [1994] 1 FCR 104, [1993] 2 FLR 645, CA.
2 For the meaning of which see *Clarke Hall and Morrison*, paras 3[251] et seq.
3 It should be noted that provision for contact can only be made under s 8 since s 12(6) of the Adoption Act 1976 has no application to freeing orders.
4 See *Re P (minors) (adoption: freeing order)* [1994] 2 FCR 1306, [1994] 2 FLR 1000, CA and *Re H (a minor) (adoption proceedings)* [1994] 2 FCR 437, [1993] 2 FLR 325, CA.

5.68 Once a freeing order has been made together with contact then unless an application for an adoption order has been made there are no proceedings on foot which means that the court has no power subsequently to vary the order.[1] Furthermore because of s 9(2)[2] the local authority is not entitled to apply to vary the order. In other words unless the person in whose favour the order has been made chooses to apply it is not normally possible to vary the contact order ahead of the adoption proceedings.[3]

1 *Re C (Minors) (Contact: Jurisdiction)* [1996] Fam 79, [1995] 2 FCR 701, [1995] 1 FLR 777, CA. On the facts, however, it was held that the Court of Appeal could, by exercising the powers of the High Court, vary the order. Sed quaere?
2 Discussed post, para 5.98.
3 Query whether the court should consider making a specific issue order rather than a contact order under s 8? This would then allow a local authority to apply, with leave, to vary the order, s 9(2) having no application to specific issue orders.

5.69 The precise nature of a contact order in relation to freeing might be speculated upon. If it is regarded as an order directing the person with whom the child lives or is to live to allow contact,[1] is such an order directed against the agency or the person who is actually looking after the child? If it is the latter what is the position if the child is subsequently placed with prospective adopters?

1 But see the arguments at para 5.47.

3. Prohibited steps order

5.70 A prohibited steps order:

'means an order that no step which could be taken by a parent in meeting his parental responsibility for a child, and which is of a kind specified in the order, shall be taken by any person without the consent of the court.'

This is one of the two orders under the CA 1989 (the other being a specific issue order, discussed below) modelled on the wardship jurisdiction and intended to broaden all courts' powers when dealing with children.

5.71 A prohibited steps order empowers a court to place a specific embargo upon the exercise of parental responsibility. This is in contrast to the vague requirement in wardship that no important step in the child's life be taken without the court's prior consent.[1] This order can be put to a variety of uses. It can, for example, be used to prohibit contact with a parent or someone else (discussed further below), restrain a particular operation, including the circumcision of a boy without the consent of the other parent or the court,[2] prevent the child's schooling or religion from being changed or to stop a parent from changing the child's name.[3] Another example, instanced by the Law Commission,[4] is to impose an embargo that the child should not be removed from the United Kingdom which they said might be useful in cases where no residence order had been made so that the automatic restrictions against removal under s 13 do not apply.[5] Even where the s 13 restrictions do apply it might still be possible to obtain a prohibited steps order to prevent repeated removal of children outside the United Kingdom for periods of less than one month by the residential parent. Furthermore since, s 13 only prevents removing a child outside the United Kingdom, if it is sought to prevent relocations *within* the country then a prohibited steps order must be sought, though as the Court of Appeal have emphasised in *Re S (a child) (residence order: condition)*[6] and *Re H (children) (residence order: condition)*[7] such orders will only be justified in exceptional circumstances.

1 Wardship is discussed in ch 12. It is assumed that an order as vague as prohibiting any important step could not be made as a prohibited steps order.
2 *Re J (child's religious upbringing and circumcision)* [1999] 2 FCR 345, sub nom *Re J (Specific Issue Orders: Muslim Upbringing and Circumcision)* [1999] 2 FLR 678, per Wall J, upheld an appeal at [2000] 1 FCR 307, [2000] 1 FLR 571, CA.
3 Note that under s 13(1)(a) a person with residence is not allowed to change the child's name without the consent of all those having parental responsibility or with leave of the court, see the discussion at paras 5.27 et seq.
4 Law Com No 172, para 4.20. This comment is repeated by the Department of Health's Guidance and Regulations, Vol 1, Court Orders, at para 2.31.
5 The embargo under s 13(1)(b) and (2) is discussed at paras 5.35 et seq. In the absence of a residence order the unilateral removal by a joint holder of parental responsibility can be an offence under the Child Abduction Act 1984.
6 [2001] EWCA Civ 847, [2001] 3 FCR 154, CA, discussed at para 5.44.
7 [2001] EWCA Civ 1338, [2001] 3 FCR 182, [2001] 2 FLR 1277, CA, discussed at para 5.44.

5.72 Although the order itself must relate to parental responsibility[1] it can be made against anyone regardless of whether they have parental responsibility. A prohibited steps order can, for example, be made against an unmarried father whether or not he has parental responsibility or against a third party, for example to restrain a former cohabitant from contacting or seeking to have contact.[2] An order can be made against non parties.[3] Provided the order is of some value to the applicant it can be made even though the child is abroad.[4] Applications for prohibited steps orders can be made ex parte[5] and an order may be made either in conjunction with another s 8 order or on its own.

1 See paras 5.75 et seq.
2 *Re H (minors) (prohibited steps order)* [1995] 4 All ER 110, [1995] 1 WLR 667, CA.
3 *Re H*, supra. Nevertheless such an order could not be enforced until it has been specifically served.
4 See *Re D (a minor) (child: removal from jurisdiction)* [1992] 1 All ER 892, [1992] 1 WLR 315, CA.
5 FPR 1991, r 4.4(4); FPC (Children Act 1989) R 1991, r 4(4). Such orders are sometimes made in the context of international child abduction, often at the request of the abducting parent, to prevent removal by the other. See eg *Re AZ (a minor) (abduction: acquiescence)* [1993] 1

FCR 733, [1993] 1 FLR 682; *Re B (Minors) (Abduction) (No 2)* [1993] 1 FLR 993; *D v D (child abduction: non convention country)* [1994] 1 FCR 654, [1994] 1 FLR 137 and *Re S (minors) (abduction)* [1993] 2 FCR 499, [1994] 1 FLR 297.

4. Specific issue order

5.73 A specific issue order:

> 'means an order giving directions for the purpose of determining a specific question which has arisen, or which may arise, in connection with any aspect of parental responsibility for a child.'

These orders enable a specific question relating to the child to be brought before the court, the aim of which is not to give one parent or the other a general 'right' to make decisions in a particular respect but to enable a particular issue to be settled.[1] It was held in *Re HG (a minor) (application for sterilisation)*[2] that there is no necessity for there to be a dispute between the parties before the power arises to make a specific issue order; it is sufficient that there is a question to be answered. In that case an unopposed application[3] for a specific issue order was granted giving High Court sanction for the sterilisation of a 17-year-old mentally subnormal child.

1   Department of Health's Guidance and Regulations, Vol 1, Court Orders, para 2.32.
2   [1993] 1 FCR 533, sub nom *Re HG (Specific Issue Order: Sterilisation)* [1993] 1 FLR 587.
3   The application was thought necessary in view of Lord Templeman's lone dictum in *Re B (a Minor) (Wardship: Sterilisation)* [1988] AC 199 at 205, [1987] 2 All ER 206 at 214 that High Court sanction is always required for a child's sterilisation. See also *Practice Note* [1993] 3 All ER 222.

5.74 Applications for specific issue orders may be made ex parte[1] and orders may be made either in conjunction with another s 8 order or on their own. Examples of specific issue orders include *Re R (a minor) (medical treatment)*[2] in which the court ordered inter alia that in an imminently life-threatening situation, the child in question be given a blood transfusion without the consent of her parents who were Jehovah's Witnesses; *Re F (minors) (solicitors' interviews)*,[3] in which an order was made permitting a defence solicitor to interview children for the purpose of providing evidence in criminal proceedings against their father; *Re D (a minor) (child removal from jurisdiction)*[4] in which a mother was ordered to return the child to the jurisdiction, and *Re A (children) (specific issue order: parental dispute)*,[5] in which the court made a specific issue order at the French father's request that notwithstanding that following the parent's separation they were now living with their English mother in England, the two children should attend the Lycée Français in London. Specific issue orders can also be brought to resolve disputes over a child's religious upbringing,[6] to inform children about their father's paternity and even very existence,[7] and, provided no residence order is in force,[8] to obtain court leave to change a child's name[9] or to take the child out of the United Kingdom.[10]

1   FPR 1991, r 4.4(4); FPC (Children Act 1989) R 1991, r 4(4). For an example of an order being made ex parte see *Re D (a minor) (child removal from jurisdiction)* [1992] 1 All ER 892, [1992] 1 WLR 315, CA.
2   [1993] 2 FCR 544, sub nom *Re R (A Minor) (Blood Transfusion)* [1993] 2 FLR 757. See also *Re C (HIV Test)* [1999] 2 FLR 1004, CA – in which a specific issue order was granted that a baby be tested for HIV.

3 [1995] 2 FCR 200, sub nom *Re F (Specific Issue: Child Interview)* [1995] 1 FLR 819, CA. See also *Re M (minors) (solicitors' interviews)* [1995] 2 FCR 643, sub nom *Re M (Care: Leave to Interview Child)* [1995] 1 FLR 825, discussed at para 3.25.
4 Supra.
5 [2001] 1 FCR 210, [2001] 1 FLR 121, CA. For a pre-Children Act example of a dispute about a child's education that would now be resolved by a specific issue order see *Re P (A Minor) (Education)* [1992] 1 FLR 316, CA.
6 See eg *Re J (child's religious upbringing and circumcision)* [1999] FCR 345, sub nom *Re J (Specific Issue Orders: Muslim Upbringing and Circumcision)* [1999] 2 FLR 678 in which a father unsuccessfully sought a specific issue order requiring the non Muslim mother to raise the child as a Muslim – not appealed on this point see [2000] 1 FCR 307, [2000] 1 FLR 571, CA.
7 See *Re K (Specific Issue Order)* [1999] 2 FLR 280, in which the application was unsuccessful.
8 Note where there is a residence order in force, then leave applications should be made under s 13, see *Re B (minors) (change of surname)* [1996] 2 FCR 304, [1996] 1 FLR 791, CA, discussed at para 5.29.
9 See eg *Dawson v Wearmouth* [1999] 2 AC 308, [1999] 2 All ER 353, HL and *Re W (A Child) (Illegitimate Child: Change of Surname)* [2001] Fam 1, [2000] 2 WLR 258, CA, discussed at paras 5.30 et seq.
10 *Re D (a minor) (child: removal from jurisdiction)* [1992] 1 All ER 892, [1992] 1 WLR 667 and see paras 5.35 et seq.

5. Limits on the court's powers to make prohibited steps and specific issue orders

Orders must relate to parental responsibility

5.75 An important limitation both on prohibited steps and specific issue orders is that they must concern an aspect of parental responsibility. Courts cannot, therefore, make a prohibited steps order forbidding contact between parents,[1] or protecting one parent from being assaulted by the other[2] nor can a specific issue order be made to compel a local authority to provide support services,[3] since neither contact between adults nor the provision of support services has anything to do with parental responsibility.

1 *Croydon London Borough Council v A* [1992] Fam 169, [1992] 3 All ER 788, but see *F v R (Contact)* [1995] 1 FLR 227 in which Wall J accepted that such an embargo could nevertheless be incorporated as a condition to a residence or contact order under s 11(7), though this decision is now difficult to square with *Re D (a minor) (contact: conditions)* [1997] 3 FCR 721, sub nom *D v N (Contact Order: Conditions)* [1997] 2 FLR 797, CA, discussed at para 5.94.
2 *M v M (Residence Order: Ancillary Jurisdiction)* [1994] Fam Law 440 but note that Johnson J also held that an injunction could nevertheless be sought under the appropriate family protection legislation, as an ancillary action to the Children Act application. Note that by s 42(1)(b) of the Family Law Act 1996, the court has power to make a non-molestation order of its own notion in any 'family proceedings', which by s 63 includes proceedings under Pt I, II and IV of the Children Act 1989.
3 *Re J (specific issue order: leave to apply)* [1995] 3 FCR 799, [1995] 1 FLR 669.

5.76 The initial assumption[1] that neither a prohibited steps order restricting, nor a specific issue order sanctioning publicity about a child could be made, since that could not be considered to be an aspect of parental responsibility, was reflected in the majority view in *Re W (minors) (continuation of wardship).*[2] However, this view has not gone unchallenged. In particular, note needs to be taken of Hobhouse LJ's well-reasoned dissenting judgment in *Re W*[3] that determinig whether an immature child should become involved with the media 'falls within the scope of the proper discharge of parental duties', and of the Court of Appeal decision in *Re Z (A Minor) (Identification: Restriction on Publication)*,[4] in which a prohibited steps order restraining publicity was made upon the basis that the mother's waiver of the child's right of confidentiality to the particular information (viz the attendance at a specialist unit dealing with children's educational needs) was an aspect of parental responsibility.

1 See Department of Health's *Guidance and Regulations*, Vol, *Court Orders* at para 2.31, and more recently, the *Guidance* to the Northern Ireland Order, Vol 1, *Court Orders and Other Legal Issues,* para 5.17.
2 [1996] 1 FCR 393, sub nom *Re W (Wardship: Discharge: Publicity)* [1995] 2 FLR 466.
3 Above at 404 and 476 respectively.
4 [1997] Fam 1, sub nom *Re Z (a minor) (freedom of publication)* [1995] 4 All ER 961, CA. For analysis of this decision, see inter alia, *Kelly v BBC* [2001] Fam 59, [2001] 1 All ER 323 [2001] 2 WLR 253, per Munby J and *Medway Council v BBC* [2001] 1 FLR 104, per Wilson J.

No power to make ouster or occupation orders

5.77 In *Nottingham County Council v P* Sir Stephen Brown P commented that 'it is very doubtful indeed whether a prohibited steps order could in any circumstances be used to 'oust' a father from a matrimonial home.'[1] Similarly, in *Pearson v Franklin*[2] Nourse LJ commented that Parliament could not have intended that ouster orders are capable of being made under the guise of specific issue orders. It was therefore held that a specific issue order (and by implication a prohibited steps order) could not be used to interfere with rights of occupation. In *Re M (minors) (disclosure of evidence)*,[3] *Nottingham* was taken to have established that there is no jurisdiction under the Children Act to exclude a parent from the home for the protection of the child, and in *D v D (ouster order)*[4] Ward LJ clearly stated that there is no jurisdiction to make an ouster order under the Children Act.[5] Aside from justifying this position as a matter of policy (ie that because of their draconian effect Parliament should be taken to confer the power to make ouster orders only where a statute clearly so provides) a possible theoretical justification for this lack of power is that ouster orders relate to matters of occupation rather than parental responsibility.[6]

1 [1994] Fam 18 at 39 E–F, [1993] 3 All ER 815 at 825b, CA.
2 [1994] 2 All ER 137, [1994] 1 WLR 370, CA.
3 [1995] 2 FCR 1, [1994] 1 FLR 760, CA.
4 [1996] 2 FCR 496, sub nom [1996] 2 FLR 281. Both these *Re D (Prohibited Steps Order)* [1996] 2 FLR 273, CA. See also *Re D (Minors) (Residence: Conditions)*[1996] 2 FCR 820,cases also establish that the inability to make an ouster order cannot be overcome by using s 11(7), see below at paras 5.88 et seq. See also *Re D (a Minor) (Contact Orders: Conditions)* [1997] 3 FCR 721, sub nom *Re D (a Minor) (Contact Orders: Conditions)* [1997] 3 FLR 797, CA, discussed at para 5.90.
5 Though probably an application for an application for an occupation order under Pt IV of the Family Law Act 1996 can be brought as an ancillary action to the Children Act application – cf *M v M (Residence Order: Ancillary Injunction)* [1994] Fam Law 440, discussed above at paras 5.75, n2. For the power to make an ouster order under the High Court's inherent jurisdiction see para 12.32, and upon making an emergency protection or interim care order, see paras 7.47–7.48 and 8.32–8.33 respectively.
6 This line of argument was hinted at by Nourse LJ in *Pearson v Franklin*, supra, but it is not beyond question since ouster orders are viewed as being primarily about protection and only incidentally about occupation.

No power to make disguised residence or contact orders

5.78 Section 9(5)(a) prevents the court from making a specific issue or a prohibited steps order 'with a view to achieving a result which could be achieved by a residence or contact order.' This provision was made to guard against the slight risk, particularly in uncontested cases, that the orders might be used to achieve the same practical results as residence or contact orders but without the same legal effects.[1]

1 Law Com No 172, para 4.19. Department of Health's Guidance and Regulations, Vol 1, Court Orders, para 2.34.

5.79 A clear example of the type of order forbidden by s 9(5)(a) is *M v C (children orders: reasons)*[1] in which justices purported to make a specific issue order returning the children to their mother which could and should have been achieved by a residence order. However, other examples are less obvious. For instance, in *Re B (Minors) (Residence Order)*[2] it was held that s 9(5)(a) operates to prevent the making of a specific issue order to return a child to a parent in the case of a snatch since such an order could be made by means of a residence order with appropriate conditions attached under s 11(7).[3] In *Nottingham County Council v P*[4] it was held to be contrary to s 9(5)(a) to order, upon a local authority application under s 8, that a father vacate the household and that the child should have no further contact with him save under local authority supervision since the application patently sought to determine the residence of the children (that is, by regulating who could live in the household) and the degree of contact which the children might have with the father. In this latter regard the Court of Appeal rejected the argument that an order for 'no contact' could not be made as a contact order under s 8.[5] However, in *Re H (minors) (prohibited steps orders)*,[6] the Court of Appeal subsequently held that a prohibited steps order restricting a former cohabitant from contacting or seeking contact with the children did not contravene s 9(5) since unlike an order for no contact under s 8 it could properly be directed and enforced against the man rather than the mother.

1 [1993] 1 FCR 264, [1993] 2 FLR 584.
2 [1992] Fam 162, [1992] 3 All ER 867, CA. Cf *Re D (a Minor) (Child: Removal From Jurisdiction)* [1992] 1 All ER 892, [1992] 1 WLR 315 in which a specific issue order was made ordering a parent abroad to return the child to the jurisdiction.
3 The power to add conditions etc under s 11(7) is discussed at paras 5.84 et seq.
4 [1994] Fam 18, [1993] 3 All ER 815, CA.
5 See para 5.53.
6 [1995] 4 All ER 110, [1995] 1 WLR 667, CA.

No power to make orders that are denied to the High Court acting under its inherent jurisdiction

5.80 Section 9(5)(b) prevents the court from exercising its power to make a specific issue or prohibited steps order 'in any way which is denied to the High Court (by s 100(2)) in the exercise of its inherent jurisdiction.'[1] According to the Department of Health's Guidance and Regulations,[2] s 9(5)(b) prevents local authorities applying for a prohibited steps or specific issue order as a way of obtaining (a) the care or supervision of a child; (b) an order that the child be accommodated by them or (c) any aspect of parental responsibility. In *Re S and D (Child Care: Powers of Court)*[3] it was held that by reason of s 9(5)(b) and s 100(2)(b) there was no power to restrain a parent from removing the child from local authority accommodation[4] pursuant to the rights conferred by s 20(7). It must also follow that there is similarly no power to restrain a parent from objecting to his child being accommodated in the first place pursuant to the right conferred by s 20(7).[5]

1 The inherent jurisdiction is discussed in ch 12.
2 Vol 1, Court Orders, para 2.33.
3 [1995] 1 FCR 626, sub nom *Re S and D (Children: Powers of Court)* [1995] 2 FLR 456, CA.
4 Accommodation is discussed in ch 6. For the position where one parent seeks to prevent the other from objecting see para 5.160.
5 Discussed at para 6.33. Query whether it is possible for a prohibited steps order to be made upon the parent's application to prevent the other parent from objecting to the child's accommodation?

Local authorities not to regard prohibited steps or specific issue orders as a substitute for an order under part iv' the 'nottingham' decision

5.81 Notwithstanding their entitlement to seek leave to apply for a prohibited steps or specific issue order in respect of a child *not* in their care,[1] *Nottingham County Council v P*[2] establishes that where intervention is thought necessary to protect children from significant harm authorities must take direct action under Pt IV of the CA 1989[3] rather than seeking to invoke the court's powers under Pt II. In that case, following allegations of sexual abuse made against her father by the eldest daughter, the local authority obtained emergency protection orders in respect of two younger children. The father voluntarily left the family home leaving the two girls residing with their mother. The local authority, resisting judicial encouragement to bring care proceedings,[4] persisted in their application for a prohibited steps order[5] requiring the father neither to reside in the same household as the girls nor to have any contact with them unless they wished it. In rejecting their application, Sir Stephen Brown P commented:[6]

> 'We consider that this court should make it clear that the route chosen by the local authority in this case was wholly inappropriate. In cases where children are found to be at risk of suffering significant harm within the meaning of s 31 of the Children Act 1989 a clear duty arises on the part of local authorities to take steps to protect them. In such circumstances a local authority is required to assume responsibility and to intervene in the family arrangements in order to protect the child. A prohibited steps order would not afford the local authority any authority as to how it might deal with the children. There may be situations for example, where a child is accommodated by a local authority, where it would be appropriate to seek a prohibited steps order for some particular purpose. However, it could not in any circumstances be regarded as providing a substitute for an order under Pt IV of the CA 1989.'

1 See post, para 5.98.
2 [1994] Fam 18, [1993] 3 All ER 815, CA.
3 Ie by initiating care proceedings, for which see ch 8.
4 Both Judge Heald, at first instance, and Ward J had made s 37 directions.
5 For which they had been granted leave to apply.
6 [1994] Fam at 39, [1993] 3 All ER at 824. In any event it was doubted whether there was any power to make an ouster order under s 8. For a critique of this decision see inter alia Cobley and Lowe: 'Ousting Abusers'Public or Private Law Solution?' (1994) 110 LQR 38.

5.82 In *F v Cambridgeshire County Council*[1] a father, a Sch 1 offender, sought limited contact with his children who were living with their mother. The local authority were opposed to the father having contact but did not themselves seek a care order since they accepted that the mother was able to look after the children properly. Stuart-White J held, following Nottingham, that unless and until the s 31 threshold had been met, the local authority could not intervene in family life and hence leave to join as a party to private law proceedings should be refused.

1 [1995] 2 FCR 804, [1995] 1 FLR 516. Query whether this embargo could be overcome by invoking wardship proceedings? Cf *Re RJ (Minors) (Fostering: Wardship)* [1999] 3 FCR 646, [1999] 1 FLR 618, discussed at para 12.18.

5.83 Although the *Nottingham* ruling clearly restricts local authorities seeking prohibited steps or specific issue orders even in respect of children they are 'looking after' but who are not in care, it should not be read as establishing that such orders should never be sought. They might be appropriate, for example, where there is concern about a specific aspect of a parent's care of a child and the authority while not wanting to seek a care order nevertheless wishes to protect the child.[1] The classic example is where the authority is concerned about the child's medical treatment. In *Re C (HIV Test)*,[2] the local authority successfully applied for a specific issue order that a baby born to an HIV positive mother be tested for HIV. Similarly, in *Re R (a Minor) (Medical Treatment)*[3] in which a local authority successfully applied for a specific issue order to sanction a blood transfusion for a child contrary to his parent's (who were Jehovah's Witnesses) wishes.

1 See eg Herring *Family Law* 496.
2 [1999] 2 FLR 1004, CA.
3 [1993] 2 FCR 544, sub nom *Re R (a Minor) (Blood Transfusion)* [1993] 2 FLR 757, discussed also at para 12.35.

6. Additional directions and conditions

5.84 The power to make interim orders, to delay implementation or to attach other special conditions is contained in s 11(7),[1] which provides that a s 8 order may:

(a) contain directions as to how the order is to be carried out;
(b) impose conditions to be complied with by any person in whose favour the order has been made or any parent or any non-parent who has parental responsibility, or any parent with whom the child is living;
(c) specify the period for which the order or any provision in it is to have effect; and
(d) make such incidental, supplemental or consequential provision as the court thinks fit.

These powers are exercisable by any court making a s 8 order.

1 Occasionally, however, courts accept undertakings rather than imposing conditions. See eg *Re R (a Minor) (Religious Sect)* [1993] 2 FCR 525, sub nom *Re R (a Minor) (Residence: Religion)*, [1993] 2 FLR 163, CA, aunt granted contact on the undertaking that she would not speak or communicate with the child in any way in relation to religious or spiritual matters.

Directions and limited duration orders

5.85 The power under s 11(7)(a) to give directions as to how an order is to be put into effect is designed[1] to enable the court to smooth the transition in cases, for example, where the child's residence is changed or to define more precisely what contact is to take place under a contact order. It also provides a means by which a first instance court can stay an order, for example by directing that any transfer of residence be delayed pending an appeal.[2]

1 See Law Com, No 172, para 4.22.
2 See *Re J (a Minor) (Residence)* [1993] 2 FCR 636 at 642,[1994] 1 FLR 369 at 375, per Singer J.

5.86 The power under s 11(7)(c) to specify the period for which a s 8 order, or any provision in it, is to have effect is intended[1] to empower the court inter alia to make what are effectively interim orders (although the Act itself does not make a rigid distinction between 'interim' and 'final' orders under s 8).[2] Accordingly, the court can make an order for a limited duration coupled with a direction that the matter be brought back to court at a later specific date. This type of order could be useful in cases where more information is required[3] or to allow time to monitor the effectiveness of, for example, contact arrangements.[4] Another use of a limited duration order might be to make a holding order pending an appeal.

1 Law Com No 172, para 4.24.
2 See, for example, para 5.20 for discussion of 'interim' residence orders.
3 Under s 11(3) courts can make a s 8 order even though they are not in a position finally to dispose of proceedings.
4 As in *Re B (a Minor) (Interim Order for Contact)* [1994] 1 FCR 905, [1994] 2 FLR 269.

Conditions and other supplemental orders

5.87 At first sight, the power under s 11(7)(b) and (d) to add conditions and to make such incidental, supplemental or consequential provision as is thought fit gives the court considerable scope for making a wide range of supporting provisions for s 8 orders. However, in recommending what were described as 'supplemental provisions' the Law Commission specifically said[1] that they did 'not expect these supplemental powers to be used at all frequently, as most cases will not require them and all are subject to the general rule that orders should only be made where they are the most effective means of safeguarding or promoting the child's welfare. The Commission instanced[2] three examples of when they could be useful, namely:

(1) in the case of a dispute about which school the child should attend, making it a condition of a residence order that the child attend a particular school;
(2) where there is a real fear that on a contact visit the parent will remove the child from the country and not return him, making it a condition of the contact order that any such removal is prohibited;[3] and
(3) where there is real concern that the person with whom the child will live will not agree to a blood transfusion, making it a condition of the residence order to require the parent to inform the other parent so that the latter can agree to it.[4]

1   Law Com No 178, para 4.21. All that the *Guidance and Regulations,* Vol 1, *Court Orders* at
    para 2.22 states is that the supplemental etc powers 'enable the new orders [ie s 8 orders] to be
    as flexible as possible and so reduce or remove the need to resort to wardship.'.
2   Above, at para 4.23.
3   Lord Mackay LC at 505 HL Official Report (5th Series) col 345 envisaged conditions being
    imposed forbidding a parent from moving the child to another town. But cf *Re S (a Child)
    (Residence Order: Condition)* [2001] EWCA Civ 847, [2001] 3 FCR 154, CA and *Re E
    (Minors) (Residence: Conditions)* [1997] 3 FCR 245, [1997] 2 FLR 638, CA, discussed below
    at para 5.91.
4   Cf the pre-Children Act decision, *Jane v Jane* (1983) 4 FLR 712, CA, in which effectively the
    father was given the power to consent to medical treatment but the mother (a Jehovah's
    Witness) looked after the child.

5.88   Notwithstanding the intention that they should have a limited role,
these provisions have generated considerable case law and even now their
full ambit cannot be stated with certainty. Indeed, in *Re D (a Minor)
(Contact: Conditions)*[1]Sir Stephen Brown P commented (in the context of
imposing conditions on a contact order) 'that it may be necessary for a court in
the future to give further consideration to the true nature, meaning and effect
of conditions imposed under s 11(7)'. Nevertheless certain things are clear.
First, s 11(7) only vests ancillary or supportive powers to those under s 8. It does
not therefore give completely novel and independent powers to make, for example,
conditions about the parties' finances or property ownership. It is on this basis,
for instance, that it is established that s 11(7) cannot be used to interfere with
rights of occupation, for, as Ward LJ said in *D v D (Ouster Order)*[2]

> 'Section 11(7), in my judgment, is ancillary to the making of a s 8 order. It is gov-
> erned by the provisions for the making of a s 8 order and does not allow the
> importation by the back door of the matters laid down in the Matrimonial Homes
> Act[3] or proper adjustment or rights of occupation.'

Secondly, as with all Pt II powers, s 11(7) is governed by the paramountcy
principle and should only be invoked where the child's welfare requires.[4]
Thirdly, as s 11(7)(b) itself expressly states, conditions may only be imposed
on the persons there listed and, according to Booth J in *Leeds County Council
v C*[5] the power to make incidental etc orders under s 11(7)(d) is similarly confined.[6] Consequently as they are not listed, there is no power under s 11(7) to
order contact to be supervised by a local authority. Nevertheless, the list is
wide and enables the courts to impose obligations not only upon the person
in whose favour the s 8 order is made, but also upon any parent,[9] any other
person who has parental responsibility, or any other person with whom the
child is living. Furthermore, provided the person is included in the list it is no
objection that he is not a party.[9]

1   [1997] 3 FCR 721 at 726–727, sub nom *D v N (Contact Order: Conditions)* [1997] 2 FLR 797
    at 802, CA.
2   [1996] 2 FCR 496, at 502–503, sub nom *Re D (Prohibited Steps Order)* [1996] 2 FLR 273 at
    279, CA.
3   Now repealed and replaced by Pt IV of the Family Law Act 1996.
4   See Law Com No. 172 at para 4.21.
5   [1993] 1 FCR 585, [1993] 1 FLR 269. See also *Re M (Judge's Discretion)* [2001] EWCA Civ
    1428, [2002] 1 FLR 730, CA.
6   As Booth J pointed out, above at 590 and 273 respectively, if it were not, then s 11(7)(b)
    would be unnecessary. See also *Re DH (a Minor) (Care Proceedings: Evidence and Orders)*
    [1994] 2 FCR 3 at 41, sub nom *Re DH (a Minor) (Child Abuse)* [1994] 1 FLR 679 at 700–1,
    per Wall J.
7   In Booth J's view the appropriate remedy is a family assistance order, discussed post, paras
    5.143 et seq.

8 Including, therefore, the unmarried father who does not have parental responsibility for the child.
9 See *Re H and Others (Minors) (Prohibited Steps Order)* [1995] 4 All ER 110, [1995] 1 WLR 667, discussed at para 5.53, in which it was held that when making a prohibited steps order against a non-party there was power under s 11(7)(d) to give that person liberty to apply on notice to vary or discharge the order.

5.89 With regard to residence orders courts seemed at first prepared to interpret s 11(7) widely. *In Re B (a Minor) (Residence Order)*,[1] Butler-Sloss LJ, having referred to the powers under s 11(7)(a) to add directions, commented:

> 'Speaking for myself, I read that very broadly as giving the judge who makes a residence order the jurisdiction to attach conditions or directions which I think are very much the same thing, as to how the children should be cared for and where they should be once the residence order has been made.'

She accordingly held that s 11(7) empowered a court, when making a residence order, to require a child to be returned; to direct the return of the child to the former matrimonial home and to the interim care of one parent, and to direct that the child remain with that parent pending the full inter partes hearing. It has become apparent, however, that a significant restriction on the application of s 11(7) is that the condition must not be incompatible with the residence order itself. In *Birmingham City Council v H*[2], Ward J refused to make a residence order with the conditions that the mother was to live at a particular unit and that she should comply with all reasonable instructions from the unit's staff, perhaps even to hand over the child to the care of the staff. As he pointed out, this latter condition was tantamount to saying that some other person could assume parental responsibility, which was clearly inconsistent with the residence order to which the condition would have been attached.

1 [1992] Fam 162 at 165; [1992] 3 All ER 867 at 869, CA.
2 [1993] 1 FCR 247, [1992] 2 FLR 323; cf *Re C (a Minor) (Care Proceedings)* [1992] 2 FCR 341, sub nom *C v Solihull Metropolitan Borough Council* [1993] 1 FLR 290 in which Ward J made a residence order conditional upon the parents undertaking a programme of assessment, and co-operating with all reasonable requests by the local authority to participate in that programme.

5.90 The point has been developed in three Court of Appeal decisions. In the first, *Re D (Minors) (Residence: Conditions)*,[1] a consent order was made under which two children were returned to live with their mother (they had previously been living with their paternal grandmother) on condition that she did not in the interim bring the children into contact with a former partner, nor allow him to reside at her current address or such other address as she may reside with the children. Subsequently, the mother applied to the court to allow her former partner to reside at her home. At first instance, the application was refused, but on appeal the Court of Appeal considered the judge had failed to look at the matter as a contested residence application and remitted the case for a full consideration of the competing claims of the mother and the father and grandmother. In so concluding Ward LJ commented that the:[2]

> '. . . case concerned a mother seeking, as she was entitled to, to allow this man back into her life because that is the way she wished to live it. *The court was not in a position so to override her right to live her life as she chose.* What was before the court was whether, if she chose to have him back, the proper person with whom the children

should reside was herself or whether it would be better for the children that they lived with their father or with the grandmother' (emphasis added).

1 [1996] 2 FCR 820, [1996] 2 FLR 281.
2 Above at 823 and 284 respectively.

5.91 This restrictive view was followed in *Re E (Minors) (Residence: Condition)*[1], in which it was held that s 11(7) did not empower a court to impose upon the carer of a child the condition that he or she should reside at a particular address, since such a restriction 'sits uneasily with the general understanding of what is meant by a residence order'. As Butler-Sloss LJ explained:[2]

'A general imposition of conditions on residence orders was clearly not contemplated by Parliament and where the parent is entirely suitable and the court intends to make a residence order in favour of that parent, a condition of residence is in my view and unwarranted imposition upon the right of the parent to choose where he/she will live within the UK or with whom'.

However, her Ladyship added:

'There may be exceptional cases, for instance, where the court, in the private law context, has concerns about the ability of the parent to be granted a residence order to be a satisfactory carer but there is no better solution than to place the child with that parent. The court might consider it necessary to keep some control over the parent by way of conditions which include a condition of residence. Again, in public law cases involving local authorities, where a residence order may be made by the court in preference to a care order, s 11(7) conditions might be applied in somewhat different circumstances.'

1 [1997] 3 FCR 245, [1997] 2 FLR 638.
2 Above at 250 and 642 respectively.

5.92 In the third decision, *Re S (a Child) (Residence Order: Condition)*[1] Thorpe LJ considered that:

'in defining the possibility of exception [in *Re E*] Butler-Sloss LJ was guarding against the danger of never saying never in family litigation. The whole tenor of her judgment is plain to me, in that she was giving the clearest guide to courts of trial that, whereas it was not safe to say never in cases in which the imposition of such a condition would be justified, it would be highly exceptional and probably restricted to a case, as yet unforeseen and may be difficult to foresee, in which the ability of the primary carer to perform to a satisfactory level required the buttress of a s 11(7) order'.

In Thorpe LJ's view[2] Butler-Sloss LJ's judgment in *Re E* was not to be interpreted as giving trial judges a 'general latitude to strive for some sort of ideal over and above the rival proposals of the available primary carers'. It was accordingly held that the judge had been wrong to grant the mother a residence order in respect of a Down's Syndrome child coupled with a condition that she should reside in Croydon although the matter was remitted to the first instance court for further investigation.

1 [2001] EWCA Civ 847, para [24], [2001] 3 FCR 154 at 160.
2 Above at para [25].

5.93 These decisions make it clear that, in the private law context particularly, it will be difficult to justify imposing on any residence order conditions restricting the care-giver's movements and choice of where and with whom to live. Instead, the proper approach is to consider whether it is right to make the residence order in the first place. No doubt there will be some exceptional cases where such conditions could be justified. In *Re H (Children) (Residence Order: Condition)*[1] it was considered justifiable to couple a residence order with a prohibited steps order to prevent he father taking the children to Northern Ireland, inter alia, because their sense of loss of their mother as a close and regular contact would be akin to a bereavement. Furthermore, as Butler-Sloss LJ indicated in *Re E*,[2] tighter restrictions may be justified in the public law context in which, given the choice between local authority care and a residence order, it might be right to opt for the latter, provided the court is given some degree of control. In this context note might also be taken of *Re KDT (a Minor)*,[3] in which rather than make a care order the court made both a supervision order and a residence order, coupling the latter with a condition that the father was not to share a bed with the child in any circumstances. In adding the latter condition the court was aware of the practicalities of enforcing any such order, but given the rigorous scrutiny which the court was confident that the local authority would exercise, it felt that any breach was likely to come to the authority's attention and as such the condition was 'a useful addition to the child protection measures already in force.'

1   [2001] EWCA Civ 1338, [2001] 3 FCR 192, [2001] 2 FLR 1277, CA.
2   [1997] 3 FCR 245 at 250, [1997] 2 FLR 638 at 642.
3   [1994] 2 FCR 721, sub nom *Re T (a Minor) (Care Order: Conditions)* [1994] 2 FLR 423, CA.

5.94   In contrast to residence orders there seems to be a greater latitude to attach conditions to contact orders. In *Re O (a Minor) (Contact: Indirect Contact)*[1] Sir Thomas Bingham MR considered that ss 8 and 11(7) give the court a wide and comprehensive power to make orders and set conditions which effectively ensure and facilitate contact between the child and the non-residential parent. Disagreeing with an earlier decision of Wall J in *Re M (a Minor) (Contact: Conditions)*,[2] his Lordship held that whilst judges should not impose duties which parents could not realistically be expected to perform, they could compel the person with a residence order and who is hostile to contact to read the other parent's communications with the child without censorship. It was also held to be wrong to place unnecessary limits on the number of letters the absent parent could send.[3] Subsequently in *F v R (Contact: Justices' Reasons)*[4] Wall J approved an agreed condition to an indirect contact order that the father was not to contact or enter a day centre or school at which the child was a pupil without either the mother's or the court's prior permission. It might also be possible to make an order for supervised contact provided the supervisor is one of the persons listed in s 11(7)(b).[5] There are, however, limits about what can be imposed. In *Re D (a Minor) (Contact: Conditions)*[6] it was held that when making an order for defined contact it was wholly inappropriate to use s 11(7) to make orders (inter alia forbidding the father to molest the mother or her relatives, from entering or damaging certain premises belonging to those relatives, or from corresponding with the mother's employers) which related more to the protection of the mother from perceived harassment than to the management of contact.

1   [1996] 1 FCR 317, sub nom *Re O (Contact: Imposition of Conditions)* [1995] 2 FLR 124, CA.
2   [1994] 1 FCR 678, [1994] 1 FLR 272.

3 Ie disagreeing with Wall J's ruling in *Re M*, supra, that orders permitting absent parents to write to or telephone a child should be carefully defined and usually expressed by reference to a maximum 'not more than' formula.
4 [1995] 1 FLR 227.
5 See para 5.88.
6 [1997] 3 FCR 721, sub nom *D v N (Contact Order: Conditions)* [1997] 2 FLR 797, CA.

5.95 The restraints on making s 8 orders in the public law context apply equally to the exercise of the supplemental powers under s 11(7). As Balcombe LJ observed in *D v D (Child Case: Powers of Court)*:[1]

'. . . s 11, just as much as s 8, falls within Pt II (the private law part) of the CA 1989 and those words cannot be construed as giving the court a power to interfere with the exercise by other bodies[2] of their statutory or common law powers, whether derived from other parts of the CA 1989 or elsewhere.'

Similarly, as *Nottingham County Council v P*[3] shows, courts should not use their s 11(7) powers, even when acting on their own motion, effectively allowing local authorities to intervene in family life under the Act's private law provisions.

1 [1994] 3 FCR 28 at 41, sub nom *D v D (County Court: Jurisdiction: Powers of Court)* [1993] 2 FLR 802 at 813, CA.
2 Ie, in this case, the local authority and the police.
3 [1994] Fam 18, [1993] 3 All ER 815, CA, discussed ante at paras 5.81 et seq.

7.   Restrictions on making s 8 orders

(a)   Children aged sixteen or over

5.96 Section 9(7) and (6) respectively provide that a s 8 order (other than a variation or discharge) should not be made in respect of a child who has attained the age of sixteen, nor should any order be expressed to have effect beyond a child's sixteenth birthday, unless the court is satisfied that the 'circumstances' of the case are exceptional'.[1] The Act itself gives no guidance on what ranks as 'exceptional' but the Department of Health's Guidance and Regulations gives as an example a case where the child concerned is mentally handicapped.[2] In *Re M (a Minor) (Immigration: Residence Order)*[3] it was held the requirement of 'exceptional circumstances' was satisfied in the case of a child who had no relatives in this country and who needed protection into adulthood. In *Re B (a Child) (Sole Adoption by Unmarried Father)*[4] Hale LJ considered that extending an order until eighteen was most likely to be appropriate where a child is living with a person, such as a relative or foster parent who does not otherwise have parental responsibility and it is contemplated that the child will stay with that person for the rest of their childhood.[5] Orders not expressed to extend beyond the child's sixteenth birthday automatically end when he reaches sixteen.[6] Where a direction is made, the order will cease to have effect when the child reaches the age of eighteen.[7] Under the Adoption and Children Bill 2002 courts will be empowered to direct, when making a residence order (but not any other s 8 order) in favour of a person who is not the parent or guardian and at that person's request, that the order continues in force until the age of eighteen. Unlike the general power to extend an order beyond the child's sixteenth birthday this power will not be subject to the requirement that there be 'exceptional circumstances'.

1   As Butler-Sloss LJ pointed out in *Re B (Minors) (Application for Contact)* [1994] 2 FCR 812 at 818, [1994] 2 FLR 1 at 6, CA, although there is no equivalent restriction 'for contact in the public law area under s 34' in practice, a similar regime operates.
2   Vol 1, Court Orders, para 2.49. The Law Commission, above at para 3.25, whilst holding to the view that circumstances where it is right to make an order will be rare, instanced the case in which it is necessary to protect an older child from the consequences of immaturity, citing *Re SW (a Minor) (Wardship: Jurisdiction)* [1986] 1 FLR 24 where a 17 year-old girl was made a ward for the few remaining months of her minority in an attempt to control her behaviour.
3   [1995] 2 FCR 793, [1993] 2 FLR 858, per Bracewell J. Order expressed to last until child's 18th birthday.
4   [2001] 1 FCR 600, para (22) at 606–607, sub nom *Re B (Adoption by One Natural Parent to Exclusion of Other)* [2001] 1 FLR 589 at 594–595, CA. But note the decision to grant a residence order rather than the adoption was subsequently reversed by the House of Lords, see [2001] UKHL 70, [2001] 1 FCR 150, [2002] 1 FLR 196, though the point made in the text was not commented upon.
5   Though these circumstances will be accommodated by the prospective new power to extend a residence order under the amendments to be introduced by the Adoption and Children Bill 2002, discussed below.
6   Section 91(10).
7   Section 91(11).

(b)   Children in local authority care

5.97   Section 9(1) prevents the court from making a s 8 order, other than a residence order, with respect to a child who is already the subject of a local authority care order.[1] We discuss the full impact of this provision in chapter 8.

1   But note there is no embargo against a s 8 contact being made at the behest of a child in care for contact with siblings who are not in care: *Re F (a Minor) (Contact: Child in Care)* [1994] 2 FCR 1354, [1995] 1 FLR 510.

(c)   Restrictions in the case of local authorities

5.98   Section 9(2) prevents local authorities from applying for and the courts from granting them a residence or contact order.[1] The embargo is intended to prevent local authorities from obtaining parental responsibility other than by a care order under s 31. If local authorities wish to restrict contact with a child accommodated by them, they must seek a care order and have the matter dealt with in those proceedings. The combined effect of s 9(1) and (2) is that where a child is in care, a local authority cannot apply for any s 8 order. On the other hand, authorities may seek leave to obtain a prohibited steps or specific issue order in respect of a child accommodated by them, though this provision may not be used as a disguised route to seeking a residence or contact order[2] nor should local authorities seek to use Pt II powers in substitution for the public law powers under Pts IV or V of the Act.[3] Similarly, it has been held inappropriate to grant a local authority leave to intervene in private law proceedings so as to challenge contact being made with one of the parents.[4]

1   For discussion of whether local authorities can apply for orders on behalf of someone else see paras 5.127 et seq.
2   Section 9(5), discussed at para 5.78.
3   *Nottingham County Council v P* [1994] Fam 18, [1993] 3 All ER 815, CA discussed on this point at para 5.81.
4   See *F v Cambridge County Council* [1995] 2 FCR 804, [1995] 1 FLR 516, discussed ante at para 5.82. Note also *Re K (Contact: Psychiatric Report)* [1996] 1 FCR 474, [1995] 2 FLR 432, CA in which it was again emphasised that local authority's powers to become involved in private law proceedings are limited. See also the comments of Wall 'The courts and child protection – the challenge of hybrid cases' (1997) 9 CFLQ at 355–356.

(d)   Other restrictions

5.99   According to Booth J residence orders cannot be made in favour of the child applicant, at any rate, where the child is seeking to live with someone else.[1] However, it must surely be open to the court to make a residence order in favour of a mother who herself is a child in respect of her own child and there seems no objection in principle[2] to granting in appropriate cases such an order in favour of a child applicant in respect of a sibling.[3]

1   *Re SC (a Minor) (Leave to Seek Residence Order)* [1994] 1 FLR 96 at 100.
2   Ie it cannot be objected that because the making of a residence order confers parental responsibility on those who do not already have it, an order cannot be made in favour of a child since of course mothers (and married fathers) have parental responsibility even if they are minors.
3   For discussion of whether courts can make residence orders on their own motion in favour of local authority foster parents when the parties themselves are barred from doing so under s 9(3), see para 5.108.

8.   When Section 8 orders can be made

5.100   Under s 10(1) the court (ie the High Court, county court or magistrates' court)[1] is empowered to make a s 8 order in 'any family proceedings in which a question arises with respect to the welfare of the child'.

1   Section 92(7).

(a)   Family proceedings

5.101   The term 'family proceedings' is defined by s 8(3)[1] as meaning any proceedings 'under the inherent jurisdiction of the High Court in relation to children' or under the enactments listed in s 8(4). With regard to the former, which refers both to wardship and to proceedings under the general inherent jurisdiction of the High Court,[2] s 8(3) states that local authority applications for leave to invoke the High Court's inherent jurisdiction fall outside the definition.

1   Note: s 8(3) only provides the exclusive definition of 'family proceedings' for the purpose of making s 8 orders. For other purposes, eg the admission of hearsay evidence, recourse might also be had to the definition in s 92(2): *R v Oxfordshire County Council (Secure Accommodation Order)* [1992] Fam 150, sub nom *R (J) v Oxfordshire County Council* [1992] 3 All ER 660, discussed further at para 9.24.
2   Wardship and the High Court's general inherent jurisdiction are discussed in ch 12.

5.102   The enactments listed in s 8(4) are as follows:

- Pts I, II and IV of the CA 1989;
- the Matrimonial Causes Act 1973;
- the Adoption Act 1976;[1]
- the Domestic Proceedings and Magistrates' Courts Act 1978;
- the Matrimonial and Family Proceedings Act 1984, Pt III; and
- the Family Law Act 1996.

Applications for parental orders under s 30 of the Human Fertilisation and Embryology Act 1990 and for child safety orders under ss 1 and 12 of the Crime and Disorder Act 1998 also rank as 'family proceedings'.[2]

1 Prospectively this will be amended to read the Adoption and Children Act 2002.
2 Human Fertilisation and Embryology Act 1990, s 30(8)(a). (for a discussion of parental orders see *Clarke Hall and Morrison* 1[378] et seq); Crime and Disorder Act 1998, s 11(6).

5.103 Based on the Law Commission's recommendations[1] and intended to rationalise, harmonise and in some cases expand the court's previous powers, the wide ambit of the above definition is to be noted. For example, the inclusion of Pt IV of the CA 1989 means that in care proceedings the court can make s 8 orders.[2] The inclusion of adoption and family protection proceedings is also to be noted. The reason for including all these proceedings is that by extending the range of options the court will be able best to meet the child's needs.[3]

1 Law Com No 172, para 4.37.
2 But note s 9(1) prevents the court from making a s 8 order *and* a care order, though there is nothing to prevent a court making both a supervision order and a s 8 order. For discussion of the power to make s 8 orders in care proceedings see para 8.113 et seq.
3 As the Law Commission had observed it seemed 'highly artificial' for the court to be able to exclude one person from the matrimonial home at least in part for the children's sake, yet not to be able to order that the child should live with the parent remaining in the home. seq. It might be noted that in family protection proceedings the court is not obliged to consider the children and in many cases the matter will be too urgent for it to do so.

5.104 The inclusion of wardship proceedings under 'family proceedings' furthers the policy of reducing the need to resort to the jurisdiction, the strategy being[1] that if the outcome is likely to be the same as in other proceedings there will be less incentive to use it. Furthermore, even where an application is made the expectation is that, where appropriate, the court will make a s 8 order and discharge the wardship.[2]

1 See Law Com No 172, para 4.35.
2 As was done in *Re T (Minor) (Care: Representation)* [1994] Fam 49, [1993] 4 All ER 518, CA, discussed further at para 12.12 and *Re P (a Minor) (Leave to Apply: Foster Parents)* [1994] 2 FCR 1093, sub nom *C v Salford City Council* [1994] 2 FLR 926, discussed further at para 5.114.

5.105 Wide though the definition is it does not include all proceedings concerning children. In particular it does not include proceedings under Pt V of the CA 1989,[1] which means that in applications for emergency protection or child assessment orders the court has no power to make a s 8 order. There is similarly no power to make s 8 orders in international child abduction proceedings under the Child Abduction and Custody Act 1985, nor in proceedings under the Family Law Act 1986.[2]

1 Pt V is discussed in Ch 7.
2 The 1986 Act deals, inter alia, with abductions within the United Kingdom and with declarations of status.

(b) Any child

5.106 Section 10(1) empowers a court in family proceedings to make a s 8 order in respect of any child (ie a person under the age of eighteen).[1] In other words, the court's powers are not limited to 'children of the family' nor to the biological children of the parties. On the other hand, as has been discussed,[2] the power is restricted in the case of children who have reached the age of sixteen. Upon normal rules of interpretation[3] 'child' only refers to live persons. There is therefore no power to make s 8 orders in respect of unborn or deceased children.

1 Section 105(1).
2 See para 5.96.
3 See the cases cited at para 3.86, n 3.

(c)   Upon application or upon the court's own motion

5.107   Section 10(1) provides that s 8 orders can be made either upon application or, once proceedings have begun, by the court itself whenever it 'considers that the order should be made even though no such application has been made'.[1] Although the Law Commission expected[2] that orders would normally be made upon application the significance of the court's ability to make s 8 orders on their own motion should not be overlooked. It is, however, established that if a court is minded to make an order that has not been argued for, it should inform the parties of that intention and give them the opportunity to make submissions on the desirability of the proposed option.[3] It has also been said[4] that it should only be in wholly exceptional circumstances that a residence order should be imposed on unwilling recipients.

1 Section 10(1)(b).
2 Law Com No 172, para 4.38.
3 See eg *Croydon London Borough Council v A* [1992] Fam 169, [1992] 3 All ER 788 and *Devon County Council v S* [1992] Fam 176 [1992] 3 All ER 793. In both these cases the observations were made in respect of magistrates' court decisions but the principle ought to be of general application. Query the position on appeal, see eg *Re F (Minors) (Denial of Contact)* [1993] 1 FCR 945, [1993] 2 FLR 677 in which the Court of Appeal refused to make a family assistance order inter alia because the point had not been argued at first instance.
4 Per Stuart-Smith J in *Re K (Minors) (Care or Residence Orders)* [1996] 1 FCR 365 at 374, [1995] 1 FLR 675 at 683, in which devoted grandparents did not wish to have legal responsibility in respect of two grandsons (who were suffering from a muscle wasting disease) they were looking after.

5.108   In *Gloucestershire County Council v P*[1] it was held that the flexibility given to a judge by s 10(1)(b) to make a residence order upon his own initiative is not limited by the restrictions imposed by ss 9 and 10(3).[2] It was thus held to be no bar on the court granting a residence order in favour of foster parents that the parties themselves were prohibited from seeking court leave to apply for such an order though as Butler-Sloss LJ observed it would only be in 'a most exceptional' case that it would be right to make an order in favour of foster-parents who could not themselves apply. A similarly purposive interpretation was applied by Court of Appeal in *Re G (a Minor) (Leave to Appeal: Jurisdiction)*[3] when upholding a decision to make an 'interim' residence order upon an application for leave to allow a child in care to go to Scotland, even though this evaded the difficulties of Sch 2 to the CA 1989. Butler-Sloss LJ said:[4]

> 'Judges cannot dispense with the Children Act. What they can dispense with are unnecessary procedural difficulties within the general powers of the Children Act to arrive at what the judge thinks under s 1 of the Children Act to be the best interests of the child, with the child's welfare being the paramount consideration'.

1 [2000] Fam 1, [1999] 3 FCR 114, [1999] 2 FLR 61, CA (Thorpe LJ dissenting).
2 Discussed at paras 5.97 et seq.
3 [1999] 3 FCR 281, [1999] 1 FLR 771.
4 Above at 284 and 773 respectively.

9.   Who may apply for s 8 orders?

5.109   The Act adopts a so-called 'open door' policy whereby some are entitled to apply, while others can, with leave of the court, apply for s 8 orders either by intervening in existing 'family proceedings'[1] or by initiating their own proceedings. The detailed scheme provided for by s 10 (which governs both initiating and intervening in family proceedings), is described below.

1   For the meaning of which, see paras 5.101 et seq.

(a)   Persons entitled to apply without leave

5.110   Parents, guardians (and, prospectively, special guardians) and those with a residence order in their favour are entitled to apply for any s 8 order.[1] For these purposes 'parents' includes the unmarried father[2] but not 'former parents' whose child has been freed for adoption.[3] In addition certain other persons are entitled to apply for a residence order or a contact order without leave,[4] namely:[5]

(a)   any party to a marriage (whether or not subsisting) in relation to whom the child is a 'child of the family';
(b)   any person with whom the child has lived for a period of at least three years (this period need not be continuous but must not have begun more than five years before, or ended more than three months before the making of the application);[6]
(c)   any person having the consent of:
  (i)   each of the persons in whose favour a residence order is in force;
  (ii)   the local authority, if the child is subject to a care order; or
  (iii)   in any other case, each of the persons who have parental responsibility for the child.

Group (a) primarily refers to step-parents but can include any married person or persons[7] who has treated the child as a 'child of the family'.[8]

1   Section 10(4), prospectively amended by the Adoption and Children Bill 2002 to include 'special guardians'. Special guardians are discussed at para 5.161 et seq.
2   *Re C (Minors) (Adoption: Residence Order)* [1994] Fam 1, sub nom *Re C (Minors) (Parent: Residence Order)* [1993] 3 All ER 313, CA (sometimes referred to as 'the Calderdale case') reversing Johnson J's ruling that for the purposes of s 10(4) 'parents' referred only to those who have parental responsibility.
3   *Re C (Minors) (Adoption: Residence Order)*, supra. A fortiori it does not include birth parents whose child has been adopted. See, ante, para 5.66.
4   Ie leave is still required to apply for a specific issue or prohibited steps order.
5   Section 10(5).
6   Section 10(6).
7   Including grandparents: see *Re A (Child of the Family)* [1998] 1 FCR 458, [1998] 1 FLR 347, CA.
8   'Child of the family' is defined by s 105(1) as a child of both the married parents and 'any other child, not being a child who is placed with those parties as foster parents by a local authority or voluntary organisation, who has been treated by both of those parties as a child of their family'.

5.111   Those not otherwise included in the above-mentioned categories will nevertheless be entitled, pursuant to s 10(6),to apply for a variation or discharge of a s 8 order if either the order in question was made on his application or, in the case of a contact order, he is named in that order. This means, for instance, that a child named in a contact order will not need leave to apply to vary it.[1] Furthermore, s 10(7) reserves the power of rules of court to prescribe additional categories of people who may make applications without prior leave. These powers have not yet been exercised.

1   *Re W (Application For Leave: Whether Necessary)* [1996] 3 FCR 337n, Per Wilson J.

(b)   Persons entitled to apply with leave

5.112   In general anyone, including the child himself and any body, local authority or organisation professionally concerned with children, who is not entitled to apply, can seek leave of the court to apply for any s 8 order.[1] However, as already discussed,[2] local authorities cannot in any event apply for residence or contact orders, while any person 'who is, or was at any time during the last six months, a local authority foster parent' (the term 'local authority foster parent' refers to any person with whom any child is 'looked after' by a local authority within the meaning of s 22(3),[3] and therefore includes those with whom the child has been placed as prospective adopters)[4] must have the consent of the local authority to apply for the court's leave unless he is a relative of the child or the child has been living with him for at least three years preceding the application.[5] This latter period need not be continuous but must not have been more than five years before the making of the application.[6] Because of the different wording of ss 9(4) and 10(10) there can be occasions, viz where foster parents have provided a home for the child for three years but not within three months preceding the application, where consent of a local authority is not required but leave of the court still is.[7]

1   Section 10(1)(a)(ii).
2   At para 5.98.
3   Discussed at para 6.45.
4   Per Judge Foster QC, in *Re C (Adoption: Notice)* [1999] 1 FLR 384.
5   Section 9(3). But under the Adoption and Children Bill 2002 this time period will be reduced to one year. See further para 5.113.
6   Section 9(4). Consequential upon the prospective reduction of the time requirement to one year this provision will be repealed by the Adoption and Children Bill 2002.
7   Where the three-year period immediately precedes the application or has not ended more than three months before the application, the foster parents can, pursuant to s 10(5)(b), apply as of right for a residence or contact order.

5.113   According to Lord Mackay LC[1] the reason for imposing the additional restrictions on applications by local authority foster parents was to prevent premature applications unduly interfering with local authority plans for the child and so undermining their efforts to bring stability to the child's life. It is also intended to guard against the risk of deterring parents from voluntarily using the fostering services provided by local authorities which, it is argued, could easily happen if the restrictions were relaxed. However, notwithstanding the importance of these objectives[2] the time restriction lies at odds with that in adoption where foster parents can obtain an order after providing a home for the child for 12 months.[3] This discrepancy has now been acknowledged to be an unjustified anomaly and under the amendments prospectively to be made by the Adoption and Children Bill 2002, local authority foster parents will not require the local authority's consent to make a leave application if the child has been living with them for at least one year.

1   In 502 HL Official Report (5th series), cols 1221 – 1222. This provision had not been recommended by the Law Commission.

2   Though, even so, many might agree with Lord Meston's observation expressed during the passage of the Bill, (502 HL Official Reports (5th Series) col 1221, that having to obtain local authority consent and leave of the court is one hurdle too many.
3   Adoption Act 1976, s 13(1) and (2). Note also *Re C (A Minor) (Adoption)* [1994] 1 WLR 1120 at 1124 [1994] 2 FCR 839 at 842,[1994] 2 FLR 513 at 515 in which the anomalies of the current position were discussed.

5.114   Ironically, in the first case to consider s 9(3), *Re P (a Minor) (Leave to Apply: Foster Parents),*[1] parents sought to challenge the propriety of the consent given by the local authority. In that case a child suffering from Down's Syndrome had been accommodated by the local authority and placed with foster parents. Subsequently, the foster parents expressed their wish to adopt but as Roman Catholics they were unacceptable as prospective adopters to the parents who were Jewish. The foster parents accordingly, and with the consent of the local authority, sought leave to apply for a residence order. The parents argued that because of their dual function as an adoption agency and as an accommodating local social services authority the local authority should not or could not have consented to the foster parents' application. Rejecting this argument, it was held that for the purposes of s 9(3) it was the consent of the social services authority accommodating the child that was required, and that therefore the authority's role as adoption agency was not part of that consent. It was further held that because the balance of the welfare factors made the case a very difficult one, that was justification in itself in having the issues resolved by the court. Accordingly, leave to apply for a residence order was granted.

1   [1994] 2 FCR 1093, sub nom *C v Salford City Council*, [1994] 2 FLR 926, per Hale J. But note this restriction does not bar the court from making an order on its own motion see *Gloucestershire County Council v P* [2000] Fam 1, [1999] 3 FCR 114, [1999] 2 FLR 61, CA (Thorpe LJ dissenting), discussed at para 5.108.

(c)   The leave criteria

5.115   So far as the leave criteria are concerned two provisions of the CA 1989 are relevant, namely, s 10(8) and (9). At one time it was generally thought that the former applied to children seeking leave, while the latter applied to adults seeking leave. However, according to Charles J in *Re S (a Minor) (Adopted Child: Contact)*[1] it is too simplistic to say that s 10(8) applies to child applicants while s 10(9) applies to adult applicants since, as he pointed out, the application of these provisions is not dependent upon whether or not the applicant is a child but upon whether or not the applicant is 'the child concerned'. He considered that for these purposes the phrase 'the child concerned' means the child who is the subject of the application.[2] If he is not then s 10(9) applies rather than s 10(8). In *Re S* itself the child (who was adopted) was seeking contact with another sibling and could not therefore be considered the subject-matter of the action and hence not the 'child concerned'. Accordingly, s 10(9) was held to apply.

1   [1999] Fam 283, [1999] 1 All ER 648, sub nom *Re S (Adopted Child: Contact by Sibling)* [1999] 1 FCR 169, [1998] 2 FLR 897.
2   Which interpretation reflects the case law on the application of the paramountcy test as established by *Birmingham City Council v H (a Minor)* [1994] 2 AC 212, [1994] 1 All ER 12, HL, discussed at paras 2.28 et seq.

5.116   On Charles J's analysis s 10(9) can apply both to adults and children seeking leave while s 10(8), though confined to child applicants, will only apply where the child is regarded as the subject of the action, as for example, where a residence order or contact order with another adult is being sought. However, it remains to be seen whether it will become the accepted approach. One problem of applying s 10(9) to child applicants is that it might appear that the child's age and understanding (referred to in s 10(8) are not relevant. However, according to Charles J that factor can be taken into account since the criteria listed in 10(9) are not meant to be exclusive. But even if this solution is accepted there remains the difficulty that s 10(9)(b) directs the court to consider 'the applicant's connection with the child' which does not sit easily with the interpretation that s 10(9) can apply to child applicants. It should be added that regardless of whether leave is sought by the child under s 10(8) or (9), applications should be made to the High Court.[1]

1 *Practice Direction (Application by Children: Leave)* [1993] 1 All ER 920, [1993] 1 WLR 313.

(i) THE APPLICATION OF S 10(9)

5.117 Section 10(9) states:

'Where the person applying for leave to make an application for a s 8 order is not the child concerned, the court shall, in deciding whether or not to grant leave, have particular regard to:
(a) the nature of the proposed application for the s 8 order;
(b) the applicant's connection with the child;
(c) any risk there might be of that proposed application disrupting the child's life to such an extent that he would be harmed by it; and
(d) where the child is being looked after by a local authority'
   (i) the authority's plans for the child's future; and
   (ii) the wishes and feelings of the child's parents'.[1]

1 Although s 10(9) only applies where leave is sought to apply for a s 8 order, it has been held that the underlying thinking behind the provision is also applicable to an application by a non-parent for proceedings to be consolidated: *W v Wakefield City Council* [1994] 2 FCR 564, at 576, [1995] 1 FLR 170 at 179, per Wall J. But note s 10(9) does *not* apply to the question of granting leave following the making of a s 91(14) order, per Thorpe LJ in *Re A (a Minor) (Contact: Parent's Application for Leave)* [1999] 1 FCR 127, [1998] 1 FLR 1, CA. See further para 5.157.

5.118 The Court of Appeal held in *Re A (Minors) (Residence Orders: Leave to Apply)*[1] that in deciding whether to grant adult applicants leave, the paramountcy of the child's welfare principle under s 1(1) has no application for three reasons:

(1) in granting or refusing a leave application the court is not determining a question with respect to the child's upbringing. That question only arises when the court hears the substantive application.
(2) furthermore some of the guidelines, for example, s 10(9)(a), (c) and (d)(i) would be otiose if the child's welfare was paramount, while
(3) in any event there 'would have been little point in Parliament providing that the court was to have particular regard to the wishes and feelings of the child's parents, if the whole decision were to be subject to the overriding (paramount) consideration of the child's welfare'.

Notwithstanding *Re A*, s 10(9) is not to be regarded as providing the exclusive guidelines and in particular as preventing the court from considering the checklist under s 1(3). It is therefore proper to consider the child's own views,[2] and, when applying s 10(9) to child applicants, to consider the child's age and understanding.[3]

1 [1992] Fam 182, [1992] 3 All ER 872, CA.
2 *Re A (a Minor) (Residence Order: Leave to Apply)* [1993] 1 FLR 425, per Hollings J.
3 Per Charles J in *Re S (a Minor) (Adopted Child: Contact)*, supra, at para 5.116.

5.119 At one time it seemed to be accepted[1] that in deciding whether or not to grant leave the proper approach should be to enquire whether there is a 'good arguable case.' Summarising the position, Ward LJ said in *Re M (Minor) (Contact: Leave to Apply)*:[2]

'(1) If the application is frivolous or vexatious or otherwise an abuse of the process of the court, of course it will fail.

(2) If the application for leave fails to disclose that there is any eventual prospect of success, if those prospects of success are remote so that the application is obviously unsustainable, then it must also be dismissed . . .[3]

(3) The applicant must satisfy the court that there is a serious issue to try and must present a good arguable case. 'A good arguable case' has acquired a distinct meaning; see the long line of authorities setting out this as the convenient approach for the grant of leave to commence proceedings and serve out of the jurisdiction under RSC Ord 11.'

However, *Re M* has been called into question by a subsequent Court of Appeal decision, *Re P (A Child)*,[4] which pointed out that *Re M* had been decided before the Human Rights Act 1998 came into force and in the light of which a reassessment may now need to be made. Even where leave has been given, it by no means follows that an order be made.[5] The refusal to give leave is a serious issue and failure to give reasons for the decision constitutes a fundamental defect.[6]

1 Cf *G v Kirklees Metropolitan Borough Council* [1993] 1 FCR 357, [1993] 1 FLR 805, in which it had previously been held that the substantive application should have a reasonable prospect of success.
2 [1995] 3 FCR 550 at 562–563, sub nom *Re M (Care: Contact: Grandmothers Application for Leave)* [1995] 2 FLR 86 at 98. See also *Re G (Child Case: Parental Involvement)* [1996] 2 FCR 1 at 11, [1996] 1 FLR 857 at 865–866, per Butler–Sloss LJ; and *Re W (a Child) (Contact: Leave to Apply)* [2000] 1 FCR 185, [2000] 1 FLR 263.
3 See eg *Re A (a Minor) (Contact: Leave to Apply)* [1995] 3 FCR 543 in which Douglas Brown J upheld a magistrate's refusal to give a grandmother leave since, given the total opposition by the parents and the serious disharmony between them, the application had no prospect of success. See also *W v Ealing London Borough Council* [1994] 2 FLR 788 and *Cheshire County Council v M* [1993] 1 FLR 463 cited by Ward LJ in *Re M (Minors) (Sexual Abuse: Evidence)* [1993] 1 FCR 253, [1993] 1 FLR 822, CA.
4 [2002] EWCA Civ 486.
5 *Re A (Section 8 Order: Grandparent Application)* [1996] 1 FCR 467, [1995] 2 FLR 153, CA and *Re W (Contact: Application by Grandparent)* [1997] 2 FCR 463, [1997] 1 FLR 793.
6 Per Connell J in *T v W (Contact Reasons for Refusing Leave)* [1997] 1 FCR 118, [1996] 2 FLR 473; and *Re W (a Child) (Contact: Leave to Apply)* [2000] 1 FCR 185, sub nom *Re W (Contact Application: Procedure)* [2000] 1 FLR 263.

5.120 The requirement of leave is intended to act as a filter to protect the child and his family against unwarranted interference with their comfort and security, whilst ensuring that the child's interests are properly respected.[1] The more tenuous the applicant's connection with the child the harder it will be to obtain leave. Conversely, the closer the connection the more readily leave should be given. As the Law Commission put it,[2] the requirement of leave will 'scarcely be a hurdle at all to close relatives such as grandparents . . . who wish to care for or visit the child'. On the other hand, as Lord Mackay LC commented in response to attempts during the passage of the Bill to give grandparents an entitlement to apply for a residence or contact order:[3]

> '[t]here is often a close bond . . . between a grandparent and a grandchild . . . and in such cases leave, if needed, will no doubt be granted. Indeed, in many cases it will be a formality; but we would be naive if we did not accept that all interest shown by a grandparent in a child's life is not necessarily benign, even if well intentioned. Arguably, at least until we have some experience of wider rights of application, the law should provide some protection to children and their parents against unwarranted applications by grandparents when they occur'.

Since implementation another concern voiced by the court is the consequential delay in having too many parties and Butler-Sloss LJ has specifically said that it is undesirable that grandparents whose interests are identical with those of the mother should be separately represented.[4]

1 As Lord Mackay LC eloquently put it (502 HL Official Report (5th Series), col 1227): 'There is clearly a danger both in limiting and expanding the categories of persons who may apply for orders in respect of children. On the one hand, a too wide and uncontrolled gateway can expose children and families to the stress and harm of unwarranted interference and the harassment of actual or threatened proceedings. If too narrow or over-controlled the gateway may prevent applications which would benefit or safeguard a child from harm'.
2 Law Com No 172, para 4.41.
3 503 HL Official Report (5th series), col 1342.
4 *Re M (Minors) (Sexual Abuse: Evidence)* [1993] 1 FCR 253 at 257, [1993] 1 FLR 822 at 825. The difficulty in practice is that the parties themselves will not always consider their interests identical.

5.121 Careful consideration needs to be given to applications for leave by individuals in respect of children in care. In *Re A (Minors) (Residence Orders: Leave to Apply)*[1] the Court of Appeal refused leave to apply for a residence order in respect of children originally placed with the applicant for long-term fostering but who had been removed from her by the local authority nearly six months earlier.[2] The court accepted that the power under s 9(1) to make a residence order notwithstanding that the child is in care represented a fundamental change in that the so-called '*Liverpool* principle'[3] no longer had direct application but that did not mean that no weight should be given to the local authority's views. On the contrary s 10(9)(d)(i) expressly provides that the court is to have particular regard to the authority's plans for the child. Furthermore in view of the duty under s 22(3) to safeguard and promote the welfare of any child in its care, it was held that the court should approach the application for leave on the basis that 'the authority's plans for the child's future are designed to safeguard and promote the child's welfare and that any departure from those plans might well disrupt the child's life to such an extent that he would be harmed by it'.[4] In other words courts should not allow such applications to become a back door means of reviewing local authority decisions.[5]

1 [1992] Fam 182, [1992] 3 All ER 872.
2 In fact the application was made one week before the expiry of six months from the removal but it was agreed between the parties that the local authority would not object to the application as they could have done under s 9(3), and that the mother would not pursue her action for judicial review.
3 Named after *A v Liverpool City Council* [1982] AC 363, [1981] 2 All ER 385, HL which established that the appropriate means of challenging local authority decisions was via judicial review rather than wardship. See further paras 12.42 and 12.43.
4 Per Balcombe LJ [1992] Fam at 189 [1992] 3 All ER at 879.
5 See also *Re M (Prohibited Steps Order: Application for Leave)* [1993] 1 FCR 78, [1993] 1 FLR

275 in which a former guardian sought leave to challenge a local authority's decision not to take care proceedings'application remitted to justices for a re-hearing.

(II) The application of s 10(8)

5.122 Where the applicant for leave to make a s 8 application[1] is the 'child concerned', s 10(8) provides that leave can only be granted provided the court is satisfied that the child has sufficient understanding to make the proposed application. There is no hard and fast rule for determining whether the child is of sufficient age and understanding. As Sir Thomas Bingham MR said in *Re S (a Minor) (Independent Representation)*:[2]

> 'the rules eschew any arbitrary line of demarcation based on age and wisely so. Different children have differing levels of understanding at the same age. And understanding is not absolute. It has to be assessed relatively to the issues in the proceedings. Where any sound judgment on these issues calls for insight and imagination which only maturity and experience can bring, both the court and the solicitor will be slow to conclude that the child's understanding is sufficient'.

Even if the child is found to be competent, leave might not necessarily be granted. For example in *Re H (Residence Order: Child's Application For Leave)*[3] a child, of sufficient understanding to make the application, was refused leave to make it because his father could adequately represent his views to the court.

1 But note that a child who has previously been given leave and who has been named in a contact order does not need fresh leave to apply to vary that order; per Wilson J in *Re W (Application for Leave: Whether Necessary)* [1996] 3 FCR 337n, applying s 10(6), see para 5.111.
2 [1993] Fam 263 at 276, [1993] 3 All ER 36 at 43–44, CA. See also ch 10.
3 [2000] 1 FLR 780.

5.123 Apart from requiring the court to be satisfied about the child's understanding, the Act itself gives little further guidance, particularly as it seems to be accepted that the guidelines under s 10(9) do not apply where a child is seeking leave under s 10(8).[1] According to Charles J in *Re S (a Minor) (Adopted Child: Contact)*[2] this lack of guidance is indicative that the court is to have regard to the interests of the child. It is, however, generally accepted that in determining whether to grant leave the child's welfare is *not* the paramount consideration. As Booth J held in *Re SC (a Minor) (Leave to Seek Residence Order)*,[3] applying in turn *Re A (Minors) (Residence Orders: Leave to Apply)*,[4] when determining an application for leave under s 10 (whether it be under s 10(8) or (9)) the court is *not* determining a question in respect of the upbringing of the child concerned (that question only arises if leave is granted and the court determines the substantive application) and that therefore s 1(1) *does* not apply.[5] To this might be added, that not regarding the child's welfare as paramount has the merit of according a child of sufficient understanding to make the application some degree of independence which seems more in keeping with the spirit of the Act. It has been said that leave should not be granted to children if the proceedings are doomed to failure,[6] but it is submitted that as with adults the correct test now is whether the applicant has a good arguable case.[7]

1 See *Re C (Minor: Leave to Apply for Order)* [1994] 1 FCR 387, sub nom *Re C (a Minor) (Leave to Seek Section 8 Orders)* [1994] 1 FLR 26 and *Re SC (a Minor) (Leave to Seek Residence Order)* [1994] 1 FLR 96 both of which were predicated upon the view that s 10(8) applied to children seeking leave, while s 10(9) applied to adults seeking leave. But it was also

implicitly accepted by Charles J in *Re S (a Minor) (Adopted Child: Contact)* [1999] Fam 283, [1999] 1 All ER 648, who, as discussed at para 5.115, considered the application of s10(8) and (9) to be dependent upon whether or not the applicant was the child concerned.

2 Supra.
3 [1994] 1 FLR 96 at 99. See also in *Re C (Residence: Child's Application for Leave)* [1995] 1 FLR 927, per Stuart White J, *North Yorkshire County Council v G* [1994] 1 FCR 737, [1993] 2 FLR 732, per Douglas Brown J, and *Re S (a Minor) (Adopted Child: Contact)*, supra, per Charles J.
4 [1992] Fam 182, [1992] 3 All ER 872, discussed at para 5.118.
5 See the discussion at para 2.17.
6 Per Booth J in *Re SC*, above at 99C, but applying the earlier test she held that the court had 'to have regard to the likelihood of success of the proposed application.' In that case a 14-year-old girl who was in local authority care successfully sought leave to apply for a residence order in favour of a friend who agreed to care for her, notwithstanding that the application was opposed by the mother and that the friend had previously been rejected as the girl's foster mother.
7 See the discussion ante at para 5.119.

5.124 According to *Re HG (Specific Issue Order: Sterilisation)*[1] parents, at any rate when applying for leave that their child be sterilised, can apply for leave on that child's behalf in cases where the child lacks the necessary understanding to apply on his own behalf. The advantage of this ruling is that in these cases legal aid can be sought on behalf of the child rather than the parents.[2]

1 [1993] 1 FCR 553, [1993] 1 FLR 587, per Peter Singer QC (as he then was).
2 In *Re HG* the parents did not qualify for legal aid.

(III) PROCEDURE FOR SEEKING LEAVE

5.125 Any person seeking leave must file a written request setting out the reasons for the application and a draft of the application for making of which leave is sought.[1] Leave can be granted by the court or a single justice, with or without a hearing.[2] However, according to Wilson J in *Re W (a Child) (Contact Leave to Apply)*[3] it should be exceptional to grant leave ex parte.[4] Notice of an application for leave to apply should generally be given to all parties likely to be affected if leave is granted. Moreover, in almost all cases, it is appropriate for the respondent, together with the applicant, to be invited to attend the hearing for the grant of leave. Where magistrates proceed in the absence of notice to the respondent and grant leave, they should record reasons for both decisions.

1 FPR 1991, r 4.3(1); FPC (CA 1989) R 1991, r 3(1). Nevertheless the fact that an order has been made without a written request does not automatically invalidate the order: per Ewbank J in *Re O (Minors) (Leave to Seek Residence Order)* [1993] 2 FCR 482, [1994] 1 FLR 172.
2 FPR 1991, rr 4.3(2) and 3(2) respectively.
3 [2000] 1 FCR 185, sub nom *Re W (Contact Application: Procedure)* [2000] 1 FLR 263, per Wilson J. See also *Re M (Prohibited Steps Order: Application for Leave)* [1993] 1 FCR 78, 82, [1993] 1 FLR 275, 278 in which Johnson J had also emphasised that, ordinarily, applications for leave should be made on notice.
4 Wilson J said (at 189 and 266 respectively) while he could imagine a case, for example, a mature teenage child leaving home and seeking leave to apply for a residence order to secure his position in the home of another family, where an ex parte application could be justified he could not readily think of an example of a proposed application for contact where an ex parte application would be justified.

(d) Applying for orders in favour of someone else

5.126 The Act is silent on whether applications may be made for a s 8 order in favour of someone else. However, implicit in the ability of a child being able to obtain leave to apply for such orders is that they at least can seek a residence order in favour of another person.[1] This proposition was accepted by Booth J in *Re SC (a Minor) (Leave to Seek Residence Order)*[2] who commented:

> 'In my judgment the court should not fetter the statutory ability of the child to seek any s 8 order, including a residence order, if it is appropriate for such an application to be made. Although the court will undoubtedly consider why it is that the person in whose favour a proposed residence order would be made is not applying, it would in my opinion be wrong to import into the Act any requirement that only he or she should make the application.'

1 As Booth J pointed out in *Re SC (a Minor) (Leave to Seek Residence Order)* [1994] 1 FLR 96 at 100, residence orders cannot be made in favour of the child applicant himself since that would confer parental responsibility on him by reason of s 12(2).
2 Above, at 100E–F.

5.127 Whether the courts would be disposed to permit applications other than by children for residence or contact orders in favour of someone else remains to be seen. However, in the public law context it seems unlikely that local authorities would be permitted to do so[1] for even supposing that s 9(2) (which provides: 'No application may be made by a local authority for a residence order or contact order and no court shall make such an order in favour of a local authority') is interpreted as not barring residence or contact applications in favour of someone else,[2] there is still the objection that contrary to the ruling in *Nottingham County Council v P*[3] local authorities would thereby be permitted to intervene in family life via Pt II rather than Pt IV of the CA 1989.

1 They might plausibly wish to apply, for example, for a residence order in favour of grandparents who, though capable, are reluctant to apply for themselves.
2 As Lowe and Douglas *Bromley's* Family Law (9th edn) p 438, n3 points out, this could depend on whether the word 'and' is read conjunctively or disjunctively. If the former then it could be argued that all that s 9(2) prevents is local authorities applying for residence or contact orders on their own behalf.
3 [1994] Fam 18, [1993] 3 All ER 815, CA, discussed at para 5.81.

10.   Enforcing s 8 orders

5.128 Enforcing s 8 orders can be a difficult and protracted matter which in any event needs to be handled sensitively.[1] The imposition of penal sanctions for breaking court orders should not be thought of as being the norm in children cases. On the contrary, they should be sought only where all other alternatives are seen to be ineffective. Even then careful thought needs to be given to the provocative and emotional effect that applications for penal notices and committals can have in themselves. Above all it is always important not to lose sight of the child's welfare in these disputes though, as will be seen, in deciding whether to impose a penal sanction the child's welfare has been held *not* to be the paramount consideration.[2]

1 See generally Lowe 'Enforcing orders relating to children' (1992) 4 Jo of Child Law 26, and especially in relation to enforcing contact orders, see *Making Contact Work* (A Report to the Lord Chancellor by the Advisory Board on Family Law: Children Act Sub-Commtitee, 2002), ch 14.
2 *A v N (Committal: Refusal of Contact)* [1997] 2 FCR 475, [1997] 1 FLR 533, CA, discussed below at para 5.142.

Family Law Act 1986, s 34

5.129 Under s 34 of the Family Law Act 1986,[1] where a person is required by a s 8 order[2] to give up a child to another person (this will most commonly apply in the enforcement of a residence order) and the court that made the order is satisfied that the child has not been given up, it may make a 'search and recovery' order authorising an officer of the court or a constable to take charge of the child and deliver him to that other person.[3] Since this power enables such orders to be implemented without recourse to penal procedures, it should normally be preferred to those latter powers.[4] However, because an order under s 34 cannot be granted unless or until the order to give up the child has been disobeyed, it might be preferable in emergencies to obtain an ex parte order under the High Court's inherent jurisdiction[5] authorising the tipstaff to find and recover the child.[6] The court may also pre-empt an unlawful removal of a child from the care of the person with a residence order or from the jurisdiction by making an order preventing such removal and attaching a penal notice[7] thereto.

1 Discussed in more detail by Fricker and Bean: *Enforcement of Injunctions and Undertakings*, p 80 et seq and by Fricker Adams, Pearce, Salter, Stevens and Wybrow: *Emergency Remedies and Procedures* (2nd edn) p 158 et seq. Note: forms for use in applications and orders have, from 3 January 1995, been prescribed by FPR 1991, r 6.17 and FPC (Children Act 1989) R 1991, r 31A.
2 Or any existing statutory custody or care and control order.
3 Note that the police generally have a duty to assist in the handing over of a child where there is a threat of danger or a breach of the peace: *R v Chief Constable of Cheshire, ex p K* [1990] FCR 201, [1990] 1 FLR 70. Note also the power under s 33 of the 1986 Act for a court to order any person who it has reason to believe may have relevant information as to the child's whereabouts to disclose it to the court.
4 Certainly this is the view of Fricker and Bean, above and Fricker et al above.
5 This jurisdiction is discussed in ch 12.
6 See Fricker et al, above, at p 248 and Fricker, 'Injunctive Orders Relating to Children' [1993] Fam Law 226, 229–230.
7 For the meaning of which see para 5.132.

The courts' general enforcement powers

5.130 More general powers of enforcement are, in the case of the High Court and county court provided by the law of contempt, and in the case of magistrates' courts, by s 63(3) of the Magistrates' Courts Act 1980.

(i) THE HIGH COURT AND COUNTY COURT POWERS

5.131 As far as the two higher courts are concerned (in this respect the powers of the High Court are no greater than those of the county court)[1] the breaking of an order or an undertaking incorporated in an order constitutes a contempt of court for which the contemnor may be fined, imprisoned or have his property sequestered.[2] The first remedy is unusual.[3] The latter remedy (under which the contemnor's assets are frozen)[4] is useful in cases where the offender is abroad but has assets in this country.[5] The major sanction for breaking a s 8 order is by committal by which means the offender can be imprisoned.

1 See *Re F (Contact: Enforcement: Representation of Child)* [1998] 3 FCR 216, [1998] 1 FLR 691, CA.
2 These powers are briefly referred to in the CAAC Report 1992/93, ch 5 but for detailed discussion reference should be made to Borrie and Lowe's The Law of Contempt (3rd edn),

ch 14; Arlidge and Eady and Smith on *Contempt* (2ⁿᵈ edn), ch 12 and Miller: *Contempt of Court* (3rd edn) ch 14.

3 See eg Miller, op cit, at p 32.

4 There is, however, power both to order the sale of sequestered assets and to direct that money raised by the sequestrators be used to pay for the costs of tracing the child and instituting proceedings abroad, see respectively *Mir v Mir* [1992] Fam 79, [1992] 1 All ER 765 and *Richardson v Richardson* [1989] Fam 95, [1989] 3 All ER 779.

5 It is therefore particularly useful in cases of international child abduction see *Clarke Hall and Morrison*, Division 2.

5.132 Before any committal order may be made the court must be satisfied beyond reasonable doubt[1] that the defendant knowingly broke the order. It is also a fundamental requirement[2] that a penal notice (that is, a notice in writing formally warning the person against whom the order is made that failure to obey it constitutes a contempt of court for which the offender may be sent to prison) has been attached to the order in question.[3] Penal notices, however, can only be attached to injunctions or to orders that are injunctive in form.[4] In other words to be enforceable at all the order must, as the Children Act Advisory Committee states:[5] 'set out in explicit terms precisely what it is that the person in question must do, or must refrain from doing' and in the former case it must also specify the time within which the act is to be done.

1 See *Dean v Dean* [1987] 1 FLR 517, CA and *Re Bramblevale Ltd* [1970] Ch 128, [1968] 3 All ER 1062, CA.

2 CPR 1998, Sch 1, RSC Ord 45 r 7(4) (High Court) and CCR 1981 Ord 29 r 1(3) and FPR 1991, r 4.21A (county court).

3 Even so, courts are not *bound* to attach penal notices even where disobedience to an order is a real issue, see *Re F (Contact: Enforcement: Representation of Child)* [1998] 3 FCR 216, [1998] 1 FLR 691, CA where a first instance judge was held justified in not attaching a penal notice on a contact order with the father in respect of a disabled child whose mother and grandmother were against such contact. See also *Re N (a Minor) (Access: Penal Notice)* [1991] FCR 1000, [1992] 1 FLR 134, in which the Court of Appeal upheld a refusal to make a specific issue order incorporating a penal notice, where the judge had found the child no longer wished to see the father and would suffer serious emotional upset if he was forced against he will to do so.

4 See *Re P (Minors) (Custody Order: Penal Notice)* [1990] 1 WLR 613, CA and *D v D (Access: Contempt: Committal)* [1991] 2 FLR 34, CA, discussed by Lowe, op cit.

5 CAAC Report 1992/93, at p 44. For the procedure of adding a penal notice see FPR 1991, r 4.21A.

5.133 The requirement that the order be in injunctive form means that not all s 8 orders and associated directions can be enforced by committal. It is clear, for example, that the embargoes against changing the child's surname and removing him from the UK as provided for by s 13[1] and clearly stated on the face of a residence order[2] are not per se enforceable by committal orders.[3] If therefore sanctions for contempt[4] are being sought it will be necessary to obtain a prohibited steps order clearly setting out what action must be refrained from and backed by a penal notice.

1 Discussed at paras 5.27 et seq.

2 Viz Form C43.

3 Cf *Re P (Minors) (Custody Order: Penal Notice)*, supra.

4 However, because of the direction against removal, residence orders per se remain useful (though not absolutely essential) for persuading the police to issue an 'all ports warning' to prevent the child's removal from the UK by the non residential parent. See further *Clarke Hall and Morrison*, 2[12] et seq.

5.134 Since residence orders are said only to settle 'the arrangements to be made as to the person with whom a child is to live' they are clearly not injunctive in form and are not therefore enforceable in themselves in the two higher courts.[1] To make such orders prima facie enforceable courts must attach precise directions or conditions, for example that the child be returned to a specific place at a specific time,[2] pursuant to their powers under s 11(7).[3] Even in these circumstances it would seem preferable to invoke the remedy under s 34 of the Family Law Act 1986,[4] rather than having recourse to committal.

1　This at any rate is the conclusion of Fricker et al, at 483, and Lowe: Enforcing orders relating to children (1992) 4 Journal of Child Law 26, 27. The position is different with regard to orders made by magistrates' courts, see para 5.139 below.
2　For an example of this type of order see *Re B (Minors) (Residence Order)* [1992] Fam 162, [1992] 3 All ER 867, CA.
3　Discussed at paras 5.84 et seq.
4　Discussed at para 5.129.

5.135　Although in their statutory form contact orders are injunctive in terms[1] and are therefore prima facie enforceable, as *D v D (Access: Contempt: Committal)*[2] shows, an order which is declaratory in terms providing, for example for reasonable contact, cannot have a penal notice attached to it and cannot therefore be enforced by committal. As the Children Act Advisory Committee has said:[3] 'To be enforceable by committal, an order for contact . . . [has] . . . to specify when and probably where, the child [is] to be allowed contact as well as with whom.' It is similarly necessary to spell out in a prohibited steps or specific issue order precisely what is prohibited or required and in the latter case by when the act in question is required to be completed.

1　But note the discussion at para 5.47.
2　[1994] 1 FLR 34.
3　CAAC Report 1992/93, p 44.

5.136　Provided the s 8 order is enforceable by committal order, FPR 1991, r 4.21A[1] provides that:

'the judge may, on the application of the person entitled to enforce the order, direct that the proper officer shall issue a copy of the order, indorsed with or incorporating a penal notice as to the consequences of disobedience, for service . . . and no copy of the order shall be issued with any such notice indorsed or incorporated save in accordance with such a direction.'

Orders are normally only enforceable against parties to the proceedings, but it can also be a contempt for someone else knowingly to frustrate a court order.[2]

1　Introduced from 5 October 1992, SI 1992/2067.
2　See *K v K (Minors) (Incitement to Breach of Orders)* [1992] 2 FCR 161, [1992] 2 FLR 108 – solicitor held guilty of contempt for advising a client mother to break an access order, *Re S (Abduction: Sequestration)* [1995] 1 FLR 858 contempt for a friend to assist mother in abducting child. Cf *Re H (Minors) (Prohibited Steps Order)* [1995] 4 All ER 110, [1995] 1 WLR 667, CA in which it was held that an order can be made against a non-party, see ante, para 5.72.

5.137　A county court judge can initiate committal proceedings of his own motion but should only do so when it is urgent and imperative to act immediately to prevent justice being obstructed.[1] The procedure for committal applications is set out in a *Practice Direction*.[2] Contempt of court must be proved by the criminal standard of proof, ie beyond all reasonable doubt. The Children (Admissibility of Hearsay Evidence) Order 1993[3] can apply to these proceedings provided the evidence 'shows a substantial connection with the upbringing, maintenance or welfare of the child.'[4]

1   *Re M (Minors) (Breach of Contact Order: Committal)* [1999] Fam 263, [1999] 2 All ER 56, CA.
2   *Practice Direction (Family Proceedings: Committal Applications)* [2001] 2 All ER 704, [2001] 1 WLR 1253, which inter alia draws attention to the need to give full effect to the Human Rights Act 1998 and in particular to Art 6 of the Convention on Human Rights regarding a fair trial.
3   SI 1993/621.
4   *Re C and others (Minors) (Hearsay Evidence: Contempt Proceedings)* [1993] 4 All ER 690, sub nom *C v C (Contempt: Evidence)* [1993] 1 FCR 820, [1993] 1 FLR 220, discussed also at para 11.04.

(ii) MAGISTRATES' COURTS' GENERAL ENFORCEMENT POWERS

5.138   Magistrates' enforcement powers are governed by the Magistrates' Courts Act 1980, s 63(3) which provides:

'Where any person disobeys an order of a magistrates' court ... to do anything other than the payment of money or to abstain from doing anything the court may:
(a)   order him to pay a sum not exceeding £50 for every day during which he is in default or a sum not exceeding £5000; or
(b)   commit him to custody until he has remedied his default for a period not exceeding 2 months; but a person who is ordered to pay a sum for every day during which he is in default or who is committed to custody until he has remedied his default shall not by virtue of this section be ordered to pay more than [£5000[1]] or be committed for more than 2 months in all for doing or abstaining from doing the same thing contrary to the order (without prejudice to the operation of this section in relation to any subsequent default).'

1   The provision in fact still specifies £1000 but it clearly should be changed in line with the maximum fine provided by sub-s (a).

5.139   Section 14 of the CA 1989 provides that where a residence order is in force and 'any other person (including one in whose favour the order is also in force) is in breach of the arrangements settled by that order', the person named in the order, may, as soon as a copy of the residence order has been served on the other person, enforce the order under the Magistrates' Courts Act 1980, s 63(3), 'as if it were an order requiring the other person to produce the child to him'. The reason for making specific provision in respect of residence orders is because, as already discussed, without such provision such orders are likely to be regarded as declaratory only and therefore not enforceable.[1] No such difficulty attaches to the other s 8 orders (at any rate in their statutory form) and accordingly all such orders are prima facie enforceable under s 63(3).

1   Following *Webster v Southwark London Borough Council* [1983] QB 698, [1983] 2 WLR 217. Query why the opportunity was not taken to make s 14 applicable to residence orders made in the High Court and county court?

5.140   Unlike the higher courts there is no provision for adding a penal notice to a magistrates' courts' order. According to FPC(Children Act 1989)R 1991, r 24 a person (in whose favour a residence order has been made) wishing to enforce it must:

'file a written statement describing the alleged breach of the arrangements settled by the order, whereupon the justices' clerk shall fix a date, time and place for a hearing of the proceedings and give notice as soon as practicable, to the person whom it is alleged is in breach of the arrangements settled by that order, of the date fixed.'

No specific rule is laid down for the enforcement of s 8 orders other than residence orders but it seems sensible to assume that a similar procedure is applicable. To be enforceable under s 63(3) an order must specify exactly what is to be done. In *Re H (Contact: Enforcement)*[1] it was held that the failure to specify in a contact order where the hand over was to take place was fatal to the complaint.

1   [1996] 2 FCR 784, [1996] 1 FLR 614.

5.141   Section 63(3) of the 1980 Act is not happily worded and seems more apt for dealing with continuing breaches. However, as Wood J said in *P v W (Access Order: Breach)*[1] the word 'or' in both s 63(3)(a) and (b) makes it 'possible to argue that the first part of each phrase makes provision for continuing disobedience and the second half provides for punishment of a past contempt.' This latter point, however, was left open in *P v W* and has yet to be authoritatively resolved. For this reason where a party is thought likely to disobey a court order it might be better to seek orders in the higher courts.

1   [1984] Fam 32 at 40.

(iii) DETERMINING WHETHER TO IMPOSE A PENALTY

5.142   Even if the court is satisfied that an order has been knowingly broken by the defendant it should regard the enforcement powers both under contempt and under the 1980 Act to imprison or fine the offender as a remedy of the last resort. As Ormrod LJ commented in *Ansah v Ansah*.[1] 'Committal orders are remedies of last resort; in family cases they should be the very last.' Further, as Hale LJ observed in *Hale v Turner*:[2]

'Family cases, it has long been recognised, raise quite different considerations from those elsewhere in the civil law. The two most obvious are the heightened emotional tensions that arise between family members and often the need for those family members to continue to be in contact with one another because they have children together or the like . . . '

Nevertheless it would be wrong to extract any general principle from these dicta and in appropriate cases it will be right to imprison an offender.[3] Indeed following *A v N (Committal: Refusal of Contact)*,[4] in which it was held that in considering whether to commit a mother for her persistent and flagrant breach of a contact order with the father, the child's welfare was a material but not the paramount consideration, imprisonment might be more likely than in the past.[5] Although in principle similar caution should be exercised when considering the imposition of penal sanctions upon the non-residential parent there may nevertheless be less concern for the child's welfare in so doing.[6]

1   [1977] Fam 138 at 143, [1977] 2 All ER 638 at 643, CA. Note also Bennett J's comment in *Re H*, supra, that magistrates should 'take the greatest caution before proceeding with a

hearing under s 63 . . . they should proceed with the greatest possible caution to use a weapon of last resort'. See also *I v D (Access Order: Enforcement)* [1989] FCR 91, [1988] 2 FLR 286.

2 [2000] 1 WLR 2377, [2000] 3 FCR 62, [2000] 2 FLR 879, at para (25), CA. See the comments thereon by Kay (2001) 64 MLR 595, particularly at 598–601.

3 See *Jones v Jones* [1993] 2 FCR 83, [1993] 2 FLR 377, CA. See also *Hale v Tanner*, supra, in which helpful general guidance is given with regard to imposing sentences for contempt.

4 [1997] 2 FCR 475, [1997] 1 FLR 533, CA in which a mother was committed to prison for 42 days for her persistent and repeated breaches and note the discussion of this decision in *Making Contact Work*. See also *F v F (Contact: Committal)* [1999] FCR 42, [1998] 2 FLR 237, CA, committal order for seven days suspended for six months, upheld by Court of Appeal, and *Z v Z (Refusal of Contact: Committal)* [1996] 1 FCR 538, n.

5 Though this is not to say that the penal remedy should be readily resorted to, cf *Re F (Contact: Enforcement: Representation of Child)* [1998] 3 FCR 216, [1998] 1 FLR 691, CA and, note also the power to suspend committals, see CPR 1998, Sch 1, RSC Ord 52, r 7(1) on which note *Griffin v Griffin* [2000] 2 FCR 302, [2000] 2 FLR 44, CA.

6 Cf *G v C (Contempt: Committal)* [1998] 1 FCR 592, sub nom *G v C (Residence Order: Committal)* [1998] 1 FLR 43, CA in which eight months' imprisonment of a father for breaking contact conditions was held justifiable.

Family Assistance Orders

5.143 Section 16 empowers the court to make a 'family assistance order'. Such an order requires either a CAFCASS officer to be made available or the local authority to make an officer of the authority available[1] to 'advise, assist and (where appropriate) befriend any person named in the order'.[2]Those who may be named in the order are: any parent (which includes the unmarried father) or guardian, any person with whom the child is living or in whose favour a contact order is in force with respect to the child, and the child -himself.[3]

1 Subject to s 16(7); see para 5.147 below.
2 Section 16(1).
3 Section 16(2).

5.144 This new power under the CA 1989 replaced the former power to make supervision orders in private law proceedings and must in turn be distinguished from supervision orders made under s 31 of the CA 1989.[1] As the Department of Health's Guidance and Regulations puts it:[2]

'A supervision order is designed for the more serious cases, in which there is an element of child protection involved. By contrast, a family assistance order aims simply to provide short-term help to a family, to overcome the problems and conflicts associated with their separation or divorce. Help may well be focused more on the adult rather than the child.'

1 Discussed at paras 8.167 et seq.
2 Vol 1, Court Orders, para 2.50 and cited by Wall J *Re DH (a Minor) (Care Proceedings: Evidence and Orders)* [1994] 2 FCR 3 at 43, sub nom in *Re D H (a Minor) (Child Abuse)* [1994] 1 FLR 679 at 702.

When orders may be made

5.145 Family assistance orders may be made in any 'family proceedings'[1] whether or not any other order has been made.[2] The power may be exercised only by the court acting upon its own motion though there is nothing to stop parties requesting the court to make such an order during the course of family proceedings.[3] However, the lack of the right to apply for such an order means that parties cannot apply to court *solely* for a family assistance order.

1 For the definition of which see para 5.101.
2 Section 16(1).
3 Though note *Re F (Minors) (Contact)* [1993] 1 FCR 945,[1993] 2 FLR 677 in which the Court of Appeal refused to consider making a family assistance order since the point had not been argued at first instance and in the absence of being able to show that the original order was wrong had no power to make such an order or remit the case back.

5.146 Before any order can be made, the court must be satisfied that 'the circumstances of the case are exceptional'.[1] The Act itself does not define what is meant by 'exceptional circumstances' in this context but it seems clear that the order should not be made as a matter of routine. The Department of Health's Guidance and Regulations also points out[2] that 'it will be particularly important in all orders for the court to make plain at the outset why family assistance is needed and what it is hoped to achieve by it'.

1 Section 16(3)(a).
2 Vol 1, Court Orders, para 2.52. For examples of reported cases of which such orders have been made see para 5.13 below.

5.147 Before an assistance order may be made the court must be satisfied that the consent of every person named in the order, *other than the child*, has been obtained.[1] Furthermore, an order may not be made requiring a local authority to make one of its officers available unless either the authority agrees or the child concerned lives or will live in its area.[2] It is not a proper use of a family assistance order to require a local authority to provide someone for escort duty where no family member is prepared to take the children to visit their father in prison.[3]

1 Section 16(3)(b).
2 Section 16(7). But see *Re C (a Minor) (Family Assistance Order)* [1996] 3 FCR 514, [1996] 1 FLR 424 where, having made an assistance order directing the local authority to make an officer available, the local authority subsequently returned to the court to say that it did not have the resources to carry the order out. Johnson J declined to take further action.
3 *S v P (Contact Application: Family Assistance Order)* [1997] 2 FCR 185, [1997] 2 FLR 277. Cf *Re E (Family Assistance order)* [1999] 3 FCR 700, [1999] 2 FLR 512, discussed at para 5.153 below.

5.148 There is no formal requirement that the child himself consents, nor is there a statutory requirement to ascertain the child's own wishes and feelings about such an order.[1] Nevertheless there is nothing to prevent the court from discovering the child's view (nor from applying the whole checklist under s 1(3)) if it so chooses and in cases where the child is mature enough to make his own decisions, it would seem prudent to do so.

1 The enjoinder to do so by s 1(3)(a) does not apply, (see s 1(4), discussed at para 2.39).

Effect of the order

5.149 Section 16 gives no guidance as to which officer should be appointed nor is it clear whether the court is empowered to appoint a particular CAF-CASS officer or a particular type of local authority officer. In the latter case, for example, in certain circumstances it might be preferable to appoint a housing officer rather than an officer from social services.[1] In the private law context the most appropriate appointee is likely to be the Children and Family Reporter who has compiled the welfare report for the court, while in care proceedings the obvious candidate is the social worker attached to the particular case.

1 See the discussion by Coubrough at [1993] Fam Law 598–599.

5.150 Under s 16(4), a family assistance order may direct the person named in the order or, such of the persons so named as may be specified, to take such steps as may be so specified with a view to enabling the officer to be kept informed of the address of any person named in the order and to be allowed to visit each person. Provided a s 8 order is also in force, while a family assistance order is in force the officer is empowered to refer to the court the question of whether a s 8 order should be varied or discharged.[1]

1 Section 16(6).

Duration of order

5.151 A family assistance order is intended to be only a short-term remedy. Hence, s 16(5) provides that unless a shorter period is specified the order will have effect only for six months from the day on which it is made. However, there is no restriction on making any further order.[1]

1 See the Department of Health's Guidance and Regulations, Vol 1 Court Orders, para 2.52 and the implicit acceptance of that proposition by Booth J in *Leeds County Council v C* [1993] 1 FCR 585 at 589, [1993] 1 FLR 269 at 272.

Family assistance orders in practice[1]

5.152 According to the *Children Act Report 1995–1999*,[2] the 'level of Family Assistance Orders made throughout the 1990s ranged from about 600 to around 1,000 annually'. Table 10.1 of the Report gives the precise numbers of orders made in private law proceedings 1992–1998, viz:

1992	**1993**	**1994**	**1995**	**1996**	**1997**	**1998**
606	913	999	1039	1060	1009	864

1 See *Making Contact Work* (A Report to the Lord Chancellor by the Advisory Board on Family Law: Children Act Sub Committee, 2002), ch 11, Trinder and Stone 'Family assistance orders – professional aspiration and partly frustration' (1998) 10 CFLQ 291 and Seden 'Family Assistance Orders and the Children Act: Ambivalence About Intervention or a Means of Safeguarding and Promoting Children's Welfare?' (2001) 15 Int Jo of Law, Policy and the Family 226.
2 Cm 4579, January 2000.

5.153 The few reported cases show that a major role of family assistance orders is in facilitating contact. In *Re M (Contact: Parental Responsibility: McKenzie Friend)*,[1] for example, the Court of Appeal proposed (subject to obtaining the mother's consent)[2] making a family assistance order to facilitate indirect contact between the children and their father in respect of whom the mother had a genuine fear. In *Leeds County Council v C*[3] Booth J held that the only appropriate way in which a court could make provision for the supervision of contact by a local authority was by an order under s 16 and not by attaching a condition under s 11(7). However in the *Re D H (a Minor) (Care Proceedings: Evidence and Orders)*[4] Wall J observed that while:

'. . . in the conventional case a supervision order under s 31 will not be appropriate where the object is simply to achieve contact supervised by a local authority . . . where the threshold criteria under s 31 are met in relation to the necessity for contact to be supervised, it may be appropriate to make a supervision order rather than an order under s 16.'

Despite this comment it is evident that a family assistance order can have a useful role to play in providing local authority assistance to supervise contact.[5] In *Re E (Family Assistance Order)*[6] a family assistance order was made against the wishes of a local authority (into whose area the family had moved) in order to supervise contact between a child and her mother in psychiatric unit. A family assistance order was also made in *Re U (Application to Free for Adoption)*,[7] where, having rejected a local authority's application to free a child for adoption and granting instead a residence order to the grandparents, it was held that the order was a useful way of monitoring the child's placement.

1   [1999] 1 FCR 703, sub nom *Re M (Contact: Family Assistance Order)* [1999] 1 FLR 75, CA. Note also the use of the s 91(14) powers (discussed at paras 5.154 et seq) in that case to prevent the father making an application to court without leave before the expiration of the family assistance order.
2   This part of the order was directed to lie on the file for 14 days to give the mother (who was not at the appellate hearing) through her solicitors the opportunity to consent to the order being made.
3   [1993] 1 FCR 585, [1993] 1 FLR 269.
4   [1994] 2 FCR 3 at 42, sub nom *Re DH (a Minor) (Child Abuse)*, [1994] 1 FLR 679 at 702.
5   See *B v B (Procedure: Alleged Sexual Abuse)* [1994] 1 FCR 809 at 836, sub nom *B v B (Child Abuse: Contact)* [1994] 2 FLR 713 at 737–738, ironically also per Wall J. See also *Re R (a Minor) (Religious Sect)* [1993] 2 FCR 525, sub nom *Re R (a Minor) (Residence: Religion)* [1993] 2 FLR 163, CA – a case involving a father who was a member of the Exclusive Bretheren. Note also the conclusions of *Making Contact Work*, above, at paras 11.9 et seq, including the recommendation that CAFCASS prepare proposals, inter alia, for educational programmes for parenting and support packages to be operated under a family assistance order.
6   [1999] 3 FCR 700, [1999] 2 FLR 512.
7   [1993] 2 FCR 64, [1993] 2 FLR 992, CA.

Restricting further applications under Section 91(14)

5.154   Section 91(14) allows the court on 'disposing of any application for an order' under the CA 1989 to restrain future applications without the leave of the court. Although perhaps more associated with private law orders, this power can be exercised both in respect of private *and* public law proceedings.[1] It seems to be accepted[2] that in deciding whether to make a s 91(14) order the court should apply the paramountcy principle under s 1(1). Accordingly, restrictions on applications by a parent who wishes to raise issues concerning the child's welfare should only be imposed where the welfare of the child so requires.[3]

1   See *Re P (Children Act 1989, ss 22 and 26: Local Authority Compliance)* [2000] 2 FLR 910. But note s 91(15) imposes an automatic leave requirement to make further applications within six months of a previous application to discharge a care, supervision or education supervision order or for the substitution of a supervision order for a care order or a child assessment order and similarly s 91(17) does so following the refusal of a contact application under s 34.
2   See *Re P (a Minor) (Residence Order: Child's Welfare)* [2000] Fam 15 at 17, sub nom *Re P (a Minor) (Residence Order: Restriction Order)* [1999] 3 All ER 734 at 752, but note the discussion above at para 2.12.
3   *B v B (Residence Order: Restricting Applications* [1997] 2 FCR 518, [1997] 2 FCR 518, [1997]

1 FLR 139, CA; confirmed in *Re R (a Minor) (Leave to Make Applications)* [1998] 2 FCR 129, sub nom *Re R (Residence: Contact: Restricting Applications)* [1998] 1 FLR 749, CA, in which a restricting order was made together with a contact order after a renewed residence application had been made with no fresh evidence. In *Re M (Contact: Family Assistance: McKenzie Friend)* [1999] 1 FCR 703, [1999] 1 FLR 75, the Court of Appeal proposed making a s 91(14) order to last as long as the family assistance order (made in order to facilitate indirect contact) was in existence.

5.155 Section 91(14) orders represent a substantial interference with a citizen's right of unrestricted access to the courts and how this should be balanced against the child's welfare was carefully considered in *Re P (a Minor) (Residence Order: Child's Welfare)*.[1] Butler-Sloss LJ commented:

'A number of guidelines might be drawn from the cases . . . It is, however, important to remember that these are only guidelines intended to assist and not to replace the wording of the section . . .

(1) Section 91(14) should be read in conjunction with section 1(1) of the CA 1989 which made the welfare of the child the paramount consideration.

(2) The power to restrict applications to the court was discretionary and in the exercise of its discretion the court had to weigh in the balance all the relevant circumstances.

(3) An important consideration was that to impose a restriction was a statutory intrusion into the right of a party to bring proceedings before the court and to be heard in matters affecting his/her child.

(4) The power was therefore to be used with great care and sparingly: the exception and not the rule.

(5) It was generally to be seen as a useful weapon of last resort in cases of repeated and unreasonable applications.

(6) In suitable circumstances, and on clear evidence, a court might impose the leave restriction in cases where the welfare of the child required it, although there was no past history of making unreasonable applications.

(7) In cases under paragraph 6 above, the court would need to be satisfied: first, that the facts went beyond the commonly encountered need for a time to settle to a regime ordered by the court and the all too common situation where there was animosity between the adults in dispute or between the local authority and the family and; second, that there was a serious risk that, without the imposition of the restriction, the child or the primary carers would be subject to unacceptable strain.

(8) A court might impose the restriction on making applications in the absence of a request from any of the parties, subject, of course, to the rules of natural justice such as an opportunity for the parties to be heard.

(9) A restriction might be imposed with or without limitation of time.

(10) The degree of restriction should be proportionate to the harm it was intended to avoid. Therefore the court imposing the restriction should carefully consider the extent of the restriction to be imposed and specify, where appropriate, the type of application to be restrained and the duration of the order.

(11) It would be undesirable in other than the most exceptional cases to make the order ex parte.'

Her Ladyship continued:

'It was suggested to us that s 91(14) may infringe the Human Rights Act 1998 and European Convention for the Protection of Human Rights and Fundamental Freedoms 1950, Art 6(1), by depriving a litigant of the right to a fair trial. I do not consider that submission to be correct. The applicant is not denied access to the court. It is a partial restriction[2] in that it does not allow him the right to an immediate inter partes hearing. It thereby protects the other parties and the child from being drawn into the proposed proceedings unless or until a court had ruled that the application should be allowed to proceed.'

1 [2000] Fam 15 at 37–38, sub nom *Re P (a Minor) (Residence Order: Restriction Order)* [1999] 3 All ER 734 at 752–753, CA and the cases there cited.
2 It is, however, possible to impose an absolute prohibition under the inherent jurisdiction, see *Re R (a Minor) (Leave to Make Application)* [1998] 2 FCR 129, sub nom *Re R (Residence: Contact: Restricting Applications)* [1998] 1 FLR 749.

5.156 The appropriate procedure for applying to discharge the order or for applying for leave, notwithstanding a s 91(14) order, is to issue the application on Form C2. If the application is successful, then Form C1 should be issued. While the court may make a s 91(14) order of its own motion, the parties should be warned so as to allow a proper opportunity for representations.[1]

1 *Re S (Contact: Prohibition of Applications)* [1995] 1 FCR 617, [1994] 2 FLR 1057, where it was also doubted whether the court could impose a condition eg for psychiatric support for any further application.

5.157 Where a s 91(14) order has been made, leave to make a further application should not be granted lightly and generally only inter partes.[1] Such applications are not governed by the criteria set out in s 10(9),[2] rather the test is simply whether the applicant has demonstrated any need for renewed judicial investigations.[3]

1 *Re N (a Minor) (Residence Order: Appeal)* [1996] 2 FCR 377, sub nom *Re N (S 91(14) Order)* [1996] 1 FLR 356.
2 Discussed at paras 5.117 et seq.
3 *Re A (Application for Leave)* [1999] 1 FCR 127, [1998] 1 FLR 1, CA, per Thorpe LJ, doubting *Re G (Child Case: Parental Involvement)* [1996] 2 FCR 1, [1996] 1 FLR 857 in which the test was said to be whether there was an arguable case, and not whether there was a reasonable likelihood that the substantive action would succeed.

Court ordered investigation under s 37

5.158 Under s 37 where, in any family proceedings[1] it appears to the court that it may be appropriate to make a care or supervision order under s 31, the court may direct a local authority to investigate the child's circumstances. This does not allow the court to make a public law order in private law proceedings,[2] and the court should only order a local authority investigation where it appears that it might be appropriate to make a public law order.[3]

1 For the meaning of which see paras 5.101–5.102.
2 *Re CE (a Minor) (Appointment of Guardian ad Litem)* [1995] 1 FCR 387, sub nom *Re CE (Section 37 Direction)* [1995] 1 FLR 26. See also *Re M (a Minor) (Official Solicitor's Role)* [1998] 3 FCR 315, [1998] 2 FLR 815, CA – inappropriate to use s 37 if the Official Solicitor is invited to investigate; and *Re H (Child's Circumstances: Direction to Investigate)* [1993] 2 FCR 277, sub nom *Re H (a Minor) (Section 37 Direction)* [1993] 2 FLR 541.
3 *Re L (a Minor) (Section 37 Direction)* [1999] 3 FCR 642, [1999] 1 FLR 984, CA.

The relationship between private law orders and public law proceedings

5.159 The relationship between the powers under Pt II and the operation of other Parts, in particular Pts III and IV of the CA 1989 has still to be fully developed. However, notwithstanding that the Act itself provides for some interplay between the different parts[1] (for example, the duty of the courts in care proceedings to consider whether to make a s 8 order instead of a care

order or in addition to a supervision order; the ability of individuals to seek
a discharge of a care order by means of an application for a residence order
rather than an application under s 39;[2] the power of the courts to order a local
authority to supervise a s 8 contact order by means of a family assistance
order;[3] and the power in any family proceedings to direct a local authority to
investigate the child's circumstances),[4] it has become evident that the courts
themselves still consider that a clear distinction should be drawn between the
so-called 'private law' and 'public law' provisions of the CA 1989. As
Balcombe LJ put it in *D v D (Child Care: Powers of Court)*,[5] 'There is no
statutory link between the private and public law parts of the CA 1989'.

1 See paras 2.61–2.63 of the Department of Health's Guidance and Regulations, Vol 1, Court
  Orders.
2 See further para 8.125.
3 See *Leeds County Council v C* [1993] 1 FCR 585, [1993] 1 FLR 269.
4 Viz under s 37, discussed above at para 5.158.
5 [1994] 3 FCR 28 at 158, sub nom *D v D (County Court Jurisdiction: Injunction)* [1993] 2 FLR
  802 at 812, CA.

5.160 The rulings in *Nottingham County Council v P*[1] and *D v D (Child
Care: Powers of Court)*[2] taken together with other limitations on the power to
make prohibited steps or specific issue orders, namely, that the orders themselves must relate to an aspect of parental responsibility[3] and cannot be used
so as to confer any aspect of parental responsibility upon a local authority
that it does not already have,[4] effectively means that Pt II cannot be looked to
either as means of forcing local authorities to act under Pts III to V[5] nor to
prevent them from so doing. What remains unclear, however, is the extent to
which orders can be made against individuals which have a direct impact on
public law powers. Hence, while it seems clear that the court cannot under a
Pt II order require a local authority to provide accommodation against the
wishes of a parent,[6] it remains a moot point whether one parent could obtain
a prohibited steps order preventing the other from objecting to the child
being accommodated. However on the strength of the decision in *Re S and D
(Child Case: Powers of Court)*[7] which held that the court had no power to
restrain a mother from removing her children from accommodation, it seems
unlikely that such an order could be made. On the other hand note might also
be taken of Balcombe LJ's comments in *D v D*[8] that while there was no direct
power under Pt II to prevent local authorities from investigating the child's
circumstances under s 47, nevertheless if satisfied:

> 'that a person with parental responsibility for a child was exercising the rights
> attaching to that responsibility in a way which would be detrimental to the child's
> welfare, eg. by permitting the child to be exposed to unnecessary interviews or
> examinations, *the court in the exercise of its private law jurisdiction could make a pro-
> hibited steps order under s 8 restraining that person from exercising those rights.* Once
> such an order had been made neither the Council nor the police (except in the exer-
> cise of their emergency powers under s 46 so far as those extend) could have taken
> any step invasive of the lives of these children without first applying to the court'.
> [Emphasis added.]

In other words Pt II orders can apparently be made against individuals which
directly impact upon local authority powers under other Parts of the CA
1989.

1 [1994] Fam 18, [1993] 3 All ER 815, CA, discussed at para 5.81.
2 [1994] 3 FCR 28, [1993] 2 FLR 802, CA, discussed at para 5.95.

3   See para 5.75.
4   See s 9(5)(b), discussed at para 5.80.
5   Eg to force local authorities to accommodate children or to bring care proceedings: see *Re J (a Minor) (Specific Issue Order: Leave To Apply)* [1995] 3 FCR 799, [1995] 1 FLR 669.
6   This would seem to be the result of s 9(5)(b).
7   [1995] 1 FCR 626, sub nom *Re S and D (Children: Powers of Court)* [1995] 2 FLR 456, CA.
8   [1994] 3 FCR 28 at 40, sub nom *D v D (County Court Jurisdiction: Injunctions)* [1993] 2 FLR 802 at 812–813.

SPECIAL GUARDIANSHIP

Introduction

5.161   The Adoption and Children Bill 2002 makes provision for a new status to be known as 'special guardianship'. Special guardianship orders are intended to provide a more permanent status for non parents than that provided by a residence order but unlike adoption they will not extinguish the legal relationship between the child and his or her birth family. In other words these new orders are intended to meet the needs of children for whom adoption is not appropriate (eg older children who do not wish to be adopted) but who cannot return to their birth parents and who 'would benefit from the permanence provided by a legally secure family placement'.[1] Special guardians will be distinguishable from guardians since unlike the latter, who as we have seen replace the deceased parents, they take office during the parents' life-time. Furthermore unlike guardians, special guardians have to be appointed by court, ie there is no power to make private appointments.

1   See the Explanatory Notes to the Bill para 17.

5.162   The proposal to have a new form of guardianship was first made in the Consultative Document on Adoption Law in 1992.[1] At that stage it was proposed that there should be power to appoint what were to be called the child's 'inter vivos guardian'. Such guardians were to have all the rights, duties and powers of a guardian under s 5 of the CA 1989 save for the power to agree to the child's adoption.[2] This proposal was not, however, included in the draft Adoption Bill 1996. The proposal in the 2002 Bill does not make reference to the guardianship provisions but will insert an entirely new set of provisions, the proposed ss 14A to 14G, into the CA 1989.

1   Department of Health, para 6.5.
2   Published as part of a government White Paper: 'Adoption – A Service for Children' (Department of Health and Welsh Office).

The power to make special guardianship orders

5.163   A special guardianship order is an order appointing one or more individuals to be a child's special guardian, or special guardians.[1] By confining the power to appoint 'individuals' it is clear that the court cannot appoint a body such as a local authority nor what has been described as an 'artificial individual' such as a director of social services.[2] Only non parents can be appointed.[3] Individuals must be aged 18 or over.[4]

1   See the prospective s 14A(1).
2   See the similar restriction in appointing guardians under s 5 of the CA 1989 and applied in
    Re SH (Care Order: Orphan) [1995] 1 FLR 746, discussed at para 3.101.
3   See s 14A(2)(b).
4   Section 14A(2)(a).

5.164   The court (ie the High Court, county court or magistrates' court)[1] may
make a special guardianship order either upon application or upon its own
motion in any 'family proceedings'.[2] Guardians, those with a residence order
in their favour, those with whom the child has lived for a period of at least
three years[3] and any person having the consent of (i) each of the persons in
whose favour a residence order is in force (ii) the local authority if the
child is subject to a care order; or (iii) in any other case, each of the persons
who have parental responsibility for the child, are *entitled* to apply for a
special guardianship order.[4] Anyone else, for example, grandparents who
have not provided a home for the child, must obtain court leave.[5] Local
authority foster parents (unless relatives) will additionally need the consent
of the local authority, if the child has not lived with them for one year.[6]

1   This is made clear both in the Bill and in the CA 1989 (s 105).
2   Section 14A(6)(b). 'Family proceedings' are defined by s 8(3),(4) of the CA 1989, see paras
    5.101 et seq. Inter alia this will mean the court has power to make special guardianship
    orders in adoption proceedings.
3   The period of three years need not be continuous but must not have begun more than five
    years before nor ended three months before the making of the application: S 14A(50(c)
    applying s 10(10) of the CA 1989.
4   Section 14A(5).
5   Section 14A(3)(b).
6   Section 14A(4) applying s 9(3) (as amended) of the CA 1989.

5.165   A prerequisite of applying is the need for applicants to give three
months' written notice to the local authority of their intention to apply for
such an order.[1] The local authority[2] must then investigate the matter and
prepare a report for the court about the suitability of the applicant and any
other relevant matters.[3] The court, too, has power to direct a local authority
to make such an investigation and report[4] and indeed must do so if it wishes
to make such an order.[5]

1   Section 14A(7).
2   But they can arrange for someone else to carry out the investigation: s 14A(10).
3   Section 14A(8). Regulations may prescribe matters to be covered in the report.
4   Section 14A(9).
5   Section 14A(11).

5.166   In deciding whether or not to make a special guardianship order the
court must regard the child's welfare as the paramount consideration and be
satisfied that making an order is better than making no order at all.[1] It must
also apply the welfare checklist under s 1(3).[2] It is also obliged to be mindful
of the general principle[3] that delay is likely to prejudice the child's welfare and
to that end courts are empowered to set timescales for proceedings involving
special guardianship applications.[4]

1   Section 1(1) and (5) of the CA 1989.
2   See the specific amendment by s 14G(3) to s 1(4)(b) of the CA 1989.
3   Under s 1(2) of the CA 1989, discussed at paras 2.58 et seq.
4   See s 14E.

5.167 Before making an order the court must consider whether a contact order (for example, to enable continued contact with the both parents or other members of the family) should be made at the same time.[1] This latter power signals that unlike adoption orders, special guardianship with contact is not be regarded as unusual. There is no restriction comparable to that under s 9(6) with respect to s 8 orders, that orders relating to 16 or 17-year-olds should only be made in exceptional circumstances.

1 Section 14B(1).

5.168 On making a special guardianship order the court may also give leave for the child to be known by a new surname.[1] This express power will no doubt encourage such applications and signals the difference between these orders and adoption, where a new surname is automatic, and a residence order where a change of name is not encouraged.[2] This is not to say, however, that such orders should always be made. It would not be appropriate to do so, for example, in the face of opposition from a child anxious to preserve his or her identity. The court can also give permission for the child to be taken outside the United Kingdom for more than three months.[3] As with s 8 orders the court will be empowered to add directions and conditions to any special guardianship order,[4] and to make provisions which have effect for a specified period.[5]

1 Section 14A(2)(a).
2 See paras 5.27 et seq.
3 Section 14A(2)(b). See further para 5.169 below.
4 Section 14E(4).
5 Section 14E(5), applying s 11(7) of the CA 1989, save s 11(7)(c) under which there is a general power to make an order for a specified time.

5.169 Special guardians will, for the duration of the order, have parental responsibility for the child which, for the most part, they will be able to exercise to the exclusion of anyone else, apart from another special guardian.[1] The exceptions to the power to exercise responsibility independently are: (1) circumstances where the law requires the consent of *all* parties with parental responsibility,[2] for example, sterilisation,[3] ritual circumcision,[4] changes in the child's education;[5] (2) consenting to the child's adoption or placement for adoption;[6] (3) causing the child to be known by a new surname[7] or removing him from the United Kingdom for a period of more than three months.[8] Special guardians will, however, have the power to appoint a guardian to take their place upon their death.[9] Conversely, they will have an obligation to take reasonable steps to inform parents with parental responsibility and guardians that the child has died.[10] A special guardianship order discharges any existing care order, related contact order or any s 8 order.[11]

1 Section 14C(1).
2 Section 14C(2)(a).
3 This example is given in the Explanatory Notes to the Bill, op cit, at para 235.
4 Cf *Re J (Child's Religious Upbringing and Circumcision)* [2000] 1 FCR 307, sub nom *Re J (Specific Issue Orders) (Muslim Upbringing and Circumcision)* [2000] 1 FLR 571, CA, discussed at para 3.92.
5 Cf *Re G (a Minor) (Parental Responsibility: Education)* [1995] 2 FCR 53, [1994] 2 FLR 964, CA, discussed at para 3.92.
6 Section 14C(2)(b).
7 Section 14C(3)(a).
8 Section 14C(3)(b) and (4). It will be noted that unlike residence orders which entitles a residence holder to remove a child from the UK for a period of less than one month, special guardians are entitled to remove the child from the UK for a period of *three* months.

9 Section 5(4) of the CA 1989, as amended by s 14G(4)(b).
10 Section 14C(5).
11 CA 1989, s 91(5A) to be added by Sch 3, to the 2002 Bill.

5.170 As the Explanatory Notes to the Bill explain:[1]

'The intention is that the special guardian has a clear responsibility for all the day to day decisions about caring for the child or young person and for taking decisions about his upbringing. But the order retains the basic link with the birth parents, unlike adoption. They remain legally the child's parents, though their ability to exercise their parental responsibility is limited. They retain the right to consent or not to the child's adoption or placement for adoption'.

1 See para 236.

Variation and Discharge

5.171 Unlike adoption orders, special guardianship orders may be varied or discharged, either upon application[1] or upon the court's own motion.[2] Those entitled to apply[3] are (a) the special guardian; (b) any parent or guardian of the child (but only one year after the order has been made and with leave of the court, which may only be given if it is satisfied that there has been a significant change of circumstances since the making of the order);[4] (c) the child, subject to leave of the court, which may only be granted if it is satisfied that the child has sufficient understanding to make the application;[5] (d) if a residence order is subsequently made, the person in whose favour it is made, and (e) if a care order is subsequently made, the designated local authority.

1 Section 14D(1).
2 Section 14D(2).
3 Section 14D(1)(a)–(e).
4 Section 14D(3), (5) and (6). These safeguards are intended to provide additional security for special guardians.
5 Section 14D(3), (4).

Special Guardianship Support Services

5.172 Section 14F makes important provision requiring local authorities to make arrangements within their area of what is to be known as special guardianship support services, namely, to provide counselling, advice and information and any other services as prescribed in regulations. The intention[1] is to ensure that local authorities put in place a range of support services, including financial support, to be available where appropriate for special guardians and their children. These provisions will be given additional teeth by the obligation under s 14G for local authorities to establish a procedure for considering representations (including complaints) made to them in respect of these support services by either special guardians or their children.

1 See the Explanatory Notes, para 240.

Commentary

5.173 Although these provisions are reminiscent of the former custodianship provisions,[1] which did not prove successful, there is every reason to believe that they will prove to be more useful. Certainly the name is better, while the provisions themselves are much more straightforward. Moreover, special guardianship clearly offers more security than residence orders while the provisions governing support are likely to be a further inducement to potential applicants. Prima facie one would expect the main users to be relatives, particularly grandparents and foster parents, particularly of older children. One issue, however, that might detract from their widespread use by relatives is the requirement to notify and be investigated by local authority.

1 Viz those provided under the Children Act 1975, Pt II (brought into force in December 1985) which were repealed by the CA 1989.

Chapter 6

Local authority support for children and families

INTRODUCTION

6.1 A central concept of the CA 1989 is that family life should be independent and free from unjustified interference. This is established by the concept of parental responsibility and reinforced by the presumption that no court order should be made unless it is for the child's welfare. It is also reinforced by the concept that local authorities should work to support these aims. This work should be undertaken with those having parental responsibility, as a partnership[1] between them.

1   The concept of partnership was introduced in the Guidance to the Act. See the Care of Children: Principles and Practice in Regulations and Guidance (HMSO 1989).

6.2 Part III of the CA 1989 sets out the duties imposed on local authorities in respect of the services which they must or may provide for children and their families. The provisions are intended to enable authorities to support family life in furtherance of the key concepts of the Act. The services relate to children in need and children with a disability. They may in certain circumstances charge for the services.

6.3 The scheme of Pt III is to impose a general duty in relation to the welfare of children in need, specific duties and powers in relation to day care and the accommodation of children looked after by a local authority. There are further specific duties and powers contained in Sch 2 aimed at facilitating the general duty. Wide-ranging advice on the whole of Pt III of the Act is given in the Department of Health's publications, the Children Act 1989 Guidance and Regulations, in Volume 3 on Family Placements, Volume 4 on Residential Care, the Framework Document on the Assessment of Children in Need and their Families[1] and the National Minimum Standards for Fostering Services.[2] The most comprehensive discussion of the implementation of these provisions is contained in Children Act Now: Messages from Research.[3]

1   Department of Health (The Stationery Office, 2000).
2   Department of Health (The Stationery Office, 2002).
3   The Stationery Office (2001).

GENERAL DUTY TO CHILDREN IN NEED

6.4 Section 17 imposes on every authority a general duty to safeguard and promote the welfare of children in their area[1] who are 'in need' and, so far as is consistent with that duty, to promote the upbringing of such children by their families by providing a range and level of services appropriate to those children's needs.[2] This is an important provision, intended to underpin a central philosophy of the legislation, that children should, wherever possible, be brought up by their families. Services should be available so as to alleviate the suffering of children and to avoid, if possible, the removal of children from their families. Nonetheless it is a general duty, not enforceable by an individual.[3] On the other hand an authority may not discriminate against an individual for no good reason and on that basis the authority must at least carry out an adequate assessment of the need in each case, so that they can establish whether the degree of need requires a service.[4] This would appear to leave open the prospect that a local authority accepts that there is a duty to assess the needs of a child but, even if it finds that those needs are substantial, it could still say to a family that those needs will not be met.

1 The meaning of the words 'in their area' is that physical presence is the only requirement: *R(S) v London Borough of Wandsworth, London Borough of Hammersmith and Fulham, London Borough of Lambeth* [2001] EWHC Admin 709, [2002] 1 FLR 469.
2 Section 17(1).
3 *A v Lambeth London Borough Council* [2001] EWCA Civ 1264, [2001] 3 FCR 678, [2002] 1 FLR 353.
4 *R(AB & SD) v Nottinghamshire County Council* [2001] EWHC Admin 235, [2001] 3 FCR 530.

6.5 The duty under s 17 is not directed to the provision of accommodation, so that where a child remains with his family, but his needs indicate a requirement for a particular kind of accommodation, provision should be made under the housing legislation.[1] The Court of Appeal has, however, held that a local authority has the power to provide accommodation for the family of a child in need.[2]

1 Housing Act 1988 and 1996. See *(R) A v Lambeth London Borough Council* [2001] EWCA Civ 1264, [2001] 3 FCR 678, [2002] 1 FLR 353 and paras 6.11 and 6.41.
2 *R (W) v Lambeth London Borough Council* [2002] EWCA Civ 613, [2002] 2 FLR 327.

1. Definitions

(a) 'In need'

6.6 A child[1] is defined as being 'in need' if he is unlikely to achieve or maintain, or to have the opportunity of achieving or maintaining, a reasonable standard of health or development without the provision for him of services by a local authority under Pt III, or his health or development is likely to be significantly impaired or further impaired, without the provision for him of such services, or he is disabled.[2] The incorporation of provision for disabled children within the general concept of children in need was an important development in the Children Act.

1 A person under 18: s 105(1)
2 Section 17(10).

(b) 'Health' and 'development'

6.7 'Health' means physical or mental health and 'development' means physical, intellectual, emotional, social or behavioural development.[1]

1   Section 17(11). The same definitions are provided in s 31(9). See para 8.41.

(c) 'Family'

6.8 'Family' includes any person who has parental responsibility for the child and any other person with whom he has been living and thus is not limited to relatives.[1] A local authority service may be provided for a family if with a view to safeguarding or promoting the child's welfare.[2]

1   Section 17(10).
2   Section 17(3).

6.9 Authorities are required to facilitate the provision of Pt III services by others, in particular voluntary organisations, and may make such arrangements as they see fit for others to provide such services (for example, day care or fostering services).[1]

1   Section 17(5). See also 'Family Support, Day Care and Educational Provision for Young Children', Guidance, Volume 2 (Dept of Health, 1991) at para 2.11.

2. Co-operation between authorities

6.10 A social services authority may request the help of another authority, including an education authority, a housing authority, or a health authority or special health authority, Primary Care Trust or National Health Service Trust, to carry out duties under Pt III. An authority so requested shall comply with the request if it is compatible with their own statutory or other duties and obligations and does not unduly prejudice the discharge of any of their functions.[1] A housing authority is not obliged to provide accommodation, but it does have a duty to ascertain whether it could provide a solution to the problems of homeless families so as to prevent children suffering from lack of accommodation.[2]

1   Section 27.
2   *R v Northavon District Council, ex p Smith* [1994] 2 AC 402, HL. See para 6.41.

6.11 Services provided under Pt III may include giving assistance in kind or in exceptional circumstances in cash, unconditionally or conditionally as to repayment.[1] There is no duty to provide assistance, in order to provide accommodation for a child and parent.[2] The authority may provide cash to assist with accommodation under s 17 and has a general discretion to make provision for the economic or social well-being of its area under s 2 of the Local Government Act 2000.[3]

1   Section 17(6) and (7). This includes the power to give assistance with the provision of accommodation: *R (W) v Lambeth London Borough Council* [2002] EWCA Civ 613, [2002] 2 FLR 327.
2   *R (G) v Barnet London Borough Council* [2001] EWCA Civ 540, [2001] 2 FCR 193, [2001] 2 FLR 877. The Court of Appeal held the offer of assistance to the mother to return to the Netherlands was lawful.
3   *R(J) v London Borough of Enfield* [2002] EWHC 432 (Admin).

6.12 Authorities are required to have regard to the means of the child and each of his parents, although no person is liable for repayment at any time when he is in receipt of income support, family credit or disability working allowance.[1] This would suggest that an authority must consider individual means before giving assistance or cash and must not have a blanket policy in relation to any group, and that authorities could impose a condition as to repayment when a person became able to pay. An authority may also contribute to the cost of looking after a child who is living with a person under a residence order, such as a relative or foster parent, except where that person is a parent or step-parent.[2]

1 Section 17(8) and (9).
2 Sch 1, para 15.

6.13 Co-ordinated assessments should be carried out in accordance with the Assessment Framework considered in chapter 7. Interventions may be short term but should be geared to the long-term interests of the child. They should also take account of the capacity of the whole community to support a family and not just the social services department. Services provided under s 17 should work alongside other services, notably health and education, to promote the well-being of children and young people. This community approach is particularly important given the prevalence of mental disorders in children aged 5 to 15.[1] Boys from low-income families are most at risk and provide the populations of prisons, long term care and unemployment.

1 The mental health of children and adolescents in Great Britain (Office of National Statistics, March 2000). This report showed a prevalence of mental disorder of 1 in 10 for this age group.

SERVICES FOR CHILDREN WITH DISABILITIES

6.14 A child is disabled if 'he is blind, deaf or dumb or suffers from mental disorder of any kind or is substantially and permanently handicapped by illness, injury or congenital deformity or such other disability as may be prescribed'.[1] The definition is that used for adults under the National Assistance Act 1948 and covers children affected by physical disability, chronic sickness, mental disability, sensory disability, communication impairment and mental illness.

1 Section 17(11). For research on this subject see Making Progress; Change and Development in Services to Disabled Children under the Children Act 1989, Robinson C, Weston C and Minkes J, (University of Bristol, 1995).

6.15 As children in need, disabled children will be able to benefit from the same services as other children. Additionally, the Act imposes on local authorities a duty to provide services for children with disabilities so as to minimise the effect of their disabilities and give such children the opportunity to lead lives which are as normal as possible.[1] The Children Act Report 2000 noted that about 12% of children in need receiving services were disabled.[2] Instead of providing services, an authority may make payments to a person with parental responsibility for a disabled child or to a disabled child aged 16 or 17 to enable them to obtain the provision of services which the authority would otherwise have provided.[3]

1   Sch 2, para 3.
2   Department of Health (2001).
3   Section 17A, inserted by the Carers and Disabled Children Act 2000, s 7. See also the requirement under s 6 of that Act to carry out an assessment and the Disabled Children (Direct Payments) (England) Regulations 2001, SI 2001/442.

SPECIFIC POWERS AND DUTIES

6.16   In pursuance of the general duty, authorities have specific duties and powers.[1] These may be amended or added to by the Secretary of State, which enables the government to ensure the development of good local authority practice without recourse to Parliament. As the provisions exist at present, they leave wide discretion to the local authority, since duties are expressed in terms of 'taking reasonable steps' or providing 'as they consider appropriate'. There are only three absolute duties: to publish information about services provided, to open and maintain a register of disabled children and to establish a complaints procedure.[2]

1   See Sch 2 generally.
2   See s 26 and paras 13.46 et seq.

1.   Identification of children in need

6.17   Every local authority must take reasonable steps to identify the extent to which there are children in need in their area. They are required to publish information[1] about the services they provide under the general duty, day care services under s 18, accommodation for children under s 20, and their duties to children leaving or who have left care.[2] Where they consider it appropriate, they must publish information about similar services provided by others. They must also take such steps as are reasonably practicable to ensure that those who might benefit from the services receive the information relevant to them.

1   Sch 2, para 1.
2   See paras 6.56 et seq.

2.   Promoting the upbringing of children by their families

6.18   In order to discharge the general duty to promote the upbringing of children by their families, local authorities are given a number of duties in relation to what might broadly be described as family support mechanisms. They should make provision for advice, guidance, counselling and home help. Occupational, social, cultural or recreational activities or assistance with holidays may be provided.[1]

1   Sch 2, para 8.

6.19   Every authority shall provide such family centres as they consider appropriate in relation to children within their area.[1] Although many authorities have provided a wide range of family centres, as an important part of their service to children in need, they had not previously been under any duty to make such a provision. A 'family centre' is a centre at which a child, his parents, a person with parental responsibility for him or any other person looking after him may attend for (a) occupational, cultural, social or recreational activities; or (b) advice, guidance or counselling; and, in case (b), may be accommodated at the same time.

1 Sch 2, para 9.

3.   Prevention of abuse and neglect

6.20   Every authority shall take reasonable steps through the provision of Pt III services to prevent children in their area suffering ill-treatment or neglect. There is a duty to inform another authority if a child who the authority believes is likely to suffer harm, lives or proposes to live in the area of that authority.[1] There is a connected duty to take reasonable steps, through the provision of Pt III services, to reduce the need to bring proceedings for care or supervision orders, family or other proceedings which might lead to placement in care, High Court proceedings under the inherent jurisdiction or criminal proceedings in respect of children. Authorities should also encourage children not to commit criminal offences and avoid the need for placing them in secure accommodation.[2] This paragraph would appear to be a general encouragement to local authorities to offer services to families which may be breaking up, so as to try to avoid the worst effects of marital disharmony.

1 Sch 2, para 4.
2 Above, para 6.

4.   Provision of accommodation to third party to protect children

6.21   Where it appears to an authority that a child is suffering or is likely to suffer ill-treatment at the hands of another person living at the same premises and that other person proposes to move from those premises, the authority may assist that other person to obtain alternative accommodation, including assistance in kind,[1] on conditions as to repayment if applicable.

1 Sch 2, para 5.

6.22   This provision is a response to concern expressed in the Report of the Enquiry into Child Abuse in Cleveland 1987[1] that children, who were allegedly sexually abused, were removed from the family home, when it might have been in their interests for the alleged abuser to have left, if he could have been provided with alternative accommodation. It is intended to allow local authorities to assist those who are willing to leave voluntarily.

1 CM 412, 1988. See also provisions on exclusion of individuals under emergency protection orders and interim care orders: paras 7.47 and 8.32.

5. Duty to consider racial groups

6.23 In making any arrangements either for the provision of day care or designed to encourage persons to act as local authority foster parents, the authority shall have regard to the different racial groups to which children in need in their area belong.[1]

1 Sch 2, para 11.

DAY CARE

6.24 Every local authority is required[1] to provide such day care as is appropriate for children in need within their area who are five and under and not yet attending school. Day care is defined as any form of care or supervised activity provided for children during the day, whether or not on a regular basis. The authority may provide day care for such children even though they are not in need. They may also provide facilities including training, advice, guidance and counselling for those caring for children in day care or who accompany children in day care. An authority is required to provide for children in need who are attending school, such care or activities supervised by a responsible person, as is appropriate outside school hours or during school holidays and may make such provision for children who are not in need.

1 Section 18. A comprehensive regime for the registration and inspection of day care and childminding services is contained in Pts X and XA of the 1989 Act, as inserted by the Care Standards Act 2000, s 79. These services are not the subject of consideration in this work.

6.25 Authorities are required to review their day care provision.[1] Department of Health Guidance makes detailed observations on the development of services and states that local authorities should have an agreed policy for discharging their general duty to provide day care for children in need.[2] Research suggests that, while there was enthusiasm for the provisions of the Act which gave some prominence to day care services, there has been little progress in coordinated action, identification of levels of need or increase in provision. Lack of resources had made it difficult to develop or expand day care for children in need or other children.[3]

1 Section 19.
2 Volume 2, 'Family Support, Day Care and Educational Provision for Young Children,'(Dept of Health, 1991).
3 Implementing the Children Act for Children under 8: Thomas Coram Research Unit (HMSO, 1994). See also Play and Care out of School, Petrie P, Poland G and Wayne S (HMSO 1994) and Out-of-school Services, Out-of-school Lives, Petrie P, Egharevba I, Oliver C and Poland G, (The Stationery Office 2000).

ACCOMMODATING CHILDREN

1. Duty to accommodate

6.26 Subject as set out below local authorities must provide accommodation for a child in need who requires it as a result of there being no person with parental responsibility for him, or because he is lost or abandoned, or because the person who has been caring for him is prevented (whether or not permanently and for whatever reason) from providing suitable accommodation or care.[1] The words 'for whatever reason' clarify that accommodation may be provided because of the disability of the child as well as that of the parent.

1   Section 20(1). See para 13.44 for consideration of whether this duty is enforceable.

6.27   Authorities have a discretion to provide accommodation for any child if they consider that to do so would safeguard or promote his welfare.[1]

1   Section 20(4).

6.28   Before providing accommodation under s 20, the authority must, as far as is reasonably practicable and consistent with the child's welfare, ascertain the child's wishes regarding the provision of accommodation and give due consideration to them having regard to his age and understanding.[1]

1   Section 20(6).

6.29   If there is no person with parental responsibility, accommodation should normally be a short-term solution. The authority cannot obtain parental responsibility without a care order but, for a young child, someone should be exercising parental responsibility.[1] The authority could seek a guardian or person who would obtain a residence order for the child. If the child is temporarily lost, he needs to be looked after, and his parent will resume care as soon as he is found.

1   See para 8.68 for discussion of taking care proceedings in respect of orphans.

6.30   'Abandoned' was not defined in previous child-care legislation, but it has been held that in adoption legislation it means 'leaving the child to its fate'.[1] Such a child should not be accommodated for more than the shortest period. Either the parent will come forward and the child returned or an agreement for looking after the child will be reached in partnership with the parent, or more secure plans will be made for the child's future.

1   *Watson v Nikolaisen* [1955] 2QB 286, [1955] 2 All ER 427.

6.31   Where a person is prevented from providing a child with suitable accommodation or care, whether an agreement for the child to be accommodated or care proceedings is the more appropriate must depend on the circumstances. If the child is suffering significant harm, the authority will have to consider carefully, in consultation with those having parental responsibility, whether the welfare of the child requires a care order rather than an agreement for accommodation.

6.32   Authorities must provide[1] for the reception and accommodation of children removed or kept away from home under Pt V of the Act.[2] The duty to provide accommodation for a child arises where he:

(a)   has been removed into police protection and the authority is requested to provide accommodation under s 46(3)(f);
(b)   has been kept in police detention and arrangements are made for him to be accommodated under the Police and Criminal Evidence Act 1984, s 38(6);

(c) is on remand under paragraph 7(5) of Sch 7 to the Powers of Criminal Courts (Sentencing) Act 2000 or S 23(1) of the Children and Young Persons Act 1969;

(d) is the subject of a supervision order imposing a residence requirement under paragraph 5 of Sch 6 to the Act of 2000; or

(e) is in the care of a local authority under s 31.

1 Section 21.
2 Ie under an emergency protection order under s 44 or police protection under s 47.

2. Limits on providing accommodation

6.33 A local authority may not provide accommodation if any person with parental responsibility for the child, who is willing and able to provide or arrange accommodation, objects to the authority so doing.[1] Any person who has parental responsibility may remove the child at any time.[2] These provisions do not apply where a child of 16 or over agrees to being provided with accommodation.[3] The effect of the provisions is that if one parent places the child in accommodation the other parent can remove him, if he has parental responsibility. This is limited insofar as, if a person with a residence order, or a person who has care of the child pursuant to an order under the High Court's inherent jurisdiction, or all of them if there are more than one, agrees to the child being accommodated, another person with parental responsibility may not object or remove the child.[4]

1 Section 20(7).
2 Section 20(8).On whether the court may restrict removal under a prohibited steps order, see para 5.98.
3 Section 20(11).
4 Section 20(9).

3. Restricting removal from accommodation

6.34 Local authorities should ensure that they involve all those with parental responsibility in the initial negotiations and written agreements on the provision of accommodation, and consider carefully whether accommodation is in the child's interests, given the nature of the agreement which may be reached. It may be necessary to suggest to some parents that they seek a residence order, even though the child is being accommodated, to ensure that the other person does not arbitrarily remove the child.

6.35 There is no requirement, as under previous legislation,[1] that the parent has to give notice of intention to remove the child from accommodation after a specified period. A person who does not have parental responsibility but has care of a child may (subject to other provisions of the Act) do what is reasonable in all the circumstances of the case for the purpose of safeguarding or promoting the child's welfare.[2] The primary purpose of the provision is to enable a de facto carer to make routine or urgent decisions, such as consenting to medical treatment in the interests of the child, provided they are not controversial. The provision would allow a foster parent or local authority to refuse to hand over the child to an inebriated parent.

1 Child Care Act 1980, s 13(2)
2 Section 3(5).

4. Agreements with parents

6.36 It is central to the philosophy of the Act that an authority should seek to reach agreement with the parent or other person with parental responsibility on such matters as the purpose of accommodating the child and the period for which it might be provided, schooling and contact with the child. This is consistent with the concept of partnership developed in Guidance.[1] The authority cannot move an accommodated child without the consent of the persons having parental responsibility. If a parent refused to agree to a necessary move, the authority would have to consider whether to seek a care order.[2]

1   See Guidance Volume 3, para 2.10 and 'The Challenge of Partnership in Child Protection: Practice Guide' (HMSO, 1995).
2   *R v Tameside Metropolitan Borough Council, ex p J* [2000] 1 FCR 173: see also para 3.96.

6.37 The Arrangements for Placement of Children (General) Regulations 1991 set out requirements to ensure appropriate consultation. Before they place a child, the local authority shall[1] so far as reasonably practicable make immediate and long-term arrangements for the placement and for promoting the welfare of the child to be placed. If it is not practicable to make arrangements before placement they shall be made as soon as reasonably practicable thereafter. The arrangements must be recorded in writing.

1   SI 1991/ 890, reg 3.

6.38 Although the agreement may include reference to the intended period of accommodation, this can be of no more than persuasive effect. It cannot be binding on the parent, who may still exercise his right of removal under s 20. In some cases breach of the agreement might provide evidence for an application for an emergency protection order or care proceedings. If the authority were seeking to foster an accommodated child, this would be part of the agreement, and if a parent refused to agree to fostering or expressed a wish for a child to be moved, the authority would have to consider whether to offer accommodation or whether the care criteria could apply.[1]

1   The care criteria could apply even though the child had previously been accommodated: *Re M (A Minor) (Care Order: Threshold Conditions)* [1994] AC 424, HL.

ACCOMMODATION AND HOUSING PROVISION

1. Homeless families

6.39 In spite of the duty placed on a local authority to provide accommodation for a child, where the person caring for him is prevented from providing him with suitable accommodation for whatever reason,[1] the provisions were not intended to be used to look after children where their parents are homeless. Although there may be circumstances where that would be necessary in an emergency, the principal responsibility for accommodating homeless families lies with the housing authority under the Housing Act 1996, Pt VII.

1   Section 20(1)(c).

6.40 The authority may request the help of the housing authority to enable it to carry out its functions under Pt III of the Act. The authority is obliged to assist with the request if it is compatible with their own statutory or other duties and obligations, and if it does not prejudice the discharge of any of their functions.[1]

1 Section 27.

6.41 If the parents have made themselves intentionally homeless within the terms of the Housing Act 1996 Pt VII, the housing authority could decline to help, on the grounds that giving priority to such a family would unduly prejudice the discharge of its functions. In *R v Northavon District Council, ex p Smith*[1] the House of Lords held that the nature and scope of the functions of housing and social services departments were not intended to change as a result of the duty to co-operate. The burden of accommodating the children of intentionally homeless parents was placed on social services and not to be transferred to the housing authority. This approach has been followed by the Court of Appeal[2] where it was held that s 20 was not engaged if the child remained in a family unit with a parent or parents. This leaves open the possibility that an authority will accommodate a child apart from his family, where the child's needs for accommodation can be met as an individual but not as part of his family because of the limits of the housing stock.

1 [1994] 2 AC 402. The courts have sought to avoid any undermining of housing policy. In *R v Oldham Metropolitan Borough Council, ex p Garlick* [1993] AC 509, [1993] 2 All ER 65, HL, the court declined to allow an application from a four-year-old whose parents were intentionally homeless.
2 *R(A) v Lambeth London Borough Council* [2001] EWCA Civ 1624, [2001] 3 FCR 678, [2002] 1 FLR 353. At the time of writing this case is under appeal to the House of Lords. See discussion at paras 6.5 and 6.11 in relation to s17. See also *R(W) v Lambeth London Borough Council* [2002] EWCA Civ 613, [2002] 2 FLR 327.

2. Homeless adolescents

6.42 A local authority has duties and powers relating to accommodation in respect of young persons found in their area[1] who are between 16 and 21-years old. They are required to provide accommodation for 16 and 17-year-olds in need, if they consider their welfare is likely to be seriously prejudiced if they are not provided with accommodation.[2] The authority may provide accommodation in a community home for any person between 16 and 21-years old, if they consider that it would safeguard or promote that person's welfare.[3]

1 In relation to s17, the words 'in their area' have been held to mean that physical presence is the only requirement: *R(S) v London Borough of Wandsworth, London Borough of Hammersmith and Fulham, London Borough of Lambeth* [2001] EWHC Admin 709, [2002] 1 FLR 469.
2 Section 20(3).
3 Section 20(5). See also paras 6.56 et seq on duties to care leavers.

3. Ordinary residence

6.43 If the child is ordinarily resident in another authority, that authority may take over the provision.[1] In determining the 'ordinary residence' of a child for any purpose of the Act:

'. . . there shall be disregarded any period in which he lives in any place'

(a) which is a school or other institution;
(b) in accordance with the requirements of a supervision order under this Act or an order under S 63(1) of the Powers of Criminal Courts (Sentencing) Act 2000; or
(c) while he is being provided with accommodation by or on behalf of a local authority.'[2]

1 Section 20(2).
2 Section 105(6). 'Ordinarily resident' refers to a man's abode in a particular place or country which he has adopted voluntarily and for settled purposes as part of the regular order of his life for the time being, whether of short or long duration': *Shah v Barnet London Borough Council* [1983] 1 All ER 226 at 235, HL.

DUTIES TO CHILDREN 'LOOKED AFTER'

6.44 Children who are in the care of the local authority or who are provided with accommodation (for a continuous period of more than 24 hours) pursuant to any of the functions of a social services authority,[1] are 'looked after' by the authority.[2] Children may also be looked after by or on behalf of a voluntary organisation.[3]

1 As provided for by the Local Authority Social Services Act 1970.
2 Section 22(2). The Department of Health provides extensive guidance: see 'Looking After Children' (HMSO, 1995) to be coordinated with the Assessment Framework (see chapter 9) to create the 'Integrated Children's System'.
3 Section 59.

6.45 Section 22(3) imposes the duty on a local authority[1] looking after a child to safeguard and promote his welfare and to make such use of services available for children cared for by their parents[2] as appears to the authority to be reasonable in his case. Before making any decision with respect to a child they are looking after, or propose to look after, the authority must ascertain, as far as practicable, the wishes and feelings of the child, his parents, any other person who has parental responsibility and any other person the authority consider to be relevant.[3] They must also give due consideration, having regard to his age and understanding, to such wishes and feelings of the child as the authority have been able to ascertain, and to his religious persuasion, racial origin and cultural and linguistic background and to such wishes and feelings of any person as mentioned above.[4]

1 There are similar duties in s61 for a child is accommodated by or on behalf of a voluntary organisation.
2 Ie under Pt III and Sch 2.
3 Section 22(4).
4 Section 22(5).

6.46 A local authority has a duty to carry out an assessment of the needs of an 'eligible child'[1] with a view to determining what advice, assistance and support it would be appropriate to provide while they are still looking after him, and after they cease to look after him. They must prepare a pathway plan and keep it under regular review and arrange for the child to have a personal adviser.[2]

1 An 'eligible child' is one aged 16 or 17, who has been looked after by a local authority for a period (prescribed under the regulations as thirteen weeks), or periods amounting in all to that period, which began after he reached fourteen years of age and ended after he reached

the age of sixteen: Sch 2 para 19A and the Children (Leaving Care) Regulations 2001 (SI 2001/2874).
2   See para 6.66

1.   Duty in respect of rehabilitation

6.47   Unless to do so would not be reasonably practicable or consistent with the child's welfare, the authority must make arrangements to enable him to live with his parents or other person with parental responsibility or a relative, friend or other person connected with him.[1] As far as is reasonably practicable and consistent with the welfare of the child, the authority must secure that the accommodation is near to his home and that siblings are accommodated together.[2]

1   Section 23(4), but see para 6.50 below.
2   Section 23(7).

2.   Promotion of contact

6.48   The duties relating to rehabilitation are further reinforced in that, when a child is being looked after by a local authority, the authority shall, unless it is not reasonably practicable or consistent with his welfare, endeavour to promote contact between the child and his family and shall ensure that they are kept informed of where he is being accommodated.[1] The authority is not required to disclose the whereabouts of the child if he is in care and the authority has reasonable cause to believe that disclosure would prejudice the child's welfare.[2] Expenses may be paid for visits to or by children.[3]

1   Sch 2, para 15(1).
2   Above, para 15(4).
3   Above, para 16.

6.49   If the child is neither living with his family,[1] nor being looked after[2] by the local authority, such steps as are reasonably practicable should be taken to enable the child to live with his family or to promote contact between him and his family, if it is necessary, in the authority's opinion, to do so in order to safeguard or promote his welfare.[3]

1   Section 17(10): see para 6.46.
2   Section 22(1): see para 6.39.
3   Sch 2, para 10.

PLACEMENT OF CHILDREN

6.50   When an authority is looking after a child, they must[1] provide him with accommodation while he is in their care and must maintain him. In carrying out this duty the authority may place the child with a family, a relative of his or any other suitable person, on such terms as to payment or otherwise as the authority determines. Placement may also be made in an appropriate children's home or by making such other arrangements as seem appropriate to the authority and comply with regulations.[2] The Arrangements for Placement of Children (General) Regulations 1991 apply to all these placements, including those by a local authority or a voluntary organisation or in an appropriate children's home.[3] They require the local authority to plan by making immediate and long term arrangements for the placement and provide for the content of those arrangements and who should be consulted about them. In relation to a disabled child, accommodation should not be unsuitable to his particular needs.[4]

1   Section 23(1).
2   Children's Homes Regulations 2001, SI 2001/3967: see *Clarke Hall and Morrison* 1[11491]. These regulations apply only to England but there are comparable regulations for Wales. 'Appropriate children's home' means a children's home in respect of which a person is registered under Pt II of the Care Standards Act 2000; and an establishment is a children's home (subject to reservations) if it provides care and accommodation wholly or mainly for children': Care Standards Act 2000, s1.
3   SI 1991/890: see *Clarke Hall and Morrison* 1[7401].
4   Section 23(8).

6.51   The placement of a child looked after by a local authority with a family[1] is with a 'foster parent'[2] and will be subject to the Fostering Services Regulations 2002.[3] The Regulations provide for the registration and duties of fostering agencies, approval of foster parents and the requirements to be satisfied on and after placement of a child with a local authority foster parent. A fostering agency may be either a local authority or an independent fostering agency, which can include a voluntary organisation.[4] A local authority may make arrangements for its fostering functions to be delegated to an independent fostering agency, save that it must be satisfied that a placement with a foster parent is the most suitable way of performing its duties of placement for a child.[5]

1   Unless placed with the child's family: s 23(3)–(4).
2   A foster parent means a person with whom a child is placed or may be placed under the Fostering Services Regulations 2002: reg 2(1). A foster parent may not be approved by more than one agency: reg 28(1). These regulations apply only to England.
3   Section 23(2): Fostering Services Regulations 2002, SI 2002/57: see *Clarke Hall and Morrison* 1[11591] and see generally Fostering Services, National Minimum Standards, Department of Health (The Stationery Office, 2002).
4   Care Standards Act 2000, S 4(4).
5   Fostering Services Regulations, reg 40. Note that the court can still make a residence order in favour of a disqualified person, or continue wardship and grant care and control: *Re RJ (Minors) (Fostering: Person Disqualified)* [1999] 1 FLR 605 and *Re RJ (Minors) (Fostering: Wardship)* [1999] 1 FLR 618 and see *Re S (Foster Placement (Children) (Regulations 1991)* [2001] 1 FLR 648.

6.52   In respect of a child subject to a care order, the local authority may only allow him to live with a parent or other person with parental responsibility for him, or with a person in whose favour there was a residence order immediately before the care order was made,[1] after the local authority has carried out the requirements contained in the Placement of Children with Parents etc Regulations 1991.[2] These include provisions as to who must be consulted and notified about the decision, the supervision and medical examination of the child and the circumstances in which he may be removed from home. In this case the Fostering Services Regulations 2002 do not apply.

1   Section 23(4).
2   SI 1991/893: see *Clarke Hall and Morrison* 1[7753].

6.53   If it is proposed to place the children in an establishment providing education, the authority must, as far as reasonably practicable, consult the education authority before doing so.[1] In relation to a child with special educational needs, who is 'statemented' under the Education Act 1996,[2] the authority to be consulted is that which maintains the statement.[3]

1 Section 28.
2 See *Clarke Hall and Morrison* 6[2101].
3 Section 28(4).

1. Placement with own family

6.54 If a child not subject to a care order is accommodated, he may simply be returned to his own family, and the authority then has no further legal responsibility (other than the general duty under s 17). If the child is placed with a relative[1] or friend, he could be discharged from accommodation at the request of a person with parental responsibility,[2] or be placed with a relative under the Arrangements for Placement of Children (General) Regulations 1991[3] and the Fostering Services Regulations 2002.[4] If he is in care, he could be placed with a relative under those regulations or be placed under the Placement with Parents etc Regulations 1991.

1 As defined by s 105(1).
2 Subject to s 20(9).
3 SI 1991/890.
4 SI 2002/57.

2. Residential placements

6.55 The Care Standards Act 2000 and the Children's Homes Regulations 2001 provide for the welfare of children placed in children's homes.[1] These provisions are not dealt with in this work.

1 An establishment is a children's home (subject to exceptions) if it provides care and accommodation wholly or mainly for children: Care Standards Act 2000, s 1. Reference should be made to Children's Homes Guidance and Regulations. See *Clarke Hall and Morrison* 1[11491]–[11560] and 4[1701]   [2100]. See also 'Choosing with Care' (HMSO, 1992) which contains detailed information and recommendations on the workings of children's homes.

AFTER-CARE

6.56 Concerns for the welfare of children formerly looked after by a local authority[1] have led to much enhanced duties being imposed on local authorities.[2] Studies found that children were unprepared for leaving care, they had poor contact with their family networks, they had poor employment opportunities and they were over-represented in the prison system.

1 See for example *Moving On: Young People and Leaving Care Schemes*, Biehal et al (HMSO 1995) and *Leaving Care in Partnership: Family Involvement with Care Leavers*, Marsh and Peel (The Stationery Office 1999).
2 Amendments to the Children Act provisions are made by the Children (Leaving Care) Act 2000.

6.57 It is the duty of the local authority looking after a child to advise, assist and befriend him with a view to promoting his welfare when they have ceased looking after him.[1]

1 Sch 2 para 19A.

6.58 The responsible local authority has a duty to assess and meet the care and support needs of *eligible* and *relevant* children and young people and to assist *former relevant children*, in particular in respect of their employment, education and training.

1. Duties to 'eligible child' being looked after

6.59 An 'eligible child' is one aged 16 or 17, who has been looked after by a local authority for 13 weeks, or periods amounting to that, which began after he reached the age of 14 and ended after he reached the age of 16.[1] A child does not come within the definition if the local authority has arranged to place him in a pre-planned series of short-term placements, none of which individually exceeds four weeks (even though they may amount in all to the prescribed period) and at the end of each such placement the child returns to the care of his parent, or a person who is not a parent but who has parental responsibility for him.[2]

1 Sch 2 para 19B and the Children (Leaving Care) Regulations 2001, reg 4 (SI 2000/2784).
2 Above, reg 5.

6.60 In respect of an eligible child the authority must, in addition to its other duties to looked after children:

(i) carry out an assessment of his needs with a view to determining what advice, assistance and support it would be appropriate for them to provide him
  (a) while they are still looking after him; and
  (b) after they cease to look after him.

2. Duties to 'relevant children'

6.61 A 'relevant child' is one, aged 16 or 17, who is not being looked after by a local authority, but was, before last ceasing to be looked after, an eligible child. A child who has returned home for a continuous period of six months is not to be treated as a relevant child unless the placement breaks down.[1] In respect of a relevant child the authority must:[2]

(i) take reasonable steps to keep in touch;
(ii) appoint a personal adviser;
(iii) prepare a pathway plan;
(iv) carry out an assessment of his needs with a view to determining what advice, assistance and support it would be appropriate to provide;
(v) safeguard and promote the child's welfare;
(vi) unless satisfied that his welfare does not require it, support him by maintaining him or providing or maintaining him in suitable accommodation; and
(vi) take reasonable steps to keep in touch with him, and if contact is lost without delay consider how to re-establish contact, take reasonable steps to do so and continue to take such steps until they succeed.

1 Reg 5(5) and (7). Given the likely vulnerability of children returning to their families, this provision does appear to fly in the face of the overall positive effect of the Regulations.
2 Sections 23A and 23B.

3. Duties to former relevant children

6.62 A former relevant child is a person who has been a relevant child (and would be one if he were under 18) and a person who was being looked after by an authority when he attained the age of 18, and immediately before ceasing to be looked after was an eligible child.[1] In relation to such a child the authority must take reasonable steps to keep in touch, and if they lose touch with him, seek to re-establish contact. They must continue the appointment of a personal adviser and continue to keep the pathway plan under regular review. They must give a former relevant child assistance to the extent that his welfare and his educational or training needs require it. These duties subsist until the child reaches the age of twenty-one, or until the end of a programme for education and training.

1 Section 23C.

4. Persons qualifying for advice and assistance

6.63 A young person who is under 21 qualifies for advice and assistance[1] if at any time after reaching the age of 16 but while still a child, he was but is no longer, looked after, accommodated or fostered (whether privately or otherwise) by a local authority or a voluntary organisation, in a private children's home or in any accommodation provided (for three months) by an education authority, Health Authority, Special Health Authority, Primary Care or National Health Service Trust or in a care home or independent hospital. The responsible local authority is that which last looked after him, wherever he is living in England or Wales. If he was not looked after by an authority, the authority where he resides is responsible.[2]

1 Section 24 (1)–(3).
2 Section 24(5).

6.64 The authority must[1] take such steps as they think appropriate to contact him at such times as they think appropriate to discharge their duties. They must consider whether he needs help by way of advice or assistance. If he does they must advise and befriend him if he was being looked after by a local authority or was accommodated by or on behalf of a voluntary organisation. If he was otherwise accommodated they may advise and befriend him, and in either case may give assistance in kind or, exceptionally, in cash. They may give assistance by contributing to expenses incurred in living near the place where employed or seeking employment and may make a grant to meet expenses connected with his education or training. The duties apply to a person under twenty-four. If the person proposes to live, or is living, in the area of another local authority they must inform that other authority.

1 Section 24A.

5. Pathway Plans

6.65 All eligible and relevant and former relevant children must have a Pathway Plan.[1] It is required to set out the advice, assistance and support which the authority intend to provide while looking after and when ceasing to look after the child. It must be maintained and reviewed until the young person is at least 21, and longer if it is to cover education, training, career plans and support.

1 Section 23E. Detailed provision about content is contained in the Children (Leaving Care) Regulations 2001. The pathway plan, which must be in writing and provided to the young person, must set out the manner in which the responsible authority proposes to meet the needs of the child, and the date by which, and by whom, any action required to implement any aspect of the plan, will be carried out: reg 8.

6.   Personal Adviser

6.66   All eligible, relevant and former relevant children must have a Personal Adviser,[1] whose responsibility it is to help draw up the Pathway Plan. He must ensure that the plan is implemented and developed with the young person's changing needs. He must keep in touch until the young person is 21 and ensure the provision of advice and support.

1 Section 23D. Detailed duties are set out in the Children (Leaving Care) Regulations 2001.

7.   Financial support

6.67   Relevant children[1] and former relevant children are removed from entitlement to means-tested benefits. They remain the responsibility of the local authority, who have to ensure that the vulnerable young people they have looked after receive the care and help they need to grow into independence. They must continue to ensure that young people in and leaving care are suitably accommodated, supported and advised according to their needs.[2]

1 Section 23B(8).
2 Section 23C(4).

8.   Employment, education and training support.

6.68   The local authority has a duty[1] to give a former relevant child assistance (and may assist other care leavers), to the extent that his welfare requires it, by contributing to expenses incurred in living near the place where he is or will be employed or where he is seeking employment. Similarly to the extent that his welfare and his educational or training needs require it, the authority has a duty to assist in kind or, in exceptional circumstances, in cash until he reaches the age of twenty-one, or longer if his pathway plan sets out a programme of education or training which extends beyond his twenty-first birthday.

1 Section 23C(4).

REFUGES FOR CHILDREN AT RISK

6.69   Section 51 enables organisations, which provide refuges for runaway youngsters, to be exempted by certificate of the Secretary of State from prosecution for assisting or inducing youngsters to run away or stay away or for harbouring them or for child abduction. Regulations relating to certificates and the requirements to be complied with while a certificate is in force are contained in the Refuges (Children's Homes and Foster Placements) Regulations 1991.[1]

1   SI 1991/1507.

6.70   A child may not be provided with a refuge unless it appears to the person providing the refuge that the child is at risk of harm unless the child is or continues to be provided with a refuge.[1]

1   Above, reg 3(2).

6.71   The Secretary of State may issue a certificate with respect to a home or approved foster parents.[1] The certificate has the effect that the home or foster parent are exempt from prosecution for:

(a) abduction of children in care;[2]
(b) abduction of child by persons other than parent;[3]
(c) compelling, persuading, inciting or assisting any person to be absent from detention;[4]
(d) harbouring children who have absconded from residential establishments.[5]

1   Section 51(1) and (2).
2   Section 49.
3   CAA 1984, s 2.
4   CYPA 1969, s 32(3).
5   Children (Scotland) Act 1995, ss 82 and 83.

6.72   Any applicant for a certificate will normally be expected first to have registered the home as a children's home or have made an application in respect of a foster parent approved under the Fostering Services Regulations 2002.[1] The objectives of the project will be expected to include the rehabilitation of the young person with his or her parent(s) or whoever else is responsible for the young person, provided this is consistent with the welfare of the child.[2]

1   SI 2002/57.
2   Guidance, Volume 4, Residential Care, paras 9.5, 9.7.

6.73   Regulation 3 sets out a number of requirements. As soon as is reasonably practicable after admitting a child to a home for the purpose of providing a refuge or after a foster parent provides a refuge for a child, and in any event within 24 hours of such provision, the person providing the refuge for the child shall notify the 'designated officer'[1] that a child has been admitted to the home, or provided with refuge by a foster parent, together with the telephone number by which the person providing the refuge for the child may be contacted. The child's name and address must be given if known. He must also give the name and address of the 'responsible person'.

1   'Designated officer' means a police officer designated for the purposes of the Regulations: reg 2(1).

6.74   Where a child ceases to be provided with a refuge, the person who provided him with the refuge shall notify the designated officer. Where a child remains in the refuge for more than 14 consecutive days, or more than 21 days in any period of three months, the protection from prosecution which a certificate provides will apply but the certificate can be withdrawn from the refuge. This emphasises the short-term aims of the provisions.

6.75 Protection from prosecution extends to the organisation itself and to those persons providing the home in which the refuge is situated, or the foster parent providing the refuge, but not those involved in outreach work, whether or not they are employed by the refuge.[1] Such a person would have, at the least, to 'assist or incite' in the absence of the refugee from detention to be vulnerable to prosecution, so that responsible counselling should not be criminal behaviour.

1   Department of Health Guidance, Volume 4, Residential Care, paras 9, 10.

6.76 Notice must be given to the person who is providing the refuge, in any proceedings under the Act where it is alleged that the child is in a refuge.[1] The person providing the refuge can seek leave to be joined as a party should he wish to challenge the application, apply for an emergency protection order, or ask the police to take the child into police protection, if they believe the child would suffer significant harm by being removed from the refuge.

1   FPR 1991, Appendix 3 and FPCR 1991, Sch 2.

IMPLEMENTATION OF PART III SERVICES

6.77 The Children Act Report 1992 stated: 'most authorities are providing a range of services commensurate with the purposes of the Children Act'.[1] Closer analysis of the information threw doubt on that statement even at that time. Only 55% of authorities responded; they were likely to be those providing better services. The 1993 Report stated:[2] 'most authorities are providing most relevant services and were planning to develop missing services or improve existing ones'. The response rate had increased to 76% but it was still a matter for concern that the Report appeared to express satisfaction that in addition to advice, child protection, accommodation and fostering, over two thirds of authorities 'also provided a range of other services'.[3]

1   Cm 2144, para 3.15.
2   Cm 2584, para 2.15.
3   Above.

6.78 Later studies[1] showed a different picture. Information about children in need was limited. Definitions of need were limited. Although practitioners would have liked to give a higher priority to proactive, preventive work, in practice resources were shown to be focused on 'high risk' cases. This was at the expense of promoting the welfare of a broader group of children through the provision of family support services. There was a considerable level of unmet need and many families struggled for a long time before any assistance was available from social services. A particular problem was the lack of services for children with emotional and behavioural difficulties in the 7 to 12 age group, a group likely to create more serious problems in subsequent years.

1   See Making Sense of S 17: Implementing Services for Children in Need within the Children
     Act 1989, Aldgate and Tunstill (HMSO, 1995), Children in Need: Family Support under the
     Children Act 1989, Colton et al (Gower, 1995) and Services for Children in Need: from
     Policy to Practice (Tunstill and Aldgate (Stationery Office, 2000) and most recently the
     Children Act Report 2000 (Department of Health, 2001).

6.79   Until 2000 there had been little information about children in need
apart from those looked after by authorities or whose names appeared on
child protection registers. The Children Act Report 2000[1] notes the advent of
a statistical collection called the Children in Need (CiN) census. Information
is collected by means of a census of activity and expenditure over seven consecutive working days. In the first year of collection, the Department of
Health received returns from all but five councils. The data only provides
information about the needs of those children who are in receipt of social services, how they are responded to and what costs are involved. There is as yet
no means of capturing the outcomes for children of social care intervention.
It is planned that this will be possible following development work and implementation of the Integrated Children's System. More importantly perhaps
there is no means of capturing the unmet need.

1   Department of Health (2001).

6.80   The data produced an estimate that, at any one time, councils in
England have a commitment to about 400,000 children in need. In a census
week there were about 230,000 children in need in receipt of a service of
some kind from social services departments. Of these 25% (some 57,900)
were looked after and 75% were in families or living independently. This is
equivalent to about 19 children in need per 1,000 of the population under 18.

6.81   It is clear beyond any doubt, and the Government's own reports show
it, that the major weaknesses of the Children Act still lie in the failure to
resource Pt III provision or to coordinate services for children throughout
social services, education, including special needs, physical and mental health
and the criminal and civil justice system. Without that it is inevitable that
more children will enter the care system long term, be involved in the criminal justice system, be unemployed and suffer mental health problems. It is
equally clear that diversion of resources away from child protection and planning for children who are the responsibility of the local authority will not
provide an overall remedy. The Integrated Children's System which provides
a model for assessment, planning, intervention and reviewing all children in
need should provide a better structure. Whether it can meet the level of need
remains in question.

Chapter 7

Assessment, investigation and emergency protection

INTRODUCTION

7.1 Every local social services authority has a general duty to safeguard and promote the welfare of children in their area who are 'in need' and, so far as is consistent with that duty, to promote the upbringing of such children by their families by providing a range and level of services appropriate to those children's needs.[1] For that purpose they have to carry out an assessment of the child, which will require making sense of the facts and information available to them. In most cases that duty can be carried out in conjunction with the family who may require the service. In some cases it may appear that a child is in need of protection from harm. It may then be necessary to carry out an investigation to establish the facts before a proper assessment can be made. It may also be necessary to take legal proceedings to protect the child and enable appropriate plans to be made in the interests of the child.

1 Section 17. See generally paras 6.4 et seq.

7.2 The statutory duties are set out in ss 17, 37 and 47 and require a local authority considering a case of alleged harm to a child to:

(a) make enquiries, calling on other authorities to assist where necessary;
(b) make an assessment of the facts and consider the needs of the child and how they might be met;
(c) ensure that the child is adequately protected, whether by the provision of services under Pt III or otherwise; and
(d) where it is in the interests of the child to do so, make an application to court for an order appropriate to the short and long term circumstances.

Investigation and assessment work should be undertaken in partnership with family members who are being investigated or assessed. Where a child is alleged to have been harmed or be likely to be harmed the same approach should be adopted wherever possible, although the safety of the child should not be compromised.

7.3 To assist in the execution of these duties, there has been a number of important Government publications:

(a) *Working Together to Safeguard Children.*[1] This is subtitled 'A guide to inter-agency working to safeguard and promote the welfare of children'. It provides a basis for practice and for administrative procedures. It requires the setting up of Child Protection Committees in each area. They are inter-agency bodies responsible for the development of local guidance.

(b) *Framework for the Assessment of Children in Need and their Families.*[2] This is a comprehensive Government guide to work to be undertaken in assessing families.

(c) *Communicating with Children.*[3] This provides guidance for interviewing children about adverse experiences and can be used as a basis for treatment.

(d) *Achieving Best Evidence in Criminal Proceedings: Guidance for Vulnerable or Intimidated Witnesses, including Children.*[4]

1 The Stationery Office, 1999: as guidance published by the Department of Health, the Home Office and the Department for Education and Employment under s 7 of the Local Authority Social Services Act 1970, which requires local authorities in their social services functions to act under the general guidance of the Secretary of State. As such this document does not have the full force of statute, but it should be complied with unless local circumstances indicate exceptional reasons, which justify a variation. See also the Challenge of Partnership in Child Protection: Practice Guide (HMSO, 1995). See also the supplementary guidance 'Safeguarding Children in whom illness is fabricated or induced' (Department of Health, August 2002).

2 The Stationery Office, 2000: from 1 April 2001 as guidance published by the Department of Health, the Home Office and the Department for Education and Employment under S 7 of the Local Authority Social Services Act 1970 see above. This Guidance should be followed when carrying out assessments whether for the purposes of ss17, 37 or 47.

3 The Stationery Office, 2002: Department of Health, in publication.

4 The Stationery Office, 2002: guidance published by the Home Office, the Lord Chancellor's Department, the Department of Health, the National Assembly for Wales and the Crown Prosecution Service. See para 7.18. See also Talking with Vulnerable Children: A handbook for Social Work and Health Care Professionals, (Jones, D., Department of Health, 2002).

7.4   The Government issued the *Framework for the Assessment of Children in Need and their Families* for the purpose of assessments carried out under s 17, 37 and 47 of Children Act 1989. The three areas to be covered in an assessment are the child's developmental needs, parenting capacity, and family and environmental factors. These are represented diagrammatically by the 'Assessment Framework' triangle shown in the diagram opposite. Social Services Departments have lead responsibility for assessments of children in need, but under s 27 other Local Authority services and Health Authorities have a duty to assist Social Services in carrying out this function.

INVESTIGATION

1.   Court-directed investigation

7.5   The need for an investigation may arise as a result of an initiative by the court which is considering the welfare of the child in other family proceedings. Where it appears to the court that it might be appropriate for a care or supervision order to be made with respect to a child, the court may direct an authority to investigate the child's circumstances[1] but

A The Assessment Framework

it should not fetter the discretion of the authority conducting the investigation.[2]

1 Section 37(1). The court should not order an investigation unless it appeared that it might be appropriate to make a public law order: *Re L (Section 37 Direction)* [1999] 1 FLR 984, CA.
2 *Re M (a Minor) (Official Solicitor: Role)* [1998] 3 FCR 315.

7.6 The court may make an interim care or supervision order pending the investigation.[1] This is the only circumstance in which the court may make such an order without an application by the authority. The court must still be satisfied as to the criteria in s 38.[2] The authority are required to consider whether to apply for a care or supervision order or to provide services or assistance for the child or his family or whether to take any other action with respect to the child[3] but the court has no power to order the authority to take proceedings.[4]

1 Section 38(1).
2 Section 37(2) and see para 8.19 on interim orders.
3 Section 38(3).
4 See para 8.5.

7.7 When the court has directed the local authority to investigate, on the basis that it is considering making an interim care or supervision order, the proceedings are 'specified' for the purposes of s 41.[1] In specified proceedings it is normal for the court to appoint a children's guardian. It has been said that in such cases the appointment of a guardian should not be automatic. If the case required an urgent child protection investigation, the guardian might not be able to play any useful role at that stage, unless the court had actually made an interim care order which involved a change of carer. If the case involved a longer assessment, the court should consider precisely what the role of a guardian would be and whether the work would be better done by a court welfare officer. If there was no public law element the latter would provide continuity.[2]

1 Section 41(6)(b).
2 See *Re CE (A Minor) (Section 37 direction)* [1995] 1 FLR 26.

2. Investigation of information given to the local authority

7.8 A local authority has duties under s 47 to investigate the child's circumstances, in order, where necessary, to provide for the protection of children. Section 47 provides that where an authority:

(a) have obtained an emergency protection order; or
(b) are informed that a child who lives or is found in their area is the subject of an emergency protection order or is in police protection; or
(c) have reasonable cause to suspect that a child who lives or is found in their area is suffering or is likely to suffer significant harm.

They must make, or cause to be made, such enquiries as they consider necessary to enable them to consider what action they should take.

There are distinctions between the standard of 'reasonable cause to suspect' in this provision, by contrast with the power of police protection where the constable must have 'reasonable cause to believe that a child would be likely to suffer significant harm',[1] the court's power to make an emergency protection order[2] where there must be 'reasonable cause to believe that the child is likely to suffer significant harm' and the court's power to make an interim care order[3] where it must be satisfied that 'there are reasonable grounds for believing that' the necessary criteria are made out. Suspicion is a lower standard and it was not necessary to establish facts on a balance of probabilities[4] but there must still be objectively reasonable grounds and not simply what the decision-maker thinks reasonable.[5]

1 Section 46(1). See para 7.61.
2 Section 47. See para 7.31.
3 Section 38. See para 8.19.
4 *R (on the application of S) v Swindon Borough Council* [2001] 3 FCR 702.
5 *Gogay v Hertfordshire County Council* [2001] 1 FCR 455.

7.9 The Assessment Framework recognises that an initial referral may require responses under different sections of the Children Act 1989 and a range of services depending on the findings of the assessment. An initial assessment should determine if a child is in need and if so what services should be provided, by whom and within what timescales. The authority should consider whether any action is necessary for further assessment of the child or for his immediate protection under Pt V. The authority may decide that in order to promote the interests of the child, they should initiate court proceedings under Pt IV. With that in mind it is important to ensure that the investigation is conducted in such a way as to provide evidence acceptable in proceedings under s 31.[1]

7.10   In chapter 3 of the Assessment Framework 'the Process of Assessing Children in Need' it is stated that a decision should be taken about what response is required within one working day of receiving a referral or new information being provided about an open case. Parents' permission should be sought before discussing a referral about them with other agencies, unless permission-seeking may itself place a child at risk of significant harm. Initially the authority should normally expect to seek the co-operation of those persons having parental responsibility, but applications may be made to the court for a child assessment order, or an emergency protection order if the child requires immediate protection. An initial assessment, which is a brief assessment of each child, should be undertaken within a maximum of seven working days. The outcome of the initial assessment should include consideration of whether there are substantiated concerns that a child may be suffering or at risk of suffering significant harm. Where there are no substantiated concerns, a local authority may decide whether or not to proceed with a 'core assessment', so as to undertake an in-depth assessment of the developmental needs of the child and what services may be required.

7.11   Where there are substantiated concerns about a child's safety, the Social Services Department must arrange a strategy discussion. The prime tasks are to:[1]

* share available information;
* decide whether s 47 enquiries should be initiated or continued;
* plan how enquiries should be handled;
* agree what action is needed immediately to safeguard the child, and/or provide interim services and support;
* decide what information about the strategy discussion will be shared with the family, unless that might place a child at risk of harm or jeopardise a police investigation into an offence.

1   Working Together to Safeguard Children, para 5.28. See also The Challenge of Partnership in Child Protection: Practice Guide (HMSO, 1995). A s 47 investigation may be carried out even though the child is being looked after by a local authority: *Gogay v Hertfordshire County Council* [2001] 1 FCR 455, but this should not be confused with any disciplinary action taken in relation to staff.

7.12   The point at which a s 47 enquiry has commenced is the point when the Social Services Department should commence its 'core assessment' under the Assessment Framework. Guidance recommends that a Social Services Department has a maximum of thirty-five working days to complete this assessment.[1]

1   The Assessment Framework, para 3.12.

7.13   The outcome of the s 47 enquiries may be that the original concerns are not substantiated and no further action is necessary. It may be appropriate to continue the core assessment to assist the process of deciding what services the child and family require. The concerns may be substantiated but the child be judged not to be at risk of continuing significant harm.

Judgments will be taken as to whether or not to hold an initial child protection conference and the decision may be taken to continue with the core assessment.

7.14 Where concerns have been substantiated and the child is judged to be at continuing risk of significant harm, an initial child protection conference must be held. The timing of the conference will depend on the urgency of the case but should always take place within fifteen days of the strategy discussion at which s 47 enquiries were instigated.[1] The Social Services Department and other agencies are required to prepare reports for the initial child protection conference. The information gathering for the purposes of the core assessment informs the report to the conference. The conference is required to take a decision whether the child is at continuing risk of significant harm and if so formulate an outline child protection plan and determine the category of abuse under which the child's name should be registered on the child protection register.[2] The child protection plan should include the name of a key worker from the Social Services Department and clarify whether, in addition to the core assessment, any specialist assessments of the child and family are required. The child protection plan should identify the professionals and agencies who should work together with the family, known as the core group, who must meet within ten days of the child protection conference to flesh out the child protection plan and decide what steps need to be taken and by whom and within what timescales to complete the core assessment and provide planned services.

1 *Working Together to Safeguard Children*, para 5.45 which considers the outcome of enquiries.
2 Para 5.99 considers the child protection register. For research on the workings of the register and the child protection system generally see Gibbons, Conroy and Bell, Operating the Child Protection System (HMSO, 1995) and Farmer and Owen, Child Protection Practice: Private Risks and Public Remedies (HMSO, 1995).

7.15 Throughout the s 47 enquiry, a Social Services Department should consider whether statutory intervention is required. Where there is considered to be a risk to the life of a child or a likelihood of serious immediate harm, emergency action can take place following an immediate strategy discussion between Police, Social Services and other agencies as appropriate. Where a single agency has to act immediately to protect a child, a strategy discussion should take place as soon as possible after such action has been taken. The initial child protection conference should also consider this although the initiation of proceedings remains a decision of the Social Services Department.

7.16 The authority should try to ensure that the child is seen unless they are satisfied that they already have enough information to decide what action to take.[1] In making enquiries the local authority must take such steps as are reasonably practicable (unless they are satisfied that they already have sufficient information) to obtain access to the child or to ensure that access to him is obtained on their behalf by a person authorised by them for the purpose. These enquiries should be made with a view to enabling the local authority to determine what action to take to safeguard or promote the child's welfare,[2] and whether they should make application to the court or exercise any of their powers under the Act or section 11 of the Crime and Disorder Act 1998.[3]

1   Section 47(4).
2   Section 47(2).
3   Section 47(3). Section 11 provides for local authorities to apply for a child safety order, which is aimed at children under ten years old and is designed to prevent them becoming involved in criminal or anti-social behaviour. See the Crime and Disorder Act Guidance Document: Child Safety Orders, Home Office, June 2000.

7.17   If the authority are refused access to the child or are denied information as to his whereabouts, the authority should apply for an emergency protection order, a child assessment order, a care order or a supervision order, unless satisfied that his welfare can be safeguarded without such an order.[1] If at the end of their enquiries they decide not to make an application for a court order, they must consider whether to review the case and, if so, fix a date for the review.[2]

1   Section 47(6).
2   Section 47(7).

3.   Investigative interviewing

7.18   In many cases where there is an allegation of significant harm to a child, there will be a joint investigation conducted by the police and social services department, since there may be questions involving both the civil and criminal law. If he is old enough, it is probable that the child will be interviewed jointly by a police officer and social worker in accordance with the guidance in 'Achieving Best Evidence in Criminal Proceedings: Guidance for Vulnerable or Intimidated Witnesses, including Children'.[1] This provides guidance for interviewing children about harm they may have suffered, where their evidence may be required for the purpose of criminal proceedings. The standards of procedure and interviewing set out are considered to provide the most reliable evidence. If there is a reasonable prospect that criminal proceedings will follow, it is likely that a video recording of the interview with the child witness will be made. Even if the child's evidence will not be used for the purposes of criminal proceedings, the interviewing methods adopted should be followed where possible, as they provide the best source of information for civil proceedings.

1   The Stationery Office, 2002; see para 7.3. Issued under Circular HOC 06/2002 the Guidance provides that with effect from 24 May 2002 it replaces the 'Memorandum of Good Practice on Interviewing Children' (Home Office, 1992).

7.19   A video-recorded interview serves two purposes for criminal proceedings, the gathering of evidence and the examination in chief of a child witness. Most importantly for child protection purposes any relevant information gained during the interview can be used to inform s 47 enquiries. The Guidance sets out a number of considerations which should be taken into account in deciding whether or not to record an interview:

- the needs and circumstances of the child;
- whether it is likely to maximise the quality of the child's evidence;
- the type and seriousness of the offence;
- the circumstances of the offence;
- the child's state of mind;
- perceived fears about intimidation and recrimination;

- the purpose and likely value of a video recorded interview;
- the competency, compellability and availability of the child for cross-examination; and
- the child's ability and willingness to talk in a formal setting.

1 Achieving Best Evidence, paras 2.27 and 2.28.

7.20 Joint interviewing has come to dominate investigation practice in child protection, where the child is old enough to communicate, not least because it provides the most effective evidence. The focus in 'Achieving Best Evidence' is on the criminal procedure and care must be taken that this does not limit the wider investigation of significant harm to children generally. Although Working Together gives extensive guidance on protection of the child and emphasises the importance of both the civil and criminal aspects of the investigation,[1] there is a risk that the criminal aspects of child protection will predominate and an investigation be carried out solely with the criminal standard of proof in mind. This may be heightened by other factors. Working Together procedures require the attendance of the police at child protection conferences. When the police are informed of an alleged offence, they may undertake an interview of anyone suspected of a crime in accordance with the Police and Criminal Evidence Act 1984 (a PACE interview), without a social worker being present. Indeed many areas now have guidance on when cases should be referred to the police for them to consider whether to carry out an investigation.

1 Working Together, para 5.47.

7.21 In spite of the importance of proper interviewing techniques it is essential to remember that proof of the tests for taking steps to protect children are not dependent on criminal standards. Local authorities have to be alert to ensure that their enquiries are conducted with the civil standard of proof in mind.[1] In those cases which raise complex questions about whether or how the child has been harmed, an early forensic analysis with the civil tests in mind, undertaken by suitable experts from all necessary disciplines, may be crucial not only to the short term investigation, but also to the longer term protection of the child through court proceedings.

1 See paras 8.52 and 11.9.

7.22 Where there are long-running concerns about the care of children, judicial guidance has suggested the following:[1]

(1) Every social work file should have as the top document a running chronology of significant events which was kept up-to-date as events unfolded; it would then be relatively straightforward to identify serious and deep rooted problems rather than the circumstances triggering the instant referral.
(2) Lack of parental co-operation was never a reason to close a file or remove a child from a protection register; on the contrary it was a reason to investigate in greater depth.
(3) Referrals by professionals such as health visitors and teachers should be given great weight and investigated thoroughly; they were a potential source of valuable information.
(4) Line managers and those with power of decision making should never

make a judgment to take no action without having full knowledge of the file and consulting those professionals who knew the family.

(5) Children who were part of a sibling group should not be considered in isolation but in the context of family history; where previous children had been brought to the attention of social services the details of their cases should be considered in assessing what had gone wrong historically and whether appropriate change had been effected.

(6) In order to avoid drift, work with families had to be time limited so that an effective timetable could be laid down within which changes needed to be achieved.'

1   *Re E (care proceedings: social work practice)* [2000] 2 FCR 297,[2000] 2 FLR 254.

CHILD ASSESSMENT ORDERS

7.23   The local authority may feel that it is unable to conduct its investigation sufficiently to establish whether further action should be taken in respect of the child. In such a case the authority (or an authorised person) may apply to the court for a child assessment order under s 43. The court must be satisfied that:

(a) the applicant has reasonable cause to suspect that a child is suffering, or is likely to suffer, significant harm;

(b) an assessment of the state of the child's health or development, or of the way in which he has been treated, is required to enable the applicant to determine whether or not the child is suffering, or is likely to suffer, significant harm; and

(c) it is unlikely that such an assessment will be made, or be satisfactory, in the absence of a child assessment order.

7.24   These proceedings, under Pt V of the Act, are not 'family proceedings',[1] so that the court must either make or refuse the order sought and cannot, of its own motion, make an order under Pt II or IV. Although the checklist in s 1(3) is not applicable, the court must have regard to the principle that the welfare of the child is paramount and that the court should not make an order unless it is better for the child than making no order.[2]

1   See s 8(4).
2   See s 1(1) and (5): see ch 2.

7.25   A child assessment order is an application made on notice and is specified proceedings for the purpose of appointing a children's guardian.[1] The order is not intended to be used in an emergency nor as a substitute for an emergency protection order. The child assessment order is appropriate where attempts to achieve an assessment have been frustrated. Guidance 'Court Orders' suggests:

'A child assessment order will usually be most appropriate where the harm to the child is long-term and cumulative rather than sudden and severe. The circumstances may be nagging concern about a child who appears to be failing to thrive; or the parents are ignorant of or unwilling to face up to possible harm to their child because of the state of his health or development; or it appears that the child may be subject to wilful neglect or abuse but not to such an extent as to place him at serious immediate risk.'[2]

1   Section 41(6)(g).
2   See para 4.9.

Effect of order

7.26 Section 43 provides that any person who is in a position to produce the child is under a duty to produce him to the person named in the order and to comply with such directions relating to the assessment of the child as may be specified in the order. The order shall specify the date by which the assessment is to begin and shall have effect for such period not exceeding seven days beginning with the date specified in the order. The child may be kept away from home, but only if it is necessary for the purposes of the assessment and then for such periods as are specified in the order. The person who is required to produce the child may be required to comply with such directions as the court thinks fit to specify.

7.27 The technical requirements of the section make it difficult to operate and there has been little use of it in practice.[1] Even though the period of seven days need not commence on the making of the order, that time may not be sufficient for an assessment. It is likely to require the participation of the parents, although court directions can only be given in relation to the child.

1 See 'Assessment and the Control of Social Work: an Analysis of Reasons for the Non-Use of the Child Assessment Order, Dickens [1993] JSWFL 88. Department of Health statistics for March 2001 show no children subject to a child assessment order.

7.28 Whether or not to apply for a child assessment order must largely depend on the evidence available to the applicant and the attitude of the parents or other person with parental responsibility. If there is evidence of harm but the local authority is doubtful as to the proper course of action, perhaps because of the lack of co-operation of the parent, an application for a child assessment order may be helpful, but the complexities of the application and the limited scope of the order have discouraged local authorities from using the provisions.

EMERGENCY PROTECTION ORDERS

1. Introduction

7.29 Provisions are contained in s 44 in respect of an emergency protection order, the purpose of which is to provide for the immediate removal or retention of a child in a genuine emergency. The provisions are based on the recommendations of the Review of Child Care Law[1] following widespread criticism of place of safety orders which they replaced.

1 DHSS, 1985, Ch 13.

7.30 By s 44 the court[1] is empowered to make an emergency protection order, initially limited to eight days, to ensure the safety of a child where he is otherwise likely to suffer significant harm. Guidance on the use of these powers is contained in 'Working Together to Safeguard Children'.[2]

1 'Court' includes a single justice on an ex parte application for an emergency protection order: FPC (CA 1989) R 1991, rr 1(1) and 2(5).
2 The Stationery Office, 2000, para 5.23.

2. Grounds for an emergency protection order

(a) Likely to suffer harm

7.31 The court may make an emergency protection order on the application of any person, if it is satisfied that there is reasonable cause to believe that the child is likely to suffer significant harm if he:

(a) is not removed to accommodation provided by or on behalf of the applicant; or

(b) does not remain in the place where he is being accommodated.[1]

1 Section 44(1)(a).

7.32 While the application is usually made by a local authority or an authorised person,[1] other people such as a police officer or hospital worker, or a parent or relative in a family dispute can apply. If the applicant is not the local authority where the child is ordinarily resident, that authority may have transferred to them the responsibilities under the order.[2] Since only a local authority can apply to extend an order,[3] it may be necessary for the authority to assume responsibility where an application has been made by an individual, unless that person has meanwhile obtained a residence order.

1 Ie the NSPCC. See note at para 8.10.
2 Emergency Protection Orders (Transfer of Responsibilities) Regulations 1991 SI 1991/1414.
3 Section 45(4), discussed further at para 7.44.

7.33 The court has to be satisfied that there is reasonable cause to believe that significant harm is likely to occur. This is a forward looking test. Evidence of harm which was occurring at the time of the application or has occurred in the past is not sufficient unless it gives cause to believe that harm is likely to occur in the future. Nonetheless harm need not actually have occurred. 'Likely' may be used in different senses and not necessarily on the balance of probabilities. It is a matter for the court's discretion how to apply it, if there is a real significant likelihood of the child suffering significant harm.[1]

1 See discussion at para 8.51. Note in *P, C and S v the United Kingdom*, [2002] 3 FCR1, ECtHR it was held that there must be extraordinarily compelling reasons before a baby can be physically removed from its mother immediately after birth.

(b) Denial of access to the child

7.34 A local authority may also apply for an order,[1] where they are making enquiries, for example, because they[2] have reasonable cause to suspect that a child is suffering, or is likely to suffer, significant harm, and those enquiries are being frustrated by access to the child being unreasonably refused to a person authorised to seek access and they have reasonable cause to believe that access to the child is required as a matter of urgency. This provision was introduced in response to a recommendation in one child death inquiry;[3] it was introduced late and little debated in Parliament. Not surprisingly there seems to have been little need for it.

1 Section 44(1)(b). There is an additional similar power in s 44(1)(c) where the investigation is being carried out by an authorised person.
2 Under this provision it is the applicant who has to be satisfied, rather than the court.
3 A Child in Mind (1987), para 7.24.

7.35 An important part of this test will obviously be whether the refusal to allow the child to be seen is unreasonable. Guidance 'Court Orders' comments:

'The hypothesis of the grounds at S 44(1)(b) and (c) is that this combination of factors is evidence of an emergency or the likelihood of an emergency. The court will have to decide whether the refusal of access to the child was unreasonable in the circumstances. It might consider a refusal unreasonable if the person refusing had had explained to him the reason for the enquiries and the request for access, the request itself was reasonable, and he had failed to respond positively in some other suitable way, by arranging for the child to be seen immediately by his GP, for example. Refusal of a request to see a sleeping child in the middle of the night may not be unreasonable, but refusal to allow access at a reasonable time without good reason could well be. The parent who refuses immediate access but offers to take the child to a local clinic the following morning may not be making a reasonable refusal where the risk to the child is believed to be imminent or where previous voluntary arrangements have broken down.'[1]

1 See para 4.39.

3. Application for an emergency protection order

7.36 Even if one of the conditions in s 44 applies, the court will not automatically make an emergency protection order. Although the court is not required to apply the checklist under s 1(3), other provisions of s 1 are applied, so that the court must make the welfare of the child its paramount consideration and not make an order unless it is better for the child to do so.[1]

1 Section 1(1) and (5).

7.37 The court will wish to know what it is that makes it necessary to remove or prevent the removal of the child as a matter of urgency. Why take the risk of separating the child from the carer immediately? If removal is necessary, can the child go to a relative or be accommodated with the co-operation of the parents? If the child is in a safe place, is there a real risk that an attempt will be made to remove?

7.38 The application may be made without notice with the consent of the justices' clerk[1] and in most cases the order will be made without the parents being present. The court will, however, wish to know why the decision cannot wait until the parents have had an opportunity to put their case at a hearing of which they have been given notice or until all the relevant evidence is available and an independent report from a children's guardian. The court has the power to refuse an application and require that it is heard on notice,[2] but it should appreciate that if there are grounds for an order, putting the parents on notice of the application might place the child in greater danger. The court should ensure that the order is not being used as a routine way of starting care proceedings.

1 FPR 1991, r 4.4(4) and FPC (CA 1989) R 1991, r 4(4). It is accepted that these provisions are compliant with Article 8 of the European Convention on Human Rights: see *K and T v Finland* [2001] 2 FCR 673, Ect HR, Grand Chamber, [2001] 2 FLR 707.
2 Above, r 4.4(5) and r 4(5).

7.39 The court may take account of any statement contained in any report made to the court in the course of, or in connection with, the hearing or any evidence given during the hearing, which is in the opinion of the court relevant to the application.[1] This enables the court to give proper weight to hearsay, opinions, health visiting or social work records and medical reports.

1 Section 45(7).

7.40 An application for an emergency protection order must be made in the family proceedings court and may be made to a single justice,[1] and if made without notice, must be with the permission of the justices' clerk.[2] The application may not be transferred to a higher court.[3] If the application arises out of a direction under s 37 to the local authority to investigate, the application should be made in the court which gave the direction, if that court is the High Court or the care centre, or in the care centre as directed.[4]

1 FPC (CA 1989) R 1991, r 2(5)(a).
2 FPR 1991, r 4.4(4) and FPC (CA 1989) R 1991 r 4(4).
3 Children (Allocation of Proceedings) Order 1991, r 7(2).
4 FPR 1991 r 4.3(2) and FPC (CA 1989) R 1991, r 3(2).

4. Effect of emergency protection order

7.41 An emergency protection order operates as a direction to any person who is in a position to do so to comply with any request to produce the child to the applicant and authorises removal to or prevention of removal from accommodation provided by or on behalf of the applicant.[1] This would include, for example, a hospital. The court may authorise an applicant to enter specified premises and search for a child and may include another child in the order, if it believed there might be another child on the premises.[2] Guidance, 'Court Orders', suggests that authority for entry and search should be asked for as a matter of course.[3] This does not give the power to make a forced entry. If the applicant is refused or likely to be refused entry the court may issue a warrant authorising a constable to assist in the execution of the order using reasonable force if necessary.[4]

1 Section 44(4).
2 Section 48(3) and (4).
3 Volume 1, para 4.52.
4 Section 48(9).

7.42 An emergency protection order gives the applicant parental responsibility for the child, but this is limited insofar as the applicant shall exercise the power to remove or prevent removal only in order to safeguard and promote the welfare of the child. If an applicant gains access and finds that the child is not harmed or likely to be harmed, he may not remove the child.[1] If during the period of the order, a return home to a parent or other connected person appears to be safe, then the applicant is required to carry that out.[2] The power of removal may be exercised again while the order remains in force if a change in circumstances makes it necessary.[3] Parental responsibility is to be exercised only as far as is reasonably required to safeguard or promote the welfare of the child, having regard in particular to the duration of the order.[4] It would not be appropriate to make any changes in the child's life, which would have a long-lasting effect.

1 Section 44(5).
2 Section 44(10).
3 Section 44(12.
4 Section 44(5).

7.43 The timing of the execution of an emergency protection order may be important. Working Together recommends[1] that unless the child is in acute physical danger, removal should be agreed following consultation with all appropriate professionals at a strategy meeting. It is necessary to balance the possible harm of a sudden removal, for example in a 'dawn raid', the risk of harm to the child if not removed, and perhaps the need to obtain evidence of criminal offences.

1 Op cit para 5.24.

5. Duration of emergency protection order

7.44 The order may be granted for up to eight days,[1] though the court may order one extension for up to seven days, on the application of a person entitled to apply for a care order,[2] if it has reasonable cause to believe that the child is likely to suffer significant harm if the order is not extended.[3] If the eighth day of the order is a public holiday or Sunday the court may specify a period for the order which has the effect of extending it to noon on the first later day which is not such a holiday or a Sunday.[4] Where the child is in police protection and the designated officer applies for an emergency protection order the period of eight days of any emergency protection order granted starts from the date that the child was taken into police protection and not from the date of the emergency protection order application.[5]

1 Section 45(1).
2 Section 45(4).
3 Section 45(5).
4 Section 45(2).
5 Section 45(3).

7.45 If there has been a genuine emergency and the authority believe care proceedings should follow, it should normally be possible to deal with the application for an interim care order[1] within the initial eight-day period. Since a first interim care order may be made for up to eight weeks, opposition to the initial order may occur more frequently and more vigorously, so that close attention should be paid to whether the parties are ready for an interim application or whether an extension of the emergency order would be preferable. In practice what has often happened is that the first interim order in care proceedings has been made for perhaps two weeks to allow time for the parties to prepare their position.

1 See paras 8.19 et seq.

7.46 There is no appeal against the making of or refusal to make an emergency protection order.[1] Local authorities which are dissatisfied with a decision will have to consider whether police protection is justified or whether to start care proceedings and seek an interim order.

1   Section 45(10) and *Essex County Council v F* [1993] 1 FLR 847.

6. Exclusion orders

7.47 During discussion of the Children Bill consideration was given to providing powers to exclude a person thought to have abused a child, especially for example a cohabitee of a parent. The powers were then limited to the provision of assistance in moving out.[1] This was extended by the Family Law Act 1996 with effect from 1 October 1997 to give the court power to order the exclusion of another person from the home rather than the child who is at risk of harm. To include an exclusion requirement in an emergency protection order the court has to be satisfied that:[2]

(a) there is reasonable cause to believe that if the person is excluded from the home in which the child lives, the child will cease to suffer, or cease to be likely to suffer, significant harm; and

(b) another person living in the home is able and willing to give the child the care which it would be reasonable to expect a parent to give, and consents to the exclusion requirement. Consent must be in writing or given orally to the court.[3]

1   See Sch 2, para 5, noted at para 6.21.
2   Section 44A.
3   FPR 1991, r 4.24; FP(CA 1989)R 1991, r 25.

7.48 The exclusion requirement is a provision requiring the relevant person to leave a dwelling house in which he is living with the child, prohibiting him from entering a dwelling house in which the child is living or excluding the relevant person from a defined area around the dwelling house. A power of arrest may be attached to the exclusion requirement.[1] The exclusion requirement and the power of arrest may be ordered for periods shorter than the substantive order. A person who is not entitled to apply for discharge of an emergency protection order, but to whom the exclusion requirement applies, may apply for variation of the requirement.[2] If the child is removed from the dwelling house, the requirement shall cease to have effect. The court may accept an undertaking, which is enforceable as if it were an order of the court, but no power of arrest can be attached.[3] The undertaking ceases to have effect if the applicant for the order removes the child from the house from which the person is excluded to other accommodation for a continuous period of more than 24 hours.[4]

1   On the operation of the power of arrest see *President's Direction* [1998] 1 FLR 495.
2   Section 45(8B).
3   Section 44B(2).
4   Section 44B(3).

7. Discharge of the order

7.49 Although there is no provision for an appeal against an emergency protection order, an application to discharge the order may be made. It may only be heard between 72 hours and eight days after the making of the order. The application may be made by the child, a parent, any other person with parental responsibility or any person with whom he was living immediately before the making of the order, except where that person was present at and given notice of the hearing.[1] In practice this provision seems to have had very little use. Local authorities may themselves only be seeking emergency protection orders, where they have good evidence of the need for an order. In any event most legal advisers of those applying for discharge would probably want to have more time to prepare a case than the 72 hours. If an application for an extension is being sought after eight days, that provides a suitable opportunity for retention of the child by the local authority to be opposed.

1 Section 45(8)–(11).

8. Experience of emergency protection orders

7.50 The changes in the emergency provisions have led to a reduction in the number of applications, especially because it is no longer a routine method of starting care proceedings. Compared with a pre-Act annual figure of about 5,000, the number of emergency protection orders initially dropped to 2,300 in 1993.[1] Although they increased to around 3,000 in 1994 and 1995, in 1999 they had dropped to just over 1,500. In 2000 they had increased again to just over 2,200,[2] still a significant decrease. This is not dissimilar to care proceedings, although, having initially dropped, they have shown a greater increase in the last two years.[3]

1 Children Act Advisory Committee Annual Report 1993/94, p 68.
2 Children Act Report 2000.
3 See para 8.9.

7.51 The overall decrease can be explained by changes in the practice of local authorities. They have been able to make other arrangements in the short term, whether placement with relatives, accommodation by agreement, without prejudice to care proceedings, or because a suspected abuser has left the home. Provided the child was safe, those arrangements would have the advantage of leaving him in familiar surroundings and working in partnership with parents.

7.52 A contributory factor to the drop in applications may be more frequent initial use of police protection.[1] *The Children Act Report 1992* suggested that this was not so in the first six months of the Act but since then there are no available statistics. Police protection avoids the emergency use of the court, which has the risk of refusal of the application, possible delay while a justices' clerk and a magistrate are found and the need to put together an argument sufficient to convince the magistrate. The police officer can study the position for himself. Although some authorities have internal guidance which requires that application to the court should be the norm, practice in this respect is patchy.

1 See para 7.56.

9. Contact during emergency protection order

7.53 The applicant must allow the child reasonable contact, during the period of an order, subject to the directions of the court, with his parents, any other person with parental responsibility, any person with whom he was living immediately before the court, any person in whose favour there is a contact order in relation to him and any person acting on behalf of those persons.[1] The court may (not must), on making the order, and at any time while it is force, give such directions, and impose conditions, as it considers appropriate in relation to contact between the child and any named person.[2] The direction can be varied at any time on the application of the parties to the application, the children's guardian, the local authority and any person named in the directions.[3] Guidance Court Orders' states:[4]

> 'It is anticipated that where the applicant is the local authority the court will leave contact to the discretion of the authority or order that reasonable contact be negotiated between the parties, unless the issue is disputed'.

1 Section 44(13).
2 Section 44(6) and (8).
3 FPC (CA 1989) R 1991, r 2(4).
4 Volume 1, para 4.62.

10. Medical or psychiatric examination or assessment

7.54 The court may give directions as to a medical or psychiatric examination or other assessment of the child[1] and may direct that there is to be no such examination or assessment.[2] The court should, given the combination of this provision and the requirement that no child shall have such an assessment for use in proceedings without the leave of the court,[3] be able to exert some control over excessive examinations of the child. In practice it is likely that the local authority will have had an examination or assessment carried out with the consent of a parent, or a child if '*Gillick* competent',[4] before proceedings or it can await a direction when care proceedings have started. If there is an emergency requiring examination for medical reasons, the primary purpose of the examination is not for proceedings, and it should proceed without the need for an order.

1 Section 44(6).
2 Section 44(8).
3 FPR 1991, r 4.18, FPC (Children Act 1989) R 1991, r 18.
4 In accordance with the so-called *Gillick* principles: discussed at para 3.32.

7.55 A child who is of sufficient understanding to make an informed decision, may refuse to submit to an examination or assessment.[1] On the face of it the court may not overrule a child who is capable of making an informed decision, but it has been held that the court could give consent by virtue of its inherent jurisdiction.[2] In practice the decision will ultimately be taken by the doctor, and he must consider, after discussion with the child and those having parental responsibility, whether to act on any other exercise of parental responsibility.

1 Section 44(7). The provision is the same as that in relation to interim care or supervision orders under s 38 and a child assessment order under s 43.
2 See *South Glamorgan County Council v W and B* [1993] 1 FLR 574. For a criticism of this decision see para 12.31.

11. Discovery of children

7.56 The whereabouts of a child who may be in need of emergency protection are not always known. The court has power to include provision in an emergency protection order, if it appears to the court that information as to the child's whereabouts is available to a person, requiring that person to disclose, if asked to do so by the applicant, any information he may have.[1] The order may also authorise an applicant to enter premises specified by an order and search for the child with respect to whom the order was made.[2] It is an offence to obstruct the exercise of this power.[3] Although, where it is necessary in the execution of the order, this provision authorises entry to premises, it does not permit forced entry and may be used only where there is co-operation. In practice the powers described in paragraph 7.52 will usually be sufficient.

1 Section 48(1).
2 Section 48(3).
3 Section 48(7).

12. Warrant to enter and search

7.57 If a person has been prevented from exercising powers under an emergency protection order, by being refused entry to premises or access to the child, or it appears to the court that he is likely to be prevented from doing so, a warrant may be issued authorising a constable to assist the entry and search, using reasonable force if necessary.[1] It would seem to be wise to obtain a warrant if difficulties in gaining entry are foreseen or there is a likelihood of threatening or intimidatory behaviour. The court may direct that the constable be accompanied by a registered medical practitioner, nurse or health visitor.[2]

1 Section 48(9). The procedure is set out under the FPC (CA 1989) R 1991, r 4(4).
2 Section 48(11).

13. Discovering other children

7.58 If the applicant believes there may be another child on the premises to be searched who ought also to be the subject of an emergency protection order, he may seek an order authorising a search for him.[1] If such an order is made and the child is found on the premises, and the applicant is satisfied that the grounds for making an emergency protection order exist, the order authorising the search has effect as if it were an emergency protection order.[2] The applicant must inform the court of the effect of an order authorising a search.[3]

1 Section 48(4).
2 Section 48(5).
3 Section 48(6).

7.59 This provision is intended to cover circumstances where an applicant believes there may be more than one child in the family or on premises, who is likely to suffer significant harm. Although in many cases the applicant will be aware of the existence of other children, and should, if there are grounds, seek an individual emergency protection order for each child, this provision is of importance in two situations. First, the applicant may not be able to identify the specific child or children,[1] but may want to check on the well-being of children in the same circumstances as the child in respect of whom the order is made. Secondly, if the police were, for example, to discover a sex ring, they might not know the number or identity of children involved.

1 As required by s 44(14).

14. Recovery orders

7.60 A court may make a recovery order[1] in respect of a child who is in care, or is the subject of an emergency protection order or in police protection, if there is reason to believe that he has been unlawfully taken away from the 'responsible person', has run away or is staying away from the responsible person or is missing. A responsible person is anyone who has care of the child by virtue of a care order, emergency protection order or police protection.[2] The local authority may designate the responsible person and can specify who that person should be at any given time. A recovery order operates as a direction to produce the child or disclose his whereabouts and authorises a constable to enter named premises and search for the child using reasonable force if necessary. Reasonable force extends not only to entry and search, but also to the removal of the child.[3] The application may be made without notice.[4]

1 Section 50.
2 Section 49(2).
3 *Re R (Recovery Orders)* [1998] 2 FLR 401.
4 FPC (CA 1989) R 1991, r 4(4).

POLICE PROTECTION

7.61 A constable has powers to take a child 'into police protection' for up to 72 hours, if he has reasonable cause to believe that a child would be likely to suffer significant harm if he did not remove the child to suitable accommodation, or take steps to prevent removal from a hospital or other place where the child is being accommodated.[1] The provision can only be used where the police officer has found the child, since the section has no powers of search attached. The section is the successor to s 28(2) of the 1969 Act, which was most frequently used by the police to hold children such as runaways or glue sniffers or whose parents have abandoned them. It may also be used by a police officer who attends a domestic dispute and finds the parents drunk, or for a child living in unhygienic conditions or the newborn in hospital. Consideration should always be given to whether the child's interests will be protected by an application to the court for an emergency protection order.

1 Section 46 (1). For analysis of recent research on the provision, see Masson 'Police Protection-Protecting Whom' JSWFL 24(2) 2002: 157–173. See also Borkowski 'Police Protection and s 46' [1995] Fam Law 204.

7.62 The police have powers to enter and search premises without a warrant for the purpose of saving life or limb,[1] but this provision appears to be rarely used and is limited to emergencies. The police may enter premises in order to arrest a person for an arrestable offence and to deal with or prevent a breach of the peace. They may arrest without a warrant any person who has committed any offence where the arrest is necessary to protect the child from that person.[2] They can obtain a warrant to enter premises and search for children.[3]

1 PACE 1984, s 17.
2 Above, s 25(3)(e).
3 Children Act 1989, s 102.

7.63 The police do not acquire parental responsibility but must do what is reasonable in all the circumstances of the case for the purpose of safeguarding or promoting the child's welfare, having regard in particular to the length of the period during which the child will be in police protection.[1] The extent of this duty is unclear but taken in conjunction with the duty to discover the wishes and feelings of the child, it clearly gives authority to take preliminary steps to establish what has happened to the child. It should not be taken as authority to conduct a detailed interview or assessment, nor a medical examination, unless the circumstances require it.

1 Section 46(9).

PROTECTION OF CHILDREN'S RIGHTS

7.64 Section 37 of the Supreme Court Act 1981 provides that 'the High Court may by order (whether interlocutory or final) grant an injunction . . . in all cases in which it appears to the court to be just and convenient to do so'. Any such order may be made either unconditionally or on such terms and conditions as the court thinks just. It has been held that this is an independent power in the High Court. It is not part of the inherent jurisdiction and therefore not restricted by s 100 of the CA 1989.[1] It can be used to protect an established legal or equitable right independently of the CA 1989 scheme. The test is not the paramountcy of the child's welfare but the protection of the child's right. Section 37 has been used to prohibit parents from obstructing a child's attendance at school by an injunction made ancillary to a care order under the CA 1989.[2]

1 See chapter 12.
2 *Re P (Care Orders: Injunctive Relief)* [2000] 2 FLR 385.

Chapter 8

The care system

INTRODUCTION

8.1 This chapter considers the system established by the Children Act, by which local authorities are empowered to take care proceedings in respect of children. Since implementation of the Act there have been marked differences of opinion and practice about the care of children who may be being harmed, both in different parts of the country and at different times of the last decade. This has resulted in fluctuations in the number of proceedings, the outcomes of proceedings and how they are managed.

8.2 The chapter considers the criteria to be satisfied in proceedings, the orders available to the court, and the way in which plans can be implemented and supervised. A child can only be in care if the court makes a care order.[1] As a local authority cannot apply for a residence order,[2] it can only acquire parental responsibility in respect of a child by way of a care order or emergency protection order.

1   Under the repealed Child Care Act 1980 a child could have been in care without a court order. The court may not require a local authority to take proceedings and cannot make an order under s 31, unless the authority has made an application: *Nottinghamshire County Council v P* [1994] Fam 18, [1993] 3 All ER 815, CA.
2   Section 9(2), discussed at para 5.98.

8.3 A local authority only has the power to intervene in the care and upbringing of a child, against the wishes of a person having parental responsibility, where an authorised court has made a care or supervision order in proceedings under s 31.[1] The concept of significant harm is central to any proceedings to protect the child.

1   Save in proceedings for a child assessment order or emergency protection order, described in chapter 7, and prospectively where there is an adoption placement order under the Adoption and Children Bill 2002. A local authority cannot use s 8 proceedings for the purpose of retaining control of a child: *Nottinghamshire County Council v P* [1994] Fam 18, [1993] 3 All ER 815, CA.

CONSIDERING WHETHER TO APPLY FOR AN ORDER

8.4 There are a number of considerations which the applicant must have in mind when deciding whether to institute proceedings under s 31.

(a) Can satisfactory arrangements for the welfare of the child be achieved without recourse to proceedings?
(b) Are the threshold criteria satisfied?
(c) What would be achieved by an order under s 31 that could not be achieved without an order?
(d) What is in the interests of the child?
(e) What are the plans for the child?
(f) Should an application for a freeing order be made simultaneously?[1]

1 Or on implementation of the Adoption and Children Bill 2002 should an application be made for a placement order.

8.5 Before taking proceedings, the local authority must consider the position carefully.[1] Applications should be part of a carefully planned process, with liaison during the stages of investigation and assessment, and following the commencement of proceedings. Some cases require the early initiation of care proceedings, and perhaps a split hearing, especially where there are unresolved fundamental issues of fact.[2] The authority cannot be compelled by judicial review to institute care proceedings.[3]

1 See *Handbook of Best Practice in Children Act Cases* (Children Act Advisory Committee, June 1997) in *Clarke Hall and Morrison* 1[20001].
2 See para 8.78 and *Re CD and MD (Care Proceedings; Practice)* [1998] 1 FLR 825.
3 *R v East Sussex County Council, ex p W* [1998] 2 FLR 1082.

8.6 Where possible, services should be provided to the child and his family on a voluntary basis, but such an approach can only be satisfactory, if it provides the child, who is suffering or likely to suffer significant harm, with adequate protection. A care or supervision order should be sought when there appears to be no better way of safeguarding and promoting the welfare of such a child. The implementation of the Human Rights Act 1998 and in particular Art 8 of the European Convention on Human Rights, has led to emphasis of the principle that throughout the proceedings intervention must be a proportionate response to the nature and gravity of the feared harm and proportionate to the legitimate aim of protecting the child.[1]

1 See for example *Re C and B (Care Order: Future Harm)* [2001] 1 FLR 611, *Re O (Supervision Order)* [2001] EWCA Civ 16, [2001] 1 FLR 923, [2001] 1 FCR 289 and *P, C and S v United Kingdom*, [2002] 3 FCR1, ECtHR.

8.7 In the initial period after implementation of the Children Act there was a substantial drop in the number of applications for orders under s 31. By comparison with about 2,900 care orders in the year to 31 March 1991, there were about 1,600 in the year to 30 September 1992.[1] The requirement that the court should make no order unless it is better for the child to make an order,[2] became interpreted as a 'no order' principle. Proceedings were not taken until all alternatives had been exhausted and even though a child had suffered serious harm, simply on the basis that the parent accepted that the local authority would look after the child.

1 Judicial statistics 1992.
2 S 1(5).

8.8 The decrease was so marked that in the Children Act Report 1992 the Department of Health advised:

'Where a local authority determines that control of the child's circumstances is necessary to promote his welfare then compulsory intervention, as part of a carefully planned process, will always be the appropriate remedy. Local authorities should not feel inhibited by the working in partnership provisions of the Children Act from seeking appropriate court orders . . . Equally, the existence of a court order should not of itself impede a local authority from continuing its efforts at working in partnership with the families of children in need. The two processes are not mutually exclusive. Each has a role to play, often simultaneously, in the case management of a child at risk.'

8.9   There was then a gradual upturn in applications, although in the second edition we noted that it appeared to have levelled off by the end of 1994.[1] The most recent figures indicate a marked increase in the number of public law applications from 17,284 in 1998 to 22,000 in 2000[2] and in care orders from 4,124 in 1999 to 6,298 in 2000.[3] In that time the number of children subject to a care order has fluctuated from 37,000 in 1991, down to 28,500 in 1995 and back up to 37,600 in 2001.[4] In the same period the number of children looked after by local authorities has fluctuated from 59,800 in 1991 down to 49,500 in 1995 and back up to 58,900 in 2001. Accordingly the increase is almost entirely in respect of children subject to care orders. The reasons for these variations are not known, but may be a reflection of the limited practical success of Part III of the Act, a recognition of problems as children grow older and a function of the changing purposes for which proceedings are used. These questions are considered in the conclusions to this chapter.

1   See the Children Act Report 1993, paras 3.5–3.9 and the Children Act Advisory Committee Annual Report 1993/94, pp 70–71.
2   See the *Scoping Study on Delay in Children Act Cases* (Lord Chancellor's Dept 2002).
3   Children Act Report 2000.
4   Children looked after by local authorities year ending March 2001, Department of Health.

CARE PROCEEDINGS

1   Procedures in the initial stages

APPLICANTS

8.10   Application to the court for an order under s 31 may be made only by a local authority or an 'authorised person' or a person authorised[1] by the Secretary of State. The court may not require a local authority to take proceedings and cannot make an order under s 31, unless the authority has made an application.[2]

1   The NSPCC is authorised by s 31(9). There is no other authorised person. The NSPCC has only made one application in recent years, but uses its status as an authorised person to carry out special investigations of child abuse (personal communication).
2   *Nottinghamshire County Council v P* [1994] Fam 18, [1993] 3 All ER 815, CA.

APPLICATION

8.11   Application must be made on the prescribed form.[1] Proceedings under Pts IV and V of the CA 1989 must be commenced in the family proceedings court,[2] unless they arise out of a direction for an investigation under s 37 or there are proceedings pending in another court. If the court has made an interim care order, the local authority may make simultaneous applications for a care order and an order freeing a child for adoption.[3] In such cases the court should decide the care application first.[4] If it were to do otherwise the court would in effect be seeking to control the care plan of the authority.

1   FPC(CA 1989)R 1991, Sch 1. In the rare case when an application is made in a higher court the form is the same under the FPR 1991.
2   Children (Allocation of Proceedings) Order 1991, SI 1991/1677, art 3.
3   Under the Adoption and Children Bill 2002 the local authority will be obliged to make application for a placement order, if the care plan is for the child to be placed for adoption.
4   *Re D (Simultaneous Applications for Care Order and Freeing Order)* [1999] 2 FLR 49.

8.12   Witness statements setting out the evidence in support of the application must be filed in the court and served on the parties.[1] The applicant will be required to submit details of plans for the immediate care of the child and any requests for directions, including restrictions on contact.[2] The level of details given will be determined to some extent by the stage reached in the investigation of the child's circumstances,[3] but it should be sufficient to justify the application. Any plan should consider the welfare checklist of factors and why an order is necessary.

1   FPC (CA 1989)R 1991, r 17.
2   The care plan will be updated as the proceedings develop, until a care plan is filed for the final hearing: see para 8.83. At the time of writing there is no statutory requirement for a care plan, but there will be on implementation of the relevant part of the Adoption and Children Bill 2002.
3   *Re G (child case: parental involvement)* [1996] 2 FCR 1, [1996] 1 FLR 857, CA.

PARTIES

8.13   The child and any person with parental responsibility for the child will automatically be given party status.[1] The applicant for a care or supervision order must serve a copy of the application on all the parties to the proceedings[2] and on every person who the applicant believes to be a parent without parental responsibility.[3] The court may direct that a father not having parental responsibility should not be served with notice[4] or that he be discharged from the proceedings.[5] If a father without parental responsibility wishes to participate in the proceedings, he should be permitted to do so, unless there is some justifiable reason for not joining him as a party.[6] A father without parental responsibility who has been given notice of the proceedings but who delays an application to be joined until the final directions hearing may be refused if that would delay the resolution of the care hearing. The father's right to access to the court has to be balanced with the right of the child to an early determination of his future, so that neither Arts 6 nor 8 of the ECHR are breached by refusing the father's application.[7]

1   FPC(CA 1989)R 1991, Sch 2.
2   FPC(CA 1989)R 1991, r 4.
3   FPC(CA 1989)R 1991 Sch 4
4   *Re X (care: notice of proceedings)* [1996] 3 FCR 91, [1996] 1 FLR 186.
5   *Re W (Discharge of Party to Proceedings)* [1997] 1 FLR 128.
6   *Re B (Care Proceedings: Notification of Father Without Parental Responsibility)*[1999] 2 FLR 408.
7   *Re P (Care Proceedings: Father's Application to be Joined as a Party)* [2001] 1 FLR 781; see also *Re B & T (Care Proceedings: Legal Representation)* [2001] 1 FLR 485, CA, in which it was held that it was not a breach of human rights for a parent not to have legal representation. In *P, C and S v United Kingdom*, [2002] 3 FCR 1, ECtHR the court, considering an application in respect of this case, concluded that the assistance of a lawyer during the hearings

of applications with such crucial consequences, was an indispensable requirement without which there was a breach of Art 6. Sed quaere when lawyers had withdrawn because they were required to conduct the case in an unreasonable manner? For a wider discussion of representation in care proceedings see Lindley, Richards and Freeman 'Advice and advocacy for parents in child protection cases', CFLQ [2001] 167 and 311.

DIRECTIONS APPOINTMENTS

8.14 On receipt of the application, the clerk of the court will consider whether a directions appointment should be held in advance of the first hearing. At a directions appointment, which may be held at any time during the course of the proceedings, directions may be issued for the conduct of the proceedings including:[1]

(a) the timetable for the proceedings and variation of any time limits in the Rules;
(b) the attendance of the child;
(c) the appointment of a children's guardian and/or solicitor;
(d) the submission of evidence including experts' reports.

Decisions will also have to be taken about where the child is to live in the course of the proceedings, with whom he has contact during that time, what evidence is to be filed, what assessments are to be undertaken, how the proceedings are to be managed and whether there is a need to separate the stages of proving the threshold criteria and deciding on the appropriate order.

1   FPC(CA 1989) R 1991, r 14(2).

TIMETABLE FOR PROCEEDINGS

8.15 Section 32 requires a court hearing an application under Pt IV to draw up a timetable with a view to disposing of the application without delay and to give such directions as it considers appropriate for the purpose of ensuring, so far as is reasonably practicable, that the timetable is adhered to. The court should control the progress of care proceedings and for that purpose directions appointments are an integral part of the process. They should not be formalities.[1] This is an extension of the duty of the court to have regard to the general principle that any delay in determining the question is likely to prejudice the welfare of the child.[2] Courts and practitioners should ensure that a timetable acts as an encouragement to bring the matter before the court expeditiously, while not discouraging sensible negotiation. Equally important the court must ensure the proper conduct of the proceedings in a way that is fair to all parties.

1   Detailed guidance is given in *Re MD and TD (Minors) (Time Estimates)* [1994] 2 FLR 336n. See also *Re A and B (Minors) (No 2)* [1995] 1 FLR 351. See also paras 4.1 et seq. Note some court areas have protocols to be followed for directions.
2   Section 1(2). Delay is ordinarily inimical to the welfare of the child but planned and purposeful delay may be beneficial: *C v Solihull Metropolitan Borough Council* [1993] 1 FLR 290. See paras 2.58 et seq.

THIRD PARTY APPLICATIONS

8.16 The court may direct that others be joined to the proceedings. There is concern about the number of parties who become involved in care proceedings, which can cause unnecessary delay and waste of costs. The court should be particularly cautious about giving leave to relatives whose interests are the same as the parents, and are simply standing behind them.[1] The court can consider an application for a residence order by a third party as an alternative to a care order, whether or not the threshold criteria are satisfied, but it will scrutinise carefully the need for the third party to be fully involved in the care proceedings. The guidelines for leave applications set out in s 10(9) are applicable.[2] A person against whom allegations are made (but who is not a party) could be given leave to intervene and permitted to take part in the proceedings to the limited extent of his involvement,[3] but has no right to be made a party.[4]

1 *Re M (minors) (sexual abuse: evidence)* [1993] 1 FCR 253, [1993] 1 FLR 822, discussed at para 5.120. See also *North Yorkshire County Council v G* [1994] 1 FCR 737, in which a brother was refused leave to become a party to care proceedings on the basis that his case was the same as that of his mother.
2 See *Re p (a child) (residence: grandmothers application for leave)* [2002] EWCA Civ 846 and [2002] All ER (D) 554 (May) and discussion at paras 5.117 to 5.121.
3 *Re S (Care: Residence: Intervener)* [1997] 1 FLR 497, CA.
4 *Re H (Care Proceedings: Intervener)* [2000] 1 FLR 775.

Interim procedures

8.17 Once care proceedings have been started, the court has the option of making:

(a) no order;
(b) a residence order and other s 8 orders for a limited period;
(c) with or without an interim supervision order; or
(d) an interim care order.

8.18 An order under s 8 may be made for a specified period and may impose conditions.[1] Orders may be made even though the court is not in a position to dispose of the proceedings.[2] Thus the court has power to make interim orders similar to those it could make as a final disposal in care proceedings. It could make a residence order until the next hearing in favour of a relative, and control the child's contact with a parent for the time being, through a contact order or a prohibited steps order.[3] The court cannot, however, make a contact order in favour of a local authority because of the restriction contained in s 9(2).[4]

1 Section 11(7), see para 5.87 et seq.
2 Section 11(3), see para 5.86.
3 See para 5.5 et seq.
4 See para 5.98.

8.19 Where, on an application for a care or supervision order, the proceedings are adjourned or where the court in any proceedings gives a direction for an authority to investigate the child's circumstances,[1] the court may make an interim care or supervision order.[2] It may not make the order unless satisfied that there are reasonable grounds for believing that the threshold criteria are satisfied.[3] If the court makes a residence order on an application for a care or supervision order, it must make an interim supervision order unless satisfied that the child's welfare will be satisfactorily safeguarded without it.[4] The court must still apply the overriding principles in s 1 that the welfare of the child is paramount and that no order should be made unless it is better for the child than making no order.[5]

1   Under s 37: see para 7.4.
2   Section 38(1).
3   Section 38(2). For the threshold criteria see para 8.38.
4   Section 38(3).
5   *Hampshire County Council v S* [1993] 1 FLR 559.

GUIDANCE ON INTERIM APPLICATIONS

8.20   The following guidance is still important when courts are dealing with interim applications.[1]

(1)   Justices should bear in mind that they are not, at an interim hearing, required to make a final conclusion; indeed it is because they are unable to reach a final conclusion that they are empowered to make an interim order. An interim order or decision will usually be required so as to establish a holding position, after weighing all the relevant risks, pending the final hearing . . .

(2)   If justices find that they are unable to provide the appropriate hearing time, be it through pressures of work or for some other reason, they must, when an urgent interim order may have to be made, consider taking steps pursuant to r 14(2)(h) by transferring the proceedings laterally to an adjacent family proceedings court.

(3)   At the start of a hearing which is concerned with interim relief, justices will usually be called upon to exercise their discretion under r 21(2) as to the order of speeches and evidence. Circumstances prevailing will almost certainly not permit full evidence to be heard. Accordingly, in such proceedings, justices should rarely make findings as to disputed facts.[2] These will have to be left over for the final hearing.

(4)   Justices must bear in mind that the greater the extent to which an interim order deviates from a previous order or the status quo, the more acute the need is likely to be for an early final hearing date. Any disruption in a child's life almost invariably requires early resolution. Justices should be cautious about changing a child's residence under an interim order. The preferred course should be to leave the child where it is, with a direction for safeguards and the earliest possible hearing date.

(5)   When an interim order may be made which will lead to a substantial change in a child's position, justices should consider permitting limited oral evidence to be led and challenged by way of cross-examination. However, it will necessarily follow that, in cross-examination, the evidence will have to be restricted to the issues which are essential at the interim stage. To this end the court may well have to intervene to ensure that this course is followed and that there is not a 'dress rehearsal' of the full hearing.

(6)   Justices should, if possible, ensure that they have before them the written advice from the children's guardian. When there are substantial issues between the parties the guardian should, if possible, be at court to give oral advice. A party who is opposed to a recommendation made by the guardian should normally be given an opportunity to put questions to him or her in regard to advice given to the court.

1   *Hampshire County Council v S* [1993] 1 FLR 559.
2   The court will have to make findings of fact and give reasons sufficient for the orders being made: *Hertfordshire County Council v W* [1992] 2 FCR 885, [1993] 1 FLR 118. The action taken must be a proportionate response to the nature and gravity of the feared harm: *Re C and B (Care Order: Future Harm)* [2001] 1 FLR 611. See paras 8.6 and 8.168.

8.21 Failure to oppose an interim care order on the basis that the child was to be placed with the parent where that does not happen is not a basis for appeal.[1] Negotiation on the basis of undertakings or understandings should therefore be approached with caution.

1   *Re M (Minors)* [1993] 2 FLR 406.

DIRECTIONS FOR ASSESSMENT

8.22 Where a medical examination or other assessment is proposed for evidential purposes, the leave of the court is required.[1] The power to make directions enables the court to control the investigation of suspected harm, where proceedings have been commenced. The court could direct a joint medical assessment or prevent a particular type of assessment. This provision clearly has implications for the examination of children whose medical condition requires consideration and the interviewing of children alleged to have been sexually abused, unless the work has been undertaken prior to the commencement of proceedings. Evidence of the desirability or otherwise of an examination or interview will have to be produced at an early stage of proceedings.[2]

1   FPR 1991, r 4.18 and FPC (CA 1989) R 1991, r 18.
2   In *Re B (A Minor) (Care Order: Criteria)* [1993] 1 FLR 815 there was evidence before the court to satisfy the test that a girl was likely to suffer significant harm, but difficulty arose over the attribution of that harm. An assessment was crucial to that and an interim care order was made which ensured that it could be properly carried out.

8.23 Section 38 provides that where a court makes an interim care or supervision order it may give such directions as it considers appropriate with regard to medical or psychiatric examination or other assessment of the child and may direct that no examination or assessment is to take place at all or unless the court directs.[1] A direction may be given or varied at any time during the period of an interim order. In deciding what directions should be given, the welfare of the child is not the court's paramount consideration.[2]

1   Section 38(6).
2   See para 2.18.

8.24 A parent who opposes the making of a care order is likely to make an application for an assessment, because without it the court may have no professional or expert evidence other than that of the local authority on which to base its decision. Thus that application can be determinative of the outcome of the care proceedings. Initially authorities argued that the courts had no power to order an assessment a) which dictated the place at which the assessment should be undertaken, because residence was a matter for the local authority to decide if it had an interim care order; or b) that the authority should fund it. Latterly the courts have developed a greater willingness to direct the local authority to carry out an assessment and contribute to the funding of it.

8.25 In *Re C (A Minor) (Interim Care Order: Residential Assessment)* the House of Lords held that a court could dictate the placement of the child during an interim care order for the purpose of an assessment.[1] Although s 38 refers to the examination or assessment of the child, a child cannot be divorced from its environment, so that another person can be included.[2]

There may be a direction to reside in a mother and baby unit, if that management was the better course for the case.[3] The court may not order that a child live at home with its parent during the course of an interim care order, which is a discretion vested in the local authority.[4] Although s 38 is wide enough to give the court jurisdiction to name the person to carry out an assessment, the court should not direct an individual who is unwilling to do so.[5]

1   [1997] AC 489, [1997] 1 FCR 149, HL.
2   But not it would seem without the child: See Posner, Section 3 (8)(6) Assessment Reassessed [2001] Fam Law 544.
3   *Re B (Interim Care Order: Directions)* [2002] EWCA Civ 25, [2002] 1 FLR 545.
4   *Re L (a minor)* [1996] 2 FCR 706, CA.
5   *Re W (a minor) (care proceedings: assessment)* [1998] 1 FCR 287, CA and *Re B (Psychiatric Therapy for Parents)* [1999] 1 FLR 701. Note also that the court cannot direct the provision of services: *Re J (a Minor) (Specific Issue Order: Leave to Apply)* [1995] 1 FLR 669. See also *Berkshire County Council v C* [1993] Fam 205,[1993] 1 FLR 569. The court can order an HIV test under s 38(6) at the interim stage of care proceedings but application for leave should be made to the High Court: *Re X (a minor)* [1994] 2 FCR 1110, sub nom *Re HIV Tests* [1994] 2 FLR 116n and see *Re W (a minor)* [1995] 2 FCR 184.

8.26   In *Re C (A Minor) (Interim Care Order: Residential Assessment)* the House of Lords also held that the court can direct the authority to fund any necessary placement, although it would take into account the cost and the fact that local authority resources were limited. It might be necessary to consider the impact of the cost compared to the ability of the authority to provide other services for children.[1] For that purpose an authority should consider whether to provide budgetary evidence. It is important to distinguish for the purposes of this provision between an examination or assessment on the one hand and treatment on the other. The latter did not come within the provision and the authority could not be directed to pay for that.

1   [1997] AC 489, [1997] 1 FCR 149, [1997] 1 FLR 1, HL and see *Re C (children) (residential assessment)* [2001] 3 FCR 164. A direction can be appealed but it must otherwise be obeyed. Lack of resources is no excuse: *Re O (Minors) (Medical Examination)* [1993] 1 FLR 860 and *Berkshire County Council v C* [1993] 1 FLR 569.

8.27   Where there is no interim order in force, a party may still obtain leave to file a report, but the court has jurisdiction to order or prohibit any assessment that involves the participation of the child.[1] If a direction is given for a medical report on a parent or the child, no party will then be able to withhold the report because it is not favourable to their case.[2] A direction to carry out an assessment is a requirement and not permission to do so.[3] It is a direction to providing the court with the material that, in the view of the court, was required to enable it to reach a proper decision at the final hearing of the application for a care order.[4]

1   FPR 1991, r 4.18 and FPC (CA 1989) R 1991, r 18.
2   See paras 11.55 to 11.59.
3   S 38(6).
4   *Re B (Interim Care Order: Directions)* [2002] EWCA Civ 25, [2002] 1 FLR 545.

8.28   If the child is of sufficient understanding to make an informed decision, he may refuse to submit to an examination or assessment.[1] The level of understanding that enables a child to make an informed decision whether to refuse to submit to a psychiatric examination is a much higher level of understanding than is required to enable him to give instructions to a solicitor on his behalf.[2] It has been held, questionably, that the High Court can, in the exercise of its inherent jurisdiction,[3] override the refusal of a child to submit to an examination or assessment.[4]

1　Section 38(6). Similar provisions apply in relation to applications for a child assessment order under s 43 or an emergency protection order under s 44.
2　*Re H (A Minor) (Care Proceedings)* [1993] 1 FLR 440.
3　See ch 12.
4　*South Glamorgan County Council v W and B* [1993] 1 FLR 574, for discussion of which see para 12.31, fn1.

DURATION OF INTERIM ORDERS

8.29　An interim care or supervision order may be made for such period as the court orders but may not last longer than eight weeks in the case of an initial order or 'the relevant period' in the case of a second or subsequent order.[1] The relevant period is four weeks, or eight weeks from the date of the first order if that is longer.[2] Thus, if the first order was made for two weeks, the second order could be made for six weeks. If the first two orders were made respectively for one week and two weeks, the third order could be made for five weeks. When deciding the period, the court must consider whether a party who was or might have been opposing the order was in a position to argue the case in full.[3]

1　Section 38(4).
2　Section 38(5).
3　Section 38(10).

8.30　If the court orders an investigation by a local authority under s 37(1), a care or supervision order may be made for no longer than the period within which the authority must report to the court. The maximum period is eight weeks.[1] The authority may decide within that period to commence and obtain an order.

1　Section 37(4).

RENEWAL OF INTERIM ORDERS

8.31　There is no limit in principle to the number of repeated interim orders which the court can make, provided they are made before the expiry of the relevant period.[1] Where an initial interim care order has been made and a date fixed for a full hearing, there will probably be no further contested interim applications unless circumstances change. Agreed interim care orders may be made in the family proceedings court under the following conditions:[2]

(a)　a written request for such an order has been made to which the other parties and any children's guardian consent, and which they or their representative have signed;
(b)　a previous such order has been made in the same proceedings; and
(c)　the terms of the order sought are the same as those of the last such order made.

Although family proceedings courts are encouraged to make interim care orders in accordance with these provisions, there is no similar provision in the Family Proceedings Rules 1991 but in general care centres appear to adopt a similar approach. Courts sometimes require the local authority to attend on the renewal application. In London some local authorities have developed the practice of seeking the agreement of other parties to ongoing approval to renewal of orders.

1 *Gateshead Metropolitan Borough Council v N* [1993] 1 FLR 811.
2 FPC (CA 1989) R 1991, r 28.

ATTACHING EXCLUSION REQUIREMENT TO AN INTERIM CARE ORDER

8.32 A court may include an exclusion requirement in an interim care order.[1] (This does not include a case which is based on the child being beyond parental control).[2] The court must be satisfied of three conditions:

(a) that there is reasonable cause to believe that if a person (the relevant person) is excluded from a dwelling house in which the child lives, the child will cease to suffer or cease to be likely to suffer significant harm; and
(b) that a person living in the dwelling house, whether a parent or some other person, is able and willing to give the child the care which it would be reasonable to expect a parent to give; and
(c) that that person consents to the inclusion of the exclusion requirement. Consent must be in writing or given orally to the court.[3]

1 CA 1989, s 38A. There are no available statistics in respect of such orders, but practical experience suggests they are rare.
2 That part of the threshold criteria is specifically excluded: s 38A(1)(a)
3 FPR 1991, r 4.24 and FP(CA 1989)R 1991, r 25. See also *President's Direction* [1998] 1 FLR 495. For the procedure to be followed and evidence required see *W v A Local Authority (exclusion requirement)* [2000] 2 FCR 662, [2001] 2 FLR 666.

8.33 An exclusion requirement may be one or more of the following provisions:

(a) requiring the relevant person to leave a dwelling house in which he is living with the child;
(b) prohibiting him from entering a dwelling house in which the child is living; or
(c) excluding the relevant person from a defined area around the dwelling house.

A power of arrest may be attached to the exclusion requirement. The exclusion requirement and the power of arrest may be ordered for periods shorter than the substantive order. If the child is removed from the dwelling house, the requirement shall cease to have effect. The court may accept an undertaking in similar terms but a power of arrest cannot be attached.[1] A person who is not entitled to apply for variation or discharge of an interim care order, but to whom the exclusion requirement applies, may apply for variation of the requirement.[2]

1 CA 1989, s 38B.
2 CA 1989, s 39(3A)

CONCURRENT CARE AND CRIMINAL PROCEEDINGS

8.34 The decision whether to adjourn care proceedings, and have repeated interim care orders, may cause difficulty when there are concurrent criminal proceedings pending. The family court should ensure that there is co-ordination between the different courts.[1] Prior to the Children Act, there was reluctance to adjourn care proceedings for the outcome of criminal proceedings.[2] In a case where parents faced a murder charge, the Court of Appeal had held that it was preferable for the criminal trial to be heard before care proceedings, unless there were exceptional circumstances requiring the child's long-term future to be arranged without delay.[3] Subsequently the Court of Appeal has held[4] that a pending criminal trial was not of itself sufficient to delay care proceedings and that the welfare of the child had to take precedence over detriment to the family.

1 *Re A and B (Minors) (No 2)* [1995] 1 FLR 351.
2 See *R v Inner London Juvenile Court, ex p G* [1988] FCR 316, [1988] 2 FLR 58; *R v Exeter Juvenile Court, ex p RKH, R v Waltham Forest Juvenile Court, ex p KB* [1988] FCR 474, [1988] 2 FLR 214.
3 *Re S (Care Order: Criminal Proceedings)* [1995] 1 FLR 151.
4 *Re T-B (Care Proceedings: Criminal Trial)* [1995] 2 FLR 801, CA.

8.35 Whether the care hearing should proceed still requires careful considera-tion. Parents may be prejudiced if the care proceedings go ahead, because the court will not know whether they will be at liberty. Additionally the parents may feel constrained about the evidence they are able to give.[1] On the other hand the delay in securing the child's future may be damaging. Where there is likely to be a lengthy criminal trial on issues which will also be relevant to care proceedings, the care court should ensure that there is coordination with the criminal court, so that where possible interlinked directions are given.[2]

1 See discussion of s 98 at paras 11.64 et seq.
2 In London there is a *Practice Direction 'Linked Criminal and Care Directions Hearings'* 21 December 1998. Originally for a trial period, the Direction was extended in 2000. Although the number of cases involved is not high, the practice established is considered to be effective and useful. Enquiries for further information about the scheme will be available from the Principal Registry of the Family Division and the Central Criminal Court.

WITHDRAWING CARE PROCEEDINGS

8.36 The leave of the court is required before an application under s 31 can be withdrawn.[1] A person seeking leave to withdraw shall file and serve on the parties a written request setting out the reasons for the request. Application may be made orally if the parties and the children's guardian are present.[2] If all these consent in writing and the court thinks fit, it shall grant the request or it may fix a date for hearing the application. The welfare of the child is paramount.[3] Prior to the Children Act it was held that the action of a local authority in offering no evidence when refused leave to withdraw was highly questionable.[4]

1 FPR 1991, r 4.5, FPC(CA 1989)R 1991, r 5; and see *Re N (Leave to Withdraw Care Proceedings)* [2000] 1 FLR 134.
2 *Re F (a minor) (care order: withdrawal of application)* [1993] 1 FCR 389, [1993] 2 FLR 9.
3 *Southwark London Borough v B* [1993] 2 FLR 559, CA.
4 *R v Birmingham Juvenile Court, ex p G and R* [1988] 3 All ER 726, [1989] 1 WLR 950; affd in the Court of Appeal [1990] 2 QB 573, [1989] 3 All ER 336, [1989] FCR 460.

2.   The final stages of care proceedings

8.37 There are a number of elements which have to be considered in the final stages of care proceedings:

(a) What are the threshold criteria?
(b) How should the proceedings be managed?
(c) Should there be a final order?
(d) What are the options for the final order?
(e) What can happen after a final order?

The threshold criteria

8.38 Section 31 empowers the court to make a care order or a supervision order, in respect of a child under 17 (or 16 if married), only if it[1] is satisfied that:

(a) the child concerned is suffering significant harm, or is likely to suffer significant harm; and
(b) the harm or likelihood of harm is attributable to
  (i) the care given to the child, or likely to be given to him if the order were not made, not being what it would be reasonable to expect a parent to give to him; or
  (ii) the child's being beyond parental control.

The burden of proving these criteria rests on the local authority; the standard of proof is the civil test of the balance of probabilities.[2]

1 The court must satisfy itself, and is not relieved of the duty because the parties agree: *Re G (A Minor) (Care Order: Threshold Conditions)* [1995] Fam 16, sub nom *Re G (A Minor) (Care Proceedings)* [1994] 2 FLR 69. See para 8.119.
2 *Re H (Minors) (Sexual Abuse: Standard of Proof)* [1996] AC 563, [1996] 1 All ER 1, HL.

8.39 The conditions have come to be known as the 'threshold criteria', because they are not in themselves grounds or reasons for making a care or supervision order. As the then Lord Chancellor, Lord Mackay, said of the provisions:[1]

'Those conditions are the minimum circumstances which the Government considers should always be found to exist before it can ever be justified for a court even to begin to contemplate whether the State should be enabled to intervene compulsorily in family life . . . Wherever rules of law apply there will always be borderline cases where it may be difficult both as a matter of law and on the merits to say whether a case falls or indeed should fall within or without a rule. The only means of avoiding borderline cases is to avoid rules and to operate a discretion . . . once the court becomes involved in intervention from outside the family, and especially where State intervention is proposed, I do not believe that a broad discretion without defined minimum criteria, whatever its guiding principle, can be justified . . . Unless there is evidence that a child is being, or is likely to be, positively harmed because of a failure in the family, the State, whether in the guise of a local authority or a court, should not interfere.'

1 Joseph Jackson Memorial Lecture (1989) 139 NLJ 505.

8.40 The threshold criteria have a number of aspects, which can conveniently be described as in the chart at figure 1, though as a matter of practice the court should not treat one of several issues as a preliminary point.

Significant harm

8.41 The central concept of the criteria is whether there is harm, which is significant. Harm is defined as ill-treatment or the impairment of health or development.[1] Ill-treatment is defined as including sexual abuse and forms of ill-treatment which are not physical, though it must by implication include physical abuse. Health is defined as physical or mental health, and development as physical, intellectual, emotional, social or behavioural development. Where the question of whether harm suffered by a child is significant turns on the child's health or development, his health or development is to be compared with that which could be reasonably be expected of a similar child.[2] It has been held that a child who persistently refuses to attend school and thereby misses education is suffering harm, in relation to her intellectual and social development.[3]

1　Section 31(9). By virtue of s 105(1) these definitions apply throughout the Act. They also interlink with the definition of a child 'in need' in Pt III: see para 6.6. The Adoption and Children Bill 2002 provides for an extension of the definition of harm by the addition of the clause 'including, for example, impairment suffered from seeing or hearing the ill-treatment of another'.
2　See para 8.44
3　*Re O (a minor) (care order: education procedure)* [1992] 4 All ER 905, [1992] 2 FLR 7.

Is the harm significant?

8.42　The court must consider whether the harm caused is significant. The word is not defined in the Act: a common sense definition should be applied. Significant is defined by the Oxford English Dictionary as 'considerable, noteworthy or important'. 'Minor shortcomings in health care or minor deficits in physical, psychological or social development should not require compulsory intervention, unless cumulatively they are having, or are likely to have, serious and lasting effects upon the child.'[1]

1　Department of Health Guidance, 'Court Orders', para 3.12.

8.43　These are clearly matters of fact for the court, but it would appear that the significance could relate to the seriousness of the harm or the implications of it. For example, a broken leg would be a serious injury, but, depending on causation or attribution, the implications of a small cigarette burn might be more significant.

Comparison with 'similar child'

8.44　Where the facts relate to impairment of health or development, it is necessary to compare the health or development with what could reasonably be expected of a similar child.[1] How should the test of 'similar child' be applied? It has been held,[2] in relation to a truanting child, that the comparison should be made with a child who is attending school rather than one who is not, but other comparisons remain to be considered. It would seem that in relation to children with learning difficulties or similar medical problems, the court should compare the child with another child who has similar difficulties. There is no authority on whether comparisons should be made between similar children in the same neighbourhood or between children from different ethnic backgrounds, whose developmental rates may vary, but evidence is likely to draw attention to differences.

1　Section 31(10). Note that the provision does not apply where the facts relate to alleged ill-treatment.
2　*Re O (a minor) (care order: education procedure)* [1992] 4 All ER 905, [1992] 2 FLR 7.

THRESHOLD CRITERIA

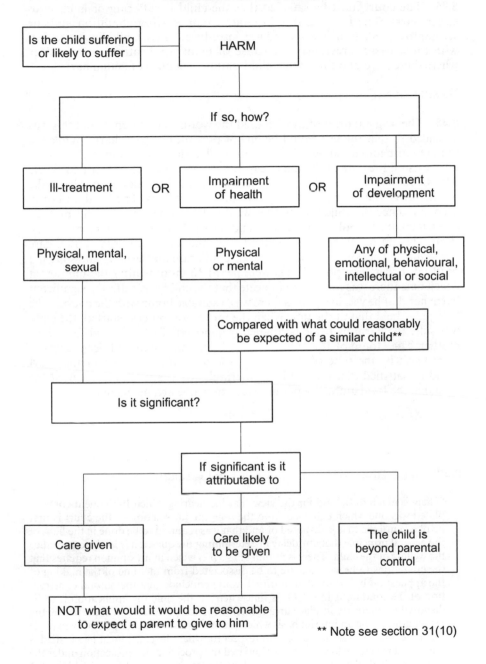

FIGURE 1

Is the child suffering or likely to suffer harm?

8.45 The court must be satisfied that the child is suffering or is likely to suffer harm. The first leg should relate to an existing condition and the second to a prediction. The second was introduced in the Children Act to deal with those cases, previously the cause of many applications in wardship, where there were grave risks to a child, but no evidence of actual harm.

'Is suffering'

8.46 The original draft of the Bill used the words 'has suffered', but this was amended so that the test would be one of present, not past, harm. While the present tense implies an existing condition, that does not mean that the state must exist at the date of the final hearing for the criteria to be satisfied. In *Re M (A Minor) (Care Order: Threshold Conditions)*[1] the father murdered the mother of a four month old baby and his half-siblings. The local authority accommodated the children and they went to live with a cousin of the mother. She felt unable to look after the baby and he was fostered. Seven months later, shortly before the father was to stand trial, the local authority started care proceedings. The cousin then felt that she could care for the child and sought a residence order. The proceedings were heard 16 months after the murder, at which time there was nothing to indicate that the child was suffering significant harm nor that he was likely to as there was a suitable home with the cousin. The trial judge held that at the time when the protection process started, the child was suffering harm by being permanently deprived of the love and care of his mother. The House of Lords held that although the child had been removed from harm by the time of the hearing, the question was whether the court could be satisfied that the child 'is suffering', because there was harm at the time that the local authority put in place protective arrangements.

1   [1994] 2 AC 424, [1994] 2 FLR 577, HL.

What are protective arrangements?

8.47   In the House of Lords Lord Mackay LC said:[1]

'There is much to be said for the view that the hearing which Parliament contemplated was one which extended from the time the jurisdiction of the court is first invoked until the case is disposed of and that was required to be done in the light of the general principle that any delay in determining the question is likely to prejudice the welfare of the child. There is nothing in s 31(2) which in my opinion requires that the conditions to be satisfied are to be dissociated from the time of the making of the application by the local authority. I would conclude that the natural construction of the conditions in s 31(2) is that where, at the time the application is to be disposed of, there are in place arrangements for the protection of the child by the local authority on an interim basis which protection has been continuously in place for some time, the relevant date with respect to which the court must be satisfied is the date at which the local authority initiated the procedure for protection under the Act from which these arrangements follow. If after a local authority had initiated protective arrangements the need for these had terminated, because the child's welfare had been satisfactorily provided for otherwise, in any subsequent proceedings it would not be possible to found jurisdiction on the situation at the time of initiation of these arrangements.'

1   [1994] 2 FLR 577 at 583.

8.48 Lord Mackay placed the time at which the criteria should be applied, when there were 'arrangements for the protection of the child by the local authority on an interim basis which protection has been continuously in place'. He affirmed the judgment of Ewbank J in *Northamptonshire County Council v S*,[1] when he said that the court had 'to consider the position immediately before an emergency protection order, if there was one, or an interim care order, if that was the initiation of protection, or as in this case, when the child went into voluntary care'. The position is not without doubt. In *Re G (children) (care order: evidence)*[2] the Court of Appeal stated that it was common ground that the threshold had to be crossed when the authority first intervened to protect the child: 'that is, either the date of the application or, if child protection measures (police protection or emergency protection order) have been *continuously* (emphasis added) in place since before then, the date when those began'. The Northamptonshire case was not referred to. If the authority accommodated the child as a protection measure, even though it should perhaps have sought an order, there seems to be no good reason why the period of intervention should not be deemed to have started at that time, provided it is continuous. How far the court is prepared to go into the past must be a matter for evidence and the exercise of judicial discretion.

1   [1993] Fam 136 at 140. See also *Southwark London Borough Council v B* [1999] 1 FCR 550, [1998] 2 FLR 1095, noted at para 8.57 fn 2.
2   [2001] EWCA Civ 968, [2001] 2 FCR 757 at 761.

8.49 Evidence accumulated during the course of the proceedings could still be used in support of the application, but it should not be the case that an application was made without evidence on the basis that subsequent investigation would substantiate the case.[1]

1   *Re G (children) (care order: evidence)* [2001] EWCA Civ 968, [2001] 2 FCR 757.

'IS LIKELY TO SUFFER'

8.50 The phrase 'is likely to suffer' was introduced with the intention of providing a remedy where harm had not occurred but there were considerable future risks for the child. Such cases arise where the child is in danger from birth, where the parents are mentally ill or drug addicted, where an abuser returns to the household, or where a previous child has died in the household.

8.51 It is necessary to consider the standard to be applied to the test 'is likely to suffer significant harm'. In *Re H (Minors) (Sexual Abuse: Threshold Conditions)*[1] the case was based solely on an allegation by a child that she had been sexually abused by her mother's partner and that as a result it was likely that her younger children would suffer harm. The House of Lords unanimously took the view that the word 'likely' was being used in the sense of a real possibility, a possibility that could not sensibly be ignored having regard to the nature and gravity of the feared harm in the particular case, rather than in the sense of more likely than not.

1   [1996] AC 563, [1996] 1 All ER 1, HL.

8.52 Their Lordships agreed that the standard of proof to be applied was the civil standard of the balance of probabilities, but Lord Nicholls (who delivered the majority judgment) also approved the statement that:

'The more serious the allegation the more cogent is the evidence required to over-come the unlikelihood of what is alleged and thus to prove it.'[1]

Lord Lloyd (who dissented) preferred a simple balance of probabilities test, pointing out that Lord Nicholls' approach would lead to the result that the more serious the anticipated injury the more difficult it would become for the local authority to satisfy the burden of proof and secure protection for the child.

1 Above at 570 and 7.

8.53 Further difficulties arise when considering how that standard should be satisfied. Lord Nicholls held that the court had to apply a two stage test. Where the likelihood was based on events which were alleged to have occurred previously, those facts had to be proved on the balance of probabilities. Based on those findings the court had then to assess whether a risk of future harm was a real possibility. Lord Nicholls upheld the view of the majority of the Court of Appeal, where Millet LJ said:

'. . . if the likelihood of the child suffering harm in the future depends upon the truth of disputed allegations, the Court must investigate the allegations and determine, on the balance of probabilities, whether they are true or false. It is not sufficient that there is a real possibility that the allegations may be true if the probability is that they are not.'[1]

1 *Re H* [1995] 2 FCR 384, [1993] 1 FLR 643.

8.54 The court could not base a finding of a risk of harm on mere suspicions. Lord Nicholls went on:[1]

'[That] would mean that once apparently credible evidence of misconduct has been given, those against whom the allegations are made must disprove them. Otherwise it would be open to a court to hold that, although the misconduct has not been proved, it has not been disproved and there is a real possibility that the misconduct did occur. Accordingly, there is a real possibility that the child will suffer harm in the future, and, hence the threshold criteria are met.'

1 Above at 591 and 21.

8.55 Lord Nicholls also noted that the range of factors which might be taken into account was infinite, including the history of members of a family, the state of relationships within a family, proposed changes within the member-ship of a family, parental attitudes, and omissions which might not reasonably have been expected, just as much as actual physical assault. They included threats and abnormal behaviour by a child and unsatisfactory parental responses to complaints or allegations and facts which might be minor in iso-lation but when taken together might suffice to satisfy the court of the likelihood of future harm. That was not the case in *Re H*, because the only allegation was that the cohabitant had sexually abused the eldest child.[1] Lord Nicholls concluded that although the threshold was comparatively low,[2] it did require proof of the relevant facts.

1 See also *Re P (a minor) (care: evidence)* [1995] 1 FCR 583, [1994] 2 FLR 751, where the only matter relied on was the death of a previous child while in the care of the parents. Since the authority could not prove that the death was non-accidental, there was no factual basis for a finding of likelihood of harm to the surviving child. In the light of *Lancashire v A* (see para 8.62) it may be that this case would now be decided differently.

2   It has been held that the likelihood test would be satisfied if the parent or carer would be unlikely to satisfy the emotional needs of the child, even some years in the future: *Re H (A Minor) (Section 37 Direction)* [1993] 2 FLR 541.

8.56   The minority view was that the two stage test was wrong and over-complicated. Lord Lloyd disagreed with Lord Nicholls holding that there was a simple test to be satisfied, namely whether the court was satisfied that there was a serious risk of significant harm. As Lord Browne-Wilkinson put it:

'To be satisfied of the existence of risk does not require proof of the occurrence of past historical events but proof of facts which are relevant to the making of a prognosis.'[1]

In their view there were sufficient worrying features to justify the finding of a likelihood of harm.

1   Above at 572 and 3.

8.57   It is also necessary to consider how the court should approach a case where proceedings are commenced on the basis that the child is likely to suffer significant harm when with the carer who has the care at that time, but that carer then proposes that a suitable relative should look after the child. When should the test be applied in a case dependent on future harm? In *Oldham Metropolitan Borough Council v E*[1] the Court of Appeal held that the criteria were not satisfied. Although the House of Lords overruled the *Oldham* case in *Re M*, it is not clear that they were doing so in relation to the future test as well as the current test. The Court of Appeal has addressed this problem. Hale LJ noted in *Re G*[2]: 'It would be odd indeed if actual and likely harm had to be judged at different dates. Further the policy considerations [of giving the court a wide discretion to protect children] are equally strong in each case.' The better view must be that in this situation the court should consider the position as at the time of intervention, and leave questions of outcome to the welfare stage of the proceedings. The correct approach is surely well expressed by Ewbank J in *Northamptonshire County Council v S*:[3]

'The threshold test relates to the parent or other carer whose lack of care has caused the harm referred to in s 31(2)(a). The care which other carers might give to the child [in the future] only becomes relevant if the threshold test is met.'

1   [1994] 1 FLR 568, CA
2   *Re G (children) (care order: evidence)* [2001] 2 FCR 757 at 762. Note also *Southwark London Borough Council v B* [1999] 1 FCR 550, [1998] 2 FLR 1095 in which it was held that 'likelihood' was to be assessed at the date of the intervention.
3   [1993] Fam 136.

8.58   Where there is a real possibility of future harm to a child which could not sensibly be ignored, the action taken by the local authority in response had to be proportionate to the nature and gravity of that feared harm.[1] The principle had to be that the local authority worked to support, and eventually to reunite, the family, unless the risks were so high that the child's welfare required alternative family care. Cases where intervention would be appropriate to protect the child from future harm were likely to involve long-standing problems interfering with the capacity to provide even 'good enough' parenting in a serious way, such as serious mental illness, or a serious personality disorder, or intractable substance abuse, or evidence of past chronic neglect, or abuse, or evidence of serious ill-treatment and physical harm.

1   *Re C and B (children) (care order: future harm)* [2000] 2 FCR 611, [2001] 1 FLR 611. See also *P, C and S v United Kingdom* [2002] 3 FCR 1, ECtHR.

8.59   The court could be satisfied as to the existence of the threshold criteria, if harm would be likely to occur during contact between the child and the non-residential parent.[1] This would enable the court to impose a supervision order to ensure some oversight during contact.

1   *Re DH (A Minor) (Child Abuse)* [1994] 1 FLR 679.

Is the harm attributable to care given or likely to be given?

8.60   Having satisfied itself that the harm is significant, the court has also to be satisfied that it is attributable to the care given, or that the likelihood of harm is attributable to the care likely to be given to the child, not being what a parent would give to the child. Harm caused solely by a third party would normally be excluded, unless the parent has failed to prevent it. This could have caused difficulties in cases where the authority was not able to prove who was responsible for injuries suffered by a child, either where parents blame each other or where the child has been injured at a time during some of which the child has been looked after by a third party.

8.61   It is now established that it is not necessary to prove that harm actually suffered is attributable to the failure of an identified individual. Although 'care given' is normally that of the parents or primary caregivers, if the court is unable to identify which of a number of carers provided the deficient care, the words can include the care of any of the carers. In *Re CB and JB (minors) (care proceedings: case conduct)*[1] it was found that one child had suffered a non-accidental injury which must have been attributable to one of the parents; it was held that their other child was likely to suffer harm, notwithstanding that they were no longer living together.

1   [1998] 2 FCR 313.

8.62   This question has been further explored in *Lancashire County Council v A*[1]. A baby of six months was looked after by a child-minder, whilst her parents were at work. She sustained serious, non-accidental head injuries. It was not possible for the court to be satisfied which of several people had been responsible for the injuries suffered by the child. The local authority commenced care proceedings, relying exclusively on the injuries sustained by the baby in a two month period during which the child-minder cared for the baby. The House of Lords held that the criteria were met where the court was satisfied that a child, whose care was shared between the parents and a child-minder whilst the parents were at work, had suffered significant harm, even though the court was unable to identify which of the carers had inflicted the injuries, and there was no more than a possibility that the parents were responsible for inflicting those injuries. The absence of a reasonable standard of care need not imply fault. In the particular case the principle was not extended to the child of the person, who had been the child-minder of the injured child. In summary, although 'attributable' denotes a causal connection, it need not be the sole, dominant or direct cause and effect; a contributory causal connection will suffice.[1]

1   [2000] 2 AC 147, [2000] 2 WLR 590, [2000] 1 FCR 509.

8.63 Although proceedings were also initially taken in respect of the child-minder's child, on the basis that there was a likelihood of him suffering significant harm, the Court of Appeal held that the threshold criteria were not satisfied.[1]

1 See *Lancashire County Council v B* [2000] 2 WLR 346, sub nom *Re B and W* [1999] 2 FLR 835.

8.64 Care is not defined in the Act, but it must be more than mere physical care and include emotional care. In the case of a sexually abused child it includes listening to the child and monitoring its words and actions so that a professional assessment can be carried out.[1]

1 *Re B (A Minor) (Care Order: Criteria)* [1993] 1 FLR 815.

8.65 If the child is being accommodated at the time of the proceedings, the test to be applied would be in relation to the care likely to be given to the child without the making of an order. This could apply if the parent is looking to resume care or if the local authority wanted to make plans for the child with which the parent did not agree. If the lack of security of the child in the placement causes the child to suffer significant harm, although the parent is not going to resume care, the authority may wish to seek an order so as to make suitable arrangements.[1] In this context, care must include love and attention, without which it could be argued that the child will suffer harm even though not returned home. The court will have to consider the plans of the parent, their behaviour and attitude to the child, any agreements which have been reached, what the parents have been told about the importance of carrying them out, and the extent to which they have been carried out. The question of degree is a matter of fact for the court, but a failure to exercise parental responsibility must be relevant to proof of the threshold criteria.

1 *R v Tameside Metropolitan Borough Council, ex p J* [2000] 1 FCR 193.

CARE OF THE REASONABLE PARENT

8.66 The care given or likely to be given must be 'not what it would be reasonable to expect a parent to give the child'. This requires a test to be applied as to whether a hypothetical reasonable parent would provide adequate care, so that parents cannot argue that they have particular problems, that they are feckless, unintelligent, irresponsible, alcoholic, drug abusers, poor or otherwise disadvantaged, which justify them in providing a lower standard of care. Those matters might be relevant to the question of whether an order should be made, if their problems could be ameliorated by the provision of other services by the local authority, but they will not enable them to avoid fulfilling the threshold criteria. Guidance[1] suggests that the court will wish to see professional evidence on the standard of care which reasonable parents could be expected to provide with support from community-wide services as appropriate, where the child's needs are complex or demanding, or the lack of reasonable care is not immediately obvious.

1 Children Act 1989 Guidance, Volume 1, para 3.23.

CARE OF THE CHILD IN QUESTION

8.67 The court has to consider the care which should be given to the child in question rather than an average child. If the child has particular difficulties, say in relation to his behaviour or handicap, the court should consider what a reasonable parent would provide for him. This could require a higher or different standard of care than for an average child.

ORPHANS

8.68 Where orphan children who were being accommodated were leading well settled lives, it was held that it would be a distortion of the threshold criteria, to find a theoretical risk of significant harm.[1] Thorpe J considered that the local authority had adequate powers to safeguard and promote the children's interests without the making of a care order. On the other hand the court did find the criteria satisfied when the 'rescue operation' began before the parents died.[2] The child was accommodated at the time of the parents' death, but Hollis J held that at the date of the initial intervention he was suffering harm. In contrast to the previous case he held that it was in the interests for a care order to be made, because without it the authority might have difficulties in carrying out what they thought was in his interests. In a third case Cazalet J held that an abandoned baby was suffering significant harm immediately before he was found, since the complete dereliction of parental responsibility constituted ill-treatment[3] and that he was likely to suffer significant harm as a result of the abandonment. Like Hollis J he held that it was essential that the authority had full powers to make decisions and accordingly made a care order. The consequence of these cases is that the threshold criteria can be satisfied even though the parents are dead, and it may be that if parents have failed to make arrangements for the care of their child in the event of their death, the child could be considered as likely to suffer harm. Satisfaction of the criteria does not mean that a care order necessarily has to be made. If a suitable carer emerges, the court can decline to make a care order and consider whether to make a residence order.

1 *Birmingham City Council v D and Birmingham City Council v M* [1994] 2 FCR 245, [1994] 2 FLR 502.
2 *Re SH (Care: Orphan)* [1995] 1 FLR 746.
3 *Re MM (care order: abandoned baby)* [1996] 2 FCR 521, sub nom *Re M (Care Order: Parental Responsibility)* [1996] 2 FLR 84.

BEYOND CONTROL

8.69 The criteria can also be satisfied if the child is suffering or likely to suffer significant harm which is attributable to the child being beyond parental control.[1]

1 For an example of the circumstances see *M v Birmingham City Council* [1994] 2 FLR 141.

Commentary on the threshold criteria

8.70 By their decision in *Re M* the House of Lords maintained a flexible approach to the threshold criteria. It has, however, been argued that their decision 'realigns the balance between the family and the state in a way which substantially weakens the family's power to withstand state intervention'.[1] It can equally be argued that if the House of Lords had interpreted the phrase 'is suffering' in any other way, the protective intention of the provision would have been nullified and planning for the child's future would have been more difficult. Whenever a child had been removed from harm, the authority would have had to satisfy the court in respect of the more uncertain provision that the child would be likely to suffer harm. That was not the intention behind the introduction of the 'likely to suffer' clause.[2]

1   Masson J 'Social engineering in the House of Lords : *Re M* [1994] 6 JCL 170.
2   See para 8.50.

8.71   It is submitted that in *Re M* the House of Lords correctly decided that it was necessary to apply the s 31 criteria at an earlier stage than the final hearing. Any other interpretation would have rendered the first limb of the provision meaningless. As a matter of law the court can trace events back to any point of intervention by the local authority provided there is continuity of intervention. While this limits the application of the test that the child is likely to suffer harm, it does mean that applications are more commonly based on established facts. In any event limitation of the application of the first limb is not necessary. As Lord Mackay emphasised, being satisfied as to the criteria did not preclude the court from taking into account all the circumstances at the date of the hearing. It is an entry to the use of powers and does not necessitate intervention. If another family member was available the court could make orders other than those under s 31 or no order at all.

8.72   Neither the Court of Appeal nor the House of Lords considered in *Re M* whether the murder of the child's mother was ill treatment of the child. It has been suggested that the statutory definition requires the harm to result from an act directed at the child and not at someone else.[1] It is submitted that this view is wrong. Surely it is ill-treatment of the child to deprive him permanently of his mother. A parent who acts in such a way must be taken to understand the consequences for the child, even if the act was not aimed at him. It necessarily entails a failure of care of the child. This argument is strengthened by recognition that children can be harmed by seeing or hearing ill-treatment of another.[2]

1   Whybrow J, 'Re M – past, present and future harm' (1994) 6 JCL 88.
2   See para 8.41, fn 1.

8.73   The courts have been concerned with the standard of proof required for the threshold criteria.[1] There is agreement that it is the balance of probabilities, but this has been obscured by the statement that the more serious the allegation, the more cogent the evidence must be to prove it. The combination of this with the requirement to prove the two-stage test to satisfy the criteria of the likelihood of harm could present problems for a local authority, especially in cases reliant on a single issue. Certainly this demonstrates the importance to local authorities of seeking to establish a range of evidence, and wherever possible not relying on a single issue.

1   *Re H (Minors) (Sexual Abuse: Standard of Proof)* [1996] AC 563, [1996] 1 All ER 1, HL: See paras 8.51 and 11.11.

8.74 Where there is actual harm, the *Lancashire* case appears to provide the court with adequate power to make findings sufficient to justify the threshold criteria where necessary. It is a difficult balance to find. As Hayes has said:

'The dilemma to be resolved is how far the legal framework, and the legal process, can best reconcile safeguarding children from suffering harm with the obligation to respect parental autonomy and family privacy.'[1]

Whilst the interpretation of the attributable condition means that parents, who might be wholly innocent and whose care might not have fallen below that of a reasonable parent, could face the possibility of losing their child with all the pain and distress that caused, so far as the threshold criteria are concerned, the factor which outweighs all others is the prospect that any unidentified, and unidentifiable, carer might inflict further injury on a child he or she had already severely damaged. It is a necessary interpretation of the provisions since an authority would otherwise have to prove who was responsible for the injury, rather than simply that the child was receiving inadequate care. As described above the finding does not necessitate an order.

1 'Reconciling protection of children with justice for parents in cases of alleged child abuse ' (1997) 17 Legal Studies 1.

8.75 There remain potential problems where the case is based on possible future harm. While it must be right that a likelihood of harm cannot be substantiated on the basis of mere suspicion, it must be questionable whether the court should exclude its powers, where the evidence shows a real risk to the child, but one which the court discounts because the local authority is unable to satisfy the test on the balance of possibilities, on the basis that there is insufficient cogent evidence commensurate with the need to satisfy the court of a serious allegation. The alternative, however, could undermine parental autonomy. If the evidence is that an allegation is more likely to be untrue than true, it is difficult to justify findings which might lead to the removal of the child. On the facts of *Re H*, one might have thought that intervention was justified, which emphasises the importance of expertise in handling these cases.

8.76 There is in fact little evidence that children are being left at home in danger for want of protective measures. The number of care orders has increased. There is no evidence that children who are injured have been sent home by the courts because they have not been satisfied of the threshold criteria. On the other hand there is still a feeling that local authorities leave cases too late, whether it is because they dislike the court arena, because they lack confidence in their ability to prove cases or from concern as to whether they can provide anything better. Ultimately it is a matter of politics and professional judgement whether you err on the side of running the risks of leaving a child in an uncertain situation or the risks inherent in local authority care.

Final hearing: procedure

8.77 Before the final hearing the local authority should make a clear statement of the facts which they wish the court to find, and the basis on which they allege that the threshold has been crossed.[1]

1 *Re G (Care Proceedings: Threshold Conditions)* [2001] EWCA Civ 968, [2001] 2 FLR 1111 and see also *Re R (Care: Disclosure; Nature of Proceedings)* [2002] 1 FLR 755 at 773.

SPLIT HEARINGS

8.78   In some cases where there is a clear issue as to sexual or physical abuse, the court should consider whether to have a preliminary hearing to obtain findings of fact on those issues. The substantive hearing focussing on the child's welfare could then proceed more speedily.[1] Wall J has said[2] in relation to the conduct of split hearings:

> 'The essence of a split hearing is the clear identification of the issue to be tried first . . . Evidence which is relevant to the assessment of the parents or other family members if and when the threshold criteria are established should not be permitted unless for some reason it is of direct relevance to the factual issue being tried. It is the essence of a split hearing that assessments of the parties and their capacity to parent their children need to be carried out on the basis of the facts found by the court. Ex hypothesi that can only be done after the court has decided both that the threshold criteria have been satisfied and the factual basis upon which they have been satisfied . . . Evidence of propensity or a psychiatric or psychological assessment of one of the parties is unlikely to be of any assistance in resolving a purely factual issue. There will in any event be before the court evidence from the local authority and the parents relating to the history of the case and the backgrounds of each of the parents.'

1   *Re S (Care Proceedings: Split Hearing)* [1996] 2 FLR 773.
2   *Re CB and JB (Minors) (Care proceedings: Case Conduct)* [1998] 2 FLR 211,[1998] 2 FCR 313. See also *Re CD and MD (Care Proceedings: Practice)* [1998] 1 FLR 825 and Handbook of Best Practice in Children Act Cases (Children Act Advisory Committee, June 1997).

8.79   The courts have made no clear distinction between findings of fact and the threshold criteria on which they should be based. Is a split hearing intended to establish whether the threshold criteria are satisfied or solely whether certain disputed facts are proved? If the latter, then that would raise the possibility of three stages in the proceedings. If the purpose of a split hearing is to establish whether the threshold criteria can be proved, then an assessment could contribute to the question of whether a parent has a tendency to behaviour which might cause significant harm.

8.80   There is jurisdiction to hear an appeal against findings of fact on preliminary issues made at a split hearing.[1] The effect of this is that there does not have to be a decision before a party can appeal against findings which would be detrimental to their case.

1   *Re B (split hearings: Jurisdiction)* [2000] 1 FCR 297, [2000] 1 FLR 334, CA. Where possible the same judge should hear both parts of the hearing: *Re G* [2001] 1 FCR 165, [2001] 1 FLR 822. See also *Practice Direction-Judicial Contiuity* [2002] 3 All ER 603, [2002] 2 FCR 667, [2002] 2 FLR 367, FD.

THE WELFARE STAGE

8.81   When the court is satisfied of the threshold criteria, it must as a separate matter, decide what order, if any, to make.[1] It must then apply the principles contained in s 1, that the welfare of the child is the paramount consideration, have regard to fact that delaying a decision is likely to prejudice the welfare of the child and to the checklist[2], and not make an order unless it considers that doing so would be better for the child than making no order at all.[3] The local authority's intentions for the child are of the utmost importance, since they justify the making of an order.

1 *Humberside County Council v B* [1993] 1 FLR 257.
2 Section 1(4)(b)
3 Section 1(5)

8.82 The welfare principle applies to the child who is the subject of the proceedings, and not the mother where she is also a child.[1]

1 *F v Leeds City Council* [1994] 2 FLR 60, CA and see *Birmingham City Council v H (No 3)* [1994] 2 AC 212, [1994] 1 All ER 12, HL discussed at para 2.28.

CARE PLANS

8.83 In practice the application of the welfare principle means that the court must be satisfied that the outcome of the proceedings provides the best available arrangements, having applied the statutory checklist and considered what would happen if no order were to be made. In order to satisfy the court that it is better for the child to make an order, the authority should be able to indicate what plans will be put into effect as a result of the order. There are three issues to consider in relation to care plans: their content, what to do in the event of a dispute about the plan and what can happen if the care plan is not implemented.

8.84 Although at the time of writing there is no statutory provision for the local authority to file a care plan,[1] there is ample authority requiring them to do so. The application form for an order under s31 contains a requirement that the plans of the applicant are set out. It has been held[2] that care plans should follow the headings set out in Guidance on Family Placements.[3] The Department of Health has issued guidance which authorities should follow unless there is good reason for not doing so.[4]

1 The Adoption and Children Bill 2002 puts care plans on a statutory basis. Clause 118 inserts as s 31(3A) that 'no care order may be made with respect to a child until the court has considered a s 31A plan'. The local authority must prepare a care plan and, while the application is pending, keep it under review. If a change is required they must revise the plan. If the authority cannot implement its care plan after the making of a care order, they will have to consider whether to refer the matter to CAFCASS. There is no indication on the face of the bill of what CAFCASS should do, but clause 116 (2C) empowers the Lord Chancellor to make regulations extending the function of officers.
2 *Manchester City Council v F* [1993] 1 FLR 419n.
3 Department of Health, Vol 3, para 2.62. See also *Handbook of Best Practice in Children Act Cases* (Children Act Advisory Committee, June 1997) *Clarke Hall and Morrison* 1 [20004].
4 See Circular LAC 99(20) issued under s 7 of the Local Authority Social Services Act 1970.

8.85 Where the local authority has ruled out rehabilitation or placement with relatives and has confirmed adoption as the preferred option, the following should be addressed in the care plan:[1]

(a) appropriate steps should be taken within the local authority to co-ordinate information between the teams responsible for the care proceedings application and those responsible for family finding and to allocate responsibilities for carrying out the necessary work;

(b) BAAF Form E (details about the child) should be completed as far as possible, including obtaining from the parent(s) relevant medical and other details, although there may be difficulty in obtaining the necessary medical and other information from the parents;

(c) the adoption panel should consider the case, with a view to making a recommendation on whether adoption is in the child's best interests;

(d) the local authority should have identified the key steps and timetable, including family finding any necessary therapy, and issues of contact (for inclusion in the care plan) which would lead to an adoptive placement, if the court made a care order;

(e) the care plan should include a contingency plan for use in specified circumstances if the preferred option for adoption cannot be achieved;

(f) consideration should be given as to whether a freeing application is appropriate.

1 See LAC(99)29 and discussion at para 8.86. See also *Re D and K (Care Plan: Twin Track Planning)* [1999] 3 FCR 109, [1999] 2 FLR 872. When the local authority makes its report to the adoption panel, it should make the views of the children's guardian known: *Re R (Minors) (Adoption) (Disclosure)* [1999] 2 FLR 1123.

8.86 Two issues have arisen concerning the making of a care order and its relationship with the care plan. First can the court decline to make a final order and continue to make interim orders, so as to keep control of the case, where it does not agree with the proposed care plan or it is not confident about the willingness or ability of the authority to carry out the plan? Secondly if a care order is made, is there any way in which the court can control the case thereafter? These questions have been considered in some detail by the House of Lords[1] in two cases heard together at the end of 2001.

1 *Re S (Minors) (Care Order: Implementation of Care Plan)*; *Re W (Minors) (Care Order: Adequacy of Care Plan)* [2002] UKHL 10, [2002] 2 WLR 720, [2002] 1 FLR 815.

MAKING AN INTERIM CARE ORDER AFTER A FULL HEARING

8.87 In *Re W*, Bedfordshire took care proceedings in respect of J and A, aged 12 and 10 years old. The final care plan was that the children should be placed with the maternal grandparents, with continuing direct contact with both parents. The grandparents lived in the United States. They agreed to move to England to care for the children. The judge concluded that the children were unable to return safely to the joint care of their parents: 'possibly, or even probably, it may be appropriate in twelve to eighteen months, but not now'. All the parties agreed that the maternal grandparents would be suitable carers, although the evidence that they would be able to come here was 'exiguous in the extreme'. The judge described the care plan as inchoate, because of all the uncertainties involved, but nonetheless made care orders for both children.

8.88 The Court of Appeal held it was clear that the care plan was insufficiently mature but the judge had been constrained by the case law to make the full care order. They held that the judge should have insisted on more information before making the order, or on a report back if things did not turn out as expected. The court allowed the appeal in this case, replacing the care order with an interim care order and remitting the case for further consideration.

8.89 It is difficult to improve on the analysis of Lord Nicholls in the House of Lords, when he said:
'[90] From a reading of s 38 as a whole it is abundantly clear that the purpose of an interim care order, so far as presently material, is to enable the court to safeguard the welfare of a child until such time as the court is in a position to decide whether

or not it is in the best interests of the child to make a care order. When that time arrives depends on the circumstances of the case and is a matter for the judgment of the trial judge. That is the general, guiding principle. The corollary to this principle is that an interim care order is not intended to be used as a means by which the court may continue to exercise a supervisory role over the local authority in cases where it is in the best interests of a child that a care order should be made.'

'[91] An interim care order, thus, is a temporary 'holding' measure. Inevitably, time is needed before an application for a care order is ready for decision. Several parties are usually involved: parents, the child's guardian, the local authority, perhaps others. Evidence has to be prepared, parents and other people interviewed, investigations may be required, assessments made, and the local authority must produce its care plan for the child in accordance with the guidance contained in local authority circular LAC(99)29. Although the Children Act itself makes no mention of a care plan, in practice this is a document of key importance. It enables the court and everyone else to know, and consider, the local authority's plans for the future of the child if a care order is made.'

'[92] When a local authority formulates a care plan in connection with an application for a care order, there are bound to be uncertainties. Even the basic shape of the future life of the child may be far from clear. Over the last ten years problems have arisen about how far courts should go in attempting to resolve these uncertainties before making a care order and passing responsibility to the local authority. Once a final care order is made, the resolution of the uncertainties will be a matter for the authority, not the court.'

'[93] In terms of legal principle one type of uncertainty is straightforward. This is the case where the uncertainty needs to be resolved before the court can decide whether it is in the best interests of the child to make a care order at all. In *C v Solihull Metropolitan Borough Council* [1993] 1 FLR 290 the court could not decide whether a care order was in the best interests of a child, there a 'battered baby', without knowing the result of a parental assessment. Ward J made an appropriate interim order. In such a case the court should finally dispose of the matter only when the material facts are as clearly known as can be hoped. Booth J adopted a similar approach, for a similar reason, in *Hounslow London Borough Council v A* [1993] 1 FLR 702.'

'[94] More difficult, as a matter of legal principle, are cases where it is obvious that a care order is in the best interests of the child but the immediate way ahead thereafter is unsatisfactorily obscure. These cases exemplify a problem, or a 'tension', inherent in the scheme of the Children Act. What should the judge do when a care order is clearly in the best interests of the child but the judge does not approve of the care plan? This judicial dilemma was described by Balcombe LJ *in Re S and D (Children: Powers of Court)* [1995] 2 FLR 456, 464, perhaps rather too bleakly, as the judge having to choose between 'the lesser of two evils'.'

'[95] In this context there are sometimes uncertainties whose nature is such that they are suitable for immediate resolution, in whole or in part, by the court in the course of disposing of the care order application. The uncertainty may be of such a character that it can, and should, be resolved so far as possible before the court proceeds to make the care order. Then, a limited period of 'planned and purposeful' delay can readily be justified as the sensible and practical way to deal with an existing problem.'

8.90 Lord Nicholls noted the Court of Appeal decision in *Re CH (Care or Interim Care Order)*,[1] where it was held that the fact that a care order was the inevitable outcome should not have deflected the judge from hearing expert evidence on this issue. Even if the issue could not be finally resolved before a care order was made, it was obviously sensible and desirable that, in the circumstances of the case, the local authority should have the benefit of the judge's observations on the point. He also approved of *Re J (Minors) (Care: Care Plan)* in which Wall J said:

'there are cases (of which this is one) in which the action which requires to be taken in the interests of children necessarily involves steps into the unknown . . . provided the court is satisfied that the local authority is alert to the difficulties which may arise in the execution of the care plan, the function of the court is not to seek to oversee the plan but to entrust its execution to the local authority.'[2]

1   [1998] 1 FLR 402. See also *Re H (Care: Change in Care Plan)* [1998] 1 FLR 193, CA, in which it was said that if the care order was based on a flawed care plan the parent was entitled to have it reconsidered, even if the order remained in force. On the other hand, it has been held that if all the facts are known, it can seldom, if ever, be right for the court to continue adjourning a case: *Re P (Minors) (Interim Order)* [1993] 2 FLR 742, CA, *Re R (Care Proceedings: Adjournment)* [1998] 2 FLR 390, CA.
2   [1994] 1 FLR 253 at 265. See also *Re L (Sexual Abuse: Standard of Proof)* [1996] 1 FLR 116 and *Re R (Care Proceedings: Adjournment)* [1998] 2 FLR 390.

8.91   Lord Nicholls continued (at para 99):

'Despite all the inevitable uncertainties, when deciding whether to make a care order the court should normally have before it a care plan which is sufficiently firm and particularised for all concerned to have a reasonably clear picture of the likely way ahead for the child for the foreseeable future. The degree of firmness to be expected, as well as the amount of detail in the plan, will vary from case to case depending on how far the local authority can foresee what will be best for the child at that time. This is necessarily so. But making a care order is always a serious interference in the lives of the child and his parents. Although Art 8 contains no explicit procedural requirements, the decision making process leading to a care order must be fair and such as to afford due respect to the interests safeguarded by Art 8: see *TP and KM v United Kingdom* [2001] 2 FLR 549, 569, paragraph 72. If the parents and the child's guardian are to have a fair and adequate opportunity to make representations to the court on whether a care order should be made, the care plan must be appropriately specific.'

8.92   He noted that in the Court of Appeal Thorpe LJ[1] had expressed the view that in certain circumstances the judge at the trial should have a 'wider discretion' to make an interim care order: 'where the care plan seems inchoate or where the passage of a relatively brief period seems bound to see the fulfilment of some event or process vital to planning and deciding the future'. In an appropriate case, a judge must be free to defer making a care order until he is satisfied that the way ahead 'is no longer obscured by an uncertainty that is neither inevitable nor chronic.'

1   *Re W and B (children: care plan)* [2001] EWCA 757 at para 29, [2001] 2 FCR 450, [2001] 2 FLR 582.

8.93   Lord Nicholls considered that his analysis 'adheres faithfully to the scheme of the Children Act and conforms to the procedural requirements of Art 8 of the Convention'. It afforded the degree of flexibility sought by Thorpe LJ, while at the same time enabling the court to maintain a proper balance between the need to satisfy itself about the appropriateness of the care plan and the avoidance of 'over-zealous investigation into matters which are properly within the administrative discretion of the local authority'.

SUPERVISING CARE PLANS

8.94   The House of Lords considered the question of supervising or reviewing care plans after the making of a care order in *Re S*. A mother had three children, P aged 14, M aged 11 and J aged 10 years. Torbay, the local authority, sought care orders in respect of all three children. Its care plan for P was that he should remain in foster care, which was agreed. The care plan for M and J was that an attempt should be made to rehabilitate them with their mother. Counsel for the mother submitted that a care order should not be made because the mother was sceptical about whether Torbay would carry out the care plan. The mother contended that interim care orders should be made. The judge made final care orders in respect of all three children, expressing confidence that Torbay would implement the care plan. This confidence proved to be misplaced. There were serious failings principally because of a financial crisis within Torbay leading to substantial cuts in the social services budget.

8.95 The Court of Appeal had held[1] that courts should not be prevented from reviewing the implementation of care plans on which the decision to make a care orders was based. It proposed a scheme of making starred care plans. It was held that only by such a mechanism could the provisions relating to care orders be considered consistent with the Human Rights Act 1998, in those cases where rights under the Convention were being abused.

1   *Re W and B (children: care plan)* [2001] EWCA 757, [2001] 2 FCR 450, [2001] 2 FLR 582.

8.96 Thorpe LJ analysed whether justice was done by the division of roles between the judge and the local authority at each of three stages: pre-trial and trial, judgment and the period after a care order. He expressed the view that there was no problem at the first stage. He noted that there could be a difficulty at judgment stage because the judge had a duty to make the child's welfare paramount. How could the judge discharge this duty if his evaluation conflicted with the outcome to which the order would lead? At the third stage he accepted that the statutory rights of adult respondents provided a sufficient remedy where there was a fundamental failure to implement the care plan. But he was not satisfied that the child was protected, because the guardian had to drop out and no one had either the locus or funds to apply on behalf of the child.

8.97 Thorpe LJ said: 'the most general concentration of misgiving, certainly in the minds of guardians and forensic experts, was the absence of any overriding mechanism for intervention in those cases where the care plan approved at trial was frustrated by unforeseen change of circumstance, lack of resources, neglect or by any other factor'. He concluded: 'A failure to reach a starred milestone within a reasonable time of the date set at trial should reactivate the interdisciplinary process that contributed to the creation of the care plan. At a minimum the authority must inform the children's guardian of the failure. Either the guardian or the authority should then be able to apply for further directions.' In order to protect the parents' rights, they would have to have the same opportunity of application.

8.98 In his comprehensive judgment Lord Nicholls addressed the proposal of the Court of Appeal for starred care plans and the compatibility of the Children Act provisions in respect of a care order with Arts 6 and 8 of the Convention. He observed:

> '[17] . . . The Court of Appeal propounded a new procedure, by which at the trial the essential milestones of a care plan would be identified and elevated to a 'starred status'. If a starred milestone was not achieved within a reasonable time after the date set at trial, the local authority was obliged to 'reactivate the interdisciplinary

process that contributed to the creation of the care plan'. At the least the local authority must inform the child's guardian of the position. Either the guardian or the local authority would then have the right to apply to the court for further directions: see the judgment of Thorpe LJ ([2000] EWCA Civ 757, at paragraphs 29 and 30).'

'[18] . . . The Court of Appeal regarded the outcome of the appeal in the Torbay case as finely balanced. The court declined to disturb the judge's order. The court also dismissed the application by the children's guardian for directions for trial under s 7 of the Human Rights Act. Progress had been sufficient to make referral to the High Court an unnecessary distraction from the main business of getting on with the care plan. An application for 'starring' of the care plan was referred to the judge . . . [who starred various items in the final care plan].'

8.99 Lord Nicholls analysed the social, legislative and case law background to the provisions:

'[20] . . . First, a cardinal principle of the Children Act is that when the court makes a care order it becomes the duty of the local authority designated by the order to receive the child into its care while the order remains in force. So long as the care order is in force the authority has parental responsibility for the child. The authority also has power to decide the extent to which a parent of the child may meet his responsibility for him: s 33 . . . '

'[26] Consistently with this, in *Kent County Council v C* [1993] Fam 57 Ewbank J decided that the court has no power to add to a care order a direction to the authority that the child's guardian ad litem should be allowed to have a continuing involvement, with a view to his applying to the court in due course if thought appropriate. In *Re T (A Minor) (Care Order: Conditions)* [1994] 2 FLR 423 the Court of Appeal rightly approved this decision and held that the court has no power to impose conditions in a care order. There the condition sought by the child's guardian was that the child should reside at home.'

'[27] This cardinal principle of the Children Act represented a change in the law. Before the Children Act came into operation the court, in exercise of its wardship jurisdiction, retained power in limited circumstances to give directions to a local authority regarding children in its care. The limits of this jurisdiction were considered by your Lordships' House in *A v Liverpool City Council* [1982] AC 363 and In *Re W (A Minor) (Wardship: Jurisdiction)* [1985] AC 791. The change brought about by the Children Act gave effect to a policy decision on the appropriate division of responsibilities between the courts and local authorities. This was one of the matters widely discussed at the time. A report made to ministers by an interdepartmental working party 'Review of Child Care Law' (September 1985) drew attention to some of the policy considerations. The particular strength of the courts lies in the resolution of disputes: its ability to hear all sides of a case, to decide issues of fact and law, and to make a firm decision on a particular issue at a particular time. But a court cannot have day to day responsibility for a child. The court cannot deliver the services which may best serve a child's needs. Unlike a local authority, a court does not have close, personal and continuing knowledge of the child. The court cannot respond with immediacy and informality to practical problems and changed circumstances as they arise. Supervision by the court would encourage 'drift' in decision making, a perennial problem in children cases. Nor does a court have the task of managing the financial and human resources available to a local authority for dealing with all children in need in its area. The authority must manage these resources in the best interests of all the children for whom it is responsible.'

'[28] The Children Act, embodying what I have described as a cardinal principle, represents the assessment made by Parliament of the division of responsibility which would best promote the interests of children within the overall care system. The court operates as the gateway into care, and makes the necessary care order when the threshold conditions are satisfied and the court considers a care order would be in the best interests of the child. That is the responsibility of the court.

Thereafter the court has no continuing role in relation to the care order. Then it is the responsibility of the local authority to decide how the child should be cared for.'

'[29] My second preliminary point is this. The Children Act has now been in operation for ten years. Over the last six years there has been a steady increase in the number of children looked after by local authorities in England and Wales. At present there are 36,400 children accommodated under care orders, compared with 28,500 in 1995, an increase of 27 percent. In addition local authorities provide accommodation for nearly 20,000 children under s 20 orders (children in need of accommodation). A decade's experience in the operation of the Act, at a time of increasing demands on local authorities, has shown that there are occasions when, with the best will in the world, local authorities' discharge of their parental responsibilities has not been satisfactory. The system does not always work well. Shortages of money, of suitable trained staff and of suitable foster carers and prospective adopters for difficult children are among the reasons. There have been delays in placing children in accordance with their care plans, unsatisfactory breakdown rates and delays in finding substitute placements . . . '

'[31] In autumn 1998 the Government published its response to the children's safeguards review (Cm 4105) and launched its 'Quality Protects' programme, aimed at improving the public care system for children. Conferences have also been held, and many research studies undertaken, both private and public, on particular aspects of the problems. Some of the problems were discussed at the bi-annual President's Interdisciplinary Conference on family law 1997, attended by judges, child psychiatrists, social workers, social services personnel and other experts. The proceedings of the conference were subsequently published in book form, '*Divided Duties*' (1998). The sharpness of the divide between the court's powers before and after the making of a care order attracted criticism. The matters discussed included the need for a care plan to be open to review by the court in exceptional cases. One suggestion was that a court review could be triggered by failure to implement 'starred' key factors in the care plan within specified time-scales. The guardian ad litem would be the appropriate person to intervene.'

'[32] This was the source of the innovation which found expression in the judgments of the Court of Appeal in the present appeals. The House was informed by counsel that the starred milestones guidance given by the Court of Appeal was not canvassed in argument before the court. This guidance appeared for the first time in the judgments of the court.'

8.100   Lord Nicholls noted that the jurisprudential route by which the Court of Appeal found itself able to bring about this development was primarily by recourse to s 3 of the Human Rights Act, quoting Hale LJ, at paragraphs 79–80:

'Where elements of the care plan are so fundamental that there is a real risk of a breach of Convention rights if they are not fulfilled, and where there is some reason to fear that they may not be fulfilled, it must be justifiable *to read into the Children Act* a power in the court to require a report on progress . . . the court would require a report, either to the court or to CAFCASS . . . who could then decide whether it was appropriate to return the case to court . . . [W]hen making a care order, the court is being asked to interfere in family life. If it perceives that the consequence of doing so will be to put at risk the Convention rights of either the parents or the child, the court *should be able* to impose this very limited requirement as a condition of its own interference.' (emphasis added)

8.101   Lord Nicholls set the scene for the approach of the Court of Appeal:
'[34] [The judgments] are a clear and forceful statement of the continuing existence of serious problems in this field. In the nature of things, courts are likely to see more of the cases which go wrong. But the view, widespread among family judges, is that all too often local authorities' discharge of their parental responsibilities falls

short of an acceptable standard. A disturbing instance can be found in the recent case of *F v London Borough of* Lambeth [2002] 1 FLR 217, where Munby J said, in paragraph 38 of his judgment, that the 'blunt truth is that in this case the state has failed these parents and these boys'.

'[35] It is entirely understandable that the Court of Appeal should seek some means to alleviate these problems: some means by which the courts may assist children where care orders have been made but subsequently, for whatever reason, care plans have not been implemented as envisaged and, as a result, the welfare of the children is being prejudiced. This is entirely understandable. The courts, notably through their wardship jurisdiction, have long discharged an invaluable role in safeguarding the interests of children. But the question before the House is much more confined. The question is whether the courts have power to introduce into the working of the Children Act a range of rights and liabilities not sanctioned by Parliament.'

8.102 On this point the House of Lords disagreed with the Court of Appeal on the basis that the court's introduction of a 'starring system' could not be justified as a legitimate exercise in interpretation of the Children Act in accordance with s 3 of the Human Rights Act.[1] The starring system would create a new supervisory function, an amendment of statute, which was a matter for Parliament.

1 For further discussion see para 1.46.

8.103 Lord Nicholls also considered whether the Children Act was incompatible with Art 8 of the European Convention. In his opinion the Act was not incompatible; the problem was the way in which a local authority discharged its responsibilities. He said:

'[54] Clearly, if matters go seriously awry, the manner in which a local authority discharges its parental responsibilities to a child in its care may violate the rights of the child or his parents under this article. The local authority's intervention in the life of the child, justified at the outset when the care order was made, may cease to be justifiable under Art 8(2) . . . A care order which keeps a child away from his family for purposes which, as time goes by, are not being realised will sooner or later become a disproportionate interference with the child's primary Art 8 rights . . . '

'[57] If an authority duly carries out these statutory duties, [for example in respect of ascertaining wishes and feelings,[1] carrying out reviews and considering representation and complaints[2]] there should be no question of infringement by the local authority of the Art 8 rights of the child or his parents. Questions of infringement are only likely to arise if a local authority fails properly to discharge its statutory responsibilities. Infringement which then occurs is not brought about, in any meaningful sense, by the Children Act. Quite the reverse. Far from the infringement being compelled, or even countenanced, by the provisions of the Children Act, the infringement flows from the local authority's failure to comply with its obligations under the Act. True, it is the Children Act which entrusts responsibility for the child's care to the local authority. But that is not inconsistent with Art 8. Local authorities are responsible public authorities, with considerable experience in this field. Entrusting a local authority with the sole responsibility for a child's care, once the 'significant harm' threshold has been established, is not of itself an infringement of Art 8. There is no suggestion in the Strasbourg jurisprudence that absence of court supervision of a local authority's discharge of its parental responsibilities is itself an infringement of Art 8.'

'[58] Where, then, is the inconsistency which is alleged to exist? As I understand it, the principal contention is that the incompatibility lies in the absence from the Children Act of an adequate remedy if a local authority fails to discharge its parental responsibilities properly and, as a direct result, the rights of the child or his parents under Art 8 are violated. The Children Act authorises the state to interfere with family life. The Act empowers courts to make care orders whose effect is to entrust the care of children to a public authority. But the selfsame Act, while conferring these wide powers of interference in family life, omits to provide any sufficient remedy, by way of a mechanism for controlling an erring local authority's conduct, if things go seriously wrong with the authority's care of the child. It is only to be expected, the submission runs, that there will be occasions when the conduct of a local authority falls short of the appropriate standards. An Act which authorises state interference but makes no provision for external control when the body entrusted with parental responsibility fails in its responsibilities is not compatible with Art 8 . . . '

'[59]   In my view this line of argument is misconceived. Failure by the state to provide an effective remedy for a violation of Art 8 is not itself a violation of Art 8. This is self-evident. So, even if the Children Act does fail to provide an adequate remedy, the Act is not for that reason incompatible with Art 8. This is the short and conclusive answer to this point.'

1   Section 22.
2   Section 26.

8.104   Lord Nicholls said that ss 7 and 8 sought to provide the remedy:[1]

'[62] . . . if a local authority fails to discharge its parental responsibilities properly, and in consequence the rights of the parents under Art 8 are violated, the parents may, as a longstop, bring proceedings against the authority under s 7 . . . I say 'as a longstop', because other remedies, both of an administrative nature and by way of court proceedings, may also be available in the particular case . . . Sometimes court proceedings by way of judicial review of a decision of a local authority may be the appropriate way to proceed. In a suitable case an application for discharge of the care order is available. One would not expect proceedings to be launched under s 7 until any other appropriate remedial routes have first been explored.'

1   See paras 13.72 where the possibility of a free-standing application under s 7 is considered, as in *Re M (Care: Challenging Decisions by Local Authority)* [2001] 2 FLR 1300.

8.105   Lord Nicholls noted that the jurisprudence of the European Court of Human Rights did not hold that Art 6(1) required that all administrative decisions should be susceptible of substantive appeal to a court, with the court substituting its views for the decision made by the administrator. 'The extent of judicial control required depends on the subject matter of the decision and the extent to which this lends itself to judicial decision.'[1] 'This principle that, the required degree of judicial control varies according to the subject matter of the impugned decision, is important in the context of the Children Act . . . [2] 'Hence the extent to which decisions by an authority affect the private law rights of parents and children also varies widely. Some affect the continuing parental responsibility of a parent, others do not.[3]

1   See para 74.
2   See para 75.
3   See para 77.

8.106   Lord Nicholls said:

'[79]   it is notable that when a care order is made questions of a most fundamental nature regarding the child's future may remain still to be decided by the local authority; for example, whether rehabilitation is still a realistic possibility. Consistently with the Strasbourg jurisprudence such decisions attract a high degree of judicial control. It must be doubtful whether judicial review will always meet this standard . . . '

8.107   Lord Nicholls concluded that there may be circumstances when English law would not satisfy the requirements of Art 6(1) regarding some child care decisions made by local authorities. 'The guarantee provided by Art 6(1) can hardly be said to be satisfied in the case of a young child who, in practice, has no way of initiating judicial review proceedings to challenge a local authority's decision affecting his civil rights.'[1] It was equally true that 'where there is no parent able and willing to become involved, the Art 8 rights of a young child may be violated by a local authority without anyone outside the local authority becoming aware of the violation, which might leave a child without an effective remedy'.[2] He did not consider that this meant that the Children Act was incompatible with the Convention but it might signify the existence of a lacuna in the statute.

1   See para 82.
2   See para 64.

Commentary

8.108   It has always been a principle of the Children Act that there is a clear demarcation between the role of the courts and the role of local authorities in care cases ' . . . the court should be able to determine major issues such as the transfer of parental rights and duties where there is or may be a dispute between parents and local authorities, while the management of the case should be the responsibility of the local authority.'[1]

1   Review of Child Care Law (1985), para 2.20.

8.109   As we commented in the second edition[1] there are problems with a rigid application of this principle. In two particular cases, this may lead to an unsatisfactory outcome. First a care plan may be unacceptable to all involved in court proceedings, save an authority which is determined not to be influenced by others, whether CAFCASS or the court. Secondly a care order may be made on the basis of a care plan approved by the court but it is not implemented either because of a change of mind or a lack of resources, whether financial professional or appropriate carers. The courts have had such concern, especially in relation to some authorities, that they have sought to find remedies.

1   At paras 8.86 and 8.87.

8.110   The decision in *Re S* does confirm that it is legitimate to make an interim care order rather than a final care order, where the care plan is inchoate or capable of early resolution, but not simply because the court does not agree with the care plan and wishes to supervise or review it. If the plan is such that it may be considered an interference with the rights of the child or the parents, because it is not necessary or proportionate, why should that reason not be used to justify the refusal of a final order? This should be an area for the exercise of judicial discretion, but it will have to be used wisely if the courts are not to be flooded with hearings leading to further delay.

8.111   The further control approved by the House of Lords arises in cases where an authority is held to have acted unfairly by not involving the parents to a degree sufficient to protect their interests and right to family life.[1] Applications can be made under the Human Rights Act 1998, s 7 in existing or fresh proceedings and the court has wide powers under s 8. The extent to which these provisions will provide solutions remains to be seen.

1 See *Re M (Care: Challenging Decisions by Local Authority)* [2001] 2 FLR 1300 discussed at para 13.72.

8.112 While the child has the same rights under ss 7 and 8, at the time of writing there is nobody to assert that right on behalf of a young child, so that there remains a gap where there is a failure to implement the care plan. Lord Nicholls held that the idea of 'starred care plans' went beyond the permissible limits of statutory interpretation and that it was not the Act which was incompatible with the Convention, but rather the actions of the local authority, for which there was no absolute obligation to provide a remedy. Nonetheless, the House of Lords was trenchant in its criticism of the present position. Given the effect on children of the lack of a remedy, it might be considered equally reasonable for the court to provide a remedy, which is within the spirit of the legislation and not contrary to any specific provision. The problem has been considered in the course of debate on the Adoption and Children Bill 2002. Whether the amendments proposed at the time of writing[1] will resolve the problems, must at this stage of their development be considered doubtful, since they rely primarily not on a requirement to bring the matter back before the court, but on the willingness of a person working within the local authority to refer the matter to CAFCASS and on expeditious work on the part of CAFCASS.

1 See para 8.84 fn 1.

3 Orders available to the court

8.113 On an application under s 31 the court has power to make a care or supervision order if the threshold criteria are satisfied, but is not required to do so. Whether or not the threshold criteria are satisfied, the court may make any of the range of s 8 orders. They can be useful at the interim stage of proceedings, where the court can make orders to assist the protection of the child, while retaining control over placement of the child.[1] In accordance with decisions relating to Art 8 of the European Convention on Human Rights a care order is normally to be regarded as a temporary measure, consistent with the ultimate aim of reuniting birth parents and child, but this is subject to the best interests of the child. The interference in family life must be proportionate and necessary in a democratic society.[2]

1 See for example *C v Solihull Metropolitan Borough Council* [1993] 1 FLR 290 and *Croydon London Borough Council v A* [1992] Fam 169, [1992] 2 FLR 341.
2 See, for example, *K and T v Finland* [2001] 2 FCR 673, [2001] 2 FLR 707, ECt HR decision of the Grand Chamber upholding the earlier Chamber decision at [2000] 3 FCR 248, [2000] 2 FLR 79, but see also *Re O (Supervision Order)* [2001] EWCA Civ 16, [2001] 1 FCR 289, [2001] 1 FLR 923.

8.114 Before making a care order, the court must also consider the arrangements which the authority have made, or propose to make, for affording any person contact with a child and invite the parties to the proceedings to comment on the arrangements.[1]

1 Section 34(11).

Kinship care

8.115 When local authorities assess the needs of a child for alternative family placement, they must consider the possibility of placement with the extended family. Kinship care, as it has come to be known, can make for successful placement,[1] provided they are carefully managed. It is likely to ensure better continuity of care and speedier placement, but these factors need to be balanced with an adequate assessment of whether the relatives will protect the child, where necessary, and facilitate contact appropriately.

1   See Harwin and Owen 'A Study of Care Plans and their Implementation', in *Delight and Dole* (eds Thorpe and Cowton), Jordans 2002.

8.116 The funding of placements with relatives can be problematic. The court will have to decide whether to make the placement under a care order, a residence order or whether any order is necessary. A care order could have financial benefits and if that would materially contribute to the welfare of the child, that would be a relevant reason for making a care order.[1] Although there is provision for the payment of allowances,[2] local authorities may be reluctant to equate this to fostering allowances, if they consider that the child should be the responsibility of the family.[3]

1   *Re K (Care or Residence Order)* [1995] 1 FLR 675.
2   As a foster parent if the child is in care, or if there is a residence order under Sch 1 para 15.
3   In *R (on the Application of L) and others v Manchester City Council; R (on the Application of R) and another* [2001] EWHC Admin 707, [2002] 1 FLR 43 the court held that the authority had a duty to pay a relative fostering a child at the same rate as any other foster parent. This may not resolve the position where the interests of the child would be better served by the making of a residence order in favour of the relative.

Appropriate order if child remains at home

8.117 The court may make a care order or a supervision order where the local authority intends to place the child with a parent[1] or with members of the extended family,[2] but there are important differences between the orders. The purpose of a supervision order is to help and assist a child, leaving full responsibility with the parents. Any conditions attached cannot be enforced by the court[3]. The limitations of the order do not address the problems of parents who continue to exercise their responsibilities inadequately. A care order, on the other hand, places a positive duty on the local authority, through the acquisition of parental responsibility, to ensure the welfare of the child and protect it from inadequate parenting. This is not inconsistent with seeking to work in partnership with parents, since s 23 of the CA 1989 envisages that the local authority could place a child with his parents under a care order. The court should not impose a care order which is not in the interests of the child simply to encourage a local authority to perform its statutory duties towards children in need.[4] There could well be circumstances where the making of a care order was the only way to protect children placed with relatives from significant harm, even though the local authority did not want an order. The court cannot, if it disapproves a local authority care plan, make an injunction to prevent a course of action[5] nor can it accept undertakings from a parent to strengthen a supervision order.[6]

1   *Re T (a minor) (care or supervision order)* [1994] 1 FCR 663, [1994] 1 FLR 103, CA;. See also *Re D (care proceedings: appropriate order)* [1993] 2 FCR 88, [1993] 2 FLR 423; *Re S (J) (A*

Minor) (Care or Supervision Order) [1993] 2 FLR 919. *Re B (Care or Supervision Order)* [1996] 2 FLR 693, *Re O (Care or Supervision Order)* [1996] 2 FLR 755, *Re K* [1999] 1 FCR 337 and *Re C (Care or Supervision Order)* [1999] 2 FLR 621.
2   *Re K (minors)* [1996] 1 FCR 365, [1995] 1 FLR 675.
3   *Re V (care or supervision order)* [1996] 2 FCR 555, [1996] 1 FLR 776, CA, followed in *Re S (care or supervision order)* [1996] 2 FCR 719, [1996] 1 FLR 753, CA. See paras 8.167 to 8.179.
4   *Oxfordshire County Council v L (Care or Supervision Order)* [1998] 1 FLR 70.
5   *Re S and D* [1995] 2 FLR 456.
6   *Re B (a minor) (supervision order: parental undertaking)* [1996] 3 FCR 446, CA.

8.118   The doctrine of proportionality under Art 8 of the ECHR in this context was emphasised by Hale LJ in *Re O (Supervision Order)*[1] in relation to whether to make a care or supervision order. As Hale LJ pointed out a supervision order is quite different to a care order – not least in who has control of the child. In *Re O* a mentally ill mother and her new partner were co-operating with the local authority. The threshold criteria were satisfied, but it was held that a care order was not justified. The authority was not seeking to remove the child and the situation was unlikely to deteriorate so quickly that the child would need to be removed without a court order. On the other hand, some order needed to be made both because of the possibility that the parents might cease to co-operate and of a deterioration in the mother's health.

1   [2001] EWCA Civ 16, [2001] 1 FCR 289, [2001] 1 FLR 923.

CONSENT ORDERS

8.119   Care proceedings frequently lead to a negotiated solution in which the threshold criteria may be agreed and the order itself may be agreed. The court should not waste time but it still has a duty to investigate, where it is being asked to make an order under s 31, and to satisfy itself that findings of fact are appropriate.[1] A judgment may be important to the future management of the case. Although the court has a duty to consider whether any order should be made, the extent of an investigation by the court should reflect the fact that there is consensus among the parties especially if they include a public authority and a children's guardian.[2] If the parties are agreed that a care order should be made, the investigation could properly be limited to a perusal of documentation and approval of an agreed order.

1   Note that the local authority should file a statement of the findings it wishes the court to make and where possible this should be agreed with the other parties: *Re G (children) (care order: evidence)* [2001] EWCA 969, [2001] 2 FCR 757.
2   *Devon County Council v S* [1992] Fam 176, [1992] 3 All ER 793.

8.120   If the factual basis is not agreed, the court should limit its investigation to those parts of the evidence which are relevant to the issue of significant harm and necessary for the proper disposal of the case.[1] Where a parent concedes sufficiently to satisfy the threshold criteria and the order sought, it may not be necessary to proceed with a long trial.[2] If the concessions were not sufficient to give a proper understanding of allegations of sexual abuse and the care plan depended on the harm which had actually occurred, or where the credibility of the children was impugned, the circumstances might warrant further investigation.[3] The court is not subsequently barred from reinvestigating a concession (ie issue estoppel is inapplicable).[4] Where concessions are found to be inadequate, for example because no responsibility was accepted for the children's sexualised behaviour, the case can be remitted for rehearing.[5]

1 *Re G (A Minor) (Care Order: Threshold Conditions)* [1995] Fam 16, sub nom *Re G (A Minor) (Care Proceedings)* [1994] 2 FLR 69 and *Stockport Metropolitan Borough Council v D* [1995] 1 FLR 873.
2 *Re B (Agreed Findings of Fact)* [1998] 2 FLR 968. In this case there were pending criminal proceedings on the same issues.
3 *Re M (Threshold Criteria: Parental Concessions)* [1999] 2 FLR 728, CA.
4 *Re D (a child) (threshold criteria: issue estoppel)* [2001] 1 FCR 124, [2001] 1 FLR 274, CA.
5 *Re W (a child) (threshold criteria: parental concessions)* [2001] 1 FCR 139, CA.

VARIATION OF CARE OR SUPERVISION ORDER

8.121 The court may substitute a supervision order for a care order on the application of any person who has parental responsibility, the child himself or the designated local authority.[1] On such an application the court may disregard the requirements to satisfy the threshold criteria.[2] There is no similar provision relating to substitution of a care order for a supervision order, so that a fresh application by the local authority is required and the court must be satisfied as to the threshold criteria.[3] The court cannot of its own volition substitute a care order on an application to extend a supervision order.

1 Section 39(4).
2 Section 39(5).
3 *Re A (Supervision Order: Extension)* [1995] 1 FLR 335, CA.

THE EFFECT OF A CARE ORDER ON OTHER COURT ORDERS

8.122 The making of a care order discharges any s 8 order, so that no parent could continue to have a residence order. It also operates to dismiss an application for a residence order, so the court should consider any such application carefully before making a care order.[1] A care order discharges a supervision order and a school attendance order and brings wardship to an end.[2]

1 *Hounslow London Borough Council v A* [1993] 1 WLR 291, [1993] 1 FLR 702.
2 Section 91.

8.123 The court cannot make a s 8 order, other than a residence order, with respect to a child who is in care.[1] If the court does make a residence order, the care order is discharged. There is no embargo on the court combining a supervision order with a s 8 order, with supplementary directions or conditions, provided the threshold criteria apply. Nor is the court prevented from making a s 8 order in respect of a child who is accommodated.

1 Section 9(1) and see para 5.97.

APPEALS[1]

8.124 All parties can appeal against the making of a care order.[2] The local authority can appeal against the refusal to make a care order.[3] In each case the principle of *G v G (Minors: Custody Appeal)*[4]applies, but there might be slightly more flexibility in care cases.[5]

1 See further para 13.1 et seq.
2 Section 94(1)(a).
3 Section 94(1)(b).
4 [1985] FLR 894, HL.
5 See for example *Re G (A Minor) (Care: Evidence)* [1994] 2 FLR 785, CA and see para 13.26 et seq.

DISCHARGE OF CARE ORDER

8.125 Application for discharge of a care order may be made by any person who has parental responsibility for the child, the child himself[1] or the local authority.[2] No application may be made without the leave of the court within six months of the disposal of a previous application.[3] The court may substitute a supervision order on such an application. It needs to consider only the welfare principles and need not satisfy itself again as to the threshold criteria.[4] If the authority is seeking a care order in substitution for a supervision order, the authority must satisfy the threshold criteria.[5] The court does not have power to postpone discharge of a care order to allow for a gradual return of a child to his family over a period of time, but it can vary the contact provisions consistent with a plan for return. It can also make a residence order with appropriate directions and conditions under s 11(7) of the CA 1989 coupled with a supervision order.

1 The child does not require leave: *Re A (care: discharge application by child)* [1995] 2 FCR 686, [1995] 1 FLR 599.
2 Section 39(1).
3 Section 91(15).
4 Section 39(5).
5 *Re O (Care: Discharge of Care Order)* [1999] 2 FLR 119.

8.126 Local authorities are required by the Review of Children's Cases Regulations 1991[1] to consider on at least every statutory review of a case of a child in care whether to apply for discharge of the care order. As part of each review the child has to be informed of steps he may take himself, which include applying for discharge of the order, applying for a contact order or variation of an existing contact order or for leave to apply for a residence order.

1 SI 1991/895, Sch 2. The Adoption and Children Bill 2002 will impose a duty on the authority to consider a care plan filed in care proceedings in the course of a review under these regulations and if the plan has not been implemented it must consider whether to inform CAFCASS. See para 8.84 fn 1.

8.127 In general family courts should be alert to see that no one is allowed to litigate afresh issues already determined. A court hearing an application to discharge a care order has discretion as to whether issues decided at an earlier hearing should be reconsidered.[1] Although the doctrine of estoppel applies, it might need to be overridden in order to ascertain the truth in the interests of the children.[2] The courts are generally reluctant to allow issue estoppel to impede their ability to determine what is in the interests of a child. A judge has a discretion to re-open a conceded issue where necessary in the interests of a child and such a course is better characterised as case management than estoppel.[3] Having heard a parent's oral evidence and submissions from the parties, it was not a denial of justice for a court to decide at that stage that there was no realistic prospect of the care order being discharged.[4]

1 *Re S (Discharge of Care Order)* [1995] 2 FLR 639, CA. See chapter 11.
2 *K v P* [1995] 2 FCR 457, [1995] 1 FLR 248.
3 *Re D (a child) (threshold criteria: issue estoppel)* [2001] 1 FCR 124, CA.
4 *Re S and P (Discharge of Care Order)* [1995] 2 FLR 782, sub nom *P v Bradford Metropolitan Borough Council* [1996] 2 FCR 227.

8.128   Where an application has been made for discharge of a care order (or supervision order), no further application may be made without the leave of the court unless the period between disposal of the application and the making of the further application exceeds six months.[1] The court has power to order that no application under the Act of any specified kind, including an application to discharge, may be made with respect to the child concerned by any named person without the leave of the court.[2] The courts have held that this order should be used sparingly, for example where there had been frequent applications or where there had been a full hearing and a subsequent application would have no prospect of success.[3]

1   Section 91(15).
2   Section 91(14).
3   See *Re F* [1992] 2 FCR 433, sub nom *F v Kent County Council* [1993] 1 FLR 432, *Re Y (Child Orders: Restricting Applications)* [1994] 2 FLR 699 and *Re N (Section 91(14) Order)* [1996] 1 FLR 356.

8.129   A third party such as a relative or foster parent who wishes a care order to be discharged, can seek a residence order. The making of such an order discharges the care order.[1] A person is entitled to apply for a residence order if they have the consent:[2]

(a)   of the local authority if the child is in care; or
(b)   of each of those people with parental responsibility; or
(c)   the child has lived with them for at least three years.

If they are or have been a local authority foster parent within the last six months, they require the consent of the local authority they are a relative or the child has been with them for at least three years.[3]

1   Section 91(1).
2   Section 10(5).
3   Section 9(3): to be reduced to one year under the Adoption and Children Bill 2002.

ORDERS PENDING APPEAL

8.130   If the court dismisses an application for a care or supervision order, and an interim care or supervision order is in force at the time of the dismissal, it may make a care or supervision order for a specific appeal period.[1] If the court grants an application to discharge a care or supervision order, it may order that the decision shall have no effect for the appeal period.[2] There are limitations to these provisions. They do not apply if there is no previous order in force, so they cannot assist in respect of a first application. There is no corresponding provision to enable a stay of execution on the application of a parent. The proper course is said to be to apply to the High Court, where the judge had power to order a stay under the inherent jurisdiction.[3] It has been argued that justices do have a common law power to grant a stay.[4] In an appropriate case it would seem to be sensible to consider maintaining the status quo pending an appeal.

1   Section 40(1).
2   Section 40(2).
3   *Re O (a minor) (care order: education: procedure)* [1992] 4 All ER 905, [1992] 2 FLR 7.
4   See 'In context: Stay of Execution pending appeal' [1992] 2 FCR 896.

DESIGNATED CARE AUTHORITY

8.131 The local authority designated in a care order must be:[1]

(a) the authority in whose area the child is ordinarily resident;[2] or
(b) where the child does not reside[3] in a local authority area, the authority in whose area any circumstances arose in consequence of which the order is being made.

There has been conflict about how the designated authority should be chosen, but the Court of Appeal has now held that the provisions should be given the construction which achieves a simple mechanism to determine which authority should be responsible for implementing the care order and the care plan.[4] Where the mother had moved after the commencement of care proceedings, it was held that for the purposes of deciding which should be the designated care authority, the child's ordinary residence should be judged as at the time when the authority first intervened.[5] Where a child had no recent connection with the authority which would have been designated on a strict interpretation of the CA 1989, s 105, it was held that the court had a discretion to designate an authority, because the child was not ordinarily resident in any authority.[6] If it is intended that a care order will designate an authority other than that which applied for the order, there should be early liaison between the authorities. A care plan should be prepared in co-operation between them. An authorised representative should attend court to give assurances about the authority's commitment to the plan.[7]

1 CA 1989, s 31(8). The designation of an authority in respect of a supervision order is to the authority where the child lives or will live, unless another authority agrees to accept the order: Sch 3, para 9.
2 In determining ordinary residence, there shall be disregarded any period during which the child lives at school or in any institution or while he is being accommodated by or on behalf of a local authority: s 105(6). If the child has been placed at home under an interim care order, he is not regarded as being accommodated under s 23, so the disregard under s 105(6) does not apply: *Re P (Care Proceedings: Designated Authority)* [1998] 1 FLR 80. This decision contains a review of all the relevant cases to that date.
3 This should be read as including the word 'ordinary' before reside: *Gateshead Metropolitan Borough Council v L* [1996] 2 FLR 179,[1996] Fam Law 401.
4 *Northamptonshire County Council v Islington London Borough Council* [1999] 3 FCR 385, CA; and *see C (A Child) v Plymouth City Council* [2000] 1 FLR 875, CA.
5 *Re BC (a minor) (care order: appropriate local authority)* [1995] 3 FCR 598.
6 *Gateshead Metropolitan Borough Council v L* [1996] 2 FLR 179. See also *Re C (Care Order: Appropriate Local Authority)* [1997] 1 FLR 544.
7 *L v London Borough of Bexley* [1996] 2 FLR 595.

The care order

EFFECTS

8.132 By s 91 the making of a care order discharges any s 8 order so that no parent could continue to have a residence order. It also discharges a supervision order and a school attendance order and brings wardship to an end.

8.133 A care order lasts until the child is eighteen,[1] unless it is brought to an end earlier by a residence order or by its discharge.[2] The making of an adoption or freeing for adoption order extinguishes any order under the CA 1989.[3]

1   Section 91(12).
2   See paras 8.125 to 8.129.
3   AA 1976, ss 12(3) and 18(5) as amended by Sch 10, paras 3(3) and 6(2).

8.134   Section 33 sets out the powers and duties acquired by a local authority under a care order, but this must be read in conjunction with s 2.[1] The local authority is required to receive the child and keep him in their care while the order is in force. The authority acquires parental responsibility, but the parent does not cease to have parental responsibility solely because some other person acquires it.[2] The local authority has no power to prevent a mother from entering into a parental responsibility agreement in relation to a child subject to a care order.[3] A person with parental responsibility is not entitled to act in a way which would be incompatible with any order made under the Act,[4] so that a parent is not entitled to exercise parental responsibility in contravention of the care order.

1   See ch 3.
2   Section 2(6) see para 3.93.
3   *Re X (Minors) (Care Proceedings: Parental Responsibility)* [2000] 2 All ER 66, sub nom *Re X (Parental Responsibility Agreement: Children in care)* [2000] 1 FCR 379, [2000] 1 FLR 517.
4   Section 2(8).

8.135   The authority has the power to determine the extent to which a parent or guardian may meet his parental responsibility insofar as it is necessary to do so to safeguard or promote the child's welfare,[1] but this is subject to a number of reservations. Issues about contact may be referred to the court.[2] Other decisions taken by a local authority may range from the trivial to those of fundamental importance to parents and children. In *Re S* Lord Nicholls drew a distinction between 'rights in respect of the control of the day to day care of the child [which] were decided by the making of the care order and the grant of parental responsibility to the local authority' and a responsibility which may be 'of fundamental importance, for example, whether rehabilitation is still a realistic possibility'.[3] The House of Lords approved the decision in *Re M (Care: Challenging Decisions By Local Authority)*[4] in which a local authority ruled out rehabilitation but was held to have acted unfairly by not involving the parents to a degree sufficient to provide their interests with the requisite protection.

1   Section 33(3)(b).
2   See para 8.141 et seq.
3   *Re S (Minors) (Care Order: Implementation of Care Plan)*; *Re W (Minors) (Care Order: Adequacy of Care Plan)* [2002] UKHL 10, [2002] 2 WLR 720, [2002] 1 FLR 815 at para 79.
4   [2001] 2 FLR 1300. See also *Re C (care proceedings: disclosure of local authority's decision making process)* [2002] EWHC 1379 (Fam) [2002] 2 FCR 673 for a similar issue raised in the cause of care proceedings.

8.136   A parent or guardian is still entitled to do what is reasonable in all the circumstances of the case for the purpose of safeguarding or promoting the child's welfare[1] and retains any right, duty, power, responsibility or authority in relation to the child and his property under any other enactment.[2] These would include the right to consent to the child's marriage, rights under the Education Act 1996 in relation to the child's special educational needs, financial responsibility for the child and some responsibility for his acts if he is in the parent's charge and control. It has been held that the court could grant an order under s 37 of the Supreme Court Act 1981 in support of the statutory duties of the authority towards a child in its care, in the particular case to require a parent to allow a child to attend a college for education.[3]

1 Section 33(5).
2 Section 33(9).
3 *Re P (Care Orders: Injunctive Relief)* [2000] 2 FLR 385.

8.137 The local authority is not allowed to cause the child to be brought up in any religious persuasion other than that in which he would have been brought up if no order had been made. They do not have the right to consent, or refuse to consent, to the making of an application for a freeing for adoption order or to agree, or refuse to agree, to an adoption order or a proposed foreign adoption order. An authority may not appoint a guardian.[1]

1 Section 33(6).

CHANGE OF NAME

8.138 While a care order is in force no person may cause the child to be known by a new surname without the written consent of every person with parental responsibility.[1] For most children in care this would be the normal expectation, but the provision can cause difficulty for that small group of children being placed for adoption without parental consent. At some point after placement, but often before the formal adoption order, it may be in the child's interests to assume the name of the substitute family, especially, for example, if the child is about to start school. It might be thought that assumption of a new name should not occur until it is clear by adoption that the placement is permanent, but that does not necessarily recognise the importance for some children of being identified with the new family at an earlier stage or the risks of losing anonymity if the original name is used. In some cases it may be necessary for the child to be known by the new name, even though formal records retain the original name.

1 Section 33(7)(a).

8.139 The court can give leave under s 33(7) for a change of name. This will depend on circumstances, but if it is a case where the local authority has made an application under s 34 to refuse contact, it may be that consideration should be given to a contemporaneous application for leave of the court for a change of name at a suitable time. A local authority successfully applied for a change of name for five children in care to allay their fears of their parents or other members of an itinerant community of removing them from their foster-carers and spiriting them away to the anonymity of their community.[1] Children in care aged 16 and 15, who were living with their maternal aunt and uncle, successfully applied to change their surname from that of their father to that of their mother's family. The Court of Appeal held that on an application by a *Gillick* competent child to determine his or her surname the child's welfare was the paramount consideration and the judge should give very careful consideration to the wishes, feelings, needs and objectives of the child.[2] In an appropriate case the order may be granted ex parte.[3]

1 *Re M, T, P, K and B (Care: Change of Name)* [2000] 2 FLR 645.
2 *Re S (a minor) (change of name)* [1999] 1 FCR 304,[1999] 1 FLR 672, CA.
3 *Re J (A Minor) (Child: Change of Name)* [1993] 1 FLR 699.

TEMPORARY REMOVAL FROM THE JURISDICTION

8.140 A child in care may not be removed from the United Kingdom[1] without the written consent of every person having parental responsibility or the leave of the court.[2] This does not prevent the local authority having the care of the child arranging for a temporary removal for no more than a month.[3] This could cover a holiday or a trip to relatives to see if a longer term residence abroad would be suitable.

1 That is England, Wales, Scotland and Northern Ireland: see *Re H (children) (residence order: condition)* [2001] EWCA Civ 1338, [2001] 3 FCR 182, [2001] 2 FLR 1277, discussed at para 5.35.
2 Section 33(7).
3 Section 33(8)(a).

ARRANGING FOR LIVING OUTSIDE ENGLAND AND WALES

8.141 If the authority wish to arrange for a child to live outside England and Wales, they must have the written consent of every person with parental responsibility or the leave of the court.[1] The approval of the court is required under the system set out in paragraph 19 of Schedule 2. If consent is withheld the court has power to dispense with it. The proper approach was to look at the broad band within which a reasonable person might exercise a responsible choice, taking into account the sacrifice contemplated. The band for objection is narrow because, unlike in adoption, the parent would not lose parental responsibility.[2]

1 Section 33(8).
2 *Re G (Minors) (Care: Leave to Place Outside Jurisdiction)* [1994] 2 FLR 301. See also *Re G (Leave to Appeal: Jurisdiction)* [1999] 1 FLR 771, CA and *Re J (Freeing for Adoption)* [2000] 2 FLR 58 at 67.

Contact with children in care

Outline scheme

8.142 The Children Act established a structure in relation to contact with children looked after[1] by a local authority, distinct from the provisions regulating visiting or staying in the private law. There are duties to all children looked after, and further provisions in respect of children who are subject to a care order. The court has power to make what may conveniently be described as a care contact order. Unlike the position prior to the CA 1989, when the local authority had discretion to make decisions about contact with children in care, those decisions are now ultimately a matter for the court. As the Contact Orders Study[2] points out, 'proposals from the local authority now have to face the rigours of legal challenge'.

1 Defined to include children accommodated and children subject to a care order: s 22(1). See para 6.39.
2 Department of Health Social Services Inspectorate A Study of Local Authority Decision Making Around Contact Applications Under S 34 (1994).

Duty to promote contact

8.143 Where a child is being looked after by a local authority, whether subject to a care order or not, the authority shall, unless it is not reasonably practicable or consistent with his welfare, endeavour to promote contact between the child and his parents, others who have parental responsibility and relatives, friends and others.[1] They must take reasonable steps to keep parents and others with parental responsibility informed of his whereabouts, unless the authority have reasonable cause for believing that giving that information would be prejudicial to the child's welfare. Information must also be given where another authority takes over the provision of accommodation. Information about the child may only be withheld where it is essential to the welfare of the child, and where the child is in the care of the local authority.

1   CA 1989, Sch 2, para 15.

8.144 The local authority may promote contact by helping with costs incurred in making visits.[1] This help may be given to the parent (or other person who is entitled to contact with the child) or to the child. The local authority should ensure that the parents and child are aware that such assistance is available when plans for contact are being discussed. *Guidance* 'Court Orders' states:

> 'Children with special needs, or who have difficulty in communicating, may need extra local authority support to help them to maintain contact when placed at a distance from their home area. Contact includes communication by letter and telephone, and some children may need special provisions to facilitate this type of contact. Particular consideration must also be given to the needs of children for whom their first language (or that of their parent) is not English'.

1   CA 1989, Sch 2, para 16.
2   See para 3.86

Duty to child in care

8.145 Section 34(1) requires the local authority to allow a child, who is subject to a care order, reasonable contact with his parents[1] or guardian, a person in whose favour there was a residence order immediately before the making of the care order, or a person who had the care of the child by virtue of an order under the inherent jurisdiction of the High Court. Reasonable contact is not the same as contact at the discretion of the local authority. 'Reasonable' implies contact which is agreed between the local authority and the parents or in the absence of an agreement, contact which is objectively reasonable.[2]

1   Parent includes the unmarried father even if he does not have parental responsibility: Family Law Reform Act 1987, s 1.
2   *Re P (Minors) (Contact With Children In Care)* [1993] 2 FLR 156.

The care contact order

8.146 Those persons referred to in the preceding paragraph may apply to the court as of right for a care contact order with regard to the contact they are to be allowed with a child in care.[1] Applications may also be made by any person, such as a relative, who has obtained the leave of the court.[2] The care contact order differs from a contact order under s 8, which is an order requiring the person with whom the child lives to allow contact. Under s 34 the order is described in terms of the contact which is to be allowed between the child and the applicant. The same interpretation as in s 8 may, however, be placed on the concept of contact, which includes visiting, staying or other contact, for example, by letter or telephone. The court may impose such conditions as it considers appropriate.[3] This may include restriction of contact to specific periods or places.

1 Section 34(3)(a).
2 Section 34(3)(b).
3 Section 34(7).

8.147 A care contact order can only exist if there is a care order in force. If the child is in care, no court can make a s 8 contact order,[1] save on an application of a child in care for contact with siblings who were not in care.[2] If there is a contact order under s 8 in existence, it is discharged on the making of a care order.[3] If the court considers that contact with a named person should continue, it must make a new order under s 34.

1 Section 9(1). The court can make a s 8 order in respect of a child who is accommodated but not subject to a care order.
2 *Re F (Contact: Child in Care)* [1995] 1 FLR 510.
3 Section 91(2).

8.148 In deciding whether to grant leave to a third party to make an application for contact under s 34(3), the court should take account of the criteria set out in s 10(9).[1] In *Re M (Minors in Care) (Contact: Grandmother's Application)*[2] it was held that it would be anomalous not to do so, since they were apposite to leave applications under s 34(3). The court should at least have regard to:

(a) the nature of the contact being sought;
(b) the connection of the applicant to the child: the more meaningful the connection, the greater the weight to be given. Although contact between grandparents and children was assumed by paragraph 15 of Schedule 3 to be beneficial, they still required leave to apply;
(c) whether the child's need for security and stability would be disrupted; and
(d) the wishes of the parents and the local authority were material.

In deciding whether or not to grant leave the court should adopt the following approach:

(1) If the application was vexatious or frivolous or an abuse of process, it would fail.
(2) If the application failed to disclose any eventual real prospect of success, it should be dismissed.
(3) The applicant had to satisfy the court that there was a serious issue to try, and present a good arguable case.

1 See paras 5.117–5.121.
2 [1995] 3 FCR 550, [1995] 2 FLR 86, CA. But see also *Re P (a child) (residence: grand-mother's application for leave)* [2002] EWCA Civ 846, [2002] All ER (D) 554 (May).

8.149 Since a wide range of interested persons may seek the leave of the court to apply for a contact order, the authority must give careful consideration to its duty to allow the child to have contact with any relevant person. The outline arrangements will have been submitted to the court at the care proceedings.[1] In view of the continuing responsibility vested in a parent after a care order, where possible the local authority should, in a spirit of partnership, seek to reach a written agreement on the terms for the contact and other arrangements while the child is in care.[2]

1 Section 34(11).
2 See Guidance and Regulations, Family Placement, Volume 3, para 6.33.

8.150 An application specifying the contact which is to be allowed between the child and any named person may be made by the local authority.[1] If it is thought that contact with a particular person is not in the interests of the child or the authority understand that he does not wish to have contact with the person, the authority may make the application and seek a defined contact order. The court should not make an order under this provision phasing out contact, if that was not consistent with the local authority care plan.[2] This contrasts with the position where the authority's plan is to phase out contact, when the court does have power to override the plan.[3]

1 Section 34(2).
2 *Re D and H (Children in Care: Termination of Contact)*[1997] 1 FLR 841, CA.
3 See paras 8.139 to 8.141.

8.151 A child in care has a right to make an application for defined contact which is to be allowed with any named person.[1] This provision has created some complex dilemmas in relationships between siblings, whose interests may differ. In most cases it would be desirable for the authority to take the proceedings if so requested by the child, but the authority may consider an application undesirable. The child may wish to take the initiative. If an applicant child in care is seeking contact with other children who are willing to see him, the interests of the applicant child are paramount, but if those children were in care, the applicant child would be the person named, and the other children would be the subject of the application, whose interests were paramount.[2]

1 Section 34(2).
2 *Re F (Contact: Child in Care)* [1995] 1 FLR 510, discussed also at para 2.81.

8.152 There are emergency arrangements which permit an authority to refuse to allow contact, where they would otherwise be obliged to do so, for no more than seven days, if they are satisfied that it is necessary to do so in order to safeguard or promote the child's welfare.[1] Where an authority decides as a matter of urgency to refuse contact that they would otherwise be required to promote or allow in accordance with an order under s 34, it must give certain persons specified information. These include the child if he is of sufficient understanding, other persons with parental responsibility, and others whose wishes and feelings the authority consider to be relevant.[2] The Schedule to the Contact with Children Regulations 1991 includes information as follows: the decision, its date and the reasons for it, the duration and the remedies available in case of dissatisfaction. Where arrangements have been made and are then varied or suspended, the person concerned must also be given written notice.[3]

1 Section 34(6).
2 SI 1991/891, reg 2.
3 Above, reg 4.

POWERS OF THE COURT

8.153 In determining contact applications under s34 the welfare of the child is the paramount consideration.[1] The court must also consider the checklist under s 1(3) and whether making no order is better than making any order at all under s 1(5). Where an application for contact to a child in care is made by a parent who is also a minor, the person whose upbringing is in question is the son or daughter of the parent and it is that child's welfare which is the paramount consideration.[2]

1 *Re B (Minors) (Termination of Contact: Paramount Consideration)* [1993] Fam 301, [1993] 3 All ER 524.
2 *Birmingham City Council v H (No 3)* [1994] 2 AC 212, [1994] 1 All ER 12, HL, discussed at para 2.28. See also *Re F (Contact: Child in Care)* [1995] 1 FLR 510.

8.154 The court may make such order and impose such conditions as it thinks appropriate.[1] It has power to make an interim contact order at the same time as a care order with a provision for a further hearing on contact.[2] The court cannot, however, make a contact order with a direction to the children's guardian 'to keep an eye on the case',[3] nor that a guardian should have contact with a child after a care order.[4] The court does not have power to make an order prohibiting a local authority from allowing contact between child and parent.[5] The court should be careful on an interim application not to prejudice the main application.[6]

1 S 34(7).
2 *Re B (A Minor) (Care Order: Review)* [1993] 1 FLR 421.
3 *Re S (A Minor) (Care: Contact Order)* [1994] 2 FLR 222, CA.
4 *Kent County Council v C* [1993] Fam 57, [1993] 1 FLR 308. In *Re MH (a child) (supervision orders), Re SB (children) (supervision orders)* [2002] 1 FCR 251 it was held that a continuing role could be imposed on a children's guardian who had been appointed (rather than CAFCASS as a service) during the period of a supervision order, but this will be repealed by the Adoption and Children Bill 2002.
5 *Re W (Parental Contact: Prohibition)* [2000] 1 FLR 502, CA.
6 *A v M and Walsall Metropolitan Borough Council* [1994] 1 FCR 606,[1993] 2 FLR 244.

8.155 These provisions give the court power to influence the future direction of a case, although the arrangements for contact which an authority may in practice make will have to be taken into account. An authority seeking a care order or opposing discharge of an order will be obliged to consider carefully the arrangements, arguments and evidence in relation to contact with the child in respect of any connected person. Those arrangements must be discussed with the child if old enough[1] and with those connected with the child.

1 Section 22(4).

8.156 The court has power where a child is in care, to make an order about contact under s 34 in any family proceedings,[1] which concern the same child. This includes domestic violence, divorce and adoption cases. Authorities will have to be on the alert constantly for questions about contact with the whole range of people who might be interested in the child.

1 As defined by s 8(3) provided of course that the judge or court is authorised to deal with care cases.

VARIATION OF CONTACT ORDER

8.157 The court may vary or discharge an order on the application of the authority, the child or the person named in the order.[1] Although the Act is not specific on the point, the making of a residence order under s 8 must discharge a s 34 order since it is dependent upon the existence of the care order which is itself discharged by virtue of s 91(1). The court should make an appropriate contact order under s 8.

1 Section 34(9).

8.158 The Contact with Children Regulations 1991 provide that an authority can depart from the terms of a court order by agreement with the person to whom the order relates, subject to agreement with the child if he is of sufficient understanding, and subject to the sending of a written notice within seven days of the agreement to depart from the terms of the order.[1] The notice must be sent to the child, his parents or guardian, a person who had a residence order before a care order was made, a person who had the care of the child under an order in the exercise of the High Court's inherent jurisdiction, and any other person whose wishes and feelings the authority consider to be relevant.[2] The notice must contain information as to the decision, the date of and reasons for it, its duration and the remedies available in case of dissatisfaction.[3] The idea behind the provisions is to allow for flexibility and obviate the need to return to court where all are agreed with the revised arrangement. That would suggest that although the scope of the power is wide, it should in practice probably be limited to minor variations. If there was a major change in contact arrangements, on which plans for the child relied, and subsequently the parent objected, there would be a risk of them being reversed on application to the court.

1 Regulation 3.
2 Above.
3 Sch 3 to the regulations.

PHASING OUT OR REFUSAL OF CONTACT

8.159 The authority or the child may also apply for an order authorising the authority to refuse to allow contact with any person with whom the authority would otherwise be required to allow the child to have contact.[1] This includes making an order on an interim basis.[2] The court should be careful on an interim application not to prejudice the main application.[3] Provided the section is used as part of a care plan approved by the court, and as a means of avoiding drift or delay in the interests of the child concerned, the section is compliant with the European Convention on Human Rights.[4]

1 Section 34(4). But note this is not a termination of contact: see paras 8.161 and 8.162.
2 *West Glamorgan County Council v P* [1992] 2 FLR 369.
3 *A v M and Walsall Metropolitan Borough Council* [1994] 1 FCR 606, [1993] 2 FLR 244
4 *Re F (Care: Termination of Contact)* [2000] 2 FCR 481.

8.160 As in all contact applications, when the court is considering whether to authorise the local authority to refuse to allow contact, the child's welfare is the paramount consideration pursuant to s 1. Although a court should not readily make an order contrary to the plans of the local authority, it must still apply the welfare principle.

8.161 In *Re B (Minors) (Termination of Contact: Paramount Consideration)*,[1] Butler-Sloss LJ said:

'Contact applications fall into two categories, those which ask for contact as such, and those which are attempts to set aside the care order itself. In the first category there is no suggestion that the applicant wishes to take over the care of the child and the issue of contact often depends on whether contact would frustrate long-term plans for the child in a substitute home, such as adoption where continuing contact may not be for the long term welfare of the child. The presumption of contact which has to be for the benefit of the child, has always to be balanced against the long-term welfare of the child and particularly where he will live in the future. Contact must not be allowed to destabilise or endanger the arrangements for the child and in many cases the plans for the child will be decisive of the contact application . . .

The proposals of the local authority, based on their appreciation of the best interests of the child, must command the greatest respect and consideration from the court, but Parliament has given to the court, and not to the local authority, the duty to decide on contact between the child and those named in s 34(1). Consequently the court may have the task of requiring the local authority to justify their long-term plans to the extent only that those plans exclude contact between parent and child.

In the second category contact applications may be made by parents by way of another attempt to obtain the return of the children. In such a case the court is obviously entitled to take into account the failure to apply to discharge the care order, and in the majority of cases the court will have little difficulty in coming to the conclusion that the application cannot demonstrate that contact with a view to rehabilitation with the parent is a viable proposition at that stage, particularly if it had already been rejected at the earlier hearing when the child was placed in care.'

1   [1993] Fam 301, [1993] 3 All ER 524, CA.

8.162 The relationship of decision-making between the courts and the local authority has been explored further by the Court of Appeal, in *Re E (A Minor) (Care Order: Contact)* where Simon Brown LJ said:[1]

'if on a s 34(4) application the judge concludes that the benefits of contact outweigh the disadvantages of disrupting any of the local authority's long term plans which are inconsistent with such contact then . . . he must give effect to it by refusing the local authority's application to terminate the contact.'

1   [1994] 1 FLR 146, CA.

8.163 In *Kent County Council v C*[1] Ewbank J commented on the form of order where the court takes the view there should be no contact to a child in care. He held that, although the court can order that there should be no contact, in ordinary cases it would be better to make no order for contact, as the Contact with Children Regulations 1991 permit parents and the local authority to agree to vary a court order without recourse to court. The problem with making no order is that the authority would continue to be under a duty to afford reasonable contact.

1   [1993] Fam 57, [1993] 1 All ER 719.

8.164 Where the mother is a child, the application of the welfare test to refusal of contact is in respect of the child whose upbringing is in question. Since s 34(4) relates to that child, no question falls to be determined as to the upbringing of the parent, even though she is a child.[1]

1   *Birmingham City Council v H (A Minor)* [1994] 2 AC 212, [1994] 1 All ER 12, HL, discussed further at para 2.28.

8.165 Where an applicant has been refused an order under s 34, he may not make another such application within six months without the leave of the court.[1] There is, however, a further provision which empowers the court to order that no application for an order under the Act may be made by a named person without the leave of the court.[2] It has been said that the order should be used sparingly.[3] It should not be made without giving the party affected due notice.[4] It would be appropriate where a party or child were suffering from too frequent applications or where there had been a full hearing and a subsequent application would have no prospect of success.[5]

1 Section 91(17).
2 Section 91(14).
3 *R v West Glamorgan County Council, ex p T* [1990] 1 FLR 339.
4 *Re S (Contact) (Prohibition of Applications)* [1994] 2 FLR 1057, CA.
5 *Re F* [1992] 2 FCR 433 [1993] 1 FLR 432; *Re Y (Child Orders: Restricting Applications)* [1994] 2 FLR 699. See also *Re N (Section 91(14) Order)* [1996] 1 FLR 356; and *Re R (Residence: Contact: Restricting applications)* [1998] 1 FLR 749.

8.166 The grant of an order authorising a local authority to refuse contact will not bring about a final termination of contact – only adoption will achieve that. An application for contact which is fundamentally inconsistent with an earlier order giving leave to place for adoption should not be allowed to proceed.[1] If the local authority fails to carry out a care plan for adoption within a reasonable period of time, it may be that there will have been a change of circumstances.[2]

1 *Cheshire County Council v M* [1992] 2 FCR 817, [1993] 1 FLR 463.
2 See para 8.84 fn 1 and *Re S (Minors) (Care Order: Implementation of Care Plan)*; *Re W (Minors) (Care Order: Adequacy of Care Plan)* [2002] UKHL 10, [2002] 2 WLR 720, [2002] 1 FLR 815.

The supervision order

8.167 The power to make a supervision order is contained in s 31 and an order may only be made if the criteria contained in that section are satisfied.[1] Section 35 and Sch 3 make further provision. The order puts the child under the supervision of a designated local authority, but does not give them parental responsibility.[2] The duties of the supervisor are:

(a) to advise, assist and befriend the supervised child;
(b) to take such steps as are reasonably necessary to give effect to the order; and
(c) where (i) the order is not wholly complied with; or (ii) the supervisor considers that the order may no longer be necessary, to consider whether or not to apply to the court for its variation or discharge.

These basic duties are substantially expanded by Sch 3 by the importing of a scheme which had previously been used primarily for the intermediate treatment of adolescents into the general scheme under which supervision orders can be made. A parent can be required to reside at a particular place under the terms of a supervision order.[3] The provisions are not enforceable. Because the local authority does not have parental responsibility, it can only bring the matter back to the court for variation.[4]

1 As provided by s 31. Note if a care order has already been made, a supervision order may be substituted without further proof of the criteria: s 39(4).

2 See Sch 3, para 9.
3 *Croydon London Borough v A and B* [1992] 2 FCR 481,[1992] 2 FLR 350.
4 See s 35(1)(c) and *Re R and G (Minors) (Interim Care or Supervision Orders)* [1994] 1 FLR 793.

8.168 The question of whether a care order or a supervision order is the more appropriate in all the circumstances will be informed by whether there is evidence of immediate risk or actual harm as opposed to a real possibility of future harm. If the evidence is restricted to future rather than immediate risk a supervision order is more likely to be appropriate having regard to the principle that the intervention of the State has to be proportionate to the legitimate aim of protecting family life.[1]

1 *Re C & B (children) (care order: future harm)* [2000] 2 FCR 614, CA; and *Re O (Supervision Order)* [2001] 1 FLR 923, CA. See also *K & T v Finland* [2001] 2 FCR 673, [2001] 2 FLR 707, Grand Chamber.

DURATION OF A SUPERVISION ORDER

8.169 A supervision order lasts for up to one year, though it may be made for a shorter period.[1] It is subject to discharge[2] and extension by the court for up to a total of three years.[3] Application to extend is not like an original application for an order, so the court's decision is governed by the welfare principle. The court does not have power to vary the order to a care order without further proof of the threshold criteria on an application by the local authority.[4]

1 *M v Warwickshire County Council* [1994] 2 FLR 593.
2 Under s 39. The provisions are the same as for discharge of a care order: see para 8.125.
3 See Sch 3, para 6.
4 *Re A (Supervision Order: Extension)* [1995] 1 FLR 335, CA.

PURPOSE OF A SUPERVISION ORDER

8.170 A supervision order should not be used for the purpose of supervising contact. A family assistance order could be used for that purpose.[1] If there is a child protection element during contact sufficient to justify the court being satisfied as to the threshold criteria a supervision order might be appropriate.[2] This might arise where a parent was making false allegations about the other parent in order to influence the children against contact.[3]

1 *Leeds City Council v C* [1993] 1 FCR 585,[1993] 1 FLR 269.
2 *Re DH (a minor) (child abuse)* [1994] 2 FCR 3,[1994] 1 FLR 679.
3 *Re Z and A (Contact: Supervision Order)* [2000] 2 FLR 406.

Requirements imposed under a supervision order

THE SUPERVISED CHILD

8.171 A supervision order may require the supervised child to comply with any directions given from time to time by the supervisor which require him to:

(a) live at a place or places specified in the directions for a specified period or periods;

(b) present himself to a specified person at a place and on a day specified;
(c) participate in specified activities, such as education or training.

The precise directions are a matter for the supervisor and not the court. He shall decide whether and to what extent and in what form he shall exercise this power. The provision does not confer on him the power to give directions in respect of any medical or psychiatric examination or treatment.[1] The court may not accept an undertaking in conjunction with a supervision order[2] nor can conditions be imposed on a supervision order.[3]

1 See Sch 3, para 2(2) and (3).
2 *Re B (A Minor) (Supervision Orders: Parental Undertakings)* [1996] 1 WLR 716, [1996] 1 FLR 676, CA.
3 *Re V (Care or Supervision Order)* [1996] 2 FCR 555, [1996] 1 FLR 776, CA. See also *Re S* [1996] 2 FCR 719, [1996] 1 FLR 753, CA.

THE RESPONSIBLE PERSON

8.172 A supervision order may include requirements, with the consent of and in relation to a 'responsible person' (that is a person with parental responsibility or with whom the child is living).[1] The requirements may be that the responsible person take all reasonable steps to ensure that the child complies with any direction given by the supervisor, that he takes all reasonable steps to ensure that the child complies with any requirement in relation to psychiatric and medical examination or treatment and that he complies with the supervisor's directions on attending at a specified place.

1 See Sch 3, para 1.

8.173 Paragraph 3 of Sch 3 contains provisions whereby a responsible person can be required to comply with directions to attend at a specified place for the purpose of taking part in specified activities. Such directions have to be given by the supervisor. Under this provision a responsible person could be required to comply with directions as to treatment, but these provisions are a matter for the supervisor and not for the court.[1] It has been held that a parent can be required to reside at a particular place under the terms of a supervision order.[2] The wording of paragraph 3 makes it clear that the directions are a matter for the supervisor and not the court, though it might be possible, where appropriate, for the court to make a residence order, conditional on the person living with the child at a specific place.

1 *Re H (Supervision Order)* [1994] 2 FLR 979.
2 *Croydon London Borough v A (No 3)* [1992] 2 FCR 481, [1992] 2 FLR 350.

8.174 A supervision order can exist at the same time as a s 8 order. Thus in appropriate cases the court can consider making a residence order in combination with a contact order or prohibited steps order, and a supervision order. Where directions are within the ambit of Sch 3, they should be made under that Schedule, rather than under s 11(7), since that provision is for the purpose of implementing s 8 orders.

MEDICAL OR PSYCHIATRIC EXAMINATION OR TREATMENT

8.175 A supervision order (but not an interim supervision order)[1] may require the supervised child to:

(a) submit to a medical or psychiatric examination;
(b) submit to such an examination from time to time as directed by the supervisor;
(c) submit to specified treatment in relation to his mental or physical condition.

1   Section 38(9).

8.176   Paragraphs 3 and 4 of Sch 3 contain detailed provisions which have to be satisfied before a requirement can be imposed as to examination and treatment. Both are subject to the conditions that the child, of sufficient understanding to make an informed decision, must consent to the inclusion of the requirement in the supervision order.[1]

1   Sch 3, para 4(4).

8.177   It would usually be preferable to make a family assistance order[1] to achieve supervised contact, but in cases involving an element of child protection, where the local authority made a s 31 application and the criteria were satisfied, a supervision order could be made.[2]

1   *Leeds City Council v C* [1993] 1 FLR 269.
2   *Re DH (A Minor) (Child Abuse)* [1994] 1 FLR 679.

ENFORCEMENT OF SUPERVISION ORDERS

8.178   The terms of a supervision order are not enforceable. The only remedy for the supervisor is to bring the matter back before the court.[1]

1   *Re R and G (Minors) (Interim Care or Supervision Orders)* [1994] 1 FLR 793.

USE OF SUPERVISION ORDERS

8.179   Supervision orders are sought and made less frequently than care orders.[1] Applications are rarely made for a supervision order but may be made by the courts as an alternative to what may be seen as a draconian care order. Local authorities may be reluctant to invest in proceedings to obtain an order which has no powers of enforcement, and where the case is less serious. On the other hand the finding that the threshold criteria are satisfied may be a powerful statement in a suitable case. Combined with the authority to direct a treatment programme for the child and the responsible person, this can make the order a powerful tool. In the light of observations about the need to ensure that an order is proportionate to the circumstances of the case, local authorities are likely to have to consider how to use supervision orders more constructively.[2]

1   See para 8.9 for the numbers of care orders. The figures for supervision orders are 1993–1203, 1994–1325, 1995–1318, 1996–1161, 1997–1072, 1998–829, 1999–787, 2000–1,326 (the *Children Act Report 2000*, Department of Health).
2   A more imaginative use of Schedule 3 might assist, but these provision (see para 8.171) provide for directions given by the supervisor to the child, and not by the court, nor to the parent. This was what was envisaged by the Review of Child Care Law (HMSO, 1985) and should perhaps be revisited in the light of current experience.

EDUCATION SUPERVISION

8.180   If it appears to an education authority that a child is not receiving suitable education, they may serve a notice on the parent requiring him to satisfy the authority that the child is receiving such education. If a parent on whom a notice has been served fails to satisfy the authority that the child is receiving suitable education or in the opinion of the authority it is expedient for the child to attend school, they shall serve on the parent a school attendance order.[1] If the parent fails to comply with the order, the parent commits an offence, unless he can show that the child is receiving suitable education.[2] There is a separate offence, if a child of compulsory school age who is a registered pupil, fails to attend school regularly.[3] In either case, before the authority institutes proceedings, it must consider whether it would be appropriate to apply instead, or in addition, for an education supervision order under s 36.[4] A court by which a person is convicted of failing to comply with a school attendance order, or before which a person is charged with failing to secure a child's regular attendance at school, may direct the education authority to apply for an education supervision order[5] and may make a parenting order.[6]

1 EA 1996, s 437.
2 Section 443.
3 Section 444.
4 Section 447(1).
5 Section 447(2).
6 See Crime and Disorder Act 1998, s 8 (Clarke, Hall and Morrison 7 [2203]).

8.181 Before instituting proceedings for an education supervision order, the education authority must consult the appropriate social services authority.[1] That authority may decide to provide support for the child and his family under Pt III[2] or to apply for a compulsory order under Pt IV of the CA 1989.

1 Section 36(8) and (9).
2 See ch 6.

8.182 An education authority may apply for an education supervision order on the ground that the child concerned is of compulsory school age and is not being properly educated, that is, he is not receiving efficient full-time education suitable to his age, ability and aptitude and any special education needs he may have.[1] This ground is deemed to be satisfied, unless it is proved to the contrary, where a school attendance order in force under s 437 of the Education Act 1996 is not complied with, or he is a registered pupil at a school and is not attending regularly within the meaning of s 444 of that Act.[2]

1 Section 36(3) and (4).
2 Section 36(5).

8.183 The scheme encourages education authorities to consider whether an education supervision order or prosecution or both is likely to provide the more effective approach. Supervision might be more effective for parents who find it difficult to exercise proper influence over a child who has developed a pattern of poor attendance, whereas parental hostility to intervention or a structured programme of work might suggest that prosecution would be necessary.[1]

1 Guidance and Regulations, Volume 7, paras 3.07 and 3.08.

8.184 The proceedings are not specified for the purposes of s 41,[1] so that a children's guardian is not appointed. The court must state any findings of fact and give reasons, when determining an application for an education supervision order.[2] The order cannot be made in respect of a child in care.[3]

1 See para 10.26.
2 See *Essex County Council v B* [1993] 1 FLR 866.
3 Section 36(6).

8.185 An education supervision order may last for up to one year but may be extended for up to a further three years at a time.[1] It shall cease to have effect when the child reaches compulsory school leaving age or when he becomes the subject of a care order. The order may be discharged on the application of the child, parent or the education authority. The supervisor has a duty to advise, assist and befriend and give directions to the child and the parents so as to secure that the child is properly educated. If directions are not complied with, the supervisor must consider what further steps to take. He may seek new directions or apply for discharge of the order. A parent who persistently fails to comply with a direction shall be guilty of an offence. If a child persistently fails to comply with a direction, the education authority must notify the social services authority, which is obliged to investigate the circumstances of the child.

1 See Sch 3, Pt III

Conclusions

8.186 There remains a tension over when to take care proceedings. Local authorities have to take into account a wide range of welfare, social, political, resource and jurisprudential factors. There are some real dilemmas in achieving the right balance in making decisions about when and whether to take care proceedings. The sometimes uneasy relationship between local authorities and the courts and the siting of the boundary between them can lead to impairment of the service provided in both arenas. This conflict can be seen in decisions about whether support services could be mandated, when proceedings should be initiated, the evidence required to satisfy a case, when there should be an assessment, who should be responsible for it, whether there should be court control of the care plan, whether to make an interim or final care order and whether the court should have review powers.

8.187 If the local authority is able to provide resources which are truly supportive of the family, this will often be preferable to taking proceedings. Since local authorities cannot be required to provide services, a child may suffer significant harm with the effect that the threshold criteria come to be satisfied as a result of their failures or lack of resources. Unfortunately the evidence suggests that so far the balance between family support and compulsory intervention has been difficult to find, not least because successive governments have not made available the resources to fund the proper implementation of Pt III of the Act. In those circumstances many local authorities will continue to provide primarily a fire-fighting service to protect children, with or without an effective use of both Pts III and IV of the Act. The shortage of staff, especially in the metropolitan areas, compounds these problems. It remains to be seen whether the 'Quality Protects' project introduced in 1998 will lead to the delivery of more family support services.

8.188 Care proceedings can be expensive, time consuming and threatening (to parents and professionals) and the possible trauma involved can have an adverse impact on the family, especially if proceedings are not well managed by the court and by the professionals involved. Proceedings may nonetheless be essential to protect the child; the irony is that those most seriously damaged children will suffer further harm as a result of the delays currently being experienced in bringing about a satisfactory conclusion to the proceedings. As a society we still seem to have failed to grasp the concept that management of the removal of a child from harm in his own family and providing alternative care is comparable to, and perhaps for the child a worse and less explicable experience than, suffering a physical illness.

8.189 Used constructively proceedings can achieve a structure and a benchmark from which to work for the future. They can provide a framework for informed discussion in which the parents will feel heard, care plans will be carefully examined and a good guardian can act as an independent mediator. It remains a sad fact that the resources required for many children suffering harm and the expertise needed to achieve satisfactory planning will only be made available if they become the subject of care proceedings. This may be equally true for obtaining advice from a well-informed third party such as a guardian, the input of an expert such as a child and family psychiatrist and the commitment of the family to take seriously social services' concerns.

8.190 In spite of these potential advantages local authorities cannot be required to take care proceedings, since, even assuming the court becomes aware of a problem, its powers are restricted to requiring the authority to carry out an investigation. This can lead to children continuing to suffer abuse and neglect at home, or to them having unplanned careers in local authority accommodation.

8.191 Initially care proceedings were perceived as an 'event', the purpose of which was to obtain a court order in order to carry out a pre-conceived plan. The local authority would have formed a clear view that the only means of securing the welfare of the child was to bring care proceedings. Although local authorities do seem to explore options for supporting children within their families more thoroughly before applying for a court order, in the majority of cases in which proceedings are brought, the local authorities' goals are not fully formed. Care proceedings appear to have become a more dynamic process, in what has been described as a 'legally protected space within which to assess, and if possible work towards, a resolution of family difficulties or to demonstrate that that was not possible'.[1] The outcome of this emphasis on resolution rather than adjudication is that only 40% of care proceedings result in a contested hearing. Those cases which do require adjudication may be different from those for which the proceedings are a dynamic process.

1 See Hunt and Macleod *Statutory Intervention in Child Protection; the Impact of the Children Act 1989*, (1998); Hunt, Macleod and Thomas *the Last Resort: Child Protection, the Courts and the Children Act 1989* (Stationery Office, 1999); Hunt 'A moving target: care proceedings as a dynamic process', [1998] CFLQ 281.

8.192 Directions are a means of managing the process to bring proceedings to a conclusion with the avoidance of delay, but the setting of a timetable for the progress of proceedings does not by itself reduce delay.[1] The *Children*

Act Scoping Study[2] suggests that causes of delay are lack of experts, inflexibility of jurisdiction leading to problems with judicial availability, and judicial case management.[3] Regrettably these problems have not been addressed since they were first identified in the Booth Report in 1995. As a result of that failure the problems may now have been compounded by additional, more fundamental causes for the lengthening period for which care cases are before the court.[4] Whilst a narrow legalistic approach to care proceedings was discouraged, proceedings were initially still viewed in the usual legal form as the local authority bringing a 'case', the court adjudicating on the merits of the case, followed by the making of an order appropriate to the adjudication. The 'resolution' process is likely to lead to longer cases and more delays, exacerbated by the inexperience of local authority and CAFCASS staff and the consequent reliance on experts.

1 See Plotnikoff *The Timetabling of Care Proceedings before the Implementation of the Children Act 1989*, (Department of Health, 1991).
2 Lord Chancellor's Department, March 2002.
3 See A Review of Case Administration in Family Proceedings Courts (Magistrates' Courts Service Inspectorate, May 2001).
4 Such as those described in paras 8.186 and 8.189.

8.193 Significant decisions, which have a bearing on the eventual outcome of the proceedings, may be made at early directions appointments. In particular, a noticeable feature of care proceedings which has grown in significance, consistent with the 'resolution' process, is the direction that there be an assessment of the ability of the parents to demonstrate adequate parenting skills and thereby avoid the need for a statutory order. In the light of the changing nature of care proceedings and their increasing complexity early judicial statements on the purpose of directions hearings may need to be reconsidered. Three significant stages have emerged at which vital elements of the proceedings will be settled:

(a) the first substantive directions appointment at which, if possible, the direction of the case will be agreed;[1]
(b) an appointment, when the parties are clear about their initial positions, at which disputes about the scope of assessments are determined;
(c) pre-trial appointment to review the position before the final hearing.

1 *Practice Direction (Judicial Continuity)* [2002] 2 FLR 367 recognises this with the requirement of an early Case Management Conference but it applies only to care proceedings in the Royal Courts of Justice in London.

8.194 The original model of proceedings which assumed a defined period for the conduct of the hearing may not be a sound basis for a more fluid and dynamic process. The challenge for the court is to provide an effective vehicle for this process and directions hearings may need an emphasis different from management of the 'case' in the familiar sense. The court has to assist in facilitating the process of 'problem resolution' as the case evolves. The Practice Direction[1] should extend beyond the High Court for which it was originally designed. Practice will need to remain flexible and ensure that distinctions are drawn where necessary between those cases, for example involving babies, where there should be early hearings and early conclusions and those where the continued oversight of the court may benefit the child.

1 See para 8.193 fn 1.

8.195 The role of the children's guardian in moderating this process has become a key feature of care proceedings.[1] This process will require CAF-CASS to play an effective role, but whether the organisation will be equipped to respond to the demands remains to be seen.

1 See para 10.7.

AFTER THE CARE ORDER

8.196 As we commented in the second edition the provisions for ensuring the implementation of care plans are unsatisfactory. The inadequacies of the system are well illustrated earlier in this chapter. There has been no progress in this respect since 1995 and little attention given by Government until the problem was considered in the House of Lords in *Re S* and *Re W*.[1] There has been great frustration because the courts have been unable to impose specific action on a local authority or be confident that the care plan on which the making of a care order was based would be implemented. Although day to day decisions about the welfare of the child must ultimately be for the local authority, when they are more fundamental to the future of the child, it has proved to be unsatisfactory to leave decisions entirely in the hands of some local authorities. Although at the time of writing the Government is bringing forward statutory provisions in an attempt to deal with these problems, whether they will do more than add a sticking plaster is doubtful.[2]

1 *Re S (Minors) (Care Order: Implementation of Care Plan)*; *Re W (Minors) (Care Order: Adequacy of Care Plan)* [2002] UKHL 10, [2002] 2 WLR 720. See paras 8.86–8.107.
2 See para 8.84 fn 1 and 8.111.

8.197 The courts can, nonetheless, only influence a small proportion of cases. Improvements in planning for children in care must be dependent on solutions to a wider range of problems than are obvious from court proceedings. Contributory factors within the social services field are the poor status of social work and residential care over a long period of time, now heightened by the equally poor status given to CAFCASS employees, consequential reluctance to engage in painful work with impoverished parents, all leading to staff shortages, inadequate training in areas such as child attachment and the law, a shortage of carers with the necessary skills to parent troubled children, and not least and in spite of all the rhetoric to the contrary, an overall lack of investment in child welfare and related areas of work.

Chapter 9

Secure accommodation

INTRODUCTION

9.1 Any infringement of personal liberty is a tort (and in some circumstances a crime) unless authorised by law. Domestic law has recognised some circumstances where the liberty of a child may be restrained as part of the exercise of parental responsibility in the child's upbringing and for his welfare. These have been extended to a limited extent to those acting in *locus parentis* such as teachers and public authorities exercising statutory responsibilities for a child eg social services departments having parental authority under a care order. Public authorities must act in accordance with the European Convention for the Protection of Human Rights and Fundamental Freedoms[1] (the 'Convention') and the use of accommodation by local authorities for the purpose of restricting a child's liberty is specifically restricted by s 25 of the CA 1989 supplemented by the Children (Secure Accommodation) Regulations 1991[2] and the Children (Secure Accommodation) (No 2) Regulations 1991.[3]

Except in relation to certain remands to local authority accommodation in criminal proceedings,[4] a child may only be kept by a local authority in secure accommodation for the purpose of restricting liberty in accordance with a secure accommodation order made by a court, except for a short period where prescribed criteria are fulfilled.[5] An attempt was made in the CA 1989, which was only partially successful, to distinguish between secure accommodation orders made in respect of children accommodated under civil provisions and those remanded in criminal proceedings. Jurisdiction in civil cases was transferred from the former juvenile (now youth) courts to the family proceedings courts, and, in circumstances prescribed in the Children (Allocation of Proceedings) Order 1991,[6] county courts and the High Court. In criminal proceedings jurisdiction was retained in the youth court and extended to the adult magistrates' court but not to the Crown Court.[7]

1 Rome 4 November 1950; TS 71 (1953); Cmd 8969.
2 SI 1191/1505, amended by SI 1992/2117, SI 1995/1398, SI 1996/692, SI 2000/694 and SI 2002/546.
3 SI 1991/2034 amended by SI 2000/694 and SI 2002/546.
4 See para 9.32.
5 See para 9.10 and 9.13.
6 SI 1991/1677 amended by SI 1993/624, SI 1994/2164 and 3138 SI 1996/1649, SI 1997/1897, SI 1998/2166, SI 1999/524 and SI 2000/2670.
7 See para 9.40.

Deprivation of liberty

9.2 Article 5.1 of the European Convention for the Protection of Human Rights and Fundamental Freedoms[1] (the 'Convention') provides inter alia that:

> 'Everyone has the right to liberty and security of person. No-one shall be deprived of his liberty save in the following cases and in accordance with a procedure prescribed by law:
>
> ... (d) the detention of a minor by lawful order for the purpose of educational supervision or his lawful detention for the purpose of bringing him before the competent legal authority.'

1   Rome 4 November 1950; TS 71 (1953); Cmd 8969.

9.3 Deprivation of liberty in criminal proceedings is usually clearly defined eg remands[1] or proceedings for contempt.[2] Defendants in criminal proceedings may be the subject of a custodial sentence where the prescribed conditions are met, for example, detention of children and young persons sentenced to a detention and training order or long term detention under ss 100 and 91 respectively of the Powers of Criminal Courts (Sentencing) Act 2000. Any such order made within jurisdiction will not be a false imprisonment. Patients may, in circumstances prescribed under the Mental Health Act 1983, be detained for their own welfare.

1   Magistrates Courts Act 1980, ss 5(1), 10(4), 17C and 18(4); and see the Supreme Court Act 1981, s 81 for the power of the Crown Court to grant bail.
2   Contempt of Court Act 1981, ss 12 and 14.

Parents and others in loco parentis

9.4 It is not every restriction on the freedom of movement of a child which will amount to a 'deprivation of liberty' within the meaning of Art 5 of the Convention as this right of the child must be balanced against the rights of parents under Art 8 which guarantees respect for private and family life. A fundamental element of family life, which is protected by the Convention, is the right of parents to exercise parental authority over their children having regard to their corresponding parental responsibilities.[1]

> 'The care and upbringing of children normally and necessarily require that the parents or only parent decide where the child must reside and also impose, or authorise others to impose, various restrictions on a child's liberty. Thus the children in a school or other educational or recreational institution must abide by certain rules which limit their freedom of movement and their liberty in other respects'[2]

Domestic law has long recognised the discretion of parents to use reasonable and moderate methods to control and discipline their children.[3] Teachers, acting in loco parentis, might use detention provided it was just and reasonable[4] otherwise a writ of habeas corpus would lie.[5] The position of educational establishments has been clarified by statute. The Education Act 1996 provides that teachers may not use corporal punishment by virtue of their position as members of staff, and defines the situations in which force may be used to control or restrain a pupil and the circumstances in which a pupil may be subject to detention outside school hours despite the absence of parental consent.[6] Nevertheless, as regards residential accommodation, there had been some uncertainty as to what powers of restraint were permissible[7] and additional guidance has been issued.[8]

1   *Nielsen v Denmark* (1988) 11 EHHR 175.
2   *Nielsen v Denmark* (1989) 11 EHHR 175 at 191–192.
3   See the discussion at para 3.20.
4   *Mansell v Griffin* [1908] 1 KB 947, 72 JP 179, CA.
5   *Price v Wilkins* (1888) 58 LT 680, 4 TLR 231.
6   Education Act 1996, ss 548–550B. See also DfEE Circulars 10/98 *S 550A of the Education Act 1996: The Use of Force to Control or Restrain Pupils*; 10/99 *Social Inclusion: Pupil Support* in *Clarke Hall and Morrison* at paras 6[10151]ff and 6[10181]ff.
7   See eg Guidance Volume 4, Residential Care; Guidance Volume 5; Independent Schools; para 3.10.3.
8   Local Authority Circular (93)13 *Guidance of Permissible Forms of Control in Children's Residental Care* in *Clarke Hall and Morrison* at paras 1[14291]ff and see the Children's Homes Regulations 2001, SI 2001/3937 amended by SI 2002/865 and the Children's Homes (Wales) Regulations 2002, SI 2002/327 amended by SI 2002/865 reg 17.

9.5   There is a point where restraint on a child's liberty exceeds ordinary acceptable parental restrictions and amounts to 'deprivation of liberty' within the meaning of Art 5 of the Convention. Deprivation of liberty is only lawful in accordance with Art 5 if it falls within an exception in Art 5.1. In determining whether there is a deprivation of liberty, the approach of the European Court of Human Rights is to have regard to the actual situation in which the child is and account is taken of a whole range of criteria, such as the type, duration, effects and manner of implementation of the measure in question, ie the distinction between deprivation and restriction is one of fact and degree, and not one of nature or substance.[1]

1   *Guzzardi v Italy* (1980) 3 EHHR 333.

9.6   In *Re K (a child) (secure accommodation order: right to liberty)*,[1] K was a 15-year-old boy with learning difficulties and a long history of problems who from a young age had displayed aggressive, sexualized and abusive behaviour towards others and had faced a number of criminal charges. He appealed against a secure accommodation order on the basis that s 25 of the Children Act 1989 under which the order had been made was incompatible with Art 5 of the Convention on the basis that although the exception in Art 5(1)(d) allowed the detention of a minor by lawful order for the purpose of educational supervision, the criteria in s 25 did not include any such purpose. Furthermore, as domestic legislation required the court's authorisation for a secure placement that extended beyond 72 hours within a 28-day period, a secure accommodation order went beyond the extent to which a parent or an authority with parental responsibilities could lawfully restrain a child and as such was a deprivation of liberty which required justification within the narrow exceptions in Art 5(1). He argued that s 25 did not fall within the exception in Art 5(1)(d) as there was no express provision for education and although the Education Act 1996 required the local authority to provide an education for any child under 16, it was possible that a child over 16 could be detained and offered no education. This possibility was sufficient to vitiate the entire section.

Butler-Sloss P giving the leading judgment in the Court of Appeal accepted that a secure accommodation order was a deprivation of liberty and the fact that the statute imposes a limit of 72 hours on a local authority keeping a child in secure accommodation without court authorisation, even in the most extreme case, was regarded as significant support for the argument that a secure accommodation order was an extreme measure and not within the ordinary and acceptable parental restrictions upon the movements of a child. However, the Her Ladyship noted that K was in fact receiving education which was carefully supervised and from which he was clearly benefiting. Although education was not one of the criteria in the section, it was not necessary for it to be expressly stated as the Education Act 1996 makes education compulsory for any child under 16 and a secure unit is under a statutory obligation to provide a child with education. Furthermore, 'educational supervision' is broader than formal academic lessons in the classroom and an order might be justified even in the case of a child over compulsory school age where on the facts the 'educational supervision' offered embraced other aspects of the exercise, by the local authority, of parental rights for the benefit and protection of the person concerned. In theory there might be circumstances in secure accommodation proceedings where the words 'for the purpose of educational supervision' do not cover the facts of the particular case and although in these circumstances, detention under a secure accommodation order would contravene Art 5, it would be the application of a s 25 order in that situation which would be a breach of a Convention right. However, that such a situation could arise does not entail the statutory provision itself being in breach of the Convention.

Thorpe LJ whilst holding that the appeal 'fails comprehensively',[2] did so on grounds different to those of the majority. In his Lordship's view the right to liberty was not absolute and has a counterbalancing duty to refrain from behaviour that is both anti-social and criminal. The right is in some circumstances qualified and those circumstances are not confined to the exceptions defined in Art 5(1). Not all restrictions on liberty amount to a deprivation of liberty. Parents, for example, have a right and a responsibility to restrict the liberty of their children, not only for protective and corrective purposes, but also sometimes for a punitive purpose. In the case of K, the order restricting liberty was made on the ground that, if kept in any other accommodation, he was likely to injure himself or other persons. The primary purpose was protective and the secondary purpose was to teach K to modify his anti-social tendencies; there was no punitive purpose or element. The restriction was vital for the promotion of his welfare. Whether such a secure accommodation order amounts to a deprivation of liberty depends on whether those applying the regime exercise proper responsibility in ensuring that statutory or common law safeguards are not breached and whether they remain faithful to the primary protective purpose of the regime. In any event, His Lordship agreed with the majority that the making of the secure accommodation order in respect of K was justified by the exception in Art 5(1)(d).

1 [2001] 2 All ER 719, [2001] 1 FCR 249, [2001] 1 FLR 526, CA. See also *Sweet and Tender Hooligans – Secure Accommodation and Human Rights* A Pack [2001] Family Law 140 and Securing Human Rights for Children and Young People in Secure Accommodation J Masson Child and Family Law Quarterly Vol 14 p 77.
2 [2001] 2 All ER 719, [2001] 1 FCR 249, [2001] 1 FLR 526, CA at para [48].

9.7 A child who is subject to proceedings for a secure accommodation order has the protection of the fair trial provisions in Art 6(1) of the Convention and while it has not been decided whether such proceedings should be categorised as civil or criminal in nature for the purpose of the Convention, such a child should be afforded the five specific minimum rights guaranteed under Art 6(3) to everyone charged with a criminal offence.[1]

1   *Re M (a child) (secure accommodation)* [2001] EWCA Civ 458, [2001] 1 FCR 692, sub nom *Re C (Secure Accommodation Order: Representation)* [2001] 2 FLR 169, CA.

CHILDREN LOOKED AFTER BY LOCAL AUTHORITIES AND OTHER ORGANISATIONS

Restriction on the use of secure accommodation

9.8   Apart from courts ordering detention in criminal proceedings, the need to impose any restriction on a child's movements to the extent that it would amount to a deprivation of liberty is likely to arise in a situation where a local authority or body providing residential accommodation is accommodating them. The deprivation of a child's liberty is an extreme step and a parent would have difficulty in justifying any detention for more than a period of a few days.[1] A local authority or other body requiring to use accommodation which deprives a child of his liberty for more than the few days justified in the case of a parent[2] would need to establish that their action was authorised by domestic law and was for a purpose which was permissible within the terms of Art 5 of the Convention.

In the case of bodies providing residential accommodation, secure accommodation may not be used unless it is authorised by the Act.[3] Those bodies accommodating children which are specified in s 25 of the Act (viz a local authority) or the regulations (viz health authorities, Primary Care Trusts, National Health Service Trusts or local education authorities, and those providing accommodation in care homes or independent hospitals)[4] may not use secure accommodation unless the criteria in s 25 are met. The criteria applicable to a local authority are set out in s 25(1)[5] and are suitably modified for other agencies by the Children (Secure Accommodation) Regulations 1991.[6]

The restriction on the use of secure accommodation in s 25 of the Act does not apply to children detained under the provisions of the Mental Health Act 1983 or the Children and Young Persons Act 1933, s 53 (now the Powers of Criminal Courts (Sentencing) Act 2000, ss 90, 91 – long term detention as punishment for certain grave crimes)[7] since their detention is regulated by those statutory provisions.[8]

1   See *Re K (a child) (secure accommodation order: right to liberty)* [2001] 2 All ER 719, [2001] 1 FCR 249, [2001] 1 FLR 526, CA at para [29], per Butler-Sloss P.
2   In any event, a local authority or other body providing residential accommodation may only use secure accommodation where the criteria in s 25 are met but may do so without the authority of a court where the period is less than 72 hours in any consecutive period of 28 days: Children (Secure Accommodation) Regulations 1991, SI 1991/1505, reg. 10(1).
3   In reality the legislation is framed in such a way as to impose a restriction on a power which is assumed already to exist since 25 reproduces in essence the terms of s 21A of the Child Care Act 1980. That Act made express provision that a local authority had the same duties and powers in respect of a child in their care as a parent and might restrict the child's liberty as appropriate. Such a power is now assumed to be an ordinary incident of parental responsibility, see the comments of Hoffmann LJ in *Re M (A Minor)* [1995] 1 FLR 418 at 425 and Butler-Sloss P in *Re K (a child) (secure accommodation order: right to liberty)*

[2001] 2 All ER 719, [2001] 1 FCR 249, [2001] 1 FLR 526, CA and see the discussion at para 3.20.
4 Children (Secure Accommodation) Regulations 1991, reg 7. Application to court may be made by such authorities or persons by virtue of the Children (Secure Accommodation) (No 2) Regulations 1991, reg 2.
5 See para 9.11.
6 SI 1991/1505, amended by SI 1992/2117, SI 1995/1398, SI 1996/692, SI 2000/694 and SI 2002/546.
7 Children (Secure Accommodation) Regulations 1991, reg 5.
8 But this does not preclude the local authority making an application in respect of such a child who has been released on leave as 'detained' is to be given its literal meaning. See, for an example, *Hereford and Worcester County Council v S* [1993] 2 FLR 360, where on release, the local authority would accommodate the child and considered it necessary to use secure accommodation.

(a) Definition of secure accommodation

9.9 Secure accommodation is defined by the Act as 'accommodation provided for the purpose of restricting liberty'.[1] The Children Act 1989 Guidance and Regulations, Volume 4, Residential Care[2] supplemented the statutory provisions whilst recognizing that the interpretation of this term was ultimately a matter for the court. The definition in the initial guidance issued with the commencement of the Act was too cautious:

'However, it is important to recognize that any practice or measure which prevents a child from leaving a room or building of his own free will may be deemed by the court to constitute 'restriction of liberty'. For example, while it is clear that the locking of a child in a room, or part of a building, to prevent him leaving voluntarily is caught by the statutory definition, other practices which place restrictions on freedom of mobility (for example, creating a human barrier), are not so clear cut . . . '[3]

Whilst the original advice addressed the definition of restricting liberty, it was incomplete in that it did not deal with the balance between the rights of the child and the rights and responsibilities of parents and professionals in supervising them,[4] a balance which is highlighted when issues arising from Art 5 of the Convention are considered.[5] The current regulations provide that measures of control, restraint or discipline may be used in children's homes provided they are not excessive or unreasonable and do not comprise any form of prohibited measure such as corporal punishment.[6]

1 CA 1989, s 25(1).
2 Department of Health 1991.
3 Guidance, Volume 4, Residential Care, para 8.10 (part).
4 See Local Authority Circular (93)13 in *Clarke Hall and Morrison* at para 1[14291].
5 As in *Re K (a child) (secure accommodation order: right to liberty)* [2001] 2 All ER 719, [2001] 1 FCR 249, [2001] 1 FLR 526, CA.
6 See the Children's Homes Regulations 2001, SI 2001/3967 amended by SI 2002/865 reg 17(1) (5) and for the duty to record details of any measures taken, see reg 17(4). *Restraint* means 'Use of reasonable physical intervention or force to prevent injury or serious damage to property.' *Measure of Control* means 'A means used to maintain acceptable behaviour by children, including supervision, guidance, reward, physical restraint and disciplinary measures or punishments.' *Children's Homes – National Minimum Standards Appendix 3.*

9.10 Secure accommodation is not limited to accommodation provided with the approval of the Secretary of State; it is the restriction of liberty which is the essential factor. A unit for the treatment of mentally disturbed children was secure accommodation, as its purpose was to restrict the liberty of children there with a view to modifying their behaviour.[1] However, it is not so much the *purpose* for which the accommodation is used as whether, on the facts, it is actually secure accommodation. Accordingly, in *A Metropolitan Borough Council v DB*[2] the patient was in a maternity ward at a hospital to which entry and exit could only be effected by the use of a key or pass. As the nursing staff were instructed to prevent the patient leaving so that her health and life were not seriously endangered, the court held that the ward should be regarded as secure accommodation within the meaning of s 25. In contrast, in *Re C (Medical treatment)*[3] the patient was in a ward which was not equipped with any devices which restricted entry or exit. In deciding that the patient was not held in secure accommodation, the court referred to the primary purpose of the clinic which was to provide treatment for eating disorders but also to the fact that in exercising its parens patriae jurisdiction, the court has the power to direct that the clinic should detain the patient as an in-patient, using reasonable force if necessary. If the ward was secure accommodation, the common law jurisdiction of the court would be ousted and the requirements of s 25 would apply.

1   *R v Northampton Juvenile Court, ex p London Borough of Hammersmith and Fulham* [1985] FLR 193.
2   [1997] 1 FLR 767, sub nom *Re B (a minor) (treatment and secure accommodation)* [1997] 1 FCR 618.
3   [1998] 1 FLR 384, [1997] Fam Law 474, FD.

(b)   *Authorisation to use secure accommodation*

9.11   Under s 25(1):

'. . . a child who is being looked after by a local authority may not be placed . . . in (secure accommodation) unless it appears:
(a) that
   (i)   he has a history[1] of absconding and is likely to abscond from any other description of accommodation;[2] and
   (ii) if he absconds, he is likely to suffer significant harm; or[3]
(b) that if he is kept in any other description of accommodation he is likely to injure himself or other persons.'

It should be noted that s 25(1) applies to children looked after by a local authority. This is defined as children in their care (ie under a care order or a deemed care order)[4] or who are provided with accommodation under any functions referred to the Social Services Committee[5] and which is accommodation which is provided for a continuous period of more than 24 hours.[6] The provisions do not apply to (and secure accommodation may not be used in respect of):

*   children accommodated for 24 hours or less;[7]
*   children over 16 years[8] accommodated under s 20(5) of the Act;[9]
*   a child kept away from home under a child assessment order made under s 43 of the Act.[10]

These criteria are modified in certain criminal proceedings and are considered separately below.[11] The interpretation of 'likely' and 'significant harm' will be the same as in Pt IV of the Act (care proceedings).[12]

1   One previous absconding is sufficient to amount to a 'history' of absconding: *R v Calder Justices, ex p C* (4 May 1993, unreported).

2   For the purpose of deciding this issue, a children's guardian is entitled to enquire into alternative local authority placements and the court is required to do so as the position is distinct from that in care proceedings: *Hereford and Worcester County Council v S* [1993] 1 FCR 618, [1993] 2 FLR 360.
3   The grounds in paras (a) and (b) are disjunctive rather than conjunctive: *Re D (Secure Accommodation Order)* [1997] 1 FLR 197.
4   CA 1989, s 105(4).
5   Apart from functions under ss 24A, 24B of the Act as inserted by the Children (Leaving Care) Act 2000, s 4 when in force.
6   Above, s 22 (1)(2). These provisions include a child who is being looked after by a local authority as a condition of bail: *Re C (secure accommodation: bail)* [1994] 2 FCR 1153, [1994]2 FLR 992. In these circumstances application for a secure accommodation order may be made to a family proceedings court: *Re W (a minor) (secure accommodation: jurisdiction)* [1995] 2 FCR 708.
7   Above, s 22 (2).
8   Where the criteria have been met, the court is not inhibited from making a secure accommodation order in respect of a child aged 15 which will extend beyond the child's sixteenth birthday: *Re G (a child) (secure accommodation order)* [2000] 2 FCR 386, [2000] 2 FLR 259, CA.
9   Children (Secure Accommodation) Regulations 1991, reg 5(2)(a).
10 Above, reg 5(2)(b).
11 See para 9.32.
12 See paras 8.41 and 8.51.

9.12   Secure accommodation in a community home must be approved by the Secretary of State[1] and the placing of a child under the age of 13 years in secure accommodation in a community home must have the prior approval of the Secretary of State and is subject to any terms and conditions that he sees fit.[2]

Formerly (that is until 23 June 1995) the use of secure accommodation in voluntary homes and registered (private) children's homes was prohibited[3] but as part of the overall scheme for phasing out the use of prison establishments for children under 17 years in criminal proceedings, s 19 of the Criminal Justice and Public Order Act 1994, which amended Schs 5 and 6 of the CA 1989, enabled the Secretary of State to approve the use of secure accommodation in voluntary homes and registered children's homes subject to any requirements in regulations to be made which may include obtaining the prior permission of the local authority.

1   Children (Secure Accommodation) Regulations 1991, reg 3.
2   Above, reg 4.
3   Children (Secure Accommodation) Amendment Regulations 1995, SI 1995/1398, reg 6.

9.13   National minimum standards for children's homes provide that apart from the measures necessary to the home's status as a secure unit, children resident in secure units should receive the same care services as they should in other children's homes and should be cared for consistently with these national minimum standards, with only those adaptations essential in the home concerned for the maintenance of security.[1]

However, such is the pressure on secure places that as from 1 December 2001 s 133 of the Criminal Justice and Police Act 2001 has enabled local authorities to arrange for 12–16-year-olds who are remanded by the courts to local authority secure accommodation under s 23 of the 1969 Act to be placed in secure training centres at the request of the local authority with the consent of the Secretary of State.[2]

1   *Children's Homes – National Minimum Standards* (Dept of Health 2002) published by the Secretary of State under s 23(1) of the Care Standards Act 2000.
2   Criminal Justice and Police Act 2001 (Commencement No 3) Order 2001, SI 2001/3736.

(c)   Using secure accommodation without the authorisation of a court

9.14   The in criteria in s 25[1] must be satisfied before a child may be kept in secure accommodation. The order of a court is not needed where the use is for not more than 72 hours in aggregate in any period of 28 days[2] and it will be for the authority itself to determine whether any of the criteria are met. If a child is in secure accommodation between 12.00 midday on the day before and 12.00 midday on the day after a public holiday or a Sunday and the child had in the 27 days before the day on which he was placed in secure accommodation, been placed and kept in secure accommodation for an aggregate of more than 48 hours, where the maximum period would otherwise have expired in this period, it will extend until 12.00 midday on the first day which is not itself a public holiday or a Sunday, after the public holiday or Sunday.[3] Time limits will run afresh after the making of any intervening court order.[4]

Where a child is placed in secure accommodation in a community home other than that which is looking after him, that authority must be notified with a view to obtaining their authority to continue to keep him there if necessary.[5]

1   See para 9.11.
2   Children (Secure Accommodation) Regulations 1991, reg 10(1).
3   Above, reg 10(3).
4   Above, reg 10(2).
5   Children (Secure Accommodation) Regulations 1991, reg 9.

9.15   There was some criticism that under the previous legislation viz the Child Care Act 1980, there might be a tendency to see secure accommodation as a convenient method of treatment or as a means of making use of facilities available in a secure establishment after a secure environment was no longer needed. Guidance from the Department of Health makes the current position plain:

'Restricting the liberty of children is a serious step which must be taken only when there is no appropriate alternative. It must be a 'last resort' in the sense that all else must first have been comprehensively considered and rejected, never because no other placement was available at the relevant time, because of inadequacies in staffing, because the child is simply being a nuisance or runs away from his accommodation and is not likely to suffer significant harm in doing so, and never as a form of punishment . . . Secure placements, once made, should be only for so long as is necessary and unavoidable. Care should be taken to ensure that children are not retained in security simply to complete a pre-determined assessment or 'treatment' programme.'[1]

1   Guidance, Volume 4, Residential Care, para 8.5 (part).

PROCEEDINGS FOR A SECURE ACCOMMODATION ORDER (CIVIL)

9.16   As it is not usually possible to predict accurately the need for secure accommodation, the short term provisions outlined above will enable the authority to deal with the situation when it arises. In this period consideration should be given to whether secure accommodation needs to be available as a longer term option. If so, an application to the court will be required. Applications are generally made to a family proceedings court[1] except that an application may be made to a county court (care centre) or the High Court where other proceedings specified in the Children (Allocation of Proceedings) Order 1991[2] are pending in respect of the same child.

1 CA 1989, s 92(6)(7), Sch 11, Pt I and the Children (Allocation of Proceedings) Order 1991, SI 1991/1677, art 3(1)(a).
2 Article 3(3), ie under the following provisions: s 31 (care and supervision orders), s 37 (leave to change name of or remove from United Kingdom child in care), s 34 (parental contact), s 36 (education supervision orders), s 43 (child assessment orders), s 44 (emergency protection orders), s 45 (duration of emergency protection orders etc), s 46(7) (application for emergency protection order by police officer), s 48 (powers to assist discovery of children etc), s 102 (powers of constable to assist etc) and para 19 of Sch 2 (approval of arrangements to assist child to live abroad).

1. Applicant

9.17 The applicant is the local authority looking after the child,[1] or where the child is not being looked after by a local authority, the health authority, Primary Care Trust, National Health Service Trust, local education authority, or the person carrying on the independent care home or hospital as the case may be.[2] Application Form C1 and supplement C20 must be filed in respect of the child together with a copy for the respondents ie each person believed to have parental responsibility, and the child himself.[3] Copies of the application must be served not less than one day before the hearing or directions appointment.[4] Notice of the application must also be given to the persons caring for the child at the time when the proceedings are commenced.[5]

1 Children (Secure Accommodation) Regulations 1991, reg 8.
2 Children (Secure Accommodation) (No 2) Regulations 1991, reg 2.
3 FPR 1991, r 4.4 and Appendix 3, FPC (CA 1989) R 1991, r 4 and Sch 2.
4 Above.
5 Above.

2. Transfer

9.18 The transfer provisions of the Children (Allocation of Proceedings) Order 1991 apply to transfers to another magistrates' court, or to a county court (care centre), or to the High Court.[1] Proceedings are generally commenced in the family proceedings court for the area in which the child normally has his home, otherwise there would be a potential burden on that court which had a secure unit in its area and a problem in providing the services of children's guardians if they were all drawn from the area containing the secure unit.

1 See para 4.15ff.

3. Children's guardian

9.19 Proceedings under s 25 are 'specified proceedings' for the purpose of s 41 of the Children Act[1] and after the commencement of the proceedings, the court (or, in a family proceedings court, the justices' clerk) must appoint a children's guardian for the child unless it is considered unnecessary.[2] The guardian will appoint and instruct a solicitor for the child in accordance with the normal powers and duties prescribed by rules of court[3] and the solicitor will represent the child in accordance with rule 12 as in other specified proceedings.[4] The guardian's general duties will be adapted to the specific requirements of an application having regard to the nature of the welfare criterion in secure accommodation cases.[5]

1   FPR 1991, r 4.2; FPC (CA 1989) R 1991, r 2(2).
2   FPR 1991, r 4.10(1); FPC (CA 1989) R 1991, r 10(1).
3   FPR 1991, r 4.11; FPC (CA 1989) R 1991, r 11. See generally, para 10.21ff.
4   See para 10.40ff.
5   See *Re M (Secure Accommodation Order)* [1995] FLR 418, and see para 9.25ff.

4.   Legal representation

9.20   Although the court has a discretion not to appoint a guardian, it cannot make a secure accommodation order in respect of a child who is not legally represented unless the child has been informed of his right to apply for representation funded by the Legal Services Commission as part of the Community Legal Service and, having had the opportunity to do so, has refused or failed to apply.[1] A right to representation is granted under Pt I of the Access to Justice Act 1999 and is not subject to any financial contribution from the client.[2]

1   CA 1989, s 25(6).
2   Community Legal Service (Financial) Regulations 2000, SI 2000/516, reg. 3(1)(c).

5.   Directions

9.21   On filing the application the court may fix a directions appointment.[1] Although on an initial application, the time scale will generally restrict the work undertaken by the guardian before the hearing itself,[2] the court may adjourn the proceedings and make an interim order.[3]

1   For directions appointments, see paras 4.34ff.
2   FPR 1991, r 4.14; FPC (CA 1989) R 1991, r 14.
3   See para 9.26.

THE HEARING (CIVIL PROCEEDINGS)

9.22   These are family proceedings to which the Family Proceedings Rules 1991 and the Family Proceedings Courts (Children Act 1989) Rules 1991 apply and therefore the rules regulating the provision of written statements, recording of evidence and giving of reasons apply.[1]

The court (or, in a family proceedings court, the justices' clerk) may give directions as to the order of speeches but subject to this, evidence is normally given first by the applicant, any party with parental responsibility and then the child and his guardian.[2]

1   FPR 1991, r 4.17, 4.20 and 4.22; FPC (CA 1989) R 1991, rr 17, 20 and 21, and see generally
    ch 4.
2   FPR 1991, r 4.21(2); FPC (CA 1989) R 1991, r 21(3).

1.   Presence of the child

9.23   Although it has been stated that the court must be scrupulous to ensure that the statutory criteria are met before it may make an order since the liberty of the subject is at stake,[1] Ewbank J expressed the view that the making of the order did not by itself curtail the liberty of the child so that natural justice required the presence of the child at the hearing. As distinct from the criminal law, the jurisdiction of the family courts is benign and for the interests of the child. The court can allow the child to be in court but should bear in mind that attendance at court is likely to be harmful to the child. Indeed, the court should only allow attendance where it is satisfied it is in the interests of the child. Even then, where the court is of the view that the child could be unruly, it can refuse to allow the child into court.[2] In *Re D (Secure Accommodation Order)*[3] Singer J expressed the view that it was unusual for a 14-year-old child to give evidence on a secure accommodation application and that if it could be avoided it should be. As yet, these decisions have not yet been tested against the 'fair trial' provisions in Art 6 of the Convention, particularly in the case of older children; we would suggest that it is necessary to consider the context of the particular case before the court and the safeguards present to ensure a fair trial such as representation balanced against the potential harm to the child which would be caused by his attending the hearing.

1   *W v North Yorkshire County Council* [1993] FCR 693 sub nom *Re W (A Minor) (Secure Accommodation Order)* [1993] 1 FLR 692, FD and see *C v Humberside County Council* [1994] 2 FLR 759, per Bracewell J.
2   *Re W (a minor) (secure accommodation: attendance at court)* [1994] 3 FCR 248, [1994] 2 FLR 1092, FD.
3   [1997] 1 FLR 197, [1996] 2 FCR 452, FD.

2.   Evidence

9.24   The Children (Admissibility of Hearsay Evidence) Order 1993[1] provides for the admission of hearsay evidence in civil proceedings in the High Court and county courts and in family proceedings in magistrates' courts in connexion with the upbringing, maintenance and welfare of a child. In *R v Oxfordshire County Council (Secure Accommodation Order)*[2] it was confirmed that 'family proceedings' means family proceedings under the CA 1989[3] and include any proceedings for a secure accommodation order.[4] In proceedings for a secure accommodation order psychiatric evidence will often be required.[5] In considering the likelihood of self-harm or threats when at large, Douglas Brown J doubted whether evidence simpliciter of an attempt at self injury and threats to others whilst in secure accommodation could be evidence on which the likelihood of self-harm or threats when at large could be assessed; psychiatric evidence would be helpful in determining this.[6] Except where matters proceed by agreement between the parties, sworn evidence must be heard so that the court may make clear recordings of facts as found by the court.[7]

1 SI 1993/621.
2 [1992] Fam 150, [1992] 3 All ER 660
3 Section 92(2).
4 *R v Oxfordshire County Council (Secure Accommodation Order)* [1992] Fam 150, [1992] 3 All ER 660.
5 *R v Oxfordshire County Council (Secure Accommodation Order)*, supra.
6 Above.
7 *Re AS (secure accommodation order)* [1999] 2 FCR 749, [1999] 1 FLR 103, FD.

3. Welfare criterion

9.25 If the court determines that the criteria in s 25 are satisfied, the terms of s 25(4) of the Act provide that the court shall make an order. However this has to be read subject to the power to make an interim order under s 25(5).[1] There was some initial uncertainty whether the court must have regard to the 'welfare principle' in s 1(1) and the 'no order' principle in s 1(5).[2]

1 *Hereford and Worcester County Council v S* [1993] 1 FCR 653, [1993] 2 FLR 360.
2 See *R v Oxfordshire County Council (Secure Accommodation Order)* [1992] Fam 150, [1992] 3 All ER 660 and *Re W (A Minor) Secure Accommodation Order)* [1993] 1 FLR 692 and *M v Birmingham City Council* [1994] 2 FLR 141.

9.26 The Court of Appeal decision *Re M (Secure Accommodation Order)*[1] has now resolved the matter and has held that the 'welfare principle' and the 'no order' principles in s 1 of the Children Act 1989 do not apply.[2] However, the welfare of the child is a relevant but not the paramount consideration. Under Pt III of the Act the general duty of a local authority is to safeguard and promote the child's welfare. In coming to a decision to hold a child in secure accommodation without a court order, the local authority has to satisfy the terms of s 25(1) and must also have regard to its duty under s 22(3) to safeguard and promote the welfare of the child who is being looked after by them. In *Re M* the Court of Appeal was of the view that the court has the same duty when considering an application under s 25:

> 'In coming to the decision to restrict the liberty of a child the local authority will also have regard to their duty to safeguard and promote the welfare of a child who is looked after by them (s 22(3)). The welfare principle is rightly to be considered by the local authority in coming to so serious and Draconian a decision as the restriction upon the liberty of the child. They have the power, however, to place him in secure accommodation if he is likely to injure others rather than himself (s 25(1)(b)). This power may be inconsistent with the concept of the child's welfare being paramount. The jurisdiction of the court is to be found in the same section and the court applies the same criteria in s 25(1) as the local authority . . .'[3]

The court's duty is to determine whether any relevant criteria in s 25(1) have been satisfied which include the welfare of the child. Where the court has found the relevant criteria to be satisfied there is a mandatory requirement for the court to make an order authorising the use of secure accommodation.[4]

1 *Re M (Secure Accommodation Order)* [1995] 1 FLR 418, CA and see *Re B (A Minor) (Secure Accommodation)* [1994] 2 FLR 707, CA.
2 See the discussion at para 2.15ff. See also *Re K (a child) (secure accommodation order: right to liberty)* [2001] 2 All ER 719, [2001] 1 FCR 249, [2001] 1 FLR 526, CA where it was made clear that the purpose of the order had to be for the educational supervision of children.
3 Per Butler-Sloss LJ at 423-442.
4 Above.

4. Interim orders

9.27 Where the court is not in a position to decide whether the criteria in s 25(1) are met and adjourns consideration of the application, it may make an interim order authorising the child to be kept in secure accommodation.[1] The making of an interim order is not justified by a desire to continue the involvement of a children's guardian.[2]

1 Section 25(5) and *Re M (a child) (secure accommodation)* [2001] EWCA Civ 458, [2001] 1 FCR 692, sub nom *Re C (Secure Accommodation Order: Representation)* [2001] 2 FLR 169, CA. See also *Re A (Secure Accommodation Order)* [2001] Fam Law 806, FD and *Re G (Secure Accommodation Order)* [2001] 1 FLR 884, FD.
2 *Re B (A Minor) (Secure Accommodation)* [1994] 2 FLR 707, CA. See *Re M (a child) (secure accommodation)* [2001] EWCA Civ 458, [2001] 1 FCR 692, sub nom *Re C (Secure Accommodation Order: Representation)* [2001] 2 FLR 169, CA where an interim order was made to enable a solicitor appointed by the child to take instructions.

5. Length of order

9.28 In determining the length of the order the court will have regard to the duty imposed on the local authority by s 22(3) of the CA 1989 to safeguard and promote the welfare of the child.[1] 'Secure placements once made, should only be for so long as is necessary and unavoidable.'[2] Furthermore, any interference with the Convention rights of the child under Art 8 must be 'proportionate.'[3] In any event, the court must consider carefully the purpose to be achieved by the order and must assess as best it can the time this is likely to take. It has a duty to explain carefully why it does so and make findings of fact and give reasons for specifying whatever is held to be the maximum period of time for which the order may take effect. Although the order is permissive, the court may not delegate to the local authority its decision as to the appropriate length[4] and may be assisted in its determination by the recommendation of the guardian. If the court departs from his recommendation, it must explain carefully why it does so.[5]

The maximum length of the order initially is three months.[6] This will include the period of a prior interim order[7] and the time limit runs from the making of the order not from the date when a child is subsequently placed in secure accommodation.[8] Orders may be renewed on further application for periods of up to six months at a time.[9]

1 *Re M (A Minor)* [1995] FLR 418, CA.
2 Guidance, Volume 1, Court Orders, para 5(1) approved in *R v Oxfordshire County Council (Secure Accommodation Order)* [1992] Fam 150, [1992] 3 All ER 660.
3 See, for the need to safeguard the child's Convention rights: *Re M (a child) (secure accommodation)* [2001] EWCA Civ 458, [2001] 1 FCR 692, sub nom *Re C (Secure Accommodation Order: Representation)* [2001] 2 FLR 169, CA
4 *Re W (A Minor) (Secure Accommodation Order)* [1993] 1 FLR 692.
5 Above.
6 Children (Secure Accommodation) Regulations 1991, reg 11.
7 *C v Humberside County Council* [1994] 2 FLR 759.
8 *Re B (A Minor) (Secure Accommodation)* [1994] 2 FLR 707.
9 The Children (Secure Accommodation) Regulations 1991, reg 12.

6. Effect of the order

9.29 The order is permissive, ie the authority are not required to use secure accommodation; they are authorised to use it when necessary and may only do so for as long as the statutory criteria are satisfied. A local authority looking after a child in secure accommodation in a children's home must appoint at least three persons, at least one of whom is independent of the authority, to review the keeping of the child in such accommodation within the first month and thereafter at intervals not exceeding three months.[1] Their duty is to satisfy themselves whether the criteria still apply and whether another placement would be practicable having regard to the wishes and feelings of the child, his parents and others responsible for his case.[2] If it ceases to appear to the local authority that the criteria are satisfied, they must cease to keep the child in secure accommodation. In *LM v Essex County Council*[3] a 15-year-old girl had been subject to a series of secure accommodation orders. A review panel had been appointed[4] to review her placement which subsequently concluded that the criteria for keeping her in secure accommodation had ceased to apply and that the authority should make immediate arrangements to remove her. However, the authority was unable to make alternative arrangements for her care and intended to keep her in a secure unit until the secure accommodation order expired. In granting a writ of habeas corpus, Holman J left open whether it was incumbent on the authority to release the child at once, as this issue no longer fell to be decided on the facts although, as has been argued,[5] Art 5 of the Convention would suggest that this is the case.[6]

Where it appears that application will be required for renewal of the order, such application, it is suggested, should be made in good time to allow for the appointment of the children's guardian and solicitor and for them to make adequate inquiries and take instructions. When appointing the children's guardian, the court (or in a family proceedings court, the justices' clerk) is required to consider the appointment of the same children's guardian who has previously acted for the child.[7]

1 Children (Secure Accommodation) Regulations 1991, reg 16 as amended by SI 1995/1398.
2 Above, reg 17.
3 *LM v Essex County Council* [1999] 1 FCR 673, [1999] 1 FLR 988, FD.
4 In accordance with the Children (Secure Accommodation) Regulations 1991, SI 1991/1505.
5 G Douglas [1999] Family Law 312.
6 Human Rights Act 1998, s 6(1).
7 FPR 1991, r 4.10(8); FPC (CA 1989) R 1991, r 10(8).

7. Appeal

9.30 Any appeal against the making of or refusal to make, an order by the family proceedings court lies to the Family Division of the High Court.[1] Detailed provision for appeals is made by Pt 52 of the Civil Procedure Rules 1998.[2] Since the liberty of the subject is in issue, any appeal should be listed as a matter of urgency and it is the duty of the appellant's solicitor to make the district registry aware of the need for urgency and to invite the district registry or the district judge to list the matter at the nearest court where an early hearing can take place before a High Court judge.[3] Where a secure accommodation order has been validly made by a court but subsequently it is alleged that the criteria no longer apply, there is no provision for an application to be made to the court to discharge the order and the court which made the order is functus officio. If the local authority decline to remove the child from the secure placement, the child must apply to the High Court for a writ of habeas corpus (where the local authority agree the criteria are not met) or judicial review (where the local authority dispute whether the criteria are satisfied).[4]

Further appeal lies to the Court of Appeal. Contrary to the normal rule, no leave is required where the appeal is in relation to a secure accommodation order made under s 25 of the Children Act 1989.[5]

1   Children Act 1989, s 94(1).
2   SI 1998/3132. Pt 52 was added by the Civil Procedure (Amendment No 4) Rules 2000, SI 2000/2092.
3   *R v Oxfordshire County Council (Secure Accommodation Order)* [1992] Fam 150, [1992] 3 All ER 660.
4   *LM v Essex County Council, supra.*
5   CPR 1998, r 52.3(1)(a)(iii).

CRIMINAL PROCEEDINGS

9.31   Applications for secure accommodation orders in criminal proceedings have been described as a 'legal labyrinth'[1] and with some justification. The complexity arises from the imperfect interrelationship between the family and criminal legislation. However, the complexity of making a placement of a child or young person the subject of criminal proceedings in secure accommodation has been reduced by the power of a criminal court to make, in certain circumstances, a 'security requirement' that the defendant be kept in secure accommodation without the need for a separate application for a secure accommodation order. Nevertheless, the demand for secure places in the criminal justice system has put a severe strain on the availability of resources so that it has been necessary to provide that local authorities may place 12 to 16-year-olds who are remanded by the courts to local authority secure accommodation under s 23 of the 1969 Act in secure training centres at the request of the local authority with the consent of the Secretary of State.[2]

1   Dawson and Stevens 'Applications for Secure Accommodation: The Legal Labyrinth' (1991) 155 JPN 777.
2   Criminal Justice and Police Act 2001, s133.

1.   Criminal remands

9.32   The complex provisions for remands in criminal proceedings may be summarised as follows.[1] When remanding[2] a child or young person under the age of 17 years, the court may grant him bail with or without conditions, or refuse bail. The decision to grant or refuse bail is made in accordance with the criteria in the Bail Act 1976.

Where a defendant is granted bail with a condition of residence where directed by the local authority, he is being 'looked after' by a local authority for the purposes of s 22(1) of the CA 1989.[3] Any application for a secure accommodation order will be made to a family proceedings court in accordance with the procedure for civil proceedings. Similarly, an application for a secure accommodation order in proceedings on an *adjourned*[4] hearing before the Crown Court is also made to the family proceedings court.

1 For the power to remand a juvenile, see generally *Clarke Hall and Morrison* paras 7[136]ff.
2 'Remand' includes a committal.
3 *Re C (A Minor) (Secure Accommodation Order: Bail)* [1994] 2 FLR 922.
4 An application must be made to the youth court in respect of a juvenile initially remanded or committed to the Crown Court: Criminal Justice Act 1991, s 60(3).

2. Security Requirement

9.33 If bail is refused, the remand is generally to local authority accommodation.[1] Such local authority accommodation is not secure and the defendant may be returned home to his parents although he is still being accommodated by the local authority. Where, however, the criteria in ss 23(4)–(5) of the Children and Young Persons Act 1969 are satisfied, there is provision for the court to require the authority to comply with a 'security requirement', ie a requirement that the person in question be placed and kept in secure accommodation.

The criteria ss 23(4)–(5) of the Children and Young Persons Act 1969 are that the local authority has been consulted and the defendant is:
'(a) charged with or has been convicted of a violent or sexual offence, or an offence punishable in the case of an adult with imprisonment for a term of fourteen years or more;'
(b) he is charged with or has been convicted of one or more imprisonable offences which, together with any other imprisonable offences of which he has been convicted in any proceedings
(i) amount, or
(ii) would, if he were convicted of the offences with which he is charged, amount, to a recent history of repeatedly committing imprisonable offences while remanded on bail or to local authority accommodation,
and (in either case) the court is of the opinion, after considering all the options for the remand of the person, that only remanding him to local authority accommodation with a security requirement would be adequate to protect the public from serious harm from him; or to prevent the commission by him of imprisonable offences'.

These provisions apply to females 12–16 years and males 12–14 years. In respect of males aged 15–16 a modified[2] s 23 of the Children and Young Persons Act 1969 Act applies and the court may make a security requirement in the case of a male aged 15–16 whom the court has declared meets the criteria in s 23(5) as modified[3] and in particular the 'vulnerability' criterion in s 23(5A).[4] At present the criminal court must remand a male offender aged 15–16 years who has met the criteria in s 23(5) as modified but who has not been declared to be a 'vulnerable person' to prison accommodation.[5]

1 Children and Young Persons Act 1969, s 23(1). The court has no power to specify the particular accommodation to be used by the local authority: *Cleveland County Council v DPP* [1995] 06 LS Gaz R 37.
2 By the Criminal Justice Act 1991, s 98.
3 Ie in addition to the criteria (a) and (b), there is secure accommodation available for him and the court is of opinion that only remanding him to a remand centre or prison, or to local authority accommodation with a requirement that he be placed and kept in secure accommodation, would be adequate to protect the public from serious harm from him.
4 'If the court is of opinion that, by reason of his physical or emotional immaturity or a propensity of his to harm himself, it would be undesirable for him to be remanded to a . . . prison.'
5 This power will be abolished when the transitory provisions of s 62 of the Criminal Justice Act 1991cease to have effect into effect and there is sufficient secure accommodation for all remanded juveniles.

3. Application for secure accommodation order

9.34 In the case of offenders aged 10 and 11 the court may not make a security requirement. Accordingly, if it is necessary for secure accommodation to be used, the local authority itself must make an application for a secure accommodation order. A local authority may similarly make such an application to a youth court where an offender has initially been remanded into non-secure local authority accommodation, but it subsequently appears to the authority that secure accommodation is required. This was the situation in *Re G (Secure Accommodation Order)*[1] where a 13-year-old girl had, with her mother's consent been placed in a residential unit. She made appearances before a youth court in criminal proceedings and was remanded in those proceedings. She continued to abscond from the residential unit where she was being accommodated but had not committed an offence during the period of her absconding. Although the criteria in reg 6(1)(b) (the criteria as modified for defendants in criminal proceedings)[2] had not been met, the youth court was not precluded from considering whether the criteria in s 25(1) of the CA 1989 had been satisfied.

1   [2001] 1 FLR 884, FD.
2   See para 9.33.

4. The court to which application is made

9.35 Section 60(3) of the Criminal Justice Act 1991 provides that: 'In the case of a child or young person who has been remanded or committed to local authority accommodation by a youth court or a magistrates' court other than a youth court, any application under s 25 of the Children Act 1989 . . . shall, notwithstanding anything in s 92(2) of that Act or s 65 of the 1980 Act,[1] be made to that[2] court.'

1   Magistrates' Courts Act 1980 – meaning of family proceedings.
2   This means a youth (or magistrates') court as distinct from a family proceedings court. A local youth court therefore has jurisdiction to make an order in respect of a youth remanded into local authority accommodation by a youth court outside the authority's boundary: *Liverpool City Council v B* [1995] 1 WLR 505, [1995] 2 FCR 105.

5. Criteria

9.36 The criteria in s 25(1) of the Children Act are modified in respect of more serious offences by the Children (Secure Accommodation) Regulations 1991[1] so that children[2] of the following descriptions:

(a) children detained under s 38(6) of the Police and Criminal Evidence Act 1984 (detained children), and
(b) children remanded to local authority accommodation under s 23 of the Children and Young Persons Act 1969 (remand to local authority accommodation) but only if:
  (i)   the child is charged with or has been convicted of a violent or sexual offence, or of an offence punishable in the case of an adult with imprisonment for a term of 14 years or more, or
  (ii) the child has a recent history of absconding while remanded to local authority accommodation, and is charged with or has been convicted of

an imprisonable offence alleged or found to have been committed while he was so remanded, may be placed in secure accommodation if they are likely to abscond from non secure accommodation, or are likely to injure themselves or other people if kept in any other accommodation.[3]

The modification makes it sufficient in the case of a serious offence (or a less serious offence where there is a recent history of absconding), for the court to be satisfied that the child is likely to abscond from non-secure accommodation. The court is not required to assess whether he is likely to suffer significant harm. There appears to be greater emphasis on the protection of the public, a factor not present in civil proceedings or for criminal offences where the criteria are not modified.[4] Moreover, the jurisdiction of the youth court is not dependent on the case falling within reg 6(1), (2) of the 1991 regulations. If a child is in local authority accommodation because he has been remanded by a youth court, the youth court has exclusive jurisdiction to make a secure accommodation order where either the conditions in reg 6 are met or if they are not so satisfied, as for example where the offence does not carry more than 14 years imprisonment in the case of an adult or is a violent offence, where the criteria in s 25 are satisfied.[5]

1 See reg 6.
2 Ie persons under 18 years : CA 1989, s 105(1). For the purpose of the Children and Young Persons Acts a child is defined as a person under the age of 14 years : CYPA 1933, s 107(1).
3 Children (Secure Accommodation) Regulations 1991, reg 6.
4 See *Re G (Secure Accommodation Order)* [2001] 1 FLR 884, FD.
5 *Re G (Secure Accommodation Order)* supra.

6. Procedure

9.37 The procedure in the youth and the adult magistrates' court is prescribed by the Magistrates' Courts (Children and Young Persons) Rules 1992, Pt III.[1] Since the Family Proceedings Courts (Children Act 1989) Rules 1991, are inapplicable to the criminal courts these are not 'specified proceedings' for the purpose of s 41 of the Children Act 1989 and a children's guardian may not be appointed.[2] Nor are statements to be filed. A criminal court is obliged to give reasons for refusing bail[3] or for imposing a custodial sentence[4] and while there is no general statutory obligation on criminal courts corresponding to that on family proceedings courts to give reasons for their decisions,[5] Art 6 of the Convention requires any court to explain its decision. It is therefore incumbent on the court to give some reasons for its decision and to indicate that it has considered whether there is any alternative to making to order.

1 SI 1992/2071 and see *AE v Staffordshire County Council* [1995] 2 FCR 84.
2 Secure accommodation applications are specified proceedings by virtue of the FPR 1991, r 4.2(2); FPC (CA 1989) R 1991, r 2(2).
3 Bail Act 1976, s 4.
4 Powers of Criminal Courts (Sentencing) Act 2000, s 79(4).
5 See para 9.21.

7. Evidence

9.38 Remand hearings in criminal courts are usually conducted by representations although evidence may be called if required. In secure accommodation proceedings evidence or statements will be required to establish the criteria but as they are, for these purposes, classified as 'family proceedings'[1] hearsay will be admissible.[2]

1 See para 5.101.
2 Children (Admissibility of Hearsay Evidence) Order 1993, SI 1993/621, and see *R v Oxfordshire County Council (Secure Accommodation Order)* [1992] Fam 150, [1992] 3 All ER 660.

8. Length of order

9.39 In the case of a child before the court in criminal proceedings who is not accommodated by a local authority other than by virtue of the remand, the maximum period of authorisation is the period of the remand[1] which includes a committal.[2] In any event the period of the order shall not exceed 28 days on any one occasion without further court authorisation.[3] The terms of reg 13 would appear to bind a family court exercising jurisdiction over a child remanded to local authority accommodation where it and not a youth court has jurisdiction ie where application is made in respect of a child who has been refused bail by the Crown Court.[4] In the case of a child remanded on bail to live where directed by the local authority in the circumstances in *Re C (A Minor) (Secure Accommodation: Bail)*[5] reg 13 may be felt not to apply following the reasoning in *Re W (a minor) (secure accommodation: jurisdiction)*,[6] in which case the time limits applicable to civil cases would apply. Whichever court is considering the matter will be bound to include the welfare of the child in its considerations and the length of any order must be for no longer than is necessary.[7]

1 Children (Secure Accommodation) Order 1991, reg 13(1).
2 Children and Young Persons Act 1969, s 23(1).
3 Children (Secure Accommodation) Order 1991, reg 13(2).
4 Where a family court exercises jurisdiction the FPR 1991 and the FPC (CA 1989) R 1991 apply and a children's guardian may be appointed, see para 9.18.
5 [1994] 2 FLR 922. See n 6 to para 9.10.
6 [1995] 2 FCR 708n.
7 See paras 9.25 and 9.26.

9. Renewals

9.40 An order may be renewed by further application to the court.[1] The reference to 'that court' in s 60(3) of the Criminal Justice Act 1991 was originally interpreted as referring to the court which remanded or committed him[2] but is now held to refer generically to the type of court ie youth or adult magistrates' court.[3]

1 Children (Secure Accommodation) Order 1991, SI 1991/1505, reg 12.
2 Guidance, Volume 7, Guardians ad litem and other Court Related Issues, para 5.5.
3 See *Liverpool City Council v B* [1995] 1 WLR 505, [1995] 2 FCR 105.

10. Crown Court

9.41 The Crown Court has no jurisdiction to make a secure accommodation order as it is not included within the terms of s 60(3). On transfer for trial or committal for sentence the youth or adult magistrates' court which remanded or committed him may have made an order for a period of up to 28 days. A renewal of such an order will be to the respective youth or magistrates' court. Where the Crown Court has further remanded the child or young person, the position is unclear. It has been cogently argued[1] that an application in these circumstances must be made to a family proceedings court in which case the procedural provisions in civil proceedings apply including the appointment of a guardian, the filing of statements and the giving of reasons but a more attractive proposal would be for the Crown Court to have the power to make such an order.

1 Dawson and Stevens op cit.

11. Appeal

9.42 Appeal against the making of or refusal to make an order by an adult magistrates' court or a youth court is to the Family Division of the High Court as for orders made in civil proceedings.[1]

1 CA 1989, s 94(1) and see *AE v Staffordshire County Council* [1995] 2 FCR 84. For procedure, see para 9.30.

Chapter 10

Child representation and welfare reporting

INTRODUCTION

10.1   In cases concerning children the court may be provided with welfare reports and in some instances the child may be represented. The way in which this is effected has evolved over the last thirty years, as greater emphasis has been given, first to the welfare of the child and more recently his right to express his wishes and feelings and be represented in so doing. The statutory principles are set out in s 1 of the CA 1989.[1] The way in which these principles are implemented is the subject of this chapter.

1   See chapter 2.

10.2   Given their increasing influence international conventions must be considered. Art 12 of the UN Convention on the Rights of the Child 1989 states:

> 'States Parties shall ensure to the child who is capable of forming his or her own views the right to express those views freely in all matters affecting the child, the views of the child being given weight in accordance with the age and maturity of the child . . . The child shall in particular be provided with the opportunity to be heard in any judicial and administrative proceedings affecting the child, either directly, or through a representative or appropriate body, in a manner consistent with procedural rules of national law.'

10.3   The European Convention on the Exercise of Children's Rights 1996, though not ratified by the United Kingdom, makes further provision. Article 3 states, in respect of a child considered to have sufficient understanding, that he is entitled:

(a)   to receive all relevant information;
(b)   to be consulted and express his views; and
(c)   to be informed of the possible consequences of compliance with these views and the possible consequences of any decision.'

Article 4 states that a child has the right 'to apply, in person or through other persons or bodies, for a special representative in proceedings before a judicial authority affecting the child where internal law precludes the holders of parental responsibilities from representing the child as a result of a conflict of interest with the latter.'

10.4   The European Convention for the Protection of Human Rights and Fundamental Freedoms 1950, which became part of domestic law following the implementation of the Human Rights Act 1998 on 2 October 2000, though as yet untested in this area, may provide further opportunity for consideration of how children participate in proceedings. Article 6 provides that 'in the determination of his civil rights and obligations . . . everyone is entitled to a fair and public hearing within a reasonable time by an independent and impartial tribunal established by law.'

CAFCASS

10.5 These principles provide a context; what has happened in practice? In the Autumn of 1997, a review conducted jointly by the Home Office, the Lord Chancellor's Department, the Department of Health and the Welsh Office of the provision of court welfare services then provided by Family Court Welfare (FCW), the Guardian ad litem and Reporting Officer (GALRO) Service and the Children's Division of the Official Solicitor's (OS) Department, concluded that an integrated service subsuming the work of each of the above services could:

- provide an improved service to the courts;
- better safeguard the interests of children; and
- reduce wasteful overlaps and increase efficiency.

The Lord Chancellor announced the decision to set up the Children and Family Court Advisory and Support Service (CAFCASS) in April 2000. It is a Non-Departmental Public Body answerable through its Board to the Lord Chancellor. This relationship is controlled by a 'Framework Document', which vests ultimate power in the Lord Chancellor's Department for controlling the range of CAFCASS work and the way in which it is carried out. The new service commenced on 2 April 2001,[1] which left little time for planning implementation of their services.

1 CAFCASS Head Office is at 16 Palace Street, London SW1E 5LX (Tel: 020–7210–4400; Fax: 020–7210–4422; website: http://www.cafcass.gov.uk).

10.6 The statutory functions[1] of CAFCASS are to:

(a) safeguard and promote the welfare of children;
(b) give advice to any court about any application made to it in any such [family] proceedings;
(c) make provision for the children to be represented in such proceedings; and
(d) provide information, advice and other support for the children and their families.

These functions are limited to 'family proceedings',[2] but in the light of (d) and the support element of the title may extend to associated activities outside the court. In its Corporate Plan for 2002–2006 CAFCASS has set out its key objectives to:

- represent, safeguard and promote the welfare of children involved in family court proceedings;
- improve the services offered to the family courts;
- improve the efficiency and effectiveness of the services offered through increased value for money;

- improve the services offered to families and other key stakeholders;
- develop the skills of staff; and
- play a full role in delivering the wider Government agenda of improvements in service.

1 The Criminal Justice and Court Services Act 2000, s12(1). As a statutory body it cannot undertake work outside its statutory functions.
2 Section 12(5).

10.7 CAFCASS may make arrangements with organisations or individuals to perform the functions of the Service. Initial plans were for former employees of the Court Welfare Service and the Official Solicitor's Department to become CAFCASS employees and for members of Panels of Guardians ad litem and Reporting Officers to be offered employment or contracts for self-employment. The offer of self-employment was unexpectedly withdrawn in July 2001 in order to centralise management of staff and improve budgetary control. On an application for judicial review, CAFCASS was ordered to reconsider the decision[1] and offered guardians self-employed contracts. This is not the place to analyse the political thinking in relation to the new agency, but it is beyond doubt that the dispute caused considerable problems for the new organisation, with shortages of staff and lack of experience, and consequent delay in the allocation of cases.

1 *The Queen on the Application of the National Association of Guardians ad Litem and Reporting Officers v Children and Family Court Advisory and Support Service* [2001] EWHC Admin 693, [2002] 1 FLR 255.

10.8 CAFCASS has published a Consultation Paper setting out a draft policy 'Principles and National Standards.[1] They are stated (at para 1.18) to be for:

(a) children and families who use CAFCASS's services;
(b) all parties to family proceedings and their legal representatives;
(c) practitioners and local managers, administrators and support staff;
(d) Family Courts;
(e) the CAFCASS Board, Executive Team and Regional Managers;
(f) any organisation or person performing functions of CAFCASS on its behalf; and
(g) other statutory agencies and agencies working in partnership with CAFCASS.

Inspectors of the magistrates' court service (MCSI) are responsible for inspecting and reporting to the Lord Chancellor on the performance of CAFCASS and its officers.[2] They too will work to the Principles and Standards when carrying out their inspections.

1 May 2002. For the draft Standards see para 10.18. See also the CAFCASS Service Standards which regulate the work of CAFCASS officers. Both documents are available on the CAFCASS website at www.cafcass.gov.uk
2 CJCSA 2000, s 17.

10.9 The name given to an officer of CAFCASS will depend on the function they are fulfilling:

- an officer appointed to prepare a welfare report is a 'child and family reporter';

- an officer appointed to represent a child in public law proceedings or adoption proceedings is a 'children's guardian';
- an officer appointed to receive the consent of the parent(s) who hold parental responsibility in adoption proceedings is a 'reporting officer';
- an officer appointed in Human Fertilisation and Embryology proceedings (parental orders) is a 'parental order reporter'; and
- The Court may ask a local authority to prepare a welfare report. An officer appointed by a local authority to prepare a welfare report is a 'welfare officer'.

A children and family reporter reports to the court about the child's background; a children's guardian represents the child, who may also have legal representation. Because their functions are different, the appointment of one does not ipso facto preclude the appointment of the other, although given the scarcity of resources, the court should consider carefully what would be gained by appointing both. All officers are required to make such investigations as may be necessary to carry out their duties and in particular, contact or seek to interview such persons as he thinks appropriate or as the court directs, and obtain such professional assistance as is available to him or the court directs.[1]

1   FPR 1991, r 4.11(2).

10.10   The distinction between a welfare officer and a guardian ad litem (as then were) has been judicially considered:

> 'The functions of the court welfare officer and those of the guardian are not identical although they do have many features in common: each has a duty to report to the court; each has a duty to consider the welfare or the interests of the child; each may be cross-examined on any report which they give. However, a court welfare officer is not a party in the proceedings, whereas the guardian ad litem, through his representation on behalf of the child, is. Nonetheless, each has a similar duty to the court, which is to advise the court as to what is best for the child independently of the other parties to the proceedings and each of them is independent of all other parties in the proceedings. Therefore the reports of both the court welfare officer and the guardian should be given the same consideration by the court receiving such reports.'

It was therefore held that it was only in exceptional circumstances that it would be justified in appointing both a welfare officer and a guardian ad litem to report in the same proceedings.

1   *Re S (a minor) (guardian ad litem/welfare officer)* [1992] 2 FCR 554, [1993] 1 FLR 110, CA.

Welfare reports

10.11   A court may, when considering *any* question with respect to a child under the Act, ask either CAFCASS or a local authority to report to the court 'on such matters relating to the welfare of that child as are required to be dealt with in the report'.[1] The power to ask for a report arises in relation to *any* issue under the CA 1989, but since a children's guardian will almost invariably be appointed in public law proceedings, these provisions relate primarily to private law proceedings. Guidance given in the 'Best practice note for the judiciary and family proceedings courts when ordering a court welfare officer's report'[2] should now be routinely followed by all courts, though there are likely to be local variations.

1 Section 7. The court will not order both a welfare report and S 37 report at the same time, although the latter may follow the former.
2 First published in the Committee's annual report for 1993/94 and re-published in Handbook of Best Practice in Children Act Cases (Children Act Advisory Committee, June 1997).

10.12 Before a welfare report is ordered consideration should be given to the court's power to refer parties to mediation (with the consent of the parties). In some areas parties will not be granted a public funding certificate to issue proceedings, unless they have attended mediation or there are good reasons for mediation not to take place. Referral may be to a mediation service or the court welfare officer, depending on local arrangements. This is not a welfare report and a welfare officer involved in mediation should not be the officer who undertakes the preparation of a welfare report.

10.13 The ordering of a welfare officer's report is a judicial act requiring inquiry into the circumstances of the child. A report should never be ordered when there is no live issue under the Children Act before the court. Although the exact procedures in different courts vary, there will always be some kind of preliminary appointment or hearing before the district judge, justices' clerk or family proceedings court in children's cases, perhaps in conjunction with a CAFCASS officer. The attendance of the parties and their solicitors is required at this time to enable the court properly to consider whether the matter can be dealt with without a report and if necessary to inquire into the issues to be covered in the report.

10.14 The court is not bound to order welfare reports in every case. If delay would prejudice the child's welfare, the court might have to balance the advantages to be gained from a report against the disadvantage of the time it takes to obtain it.[1] It has been held that the decision whether to ask for a welfare report lies within the judge's discretion and cannot be appealed.[2] On the other hand it is the general practice for a welfare report to be ordered where the matter remains contested. Whenever possible there should be one report made by one officer recording his own observations especially where the parties lived or the proposed homes are near each other, although it is recognised that it is sometimes impossible if it would cause unacceptable delay or expense. If a report is ordered, the court should ascertain when the report can be expected and fix a specific date in the light of that information[3] and must notify the reporter of any decisions made during the course of the proceedings and of the date for hearings.[4]

1 Cf *Re H (Minors) (Welfare Reports)* [1990] 2 FLR 172, CA.
2 *Re W (Welfare Reports)* [1995] 2 FLR 142, CA.
3 *B v B (Minors) (Interviews and Listing Arrangements)* [1994] 2 FLR 489, sub nom *B v B (minors: residence and care disputes)* [1994] 2 FCR 667.
4 FPR 1991, r 4.5; FPC(CA 1989)R 1991, r 5.

10.15 When a welfare report is ordered the court should explain to the parties what will be involved and should emphasise the need to co-operate with the welfare officer and specifically to keep any appointments made. In particular, when the principle of contact is in dispute the parties should be told that the welfare officer will probably wish to see the applicant parent alone with the child. It should also be emphasised that the report, when received, is a confidential document and must not be shown to anyone who is not a named party to the application.

10.16 The court may, in private law proceedings, ask a local authority to report rather than a children and family reporter. This can provide a useful bridge between private and public law proceedings. If a local authority has already been involved applications can properly be made to the court hearing the private law proceedings for a report, which a local authority is duty bound to provide.[1] Where there are both private law proceedings and investigations being carried out by the police and social services, the local authority should report to the court on the nature, progress and outcome of the investigations. In this way the court can ensure the co-ordination of the private law proceedings with the statutory local authority child abuse investigations.[2] Where the court decides to ask the local authority to report, it can ask them to arrange for it to be done either by one of their officers or such other person (other than a probation officer) as the authority consider appropriate, but there is no power to order a local authority to instruct a child psychiatrist to prepare a report for the court.[3]

1 *W v Wakefield City Council* [1994] 2 FCR 564, [1995] 1 FLR 170.
2 *Re A and B (Minors) (No 2)* [1995] 1 FLR 351 at 368–369.
3 *Re K (Contact: Psychiatric Report)* [1995] 2 FLR 432, CA.

10.17 There is concern at the ability of child and family reporters to 'sufficiently see and hear' the child,[1] especially where there is a conflict of interest between parents and child. There is no automatic right for the child to be represented in private family law proceedings, but increasingly the courts recognise the need for representation. The reporter is under a duty to consider whether it is in the best interests of the child to be made a party to proceedings and notify the court of that opinion and the reasons for it.[2] The *Practice Note* suggests that such cases should in future be referred to CAFCASS Legal,[3] but they are unlikely to be able to manage the volume of cases which could require representation. If the officer is authorised by CAFCASS, he can conduct the proceedings on behalf of the child himself, unless the child wishes to instruct a solicitor direct, and the court and the guardian consider that he is of sufficient understanding to do so. It remains to be seen how we shall meet the recognised need for children to be represented where their interests are affected in private family law proceedings.

1 *Re A (A Child) (Contact: Separate Representation)* [2001] FLR 715, CA.
2 FPR 1991, r 4.13(3A)
3 *CAFCASS Practice Note: Officers of CAFCASS Legal Services and Special Casework: Appointment in Family Proceedings* [2001] 2 FCR 562.

The National Standards of Practice

10.18 National standards for work previously undertaken by probation officers were issued by the Home Office in a document entitled *National Standards for Probation Service Family Court Welfare Work.*[1] Advice for guardians ad litem under the former panel system was available under the title *Manual of Practice Guidance for Guardians ad litem and Reporting Officers,*[2] *A Guide for Guardians ad Litem in Public Law Proceedings under the Children Act 1989*[3] and the *National Standards for the Guardian ad Litem and Reporting Officer Service.*[4]

1 HMSO, 1994.
2 HMSO, 1992.
3 HMSO 1995.
4 Department of Health and the Welsh Office; copies can be obtained from DOH, Publications Unit, PO Box 410, Wetherby LS23 7LN.

10.19 CAFCASS will replace these standards and issued a Consultation Paper setting out its proposals. Although at the time of writing this is only a Consultation Paper, it may be anticipated that work will be undertaken in accordance with the Paper, which will be amended as and when necessary. The draft provisions (at para 3) are:

'**General**
3.1 The Practitioner will perform his/her responsibilities in each case in accordance with:
    3.1.1 the relevant Rules of Court (in particular Rules 4.10,4.11 and 4.11A Family Proceedings Rules 1991, as amended); and
    3.1.2 the timetable set and any other directions given by the Court.
3.2 The Practitioner will maintain all records and provide all information in the manner required by CAFCASS.

Referral and allocation
3.3 CAFCASS will enter all new cases into its systems within two working days of receiving the referral from the Court.
3.4 CAFCASS will allocate all new cases within ten working days of receiving the referral from the Court.
3.5 On being allocated a case, the Practitioner will:
    3.5.1 ensure that s/he has the necessary skills, knowledge and experience to undertake the work effectively; and
    3.5.2 consider whether there is any conflict of interests and will inform his/her manager if there is any reason why it is not appropriate for him/ her to deal with the case.

Enquiries
3.6 The Practitioner will contact all parties within five working days of the case being allocated to him/her. If the Practitioner is unable to do so s/he will record the reasons.
3.7 The Practitioner will always see any child who is the subject of proceedings and will do so in a child-friendly venue.
3.8 The Practitioner will see all the other parties unless directed otherwise by the Court.
3.9 The Practitioner will ensure at an early stage in his/her enquiries, information leaflets, including those about CAFCASS's Complaints Policy, are given to any children (if appropriate) and all (other) parties to the case.
3.10 The Practitioner will:
    3.10.1 prepare and regularly update a detailed case plan, identifying the issues raised in the particular case, the enquiries to be made and any issues of diversity;
    3.10.2 take a positive approach to enable the Court to fix and implement the timetable most likely to meet the needs of the child; and
    3.10.3 consider throughout whether the case should be transferred to a Court of a different level or in a different location.
3.11 The Practitioner will make appropriate enquiries about all issues:
    3.11.1 identified by the Court;
    3.11.2 raised by the parties and believed by the Practitioner to be relevant; and
    3.11.3 any other issues identified by the Practitioner which s/he believes to be relevant.

Reporting, Attending Court and Giving Evidence
3.12 Reports will comply with the standard CAFCASS format and guidelines.
3.13 Reports will:
    3.13.1 set out all relevant information which the Practitioner has acquired through his/her enquiries, making clear from what source the information has been obtained and distinguishing between matters of fact and matters of opinion;
    3.13.2 make clear recommendations (or explain why recommendations cannot be made); and

    3.13.3 explain the basis upon which those recommendations have been made, including reasons both for and against those recommendations.

3.14 The Practitioner will usually share the recommendations contained in his/her report with any child who is the subject of proceedings and will do so in a manner that is appropriate to the child's age and understanding. If the Practitioner decides not to do so s/he will record his/her reasons.

3.15 Reports will be filed within the timescale set by the Court.

3.16 The Practitioner will consider whether to recommend that the Court makes an order or direction in addition to, or instead of, the orders applied for by the parties (including the making of a family assistance order, an order pursuant to s 91(14) and for the disclosure of any documents in the proceedings to relevant third parties for identified purposes).

3.17 The Practitioner will attend all Court hearings in accordance with the Court rules unless s/he is not required to do so by a local practice direction or a direction given in the particular case.

3.18 The Practitioner will present as a credible witness in oral evidence, demonstrating a thorough knowledge of the issues of the case and the factors affecting them.

Closure of the Case

3.19 In any proceedings in which s/he represents a child, the Practitioner will consider whether it may be appropriate to appeal against any order made and, if so, will immediately discuss this with any solicitor for the child and/or his/her manager.

3.20 The Practitioner will usually see any child who is the subject of proceedings and explain to the child the outcome of the proceedings in a manner that is appropriate to the child's age and understanding. If the Practitioner decides not to do so, s/he will record his/her reasons.

3.21 The Practitioner will provide all information required by CAFCASS for information and monitoring purposes within four weeks of the conclusion of the case.

3.22 The Practitioner will prepare all case papers and submit them for safe storage in accordance with CAFCASS's procedures for the retention of case files'.

10.20   The Standards are notable for imposing requirements on the individual CAFCASS officer.[1] They will require support to achieve them. In a number of respects, for example time limits (in paras 3.3 and 3.4) where there are urgent cases, the standards may be inadequate and suggest a response more attuned to the resources of the agency than a reflection of the needs of the child. The previous standards specifically required that consideration be given to what issues, if any, are in dispute; whether there is any measure of agreement between the parties; what course of action might achieve it; and whether there is any prospect of agreement being reached without the continued involvement of the court. Consultation may lead to their restoration.

1   See para 10.8 and the CAFCASS website at (www.cafcass.gov.uk).

Children's guardian in specified proceedings

10.21   In specified proceedings[1] the child is a respondent[2] and the court is required to appoint an officer of CAFCASS, known as a children's guardian to represent the child, unless satisfied that it is not necessary to do so in order to safeguard his interests. The courts have continued to adopt an approach expressed under previous legislation.[3] The specified proceedings are:

(a) applications for the making, variation or discharge of a care or supervision order and related appeals;

(b) where a direction for the local authority to investigate has been given and the court has made, or is considering making, an interim care order;[4]
(c) where the court is considering making a residence order with respect to a child who is the subject of a care order and related appeals;
(d) applications in respect of contact between a child in care and any person and related appeals; and
(e) applications for a child assessment order or other proceedings under Pt V of the Act, which would include an application to discharge an emergency protection order and related appeals.

Further proceedings may be specified by rules of court. Education supervision orders and orders under Pt II are not provided for except under (c) above. The Rules[5] add:

(a) family proceedings under s 25 for a child to be kept in secure accommodation;
(b) application under s 33(7) enabling a child to be known by a new surname or removed from the United Kingdom;
(c) proceedings under Sch 3, para 19(1) to approve a child in care living abroad; and
(d) applications under Sch 3, para 6(3) for extension of a supervision order.

1   CA 1989, s 41(6).
2   FPR 1991; FPC(CA 1989)R 1991, App 3.
3   The appointment of a guardian ad litem (under previous legislation) who could make a close independent investigation of the facts and circumstances would be in the child's best interests: *R v Plymouth Juvenile Court, ex p F* [1987] 1 FLR 169.
4   The proceedings are no longer specified when the local authority decides not to make an application under the CA 1989, s 31.
5   FPR 1991, r 4.2; FPC(CA 1989)R 1991, r 2(2).

Appointment of children's guardian

10.22   A children's guardian is appointed in accordance with rules of court which provide that the appointment shall be made as soon as practicable after the commencement of proceedings, unless the court considers such an appointment is not necessary to safeguard the interests of the child.[1]

1   FPR 1991, r 4.10(7); FPC(CA 1989)R 1991, r 10(7).

10.23   Proceedings may cease to be specified proceedings, such as where a local authority, having conducted an investigation under s 37, decides not to make an application for a care or supervision order. The appointment of the guardian should then be terminated by a judicial rather than an administrative act.[1] There may be cases where, subject to consent and the availability of funding, it would be appropriate for the guardian to continue.[2] Prior to the existence of CAFCASS there would have been no funding for the guardian, but this difficulty is now resolved.

1   See the FPR 1991, r 4.10(9); FPC(CA 1989)R 1991, r 10(9); and *Re M (Terminating Appointment of Guardian Ad Litem)* [1999] 2 FLR 717.
2   *Re CE (A Minor) (Section 37 Direction)* [1995] 1 FLR 26. See also *Oxfordshire County Council v L and F* [1997] 1 FLR 235 where it was held desirable for the child to be represented after the termination of care proceedings on an application for disclosure of documents.

Duties of the children's guardian in specified proceedings

10.24 The duties of a children's guardian have not been radically changed and accordingly pre-existing case law and guidance is likely to remain relevant. The guardian is under a duty to safeguard the interests of the child as prescribed by rules of court.[1] These require him to have regard to the welfare principles. The guardian must,[2] unless excused, attend all directions appointments and hearings of proceedings and shall advise on the following matters:

(a) whether the child is of sufficient understanding for any purpose including the child's refusal to submit to a medical or psychiatric examination or other assessment that the court has power to require, direct or order;
(b) the wishes of the child in respect of any matter relevant to the proceedings, including his attendance at court;
(c) the appropriate forum for the proceedings;
(d) the appropriate timing of the proceedings or any part of them;
(e) the options available to it in respect of the child and the suitability of each such option including what order should be made in determining the application;
(f) any other matter on which the court seeks his advice or about which he considers that the court should be informed.[2]

1 CA 1989, s 41(2).
2 FPR 1991, r 4.11; FPC(CA 1989)R, r 11(4).

10.25 Since the guardian will be appointed at an early stage of the proceedings, he should be able to advise the court about:

(a) discharge of an emergency protection order;
(b) variation of directions attached to such an order;
(c) the making or extension of an interim care or supervision order;
(d) directions for the conduct of proceedings; and
(e) the option of s 8 orders.

The rules[1] provide for the children's guardian to:

(a) investigate the case;
(b) consider arrangements for contact;
(c) seek to interview such persons as he thinks appropriate or as the court directs;
(d) inspect appropriate records[2] and bring to the attention of the court, such records and documents which may, in his opinion, assist in the proper determination of the proceedings; and
(e) obtain such professional assistance as is available to him which he thinks appropriate or which the court directs him to obtain.

Unless otherwise directed, the guardian shall file a written report advising on the interests of the child not less than seven days before the date fixed for the final hearing.

1 FPR 1991, r 4.11 and 4.11A; FPC(CA 1989)R, r 11 and 11A.
2 Section 42. See para 10.30.

10.26 A children's guardian should not promise a child to withhold information from the court,[1] but may apply to the court for directions that information should not be revealed to another party.[2]

1 *Re D (minors)* [1995] 4 All ER 385, [1995] 2 FLR 687, HL.
2 *Re C (Disclosure)* [1996] 1 FLR 797.

10.27 The *Manual of Practice for Guardians ad litem and Reporting Officers*[1] advises that:

'The guardian should not attempt to appear in court as an expert witness in matters on which he is not competent and credible in the court's eyes, as this can only undermine the child's case.'

The guardian has to decide in the exercise of his duty to safeguard the interests of the child, whether or not he believes the child.[2] Guardians will have to be careful not to confuse their roles. They cannot, and should not attempt to be, experts in all matters about which they have to report. Nonetheless as experienced social workers they may well have considerable expertise in a particular area.

1 See para 10.18.
2 *Re N (Child Abuse: Evidence)* [1996] 2 FLR 214, CA.

10.28 The court cannot order that a children's guardian should have contact with a child after a care order has been made.[1] A desire on the part of the court to monitor a rehabilitation process under a care order is not a matter for the children's guardian.[2] However if the court makes a care contact order and adjourns the application, it may require the guardian to report further on the adjourned hearing. If a local authority decides to remove a child from a foster parent during the course of proceedings, it has a duty to consult the guardian and the foster parent before making the decision.[3]

1 *Kent County Council v C* [1993] Fam 57, [1993] 1 FLR 308.
2 See *Re S (Care Order: Implementation of Care Plan)* [2002] 2 WLR 720. For a full discussion of this case see para 8.00. It is the intention of the Government to provide in the Adoption and Children Bill 2002 for the power of referral of cases to a CAFCASS officer where a care plan has not been carried out: see para 8.00.
3 *R v Hereford and Worcester County Council, ex p D* [1992] 1 FCR 497, [1992] 1 FLR 448.

10.29 Where the court makes a supervision order, the proceedings are defined to continue until the order ends.[1] It has been held that since these are continuing proceedings the role of the children's guardian will continue.[2]

1 Criminal Justice and Court Services Act, s 12.
2 *Re MH (A Child); and Re SB and MB (Children)* [2001] 2 FLR 134. The Government has indicated that this provision was a 'slip of the pen' and will be deleted by the Adoption and Children Bill 2002, to clarify that the guardian's responsibilities do not continue during the period of a supervision order.

Guardian's right to inspect records

10.30 A children's guardian appointed for the purpose of specified proceedings has a right at all reasonable times to examine and take copies of any records of or held by a local authority or other authorised persons compiled in connection with the making or proposed making by any person of any application under the CA 1989 with respect to the child he represents and any other records of or held by an authority in relation to the child and compiled in connection with any function of the social services committee under the Local Authority Social Services Act 1970.[1] The provision is wide enough to include case conference minutes. It includes files compiled with a view to adoption[2] and a report prepared under Pt 8 of Working Together for an Area Child Protection Committee.[3] The provision is limited to the local authority or any authorised person. The Arrangements for Placement of Children (General) Regulations 1991 make additional provision so that each voluntary organisation, where it is not acting as an authorised person, and every person carrying on a registered children's home, shall provide a guardian with access to the case records and registers and information from and copies of such records or registers held in whatever form (such as by means of computer). The guardian has no right to inspect records of the Crown Prosecution Service, but disclosure can be ordered if documents are of real importance to a care case.[4]

1 Section 42.
2 *Re T (A Minor) (Guardian Ad Litem: Case Record)* [1994] 1 FLR 632, CA.
3 *Re R (Care Proceedings: Disclosure)* [2000] 2 FLR 751.
4 *Nottinghamshire County Council v H* [1995] 1 FLR 115.

10.31 Where copies of records are taken they are admissible as evidence in proceedings, regardless of any enactment or rule of law which would otherwise prevent the record in question being admissible in evidence.[1] This would appear to be wide enough to counteract any claim for public interest immunity, but it has been said that where records may be immune from disclosure, the guardian should draw this to the attention of the court.[2]

1 CA 1989, s 42(2), (3).
2 *Re C (Children Act 1989: Expert Evidence)* [1995] 1 FLR 204 and see para 11.48.

Cross examination of CAFCASS officers

10.32 A party may question an officer of CAFCASS about oral or written evidence tendered by him to the court.[1] Although it has been suggested that welfare officers are not witnesses on oath since they are officers of the court,[2] this argument is now difficult to sustain in the light of this new rule. The same considerations apply to a guardian as to a children and family reporter.

1 FPR 1991, r 4.11(4), but the court has power to limit cross-examination.
2 *Re I and H (Contact: Right to Give Evidence)* [1998] 1 FLR 876, CA and see *Re B (Residence Order: Status Quo)* [1998] 1 FLR 368.

10.33 The Service may authorise an officer of the Service of a prescribed description to conduct litigation in relation to any proceedings in any court and to exercise a right of audience in any proceedings before any court in the exercise of the functions of the Service.[1] An officer of the Service may be cross-examined in any proceedings to the same extent as any witness but may not be cross-examined merely because he is exercising a right to conduct litigation or a right of audience.[2]

1 CJCSA 2000, s 15.
2 CJCSA 2000, s 16.

Recommendations

10.34 The court is not bound by any recommendation in welfare reports, but if it departs from a recommendation the court should give its reasons for doing so.[1] On the other hand provided the reasons given by a judge constitute a sound basis for the exercise of his discretion and for dissenting from the court welfare officer's recommendation, the failure to state expressly his reasons for not following the latter's recommendation does not vitiate the decision. Normally, clear cut recommendations should only be rejected after hearing the welfare officer's oral evidence.[2] However, bearing in mind the principle of delay, it is within the court's power to depart from a recommendation even where the officer does not attend the hearing.[3]

1 *Re L (Residence: Justices Reasons)* [1995] 2 FLR 445; *Re T (A Minor) (Welfare Report Recommendation)* [1977] 1 FLR 59 and *Re W (Residence)* [1999] 2 FLR 390, [1999] 3 FCR 274, CA.
2 *Re CB (Access: Court Welfare Report)* [1995] 1 FLR 622, CA. See also *Re F (minors) (contact: appeal)* [1997] 1 FCR 523, CA and *Re W (residence)* [1999] 3 FCR 274, [1999] 2 FLR 390, CA.
3 *Re C (Section 8 Order: Court Welfare Officer)* [1995] 1 FLR 617, CA.

Legal Representation

10.35 Historically children who are parties to proceedings are regarded as being under a disability and must act through a next friend or guardian ad litem. In most cases that person will instruct a solicitor. In the High Court and in some county court cases the Official Solicitor has carried out both functions. CAFCASS has issued a *Practice Note*[1] in relation to that part of the Service which will provide legal advice and representation in much the same way as did the Children's Branch of the Official Solicitor's Department. It is known as CAFCASS Legal Services and Special Casework and deals with complex cases and those where a child requires representation.

1 *CAFCASS Practice Note, Officers of CAFCASS Legal Services and Special Casework: Appointment in Family Proceedings* [2001] 2 FCR 562; *Practice Note: The Official Solicitor: Appointment in Family Proceedings* [2001] 2 FCR 566.

Private family proceedings

10.36 Except as otherwise provided a child may begin and prosecute any family proceedings only by a next friend and may defend such proceedings only by a guardian ad litem.[1] In any family proceedings where it appears to the court that the child should be separately represented, the court has in the past appointed the Official Solicitor or some other proper person, provided in either case he consents to be the guardian ad litem of the child.[2] A solicitor on the Law Society Children Panel would be a proper person.[3] In such a case the child should be made a party. From 1 April 2001 where it is considered appropriate for the child to be made a party, the court will normally refer the matter to CAFCASS Legal.

1 FPR 1991, r 9.2 and still referred to as a guardian ad litem in this context.

2 FPR 1991, r 9.5 and see Practice Direction [1999] 1 FCR 1. This Practice Direction has now
   been superseded (see below).
3 *L v L (minors) (separate representation)* [1994] 1 FCR 890, [1994] 1 FLR 156, CA. See also
   Re K (Replacement of Guardian Ad Litem) [2001] 1 FLR 663.

10.37 CAFCASS has established CAFCASS Legal Services and Special
Casework (known as CAFCASS Legal) principally to take over the responsibilities of the Official Solicitor for representing children who are the subject
of family proceedings. The CAFCASS *Practice Note*[1] sets out guidance for
the work of this division. The involvement of CAFCASS Legal will generally
only arise where it appears to the court that the child ought to have party
status and be legally represented. CAFCASS Legal may not represent a child
in the family proceedings court. An officer of the Service may be authorised
to conduct litigation in relation to any proceedings in any court and to exercise a right of audience in any proceedings before any court in the exercise of
the functions of the Service.[2]

1 *CAFCASS Practice Note: Officers of CAFCASS Legal Services and Special Casework:
   Appointment in Family Proceedings* [2001] 2 FCR 562.
2 CJCSA 2000, s 15. The Government has undertaken that this power will only be used in lim-
   ited circumstances, so that most children will continue to be represented by an independent
   Children Panel solicitor, but the rule is clearly capable of wider application. See also
   'Comment', Hinchcliffe M, September [2001] Fam Law.

10.38 The cases which may require representation arise where the child
needs someone to orchestrate an investigation of the case on their behalf.[1]
Particular examples are where:

(a) there is a significant foreign element such as a challenge to the English
     court's jurisdiction or a need for enquiries to be conducted abroad;
(b) there is a need for expert medical or other evidence to be adduced on
     behalf of the child in circumstances where a joint instruction by the par-
     ties is impossible;
(c) where a child wants to instruct a solicitor direct but has been refused
     leave to instruct a solicitor in accordance with the Family Proceedings
     Rules 1991, r 9.2A;
(d) an application is made for leave to seek contact with an adopted child; and
(e) there are exceptionally difficult, unusual or sensitive issues (usually dealt
     with in the High Court) making it necessary for the child to be granted
     party status within the proceedings.

CAFCASS Legal may be invited to act or instruct counsel to appear as
amicus curiae in proceedings under the Act in which, in the opinion of the
court, an issue of general public importance has arisen or is likely to arise.

1 *Re A (Contact: Separate Representation)* [2001] 1 FLR 715.

Right of child to instruct solicitor

10.39 A child may begin, prosecute or defend proceedings under the
Children Act or the inherent jurisdiction with respect to children without a
next friend or guardian ad litem, where he has obtained the leave of the
court to do so, or where a solicitor considers that the child is able, having
regard to his understanding, to give instructions in relation to the proceedings and has accepted instructions from the child to act for him and where

the proceedings have begun is so acting.[1] Before granting leave to the child, the court had to be satisfied that the child had sufficient understanding to participate as a party in the context of the particular proceedings without a next friend or guardian ad litem.[2] Where the court considers that the child does not have the capacity, including where a solicitor's assessment of a child's capacity to instruct him is unsustainable, the court could appoint a next friend or guardian ad litem.[3] This will now be done by reference to CAFCASS Legal.[4]

1 FPR 1991, r 9.2A. See also 'Acting for Children': (Solicitors Family Law Association, 2002). Applications by a child for a s 8 order should be transferred to the High Court for hearing: Even though the child is competent to give instructions, the court may decline to give leave: *Practice Direction* [1993] 1 All ER 820, [1993] 1 FLR 668.
2 *Re S (A Minor) (Representation)* [1993] 2 FLR 437, CA; *Re H (A Minor) (Role of Official Solicitor)* [1993] 2 FLR 552; and *Re M (Minors)* [1994] 1 FLR 749.
3 FPR 1991, r 9.2A(10) and see *Re T* [1994] Fam 49, [1993] 2 FCR 445, sub nom *Re CT (A Minor) (Wardship Representation)* [1993] 2 FLR 278, CA.
4 See CAFCASS *Practice Note* [2001] 2 FCR 562.

Appointment of a solicitor for the child in specified proceedings

10.40 The guardian is required to appoint a solicitor to act for the child, unless already appointed, and shall instruct the solicitor on all matters relevant to the interests of the child, including appeal, in the course of proceedings.[1] Where the children's guardian is an officer of the Service authorised to conduct litigation, he is not required to instruct a solicitor if he intends to have conduct of the proceedings on behalf of the child, unless the child wishes to instruct a solicitor direct and the children's guardian or the court considers that he is of sufficient understanding to do so.[2] Notwithstanding the duty to instruct a solicitor, the Legal Services Commission may decide that the merits of a case do not warrant legal representation and refuse legal aid.[3] The court may appoint a solicitor if there is no guardian or if the child has sufficient understanding to instruct a solicitor and wishes to do so or if it appears to the court that it is in the child's interests for him to be represented by a solicitor.[4] Where it appears to the guardian that the child is instructing his solicitor direct, or intends to, and is capable of, conducting the proceedings on his own behalf, the guardian must inform the court. He then carries on with his duties, save for instructing the solicitor, but may, with leave, have legal representation.[5]

1 FPR 1991, r 4.11(2); FPC(CA 1989)R, r 11(2). See the Protocol for the Working Relationship between Children Panel solicitors and Guardians ad Litem (Law Society, March 2000).
2 FPR 1991, r 4.11A(2). But see para 10.37 fn 2.
3 While the LSC may seek to avoid public funding, they should take account of the mandatory requirement placed on the guardian to appoint a solicitor: *R v Legal Aid Board, ex p W* [2000] 3 FCR 352, [2000] 2 FLR 821 and Focus 32, September 2000.
4 CA 1989, s 41(3), (4). As a result of the shortage of guardians and the delay in their allocation, some courts are appointing solicitors who will conduct the case for the child on their own initiative pending instructions from a guardian: see 'The Dilemmas of a Panel Solicitor who has no Children's Guardian' Winter D, [2001] Fam Law 904.
5 FPR 1991, r 4.11A(3); FPC(CA 1989)R, r 11A(3).

Duties of the solicitor for the child

10.41 As for the children's guardian, the duties of a solicitor appointed to represent the child in specified proceedings are specific and they must:[1]

(a) act in accordance with instructions received from the children's guardian;
(b) conduct the proceedings in accordance with instructions received from the child, if the solicitor considers, having taken into account the views of the children's guardian and any direction of the court under the FPC(CA 1989)R, r 11A(3), that the child wishes to give instructions which conflict with those of the children's guardian and that he is able, having regard to his understanding, to give such instructions on his own behalf;
(c) act in accordance with instructions received from the child, if no children's guardian has been appointed for the child and the child has sufficient understanding to instruct a solicitor and wishes to do so;
(d) in default of any instructions, act in furtherance of the best interests of the child;[2]
(e) inform the court and other parties how the child was to be represented and what views he was expressing;[3] and
(f) not advance a local authority care plan when representing one child and at the same time represent a child, capable of giving instructions, who is opposed to the care plan.[4]

1   FPR 1991, r 4.12; FPC(CA 1989)R, r 12.
2   The solicitor for the child is not functus officio at the conclusion of proceedings and has a duty to consider the question of appeal and to serve notice of appeal if appropriate: *R v Plymouth Juvenile Court, ex p F* [1987] 1 FLR 169.
3   *Re M (minors) (care proceedings: child's wishes)* [1994] 1 FCR 866, [1994] 1 FLR 749.
4   *Re P (Minors) (Representation)* (1995) Times, 30 November.

Instructions from the child in specified proceedings

10.42   The solicitor should be careful to take full instructions from an intelligent and articulate, even though, disturbed child.[1] If a child is suffering emotional disturbance, his ability to instruct a solicitor depends on whether the level of disturbance is such as to remove the level of understanding required for giving rational instructions. If such a question arises it is a matter for expert opinion.[2]

1   *Re H (a minor) (care proceedings: child's wishes)* [1992] 2 FCR 330, [1993] 1 FLR 440.
2   *Re M (minors) (care proceedings: child's wishes)* [1994] 1 FCR 866, [1994] 1 FLR 749.

Termination of solicitor's instructions

10.43   Where the child or the children's guardian wishes an appointment of a solicitor to be terminated, he may apply to the court for an order terminating the appointment. The solicitor and the child or children's guardian shall be given an opportunity to make representations.[1] A solicitor whose firm had acted previously in unrelated matters for a party in family proceedings was not required to stand down unless there was a real risk of disclosure of confidential information.[2] Where solicitors representing parties in proceedings have a close personal relationship, one of them should stand down.[3]

1   FPR 1991, r 4.12; FPC(CA 1989)R, r 12(3).
2   *Re T and A* [2000] 1 FLR 859.
3   *Re L (Children) (Care Proceedings: Cohabiting Solicitors)* [2000] 3 FCR 71.

Attendance of child at hearings

10.44   The child is a party to specified proceedings, but has no absolute right to attend the hearing. The Rules provide[1] that it shall take place in the absence of the child if the court considers it in the interests of the child, having regard to the matters to be discussed or the evidence likely to be given, and the child is represented by a children's guardian or solicitor. It should not be routine practice for children to be in the court throughout care proceedings. Children's guardians should think carefully about arrangements for children to be present and be prepared to explain them to the court.[2] If a child is likely to be unruly the court could refuse to allow him to attend.[3] The decision whether or not to see the child is a matter for the discretion of the judge.[4]

1   FPR 1991, r 4.16(2); FPC(CA 1989)R 1991, r 16(2), (7).
2   *Re C (A Minor) (Care: Child's Wishes)* [1993] 1 FLR 832.
3   *Re W (A Minor) (Secure Accommodation Order: Attendance at Court)* [1994] 2 FLR 1092.
4   *Re C (Section 8 order: Court Welfare Officer)* [1995] 1 FLR 617 and *Re CB (Access: Court Welfare Report)* [1995] 1 FLR 622.

The Official Solicitor

10.45   Cases in which the Official Solicitor may represent children fall into two main groups. First there are those in which relief is sought for or against a child in general litigation (claims for damages, inheritance claims, construction summonses, etc). The Official Solicitor may then accept the client role and entrust the conduct of the proceedings on the child's behalf to solicitors in private practice. If a child's welfare is the subject of dispute and it is appropriate that the child should be separately represented, he may represent the child but only if the circumstances are exceptional and he has consulted with CAFCASS. He would then act not only as guardian ad litem but also as his own solicitor. The Official Solicitor will in the absence of another suitable person act as next friend or guardian ad litem of an adult party under a disability or a child party whose own welfare is not the subject of the proceedings.

1   See *Practice Note, The Official Solicitor: Appointment in Family Proceedings* [2001] 2 FCR 566; and *CAFCASS Practice Note: Officers of CAFCASS Legal Services and Special Casework: Appointment in Family Proceedings* [2001] 2 FCR 562.

Chapter 11

Evidence

INTRODUCTION

11.1 Evidence in proceedings relating to children raises complex issues. It is necessary to consider how the court is to be satisfied of the basis for making an order, the nature of evidence required by the courts, rules of evidence peculiar to children's proceedings, the sources of evidence, the way in which that evidence is obtained, in particular from experts, disclosure of information and documents for the purpose of proceedings, withholding of information or documents on the basis of confidentiality, privilege or self incrimination.

11.2 This chapter explores these issues as they have developed in proceedings under the Children Act. Although the principles have been considered primarily in the public law field, and indeed frequently in sex abuse cases, they are fundamentally the same and applicable to other types of harm, such as head injuries, and to private law cases where appropriate. The issues are:

(a) the basis for proving the case;
(b) evidence from experts;
(c) evidence from the child;
(d) disclosure of documents and information in proceedings:
  - general duty
  - reasons for withholding
  - public interest immunity
  - privilege
  - real harm to the child
  - immunity from self incrimination
  - disclosure to third parties
(e) disclosure where there are no proceedings.

PROVING THE CASE

11.3 Evidence in private and public law proceedings is likely to be a mixture of factual information, professional observation and expert opinion. It can be produced by way of written statement or oral evidence. It is likely to be accumulated over a period of time through assessment and questioning of the parties and the child outside of the hearing. As a result there is likely to be a substantial amount of hearsay evidence, especially in care proceedings.

11.4 The Children (Admissibility of Hearsay Evidence) Order 1993 provides that in civil proceedings before the High Court, county court and in 'family proceedings',[1] and civil proceedings under the CSA 1991 before a magistrates' court, evidence given in connection with the upbringing, maintenance or welfare of a child is admissible notwithstanding any rule of law relating to hearsay.[2] Hearsay evidence is also admissible under the Civil Evidence Act 1995 but there are procedural safeguards.[3] As a result the provisions appear to be little used in proceedings relating to children.

1 Defined for this purpose by the CA 1989, s 92(2).
2 SI 1993/621.
3 Section 1. For the implementation of these provisions in magistrates' courts see the Magistrates' Courts (Hearsay Evidence in Civil Proceedings) Rules 1999, SI 1999/681. Note also that a document which is shown to form part of the records of a public authority may be received in evidence in civil proceedings without further proof: s 9(1).

11.5 The weight to be given to hearsay evidence is a matter for the court, but under the Civil Evidence Act it must have regard to any circumstances from which any inference can reasonably be drawn as to the reliability or otherwise of the evidence,[1] and in particular to:

(a) whether it would have been reasonable and practicable for the party by whom the evidence was adduced to have produced the maker of the original statement as a witness;
(b) whether the original statement was made contemporaneously with the occurrence or existence of the matters stated;
(c) whether the evidence involves multiple hearsay;
(d) whether any person involved had any motive to conceal or misrepresent matters;
(e) whether the original statement was an edited account, or was made in collaboration with another or for a particular purpose; and
(f) whether the circumstances in which the evidence is adduced as hearsay are such as to suggest an attempt to prevent proper evaluation of its weight.

1 CEA 1995, s 4.

11.6 Subject to the following paragraph parties must file and serve on the parties and any welfare officer:

(a) written statements of the substance of the oral evidence which the party intends to adduce at the hearing or directions appointment; and
(b) copies of any documents, including experts' reports upon which the party intends to rely, at or by such time as the court directs.[1]

1 FPR 1991, r 4.17(1); FPC(CA 1989)R 1991, r 17(1).

11.7 In proceedings for a s 8 order no statement or copy may be filed until such time as the court directs,[1] and no file, document, information or statement, other than those required or authorised by the Rules, should be served or made without leave of the court. Subject to any direction of the court about the timing of statements, supplementary statements may be filed, as can, with leave, written amendments to the documents already served. Evidence or documents not filed in accordance with the Rules cannot be adduced or relied upon at the subsequent directions appointment or hearing without leave of the court: rr 4.17(4) and 17(4). For hearings preparation of court bundles is essential and regard should be had to *Practice Note (Case Management)*,[4] *B v B (Court Bundles: Video Evidence)*[5], *Practice Note*

(Family Proceedings: Court Bundles)[6] and *President's Direction: Judicial Continuity.*[7]

1 See rr 4.17(5) and 17(5)
2 See rr 4.17(4) and 17(4).
3 See rr 4.17(2), 4.19 and rr 17(2) and 19.
4 [1995] 1 All ER 586, [1995] 2 FCR 340, [1995] 1 FLR 456, see para 4.36.
5 [1994] 1 FCR 805, [1994] 1 FLR 323n.
6 [2000] 1 FCR 521, [2000] 1 FLR 536.
7 [2002] 2 FLR 367. See chapter 4 and p 729.

Burden of proof

11.8 The legal burden of establishing the existence of the threshold criteria rests on the applicant for a care order. The general principle is that he who asserts must prove. The applicant must establish the existence of the pre-conditions and the facts entitling him to the order he seeks.[1]

1 *Re H (Minors) (Sexual Abuse: Standard of Proof)* [1996] AC 563, [1996] 1 All ER 1, [1996] 1 FCR 509, HL.

Standard of proof

11.9 In care proceedings the court has to consider whether the child is suffering significant harm, what any harm is attributable to, what its likely effect is, and in relation to each decide whether the evidence is sufficient to justify the serious decision about the future of the child. The standard in civil proceedings is the balance of probabilities, as distinct from the criminal standard of beyond reasonable doubt. This has generally been interpreted as a 'more likely than not' test, especially in wardship proceedings. However the courts have been less than clear in deciding whether some additional test has to be applied, especially where a case is based on serious allegations.

11.10 Once the judge is satisfied that the child has suffered harm, it will usually be necessary to see whether it is possible to come to some conclusion as to the identity of the abuser or abusers, who may be another child or an adult, inside or outside the household. This will establish the test of whether the harm is attributable to parental care or a lack of it.

11.11 It is established by the House of Lords decision in *Re H*[1] that the standard of proof required in care proceedings is the balance of probability, which meant that a court was satisfied an event occurred if it considered that, on the evidence, the occurrence of the event was more likely than not. When assessing the probabilities the court should have in mind as a factor, to whatever extent was appropriate in the particular case, that the more serious the allegation, the less likely that the event occurred and, hence, the stronger should be the evidence before the court concluded that the allegation was established on the balance of probability. There remained in assessing the probability a generous degree of flexibility in respect of the seriousness of the allegation. This did not mean that where a serious allegation was in issue the standard of proof required was higher. It meant only that the inherent probability or improbability of an event was itself a matter to be taken into account when weighing the probabilities and deciding whether, on balance, the event occurred. The more improbable the event, the stronger must be the evidence that it did occur before, on the balance of probability, the occurrence would be established.

1   *Re H (Minors) (Sexual Abuse: Standard of Proof)* [1996] AC 563, [1996] 1 All ER 1, [1996] [1996] 1 FCR 509, HL. The same test should be applied to findings as to the threshold criteria and the question of whether a particular person is the perpetrator of harm: *Re G (a Child) (Non-Accidental Injury: Standard of Proof)* [2001] 1 FCR 97. See also para 8.60.

11.12   Where the court has correctly applied the test, it is not necessary to repeat the formulation for the standard of proof.[1] The criteria could be satisfied where, for example, the medical evidence has eliminated medical causes for a baby appearing nearly to have suffocated.[2] If one of two parents must have caused the injuries to a child but the court is unable to decide which on the *Re H* standard, the threshold criteria could still be satisfied on the basis that the child remains at risk of harm.[3] The opinion of an expert is by itself insufficient to satisfy the test.[4]

1   *Re L (Minors) (Sexual Abuse: Standard of Proof)* [1996] 1 FLR 116, CA.
2   *Re P (Emergency Protection Order)* [1996] 1 FLR 482; see also *Manchester City Council v B* [1996] 1 FLR 324.
3   *Re CB and JB (minors) (care proceedings: case conduct)* [1998] 2 FCR 313.
4   *Re M (Sexual Abuse Allegations: Interviewing Techniques)* [1999] 2 FLR 92.

11.13   The same standard of proof as in *Re H* applies to s 1(3)(*e*) when the court is considering any harm that the child is at risk of suffering.[1]

1   *Re M and R (Child Abuse: Evidence)* [1996] 2 FLR 195; and see *Re W (Residence Order)* [1999] 1 FLR 869.

Commentary

11.14   The recent increase in the number of care proceedings does not suggest that the standard has created major difficulties, although there may be a few isolated, single issue, cases where problems arise because there is no supporting evidence.[1] It is a matter for concern that practice experience suggests that sexual abuse is identified in fewer cases, at least until the behaviour of children becomes more seriously disturbed. Whether this comes about as a result of the reluctance of the courts to accept the evidence or the failure of professionals to evaluate the evidence adequately is not clear. The court must take a realistic view of the evidence, but if it is more likely than not that there has been no abuse, it is difficult to justify intervention.

1   See paras 8.51 and 8.73. For further review of the problems see: Hayes 'Reconciling protection of children with justice for parents in cases of alleged child abuse' [1997] 1 Legal Studies 1, Keating 'Shifting standards in the House of Lords – *Re H and others (Minors) (Sexual Abuse: Standard of Proof)* (1996) 8 CFLQ 157, Victor Smith, 'Sexual Abuse: Standard of Proof' [1994] Family Law 626 and John Spencer 'Evidence in child abuse cases – too high a price for too high a standard?' (1994) 6 JCL 160.

11.15   The test may present a greater problem in contact proceedings between parents where allegations of abuse cannot be proved to the satisfaction of the court, although the child appears to be convinced he has been abused. The court will deal with contact on the basis of its findings, which may be contrary to the beliefs of the child.[1]

1   See, for example, *Re M and R* [1996] 2 FCR 617.

Estoppel

11.16 The question arises as to the application of the doctrine of estoppel per rem judicatam in Children Act proceedings. In order to create an estoppel the judgment in the earlier action relied on as creating an estoppel must be:

(a) of a court of competent jurisdiction;
(b) final and conclusive;
(c) on the merits;
(d) the parties in the earlier action and those in the later action in which that estoppel is raised must be the same; and
(e) the issue in the later action in which the estoppel is raised must be the same issue as that decided by the judgment in the earlier action.[1]

This is consistent with the practical need for family courts to be cautious about allowing parties to litigate afresh issues of fact already determined.

1 *K v P (Children Act Proceedings: Estoppel)* [1995] 1 FLR 248.

11.17 Where a finding of abuse has been made against a party in previous proceedings, that party will rarely be allowed to challenge the finding in subsequent proceedings.[1] The court is not, however, bound by the doctrine of estoppel and has a discretion to decide whether issues should be reconsidered.[2]The court should bear in mind considerations of public policy such as:

* finality of litigation;
* the prejudicial effect of delay on the welfare of the child balanced against the likely effect of reliance on findings of fact that might turn out to have been erroneous;
* what form the previous hearings had taken;
* the importance of previous findings in the context of the present proceedings; and
* whether a rehearing of the issue would result in any substantially different finding.

1 *Re S, S and A (Care Proceedings: Issue Estoppel)* [1995] 2 FLR 244; *Re S (Minors) (Discharge of Care Order)* [1995] 2 FLR 639,CA; *C v Hackney London Borough Council* [1996] 1 FLR 427, CA; and *Re S (a minor) (contact: evidence)* [1998] 3 FCR 70.
2 *Re B (children act proceedings) (issue estoppel)* [1997] 1 FCR 477, [1997] 1 FLR 285.

11.18 In *Re D (a child) (threshold criteria: issue estoppel)*[1] the parties had entered into an agreement on a finding that a mother had failed to exercise proper supervision of her child. Subsequently in proceedings relating to a younger child, it was seen that the key question was whether she had been careless or a deliberate abuser. The Court of Appeal held that the court must retain a discretion to have the matter reopened and held that, the welfare of the child being the paramount consideration, the doctrine of estoppel had no application.

1 [2001] 1 FCR 124, CA. None of the earlier authorities appear to have been considered.

Covert video surveillance

11.19   Evidence may be obtained by covert video surveillance, for example if a parent is suspected of injuring a child.[1] Although it might be desirable to obtain the consent of the parent not suspected or the court, if there was a risk of more than transient harm, there should be no delay in operating the surveillance.[2] The Regulation of Investigatory Powers Act 2000, which seeks to ensure that investigatory powers are used in accordance with human rights, covers covert video surveillance. There are designated authorities empowered to carry out such investigations, including the police, local authorities and health authorities. The guidance suggests[3] that where there is any potential for use of covert video surveillance the police should be informed and, within the multi-agency team, take the lead in coordinating such action. Area Child Protection Committee procedures should include guidance on fabricated or induced illness in children and on the use of covert video surveillance.

1   See Safeguarding Children in whom Illness is Induced or Fabricated by Carers with Parenting Responsibilities: Supplementary Guidance to Working Together to Safeguard Children, Department of Health, Home Office and Department for Education and Skills, August 2002, paras 6.46–6.51. For earlier guidance see Guidelines for the multi-agency management of patients suspected or at risk of suffering from life threatening abuse resulting in cyanotic apnoeic episodes Staffordshire Area Child Protection Committee January 1994.
2   *Re DH (a minor) (child abuse)* [1994] 2 FCR 3,[1994] 1 FLR 679.
3   At paras 1.20 and 1.21.

Evidence

Evidence of harm

11.20   The following matters are typical of relevant evidence:

(a)   perpetrators' admission;
(b)   third party witness to ill-treatment;
(c)   physical indicators, through height or weight charts, X-rays;
(d)   behavioural indicators;
(e)   educational problems in school age children;
(f)   behaviour in older children;
(g)   expert opinion as to the nature and cause of harm;
(h)   opportunity and circumstances;
(i)   social assessment of family;
(j)   child's complaint eg to teacher, especially if spontaneous;
(k)   exposure to pornographic material especially involving children;
(l)   interview of the child; and
(m) family history.
Evidence should be regulated 'by way of weight rather than admissibility'.[1]

1   *H v West Sussex County Council* [1998] 1 FLR 862 and see para 11.04.

Certificate of conviction

11.21   A conviction is prima facie evidence of the offence to which it relates.[1] A father's conviction for violence against his child, for example, is admissible to prove the commission of that offence. A conviction may be proved by a certified extract from a court register.[2]

1   Civil Evidence Act 1968, s 11.
2   MCR 1981, SI 1981/552, r 68.

Expert evidence

11.22   Evidence from experts may be required in relation to the welfare of the child, the existence of specific harm, or as to its likelihood or its effect. If an allegation relates to ill-treatment, unless there is physical evidence, it is likely to depend on statements of the child. If the harm relates to health or development, expert opinion will be required as to existence of the harm, and how the child compares with a similar child. Whether the evidence comes from a social worker, health visitor, psychologist or child and family psychiatrist or other experienced person will depend on the expertise of the individual and the facts of the case.[1] Evidence of a diagnosis of sexual abuse calls for a very high level of expertise. For the court to rely on opinion evidence, even to admit it, the qualifications of the witness must extend beyond experience gained as a social worker and require clinical experience as or akin to a child psychologist or child psychiatrist.[2] The opinion of an expert, however eminent, is not sufficient, since ultimately findings are a matter for the court.[3]

1   As to experts generally, see Cross on Evidence (7th Edn, Butterworths, 1994) p 593. The Children Act Advisory Committee advised that all experts should have certain basic skills, which are set out in a core CV in the 1993/94 report at p 24. See also A Handbook for Expert Witnesses in Children Act Cases, Wall N and Hamilton I, (Family Law 2000); Expert Reporting in Public Law Cases: Position Statement of the Association of Directors of Social Services, published in 'Delight and Dole', eds Thorpe M and Cowton C, (Jordans 2002); Reporting to Court under the Children Act, Plotnikoff J and Woolfson R (Department of Health, 1996); Expert Evidence in Child Protection Litigation, Brophy J (Stationery Office, 1999) and Child Psychiatry and Child Protection Litigation, Brophy J (Gaskell, 2001).
2   *Re N (a minor) (child abuse: evidence)* [1996] 2 FCR 572, [1996] 2 FLR 214, CA.
3   *Re M and R (minors)* [1996] 2 FCR 617, [1996] 2 FLR 195, CA.

11.23   The need for there to be an impartial opinion will often arise and this cannot be provided by an expert who is treating the child or family. The role of the expert to treat must not be confused with the role of the expert to report. Instructions for a forensic report were impartial and, wherever possible, were joint and agreed with the other side, a unilateral appeal to an expert for a partial report. Although in *Re B*[1] Thorpe LJ stated that the treating clinician could make *no* forensic contribution, it must be doubted whether that can be taken literally. It may be essential for there to be evidence on the presenting medical history and diagnosis. An independent forensic expert, instructed jointly or by the guardian, can then comment on the diagnosis and such issues as reliability and suggestibility.

1   *Re B (Sexual Abuse: Expert's Report)* [2000] 2 FCR 8, [2000] 1 FLR 871, CA.

Leave for expert evidence

11.24   If the evidence to be given requires the child to be medically or psychiatrically examined or otherwise assessed, the leave of the court or the justices' clerk must be obtained.[1] Without leave no evidence arising out of the examination or assessment may be adduced.[2] Documents relating to the proceedings may be disclosed to an expert whose instruction by a party has been authorised by the court.[3]

1   FPR 1991, r 4.18(1), FPC (CA 1989) R 1991, r 18(1).
2   Above r 4.18(3), r 18(3).
3   R 4.23(1)(f).

11.25   The court has a proactive role in the grant of leave. The court has the duty to analyse the evidence and decide the areas in which expert evidence is necessary and both the power and the duty to limit expert evidence to given categories of expertise and to specify the numbers of experts to be called. The court should be proactive:

(a)   in laying down a timetable for the filing of evidence;
(b)   in making arrangements for the dissemination of reports; and
(c)   in giving directions for the experts to confer.[1]
The court should not give leave for an assessment, where there was no issue before the court on which the assessment was likely to assist.[2] Detailed guidance on the instruction of experts is given in the Handbook of Best Practice in Children Act Cases.[3] Parties should consider whether evidence can properly be obtained by joint instruction to an expert. This may put parents at a disadvantage if they are then constrained by the evidence of that expert. An alternative is to consider whether an expert should initially be instructed by the children's guardian. Parents will have to consider whether they would be permitted to obtain another report, if that report proved unacceptable. In any event a party instructing an expert should try to agree the terms of the letter of instruction and the letter should be in the court bundle.[4] All instructions to experts should be impartial.[5]

1   *Re G (minors)* [1994] 2 FCR 106, [1994] 2 FLR 291. See also *Practice Direction (Case Management)* [1995] 1 FLR 456 and *Re R (child abuse: video evidence)* [1995] 2 FCR 573, [1995] 1 FLR 451.
2   *Re F (a minor) (care proceedings: directions)* [1995] 3 FCR 601 and *H v Cambridgeshire County Council* [1996] 2 FLR 566.
3   Children Act Advisory Committee, June 1997. See also *Re CS (Expert Witnesses)* [1996] 2 FLR 115.
4   *Re CB and JB (minors) (care proceedings: case conduct)* [1998] 2 FCR 313.
5   *Re B (a minor) (sexual abuse: expert's report)* [2000] 2 FCR 8, [2000] 1 FLR 871, CA.

Commentary

11.26   All reports on the progress of the Children Act have concluded that delays in proceedings are compounded by the lack of availability of expert witnesses. This is in turn compounded by reluctance to accept the evidence of social workers, which in its turn has deteriorated with the decrease in their skills and numbers. It is a vicious circle. Following the Report on the Scoping Study[1] the Lord Chancellor's Department has announced its intention to track cases to seek to analyse where the problems arise and how they can be tackled.

1   Lord Chancellor's Department, March 2002.

The duties of expert witnesses

11.27 In *Re AB (Child Abuse: Expert Witnesses)*[1] Wall J, adopting the approach in commercial cases,[2] set out the duties and responsibilities of experts:

(1) Expert evidence presented to the court should be and should be seen to be the independent product of the expert uninfluenced as to form or content by the exigencies of litigation.
(2) An expert witness should provide independent assistance to the court by way of objective unbiased opinion in relation to matters within his expertise. An expert witness in the High Court should never assume the role of advocate.
(3) An expert witness should state the facts or assumptions on which his opinion is based. He should not omit to consider material facts which detract from his concluded opinion.
(4) An expert witness should make it clear when a particular question falls outside his expertise.
(5) If an expert's opinion is not properly researched because he considers that insufficient data is available then this must be stated with an indication that the opinion is no more than a provisional one.
(6) If after exchange of reports, an expert witness changes his view on a material matter, such change of view should be communicated . . . to the other side without delay and when appropriate to the court.
(7) Where expert evidence refers to photographs, plans, calculations . . . survey reports or other similar documents these must be provided to the opposite party at the same time as the exchange of reports.

1 [1995] 1 FLR 181. See also *Re R (A Minor) (Experts' Evidence)* [1991] 1 FLR 291n.
2 *National Justice Compania Naviera SA v Prudential Assurance Co Ltd, the Ikarian Reefer* [1993] 2 Lloyd's Rep 68.

11.28 In *Re AB* it was emphasised that experts have a privileged position as only they can give opinion evidence, and because they bring to court an expertise on which the court is dependent. They must only express opinions which they genuinely hold and which are not biased in favour of one party. If an expert does seek to promote a particular case, the report must make that clear, but that approach should be avoided. A misleading opinion may well inhibit a proper assessment of the case by non-medical professional advisers, increase costs and lead parties, and in particular parents, to false views and hopes.

11.29 Experts should be instructed to hold discussions with the other experts instructed in the same field. They may be able to prepare an agreed report, but if not they should set out in writing the areas of disagreement and give their opinions on the facts. A coordinator, either the guardian ad litem or the local authority, should collate expert reports.[1]

1 *Re C (Expert Evidence: Disclosure: Practice)* [1995] 1 FLR 204. See also *Re R (Child Abuse: Video Evidence)* [1995] 1 FLR 451. For a proposed form of directions see Children Act Advisory Committee Report 1993/94, p 26.

Evidence from the child

11.30 Although it is well established that the High Court and county court judges have the power to interview children in private, there are no specific rules governing when they should do so. In *Re R (A Minor) (Residence: Religion)*,[1] Balcombe LJ commented that 'a judge's decision whether or not personally to interview a child must above all be a question for the exercise of judicial discretion'.

1 [1993] 2 FLR 163, CA. For a case where it was held appropriate to see a child in private, see *Re F (Minors) (Denial of Contact)* [1993] 2 FLR 677, CA.

11.31 It is established that if a judge does interview a child in private he cannot promise confidentiality and for that very reason should be cautious in agreeing to see the child in such circumstances.[1] Before the CA 1989 it was established that magistrates had no powers to interview children in private,[2] but in *Re M (a minor) (justices' discretion)*[3] Booth J held that in exceptional circumstances magistrates could see a child in private.

1 Per Wall J in *B v B (Minors) (Interviews and Listing Arrangements)* [1994] 2 FLR 489 at 496, sub nom *B v B (minors: residence and custody orders)* [1994] 2 FCR 667 at 675, CA. See also *Elder v Elder* [1986] 1 FLR 610, CA.
2 *Re W (Minors)* (1980) 10 Fam Law 120; *Re T (A Minor) (Welfare Report Recommendations)* [1977] 1 FLR 59.
3 [1993] 2 FCR 721, [1993] 2 FLR 706. See also *Re W (child: contact)* [1993] 2 FCR 731, [1994] 1 FLR 843 and *Re K (A Minor) (Contact)* [1993] Fam Law 552.

11.32 If it is alleged that a child has been the victim of abuse, a child who is old enough may be the best source of information, especially in sexual abuse cases, where there is no physical evidence. The child's evidence may be heard directly by the court if, in its opinion, he understands that it his duty to speak the truth and he has sufficient understanding to justify his evidence being heard.[1] It is rare for a child to give evidence directly. If the child is too young or too frightened to give evidence, or where there has been a criminal investigation, hearsay evidence will be given by an interviewer, possibly in accordance with Achieving Best Evidence.[2]

1 CA 1989, s 96(2). The child should not be asked to swear an affidavit to boost the chances of a parent on an appeal: *Re M (a minor)* [1995] 2 FCR 90, CA.
2 Home Office, 2002, see para 7.16.

11.33 The following issues should be considered where evidence is being given by a witness of an interview with a child:[1]

- should the child be called to give evidence personally;
- has the child and/or a parent given informed consent to the interview;
- has the interview been video or audiotaped and is a transcript available, and if not why not;
- where appropriate has the leave of the court been given;
- what was the purpose of the interview: forensic, diagnostic, therapeutic;
- was/were appropriate person(s) conducting the interview: police, child psychiatrist, social worker and what was their experience;
- were the venue and time suitable; and
- how many and how long were the interviews;[2]

(It must be recognised that there is a danger of pressurising the child by lengthy or repeated interviews, and yet the child may not reveal the whole story on one occasion, and may only do so when she feels safe.)

- has there been a spontaneous statement by child;
- is the child's sexual knowledge appropriate to age and development;
- is there information suggestive of sexual knowledge or experience, eg smell, touch, pain;
- have there been leading or hypothetical questions, and if so were they inappropriate;[3]
- has the child been given an opportunity to deny that abuse has taken place or provide an alternative explanation of established facts;
- has the interviewer avoided presuming that abuse has taken place;[4]
- has the interviewer taken the child seriously, and not made promises about believing or not revealing what the child has said; and
- if dolls, puppets, drawings or other aids to communication have been used, has this been appropriate.

1 See generally *Re M (Sexual Abuse Allegations: Interviewing Techniques)* [1999] 2 FLR 92.
2 *H v H (Minor) (Child Abuse: Evidence)* [1990] Fam 86, [1989] 3 All ER 740, CA.
3 *C v C (Child Abuse: Access)* [1988] 1 FLR 462 at 465.
4 *Re E (a minor)* [1987] FCR 169, [1987] 1 FLR 269 and *Re D (Child Abuse: Investigation Procedure)* [1995] 3 FCR 581.

11.34 In the light of the standard of proof and the importance of not focussing exclusively on specific allegations, it is important for the court to be presented with a comprehensive picture about the child. Reliance solely on children's evidence can present problems of credibility, suggestibility, retraction and confusion of events and detail, especially where there have been delays. Nonetheless children are now not necessarily regarded as less reliable than adults, although the courts will exercise caution. The need for caution was emphasised in pre-Children Act proceedings, but the same principles still apply.

11.35 Although it is likely that evidence will be sought from a formal interview of the child, especially in view of the standard of proof in relation to allegations of abuse, other sources may still be relevant, in particular where they would contribute to a range of concerns about the care of the child. Although there was a sexual abuse context to the case, there is no reason why the observations of Butler-Sloss LJ should not remain relevant, when she said in *Re W (Minors) (Wardship: Evidence)*:[1]

'In wardship, therefore, the rules as to the reception of statements made by children to others, whether doctors, police officers, social workers, welfare officers, foster-mothers, teachers or others, may be relaxed and the information may be received by the judge. He has a duty to look at it and consider what weight, if any, he should give to it. The weight which he places upon the information is a matter for the exercise of his discretion. He may totally disregard it. He may wish to rely upon some or all of it. Unless uncontroversial it must be regarded with great caution. In considering the extent to which, if at all, a judge would rely on the statements of a child made to others, the age of the child, the context in which the statement was made, the surrounding circumstances, previous behaviour of the child, opportunities for the child to have knowledge from other sources, any knowledge, as in this case, of a child's predisposition to tell untruths or to fantasise, are among the relevant considerations.'

1 [1990] 1 FLR 203 at 214, CA. She referred to a number of decisions about the court's view of interviews with children for the purpose of 'disclosures'. See the [1987] Family Law Reports, principally, Latey J in *Re M (A Minor) (Child Abuse: Evidence)* [1987] 1 FLR 293n. Where an allegation was made by an adult in respect of incidents alleged to have occurred when the person was a child, oral evidence should normally be given by that person: *Re D (Sexual Abuse Allegations: Evidence of Adult Victim)* [2002] 1 FLR 723.

11.36 In relation specifically to sexual abuse great care will be exercised as the judge emphasised:

'Allegations of sexual abuse made in a statement by a child naming a perpetrator presented considerable problems and would, unsupported, rarely be sufficiently cogent and reliable for a court to be satisfied on the balance of probabilities, that the person named was the perpetrator. The evidence may, however, reveal a clear indication that the child has been exposed to inappropriate sexual activities and may be sufficiently compelling to satisfy the judge that the child has been subjected to serious sexual abuse.'[1]

1 *Re W*, supra.

11.37 The difficulties inherent in the investigation and proof of allegations of child sexual abuse have been highlighted in many cases which have considered the forensic implications of the therapeutic interviewing techniques sometimes used where children are alleged to have been sexually abused. The courts have frequently drawn attention to the Report of the Inquiry into Child Abuse in Cleveland 1987 known as 'The Cleveland Report',[1] for the guidance it contains on investigating allegations of sexual abuse.

1 HMSO 1988, CM 412. See *Re A (a minor) (child abuse: guidelines) (practice note)* [1992] 1 All ER 153, [1991] 1 WLR 1026.

11.38 In *Re M (minors)*[1] Butler-Sloss LJ said:

'It is important to draw distinctions between interviews with young children for the purposes of investigation, assessment and therapy. It would be rare, I would assume, that interviews for a specifically therapeutic purpose would be provided for use in court. Generally it is desirable that interviews with young children should be conducted as soon as possible after the allegations are first raised, should be few in number and should have investigation as their primary purpose. However, an expert interview of a child at a later stage, if conducted in such a way as to satisfy the court that the child has given information after acceptable questioning, may be a valuable part of the evidence for consideration as to whether abuse has occurred. No rigid rules can be laid down and it is for the court to decide whether such evidence is or is not of assistance.'

1 [1993] 1 FCR 253, [1993] 1 FLR 822, CA.

Recording interviews

11.39 The practice of video recording interviews of children now seems well established, especially if there is an allegation of a criminal offence. Provided they are conducted in accordance with guidance[1] they will be useful in civil proceedings, though there may be argument about how the interview is conducted, the value of what the video shows and its relevance to other evidence. Although the video is usually the property of the police, they can be required to produce it by sub poena duces tecum. It should be disclosed subject to proper controls about who has access to it.[2] The solicitor representing the child may be asked to co-ordinate the use of the video.[3]

1   Achieving Best Evidence (Home Office, 2002) see para 7.18.
2   *Re M (Child Abuse: Video Evidence)* [1995] 2 FLR 571. If the question of disclosure of the video and its transcript is not submitted promptly to the court for a decision, there may be a breach of Art 8: *TP and KM v United Kingdom* [2001] 2 FCR 289, ECtHR.
3   *Re R (Child Abuse: Video Evidence)* [1995] 1 FLR 451.

Witness credibility

11.40   An expert may give evidence of opinion as to the truthfulness of a witness or reporter of events which are in dispute but it is the judge's duty to decide whether or not a child should be believed.[1] It should be rare to extend this to a parent.[2] Earlier observations of the Court of Appeal made in relation to video recorded evidence[3] appear to remain relevant:

'(1)   The recording was admitted as a form of hearsay evidence. It was for the judge to decide its weight and credibility. He would judge the internal consistency and inconsistency of the story. He would look for any inherent improbabilities in the truth of what the child related and would decide what part, if any, he could believe.

(2)   The judge would receive expert evidence to explain and interpret the video. This would cover such things as the nuances of emotion and behaviour, the gestures and the body movements, the use or non-use of language and its imagery, the vocal inflections and intonations, the pace and pressure of the interview, the child's intellectual and verbal abilities, or lack of them, and any signs or the absence of signs of fantasising.

(3)   It was for the judge to separate admissible from inadmissible expert evidence. Proper evidence from an expert would be couched in terms that a particular fact was consistent or inconsistent with sexual abuse, and that it rendered the child's evidence capable or incapable of being accepted by the judge as true.'

1   *Re M and R (minors)* [1996] 2 FCR 617, [1996] 2 FLR 195, CA. See also *Re S and B (minors) (child abuse: evidence)* [1991] FCR 175, [1990] 2 FLR 489, CA and *Re FS (minors) (child abuse: evidence)* [1996] 1 FCR 666, [1996] 2 FLR 158, CA.
2   *Re CB and JB (minors) (care proceedings: case conduct)* [1998] 2 FCR 313.
3   *Re N (a minor) (child abuse: evidence)* [1996] 2 FCR 572, [1996] 2 FLR 214, CA.

Disclosure

General duty

11.41   'It is a duty owed to the court both by the parties and by their legal representatives to give full and frank disclosure . . . in all matters in respect of children.'[1] This duty of disclosure has to be considered in conjunction with the practical need to present the case in a way which is comprehensible to the court and fair to the parties.

1   *Practice Direction: Case Management* [1995] 1 FLR 456.

11.42   A local authority which brings care proceedings has a duty to disclose all relevant information in its possession or power which might assist parents to rebut allegations made against them. In *R v Hampshire County Council, ex p K*[1] a child who had allegedly been sexually abused was examined by a police surgeon who found no physical evidence of abuse but because of what the child had said, sexual abuse was suspected. After a further examination two months later, another paediatrician concluded there had been sexual abuse. The court held that local authorities:

'had a high duty in law, not only on grounds of general fairness but also in the direct interests of a child whose welfare they served, to be open in the disclosure of all relevant material affecting that child in their possession or power (excluding documents protected on established grounds of public immunity) which might be of assistance to the natural parent or parents in rebutting charges against one or both of them of in any way ill-treating the child'.

1 [1990] 2 QB 71, [1990] 2 All ER 129, [1990] 1 FLR 330.

11.43 More recently it has been noted by Charles J in *Re R (Care: Disclosure: Nature of Proceedings)*[1] that:

'there seems to be a general reluctance of many involved in family proceedings to disclose documents'. He noted that this was often 'incorrectly based on views relating to confidentiality and an assertion that records of the local authority are subject to public interest immunity'. He suggested that 'local authorities and guardians should be more willing than they seem to be to exhibit their notes of relevant conversations and incidents that are relied on for findings'. As he noted this is the practice which was formerly adopted by the Official Solicitor.

1 [2002] 1 FLR 755 per Charles J.

Reasons for withholding information – the local authority

PUBLIC INTEREST IMMUNITY

11.44 The House of Lords has held that in principle, social work and analogous records are immune from disclosure,[1] but there is no absolute rule providing immunity. If records appear to be protected by public interest immunity, the local authority should draw the existence of the document to the attention of the other parties, so that they can apply for it to be disclosed.[2] The difficulty is that the authorities do not state explicitly which records attract immunity. It would appear that the public interest immunity is based on the duty owed to children that what they say in confidence will not be disclosed without good reason. Ultimately the question of disclosure is a matter for the court and certainly a child should not be given an undertaking that what they say will remain confidential.[3]

1 *D v NSPCC* [1978] AC 178, HL a case which applied to immunity from disclosure of the identity of informants. In *Re R (Care: Disclosure: Nature of Proceedings)* [2002] 1 FLR 755 Charles J commented that any case on public interest immunity prior to *Wiley* in 1995 (see below) should be regarded with caution and carefully reconsidered.
2 *Re C (Expert Evidence: Disclosure: Practice)* [1995] 1 FLR 204.
3 *Re G (Minors) (Welfare Report: Disclosure)* [1993] 2 FLR 293, CA.

11.45 As a matter of practice non-disclosure of information by a professional to a parent and/or his legal advisors should only occur in exceptional cases and on the basis of the need not to disclose specific documents because of their contents rather than because of the type or class of document.[1] This is consistent with the Data Protection Act 1998, under which a parent would be entitled to disclosure of records relating to their child unless disclosure would be likely to cause serious harm.[2]

1 *R v Chief Constable of West Midlands Police ex parte Wiley; R v Chief Constable of Nottinghamshire Police ex parte Sunderland* [1995] 1 AC 274.
2 An individual is entitled to have communicated to him in an intelligible form personal data of which that individual is the data subject: DPA 1998, s 7. The Information Commissioner

takes the view that an individual can exercise parental responsibility in relation to his child in this regard. Data is exempt from disclosure if the supply of the information to the data subject would be likely to cause serious harm to his or any other person's physical or mental health or condition: Data Protection (Subject Access Modification) (Social Work) Order 2000, SI 2000/415. See also Data Protection (Subject Access Modification) (Health) Order 2000, SI 2000/413 and Data Protection (Subject Access Modification) (Education) Order 2000, SI 2000/414 for similar provisions.

11.46 The child's interests must be balanced against the principle of justice that parties are entitled to know the evidence in the case.[1] Although the right to a fair trial under Art 6 is absolute, that does not mean that there is an absolute and unqualified right to see all the documents. The interests of anyone who could demonstrate a right to family life under Art 8 were capable of denying a litigant access to documents.[2]

1 *Re M (Disclosure)* [1998] 2 FLR 1028, CA in which a guardian ad litem sought leave to withhold information from a mother and her legal advisers. The appropriate procedure in these cases is set out in *Re C (child cases: evidence and disclosure)* [1995] 2 FCR 97, [1997] 1 FLR 204.
2 *Re B (Disclosure to Other Parties)* [2001] 2 FLR 1017. This analysis was approved by the Court of Appeal in *Re X (Children) (Adoption Reports: Confidentiality)* [2002] All ER (D) 489 (May).

11.47 A children's guardian has the right to examine and take copies of any records held by a local authority or authorised person which were compiled in connection with the making or proposed making of an application under the Act with respect to the child concerned.[1] Any copy shall be admissible as evidence of the matter referred to,[2] and that rule applies regardless of any enactment or rule of law which would prevent the record being admissible.[3] The local authority should draw to the attention of the guardian any concerns within its records. If in the course of inspecting records, the guardian found relevant records which had not been disclosed, he should invite disclosure by the local authority. The guardian cannot disclose documents covered by public interest immunity and should seek an order of the court if necessary.[4]

1 Section 41(1).
2 Section 41(2).
3 Section 41(3)
4 *Re C (Expert Evidence: Disclosure: Practice)* [1995] 1 FLR 204. In *Re R (Care Proceedings: Disclosure)* [2000] 2 FLR 751, CA it was held that a children's guardian had the right to an area child protection committee report on the child's half-sibling.

11.48 Under the Civil Procedure Rules 1998 standard disclosure requires a party to disclose only a) the documents on which he relies; b) the documents which adversely affect his own or another party's case or support his own case; and c) documents which he is required to disclose by a relevant practice direction.[1] A person may apply, without notice, for an order permitting him to withhold disclosure of a document on the ground that disclosure would damage the public interest.[2] These rules do not apply to children's proceedings and the FPR 1991 have no similar provision but the principles are helpful. A local authority taking care proceedings does have a duty to disclose all relevant information which might assist parents to rebut allegations made against them, except that which is protected by public interest immunity. If records appear to be covered by public interest immunity, the local authority should draw the existence of the document to the other parties, so that they can apply for it to be disclosed.[3]

1   CPR 1998, r 31.6.
2   Above, r 31.19.
3   *Re C (Expert Evidence: Disclosure: Practice)* [1995] 1 FLR 204.

11.49   Where an application for disclosure is made the court must exercise its discretion by carrying out a balancing exercise between the public interest in protecting the confidentiality of social work records and the public interest in the fair administration of justice, so that a party may have access to information he requires to obtain legal redress. The party seeking disclosure must establish that production of the documents, otherwise covered by public interest immunity, is necessary (ie that they are relevant, material and admissible) as containing material of real importance to him.[1] The court may inspect the documents in order to decide whether to order disclosure.

1   *Re M (A Minor) (Disclosure of Material)* [1990] 2 FLR 36. In *Re R (Care Disclosure: Nature of Proceedings)* [2002] 1 FLR 755, Charles J commented that this decision should now be treated with caution.

11.50   While issues of public interest immunity in children's cases will usually relate to local authority records, the issue may also apply to documents in the possession of the police or Crown Prosecution Service,[1] for example as a result of sharing of information under child protection procedures. Disclosure of confidential adoption records raises separate considerations.[2]

1   *Nottinghamshire County Council v H* [1995] 1 FLR 115.
2   *Re K (Adoption: Disclosure of Information)* [1997] 2 FLR 74.

11.51   Guidance as to the procedure where documents may be subject to public interest immunity is set out in *Re C (Expert Evidence: Disclosure: Practice)*:[1]

> 'It is the responsibility of the local authority actively to consider what documents they have in their possession which are or may be relevant to the issues as they affect the child, its family and any other person who is relevant in regard to an allegation of significant harm, and to the care and upbringing of the child in the context of the welfare check-list issues. The local authority should not content themselves with disclosing the documents which support their case, but must consider themselves under a duty to disclose in the interests of the child and of justice documents which may modify or cast doubt on their case. The particular concern should relate to those documents which actually help the case of an opposing party. If there is any doubt about whether the information is relevant, consideration should be given to notifying the affected parties of the existence of the material. Whilst the temptation to invite costly, intrusive and pointless fishing expeditions should be avoided, there should be a presumption in favour of disclosure of potentially helpful information. If documents are obviously relevant and not protected from disclosure by public interest immunity, then the local authority should initiate disclosure. The parties should endeavour to agree some sensible arrangement for the costs incurred in photocopying of documents.
>
> If documents are apparently relevant but appear to be protected by public interest immunity from disclosure, a letter should be written by the local authority to the parties' legal advisers and to the guardian drawing general attention to the existence of the documents and inviting an application to the court if disclosure of the relevant documents is required.
>
> In all cases it is particularly important that the local authority should draw the guardian ad litem's attention to any matters of concern within the documents. Whilst it is the court's task to decide any contested disclosure matter, the guardian ad litem's full knowledge of the material may enable him to assist the court as to its relevance.'

1   [1995] 1 FLR 204.

11.52 'It is a fundamental principle of fairness that a party is entitled to the disclosure of all materials which may be taken into account by the court when reaching a decision adverse to that party.'[1]

1   *Re D (Minors) (Adoption Reports: Confidentiality)* [1996] AC 593, [1996] 1 FCR 205.

REAL HARM

11.53 Although evidence filed in proceedings relating to children should normally be disclosed to the parties, the court has a long established power to withhold evidence from a party in exceptional cases.[1] In *Re M (A Minor) (Disclosure of Evidence)*[2] the Court of Appeal held that the test is whether real harm to the child would ensue. In *Re B (Disclosure to Other Parties)*[3] it was held that although under Art 6 a litigant was prima facie entitled to disclosure of all materials which might be taken into account by the court, the rights of other parties to the proceedings, including children, had to be afforded due respect. Non-disclosure had to be limited to what the situation demanded. The court had to be rigorous in its examination of the feared harm.

1   *Official Solicitor v K* [1965] AC 201, applied in *Re B (A Minor) (Disclosure of Evidence)* [1993] Fam 142, [1993] 1 All ER 931, CA and *Re C (A Minor) (Irregularity of Practice)* [1991] 2 FLR 438.
2   [1994] 1 FLR 760.
3   [2001] 2 FLR 1017.

Commentary

11.54 Although historically the case law has encouraged the withholding of social work records, the authorities have recently moved in the direction of requiring specific justification for non-disclosure, which should be based on serious harm to the child. This is a development to be welcomed, since it is consistent with a more open approach to work with parents and a fairer basis for the conduct of cases. This does bring together the principles of the Data Protection Act and is consistent with Art 6 of the European Convention. Nonetheless the courts will have to ensure that this approach is not used as an excuse to conduct a fishing expedition of records looking for the slightest inconsistency nor an opportunity to flood the court with a volume of irrelevant material.

Withholding information – by parents

11.55 Material held by or on behalf of parents may come within a number of categories:

(a) reports prepared on their behalf with or without the permission of the court and whether specifically for the purpose of children's or other proceedings;
(b) communications between client and solicitor;
(c) statements or admissions made by parents in the course of investigations for the purposes of the proceedings in respect of themselves or others; and
(d) material acquired by the solicitor in the course of representation of the client.

11.56 The Practice Direction on Case Management[1] requires disclosure by all parties and their legal advisers but consideration has to be given as to the extent this applies to parents in relation to whether:

(a) disclosure can and should be ordered by the court for the purposes of children's proceedings; and
(b) disclosure can and should be ordered to a third party for other purposes, such as criminal proceedings.

1 [1995] 1 FLR 456.

11.57 The extent of the duty of the parents or their advisers to disclose material in their possession has been the subject of much litigation. It was held in *Barking and Dagenham London Borough Council v O*[1] that parties could only be required to disclose reports on which they were intending to rely. Subsequently it was held in *Essex County Council v R (Legal Professional Privilege)*[2] that legal representatives having reports relevant to the determination of a matter concerning children, but contrary to the interests of their client, had a positive duty to disclose the reports to all the parties and to the courts. In *Oxfordshire County Council v M*[3] the Court of Appeal approved the Essex decision, but the case concerned the disclosure of experts' reports obtained in care proceedings. That left open the question of reports in the parties' possession not obtained with the leave of the court or for the purpose of other proceedings. In *Vernon v Bosley (No 2)*[4] Thorpe LJ confirmed his approach when he stated: 'The court's inquiry cannot be deflected, inhibited or disadvantaged by litigation privilege.'

1 *Barking and Dagenham London Borough Council v O* [1993] Fam 295, [1993] 4 All ER 59,[1993] 2 FLR 651.
2 *Re R (a minor) (disclosure of privileged material)* [1993] 4 All ER 702, sub nom *Essex County Council v R* [1994] Fam 167,[1993] 2 FLR 826.
3 [1994] Fam 151, [1994] 2 All ER 269, [1994] 1 FLR 175.
4 [1999] QB 18.

11.58 In *R v Derby Magistrates' Court, ex p B*[1] the House of Lords were considering the privilege attaching to communications between solicitor and client and held that 'no exception should be allowed to the absolute nature of legal professional privilege once established'. In *Re L (a Minor) (Police investigation: Privilege)*[2] the House of Lords held by a majority that there was a distinction between legal professional privilege attaching to communications between solicitor and client and that attaching to reports by third parties prepared on the instructions of a client for the purposes of litigation and upheld their disclosure. The European Court of Human Rights upheld[3] the House of Lords decision in *Re L* by ruling inadmissible a claim that the requirement to disclose an adverse medical report in Children Act proceedings was a breach of Art 6 of the Convention (right to a fair trial).

1 [1996] AC 487, [1995] 4 All ER 526, HL.
2 [1997] AC 16, [1996] 2 All ER 78, HL.
3 *L v United Kingdom (disclosure of expert evidence)* [2000] 2 FCR 145, ECtHR.

11.59 In *S County Council v B*[1] Charles J, in a detailed study of the law in this area, considered the potential conflict between the principles in *Re L* and the *Derby Magistrates' Court* case. He considered that the *Derby* case applied both to privilege between solicitor and client, and to communications with third parties for the purposes of litigation, the latter known as 'litigation privilege'. He interpreted *Re L* as a case in which litigation privilege never arose. He defined the ratio of the case as follows:

'In proceedings under Pt IV of the CA 1989 where the welfare of children is paramount and thus the proceedings are essentially non-adversarial, legal professional privilege does not arise in respect of the reports of an expert based on the papers disclosed in the proceedings and which the court has given leave to a party to disclose to that expert.'

Accordingly he held that the absolute right to legal professional privilege meant that a father, who had instructed different medical experts in criminal proceedings from those in the care proceedings, could refuse and should not be ordered to disclose any communications with, and the reports of, those medical experts, nor even to disclose the names of the experts he instructed for the purpose of the criminal proceedings.

1   [2000] 1 FCR 536, [2000] 2 FLR 161, FD. Charles J regarded the observations of Thorpe LJ in *Vernon v Bosley*, cited in para 11.57, as obiter. For consideration of this problem see 'Legal Professional Privilege in Children Act Cases', Power E, Fam Law [2002] 465.

11.60   Threats of criminal acts do not come within the scope of legal professional privilege.[1] An affidavit sworn by a husband's former solicitors in support of their application to be removed from the record could be used by the wife in proceedings relating to the welfare of the child, even though the affidavit had been sent to the solicitors inadvertently, because it showed the husband had made grossly indecent, obscene and menacing statements in telephone calls to his solicitors.

1   *C v C (evidence: privilege)* [2001] 1 FCR 756, [2001] 2 FLR 184, CA.

11.61   In practice it may be academic whether the court can order disclosure. An expert who had provided a report could be subpoenaed, provided his identity was known, and would be in difficulty declining to answer questions. If a party knows of the existence of reports, it is unlikely that the other will decline to produce them, if parenting competence is in question. If reports are withheld, the court may draw its own conclusions. The difficulty arises where documents are in the possession of solicitors, unknown to other parties. Thorpe J gave a clear view in the Essex case that the duty to the child overrode professional confidence.[1] In *S County Council v B* Charles J expressed the view that this was limited to those reports which had been prepared for proceedings relating to the child. For practitioners there remains uncertainty. It is suggested that this can only be resolved by recourse to the principles set out below.[2]

1   See also *Re DH (A Minor)* [1994] 1 FLR 679; *Re A and B (Minors) (No 2)* [1995] 1 FLR 351 and *Oxfordshire County Council v P* [1995] 1 FLR 551.
2   See para 11.82.

Court ordered disclosure for other proceedings

11.62   There have been similar difficulties in settling the issue of whether material which might be useful for purposes other than the care proceedings should be disclosed. This can arise in two ways, either through material which has been filed in the children proceedings, or through statements which might be made if the parents could be confident that they would not be disclosed, for example to the police for the purposes of investigation of an alleged crime. There are two relevant statutory provisions.

11.63 No document, other than a record of an order, held by a court and relating to relevant proceedings shall be disclosed, other than to a party, the legal representative of a party, the children's guardian, the Legal Services Commission, or a CAFCASS officer, without leave of the court.[1] The purpose of the rule is to impose confidentiality on the parties so that no improper disclosure of documents is made to a third party. The rule applies generally, whether proceedings are pending or concluded.[2]

1   FPR 1991, rr 4.23(1) and 10.20(3); FPC (CA 1989) R 1991, r 23(1).
2   *Re A (a minor) (disclosure of medical records to the GMC)* [1999] 1 FCR 30.

11.64 In any proceedings under Pts IV or V of the CA 1989, no person shall be excused from giving evidence on any matter or answering any question put to him in the course of his giving evidence, on the ground that doing so might incriminate him or his spouse of an offence.[1] A statement or admission made in such proceedings shall not be admissible in evidence against the person making it or his spouse in proceedings for an offence other than perjury.[2] This section was intended to protect parents against incriminating themselves or their spouses when giving evidence in civil proceedings, so as to encourage them to be truthful, without exposing themselves to prosecution.

1   Section 98(1).
2   Section 98(2).

11.65 In *Oxfordshire County Council v P*[1] Ward J (as he then was) held that statements made to a guardian ad litem in the course of her enquiries come within the term 'statement or admission' in s 98 and should not be disclosed to the police without the leave of the court. He suggested that 'a practice could quickly be developed permitting the free exchange of information between the social services and police on a basis that the information was treated by the police as confidential and might be used for investigation but not as evidence in any criminal proceedings which might follow, and if the police wished to use as evidence information arising in care proceedings they must seek the court's leave'.

1   [1995] 1 FLR 552.

11.66 In *Cleveland County Council v F*[1] Hale J held that this approach should extend to statements made to social workers in the course of their investigations. She expressed the hope that this afforded parents protection and an incentive to co-operate with the investigation and assessment in the interests of the children. If the parents were married, the protection extended to the spouse. In the Cleveland case they were not and the mother sought an order of the court that any statement she might make should be protected from disclosure.

1   [1995] 2 All ER 236. See also *Re G (minor) (social worker: disclosure)* [1996] 2 All ER 65, [1996] 1 FLR 276.

11.67 In *Re L (A Minor) (Police investigation: Privilege)*[1] the House of Lords considered s 98. It was said that the court should not make an order for disclosure, compliance with which was likely to involve the danger of self-incrimination. On the other hand it was also said that it would be most unsatisfactory if the court had information that a mother might have a committed a serious offence against a child but was disabled from disclosing such information to an investigating authority.

1   [1997] AC 16, [1996] 2 All ER 78, HL.

11.68   The Court of Appeal has now held[1] that s 98(2) only gave protection against statements being admissible evidence in criminal proceedings (unless for perjury). This did not cover a police enquiry into the commission of an offence. Nothing in the subsection detracted from the power of the judge to order disclosure of any part of the proceedings in appropriate circumstances, including material covered by s 98(2). The judge should consider:

(a)   the welfare and interest of the child concerned and of other children generally;
(b)   the maintenance of confidentiality in children's cases and the importance of encouraging frankness;
(c)   the public interest in the administration of justice and the prosecution of serious crime;
(d)   the gravity of the alleged offence and the relevance of the evidence to it;
(e)   the desirability of co-operation between the various agencies concerned with the welfare of children;
(f)   fairness to the person who had incriminated himself and any others affected by the incriminating statement; and
(g)   any other material disclosure which had taken place.

1   *Re C (A Minor) (Care Proceedings: Disclosure)* [1997] Fam 76, [1996] 2 FLR 725. *See also Oxfordshire County Council v L and F* [1997] 1 FLR 235, *Re B (Hearing in Open Court)* noted at [1997] Fam Law Brief 508 where Hale J refused the application of the Crown Prosecution Service that a case should be heard in open court, so that the police could hear the evidence to enable the prosecution to consider more fully the criminal case against the father; and *Re L (Care: Confidentiality)* [1999] 1 FLR 165 where Johnson J commented that the protection provided by s 98(2) could not be absolute and might offend against the requirements of a fair trial under art 6 of the European Convention on Human Rights. See *Re W (Minors) (Social Workers: Disclosure)* 1999] 1 WLR 205, [1998] 2 FCR 405, CA, where leave was given for the police to have a copy of an assessment report from child protection investigations which had been filed with the court and *Re M (disclosure: police investigation)* [2002] 1 FCR 655, [2001] 2 FLR 1316 for a case in which the court decided that the balance was tipped against disclosure of incriminating statements made by the mother in the course of care proceedings.

11.69   If the police want disclosure of potentially incriminating statements, they have to apply to the court hearing the care proceedings. The court will then have to carry out the exercise of balancing competing public interests to ensure that justice is served in the circumstances of the particular case. It is debatable whether the original purpose of the section can be achieved and whether the protection now afforded by s 98 will encourage candour on the part of parents. Casual or unguarded statements made to the guardian or social worker, or indeed doctor, may be protected from use as evidence in a prosecution but still be used for investigation. Parents who fear a criminal prosecution are unlikely to make statements on the subtle basis that they could be used for investigation but not for evidence in criminal proceedings. A solicitor advising a parent would be failing in his duty not to advise of the risks in speaking to anyone, no matter what the purpose of the interview.

11.70 The Family Proceedings Rules require an application for disclosure in other circumstances and require the court to consider whether disclosure is appropriate. These circumstances include:

- the address of the parent, even though that person has been found in care proceedings to have abused a child;[1]
- any transcript of the oral evidence and of the judgment, all medical evidence given in the case, any of the child's medical records submitted in the proceedings, copies of all material supplied to doctors to enable them to prepare their reports and give evidence, and any other document on the court file;[2]
- the disclosure of a document prepared by an officer of CAFCASS for the purpose of enabling a person to perform inspection functions or assisting a CAFCASS officer appointed by the court under any enactment to perform statutory functions. Disclosure of any document relating to proceedings by one CAFCASS officer to another is permitted, unless that other officer is involved in the same proceedings on behalf of a different party.[3]

Where a report has been filed in one set of civil proceedings, it may be disclosed in another.[4]

1 *Re V (sexual abuse: disclosure); Re L (sexual abuse: disclosure)* [1999] 1 FCR 308, [1999] 1 FLR 267.
2 *Re A (a minor) (disclosure of medical records to the GMC)* [1999] 1 FCR 30. See also *A County Council v W (Disclosure)* [1997] 1 FLR 574, [1996] 3 FCR 728 for a case relating to disciplinary proceedings before the General Medical Council and *Re L (Care Proceedings: Disclosure to Third Party)* [2000] 1 FLR 913: disclosure of the court's judgment, expert medical reports and minutes of the experts' meetings, was allowed to the UK Central Council for Nursing, Midwifery and Health Visiting where the mother was a nurse who had been deprived of caring for her own child. The court may attach conditions to an order for disclosure: *A Health Authority v X* [2002] EWCA Civ 2014, [2002] 1 FLR 1045.
3 FPR 1991, r 4.23, FPC (CA 1989) R 1991, r 23. The Court of Appeal held in *Re M (a child) (disclosure: children and family reporter)* [2002] All ER (D) 482 (Jul) that where a Children and Family Reporter had concerns about child abuse he did not have to seek the permission of the court before acting on the concerns and reporting them to social services. Documents may be disclosed to an expert whose instruction by a party has been authorised by the court.
4 *Re C (A Minor) (Disclosure of Adoption Reports)* [1994] 2 FLR 525.

Disclosure where there are no proceedings

11.71 *Working Together* comments:

'Professionals can only work together to safeguard children if there is an exchange of relevant information between them.'[1]

Disclosure should be appropriate for the purpose and only to the extent necessary to achieve that purpose.[2] In child protection work the degree of confidentiality will be governed by the need to protect the child.[3] Social workers and others working with a child and family must make clear to those providing information that confidentiality may not be maintained if the withholding of the information will prejudice the welfare of a child. *Working Together* recommends information sharing protocols,[4] while requiring regard for the law.[5]

1 *Working Together under the Children Act 1989*, para 7.29 (The Stationery Office, 1999), which notes Re G [1996] 2 All ER 65.

2   See para 7.36.
3   See paras 7.22 and 7.23.
4   See para 7.31 and App 4.
5   In *Re W (Minors) (Social Workers: Disclosure)* [1999] 1 WLR 205, [1999] 2 FCR 405, CA, it was pointed out that notes and preparatory documents in child protection investigations, while covered by confidentiality, could be shared with the police as part of the co-operation required by Working Together but the court's leave was required for an assessment report filed with the court.

11.72   All the professional bodies have published guidance on the disclosure of confidential information, which in general terms provide for disclosure only where the person to whom the confidence is owed has given consent to disclosure or there is an order of the court or there is an overriding need for disclosure in the public interest, which includes the prevention of child abuse[1].

1   See for example *Confidentiality* (General Medical Council, 1995) and *Guidelines for Professional Practice* (United Kingdom Central Council for Nursing, Midwifery and Health Visiting, 1996). See also *Child Protection: Medical Responsibilities* (HMSO, 1994); and see *Re A (a minor) (disclosure of medical records to the GMC)* [1999] 1 FCR 29.

11.73   In spite of the general principle that information should be shared to protect children, the Court of Appeal has held that a local authority has no duty to disclose to another local authority the name of a person found in care proceedings to have abused a child, and accordingly his address would not be disclosed by the court.[1]

1   *Re V (Sexual Abuse: Disclosure)*; *Re L (Sexual Abuse: Disclosure)* [1999] 1 FLR 267.

11.74   Records of allegations of abuse held by the police and/or a local authority may be subsequently disclosed where it was genuinely and reasonably believed that this was necessary to protect children.[1] Such disclosure should only take place if there was 'a pressing need' for it, having taken into account relevant considerations of the authority's belief as to the truth of the allegations, the interest of the third party in obtaining the information, and the degree of risk posed if the information is not disclosed.[2] Principles on disclosure of such sensitive information are established by Data Protection (Processing of Sensitive Personal Data) Order 2000.

1   *R v Local Authority in the Midlands, ex p LM* [2000] 1 FCR 736,[2000] 1 FLR 612, QBD; following *R v Chief Constable of North Wales Police, ex p AB* [1998] 3 FCR 371 and *Woolgar v Chief Constable of the Sussex Police* [1999] 3 All ER 604. See also *Re C (sexual abuse: disclosure)* [2002] EWCH 234 (Fam), [2002] 2 FCR 385.
2   *R v Chief Constables of C and D, ex parte A* [2001] 2 FCR 431, where it was held that the police were justified in passing information to another police force about their investigation of alleged sexual offences by a schoolteacher, even though he was not prosecuted. A duty of care is still owed to the suspected abuser as well as the child: *L v Reading Borough Council* [2001] EWCA Civ 346, [2001] 1 FCR 673.

Disclosure by solicitors

11.75   Guidance has been given by the Law Society on cases where a solicitor receives information from a client which is or might be privileged, but which if revealed might protect a child from harm. The following guidance sets out general principles to which a practitioner should have regard. The guidance is also applicable in child abduction cases.

'General principles:
(1) The Law Society committees take the view that child abduction is merely one example of child abuse and, therefore, any guidance given applies equally to cases of abuse and abduction.
(2) A solicitor has two basic duties to a client, whether parent or child:

The duty to act in the client's best interests

Clearly, the nature of this duty depends on who the client is. In considering the duty to act in the client's best interests, the solicitor will need to draw a distinction between those children who are competent to give instructions and those who are not. A child who is competent to give instructions should be represented in accordance with those instructions. If a child is not competent to give instructions the solicitor should act in the child's best interests.

The duty of confidentiality

A number of preliminary points can be made before considering how the situation is affected by the question of who the client is:
(1) Is the information confidential? It has been held at common law that when communications are made by a client to his or her solicitor before the commission of a crime, for the purpose of being guided or helped in the commission of it, this constitutes a move outside the solicitor/client relationship and any communications made are not confidential and the solicitor is free to pass them on to a third party. The solicitor will, therefore, need to consider whether or not the proposed action is in fact a crime and reference should be made to the appropriate provisions, for example the common law offence of kidnapping or the provisions of the CAA 1984 and the CACA 1985 and provisions relating to child abuse.[1]
(2) Assuming that the information received is confidential, which will usually be the case, a solicitor also has a duty to the court (as opposed to the client). As a result, the solicitor may still be ordered by the court to disclose the information – for instance in a wardship case.[2] In all cases it is the solicitor's duty not to mislead the court.[3]
(3) In circumstances other than those outlined above the committees are in favour of the principle of absolute confidentiality being maintained save in truly exceptional circumstances. Any solicitor considering the disclosure of confidential information, should bear in mind that he or she is bound by a duty of confidentiality and may only be entitled to depart from this duty in exceptional circumstances.
In considering what might constitute exceptional circumstances a solicitor must consider what would be in the public interest. There is a public interest in maintaining the duty of confidentiality. Without this, the public interest in being able to confide in professional advisers would be harmed and the duty of confidentiality would be brought into disrepute. There is also a public interest in protecting children at risk from serious harm. Only in cases where the solicitor believes that the public interest in protecting children at risk outweighs the public interest in maintaining the duty of confidentiality does the solicitor have a discretion to disclose confidential information.
(4) If a solicitor, having considered the arguments set out above, feels that he or she may be entitled to disclose confidential information he or she should, in addition, consider the following points:
(a) is there any way of remedying the situation other than revealing the information? If so, thought should be given as to whether this course would have the desired effect of protecting the child and, if so, whether it should be taken;
(b) if the information is or is not disclosed, will the solicitor involved be able to justify his or her actions if called upon to do so by the court or Solicitors Complaints Bureau? Before revealing any information a junior solicitor or

member of the solicitor's staff should always consult with his or her principal on the appropriate course of action to take.'

1   This may be better described as a move outside the relationship of privilege: see, for example, *C v C (Evidence: Privilege)* [2001] 1 FCR 756, [2001] 2 FLR 184, CA at para 11.60.
2   *Ramsbottom v Senior* (1869) LR 8 Esq 575 (Rayden and Jackson on Divorce and Family Matters, 17th edn), para 42.22.
3   Chapter 14 of the Guide to the Professional Conduct of Solicitors.

'Who is the client?

Five different situations have been considered:

An adult

(1)   An adult (parent or otherwise) who is not an abuser but is asserting that a third party is abusing a child. In this situation a solicitor's duty to act in the best interests of his client might entail suggesting that the client alerts a relevant agency, for example the police or a social services department, him or herself or accepting instructions to do so. If the client does not wish to alert a relevant agency or does not give the solicitor instructions to do so, the solicitor must accept the client's decision and may remain bound by the duty of confidentiality. A solicitor in this position should explain the legal position and can seek to persuade the client to disclose the abuse or allow the solicitor to do so. If the client refuses to follow either of these courses of action, the solicitor may still exercise his or her discretion and reveal the information. This will only be the case if the public interest in revealing the information outweighs that of keeping it confidential.

(2)   An adult who is abusing or whom the solicitor believes will abuse a child. Where the client is an abuser or potential abuser it becomes necessary to consider not only the duty to act in the client's best interests and the duty of confidentiality, but also whether or not any distinction should be made between continuing and future abuse and how and when a solicitor should explain his duty of confidentiality and any possible limitations to it.

Where a client is continuing to commit an offence or is proposing to commit an offence, the duty to act in the client's best interests means that a solicitor should explain the legal implications of what a client has done, is doing or is proposing to do. For example, a client who tells a solicitor that he has or is proposing to abduct a child should be told about the common law offence of kidnapping, the provisions of the CAA 1984, the CACA 1985 and the client's duty to obey orders of the court, if there are any which are relevant. Similar steps should be taken in relation to cases of child abuse.

In the case of future abuse if, after receiving the solicitor's advice on the legal position, the client is dissuaded from his criminal course of action the solicitor's duty of confidentiality is absolute. In the case of a continuing offence, which as a result of the advice then ceases, this is equally the case.

In the case of a continuing crime which does not cease as a result of the advice given, or a future crime which the solicitor understands from the client may or will take place, the solicitor must then go on to consider whether or not it is justifiable to breach his or her duty of confidentiality bearing in mind the guidance set out above. In addition, it may be appropriate for the solicitor to point out that he or she has a discretion to inform a third party of the offence that is, will or may be committed.

(3)   An adult who has been abused or is being abused. As above, where the client is an adult who has been or is being abused, the duty to act in the client's best interests would entail outlining the legal position and suggesting where the client, or the solicitor on the client's behalf, could go for help. A solicitor in these circumstances is absolutely bound by the duty of confidentiality to the client but it is always permissible to try to persuade the client to reveal the abuse.

A child

The extent of a solicitor's potential entitlement to breach the duty of confidentiality will depend on whether the child is mature or immature. It will often be difficult for a solicitor to judge the maturity of a child and he or she will need to make a judgment on the basis of the child's understanding. Reference should be made to the principles in *Gillick v West Norfolk and Wisbech Area Health Authority and Department of Health and Social Security*[1] and the CA 1989. In difficult cases it may be appropriate for a solicitor to approach a third party with knowledge of the child and expertise in this area, for instance the guardian ad litem involved in the case (if any). A solicitor should never breach the duty of confidentiality unless he or she strongly suspects or knows that abuse has taken, is taking, or will take place.

(4) A mature child who is being abused. Where a mature child is the client the guidance in (3) above applies except that a solicitor may have a discretion to breach the duty of confidentiality where he or she knows or strongly suspects that younger siblings are being abused or where the child is in fear of his or her life or of serious injury.

(5) An immature child who is being abused. Where an immature child is the client, the solicitor's duty is as in (3) above in relation to doing the best for the client. A solicitor can try to persuade the client to reveal the abuse. If the client refuses, the solicitor is not absolutely bound by the duty of confidentiality and may feel, bearing the above arguments in mind, that he or she is entitled to disclose what the child has told him or her to a third party. This should only be done if it is in the public interest and there is no other less oppressive method of dealing with the situation (such as a guardian ad litem disclosing the abuse).

Where the client is an immature child, the solicitor may need to consider whether or not he or she should reveal any disclosures to the child's parents. It may be that a disclosure of information to another third party, such as the police or a social services department, would best serve the interests of the client.'

1 [1986] AC 112, [1986] 1 FLR 224, HL.

'The decision to disclose and possible consequences

Any client, whether child or adult, has a right to be made aware of when and in what circumstances the solicitor's duty of confidentiality may be breached. The decision of when and how to tell the client of the solicitor's decision will clearly be a difficult one, although it is thought to be preferable to make the position clear during the first interview. This will present the solicitor with a dilemma – if he or she fails to disclose the abuse, he or she will not be in a position to help protect the child from further abuse. On the other hand, if the solicitor tells the child he or she may breach the duty of confidentiality, there is a risk that further disclosures will not be forthcoming from the child. Despite this, if a solicitor is about to breach his or her duty of confidentiality there is a high expectation that the solicitor will tell the client of his or her decision and explore with the client how this should be done. However, in the end it is for the solicitor to exercise his or her professional judgment about when and how to explain the duty of confidentiality to any client; it is impossible to formulate a rule that can be applied in all circumstances.

Any solicitor who tells the client that the solicitor will breach the duty of confidentiality should inform the client that he or she is entitled to terminate the solicitor's retainer if such disclosure is contrary to the client's wishes. However, it is almost inevitable that the breaching of the duty of confidentiality by the solicitor will cause the client to terminate the solicitor's retainer whether or not the client is informed by the solicitor of his or her intentions. Upon the termination of the retainer the duty of confidentiality still remains, subject to the solicitor being able to justify a breach of the duty in the exceptional circumstances referred to in *The duty of confidentiality* above.'

Conclusions on Disclosure

11.76 The law on disclosure of information which could influence the future welfare of the child and for the purpose of proceedings is complex and intricate, especially in relation to disclosure by parents. The detailed analysis by Charles J in *S County Council v B*,[1] and his rationale of the leading House of Lords cases, the uncertainty of the application of the principles in *Re C (A Minor) (Care Proceedings: Disclosure)*[2] and the observations of Munby J in *Re B (Disclosure to Other Parties)*[3] and of Charles J in *Re R (Care: Disclosure: Nature of Proceedings)*[4] illustrate the difficulties.

1 [2000] 1 FCR 536, [2000] 2 FLR 161: see para 11.69.
2 [1997] Fam 76, [1996] 2 FLR 725: see para 11.69.
3 [2001] 2 FLR 1017. See para 11.53.
4 [2002] 1 FLR 755: see para 11.43.

11.77 Some principles can be elicited:

(1) Local authorities have a high duty of disclosure of all relevant information;
(2) Parents have absolute privilege in respect of communications between themselves and their lawyers;
(3) The permission of the court is required before documents filed in proceedings relating to a child can be disclosed to a third party; and
(4) The court has power to order disclosure of reports prepared for the purposes of proceedings relating to children.

11.78 At the least for the purpose of children proceedings there is uncertainty about:

(1) when absolute privilege arises;
(2) the scope of public interest immunity, legal professional privilege and litigation privilege;
(3) whether privilege extends to communications such as the seeking of advice from experts;
(4) whether the court can order disclosure of the identity of experts, and whether, if identified, they could be required to give evidence;
(5) whether the court can order disclosure of reports not filed in proceedings relating to the children;
(6) when the court should order disclosure of papers or reports, which may incriminate the person making the statement or the person to whom the report relates;
(7) when local authorities can legitimately withhold information from parties to proceedings;
(8) whether professional guidance on disclosure is binding; and
(9) whether and when legal advisers have a duty to disclose material in their possession, relevant to the proceedings, whether or not it suggests the risk of harm to a child.

11.79 These uncertainties act to the detriment of the conduct of proceedings. The battleground lies between those who believe that, in order to ensure that the welfare of the child can be made paramount, the court should have access to all information which might be relevant to the future welfare of the child, and those who believe that the administration of justice and fairness to other parties requires that there are circumstances where they should be entitled to withhold information.

11.80 During the 1990s the overriding consideration was the welfare of the child. Rules of evidence have in general been interpreted in a lax fashion, giving the court a wide discretion to do what it believes to be in the interests of the child. More recently a stricter approach has been adopted, consistent perhaps with a concern for adherence to the principles of a right to a fair trial in Art 6 and the right to family life in Art 8 of the European Convention on Human Rights. In disclosure cases as yet, little attention appears to have been given to whether the child has a right under the Convention to information contained within the family, in order that his future can be properly protected.

11.81 Charles J may well be correct when he says in *S County Council v B*[1] that the principles relating to privilege can only be changed by statute. Certainly this area of the law would benefit from a thorough and authoritative analysis, so that courts can concentrate on taking decisions about the welfare of the child rather than the way in which proceedings have to be conducted.

1   [2000] 1 FCR 536, [2000] 2 FLR 161.

Chapter 12

Wardship and the High Court's inherent jurisdiction

INTRODUCTION

12.1 Lord Mackay LC said, when introducing the Bill,[1] that subject to one important exception it was not sought to reform wardship as such although 'many of the reforms both in the private and public statute law should substantially reduce the need to invoke the High Court's inherent jurisdiction'. That 'one important exception', now contained in s 100, was intended to end local authority use of wardship. The inclusion of this restriction on the use of wardship was one of the surprises of the original Children Bill[2] since it had neither been recommended by the Review of Child Care Law nor by the Law Commission and indeed flew directly in the face of a recommendation to the contrary by the Cleveland Inquiry Report.[3] Admittedly in its earlier Working Paper on Wards of Court[4] the Law Commission had canvassed abolishing the jurisdiction altogether but its final report on Guardianship and Custody the Commission[5] expressly postponed making any substantial recommendations for the reform of wardship.

1   502 HL Official Report (5th Series) col 493.
2   Lord Mackay LC explained in his Joseph Jackson Memorial Lecture (1989) 139 NLJ at 507, that the government's decision to restrict its use was taken late in the day.
3   Cm 412, 1988, para 16.37.
4   Working Paper No 101, 1987.
5   Law Com No 172, 1988, para 1.4.

12.2 Although s 100 prevents local authorities from using wardship in respect of any child already in care,[1] it nevertheless permits them, in appropriate cases,[2] to invoke the High Court's general inherent jurisdiction to resolve specific issues concerning children provided there is no alternative statutory procedure and is a likelihood of substantial harm to the child. This was explained by Lord Mackay in his Joseph Jackson Memorial Lecture when he commented:[3]

> 'In the Government's view, wardship is only one use of the High Court's inherent parens patriae jurisdiction. We believe therefore, it is open to the High Court to make orders under its inherent jurisdiction in respect of children other than through wardship'.

Thus s 100 of the CA 1989 is based on the premise that the High Court's inherent jurisdiction comprises both wardship and the general or residual inherent jurisdiction[4] but that it is to the latter that local authorities must now look whenever they wish to obtain a High Court order in respect of children already in their care. Although there was some pre CA 1989 authority for the High Court having a general inherent power to protect children outside wardship[5] it was seldom used[6] and largely unfamiliar.[7]

1 See paras 12.4 et seq.
2 See paras 12.34 et seq.
3 (1989) 139 NLJ 505 at 507.
4 But as Parry: The Children Act 1989: Local Authorities, Wardship and the Revival of the Inherent Jurisdiction' [1992] JSWFL 212, 213 observes: 's 100 has the marginal heading for guidance, 'Restrictions on use of wardship jurisdiction,' whereas the substance of the section relates to the inherent jurisdiction as much as to wardship'.
5 Viz *Re M and N (Wardship: Publication of Information)* [1990] Fam 211 at 223 [1990] 1 All ER 205 at 210, per Butler-Sloss LJ; *Re C (A Minor) (Wardship: Medical Treatment) (No 2)* [1990] Fam 39 at 46, [1989] 2 All ER 791 at 793, CA, per Lord Donaldson MR; *Re L (an infant)* [1968] P 119 at 156-157, [1968] 1 All ER 20 at 24-25, per Lord Denning MR and *Re N (infants)* [1967] Ch 512, [1967] 1 All ER 161, per Stamp J.
6 See eg Lowe and White: *Wards of Court* (2nd edn) who stated at para 1-5 'the general view seems to be taken that the inherent jurisdiction to protect children is not exclusively vested in the wardship jurisdiction but that that jurisdiction is a convenient machinery for administering it'. Note also Munby J's analysis in *A (A Patient) v A Health Authority; Re J; The Queen on the Application of S v Secretary of the State for the Home Department* [2002] EWHC 18 (Fam/Admin), para 31, [2002] 1 FLR 845. For a detailed examination of the history of the parens patriae jurisdiction see Seymour: 'Parens Patriae and Wardship Powers: Their Nature and Origins' (1994) 14 Oxford Journal of Legal Studies 159, and Lowe and White: *Wards of Court*, chs 1 and 7.
7 See eg the discussion in *Clarke Hall and Morrison* 1[881] et seq and Lowe and Douglas *Bromley's* Family Law (9th edn), p 701 et seq.

12.3 Although the Court of Appeal has said both that the High Court's inherent jurisdiction is equally exercisable whether the child is or is not a ward of court[1] and that 'for all practicable purposes the jurisdiction in wardship and the inherent jurisdiction over children is one and the same',[2] wardship and the inherent jurisdiction are not synonymous. Unlike wardship, the exercise of the inherent jurisdiction does *not* place the child under the ultimate responsibility of the court. The inherent jurisdiction empowers the High Court to make orders dealing with particular aspects of the child's welfare whereas wardship additionally vests in the court both an immediate and a continuing supervisory function over the child.[3]

1 Per Lord Donaldson MR in *Re W (a Minor) (Medical Treatment: Court's Jurisdiction)* [1993] Fam 64 at 73 F-G, [1992] 4 All ER 627 at 631d,
2 Per Ward LJ in *Re Z (A Minor) (Identification: Restrictions on Publication)* [1997] Fam 1 at 14, sub nom *Re Z (a Minor) (Freedom of Publication)* [1995] 4 All ER 961 at 968.
3 Per Lord Donaldson MR in *Re W*, above.

THE IMPACT OF THE 1989 ACT ON THE WARDSHIP JURISDICTION[1]

1. Public law

(a) No independent power to commit wards of court into care or supervision of a local authority

12.4 Before the Children Act 1989 local authorities frequently looked to the wardship jurisdiction rather than to the statutory scheme under the Children and Young Persons Act 1969 as a means of having children committed into their care.[2] The continued existence of such an alternative, however, ran counter to the philosophy of having a single route into care based on the s 31 threshold which had been carefully designed to provide the minimum circumstances justifying state intervention. Accordingly, s 100(1) repealed the former statutory power under s 7 of the Family Law Reform Act 1969 to commit a ward of court into the care or supervision of a local authority. Similarly, s 100(2) expressly prevents the High Court from exercising its inherent jurisdiction to require a child to be placed in the care, or to be put under the supervision of, a local authority, or to require a child to be accommodated by or on behalf of a local authority.[3]

1   See the excellent articles by District Judge John Mitchell: 'Whatever happened to Wardship? Part I and Part II' [2001] Fam Law 130 and 212.
2   In 1991, for example, of the 4,961 originating summonses issued in wardship, 2,725 (55.5%) were taken out by local authorities: Judicial Statistics 1991. For a detailed account of the way in which local authorities formerly used wardship see eg Lowe and White, *Wards of Court* (2nd edn) ch 16, Masson and Morton, 'The Use of Wardship by Local Authorities' (1989) 52 MLR 762, and Hunt, 'Local Authority Wardship before the Children Act: The Baby or the Bathwater' (HMSO, 1993).
3   Upon implementation of Pt IV (ie from 14 October 1991) wards of court already committed into local authority care ceased to be wards: Sch 14, para 16A(1), and those committed on an interim basis as at 14 October 1991 ceased to be wards on 13 October 1992: Sch 14, para 1A. Hence it is now no longer possible for a child to be both in local authority care and be a ward of court. Upon the cessation of wardship the child is deemed to be in care under s 31: Sch 14, para 15(1). Nevertheless any directions or orders made in the wardship proceedings continue to be in force until varied or discharged by the court. Sch 14, para 16(5)(c) and *Re O (minors) (adoption: injunction)* [1993] 2 FCR 746, [1993] 2 FLR 737. However, where a former wardship case does come before the court it should always review any continuing directions, discharge those which are no longer necessary and generally be cautious about varying them so that they are continued indefinitely – see the President's Letter in 1991 (reproduced in *Clarke Hall and Morrison* at 1 [13085]). For further details see *Clarke Hall and Morrison* 1[848] et seq.

12.5   If, in wardship proceedings it appears to the court that a care or supervision order might be appropriate then, like any other court in 'family proceedings',[1] it can, pursuant to the powers under s 37,[2] direct a local authority to investigate the child's circumstances with a view to the authority making an application. In the event of such an application being made[3] a care or supervision order can only be made provided the threshold criteria under s 31 are satisfied.

1   Wardship proceedings are 'family proceedings' by reason of s 8(3)(a), see para 5.101.
2   Discussed at paras 5.158 and 7.5.
3   But there is no power to force the local authority to apply: see eg *Nottingham County Council v P* [1994] Fam 18, [1993] 3 All ER 815, discussed at para 12.46.

(b)   Wardship and care incompatible

12.6   The Act makes wardship and local authority care incompatible. Section 91(4) provides that the making of a care order with respect to a child who is already a ward of court brings that wardship to an end, while s 100(2)(c) states that the High Court cannot exercise its inherent jurisdiction 'so as to make a child who is the subject of a care order a ward of court'.[1] Section 41(2A) of the Supreme Court Act 1981[2] also provides that a child in care does not become a ward of court upon the making of a wardship application.[3]

1   A point emphasised by Hale J in *Re W and B, Re W (care plan)* [2001] EWCA Civ 751 at para [76], [2001] 2 FCR 450, [2001] 2 FLR 582, not commented upon by the House of Lords.

2 Added by CA 1989, Sch 13, para 45(2).
3 This is contrary to the normal rule that immediately upon the issue of the originating summons the child becomes a ward of court; see Supreme Court Act 1981, s 41(2) and *Clarke Hall and Morrison* at 1[776].

12.7 These restrictions mean that the High Court cannot use wardship to keep control of a child committed to the care of a local authority.[1] Similarly, a local authority cannot look to wardship to obtain a High Court order in respect of a child already in their care. In this latter case, however, they can seek to invoke the High Court's inherent jurisdiction.[2]

1 This means, for example, that wardship cannot be used to get round the embargo (see *Re KDT (a minor) (care order: conditions)* [1994] 2 FCR 72, sub nom *Re T (A Minor) (Care Order: Conditions)* 1 [1994] 2 FLR 423 and *Kent County Council v C* [1993] Fam 57, [1993] 1 All ER 719) against making conditional care orders.
2 See post paras 12.24 et seq. For the position of individuals seeking to challenge a local authority's decision in respect of a child in care, see post, paras 12.42 and 12.43.

(c) Circumstances in which local authorities might still look to wardship

12.8 Recourse to the prerogative jurisdiction remains a possible option in respect of children not in local authority care including those being accommodated by them. Although wardship cannot be used initially to bring about such an arrangement,[1] unlike care, accommodation is not incompatible with wardship. However, to invoke wardship local authorities must first obtain court leave to invoke the jurisdiction,[2] which may only be given upon the court being satisfied that (a) the result sought to be achieved cannot be achieved by the making of a s 8 order,[3] (in this regard it must be remembered that it is also open to an authority to apply with court leave for a prohibited steps or specific issue order);[4] and (b) that 'if the court's inherent jurisdiction[5] is not exercised with respect to the child he is likely to suffer significant harm.'[6] Even if leave is given, s 100(2)(d)[7] prevents the courts from making orders the effect of which is to confer upon authorities aspects of parental responsibility that they do not already have.

1 See s 100(2)(b). See also *Re G (a child) (secure accommodation order)* [2000] 2 FCR 385, [2000] 2 FLR 259, in which the first instance judge was held to be in 'plain breach' of s 100(2) in requiring a local authority to accommodate a child.
2 Pursuant to s 100(3).
3 Section 100(4)(a), discussed further at para 12.35.
4 See para 5.70.
5 Which, for these purposes, applies to wardship proceedings as well.
6 Section 100(4)(b), discussed in more detail at para 12.36.
7 Discussed in detail at para 12.28.

12.9 Since s 8 orders do not cover every situation in cases where the local authority is not itself seeking care but is nevertheless concerned about a child's well-being,[1] wardship might be the right solution, at any rate, where there is thought to be a need for the court's continuing control.[2] In *Re R (a minor) (contempt)*,[3] for example, a local authority warded a 14-year-old child accommodated by them to protect her from a relationship with a 33-year-old man. A local authority has also been known to ward children to protect them from being identified in a television programme about alleged paedophiles.[4] Wardship might also offer the best and sometimes the only means open to a local authority seeking to protect 17-year-olds when most of the public law options are unavailable.[5] Other possible examples are safe-guarding the interests of orphans[6] and cases where a local authority are concerned about the child's welfare but are not themselves seeking care as for example supporting foster parents' applications for care and control,[7] and upon learning of a surrogacy arrangement[8] or of a parental refusal to consent to a child's medical treatment.[9] In this latter context one advantage of ward-ship is the immediacy of its effect, that is, the moment the child becomes a ward, no important step may be taken without the court's consent, and hence leave to carry out the proposed operation will be required. Nevertheless unless the continuing control of the court is desirable or useful[10] then it is unlikely that the wardship would be continued by the court. In any event it is usually equally effective simply to seek a prohibited steps or specific issue order.[11]

1   See ante, paras 5.75 et seq.
2   Cf Bainham, Children: *The Modern Law* (2nd edn) p 406, who submits that wardship (as dis-tinct from the inherent jurisdiction) is redundant in public law cases.
3   [1994] 2 All ER 144, [1994] 1 WLR 487, CA. Query whether a prohibited steps order could have been made in this case? Cf *Re C (HIV Test)* [1997] 2 FLR 1004 in which, following local authority intervention, a specific issue order was granted, ordering a baby to be tested for HIV.
4   *Cornwall County Council v BBC* (1994) unreported. But note the restrictions on obtaining orders restricting publicity following *R v Central Independent Television plc* [1994] Fam 192, [1994] 3 All ER 641, CA and *Re R (A Minor) (Wardship: Restrictions on Publication)* [1994] Fam 254, [1994] 3 All ER 658, CA, discussed post at para 12.29 and note also *Kelly v BBC* [2001] Fam 59, [2000] 3 FCR 509, [2001] 1 FLR 197, in the absence of an express order to the contrary, no contempt by media interviewing a boy known to be a ward. For a comment on this decision, see Woods [2001] CFLQ 209.
5   See eg *Re F (mental health act guardianship)* [2000] 1 FCR 11, [2000] 1 FLR 192, CA, dis-cussed further at para 12.19 and *Re D (a child) (wardship: evidence of abuse)* [2001] 1 FCR 707, CA, which concerned allegations made by a 17-year-old with a mental age of 2 and who lived in a special care unit that he had been sexually abused by his father. In the event these allegations were not proved and the wardship was discharged.
6   Cf *Birmingham City Council v D, Birmingham City Council v M* [1994] 2 FCR 245, [1994] 2 FLR 502 in which a local authority unsuccessfully sought a care order in respect of two orphan children accommodated by them essentially to obtain parental responsibility. It is submitted that in that instance, by providing for the court's continuing control, wardship could have provided a better solution. But note the criticism of this case in Lowe and Douglas' *Bromley's Family Law* (9th edn) at 548 and contrast *Re S H (care order: orphan)* [1996] 1 FCR 1, [1995] 1 FLR 746 and *Re MM (care order: abandoned baby)* [1996] 2 FCR 521, sub nom *Re M (Care Order: Parental Responsibility)* [1996] 2 FLR 84 in which a care orders were made.
7   As in *Re RJ (minors) (fostering: wardship)* [1999] 3 FCR 646, [1999] 1 FLR 618, discussed at para 12.18.
8   Cf *Re C (A Minor) (Wardship: Surrogacy)* [1985] FLR 846, and Local Authority Circular (85) 12.
9   Cf *Re B (A Minor) (Wardship: Medical Treatment)* [1981] 1 WLR 1421, (1981) 3 FLR 117, CA.
10 As in *Re C (a baby)* [1998] 2 FCR 269, [1996] 2 FCR 43 and *R v Portsmouth Hospitals NHS Trust, ex p Glass* [1999] 3 FCR 145, [1999] 2 FLR 905, discussed below at para 12.17.
11 See eg *Re C (HIV Test)* above.

2.   Private law

12.10   Although the CA 1989 places no express restraint on the use of ward-ship by individuals, the expectation and indeed the object[1] was that there would be a substantial decline in the private law use of the jurisdiction. As the Department of Health's Guidance and Regulations[2] put it:

'By incorporating many of the beneficial aspects of wardship such as the 'open door' policy, and a flexible range of orders, the Act will substantially reduce the need to have recourse to the High Court.'

As a result of these changes, relatives who formerly were often forced to use wardship and who before implementation initiated about 13 % of all wardships,[3] are now generally better advised to seek, albeit with leave, s 8 orders[4] in the lower courts. Similarly, in most cases,[5] it is difficult to see what parents can now gain from wardship as against pursuing remedies under the CA 1989.

1 See para 12.1.
2 Vol 1, Court Orders, para 3.98.
3 Law Com Working Paper No. 101, Wardship, para 3.3.
4 Or, prospectively, special guardianship, see paras 5.161 et seq.
5 But see paras 12.15 et seq below.

12.11 The statistics, insofar as they are available, do bear evidence of the dramatic decline in the private use of wardship. In 1991, the final year running up to implementation, 2209 (accounting for 44.5% of the record number of wardship applications made in that year) originating summonses were taken out by individuals.[1] In contrast in 1992 the total number of summonses issued was 492, declining to 269 in 1993.[2] The numbers, however, have since risen to 437 in 1996, 437 in 1997, 431 in 1998, and 418 in 1999.[3]

1 Judicial Statistics for 1991 (Cm 1991), Table 5.8.
2 CAAC Report 1992/93, p 25. According to that report, in 1993 141 originating summonses for wardship were issued between January and July but we understand from the Information Management Unit of the Lord Chancellor's Department that a total of 269 summonses were issued in 1993.
3 See the figures quoted by Mitchell at [2001] Fam Law 130 and obtained from the Statistical Support Office of the Court Service. There are no other published statistics, such information not being included in *Judicial Statistics* Annual Reports (why not?) since 1991. According to Mitchell, three-quarters of all originating summonses were issued in the Principal Registry. It is unknown how many of these summonses were issued by individuals but given the embargo on the public law use of wardship it is reasonable to assume that the vast majority were issued in the private law context.

(a)   The ruling in Re T

12.12 The first post-Children Act case to consider the continuing role of wardship in private law proceedings was *Re T (A Minor) (Child: Representation)*[1] which concerned an adopted child who wished to live permanently with her natural paternal aunt. The child's solicitor considering her able, having regard to her understanding, to instruct him without the need for a next friend pursuant to FPR 1991, r 9.2A,[2] issued an application on her instructions for leave to apply for a residence order. At the first instance, however, Thorpe J, following an undertaking by the adoptive parents (who opposed the child's application) to institute wardship proceedings, directed inter alia that the child be made a ward and the Official Solicitor be appointed as the child's guardian. On appeal, however, the Court of Appeal ruled that FPR 1991, r 9.2A applied to all 'family proceedings' and that accordingly in wardship, as in any other family proceedings, provided the child has sufficient understanding to bring or defend proceedings on his or her own behalf, the court has no power to impose a guardian ad litem on such a child against his or her wishes. It was further held that given that there were no advantages either to the child or to the adoptive parents that were not also available in ordinary family proceedings under Pt II of the CA 1989, there was nothing which, in the words of Waite LJ, would justify giving the child 'the status, an exceptional status under the modern law as it must now be applied, of a ward of court'.[3]

1 [1994] Fam 49, [1993] 4 All ER 518, [1993] 2 FCR 445, sub nom *Re CT (A Minor) (Wardship: Representation)* [1993] 2 FLR 278, CA.
2 Ie pursuant to FPR 1991, r 9.2A, discussed ante at para 10.39.

3 [1994] Fam at 65D, [1993] 4 All ER at 528. See also *Re P (a minor) (leave to apply: foster parents)* [1994] 2 FCR 1093, sub nom *C v Salford City Council* [1994] 2 FLR 926, in which Hale J could see no advantage in continuing the wardship.

12.13 In concluding that the continuation of wardship was inappropriate, Waite LJ commented:

That while it survives as an independent jurisdiction, the

'courts' undoubted discretion to allow wardship to go forward in a suitable case is subject to their clear duty, in loyalty to the scheme and purpose of the Children Act legislation, to permit recourse to wardship only when it becomes apparent to the judge in any particular case that the question which the court is determining in regard to the minor's upbringing or property cannot be resolved under the statutory procedures in Pt II of the Act in a way that secures the best interests of the child; or where the minor's person is in a state of jeopardy from which he can only be protected by giving him the status of a ward of court; or where the court's functions need to be secured from the effects potentially injurious to the child, of external influences (intrusive publicity for example) and it is decided that conferring on the child the status of a ward will prove a more efficient deterrent than the ordinary sanctions of a contempt of court which already protect all family proceedings'.[1]

1 [1994] Fam 49 at 60, [1993] 4 All ER 518 at 524.

(b) Some possible remaining uses of wardship

12.14 Given that no material changes have been made to the rules governing the issue of an originating summons,[1] it is submitted that Waite LJ's comments in *Re T* ought not to be taken as restricting individuals' ability to make a child a ward of court in the first instance, though clearly, the courts will require special justification to continue the wardship once the case comes before them. It remains now to consider what advantages there may be in issuing an originating summons and when the court might consider continuing the wardship.

1 The current procedure is governed by FPR 1991, r 5.1 which replaced RSC Ord 90, r 1(3).

12.15 One important feature of the wardship jurisdiction is its immediacy: as soon as the originating summons is issued the child becomes a ward and no important step may then be taken without prior court sanction.[1] In effect the issuing of the originating summons provides a unique quasi-administrative mechanism by which the child's legal position can be immediately frozen, which is useful when dealing with emergencies, such as threatened child abduction, particularly when an international element is involved.[2] Invoking wardship can also be an effective way of halting a proposed medical operation on the child and can provide a usefully speedy means by which non parents, who would otherwise have to seek leave to apply for a s 8 order can safeguard their position, for example, by preventing parents from removing the child from their care pending a court hearing.

1   *Re S (infants)* [1967] 1 All ER 202, [1967] 1 WLR 396, per Cross J.
2   See further paras 12.20 et seq below.

12.16   The court's wardship powers are wider than those under s 8 and where advantage needs to be taken of this it would be proper both to invoke and to continue the wardship. In *Re T (A Minor) (Child: Representation)*[1] Waite LJ instanced the example of protecting the child from publicity though the Court of Appeal has subsequently taken a more restrictive view of its inherent powers in that regard.[2] However, in *Re W (minors) (continuation of wardship)*[3] a father's request to discharge an earlier wardship was refused. In that case the father, having been granted care and control of four sons in pre CA 1989 wardship proceedings, had unilaterally changed their schooling and acquiesced in them talking to the press about their 'fight to stay with their Dad'. In the Court of Appeal's view the continuation of the wardship was justified because no comparable protection could be achieved under the CA 1989 since it was impossible to make a prohibited steps order which could anticipate how the father might act and because a prohibited steps order might not be appropriate to prevent the publishing of information about the children.[4] Furthermore the continuing nature of the wardship meant that the Official Solicitor could remain involved and act as a buffer between the parents. The case could also be reserved to the same judge.

1   [1994] Fam 49 at 60, [1993] 4 All ER 518 at 524, CA.
2   See *R v Central Independent Television plc* [1994] Fam 192, [1994] 3 All ER CA 641, CA, *Kelly v BBC* [2001] Fam 59, [2000] 3 FCR 509, [2001] 1 FLR 197 and *Medway Council v BBC* [2002] 1 FLR 105.
3   [1996] 1 FCR 393, sub nom *Re W (Wardship: Discharge: Publicity)* [1995] 2 FLR 466, CA.
4   But note Hobhouse LJ's dissenting judgment and the subsequent decision in *Re Z (A Minor) (Identification: Restrictions on Publication)* [1997] Fam 1, sub nom *Re Z (a minor) (freedom of publication)* [1995] 4 All ER 961, CA.

12.17   The court's overall control of its wards may also be thought advantageous, for example, in the case of an abandoned child, where no-one looking after him has parental responsibility. Alternatively, it can be appropriate for a court to assist with taking responsibility in cases of grave anxiety. For example, in *Re C (a baby)*,[1] a child developed meningitis which left her brain-damaged and unable to survive without artificial ventilation and likely to suffer increasing pain and distress with no hope of recovery. Sir Stephen Brown P commented:

'It appeared appropriate that the courts should take responsibility for this child and relieve the parents in some measure of the grave responsibility which they have borne since her birth.'

The jurisdiction could also provide an effective means of protecting and managing a child's property interests in the event of the parents' death.

1   [1996] 2 FCR 569, [1996] 2 FLR 43. See also *R v Portsmouth Hospitals NH Trust, ex p Glass* [1999] 3 FCR 145, [1999] 2 FLR 905, CA, which concerned a 12-year-old severely disabled boy with only a limited lifespan. Trust between the mother and the hospital had completely

broken down and following her unsuccessful appeal against the dismissal of her action for judicial review, the mother was urged to ward her son so as to allow the Official Solicitor to be continuously involved in the case. *Note* as from 1 April 2001 the Official Solicitor's role in wardship has now largely been taken over by CAFCASS see *Practice Notes* [2001] 2 FCR 562 and [2001] 2 FCR 566, [2001] 2 FLR 155.

12.18   Wardship was found advantageous both in short and long term in *Re RJ (Minors) (Fostering: Person Disqualified)*[1] and *Re RJ (minors) (fostering: wardship)*.[2] These decisions concerned three children who though happily placed with foster carers could not remain there following the implementation of the Children (Protection From Offenders)(Miscellaneous Amendments) Regulations 1997,[3] since the foster-father had previously been formally cautioned for actual bodily harm to another foster child who was now adopted by him and his wife. Following the foster parents' intervention in care proceedings at which the mother was still seeking her children's return, the Court of Appeal in the first mentioned decision, held that although the 1997 Regulations did not prevent the court from making a residence order, in this case the preferable course was to discharge the interim care orders, make the children wards of court and grant interim care and control to the foster parents. In this way the status quo could be preserved as nearly as possible pending the full hearing and, by not granting even interim residence orders which would have vested parental responsibility in the foster parent, any perception of prejudice by the mother could be avoided. At the subsequent full hearing (the second mentioned decision) it was held that, given the exceptional circumstances, the appropriate long-term solution was as to continue the wardship and to grant care and control to the foster carers. The advantages of this solution were thought to be:

(1)   giving ultimate control to the court would be reassuring to the foster carer (who would otherwise have shared parental responsibility with the mother had they been granted residence orders);

(2)   it placed the children in a neutral setting, removing them to some extent from the pressure of the more adversarial nature of Children Act proceedings;[4]

(3)   it was only by this means that the local authority could remain involved in what had become a private law case and would therefore enable the authority to apply for certain orders which might not have otherwise been available to them given the prohibition against local authorities applying for s 8 orders;[5] and

(4)   it would similarly allow the children's guardian to continue to be involved.

As Cazalet J put it 'the use of wardship will enable this case to be managed appropriately for the future'.

1   [1999] 1 WLR 581, [1998] 3 FCR 579, [1999] 1 FLR 605, CA.
2   [1999] 3 FCR 646, [1999] 1 FLR 618.
3   SI 1997/2308. This Regulation was intended to prevent paedophiles from becoming foster parents.
4   Query if this reason would generally be thought to be justifiable?
5   Cf *F v Cambridgeshire County Council* [1995] 2 FCR 804, [1995] 1 FLR 516, discussed at para 5.82.

12.19   Wardship was thought to provide a preferable means of protecting a mentally impaired 17-year-old child rather than guardianship under the Mental Health Act 1983. In *Re F (mental health act: guardianship)*[1] a 17-year-old, who had a mental age of between 5 and 8 had been accommodated by a local authority because of chronic neglect. (Her seven siblings were taken into interim care for the same reason).[2] Her parents sought her return. Care proceedings were not possible because of the child's age and the local authority instead obtained a guardianship order under the Mental Health Act 1983. The Court of Appeal held that wardship was the more appropriate remedy not least because the 1983 Act was not a child centred jurisdiction and the child lacked the benefit of independent representation. Furthermore, on the particular facts wardship would enable a single judge to consider the interests both of the child in question and her seven siblings.

1   [2000] 1 FCR 11, [2000] 1 FLR 192, CA.
2   This option could not be exercised over the child in question since she was already aged 17.

(c)   *The use of wardship when dealing with child abduction*

12.20   Although there are no published statistics on the current use of wardship it seems likely that a substantial proportion of applications are made in connection with child abduction.[1] This has long been a key role of the jurisdiction and although there are no longer any jurisdictional advantages in invoking wardship[2] and while many of the powers that were formerly unique to it are now more generally available, wardship remains a useful option because of the immediate and all round protection that it offers, in particular the embargo against the child's removal from England and Wales without court leave which automatically arises immediately that the child is warded. Applications are commonly of three types, namely, those aimed at preventing children from being wrongfully removed from England and Wales, those made by left-behind parents in respect of children abducted abroad and those, usually made by the abducting parent, in connection with children brought to this country from overseas. With regard to the first use, since under the Child Abduction Act 1984 it is a crime wrongfully to take a child outside the United Kingdom,[3] it is not necessary to have a court order to obtain police help to obtain an all ports warning.[4] Nevertheless wardship remains a useful device for convincing the police to intervene. Furthermore, a court order is advantageous if the child is missing since it enables the applicant to enlist the aid of government agencies to trace the child.[5] The court can make 'seek and find' orders and although the inherent seek and find powers are little different to those granted under s 34 of the Family Law Act 1986 there is some evidence that wardship cases are given higher priority by the police.[6] A court can order individuals, including solicitors, to disclose the whereabouts both of the child and proposed defendant. Moreover, in appropriate cases, it can also order solicitors not to reveal the making, content or service of the whereabouts order.[7] Alternatively, the court can order publicity to help trace a ward.[8] Wardship can also help to prevent abduction, inter alia, because a court can order the surrender of a British[9] or even a foreign passport.[10]

1   CAAC Report 1993/4, p 33. According to Mitchell [2001] Fam Law 212 at 214, a third of all wardship cases reported in *Family Law* since the implementation of the CA 1989, have concerned child abduction.
2   Jurisdiction in children cases is generally governed by the Family Law Act 1986 Pt I (as amended to take account of the so called Brussels II Regulation) see *Clarke Hall and Morrison* 1 [577] et seq, and the Court of Appeal has ruled in *Al Habtoor v Fotheringham* [2001] EWCA Civ 186, [2001] 1 FCR 385, [2001] 1 FLR 951 that English courts should not seek to take jurisdiction on any wider basis.
3   For a discussion of the operation of the 1984 Act see *Clarke Hall and Morrison* 2[11].

4 See *Clarke Hall and Morrison* 2[12].
5 *Practice Direction (disclosure of addresses)* [1989] 1 All ER 765, [1989] 1 WLR 219.
6 *Re B (minors) (wardship: power to detain)* [1994] 2 FCR 1142 at 1146, [1994] 2 FLR 479 at 482, per Butler-Sloss LJ.
7 See *Re H (child abduction: whereabouts order to solicitors)* [2000] 1 FCR 499, [2000] 1 FLR 766.
8 *Re R (MJ) (A Minor) (Publication of Transcript)* [1975] Fam 89 and *Practice Note* [1980] 2 All ER 806, discussed in *Clarke Hall and Morrison* 2[22].
9 This power, formerly exclusively an inherent power, is now conferred on all courts by s 37 of the Family Law Act 1986.
10 See *Re A-K (minors) (contact)* [1997] 2 FCR 563, sub nom *Re AK (Foreign Passport: Jurisdiction)* [1997] 2 FLR 569, CA.

12.21 Apart from being useful both to prevent abductions and trace children within the United Kingdom, wardship can be advantageous in cases where children are subsequently taken abroad particularly to so-called non Convention countries, that is, states that have implemented neither the 1980 Hague Convention on the Civil Aspects of International Child Abduction nor the 1980 European (or Luxembourg) Convention on Recognition and Enforcement of Decisions Concerning Custody of Children.[1] Although in non Convention cases it is ultimately better in most cases to institute proceedings in the State to which the child has been taken, the respect that wardship commands abroad is not to be underestimated. A good example is *Re KR (a child) (abduction: forcible removal by parents)*[2] in which a 16 year-old Sikh girl living in England was taken to the Punjab by her parents for an arranged marriage. Her elder sister issued wardship proceedings and, following what has been described[3] as 'an imaginative order, replete with recitals' by Singer J which secured in the co-operation of the Indian authorities, the ward was returned. Wardship can even be useful in cases where children are subsequently removed to Convention countries since it can enable those who do not otherwise have 'rights of custody'[4] to be able to apply under the 1980 Hague Convention[5] while an order giving residence or contact is enforceable under either the 1980 European Convention[6] or the Brussels II Regulation.[7]

1 For a list of Contracting States see *Clarke Hall and Morrison* 2[2104].
2 [1999] 4 All ER 954, [1999] 2 FCR 337, [1999] 2 FLR 542.
3 Mitchell, [2001] Fam Law 212 at 215.
4 See Art 3 of the Hague Convention, discussed in *Clarke Hall and Morrison* 2 [51].
5 See *Re J (Minor: Abduction: Ward of Court)* [1989] Fam 85, [1989] 3 All ER 590; *Re B M (Wardship: Jurisdiction)* [1993] 1 FLR 979 and *Re R (Wardship: Child Abduction) (No.2)* [1993] 1 FLR 249, discussed by Lowe and Nicholls, 'Child Abduction, The Wardship Jurisdiction and the Hague Convention' [1994] Fam Law 191.
6 See *Clarke Hall and Morrison* at 2 [351] ff.
7 See *Clarke Hall and Morrison* at 2 [74] ff.

12.22 With regard to children wrongfully brought into this country a distinction needs to be made between non Convention applications and those made under the Hague or European Conventions. In the former case the court is free in wardship proceedings to determine the dispute on the merits though in practice, provided the application is brought quickly, the court will order the child's immediate return to the state whence he came provided it is satisfied that:

(a) (where relevant)[1] the foreign court in question will apply principles acceptable to the English court;[2] and
(b) there are no contra indicators such as those referred to in Art 13 of the Hague Convention.[3] A Convention application takes precedence over the

wardship,[4] but the latter jurisdiction will come into play if the Convention application fails.[5] Wardship has also proved useful as a means of dealing with questions concerning contact abroad.[6]

1 See *T v T (child abduction: non-convention country)* [1999] 2 FCR 70, [1998] 2 FLR 1110 in which it was held to be in the children's welfare to be returned to the mother in the United Emirates without the need for further enquiry by any court.
2 There is, however, a conflict of view as to what enquiries need to be made of the foreign regime – cf *Re M (minors) (abduction: peremptory return order)* [1996] 1 FCR 557, sub nom *Re M (Abduction: Non-Convention Country)* [1995] 1 FLR 89, CA and *Re E (child abduction: non-convention country)* [1999] 3 FCR 497, [1999] 2 FLR 642, CA which favoured the view that foreign regimes can be assumed, unless the country is proved, to apply acceptable principles – with *Re JA (a minor) (child abduction: non-convention country)* [1998] 2 FCR 159, [1998] 1 FLR 231, CA which held that evidence needs to be had that the regime in question applies the principle that the child's welfare is paramount. It seems clear, however, that courts should be slow to find that a foreign law's principles are repugnant to English law, at any rate where the children have a close connection with the state in question; see *Re E*, supra and *Al Habtoor v Fotheringham* [2001] EWCA Civ 186, [2001] 1 FCR 385, [2001] 1 FLR 951, CA. See further *Clarke Hall and Morrison* 2 [33] ff.
3 *Re F (A Minor: Abduction: Jurisdiction)* [1991] Fam 25, [1990] 3 All ER 97, CA, *D v D (child abduction: non convention country)* [1994] 1 FCR 654, [1994] 1 FLR 137, CA and *Re Z (a minor) (abduction: non-convention country)* [1999] 1 FCR 251, [1999] 1 FLR 1270, discussed in *Clarke Hall and Morrison* at 2 [33.2].
4 Child Abduction and Custody Act 1985, ss 9 (Hague) and 27 (European) and FPR 1991, r 6.11(4).
5 *Re A (Minors) (Abduction: Custody Rights)* [1992] Fam 106 at 124, sub nom *Re A (minors) (abduction: acquiescence)* [1992] 1 All ER 929 at 943, *Re M (Child Abduction: Child's Objection to Return)* [1995] 1 FLR 170, sub nom *Re M (A Minor) (Abduction: Child's Objections)* [1994] 2 FLR 126, CA and *Re M (abduction: psychological harm)* [1998] 2 FCR 488, [1997] 2 FLR 690, CA.
6 See eg *Re T (staying contact in non-convention country)* [1998] 3 FCR 574 n, [1999] 1 FLR 262 n.

(d)   Other cases involving an international element

12.23   Wardship has been found useful in cases involving an international element following a refusal to make an adoption order. One such case, *Re M (child's upbringing)*,[1] concerned a boy born in South Africa to Zulu parents, who, with his parents' consent, was brought to England by a white woman who later applied to adopt him. The parents objected to the adoption and the child was warded. The adoption application was refused and the child was ordered to be returned to his parents but the wardship was continued. The boy's return proved unsuccessful and he is now back in England living with the applicant under a wardship order.[2] In a second case, *Re K (adoption: foreign child)*[3] a Bosnian Muslim orphan baby was brought to England by an English couple initially to receive medical treatment. The couple were later granted an adoption order. However, because they had failed to reveal to the court that the child had relatives in Switzerland who wished to look after her, the adoption was set aside, but the court felt that she should nevertheless remain with the couple because of her psychological bond with them. Accordingly the couple were granted care and control, with substantial access being granted to the relatives. The wardship was continued.

1 [1996] 2 FCR 473, [1996] 2 FLR 441, CA.
2 See *Re O (family appeals: management)* [1998] 3 FCR 226, [1998] 1 FLR 431 n.
3 [1997] 2 FCR 389, sub nom *Re K (Adoption and Wardship)* [1997] 2 FLR 221. See also *Re R (Inter-Country Adoption)* [1999] 1 FCR 385, [1999] 1 FLR 1014.

THE INHERENT JURISDICTION[1]

1. Procedure

12.24 The inherent jurisdiction can be invoked either upon specific application or by the court itself in cases where it is already seized of proceedings.[2] In that latter case the power is confined to the High Court[3] since it is established that county courts (and a fortiori magistrates' courts) have no inherent powers to protect children.[4] Applications for declarations may also be made under the inherent jurisdiction,[5] and it is now possible to obtain interim declarations.[6]

1 See generally *Clarke Hall and Morrison* 1 [881] ff.
2 See Charles J's analysis in *Re P (care orders: injunctive relief)* [2000] 3 FCR 426, [2000] 2 FLR 385. For an example of its exercise upon the court's initiative see *Re X (A Minor) (Adoption Details: Disclosure)* [1994] Fam 174, [1994] 3 All ER 372, CA, in which it was held to be an appropriate use of the inherent jurisdiction by the High Court hearing an adoption application to order that during the minority of the child in question the Registrar General should not disclose to any person without leave of the court the details of the adoption entered in the Adopted Children Register. Note following *Re P*, supra, a distinction may have to be made between exercising the powers to support an order under s 37 of the Supreme Court Act 1981 and those under the inherent jurisdiction.
3 Unless proceedings have been transferred from the High Court to the county court under the Matrimonial and Family Proceedings Act 1984, s 38.
4 *D v D (child case: powers of court)* [1994] 3 FCR 28, sub nom *D v D (County Court Jurisdiction: Injunctions)* [1993] 2 FLR 802, CA, *Devon County Council v B* [1997] 3 FCR 33, [1997] 1 FLR 591, CA and *Re S and D (children: powers of the court)* [1995] 1 FCR 626, [1995] 2 FLR 456, CA. It will be noted, however, that where a county court has jurisdiction over the subject matter then under the County Courts Act 1984, s 38 the courts can exercise the same powers as the High Court to grant an injunction. See Fricker, 'Injunctive Orders relating to the Children' [1993] Fam Law 141, 142, para 1.4.
5 CPR 1998 r 40.20 (in force since March 2001).
6 CPR 1998, r 25.1(9).

12.25 Applications to invoke the inherent jurisdiction must be made to the High Court (such proceedings are assigned to the Family Division)[1] but proceedings can subsequently be transferred to the county court.[2] Although no specific procedure is prescribed by the FPR 1991, in practice, application is made by originating summons and is headed 'In the Matter of the Supreme Court Act 1981'.[3] Like wardship, the plaintiff should, unless directed otherwise, file an affidavit in support of the application when the summons is issued. Local authorities wishing to invoke the inherent jurisdiction must first obtain leave of the court.[4]

1 Supreme Court Act 1981, Sch 1 para 3(b)(ii), as amended by CA 1989, Sch 13, para 45(3).
2 Ie in accordance with the Matrimonial and Family Proceedings Act 1984, s 38.
3 See *Re Z (A Minor) (Identification: Restrictions on Publication)* [1997] Fam 1 at 14 sub nom *Re Z (a minor) (freedom of Publication)* [1995] 4 All ER 961 at 968, per Ward LJ.
4 CA 1989, s 100(3), discussed at paras 12.34 et seq.

2. Jurisdiction

12.26 Jurisdiction to make orders giving care of a child to any person or providing for contact with, or the education of a child within the meaning of the Family Law Act 1986 s 1(1)(d), is governed by the 1986 Act and is generally confined to where the child is either habitually resident in England and Wales or physically present here and not habitually resident in another part of the United Kingdom or Isle of Man.[1] Exceptionally, where the court considers that the immediate exercise of its powers are necessary for the child's protection, the child's physical presence in England and Wales will suffice to give jurisdiction.[2] Even if there is a residual jurisdiction based on the child's allegiance to the Crown to make orders not caught by s 1(1)(d),[3] it now seems unlikely that the courts will be prepared to take jurisdiction on that basis.[4]

1 FLA 1986, s 3(1). The initial burden of proof lies on the applicant to satisfy the court that it has jurisdiction but once this has been discharged the burden shifts to the defendant to show that jurisdiction has subsequently been lost by establishing, for example, that the child is no longer habitually resident in the country: *Re E (child abduction)* [1992] 1 FCR 541, sub nom *F v S (Wardship: Jurisdiction)* [1993] 2 FLR 686, CA (decided in 1991) and *Re EW* [1992] 2 FCR 441, sub nom *Re R (Wardship: Child Abduction)* [1992] 2 FLR 481, CA.
2 FLA 1986, s 2(3)(b).
3 As accepted by Ward J in *F v S (wardship: jurisdiction)* [1991] FCR 631, [1991] 2 FLR 349, not commented upon on the point by the Court of Appeal. Following *Re F (In Utero)* [1988] Fam 122, [1988] 2 All ER 193, CA, there would appear to be no jurisdiction to protect an unborn child.
4 See *Al Habtoor v Fotheringham* [2001] EWCA Civ 186, [2001] 1 FCR 385, [2001] 1 FLR 951, CA.

3. Powers

(a) The general extent of the inherent powers

12.27 Proceedings under the inherent jurisdiction rank as 'family proceedings'[1] so that the court is empowered either upon application or its own motion to make any s 8 order.[2] The powers under the general inherent jurisdiction are coextensive with those under wardship. As Lord Donaldson MR put it in *Re W (A Minor) (Medical Treatment: Court's Jurisdiction)*:[3]

'Since there seems to be some doubt about the matter, it should be made clear that the High Court's inherent jurisdiction in relation to children the parens patriae jurisdiction' is equally exercisable whether the child is or is not a ward of court . . .'

1 CA 1989, s 8(3)(a).
2 S 10(1).
3 [1993] Fam 64 at 73F, [1992] 4 All ER 627 at 641c. See also Balcombe LJ at 85 and 640 respectively. Query whether the power to restrict publicity about a child is wider under wardship than under the inherent jurisdiction because of the court's continuing supervisory role in the former case? Cf *R v Central Independent Television plc* [1994] Fam 192, at 208, [1994] 3 All ER 641 at 657, per Waite LJ, and note the analysis by Wilson J in *Medway Council v BBC* [2002] 1 FLR 105.

(b) Express restriction of powers under the CA 1989

12.28 Section 100(2)(d) of the CA 1989 prevents the High Court from exercising its inherent jurisdiction[1] 'for the purposes of conferring on any local authority power to determine any question which has arisen, or which may arise, in connection with any aspect of parental responsibility for a child'. This provision does not prevent the High Court from making orders under its inherent jurisdiction in respect of a child but, in doing so, it must not confer any aspect of parental responsibility upon a local authority that the authority does not already have.[2] If the child is in care, then the local authority will already have parental responsibility and so the determination of a particular question by the court, for example, obtaining a return order against abducting parents, will not be contrary to s 100(2)(d).[3] Similarly, the court is free to determine the scope and extent of parental responsibility and can, for instance, make orders giving leave for a child in care to be interviewed by the father's solicitor to prepare a defence to criminal charges.[4] If the local authority do not have parental responsibility for the child, the High Court may not under its inherent jurisdiction make orders which in any way confer parental responsibility upon the authority. Hence, for example, while the court could sanction a named couple to look after the child[5] it could not authorise a local authority to place the child, nor a fortiori, to place the child 'with a view to adoption'. It has, however, been held wrong that s 100 be restrictively interpreted and that it is perfectly proper for a local authority to invite the court to exercise its inherent jurisdiction to protect children even if the exercise of that power would be an invasion of a person's parental responsibility, for example, by restricting a non-family member from contacting or communicating with the children in question.[6]

1   Which, for these purposes, also includes the wardship jurisdiction.
2   See eg Guidance, Vol 1, Court Orders, para 3.102.
3   See *Re DB and CB (minors)* [1993] 2 FCR 607, sub nom *Southwark London Borough v B* [1993] 2 FLR 559 at 571 per Waite LJ.
4   Per Hale J in *Re M (minors) (care: leave to interview child)* [1995] 2 FCR 643, [1995] 1 FLR 825.
5   See eg *Re RJ (minors) (fostering: wardship)* [1999] 3 FCR 646, [1999] 1 FLR 618 in which foster parents were granted care and control of three children – discussed further at para 12.18. Note also the much publicised case in which notwithstanding absconding to Ireland to prevent the local authority from removing two children who, being freed for adoption, had been placed for adoption with them, a couple were granted care and control in subsequent wardship proceedings.
6   Per Thorpe J in *Devon County Council v S* [1994] Fam 169, accepting the argument that the local authority were not seeking leave to apply to the court to confer any power upon themselves but were asking the court to exercise its own powers.

(c)   Other restrictions on the exercise of inherent powers[1]

12.29   Courts have traditionally declined to define the limits of their inherent powers to protect children which have been frequently described as theoretically unlimited.[2] Nevertheless although it is accepted that the High Court's inherent power to protect children is wider than that of a parent,[3] it is equally well established that whatever may be the theoretical position, there are 'far-reaching limitations in principle' on the exercise of that jurisdiction.[4] As Ward LJ put it in *Re Z (A Minor) (Identification: Restrictions on Publication)*:[5]

'The wardship or inherent jurisdiction of the court to cast its cloak of protection over minors whose interests are at risk of harm is unlimited in theory though in practice the judges who exercise the jurisdiction have created classes of cases in which the court will not exercise its powers'.

However, because of the court's tendency to approach the issue on a case-by-case basis rather than by laying down general guidance the precise ambit of these limits is still far from clear. Nevertheless the courts seem to be moving to a position of saying that the inherent jurisdiction should not be exercised so as to exempt the child from the general law or to obtain rights and privileges for a specific child that are not generally available to all children.[6]

1   For a detailed discussion see Lowe and Douglas' *Bromley's Family Law* (9th edn) 704 ff.
2   See eg *Re W (A Minor) (Medical Treatment: Court's Jurisdiction)* [1993] Fam 64, [1992] 4 All ER 627 per Lord Donaldson MR and Balcombe LJ and *Re R (A Minor) (Wardship:*

Restrictions on Publication) [1994] Fam 254 at 271, [1994] 3 All ER 658 at 672, per Millett LJ; and *Re B (child abduction: wardship: power to detain)* [1994] 2 FCR 1142, [1994] 1 FLR 479 at 483 (per Butler-Sloss LJ) and 487 (per Hobhouse LJ).

3 See *Re R (A Minor) (Wardship: Consent to Medical Treatment)* [1992] Fam 11 at 25B and 28G and *Re W (A Minor) (Medical Treatment: Court's Jurisdiction)*, supra. Note also that a similar standpoint has been taken by the Australian High Court in *Department of Health and Community Services v JWB and SMB* (1992) 66 ALJR 300.

4 Per Balcombe LJ in *Re W*, supra, at 85 and 640 respectively, citing Sir John Pennycuick in *Re X (A Minor) (Wardship: Jurisdiction)* [1975] Fam 47 at 61, CA.

5 [1997] Fam 1 at 23, sub nom *Re Z (a minor) (freedom of publication)* [1995] All ER 961 at 977.

6 See eg *Re R (A Minor) (Wardship: Restrictions on Publication)* [1994] Fam 254 at 271, [1994] 3 All ER 658 at 672-673 per Millett LJ and *R v Central Independent Television plc* [1994] Fam 192, [1994] 3 All ER 641, CA.

12.30 Among the more important specific limitations established in wardship and therefore by implication under the inherent jurisdiction are that the court will not interfere with the exercise of powers clearly vested in other bodies such as local authorities,[1] the immigration service[2] or the lower courts.[3] The inherent powers cannot be used to interfere with the normal criminal process[4] nor with the normal operation of military law.[5] It has also been held that there is no inherent power to order a doctor directly or indirectly to treat a child in a manner contrary to his or her clinical judgment.[6] The court has also refused to grant a mandatory injunction against a school to educate a child against its wishes.[7]

1 *A v Liverpool City Council* [1982] AC 363, [1981] 2 All ER 385, HL, discussed at para 12.42.
2 *Re Mohamed Arif An Infant), Re Nirbhai Singh (An Infant)* [1968] Ch 643, [1988] 2 All ER 145, CA, *Re F (A Minor) (Immigration: Wardship)* [1990] Fam 125, [1989] 1 All ER 1155, CA.
3 See eg *Re A-H (Infants)* [1963] Ch 232 and *Re P(AJ) (An Infant)* [1968] 1 WLR 1976.
4 See eg *Re K (a minor) (wardship: criminal proceedings)* [1988] 1 All ER 214.
5 *Re JS (A Minor) (Wardship: Boy Soldier)* [1990] Fam 182, [1990] 2 All ER 861.
6 *Re J (A Minor) (Child in Care: Medical Treatment)* [1993] Fam 15, [1992] 4 All ER 614, CA.
7 *Re C (a minor) (wardship: jurisdiction)* [1991] FCR 1018, [1991] 2 FLR 168, CA.

12.31 The inherent jurisdiction cannot, as a matter of principle, be exercised to override a statutory provision,[1] though it can be a matter of fine judgment to determine what the legislative intention is.[2] It is accepted that the jurisdiction can be used to fill unintended lacunas in legislative schemes.[3]

1 See *Re O (A Minor) (Blood Tests: Constraint)* [2000] Fam 137, [2000] 2 All ER 29 in which Wall J refused to exercise the inherent jurisdiction to override the refusal of a parent with care and control to consent to a blood sample being taken from her child as she was then entitled to do under the Family Law Reform Act 1969, s 21 (since amended by the Child Support, Pensions and Social Security Act 2000, s 82). It is on this ground that Douglas Brown J's decision in *South Glamorgan County Council v W and B* [1993] 1 FCR 626, [1993] 1 FLR 574 that the High Court has an inherent power to override a child's refusal to submit an examination when placed inter alia in interim care can be criticised, since there is a clear statutory power (see eg s 38(6)) to do so.
2 Compare, for example, *Re RJ (foster placement)* [1998] 3 FCR 579, [1998] 2 FLR 110 in which Brown P considered granting care and control to disqualified foster parents would subvert the policy behind the Children (Protection From Offenders) Miscellaneous Amendments Regulations 1997, with that of the Court of Appeal at [1999] 1 WLR 581, [1998] 3 FCR 579, [1999] 1 FLR 605, which was content to say that the Regulations were not directed at the courts.
3 See eg *Re C (A Minor) (Adoption: Freeing Orders)* [1999] Fam 43, 2 WLR 1079, [1999] 1 FCR 145, [1999] 1 FLR 348, discussed at para 12.40.

(d) Exclusion from the family home

12.32 There is uncertainty about whether there is an inherent power to exclude persons from the family home, which is important given that local authorities cannot look to Pt II of the CA 1989 to obtain such a remedy.[1] Prior to *Richards v Richards*[2] there was authority for saying that what were then known as ouster orders could be made broadly on the basis of what was best for the child and it was not unknown for such orders to be made in wardship proceedings.[3] *Richards*, however, seemed to put an end to such a line of reasoning, and in particular seemed to doubt the existence of an independent jurisdiction (ie outside that provided by the family protection legislation) to protect children by means of ouster orders.[4] However, in attempting to reconcile certain post *Richards* decisions, the Court of Appeal in *Pearson v Franklin*[5] concluded that distinctions have to be drawn according to whether the adult parties were spouses, former spouses, cohabitants or former cohabitants. Only if the adult parties were former spouses whose marriage has been dissolved by the decree absolute is there an inherent power to make ouster orders.[6]

1   See *D v D (ouster order)* [1996] 2 FCR 496, sub nom *Re D (Prohibited Steps Order)* [1996] 2 FLR 273 CA, discussed at para 5.77.
2   [1984] AC 174, [1983] 2 All ER 807, HL.
3   See *Re V (A Minor) (Wardship)* (1979) 123 Sol Jo 201 and *Rennick v Rennick* [1978] 1 All ER 817 at 819 and *Spindlow v Spindlow* [1979] Fam 52 at 58 in which Ormrod LJ assumed there was such a power. The matter was not beyond doubt, however: see to the contrary *Re D (Minors)* (1983) 13 Fam Law 111.
4   See eg Lowe and White, *Wards of Court* (2nd edn) pp 6-51.
5   [1994] 2 All ER 137, [1994] 1 WLR 370. In doing so Nourse LJ acknowledged that the distinctions between couples who are or have been married and unmarried couples who are or have been living together 'may not, on a long view, be satisfactorily explicable'. See also the critical commentary at [1994] Fam Law 379-380.
6   Following *Webb v Webb* [1986] 1 FLR 541, and *Wilde v Wilde* [1988] FCR 551, [1988] 2 FLR 83, CA, each in turn applying *Quinn v Quinn* (1983) 4 FLR 394, CA.

12.33 Since *Pearson*, however, there have been two first instance decisions suggesting that the inherent powers may be wider. In the first, *Re S (minors) (inherent jurisdiction: ouster)*[1] Connell J, granted a local authority's request under s 100 for leave to pursue an application to exclude a father from the matrimonial home, while in the second, *C v K (ouster order: non parent)*,[2] Wall J also concluded there remained an inherent power to protect children by means of an ouster order. Whether the appellate courts will be disposed to uphold either decision remains to be seen but so far as the former is concerned the need to do has been undermined by the power to include exclusion requirements in interim care orders and emergency protection orders introduced by the Family Law Act 1996.[3]

1   [1994] 2 FCR 986, sub nom *C v K (Inherent Powers: Exclusion Order)* [1994] 1 FLR 623.
2   [1996] 3 FCR 488, [1996] 2 FLR 506. See also *Devon County Council v S* [1994] Fam 169, [1995] 1 All ER 243 in which Thorpe J acted under the inherent jurisdiction to exclude a family friend (see further para 12.39). See the analysis by Judge Fricker QC at [1994] Fam Law 629.
3   Viz under ss 38A (discussed at paras 8.32–8.33) and 44A (discussed at paras 7.47–7.48) of the CA 1989. Query whether it is implicit in these reforms that Parliament was anticipating courts to apply the Family Law Act 1996 when making exclusion orders?

4. Local authority use of the jurisdiction

(a) The need to obtain leave

12.34 Although local authorities cannot look to the inherent jurisdiction as a means of putting them in charge of the child's living arrangements[1] they can nevertheless seek to use it to resolve specific questions about the child's future. Indeed, because of the unavailability of wardship[2] and of s 8 orders (by reason of the embargoes in s 9(1) and (2))[3] they must do so if the child is in their care. Nevertheless, this avenue is fettered because under s 100(3) of the CA 1989 local authorities must first obtain the court's leave to apply for any exercise of the High Court's inherent jurisdiction.[4]

1 See CA 1989, s 100(2).
2 See paras 12.6-12.7.
3 Discussed at para 5.98.
4 See eg *Devon County Council v B* [1997] 3 FCR 333, [1997] 1 FLR 591, CA. But note that according to *Re P (care orders: injunctive relief)* [2000] 3 FCR 426, [2000] 2 FLR 385 insofar as powers are sought under s 37 of the Supreme Court Act 1981 (viz injunctive relief to support rights conferred by the Children Act 1989) leave is not required.

(b) Criteria for granting leave

12.35 Before granting leave, the court must first be satisfied that the result sought to be achieved cannot be achieved under any statutory jurisdiction.[1] This bar will operate even where the statutory remedy is contingent upon the local authority having first to obtain leave before being able to seek an order.[2] This restriction makes it particularly difficult for an authority to obtain leave for the exercise of the inherent jurisdiction in respect of a child not in their care, since in those circumstances they could seek to obtain a prohibited steps or specific issue order under s 8,[3] or possibly injunctive relief under s 37 of the Supreme Court Act 1981.[4] In *Re R (a minor) (blood transfusion)*[5] a local authority wishing to obtain sanction for a blood transfusion for a child contrary to his parents' (who were Jehovah's Witnesses) wishes, were refused leave because, as the child was not in care, an appropriate remedy could be obtained under s 8.[6] One example, however, where leave might be given is where it is sought to restrain publicity about a child, since that seems to fall outside the scope of s 8.[7]

1 CA 1989, s 100(4)(a).
2 S 100(5)(b).
3 *Re C (a child) (HIV test)* [1999] 3 FCR 289, [1999] 2 FLR 1004 where a local authority successfully applied for a specific issue order to have a baby tested for HIV.
4 See *Re P (care orders: injunctive relief)* [2000] 3 FCR 426, [2000] 1 FLR 385 – injunction granted under the CA 1989 to require parents to allow the child (who was being fostered) to attend school without interference.
5 [1993] 2 FCR 544, [1993] 2 FLR 757, per Booth J. This point was apparently overlooked by Thorpe J in *Re S (a minor) (Medical Treatment)* [1993] 1 FLR 376. Cf *Re O (a minor) (medical treatment)* [1993] 1 FCR 925, [1993] 2 FLR 149.
6 Though Booth J was doubtful about whether a specific issue order should be granted ex parte. Sed quaere?
7 See para 5.76. For an example of the exercise of the inherent jurisdiction in this context, see *Nottingham City Council v October Films Ltd* [1999] 2 FCR 529, [1999] 2 FLR 347. Cf *Medway Council v BBC* [2002] 1 FLR 104.

12.36 Even if there is no alternative remedy, before granting leave, the court must be satisfied that 'there is reasonable cause to believe that if the court's inherent jurisdiction is not exercised with respect to the child he is likely to suffer significant harm'.[1] It has been accepted[2] that cases determining the meaning of 'likely to suffer significant harm' for the purposes of s 31[3] are also relevant to its meaning under s 100(4)(b). This potentially stringent requirement has been criticised as being too restrictive. Since a local authority must of necessity not be seeking to acquire full parental responsibility but to have some specific matter of upbringing determined, the less onerous welfare test would surely have been appropriate.[4]

1 CA 1989, s 100(4)(b).
2 Per Connell J in *Essex County Council v Mirror Group Newspapers Ltd* [1996] 2 FCR 831, [1996] 1 FLR 585. Leave was refused in that case. But as Bainham, *Children – The Modern Law* (2nd edn) 407, points out, unlike s 31, s 100(4)(b) only requires the court to be 'reasonably satisfied' that significant harm might result in the jurisdiction is not exercised. But see *Medway Council v BBC* [2002] 1 FLR 104, in which Wilson J could not find that there was even a 'reasonable cause' to believe that in the absence of restraint of a 30 second broadcast, the boy in question was likely to suffer significant harm.
3 Discussed at paras 8.38 et seq.
4 See Eekelaar and Dingwall (1989) 139 NLJ 217, 218; Lowe (1989) 139 NLJ 87, 88 407. Cf Bainham, above at 407.

(c) Circumstances when the leave criteria have been or might be satisfied

12.37 Local authorities were not expected to make frequent use of the inherent jurisdiction.[1] In cases where a child is in care the local authority will have parental responsibility and should normally make any necessary decisions themselves and in cases where the child is not in care, specific issue or prohibited steps orders under s 8 will normally provide an appropriate remedy. Nevertheless, there will be occasions when recourse to the High Court will be appropriate. Lord Mackay instanced[2] the exercise of the inherent power to sanction or forbid an abortion being carried out on a child in care, where there are no other statutory means of seeking a court order and the decision, if wrong, is clearly likely to cause significant harm. In *Re W (A Minor) (Medical Treatment: Court's Jurisdiction)*,[3] for example, it was thought right to invoke the inherent jurisdiction to overcome the refusal of a 16 year-old anorexic child in care to consent to medical treatment. Other examples of medical treatment where leave is likely to be given include sterilisation[4] and contested cases involving emergency medical treatment of a child in care.[5]

1 See the Department of Health, Guidance and Regulations, Vol 1, Court Orders, paras 3.100 and 101.
2 (1989) 139 NLJ at 507.
3 [1993] Fam 64, [1992] 4 All ER 627, CA. See also *Re C (a minor) (detention for medical treatment)* [1997] 3 FCR 49, [1997] 2 FLR 180 and *Re L (medical treatment: Gillick competence)* [1999] 2 FCR 524, [1998] 2 FLR 810. Note also *South Glamorgan County Council v W and B* [1993] 1 FLR 574, in which Douglas Brown J held (dubiously it is submitted, see para 12.31, n1) that the High Court could under its inherent power override the statutory right under the CA 1989, ss 38(6), 43(8) and 44(7) of a child of sufficient understanding to make an informed decision to refuse to submit to an examination or other assessment.
4 *Practice Note: (minors and mental health patients: sterilisation)* [1993] 3 All ER 222, [1993] 2 FLR 222.
5 See *Re O (a minor) (medical treatment)* [1993] 1 FCR 925, [1993] 2 FLR 149, per Johnson J, as explained by Booth J in *Re R (a minor) (blood transfusion)* [1993] 2 FCR 544, [1993] 2 FLR 757.

12.38 Another issue where High Court help might be justified is whether a mentally or physically handicapped child should have a life-saving or life-prolonging operation. While such an issue is obviously crucial to the child concerned, it must not be assumed that leave will always be given. For example, if as in *Re C (A Minor) (Wardship: Medical Treatment)*,[1] a baby is terminally ill and the medical team considers that the goal should be to ease the baby's suffering rather than to achieve a short prolongation of life, then even if the local authority disagree, it is not at all certain that they would satisfy the criterion set out in s 100(4)(b). In practice, the argument of substance may well take place on the application for leave.

1 [1990] Fam 26, [1989] 2 All ER 782, CA. See also *Re C (a minor) (medical treatment)* [1998] 1 FCR 1, [1998] 1 FLR 384, in which, contrary to the parents' wishes, leave was given to take a 16-month-old child suffering from a fatal disease off ventilation. Cf *Re T (a minor) (wardship: medical treatment)* [1997] 1 All ER 906, [1997] 1 WLR 242, CA, in which the court upheld a parental refusal to consent to a life-serving liver transplant for their 18-month-old child.

12.39 The above medical problems are extreme examples of situations when High Court intervention might be justified, but circumstances do not always have to be so extraordinary. In *Re DB and CB (minors)*[1] leave was granted to a local authority first to seek an order for the return of a child in their care and then to seek to enforce that order. In other cases, for example, where a local authority seeks an injunction to prevent a violent father from discovering his child's whereabouts,[2] or from molesting his child[3] or, to restrain harmful publicity about the child[4] then, as the inherent jurisdiction is the only means of obtaining a remedy, it should not be too difficult to satisfy the leave criteria. In *Devon County Council v S*[5] it was held appropriate to exercise the inherent jurisdiction to prevent a family friend (a Sch 1 offender and a paedophile) from having contact with the children and to prevent the mother from allowing the children to have contact with him since there was no other means of obtaining such a remedy. In *Re M (Care: Leave to Interview Child)*[6] the jurisdiction was successfully invoked to permit a child in care to be interviewed by the father's solicitor with a view to preparing evidence in the father's defence in furthering criminal proceedings against him.

1 [1993] 2 FCR 607, sub nom *Southwark London Borough v B* [1993] 2 FLR 559, CA.
2 *Re JT (A Minor)* [1986] 2 FLR 107.
3 Cf *Re B (A Minor) (Wardship: Child in Care)* [1975] Fam 36, [1974] 3 All ER 915.
4 See eg *Nottingham City Council v October Films Ltd* [1999] 2 FCR 529, [1999] 2 FLR 347.
5 [1994] Fam 169, [1995] 1 All ER 243, per Thorpe J.
6 [1995] 2 FCR 643, [1995] 1 FLR 825, per Hale J.

12.40 Another example of where the court has exercised its inherent jurisdiction at the behest of a local authority is in relation to revoking freeing for adoption orders. A key case is *Re C (A Minor) (Adoption: Freeing Order)*[1] in which notwithstanding a previous freeing order there was no longer any prospect of the 15-year-old child being adopted. Under the 1976 Adoption Act, adoption agencies have no power to seek to revoke a freeing order and in this case, because she had made a s 18(6) declaration that she no longer wished to be involved, the mother had no right to seek a revocation. Accordingly, on its face it was not possible to discharge the freeing order.[2] However, in Wall J's view, Parliament could not have intended such a result and, relying on *Re J (A Minor) (Wardship: Jurisdiction)*[3] (which in turn relied upon dicta by Lord Wilberforce in *A v Liverpool City Council*)[4], held that he could exercise his inherent jurisdiction to fill the unintended lacuna. Although it could be argued that there was no *unintended* lacuna,[5] *Re C* has been followed on at least two occasions[6] and is now unlikely to be challenged especially since freeing will be replaced by placement orders under the Adoption and Children Bill 2002 currently before Parliament.

1 [1999] Fam 240, [1999] 2 WLR 1079, [1999] 1 FCR 145, [1999] 1 FLR 348.
2 It was for this reason that Wall J was unable to apply the reasoning in *Re G (A Minor) (Adoption: Freeing Order)* [1997] AC 613, [1997] 2 All ER 534, HL.
3 [1984] 1 WLR 81, [1984] 1 All ER 29.
4 [1982] AC 363 at 372-373, [1981] 2 All ER 385 at 388-389.
5 See eg Spon Smith 'Inherent Jurisdiction and Freeing Orders' [2000] Fam Law 43.
6 Viz *Re J (Adoption: Revocation of Freeing Order)* [2000] 2 FCR 133, [2000] 2 FLR 58 and *Oldham Metropolitan Borough Council v D* [2000] 2 FLR 382.

12.41 Although in theory the granting of leave does not automatically mean that the court must exercise its jurisdiction, given that it must be satisfied that the child is likely to suffer significant harm if the jurisdiction is not exercised[1] it would be an unusual case where leave was given and the jurisdiction not subsequently exercised.

1 This requirement distinguishes s 100 from leave under s 10 to apply for a s 8 order, where it by no means follows that an order be made following the granting of leave. See para 5.119.

5. Individual's use of the jurisdiction

12.42 Although individuals can invoke the inherent jurisdiction there is normally little advantage in doing so, not least because of the continued availability of wardship. However, as wardship cannot be invoked, where the child is in local authority care, if it is sought to invoke the High Court's inherent powers to challenge a local authority decision in relation to a child in care, it can only be done, if at all, under the wider inherent jurisdiction. However, before the Children Act 1989 it was well settled that the High Court would not allow the prerogative jurisdiction to be used as a means of challenging authorities' decisions over children in care. The basic rationale for what became known as the '*Liverpool* principle' was that as Parliament had vouchsafed a wide discretion in local authorities over the management of children in care, it was not for the courts to subvert that intention by allowing parents and others a right of challenge through wardship and therefore outside the statutory system. As Lord Wilberforce said in *A v Liverpool City Council*:[1]

'In my opinion the court has no such reviewing power. Parliament has by statute entrusted a local authority the power and duty to make decisions as to the welfare of children without any reservation of reviewing power to the court.'

1 [1982] AC 363, [1981] 2 All ER 385, HL. See also *Re W (A Minor) (Wardship: Jurisdiction)* [1985] AC 791, [1985] 2 All ER 301, HL.

12.43 Nothing in the Children Act 1989 can be taken to have altered the pre-Act standpoint. This was made clear by Butler-Sloss LJ in *Re B (Minors) (Termination of Contact: Paramount Consideration)*[1] who commented:

'*A v Liverpool City Council* is still, in my opinion, of the greatest relevance beyond the confines of child care law and the principle set out by Lord Wilberforce is equally applicable today, that the court has no reviewing power over the exercise of the local authority's discretionary decisions in carrying out its statutory role.'

She further observed that the principal judicial remedy for an abuse of power is judicial review.[2]

1 [1993] Fam 301 at 309, [1993] 3 All ER 524 at 529 – 530. See also *Re P (a minor) (leave to apply: foster parents)* [1994] 2 FCR 1093, sub nom *C v Salford City Council* [1994] 2 FLR 926, per Hale J. Note also the comments in *Re A (Minors) (Residence Orders: Leave to Apply)* [1992] Fam 182, [1992] 3 All ER 872, CA, per Balcombe LJ, and *Kent County Council v C* [1993] Fam 57, [1993] 1 All ER 719, per Ewbank J.
2 Though other remedies include invoking the local authority's complaints procedure, invoking the Secretary of State's default powers, complaining to the 'local government ombudsman' or seeking a remedy at the European Court of Human Rights. See Ch 13.

COMMENTARY

12.44 During the passage of the Bill anxieties were expressed about the wisdom of curtailing the use of wardship by local authorities.[1] In particular there was concern that it was potentially detrimental to the interests of the children:

(1) to deprive local authorities, through the removal of the wardship option, from having direct access to the High Court;
(2) to remove the wardship safety net underpinning the statutory scheme for obtaining care or supervision orders;
(3) to curtail the power formerly enjoyed, inter alia, under the wardship jurisdiction to commit children into care on the court's own motion; and
(4) to deprive the court of being able to use its flexible powers under wardship when making care or supervision orders.

1 See, inter alia, Lowe: (1989) 139 NLJ 87, but note the reply by Eekelaar and Dingwall at (1989) NLJ 217.

12.45 Not all the above-mentioned concerns have proved to be well founded in practice. In particular, the lack of direct access to the High Court in care cases has not proved problematic inasmuch as there is little or no evidence to suggest that cases that should be heard by the High Court are not in fact being heard at that level.[1] Similarly, while there might be some misgivings as to the majority's interpretation in *Re H (Minors) (Sexual Abuse: Standard of Proof)*,[2] given the House of Lords more generous interpretation both in *Re M (a Minor) (Care Order: Threshold Conditions)*[3] and in *Lancashire County Council v B*,[4] the threshold provisions under s 31 have so far stood the test of time reasonably well.

1 There are, however, problems caused by transfers made late in proceedings. See further ch 4.
2 [1996] AC 563, [1996] 1 All ER 1, HL, discussed at paras 8.51 et seq.
3 [1994] 2 AC 424, [1994] 3 All ER 298, HL, discussed at paras 8.46 et seq.
4 [2000] 2 AC 147, [2000] 2 All ER 97, HL, discussed at paras 8.62 et seq.

12.46 On the other hand concern has been expressed about the court's inability even to direct that the local authority institute care proceedings.[1] In *Nottingham County Council v P*[2] Sir Stephen Brown P said:

'This court is deeply concerned at the absence of any power to direct the authority to take steps to protect the children. In the former wardship jurisdiction it might well have been able to do so. The operation of the Children Act 1989 is entirely dependent upon the full co-operation of all those involved. This includes the courts, local authorities, social workers, and all who have to deal with children. Unfortunately, as appears from this case, if a local authority doggedly resists taking the steps which are appropriate to the case of children at risk of suffering significant harm it appears that the court is powerless.'

The former flexible powers under wardship when making care or supervision orders seem also to be missed in particular in being able to provide a regime under which the court can monitor the local authority's care plan,[3] which, as we have seen,[4] was the subject of prominent litigation ending with the House of Lords' decision in *Re S (Minors) (Care Order: Implementation of Care Plan, Re W (Minors) (Care Order: Adequacy of Care Plan).*[5] This issue, however, is likely to be addressed in the Adoption and Children Bill 2002.

1 All the court can do is to make a direction under s 37 (discussed at paras 5.158 and 7.4) that a local authority investigate the child's circumstances.
2 [1994] Fam 18 at 43, [1993] 3 All ER 815 at 828, CA.
3 See the discussion in *Divided Duties: Care Planning for Children within the Family Justice System* (eds Thorpe and Clarke).
4 See paras 8.94 et seq.
5 [2002] UKHL 10, [2002] 2 WLR 720, [2002] 2 All ER 192, [2002] 1 FCR 577, [2002] 1 FLR 815, discussed at paras 8.94 et seq.

12.47   Both the wardship and inherent jurisdictions have proved remarkably enduring and it is evident that they continue to play a small but not unimportant role notwithstanding the Children Act 1989.

Chapter 13

Challenging decisions

APPEALS

1. Generally

13.1 In line with the policy of creating concurrent jurisdiction the CA 1989 provides the same right and avenue of appeal for all proceedings under the Act regardless of whether they are private or public law cases. Although with regard to the former the substantive provisions are essentially the same as under the pre-1989 Act law, the CA 1989 made fundamental changes to the public law position allowing for the first time local authorities a general right of appeal against the refusal of a care or supervision order.[1] Since the Act there has been an important procedural change in that in most cases an appeal to the Court of Appeal requires court permission.[2] The right and avenue of appeal under the CA 1989 is the same as in other proceedings concerning children.[3]

1 Formerly appeals were only permitted on points of law.
2 See Civil Procedure Rules (CPR) 1998 r 52.3, which came into force on 2 May 2000, and which replaced, pursuant to the powers conferred by the Access to Justice Act 1999, RSC Orders 55 and 59, discussed at para 13.11.
3 A uniform system of appeals is provided for by CPR 1998, Pt 52.

13.2 With certain exceptions and subject to permission when appealing to the Court of Appeal, there is a general right of appeal against the making or refusal to make orders (including 'no orders') under the CA 1989.[1] In the private law context, any party can appeal against the making or refusal to make, for example, s 8 orders, directions under s 13, parental responsibility orders under s 4 or guardianship orders under s 5. Similarly, in the public law context anyone who had party status (including, therefore, local authorities) in the original proceedings may appeal against the making of a care or supervision order (including an interim order) or of an order varying or discharging such an order, or against the court's refusal to make such order.[2] This includes a direction made under s 38(6).[3]

1 S 94(1).
2 But note Johnson J's comment in *Re M (prohibited steps order: application for leave)* [1993] 1 FCR 78, [1993] 1 FLR 275 that CA 1989, s 94(1) should not be read as limiting the class of those entitled to appeal. Hence in that case the local authority could appeal even though they were not a party to the original proceedings.
3 *Re O (minors) (medical examination)* [1992] 2 FCR 394, [1993] 1 FLR 860.

13.3 Although as a matter of principle there is no automatic embargo against appealing against a consent order, normally such an appeal will only be entertained where it is made with the leave of the court that made the order.[1] The exception to this is where it is alleged that the judge brought improper pressure upon a party to reach a settlement[2] or so conducted the case as to prevent the party from putting his case properly.[3] Where the consent order has been reached by the parties without involvement of the judge at all then, unless leave to appeal has been given, the proper procedure is to apply to the first instance court to vary the order.[4]

1 See *Re R (A Minor) (Consent Order: Appeal)* [1995] 1 WLR 184, [1994] 2 FCR 1251, sub nom *Re R (Contact: Consent Order)* [1995] 1 FLR 123, CA and the SCA 1981, s 18(1).
2 See *Re R* Above, respectively at 190, 1257–1258 and 123 at 129, CA, per Stuart-Smith LJ.
3 See *Jones v National Coal Board* [1957] 2 QB 55, [1957] 2 All ER 155, CA.
4 *Re F (a minor) (appeal)* [1992] 1 FCR 167, sub nom *Re F (A Minor) (Custody: Consent Order: Procedure)* [1992] 1 FLR 561, CA.

13.4 Notwithstanding the aforesaid general right of appeal there are some limitations:

- There is no right of appeal against the making of or refusal to make an emergency protection order.[1]
- There is no right of appeal against a magistrates' court decision to decline jurisdiction (where it has power to do so) because it considers that the case can be more conveniently dealt with by another court.[2]

Furthermore, because it is a matter of judicial discretion, there is effectively no right of appeal. against a decision not to interview a child in private,[3] or against whether or not to ask for a welfare report.[4] It has also been said that an application to discharge a care order should be made, rather than an application for an extension to appeal out of time.[5]

1 S 45(10) but note the criticisms in *Re P (emergency protection order)* [1996] 3 FCR 637, [1996] 1 FLR 482 and in *Essex County Council v F* [1993] 2 FCR 289, [1993] 1 FLR 847.
2 S 94(2). Note also there is no right of appeal in relation to an interim order for periodical payments under Sch 1 to the CA 1989: CA 1989, s 94(3), see *Clarke Hall and Morrison* at 4[14].
3 See *Re R (a minor) (religious sect)* [1993] 2 FCR 525, sub nom *Re R (A Minor) (Residence: Religion)* [1993] 2 FCR 163, CA.
4 *Re W (a minor) (welfare reports)* [1995] 3 FCR 793, [1995] 2 FLR 142, CA.
5 *Re S (minors) (care orders: appeal out of time)* [1996] 2 FCR 838, sub nom *Re S (Minors) (Discharge of Care Order)* [1995] 2 FLR 639, CA.

13.5 The comparatively unrestricted right of appeal, at least to the High Court from a family proceedings court, imposes a duty on advocates not to advise or encourage an appeal in cases with no hope of succeeding, however dissatisfied the party may be with the decision.[1] Legal advisers have been warned not to be carried away by the enthusiasm, frustration and hurt of their lay clients, it being observed that hopeless family appeals which have been brought without leave on public funds were all too frequent examples of public money spent to no good effect and as having an adverse effect upon the children concerned.[2]

1 *Re D (minors) (family appeals)* [1995] 1 FCR 301, CA, per Butler-Sloss LJ. See also Handbook of Best Practice in Children Act Cases (Children Act Advisory Committee, June 1997) para 89(a). Note also the comment in *Practice Note* [1999] 1 All ER 186, at para 7.
2 *Re N (minors) (residence orders: sexual abuse)* [1996] 1 FCR 244, sub nom *Re N (Residence: Hopeless Appeals)* [1995] 2 FLR 230, CA, per Butler-Sloss LJ. The courts have also warned legal advisers of hopeless appeals that they might make wasted costed orders against them.

See *Re G (A Minor) (Role of Appellate Court)* [1987] 1 FLR 164, CA and *Re O (a minor) (legal aid costs)* [1997] 1 FCR 159, sub nom *Re O (Costs: Liability of Legal Aid Board)* [1997] 1 FLR 465, CA. Cf *B v B (wasted costs order)* [2001] 3 FCR 724, [2001] 1 FLR 743.

13.6 In cases before the family proceedings court, advocates must not take an adversarial view of the proceedings. Accordingly, if the justices are in the process of making or appear likely to make a decision which is procedurally plainly wrong, it is the duty of the advocates, and notably those acting for the children's guardian and the local authority, to advise the justices that they are about to make a fundamental error of law.[1]

1   *Re F (interim care order: evidence)* [1994] 1 FCR 729, sub nom *Re F (A Minor) (Care Order: Procedure)* [1994] 1 FLR 240.

2. Routes of appeal and procedure

(a)   Appeals from the magistrates' courts

13.7 The general rule, provided by, s 94(1) of the CA 1989, is that an appeal lies to the High Court against both the making and the refusal to make any order by a magistrates' court. Appeals lie to a single judge of the Family Division unless the President otherwise directs.[1] Save in the case of consent orders,[2] leave to appeal is not required.

1   Handbook of Best Practice in Children Act Cases (Children Act Advisory Committee, June 1997) para 87.
2   See para 13.3.

13.8 The procedure for appealing is governed by the FPR 1991, r 4.22 (which also applies to appeals against any decision of a district judge). The appellant must file and serve on the parties:

* written notice of appeal setting out the grounds relied upon;
* a certified copy of the order appealed against and of any order staying its execution;
* copies of any notes of evidence; and
* copies of any reasons for the decision.

Notice of appeal must be filed and served within 14 days after the determination against which the appeal is brought or seven days where the appeal is against an interim care order or interim supervision order. Although these periods for service may be altered[1] by the High Court upon application, these time limits are strict and extensions of time will not be granted without good reason which advocates will be expected to justify.[2] Similar strict time limits[3] are laid down for respondents wishing to cross appeal or to seek a variation, or an affirmation of the decision on grounds other than those relied upon by the magistrates. No notice may be filed or served in an appeal against an order under s 38 of the CA 1989.[4]

1   Viz to a longer or shorter period: FPR 1991, r 4.22(3)(c).
2   See Handbook of Best Practice in Children Act Cases (Children Act Advisory Committee, June 1997) para 89(b).
3   Viz 14 days of receipt of the notice of appeal: FPR 1991, r 4.22(5).
4   FPR 1991, r 4.22(6).

13.9   Ideally, appeals should take place at the nearest convenient High Court centre.[1] It is vital, however, that the appeal be set down promptly and where it is unlikely that a case can be listed without delay on Circuit, arrangements will be made for the appeal to be heard in London.[2] Appellants should file a paginated bundle with a chronology together (save in the most simple cases) with a skeleton argument in advance of the hearing. Advocates must also file in advance an accurate estimate of the length of the hearing and keep the court informed of any change to that estimate.[3]

1   *Practice Direction* [1992] 1 All ER 864 [1992] 1 WLR 261, as supplemented by the *Procedural Directive* [1992] 2 FLR 503, but cf *R v Oxfordshire County Council (Secure Accommodation Order)* [1992] Fam 150, sub nom *R (J) v Oxfordshire County Council* [1992] 3 All ER 660.
2   Handbook of Best Practice in Children Act Cases (Children Act Advisory Committee, June 1997) para 90.
3   Handbook of Best Practice in Children Act Cases (Children Act Advisory Committee, June 1997) para 91.

13.10   Upon an appeal, the High Court may make such orders as may be necessary to give effect to its determination of the appeal and such incidental and consequential orders as appear just.[1] Any order made on appeal, other than that directing the application to be reheard by the magistrates, for the purposes of enforcement[2] and any power to vary, revive or discharge the order, shall be treated as if it were an order of the original magistrates' court and not the High Court.[3]

1   S 94(5) and (6).
2   Ie MCA 1980, s 63(3), applies, see *B (BPM) v B (MM)* [1969] P 103, sub nom *B (B) v B (M)* [1969] 1 All ER 891.
3   CA 1989, s 94(9).

(b)   Appeals from county courts and the High Court

13.11   Appeals generally lie to the Court of Appeal.[1] The procedure is now governed by CPR 1998, Pt 52 and the accompanying *Practice Direction*.

1   County Courts Act 1984, s 77(1); Supreme Court Act 1981, s 16. But note so far as County Courts are concerned (1) there is a power in the original tribunal to review interim orders and also to order a rehearing if new evidence comes to light: County Court Rules 1991 Ord 37, r 1 (not revoked in relation to family proceedings: CPR 1998, r 2.1), and (2) appeals from district judges normally lie to a circuit judge unless he is sitting in the Principal Registry when it lies to the High Court, see *Re S (a minor) (appeals from the principal registry)* [1997] 2 FCR 119, [1997] 2 FLR 856.

(c)   Permission to appeal

13.12   Both the appellant and the respondent require permission to appeal save where the appeal is against:

- a committal order;
- a refusal to grant habeas corpus;
- a secure accommodation order made under the CA 1989, s 25; or
- as provided by the relevant practice direction.[1]

Where the appeal is from a decision which itself was the determination of an appeal (ie a 'second appeal') permission to appeal is required from the Court of Appeal which will not be given unless it raises an important principle or practice or there is some other compelling reason.[2]

1   CPR 1998, r 52.3(1).
2   CPR 1998, r 52.13, *Practice Direction* 52, para 4.9.

13.13   Save in the case of second appeals, where permission *must* be sought from the Court of Appeal,[1] permission to appeal should normally be sought from the lower court first[2] but if that application is refused or if no application was made at the first instance hearing, permission can then be sought from the Court of Appeal.[3] If the appeal court refuses permission without a hearing the applicant has the right to ask for an oral hearing.[4] There is, however, no appeal from a decision of the appeal court made at an oral hearing either to allow or to refuse permission to appeal to that court.[5]

1   See para 13.12.
2   *Practice Direction* 52 para 4.6 the rationale being that because the first instance court is usually in the best position to determine whether leave to appeal should be given, where the parties are present for the delivery of the judgment it should be routine for the judge below (a) to ask whether either party wants leave to appeal and (b) to deal with the matter there and then. Applications should be made orally.
3   CPR 1998, r 52.3(2), (3) and *Practice Direction* 52, para 4.7.
4   CPR 1998, r 52.3(4).
5   *Practice Direction* 52, para 4.8 referring to s 54(4) of the Access to Justice Act 1999.

13.14   In the case of first appeals, permission to appeal will only be given where:
  '(a) the court considers that the appeal would have a real prospect of success; or
  (b)   there is some other compelling reason why the appeal should be heard'.[1]

In the case of second appeals the test is more stringent in that the court should not give permission unless it considers that:
  '(a) the appeal would raise an important point of principle or practice; or
  (b)   there is some other compelling reason for the Court of Appeal to hear it'.[2]

An order giving permission may limit the issues to be heard and be made subject to conditions.[3]

1   CPR 1998, r 52.3(6).
2   CPR 1998, r 52.13(2).
3   CPR 1998, r 52.3(7).

13.15   Applications for permission to appeal should be made orally to the lower court at the hearing at which the decision to be appealed is made[1] or to the appeal court in an appeal notice.[2] Applications for permission may be considered by the appeal court without a hearing.[3] If granted the parties will be notified of that decision.[4] If refused, the parties will be informed of the reasons but this latter decision is subject to the appellant's right to have it reconsidered at an oral hearing.[5] A request for reconsideration must be filed at the appeal court within seven days after service of the notice that permission has been refused and a copy of the request must be served by the appellant on the respondent at the same time.[6]

1   *Practice Direction* 52, para 4.6.
2   CPR 1998, r 52.3(2)(b), and see para [13.16] below.
3   *Practice Direction* 52, para 4.11. Unless the court directs otherwise such applications need not be on notice. However, such directions will usually be given if the appellant is seeking a remedy against the respondent pending the appeal: *Practice Direction* 52, para 4.15.
4   *Practice Direction* 52, para 4.12.
5   *Practice Direction* 52, para 4.13.

6 *Practice Direction* 52, para 4.14. If no request is made for the decision to be reconsidered, the refusal becomes binding once the time limits have expired. In children cases it is not uncommon for the Court of Appeal to adjourn the application for an oral hearing on notice with an appeal to follow if permission is granted.

13.16 Where the appellant seeks permission from the appeal court it must be requested in the appellant's notice.[1] This notice should be filed at the appeal court within such a period as may be directed by the lower court or, in the absence of any such direction, within 14 days of the date of the lower court's decision that is being appealed. If an extension of time for filing is required, the application should be made in the appellant's notice,[2] stating the reason for the delay and the steps taken before the making of the application. This appeal notice should, unless the appeal court otherwise orders, be served on each respondent as soon as practicable and in any event not later than seven days after it is filed. Similarly, where the respondent seeks permission it must be requested in the respondent's notice and filed within such period as directed by the lower court or, in the absence of any such direction, within 14 days of the date when the respondent:

(a) is served with the appellant's notice; or
(b) receives notification that the appeal court has given the appellant permission to appeal; or
(c) receives notification that the application for permission to appeal and the appeal itself are to be heard together.

This notice should, unless the appeal court otherwise directs, be served on the appellant or any other respondent as soon as practicable and in any event not later than seven days after it is filed.[3] An appeal notice may not be amended without the appeal court's permission.[4]

1 CPR 1998, r 52.4(1), and see Form N161.
2 See respectively CPR 1998, r 52.4(2), r 52.6 and *Practice Direction* 52, para 5.2 and r 52.4(3).
3 CPR 1998, r 52.5(1), (5), (6).
4 CPR 1998, r 52.8.

13.17 The granting of permission to appeal does not operate to stay the order which is the subject of appeal. Instead a specific application to stay must be made.[1] Similarly, separate applications should also be made for other remedies incidental to the appeal, eg an interim remedy or security for costs.[2]

1 CPR 1998, r 52.7.
2 *Practice Direction* 52, para 5.5.

(d) Documents to be included with the appellant's notice

13.18 Except where it relates to a refusal of permission to apply for judicial review,[1] the appellant must lodge the following documents with his notice:

'(1) one additional copy of the appellant's notice for the appeal court;
(2) one copy of the appellant's notice for each of the respondents;
(3) one copy of any skeleton argument . . . ;
(4) a sealed copy of the order being appealed;
(5) any order giving or refusing permission to appeal, together with a copy of the reasons for that decision;
(6) any witness statements or affidavits in support of any application included in the appellant's notice; and

(7) a bundle of documents in support of the appeal – this should include copies of the documents referred to in paragraphs (1) to (6) and any other documents which the appellant reasonably considers necessary to enable the appeal court to reach its decision on the hearing of the application or appeal. Documents which are extraneous to the issues to be considered should be excluded. The other documents will, subject to paragraph 5.7, include –

   (a) any affidavit or witness statement filed in support of the application for permission to appeal or the appeal;

   (b) a suitable record of the reasons for judgment of the lower court . . . ;

   (c) where permission to appeal has been given or permission is not required; any relevant transcript or note of evidence . . . ;

   (d) statements of case;

   (e) any application notice (or case management documentation) relevant to the subject of the appeal;

   (f) in cases where the decision appealed was itself made on appeal, the first order, the reasons given and the appellant's notice of appeal from that order;

   (g) in cases where the appeal is from a tribunal, a copy of the tribunal's reasons for the decision, a copy of the decision reviewed by the tribunal and the reasons for the original decision;

   (h) in the case of judicial review or a statutory appeal, the original decision which was the subject of the application to the lower court;

   (i) relevant affidavits, witness statements, summaries, experts' reports and exhibits;

   (j) any skeleton arguments relied on in the lower court; and

   (k) such other documents as the court may direct.'[2]

1 *Practice Direction* 52, para 15.3.
2 *Practice Direction* 52, para 5.6.

(e) *Skeleton arguments*

13.19 The appellant's notice must either be accompanied by a skeleton argument or such an argument may be included in the notice unless:

(a) it is impracticable to do so, in which case it must be lodged and served on all respondents within 14 days of the filing of the notice; or

(*b*) the appellant is unrepresented (though even unrepresented litigants are encouraged to do so since this is helpful to the court).[1]

1 *Practice Direction* 52, para 5.9.

13.20 Skeleton arguments for the appeal court should contain a numbered list of points of no more than a few sentences which should both define and confine the areas of controversy. Each point should be followed by references to any documentation on which the appellant seeks to rely.[1] The appellant should also consider what other information the appeal court will need, for example, a list of persons who feature in the case or glossaries of technical terms. In most appeals a chronology of relevant events will be necessary. In relation to points of law, authorities relied upon should be cited with reference to the particular pages where the principle concerned is set out.[2]

1 *Practice Direction* 52, para 5.10. In practice this requirement seems more honoured in the breach than in the observance.
2 *Practice Direction* 52, para 5.11.

(f) Procedure after permission is granted

13.21 Where the appeal court gives permission to appeal, copies of all the documents must be served on the respondent within seven days of receiving the order giving permission to appeal.[1] The Court of Appeal will send the parties notification of either the date of the hearing or the period of time (the 'listing window') during which the appeal is likely to be heard and the date by which the appeal will be heard.[2] In addition it will send the parties a questionnaire which must be completed and lodged within 14 days of the date of the letter of notification and which must include, if the appellant is legally represented, the advocate's time estimate for the hearing and details of the preparation of documents.[3]

1 *Practice Direction* 52, para 6.2
2 *Practice Direction* 52, para 6.3. In Children's cases hearing dates are normally listed within 3 months of permission being granted.
3 *Practice Direction* 52, paras 6.4–6.6.

3. The position pending appeal

13.22 Under the general powers to impose directions and conditions in private law orders under the CA 1989, s 11(7)[1] the operation of any s 8 order can be postponed pending an appeal, or other interim arrangements can be made. Stays, may be granted at first instance both in the county court and High Court.[2] In these cases any stays or other interim arrangements pending an appeal imposed under s 11(7) should be made before the parties leave the court since once they have left the court and an appeal is lodged the court at first instance ceases to have jurisdiction.[3]

1 Discussed at paras 5.85 et seq.
2 In cases of urgency stays can be granted over the telephone, see eg *Re R (a minor) (recovery order)* [1998] 3 FCR 321 at 328, [1998] 2 FLR 401 at 406. According to Wood J in the pre Children Act decision, *Hereford and Worcester County Council v EH* [1985] FLR 975 at 977, stays should not normally be granted for more than 14 days.
3 Per Singer J in *Re J (a minor) (residence)* [1993] 2 FCR 636 at 642, [1994] 1 FLR 369 at 375. For the position regarding magistrates' powers see para 13.24 below.

13.23 In public law cases the court may, if it dismisses an application for a care order and at the time of dismissal the child is the subject of an interim care or supervision order, make either a care or supervision order, as the case may be, for a limited duration pending an appeal.[1] Similarly, upon granting a discharge, the court may order either that its decision is not to have effect or that the care or supervision order is to continue, pending the appeal.[2] In each case these orders may have effect only for the 'appeal period', that is, either between the lodging of an appeal and the determination of it, or the time during which an appeal may be made.[3]

1 Section 40(1), (2).
2 Section 40(3).
3 Section 40(4) and (6).

13.24 Justices have no statutory power to grant a stay of a care order. If an appeal is being considered and a stay required, the proper course is to apply to the High Court where the judge has such power under his inherent jurisdiction.[1] It may be, however, that justices have a common law power to grant a stay of execution, which has not been affected by, s 40. In an appropriate case the court should consider the welfare of the child and the effect of a move pending appeal.[2]

1   *Re O (a minor) (care order: education: procedure)* [1992] 4 All ER 905, [1992] 2 FLR 7. Applications for stays pending a s 94 appeal can be heard by the High Court without the involvement of the magistrates court: *Re J (a minor) (residence)* [1993] 2 FCR 636 at 643, [1994] 1 FLR 369 at 376, per Singer J.
2   See *Re M (a minor) (appeal: interim order)* [1994] 1 FCR 1, [1994] 1 FLR 54. See also In context: *Stay of Execution pending Appeal* [1992] 2 FCR 896.

4.   The powers of appellate courts – the general position

13.25   An appellate court may grant or dismiss the appeal.[1] Alternatively, if it is satisfied that the original order was wrong but is unsure upon the evidence what order should be made, it can remit the case for a rehearing and in the meantime give appropriate directions. This power of remittal, at any rate in cases where the order appealed from is a final order, includes the power to remit the case to a different court level from that of first instance.[2]

1   Where an appeal is granted it may make such incidental or consequential orders as it thinks just (CA 1989, s 94(5)).
2   See *Suffolk County Council v C* [1999] 1 FCR 473n, [1999] 1 FLR 259n, per Holman J explaining and distinguishing *Leicestershire County Council v G* [1995] 1 FCR 205, [1994] 2 FLR 329. See also *D v D (application for contact)* [1994] 1 FCR 694.

13.26   The appeal court has 'a wide ranging power to consider and deal with the way in which the court below came to its decision but it is not empowered to hear evidence, except in certain circumstances.'[1] It can, however hear fresh evidence to resolve its doubts about the original decision.[2] The admission of such evidence is at the appellate court's discretion,[3] though it is normally admitted if it relates to relevant circumstances occurring between the first instance hearing and the appeal hearing. In the private law context it has been held[4] that appeals concerning children do not automatically call for an up-to-date welfare report. If fresh evidence is admitted, the appellate court will look to see if it invalidates the first instance decision, and if that decision is found wrong on the material before the court the appeal will normally be allowed.[5] Conversely, the admission of fresh evidence may justify upholding the original decision even though it has been held to be plainly wrong.[6]

1   See *Croydon London Borough v A* [1992] Fam 169, [1992] 3 All ER 788.
2   See Lord Scarman in *B v W (wardship: appeal)* [1979] 3 All ER 83 at 95–6, HL. But note Waite LJ's comments in *Re G (A Minor) (Care: Evidence)* [1994] 2 FLR 785, 797, CA that so the so-called rule in *Ladd v Marshall* [1954] 3 All ER 745, [1954] 1 WLR 1489, is applied less rigorously in children cases.
3   *A v A (Custody Appeal: Role of Appellate Court)* [1988] 1 FLR 193, CA; *M v M (Minor: Custody Appeal)* [1987] 1 WLR 404, CA; *Re C (A Minor) (Wardship: Proceedings)* [1984] FLR 419, CA and *Ladd v Marshall*, supra
4   *M v M (Welfare Report)* [1989] 2 FLR 354, CA.
5   *Re C (A Minor) (Care: Child's Wishes)* [1993] 1 FLR 832, sub nom *Re G (a minor) (appeal)* [1993] 1 FCR 810; *Croydon London Borough v A* [1992] Fam 169, [1992] 3 All ER 788.
6   *M v M (Minor: Custody Appeal)* [1987] 1 WLR 404, CA.

13.27   In deciding whether to allow an appeal, there are no special rules governing cases involving children. In *G v G*[1] the House of Lords held that an appellate court cannot overturn a first instance decision merely upon the basis that it disagrees with it. Rather it must be satisfied that either the judge has erred as a matter of law (ie he applied the wrong principle) or that he relied upon evidence that he should have ignored or ignored evidence that he should have taken into account, or that the decision was so 'plainly wrong' that the only legitimate conclusion was that the judge had erred in the exercise of his discretion. Applying *G v G*, Lord Nicholls has forcibly observed:[2]

> 'The Court of Appeal is not intended to be a forum in which unsuccessful litigants, where no error occurred at first instance, may have a second trial of the same issue by different judges under the guise of an appeal. The mere fact that appellate judges might have reached a different conclusion had they been carrying out the evaluation and balancing exercise does not mean that the first instance judge fall into error'.

This approach applies equally to appeals against private law or public law decisions[3] or those made in wardship[4] and regardless of whether, for example, the appeal is to the High Court from a magistrates' court decision, to a circuit judge from a district judge or to the Court of Appeal from a judge.[5]

1   [1985] 2 All ER 225, [1985] 1 WLR 647, HL.
2   *Re B (a child) (sole adoption by unmarried father)* [2001] UKHL 70, para [17], [2002] 1 FCR 150, [2002] 1 FLR 196. See also *Re C (leave to remove from jurisdiction)* [2000] 2 FCR 40, [2000] 2 FLR 457, CA.
3   See eg *Croydon London Borough Council v A* [1992] Fam 169, [1992] 3 All ER 788, *Re G (a Minor) (Care: Evidence)* [1995] 2 FCR 120, [1994] 2 FLR 785, CA and *Re S (Appeal from Principal Registry: Procedure)*[1998] 1 FCR 119, [1997] 2 FLR 856.
4   See *B v W (Wardship: Appeal)* [1979] 3 All ER 83, [1979] 1 WLR 1041, HL.
5   Per Butler-Sloss LJ in *Re W (A Child) (Illegitimate Child: Change of Surname)* [2001] Fam 1 at para [23], [2000] 2 WLR 258, [1999] 3 FCR 337, [1999] 2 FLR 930, CA. See also *Re M (Section 94 Appeals)* [1995] 1 FLR 546, sub nom *Re M (a minor) (contact)* [1995] 2 FCR 435, CA.

5.   The powers of the Court of Appeal

13.28   In respect of appeals against orders made on or after 2 May 2000 it is now expressly provided by CPR 1998, r 52.10 that the Court of Appeal has, in general, all the powers of the lower court and in particular can:

* affirm, set aside or vary any order or judgment made by the lower court;
* refer any claim or issue for determination by the lower court;
* order a new trial or hearing;
* make orders for the payment of interest; and
* make a costs order.

13.29   Appeals are limited to a review of the lower court's decision unless the Court of Appeal considers that in the particular case it is in the interests of justice that there be a rehearing.[1] Unless it orders otherwise the appeal court will not receive oral evidence or evidence which was not before the lower court.[2] At the appeal hearing a party may not rely on a matter that is not contained in the notice of appeal unless the appeal court gives permission.[3]

1   CPR 1998, r 52.11(1).
2   CPR 1998, r 52.11(2). But see also para 13.26.
3   CPR 1998, r 52.11(5).

13.30   The Court of Appeal will allow an appeal where the lower court's decision was:

'(a) wrong; or
(b) unjust because of a serious procedural or other irregularity in the proceedings in the lower court'.[1]

It may draw any inference of fact which it considers justified on the evidence.[2]

1 CPR 1998, r 52.11(3).
2 CPR 1998, r 52.11(4).

13.31 In all cases it is desirable that appeals should be heard as quickly as possible.[1] Failure by barristers and solicitors to exercise the greatest possible diligence in complying with time limits imposed by the courts for the preparation of appeals may be regarded as professional misconduct.[2]

1 See Handbook of Best Practice in Children Act Cases (Children Act Advisory Committee, June 1997) para 90.
2 *Re M (A Minor)* (1989) Times, 29 December, CA.

JUDICIAL REVIEW

1. Nature of the remedy

13.32 Judicial review is the standard administrative law remedy for correcting decisions taken by inferior courts, tribunals and other bodies. Applications are now made to the Administrative Court. As Civil Procedure Rules ('CPR') 1998, r 54.1(2)(a) states:

'a "claim for judicial review" means a claim to review the lawfulness of
(i) an enactment; or
(ii) a decision, action or failure to act in relation to the exercise of a public function'.

13.33 A claim for judicial review may only be made in respect of a decision, action or failure to act in relation to the exercise of a *public* function. It cannot be made merely to enforce private law rights against a public body.[1] Any person with a sufficient interest in the matter may bring a claim.[2]

1 *R v East Berkshire Health Authority ex p Walsh* [1985] QB 152 at 162, [1984] 3 All ER 425 at 429, per Lord Donaldson MR.
2 Supreme Court Act 1981, s 31(3). For further discussion see *Court Procedure: The White Book Service 2001* at 54.1.22 et seq.

13.34 No special rules apply in judicial review of children cases.[1] The function of the court, as Scott Baker J neatly expressed it, is 'to consider in each case not whether the decision itself is right or fair but whether the manner in which the decision is made is fair'.[2] There are three principal remedies, namely, what are now called:[3]

- *mandatory orders* (formerly mandamus), that is, where a body is ordered to comply with statutory duty, for example, that the local authority provide some specific support service provided for in Pt III of Sch 2 to the CA 1989,[4] or to set up a complaints procedure that complies with the regulations issued under s 26;[5]
- *quashing orders* (formerly certiorari), that is, that the original order or decision be quashed as, for example, a Director of Social Services decision

not to ratify a complaints panel decision that a 17-year-old should be accommodated;[6] and

- *prohibiting orders* (formerly prohibition), that is, restraining a body from acting unlawfully.

1 But this is not to say that in judging the reasonableness of a local authority's action in respect of children in their care attention should not be paid to the authority's duty to safeguard the child's interests; cf *R v Harrow London Borough Council, ex p D* [1990] Fam 133, [1990] 3 All ER 12, CA, per Butler-Sloss LJ.
2 *R v Hereford and Worcester County Council, ex p D* [1992] 1 FLR 448 at 457. 'Fairness' is judged in this context against the criteria of legality, rationality and procedural propriety, see para 13.39 below.
3 The former so-called prerogative remedies were renamed by Pt 54 of the CPR 1998 which came into force in October 2000, under the Civil Procedure (Amendment No. 4) Rules 2000, SI 2000/2092. However, the remedies are still referred to by the former name in the Supreme Court Act 1981, s 29.
4 See *R (on the Application of S) v London Borough of Wandsworth, London Borough of Hammersmith and Fulham, London Borough of Lambeth* [2001] EWHC Admin 209, [2002] 1 FLR 469, in which Lambeth and Wandsworth were ordered to make an assessment of whether the children concerned were in 'need'.
5 See *R v London Borough of Barnet, ex p B* [1994] 2 FCR 781 at 788, [1994] 1 FLR 592 at 598, per Auld J. The complaints procedure is discussed at para 13.50 et seq.
6 See eg *Re T (accommodation by local authority)* [1995] 1 FCR 517, [1995] 1 FLR 159. If a quashing order is made the court may remit the matter to the decision-maker and direct it to reconsider the matter but if it feels there is no purpose in remitting, the court can take the decision itself: CPR 1998 r 54.19.

13.35 In addition to these three remedies it is possible to obtain a declaration, for example, that an action or policy is unlawful[1] and/or an injunction to prevent an unlawful act taking place or to prevent an unlawful policy from continuing.[2] It is also possible to include in a claim for judicial review a claim for damages but not to seek damages alone.[3] The court may at any time during the course of judicial review proceedings grant interim relief.[4]

1 See eg *R v Cornwall County Council, ex p LH* [2000] 1 FCR 460, [2000] 1 FLR 236, *R v Thameside Metropolitan Borough Council, ex p J* [2000] 1 FCR 173, [2000] 1 FLR 942, *R v Hampshire County Council ex p H* [1999] 3 FCR 129, [1999] 2 FLR 359, CA, and *R v Birmingham City Council ex p A* [1997] 2 FCR 357, [1997] 2 FLR 841.
2 Unlike when seeking a mandatory, prohibiting or quashing order, it is not mandatory to use the judicial review procedure laid down in CPR 1998 Pt 54, see r 54.3. Note it is not unknown for mandatory injunctions to be sought.
3 CPR 1998, r 54.3(2).
4 CPR 1998, Pt 25.

2. The requirements for judicial review

13.36 A prerequisite for a claim for judicial review is that there must be a reviewable 'decision'. In *R v Devon County Council ex p L*,[1] for example, it was held that a social worker's letter informing the applicant's cohabitant that he was suspected of sexual abuse did not amount to a 'decision' so that the action for judicial review failed at the outset. Even if there is a reviewable 'decision' applicants must first obtain the court's permission to proceed.[2] The procedure for applying for that permission is now governed by CPR 1998, Pt 54. The claimant must first file a claim form in the Administrative Court Office. Claim forms must be filed promptly and in any event not later than 3 months after the grounds to make the claim first arose.[3] Claims must inter alia state any remedy (including any interim remedy) being sought, and provide a detailed statement of the grounds for bringing the claim (accompanied by any written evidence in support) and a time estimate for the substantive hearing of the application for judicial review, should permission be granted.[4]

1 [1991] 2 FLR 541. Cf *R v Chief Constable of North Wales ex p Thorpe* [1999] QB 396, [1998] 2 FLR 571, sub nom *R v Chief Constable of North Wales Police ex p AB*, [1998] 3 All ER 310, [1998] 3 FCR 371, CA – decision of police to reveal applicant's identity (the applicant having served sentences for rape and indecent assault) was amenable to judicial review – but the action failed on facts.
2 CPR 1998, r 54.4.
3 Rule 54.5. Although this time limit cannot be extended simply by agreement between the parties a court may grant an extension subject to a good reason being adduced. But see *Re S (Application for Judicial Review)* [1998] 1 FCR 368, [1998] 1 FLR 790, CA, where leave was refused the application being made four months after the expiration of the time limit.
4 See generally CPR 1998, r 8.2 and 54.2 and the accompanying Practice Direction – Judicial Review paras 5.1, 5.6 and 5.7.

13.37 Applications for permission are generally considered on the papers alone.[1] The claimant does not have a right to have the permission determined at an oral hearing. However, there is a right to request that any decision to refuse or limit the grant of permission be reconsidered at an oral hearing.[2]

1 *Practice Direction* 54, op cit, at para 8.4.
2 CPR 1998, r 54.12(3).

13.38 The requirement to obtain permission is not a formality for, as Balcombe LJ said in *R v Lancashire County Council ex p M*,[1] there must be a reasonable prospect of the court coming to the decision that the local authority's conclusion was so unreasonable that no reasonable local authority could ever have come to it. In any event in some cases it is likely to be held that the preferable remedy is to invoke the complaints procedure.[2] It has been held,[3] for instance, that where neither fact nor law is in dispute but rather the way the local authority carried out its duty, the proper remedy is under the complaints procedure and not by judicial review. Nevertheless the availability of an alternative remedy cannot be said as a matter of principle to mean that there cannot be a judicial review.[4]

1 [1992] 1 FLR 109 at 113, CA. See also *R v Cornwall County Council, ex p E* [1999] 2 FCR 685, [1999] 1 FLR 1055, CA in which leave was refused.
2 Note Ward J's observation in *R v Royal Borough of Kingston-upon-Thomas ex p T* [1994] 1 FLR 798 that it is the clear broad legislative purpose that the complaints procedure should be invoked in preference to judicial review. See further para 13.54. But cf *Re R (recovery orders)* [1998] 3 FCR 321 at 330, [1998] 2 FLR 401 at 409 in which Wall J suggested that judicial review is the only means of challenging a local authority decision to change a 'responsible person' under a care or emergency protection order.
3 *R v Birmingham City Council ex p A* [1997] 2 FCR 357, [1997] 2 FLR 841, per Sir Stephen Brown P (see further para 13.51) and *R v East Sussex County Council ex p W* [1999] 1 FCR 536; [1998] 2 FLR 1082.
4 Per Cazalet J in *R v High Peak Magistrates' Court ex p B* [1995] 3 FCR 237, [1995] 1 FLR 568.

13.39 To substantiate a claim for judicial review, the applicant must be able to bring himself within the so-called *Wednesbury* principle[1] as interpreted by the House of Lords in *Council of Civil Service Unions v Minister for Civil Defence*.[2] According to Lord Diplock in that case,[3] there are three main heads under which court intervention may be justified:

- 'illegality' (where there was an error of law in reaching the relevant decision);
- 'procedural impropriety' (where the relevant rules have not been complied with); and

- 'irrationality' (where a decision 'is so outrageous in its defiance of logic or of accepted moral standards that no sensible person who had applied his mind to the question to be decided could have arrived at it').

1 Following *Associated Provincial Picture Houses Ltd v Wednesbury Corpn* [1948] 1 KB 223, [1947] 2 All ER 680, CA.
2 [1985] AC 374, [1984] 3 All ER 935, HL.
3 [1985] AC 374 at 410, [1984] 3 All ER 935 at 950, HL.

3. Circumstances in which judicial review has been sought

13.40 In the context of disputing local authority decisions,[1] claimants are commonly parents, foster parents, prospective adopters and the children themselves. However, there is no reason why others such as relatives or guardians,[2] should not seek judicial review.

1 Of course claims, concerning children, can be made against bodies other than local authorities, see eg *R (on the application of P) v Secretary of State for the Home Department*; *R (on the application of Q) v Secretary of State for the Home Department* [2001] EWCA Civ 1151, [2001] 3 FCR 416, [2001] 2 FLR 1122, CA, in which claims (one successful and one unsuccessful) and one made against the Prison Service in respect of their policy only to allow babies up to the age of 18 months to remain in prison with their mothers. See also *R (on the Application of the National Association of Guardians ad Litem and Reporting Officers) v Children and Family Court Advisory and Support Service* [2001] EWHC Admin 693, [2002] 1 FLR 255 in which the decision of the CAFCASS board not to proceed with the offer of self employment to guardians ad litem was quashed.
2 See eg *R v Cornwall County Council* [1992] 2 All ER 471, in which the authority's attempt to prescribe maximum hours a guardian could work on a particular case without express authorisation from the council was successfully challenged.

13.41 Although complaints have been made about a variety of local authority decisions by no means were all successful; indeed a significant proportion failed (see the chart at para 13.45 below). A number failed either because the local authority were not under a *duty* to provide the service complained about[1] or because it would have been preferable to have used the local authority complaints procedure.[2] Quite commonly the action will fail because the authority was acting lawfully and reasonably.[3] In this respect it should be appreciated that it is not enough to question the wisdom of a decision, rather the claimant must discharge the heavy onus of showing that no reasonable authority could have reached the particular decision complained of.

1 See eg *A v Lambeth London Borough Council* [2001] EWCA Civ 1624, [2001] 3 FCR 678, [2002] 1 FLR 353, CA, no duty under the CA 1989 to rehouse mother and children notwithstanding the family had been accorded 'overriding priority'; and *R (on the application of G) v London Borough of Barnet)* [2000] EWCA Civ 540, [2001] 2 FCR 193, [2001] 2 FLR 877, CA, no duty, only a power to provide accommodation for mother and child under s 17 of the CA 1989. But both these decisions must now be regarded as wrongly decided see *R (on the Application of W) v Lambeth London Borough Council* [2002] EWCA Civ 613, [2002] 2 FLR 327 and *R (on the Application of J) v Enfield London Borough Council* [2002] EWHC 432 (Admin), [2002] 2 FLR 1. See further ch 6 and the chart below at para 13.45.
2 See eg *R v East Sussex County Council, ex p W* [1999] 1 FCR 536, [1998] 2 FLR 1082, *R v Birmingham City Council, ex p A* [1997] 2 FCR 357, [1997] 2 FLR 841 and *R v Royal Borough of Kingston-upon-Thames, ex p T* [1994] 1 FLR 798, discussed further at para 13.51. But cf *Re R (recovery orders)* [1998] 3 FCR 321, [1998] 2 FLR 401, discussed at para 13.38, n 2.
3 See eg *R (on the Application of S) v Swindon Borough Council* [2001] EWHC Admin 334, [2001] 3 FCR 702, [2001] 2 FLR 776 – only a low threshold viz reasonable cause to suspect abuse to trigger duty under s 47 to investigate and monitor family. See also *R v Hertfordshire County Council, ex p B* [1987] 1 FLR 229, in which an unsuccessful attempt was made by the mother to challenge the local authority's removal of her child at home on trial with her.

13.42 Of those actions that were successful one important factor was the failure of the local authority either to allow the complainant to put his side of the case or otherwise to explain their reasoning. In *R v Devon County Council, ex p O (Adoption),*[1] for example, which involved the removal of a child placed for adoption with the applicants, judicial review succeeded because the local authority failed to consult or give the applicants an opportunity to be heard. Another striking example is *R v Norfolk County Council, ex p M,*[2] which concerned a plumber working in a house where a teenage girl made allegations that she was sexually abused by him. She had twice previously been the victim of sexual abuse and a few days later made similar allegations against another man. After a case conference the plumber's name was entered on the Child Abuse Register as an abuser. His employers were informed and they suspended him pending a fully enquiry. The plumber first learned of these allegations through a letter informing him of the decision to place his name on the register. Waite J held that, given the serious consequences of registration for the plumber, the local authority had a duty to act fairly, which they had manifestly failed to do by not giving him an opportunity to meet the allegations.

1 [1997] 2 FLR 388. Cf *R v Avon County Council, ex p Crabtree* [1996] 1 FLR 502, CA, where the de-registration of an approved foster parent was only made after careful consideration and consultation. Consequently the action failed.
2 [1989] QB 619, [1989] 2 All ER 359.

13.43 The *Norfolk*[1] case was exceptional and, as Butler-Sloss LJ said in *R v Harrow London Borough Council, ex p D,*[2] recourse to judicial review in respect of placing a name on the Child Protection Register ought to be rare. She further held that courts should not encourage applications to review case conference decisions or recommendations because it was important for those involved in this difficult area to 'be allowed to perform their task without having to look over their shoulder all the time for the possible intervention of the court'. She pointed out that in 'balancing adequate protection for the child and the fairness to an adult, the interest of an adult may have to take second place to the needs of the child'.[3] Notwithstanding these observations, there may still be some occasions when judicial review is appropriate, even of a decision to place a child's name on the Protection Register.[4] More recently an action for judicial review succeeded against Cornwall County Council in respect of their policy (a) not to permit solicitors to attend child protection case conferences on behalf of parents, other than to read out a prepared statement, and (b) not to provide parents attending such conferences with a copy of the minutes.[5]

1 *R v Norfolk County Council, ex p M* [1989] QB 619, [1989] 2 All ER 359.
2 [1990] Fam 133, [1990] 2 All ER 12, CA.
3 Above at 138 and 17 respectively. See also *R v London Borough of Wandsworth, ex p P* [1989] 1 FLR 387 at 308 in which Ewbank J said 'Foster-parents have to accept that their interests may have to be subordinated to the children they care for. Accordingly, provided the rules of fairness are complied with, the decision as to whether there is a risk or not, is one that has to be taken by the local authority. In the ordinary way, provided the rules of natural justice are complied with the foster parents have no redress'.
4 See eg *R v Hampshire County Council, ex p H* [1999] 2 FLR 359, CA.
5 *R v Cornwall County Council, ex p LH* [2000] 1 FLR 236, [2000] 1 FCR 460. As Scott Baker J commented (at 243 and 469 respectively) what was complained about in this case was not 'the decision of the conference but the manner in which its deliberations were conducted'.

13.44 Another example of where judicial review succeeded is *Re T (Accommodation by Local Authority),*[1] in which the court quashed the Director of Social Services' decision not to ratify the decision of complaints panel that a 17-year-old child should be accommodated under the CA 1989, s 20(3), on the basis that her welfare would otherwise be seriously prejudiced. In that case the Director was held to have erred when he decided that past provision of support given to her under s 17 of the CA 1989 made it unlikely that the child's future welfare would be seriously prejudiced if she were not provided with accommodation.

1 [1995] 1 FLR 159. For other successful judicial review actions see *R v Avon County Council ex p M* [1994] 2 FLR 1006, *R (on the Application of) Stewart v London Borough of Wandsworth, London Borough of Hammersmith and Fulham, London Borough of Lambeth* [2001] EWHC Admin 709, [2002] 1 FLR 469 and *R v Cornwall County Council* [1992] 2 All ER 471, summarised in the chart below.

(d)   Summary of reported judicial review cases involving children and local authorities 1992–2002

13.44A

Case	Subject-matter	Result
R (on the Application of W) v Lambeth London Borough [2002] EWCA Civ 613, [2002] 2 FLR 327.	Mother of two children evicted for being in arrears with rent, applied to Social Services for assistance in securing private accommodation for herself and her children which was refused.	Failed: Although Social Services had power under s 17 of the Children Act 1989 to provide accommodation for a family in need when not otherwise entitled to help from the local housing authority, the local authority was nevertheless entitled to reserve the use of that power to cope with extreme cases. The court refused to quash the local authority decision but nevertheless hoped that it might reconsider it.
R (on the Application of J) v Enfield London Borough Council [2002] EWHC 432 (Admin), [2002] 2 FLR 1.	A Ghanian mother diagnosed with HIV and who had over stayed her permission to remain in the UK claimed that she should be provided with accommodation or that she and her two-year-old daughter be provided with financial assistance to enable them to secure accommodation.	Succeeded: Although there is no duty under s 17 of the CA 1989 to provide financial assistance to secure accommodation there was a duty to do so under s 2 of the Local Government Act 2000. A refusal to provide such assistance would amount to a breach of Art 8 of the European Convention of Human Rights inasmuch as it would cause the separation of mother and child.
R (on the Application of Stewart) v London Borough of Wandsworth, London Borough of Hammersmith and Fulham, London Borough of Lambeth [2001] EWHC Admin 709, [2002] 1 FLR 469.	After being informed that she was intentionally homeless a mother sought an assessment as to whether her children were 'in need'. She applied to Wandsworth which had temporarily housed the family; to Lambeth where the temporary accommodation was situated and to Wandsworth where the children went to school. Each authority refused to make an assessment.	Succeeded: Lambeth and Wandsworth were ordered to make an assessment; the children being physically present in the area which triggered their duty under s 17 of the CA 1989.

Case	Subject-matter	Result
R (on the Application of L) and Others v Manchester City Council; R (on the Application of R) and Another v Manchester City Council [2000] EWHC Admin 707, [2002] 1 FLR 43	Local authority policy to pay short-term foster carers who were friends or relatives of the child a significantly lower rate in respect of child's maintenance than was paid to other foster-carers.	Succeeded: policy to pay lower rate to foster carers who were friends or relatives was irrational and discriminatory against both the adults and the children concerned.
R (on the application of S) v Swindon Borough Council [2001] EWHC Admin 332, [2001] 3 FCR 702, [2001] 2 FLR 776.	Complaint that notwithstanding his acquittal on sexual abuse charges two local authorities continued to treat the claimant as posing a risk to children particularly those unrelated to him, The first authority accordingly decided that there remained a need to consider and deal with the prospect of the claimant interfering with the children, while the second authority informed the ex-husband of the claimant's new partner of their risk assessment.	Failed: each local authority had acted lawfully in the assessment of risk and their respective decisions were not perverse. The duty under s 47 of the CA 1989 was only triggered by a reasonable cause to suspect abuse – they did not have to be satisfied that it had taken place. The acquittal did not ipso facto mean that there was no risk.
R (on the application of G) v London Borough of Barnet [2001] EWCA Civ 540, [2001] 2 FCR 193, [2001] 2 FLR 877.	Decision that a 2-year-old child brought to the UK by a mother who was a Dutch national was not 'in need' because his long-term interests could best be met in settled accommodation with financial support that would be available in Holland. The mother was offered fares to return to Holland with her child. The authority also offered in the alternative to provide accommodation for the child.	Failed: Under s 17 local authorities only have a power not a duty to provide accommodation for mother and child. Here the duty was satisfied by the offer of return fares and, by offering to accommodate the child in the alternative, the authority had also fulfilled its duty under s 20. But note *Lambeth* above.
R (on the application of AB and SB) v Nottingham City Council [2001] EWHC Admin 235, [2001] 3 FCR 350.	Failure to carry out a proper core assessment based on the Framework for the Assessment of Children in Need and their Families document.	Succeeded: Failure without good cause to identify the child's needs (including housing needs); produce a care plan, and to provide identified services amounted to an impermissible departure from the Framework guidance.

Case	Subject-matter	Result
R v Somerset County Council, ex p Prospects Care Services [2000] 1 FLR 636	Decision to publish a document for promulgation to other authorities from whom enquiries were received containing information about a private fostering agency, the details of which were objected to by the agency.	Failed: the authority had acted intra vires in publishing the details and had acted reasonably in doing so.
R v Cornwall County Council, ex p LH [2000] 1 FCR 460, 2000] 1 FLR 236	Local authority policy not to (a) permit solicitors to attend child protection case conferences on behalf of parents save to read out prepared statement, and (b) give parents attending such conferences copy of the minutes.	Succeeded: Both policies declared to be unlawful.
R v Tameside Metropolitan Borough Council, ex p J [2000] 1 FCR 173, [2000] 1 FLR 942	Decision to move an 'accommodated' child from residential care to foster care without parental permission.	Succeeded: Without parental responsibility such local authority action was ultra vires.
R v Cornwall County Council, ex p E [1999] 2 FCR 685, [1999] 1 FLR 1055, CA	Decision to give foster parents (who had just given notice of their intention to apply for adoption) notice of removal under the Adoption Act 1976, s 30.	Failed: Leave refused – decision not unreasonable.
R v Hampshire County Council, ex p H [1999] 2 FLR 359, CA	Decision to place three siblings on Child Protection Register following allegations (later withdrawn) by one of the children that he had been physically abused by step-father.	Succeeded in part. Declaration granted in respect of third child since there was insufficient material to justify registration.
R v Hammersmith and Fulham London Borough Council, ex p D [1999] 1 FLR 642.	Decision not to continue to provide accommodation and a subsistence allowance for child if mother did not accept local authority offer to fund return to Sweden.	Succeeded – wrong to decide or threaten to withdraw future assistance – in clear breach of statutory duty under CA 1989, s 17.
R v East Sussex County Concil, ex p W [1999] 1 FCR 536, [1998] 2 FLR 1082.	Child complaining local authority had wrongly not sought a care order.	Failed – should have used complaints procedure.
R v Devon County Council ex p A [1997] 2 FLR 388.	Prospective adopters complaining child had wrongfully been removed.	Succeeded – insufficient consultation.

Case	Subject-matter	Result
R v Birmingham County Council ex p A [1997] 2 FCR 357, [1997] 2 FLR 841.	Child and mother seeking declaration that local authority had not acted with due diligence in placing child in appropriate accommodation.	Failed – in absence dispute of law or fact should use complaints procedure.
R v Avon County Council, ex p Crabtree [1996] 1 FLR 502, CA.	Approved foster parents complaining about their de-registration.	Failed – adequate warning and consultation.
Re T (Accommodation by Local Authority) [1995] 1 FLR 159.	17-year-old child complaining about local authority decision not to accommodate her.	Succeeded – Director of Social Services did not accept complaints panel decision – erred in assessing, on basis of past support, child's future welfare would not be prejudiced.
R v Royal Borough of Kingston-upon-Thames, ex p T [1994] 1 FLR 798.	Complaint by mother about a refusal to accommodate child at a particular home.	Failed – complaints procedure preferable – in any event decision not 'Wednesbury unreasonable'.
R v London Borough of Brent, ex p S [1994] 1 FLR 203, CA.	Child complaining about local authority failure to provide adequate accommodation.	Failed – decision not 'Wednesbury unreasonable'.
R v Secretary of State for Health, ex p Luff [1992] 1 FLR 59.	Complaint by prospective adopters about Department of Health recommendation that applicants were unsuitable to adopt Romanian orphan.	Failed – decision neither perverse nor 'Wednesbury unreasonable'.
R v Lancashire County Council, ex p M [1992] 1 FLR 109, CA.	Complaint by prospective adopters that LA (as an adoption agency) had potential adopters.	Failed – decision not perverse nor 'Wednesbury unreasonable'.
R v Cornwall County Council, ex p G [1992] 1 FLR 270.	Complaint by Guardians ad Litem about Director of Social Services' decision to put limits on number of hours to be spent on any one case.	Succeeded – decision unreasonable.

REVIEWS, COMPLAINTS AND OTHER REMEDIES

1. Generally

(a) Review of children's cases

13.45 Regulations made under s 26 require the review of the case of each child being looked after by a local authority.[1] They provide in detail for the manner, content and frequency of reviews, the considerations to which the authority is to have regard and who is to be consulted beforehand and notified of the result afterwards. The regulations apply where accommodation is provided by a voluntary organisation.[2]

1   Review of Children's Cases Regulations 1991, SI 1991/895. Note these Regulations will prospectively be widened by the Adoption and Children Bill to include reviewing care plans.
2   CA 1989, s 59(4). See also paras 8.1ff of The Children Act 1989 Guidance and Regulations Volume 3 'Family Placements' (Dept of Health, 1991).

(b)   Complaints about after-care

13.46   Every local authority must establish a procedure for considering any representations (including any complaint) made to it by a person qualifying for advice and assistance about the discharge of its functions under Pt III of the 1989 act in relation to him.[1] This allows young people to complain if they consider that the local authority has not given them adequate preparation for leaving care, or adequate aftercare.[2]

1   Section 24D(1), added by the Children (Leaving Care) Act 2000, s 5.
2   Cf *R v Lambeth London Borough Council, ex p Caddell* [1998] 2 FCR 6, [1998] 1 FLR 253. See further, para 6.56.

2.   Complaints procedures[1]

13.47   It is mandatory for all local authorities, voluntary authorities providing accommodation for the child and children's homes[2] to have a formal representation or complaints procedure in relation to their Pt III powers and functions.[3] To ensure that there is an independent element, s 26(4) provides that at least one person who is not a member or officer of the authority concerned must take part in the consideration of the complaint or representation and in any discussions held by the authority about the action to be taken. Equally importantly, under s 26(8) there is an obligation to publicise the complaints procedure. Rules governing the scope and procedure of the complaints scheme are provided by the Representations Procedure (Children) Regulations 1991.[4] The Department of Health and Social Services Inspectorate have also issued practice guidance.[5]

1   See generally Williams 'The practical operation of the Children Act complaints procedure' [2002] CFLQ 25.
2   Section 26(3) as applied by reg 11 of the Representations Procedure (Children) Regulations 1991 (SI 1991/894), issued pursuant to s 59(4), (5).
3   Failure to have a procedure or having one that fails to comply with the regulations can be remedied by invoking the Secretary of State's default powers under s 84 (see para 13.56), per Auld J in *R v London Borough of Barnet, ex p B* [1994] 2 FCR 781 at 788, [1994] 1 FLR 592 at 598. Note also that the local authorities have to make provision for complaints about community care: see LASSA 1970, s 7B. There will also a separate complaints system in relation to the CAFCASS service. The initial interim procedure is expected to be replaced by a new procedure towards the end of 2002, see *Setting up – Report of a Programme of Visits to the Children and Family Court Advisory and Support Service* (HM Magistrates' Courts Service Inspectorate, March 2002).
4   SI 1991/894.
5   *The Right to Complain – Practice Guidance on Complaints Procedures in Social Services Departments* (HMSO, 1991). Note also the subsequent Inspectorate's reports of 1993, 1994 and 1996.

(a) Who may complain?

13.48   Under s 26(3) complaints may be made against the relevant body by:

- a child who is being looked after or who is not being looked after but is in need. This is intended to ensure that children are consulted on decisions taken about them.[1] It could also assist a child who believes he should be accommodated where the body is refusing to offer the service;[2]
- a parent;[3]
- any other person (other than a parent) with parental responsibility;
- any local authority foster parent; or
- such other person as the authority consider has a sufficient interest in the child's welfare to warrant representations being considered by it about the discharge by the authority of any of their functions under Pt III in relation to the child.

1   According to the Department of Health's Guidance (Volume 3) para 10.7, the responsible authority should always check with the child (subject to his understanding) that a complaint submitted on his behalf reflects his views and that he wishes the person submitting it to act on his behalf.
2   See Ward J in *Royal Borough of Kingston-upon-Thames, ex p T* [1994] 1 FLR 798 at 812.
3   Including the unmarried father.

13.49   The procedure is available to a wide range of people. In addition to the child, parents or other persons with parental responsibility or other members of the family, who cannot achieve their objectives by applying for discharge of a care order or an application for contact with the child, are entitled to have their complaint heard. Foster parents are able to question why a child is being moved away from them or why they are being denied an enhanced fostering allowance. Other interested people can use the procedure, though this is subject to the local authority's discretion. Nevertheless while an authority may decide who it considers has a sufficient interest in the child's welfare, it would be difficult to deny that professionals in other agencies providing a service to the child would qualify.

(b) What may be complained about?

13.50   The statutory complaints procedure caters for complaints about local authority support for families and their children under Pt III of the CA 1989. This includes, as the Department of Health's *Guidance* (Volume 3) says:[1]

'... complaints about day care, services to support children within their family home, accommodation of a child, after-care and decisions relating to the placement of a child or the handling of a child's case. The processes involved in decision making or the denial of a service must also be covered by the responsible authority's arrangements.'

In *R v Birmingham City Council, ex p A*[2] judicial review was sought to challenge a local authority's apparent inability speedily to place a child with special needs with an appropriate foster parent. Sir Stephen Brown P commented that, in cases such as these where neither fact nor law was in dispute but instead the ground of complaint was the way the authority was carrying out its duty, the appropriate remedy was a complaint under, s 26. Similarly it has been held[3] that the complaints procedure would in ordinary circumstances, provide a suitable alternative remedy to judicial review to question a local authority decision not to apply for a care order.

1   Guidance (Volume 3) at para 10.8
2   [1997] 2 FLR 841.
3   Per Scott Baker J in *R v East Sussex County Council ex p W* [1999] 1 FCR 536, [1998] 2 FLR 1082.

13.51   Matters falling outside Pt III,[1] including the placing of a child's name on the Child Protection Register and complaints by private foster parents on their own behalf, do not have to be included in the scheme. However, as the Department of Health's *Guidance* says, a responsible authority should consider what other matters might appropriately be covered by the procedures to meet the requirements of the Regulations.[2]

1   Except decisions about the 'usual fostering limit' which are included under the Representations Procedure (Children) Regulations 1991, SI 1991/894, reg 12(2).
2   Guidance (Volume 3) at para 10.9.

(c)   Procedure and outcome

13.52   There is a two-stage process for handling complaints (which can be made at any time): a relatively informal stage, and, if that does not resolve matters, a formal stage before a panel. In the first instance the responsible authority and an independent person must consider the representation and formulate a response within 28 days.[1] If the claimant is dissatisfied with the responsible authority's response, he has 28 days to request in writing that the complaint be heard by the panel,[2] which in turn must meet within 28 days after the receipt by the local authority of such a request. The complainant and authority can each make written and oral submissions to the Panel.[3] The panel must make a recommendation within 24 hours of its meeting and give written notification of it to the responsible authority, the complainant, the independent person (if he is not a member of the panel) and any other interested person.[4] The responsible authority must consider what action, if any, should be taken in the light of the panel's findings and notify among others the complainant and the child (if of sufficient understanding) of their decision and reasons for taking that decision.[5]

1   Representations Procedure (Children) Regulations 1991, SI 1991/894, reg 6. But note the delay in *R v Lambeth London Borough Council, ex p Caddell* [1998] 2 FLR 6, [1998] 1 FLR 253 . The independent person can inter alia interview the child and, if different, the complainant: reg 8(1).
2   See reg 8(2). The panel, which must include at least one independent person, is appointed by the local authority for this purpose: reg 8(2)–(3) It must meet within 28 days after the receipt by the local authority of the request: reg 8(4). As the Department of Health's Guidance (Volume 3) at para 10.22 comments, this second stage of the procedure does not affect the complainant's right to complain about maladministration to the local ombudsman (discussed at paras 13.58ff), since the panel is not a decision-making body.
3   See reg 8(5).
4   See reg 9.
5   Section 26(7)(b).

13.53   Although a panel decision is not binding upon the local authority,[1] as Peter Gibson LJ said in *R v London Borough of Brent, ex p S*,[2] it would be 'an unusual case when a local authority acted otherwise than in accord with the panel's recommendations and the independent person's views'. Furthermore, ignoring or failing reasonably to consider the recommendations will lay the authority open to judicial review.[3] On the other hand, as Ward J observed in *R v Borough of Kingston-upon-Thames, ex p T*,[4] it is the clear broad legislative purpose that the complaints procedure should be invoked in preference to judicial review in respect of matters within the remit of s 26. In any event the remedy is quicker and more convenient. In *Kingston*, Ward J specifically rejected both the argument that because the panel was dominated by local authority membership it was likely to be biased, and that it was ineffective. In relation to the former argument he was satisfied that professional integrity would ensure fairness and in relation to the latter he pointed to the availability of judicial review should any recommendation simply be ignored.

1   This is implicit in, s 26(7) which requires the authority, having had due regard to the findings, to 'take such steps *as are reasonably practicable*' [emphasis added].
2   [1994] 2 FCR 996 at 1004, [1994] 1 FLR 203 at 211.
3   Per Ward J in *Royal Borough of Kingston-upon-Thames, ex p T* [1994] 1 FLR 798 at 814. For examples of where judicial review was successfully invoked see *Re T (Accommodation by Local Authority)* [1995] 1 FLR 159, and *R v Avon County Council, ex p M* [1994] 2 FCR 259.
4   [1994] 1 FLR 798.

13.54   The effectiveness of the complaints system is an important issue particularly given the lack of power of the courts to review local authority decisions in individual cases.[1] Relatively little is known about the actual use of the procedure,[2] though there is evidence that children themselves are reluctant to complain because of fear of victimisation or retaliation.[3] Research in other contexts[4] has found that parents are generally reluctant to complain either because they are tired of battling the system or cannot see the point of doing so, the damage already having been done.

1   It was moreover cited as a justification for not imposing a general duty of care upon local authorities, see *X v Bedfordshire County Council* [1995] 2 AC 633, [1995] 3 All ER 353, HL, discussed further at para 13.62. Under the Adoption and Children Bill 2002 there will prospectively be a power to review implementation of care plans.
2   But see the Inspection of the Complaints Procedures in Local Authority Social Services Departments, Social Services Inspectorate, July 1993 which found only 14% of complaints related to the Children Act. See also Williams and Jordan *The Children Act 1989 Complaints Procedure: A Study of Six Local Authority Areas*.
3   See Williams and Jordan 'Factors relating to publicity surrounding the complaints procedure under the Children Act' (1998) 8 CFLQ 337.
4   See Murch and Lowe, Borkowski, Weaver, Beckford *Supporting Adoption – Reframing the Approach* (1999) 251-252.

DEFAULT POWERS OF THE SECRETARY OF STATE

13.55   Section 84, enables[1] the Secretary of State to declare a local authority in default where he is satisfied that they have without reasonable cause, failed to comply with a *duty*[2] under the Act. Such a declaration may contain such directions as are necessary to ensure compliance within a specified period and may be enforced upon the Secretary of State's application for a mandatory order.[3]

1   Ie it is only a discretionary power, the Secretary of State is not obliged to act even if a local authority is in default, see *R v London Borough of Brent, ex p S* [1994] 2 FCR 996 at 1004, [1994] 1 FLR 203 at 211, per Peter Gibson LJ.
2   Ie not simply a power, see Peter Gibson LJ in *R v London Borough of Brent*, ex p S, supra.
3   Section 84(2), (3). Mandatory orders are discussed at para 13.34.

13.56   Although individuals aggrieved by a local authority decision (or lack of it) may make a complaint under s 84[1] it would be wrong to regard the provision as conferring, either expressly or by implication, on any individual a right so to appeal. As has been pointed out,[2] the Secretary of State's power exists irrespective of any complaint or representation. He can act of his own motion. Furthermore there appears to be no restriction on the material, or its sources, from which the Secretary of State may draw his conclusions. It accordingly follows that the existence of these default powers does not bar applications for judicial review.[3]

1   As was suggested in *R v Barnet London Borough Council, ex p B* [1994] 2 FCR 781, [1994] 1 FLR 592, where it was alleged that a local authority was failing to provide a day care service. During the debates on the Bill the Solicitor General commented that the general expectation was that the Secretary of State would exercise his powers, if at all, where an authority's failure to discharge its statutory duties affected a class as opposed to individual children, see HC Official Reports (6th Series) SC col 492 (13 June 1989).
2   Per Peter Gibson LJ in *R v London Borough of Brent, ex p S* [1994] 2 FCR 996 at 1004, [1994] 1 FLR 203 at 211.
3   See *R v London Borough of Brent*, ex p S, Above at 1007 and 214 respectively.

APPLYING TO THE LOCAL GOVERNMENT OMBUDSMAN

13.57   Another possible avenue for individuals aggrieved by a local authority decision (or the lack of it) concerning their children is to complain to the Commissioner for Local Administration ('the Local Government Ombudsman'), according to the procedure[1] set out by the Local Government Act 1974 (LGA 1974) as amended and under which investigations of written complaints of 'maladministration' may be investigated.[2]

1   A free booklet explaining the procedure is available from the Commissioner.
2   In Wales complaints can also be made to the Children's Commissioner for Wales under s 74 of the Care Standards Act 2000 (as amended by the Children's Commissioner for Wales Act 2001). See Hollingsworth and Douglas 'Creating a children's champion for Wales?' (2002) 65 MLR 58.

13.58   Before a complaint may be made, the local authority must first be given an opportunity to address it.[1] If, however, this approach has not produced a satisfactory result, a complaint can be made. Complaints can be made directly to the Commissioner or through a councillor.[2] The Commissioner cannot normally investigate complaints concerning proceedings or events that occurred more than 12 months previously.[3]

1   LGA 1974, s 26(5).
2   Formerly they had to be initially referred to a local councillor, but this was changed by LGA 1988, s 29 and Sch 3.
3   LGA 1974, s 26(4).

13.59   To find the complaint justified the Commissioner must find there has been 'maladministration'. The Court of Appeal has ruled[1] that it is not necessary for the complainant to spell out the particular maladministration which led to the injustice complained of; it is sufficient if he specifies the action alleged to be wrong. This is generally taken to refer to the procedure by which the decision is made or put into action rather than to the merits of the particular decision itself. At the conclusion of his investigation the Commissioner issues a report and, if he has found maladministration and injustice, he may recommend an ex gratia payment.[2] Although the local authority must consider these recommendations they are not *bound* to follow them and indeed, given the passage of time, may not be able to do so if that would be inconsistent with the child's welfare.

1   See *R v Local Comr for Administration for the North and East Area of England, ex p Bradford Metropolitan City Council* [1979] QB 287, [1979] 2 All ER 881, CA.
2   Awards of £1,000 have been recommended where a local authority failed to follow a case conference's recommendation, and of £2,000 where children were inappropriately interviewed about allegations of sexual abuse.

13.60   As a general mechanism for scrutinising administrative action, the main drawbacks are that:

- the central concern is with procedural propriety and not the child's welfare;
- the Commissioner may have no expertise in child matters;
- the investigation is itself a long process[1] and will probably result in delaying implementation of plans for the child's long-term future (it is in any event a process concerned to judge the past and not to manage the future); and
- even if 'maladministration' is established, there is no power to interfere with the decision taken by the authority.[2]

1   Though in *Re A Subpoena (Adoption: Comr for Local Administration)* [1996] 2 FLR 629 it was held that the Commissioner was entitled to subpoena a local authority to produce adoption documents.
2   In *Z and others v United Kingdom* [2001] 2 FCR 246, [2001] 2 FLR 614 at para [107], ECtHR, the Government accepted that in the particular circumstances of the case complaining to the Local Government Ombudsman and/or under the complaints procedure was insufficient to satisfy the requirements of Art 13 of the European Convention on Human Rights – see further para 13.70 below.

CLAIMS FOR DAMAGES FOR FAILURE BY LOCAL AUTHORITIES TO CARRY OUT THEIR STATUTORY DUTIES[1]

1.   Limited liability for negligence

13.61   At one time English domestic law set its face against superimposing a general common law duty of care on local authorities in relation to performance of their duties to protect children. The key case was *X (Minors) v Bedfordshire County Council*[2] which comprised five test cases, two of which concerned the way local authorities had dealt with child abuse. In one, *M v Newham London Borough*, the parents alleged that a child had been taken into care after an inadequate investigation into allegations of harm. In the other, *X v Bedfordshire County Council*, the position was reversed, the allegation being that the local authority failed properly to investigate reports suggesting that the children had been abused and therefore adequately to protect them. The five children concerned sought damages for personal injuries. In each case the action failed since the House of Lords held that a child had no cause of action for harm arising from:

- an alleged failure of a local authority to comply with its statutory duties under children's welfare legislation;
- careless performance of a statutory duty by an authority;
- negligence in respect of an alleged failure; and
- actions or decisions where a common law duty of care might arise, if they came within the ambit of a statutory discretion.

Furthermore, it held there was no right of action in private law for breach of statutory duty, although this did not necessarily exclude recourse being had to judicial review or complaint to the Local Government Ombudsman.

1 Cf *L v Reading Borough Council* [2001] EWCA Civ 346, [2001] 1 FCR 673, sub nom *L & P v Reading Borough Council and Chief Constable of Thames Valley Police* [2001] 2 FLR 50, CA, in which the court refused to strike out a negligence action against the police in connection with false allegations (made by the mother) of sexual abuse by the father.
2 [1995] 3 WLR 152, [1995] 2 AC 633, [1995] 3 All ER 353, HL, on which see Cane 'Suing public authorities in tort' (1996) 112 LQR 13, Oliphant 'Tort' (1996) 49 Current Legal Problems 29 and Bailey Harris and Harris 'The Immunity of local authorities in child protection functions – Is the door now ajar?' (1998) 10 CFLQ 227.

13.62 Lord Browne-Wilkinson said that a distinction had to be drawn between those alleged negligent acts or decisions which involved policy matters, which were not justiciable in tort at all, and those which did not. Where policy matters were not involved, then it had to be shown that the local authority had exercised its jurisdiction so unreasonably that it had acted outside the discretion entrusted to it by Parliament. In this latter case the plaintiff would then have to bring him or herself within the tripartite test established by *Caparo Industries v Dickman*:[1]

- Was the damage to the plaintiff reasonably foreseeable?
- Was the relationship between the plaintiff and the defendant sufficiently proximate?
- Was it just and reasonable to impose a duty of care?

1 [1990] 2 AC 605 at 616–17, HL

13.63 Although *Bedfordshire* did not establish a blanket immunity for any action taken by a local authority in respect of children, it certainly seemed to limit the possibilities of action.[1] However, a number of subsequent domestic decisions have widened the scope for action in negligence. Furthermore the House of Lords decision itself has been ruled in breach of the European Convention and the Government was ordered to pay compensation to the claimants and it is now becoming apparent that ss 7 and 8 of the Human Rights Act 1998 provide an important alternative means of seeking redress. Each of these developments will now be considered.

1 See eg *H v Norfolk County Council* [1997] 2 FCR 334, [1997] 1 FLR 384, CA in which the applicant, then aged 22, failed in his action for damages in negligence against the local authority for failing properly to monitor and supervise his foster care placement (he alleged that he had been sexually and physically abused by his foster-father) and for failing to remove him from that placement. Note that this case has since been said to have been wrongly decided, see *S v Gloucestershire County Council, L v Tower Hamlets London Borough Council* [2000] 3 All ER 346, [2001] 2 WLR 909, [2000] 2 FCR 345, [2000] 1 FLR 825, CA, discussed below at para 13.66.

2. The potential widening of liability for negligence

13.64 In *Barrett v Enfield London Borough Council*[1] the House of Lords refused to strike out a claim for negligence against the local authority for its alleged catalogue of errors during the 17 years the claimant had been in its care, which had resulted in him leaving care with deep-seated psychological and psychiatric problems. In reaching this decision their Lordships drew a distinction between deciding to take a child into care pursuant to a statutory duty, which unless it was wholly unreasonable so as not to be a real exercise of the discretion, was not normally justiciable, and looking after a child in care, when it might be easier to establish a breach of duty. However, while their Lordships were not prepared to strike out the claim,[2] the decision by no means indicated that the claim would in fact succeed. Indeed Lord Slynn expressly said that many of the allegations would be difficult to establish and were likely to fail.

1 [1999] 3 All ER 193, [1999] 3 WLR 79, [1999] 2 FCR 434, [1999] 2 FLR 426.
2 Their Lordships were mindful of the obligation under Art 6 of the European Convention on Human Rights to allow everyone to have a fair and public hearing and referred expressly to the decision in *Osman v UK* [1999] 1 FLR 193, 29 EHRR 245, ECtHR.

13.65 *Barrett* has since been applied in *S v Gloucester County Council, L v Tower Hamlets London Borough Council*[1] in which claims for negligence were brought against the local authorities by children who alleged that the foster-fathers with whom they had been placed had abused them sexually and as a result they had suffered long-term damage. In each case the foster-fathers had eventually been convicted of sexual offences with children. According to May LJ[2] the relevant law derived from *Barrett* can be summarised as follows:

'(a) depending upon the particular facts of the case, a claim in common-law negligence may be available to a person who claims to have been damaged by failings of a local authority which was responsible under statutory powers for his care and upbringing . . .

(b) the claim will not succeed if the failings alleged comprise actions or decisions by the local authority of a kind which are not justiciable. These may include, but will not necessarily be limited to, policy decisions and decisions about allocating public funds;

(c) the border line between what is justiciable and what is not may in a particular case be unclear. Its demarcation may require a more extensive investigation than is capable of being made from material in traditional pleadings alone;

(d) there may be circumstances in which it will not be just and reasonable to impose a duty of care of the kind contended for. It may often be necessary to conduct a detailed investigation of the facts to determine this question; and

(e) in considering whether a discretionary decision was negligent, the court will not substitute its view for that of the local authority upon which the state has placed the power to exercise discretion, unless the discretionary decision was plainly wrong. But decisions of, for example, social workers, are capable of being held to have been negligent by analogy with decisions of other professional people. Here again, it may well be necessary to conduct a detailed factual enquiry.'

Applying these principles it was held that the allegation that Gloucestershire had failed to deal with the abuse by the foster carer after being informed of it was actionable. However, in the case of Tower Hamlets there was held to be no real prospect of establishing negligence in their approval of the foster parents nor in their subsequent placement of the child with them and the action was struck out.

1 [2000] 3 All ER 346, [2000] 2 FCR 345, [2000] 1 FLR 825, CA.
2 Above at 369, 374 and 848–849 respectively.

13.66 In *W v Essex County Council*[1] a foster child, known by the social worker to be an active sexual abuser, sexually abused the birth children of the foster carers. The Court of Appeal held that while the foster parents' claim for negligence against the local authority should be struck out, the children's should not. The majority held that a social worker placing a child with foster parents had a duty of care to the foster parents' children to provide them, before and during the placement, with such information about the placed child as a reasonable social worker would provide in all the circumstances, and a local authority was vicariously liable for the conduct of its social worker relating to that. Although appeals were lodged on both counts, that relating to the children was not pursued but in relation to the action by the parents, the House of Lords held that that too should not be struck out on the basis that it could not be said that such a claim was unarguable.

1 [1998] 3 All ER 111, [1999] Fam 90, [1998] 3 WLR 534, CA; revsd [2000] 2 All ER 237, [2000] 2 WLR 601, [2000] 1 FCR 568, [2000] 1 FCR 568, [2000] 1 FLR 657, HL. Note a local authority might be liable for negligent misstatement under common law liability, if a decision was so unreasonable, even though it could not be liable for breach of statutory duty: *T v Surrey County Council* [1994] 2 FCR 1269, a case relating to a registered childminder held to have injured a child in her care. For liability of a local education authority for not diagnosing children's special education needs see *Phelps v Hillingdon London Borough Council* [2001] 2 AC 619, [2000] 4 All ER 504, [2000] 2 WLR 776, HL.

13.67 In *C v A Local Authority,*[1] damages were awarded against the local authority in respect of physical, emotional and sexual abuse at the hands of members of staff at the children's home in which the claimant (now aged 36) had been placed. In upholding an award of £35,000 for pain, suffering and loss of amenities, £20,000 for his loss of past earnings, £5,000 for future loss of earnings and £10,000 for the cost of future psychotherapy, the Court of Appeal doubted whether the Judicial Studies Board guidelines on damages for psychiatric harm applied to cases of abuse of children in care by their carers.

1 [2001] EWCA Civ 302, [2001] 1 FCR 614, sub nom *C v Flintshire County Council* [2001] 2 FLR 33, CA.

3. The Strasbourg Rulings

13.68 The four children denied relief by the House of Lords[1] in the *Bedfordshire* case and both the mother and child involved in the *Newham* decision, subsequently took their claims before the European Court of Human Rights. In both cases, respectively reported as *Z v United Kingdom*[2] and *TP and KM v United Kingdom,*[3] the claim that the striking out of the negligence claims by the House of Lords amounted to a breach of Art 6 of the Convention was rejected on the basis that while that Article generally safeguarded a right of access to the courts in respect of complaints of unlawful interference with civil rights, it did not guarantee a particular content of these civil rights or obligations. In other words States can properly restrict those rights provided they do so for legitimate reasons and 'there is a reasonable relationship of proportionality between the means employed and the aim sought to be achieved'. In the Court's view the UK had legitimately restricted the application of negligence. Nevertheless despite this ruling the Court found other reasons for holding the UK to be breach of the Convention in each of the two cases.

1 [1995] 2 AC 633, [1995] 3 All ER 353, [1995] 2 WLR 152, discussed at paras 13.62–13.63.
2 [2001] 2 FCR 246, [2001] 2 FLR 612, ECtHR, on which see the excellent analysis by Bailey Harris at [2001] Fam Law 584.
3 [2001] 2 FCR 289, [2001] 2 FLR 549, ECtHR.

13.69 In *Z v United Kingdom* the European Court upheld the children's claim that there had been a breach of Art 3. The local authority were found to be aware of the appalling treatment and neglect suffered over a period of years by the applicants at the hands of their parents (the UK Government did not contest the Commission's finding that the treatment suffered by the children had reached the level of severity prohibited by Art 3, ie that it amounted to inhuman and degrading treatment) but had failed, despite the powers available to take them, to take effective measures to bring it to an end. Accordingly, the State too had failed in its positive obligation under Art 3 to provide the applicants with adequate protection against inhuman and degrading treatment. The Court further held that notwithstanding the propriety of striking out the negligence claim, the absence of an effective remedy for the breach itself amounted to a breach of Art 13 (under which everyone should have an effective remedy for a violation of a Convention right). The court awarded £32,000 compensation to each applicant.

13.70 Since Art 3 was found to have been broken the Court in *Z* found it unnecessary to consider whether Art 8 had also been breached in that case. In *TP and KM v United Kingdom*, however, the Court upheld the mother and daughter's complaint that because the child had unjustifiably been taken into care and separated from her mother, both claimants' Art 8 rights had been breached. What constituted the violation in the Court's view was the local authority's failure to disclose to the mother a video of the child's disclosure interview[1] which in turn deprived the mother of an effective opportunity to deal with allegations that the child could not be safely returned to her. As in *Z* the absence of an effective domestic remedy was found to be a breach of Art 13 and each applicant was awarded £10,000 compensation.

1 There was some doubt as to whom the child was referring to in relation to the allegations of abuse.

4. Actions under ss 7 and 8 of the Human Rights Act 1998

13.71 Although the two Strasbourg rulings should not be underestimated, not least for establishing how the Convention can still be used despite the legitimate restriction of an action for negligence, such claims will now have to be brought domestically under ss 7 and 8 of the Human Rights Act 1998.[1] Section 7 enables victims to bring proceedings against public authorities (which includes both local authorities and the courts)[2] in respect of acts claimed to be incompatible with a Convention right and if successful, s 8 empowers the court to grant 'such relief or remedy, or make such order, within its powers as it considers just and appropriate'. These latter powers include awarding damages. As Lord Nicholls observed in *Re S (Care Order: Implementation of Care Plan)*,[3] 'The object of these sections is to provide in English law the very remedy Art 13 declares is the entitlement of everyone whose rights are violated'. In so doing the 1998 Act has rendered nugatory the Art 13 position in which the Strasbourg decisions ultimately turned.[4]

1 As these provisions were not then in force they could not be used by the applicants in the Strasbourg cases.
2 Section 6(3) of the 1998 Act, discussed at para 1.49.

3   [2002] UKHL 10 at para [61], [2002] 2 All ER 192, [2002] 2 WLR 720. As His Lordship said
    unlike Art 13 which makes it a 'right' to have an effective remedy, ss 7 and 8 simply provide
    a remedy for enforcing a Convention right. Note: the UK has not incorporated Art 13 into
    domestic law.
4   Though this is not to say that complaints can no longer be made to the European Court. A
    ruling that there should be no relief under s 8 could, for example, be challenged at Strasbourg.
    For guidance on how to bring actions in Strasbourg, see Clements, Mole and *Simmonds
    European human rights: taking a case under the Convention* (2nd edn, 1999).

13.72   Although had they been able to bring their action under ss 7 and 8 the
claimants in the two Strasbourg cases would clearly have obtained damages
it is less certain what the quantum would have been. It has been pointed out[1]
that the award of £32,000 to each child in *Z v United Kingdom* lay at the lower
end of the Judicial Studies Board's guidelines for severe cases.[2] On the other
hand, s 8(4) of the 1998 Act directs the court to 'take into account the principles applied by the European Court of Human Rights in relation to the
award of compensation under Art 41 of the Convention'. Furthermore, Lord
Woolf has argued extra judicially that damages under the Act should be 'on
the low side by comparison to tortuous awards'.[3] For this reason, it might still
be worthwhile seeking a remedy in negligence, at any rate in the alternative to
an action under ss 7 and 8.

1   Bailey-Harris at [2001] Fam Law at 585.
2   Furthermore, it has been held that even these guidelines might not limit the courts, see *C v A
    Local Authority* [2001] EWCA Civ 307, [2001] 1 FCR 614, sub nom *C v Flintshire County
    Council* [2001] 2 FLR 33, CA, discussed at para 13.68.
3   See 'The Human Rights Act 1998 and Remedies' in *Judicial Review in International
    Perspective* (eds Andenas and Fairgrieve) at 432 and 434.

13.73   Procedurally, actions may either be brought directly against the public
authority alleged to be at fault (sometimes referred to as 'free-standing
action') or can be raised in existing proceedings. Freestanding actions have to
be brought in an 'appropriate court or tribunal',[1] but, as Hale LJ said, in *Re
W and B (children: care plan), Re W (children) (care plan):*[2]

> 'There is no definition of the 'appropriate court or tribunal' for purpose of s 7(1)(a).
> The amended *Practice Direction* to Pt 16 of the Civil Procedure Rules 1998 requires
> any party who seeks to rely on the Human Rights Act to state that and give particu-
> lars in his statement of case. A claim against a local authority under s 7(1)(a) might
> therefore be brought as an ordinary civil claim in the county or the High Court'.

However, her Ladyship also pointed out, a parent or child can invoke existing
procedures in the CA 1989 to get the matter back before the care court and
then rely upon s 7(1)(b), though it might be preferable to get the matter
before higher courts rather than the family proceedings court since only they
can grant an injunction and award damages.[3]

1   Section 7(1)(a) of the 1998 Act . According to *C and Another v Bury Metropolitan Borough
    Council* (2002 Times, 25 July), per Butler-Sloss P, human rights challenges to care plans and
    placement of children in care should be heard in the Family Division of the High Court and,
    if possible, by judges with experience of sitting in the administrative court.
2   [2001] EWCA Civ 757 at para [74], [2001] 2 FCR 450, [2001] 2 FLR 582, not commented
    upon by HL on appeal.
3   Above at para [75].

13.74   There are important limits on the ability to invoke ss 7 and 8. First,
the claimant has to show that he or she is a 'victim', that is a person who is

directly affected by the act or omission.[1] It is therefore insufficient to be a secondary victim, which would have meant, for example, that the foster carers in *Re Z* would have had no action.[2] Secondly, the action must be brought within one year of the act complained of, although claims after that can be admitted at the court's discretion.[3] Thirdly, there must be no other appropriate remedy. Indeed, in *Re S (Care Order: Implementation of Care Plan)*[4] Lord Nicholls considered actions generally under s 7 to be a 'longstop remedy'. He commented 'One would not expect proceedings to be launched under s 7 until any other appropriate remedial routes have first been explored'. His Lordship did not explain why s 7 actions should be of 'last resort'.

1 Section 7(7) applying Art 34 of the Convention.
2 Cf *A and B v United Kingdom* [1998] 1 EHRLR 82 in which the father of a son who was beaten by his stepfather was not considered to be a victim.
3 Section 79(5). See further para 1.49.
4 [2002] UKHL 10 at para [62], [2002] 2 All ER 192, [2002] 2 WLR 720.

13.75 It remains to be seen how frequently actions under ss 7 and 8 will be resorted to. At the time of writing there has been one reported successful action, namely, *Re M (Care: Challenging Decisions By Local Authority)*[1]. In that case following a review of its care plan for a child in its care the local authority finally ruled out any further prospect of the child returning to live with her mother or of ever going to live with her father. In reaching this decision, however, the authority was held to have acted unfairly and therefore in breach of Art 8 by not involving the parents to a degree sufficient to provide their interests with the requisite protection. Exercising his powers under s 8 of the 1998 Act upon an application by the parents under s 7, Holman J set the local authority decision aside. He also gave directions for a full hearing of the review issues and of applications for the discharge of the care orders.

1 [2001] 2 FLR 1300.

13.76 Holman J's decision was specifically endorsed by Lord Nicholls in *Re S (Care Order: Implementation of Care Plan)*.[1] At the same time his Lordship emphasised that wide though the powers are under s 8 they are nevertheless confined to acts or proposed acts which the court finds are or would be unlawful. It does not confer a power to give relief in respect of acts by public authorities who have not and are not proposing to act in breach of a Convention right.[2]

1 [2002] UKHL 10 at para [46], [2002] 2 WLR 720, [2002] 2 All ER 192.
2 It was for this reason that his Lordship considered the Court of Appeal was wrong to justify the starring of care plans (discussed at paras 8.95 et seq) upon the basis of ss 7 and 8.

Chapter 14

Conclusions

OVERVIEW

14.1   The aims of the Children Act 1989 can be broadly summarised as follows:

(a)   The creation of a unified system of modern law and procedure to provide for the welfare of children;
(b)   the integration of provisions on private and public law;
(c)   the provision of local authority support for families with children in need, and where necessary, the power to take steps to protect the child; and
(d)   unification of the court system to deal with these matters.

In this Chapter we consider the extent to which these aims have been achieved and what might lie ahead.

14.2   In assessing the success of the Children Act legal critique has to be separated from political comment. The Act and its supplementary legislation necessarily remain extensive with its rules, regulations, orders and guidance. The Act has not created simplicity but it has been a major achievement to have a single structure, which is largely internally coherent. With the exception of legislation concerning adoption and abduction, all the law relating to the welfare of children is in one place. The Adoption and Children Bill 2002, when implemented, should make adoption consistent with the principles of the Children Act. The essential principles of the Act have created a framework for good practice. Nonetheless the second stage of implementation of the infrastructure in relation to work concerning children has not been adequately accomplished.

THE COURTS

14.3   The Act provided a unified jurisdiction for children's cases but not a unified court, as had been sought for many years. The system has had significant advantages in that, with a few exceptions, the High Court, the county court and the family proceedings court apply the same law and have the same powers, and each have personnel who are experienced in the application of the relevant law. Courts can interact and ensure coordination based on complexity and convenience rather than the nature of the case.

14.4   A central principle of the Act is that delay in deciding any question with respect to a child's upbringing is likely to prejudice the child's welfare. As the *Scoping Study on Delay in Children Act Cases*[1] has shown there is still substantial delay in hearings, notwithstanding the attention of the Booth Report[2] to the problem in 1995. The increasing delay in obtaining court hearings is the most serious problem in that part of the Act which affects the courts. This has led to drift rather than planned timetables operating at a pace consistent with the welfare of the child.

1   Lord Chancellor's Department, May 2002.
2   See 'Delay in Public Law Children Act Cases: Preliminary Report' (1995), a report by Dame Margaret Booth on research conducted for the Lord Chancellor's Department.

14.5   The *Scoping Study* comments that 'when the Children Act Advisory Committee was abolished in 1997 there was a vacuum in taking forward its functions in relation to the implementation of the Report of Dame Margaret Booth on delay and as a consequence some momentum was lost.' What the *Scoping Study* also showed was that, in spite of the publication of best practice proposals, 'one of the most depressing features of the study was the extent to which interagency working had foundered in some areas'. The possible introduction of a Family Justice Council, which would have the responsibility of improving outcomes for those who come into contact with the family justice system, would be welcome, in that it would help to address these problems.

14.6   The lack of available judiciary, especially in the county court, was identified as a problem in the *Scoping Study* and is a significant contribution to the problem of delay. Although delays are far more frequently brought about by the court rather than practitioners, the primary response to delay in the higher courts so far has been to introduce strict provisions on the conduct of cases and draconian threats on costs. Practice Directions have required proper arrangements for filing evidence, the use of experts, the provision of bundles of documents and a chronology, control of unnecessary examination of witnesses and preventing oral evidence, which should all be good practice in the right circumstances. Warranted as these controls on cases are, the Court Service has to make adequate provision for judges and court staff to ensure expeditious hearings and oversee the conduct of proceedings.

14.7   The different levels of courts are separately funded and administered. Magistrates' courts are fragmented by the devolution of responsibility to forty two different committees, where family business has to compete for funding in an organisation which is primarily focussed on criminal business. The argument whether magistrates' courts should continue to have a family jurisdiction is based not on whether they do the work well, which in general it is thought they do, but rather that the divided administrative structure serves to hinder the efficient dispatch of business and generate delay. Family proceedings courts should be organised to enable them to concentrate on their specialist work as has been done with Care Centres in the county court or the dedicated Inner London and City Family Proceedings Court. This would enable them to develop expertise and administrative and case management structures to support it.

14.8   The messages of the Thematic Review of the Magistrates' Courts' Service Inspectorate, a research paper from the Lord Chancellor's Department, *Professionalising Lay Justice*,[1] and the *Scoping Study* all point towards an integrated family court. But it may be that one of the most potent drivers for change will prove to be a report that is not about family courts at all. In October 2001 Lord Justice Auld published his *Review of the Criminal Courts of England and Wales*,[2] which was commissioned by the Lord Chancellor, the Home Secretary and the Attorney General. The report recommends the creation of a unified criminal court and management structure. The opportunity should not be lost to ensure that the family courts benefit equally from a coherent unified approach to their judicial and administrative structure.

1 See para 4.12 et seq.
2 See para p 729.

14.9 What we did not foresee in the second edition were the consequences of the Access to Justice Act 1999 and accompanying policy. The decreasing number of legal aid practitioners cannot continue without an adverse effect, not only on access to justice, but also on the development of child jurisprudence. The imposition of the requirement of court leave to appeal to the Court of Appeal has shifted responsibility for selecting appeals from legal advisers to the Appeal Court. The effect of this is unknown. There is no single source of reliable statistics relating to proceedings under the Act, unlike those in respect of children in care and looked after.

Parental Responsibility

14.10 One of the objectives of the private law provisions was to encourage those responsible for children to reach their own decisions, where appropriately jointly, without recourse to the courts. Yet the Act imposes no duty on the residential parent to consult, following the Law Commission view that such a duty was unworkable and undesirable.[1] However, the courts have created some exceptions, namely, changing the child's schooling[2] and name,[3] so that it is uncertain as to the extent which the parent with whom the child does not reside can or should be involved in the exercise of parental responsibility. In any event what is the scope of the responsibility of the non-residential parent, if there is no duty to consult?

1 Report on Guardianship and Custody, Law Com 1988, No. 172.
2 *Re G (a minor)(parental responsibility: education)* [1995] 2 FCR 53, [1994] 2 FLR 964, discussed at para 3.92.
3 *Re PC (Change of Surname)* [1997] 2 FLR 730, sub nom *Re C (minors)(change of surname)* [1997] 3 FCR 310. See also *Re J (child's religious upbringing and circumcision)* [2000] 1 FCR 307, sub *nom Re J (Specific Issue Orders)(Muslim Upbringing and Circumcision)* [2000] 1 FLR 571, discussed at para 3.92.

14.11 Although in terms of the overall number of unmarried fathers, not many parental responsibility agreements or orders are made, s 4 applications continue to generate considerable caselaw. Nevertheless, it remains clear that in practice courts are reluctant to deny fathers parental responsibility once they have sought it. Although distinguishing married from unmarried fathers has survived a challenge before the European Court of Human Rights,[1] the government has chosen to amend the law via the Adoption and Children Bill 2002 so as to give unmarried fathers automatic parental responsibility upon being registered as the father.[2] How this provision will work remains to be seen. Will mothers, for example, become more reluctant to name the father? However, it seems likely that in consequence there will be a sharp drop in the number of parental agreements made. Whether the reform should have gone further and given automatic parental responsibility to all fathers can be debated.[3]

1 *B v United Kingdom* [2000] 1 FCR 289, [2000] 1 FLR 612, 1 ECtHR, discussed at para 3.44.
2 See para 3.67.
3 See eg Lowe and Douglas Bromley's Family Law (9th edn) 388 et seq.

14.12 While the Adoption and Children Bill 2002 is likely to lead to a sharp diminution of parental responsibility agreements and orders in favour of fathers, another prospective change, namely, to permit agreements and orders to be made in favour of step-parents is likely to lead to an increased use of s 4. At the time of writing, the Bill proposes only to give these rights to a step-parent who is married to a parent with parental responsibility, but whether it should go further and allow applications to be made by unmarried cohabitants might be questioned.

14.13 Notwithstanding these prospective changes, it remains the case that, unlike Scotland, there is no general power to grant parental responsibility. Consequently, an individual other than a parent or step-parent can acquire parental responsibility only by means of a residence order, which the courts will not use purely to allocate responsibility.[1] While this was an intended effect of the Act, there does seem to be a case for extending the courts' powers to grant responsibility to others, even though they are not caring for the child.

1 See eg *N v B (children: order as to residence)* [1993] 1 FCR 231, sub nom *Re WB (Residence Orders)* [1995] 2 FLR 1023, where the mother's cohabitant helped bring up the child, but when a dispute arose discovered on the eve of the court hearing that he was not the father. Cf *Re H (shared residence: parental responsibility)* [1996] 3 FCR 321, [1995] 2 FLR 883, CA, discussed at para 5.11.

Other Private Law Developments

14.14 Another important amendment to the 1989 Act contained in the Adoption and Children Bill 2002 is the creation of special guardianship which is designed to provide a half way house between residence orders and adoption.[1] It is likely to be used by relatives though to what extent remains to be seen. On the one hand potential applicants might be put off by the requirement to notify the local authority which must then prepare a report, but on the other they might be encouraged to apply by the provisions for local authority support for successful applicants.

1 Discussed at paras 5.161 et seq.

14.15 The issue of making contact orders particularly in the face of allegations of domestic violence has continued to exercise the courts. It has become evident that the courts have had to re-think their position upon the realisation that violence perpetrated on one parent by the other can have harmful effects upon the child.[1] In this respect the prospective amendment to the welfare checklist by the Adoption and Children Bill 2002 that 'harm includes impairment suffered from seeing or hearing the ill-treatment of another' is likely to prove important.

1 See the discussion at paras 5.60 et seq.

The local authority context

Local authority support for children and families

14.16 The provision of services for children in need and families is a central plank of the public law provisions of the Act. The duty to safeguard and promote the welfare of children in need is vital to the proper functioning of the legislation. Unfortunately it is one of those areas which has suffered most through inadequate resources, though some would say that there never could be sufficient.

14.17 The ability to sue local authorities for their failure to carry out their statutory duties has been a major issue. When the second edition was published the House of Lords had apparently closed the door to such actions[1] but since then a series of domestic decisions[2] and those by the European Court of Human Rights[3] have seemingly opened the door for suits. It seems likely that ss 7 and 8 of the Human Rights Act 1998 will provide a profitable avenue for attack[4] but exactly how far redress will be able to be sought remains to be seen.

1 In *X (Minors) v Bedfordshire County Council* [1995] 2 AC 633, [1995] 3 All ER 353, [1995] 3 WLR 152, HL, discussed at paras 13.62 et seq.
2 Eg *Barrett v Enfield London Borough Council* [1999] 3 All ER 193, [1999] 3 WLR 79, HL, *S v Gloucestershire County Council, L v Tower Hamlets Borough Council* [2000] 3 All ER 346, [2000] 2 FCR 345, [2000] 1 FLR 825, CA *and W v Essex County Council* [2000] 2 All ER 237, [2000] 2 WLR 601, HL, discussed at paras 13.65 et seq.
3 *Z v United Kingdom* [2001] 2 FCR 246, [2001] 2 FLR 612, ECtHR *and TP and KM v United Kingdom* [2001] 2 FCR 289, [2001] 2 FLR 549, ECtHR, discussed at paras 13.69 et seq.
4 See the discussion at paras 13.72 et seq.

Care proceedings

14.18 Concerns about how the court system would work, especially in the public law, without the availability of wardship, appear to have proved unfounded. Through flexible interpretation of the threshold criteria, the courts have acquired an ability to exercise a reasonable degree of discretion in reaching solutions in care proceedings. In spite of concerns the threshold criteria seem to have achieved a suitable balance.

14.19 Another issue concerns the respective roles of the court and the local authority. Which has the greater say in deciding whether a child should be in care? The existing system provides a tension by which the court cannot require an authority to take proceedings, but may, when directing an investigation, feel that the authority is driven not to take proceedings by resource issues rather than the welfare of the individual child. The philosophy of the Act makes authorities responsible for resources, but can the court realistically be limited to deciding whether or not to authorise local authority applications under s 31 if they choose to make them?

14.20 In *Re S* the House of Lords considered the use of interim care orders. Courts have sought to use them as a means of keeping the case under review, because of a lack of confidence in the local authority's ability to carry out its care plan. If courts are to manage their business satisfactorily, they must consider carefully what are the real benefits of seeking to continue court supervision of a case. What happens in the lives of children in care after care orders have been made may depend on the success of new provisions in the Adoption and Children Bill 2002.

14.21 Concerns about the interaction of the welfare of the child and prosecution of carers have arisen in a number of ways and remain unresolved. Can both care and criminal proceedings be heard expeditiously to satisfy the needs for the welfare of children and the public interest requirement to prosecute wrongdoers? There are conflicts between children centred protection investigations, the aims of video interviewing of children for criminal proceedings and the involvement of children as witnesses. Can these be resolved by the latest guidance?[1]

1   See para 7.3.

14.22 The courts have sought to develop a philosophy of full disclosure in child welfare cases, including disclosure by those representing parties. Conflicts remain as to the boundaries. How far do lawyers' duties to their clients extend in child welfare proceedings? If disclosure of confidential information about one's own client is required, the law must be explicit and professional Codes of Conduct must reflect it.

14.23 The intention of s 98, to provide immunity from prosecution where a parent makes an admission about harming a child, seem to have limited application in practice. Closer analysis is required of what can happen if a parent wishes to make admissions for the purpose of care proceedings, without having evidence in those proceedings disclosed for the purposes of criminal investigation or proceedings.

Representation of Children and their Interests

14.24 The Act gave children the right to object to certain court directions and to apply for orders or seek leave to apply in some circumstances. The philosophy followed the approach of the House of Lords in *Gillick*.[1] What came to be known as '*Gillick*-competent' children acquired a level of self-determination or at least an opportunity to be heard. The major difficulties which have arisen relate to how that interest should be represented in private and public law.

1   *Gillick v West Norfolk and Wisbech Area Health Authority* [1986] AC 112, [1985] 3 All ER 402, HL.

14.25 There is a growing awareness of the need for child participation in proceedings. There is good evidence that children want to be treated as active participants whose thoughts about their futures are listened to and not as passive objects. Courts have always been against seeing children and this has given a wider signal which may have served to limit their involvement.

14.26 Although the 1989 Act makes provision both for the child to be heard and for his or her views to be taken into account, whether sufficient provision is made for the child's active participation in legal proceedings may be questioned.[1] There is still no provision for them even to be made a party to private law proceedings in the family proceedings court.

1   Research has increasingly pointed to the shift of emphasis so that children are no longer seen simply as passive victims of family breakdown but increasingly as participants and actors in the family justice system. See eg Lowe and Murch 'Children's participation in the family justice system – translating principles into practice'. [2001] CFLQ 137.

14.27   We said in 1995 that the Court Welfare Service was in crisis and there were problems with the guardian ad litem service. The obvious solution, which the authors first canvassed in 1985,[1] was to construct an agency with responsibility for all aspects of welfare reporting to the court. The Lord Chancellor's Department considered the options in 1987,[2] and introduced an integrated system in 2001. Regrettably the introduction of CAFCASS has caused even further deterioration in services, extending in many areas to the provision of children's guardians. We had not foreseen that, after so many years of pressure for a new service, there would be a hasty introduction of an underfunded and poorly managed organisation with little political impetus for improvement. This policy must be reversed if another negative message to and about children is to be avoided.

1   See Lowe and White, *Wards of Court* (2nd edn), para 9.31 (Barry Rose, 1986).
2   The Office of Child Protection, Lord Chancellor's Department, 1988.

14.28   Outside the court context the creation of the Children's Commissioner has been an important development in Wales. In England there has been the appointment of the Children's Director under provisions in the Care Standards Act 2000. It remains to be seen whether his more limited powers will be sufficient.

Human Rights

14.29   A key development since publication of the second edition has been the implementation of the Human Rights Act 1998, which has led to numerous arguments on the application of human rights in domestic law generally. So far, human rights challenges to the substantive provisions of the Children Act have been largely unsuccessful. This is unsurprising since the 1989 Act was drafted with the Convention very much in mind. However, that is not to say that the 1989 Act will continue to be invulnerable particularly to challenges on procedural issues such as delay, secure accommodation and the failure of representation of children, especially if CAFCASS does not succeed in providing a satisfactory service. As mentioned above, two key decisions of the European Court of Human Rights[1] have shown how the Convention might be relevant to suing local authorities for their failure to provide adequate protection, though future actions are likely to be prosecuted via ss 7 and 8 of the 1998 Act.[2] Given that these latter provisions are capable of righting wrongs it is difficult to see why as, Lord Nicholls suggested in *Re S (Care Order: Implementation of Care Plan)*,[3] they should be regarded as a 'longstop remedy'. At all events, further human rights issues seem likely to play a prominent role in the future application of the 1989 Act.

1   Viz *Z v United Kingdom*, supra and *TP and KM v United Kingdom*, supra.
2   Discussed at paras 13.72 et seq.
3   [2002] UKHL10 at para [46], [2002] 2 All ER 192, [2002] AC 291 HL.

14.30   Specific issues which are likely to require more attention are care plans, depending on the success of the proposed amendments to s 31 and the Review Regulations,[1] the denial of the right to services as potential interference with family life, especially in relation to the provision of funding under s 17 for the accommodation of a child in need with his parent and the use of s 20 to deal with homelessness of child and parent.[2]

1 See para 8.84 fn 1.
2 See chapter 6.

International Developments

14.31 International instruments are likely to play an increasing role in shaping not just so-called international family law but domestic law as well. In particular the European Union will predictably play a much greater role. The so-called Brussels II Regulation which controls jurisdiction, recognition and enforcement of decisions in relation to parental responsibility in divorce proceedings,[1] is currently under review and is likely to be extended to parental responsibility of all children. Furthermore, though not yet binding, the European Charter of Human Rights, could well lead to further attempts to harmonise domestic family law of Member States.

1 See further para 4.4.

14.32 It is possible that the United Kingdom will ratify the 1996 Hague Convention on the Protection of Children which contains important provisions for the recognition and enforcement of measures directed both to the protection of the child's person and property and to establish the necessary co-operation between the authorities of contracting states to achieve this purpose.[1]

1 For a discussion of this Convention see Lowe 'The 1996 Hague Convention on the protection of children – a fresh appraisal' [2002] CFLQ 191 and the authorities there cited.

FIT FOR THE 21ST CENTURY?

14.33 The Act has been in place for eleven years and has withstood examination fairly well in spite of restraint on the provision of resources. If the structures and support services provided under the legislation were to be adequately resourced, there is no reason to suppose the Act will not serve well for the foreseeable future. The Act remains a good basis for the law of the 21st century. There have been diverse amendments, many of major consequence such as those under the Care Standards Act 2000 and the Adoption and Children Bill and others of significance such as Leaving Care legislation and redefinition of the meaning of accommodation of children. The long term effects of the Data Protection Act 1998 and the Human Rights Act 1998 remain uncertain. Given the absence of an official up to date copy of the Act with all amendments in force, there may be a need for consolidation, but it would surprise us if by 2010 we were writing about the need for a new framework for the Act.

List of Relevant Statutory Instruments in Force

Access to Personal Files (Social Services) Regulations 1989, SI 1989/206
Arrangements for Placement of Children (General) Regulations 1991, SI 1991/890
Blood Tests (Evidence of Paternity) Regulations 1971, SI 1971/1861
Children Act (Miscellaneous Amendments) (England) Regulations 2002, SI 2002/546
Child Minding and Day Care (Application for Registration) Regulations 1991, SI 1991/1689
Child Minding and Day Care (Registration and Inspection Fees) Regulations 1991, SI 1991/2076
Children (Admissibility of Hearsay Evidence) Order 1993/621
Children and Family Court Advisory and Support Service (Conduct of Litigation and Exercise of Rights of Audience) Regulations 2001, SI 2001/698
Children (Allocation of Proceedings) Order 1991, SI 1991/1677
Children (Allocation of Proceedings) (Appeals) Order 1991, SI 1991/1801
Children's Homes Regulations 2001, SI 2001/3967
Children (Leaving Care) (England) Regulations 2001, SI 2001/2874
Children (Prescribed Orders–Northern Ireland Guernsey and Isle of Man) Regulations 1991, SI 1991/2032
Children (Private Arrangements for Fostering) Regulations 1991, SI 1991/2050
Children (Secure Accommodation) Regulations 1991, SI 1991/1505
Children (Secure Accommodation) (No 2) Regulations 1991, SI 1991/2034
Contact with Children Regulations 1991, SI 1991/891
Definition of Independent Visitors (Children) Regulations 1991, SI 1991/892
Disabled Children (Direct Payments) (England) Regulations 2001, SI 2001/442
Disqualification from Caring for Children (England) Regulations 2002, SI 2002/635
Emergency Protection Order (Transfer of Responsibilities) Regulations 1991, SI 1991/1414
Family Proceedings Courts (Children Act 1989) Rules 1991, SI 1991/1395
Family Proceedings Courts (Constitution) Rules 1991, SI 1991/1405
Family Proceedings Courts (Metropolitan Area) Rules 1991, SI 1991/1426
Family Proceedings Courts (Matrimonial Proceedings etc) Rules 1991, SI 1991/1991
Family Proceedings Fees Order 1991, SI 1991/2114
Family Proceedings Rules 1991, SI 1991/1247
Forms of Entry for Parental Orders Regulations 1994, SI 1994/2981
Fostering Services Regulations 2002, SI 2002/57
Guardians Ad Litem and Reporting Officers (Panels) Regulations 1991, SI 1991/2051
Legal Aid in Family Proceedings (Remuneration) Regulations 1991, SI 1991/2038
Parental Responsibility Agreement Regulations 1991, SI 1991/1478
Placement of Children with Parents etc Regulations 1991, SI 1991/893
Refuges (Children's Homes and Foster Placements) Regulations 1991, SI 1991/1507
Representation Procedure (Children) Regulations 1991, SI 1991/894
Review of Children's Cases Regulations 1991, SI 1991/895

Children Act 1989

(1989 c 41)

ARRANGEMENT OF SECTIONS

PART I
INTRODUCTORY

PART II
ORDERS WITH RESPECT TO CHILDREN IN FAMILY PROCEEDINGS

General

Financial relief

Family assistance orders

PART III
LOCAL AUTHORITY SUPPORT FOR CHILDREN AND FAMILIES

Provision of services for children and their families

Provision of accommodation for children

Part IV
Care and Supervision

Part V
Protection of Children

Part VI
Community Homes

Part VII
Voluntary Homes and Voluntary Organisations

Part VIII
Registered Children's Homes

Search warrants

General

SCHEDULES

*An Act to reform the law relating to children; to provide for local authority services for
children in need and others; to amend the law with respect to children's homes, community homes, voluntary homes and voluntary organisations; to make provision with
respect to fostering, child minding and day care for young children and adoption; and
for connected purposes*

[16th November 1989]

PART I
INTRODUCTORY

1 Welfare of the child

(1) When a court determines any question with respect to—

(a) the upbringing of a child; or

(b) the administration of a child's property or the application of any income arising from it,

the child's welfare shall be the court's paramount consideration.

(2) In any proceedings in which any question with respect to the upbringing of a child arises, the court shall have regard to the general principle that any delay in determining the question is likely to prejudice the welfare of the child.

(3) In the circumstances mentioned in subsection (4), a court shall have regard in particular to—

(a) the ascertainable wishes and feelings of the child concerned (considered in the light of his age and understanding);

(b) his physical, emotional and educational needs;

(c) the likely effect on him of any change in his circumstances;

(d) his age, sex, background and any characteristics of his which the court considers relevant;

(e) any harm which he has suffered or is at risk of suffering;

(f) how capable each of his parents, and any other person in relation to whom the court considers the question to be relevant, is of meeting his needs;

(g) the range of powers available to the court under this Act in the proceedings in question.

(4) The circumstances are that—

(a) the court is considering whether to make, vary or discharge a section 8 order, and the making, variation or discharge of the order is opposed by any party to the proceedings; or

(b) the court is considering whether to make, vary or discharge an order under Part IV.

(5) Where a court is considering whether or not to make one or more orders under this Act with respect to a child, it shall not make the order or any of the orders unless it considers that doing so would be better for the child than making no order at all.

Date in force
14 October 1991: SI 1991/828.

Definitions
For 'court' see s 97(7); for 'child' and 'upbringing' see s 105(1); for 'harm' see s 31(9) as applied to the whole Act by s 105(1); for 'a section 8 order' see s 8(2).

References
See generally chapter 2.2ff. For jurisdiction of courts see s 92 and Sch 11; for welfare of the child, see para 2.2ff for 'parent' see para 3.43. 'Part IV' ie ss 31-42 and Sch 3 (care and supervision). For 'family proceedings' under this Act see s 8(3), (4)(a).

Sub-s (1)
For 'paramount' see paras 2.3ff. For the impact of the European Convention on Human Rights generally, see *Re S (children: care plan)* [2002] UKHL 10, [2002] 1 All ER 192. For where the paramountcy principle does not apply, see paras 2.13ff. The paramountcy principle does not apply to determining whether to grant leave to apply for a s 8 order under s 10: *Re A (Minors) (Residence Orders: Leave to Apply)* [1992] Fam 182, [1992] 3 All ER 872, sub nom *Re A and W (Minors) (Residence Order: Leave to Apply)* [1992] 2 FLR 154, CA.

Sub-s (2)
For delay, prima facie, prejudicial to child's welfare, see paras 2.58ff.

Sub-s (3)(a)
For application of the checklist, see paras 2.41ff. Child's view does not have priority over other heads in the checklist. See *Re W (minors) (residence order)* [1992] 2 FCR 461, CA. See para 2.42.

Sub-s (5)
For the application of this principle, see para 2.62 ff. Has little or no application to applications for financial relief under Sch 1: *K v H* [1993] 1 FCR 684, [1993] 2 FLR 61. Nor to applications for secure accommodation orders: *Re M (A Minor) (Secure Accommodation Order)* [1995] Fam 108, [1995] 3 All ER 407, CA. For application to 'non-parent' applicants see *Re B (a minor) (residence order)* [1992] 2 FLR 327 and para 2.72.

2 Parental responsibility for children

(1) Where a child's father and mother were married to each other at the time of his birth, they shall each have parental responsibility for the child.

(2) Where a child's father and mother were not married to each other at the time of his birth—

(a) the mother shall have parental responsibility for the child;
(b) the father shall not have parental responsibility for the child, unless he acquires it in accordance with the provisions of this Act.

(3) References in this Act to a child whose father and mother were, or (as the case may be) were not, married to each other at the time of his birth must be read with section 1 of the Family Law Reform Act 1987 (which extends their meaning).

(4) The rule of law that a father is the natural guardian of his legitimate child is abolished.

(5) More than one person may have parental responsibility for the same child at the same time.

(6) A person who has parental responsibility for a child at any time shall not cease to have that responsibility solely because some other person subsequently acquires parental responsibility for the child.

(7) Where more than one person has parental responsibility for a child, each of them may act alone and without the other (or others) in meeting that responsibility; but nothing in this Part shall be taken to affect the operation of any enactment which requires the consent of more than one person in a matter affecting the child.

(8) The fact that a person has parental responsibility for a child shall not entitle him to act in any way which would be incompatible with any order made with respect to the child under this Act.

(9) A person who has parental responsibility for a child may not surrender or transfer any part of that responsibility to another but may arrange for some or all of it to be met by one or more persons acting on his behalf.

(10) The person with whom any such arrangement is made may himself be a person who already has parental responsibility for the child concerned.

(11) The making of any such arrangement shall not affect any liability of the person making it which may arise from any failure to meet any part of his parental responsibility for the child concerned.

Date in force
14 October 1991: SI 1991/828.

Definitions
For 'child' see s 105(1); for 'parental responsibility' see s 3.

References
See generally paras 3.43 ff. For whether a child's father and mother were married to each other at the time of his birth see sub-s (3); for father acquiring parental responsibility see s 4 and at paras 3.46 ff; for 'this part' see Part I ss 1-7.

3 Meaning of 'parental responsibility'

(1) In this Act 'parental responsibility' means all the rights, duties, powers, responsibilities and authority which by law a parent of a child has in relation to the child and his property.

(2) It also includes the rights, powers and duties which a guardian of the child's estate (appointed, before the commencement of section 5, to act generally) would have had in relation to the child and his property.

(3) The rights referred to in subsection (2) include, in particular, the right of the guardian to receive or recover in his own name, for the benefit of the child, property of whatever description and wherever situated which the child is entitled to receive or recover.

(4) The fact that a person has, or does not have, parental responsibility for a child shall not affect—

  (a) any obligation which he may have in relation to the child (such as a statutory duty to maintain the child); or

  (b) any rights which, in the event of the child's death, he (or any other person) may have in relation to the child's property.

(5) A person who—

  (a) does not have parental responsibility for a particular child; but

  (b) has care of the child,

may (subject to the provisions of this Act) do what is reasonable in all the circumstances of the case for the purpose of safeguarding or promoting the child's welfare.

Date in force
14 October 1991: SI 1991/828.

Definitions
For 'parental responsibility' see sub-s (1); for 'child' see s 105(1).

References
For the meaning and scope of parental responsibility, see paras 3.7 ff; for duration, see para 3.81 and for sharing with others, see paras 3.89 ff. For 'parent', see para 3.43; for the application of 'parental responsibility' to other enactments see s 108(5), Sch 13.

4 Acquisition of parental responsibility by father

(1) Where a child's father and mother were not married to each other at the time of his birth —

  (a) the court may, on the application of the father, order that he shall have parental responsibility for the child; or

  (b) the father and mother may by agreement ('a parental responsibility agreement') provide for the father to have parental responsibility for the child.

(2) No parental responsibility agreement shall have effect for the purposes of this Act unless—

  (a) it is made in the form prescribed by regulations made by the Lord Chancellor; and

  (b) where regulations are made by the Lord Chancellor prescribing the manner in which such agreements must be recorded, it is recorded in the prescribed manner.

(3) Subject to section 12(4), an order under subsection (1)(*a*), or a parental responsibility agreement, may only be brought to an end by an order of the court made on the application—

  (a) of any person who has parental responsibility for the child; or

  (b) with leave of the court, of the child himself.

(4) The court may only grant leave under subsection (3)(*b*) if it is satisfied that the child has sufficient understanding to make the proposed application.

Date in force
14 October 1991: SI 1991/828.

Definitions
For 'child' see s 105(1); for 'court' see s 92(7); for 'parental responsibility' see s 3; for 'parental responsibility agreement' see sub-s (1)(b); for 'prescribed' see sub-s (2).

References
See generally paras 3.46 ff. For jurisdiction of courts see s 92 and Sch 11; for appeals see s 94. For whether a child's father and mother were married to each other at the time of his birth see s 2(3), s 105(2); for duration of the order see s 12(4) (where residence order made in favour of the father) and generally s 91(7), (8); for 'family proceedings' under this Act see s 8(3), (4)(a).

Regulations
See Parental Responsibility Agreement Regulations 1991, SI 1991/1478 amended by SI 1994/3157 and SI 2001/2262.

Sub-s (1)
May make an order. For examples where an application was refused, see para 3.63. For the practical effects of an order, see para 3.72.

5   Appointment of guardians

(1) Where an application with respect to a child is made to the court by any individual, the court may by order appoint that individual to be the child's guardian if—

(a)   the child has no parent with parental responsibility for him; or

(b)   a residence order has been made with respect to the child in favour of a parent or guardian of his who has died while the order was in force.

(2) The power conferred by subsection (1) may also be exercised in any family proceedings if the court considers that the order should be made even though no application has been made for it.

(3) A parent who has parental responsibility for his child may appoint another individual to be the child's guardian in the event of his death.

(4) A guardian of a child may appoint another individual to take his place as the child's guardian in the event of his death.

(5) An appointment under subsection (3) or (4) shall not have effect unless it is made in writing, is dated and is signed by the person making the appointment or—

(a)   in the case of an appointment made by a will which is not signed by the testator, is signed at the direction of the testator in accordance with the requirements of section 9 of the Wills Act 1837; or

(b)   in any other case, is signed at the direction of the person making the appointment, in his presence and in the presence of two witnesses who each attest the signature.

(6) A person appointed as a child's guardian under this section shall have parental responsibility for the child concerned.

(7) Where—

(a)   on the death of any person making an appointment under subsection (3) or (4), the child concerned has no parent with parental responsibility for him; or

(b)   immediately before the death of any person making such an appointment, a residence order in his favour was in force with respect to the child,

the appointment shall take effect on the death of that person.

(8) Where, on the death of any person making an appointment under subsection (3) or (4)—

(a)   the child concerned has a parent with parental responsibility for him; and

(b)   subsection (7)(b) does not apply,

the appointment shall take effect when the child no longer has a parent who has parental responsibility for him.

(9) Subsections (1) and (7) do not apply if the residence order referred to in para-

graph (b) of those subsections was also made in favour of a surviving parent of the child.

(10) Nothing in this section shall be taken to prevent an appointment under subsection (3) or (4) being made by two or more persons acting jointly.

(11) Subject to any provision made by rules of court, no court shall exercise the High Court's inherent jurisdiction to appoint a guardian of the estate of any child.

(12) Where rules of court are made under subsection (11) they may prescribe the circumstances in which, and conditions subject to which, an appointment of such a guardian may be made.

(13) A guardian of a child may only be appointed in accordance with the provisions of this section.

Date in force
Sub-ss (1)-(10), (13): 14 October 1991: SI 1991/828. Sub-ss (11), (12): 1 February 1992: SI 1991/828.

Definitions
For 'child' and 'signed' see s 105(1); for 'court' see s 92(7); for 'parental responsibility' see s 3; for 'residence order' see s 8(1); for a person in whose favour a residence order is in force see s 105(3).

References
See generally paras 3.97 ff. Guardianship is discussed at para 2.131 of *The Children Act 1989 Guidance and Regulations, Volume 1, Court Orders* (Dept of Health, 1991). For jurisdiction of courts see s 92 and Sch 11; for duration of order of appointment see s 91(7), (8); for transitional provisions see s 108(6) and Sch 14, para 12; for 'family proceedings' under this Act see s 8(3), (4)(a); for other restrictions on the use of wardship jurisdiction see s 100.

6 Guardians: revocation and disclaimer

(1) An appointment under section 5(3) or (4) revokes an earlier such appointment (including one made in an unrevoked will or codicil) made by the same person in respect of the same child, unless it is clear (whether as the result of an express provision in the later appointment or by any necessary implication) that the purpose of the later appointment is to appoint an additional guardian.

(2) An appointment under section 5(3) or (4) (including one made in an unrevoked will or codicil) is revoked if the person who made the appointment revokes it by a written and dated instrument which is signed—

(a) by him; or
(b) at his direction, in his presence and in the presence of two witnesses who each attest the signature.

(3) An appointment under section 5(3) or (4) (other than one made in a will or codicil) is revoked if, with the intention of revoking the appointment, the person who made it—

(a) destroys the instrument by which it was made; or
(b) has some other person destroy that instrument in his presence.

[(3A) An appointment under section 5(3) or (4) (including one made in an unrevoked will or codicil) is revoked if the person appointed is the spouse of the person who made the appointment and either—

(a) a decree of a court of civil jurisdiction in England and Wales dissolves or annuls the marriage, or
[(a) a court of civil jurisdiction in England and Wales by order dissolves, or by decree annuls, a marriage, or]
(b) the marriage is dissolved or annulled and the divorce or annulment is entitled to recognition in England and Wales by virtue of Part II of the Family Law Act 1986,

unless a contrary intention appears by the appointment.]

(4) For the avoidance of doubt, an appointment under section 5(3) or (4) made in a will or codicil is revoked if the will or codicil is revoked.

(5) A person who is appointed as a guardian under section 5(3) or (4) may disclaim his appointment by an instrument in writing signed by him and made within a reasonable time of his first knowing that the appointment has taken effect.

(6) Where regulations are made by the Lord Chancellor prescribing the manner in which such disclaimers must be recorded, no such disclaimer shall have effect unless it is recorded in the prescribed manner.

(7) Any appointment of a guardian under section 5 may be brought to an end at any time by order of the court—

(a)　on the application of any person who has parental responsibility for the child;

(b)　on the application of the child concerned, with leave of the court; or

(c)　in any family proceedings, if the court considers that it should be brought to an end even though no application has been made.

Date in force
14 October 1991: SI 1991/828.

Amendment Sub-s (3A)
Law Reform (Succession) Act 1995, s 4.

Definitions
For 'child', and 'signed' see s 105(1); for 'court' see s 92(7); for 'parental responsibility' see s 3.

Reference
For jurisdiction of courts see s 92 and Sch 11; for 'family proceedings' under this Act see s 8(3), (4)(a).

7　Welfare reports

(1) A court considering any question with respect to a child under this Act may—

(a)　ask [an officer of the Service]; or

(b)　ask a local authority to arrange for—

(i)　an officer of the authority; or

(ii)　such other person (other than [an officer of the Service]) as the authority considers appropriate,

to report to the court on such matters relating to the welfare of that child as are required to be dealt with in the report.

(2) The Lord Chancellor may make regulations specifying matters which, unless the court orders otherwise, must be dealt with in any report under this section.

(3) The report may be made in writing, or orally, as the court requires.

(4) Regardless of any enactment or rule of law which would otherwise prevent it from doing so, the court may take account of—

(a)　any statement contained in the report; and

(b)　any evidence given in respect of the matters referred to in the report,

in so far as the statement or evidence is, in the opinion of the court, relevant to the question which it is considering.

(5) It shall be the duty of the authority or [officer of the Service] to comply with any request for a report under this section.

Date in force
14 October 1991: SI 1991/828.

Amendment
Sub-s (1): words "an officer of the Service" in square brackets in both places they occur substituted by the Criminal Justice and Court Services Act 2000, s 74, Sch 7, Pt II, paras 87, 88(a).

Sub-s (5): words "officer of the Service" in square brackets substituted by the Criminal Justice and Court Services Act 2000, s 74, Sch 7, Pt II, paras 87, 88(b).

Definitions
For 'court' see s 92(7); for 'child' and 'local authority' see s 105(1).

References
See generally chapter 10 and in particular paras 10.1 ff. For jurisdiction of courts see s 92 and Sch 11; for other evidential provisions see s 96. For the need for the court to give clear reasons for departing from the evidence of a professional witness given by way of a s 7 report, see *Re J (children) (residence: expert evidence)* [2001] 2 FCR 43 and see for where such reasons were sufficient, *Re E (children) (residence order)* [2001] EWCA Civ 567, [2001] 2 FCR 662.

To date no regulations have been issued under sub-s (2).

PART II

ORDERS WITH RESPECT TO CHILDREN IN FAMILY PROCEEDINGS

General

8 Residence, contact and other orders with respect to children

(1) In this Act—

'a contact order' means an order requiring the person with whom a child lives or is to live, to allow the child to visit or stay with the person named in the order, or for that person and the child otherwise to have contact with each other;

'a prohibited steps order' means an order that no step which could be taken by a parent in meeting his parental responsibility for a child, and which is of a kind specified in the order, shall be taken by any person without the consent of the court;

'a residence order' means an order settling the arrangements to be made as to the person with whom a child is to live; and

'a specific issue order' means an order giving directions for the purpose of determining a specific question which has arisen, or which may arise, in connection with any aspect of parental responsibility for a child.

(2) In this Act 'a section 8 order' means any of the orders mentioned in subsection (1) and any order varying or discharging such an order.

(3) For the purposes of this Act 'family proceedings' means [(subject to subsection (5))] any proceedings—

(a) under the inherent jurisdiction of the High Court in relation to children; and

(b) under the enactments mentioned in subsection (4),

but does not include proceedings on an application for leave under section 100(3).

(4) The enactments are—

(a) Parts I, II and IV of this Act;
(b) the Matrimonial Causes Act 1973;
(c) 000.
(d) the Adoption Act 1976;
(e) the Domestic Proceedings and Magistrates' Courts Act 1978;
(f) 000.
(g) Part III of the Matrimonial and Family Proceedings Act 1984.
[(h) the Family Law Act 1996.]
[(i) sections 11 and 12 of the Crime and Disorder Act 1998.]

[(5) For the purposes of any reference in this Act to family proceedings powers which under this Act are exercisable in family proceedings shall also be exercisable in relation to a child, without any such proceedings having been commenced or any application having been made to the court under this Act, if—

(a) a statement of marital breakdown under section 5 of the Family Law Act 1996 with respect to the marriage in relation to which that child is a child of the family has been received by the court; and

(b) it may, in due course, become possible for an application for a divorce order or for a separation order to be made by reference to that statement.]

Date in force
14 October 1991: SI 1991/828.

Amendments
Sub-s (4): Family Law Act 1996, s 66 and Sch 8, para 60; Crime and Disorder Act 1998 s119, and Sch 8 para 68

Definitions
For 'contact order', 'prohibited steps order', 'residence order', 'specific issue order' see sub-s (1); for 'child' see s 105(1); for 'parental responsibility' see s 3; for 'court' see s 92(7); for 'a section 8 order' see sub-s (2); for 'family proceedings' see sub-s (3).

References
See generally chapter 5. Section 8 orders are discussed at paras 2.22ff of *The Children Act 1989 Guidance and Regulations, Volume 1, Court Orders* (Dept of Health, 1991). For 'parent', see para 3.43; for jurisdiction of the courts see s 92 and Sch 11. Part I of this Act: ie ss 1-7 (introductory); Pt II, ss 8-17 and Sch 1 (orders with respect to children in family and other proceedings); Pt IV, ss 31-42 and Sch 3 (care and supervision); for the effects of orders generally see s 91.

Note
Proceedings under the HFEA 1990, s 30 also rank as 'family proceedings': HFEA 1990, s 30(3)(a) as do applications under ss 1 and 2 of the Crime and Disorder Act 1998, see paras 5.101 ff.

Residence order
See generally paras 5.10 ff. Can be made ex parte but only in exceptional circumstances: FPR 1991, SI 1991/1247, r 4.4(4); FPC (CA 1989) R 1991, SI 1991/1395, r 4(4); *Re B (minors) (residence orders)* [1992] Fam 162, [1992] 3 All ER 867, CA; *Re G (minors) (ex parte interim residence order)* [1993] 1 FLR 910, CA; *Re P (a minor) (ex parte interim residence order)* [1993] 1 FLR 915, CA, see paras 5.22 ff.

Contact order
See paras 5.45 ff. For contact and domestic violence, see paras 5.60 ff.

Prohibited steps order
See generally paras 5.70 ff. Must not be used as a disguised residence or contact order, see s 9(5) above and *Re B (minors) (residence orders)* at 165 and 869 respectively per Butler-Sloss LJ and *Nottingham County Council v P* [1993] 3 All ER 815, [1994] Fam 18 CA. There is no jurisdiction to make ouster orders: *Re D (Prohibited Steps Order)* [1996] 2 FLR 273, sub nom *D v D (Ouster Order)* [1996] 2 FCR 496, CA nor an order prohibiting parents from seeing each other as such contact is not a step which can be taken by a parent in meeting his parental responsibility towards his child: *Croydon London Borough Council v A* [1992] 3 All ER 788, [1992] 3 WLR 267, CA.. Orders can be made even though child is abroad: *Re D (a minor) (child: removal from jurisdiction)* [1992] 1 All ER 892, [1992] 1 WLR 315, CA. For prohibiting contact see *Nottingham County Council v P*, supra and *Re H (prohibited steps order)* [1995] 1 FLR 638, CA, see paras 5.53.

Specific issue order
See generally paras 5.73 ff.

9 Restrictions on making section 8 orders

(1) No court shall make any section 8 order, other than a residence order, with respect to a child who is in the care of a local authority.

(2) No application may be made by a local authority for a residence order or contact order and no court shall make such an order in favour of a local authority.

(3) A person who is, or was at any time within the last six months, a local authority

foster parent of a child may not apply for leave to apply for a section 8 order with respect to the child unless—

(a) he has the consent of the authority;

(b) he is a relative of the child; or

(c) the child has lived with him for at least three years preceding the application.

(4) The period of three years mentioned in subsection (3)(*c*) need not be continuous but must have begun not more than five years before the making of the application.

(5) No court shall exercise its powers to make a specific issue order or prohibited steps order—

(a) with a view to achieving a result which could be achieved by making a residence or contact order; or

(b) in any way which is denied to the High Court (by section 100(2)) in the exercise of its inherent jurisdiction with respect to children.

(6) No court shall make any section 8 order which is to have effect for a period which will end after the child has reached the age of sixteen unless it is satisfied that the circumstances of the case are exceptional.

(7) No court shall make any section 8 order, other than one varying or discharging such an order, with respect to a child who has reached the age of sixteen unless it is satisfied that the circumstances of the case are exceptional.

Date in force
14 October 1991: SI 1991/828.

Definitions
For 'court' see s 92(7); for 'a section 8 order' see s 8(2); for 'residence order', 'contact order', 'specific issue order' and 'prohibited steps order' see s 8(1); for 'child', 'child who is in the care of a local authority', 'local authority' and 'relative' see s 105(1); for 'local authority foster parent', see s 23(3).

References
For 'family proceedings' under this Act see s 8(3), (4)(a); for jurisdiction of courts see s 92 and Sch 11; for power of court to make s 8 orders, person who may make an application for such orders and the need for leave to apply see s 10; for the presumption that a delay in determining any question in proceedings concerning the upbringing of a child is likely to prejudice the welfare of the child concerned see s 1(2); for timetable for s 8 proceedings and supplementary provisions see s 11; for provisions connected with residence orders see ss 12, 13 and 14; for the application of s 9(1)(2) see paras 5.81 ff and 5.98 ff and for 9(5) see para 5.80 and see *Re B (Minors) (Residence Orders)* [1992] Fam 162 at 165, [1992] 3 All ER 867 at 869, per Butler-Sloss LJ and *Nottingham County Council v P* [1994] Fam 18, [1993] 3 All ER 815, [1993] 3 WLR 637, CA. Cf *Re H (Prohibited Steps Order)* [1995] 1 FLR 638, CA. A local authority may apply for leave to apply for a specific issue order in respect of a child not in care: *Re C (a child) (HIV test)* [1999] 3 FCR 289.

10   Power of court to make section 8 orders

(1) In any family proceedings in which a question arises with respect to the welfare of any child, the court may make a section 8 order with respect to the child if—

(a) an application for the order has been made by a person who—

(i)   is entitled to apply for a section 8 order with respect to the child; or

(ii) has obtained the leave of the court to make the application; or

(b) the court considers that the order should be made even though no such application has been made.

(2) The court may also make a section 8 order with respect to any child on the application of a person who—

(a) is entitled to apply for a section 8 order with respect to the child; or

(b) has obtained the leave of the court to make the application.

(3) This section is subject to the restrictions imposed by section 9.

(4) The following persons are entitled to apply to the court for any section 8 order with respect to a child—

(a) any parent or guardian of the child;

(b) any person in whose favour a residence order is in force with respect to the child.

(5) The following persons are entitled to apply for a residence or contact order with respect to a child—

(a) any party to a marriage (whether or not subsisting) in relation to whom the child is a child of the family;

(b) any person with whom the child has lived for a period of at least three years;

(c) any person—

(i) in any case where a residence order is in force with respect to the child, has the consent of each of the persons in whose favour the order was made;

(ii) in any case where the child is in the care of a local authority, has the consent of that authority; or

(iii) in any other case, has the consent of each of those (if any) who have parental responsibility for the child.

(6) A person who would not otherwise be entitled (under the previous provisions of this section) to apply for the variation or discharge of a section 8 order shall be entitled to do so if—

(a) the order was made on his application; or

(b) in the case of a contact order, he is named in the order.

(7) Any person who falls within a category of person prescribed by rules of court is entitled to apply for any such section 8 order as may be prescribed in relation to that category of person.

(8) Where the person applying for leave to make an application for a section 8 order is the child concerned, the court may only grant leave if it is satisfied that he has sufficient understanding to make the proposed application for the section 8 order.

(9) Where the person applying for leave to make an application for a section 8 order is not the child concerned, the court shall, in deciding whether or not to grant leave, have particular regard to—

(a) the nature of the proposed application for the section 8 order;

(b) the applicant's connection with the child;

(c) any risk there might be of that proposed application disrupting the child's life to such an extent that he would be harmed by it; and

(d) where the child is being looked after by a local authority—

(i) the authority's plans for the child's future; and

(ii) the wishes and feelings of the child's parents.

(10) The period of three years mentioned in subsection (5)(b) need not be continuous but must not have begun more than five years before, or ended more than three months before, the making of the application.

Date in force
14 October 1991: SI 1991/828.

Definitions
For 'family proceedings' see s 8(3); for 'child', 'guardian', 'child of the family', 'child in the care of local authority', 'local authority', 'prescribed' see s 105(1); for 'court' see s 92(7); for 'a section 8 order' see s 8(2); for 'residence order', 'contact order', see s 8(1); for a 'person in whose favour a residence order is in force' see s 105(3)(b); for 'parental responsibility' see s 3; for 'harm' see s 31(9) as applied to the whole Act by s 105(1); for 'child looked after by a local authority' see s 22(1) and s 105(4).

References
See generally para 5.107 ff. For jurisdiction of courts see s 92 and Sch 11; for appeals see s 94; for persons entitled to apply for s 8 orders see sub-ss (4), (5) and (6); for 'parent' see para 3.43; for appointment of children's guardian see s 41; for duration of orders made under this section see

s 11(5), (6) and ss 91(10), (11); for 'family proceedings' under this Act see s 8(3), (4)(a); for where the leave of the court may be required in order to make an application for an order under this section see s 91(14); for the making of family assistance orders under this Part, ie Pt II (ss 8-16 and Sch 1) see s 16; for the restrictions on the making of applications for a s 8 order see s 9; for the presumption that a delay in determining any question in proceedings concerning a s 8 order is likely to prejudice the welfare of the child concerned see s 1(2); for the timetable for such proceedings and supplementary provisions see s 11; for other provisions connected with residence orders see ss 12, 13 and 14. Unmarried fathers do not require leave, but parents whose child has been freed for adoption do require leave: Re *C (Minors) (Adoption: Residence Order)* [1994] Fam 1, sub nom *Re C (minors) (parent:residence order)* [1993] 3 All ER 313, [1993] 3 WLR 249, sub nom *M v C and Calderdale Metropolitan Borough Council* [1993] 1 FLR 505, CA. A child who is named in a contact order for whom he had previously obtained leave to apply does not need leave to apply for its subsequent variation, per Wilson J in *Re W (application for leave: whether necessary)* [1996] 3 FCR 337n. The grant of leave is a substantial judicial decision and generally, any application should be heard on notice to all likely to be affected, see *Re (minors)* [1992] 3 All ER 867, *Re G (minors) (ex p Residence Order)* [1992] 2 FCR 720 and *Re W (A Child)(Contact: Leave to Apply)* [2000] 1 FLR 263, FD. In deciding whether to grant adults leave the child's welfare is not the paramount consideration: *Re A (Minors) (Residence Orders: Leave to Apply)* [1992] Fam 182, [1992] 3 All ER 872, sub nom *Re A and W (Minors) (Residence Order) (Leave to Apply)* [1992] 2 FLR 154, [1992] Fam Law 439,CA. In the case of applications for leave by children, the criteria in s 10(9) do not apply but there is a conflict of opinion as to whether the child's welfare is the paramount consideration. See *Re C (A Minor) (Leave to Seek Section 8 Orders)* [1994] 1 FLR 26, where the child's welfare is the paramount consideration, per Johnson J, cf *Re SC (A Minor) (Leave to Seek Residence Order)* [1994] 1 FLR 96 and *Re C (Residence: Child's Application for Leave)* [1995] 1 FLR 927 in which Booth J and Stuart-White J respectively held that it was not. Although a local authority foster parent may not apply without the consent of the local authority, the court may make an order of its own motion in favour of the foster parent: *Gloucestershire County Council v P* [1999] 3 FCR 114, [1999] 2 FLR 61, CA.

---

11 General principles and supplementary provisions

(1) In proceedings in which any question of making a section 8 order, or any other question with respect to such an order, arises, the court shall (in the light of any rules made by virtue of subsection (2))—

(a) draw up a timetable with a view to determining the question without delay; and

(b) give such directions as it considers appropriate for the purpose of ensuring, so far as is reasonably practicable, that that timetable is adhered to.

(2) Rules of court may—

(a) specify periods within which specified steps must be taken in relation to proceedings in which such questions arise; and

(b) make other provision with respect to such proceedings for the purpose of ensuring, so far as is reasonably practicable, that such questions are determined without delay.

(3) Where a court has power to make a section 8 order, it may do so at any time during the course of the proceedings in question even though it is not in a position to dispose finally of those proceedings.

(4) Where a residence order is made in favour of two or more persons who do not themselves all live together, the order may specify the periods during which the child is to live in the different households concerned.

(5) Where—

(a) a residence order has been made with respect to a child; and

(b) as a result of the order the child lives, or is to live, with one of two parents who each have parental responsibility for him,

the residence order shall cease to have effect if the parents live together for a continuous period of more than six months.

(6) A contact order which requires the parent with whom a child lives to allow the child to visit, or otherwise have contact with, his other parent shall cease to have effect if the parents live together for a continuous period of more than six months.

(7) A section 8 order may—

(a) contain directions about how it is to be carried into effect;

(b) impose conditions which must be complied with by any person—

    (i) in whose favour the order is made;

    (ii) who is a parent of the child concerned;

    (iii) who is not a parent of his but who has parental responsibility for him; or

    (iv) with whom the child is living,

and to whom the conditions are expressed to apply;

(c) be made to have effect for a specified period, or contain provisions which are to have effect for a specified period;

(d) make such incidental, supplemental or consequential provision as the court thinks fit.

Date in force

14 October 1991: SI 1991/828.

Definitions

For 'a section 8 order' see s 8(2); for 'court' see s 92(7) for 'residence order' and 'contact order' see s 8(1); for 'child' see s 105(1); for a person in whose favour a residence order is made or a person with whom a child lives, or is to live, as the result of the residence order see s 105(3); for 'parental responsibility' see s 3.

References

For jurisdiction of courts see s 92 and Sch 11; for welfare of the child see chapter 2; for the presumption that a delay in determining any question in proceedings concerning the upbringing of a child is likely to prejudice the welfare of the child concerned see s 1(2); for 'parent' see para 3.43.

Sub-s (4)

Where children were de facto spending substantial amounts of time with each of their parents, a shared residence order was an appropriate order to make and there was no need to show exceptional circumstances or a positive benefit to the children, see *Re D (children) (shared residence orders)* [2001] 1 FCR 147, [2001] 1 FLR 495 explaining *Re H (a minor) (Residence Order)* [1993] 1 FCR 671 where it had been held that it would rarely be appropriate for a shared residence order to be made other than in exceptional circumstances. See also *N v B (Children: Orders as to Residence)* [1993] 1 FCR 231 (wrong to make a shared residence order solely to give an applicant parental responsibility).

Sub-s (7)

See generally paras 5.85 ff. The powers under sub s (7) are ancillary to the making of a s 8 order and are governed by the provisions for the making of a s 8 order. There is not power therefore to interfere with rights of occupation: per Ward LJ in *Re D (Prohibited Steps Order)* [1996] 2 FLR 273, sub nom *D v D (ouster order)* [1996] 2 FCR 496, CA and *Re D (Residence: Imposition of Conditions)* [1996] 2 FLR, CA. Conditions must not be inconsistent with any residence order granted: *Birmingham City Council v H* [1992] 2 FLR 323 and can only be imposed on persons listed (ie not local authorities): *Leeds County Council v C* [1993] 1 FLR 269. Section 11 cannot be used to interfere with the exercise by other bodies, such as local authorities or the police, of their statutory law powers: *D v D (County Court Jurisdiction: Injunctions)* [1993] 2 FLR 802, CA. It is highly exceptional to impose a condition of residence on a primary carer in circumstances other than the express restrictions on a removal of a child from the jurisdiction in s 13 of the Act: *Re S (a child) (residence order: condition)* [2001] EWCA Civ 847, [2001] 3 FCR 847.

---

12 Residence orders and parental responsibility

(1) Where the court makes a residence order in favour of the father of a child it shall, if the father would not otherwise have parental responsibility for the child, also make an order under section 4 giving him that responsibility.

(2) Where the court makes a residence order in favour of any person who is not the parent or guardian of the child concerned that person shall have parental responsibility for the child while the residence order remains in force.

(3) Where a person has parental responsibility for a child as a result of subsection (2), he shall not have the right—

(a) to consent, or refuse to consent, to the making of an application with respect to the child under section 18 of the Adoption Act 1976;

(b) to agree, or refuse to agree, to the making of an adoption order, or an order under section 55 of the Act of 1976, with respect to the child; or

(c) to appoint a guardian for the child.

(4) Where subsection (1) requires the court to make an order under section 4 in respect of the father of a child, the court shall not bring that order to an end at any time while the residence order concerned remains in force.

Date in force
14 October 1991: SI 1991/828.

Definitions
For 'court' see s 92(7); for 'residence order' see s 8(1); for 'child' and 'guardian of a child' see s 105(1); for 'parental responsibility' see s 3.

References
See generally paras 3.65 and 3.83. For jurisdiction of courts see s 92, and Sch 11. For 'an order under section 4' see para 3.55; for 'parent', see para 3.43; for the duration of residence orders see s 11(5), and s 91(10), (11); for 'family proceedings' under this Act see s 8(3), (4)(a).

13 Change of child's name or removal from jurisdiction

(1) Where a residence order is in force with respect to a child, no person may—

(a) cause the child to be known by a new surname; or

(b) remove him from the United Kingdom;

without either the written consent of every person who has parental responsibility for the child or the leave of the court.

(2) Subsection (1)(*b*) does not prevent the removal of a child, for a period of less than one month, by the person in whose favour the residence order is made.

(3) In making a residence order with respect to a child the court may grant the leave required by subsection (1)(*b*), either generally or for specified purposes.

Date in force
14 October 1991: SI 1991/828.

Definitions
For 'residence order' see s 8(1); for 'child' see s 105(1); for 'parental responsibility' see s 3; for 'court' see s 92(7); for 'the person in whose favour a residence order is in force' see s 105(3).

References
See generally paras 5.27 ff. For 'family proceedings' under this Act see s 8(3), (4)(a).

Sub-s (1)(a)
For the principles applying to change of names see *Dawson v Wearmouth* [1999] 2 AC 308, [1999] 2 All ER, [1999] 2 FCR 625, *Re W, Re A, Re B (Change of Surname)* [1999] 2 FLR 930, [1999] 3 FCR 357 and *Re R (a child)* [2001] EWCA Civ 1344, [2002] 1 FCR 170.

Sub-s (1)(b)
For the principles governing applications to remove a child form the jurisdiction see, see *Re K (applications to remove from jurisdiction)* [1999] 2 FCR 410. [1999] 2 FLR 1006 and see paras 5.35 ff. There is no presumption in favour of the applicant parent and the European Convention on Human Rights has not affected the principles of domestic law: *Payne v Payne* [2001] EWCA Civ 166, [2001] 1 FCR 425 see paras 5.40 ff. 'United Kingdom' includes Northern Ireland, see *Re H (children) (residence order: condition)* [2001] EWCA Civ 1338, [2001] 3 FCR 182 where exceptionally a prohibited steps order was made preventing the removal of children by their father to Northern Ireland see para 5.35.

14 Enforcement of residence orders

(1) Where—

(a) a residence order is in force with respect to a child in favour of any person; and

(b) any other person (including one in whose favour the order is also in force) is in breach of the arrangements settled by that order,

the person mentioned in paragraph (*a*) may, as soon as the requirement in subsection (2) is complied with, enforce the order under section 63(3) of the Magistrates' Courts Act 1980 as if it were an order requiring the other person to produce the child to him.

(2) The requirement is that a copy of the residence order has been served on the other person.

(3) Subsection (1) is without prejudice to any other remedy open to the person in whose favour the residence order is in force.

Date in force
14 October 1991: SI 1991/828.

Definitions
For 'residence order' see s 8(1); for 'child' see s 105(1); for 'the person in whose favour a residence order is in force' see s 105(3).

References
See generally para 5.128. For service of documents under the Act generally see s 105(8)-(10).

Financial relief

15 Orders for financial relief with respect to children

(1) Schedule 1 (which consists primarily of the re-enactment, with consequential amendments and minor modifications, of provisions of [section 6 of the Family Law Reform Act 1969] the Guardianship of Minors Acts 1971 and 1973, the Children Act 1975 and of sections 15 and 16 of the Family Law Reform Act 1987) makes provision in relation to financial relief for children.

(2) The powers of a magistrates' court under section 60 of the Magistrates' Courts Act 1980 to revoke, revive or vary an order for the periodical payment of money [and the power of the clerk of a magistrates' court to vary such an order] shall not apply in relation to an order made under Schedule 1.

Date in force
14 October 1991: SI 1991/828.

Amendment
Sub-s (1): CLSA 1990, Sch 16, para 10. Sub-s (2): MEA 1991, Sch 2, para 10.

Definition
For 'child' see s 105(1).

Reference
For 'family proceedings' under this Act see s 8(3), (4)(a).

Family assistance orders

16 Family assistance orders

(1) Where, in any family proceedings, the court has power to make an order under this Part with respect to any child, it may (whether or not it makes such an order) make an order requiring—

(a) [an officer of the Service] to be made available; or

(b) a local authority to make an officer of the authority available,

to advise, assist and (where appropriate) befriend any person named in the order.

(2) The persons who may be named in an order under this section ('a family assistance order') are—

(a) any parent or guardian of the child;
(b) any person with whom the child is living or in whose favour a contact order is in force with respect to the child;
(c) the child himself.

(3) No court may make a family assistance order unless—

(a) it is satisfied that the circumstances of the case are exceptional; and
(b) it has obtained the consent of every person to be named in the order other than the child.

(4) A family assistance order may direct—

(a) the person named in the order; or
(b) such of the persons named in the order as may be specified in the order,

to take such steps as may be so specified with a view to enabling the officer concerned to be kept informed of the address of any person named in the order and to be allowed to visit any such person.

(5) Unless it specifies a shorter period, a family assistance order shall have effect for a period of six months beginning with the day on which it is made.

(6) Where—

(a) a family assistance order is in force with respect to a child; and
(b) a section 8 order is also in force with respect to the child,

the officer concerned may refer to the court the question whether the section 8 order should be varied or discharged.

(7) A family assistance order shall not be made so as to require a local authority to make an officer of theirs available unless—

(a) the authority agree; or
(b) the child concerned lives or will live within their area.

(8) [*Repealed by the Criminal Justice and Court Services Act 2000, ss 74, 75, Sch 7, Pt II, paras 87, 89(b), Sch 8.*]

(9) [*Repealed by the Criminal Justice and Court Services Act 2000, ss 74, 75, Sch 7, Pt II, paras 87, 89(b), Sch 8.*]

Date in force
14 October 1991: SI 1991/828.

Amendment
Sub-s (1): in para (a) words "an officer of the Service" in square brackets substituted by the Criminal Justice and Court Services Act 2000, s 74, Sch 7, Pt II, paras 87, 89(a).
Sub-ss (8), (9): repealed by the Criminal Justice and Court Services Act 2000, ss 74, 75, Sch 7, Pt II, paras 87, 89(b), Sch 8.

Definitions
For 'family proceedings' see s 8(3), (4)(a); for 'court' see s 92(7); for 'child', 'local authority' and 'guardian of a child' see s 105(1); 'family assistance order' see sub-s (2); for 'contact order' see s 8(1) and 'a section 8 order' see s 8(2).

References
See generally paras 5.143 ff. For 'this Part' see Pt II ie ss 8-16 and Sch 1 (orders with respect to children in family and other proceedings); for 'parent' see para 3.43; for the ending of orders see sub-s (5) and for the duration of s 8 orders see s 91(10), (11); for the use of a family assistance order as a means by which a local authority can supervise contact: *Leeds County Council v C* [1993] 1 FLR 269; not by attaching a condition to the contact order under s 11(7). And see *Re DH (A Minor) (Child Abuse)* [1994] 1 FLR 679 and *Re E (family assistance order)* [1999] 3 FCR 700.

PART III
LOCAL AUTHORITY SUPPORT FOR CHILDREN AND FAMILIES

Provision of services for children and their families

17 Provision of services for children in need, their families and others

(1) It shall be the general duty of every local authority (in addition to the other duties imposed on them by this Part)—

(a) to safeguard and promote the welfare of children within their area who are in need; and

(b) so far as is consistent with that duty, to promote the upbringing of such children by their families,

by providing a range and level of services appropriate to those children's needs.

(2) For the purpose principally of facilitating the discharge of their general duty under this section, every local authority shall have the specific duties and powers set out in Part I of Schedule 2.

(3) Any service provided by an authority in the exercise of functions conferred on them by this section may be provided for the family of a particular child in need or for any member of his family, if it is provided with a view to safeguarding or promoting the child's welfare.

(4) The Secretary of State may by order amend any provision of Part I of Schedule 2 or add any further duty or power to those for the time being mentioned there.

(5) Every local authority—

(a) shall facilitate the provision by others (including in particular voluntary organisations) of services which the authority have power to provide by virtue of this section, or section 18, 20, [23, 23B to 23D, 24A or 24B]; and

(b) may make such arrangements as they see fit for any person to act on their behalf in the provision of any such service.

(6) The services provided by a local authority in the exercise of functions conferred on them by this section may include giving assistance in kind or, in exceptional circumstances, in cash.

(7) Assistance may be unconditional or subject to conditions as to the repayment of the assistance or of its value (in whole or in part).

(8) Before giving any assistance or imposing any conditions, a local authority shall have regard to the means of the child concerned and of each of his parents.

(9) No person shall be liable to make any repayment of assistance or of its value at any time when he is in receipt of income support[, working families' tax credit] [or disabled person's tax credit] under the [Part VII of the Social Security Contributions and Benefits Act 1992] [or of an income-based jobseeker's allowance].

(10) For the purposes of this Part a child shall be taken to be in need if—

(a) he is unlikely to achieve or maintain, or to have the opportunity of achieving or maintaining, a reasonable standard of health or development without the provision for him of services by a local authority under this Part;

(b) his health or development is likely to be significantly impaired, or further impaired, without the provision for him of such services; or

(c) he is disabled,

and 'family', in relation to such a child, includes any person who has parental responsibility for the child and any other person with whom he has been living.

(11) For the purposes of this Part, a child is disabled if he is blind, deaf or dumb or suffers from mental disorder of any kind or is substantially and permanently handicapped by illness, injury or congenital deformity or such other disability as may be prescribed; and in this Part—

'development' means physical, intellectual, emotional, social or behavioural development; and

'health' means physical or mental health.

Date in force
14 October 1991: SI 1991/828.

Amendments
Sub-s (5): Children (Leaving Care) Act 2000,s 7(1),(2). Sub-s (9): Disability Living Allowance and Disability Working Allowance Act 1991, Sch 3, para 13; Social Security (Consequential Provisions) Act 1992, Sch 2, para 108(a), Jobseekers Act 1995, s 41(4), Sch 2, para 19, Tax Credits Act 1999,s 1(2), Sch 1, paras 1,6.

Definitions
For 'local authority', 'child', 'upbringing', 'service' 'functions' and 'prescribed' see s 105(1); for 'need' and 'family' see sub-s (10); for 'voluntary organisation' see s 105(1); for 'health', 'development' and 'disabled' see sub-s (11).

References
See generally chapter 6 and *The Children Act 1989 Guidance and Regulations, Volume 2, Family Support, Day Care and Educational Provision for Young Children* (Dept of Health, 1991). For 'this Part' see Pt III ie ss 17-30 and Sch 2 (local authority support for children and families). 'Parent' ie mother and father; for the application of sub-ss (7)-(9) in relation to assistance given under s 24 see s 24(10); for the duty to publish information about the services provided under this section see Sch 2, Pt I; for co-operation between authorities see s 27; for recoupment of the cost of services see s 29; for miscellaneous supplementary provisions see s 30.

Transfer of functions
Functions of the Secretary of State, so far as exercisable in relation to Wales, transferred to the National Assembly for Wales, by the National Assembly for Wales (Transfer of Functions) Order 1999, SI 1999/672, art 2, Sch 1.

Within their area
These words have the same meaning as in other sections of the Act and physical presence is required and is sufficient to found the duty under s 17(1): *R(S) v London Borough of Wandsworth, London Borough of Hammersmith and Fulham, London Borough of Lambeth* [2001] EWHC Admin 799, [2002] 1 FLR 469.

Services
For the framework and nature of the assessment required to be undertaken by local authorities , see 'Framework for the Assessment of Children in Need (2000) (Department of Health) and also *R (on the application of AB and SB) v Nottingham City Council* [2001] EWHC Admin 235, [2001] 3 FCR 349. A local authority has a discretionary power under this provision to assist a family with dependent children which is not entitled to help from the local housing authority with the provision of accommodation but may reserve this for extreme cases, *R(W) v Lambeth London Borough Council* [2002] EWCA Civ 613, [2002] 2 All ER 901, [2002] 2 FCR 289, not *following A v Lambeth London Borough Council* [2001] EWCA Civ 1624, [2001] 3 FCR 673, [2001] 2 FLR 1201.

Sub-s (4) Order
See the Children Act 1989 (Amendment) (Children's Services Planning) Order 1996, SI 1996/785.

[17A Direct payments

(1) Instead of providing services in the exercise of functions conferred on them by section 17, a local authority may make to a person falling within subsection (2) (if he consents) a payment of such amount as, subject to subsections (5) and (6), they think fit in respect of his securing the provision of any of the services which the local authority would otherwise have provided.

(2) The following fall within this subsection—

(a) a person with parental responsibility for a disabled child;

(b) a disabled child aged 16 or 17.

(3) A payment under subsection (1) shall be subject to the condition that the person to whom it is made shall not secure the provision of the service to which it relates by a person who is of a prescribed description.

(4) The Secretary of State may by regulations provide that the power conferred by subsection (1) is not to be exercisable in relation to the provision of residential accommodation for any person for a period exceeding a prescribed period.

(5) Except as mentioned in subsection (6) of this section, subsections (2) and (6) of section 1, and subsections (1) and (2) of section 2, of the Community Care (Direct Payments) Act 1996 apply in relation to payments under subsection (1) as they apply in relation to payments under section 1(1) of that Act, but as if—

    (a)   the reference to 'subsection (4)' in section 1(6)(b) of that Act were a reference to subsection (3) of this section; and

    (b)   the references to 'the relevant community care enactment' in section 2 of that Act were to Part III of the Children Act 1989.

(6) Section 1(2) of the Community Care (Direct Payments) Act 1996 does not apply in relation to payments under subsection (1) to—

    (a)   a person with parental responsibility for a disabled child, other than a parent of such a child under the age of sixteen, in respect of a service which would otherwise have been provided for the child; or

    (b)   any person who is in receipt of income support, working families' tax credit or disabled person's tax credit under Part VII of the Social Security Contributions and Benefits Act 1992 or of an income-based jobseeker's allowance,

and in those cases the amount of any payment under subsection (1) is to be at a rate equal to the local authority's estimate of the reasonable cost of securing the provision of the service concerned.]

[(1) The Secretary of State may by regulations make provision for and in connection with requiring or authorising the responsible authority in the case of a person of a prescribed description who falls within subsection (2) to make, with that person's consent, such payments to him as they may determine in accordance with the regulations in respect of his securing the provision of the service mentioned in that subsection.

(2) A person falls within this subsection if he is—

    (a)   a person with parental responsibility for a disabled child,

    (b)   a disabled person with parental responsibility for a child, or

    (c)   a disabled child aged 16 or 17,

and a local authority ('the responsible authority') have decided for the purposes of section 17 that the child's needs (or, if he is such a disabled child, his needs) call for the provision by them of a service in exercise of functions conferred on them under that section.

(3) Subsections (3) to (5) and (7) of section 57 of the 2001 Act shall apply, with any necessary modifications, in relation to regulations under this section as they apply in relation to regulations under that section.

(4) Regulations under this section shall provide that, where payments are made under the regulations to a person falling within subsection (5)—

    (a)   the payments shall be made at the rate mentioned in subsection (4)(a) of section 57 of the 2001 Act (as applied by subsection (3)); and

    (b)   subsection (4)(b) of that section shall not apply.

(5) A person falls within this subsection if he is—

    (a)   a person falling within subsection (2)(a) or (b) and the child in question is aged 16 or 17, or

    (b)   a person who is in receipt of income support, working families' tax credit or disabled person's tax credit under Part 7 of the Social Security Contributions and Benefits Act 1992 (c 4) or of an income-based jobseeker's allowance.

(6) In this section—

'the 2001 Act' means the Health and Social Care Act 2001;

'disabled' in relation to an adult has the same meaning as that given by section 17(11) in relation to a child;

'prescribed' means specified in or determined in accordance with regulations under this section (and has the same meaning in the provisions of the 2001 Act mentioned in subsection (3) as they apply by virtue of that subsection).]

Date in force
Inserted by the Carers and Disabled Children Act 2000, s 7(1) as from 1 April 2001 (England) SI 2001/510; 1 July 2001 (Wales) SI 2001/2196.

Amendments
Substituted by the Health and Social Care Act 2001, s 58 for certain purposes as from 11 May 2001.

Definitions
For 'parental responsibility' see s 3; for 'disabled child' see s 17 and for 'disabled' in relation to an adult see sub-s (6).

Regulations
See the Disabled Children (Direct Payments) (England) Regulations 2001, SI 2001/442 and the Disabled Children (Direct Payments) (Wales) Regulations 2001, SI 2001/2192.

[17B   Vouchers for persons with parental responsibility for disabled children]

[(1) The Secretary of State may by regulations make provision for the issue by a local authority of vouchers to a person with parental responsibility for a disabled child.

(2) 'Voucher' means a document whereby, if the local authority agrees with the person with parental responsibility that it would help him care for the child if the person with parental responsibility had a break from caring, that person may secure the temporary provision of services for the child under section 17.

(3) The regulations may, in particular, provide—
(a)   for the value of a voucher to be expressed in terms of money, or of the delivery of a service for a period of time, or both;
(b)   for the person who supplies a service against a voucher, or for the arrangement under which it is supplied, to be approved by the local authority;
(c)   for a maximum period during which a service (or a service of a prescribed description) can be provided against a voucher.]

Date in force
Inserted by the Carers and Disabled Children Act 2000, s 7(1) as from a date to be appointed.

18   Day care for pre-school and other children

(1) Every local authority shall provide such day care for children in need within their area who are—

(a)   aged five or under; and
(b)   not yet attending schools,

as is appropriate.

(2) A local authority may provide day care for children within their area who satisfy the conditions mentioned in subsection (1)(*a*) and (*b*) even though they are not in need.

(3) A local authority may provide facilities (including training, advice, guidance and counselling) for those—

(a)   caring for children in day care; or
(b)   who at any time accompany such children while they are in day care.

(4) In this section 'day care' means any form of care or supervised activity provided for children during the day (whether or not it is provided on a regular basis).

(5) Every local authority shall provide for children in need within their area who are attending any school such care or supervised activities as is appropriate—

(a) outside school hours; or

(b) during school holidays.

(6) A local authority may provide such care or supervised activities for children within their area who are attending any school even though those children are not in need.

(7) In this section 'supervised activity' means an activity supervised by a responsible person.

Date in force
14 October 1991: SI 1991/828.

Definitions
For 'local authority', 'child' and 'school' see s 105(1); for 'a child in need' see s 17(19); for 'day care' see sub-s (4); for 'supervised activity' see sub-s (7).

References
See para 6.24 and The Children Act 1989 Guidance and Regulations, Volume 2, Family Support, Day Care and Educational Provision For Young Children (Dept of Health, 1991).

Note
Allegations of failure to make proper provision under this section should be dealt with by complaint under s 26 and, if that is not satisfactory, s 84.

---

19 Review of provision for day care, child minding etc

(1) Every local authority in England and Wales shall review—

(a) the provision which they make under section 18;

(b) the extent to which the services of child minders are available within their area with respect to children under the age of eight; and

(c) the provision for day care within their area made for children under the age of eight by persons other, than the authority, required to register under section 71(1)(b) [Part XA].

(2) A review under subsection (1) shall be conducted—

(a) together with the appropriate local education authority; and

(b) at least once in every review period.

(3) Every local authority in Scotland shall, at least once in every review period, review—

(a) the provision for day care within their area made for children under the age of eight by the local authority and by persons required to register under section 71(1)(b); and

(b) the extent to which the services of child minders are available within their area with respect to children under the age of eight.

(4) In conducting any such review, the two authorities or, in Scotland, the authority shall have regard to the provision made with respect to children under the age of eight in relevant establishments within their area.

(5) In this section—

'relevant establishment' means any establishment which is mentioned in paragraphs 3 and 4 of Schedule 9 (hospitals, schools and other establishments exempt from the registration requirements which apply in relation to the provision of day care); and

['relevant establishment' means—

(a) in relation to Scotland, any establishment which is mentioned in paragraphs 3 and 4 of Schedule 9 (establishments exempt from the registration requirements which apply in relation to the provision of day care in Scotland); and

(b) in relation to England and Wales, any establishment which is mentioned in paragraphs 1 and 2 of Schedule 9A (establishments exempt from the registration requirements which apply in relation to the provision of day care in England and Wales);]

'review period' means the period of one year beginning with the commencement of this section and each subsequent period of three years beginning with an anniversary of that commencement.

(6) Where a local authority have conducted a review under this section they shall publish the result of the review—

(a) as soon as is reasonably practicable;
(b) in such form as they consider appropriate; and
(c) together with any proposals they may have with respect to the matters reviewed.

(7) The authorities conducting any review under this section shall have regard to—

(a) any representations made to any one of them by any relevant [Health Authority, Special Health Authority] [, Primary Care Trust] or health board; and
(b) any other representations which they consider to be relevant.

(8) In the application of this section to Scotland, 'day care' has the same meaning as in section 79 and 'health board' has the same meaning as in the National Health Service (Scotland) Act 1978.

Date in force
14 October 1991: SI 1991/828.

Amendments
Sub-s (1): Care Standards Act 2000, s 116, Sch 4, paras 14 (in relation to England). Sub-s (5) Care Standards Act 2000, s 116, Sch 4, para 14 (in relation to England). Sub-s (7): Health Authorities Act 1995, s 2(1). Sch 1, para 118(2).and SI 2000/90.

Definitions
For 'local authority', 'child' 'local education authority', 'hospital' and 'health authority' see s 105(1); for 'child minder' see s 71 as applied to the whole Act by s 105(1); for 'day care' see s 18(4) as applied to the whole Act by s 105(1); for 'review period' and 'relevant establishment' see sub-s (5).

References
See para 6.25 and *The Children Act 1989 Guidance and Regulations, Volume 2, Family Support, Day Care and Educational Provision for Young Children* (Dept of Health, 1991). For the general duty of local authorities in connection with the welfare of children in need see s 17; for co-operation between authorities see s 27; for recoupment of the cost of services provided see s 29 and for miscellaneous supplementary provisions see s 30. For the registration of child minders and persons providing day care for young children see Pt XA (ss 79A – 79X and Sch 9A).

Provision of accommodation for children

20 Provision of accommodation for children: general

(1) Every local authority shall provide accommodation for any child in need within their area who appears to them to require accommodation as a result of—

(a) there being no person who has parental responsibility for him;
(b) his being lost or having been abandoned; or
(c) the person who has been caring for him being prevented (whether or not permanently, and for whatever reason) from providing him with suitable accommodation or care.

(2) Where a local authority provide accommodation under subsection (1) for a child who is ordinarily resident in the area of another local authority, that other local authority may take over the provision of accommodation for the child within—

(a) three months of being notified in writing that the child is being provided with accommodation; or

(b) such other longer period as may be prescribed.

(3) Every local authority shall provide accommodation for any child in need within their area who has reached the age of sixteen and whose welfare the authority consider is likely to be seriously prejudiced if they do not provide him with accommodation.

(4) A local authority may provide accommodation for any child within their area (even though a person who has parental responsibility for him is able to provide him with accommodation) if they consider that to do so would safeguard or promote the child's welfare.

(5) A local authority may provide accommodation for any person who has reached the age of sixteen but is under twenty-one in any community home which takes children who have reached the age of sixteen if they consider that to do so would safeguard or promote his welfare.

(6) Before providing accommodation under this section, a local authority shall, so far as is reasonably practicable and consistent with the child's welfare—

(a) ascertain the child's wishes regarding the provision of accommodation; and

(b) give due consideration (having regard to his age and understanding) to such wishes of the child as they have been able to ascertain.

(7) A local authority may not provide accommodation under this section for any child if any person who—

(a) has parental responsibility for him; and

(b) is willing and able to—

(i) provide accommodation for him; or

(ii) arrange for accommodation to be provided for him,

objects.

(8) Any person who has parental responsibility for a child may at any time remove the child from accommodation provided by or on behalf of the local authority under this section.

(9) Subsections (7) and (8) do not apply while any person—

(a) in whose favour a residence order is in force with respect to the child; or

(b) who has care of the child by virtue of an order made in the exercise of the High Court's inherent jurisdiction with respect to children,

agrees to the child being looked after in accommodation provided by or on behalf of the local authority.

(10) Where there is more than one such person as is mentioned in subsection (9), all of them must agree.

(11) Subsections (7) and (8) do not apply where a child who has reached the age of sixteen agrees to being provided with accommodation under this section.

Date in force
14 October 1991: SI 1991/828.

Definitions
For 'local authority', 'child' and 'prescribed' see s 105(1); for 'a child in need' see s 17(10) as applied to the whole Act by s 105(7); for 'parental responsibility' see s 3; for 'community home' see s 53: for 'residence order' see s 8(1). For a person in whose favour a residence order is in force see s 105(3).

References
See paras 6.26 ff and *The Children Act 1989 Guidance and Regulations, Volume 2, Family Support, Day Care and Educational Provision for Young Children* (Dept of Health, 1991) *and The Children Act 1989 Guidance and Regulations, Volume 3, Family Placements* (Dept of Health, 1991). For the determination of the ordinary residence of a child for the purposes of sub-s (2), 21(3) or s 29(7)-(9) see s 30(2) and s 105(6); for the general duties of local authorities in connection with the welfare of

children in need see s 17; for review of case of, and representations relating to, child being looked after by local authority see s 26 and Review of Children's Cases Regulations 1991, SI 1991/895 amended by SI 2002/546; for co-operation between authorities see s 27; for recoupment for the cost of services provided see s 29; for miscellaneous supplementary provisions see s 30.

Sub-s (1)
These criteria reflect those formerly contained in the CCA 1980, s 2. Children in care under the section shall be treated as being provided with accommodation, provided no parental rights resolution has been passed: Sch 14, para 20. As to contact with accommodated children see the Contact with Children Regulations 1991, SI 1991/891, and Sch 2, para 15. As to arrangements for the provision of accommodation see s 23 and Arrangement for Placement of Children Regulations 1991, SI 1991/890 and note the duties of other authorities to provide help for Pt III functions by virtue of s 27.

Sub-s (7)
Objections by person with parental responsibility. The local authority does not have the power to override the wishes of a parent with parental responsibility and does not have the power to place a child with foster parents against the wishes of the parents: *R v Tameside Metropolitan Borough Council, ex p J* [2000] 1 FCR 173, [2000] 1 FLR 942, QBD.

---

21 Provision for accommodation for children in police protection or detention or on remand, etc

(1) Every local authority shall make provision for the reception and accommodation of children who are removed or kept away from home under Part V.

(2) Every local authority shall receive, and provide accommodation for, children—

(a) in police protection whom they are requested to receive under section 46(3)(f);

(b) whom they are requested to receive under section 38(6) of the Police and Criminal Evidence Act 1984;

(c) who are—

   (i) on remand [(within the meaning of the section)] under [paragraph 7(5) of Schedule 7 to the Powers of Criminal Courts (Sentencing) Act 2000 or section] 23(1) of the Children and Young Persons Act 1969; or

   (ii) the subject of a supervision order imposing a [local authority residence requirement under paragraph 5 of Schedule 6 to that Act of 2000],

and with respect to whom they are the designated authority.

(3) Where a child has been—

(a) removed under Part V; or

(b) detained under section 38 of the Police and Criminal Evidence Act 1984,

and he is not being provided with accommodation by a local authority or in a hospital vested in the Secretary of State [or a Primary Care Trust,] [or otherwise made available pursuant to arrangements made by a [Health Authority]] [or a Primary Care Trust], any reasonable expenses of accommodating him shall be recoverable from the local authority in whose area he is ordinarily resident.

Date in force
14 October 1991: SI 1991/828.

Amendment
Sub-s (2): CLSA 1990, Sch 16, para 11; Powers of Criminal Courts (Sentencing) Act 2000, Sch 9. Sub-s (3): National Health Service and Community Care Act 1990, Sch 9, para 36(1); Health Authorities Act 1995, Sch 1,; SI 2000/90.

Definitions
For 'local authority', 'child' and 'hospital' see s 105(1); for 'in police protection' see s 46(2); for 'supervision order' see s 31(11); for 'designated authority' see s 31(8).

References
'Part V' ie ss 43-52 (protection of children). For the determination of the ordinary residence of a child see ss 30(2) and 105(6).

Transfer of functions
Functions of the Secretary of State, so far as exercisable in relation to Wales, transferred to the National Assembly for Wales, by the National Assembly for Wales (Transfer of Functions) Order 1999, SI 1999/672, art 2, Sch 1.

Duties of local authorities in relation to children looked after by them

22 General duty of local authority in relation to children looked after by them

(1) In this Act, any reference to a child who is looked after by a local authority is a reference to a child who is—

(a) in their care; or

(b) provided with accommodation by the authority in the exercise of any functions (in particular those under this Act) which [are social services functions within the meaning of] the Local Authority Social Services Act 1970[, apart from functions under sections 23B and 24B].

(2) In subsection (1) 'accommodation' means accommodation which is provided for a continuous period of more than 24 hours.

(3) It shall be the duty of a local authority looking after any child—

(a) to safeguard and promote his welfare; and

(b) to make such use of services available for children cared for by their own parents as appears to the authority reasonable in his case.

(4) Before making any decision with respect to a child whom they are looking after, or proposing to look after, a local authority shall, so far as is reasonably practicable, ascertain the wishes and feelings of—

(a) the child;

(b) his parents;

(c) any person who is not a parent of his but who has parental responsibility for him; and

(d) any other person whose wishes and feelings the authority consider to be relevant,

regarding the matter to be decided.

(5) In making any such decision a local authority shall give due consideration—

(a) having regard to his age and understanding, to such wishes and feelings of the child as they have been able to ascertain;

(b) to such wishes and feelings of any person mentioned in subsection (4)(b) to (d) as they have been able to ascertain; and

(c) to the child's religious persuasion, racial origin and cultural and linguistic background.

(6) If it appears to a local authority that it is necessary, for the purpose of protecting members of the public from serious injury, to exercise their powers with respect to a child whom they are looking after in a manner which may not be consistent with their duties under this section, they may do so.

(7) If the Secretary of State considers it necessary, for the purpose of protecting members of the public from serious injury, to give directions to a local authority with respect to the exercise of their powers with respect to a child whom they are looking after, he may give such directions to the authority.

(8) Where any such directions are given to an authority they shall comply with them even though doing so is inconsistent with their duties under this section.

Date in force
14 October 1991: SI 1991/828.

Amendments
Sub-s (1): Local Government Act 2000, Sch 5; Children Leaving Care Act 2000, s 2(1), (2).

Definitions
For 'child', 'local authority' and 'child in the care of a local authority' and 'service' see s 105(1); for 'looked after by a local authority' see sub-s (1); for 'accommodation' see sub-s (2); for 'parental responsibility' see s 3.

References
See paras 6.44 ff and *The Children Act 1989 Guidance and Regulations, Volume 2, Family Support, Day Care and Educational Provision for Young Children* (Dept of Health, 1991) and *The Children Act 1989 Guidance and Regulations, Volume 3, Family Placements* (Dept of Health, 1991). *The Children Act 1989 Guidance and Regulations, Volume 4, Residential Care* (Dept of Health, 1991). For inspection of premises where a child who is being looked after by a local authority is living, by a person authorised to do by the Secretary of State, see 80(1)(b); for the general duty of local authorities in connection with the welfare of children in need see s 17; for review of case of and representations relating to child being looked after by local authority see s 26 and Review of Children's Cases Regulations 1991, SI 1991/895 amended by SI 2002/546 and Representations Procedure (Children) Regulations 1991, SI 1991/894 amended by SI 2002/546; for co-operation between authorities see s 27; for recoupment of the cost of services provided see s 29; for miscellaneous supplementary provisions see s 30; for transitional provisions relating to children in care under repealed enactments see s 108(6) and Sch 14, paras 15ff.

Transfer of functions
Functions of the Secretary of State, so far as exercisable in relation to Wales, transferred to the National Assembly for Wales, by the National Assembly for Wales (Transfer of Functions) Order 1999, SI 1999/672, art 2, Sch 1.

---

23 Provision of accommodation and maintenance by local authority for children whom they are looking after

(1) It shall be the duty of any local authority looking after a child—

(a) when he is in their care, to provide accommodation for him; and

(b) to maintain him in other respects apart from providing accommodation for him.

(2) A local authority shall provide accommodation and maintenance for any child whom they are looking after by—

(a) placing him (subject to subsection (5) and any regulations made by the Secretary of State) with—

(i) a family;

(ii) a relative of his; or

(iii) any other suitable person,

on such terms as to payment by the authority and otherwise as the authority may determine;

(b) maintaining him in a community home;

(c) maintaining him in a voluntary home;

(d) maintaining him in a registered children's home;

(e) maintaining him in a home provided [in accordance with arrangements made] by the Secretary of State under section 82(5) on such terms as the Secretary of State may from time to time determine;

[(aa) maintaining him in an appropriate children's home;] or

(f) making such other arrangements as—

(i) seem appropriate to them; and

(ii) comply with any regulations made by the Secretary of State.

[(2A) Where under subsection (2)(aa) a local authority maintains a child in a home provided, equipped and maintained by the Secretary of State under section 82(5), it shall do so on such terms as the Secretary of State may from time to time determine.]

(3) Any person with whom a child has been placed under subsection (2)(*a*) is referred to in this Act as a local authority foster parent unless he falls within subsection (4).

(4) A person falls within this subsection if he is—

(a) a parent of the child;

(b) a person who is not a parent of the child but who has parental responsibility for him; or

(c) where the child is in care and there was a residence order in force with respect to him immediately before the care order was made, a person in whose favour the residence order was made.

(5) Where a child is in the care of a local authority, the authority may only allow him to live with a person who falls within subsection (4) in accordance with regulations made by the Secretary of State.

[(5A) For the purposes of subsection (5) a child shall be regarded as living with a person if he stays with that person for a continuous period of more than 24 hours].

(6) Subject to any regulations made by the Secretary of State for the purposes of this subsection, any local authority looking after a child shall make arrangements to enable him to live with—

(a) a person falling within subsection (4); or

(b) a relative, friend or other person connected with him,

unless that would not be reasonably practicable or consistent with his welfare.

(7) Where a local authority provide accommodation for a child whom they are looking after, they shall, subject to the provisions of this Part and so far as is reasonably practicable and consistent with his welfare, secure that—

(a) the accommodation is near his home; and

(b) where the authority are also providing accommodation for a sibling of his, they are accommodated together.

(8) Where a local authority provide accommodation for a child whom they are looking after and who is disabled, they shall, so far as is reasonably practicable, secure that the accommodation is not unsuitable to his particular needs.

(9) Part II of Schedule 2 shall have effect for the purposes of making further provision as to children looked after by local authorities and in particular as to the regulations that may be made under subsections (2)(*a*) and (*f*) and (5).

[(10) In this Act—

'appropriate children's home' means a children's home in respect of which a person is registered under Part II of the Care Standards Act 2000; and

'children's home' has the same meaning as in that Act.]

Date in force
14 October 1991: SI 1991/828.

Amendment
Sub-s (2): CLSA 1990, Sch 16, para 12(1). Sub-s (5A): added by the CLSA 1990, Sch 16, para 12(2).

Sub-s (2): para (aa) substituted, for paras (b)–(e) as originally enacted, by the Care Standards Act 2000, s 116, Sch 4, para 14(1), (3)(a).

Sub-s (2A): inserted by the Care Standards Act 2000, s 116, Sch 4, para 14(1), (3)(b).

Definitions
For 'local authority', 'child', 'relative', 'in the care of a local authority' see s 105(1); for 'looked after by a local authority' see s 22(1); for 'community home' see s 53; for 'voluntary home' see s 60; for 'registered children's home' see s 63(8) and for 'appropriate children's home' see Sub-s (10) as applied to the whole Act by s 105(1); for 'residence order' see s 8; for 'local authority foster parent' see s 23(3); for 'parental responsibility' see s 3; for 'disabled' see s 17(11).

References
See para 6.50 ff *and The Children Act 1989 Guidance and Regulations, Volume 3, Family Placements* (Dept of Health, 1991) *and The Children Act 1989 Guidance and Regulations, Volume*

4, Residential Care (Dept of Health, 1991). 'This Part' ie Pt III (ss 17-30 and Sch 2) (local authority support for children and families). For 'live with a person' see sub-s (5A).

Sub-s (2) Regulations
See Sch 2, paras 12 and 13, and the Arrangements for Placement of Children (General) Regulations 1991, SI 1991/890 amended by SI 1991/2033, SI 1993/3069, SI 1995/2015 and SI 2002/546, the Foster Placement (Children) Regulations 1991, SI 1991/910 amended by SI1995/2015, SI 1997/2308 , SI 1999/2768 and SI 2001/2992 (England) and 3443 (Wales) revoked in so far as they apply to England and substituted by the Fostering Services Regulations 2002, SI 2002/57 amended by SI 2002/865.

Sub-s (5) Regulations
See Sch 2, para 14 and the Placement of Children with Parents etc Regulations 1991, SI 1991/893 amended by SI 1995/2015 and SI 2002/546.

Sub-s (10) Children's home. For s 1 of the Care Standards Act, see note to s 53, post.

Transfer of functions
Functions of the Secretary of State, so far as exercisable in relation to Wales, transferred to the National Assembly for Wales, by the National Assembly for Wales (Transfer of Functions) Order 1999, SI 1999/672, art 2, Sch 1.

Advice and assistance for certain children [and young persons]

[23A   The responsible authority and relevant children]

[(1) The responsible local authority shall have the functions set out in section 23B in respect of a relevant child.

(2) In subsection (1) 'relevant child' means (subject to subsection (3)) a child who—

(a)   is not being looked after by any local authority;

(b)   was, before last ceasing to be looked after, an eligible child for the purposes of paragraph 19B of Schedule 2; and

(c)   is aged sixteen or seventeen.

(3) The Secretary of State may prescribe—

(a)   additional categories of relevant children; and

(b)   categories of children who are not to be relevant children despite falling within subsection (2).

(4) In subsection (1) the 'responsible local authority' is the one which last looked after the child.

(5) If under subsection (3)(a) the Secretary of State prescribes a category of relevant children which includes children who do not fall within subsection (2)(b) (for example, because they were being looked after by a local authority in Scotland), he may in the regulations also provide for which local authority is to be the responsible local authority for those children.]

Date in force
Inserted by the Children (Leaving Care) Act 2000, s 2(1), (2) as from 1 October 2001.

Definitions
For 'responsible local authority' see sub-s (4); for 'relevant child' see sub-s (2); for 'pathway plan' see s 23E(1).

Reference
See generally chapter 6.

Sub-s (3) Regulations
See the Children Leaving Care (Wales) Regulations 2001, SI 2001/2189 amended by SI 2002/546 and 1833 and the Children Leaving Care (England) Regulations 2001, SI 2001/2874 amended by SI 2002/546.

[23B Additional functions of the responsible authority in respect of relevant children]

[(1) It is the duty of each local authority to take reasonable steps to keep in touch with a relevant child for whom they are the responsible authority, whether he is within their area or not.

(2) It is the duty of each local authority to appoint a personal adviser for each relevant child (if they have not already done so under paragraph 19C of Schedule 2).

(3) It is the duty of each local authority, in relation to any relevant child who does not already have a pathway plan prepared for the purposes of paragraph 19B of Schedule 2—

    (a) to carry out an assessment of his needs with a view to determining what advice, assistance and support it would be appropriate for them to provide him under this Part; and

    (b) to prepare a pathway plan for him.

(4) The local authority may carry out such an assessment at the same time as any assessment of his needs is made under any enactment referred to in sub-paragraphs (a) to (c) of paragraph 3 of Schedule 2, or under any other enactment.

(5) The Secretary of State may by regulations make provision as to assessments for the purposes of subsection (3).

(6) The regulations may in particular make provision about—

    (a) who is to be consulted in relation to an assessment;

    (b) the way in which an assessment is to be carried out, by whom and when;

    (c) the recording of the results of an assessment;

    (d) the considerations to which the local authority are to have regard in carrying out an assessment.

(7) The authority shall keep the pathway plan under regular review.

(8) The responsible local authority shall safeguard and promote the child's welfare and, unless they are satisfied that his welfare does not require it, support him by—

    (a) maintaining him;

    (b) providing him with or maintaining him in suitable accommodation; and

    (c) providing support of such other descriptions as may be prescribed.

(9) Support under subsection (8) may be in cash.

(10) The Secretary of State may by regulations make provision about the meaning of 'suitable accommodation' and in particular about the suitability of landlords or other providers of accommodation.

(11) If the local authority have lost touch with a relevant child, despite taking reasonable steps to keep in touch, they must without delay—

    (a) consider how to re-establish contact; and

    (b) take reasonable steps to do so,

and while the child is still a relevant child must continue to take such steps until they succeed.

(12) Subsections (7) to (9) of section 17 apply in relation to support given under this section as they apply in relation to assistance given under that section.

(13) Subsections (4) and (5) of section 22 apply in relation to any decision by a local authority for the purposes of this section as they apply in relation to the decisions referred to in that section.]

Date in force

Inserted by the Children (Leaving Care) Act 2000, s 2(1), (2) as from 1 October 2001.

Definitions

For 'local authority' and 'child' see s 105(1); for 'relevant child' see s23A(2); for 'responsible local authority' see sub-s (4).

Sub-ss (5), (6), (8), (10) Regulations
See the Children Leaving Care (Wales) Regulations 2001, SI 2001/2189 amended by SI 2002/546 and 1855 and the Children Leaving Care (England) Regulations 2001, SI 2001/2874 amended by SI 2002/546.

[23C Continuing functions in respect of former relevant children]

[(1) Each local authority shall have the duties provided for in this section towards—

(a) a person who has been a relevant child for the purposes of section 23A (and would be one if he were under eighteen), and in relation to whom they were the last responsible authority; and

(b) a person who was being looked after by them when he attained the age of eighteen, and immediately before ceasing to be looked after was an eligible child,

and in this section such a person is referred to as a 'former relevant child'.

(2) It is the duty of the local authority to take reasonable steps—

(a) to keep in touch with a former relevant child whether he is within their area or not; and

(b) if they lose touch with him, to re-establish contact.

(3) It is the duty of the local authority—

(a) to continue the appointment of a personal adviser for a former relevant child; and

(b) to continue to keep his pathway plan under regular review.

(4) It is the duty of the local authority to give a former relevant child—

(a) assistance of the kind referred to in section 24B(1), to the extent that his welfare requires it;

(b) assistance of the kind referred to in section 24B(2), to the extent that his welfare and his educational or training needs require it;

(c) other assistance, to the extent that his welfare requires it.

(5) The assistance given under subsection (4)(c) may be in kind or, in exceptional circumstances, in cash.

(6) Subject to subsection (7), the duties set out in subsections (2), (3) and (4) subsist until the former relevant child reaches the age of twenty-one.

(7) If the former relevant child's pathway plan sets out a programme of education or training which extends beyond his twenty-first birthday—

(a) the duty set out in subsection (4)(b) continues to subsist for so long as the former relevant child continues to pursue that programme; and

(b) the duties set out in subsections (2) and (3) continue to subsist concurrently with that duty.

(8) For the purposes of subsection (7)(a) there shall be disregarded any interruption in a former relevant child's pursuance of a programme of education or training if the local authority are satisfied that he will resume it as soon as is reasonably practicable.

(9) Section 24B(5) applies in relation to a person being given assistance under subsection (4)(b) as it applies in relation to a person to whom section 24B(3) applies

(10) Subsections (7) to (9) of section 17 apply in relation to assistance given under this section as they apply in relation to assistance given under that section.]

Date in force
Inserted by the Children (Leaving Care) Act 2000, s 2(1), (2) as from 1 October 2001.

Definitions
For 'local authority' and 'child' see s 105(1); for 'relevant child' see s 23A(2); for 'former relevant child' see sub-s (1); for 'responsible local authority' see s 23A(4).

[Personal advisers and pathway plans]

[23D Personal advisers]

[(1) The Secretary of State may by regulations require local authorities to appoint a personal adviser for children or young persons of a prescribed description who have reached the age of sixteen but not the age of twenty-one who are not—

(a) children who are relevant children for the purposes of section 23A;
(b) the young persons referred to in section 23C; or
(c) the children referred to in paragraph 19C of Schedule 2.

(2) Personal advisers appointed under or by virtue of this Part shall (in addition to any other functions) have such functions as the Secretary of State prescribes.]

Date in force
Inserted by the Children (Leaving Care) Act 2000, s 3 as from 1 October 2001.

Sub-s (2) Prescribed
See the Children Leaving Care (Wales) Regulations 2001, SI 2001/2189 amended by SI 2002/546 and 1855 and the Children Leaving Care (England) Regulations 2001, SI 2001/2874 amended by SI 2002/546.

[23E Pathway plans]

[(1) In this Part, a reference to a 'pathway plan' is to a plan setting out—

(a) in the case of a plan prepared under paragraph 19B of Schedule 2—

(i) the advice, assistance and support which the local authority intend to provide a child under this Part, both while they are looking after him and later; and
(ii) when they might cease to look after him; and

(b) in the case of a plan prepared under section 23B, the advice, assistance and support which the local authority intend to provide under this Part,

and dealing with such other matters (if any) as may be prescribed.

(2) The Secretary of State may by regulations make provision about pathway plans and their review.]

Date in force
Inserted by the Children (Leaving Care) Act 2000, s 3 as from 1 October 2001.

Sub-s(1)(b) . . . sub-s(2) Regulations
See the Children Leaving Care (Wales) Regulations 2001, SI 2001/2189 amended by SI 2002/546 and 1855 and the Children Leaving Care (England) Regulations 2001, SI 2001/2874 amended by SI 2002/546.

[24 Persons qualifying for advice and assistance]

[(1) In this Part 'a person qualifying for advice and assistance' means a person who—

(a) is under twenty-one; and
(b) at any time after reaching the age of sixteen but while still a child was, but is no longer, looked after, accommodated or fostered.

(2) In subsection (1)(b), 'looked after, accommodated or fostered' means—

(a) looked after by a local authority;
(b) accommodated by or on behalf of a voluntary organisation;
(c) accommodated in a private children's home;
(d) accommodated for a consecutive period of at least three months—

(i) by any Health Authority, Special Health Authority, Primary Care Trust or local education authority, or

(ii)   in any care home or independent hospital or in any accommodation provided by a National Health Service trust; or

(e)   privately fostered.

(3) Subsection (2)(d) applies even if the period of three months mentioned there began before the child reached the age of sixteen.

(4) In the case of a person qualifying for advice and assistance by virtue of subsection (2)(a), it is the duty of the local authority which last looked after him to take such steps as they think appropriate to contact him at such times as they think appropriate with a view to discharging their functions under sections 24A and 24B.

(5) In each of sections 24A and 24B, the local authority under the duty or having the power mentioned there ('the relevant authority') is—

(a)   in the case of a person qualifying for advice and assistance by virtue of subsection (2)(a), the local authority which last looked after him; or

(b)   in the case of any other person qualifying for advice and assistance, the local authority within whose area the person is (if he has asked for help of a kind which can be given under section 24A or 24B).]

Date in force
Substituted by the Children (Leaving Care) Act 2000, s 4(1) as from 1 October 2001.

Amendments
Substituted, together with ss 24A-24C, for s 24 as originally enacted, by the children (Leaving Care) Act 2000, s 4(1). Sub-ss (2), (12): National Health Service and Community Care Act 1990, Sch 9, para 36(2); Health Authorities Act 1995, Sch 1 para 24; SI 2000/90. Sub-ss (14), (15): added by the CLSA 1990, Sch 16, para 13.

Definitions
For 'child', 'local authority', 'voluntary organisation', 'health authority', 'local education authority' 'residential care home', 'nursing home' and 'mental nursing home' see s 105(1); for 'a child who is being looked after by a local authority' see s 22(1); for 'a person qualifying for advice and assistance' see sub-s (1); for 'privately fostered' see s 66 as applied to the whole Act by s 105(1).

References
See paras 6.63 ff and *The Children Act 1989 Guidance and Regulations, Volume 2, Family Support, Day Care and Educational Provision for Young Children* (Dept of Health, 1991) and *The Children Act 1989 Guidance and Regulations, Volume 3, Family Placement* (Dept of Health, 1991). For 'after-care' see *The Children Act 1989 Guidance and Regulations, Volume 2, Family Support, Day Care and Educational Provision for Young Children* (Dept of Health, 1991) para 2.32. 'This Part' ie Pt III (ss 17-30 and Sch 2) (local authority support for children and families).

Transfer of functions
Functions of the Secretary of State, so far as exercisable in relation to Wales, transferred to the National Assembly for Wales, by the National Assembly for Wales (Transfer of Functions) Order 1999, SI 1999/672, art 2, Sch 1

[24A   Advice and assistance]

[(1) The relevant authority shall consider whether the conditions in subsection (2) are satisfied in relation to a person qualifying for advice and assistance.

(2) The conditions are that—

(a)   he needs help of a kind which they can give under this section or section 24B; and

(b)   in the case of a person who was not being looked after by any local authority, they are satisfied that the person by whom he was being looked after does not have the necessary facilities for advising or befriending him.

(3) If the conditions are satisfied—

(a)   they shall advise and befriend him if he was being looked after by a local authority or was accommodated by or on behalf of a voluntary organisation; and

(b)   in any other case they may do so.

(4) Where as a result of this section a local authority are under a duty, or are empowered, to advise and befriend a person, they may also give him assistance.

(5) The assistance may be in kind or, in exceptional circumstances, in cash.

(6) Subsections (7) to (9) of section 17 apply in relation to assistance given under this section or section 24B as they apply in relation to assistance given under that section.]

Date in force
Substituted by the Children (Leaving Care) Act 2000, s 4(1) as from 1 October 2001.

Definitions
For 'relevant authority' see s 24(5); for 'person qualifying for help and assistance' see s 24(1); for 'looked after by a local authority' see s 22(1); for 'voluntary organisation' see s 105(1).

[24B Employment, education and training]

[(1) The relevant local authority may give assistance to any person who qualifies for advice and assistance by virtue of section 24(2)(a) by contributing to expenses incurred by him in living near the place where he is, or will be, employed or seeking employment.

(2) The relevant local authority may give assistance to a person to whom subsection (3) applies by—

- (a) contributing to expenses incurred by the person in question in living near the place where he is, or will be, receiving education or training; or
- (b) making a grant to enable him to meet expenses connected with his education or training.

(3) This subsection applies to any person who—

- (a) is under twenty-four; and
- (b) qualifies for advice and assistance by virtue of section 24(2)(a), or would have done so if he were under twenty-one.

(4) Where a local authority are assisting a person under subsection (2) they may disregard any interruption in his attendance on the course if he resumes it as soon as is reasonably practicable.

(5) Where the local authority are satisfied that a person to whom subsection (3) applies who is in full-time further or higher education needs accommodation during a vacation because his term-time accommodation is not available to him then, they shall give him assistance by—

- (a) providing him with suitable accommodation during the vacation; or
- (b) paying him enough to enable him to secure such accommodation himself.

(6) The Secretary of State may prescribe the meaning of 'full-time', 'further education', 'higher education' and 'vacation' for the purposes of subsection (5).]

Date in force
Substituted by the Children (Leaving Care) Act 2000, s 4(1) as from 1 October 2001.

Definitions
For 'relevant local authority' see s 24(5); for 'person qualifying for help and assistance' see s 24(1).

[24C Information]

[(1) Where it appears to a local authority that a person—
- (a) with whom they are under a duty to keep in touch under section 23B, 23C or 24; or
- (b) whom they have been advising and befriending under section 24A; or
- (c) to whom they have been giving assistance under section 24B,

proposes to live, or is living, in the area of another local authority, they must inform that other authority.

(2) Where a child who is accommodated—

(a) by a voluntary organisation or in a private children's home;
(b) by any Health Authority, Special Health Authority, Primary Care Trust or local education authority; or
(c) in any [any residential care home, nursing home or mental nursing home] or any accommodation provided by a National Health Service trust,

ceases to be so accommodated, after reaching the age of sixteen, the organisation, authority or (as the case may be) person carrying on the home shall inform the local authority within whose area the child proposes to live.

(3) Subsection (2) only applies, by virtue of paragraph (b) or (c), if the accommodation has been provided for a consecutive period of at least three months.]

Date in force
Substituted by the Children (Leaving Care) Act 2000, s 4(1) as from 1 October 2001.

[24D   Representations: sections 23A to 24B]

[(1) Every local authority shall establish a procedure for considering representations (including complaints) made to them by—

(a) a relevant child for the purposes of section 23A or a young person falling within section 23C;
(b) a person qualifying for advice and assistance; or
(c) a person falling within section 24B(2),

about the discharge of their functions under this Part in relation to him.

(2) In considering representations under subsection (1), a local authority shall comply with regulations (if any) made by the Secretary of State for the purposes of this subsection.]

Date in force
Substituted by the Children (Leaving Care) Act 2000, s 5 as from 1 October 2001.

Reference
See para 13.47.

Sub-s(2)
Regulations.

Secure accommodation

25   Use of accommodation for restricting liberty

(1) Subject to the following provisions of this section, a child who is being looked after by a local authority may not be placed, and, if placed, may not be kept, in accommodation provided for the purpose of restricting liberty ('secure accommodation') unless it appears—

(a) that—
    (i)   he has a history of absconding and is likely to abscond from any other description of accommodation; and
    (ii) if he absconds, he is likely to suffer significant harm; or
(b) that if he is kept in any other description of accommodation he is likely to injure himself or other persons.

(2) The Secretary of State may by regulations—

(a) specify a maximum period—
    (i)   beyond which a child may not be kept in secure accommodation without the authority of the court; and
    (ii) for which the court may authorise a child to be kept in secure accommodation;

(b) empower the court from time to time to authorise a child to be kept in secure accommodation for such further period as the regulations may specify; and

(c) provide that applications to the court under this section shall be made only by local authorities.

(3) It shall be the duty of a court hearing an application under this section to determine whether any relevant criteria for keeping a child in secure accommodation are satisfied in his case.

(4) If a court determines that any such criteria are satisfied, it shall make an order authorising the child to be kept in secure accommodation and specifying the maximum period for which he may be so kept.

(5) On any adjournment of the hearing of an application under this section, a court may make an interim order permitting the child to be kept during the period of the adjournment in secure accommodation.

(6) No court shall exercise the powers conferred by this section in respect of a child who is not legally represented in that court unless, having been informed of his right to apply for [representation funded by the Legal Services Commission as part of the Community Legal Service or Criminal Defence Service] and having had the opportunity to do so, he refused or failed to apply.

(7) The Secretary of State may by regulations provide that—

(a) this section shall or shall not apply to any description of children specified in the regulations;

(b) this section shall have effect in relation to children of a description specified in the regulations subject to such modifications as may be so specified;

(c) such other provisions as may be so specified shall have effect for the purpose of determining whether a child of a description specified in the regulations may be placed or kept in secure accommodation.

(8) The giving of an authorisation under this section shall not prejudice any power of any court in England and Wales or Scotland to give directions relating to the child to whom the authorisation relates.

(9) This section is subject to section 20(8).

Date in force
14 October 1991: SI 1991/828.

Amendment
Sub-s (1) modified in relation to certain children by SI 1991/1505, regs 6, 7, see para 9.35. Sub-s (6): Access to Justice Act 1999, Sch 4, para 45.

Definitions
For 'child' and 'local authority' see s 105(1); for 'a child who is being looked after by a local authority' see s 22(1); for 'secure accommodation' see sub-s (1); for 'harm' see s 31(9) as applied to the whole Act by s 105; as to whether harm is significant see s 31(10) as applied to the whole Act by s 105(1); for 'court' see s 92(7).

References
See generally chapter 9 and *The Children Act 1989 Guidance and Regulations, Volume 4, Residential Care* (Dept of Health, 1991). For jurisdiction of courts see s 92 and Sch 11 and for orders made in criminal proceedings see the CJA 1991, the Crime and Disorder Act 1998 and para 9.33 ff.

Sub-s (6) and (7) Regulations
See the Children (Secure Accommodation) Regulations 1991, SI 1991/1505 amended by SI 1992/2117, SI 1995/1398, SI 1996/692, SI 2000/694 and SI 2002/546 and the Children (Secure Accommodation) (No 2) Regulations 1991, SI 1991/2034 amended by SI 2002/546.

Sub-s (1)
The grounds in paras (a) and (b) are disjunctive rather than conjunctive: *Re D (Secure Accommodation)* [1997] 1 FLR 197.

Supplemental

26   Review of cases and inquiries into representations

(1) The Secretary of State may make regulations requiring the case of each child who is being looked after by a local authority to be reviewed in accordance with the provisions of the regulations.

(2) The regulations may, in particular, make provision—

(a)   as to the manner in which each case is to be reviewed;

(b)   as to the considerations to which the local authority are to have regard in reviewing each case;

(c)   as to the time when each case is first to be reviewed and the frequency of subsequent reviews;

(d)   requiring the authority, before conducting any review, to seek the views of—

    (i)   the child;

    (ii)   his parents;

    (iii)   any person who is not a parent of his but who has parental responsibility for him; and

    (iv)   any other person whose views the authority consider to be relevant,

including, in particular, the views of those persons in relation to any particular matter which is to be considered in the course of the review;

(e)   requiring the authority to consider, in the case of a child who is in their care, whether an application should be made to discharge the care order;

(f)   requiring the authority to consider, in the case of a child in accommodation provided by the authority, whether the accommodation accords with the requirements of this Part;

(g)   requiring the authority to inform the child, so far as is reasonably practicable, of any steps he may take under this Act;

(h)   requiring the authority to make arrangements, including arrangements with such other bodies providing services as it considers appropriate, to implement any decision which they propose to make in the course, or as a result, of the review;

    (i)   requiring the authority to notify details of the result of the review and of any decision taken by them in consequence of the review to—

    (ii)   the child;

    (iii)   his parents;

    (iv)   any person who is not a parent of his but who has parental responsibility for him; and

(i)   any other person whom they consider ought to be notified;

(j)   requiring the authority to monitor the arrangements which they have made with a view to ensuring that they comply with the regulations.

(3) Every local authority shall establish a procedure for considering any representations (including any complaint) made to them by—

(a)   any child who is being looked after by them or who is not being looked after by them but is in need;

(b)   a parent of his;

(c)   any person who is not a parent of his but who has parental responsibility for him;

(d)   any local authority foster parent;

(e)   such other person as the authority consider has a sufficient interest in the child's welfare to warrant his representations being considered by them,

about the discharge by the authority of any of their functions under this Part in relation to the child.

(4) The procedure shall ensure that at least one person who is not a member or officer of the authority takes part in—

   (a) the consideration; and

   (b) any discussions which are held by the authority about the action (if any) to be taken in relation to the child in the light of the consideration.

(5) In carrying out any consideration of representations under this section a local authority shall comply with any regulations made by the Secretary of State for the purpose of regulating the procedure to be followed.

(6) The Secretary of State may make regulations requiring local authorities to monitor the arrangements that they have made with a view to ensuring that they comply with any regulations made for the purposes of subsection (5).

(7) Where any representation has been considered under the procedure established by a local authority under this section, the authority shall—

   (a) have due regard to the findings of those considering the representation; and

   (b) take such steps as are reasonably practicable to notify (in writing)—

      (i)   the person making the representation;

      (ii) the child (if the authority consider that he has sufficient understanding); and

      (iii) such other persons (if any) as appear to the authority to be likely to be affected,

of the authority's decision in the matter and their reasons for taking that decision and of any action which they have taken, or propose to take.

(8) Every local authority shall give such publicity to their procedure for considering representations under this section as they consider appropriate.

Date in force
14 October 1991: SI 1991/828.

Definitions
For 'child' and 'local authority' see s 105(1); for 'a child who is being looked after by a local authority see s 22(1); for 'parental responsibility' see s 3; for 'care order' see s 31(11) and s 105(1); for 'local authority foster parent' see s 23(3).

References
See paras 13.48 ff and *The Children Act 1989 Guidance and Regulations, Volume 3, Family Placements* (Dept of Health, 1991). 'This Part' ie Pt III (ss 17-30 and Sch 2) (local authority support for children and families). For the powers and duties of local authorities under this Part to provide accommodation for children see s 20, (accommodation for certain children eg those lost or abandoned), s 23 (accommodation for and maintenance of children an authority is looking after) and s 25 (use of accommodation for restricting liberty); for reviews and representations procedure see *The Children Act 1989 Guidance and Regulations, Volume 3, Family Placements* (Dept of Health, 1991).

Sub-s (1) Regulations
See the Review of Children's Cases Regulations 1991, SI 1991/895 amended by SI 1991/2033, SI 1993/3069, SI 1995/2015 and SI 2002/546.

Sub-s (3)-(6) Regulations
See the Representations Procedure (Children) Regulations 1991 SI 1991/894 amended by SI 1991/2033, SI 1993/3069 and SI 2002/546.

---

27   Co-operation between authorities

(1) Where it appears to a local authority that any authority . . . mentioned in subsection (3) could, by taking any specified action, help in the exercise of any of their functions under this Part, they may request the help of that other authority . . . specifying the action in question.

(2) An authority whose help is so requested shall comply with the request if it is compatible with their own statutory or other duties and obligations and does not unduly prejudice the discharge of any of their functions.

(3) The [authorities] are—

(a) any local authority;

(b) any local education authority;

(c) any local housing authority;

(d) any [Health Authority, Special Health Authority][, Primary Care Trust] [or National Health Service trust]; and

(e) any person authorised by the Secretary of State for the purposes of this section.

(4) . . .

Date in force
14 October 1991: SI 1991/828.

Amendments
Sub-ss (1), (3): CLSA 1990, Sch 16, para 14, Sch 20. Sub-s (3): Health Authorities Act 1995, Sch 1, para 24; SI 2000/90

Definitions
For 'local authority', 'functions', 'local education authority', 'local housing authority', 'health authority', 'special educational needs' see s 105(1).

References
See generally para 6.8 and *The Children Act 1989 Guidance and Regulations, Volume 3, Family Placement* (Dept of Health, 1991). 'This Part' ie Pt III (ss 17-30 and Sch 2) (local authority support for children and families). For the recovery of reasonable expenses by one local authority from another see s 29(7).

Note
This section does not give a social services authority power to require a housing authority to provide accommodation under the Housing Acts. The section does impose on a housing authority a duty to ascertain whether it could provide a solution for a homeless family with children: *R v Northavon District Council, ex p Smith* [1994] 3 WLR 403, HL.

Transfer of functions
Functions of the Secretary of State, so far as exercisable in relation to Wales, transferred to the National Assembly for Wales, by the National Assembly for Wales (Transfer of Functions) Order 1999, SI 1999/672, art 2, Sch 1.

---

28 Consultation with local education authorities

(1) Where—

(a) a child is being looked after by a local authority; and

(b) the authority propose to provide accommodation for him in an establishment at which education is provided for children who are accommodated there,

they shall, so far as is reasonably practicable, consult the appropriate local education authority before doing so.

(2) Where any such proposal is carried out, the local authority shall, as soon as is reasonably practicable, inform the appropriate local education authority of the arrangements that have been made for the child's accommodation.

(3) Where the child ceases to be accommodated as mentioned in subsection (1)(b), the local authority shall inform the appropriate local education authority.

(4) In this section 'the appropriate local education authority' means—

(a) the local education authority within whose area the local authority's area falls; or,

(b) where the child has special educational needs and a statement of his needs is maintained under [Part IV of the Education Act 1996], the local education authority who maintain the statement.

Date in force
14 October 1991: SI 1991/828.

Amendment
Sub-s (4): EA 1996, Sch 37 para 84.

Definitions
For 'child', 'local authority' and 'local education authority' see s 105(1); for 'a child who is being looked after by a local authority' see s 22(1); for 'the appropriate local education authority' see sub-s (4).

---

29 Recoupment of cost of providing services etc

(1) Where a local authority provide any service under section 17 or 18, other than advice, guidance or counselling, they may recover from a person specified in subsection (4) such charge for the service as they consider reasonable.

(2) Where the authority are satisfied that that person's means are insufficient for it to be reasonably practicable for him to pay the charge, they shall not require him to pay more than he can reasonably be expected to pay.

(3) No person shall be liable to pay any charge under subsection (1) [for a service provided under section 17 or section 18(1) or (5)] at any time when he is in receipt of income support[, working families' tax credit] [or disabled person's tax credit] under the [Part VII of the Social Security Contributions and Benefits Act 1992] [or of an income-based jobseeker's allowance].

[(3A) No person shall be liable to pay any charge under subsection (1) for a service provided under section 18(2) or (6) at any time when he is in receipt of income support under Part VII of the Social Security Contributions and Benefits Act 1992 or of an income-based jobseeker's allowance.]

(4) The persons are—

(a) where the service is provided for a child under sixteen, each of his parents;
(b) where it is provided for a child who has reached the age of sixteen, the child himself; and
(c) where it is provided for a member of the child's family, that member.

(5) Any charge under subsection (1) may, without prejudice to any other method of recovery, be recovered summarily as a civil debt.

(6) Part III of Schedule 2 makes provision in connection with contributions towards the maintenance of children who are being looked after by local authorities and consists of the re-enactment with modifications of provisions in Part V of the Child Care Act 1980.

(7) Where a local authority provide any accommodation under section 20(1) for a child who was (immediately before they began to look after him) ordinarily resident within the area of another local authority, they may recover from that other authority any reasonable expenses incurred by them in providing the accommodation and maintaining him.

(8) Where a local authority provide accommodation under section 21(1) or (2)(a) or (b) for a child who is ordinarily resident within the area of another local authority and they are not maintaining him in—

(a) a community home provided by them;
(b) a controlled community home; or
(c) a hospital vested in the Secretary of State [or a Primary Care Trust], [or any other hospital made available pursuant to arrangements made by a [Health Authority]] [or a Primary Care Trust,]

they may recover from that other authority any reasonable expenses incurred by them in providing the accommodation and maintaining him.

(9) [Except where subsection (10) applies,] where a local authority comply with any request under section 27(2) in relation to a child or other person who is not ordinarily resident within their area, they may recover from the local authority in whose area the child or person is ordinarily resident any [reasonable expenses] incurred by them in respect of that person.

[(10) Where a local authority ('authority A') comply with any request under section 27(2) from another local authority ('authority B') in relation to a child or other person—

(a) whose responsible authority is authority B for the purposes of section 23B or 23C; or

(b) whom authority B are advising or befriending or to whom they are giving assistance by virtue of section 24(5)(a),

authority A may recover from authority B any reasonable expenses incurred by them in respect of that person.]

Date in force
14 October 1991: SI 1991/828.

Amendments
Subs (3): Disability Living Allowance and Disability Working Allowance Act 1991, Sch 3, para 14; Social Security (Consequential Provisions) Act 1992, Sch 2, para 108(b); Jobseekers Act 1995, Sch 2, para 19; Tax Credits Act 1999, Sch 1, paras 1, 6Local Government Act 2000, s 103(1). Sub-s (3A): inserted by the Local Government Act 2000, s 103(2). Sub-s (8): National Health Service and Community Care Act 1990, Sch 9, para 36(3); SI 2000/90; Health Authorities Act 2000, Sch 1, para 118. Sub-s (9): CLSA 1990, Sch 16, para 15. Sub-ss (9) and (10): Children (Leaving Care) Act 2000, s 7.

Definitions
For 'looked after' see s 22(1); for 'local authority', 'service', 'child' and 'hospital' see s 105(1); for 'community home' and 'controlled community home' see s 53 as applied to the whole Act by s 105(1).

References
See generally *The Children Act 1989 Guidance and Regulations, Volume 2, Family Support Day Care and Educational Provision* (Dept of Health, 1991), para 238; for the determination of the ordinary residence of a child for the purposes of sub-s (7)-(9) see s 30(2) and s 105(6). For transitional provisions for contributions for maintenance of children in care under repealed enactments see s 108(6) and Sch 14, para 24; for contributions to the maintenance of accommodated children see Sch 2, Pt III.

Transfer of functions
Functions of the Secretary of State, so far as exercisable in relation to Wales, transferred to the National Assembly for Wales, by the National Assembly for Wales (Transfer of Functions) Order 1999, SI 1999/672, art 2, Sch 1.

30 Miscellaneous

(1) Nothing in this Part shall affect any duty imposed on a local authority by or under any other enactment.

(2) Any question arising under section 20(2), 21(3) or 29(7) to (9) as to the ordinary residence of a child shall be determined by agreement between the local authorities concerned or, in default of agreement, by the Secretary of State.

(3) Where the functions conferred on a local authority by this Part and the functions of a local education authority are concurrent, the Secretary of State may by regulations provide by which authority the functions are to be exercised.

(4) The Secretary of State may make regulations for determining, as respects any local education authority functions specified in the regulations, whether a child who is being looked after by a local authority is to be treated, for purposes so specified, as a child of parents of sufficient resources or as a child of parents without resources.

Date in force
14 October 1991: SI 1991/828.

Definitions
For 'local authority', 'child', 'functions', 'local education authority' see s 105(1); for 'a child who is being looked after by a local authority' see s 22(1).

References

For determination of ordinary residence of a child see sub-s (2) and s 105(6). 'This Part' ie Pt III (ss 17-30 and Sch 2) (local authority support for children and families).

PART IV
CARE AND SUPERVISION

General

31 Care and supervision orders

(1) On the application of any local authority or authorised person, the court may make an order—

(a) placing the child with respect to whom the application is made in the care of a designated local authority; or

(b) putting him under the supervision of a designated local authority . . .

(2) A court may only make a care order or supervision order if it is satisfied—

(a) that the child concerned is suffering, or is likely to suffer, significant harm; and

(b) that the harm, or likelihood of harm, is attributable to—

    (i) the care given to the child, or likely to be given to him if the order were not made, not being what it would be reasonable to expect a parent to give to him; or

    (ii) the child's being beyond parental control.

(3) No care order or supervision order may be made with respect to a child who has reached the age of seventeen (or sixteen, in the case of a child who is married).

(4) An application under this section may be made on its own or in any other family proceedings.

(5) The court may—

(a) on an application for a care order, make a supervision order;

(b) on an application for a supervision order, make a care order.

(6) Where an authorised person proposes to make an application under this section he shall—

(a) if it is reasonably practicable to do so; and

(b) before making the application,

consult the local authority appearing to him to be the authority in whose area the child concerned is ordinarily resident.

(7) An application made by an authorised person shall not be entertained by the court if, at the time when it is made, the child concerned is—

(a) the subject of an earlier application for a care order, or supervision order, which has not been disposed of; or

(b) subject to—

    (i) a care order or supervision order;

    (ii) an order under [section 63(1) of the Powers of Criminal Courts (Sentencing) Act 2000]; or

    (iii) a supervision requirement within the meaning of [Part II of the Children (Scotland) Act 1995].

(8) The local authority designated in a care order must be—

(a) the authority within whose area the child is ordinarily resident; or

(b) where the child does not reside in the area of a local authority, the authority within whose area any circumstances arose in consequence of which the order is being made.

(9) In this section—

'authorised person' means—

(a) the National Society for the Prevention of Cruelty to Children and any of its officers; and

(b) any person authorised by order of the Secretary of State to bring proceedings under this section and any officer of a body which is so authorised;

'harm' means ill-treatment or the impairment of health or development;

'development' means physical, intellectual, emotional, social or behavioural development;

'health' means physical or mental health; and

'ill-treatment' includes sexual abuse and forms of ill-treatment which are not physical.

(10) Where the question of whether harm suffered by a child is significant turns on the child's health or development, his health or development shall be compared with that which could reasonably be expected of a similar child.

(11) In this Act—

'a care order' means (subject to section 105(1)) an order under subsection (1)(a) and (except where express provision to the contrary is made) includes an interim care order made under section 38; and

'a supervision order' means an order under subsection (1)(b) and (except where express provision to the contrary is made) includes an interim supervision order made under section 38.

Date in force
14 October 1991: SI 1991/828.

Amendment
Sub-s (7): Children (Scotland) Act 1995, Sch 4 para 48; Powers of Criminal Courts (Sentencing) Act 2000, Sch 9, para 127.

Definitions
For 'local authority', 'child' see s 105(1); for 'court' see s 92(7); for 'designated local authority' see sub-s (8); for 'care order', 'supervision order' see sub-s (11); for 'harm' see sub-s (9) and as to whether harm is significant see sub-s (10); for 'authorised person', 'development', 'health', 'ill-treatment' see sub-s (9).

References
See generally chapter 8 and *The Children Act 1989 Guidance and Regulations, Volume 1, Court Orders* (Dept of Health, 1991). See also *Care Plans and Care Proceedings Under the Children Act 1989* LAC (99) 29 in Clarke Hall and Morrison at para 1[14454] and *Handbook of Best Practice in Children Act Cases* at para 1[20001] also *Re S (children: care plan)* [2002] UKHL 10, [2002] 1 All ER 192. The principles of s 1 apply. For jurisdiction of courts see s 92 and Sch 11 and paras 4.3 ff; for appeals see s 94 and orders pending appeals s 40; for determining the 'ordinary residence' of a child see s 105(6). Care proceedings must be commenced in the magistrates' court, but may be allocated to the county court or High Court: Children (Allocation of Proceedings) Order 1991, SI 1991/1677, rr 3(i)(b) and 12, see paras 4.15 and 4.27 ff; for 'family proceedings' see s 8(3); for duty of local authority to make inquiries with respect to certain children to enable them to decide whether they should take any action to safeguard or promote the child's welfare see s 47(1); for the appointment of a children's guardian see s 41; for interim care and supervision orders see s 38; for attendance of child at hearing see s 95; for evidence given by or with respect of children see s 96; for self incrimination of witness see s 98; for powers of the court when considering whether to make a care or supervision order under this section see s 37; for variation and discharge of care and supervision orders see s 39; for duration of care orders and supervision orders see s 91(12), (13); for effect of orders see generally s 91 and for further provisions relating to care orders see ss 33, 34, and for supervision orders s 35. For consent orders, see paras 8.119 ff and for the effect of a care order on other court orders, see paras 8.122 ff.

Transfer of functions
Functions of the Secretary of State, so far as exercisable in relation to Wales, transferred to the National Assembly for Wales, by the National Assembly for Wales (Transfer of Functions) Order 1999, SI 1999/672, art 2, Sch 1

Sub-s (5)(b)
But does not include the making of a care order on an application under para 6(3) of Sch 3 for

the extension of a supervision order *(Re A (a minor) (Supervision Order: Extension)* [1995] 3 All ER 401,[1995] 2 FCR 114.

Sub-s (8)
For the test of ordinary residence for these purposes see *Northampton County Council v Islington London Borough Council* [1999] 3 FCR 385, [1999] 2 FLR 881, *C v Plymouth City Council* [2000] 2 FCR 289, [2000] 2 FLR 875, CA and Re BC (a minor) (care order: appropriate local authority) [1995] 3 FCR 598. See further cases cited at para 8.131.

Sub-s (8)(b)
Should be read as if the word 'ordinarily' preceded reside': *Gateshead Metropolitan Borough Council v B* [1996] 2 FLR 179.

---

32 Period within which application for order under this Part must be disposed of

(1) A court hearing an application for an order under this Part shall (in the light of any rules made by virtue of subsection (2))—

(a) draw up a timetable with a view to disposing of the application without delay; and

(b) give such directions as it considers appropriate for the purpose of ensuring, so far as is reasonably practicable, that that timetable is adhered to.

(2) Rules of court may—

(a) specify periods within which specified steps must be taken in relation to such proceedings; and

(b) make other provisions with respect to such proceedings for the purpose of ensuring, so far as is reasonably practicable, that they are disposed of without delay.

Date in force
14 October 1991: SI 1991/828.

Definitions
For 'court' see s 92(7); for 'child' see s 105(1).

References
For jurisdiction of courts see s 92 and Sch 11, paras 4.3 ff. 'This Part' ie Pt IV (ss 31-42 and Sch 3) (care and supervision). For welfare of the child the paramount consideration see s 1(1). For family proceedings see s 8(3). For timetable see para 8.15.

Rules of Court
See the FPC (CA 1989) R 1991, r 15, and the FPR 1991, r 4.15, see paras 4.20 ff. For allocation of care proceedings see the Children (Allocation of Proceedings) Order 1991, see paras 4.15 and 4.27.

Care orders

33 Effect of care order

(1) Where a care order is made with respect to a child it shall be the duty of the local authority designated by the order to receive the child into their care and to keep him in their care while the order remains in force.

(2) Where—

(a) a care order has been made with respect to a child on the application of an authorised person; but

(b) the local authority designated by the order was not informed that that person proposed to make the application,

the child may be kept in the care of that person until received into the care of the authority.

(3) While a care order is in force with respect to a child, the local authority designated by the order shall—

(a) have parental responsibility for the child; and

(b) have the power (subject to the following provisions of this section) to determine the extent to which a parent or guardian of the child may meet his parental responsibility for him.

(4) The authority may not exercise the power in subsection (3)(b) unless they are satisfied that it is necessary to do so in order to safeguard or promote the child's welfare.

(5) Nothing in subsection (3)(b) shall prevent a parent or guardian of the child who has care of him from doing what is reasonable in all the circumstances of the case for the purpose of safeguarding or promoting his welfare.

(6) While a care order is in force with respect to a child, the local authority designated by the order shall not—

(a) cause the child to be brought up in any religious persuasion other than that in which he would have been brought up if the order had not been made; or

(b) have the right—

(i)   to consent or refuse to consent to the making of an application with respect to the child under section 18 of the Adoption Act 1976;

(ii)   to agree or refuse to agree to the making of an adoption order, or an order under section 55 of the Act of 1976, with respect to the child; or

(iii) to appoint a guardian for the child.

(7) While a care order is in force with respect to a child, no person may—

(a) cause the child to be known by a new surname; or

(b) remove him from the United Kingdom,

without either the written consent of every person who has parental responsibility for the child or the leave of the court.

(8) Subsection (7)(b) does not—

(a) prevent the removal of such a child, for a period of less than one month, by the authority in whose care he is; or

(b) apply to arrangements for such a child to live outside England and Wales (which are governed by paragraph 19 of Schedule 2).

(9) The power in subsection (3)(b) is subject (in addition to being subject to the provisions of this section) to any right, duty, power, responsibility or authority which a parent or guardian of the child has in relation to the child and his property by virtue of any other enactment.

Date in force
14 October 1991: SI 1991/828.

Definitions
For 'care order' see s 31(11) and s 105(1); for 'child', 'local authority' and 'guardian of a child' see s 105(1); for 'designated local authority' see s 31(8); for 'authorised person' see s 31(9), for 'parental responsibility' see s 3; for 'court' see s 92(7).

References
See generally chapter 8 and in particular para 8.122 ff and 8.132 ff and *The Children Act 1989 Guidance and Regulations, Volume 1, Court Orders* (Dept of Health, 1991) at paras 3.65-3.74. For appointment of children's guardian see s 41. For duration of care orders see s 91(12); for care and supervision orders generally see s 31; for further provisions in connection with care orders see s 34 and in connection with supervision orders see ss 35 and 36; for interim care and supervision orders see s 38; for the discharge and variation of care and supervision orders see s 39; for jurisdiction of courts see s 92 and Sch 11.

Sub-s (1)
A family proceedings court does not have power to stay a care order pending appeal to the High Court but application may be made to the High Court immediately for a stay: See *Re O (a minor)* [1992] 4 All ER 905.

Sub-s (7)
Cf s 13(1) where a residence order is in force. Application for leave must be commenced in the magistrates' court: Children (Allocation of Proceedings) Order 1991, r 2.

Sub-s (8)
Cf s 13(2) where a residence order is in force.

---

34   Parental contact etc with children in care

(1) Where a child is in the care of a local authority, the authority shall (subject to the provisions of this section) allow the child reasonable contact with—

(a) his parents;

(b) any guardian of his;

(c) where there was a residence order in force with respect to the child immediately before the care order was made, the person in whose favour the order was made; and

(d) where, immediately before the care order was made a person had care of the child by virtue of an order made in the exercise of the High Court's inherent jurisdiction with respect to children, that person.

(2) On an application made by the authority or the child, the court may make such order as it considers appropriate with respect to the contact which is to be allowed between the child and any named person.

(3) On an application made by—

(a) any person mentioned in paragraphs (a) to (d) of subsection (1); or

(b) any person who has obtained the leave of the court to make the application,

the court may make such order as it considers appropriate with respect to the contact which is to be allowed between the child and that person.

(4) On an application made by the authority or the child, the court may make an order authorising the authority to refuse to allow contact between the child and any person who is mentioned in paragraphs (a) to (d) of subsection (1) and named in the order.

(5) When making a care order with respect to a child, or in any family proceedings in connection with a child who is in the care of a local authority, the court may make an order under this section, even though no application for such an order has been made with respect to the child, if it considers that the order should be made.

(6) An authority may refuse to allow the contact that would otherwise be required by virtue of subsection (1) or an order under this section if—

(a) they are satisfied that it is necessary to do so in order to safeguard or promote the child's welfare; and

(b) the refusal—

(i) is decided upon as a matter of urgency; and

(ii) does not last for more than seven days.

(7) An order under this section may impose such conditions as the court considers appropriate.

(8) The Secretary of State may by regulations make provision as to—

(a) the steps to be taken by a local authority who have exercised their powers under subsection (6);

(b) the circumstances in which, and conditions subject to which, the terms of any order under this section may be departed from by agreement between the local authority and the person in relation to whom the order is made;

(c) notification by a local authority of any variation or suspension of arrangements made (otherwise than under an order under this section) with a view to affording any person contact with a child to whom this section applies.

(9) The court may vary or discharge any order made under this section on the application of the authority, the child concerned or the person named in the order.

(10) An order under this section may be made either at the same time as the care order itself or later.

(11) Before making a care order with respect to any child the court shall—

(a) consider the arrangements which the authority have made, or propose to make, for affording any person contact with a child to whom this section applies; and

(b) invite the parties to the proceedings to comment on those arrangements.

Date in force
14 October 1991: SI 1991/828.

Definitions
For 'child', 'local authority', 'guardian of a child' and 'child in the care of a local authority' see s 105(1). For 'care order' see s 31(11) and s 105(1); for 'residence order' see s 8(1); for a 'person in whose favour a residence order is in force' see s 105(3); for 'court' see s 92(7); for 'the local authority designated in a care order' see s 31(8).

References
Proceedings must be commenced in the magistrates' court: Children (Allocation of Proceedings) Order 1991, r 3, see para 4.15. See generally chapter 8 and in particular paras 8.141 ff and *The Children Act 1989 Guidance and Regulations, Volume 1, Court Orders* (Dept of Health, 1991), paras 3.75-3.86, and Volume 3 Family Placements. For welfare of the child the paramount consideration see s 1(1) and chapter 2; for appointment of a children's guardian see s 41; for care and supervision orders generally see s 31; for further provisions in connection with supervision orders see s 35 and 36; for interim care and supervision orders see s 38; for exclusion requirement in interim order, see s 38A; for the discharge and variation of care and supervisions orders see s 39; for jurisdiction of courts see s 92 and Sch 11; for refusal of contact, see para 8.158 ff.

Sub-s (3) Leave of the Court
Leave may be granted by a single justice: FPC (CA 1989) R 1991, r 2(5).

Sub-s (4)
The court may make an interim order for no contact: *West Glamorgan County Council v P* [1992] 2 FCR 378; see para 8.111.

Sub-s (8) Regulations
See the Contact with Children Regulations 1991, SI 1991/891 which provide, inter alia, for the local authority to depart from the terms of any order as to contact by agreement with the person about whom the order was made. The child must agree if of sufficient understanding and the authority must send written notification to specified persons.

Transfer of functions
Functions of the Secretary of State, so far as exercisable in relation to Wales, transferred to the National Assembly for Wales, by the National Assembly for Wales (Transfer of Functions) Order 1999, SI 1999/672, art 2, Sch 1

Supervision orders

35 Supervision orders

(1) While a supervision order is in force it shall be the duty of the supervisor—

(a) to advise, assist and befriend the supervised child;

(b) to take such steps as are reasonably necessary to give effect to the order; and

(c) where—

(i) the order is not wholly complied with; or

(ii) the supervisor considers that the order may no longer be necessary,

to consider whether or not to apply to the court for its variation or discharge.

(2) Parts I and II of Schedule 3 make further provision with respect to supervision orders.

Date in force
14 October 1991: SI 1991/828.

Definitions
For 'supervision order' see s 31(11); for 'supervisor', 'supervised child' see s 105(1).

References
See generally paras 8.17 ff and 8.167 ff and *The Children Act 1989 Guidance and Regulations, Volume 1, Court Orders* (Dept of Health, 1991), at paras 3.87-3.97. For duration of supervision orders see s 91(13) and Sch 3, para 6(1). For care and supervision orders generally see s 31; for further provisions in connection with supervision orders see s 36 and Sch 3; for interim care and supervision orders see s 38; for the discharge and variation of care and supervision orders see s 39.

Note
Before the court can make a supervision order it must be satisfied as to the provisions of s 31. Section 35 must be read with Sch 3 in view of the detailed powers contained therein.

---

36 Education supervision orders

(1) On the application of any local education authority, the court may make an order putting the child with respect to whom the application is made under the supervision of a designated local education authority.

(2) In this Act 'an education supervision order' means an order under subsection (1).

(3) A court may only make an education supervision order if it is satisfied that the child concerned is of compulsory school age and is not being properly educated.

(4) For the purposes of this section, a child is being properly educated only if he is receiving efficient full-time education suitable to his age, ability and aptitude and any special educational needs he may have.

(5) Where a child is—

(a) the subject of a school attendance order which is in force under [section 437 of the Education Act 1996] and which has not been complied with; or
(b) a registered pupil at a school which he is not attending regularly within the meaning of [section 444] of that Act,

then, unless it is proved that he is being properly educated, it shall be assumed that he is not.

(6) An education supervision order may not be made with respect to a child who is in the care of a local authority.

(7) The local education authority designated in an education supervision order must be—

(a) the authority within whose area the child concerned is living or will live; or
(b) where—

(i) the child is a registered pupil at a school; and
(ii) the authority mentioned in paragraph (a) and the authority within whose area the school is situated agree,

the latter authority.

(8) Where a local education authority propose to make an application for an education supervision order they shall, before making the application, consult the . . . appropriate local authority.

(9) The appropriate local authority is—

(a) in the case of a child who is being provided with accommodation by, or on behalf of, a local authority, that authority; and
(b) in any other case, the local authority within whose area the child concerned lives, or will live.

(10) Part III of Schedule 3 makes further provision with respect to education supervision orders.

Date in force
14 October 1991: SI 1991/828.

Amendment
Sub-s (5): Education Act 1996, Sch 37, para 85. Sub-s (8): Education Act 1993, Sch 19, para 149, Sch 21 Pt II.

Definitions
For 'local education authority', 'child', 'child who is in the care of a local authority', 'local authority' see s 105(1); for 'court' see s 92(7); for 'designated local authority' see sub-s (7); for 'education supervision order' see sub-s (2); for 'being properly educated' see sub-s (4), (5); for 'registered pupil' see s 105(1) and the EA 1996 s 434(5); for 'special educational needs' see s 105(1) and the EA 1996 s 312(1); for 'appropriate local authority' see sub-s (9); for 'accommodation provided by or on behalf of a local authority' see s 105(5).

References
See generally paras 8.180 ff. For jurisdiction of courts see s 92 and Sch 11, paras 4.3 ff; proceedings under this section must be commenced in the magistrates' court: Children (Allocation of Proceedings) Order 1991; for attendance of child at hearing see s 95; for evidence given by or with respect to children see s 96; for self incrimination of witness see s 98.

Powers of court

37 Powers of court in certain family proceedings

(1) Where, in any family proceedings in which a question arises with respect to the welfare of any child, it appears to the court that it may be appropriate for a care or supervision order to be made with respect to him, the court may direct the appropriate authority to undertake an investigation of the child's circumstances.

(2) Where the court gives a direction under this section the local authority concerned shall, when undertaking the investigation, consider whether they should—

(a) apply for a care order or for a supervision order with respect to the child;
(b) provide services or assistance for the child or his family; or
(c) take any other action with respect to the child.

(3) Where a local authority undertake an investigation under this section, and decide not to apply for a care order or supervision order with respect to the child concerned, they shall inform the court of—

(a) their reasons for so deciding;
(b) any service or assistance which they have provided, or intend to provide, for the child and his family; and
(c) any other action which they have taken, or propose to take, with respect to the child.

(4) The information shall be given to the court before the end of the period of eight weeks beginning with the date of the direction, unless the court otherwise directs.

(5) The local authority named in a direction under subsection (1) must be—

(a) the authority in whose area the child is ordinarily resident; or
(b) where the child [is not ordinarily resident] in the area of a local authority, the authority within whose area any circumstances arose in consequence of which the direction is being given.

(6) If, on the conclusion of any investigation or review under this section, the authority decide not to apply for a care order or supervision order with respect to the child—

(a) they shall consider whether it would be appropriate to review the case at a later date; and
(b) if they decide that it would be, they shall determine the date on which that review is to begin.

Date in force
14 October 1991: SI 1991/828.68

Amendment
Sub-s (5): CLSA 1990, Sch 16, para 16.

Definitions

For 'family proceedings' see s 8(3), (4)(a); for 'child', 'local authority' see s 105(1); for 'court' see s 92(7) (a single justice may make the direction: FPC (CA 1989) R 1991, r 2(5); for 'care order' see s 31(11) and s 105(1); for 'supervision order' see s 31(11); for 'appropriate authority' see sub-s (5); for 'ordinary residence' see s 105(6).

References

See generally paras 5.158 and 7.5 ff, the FPR 1991, r 4.26 and FPC (CA 1989) R 1991, r 27 and The Children Act 1989 Guidance and Regulations, Volume 1, Court Orders (Dept of Health, 1991), at paras 4.78-4.82. For welfare of the child as paramount consideration see s 1(1); for jurisdiction of courts see s 92 and Sch 11; for the bringing to an end of an interim order made under s 38 as a result of a direction by the court under sub-s (1) see s 38(4); for the appointment of a children's guardian see s 41 and para 10.21; for the provision of services and assistance by local authorities see Pt III ie ss 17-30 and Sch 2 (local authority support for children and families); for interim orders see s 38; for exclusion requirement in interim order see s 38A. For 'family proceedings' under this Act see s 8(3), (4)(a). See also s 47 for investigations by the local authority.

Investigation

A court should only order an investigation where it appears that it may be appropriate to make a public law order: *Re CE (section 37 direction)* [1995] 1 FLR 26; *Re L (a minor) (section 37 direction)* [1999] 3 FCR 642, [1999] 1 FLR 984, CA.

---

38 Interim orders

(1) Where—

(a) in any proceedings on an application for a care order or supervision order, the proceedings are adjourned; or

(b) the court gives a direction under section 37(1),

the court may make an interim care order or an interim supervision order with respect to the child concerned.

(2) A court shall not make an interim care order or interim supervision order under this section unless it is satisfied that there are reasonable grounds for believing that the circumstances with respect to the child are as mentioned in section 31(2).

(3) Where, in any proceedings on an application for a care order or supervision order, a court makes a residence order with respect to the child concerned, it shall also make an interim supervision order with respect to him unless satisfied that his welfare will be satisfactorily safeguarded without an interim order being made.

(4) An interim order made under or by virtue of this section shall have effect for such period as may be specified in the order, but shall in any event cease to have effect on whichever of the following events first occurs—

(a) the expiry of the period of eight weeks beginning with the date on which the order is made;

(b) if the order is the second or subsequent such order made with respect to the same child in the same proceedings, the expiry of the relevant period;

(c) in a case which falls within subsection (1)(a), the disposal of the application;

(d) in a case which falls within subsection (1)(b), the disposal of an application for a care order or supervision order made by the authority with respect to the child;

(e) in a case which falls within subsection (1)(b) and in which—

(i) the court has given a direction under section 37(4), but

(ii) no application for a care order or supervision order has been made with respect to the child,

the expiry of the period fixed by that direction.

(5) In subsection (4)(b) 'the relevant period' means—

(a) the period of four weeks beginning with the date on which the order in question is made; or

(b) the period of eight weeks beginning with the date on which the first order was made if that period ends later than the period mentioned in paragraph (a).

(6) Where the court makes an interim care order, or interim supervision order, it may give such directions (if any) as it considers appropriate with regard to the medical or psychiatric examination or other assessment of the child; but if the child is of sufficient understanding to make an informed decision he may refuse to submit to the examination or other assessment.

(7) A direction under subsection (6) may be to the effect that there is to be—

(a) no such examination or assessment; or

(b) no such examination or assessment unless the court directs otherwise.

(8) A direction under subsection (6) may be—

(a) given when the interim order is made or at any time while it is in force; and

(b) varied at any time on the application of any person falling within any class of person prescribed by rules of court for the purposes of this subsection.

(9) Paragraphs 4 and 5 of Schedule 3 shall not apply in relation to an interim supervision order.

(10) Where a court makes an order under or by virtue of this section it shall, in determining the period for which the order is to be in force, consider whether any party who was, or might have been, opposed to the making of the order was in a position to argue his case against the order in full.

Date in force
14 October 1991: SI 1991/828.

Definitions
For 'care order' see s 31(11) and s 105(1); for 'supervision order' see s 31(11); for 'court' see s 92(7); for 'child' see s 105(1); for 'residence order' see s 8(1); for 'the relevant period' see sub-s (5); for 'the authority' see s 37(1), (5).

References
See generally paras 8.17 ff and *The Children Act 1989 Guidance and Regulations, Volume 1, Court Orders* (Dept of Health, 1991), at paras 3.35-3.43. For application for care order or supervision order see s 31; for jurisdiction of courts see s 92 and Sch 11, paras 4.3 ff; for attendance of child at hearing see s 95 and the FPR 1991, r 4.16 and the FPC (CA 1989) R 1991, r 16; for evidence given by or with respect to children see s 96 and the Children (Admissibility of Hearsay Evidence) Order 1993, SI 1993/621; for self-incrimination of witness see s 98. For making of interim care orders after a full hearing, see paras 8.86 ff and *Re S (Minors) (Care Order: Implementation of Care Plan); Re W (Minors) (Care Orders: Adequacy of Care Plan)* [2002] UKHL 10, [2002] 2 WLR 720, [2002] 1 FLR 815.

Sub-s (1) Court
An interim order may be made by a single justice or justices' clerk in certain circumstances: FPC (CA 1989) R 1991, r 28.

Sub-s (3)
This creates a presumption that the court shall make an interim supervision order in the circumstances described, but it must also be satisfied as to sub-s (2). Even where the criteria for an interim order are satisfied, such an order may only be made where it is in the interests of the child to do so: *Re A (children) (interim care order)* [2001] 3 FCR 402. For the use of interim orders in relation to care plans, see *Re S (children: care plan)* [2002] UKHL 10, [2002] 1 All ER 192.

Sub-ss (4) and (5)
The effect of these provisions is that the court can make interim orders initially for up to eight weeks or any part thereof including any unspent period of eight weeks from the date of the first order, and thereafter for one or more periods of up to four weeks. Note s 1 on the avoidance of delay and s 32 on the requirement to establish a timetable.

Sub-s (6)
See generally para 8.22 ff. In addition to directions under this sub-s, the court can impose requirements under Sch 3, paras 1-3, on orders under s 8, in addition to a supervision order. The directions may be varied: sub-s (8) on the application of specified persons: FPR 1991, r 4.2 and FPC (CA 1989) R 1991, r 2 and subject to appeal: *Re O (minors) (medical examination)* [1992] 2 FCR 394. The court may direct a local authority to carry out an assessment even though the authority is unwilling to do so: *Re C (A Minor) (Interim Care Order: Residential Assessment)* [1997] 1 FLR 1, HL. The

order may include a direction for residency where that is in the context of a series of assessments designed to illuminate the court's ultimate conclusion: *Re B (a child: interim care order)* [2002] EWC AC iv 25, [2002] 2 FCR 367, [2002] FCR 367, [2002] FCR 545.

[38A   Power to include exclusion requirement in interim care order]

[(1) Where—

(a)   on being satisfied that there are reasonable grounds for believing that the circumstances with respect to a child are as mentioned in section 31(2)(a) and (b)(i), the court makes an interim care order with respect to a child, and
(b)   the conditions mentioned in subsection (2) are satisfied,

the court may include an exclusion requirement in the interim care order.

(2) The conditions are—

(a)   that there is reasonable cause to believe that, if a person ('the relevant person') is excluded from a dwelling-house in which the child lives, the child will cease to suffer, or cease to be likely to suffer, significant harm, and
(b)   that another person living in the dwelling-house (whether a parent of the child or some other person)—

   (i)   is able and willing to give to the child the care which it would be reasonable to expect a parent to give him, and
   (ii) consents to the inclusion of the exclusion requirement.

(3) For the purposes of this section an exclusion requirement is any one or more of the following—

(a)   a provision requiring the relevant person to leave a dwelling-house in which he is living with the child,
(b)   a provision prohibiting the relevant person from entering a dwelling-house in which the child lives, and
(c)   a provision excluding the relevant person from a defined area in which a dwelling-house in which the child lives is situated.

(4) The court may provide that the exclusion requirement is to have effect for a shorter period than the other provisions of the interim care order.

(5) Where the court makes an interim care order containing an exclusion requirement, the court may attach a power of arrest to the exclusion requirement.

(6) Where the court attaches a power of arrest to an exclusion requirement of an interim care order, it may provide that the power of arrest is to have effect for a shorter period than the exclusion requirement.

(7) Any period specified for the purposes of subsection (4) or (6) may be extended by the court (on one or more occasions) on an application to vary or discharge the interim care order.

(8) Where a power of arrest is attached to an exclusion requirement of an interim care order by virtue of subsection (5), a constable may arrest without warrant any person whom he has reasonable cause to believe to be in breach of the requirement.

(9) Sections 47(7), (11) and (12) and 48 of, and Schedule 5 to, the Family Law Act 1996 shall have effect in relation to a person arrested under subsection (8) of this section as they have effect in relation to a person arrested under section 47(6) of that Act.

(10) If, while an interim care order containing an exclusion requirement is in force, the local authority have removed the child from the dwelling-house from which the relevant person is excluded to other accommodation for a continuous period of more than 24 hours, the interim care order shall cease to have effect in so far as it imposes the exclusion requirement.]

Date in force
Inserted by the Family Law Act 1996, Sch 6, para 1 as from 1 October 1997.

Definitions
For 'child', 'local authority' see s 105(1); for 'court' see s 92(7); for 'relevant person' see sub-s (2); for 'exclusion requirement' see sub-s (3).

Reference
For interim care orders see s 38.

[38B Undertakings relating to interim care orders]

[(1) In any case where the court has power to include an exclusion requirement in an interim care order, the court may accept an undertaking from the relevant person.

(2) No power of arrest may be attached to any undertaking given under subsection (1).

(3) An undertaking given to a court under subsection (1)—

(a) shall be enforceable as if it were an order of the court, and
(b) shall cease to have effect if, while it is in force, the local authority have removed the child from the dwelling house from which the relevant person is excluded to other accommodation for a continuous period of more than 24 hours.

(4) This section has effect without prejudice to the powers of the High Court and county court apart from this section.

(5) In this section 'exclusion requirement' and 'relevant person' have the same meaning as in section 38A.]

Date in force
Inserted by the Family Law Act 1996, Sch 6, para 1 as from 1 October 1997.

Reference
For 'court' see s 92(7); for 'relevant person' and 'exclusion requirement' see sub-s (5) and s 38A(2)(3).

---

39 Discharge and variation etc of care orders and supervision orders

(1) A care order may be discharged by the court on the application of—

(a) any person who has parental responsibility for the child;
(b) the child himself; or
(c) the local authority designated by the order.

(2) A supervision order may be varied or discharged by the court on the application of—

(a) any person who has parental responsibility for the child;
(b) the child himself; or
(c) the supervisor.

(3) On the application of a person who is not entitled to apply for the order to be discharged, but who is a person with whom the child is living, a supervision order may be varied by the court in so far as it imposes a requirement which affects that person.

[(3A) On the application of a person who is not entitled to apply for the order to be discharged, but who is a person to whom an exclusion requirement contained in the order applies, an interim care order may be varied or discharged by the court in so far as it imposes the exclusion requirement.

(3B) Where a power of arrest has been attached to an exclusion requirement of an interim care order, the court may, on the application of any person entitled to apply for the discharge of the order so far as it imposes the exclusion requirement, vary or discharge the order in so far as it confers a power of arrest (whether or not any application has been made to vary or discharge any other provision of the order).]

(4) Where a care order is in force with respect to a child the court may, on the application of any person entitled to apply for the order to be discharged, substitute a supervision order for the care order.

(5) When a court is considering whether to substitute one order for another under subsection (4) any provision of this Act which would otherwise require section 31(2) to be satisfied at the time when the proposed order is substituted or made shall be disregarded.

Date in force
14 October 1991: SI 1991/828.

Amendment
Sub-ss (3A) and (3B) inserted by the Family Law Act Sch 6, para 2 as from 1 October 1997.

Definitions
For 'care order' see s 31(11) and s 105(1); for 'court' see s 92(7); for parental responsibility see s 3; for 'child', 'local authority', 'supervision' see s 105(1). For 'supervision order' see s 31(11); for 'exclusion requirement' see s 38A(3).

References
See generally paras 8.122 and 8.125 ff. For jurisdiction of courts see s 92 and Sch 11, paras 4.3 ff; for attendance of child at hearing see s 95; for evidence given by or with respect to children see s 96; for self incrimination of witness see s 98; for 'family proceedings' under this Act see s 8(3), (4)(a); for limitation on repeated applications see s 91(14)(15).

Note
This section is silent on the test to be applied, but obviously the principles of s 1 must apply. While sub-ss (4) and (5) empower the court to substitute a supervision order for a care order solely on the application of those principles, substitution of a care order for a supervision order requires the conditions in s 31(2) to be satisfied again. The making of a residence order discharges a care order: s 91(1).

Sub-s (1)(b)
There is no need for the child first to apply for leave before making an application: *Re A (Care: Discharge Application by Child)* [1995] 2 FCR 686, [1995] 1 FLR 599.

---

40   Orders pending appeals in cases about care or supervision orders

(1) Where—

(a)   a court dismisses an application for a care order; and

(b)   at the time when the court dismisses the application, the child concerned is the subject of an interim care order,

the court may make a care order with respect to the child to have effect subject to such directions (if any) as the court may see fit to include in the order.

(2) Where—

(a)   a court dismisses an application for a care order, or an application for a supervision order; and

(b)   at the time when the court dismisses the application, the child concerned is the subject of an interim supervision order,

the court may make a supervision order with respect to the child to have effect subject to such directions (if any) as the court may see fit to include in the order.

(3) Where a court grants an application to discharge a care order or supervision order, it may order that—

(a)   its decision is not to have effect; or

(b)   the care order, or supervision order, is to continue to have effect but subject to such directions as the court sees fit to include in the order.

(4) An order made under this section shall only have effect for such period, not exceeding the appeal period, as may be specified in the order.

(5) Where—

(a) an appeal is made against any decision of a court under this section; or

(b) any application is made to the appellate court in connection with a proposed appeal against that decision.

the appellate court may extend the period for which the order in question is to have effect, but not so as to extend it beyond the end of the appeal period.

(6) In this section 'the appeal period' means—

(a) where an appeal is made against the decision in question, the period between the making of that decision and the determination of the appeal; and

(b) otherwise, the period during which an appeal may be made against the decision.

Date in force
14 October 1991: SI 1991/828.

Definitions
For 'court' see s 92(7); for 'care order' see s 31(11) and s 105(1); for 'child' see s 105(1); for 'supervision order' see s 31(11); for 'appeal period' see sub-s (6).

References
See para 8.130. For interim care and supervision orders see s 38; for discharge of care or supervision orders see s 39; for appeals see s 94 and the FPR 1991. Note the court may also make an order under s 8 with directions or conditions under s 11(7), pending the outcome of an appeal. The High Court has no power to make a care order pending the determination of the appeal. But can make a care order under s 38 of the Act : *Croydon London Borough Council v A (No 2)* [1992] 1WLR 984, [1992] 2 FCR 858.

[Representation of child]

41 Representation of child and of his interests in certain proceedings

(1) For the purpose of any specified proceedings, the court shall appoint [an officer of the Service] for the child concerned unless satisfied that it is not necessary to do so in order to safeguard his interests.

(2) The [officer of the Service] shall—

(a) be appointed in accordance with the rules of court; and

(b) be under a duty to safeguard the interests of the child in the manner prescribed by such rules.

(3) Where—

(a) the child concerned is not represented by a solicitor; and

(b) any of the conditions mentioned in subsection (4) is satisfied,

the court may appoint a solicitor to represent him.

(4) The conditions are that—

(a) no [officer of the Service] has been appointed for the child;

(b) the child has sufficient understanding to instruct a solicitor and wishes to do so;

(c) it appears to the court that it would be in the child's best interests for him to be represented by a solicitor.

(5) Any solicitor appointed under or by virtue of this section shall be appointed, and shall represent the child, in accordance with rules of court.

(6) In this section 'specified proceedings' means any proceedings—

(a) on an application for a care order or supervision order;

(b) in which the court has given a direction under section 37(1) and has made, or is considering whether to make, an interim care order;

(c) on an application for the discharge of a care order or the variation or discharge of a supervision order;

(d) on an application under section 39(4);

(e) in which the court is considering whether to make a residence order with respect to a child who is the subject of a care order;

(f) with respect to contact between a child who is the subject of a care order and any other person;

(g) under Part V;

(h) on an appeal against—

    (i) the making of, or refusal to make, a care order, supervision order or any order under section 34;

    (ii) the making of, or refusal to make, a residence order with respect to a child who is the subject of a care order; or

    (iii) the variation or discharge, or refusal of an application to vary or discharge, an order of a kind mentioned in sub-paragraph (i) or (ii);

    (iv) the refusal of an application under section 39(4); or

    (v) the making of, or refusal to make, an order under Part V; or

    (vi) which are specified for the time being, for the purposes of this section, by rules of court.

(7) . . .

(8) . . .

(9) . . .

(10) Rules of court may make provision as to—

(a) the assistance which any [officer of the Service] may be required by the court to give to it;

(b) the consideration to be given by any [officer of the Service], where an order of a specified kind has been made in the proceedings in question, as to whether to apply for the variation or discharge of the order;

(c) the participation of [officers of the Service] in reviews, of a kind specified in the rules, which are conducted by the court.

(11) Regardless of any enactment or rule of law which would otherwise prevent it from doing so, the court may take account of—

(a) any statement contained in a report made by [an officer of the Service] who is appointed under this section for the purpose of the proceedings in question; and

(b) any evidence given in respect of the matters referred to in the report,

in so far as the statement or evidence is, in the opinion of the court, relevant to the question which the court is considering.

[(12) . . .]

Date in force
14 October 1991: SI 1991/828.

Amendment
Sub-ss (1),(2),(4), (7)-(12): Criminal Justice and Court Services Act 2000, Schs 7, 8. Modified except in sub-s (8): any reference to solicitors etc modified to include references to recognised bodies by SI 1991/2684, arts 4, 5, Sch 1.

Definitions
For specified proceedings' see sub-s (6); for 'court' see s 92(7); for 'child', prescribed', 'local authority' see s 105(1); for 'care order' see s 31(11) and s 105(1); for 'supervision order' see s 31(11); for 'residence order' see s 8(1).

References
See generally chapter 10 and in particular paras 10.21 ff. For the power to make interim care orders see s 38(1). Part V ie ss 43-52 (protection of children).

Sub-ss (2) and (10)
See the FPR 1991, r 4.10, and the FPC (CA 1989) R 1991, r 10. A children's guardian may be appointed by a single justice: FPC (CA 1989) R 1991, r 2(5).

Sub-s (5)
See para 10.41 for duties of the solicitor and *Re H (a minor) (care proceedings)* [1992] 2 FCR 330, [1993] 1 FLR 440, *Re M (Minors) (Care Proceedings)* [1994] 1 FCR 866, [1994] 1 FLR 749; and for duties re appeal, see *R v Plymouth Juvenile Court, ex p F* [1987] 1 FLR 169.

Sub-s (6)(i) and 10
An application under s 8 of the Act for a prohibited steps order is not a 'specified proceeding': *Re M (Prohibited Steps Order: Application for Leave)* [1993] 1 FCR 78, [1993] 1 FLR 275. For specified proceedings see also the FPR 1991, r 4.2 and the FPC (CA 1989) R 1991, r 2. As to the duties of the children's guardian see the FPR 1991, r 4.11 and the FPC (CA 1989) R 1991, r 11.

---

42 [Right of officer of the Service to have access to local authority records]

(1) Where [an officer of the Service] has been appointed [under section 41] he shall have the right at all reasonable times to examine and take copies of—

(a) any records of, or held by, a local authority [or an authorised person] which were compiled in connection with the making, or proposed making, by any person of any application under this Act with respect to the child concerned; . . .

(b) any . . . records of, or held by, a local authority which were compiled in connection with any functions which [are social services functions within the meaning of] the Local Authority Social Services Act 1970, so far as those records relate to that child [; or

(c) any records of, or held by, an authorised person which were compiled in connection with the activities of that person, so far as those records relate to that child].

(2) Where [an officer of the Service] takes a copy of any record which he is entitled to examine under this section, that copy or any part of it shall be admissible as evidence of any matter referred to in any—

(a) report which he makes to the court in the proceedings in question; or

(b) evidence which he gives in those proceedings.

(3) Subsection (2) has effect regardless of any enactment or rule of law which would otherwise prevent the record in question being admissible in evidence.

[(4) In this section 'authorised person' has the same meaning as in section 31.]

Date in force
14 October 1991: SI 1991/828.

Amendments
Provision heading substituted by the Criminal Justice and Court Services Act 2000, S 74, Sch 7, Pt II, paras 87, 92 (C). Sub-s (1): CLSA 1990, Sch 16, para 18(2), (3), Sch 20; Local Government Act 2000, Sch 5, para 20. Sub-s (4): added by the CLSA 1990, Sch 16, para 18(4).

Definitions
For 'local authority' and 'child' see s 105(1).

References
For other evidential provisions see s 96; for the right of the children's guardian to examine records, see paras 10.30 and 11.48.

Records
Include the case record relating to prospective adopters: *Re T (a minor) (Guardian ad litem: case records)* [1994] 2 All ER 526, [1994] 1 FLR 632; and a document prepared by an Area Child Protection Committee for a 'Part 8 Review' (part 8 of the *Working Together under the Children Act 1989) · Re R (Care proceedings: Disclosure)* [2000] 3 FCR 721, [2000] 2 FLR 751, CA.

PART V
PROTECTION OF CHILDREN

43 Child assessment orders

(1) On the application of a local authority or authorised person for an order to be made under this section with respect to a child, the court may make the order if, but only if, it is satisfied that—

    (a) the applicant has reasonable cause to suspect that the child is suffering, or is likely to suffer, significant harm;

    (b) an assessment of the state of the child's health or development, or of the way in which he has been treated, is required to enable the applicant to determine whether or not the child is suffering, or is likely to suffer, significant harm; and

    (c) it is unlikely that such an assessment will be made, or be satisfactory, in the absence of an order under this section.

(2) In this Act 'a child assessment order' means an order under this section.

(3) A court may treat an application under this section as an application for an emergency protection order.

(4) No court shall make a child assessment order if it is satisfied—

    (a) that there are grounds for making an emergency protection order with respect to the child; and

    (b) that it ought to make such an order rather than a child assessment order.

(5) A child assessment order shall—

    (a) specify the date by which the assessment is to begin; and

    (b) have effect for such period, not exceeding 7 days beginning with that date, as may be specified in the order.

(6) Where a child assessment order is in force with respect to a child it shall be the duty of any person who is in a position to produce the child—

    (a) to produce him to such person as may be named in the order; and

    (b) to comply with such directions relating to the assessment of the child as the court thinks fit to specify in the order.

(7) A child assessment order authorises any person carrying out the assessment, or any part of the assessment, to do so in accordance with the terms of the order.

(8) Regardless of subsection (7), if the child is of sufficient understanding to make an informed decision he may refuse to submit to a medical or psychiatric examination or other assessment.

(9) The child may only be kept away from home—

    (a) in accordance with directions specified in the order;

    (b) if it is necessary for the purposes of the assessment; and

    (c) for such period or periods as may be specified in the order.

(10) Where the child is to be kept away from home, the order shall contain such directions as the court thinks fit with regard to the contact that he must be allowed to have with other persons while away from home.

(11) Any person making an application for a child assessment order shall take such steps as are reasonably practicable to ensure that notice of the application is given to—

    (a) the child's parents;

    (b) any person who is not a parent of his but who has parental responsibility for him;

    (c) any other person caring for the child;

    (d) any person in whose favour a contact order is in force with respect to the child;

    (e) any person who is allowed to have contact with the child by virtue of an order under section 34; and

    (f) the child,

before the hearing of the application.

(12) Rules of court may make provision as to the circumstances in which—

    (a) any of the persons mentioned in subsection (11); or

    (b) such other person as may be specified in the rules,

may apply to the court for a child assessment order to be varied or discharged.

(13) In this section 'authorised person' means a person who is an authorised person for the purposes of section 31.

Date in force
14 October 1991: SI 1991/828.

Definitions
For 'local authority' and 'child' see s 105(1); for 'authorised person' see sub-s (13); for 'court' see s 92(7); for 'harm' see s 31(9) as applied to the whole Act by s 105(1) and as to whether harm is significant see s 31(10) as applied to the whole Act by s 105(1); for 'a child assessment order' see sub-s (2); for 'emergency protection order' see s 44(4) as applied to the whole Act by s 105(1); for 'parental responsibility' see s 3; for 'contact order' see s 8(1).

References
See generally chapter 7.23 ff. *The Children Act 1989 Guidance and Regulations Volume 1, Court Orders* (Dept of Health, 1991), at paras 4.6-4.27. Proceedings must be commenced in the magistrates' court: Children (Allocation of Proceedings) Order 1991, r 3, see para 4.15. For jurisdiction of courts see s 92 and Sch 11, para 4.3; for attendance of child at hearing see s 95 and the Children (Admissibility of Hearsay Evidence) Order 1991; for evidence given by or with respect to children see s 96; for self-incrimination of witness see s 98.

Rules of court
See FPC (CA 1989) R 1991, r 2(3).

44 Orders for emergency protection of children

(1) Where any person ('the applicant') applies to the court for an order to be made under this section with respect to a child, the court may make the order if, but only if, it is satisfied that—

(a) there is reasonable cause to believe that the child is likely to suffer significant harm if—

    (i) he is not removed to accommodation provided by or on behalf of the applicant; or

    (ii) he does not remain in the place in which he is then being accommodated;

(b) in the case of an application made by a local authority—

    (i) enquiries are being made with respect to the child under section 47(1)(b); and

    (ii) those enquiries are being frustrated by access to the child being unreasonably refused to a person authorised to seek access and that the applicant has reasonable cause to believe that access to the child is required as a matter of urgency; or

(c) in the case of an application made by an authorised person—

    (i) the applicant has reasonable cause to suspect that a child is suffering, or is likely to suffer, significant harm;

    (ii) the applicant is making enquiries with respect to the child's welfare; and

    (iii) those enquiries are being frustrated by access to the child being unreasonably refused to a person authorised to seek access and the applicant has reasonable cause to believe that access to the child is required as a matter of urgency.

(2) In this section—

(a) 'authorised person' means a person who is an authorised person for the purposes of section 31; and

(b) 'a person authorised to seek access' means—

    (i) in the case of an application by a local authority, an officer of the local authority or a person authorised by the authority to act on their behalf in connection with the enquiries; or

    (ii) in the case of an application by an authorised person, that person.

(3) Any person—

(a) seeking access to a child in connection with enquiries of a kind mentioned in subsection (1); and

(b) purporting to be a person authorised to do so,

shall, on being asked to do so, produce some duly authenticated document as evidence that he is such a person.

(4) While an order under this section ('an emergency protection order') is in force it—

(a) operates as a direction to any person who is in a position to do so to comply with any request to produce the child to the applicant;

(b) authorises—

(i) the removal of the child at any time to accommodation provided by or on behalf of the applicant and his being kept there; or

(ii) the prevention of the child's removal from any hospital, or other place, in which he was being accommodated immediately before the making of the order; and

(c) gives the applicant parental responsibility for the child.

(5) Where an emergency protection order is in force with respect to a child, the applicant—

(a) shall only exercise the power given by virtue of subsection (4)(b) in order to safeguard the welfare of the child;

(b) shall take, and shall only take, such action in meeting his parental responsibility for the child as is reasonably required to safeguard or promote the welfare of the child (having regard in particular to the duration of the order); and

(c) shall comply with the requirements of any regulations made by the Secretary of State for the purposes of this subsection.

(6) Where the court makes an emergency protection order, it may give such directions (if any) as it considers appropriate with respect to—

(a) the contact which is, or is not, to be allowed between the child and any named person;

(b) the medical or psychiatric examination or other assessment of the child.

(7) Where any direction is given under subsection (6)(b), the child may, if he is of sufficient understanding to make an informed decision, refuse to submit to the examination or other assessment.

(8) A direction under subsection (6)(a) may impose conditions and one under subsection (6)(b) may be to the effect that there is to be—

(a) no such examination or assessment; or

(b) no such examination or assessment unless the court directs otherwise.

(9) A direction under subsection (6) may be—

(a) given when the emergency protection order is made or at any time while it is in force; and

(b) varied at any time on the application of any person falling within any class of person prescribed by rules of court for the purposes of this subsection.

(10) Where an emergency protection order is in force with respect to a child and—

(a) the applicant has exercised the power given by subsection (4)(b)(i) but it appears to him that it is safe for the child to be returned; or

(b) the applicant has exercised the power given by subsection (4)(b)(ii) but it appears to him that it is safe for the child to be allowed to be removed from the place in question,

he shall return the child or (as the case may be) allow him to be removed.

(11) Where he is required by subsection (10) to return the child the applicant shall—

(a) return him to the care of the person from whose care he was removed; or

(b) if that is not reasonably practicable, return him to the care of—

(i) a parent of his;

(ii)   any person who is not a parent of his but who has parental responsibility for him; or

(iii) such other person as the applicant (with the agreement of the court) considers appropriate.

(12) Where the applicant has been required by subsection (10) to return the child, or to allow him to be removed, he may again exercise his powers with respect to the child (at any time while the emergency protection order remains in force) if it appears to him that a change in the circumstances of the case makes it necessary for him to do so.

(13) Where an emergency protection order has been made with respect to a child, the applicant shall, subject to any direction given under subsection (6), allow the child reasonable contact with—

(a) his parents;

(b) any person who is not a parent of his but who has parental responsibility for him;

(c) any person with whom he was living immediately before the making of the order;

(d) any person in whose favour a contact order is in force with respect to him;

(e) any person who is allowed to have contact with the child by virtue of an order under section 34; and

(f) any person acting on behalf of any of those persons.

(14) Wherever it is reasonably practicable to do so, an emergency protection order shall name the child; and where it does not name him it shall describe him as clearly as possible.

(15) A person shall be guilty of an offence if he intentionally obstructs any person exercising the power under subsection (4)(b) to remove, or prevent the removal of, a child.

(16) A person guilty of an offence under subsection (15) shall be liable on summary conviction to a fine not exceeding level 3 on the standard scale.

Date in force
14 October 1991: SI 1991/828.

Definitions
For 'court' see s 92(7); for 'child', 'local authority', 'hospital' see s 105(1); for 'harm' see s 31(9) as applied to the whole Act by s 105(1) and as to whether harm is significant see s 31(10) as applied to the whole Act by s 105(1); for 'applicant' see sub-s (1); for 'a person authorised to seek access' see sub-s (2)(b); for 'authorised person' see sub-s (2)(a); for 'emergency protection order' see sub-s (4); for 'parental responsibility' see s 3; for 'contact order' see s 8(1).

References
See generally chapter 7 and in particular paras 7.29 ff and the FPC (CA 1989) R 1991. For welfare of the child as paramount consideration see s 1(1). For jurisdiction of courts see s 92 and Sch 11, paras 4.3 ff; for attendance of child at hearing see s 95, FPR 1991, r 4.16 and FPC (CA 1989) R 1991, r 16; for evidence given by or with respect to children see s 45(7), s 96, and The Children Act 1989 Guidance and Regulations Volume 1, Court Orders (Dept of Health, 1991), paras 4.28-4.69, and the Children (Admissibility of Hearsay Evidence) Order 1993; for self-incrimination of witness see s 98; for application by the police when child is in police protection see s 46(7), (8); for duration of an emergency protection order see s 45; for duty of local authority to make inquiries with respect to certain children to enable them to decide whether they should take any action to safeguard or promote the child's welfare see s 47(1); for powers to assist in discovery of children who may be in need of emergency protection see s 48; for local authority responsibility in relation to accommodation see s 21; for 'the standard scale' see the CJA 1982, s 37(2), (3) as amended; for 'likely to suffer significant harm', see paras 7.31 and 8.41 and *Newham London Borough v AG* [1992] 2 FCR 119, CA.

Transfer of functions
Functions of the Secretary of State, so far as exercisable in relation to Wales, transferred to the National Assembly for Wales, by the National Assembly for Wales (Transfer of Functions) Order 1999, SI 1999/672, art 2, Sch 1.

Sub-s (1)
This application may be made ex parte to a single justice with the leave of the justices' clerk: FPC (CA 1989) R 1991, rr 2 and 4. Where the applicant is not the authority in whose area the child is ordinarily resident, that authority may have responsibility transferred to it: Emergency Protection Order (Transfer of Responsibilities) Regulations 1991, SI 1991/1414.

Sub-s (9) Rules
See the FPC (CA 1989) R 1991, r 2(4).

Sub-s (11) Agreement of the court
Agreement may be given by a single justice: FPC (CA 1989) R 1991, r 2(5).

[44A Power to include exclusion requirement in emergency protection order]

[(1) Where—

(a) on being satisfied as mentioned in section 44(1)(a), (b) or (c), the court makes an emergency protection order with respect to a child, and

(b) the conditions mentioned in subsection (2) are satisfied,

the court may include an exclusion requirement in the emergency protection order.

(2) The conditions are—

(a) that there is reasonable cause to believe that, if a person ('the relevant person') is excluded from a dwelling-house in which the child lives, then—

    (i) in the case of an order made on the ground mentioned in section 44(1)(a), the child will not be likely to suffer significant harm, even though the child is not removed as mentioned in section 44(1)(a)(i) or does not remain as mentioned in section 44(1)(a)(ii), or

    (ii) in the case of an order made on the ground mentioned in paragraph (b) or (c) of section 44(1), the enquiries referred to in that paragraph will cease to be frustrated, and

(b) that another person living in the dwelling-house (whether a parent of the child or some other person)—

    (i) is able and willing to give to the child the care which it would be reasonable to expect a parent to give him, and

    (ii) consents to the inclusion of the exclusion requirement.

(3) For the purposes of this section an exclusion requirement is any one or more of the following—

(a) a provision requiring the relevant person to leave a dwelling-house in which he is living with the child,

(b) a provision prohibiting the relevant person from entering a dwelling-house in which the child lives, and

(c) a provision excluding the relevant person from a defined area in which a dwelling-house in which the child lives is situated.

(4) The court may provide that the exclusion requirement is to have effect for a shorter period than the other provisions of the order.

(5) Where the court makes an emergency protection order containing an exclusion requirement, the court may attach a power of arrest to the exclusion requirement.

(6) Where the court attaches a power of arrest to an exclusion requirement of an emergency protection order, it may provide that the power of arrest is to have effect for a shorter period than the exclusion requirement.

(7) Any period specified for the purposes of subsection (4) or (6) may be extended by the court (on one or more occasions) on an application to vary or discharge the emergency protection order.

(8) Where a power of arrest is attached to an exclusion requirement of an emergency protection order by virtue of subsection (5), a constable may arrest without warrant any person whom he has reasonable cause to believe to be in breach of the requirement.

(9) Sections 47(7), (11) and (12) and 48 of, and Schedule 5 to, the Family Law Act 1996 shall have effect in relation to a person arrested under subsection (8) of this section as they have effect in relation to a person arrested under section 47(6) of that Act.

(10) If, while an emergency protection order containing an exclusion requirement is in force, the applicant has removed the child from the dwelling-house from which the relevant person is excluded to other accommodation for a continuous period of more than 24 hours, the order shall cease to have effect in so far as it imposes the exclusion requirement.]

Date in force
Inserted by the Family Law Act 1996, Sch 6, para 3.

Definitions
For 'court' see s 92(7); for 'child' see s 105(1); for 'exclusion requirement' see sub-s (3); for 'relevant person' see sub-s (2); for 'harm' see s 31(9) as applied to the whole Act by s 105(1); and as to whether harm is significant see s 31(10) as applied to the whole Act by s 105(1).

Reference
See para 7.47.

[44B Undertakings relating to emergency protection orders]

[(1) In any case where the court has power to include an exclusion requirement in an emergency protection order, the court may accept an undertaking from the relevant person.

(2) No power of arrest may be attached to any undertaking given under subsection (1).

(3) An undertaking given to a court under subsection (1)—

(a) shall be enforceable as if it were an order of the court, and

(b) shall cease to have effect if, while it is in force, the applicant has removed the child from the dwelling-house from which the relevant person is excluded to other accommodation for a continuous period of more than 24 hours.

(4) This section has effect without prejudice to the powers of the High Court and county court apart from this section.

(5) In this section 'exclusion requirement' and 'relevant person' have the same meaning as in section 44A.]

Date in force
Inserted by the Family Law Act 1996, Sch 6, para 3.

Definitions
For 'court' see s 92(7); for 'child' see s 105(1); for 'exclusion requirement' see sub-s (5); for 'relevant person' see sub-s (5).

45 Duration of emergency protection orders and other supplemental provisions

(1) An emergency protection order shall have effect for such period, not exceeding eight days, as may be specified in the order.

(2) Where—

(a) the court making an emergency protection order would, but for this subsection, specify a period of eight days as the period for which the order is to have effect; but

(b) the last of those eight days is a public holiday (that is to say, Christmas Day, Good Friday, a bank holiday or a Sunday),

the court may specify a period which ends at noon on the first later day which is not such a holiday.

(3) Where an emergency protection order is made on an application under section 46(7), the period of eight days mentioned in subsection (1) shall begin with the first day on which the child was taken into police protection under section 46.

(4) Any person who—

(a) has parental responsibility for a child as the result of an emergency protection order; and

(b) is entitled to apply for a care order with respect to the child,

may apply to the court for the period during which the emergency protection order is to have effect to be extended.

(5) On an application under subsection (4) the court may extend the period during which the order is to have effect by such period, not exceeding seven days, as it thinks fit, but may do so only if it has reasonable cause to believe that the child concerned is likely to suffer significant harm if the order is not extended.

(6) An emergency protection order may only be extended once.

(7) Regardless of any enactment or rule of law which would otherwise prevent it from doing so, a court hearing an application for, or with respect to, an emergency protection order may take account of—

(a) any statement contained in any report made to the court in the course of, or in connection with, the hearing; or

(b) any evidence given during the hearing,

which is, in the opinion of the court, relevant to the application.

(8) Any of the following may apply to the court for an emergency protection order to be discharged—

(a) the child;

(b) a parent of his;

(c) any person who is not a parent of his but who has parental responsibility for him; or

(d) any person with whom he was living immediately before the making of the order.

[(8A) On the application of a person who is not entitled to apply for the order to be discharged, but who is a person to whom an exclusion requirement contained in the order applies, an emergency protection order may be varied or discharged by the court in so far as it imposes the exclusion requirement.

(8B) Where a power of arrest has been attached to an exclusion requirement of an emergency protection order, the court may, on the application of any person entitled to apply for the discharge of the order so far as it imposes the exclusion requirement, vary or discharge the order in so far as it confers a power of arrest (whether or not any application has been made to vary or discharge any other provision of the order).]

(9) No application for the discharge of an emergency protection order shall be heard by the court before the expiry of the period of 72 hours beginning with the making of the order.

[(10) No appeal may be made against—

(a) the making of, or refusal to make, an emergency protection order;

(b) the extension of, or refusal to extend, the period during which such an order is to have effect;

(c) the discharge of, or refusal to discharge, such an order; or

(d) the giving of, or refusal to give, any direction in connection with such an order.]

(11) Subsection (8) does not apply—

(a) where the person who would otherwise be entitled to apply for the emergency protection order to be discharged—

(i) was given notice (in accordance with rules of court) of the hearing at which the order was made; and

(ii) was present at that hearing; or

(b) to any emergency protection order the effective period of which has been extended under subsection (5).

(12) A court making an emergency protection order may direct that the applicant may in exercising any powers which he has by virtue of the order, be accompanied by a registered medical practitioner, registered nurse or *registered health visitor* [registered midwife], if he so chooses.

Date in force
14 October 1991: SI 1991/828.

Amendment
Sub-ss (8A), (8B) inserted by the Family Law Act 1996, Sch 6, para 4. Sub-s (10): substituted by the CLSA 1990, Sch 16, para 19.

Definitions
For 'emergency protection order' see s 44(4); for 'court' see s 92(7); for 'bank holiday', 'child' see s 105(1); for 'parental responsibility' see s 3; for 'care order' see s 31(11); for 'harm' see s 31(9) as applied to the whole Act by s 105(1); and as to whether harm is significant see s 31(10) as applied to the whole Act by s 105(1); for 'applicant' see s 44(1); for 'exclusion requirement' see s 44A(3).

References
See generally paras 7.44 ff and The Children Act 1989 Guidance and Regulations, Volume 1, Court Orders (Dept of Health, 1991), at paras 4.28-4.69. For persons entitled to apply for care order see s 31(1)(9); for 'parent' see para 3.43; for further provisions see note to s 44; for jurisdiction of courts see s 92(7) and Sch 11, paras 4.3 ff.

Sub-s (4)
Any person other than the local authority or the NSPCC who has obtained an emergency protection order under s 44, cannot obtain an extension of the order, since they are not entitled to apply for a care order: see s 31(1) and (9).

Sub-s (10)
There is no appeal procedure under this section; refusal includes any decision not to make an order: *Essex County Council v F* [1993] 1 FLR 847, see paras 7.45 and 7.46.

46 Removal and accommodation of children by police in cases of emergency

(1) Where a constable has reasonable cause to believe that a child would otherwise be likely to suffer significant harm, he may—

(a) remove the child to suitable accommodation and keep him there; or
(b) take such steps as are reasonable to ensure that the child's removal from any hospital, or other place, in which he is then being accommodated is prevented.

(2) For the purposes of this Act, a child with respect to whom a constable has exercised his powers under this section is referred to as having been taken into police protection.

(3) As soon as is reasonably practicable after taking a child into police protection, the constable concerned shall—

(a) inform the local authority within whose area the child was found of the steps that have been, and are proposed to be, taken with respect to the child under this section and the reasons for taking them;
(b) give details to the authority within whose area the child is ordinarily resident ('the appropriate authority') of the place at which the child is being accommodated;
(c) inform the child (if he appears capable of understanding)—
    (i) of the steps that have been taken with respect to him under this section and of the reasons for taking them; and
    (ii) of the further steps that may be taken with respect to him under this section;
(d) take such steps as are reasonably practicable to discover the wishes and feelings of the child;

    (e)   secure that the case is inquired into by an officer designated for the purposes of this section by the chief officer of the police area concerned; and

    (f)   where the child was taken into police protection by being removed to accommodation which is not provided—

        (i)   by or on behalf of a local authority; or

       (ii)   as a refuge, in compliance with the requirements of section 51,

secure that he is moved to accommodation which is so provided.

(4) As soon as is reasonably practicable after taking a child into police protection, the constable concerned shall take such steps as are reasonably practicable to inform—

    (a)   the child's parents;

    (b)   every person who is not a parent of his but who has parental responsibility for him; and

    (c)   any other person with whom the child was living immediately before being taken into police protection,

of the steps that he has taken under this section with respect to the child, the reasons for taking them and the further steps that may be taken with respect to him under this section.

(5) On completing any inquiry under subsection (3)(e), the officer conducting it shall release the child from police protection unless he considers that there is still reasonable cause for believing that the child would be likely to suffer significant harm if released.

(6) No child may be kept in police protection for more than 72 hours.

(7) While a child is being kept in police protection, the designated officer may apply on behalf of the appropriate authority for an emergency protection order to be made under section 44 with respect to the child.

(8) An application may be made under subsection (7) whether or not the authority know of it or agree to its being made.

(9) While a child is being kept in police protection—

    (a)   neither the constable concerned nor the designated officer shall have parental responsibility for him; but

    (b)   the designated officer shall do what is reasonable in all the circumstances of the case for the purpose of safeguarding or promoting the child's welfare (having regard in particular to the length of the period during which the child will be so protected).

(10) Where a child has been taken into police protection, the designated officer shall allow—

    (a)   the child's parents;

    (b)   any person who is not a parent of the child but who has parental responsibility for him;

    (c)   any person with whom the child was living immediately before he was taken into police protection;

    (d)   any person in whose favour a contact order is in force with respect to the child;

    (e)   any person who is allowed to have contact with the child by virtue of an order under section 34; and

    (f)   any person acting on behalf of any of those persons,

to have such contact (if any) with the child as, in the opinion of the designated officer, is both reasonable and in the child's best interests.

(11) Where a child who has been taken into police protection is in accommodation provided by, or on behalf of, the appropriate authority, subsection (10) shall have effect as if it referred to the authority rather than to the designated officer.

Date in force
14 October 1991: SI 1991/828.

Definitions
For 'child', 'hospital' and 'local authority' see s 105(1); for 'harm' see s 31(9) as applied to the whole Act by s 105(1) and as to whether harm is significant see s 31(10) as applied to the whole Act by s 105(1); for 'police protection' see sub-s (2); for 'ordinary residence' see s 105(6); for 'appropriate authority' see sub-s (3)(b); for 'emergency protection order' see s 44(4); for 'designated officer' see sub-s (3)(e). For 'parental responsibility' see s 3; for 'contact order' see s 8(1).

References
See generally paras 7.56 ff and *The Children Act 1989 Guidance and Regulations, Volume 1, Court Orders* (Dept of Health, 1991), at paras 4.71-4.77. For 'parent' see para 3.43; for the maximum duration of an emergency protection order taken under sub-s (7) see s 45(3); for the welfare of the child the paramount consideration see s 1(1); for duty of local authority to make inquiries with respect to certain children to enable them to decide whether they should take any action to safeguard or promote the child's welfare see s 47(1); for powers to assist in discovery of children who may be in need of emergency protection see s 48; for local authority responsibility in relation to accommodation see s 21; for refuges for children at risk see s 51.

Sub-s (6)
'72 hours' in this section, the period is not extended by public holidays. Cf s 45(2).

Sub-s (7)
The maximum period of eight days for such an order begins with the first day on which the child is taken into police protection: s 45(3).

---

47 Local authority's duty to investigate

(1) Where a local authority—

(a) are informed that a child who lives, or is found, in their area—

  (i)   is the subject of an emergency protection order; or

  (ii) is in police protection; or

  [(iii) has contravened a ban imposed by a curfew notice within the meaning of Chapter I of Part I of the Crime and Disorder Act 1998; or]

(b) have reasonable cause to suspect that a child who lives, or is found, in their area is suffering, or is likely to suffer, significant harm,

the authority shall make, or cause to be made, such enquiries as they consider necessary to enable them to decide whether they should take any action to safeguard or promote the child's welfare.

[In the case of a child falling within paragraph (a)(iii) above, the enquiries shall be commenced as soon as practicable and, in any event, within 48 hours of the authority receiving the information.]

(2) Where a local authority have obtained an emergency protection order with respect to a child, they shall make, or cause to be made, such enquiries as they consider necessary to enable them to decide what action they should take to safeguard or promote the child's welfare.

(3) The enquiries shall, in particular, be directed towards establishing—

(a) whether the authority should make any application to the court, or exercise any of their other powers under this Act [or section 11 of the Crime and Disorder Act 1998 (child safety orders)], with respect to the child;

(b) whether, in the case of a child—

  (i)   with respect to whom an emergency protection order has been made; and

  (ii) who is not in accommodation provided by or on behalf of the authority,

it would be in the child's best interests (while an emergency protection order remains in force) for him to be in such accommodation; and

(c) whether, in the case of a child who has been taken into police protection, it would be in the child's best interests for the authority to ask for an application to be made under section 46(7).

(4) Where enquiries are being made under subsection (1) with respect to a child, the local authority concerned shall (with a view to enabling them to determine what action, if any, to take with respect to him) take such steps as are reasonably practicable—

(a)   to obtain access to him; or

(b)   to ensure that access to him is obtained, on their behalf, by a person authorised by them for the purpose,

unless they are satisfied that they already have sufficient information with respect to him.

(5) Where, as a result of any such enquiries, it appears to the authority that there are matters connected with the child's education which should be investigated, they shall consult the relevant local education authority.

(6) Where, in the course of enquiries made under this section—

(a)   any officer of the local authority concerned; or

(b)   any person authorised by the authority to act on their behalf in connection with those enquiries—

(i)   is refused access to the child concerned; or

(ii)   is denied information as to his whereabouts,

the authority shall apply for an emergency protection order, a child assessment order, a care order or a supervision order with respect to the child unless they are satisfied that his welfare can be satisfactorily safeguarded without their doing so.

(7) If, on the conclusion of any enquiries or review made under this section, the authority decide not to apply for an emergency protection order, a child assessment order, a care order or a supervision order they shall—

(a)   consider whether it would be appropriate to review the case at a later date; and

(b)   if they decide that it would be, determine the date on which that review is to begin.

(8) Where, as a result of complying with this section, a local authority conclude that they should take action to safeguard or promote the child's welfare they shall take that action (so far as it is both within their power and reasonably practicable for them to do so).

(9) Where a local authority are conducting enquiries under this section, it shall be the duty of any person mentioned in subsection (11) to assist them with those enquiries (in particular by providing relevant information and advice) if called upon by the authority to do so.

(10) Subsection (9) does not oblige any person to assist a local authority where doing so would be unreasonable in all the circumstances of the case.

(11) The persons are—

(a)   any local authority;

(b)   any local education authority;

(c)   any local housing authority;

(d)   any [Health Authority, Special Health Authority][, Primary Care Trust] [or National Health Service Trust]; and

(e)   any person authorised by the Secretary of State for the purposes of this section.

(12) Where a local authority are making enquiries under this section with respect to a child who appears to them to be ordinarily resident within the area of another authority, they shall consult that other authority, who may undertake the necessary enquiries in their place.

Date in force
14 October 1991: SI 1991/828.

Amendment
Sub-s (1): Crime and Disorder Act 1998, s 15. Sub-s (3): Crime and Disorder Act 1998, Sch 8, para 69. Sub-s (11): CLSA 1990, Sch 16, para 20; Health Authorities Act 1995, Sch 1, para 118; SI 2000/90.

Definitions
For 'local authority', 'child', 'local education authority', 'local housing authority', 'health authority' see s 105(1); for 'emergency protection order' see s 44(4); for 'police protection' see s 46(2); for 'harm' see s 31(9) as applied to the whole Act by s 105(1); as to whether harm is significant see s 31(10) as applied to the whole Act by s 105(1); for 'court' see s 92(7); for 'accommodation provided by or on behalf of a local authority' see s 105(5); for 'care order', 'supervision order' see s 31(11); for 'ordinary residence' see s 105(6). For 'child assessment order' see s 43(2).

References
See generally paras 7.8 ff and *The Children Act 1989 Guidance and Regulations, Volume 1, Court Orders* (Dept of Health, 1991), at paras 4.78-4.87 and *Handbook of Best Practice in Children Act Cases* in Clarke Hall and Morrison at para 1[20001]. For welfare of the child the paramount consideration see s 1(1); for emergency protection orders see s 44 and for child assessment orders see s 43.

Transfer of functions
Functions of the Secretary of State, so far as exercisable in relation to Wales, transferred to the National Assembly for Wales, by the National Assembly for Wales (Transfer of Functions) Order 1999, SI 1999/672, art 2, Sch 1.

Sub-s (1) Reasonable cause to suspect
Ie a local authority is not required to make a finding on the balance of probabilities as to past conduct before assessing risk and taking any necessary steps: *Re S (sexual abuse allegations: local authority response)* [2001] EWHC Admin 334, [2001] 3 FCR 702, [2001] 2 FLR 776.

---

48 Powers to assist in discovery of children who may be in need of emergency protection

(1) Where it appears to a court making an emergency protection order that adequate information as to the child's whereabouts—

(a) is not available to the applicant for the order; but
(b) is available to another person,

it may include in the order a provision requiring that other person to disclose, if asked to do so by the applicant, any information that he may have as to the child's whereabouts.

(2) No person shall be excused from complying with such a requirement on the ground that complying might incriminate him or his spouse of an offence; but a statement or admission made in complying shall not be admissible in evidence against either of them in proceedings for any offence other than perjury.

(3) An emergency protection order may authorise the applicant to enter premises specified by the order and search for the child with respect to whom the order is made.

(4) Where the court is satisfied that there is reasonable cause to believe that there may be another child on those premises with respect to whom an emergency protection order ought to be made, it may make an order authorising the applicant to search for that other child on those premises.

(5) Where—

(a) an order has been made under subsection (4);
(b) the child concerned has been found on the premises; and
(c) the applicant is satisfied that the grounds for making an emergency protection order exist with respect to him,

the order shall have effect as if it were an emergency protection order.

(6) Where an order has been made under subsection (4), the applicant shall notify the court of its effect.

(7) A person shall be guilty of an offence if he intentionally obstructs any person exercising the power of entry and search under subsection (3) or (4).

(8) A person guilty of an offence under subsection (7) shall be liable on summary conviction to a fine not exceeding level 3 on the standard scale.

(9) Where, on an application made by any person for a warrant under this section, it appears to the court—

    (a) that a person attempting to exercise powers under an emergency protection order has been prevented from doing so by being refused entry to the premises concerned or access to the child concerned; or

    (b) that any such person is likely to be so prevented from exercising any such powers,

it may issue a warrant authorising any constable to assist the person mentioned in paragraph (*a*) or (*b*) in the exercise of those powers, using reasonable force if necessary.

(10) Every warrant issued under this section shall be addressed to, and executed by, a constable who shall be accompanied by the person applying for the warrant if—

    (a) that person so desires; and

    (b) the court by whom the warrant is issued does not direct otherwise.

(11) A court granting an application for a warrant under this section may direct that the constable concerned may, in executing the warrant, be accompanied by a registered medical practitioner, registered nurse or *registered health visitor* [registered midwife] if he so chooses.

(12) An application for a warrant under this section shall be made in the manner and form prescribed by rules of court.

(13) Wherever it is reasonably practicable to do so, an order under subsection (4), an application for a warrant under this section and any such warrant shall name the child; and where it does not name him it shall describe him as clearly as possible.

Date in force
14 October 1991: SI 1991/828.

Definitions
For 'court' see s 92(7); for 'emergency protection order' see s 44(4); for 'child' see s 105(1); for 'applicant' see s 44(1).

References
See generally paras 7.59 ff and *The Children Act 1989 Guidance and Regulations, Volume 1, Court Orders* (Dept of Health, 1991), at paras 4.49-4.57. For grounds for making an emergency protection order see s 44(1); for 'the standard scale' see the CJA 1982, s 37(2)(3) as amended.

Sub-s (3)
Note this provision is permissive. It needs to be used with sub-s (9) if the help of the police and reasonable force to gain entry is required. See also the powers in s 50.

Sub-s (4) Court
A single justice may make this order: FPC (CA 1989) R 1991.

Sub-s (9) Court
A single justice may make this order ex parte with leave of the justices' clerk: FPC (CA 1989) R 1991, rr 2(5) and 4(4).

---

49   Abduction of children in care etc

(1) A person shall be guilty of an offence if, knowingly and without lawful authority or reasonable excuse, he—

    (a) takes a child to whom this section applies away from the responsible person;

    (b) keeps such a child away from the responsible person; or

    (c) induces, assists or incites such a child to run away or stay away from the responsible person.

(2) This section applies in relation to a child who is—

    (a) in care;

    (b) the subject of an emergency protection order; or

    (c) in police protection,

and in this section 'the responsible person' means any person who for the time being has care of him by virtue of the care order, the emergency protection order, or section 46, as the case may be.

(3) A person guilty of an offence under this section shall be liable on summary conviction to imprisonment for a term not exceeding six months, or to a fine not exceeding level 5 on the standard scale, or to both.

Date in force
14 October 1991: SI 1991/828.91.

Definitions
For 'child' and 'child who is in care' see s 105(1); for 'the responsible person' see sub-s (2); for 'emergency protection order' see s 44(4); for 'in police protection' see s 46(2).

References
See paras 4.28-4.89 of *The Children Act 1989 Guidance and Regulations, Volume 1, Court Orders* (Dept of Health, 1991). For 'the standard scale' see the CJA 1982, s 37(2) (3) as amended.

Sub-s (2)
The local authority may designate who the responsible person should be at any given time: *Re R (Recovery Orders)* [1998] 3 FCR 321, [1998] 2 FLR 401.

---

50 Recovery of abducted children etc

(1) Where it appears to the court that there is reason to believe that a child to whom this section applies—

  (a) has been unlawfully taken away or is being unlawfully kept away from the responsible person;

  (b) has run away or is staying away from the responsible person; or

  (c) is missing,

the court may make an order under this section ('a recovery order').

(2) This section applies to the same children to whom section 49 applies and in this section 'the responsible person' has the same meaning as in section 49.

(3) A recovery order—

  (a) operates as a direction to any person who is in a position to do so to produce the child on request to any authorised person;

  (b) authorises the removal of the child by any authorised person;

  (c) requires any person who has information as to the child's whereabouts to disclose that information, if asked to do so, to a constable or an officer of the court;

  (d) authorises a constable to enter any premises specified in the order and search for the child, using reasonable force if necessary.

(4) The court may make a recovery order only on the application of—

  (a) any person who has parental responsibility for the child by virtue of a care order or emergency protection order; or

  (b) where the child is in police protection, the designated officer.

(5) A recovery order shall name the child and—

  (a) any person who has parental responsibility for the child by virtue of a care order or emergency protection order; or

  (b) where the child is in police protection, the designated officer.

(6) Premises may only be specified under subsection (3)(d) if it appears to the court that there are reasonable grounds for believing the child to be on them.

(7) In this section—

'an authorised person' means—

  (a) any person specified by the court;

  (b) any constable;

(c) any person who is authorised—

    (i) after the recovery order is made; and

    (ii) by a person who has parental responsibility for the child by virtue of a care order or an emergency protection order,

to exercise any power under a recovery order; and

'the designated officer' means the officer designated for the purposes of section 46.

(8) Where a person is authorised as mentioned in subsection (7)(c)—

(a) the authorisation shall identify the recovery order; and

(b) any person claiming to be so authorised shall, if asked to do so, produce some duly authenticated document showing that he is so authorised.

(9) A person shall be guilty of an offence if he intentionally obstructs an authorised person exercising the power under subsection (3)(b) to remove a child.

(10) A person guilty of an offence under this section shall be liable on summary conviction to a fine not exceeding level 3 on the standard scale.

(11) No person shall be excused from complying with any request made under sub-section (3)(c) on the ground that complying with it might incriminate him or his spouse of an offence; but a statement or admission made in complying shall not be admissible in evidence against either of them in proceedings for an offence other than perjury.

(12) Where a child is made the subject of a recovery order whilst being looked after by a local authority, any reasonable expenses incurred by an authorised person in giving effect to the order shall be recoverable from the authority.

(13) A recovery order shall have effect in Scotland as if it had been made by the Court of Session and as if that court had had jurisdiction to make it.

(14) In this section 'the court', in relation to Northern Ireland, means a magistrates' court within the meaning of the Magistrates' Courts (Northern Ireland) Order 1981.

Date in force

14 October 1991: SI 1991/828.

Definitions

For 'court' see s 92(7) and sub-ss (13) (Scotland) and (14) (Northern Ireland); for 'child' and 'local authority' see s 105(1); for 'the responsible person' see sub-s (2) and s 49(2); for 'a recovery order' see sub-s (1); for 'authorised person' and 'designated officer' see sub-s (7); for 'parental responsibility' see s 3; for 'care order' sees s 31(11) and s 105(1); for 'emergency protection order' see s 44(4); for 'in police protection' see s 46(2); for 'child looked after by a local authority' see s 22(1).

References

See generally paras 7.63 ff, and *The Children Act 1989 Guidance and Regulations, Volume 1, Court Orders* (Dept of Health, 1991), at paras 4.90-4.98. Application may be made ex parte with the leave of the justices' clerk: FPC (CA 1989) R 1991, rr 2(5) and 4(4). For 'the standard scale' see the CJA 1982, s 37(2) (3) as amended.

---

51 Refuges for children at risk

(1) Where it is proposed to use a voluntary home or *registered* [private] children's home to provide a refuge for children who appear to be at risk of harm, the Secretary of State may issue a certificate under this section with respect to that home.

(2) Where a local authority or voluntary organisation arrange for a foster parent to provide such a refuge, the Secretary of State may issue a certificate under this section with respect to that foster parent.

(3) In subsection (2) 'foster parent' means a person who is, or who from time to time is, a local authority foster parent or a foster parent with whom children are placed by a voluntary organisation.

(4) The Secretary of State may by regulations—

(a) make provision as to the manner in which certificates may be issued;

(b) impose requirements which must be complied with while any certificate is in force; and

(c) provide for the withdrawal of certificates in prescribed circumstances.

(5) Where a certificate is in force with respect to a home, none of the provisions mentioned in subsection (7) shall apply in relation to any person providing a refuge for any child in that home.

(6) Where a certificate is in force with respect to a foster parent, none of those provisions shall apply in relation to the provision by him of a refuge for any child in accordance with arrangements made by the local authority or voluntary organisation.

(7) The provisions are—

(a) section 49;

[(b) sections 82 (recovery of certain fugitive children) and 83 (harbouring) of the Children (Scotland) Act 1995, so far as they apply in relation to anything done in England and Wales;]

(c) section 32(3) of the Children and Young Persons Act 1969 (compelling, persuading, inciting or assisting any person to be absent from detention, etc.), so far as it applies in relation to anything done in England and Wales;

(d) section 2 of the Child Abduction Act 1984.

Date in force
14 October 1991: SI 1991/828.

Amendment
Sub-s (1): word 'private' in square brackets substituted by the Care Standards Act 2000, s 116, Sch 4, para 14(1), (7). In section 51(7) (enactments which do not apply where a child is granted refuge), for paragraph (b) substitute '(b) sections 82 (recovery of certain fugitive children) and 83 (harbouring) of the Children (Scotland) Act 1995, so far as they apply in relation to anything done in England and Wales;' (Children (Scotland) Act 1995, Sch 4, para 48).'

Definitions
For 'voluntary home' see s 60(2); for 'registered children's home' see s 63(8); for 'child', 'local authority', 'private children's home' and 'voluntary organisation' see s 105(1); for 'harm' see s 31(9) as applied to the whole Act by s 105(1); for 'foster parent' see sub-s (3); for 'local authority foster parent' see s 23(3).

References
See generally para 6.69 ff and *The Children Act 1989 Guidance and Regulations, Volume 1, Court Orders* (Dept of Health, 1991), at para 4.70.

Transfer of functions
Functions of the Secretary of State, so far as exercisable in relation to Wales, transferred to the National Assembly for Wales, by the National Assembly for Wales (Transfer of Functions) Order 1999, SI 1999/672, art 2, Sch 1.

References
For 'children's home' see s 23(10) as applied to the whole Act by s 105(1) and see note to s 53, post.

Sub-s (4) Regulations
See the Refuges (Children's Homes and Foster Placements) Regulations 1991, SI 1991/1507 amended by SI 2002/546.

---

52 Rules and regulations

(1) Without prejudice to section 93 or any other power to make such rules, rules of court may be made with respect to the procedure to be followed in connection with proceedings under this Part.

(2) The rules may, in particular make provision—

(a) as to the form in which any application is to be made or direction is to be given;

(b) prescribing the persons who are to be notified of—

    (i)   the making, or extension, of an emergency protection order; or

    (ii) the making of an application under section 45(4) or (8) or 46(7); and

(c) as to the content of any such notification and the manner in which, and person by whom, it is to be given.

(3) The Secretary of State may by regulations provide that, where—

(a) an emergency protection order has been made with respect to a child;

(b) the applicant for the order was not the local authority within whose area the child is ordinarily resident; and

(c) that local authority are of the opinion that it would be in the child's best interests for the applicant's responsibilities under the order to be transferred to them,

that authority shall (subject to their having complied with any requirements imposed by the regulations) be treated, for the purposes of this Act, as though they and not the original applicant had applied for, and been granted, the order.

(4) Regulations made under subsection (3) may, in particular, make provision as to—

(a) the considerations to which the local authority shall have regard in forming an opinion as mentioned in subsection (3)(c); and

(b) the time at which responsibility under any emergency protection order is to be treated as having been transferred to a local authority.

Date in force
14 October 1991: SI 1991/828.

Definitions
For 'emergency protection order' see s 44(4); for 'child' and 'local authority' see s 105(1); for 'ordinary residence' see s 105(6).

References
See generally the FPC (CA 1989) R 1991, and the FPR 1991. 'This Part' ie Pt V (ss 43–52) (protection of children).

Transfer of functions
Functions of the Secretary of State, so far as exercisable in relation to Wales, transferred to the National Assembly for Wales, by the National Assembly for Wales (Transfer of Functions) Order 1999, SI 1999/672, art 2, Sch 1.

Regulations
See the Emergency Protection Order (Transfer of Responsibility) Regulation 1991, SI 1991/1414.

Part VI
Community Homes

53 Provision of community homes by local authorities

(1) Every local authority shall make such arrangements as they consider appropriate for securing that homes ('community homes') are available—

(a) for the care and accommodation of children looked after by them; and

(b) for purposes connected with the welfare of children (whether or not looked after by them),

and may do so jointly with one or more other local authorities.

(2) In making such arrangements, a local authority shall have regard to the need for ensuring the availability of accommodation—

(a) of different descriptions; and

(b) which is suitable for different purposes and the requirements of different descriptions of children.

(3) A community home may be a home—

(a) provided, [equipped, maintained and (subject to subsection (3A)) managed] by a local authority; or

(b) provided by a voluntary organisation but in respect of which a local authority and the organisation—

    (i) propose that, in accordance with an instrument of management, the [equipment, maintenance and (subject to subsection (3B)) management] of the home shall be the responsibility of the local authority; or

    (ii) so propose that the management, equipment and maintenance of the home shall be the responsibility of the voluntary organisation.

[(3A) A local authority may make arrangements for the management by another person of accommodation provided by the local authority for the purpose of restricting the liberty of children.

(3B) Where a local authority are to be responsible for the management of a community home provided by a voluntary organisation, the local authority may, with the consent of the body of managers constituted by the instrument of management for the home, make arrangements for the management by another person of accommodation provided for the purpose of restricting the liberty of children.]

(4) Where a local authority are to be responsible for the management of a community home provided by a voluntary organisation, the authority shall designate the home as a controlled community home.

(5) Where a voluntary organisation are to be responsible for the management of a community home provided by the organisation, the local authority shall designate the home as an assisted community home.

(6) Schedule 4 shall have effect for the purpose of supplementing the provisions of this Part.

Date in force
14 October 1991: SI 1991/828.

Amendment
Sub-s (3) amended and sub-ss (3A), (3B) inserted by the Criminal Justice and Public Order Act 1994, s 22(2)(a) and (b).

Definitions
For 'local authority', 'child', 'voluntary organisation' see s 105(1); for 'child who is looked after by a local authority' see s 22(1); for 'controlled community home' see sub-s (4) and 'assisted community home' see sub-s (5).

Reference
'This Part' ie Pt VI (ss 53-58 and Sch 4) (community homes).

Note
Part VI of the CA 1989 largely replaced, with amendments of terminology and layout, Pt IV of the CCA 1980. Section 53 of the 1989 Act corresponds with minor amendments to s 31 of the 1980 Act (as substituted by the HSSSSA 1983, s 4(1)). It gives a local authority wide discretion to make such arrangements as they consider appropriate to provide community homes for children whether looked after by them or not. They may operate jointly with one or more other local authorities. There are three types of home: a home provided, managed, equipped and maintained by the local authority; a controlled community home provided by a voluntary organisation but managed by the local authority; and an assisted community home provided and managed by the voluntary organisation. See Sch 4 for organisation and management of controlled and assisted homes. See s 82(4) for the power of the Secretary of State to pay grants to voluntary organisations for the establishment, maintenance and improvement of assisted community homes.

Conduct, registration and inspection of children's homes
The Care Standards Act 2000 Act which is being progressively implemented in England and Wales makes provision for the conduct, registration and inspection of children's homes. S 1 of the 2000 Act defines a 'children's home' as follows:

Children's homes.

(1) Subsections (2) to (6) have effect for the purposes of this Act.

(2) An establishment is a children's home (subject to the following provisions of this section) if it provides care and accommodation wholly or mainly for children.

(3) An establishment is not a children's home merely because a child is cared for and accommodated there by a parent or relative of his or by a foster parent.

(4) An establishment is not a children's home if it is-

(a) a health service hospital;
(b) an independent hospital or an independent clinic; or
(c) a residential family centre,

or if it is of a description excepted by regulations.

(5) Subject to subsection (6), an establishment is not a children's home if it is a school.

(6) A school is a children's home at any time if at that time accommodation is provided for children at the school and either-

(a) in each year that fell within the period of two years ending at that time, accommodation was provided for children, either at the school or under arrangements made by the proprietor of the school, for more than 295 days; or
(b) it is intended to provide accommodation for children, either at the school or under arrangements made by the proprietor of the school, for more than 295 days in any year;

and in this subsection 'year' means a period of twelve months.

But accommodation shall not for the purposes of paragraph (a) be regarded as provided to children for a number of days unless there is at least one child to whom it is provided for that number of days; and paragraph (b) shall be construed accordingly.

(7) For the purposes of this section a person is a foster parent in relation to a child if-

(a) he is a local authority foster parent in relation to the child;
(b) he is a foster parent with whom a child has been placed by a voluntary organisation under section 59(1)(a) of the 1989 Act; or
(c) he fosters the child privately.

This definition encompasses (subject to the exemptions in the section) community homes, voluntary homes and private (formerly registered) children's homes as defined in the Children Act 1989.

Any person who carries on or manages an establishment or agency of any description within the meaning of Part I of the CSA 2000 is required to be registered under Part II of the Act with the National Care Standards Commission or, in Wales, with the National Assembly. Failure to register in accordance with the CSA 2000 incurs criminal sanctions.

The conduct of children's homes is regulated by the Children's Homes Regulations 2001, SI 2001/3967 amended by SI 2002/865 and the Children's Homes (Wales) Regulations 2002, SI 2002/327 made under s 22 of the Care Standards Act 2000. In addition, the Secretary of State has published *Children's Homes – National Minimum Standards* (Dept of Health 2002) in accordance with s 23(1) of the 2000 Act. These standards must be taken into account in respect of Part II of the 2000 Act by the registration authority in the making of any decision, in proceedings for an emergency cancellation of registration, any appeal against cancellation of registration and any proceedings for an offence under that Part.

Sub-s (2) Shall have regard
Consider but not place any particular weight on the needs and requirements of different children.

---

54 Directions that premises be no longer used for community home *[Repealed]*

(1) Where it appears to the Secretary of State that—

(a) any premises used for the purposes of a community home are unsuitable for those purposes; or
(b) the conduct of a community home—

    (i) is not in accordance with regulations made by him under paragraph 4 of Schedule 4; or
    (ii) is otherwise unsatisfactory,

he may, by notice in writing served on the responsible body, direct that as from such date as may be specified in the notice the premises shall not be used for the purposes of a community home.

(2) Where—

(a) the Secretary of State has given a direction under subsection (1); and

(b) the direction has not been revoked,

he may at any time by order revoke the instrument of management for the home concerned.

(3) For the purposes of subsection (1), the responsible body—

(a) in relation to a community home provided by a local authority, is that local authority;

(b) in relation to a controlled community home, is the local authority specified in the home's instrument of management; and

(c) in relation to an assisted community home, is the voluntary organisation by which the home is provided.

Date in force
14 October 1991: SI 1991/828.

Amendment
Repealed by the Care Standards Act 2002, s 117(2), Sch 6

Definitions
For 'community home' see s 53; for 'the responsible body' see sub-s (3); for 'local authority' see s 105(1); for 'controlled community home' see s 53(4); for 'assisted community home' see s 53(5).

References
For service of notices under the Act generally see s 105(8)-(10); for instruments of management see Sch 4, Pt I; for the financial provisions which apply on the cessation of a community home see s 58.

Transfer of functions
Functions of the Secretary of State, so far as exercisable in relation to Wales, transferred to the National Assembly for Wales, by the National Assembly for Wales (Transfer of Functions) Order 1999, SI 1999/672, art 2, Sch 1.

55 Determination of disputes relating to controlled and assisted community homes

(1) Where any dispute relating to a controlled community home arises between the local authority specified in the home's instrument of management and—

(a) the voluntary organisation by which the home is provided; or

(b) any other local authority who have placed, or desire or are required to place, in the home a child who is looked after by them,

the dispute may be referred by either party to the Secretary of State for his determination.

(2) Where any dispute relating to an assisted community home arises between the voluntary organisation by which the home is provided and any local authority who have placed, or desire to place, in the home a child who is looked after by them, the dispute may be referred by either party to the Secretary of State for his determination.

(3) Where a dispute is referred to the Secretary of State under this section he may, in order to give effect to his determination of the dispute, give such directions as he thinks fit to the local authority or voluntary organisation concerned.

(4) This section applies even though the matter in dispute may be one which, under or by virtue of Part II of Schedule 4, is reserved for the decision, or is the responsibility, of—

(a) the local authority specified in the home's instrument of management; or

(b) (as the case may be) the voluntary organisation by which the home is provided.

(5) Where any trust deed relating to a controlled or assisted community home contains provision whereby a bishop or any other ecclesiastical or denominational authority has power to decide questions relating to religious instruction given in the home, no dispute which is capable of being dealt with in accordance with that provision shall be referred to the Secretary of State under this section.

(6) In this Part 'trust deed', in relation to a voluntary home, means any instrument (other than an instrument of management) regulating—

(a) the maintenance, management or conduct of the home; or

(b) the constitution of a body of managers or trustees of the home.

Date in force
14 October 1991: SI 1991/828.

Definitions
For 'controlled community home' see s 53(4). For 'local authority', 'voluntary organisation', 'child' see s 105(1); for 'child who is looked after by a local authority' see s 22(1); for 'assisted community home' see s 53(5); for 'trust deed' see sub-s (6).

References
For instruments of management see Sch 4, Pt I. This Part' ie Pt VI (ss 53-58 and Sch 4) (community homes).

Transfer of functions
Functions of the Secretary of State, so far as exercisable in relation to Wales, transferred to the National Assembly for Wales, by the National Assembly for Wales (Transfer of Functions) Order 1999, SI 1999/672, art 2, Sch 1.

Note
The Secretary of State is enabled to settle disputes between a local authority and a voluntary organisation about a controlled or assisted home. If the trust deed of the home gives power to an ecclesiastical authority to decide questions on religious instruction, the dispute shall not be referred to the Secretary of State.

---

56 Discontinuance by voluntary organisation of controlled or assisted community home

(1) The voluntary organisation by which a controlled or assisted community home is provided shall not cease to provide the home except after giving to the Secretary of State and the local authority specified in the home's instrument of management not less than two years' notice in writing of their intention to do so.

(2) A notice under subsection (1) shall specify the date from which the voluntary organisation intend to cease to provide the home as a community home.

(3) Where such a notice is given and is not withdrawn before the date specified in it, the home's instrument of management shall cease to have effect on that date and the home shall then cease to be a controlled or assisted community home.

(4) Where a notice is given under subsection (1) and the home's managers give notice in writing to the Secretary of State that they are unable or unwilling to continue as its managers until the date specified in the subsection (1) notice, the Secretary of State may by order—

(a) revoke the home's instrument of management; and

(b) require the local authority who were specified in that instrument to conduct the home until—

(i) the date specified in the subsection (1) notice; or

(ii) such earlier date (if any) as may be specified for the purposes of this paragraph in the order,

as if it were a community home provided by the local authority.

(5) Where the Secretary of State imposes a requirement under subsection (4)(b)—

(a) nothing in the trust deed for the home shall affect the conduct of the home by the local authority;

(b) the Secretary of State may by order direct that for the purposes of any provision specified in the direction and made by or under any enactment relating to community homes (other than this section) the home shall, until the date or earlier date specified as mentioned in subsection (4)(b), be treated as a controlled or assisted community home;

(c) except in so far as the Secretary of State so directs, the home shall until that date be treated for the purposes of any such enactment as a community home provided by the local authority; and

(d) on the date or earlier date specified as mentioned in subsection (4)(b) the home shall cease to be a community home.

Date in force
14 October 1991: SI 1991/828.

Definitions
For 'voluntary organisation', 'local authority' see s 105(1); for 'controlled community home' see s 53(4); for 'assisted community home' see s 53(5); for 'trust deed' see s 55(6).

References
For instruments of management see Sch 4, Pt I; for service of notices under the Act generally see s 105(8)-(10); for the financial provisions which apply on the cessation of a community home see s 58.

Transfer of functions
Functions of the Secretary of State, so far as exercisable in relation to Wales, transferred to the National Assembly for Wales, by the National Assembly for Wales (Transfer of Functions) Order 1999, SI 1999/672, art 2, Sch 1.

57 Closure by local authority of controlled or assisted community home

(1) The local authority specified in the instrument of management for a controlled or assisted community home may give—

(a) the Secretary of State; and

(b) the voluntary organisation by which the home is provided,

not less than two years' notice in writing of their intention to withdraw their designation of the home as a controlled or assisted community home.

(2) A notice under subsection (1) shall specify the date ('the specified date') on which the designation is to be withdrawn.

(3) Where—

(a) a notice is given under subsection (1) in respect of a controlled or assisted community home;

(b) the home's managers give notice in writing to the Secretary of State that they are unable or unwilling to continue as managers until the specified date; and

(c) the managers' notice is not withdrawn,

the Secretary of State may by order revoke the home's instrument of management from such date earlier than the specified date as may be specified in the order.

(4) Before making an order under subsection (3), the Secretary of State shall consult the local authority and the voluntary organisation.

(5) Where a notice has been given under subsection (1) and is not withdrawn, the home's instrument of management shall cease to have effect on—

(a) the specified date; or

(b) where an earlier date has been specified under subsection (3), that earlier date,

and the home shall then cease to be a community home.

Date in force
14 October 1991: SI 1991/828.

Definitions
For 'local authority', 'voluntary organisation' see s 105(1); for 'community home' see s 53; for 'controlled community home' see s 53(4); for 'assisted community home' see s 53(5); for 'the specified date' see sub-s (2).

References
For instruments of management see Sch 4, Pt I. For service of notices under the Act generally see s 105(8)-(10). For the financial provisions which apply on the cessation of a community home see s 58.

Transfer of functions
Functions of the Secretary of State, so far as exercisable in relation to Wales, transferred to the National Assembly for Wales, by the National Assembly for Wales (Transfer of Functions) Order 1999, SI 1999/672, art 2, Sch 1.

58 Financial provisions applicable on cessation of controlled or assisted community home or disposal etc of premises

(1) Where—

(a) the instrument of management for a controlled or assisted community home is revoked or otherwise ceases to have effect under section *54(2)*, 56(3) or (4)(a) or 57(3) or (5); or

(b) any premises used for the purposes of such a home are (at any time after 13th January 1987) disposed of, or put to use otherwise than for those purposes,

the proprietor shall become liable to pay compensation ('the appropriate compensation') in accordance with this section.

(2) Where the instrument of management in force at the relevant time relates—

(a) to a controlled community home; or

(b) to an assisted community home which, at any time before the instrument came into force, was a controlled community home,

the appropriate compensation is a sum equal to that part of the value of any premises which is attributable to expenditure incurred in relation to the premises, while the home was a controlled community home, by the authority who were then the responsible authority.

(3) Where the instrument of management in force at the relevant time relates—

(a) to an assisted community home; or

(b) to a controlled community home which, at any time before the instrument came into force, was an assisted community home,

the appropriate compensation is a sum equal to that part of the value of the premises which is attributable to the expenditure of money provided by way of grant under section 82, section 65 of the Children and Young Persons Act 1969 or section 82 of the Child Care Act 1980.

(4) Where the home is, at the relevant time, conducted in premises which formerly were used as an approved school or were an approved probation hostel or home, the appropriate compensation is a sum equal to that part of the value of the premises which is attributable to the expenditure—

(a) of sums paid towards the expenses of the managers of an approved school under section 104 of the Children and Young Persons Act 1933; . . .

(b) of sums paid under section 51(3)(c) of the Powers of Criminal Courts Act 1973 [or section 20(1)(c) of the Probation Service Act 1993] in relation to expenditure on approved probation hostels or homes[; or

(c) of sums paid under section 3, 5 or 9 of the Criminal Justice and Court Services Act 2000 in relation to expenditure on approved premises (within the meaning of Part I of that Act)].

(5) The appropriate compensation shall be paid—

(a) in the case of compensation payable under subsection (2), to the authority who were the responsible authority at the relevant time; and

(b) in any other case, to the Secretary of State.

(6) In this section—

'disposal' includes the grant of a tenancy and any other conveyance, assignment, transfer, grant, variation or extinguishment of an interest in or right over land, whether made by instrument or otherwise;

'premises' means any premises or part of premises (including land) used for the purposes of the home and belonging to the proprietor;

'the proprietor' means—

(a) the voluntary organisation by which the home is, at the relevant time, provided; or

(b) if the premises are not, at the relevant time, vested in that organisation, the persons in whom they are vested;

'the relevant time' means the time immediately before the liability to pay arises under subsection (1); and

'the responsible authority' means the local authority specified in the instrument of management in question.

(7) For the purposes of this section an event of a kind mentioned in subsection (1)(b) shall be taken to have occurred—

(a) in the case of a disposal, on the date on which the disposal was completed or, in the case of a disposal which is effected by a series of transactions, the date on which the last of those transactions was completed;

(b) in the case of premises which are put to different use, on the date on which they first begin to be put to their new use.

(8) The amount of any sum payable under this section shall be determined in accordance with such arrangements—

(a) as may be agreed between the voluntary organisation by which the home is, at the relevant time, provided and the responsible authority or (as the case may be) the Secretary of State; or

(b) in default of agreement, as may be determined by the Secretary of State.

(9) With the agreement of the responsible authority or (as the case may be) the Secretary of State, the liability to pay any sum under this section may be discharged, in whole or in part, by the transfer of any premises.

(10) This section has effect regardless of—

(a) anything in any trust deed for a controlled or assisted community home;

(b) the provisions of any enactment or instrument governing the disposition of the property of a voluntary organisation.

Date in force
14 October 1991: SI 1991/828. But note s 58(1)(b) for disputes after 13 January 1987.

Amendment
Sub-s (4): Probation Service Act 1993, Sch 3, para 9(2).

Definitions
For 'controlled community home' see s 53(4), for 'assisted community home' see s 53(5); for 'appropriate compensation', see sub-s (1); for 'the relevant time', 'disposal', 'premises', 'the proprietor', 'relevant premises', 'the responsible authority', see sub-s (6); for 'trust deed' see s 55(6).

References
For instruments of management see Sch 4, Pt I; for disposal or change of use of premises see sub-s (7); for the amount of any sum payable under this section see sub-s (8) and for the payment of such funds into the consolidated fund see s 106(2).

Note

Section 58 replaced former provisions in the CCA 1980, s 44 but was completely redrafted to fill a lacuna in the previous legislation. In an unreported case referred to in the Law on Child Care and Family Services (Cm 62, 1987) para 83, (*Norton v DHSS*) it had been held that under the CCA 1980, s 44 the value to be taken into account for repayment to central or local government was limited to the value of the home as it existed at the time of closure and parts of the home disposed of prior to closure could not be taken into account.

Transfer of functions

Functions of the Secretary of State, so far as exercisable in relation to Wales, transferred to the National Assembly for Wales, by the National Assembly for Wales (Transfer of Functions) Order 1999, SI 1999/672, art 2, Sch 1.

PART VII

VOLUNTARY HOMES AND VOLUNTARY ORGANISATIONS

59 Provision of accommodation by voluntary organisations

(1) Where a voluntary organisation provide accommodation for a child, they shall do so by—

(a) placing him (subject to subsection (2)) with—

    (i)   a family;

    (ii) a relative of his; or

    (iii) any other suitable person,

on such terms as to payment by the organisation and otherwise as the organisation may determine;

(b) maintaining him in a voluntary home;

(c) maintaining him in a community home;

(d) maintaining him in a registered children's home;

(e) maintaining him in a home provided by the Secretary of State under section 82(5) on such terms as the Secretary of State may from time to time determine;

[(aa) maintaining him in an appropriate children's home;] or

(f) making such other arrangements (subject to subsection (3)) as seem appropriate to them.

[(1A) Where under subsection (1)(aa) a local authority maintains a child in a home provided, equipped and maintained by the Secretary of State under section 82(5), it shall do so on such terms as the Secretary of State may from time to time determine.]

(2) The Secretary of State may make regulations as to the placing of children with foster parents by voluntary organisations and the regulations may, in particular, make provision which (with any necessary modifications) is similar to the provision that may be made under section 23(2)(a).

(3) The Secretary of State may make regulations as to the arrangements which may be made under subsection (1)(f) and the regulations may, in particular, make provision which (with any necessary modifications) is similar to the provision that may be made under section 23(2)(f).

(4) The Secretary of State may make regulations requiring any voluntary organisation who are providing accommodation for a child—

(a) to review his case; and

(b) to consider any representations (including any complaint) made to them by any person falling within a prescribed class of person,

in accordance with the provisions of the regulations.

(5) Regulations under subsection (4) may in particular make provision which (with any necessary modifications) is similar to the provision that may be made under section 26.

(6) Regulations under subsections (2) to (4) may provide that any person who, without reasonable excuse, contravenes or fails to comply with a regulation shall be guilty of an offence and liable on summary conviction to a fine not exceeding level 4 on the standard scale.

Date in force
14 October 1991: SI 1991/828.109.

Amendments
Sub-s (1): para (aa) substituted, for paras (b)–(e) as originally enacted, by the Care Standards Act 2000, s 116, Sch 4, para 14(1), (8)(a).

Definitions
For 'voluntary organisation', 'child' and 'relative' see s 105(1); for 'voluntary home' see s 60(3); for 'community home' see s 53; for 'registered children's home' see s 63(8); for 'appropriate children's home' see s 23; for 'the standard scale' see the CJA 1982, s 37(2) (3) as amended.

Note
This section places voluntary organisations in the same position as local authorities with respect to the provision of accommodation cf s 23(2). Voluntary homes are provided by not-for-profit organisations (voluntary organisations) and must be registered with the Secretary of State (for procedure, see Sch 5). For placement of a child by a voluntary organisation see s 60. For the duty on a voluntary organisation to safeguard and promote the welfare of any child it arranges or provides accommodation for see s 61. For duties on local authorities regarding any voluntary organisation within its area or any voluntary organisation outside its area providing accommodation for a child on behalf of the authority see s 62.

Registration and inspection of children's homes
See the note to s 53, ante.

Sub-s (2) Foster parents
The placing of a child with foster parents by a voluntary organisation is not private fostering and is not subject to the provisions of Part IX (ss 66-70 and Sch 8) (see Sch 8, para 2(1)(c)) although the 'usual fostering limit' will apply so that where more than three children who are not siblings with respect to each other are placed by a voluntary organisation, that placement will be treated as a placement in a children's home unless it is exempted by the local authority (Sch 7).

Regulations
See the Arrangements for Placement of Children (General) Regulations 1991, SI 1991/890 amended by SI 1991/2033, SI 1993/3069, SI 1995/2015, SI 1997/649 and SI 2002/546; the Foster Placement (Children) Regulations 1991, SI 1991/910 amended by SI 1995/2015, SI 1997/2308, SI 1999/2768 and SI 2001/2992 (England) and 3443 (Wales) revoked in so far as they apply to England and substituted by the Fostering Services Regulations 2002, SI 2002/57 amended by SI 2002/865.

Sub-s (3) Regulations
See the Arrangements for Placement of Children (General) Regulations 1991, SI 1991/890 amended by SI 1991/2033, SI 1993/3069, SI 1995/2015, SI 1997/649 and SI 2002/546.

Sub-s (4), (5) Regulations
See the Representations Procedure (Children) Regulations 1991, SI 1991/894 amended by SI 1991/2033, SI 1993/3069 and SI 2002/546; the Review of Children's Cases Regulations 1991, SI 1991/895 amended by SI 1991/2033, SI 1993/3069, SI 1995/2015, SI 1997/649 and SI 2002/546.

60 Registration and regulation of voluntary homes [Voluntary homes]

(1) No voluntary home shall be carried on unless it is registered in a register to be kept for the purposes of this section by the Secretary of State.

(2) The register may be kept by means of a computer.

(3) In this Act 'voluntary home' means any home or other institution providing care and accommodation for children which is carried on by a voluntary organisation but does not include—

    (a)   a nursing home, mental nursing home or residential care home [(other than a small home)];

    (b)   a school;

    (c)   any health service hospital;

    (d)   any community home;

    (e)   any home or other institution provided, equipped and maintained by the Secretary of State; or

    (f)   any home which is exempted by regulations made for the purposes of this section by the Secretary of State.

[(3) In this Act 'voluntary home' means a children's home which is carried on by a voluntary organisation but does not include a community home.]

(4) Schedule 5 shall have effect for the purpose of supplementing the provisions of this Part.

Date in force
14 October 1991: SI 1991/828.

Amendment
Sub-s (3): Registered Homes (Amendment) Act 1991, s 2(6). Sub-s (3): CSA 2000 Sch 4.

Definitions
For 'voluntary home' see sub-s (3); for 'child', 'voluntary organisation', 'nursing home', 'mental nursing home', 'residential care home', 'school', 'health service hospital', 'local authority' see s 105(1); for 'community home' see s 53.

References
' This Part' ie Pt VII (ss 59-62 and Sch 5) (voluntary homes and voluntary organisations). For the circumstances in which the Secretary of State may make a grant to a voluntary organisation in connection with a voluntary home see s 82(4); for the power to inspect a voluntary home and to hold inquiries into any matter connected with a voluntary home see ss 80 and 81.

Note
'Voluntary home' is defined so as to exclude establishments which are regulated by other statutory provisions. Regulations as to the conduct of voluntary homes may be made by the Secretary of State under Sch 5, Pt II to the 1989 Act. Regulations may also provide for the disqualification of persons in relation to voluntary homes (Sch 5, para 8).

Transfer of functions
Functions of the Secretary of State, so far as exercisable in relation to Wales, transferred to the National Assembly for Wales, by the National Assembly for Wales (Transfer of Functions) Order 1999, SI 1999/672, art 2, Sch 1.

Registration
For procedure see Sch 5, Pt I. Express provision is made for the register to be maintained by computer.

---

61 Duties of voluntary organisations

(1) Where a child is accommodated by or on behalf of a voluntary organisation, it shall be the duty of the organisation—

    (a)   to safeguard and promote his welfare;

    (b)   to make such use of the services and facilities available for children cared for by their own parents as appears to the organisation reasonable in his case; and

    (c)   to advise, assist and befriend him with a view to promoting his welfare when he ceases to be so accommodated.

(2) Before making any decision with respect to any such child the organisation shall, so far as is reasonably practicable, ascertain the wishes and feelings of—

    (a)   the child;

    (b)   his parents;

    (c)   any person who is not a parent of his but who has parental responsibility for him; and

(d) any other person whose wishes and feelings the organisation consider to be relevant,

regarding the matter to be decided.

(3) In making any such decision the organisation shall give due consideration—

(a) having regard to the child's age and understanding, to such wishes and feelings of his as they have been able to ascertain;

(b) to such other wishes and feelings mentioned in subsection (2) as they have been able to ascertain; and

(c) to the child's religious persuasion, racial origin and cultural and linguistic background.

Date in force
14 October 1991: SI 1991/828.

Amendments
Sub-s (6): in para (c) words "section 22 of the Care Standards Act 2000" in square brackets substituted by the Care Standards Act 2000, s 116, Sch 4, para 14(1), (10)(a). Date in force (in relation to England): 1 April 2002: see SI 2001/4150, art 3(3)(a); for transitional provisions see SI 2001/4150, arts 3(2), 4(1), (3), (4) and SI 2002/1493, art 4 (as amended by SI 2002/1493, art 6).

Sub-s (10): inserted by the Care Standards Act 2000, s 105(5).

Definitions
For 'child' and 'voluntary organisation' see s 105(1); for 'parental responsibility' see s 3.

Note
Compare the similar duties imposed on local authorities in respect of children they are looking after: s 22(2). A local authority has a duty to provide aftercare for children formerly looked after by a voluntary organisation (s 24).

Applications for orders under section 8
The embargo under s 9(2) against local authorities applying for residence or contact orders does not apply to voluntary organisations, but the circumstances in which the court will give leave to apply for such orders must be limited. By applying for such an order the applicant would be circumventing the general principle applicable to local authorities, that the 'threshold criteria' in s 31(2) must be satisfied before the authority can intervene compulsorily in family life. Although an application by a voluntary organisation may not necessarily be equated with intervention by the State, such an organisation perhaps may not be seen to be in a similar position to an individual.

---

62 Duties of local authorities

(1) Every local authority shall satisfy themselves that any voluntary organisation providing accommodation—

(a) within the authority's area for any child; or

(b) outside that area for any child on behalf of the authority,

are satisfactorily safeguarding and promoting the welfare of the children so provided with accommodation.

(2) Every local authority shall arrange for children who are accommodated within their area by or on behalf of voluntary organisations to be visited, from time to time, in the interests of their welfare.

(3) The Secretary of State may make regulations—

(a) requiring every child who is accommodated within a local authority's area, by or on behalf of a voluntary organisation, to be visited by an officer of the authority—

(i) in prescribed circumstances; and

(ii) on specified occasions or within specified periods; and

(b) imposing requirements which must be met by any local authority, or officer of a local authority, carrying out functions under this section.

(4) Subsection (2) does not apply in relation to community homes.

(5) Where a local authority are not satisfied that the welfare of any child who is accommodated by or on behalf of a voluntary organisation is being satisfactorily safeguarded or promoted they shall—

(a) unless they consider that it would not be in the best interests of the child, take such steps as are reasonably practicable to secure that the care and accommodation of the child is undertaken by—

(i) a parent of his;
(ii) any person who is not a parent of his but who has parental responsibility for him; or
(iii) a relative of his; and

(b) consider the extent to which (if at all) they should exercise any of their functions with respect to the child.

(6) Any person authorised by a local authority may, for the purpose of enabling the authority to discharge their duties under this section—

(a) enter, at any reasonable time, and inspect any premises in which children are being accommodated as mentioned in subsection (1) or (2);
(b) inspect any children there;
(c) require any person to furnish him with such records of a kind required to be kept by regulations made under *paragraph 7 of Schedule 5* [section 22 of the Care Standards Act 2000] (in whatever form they are held), or allow him to inspect such records, as he may at any time direct.

(7) Any person exercising the power conferred by subsection (6) shall, if asked to do so, produce some duly authenticated document showing his authority to do so.

(8) Any person authorised to exercise the power to inspect records conferred by subsection (6)—

(a) shall be entitled at any reasonable time to have access to, and inspect and check the operation of, any computer and any associated apparatus or material which is or has been in use in connection with the records in question; and
(b) may require—

(i) the person by whom or on whose behalf the computer is or has been so used; or
(ii) any person having charge of, or otherwise concerned with the operation of, the computer, apparatus or material,

to afford him such assistance as he may reasonably require.

(9) Any person who intentionally obstructs another in the exercise of any power conferred by subsection (6) or (8) shall be guilty of an offence and liable on summary conviction to a fine not exceeding level 3 on the standard scale.

[(10) This section does not apply in relation to any voluntary organisation which is an institution within the further education sector, as defined in section 91 of the Further and Higher Education Act 1992, or a school.]

Date in force
14 October 1991: SI 1991/828.115.

Amendment
Sub-s (6): in para (c) words "section 22 of the Care Standards Act 2000" in square brackets subsituted by the Care Standards Act 2000, s 116, Sch 4, Para 14 (1).

Definitions
For 'local authority', 'voluntary organisation', 'child', 'functions' and 'relative' see s 105(1); for 'community home' see s 53; for 'parental responsibility' see s 3.

References
For power to issue warrant to authorise a constable to assist in exercising the power under sub-ss (6) or (8) see s 102; for 'the standard scale' see the CJA 1982, s 37(2) (3) as amended.

Transfer of functions
Functions of the Secretary of State, so far as exercisable in relation to Wales, transferred to the National Assembly for Wales, by the National Assembly for Wales (Transfer of Functions) Order 1999, SI 1999/672, art 2, Sch 1

Sub-s (2) From time to time
This section is based on provisions formerly contained in the CCA 1980, s 68. The regulation making powers of the 1980 Act were not used and accordingly the frequency and nature of the visiting was left to the discretion of the local authority. At the time of writing no regulations have yet been made under s 62(3) of the 1989 Act. However, the frequency of visits by a local authority is prescribed by the Foster Placement (Children) Regulations 1991 and now the Fostering Services Regulations 2002.

Sub-s (3) Regulations
See the Foster Placement (Children) Regulations 1991, SI 1991/910 amended by SI 1995/2015, SI 1997/2308 and SI 1999/2768 revoked in so far as they apply to England and substituted by the Fostering Services Regulations 2002, SI 2002/57 amended by SI 2002/865.

Sub-s (6) May enter
If they so choose, but they cannot force entry. Their remedy is to seek a warrant under s 102(1) where entry has been prevented or refused or they are likely to be prevented from using these powers. The warrant of entry will be executed by a constable who may be accompanied by the person applying for the warrant.

Sub-s (8)
For where access is refused see s 102(1) for warrant of entry.

Sub-s (9) Intentionally obstructs
The former legislation merely required an obstruction (CCA 1980, s 68(5)). 'Obstructs' need not involve physical violence: *Hinchliffe v Sheldon* [1955] 3 All ER 406, [1955] 1 WLR 1207. Doing anything which makes it more difficult for a person to carry out his duty may amount to obstruction: *Rice v Connolly* [1966] 2 QB 414, [1966] 2 All ER 649, but standing by and doing nothing, in the absence of a legal duty to act, is not obstruction: *Swallow v LCC* [1916] 1 KB 224. For cases on 'wilful obstruction': *Hills v Ellis* [1983] QB 680, [1983] 1 All ER 667; *Moore v Green* [1983] 1 All ER 663; *Willmott v Atack* [1977] QB 498, [1976] 3 All ER 794, 141 JP 35.

PART VIII
[PRIVATE] REGISTERED CHILDREN'S HOMES

63 Children not to be cared for and accommodated in unregistered children's home [Private children's homes etc]

(1) No child shall be cared for and provided with accommodation in a children's home unless the home is registered under this Part.

(2) The register may be kept by means of a computer.

(3) For the purposes of this Part, 'a children's home'—

(a) means a home which provides (or usually provides or is intended to provide) care and accommodation wholly or mainly for [children]; but

(b) does not include a home which is exempted by or under any of the following provisions of this section or by regulations made for the purposes of this sub-section by the Secretary of State.

(4) A child is not cared for and accommodated in a children's home when he is cared for and accommodated by—

(a) a parent of his;

(b) a person who is not a parent of his but who has parental responsibility for him; or

(c) any relative of his.

(5) A home is not a children's home for the purposes of this Part if it is—

(a) a community home;
(b) a voluntary home;
(c) a residential care home [(other than a small home)], nursing home or mental nursing home;
(d) a health service hospital;
(e) a home provided, equipped and maintained by the Secretary of State; or
(f) a school (but subject to subsection (6)).

[(6) An independent school is a children's home at any time if at that time accommodation is provided for children at the school and either—

(a) in each year that fell within the period of two years ending at that time accommodation was provided for more than three of the children at the school, or under arrangements made by the proprietor of the school, for more than 295 days in that year, or
(b) it is intended to provide accommodation for more than three of the children at the school, or under arrangements made by the proprietor of the school, for more than 295 days in any year,

unless the school is approved by the Secretary of State under section 347(1) of the Education Act 1996 (approval of independent schools for children with statements); and in this subsection 'year' means a period of twelve months and 'proprietor' has the same meaning as in that Act.]

(7) A child shall not be treated as cared for and accommodated in a children's home when—

(a) any person mentioned in subsection (4)(a) or (b) is living at the home; or
(b) the person caring for him is doing so in his personal capacity and not in the course of carrying out his duties in relation to the home.

(8) In this Act 'a registered children's home' means a children's home registered under this Part.

(9) In this section 'home' includes any institution.

(10) Where any child is at any time cared for and accommodated in a children's home which is not a registered children's home, the person carrying on the home shall be—

(a) guilty of an offence; and
(b) liable to a fine not exceeding level 5 on the standard scale,

unless he has a reasonable excuse.

(11) Schedule 6 shall have effect with respect to [private] children's homes.

(12) Schedule 7 shall have effect for the purpose of setting out the circumstances in which a person may foster more than three children without being treated[, for the purposes of this Act and the Care Standards Act 2000,] as carrying on a children's home.

Date in force
14 October 1991: SI 1991/828.

Amendment
Sub-s (3): Care Standards Act 2000, s 40. Sub-s (5): Registered Homes (Amendment) Act 1991, s 2(6). Sub-s (6): Substituted by the EA 1996, Sch 37, para 86.
Sub-ss (1)–(10): repealed by the Care Standards Act 2000, s 177(2), Sch 6. Date in force (in relation to England): 1 April 2002: see SI 2001/3852, art 3(7)(j); for transitional provisions see Sch 1, paras 7, 10, 14 thereto.

Definitions
For 'child', 'local authority', 'residential care home', 'nursing home', 'mental nursing home', 'health service hospital', 'school', 'independent school', 'relative', 'private children's home see s 105(1); for 'a children's home' see sub-s (3); for 'home' see sub-s (9); for 'parental responsibility' see s 3; for 'community home' see s 53; for 'voluntary home' see s 60(3); for 'registered children's

home' see sub-s (8); for 'children's home' see s 23(10) as applied to the whole act by s 105(1) and see note to s 53, ante.

References
For 'the standard scale' see the CJA 1982, s 37(2)(3) as amended; for the inspection of registered children's homes see s 80(1)(a); for the power to hold inquiries into any matter connected with a registered children's home see s 81; for transitional provisions see s 108(6) and Sch 14, para 32.

Note
Part VIII (ss 63-65, Sch 6 and 7) replaces in a modified form the provisions of the Children's Homes Act 1982 which was never brought into force. The scheme of Pt VIII is to control homes or institutions for children which are privately run for profit.

Registration and inspection of children's homes
See the note to s 53 ante. S 40 of the Care Standards Act 2000 Act has amended s 63(3)(a) of the 1989 Act as an interim measure to require all private children's homes (and not just those accommodating 4 or more children) to be registered. At present, until the provisions of the Care Standards Act 2000 are fully in force registration is with the local authority. Thereafter registration will be with the Secretary of State. For the welfare of children in private children's homes, and the duty on the person carrying on the home to safeguard and protect the children's welfare see s 64.

Regulations
See the Children's Homes Regulations 2001, SI 2001/3967 amended by SI 2002/865 and the Children's Homes (Wales) Regulations 2002, SI 2002/327 made under the Care Standards Act 2000.

---

64 Welfare of children in children's homes

(1) Where a child is accommodated in a [private] children's home, it shall be the duty of the person carrying on the home to—

(a) safeguard and promote the child's welfare;

(b) make such use of the services and facilities available for children cared for by their own parents as appears to that person reasonable in the case of the child; and

(c) advise, assist and befriend him with a view to promoting his welfare when he ceases to be so accommodated.

(2) Before making any decision with respect to any such child the person carrying on the home shall, so far as is reasonably practicable, ascertain the wishes and feelings of—

(a) the child;

(b) his parents;

(c) any other person who is not a parent of his but who has parental responsibility for him; and

(d) any person whose wishes and feelings the person carrying on the home considers to be relevant,

regarding the matter to be decided.

(3) In making any such decision the person concerned shall give due consideration—

(a) having regard to the child's age and understanding, to such wishes and feelings of his as he has been able to ascertain;

(b) to such other wishes and feelings mentioned in subsection (2) as he has been able to ascertain; and

(c) to the child's religious persuasion, racial origin and cultural and linguistic background.

(4) Section 62, except subsection (4), shall apply in relation to any person who is carrying on a [private] children's home as it applies in relation to any voluntary organisation.

Date in force
14 October 1991: SI 1991/828.

Amendments
Sub-s (1): (word "private" in square brackets inserted by the Care Standards Act 2000, s 116, Sch 4, para 14(1), (12).
Sub-s (4): (word "private" in square brackets inserted by the Care Standards Act 2000, s 116, Sch 4, para 14(1), (12).

Definitions
For 'child', 'voluntary organisation' and 'private children's home' see s 105(1); for 'children's home' see s 63(3) and s 23(10) as applied to the whole Act by s 105(1) and see note to s 53, ante; for 'parental responsibility' see s 3.

Reference
For power to issue a warrant to authorise a constable to assist in exercising the power under sub-s (4) see s 102.

Note
Sections 64 and 65 apply whether or not a private children's home is currently registered- for example, during the period when an application for registration is being considered or where a home should be registered but is not and the welfare of the children in the home is in issue. Cf a local authority's duties under ss 22 and 24(1).

Sub-s (4)
The duties of local authorities to ensure that the welfare of the children are being satisfactorily safeguarded and promoted.

---

65   Persons disqualified from carrying on, or being employed in, children's homes

(1) A person who is disqualified (under section 68) from fostering a child privately shall not carry on, or be otherwise concerned in the management of, or have any financial interest in, a children's home unless he has—

(a)   disclosed to *the responsible authority* [the appropriate authority] the fact that he is so disqualified; and

(b)   obtained *their* [its] written consent.

(2) No person shall employ a person who is so disqualified in a children's home unless he has—

(a)   disclosed to *the responsible authority* [the appropriate authority] the fact that that person is so disqualified; and

(b)   obtained *their* [its] written consent.

(3) Where *an authority refuse to give their consent under this section, they* [the appropriate authority refuses to give its consent under this section, it] shall inform the applicant by a written notice which states—

(a)   the reason for the refusal;

[(b)   the applicant's right to appeal under section 65A against the refusal to the Tribunal established under section 9 of the Protection of Children Act 1999]; and

(c)   the time within which he may do so.

(4) Any person who contravenes subsection (1) or (2) shall be guilty of an offence and liable on summary conviction to imprisonment for a term not exceeding six months or to a fine not exceeding level 5 on the standard scale or to both.

(5) Where a person contravenes subsection (2) he shall not be guilty of an offence if he proves that he did not know, and had no reasonable grounds for believing, that the person whom he was employing was disqualified under section 68.

[(6) In this section and section 65A 'appropriate authority' means—

(a)   in relation to England, the National Care Standards Commission; and

(b)   in relation to Wales, the National Assembly for Wales.]

Date in force
14 October 1991: SI 1991/828.

Amendments
Sub-s (1), (2), (3), (5), (6) of the Care Standards Act 2000. Sub-s (1): words "the appropriate authority" and "its" in square brackets substituted by the Care Standards Act 2000, s 116, Sch 4, para 14(1), (13)(a). Date in force (in relation to England): 1 April 2002: see the Care Standards Act 2000, s 122 and SI 2002/1493, art 3(2)(b); for transitional provisions see SI 2002/1493, arts 3(1), 4.
Sub-s (2): words "the appropriate authority" and "its" in square brackets substituted by the Care Standards Act 2000, s 116, Sch 4, para 14(1), (13)(a). Date in force (in relation to England): 1 April 2002: see the Care Standards Act 2000, s 122 and SI 2002/1493, art 3(2)(b); for transitional provisions see SI 2002/1493, arts 3(1), 4.

Definitions
For 'fostering a child privately' see s 66(1)(b) as applied to the whole Act by s 105(1); for 'children's home' see s 63(3) see sub-s (6); for 'the responsible authority' see Sch 6, Pt I para 3(1); for 'the appropriate authority'.

References
For service of notices under the Act generally see s 105(8)-(10); for 'the standard scale' see the CJA 1982, s 37(2) (3) as amended.

Person disqualified
Persons disqualified from fostering privately are disqualified under s 65. The Secretary of State has power under s 68(2) to make regulations prescribing those persons who are disqualified from being private foster parents: see the Disqualification for Caring for Children Regulations 1991, SI 1991/2094 and the Disqualification for Caring for Children (England) Regulations 2002, SI 2002/635.

Sub-s (5) If he proves
On the balance of probabilities: *R v Carr-Briant* [1943] KB 607, [1943] 2 All ER 156, 107 JP 167, CCA. Under the former CHA 1982, s 10(4) the prosecution had to prove beyond reasonable doubt that the defendant knowingly employed a disqualified person. Now once the prosecution have proved that such a person was employed by the defendant, he must prove not only that he did not know of the disqualification but also a further requirement that he had no reasonable cause to know of the disqualification.

[65A   Appeal against refusal of authority to give consent under section 65]

[(1) An appeal against a decision of an appropriate authority under section 65 shall lie to the Tribunal established under section 9 of the Protection of Children Act 1999.

(2) On an appeal the Tribunal may confirm the authority's decision or direct it to give the consent in question.]

Date in force
Date to be appointed.

Amendment
Inserted by the Care Standards Act 2000, s 116, Sch 4 para 14(1), (14).

PART IX
PRIVATE ARRANGEMENTS FOR FOSTERING CHILDREN

66   Privately fostered children

(1) In this Part—

(a) 'a privately fostered child' means a child who is under the age of sixteen and who is cared for, and provided with accommodation [in their own home] by, someone other than—

    (i)   a parent of his;

    (ii)   a person who is not a parent of his but who has parental responsibility for him; or

    (iii) a relative of his; and

(b) 'to foster a child privately' means to look after the child in circumstances in which he is a privately fostered child as defined by this section.

(2) A child is not a privately fostered child if the person caring for and accommodating him—

(a) has done so for a period of less than 28 days; and

(b) does not intend to do so for any longer period.

(3) Subsection (1) is subject to—

(a) the provisions of section 63; and

(b) the exceptions made by a paragraphs 1 to 5 of Schedule 8.

(4) In the case of a child who is disabled, subsection (1)(a) shall have effect as if for 'sixteen' there were substituted 'eighteen'.

[(4A) The Secretary of State may by regulations make provision as to the circumstances in which a person who provides accommodation to a child is, or is not, to be treated as providing him with accommodation in the person's own home.]

(5) Schedule 8 shall have effect for the purposes of supplementing the provision made by this Part.

Date in force
14 October 1991: SI 1991/828.

Amendments

Sub-s (1): Care Standards Act 2000, Sch 4, para 15. Sub-s (4A): inserted by the Care Standards Act 2000, Sch 4, para 15.

Definitions
For 'a privately fostered child' see sub-s (1)(a); for 'parental responsibility' see s 3; for 'relative' see s 105(1); for 'to foster a child privately' see sub-s (1)(b); for 'disabled' see s 17(11) as applied to the whole Act by s 105(1).

References
'This Part' ie Part IX, ss 66-70 and Sch 8 (private arrangements for fostering children). For transitional provisions see s 108(6) and Sch 14, para 32.

Sub-s (1) Relative
This is defined as a 'grandparent, brother, sister, uncle or aunt (whether of the full blood or half blood or by affinity) or step-parent. The definition formerly contained in the FCA 1980, s 22 included, where the child was illegitimate, the father and his relatives. This definition is no longer necessary because references to any relationship between two persons shall, unless the contrary intention appears, be construed without regard to whether or not the father and mother of either of them have been married to each other (see the FLRA 1987, s 1), also note the inclusion of step-parents.

Note
A person may be a foster parent notwithstanding he receives no reward or financial assistance for caring for the child.

Sub-s (2) Period of less than 28 days
In Surrey County Council v Battersby [1965] 2 QB 194, [1965] 1 All ER 273, 129 JP 116, a case under the CA 1958 where the relevant period was described as 'for a period of more than 27 days' it was held that the provisions were aimed at the intention of the person taking in the child, and that intention could be inferred from the facts. In that case the parents agreed with the foster parent that the child would remain with the foster parent for an indefinite period, returning to the parents for periodical weekends. It was held that the weekends did not interrupt the overall period.

---

67 Welfare of privately fostered children

(1) It shall be the duty of every local authority to satisfy themselves that the welfare of children who are privately fostered within their area is being satisfactorily safeguarded and promoted and to secure that such advice is given to those caring for them as appears to the authority to be needed.

(2) The Secretary of State may make regulations—

(a) requiring every child who is privately fostered within a local authority's area to be visited by an officer of the authority—

    (i)   in prescribed circumstances; and

    (ii)   on specified occasions or within specified periods; and

(b) imposing requirements which are to be met by any local authority, or officer of a local authority, in carrying out functions under this section.

(3) Where any person who is authorised by a local authority to visit privately fostered children has reasonable cause to believe that—

(a) any privately fostered child is being accommodated in premises within the authority's area; or

(b) it is proposed to accommodate any such child in any such premises,

he may at any reasonable time inspect those premises and any children there.

(4) Any person exercising the power under subsection (3) shall, if so required, produce some duly authenticated document showing his authority to do so.

(5) Where a local authority are not satisfied that the welfare of any child who is privately fostered within their area is being satisfactorily safeguarded or promoted they shall—

(a) unless they consider that it would not be in the best interests of the child, take such steps as are reasonably practicable to secure that the care and accommodation of the child is undertaken by—

    (i)   a parent of his;

    (ii)   any person who is not a parent of his but who has parental responsibility for him; or

    (iii) a relative of his; and

(b) consider the extent to which (if at all) they should exercise any of their functions under this Act with respect to the child.

Date in force
14 October 1991: SI 1991/828.

Definitions
For 'local authority', 'child', 'relative', 'functions' see s 105(1); for 'a privately fostered child' see s 66(1)(a); for 'parental responsibility' see s 3.

References
For the offence of intentionally obstructing a person exercising the power under sub-s (3) see s 70(1)(c) in particular and s 70(4) concerning the punishment for such offence. For the inspection of premises where a foster child is living see s 80(1)(g). For power to issue a warrant to authorise a constable to assist in exercising the power under sub-s (3) see s 102.

Transfer of functions
Functions of the Secretary of State, so far as exercisable in relation to Wales, transferred to the National Assembly for Wales, by the National Assembly for Wales (Transfer of Functions) Order 1999, SI 1999/672, art 2, Sch 1

Sub-s (2) Regulations
See the Children (Private Arrangements for Fostering) Regulations 1991, SI 1991/2050 amended by SI 1998/646.

Premises
This will mean the whole of the premises in which the child is being accommodated not just that part in which the child has a room. The FCA 1980, s 8 referred to premises in the whole or any part of which the child was kept. This provision does not appear to have affected the position.

Sub-s (5) Local authority functions
Eg under Pt III or make application for an emergency protection order s 44, child assessment order s 43 or commence care proceedings s 31

---

68 Persons disqualified from being private foster parents

(1) Unless he has disclosed the fact to the appropriate local authority and obtained their written consent, a person shall not foster a child privately if he is disqualified from doing so by regulations made by the Secretary of State for the purposes of this section.

(2) The regulations may, in particular, provide for a person to be so disqualified where—

(a) an order of a kind specified in the regulations has been made at any time with respect to him;

(b) an order of a kind so specified has been made at any time with respect to any child who has been in his care;

(c) a requirement of a kind so specified has been imposed at any time with respect to any such child, under or by virtue of any enactment;

(d) he has been convicted of an offence of a kind specified, or [a probation order has been made in respect of him or he has been] discharged absolutely or conditionally for any such offence;

(e) a prohibition has been imposed on him at any time under section 69 or under any other specified enactment;

(f) his rights and powers with respect to a child have at any time been vested in a specified authority under a specified enactment.

(3) Unless he has disclosed the fact to the appropriate local authority and obtained their written consent, a person shall not foster a child privately if—

(a) he lives in the same household as a person who is himself prevented from fostering a child by subsection (1); or

(b) he lives in a household at which any such person is employed.

(4) Where an authority refuse to give their consent under this section, they shall inform the applicant by a written notice which states—

(a) the reason for the refusal;

(b) the applicant's right under paragraph 8 of Schedule 8 to appeal against the refusal; and

(c) the time within which he may do so.

(5) In this section—

'the appropriate authority' means the local authority within whose area it is proposed to foster the child in question; and

'enactment' means any enactment having effect, at any time, in any part of the United Kingdom.

Date in force
4 October 1991: SI 1991/828.

Definitions
For 'the appropriate local authority' and 'enactment' see sub-s (5); for 'to foster a child privately' see s 66(1)(b); for 'child', 'local authority' see s 105(1).

References
For appeal to the court by a person aggrieved by a refusal of consent under this section see Sch 8, para 8; for offences see s 70.

Regulations
See the Disqualification for Caring for Children Regulations 1991, SI 1991/2094 amended by SI 1997/2308 and the Disqualification for Caring for Children Regulations (England) Regulations 2002, SI 2002/635.

Transfer of functions
Functions of the Secretary of State, so far as exercisable in relation to Wales, transferred to the National Assembly for Wales, by the National Assembly for Wales (Transfer of Functions) Order 1999, SI 1999/672, art 2, Sch 1.

Sub-s (2)
Or has been placed on probation. A conviction followed by an absolute or conditional discharge is not normally a conviction for the purposes of any proceedings other than those in which the

order is made (PCC(S)A 2000, s 1C) and the inclusion of these words is necessary to give a local authority opportunity to consider the case. Probation had a similar effect until s 13 of the PCCA 1973 was repealed by the CJA 1991, so that a finding of guilt followed by a sentence of probation (now a 'community rehabilitation order' (Criminal Justice and Court Services Act 2000, s 74)) ranks as a conviction.

Sub-s (3)
Same household The former provisions in the FCA 1980, s 7(2) referred to persons in the 'same premises'. The new restriction seems therefore to be drawn more closely. But note the defence to a prosecution in s 70(2).

---

69 Power to prohibit private fostering

(1) This section applies where a person—

(a) proposes to foster a child privately; or
(b) is fostering a child privately.

(2) Where the local authority for the area within which the child is proposed to be, or is being, fostered are of the opinion that—

(a) he is not a suitable person to foster a child;
(b) the premises in which the child will be, or is being, accommodated are not suitable; or
(c) it would be prejudicial to the welfare of the child for him to be, or continue to be, accommodated by that person in those premises,

the authority may impose a prohibition on him under subsection (3).

(3) A prohibition imposed on any person under this subsection may prohibit him from fostering privately—

(a) any child in any premises within the area of the local authority; or
(b) any child in premises specified in the prohibition;
(c) a child identified in the prohibition, in premises specified in the prohibition.

(4) A local authority who have imposed a prohibition on any person under subsection (3) may, if they think fit, cancel the prohibition—

(a) of their own motion; or
(b) on an application made by that person,

if they are satisfied that the prohibition is no longer justified.

(5) Where a local authority impose a requirement on any person under paragraph 6 of Schedule 8, they may also impose a prohibition on him under subsection (3).

(6) Any prohibition imposed by virtue of subsection (5) shall not have effect unless—

(a) the time specified for compliance with the requirement has expired; and
(b) the requirement has not been complied with.

(7) A prohibition imposed under this section shall be imposed by notice in writing addressed to the person on whom it is imposed and informing him of—

(a) the reason for imposing the prohibition;
(b) his right under paragraph 8 of Schedule 8 to appeal against the prohibition; and
(c) the time within which he may do so.

Date in force
14 October 1991: SI 1991/828.

Definitions
For 'child', 'local authority' see s 105(1); for 'to foster a child privately' see s 66(1)(b).

References
For 'required notice' see Sch 8, para 7; for service of notices under this Act generally see s 105(8)-(10); for appeal to the court by a person aggrieved by a prohibition imposed under this section see Sch 8, para 8; for offences see s 70; for inspection of premises where a child is privately fostered see s 67(3).

Sub-s (1) Is fostering
Formerly the power of prohibition existed only where the foster parent had failed to give the authority notice of his proposal to foster. Now the power exists even where the placement had at first been deemed suitable but where circumstances may have changed and the local authority may need to act to safeguard the child.

Sub-s (2) Impose a prohibition
The prohibition appears to be effective pending appeal under Sch 8, para (1). Cf effect of an appeal on a requirement under para 6 (requirements).

Sub-s (7) Notice in writing
May be given by post, s 105(8).

70   Offences

(1) A person shall be guilty of an offence if—

  (a) being required, under any provision made by or under this Part, to give any notice or information—

    (i) he fails without reasonable excuse to give the notice within the time specified in that provision; or

    (ii) he fails without reasonable excuse to give the information within a reasonable time; or

    (iii) he makes, or causes or procures another person to make, any statement in the notice or information which he knows to be false or misleading in a material particular;

  (b) he refuses to allow a privately fostered child to be visited by a duly authorised officer of a local authority;

  (c) he intentionally obstructs another in the exercise of the power conferred by section 67(3);

  (d) he contravenes section 68;

  (e) he fails without reasonable excuse to comply with any requirement imposed by a local authority under this Part;

  (f) he accommodates a privately fostered child in any premises in contravention of a prohibition imposed by a local authority under this Part;

  (g) he knowingly causes to be published, or publishes, an advertisement which he knows contravenes paragraph 10 of Schedule 8.

(2) Where a person contravenes section 68(3), he shall not be guilty of an offence under this section if he proves that he did not know, and had no reasonable ground for believing, that any person to whom section 68(1) applies was living or employed in the premises in question.

(3) A person guilty of an offence under subsection (1)(a) shall be liable on summary conviction to a fine not exceeding level 5 on the standard scale.

(4) A person guilty of an offence under subsection (1)(b), (c) or (g) shall be liable on summary conviction to a fine not exceeding level 3 on the standard scale.

(5) A person guilty of an offence under subsection (1)(d) or (f) shall be liable on summary conviction to imprisonment for a term not exceeding six months, or to a fine not exceeding level 5 on the standard scale, or to both.

(6) A person guilty of an offence under subsection (1)(e) shall be liable on summary conviction to a fine not exceeding level 5 on the standard scale.

(7) If any person who is required, under any provision of this Part, to give a notice fails to give the notice within the time specified in that provision, proceedings for the offence may be brought at any time within six months from the date when evidence of the offence came to the knowledge of the local authority.

(8) Subsection (7) is not affected by anything in section 127(1) of the Magistrates' Courts Act 1980 (time limit for proceedings).

Date in force
14 October 1991: SI 1991/828.

Definitions
For 'a privately fostered child' see s 66(1)(a); for 'local authority' see s 105(1).

References
'This Part' ie Pt IX, s 66-70 and Sch 8 (private arrangements for fostering children). For 'the standard scale' see the CJA 1982, s 37(2)(3) as amended.

Sub-s (1)
Note that these provisions require the failure in s 70(1)(a)(i) (ii) and (e) to be without reasonable excuse and that statement in sub-s (iii) to be false in a material particular.

Intentionally obstructs
The former provision referred to 'wilfully obstructs' but the law probably remains the same.

Sub-s (2)
He proves that he did not know Ie the burden of proof is on the defendant but on the balance of probabilities: *R v Carr-Briant* [1943] KB 607, [1943] 2 All ER 156, 107 JP 167, CCA.

Sub-s (8)
The normal time limit for criminal proceedings in respect of summary offences is six months: Magistrates' Courts Act 1980, s 127(1).

PART X

CHILD MINDING AND DAY CARE FOR YOUNG CHILDREN

Part X is repealed as it applies to England and Wales (but not Scotland) by s 79 of the Care Standards Act. For the provisions of Part X, see the second edition of this work.

[PART XA

CHILD MINDING AND DAY CARE FOR CHILDREN IN ENGLAND AND WALES]

[Introductory]

[79A Child minders and day care providers]

[(1) This section and section 79B apply for the purposes of this Part.

(2) 'Act as a child minder' means (subject to the following subsections) look after one or more children under the age of eight on domestic premises for reward; and 'child minding' shall be interpreted accordingly.

(3) A person who—

(a) is the parent, or a relative, of a child;
(b) has parental responsibility for a child;
(c) is a local authority foster parent in relation to a child;
(d) is a foster parent with whom a child has been placed by a voluntary organisation; or
(e) fosters a child privately,

does not act as a child minder when looking after that child.

(4) Where a person—

(a) looks after a child for the parents ('P1'), or
(b) in addition to that work, looks after another child for different parents ('P2'),

and the work consists (in a case within paragraph (a)) of looking after the child wholly or mainly in P1's home or (in a case within paragraph (b)) of looking after the children wholly or mainly in P1's home or P2's home or both, the work is not to be treated as child minding.

(5) In subsection (4), 'parent', in relation to a child, includes—

(a) a person who is not a parent of the child but who has parental responsibility for the child;

(b) a person who is a relative of the child.

(6) 'Day care' means care provided at any time for children under the age of eight on premises other than domestic premises.

(7) This Part does not apply in relation to a person who acts as a child minder, or provides day care on any premises, unless the period, or the total of the periods, in any day which he spends looking after children or (as the case may be) during which the children are looked after on the premises exceeds two hours.

(8) In determining whether a person is required to register under this Part for child minding, any day on which he does not act as a child minder at any time between 2am and 6pm is to be disregarded.]

Date in force
2 July 2001.

Amendment
Inserted by s 79 of the Care Standards Act 2000.

Definitions
For 'act as a child minder' see sub-s (2) as applied to the whole Act by s 105(5A); for 'relative', 'child', 'voluntary organization' see 105(1); for 'domestic premises' see s 79B(6); for 'parent' see sub-s (5); for 'parental responsibility' see s 3; for 'local authority foster parent' see s 23(3); for 'fosters a child privately' see 66(1)(b); for 'day care' see sub-s (6).

Reference
'This Part' ie Part XA ss 79A-79X and Sch 9A (child minding and day care for young children).

Note
Part XA provides new definitions of child minding and day care which, particularly as regards child minding, clarifies some of the concepts which were doubtful in the former legislation (Part X of the 1989 Act) eg nannies, unless they work for more than two families are exempt from the definition of day care; 'day care' includes care given at any time of the day or night; and babysitters, provided they work for no more than 2 hours a day or between 6pm and 2 am are not 'child minders'. (See generally, the *Explanatory Notes to the Care Standards Act 2000* The Stationery Office Limited ISBN 0105614009).

In addition, provision is made for checks on the suitability of persons working with older children.

In England the responsibility for child minding and day care regulation is transferred from local authorities to Her Majesty's Chief Inspector of Schools for England (HMCIS) and in Wales to the National Assembly and the Chief Inspector of Education and Training in Wales (the 'registration authorities').

Criteria are established for applicants to be registered and for suspension or cancellation of registration. Whilst it is an offence to act as an unregistered day care provider an unregistered child minder only commits an offence if he or she acts as such without reasonable excuse whilst an enforcement notice is in effect. The register of child minders and providers of day care must be publicly available. Registration may be voluntarily given up which may assist in ensuring that information provided for parents seeking child care provision relates only to those who are currently providing these services.

A magistrates' court may make, on application by the registration authority, an emergency order in respect of a registered childminder or day care provider where the registration authority believes that a child in their care is suffering, or is likely to suffer, significant harm.

[79B Other definitions, etc]

[(1) The registration authority in relation to England is Her Majesty's Chief Inspector of Schools in England (referred to in this Part as the Chief Inspector) and references to the Chief Inspector's area are references to England.

(2) The registration authority in relation to Wales is the National Assembly for Wales (referred to in this Act as 'the Assembly').

(3) A person is qualified for registration for child minding if—

(a) he, and every other person looking after children on any premises on which he is or is likely to be child minding, is suitable to look after children under the age of eight;

(b) every person living or employed on the premises in question is suitable to be in regular contact with children under the age of eight;

(c) the premises in question are suitable to be used for looking after children under the age of eight, having regard to their condition and the condition and appropriateness of any equipment on the premises and to any other factor connected with the situation, construction or size of the premises; and

(d) he is complying with regulations under section 79C and with any conditions imposed by the registration authority.

(4) A person is qualified for registration for providing day care on particular premises if—

(a) every person looking after children on the premises is suitable to look after children under the age of eight;

(b) every person living or working on the premises is suitable to be in regular contact with children under the age of eight;

(c) the premises are suitable to be used for looking after children under the age of eight, having regard to their condition and the condition and appropriateness of any equipment on the premises and to any other factor connected with the situation, construction or size of the premises; and

(d) he is complying with regulations under section 79C and with any conditions imposed by the registration authority.

(5) For the purposes of subsection (4)(b) a person is not treated as working on the premises in question if—

(a) none of his work is done in the part of the premises in which children are looked after; or

(b) he does not work on the premises at times when children are looked after there.

(6) 'Domestic premises' means any premises which are wholly or mainly used as a private dwelling and 'premises' includes any area and any vehicle.

(7) 'Regulations' means—

(a) in relation to England, regulations made by the Secretary of State;

(b) in relation to Wales, regulations made by the Assembly.

(8) 'Tribunal' means the Tribunal established by section 9 of the Protection of Children Act 1999.

(9) Schedule 9A (which supplements the provisions of this Part) shall have effect.]

Date in force
1 July 2001

Amendment
Inserted by s 79 of the Care Standards Act 2000.

Definitions
For 'the registration authority' and 'Chief Inspector' see sub-s (1)(2); for 'the Assembly' see sub-s (2); for 'child minding' see s 79A(1) as applied to the whole Act by s 105(5A); for 'premises' see sub-s (6); for 'day care' see s 79A(6).

Reference
'This Part' ie Part XA ss 79A-79X and Sch 9A (child minding and day care for young children).

[79C Regulations etc governing child minders and day care providers]

[(1) The Secretary of State may, after consulting the Chief Inspector and any other person he considers appropriate, make regulations governing the activities of registered persons who act as child minders, or provide day care, on premises in England.

(2) The Assembly may make regulations governing the activities of registered persons who act as child minders, or provide day care, on premises in Wales.

(3) The regulations under this section may deal with the following matters (among others)—

(a) the welfare and development of the children concerned;
(b) suitability to look after, or be in regular contact with, children under the age of eight;
(c) qualifications and training;
(d) the maximum number of children who may be looked after and the number of persons required to assist in looking after them;
(e) the maintenance, safety and suitability of premises and equipment;
(f) the keeping of records;
(g) the provision of information.

(4) In relation to activities on premises in England, the power to make regulations under this section may be exercised so as to confer powers or impose duties on the Chief Inspector in the exercise of his functions under this Part.

(5) In particular they may be exercised so as to require or authorise the Chief Inspector, in exercising those functions, to have regard to or meet factors, standards and other matters prescribed by or referred to in the regulations.

(6) If the regulations require any person (other than the registration authority) to have regard to or meet factors, standards and other matters prescribed by or referred to in the regulations, they may also provide for any allegation that the person has failed to do so to be taken into account—

(a) by the registration authority in the exercise of its functions under this Part, or
(b) in any proceedings under this Part.

(7) Regulations may provide—

(a) that a registered person who without reasonable excuse contravenes, or otherwise fails to comply with, any requirement of the regulations shall be guilty of an offence; and
(b) that a person guilty of the offence shall be liable on summary conviction to a fine not exceeding level 5 on the standard scale.]

Date in force
16 March 2001

Amendment
Inserted by s 79 of the Care Standards Act 2000.

Definitions
For 'the Chief Inspector' see s 79B(1); for 'act as a child minder' see s 79A(2) as applied to the whole Act by s 105(5A); for 'day care' see s 79A(6); for 'premises' see s 79B(6); for 'the Assembly' see s 79B(2); for 'the registration authority' see s 79B(1)(2).

Reference
For 'the standard scale' see the CJA 1982 s 37(2) (3) as amended.

Without reasonable excuse
The defendant will have the evidential burden of raising the defence of reasonable excuse but the final burden of proving his guilt beyond reasonable doubt will remain with the prosecution throughout. What amounts to a reasonable excuse in the circumstances of a particular case will be for the court to decide.

Regulations
See the Day Care and Child Minding (National Standards) (England) Regulations 2001, SI 2001/1828 and the Child Minding and Day Care (Wales) Regulations 2002, SI 2002/812.

[Registration]

[79D Requirement to register]

[(1) No person shall—

(a) act as a child minder in England unless he is registered under this Part for child minding by the Chief Inspector; or

(b) act as a child minder in Wales unless he is registered under this Part for child minding by the Assembly.

(2) Where it appears to the registration authority that a person has contravened subsection (1), the authority may serve a notice ('an enforcement notice') on him.

(3) An enforcement notice shall have effect for a period of one year beginning with the date on which it is served.

(4) If a person in respect of whom an enforcement notice has effect contravenes subsection (1) without reasonable excuse (whether the contravention occurs in England or Wales), he shall be guilty of an offence.

(5) No person shall provide day care on any premises unless he is registered under this Part for providing day care on those premises by the registration authority.

(6) If any person contravenes subsection (5) without reasonable excuse, he shall be guilty of an offence.

(7) A person guilty of an offence under this section shall be liable on summary conviction to a fine not exceeding level 5 on the standard scale.]

Date in force
2 July 2001.

Amendment
Inserted by s 79 of the Care Standards Act 2000.

Definitions
For 'act as a child minder' see s 79A(2) as applied to the whole Act by s 105(5A); for 'the Chief Inspector' see s 79B(1); for 'the registration authority' see s 79B(1)(2); for 'the Assembly' see s 79B(2); for 'an enforcement notice' see sub-s (2); for 'premises' see s 79B(6); for 'day care' see s 79A(6).

References
'This Part' ie Part XA ss 79A-79X and Sch 9A (child minding and day care for young children). For 'the standard scale' see the CJA 1982 s 37(2) (3) as amended.

Without reasonable excuse
The defendant will have the evidential burden of raising the defence of reasonable excuse but the final burden of proving his guilt beyond reasonable doubt will remain with the prosecution throughout. What amounts to a reasonable excuse in the circumstances of a particular case will be for the court to decide.

[79E Applications for registration]

[(1) A person who wishes to be registered under this Part shall make an application to the registration authority.

(2) The application shall—

(a) give prescribed information about prescribed matters;

(b) give any other information which the registration authority reasonably requires the applicant to give.

(3) Where a person provides, or proposes to provide, day care on different premises, he shall make a separate application in respect of each of them.

(4) Where the registration authority has sent the applicant notice under section 79L(1) of its intention to refuse an application under this section, the application may not be withdrawn without the consent of the authority.

(5) A person who, in an application under this section, knowingly makes a statement which is false or misleading in a material particular shall be guilty of an offence and liable, on summary conviction, to a fine not exceeding level 5 on the standard scale.]

Date in force
16 March 2001.

Amendment
Inserted by s 79 of the Care Standards Act 2000.

Definitions
For 'the registration authority' see s 79B(1)(2); for 'day care' see s 79A(6); for 'premises' see s 79B(6); for 'act as a child minder' see s 79A(2) as applied to the whole Act by s 105(5A).

References
'This Part' ie Part XA ss 79A-79X and Sch 9A (child minding and day care for young children). For 'the standard scale' see the CJA 1982 s 37(2) (3) as amended.

Regulations
See the Child Minding and Day Care (Applications for Registration) (England) Regulations 2001, SI 2001/1829.

[79F   Grant or refusal of registration]

[(1) If, on an application by a person for registration for child minding—

(a)   the registration authority is of the opinion that the applicant is, and will continue to be, qualified for registration for child minding (so far as the conditions of section 79B(3) are applicable); and

(b)   the applicant pays the prescribed fee,

the authority shall grant the application; otherwise, it shall refuse it.

(2) If, on an application by any person for registration for providing day care on any premises—

(a)   the registration authority is of the opinion that the applicant is, and will continue to be, qualified for registration for providing day care on those premises (so far as the conditions of section 79B(4) are applicable); and

(b)   the applicant pays the prescribed fee,

the authority shall grant the application; otherwise, it shall refuse it.

(3) An application may, as well as being granted subject to any conditions the authority thinks necessary or expedient for the purpose of giving effect to regulations under section 79C, be granted subject to any other conditions the authority thinks fit to impose.

(4) The registration authority may as it thinks fit vary or remove any condition to which the registration is subject or impose a new condition.

(5) Any register kept by a registration authority of persons who act as child minders or provide day care shall be open to inspection by any person at all reasonable times.

(6) A registered person who without reasonable excuse contravenes, or otherwise fails to comply with, any condition imposed on his registration shall be guilty of an offence.

(7) A person guilty of an offence under subsection (6) shall be liable on summary conviction to a fine not exceeding level 5 on the standard scale.]

Date in force
16 March 2001.

Amendment
Inserted by s 79 of the Care Standards Act 2000.

Definitions
For 'child minding' see s 79A (2) as applied to the whole Act by s 105(5A); for 'the registration authority' see s 79B(1)(2); for 'day care' see s 79A(6); for 'premises' see s 79B(6).

Reference
For 'the standard scale' see the CJA 1982 s 37(2) (3) as amended.

Without reasonable excuse
The defendant will have the evidential burden of raising the defence of reasonable excuse but the final burden of proving his guilt beyond reasonable doubt will remain with the prosecution throughout. What amounts to a reasonable excuse in the circumstances of a particular case will be for the court to decide.

[79G   Cancellation of registration]

[(1) The registration authority may cancel the registration of any person if—

(a)   in the case of a person registered for child minding, the authority is of the opinion that the person has ceased or will cease to be qualified for registration for child minding;

(b)   in the case of a person registered for providing day care on any premises, the authority is of the opinion that the person has ceased or will cease to be qualified for registration for providing day care on those premises,

or if an annual fee which is due from the person has not been paid.

(2) Where a requirement to make any changes or additions to any services, equipment or premises has been imposed on a registered person under section 79F(3), his registration shall not be cancelled on the ground of any defect or insufficiency in the services, equipment or premises if—

(a)   the time set for complying with the requirements has not expired; and

(b)   it is shown that the defect or insufficiency is due to the changes or additions not having been made.

(3) Any cancellation under this section must be in writing.]

Date in force
2 July 2001

Amendment
Inserted by s 79 of the Care Standards Act 2000.

Definitions
For 'the registration authority' see s 79B(1)(2); for 'child minding' see s 79A(2) as applied to the whole Act by s 105(5A); for 'day care' see s 79A(6); for 'premises' see s 79B(6).

[79H   Suspension of registration]

[(1) Regulations may provide for the registration of any person for acting as a child minder or providing day care to be suspended for a prescribed period by the registration authority in prescribed circumstances.

(2) Any regulations made under this section shall include provision conferring on the person concerned a right of appeal to the Tribunal against suspension.]

Date in force
16 March 2001.

Amendment
Inserted by s 79 of the Care Standards Act 2000.

Definitions
For 'act as a child minder' see s 79A(2) as applied to the whole Act by s 105(5A); for 'day care' see s 79A(6); for 'the registration authority' see s 79B(1)(2); for 'the Tribunal' see s 79B(8).

[79J   Resignation of registration]

[(1) A person who is registered for acting as a child minder or providing day care may by notice in writing to the registration authority resign his registration.

(2) But a person may not give a notice under subsection (1)—

(a)   if the registration authority has sent him a notice under section 79L(1) of its intention to cancel the registration, unless the authority has decided not to take that step; or

(b)   if the registration authority has sent him a notice under section 79L(5) of its decision to cancel the registration and the time within which an appeal may be brought has not expired or, if an appeal has been brought, it has not been determined.]

Date in force
2 July 2001.

Amendment
Inserted by s 79 of the Care Standards Act 2000.

Definitions
For 'act as a child minder' see s 79A(2) as applied to the whole Act by s 105(5A); for 'day care' see s 79A(6); for 'the registration authority' see s 79B(1)(2); for 'the Tribunal' see s 79B(8).

Reference
For service of documents see s 105(8)-(10).

[79K   Protection of children in an emergency]

[(1) If, in the case of any person registered for acting as a child minder or providing day care—

(a)   the registration authority applies to a justice of the peace for an order—

(i)   cancelling the registration;

(ii)   varying or removing any condition to which the registration is subject; or

(iii)   imposing a new condition; and

(b)   it appears to the justice that a child who is being, or may be, looked after by that person, or (as the case may be) in accordance with the provision for day care made by that person, is suffering, or is likely to suffer, significant harm,

the justice may make the order.

(2) The cancellation, variation, removal or imposition shall have effect from the time when the order is made.

(3) An application under subsection (1) may be made without notice.

(4) An order under subsection (1) shall be made in writing.

(5) Where an order is made under this section, the registration authority shall serve on the registered person, as soon as is reasonably practicable after the making of the order—

(a)   a copy of the order;

(b)   a copy of any written statement of the authority's reasons for making the application for the order which supported that application; and

(c)   notice of any right of appeal conferred by section 79M.

(6) Where an order has been so made, the registration authority shall, as soon as is reasonably practicable after the making of the order, notify the local authority in whose area the person concerned acts or acted as a child minder, or provides or provided day care, of the making of the order.]

Date in force
2 July 2001.

Amendment
Inserted by s 79 of the Care Standards Act 2000.

Definitions
For 'act as a child minder' see s 79A(2) as applied to the whole Act by s 105(5A); for 'day care' see s 79A(6); for 'the registration authority' see s 79B(1)(2); for 'harm' see s 31(9) and as to whether harm is significant see s 31(10) as applied to the whole Act by s 105(1); for 'local authority' see s 105(1).

References
For 'likely to suffer significant harm' see s 31 and see generally chapter 8.

Service of documents
See s 105(8)-(10).

[79L   Notice of intention to take steps]

[(1)   Not less than 14 days before—

(a)   refusing an application for registration;
(b)   cancelling a registration;
(c)   removing or varying any condition to which a registration is subject or imposing a new condition; or
(d)   refusing to grant an application for the removal or variation of any condition to
which a registration is subject,

the registration authority shall send to the applicant, or (as the case may be) registered person, notice in writing of its intention to take the step in question.

(2)   Every such notice shall—

(a)   give the authority's reasons for proposing to take the step; and
(b)   inform the person concerned of his rights under this section.

(3)   Where the recipient of such a notice informs the authority in writing of his desire to object to the step being taken, the authority shall afford him an opportunity to do so.

(4)   Any objection made under subsection (3) may be made orally or in writing, by the recipient of the notice or a representative.

(5)   If the authority, after giving the person concerned an opportunity to object to the step being taken, decides nevertheless to take it, it shall send him written notice of its decision.

(6)   A step of a kind mentioned in subsection (1)(b) or (c) shall not take effect until the expiry of the time within which an appeal may be brought under section 79M or, where such an appeal is brought, before its determination.

(7)   Subsection (6) does not prevent a step from taking effect before the expiry of the time within which an appeal may be brought under section 79M if the person concerned notifies the registration authority in writing that he does not intend to appeal.]

Date in force
2 July 2001.

Amendment
Inserted by s 79 of the Care Standards Act 2000.

Definitions
For 'the registration authority' see s 79B(1)(2).

Service of documents
See s 105(8)-(10).

Representative
No professional qualifications are required for a representative who may, therefore, be any person nominated for the purpose.

[79M   Appeals]

[(1) An appeal against—

(a)   the taking of any step mentioned in section 79L(1); or

(b)   an order under section 79K,

shall lie to the Tribunal.

(2) On an appeal, the Tribunal may—

(a)   confirm the taking of the step or the making of the order or direct that it shall not have, or shall cease to have, effect; and

(b)   impose, vary or cancel any condition.]

Amendment
Inserted by s 79 of the Care Standards Act 2000.

Definition
For 'the Tribunal' see s 79B(8).

[Inspection: England]

[79N   General functions of the Chief Inspector]

[(1) The Chief Inspector has the general duty of keeping the Secretary of State informed about the quality and standards of child minding and day care provided by registered persons in England.

(2) When asked to do so by the Secretary of State, the Chief Inspector shall give advice or information to the Secretary of State about such matters relating to the provision of child minding or day care by registered persons in England as may be specified in the Secretary of State's request.

(3) The Chief Inspector may at any time give advice to the Secretary of State, either generally or in relation to provision by particular persons or on particular premises, on any matter connected with the provision of child minding or day care by registered persons in England.

(4) The Chief Inspector may secure the provision of training for persons who provide or assist in providing child minding or day care, or intend to do so.

(5) Regulations may confer further functions on the Chief Inspector relating to child minding and day care provided in England.

(6) The annual reports of the Chief Inspector required by subsection (7)(a) of section 2 of the School Inspections Act 1996 to be made to the Secretary of State shall include an account of the exercise of the Chief Inspector's functions under this Part, and the power conferred by subsection (7)(b) of that section to make other reports to the Secretary of State includes a power to make reports with respect to matters which fall within the scope of his functions by virtue of this Part.]

Date in force
16 March 2001.

Amendment
Inserted by s 79 of the Care Standards Act 2000.

Definitions
For 'child minding' see s 79A(2) as applied to the whole Act by s 105(5A); for 'day care' see s 79A(6); for 'premises' see s 79B(6).

[79P   Early years child care inspectorate]

[(1) The Chief Inspector shall establish and maintain a register of early years child care inspectors for England.

(2) The register may be combined with the register maintained for England under paragraph 8(1) of Schedule 26 to the School Standards and Framework Act 1998 (register of nursery education inspectors).

(3) Paragraphs 8(2) to (9), 9(1) to (4), 10 and 11 of that Schedule shall apply in relation to the register of early years child care inspectors as they apply in relation to the register maintained for England under paragraph 8(1) of that Schedule, but with the modifications set out in subsection (4).

(4) In the provisions concerned—

(a) references to registered nursery education inspectors shall be read as references to registered early years child care inspectors;

(b) references to inspections under paragraph 6 of that Schedule shall be read as references to inspections under section 79Q (and references to the functions of a registered nursery education inspector under paragraph 6 shall be interpreted accordingly);

(c) references to the registration of a person under paragraph 6 of that Schedule shall be read as references to the registration of a person under subsection (1) (and references to applications made under paragraph 6 shall be interpreted accordingly); and

(d) in paragraph 10(2), for the words from 'to a tribunal' to the end there shall be substituted 'to the Tribunal established under section 9 of the Protection of Children Act 1999.'

(5) Registered early years child care inspectors are referred to below in this Part as registered inspectors.]

Date in force
2 July 2001.

Amendment
Inserted by s 79 of the Care Standards Act 2000.

[79Q Inspection of provision of child minding and day care in England]

[(1) The Chief Inspector may at any time require any registered person to provide him with any information connected with the person's activities as a child minder, or provision of day care, which the Chief Inspector considers it necessary to have for the purposes of his functions under this Part.

(2) The Chief Inspector shall secure that any child minding provided in England by a registered person is inspected by a registered inspector at prescribed intervals.

(3) The Chief Inspector shall secure that any day care provided by a registered person on any premises in England is inspected by a registered inspector at prescribed intervals.

(4) The Chief Inspector may comply with subsection (2) or (3) either by organising inspections or by making arrangements with others for them to organise inspections.

(5) In prescribing the intervals mentioned in subsection (2) or (3) the Secretary of State may make provision as to the period within which the first inspection of child minding or day care provided by any person or at any premises is to take place.

(6) A person conducting an inspection under this section shall report on the quality and standards of the child minding or day care provided.

(7) The Chief Inspector may arrange for an inspection conducted by a registered inspector under this section to be monitored by another registered inspector.]

Date in force
16 March 2001.

Amendment
Inserted by s 79 of the Care Standards Act 2000.

Definitions
For 'act as a child minder' see s 79A(2) as applied to the whole Act by s 105(5A); for 'day care' see s 79A(6); for 'premises' see s 79B(6); for 'registered inspector' see s 79P(5).

Regulations
See the Day Care and Child Minding (Inspections) (Prescribed Matters) (England) Regulations 2001, SI 2001/2745.

[79R   Reports of inspections]

[(1) A person who has conducted an inspection under section 79Q shall report in writing on the matters inspected to the Chief Inspector within the prescribed period.

(2) The period mentioned in subsection (1) may, if the Chief Inspector considers it necessary, be extended by up to three months.

(3) Once the report of an inspection has been made to the Chief Inspector under subsection (1) he—

(a)   may send a copy of it to the Secretary of State, and shall do so without delay if the Secretary of State requests a copy;

(b)   shall send a copy of it, or of such parts of it as he considers appropriate, to any prescribed authorities or persons; and

(c)   may arrange for the report (or parts of it) to be further published in any manner he considers appropriate.

(4) Subsections (2) to (4) of section 42A of the School Inspections Act 1996 shall apply in relation to the publication of any report under subsection (3) as they apply in relation to the publication of a report under any of the provisions mentioned in subsection (2) of section 42A.]

Date in force
16 March 2001.

Amendment
Inserted by s 79 of the Care Standards Act 2000. Amended by the Education Act 2000, Sch 13, paras 4, 5.

Regulations
See the Day Care and Child Minding (Inspections) (Prescribed Matters) (England) Regulations 2001, SI 2001/2745.

[Inspection: Wales]

[79S   General functions of the Assembly]

[(1) The Assembly may secure the provision of training for persons who provide or assist in providing child minding or day care, or intend to do so.

(2) In relation to child minding and day care provided in Wales, the Assembly shall have any additional function specified in regulations made by the Assembly; but the regulations may only specify a function corresponding to a function which, by virtue of section 79N(5), is exercisable by the Chief Inspector in relation to child minding and day care provided in England.]

Date in force
1 April 2002.

Amendment
Inserted by s 79 of the Care Standards Act 2000. Amended by Education Act 2000, Sch 22.

Definitions
For 'the Assembly' see 79B(2); for 'child minding' see s 79A(2) as applied to the whole Act by s 105(5A); for 'day care' see s 79A(6).

[79T Inspection: Wales]

[(1) The Assembly may at any time require any registered person to provide it with any information connected with the person's activities as a child minder or provision of day care which the Assembly considers it necessary to have for the purposes of its functions under this Part.

(2) The Assembly may by regulations make provision—

(a) for the inspection of the quality and standards of child minding provided in Wales by registered persons and of day care provided by registered persons on premises in Wales;

(b) for the publication of reports of the inspections in such manner as the Assembly considers appropriate.

(3) The regulations may provide for the inspections to be organised by—

(a) the Assembly; or

(b) Her Majesty's Chief Inspector of Education and Training in Wales, or any other person, under arrangements made with the Assembly.

(4) The regulations may provide for subsections (2) to (4) of section 42A of the School Inspections Act 1996 to apply with modifications in relation to the publication of reports under the regulations.]

Date in force
1 April 2002.

Amendment
Inserted by s 79 of the Care Standards Act 2000.

Definitions
For 'the Assembly' see 79B(2); for 'act as a child minder' see s 79A(2) as applied to the whole Act by s 105(5A); for 'day care' see s 79A(6).

[Supplementary]

[79U Rights of entry etc]

[(1) An authorised inspector may at any reasonable time enter any premises in England or Wales on which child minding or day care is at any time provided.

(2) Where an authorised inspector has reasonable cause to believe that a child is being looked after on any premises in contravention of this Part, he may enter those premises at any reasonable time.

(3) An inspector entering premises under this section may—

(a) inspect the premises;

(b) inspect, and take copies of—

    (i)   any records kept by the person providing the child minding or day care; and

    (ii) any other documents containing information relating to its provision;

(c) seize and remove any document or other material or thing found there which he has reasonable grounds to believe may be evidence of a failure to comply with any condition or requirement imposed by or under this Part;

(d) require any person to afford him such facilities and assistance with respect to matters within the person's control as are necessary to enable him to exercise his powers under this section;

(e) take measurements and photographs or make recordings;

(f) inspect any children being looked after there, and the arrangements made for their welfare;

(g) interview in private the person providing the child minding or day care; and

(h) interview in private any person looking after children, or living or working, there who consents to be interviewed.

(4) Section 42 of the School Inspections Act 1996 (inspection of computer records for purposes of Part I of that Act) shall apply for the purposes of subsection (3) as it applies for the purposes of Part I of that Act.

(5) The registration authority may, in any case where it appears to the authority appropriate to do so, authorise a person who is not an authorised inspector to exercise any of the powers conferred by this section.

(6) A person exercising any power conferred by this section shall, if so required, produce some duly authenticated document showing his authority to do so.

(7) It shall be an offence wilfully to obstruct a person exercising any such power.

(8) Any person guilty of an offence under subsection (7) shall be liable on summary conviction to a fine not exceeding level 4 on the standard scale.

(9) In this section—

'authorised inspector' means a registered inspector or a person authorised by the Assembly or by any person with whom the Assembly has made arrangements under section 79T(3);

'documents' and 'records' each include information recorded in any form.]

Date in force
2 July 2001.

Amendment
Inserted by s 79 of the Care Standards Act 2000. Amended by Education Act 2000, Sch 22.

Definitions
For 'authorised inspector', 'documents', 'records' see sub-s (9); for 'premises' see s 79B(6); for 'child minding' see s 79A(2) as applied to the whole Act by s 105(5A); for 'day care' see s 79A(6); for 'the registration authority' see s 79B(1)(2).

References
'This Part' ie Part XA ss 79A-79X and Sch 9A (child minding and day care for young children). For 'the standard scale' see the CJA 1982 s 37(2) (3) as amended.

Wilfully obstructs
'Obstructs' need not involve physical violence: *Hinchliffe v Sheldon* [1955] 3 All ER 406, [1955] 1 WLR 1207. Doing anything which makes it more difficult for a person to carry out his duty may amount to obstruction: *Rice v Connolly* [1966] 2 QB 414, [1966] 2 All ER 649, but standing by and doing nothing, in the absence of a legal duty to act, is not obstruction: *Swallow v LCC* [1916] 1 KB 224. For cases on 'wilful obstruction': Hills v Ellis [1983] QB 680, [1983] 1 All ER 667; *Moore v Green* [1983] 1 All ER 663; *Willmott v Atack* [1977] QB 498, [1976] 3 All ER 794, 141 JP 35.

[79V Function of local authorities]

[Each local authority shall, in accordance with regulations, secure the provision—

(a) of information and advice about child minding and day care; and

(b) of training for persons who provide or assist in providing child minding or day care.]

Date in force
16 March 2001.

Amendment
Inserted by s 79 of the Care Standards Act 2000.

Definition
For 'local authority' see s 105(1).

Regulations
See the Day Care and Child Minding (Functions of Local Authorities: Information, Advice and Training) (England) Regulations 2001, SI 2001/2746.

[Checks on suitability of persons working with children over the age of seven]

[79W   Requirement for certificate of suitability]

[(1) This section applies to any person not required to register under this Part who looks after, or provides care for, children and meets the following conditions.

References in this section to children are to those under the age of 15 or (in the case of disabled children) 17.

(2) The first condition is that the period, or the total of the periods, in any week which he spends looking after children or (as the case may be) during which the children are looked after exceeds five hours.

(3) The second condition is that he would be required to register under this Part (or, as the case may be, this Part if it were subject to prescribed modifications) if the children were under the age of eight.

(4) Regulations may require a person to whom this section applies to hold a certificate issued by the registration authority as to his suitability, and the suitability of each prescribed person, to look after children.

(5) The regulations may make provision about—

(a)   applications for certificates;
(b)   the matters to be taken into account by the registration authority in determining whether to issue certificates;
(c)   the information to be contained in certificates;
(d)   the period of their validity.

(6) The regulations may provide that a person to whom this section applies shall be guilty of an offence—

(a)   if he does not hold a certificate as required by the regulations; or
(b)   if, being a person who holds such a certificate, he fails to produce it when reasonably required to do so by a prescribed person.

(7) The regulations may provide that a person who, for the purpose of obtaining such a certificate, knowingly makes a statement which is false or misleading in a material particular shall be guilty of an offence.

(8) The regulations may provide that a person guilty of an offence under the regulations shall be liable on summary conviction to a fine not exceeding level 5 on the standard scale.]

Date in force
16 March 2001.

Amendment
Inserted by s 79 of the Care Standards Act 2000.

Definitions
For 'child' see sub-s (1).

References
'This Part' ie Part XA ss 79A-79X and Sch 9A (child minding and day care for young children). For 'the standard scale' see the CJA 1982 s 37(2) (3) as amended.

[Time limit for proceedings]

[79X   Time limit for proceedings]

[Proceedings for an offence under this Part or regulations made under it may be brought within a period of six months from the date on which evidence sufficient in the opinion of the prosecutor to warrant the proceedings came to his knowledge; but no such proceedings shall be brought by virtue of this section more than three years after the commission of the offence.]

Date in force
2 July 2001.

Amendment
Inserted by s 79 of the Care Standards Act 2000.

Time limit for proceedings
The normal time limit for criminal proceedings in respect of summary offences is six months: Magistrates' Courts Act 1980, s 127(1).

PART XI
SECRETARY OF STATE'S SUPERVISORY FUNCTIONS AND RESPONSIBILITIES

80   Inspection of children's homes etc by persons authorised by Secretary of State

(1) The Secretary of State may cause to be inspected from time to time any—

(a) [private] children's home;

(b) premises in which a child who is being looked after by a local authority is living;

(c) premises in which a child who is being accommodated by or on behalf of a local education authority or voluntary organisation is living;

(d) premises in which a child who is being accommodated by or on behalf of a [Health Authority, Special Health Authority] [, Primary Care Trust] [or National Health Service trust] is living;

(e) premises in which a child is living with a person with whom he has been placed by an adoption agency;

(f) premises in which a child who is a protected child is, or will be, living;

(g) premises in which a privately fostered child, or child who is treated as a foster child by virtue of paragraph 9 of Schedule 8, is living or in which it is proposed that he will live;

(h) premises on which any person is acting as a child minder;

(i) premises with respect to which a person is registered under section 71(1)(b) [or with respect to which a person is registered for providing day care under Part XA];

(j) residential care home, nursing home or mental nursing home required to be registered under the Registered Homes Act 1984 and used to accommodate children;

[(j) care home or independent hospital used to accommodate children;]

(k) premises which are provided by a local authority and in which any service is provided by that authority under Part III;

(l) independent school [school or college] providing accommodation for any child.

(2) An inspection under this section shall be conducted by a person authorised to do so by the Secretary of State.

(3) An officer of a local authority shall not be so authorised except with the consent of that authority.

(4) The Secretary of State may require any person of a kind mentioned in subsection (5) to furnish him with such information, or allow him to inspect such records (in whatever form they are held), relating to—

(a) any premises to which subsection (1) or, in relation to Scotland, subsection (1)(h) or (i) applies;

(b) any child who is living in any such premises;

(c) the discharge by the Secretary of State of any of his functions under this Act; or

(d) the discharge by any local authority of any of their functions under this Act,

as the Secretary of State may at any time direct.

(5) The persons are any—

(a) local authority;

(b) voluntary organisation;

(c) person carrying on a [private] children's home;

(d) proprietor of an independent school [or governing body of any other school];

[(da) governing body of an institution designated under section 28 of the Further and Higher Education Act 1992;

(db) further education corporation;]

(e) person fostering any privately fostered child or providing accommodation for a child on behalf of a local authority, local education authority, [Health Authority, Special Health Authority,] [Primary Care Trust,] [National Health Service trust] or voluntary organisation;

(f) local education authority providing accommodation for any child;

(g) person employed in a teaching or administrative capacity at any educational establishment (whether or not maintained by a local education authority) at which a child is accommodated on behalf of a local authority or local education authority;

(h) person who is the occupier of any premises in which any person acts as a child minder (within the meaning of Part X) or provides day care for young children (within the meaning of that Part);

[(hh) person who is the occupier of any premises—

(i) in which any person required to be registered for child minding under Part XA acts as a child minder (within the meaning of that Part); or

(ii) with respect to which a person is required to be registered under that Part for providing day care;]

(i) person carrying on any home of a kind mentioned in subsection (1)(j)

[(j) person carrying on a fostering agency].

(6) Any person inspecting any home or other premises under this section may—

(a) inspect the children there; and

(b) make such examination into the state and management of the home or premises and the treatment of the children there as he thinks fit.

(7) Any person authorised by the Secretary of State to exercise the power to inspect records conferred by subsection (4)—

(a) shall be entitled at any reasonable time to have access to, and inspect and check the operation of, any computer and any associated apparatus or material which is or has been in use in connection with the records in question; and

(b) may require—

(i) the person by whom or on whose behalf the computer is or has been so used; or

(ii) any person having charge of, or otherwise concerned with the operation of, the computer, apparatus or material,

to afford him such reasonable assistance as he may require.

(8) A person authorised to inspect any premises under this section shall have a right to enter the premises for that purpose, and for any purpose specified in subsection (4), at any reasonable time.

(9) Any person exercising that power shall, if so required, produce some duly authenticated document showing his authority to do so.

(10) Any person who intentionally obstructs another in the exercise of that power shall be guilty of an offence and liable on summary conviction to a fine not exceeding level 3 on the standard scale.

(11) The Secretary of State may by order provide for subsections (1), (4) and (6) not to apply in relation to such homes, or other premises, as may be specified in the order.

(12) Without prejudice to section 104, any such order may make different provisions with respect to each of those subsections.

[(13) In this section—

'college' means an institution within the further education sector as defined in section 91 of the Further and Higher Education Act 1992;

'fostering agency' has the same meaning as in the Care Standards Act 2000;

'further education corporation' has the same meaning as in the Further and Higher Education Act 1992.]

Date in force
14 October 1991: SI 1991/828.

Amendments
Sub-s (1) in para (a) word "private" in square brackets inserted by the Care Standards Act 2000. Sub-ss (1): National Health Service and Community Care Act 1990, Sch 9, para 36(4); Health Authorities Act 1995, Sch 1, para 118; SI 2000/90, Sch 1 , para 24; Care Standards Act 2000. Sch 4, para 14. Sub-s (5): Health Authorities Act 1995, Sch 1, para 36; Care Standards Act 2000, Sch 4, para 14. Sub-s (1): in para (l) words "independent school" repealed and subsequent words in square brackets substituted by the Care Standards Act 2000, s 109(1), (2).

Definitions
For 'children home' see s 63(3) and s 23(10) as applied to the whole Act by s 105(1) and see note to s 53, ante; for 'child', 'local authority', 'local education authority', 'voluntary organisation', 'health authority', 'adoption agency', 'protected child', 'residential care home', 'nursing home', 'mental nursing home', 'independent school', 'school' and 'service' see s 105(1); for 'college', 'fostering agency' and 'further education corporation' see sub-s (13); for 'child who is looked after by a local authority' see s 22(1); for 'accommodation provided by or on behalf of a local authority' see s 105(5); for 'privately fostered child' see s 66(1) as applied to the whole Act by s 105(1); for 'child minder' see s 71(2)(a) as applied to the whole Act by s 105(1) and s 79A as applied to the whole Act by s 105(5A).

References
'Part III' ie ss 17-30 and Sch 2 (local authority support for children and families). For proprietor of an independent school see the EA 1996, s 579(1); for power to issue warrant to authorise a constable to assist in exercising the power under this section see s 102; for 'the standard scale' see the CJA 1982, s 37(2) (3) as amended.

Transfer of functions
Functions of the Secretary of State, so far as exercisable in relation to Wales, transferred to the National Assembly for Wales, by the National Assembly for Wales (Transfer of Functions) Order 1999, SI 1999/672, art 2, Sch 1.

Note
Part XI contains the Secretary of State's supervisory functions and responsibilities. Although it largely reproduces the pre-existing law, the CA 1989 also implemented proposals made in The Law on Child Care and Family Services (1987, Cm 62). The Government was of the view that the opportunity should be taken to bring together in child care legislation the provisions relating to general matters such as research and training and the giving of grants to voluntary organisations. Also a general power should be included for the Secretary of State through the Social Services Inspectorate to inspect the work that local authority social services departments carry out for families with children and that this would include the inspection of records. (Cm 62, para 84).

81 Inquiries

(1) The Secretary of State may cause an inquiry to be held into any matter connected with—

(a) the functions of [a local authority which are social services functions within the meaning of the Local Authority Social Services Act 1970], in so far as those functions relate to children;

(b) the functions of an adoption agency;

(c) the functions of a voluntary organisation, in so far as those functions relate to children;

(d) a [private] . . . children's home or voluntary home;

(e) *a residential care home, nursing home or mental nursing home* [a care home or independent hospital], so far as it provides accommodation for children;

(f) a home provided [in accordance with arrangements made] by the Secretary of State under section 82(5);

(g) the detention of a child under [section 92 of the Powers of Criminal Courts (Sentencing) Act 2000].

(2) Before an inquiry is begun, the Secretary of State may direct that it shall be held in private.

(3) Where no direction has been given, the person holding the inquiry may if he thinks fit hold it, or any part of it, in private.

(4) Subsections (2) to (5) of section 250 of the Local Government Act 1972 (powers in relation to local inquiries) shall apply in relation to an inquiry under this section as they apply in relation to a local inquiry under that section.

(5) In this section 'functions' includes powers and duties which a person has otherwise than by virtue of any enactment.

Date in force
14 October 1991: SI 1991/828.

Amendment
Sub-s (1): CLSA 1990, ss 116(1), 125(7), Sch 16, para 21, Sch 20; Local Government Act 2000, Sch 5, para 21; Powers of Criminal Courts (Sentencing) Act 2000, Sch 9, para 128. Sub-s (1): in para (d) word "private" in square brackets inserted by the Care Standards Act 2000, s 116, Sch 4, para 14(1), (17)(a).

Definitions
For 'functions' see sub-s (5); for 'local authority', 'child', 'adoption agency', 'voluntary organisation', 'residential care home', 'nursing home', 'mental nursing home', see s 105(1); for 'registered children's home' see s 63(8); for 'voluntary home' see s 60(3).

Children
The plural includes the singular and therefore an inquiry may be held in respect of an individual child: IA 1978, s 6(c).

---

82 Financial support by Secretary of State

(1) The Secretary of State may (with the consent of the Treasury) defray or contribute towards—

(a) any fees or expenses incurred by any person undergoing approved child care training;

(b) any fees charged, or expenses incurred, by any person providing approved child care training or preparing material for use in connection with such training; or

(c) the cost of maintaining any person undergoing such training.

(2) The Secretary of State may make grants to local authorities in respect of expenditure incurred by them in providing secure accommodation in community homes other than assisted community homes.

(3) Where—

(a) a grant has been made under subsection (2) with respect to any secure accommodation; but

(b) the grant is not used for the purpose for which it was made or the accommodation is not used as, or ceases to be used as, secure accommodation,

the Secretary of State may (with the consent of the Treasury) require the authority concerned to repay the grant, in whole or in part.

(4) The Secretary of State may make grants to voluntary organisations towards—

(a) expenditure incurred by them in connection with the establishment, maintenance or improvement of voluntary homes which, at the time when the expenditure was incurred—

    (i)   were assisted community homes; or

    (ii) were designated as such; or

(b) expenses incurred in respect of the borrowing of money to defray any such expenditure.

(5) The Secretary of State may arrange for the provision, equipment and maintenance of homes for the accommodation of children who are in need of particular facilities and services which—

(a) are or will be provided in those homes; and

(b) in the opinion of the Secretary of State, are unlikely to be readily available in community homes.

(6) In this Part—

'child care training' means training undergone by any person with a view to, or in the course of—

(a) his employment for the purposes of any of the functions mentioned in section 83(9) or in connection with the adoption of children or with the accommodation of children in a *residential care home, nursing home or mental nursing home* [care home or independent hospital]; or

(b) his employment by a voluntary organisation for similar purposes;

'approved child care training' means child care training which is approved by the Secretary of State; and

'secure accommodation' means accommodation provided for the purpose of restricting the liberty of children.

(7) Any grant made under this section shall be of such amount, and shall be subject to such conditions, as the Secretary of State may (with the consent of the Treasury) determine.

Date in force
14 October 1991: SI 1991/828.

Amendments
Sub-s (6): in definition "child care training" words "care home or independent hospital" in square brackets substituted by the Care Standards Act 2000, s 116, Sch 4, para 14(1), (18).

Definitions
For 'child care training', 'approved child care training', 'secure accommodation' see sub-s (6); for 'local authority', 'voluntary organisation' see s 105(1); for 'community home' and 'assisted community home' see s 53 as applied to the whole Act by s 105(1); for 'voluntary home' see s 60(3).

Reference
'This Part' ie Pt XI ss 80-84 (Secretary of State's supervisory functions and responsibilities).

Transfer of functions
Functions of the Secretary of State, so far as exercisable in relation to Wales, transferred to the National Assembly for Wales, by the National Assembly for Wales (Transfer of Functions) Order 1999, SI 1999/672, art 2, Sch 1

Sub-s (5)
A home under this provision (known as 'Youth Treatment Centre') is currently maintained at Glenthorne, Birmingham.

---

83   Research and returns of information

(1) The Secretary of State may conduct, or assist other persons in conducting, research into any matter connected with—

(a) his functions, or the functions of local authorities, under the enactments mentioned in subsection (9);

(b) the adoption of children; or

(c) the accommodation of children in a *residential care home, nursing home or mental nursing home* [care home or independent hospital].

(2) Any local authority may conduct, or assist other persons in conducting, research into any matter connected with—

(a) their functions under the enactments mentioned in subsection (9);

(b) the adoption of children; or

(c) the accommodation of children in a *residential care home, nursing home or mental nursing home* [care home or independent hospital].

(3) Every local authority shall, at such times and in such form as the Secretary of State may direct, transmit to him such particulars as he may require with respect to—

(a) the performance by the local authority of all or any of their functions—

  (i) under the enactments mentioned in subsection (9); or

  (ii) in connection with the accommodation of children in a *residential care home, nursing home or mental nursing home* [care home or independent hospital]; and

(b) the children in relation to whom the authority have exercised those functions.

(4) Every voluntary organisation shall, at such times and in such form as the Secretary of State may direct, transmit to him such particulars as he may require with respect to children accommodated by them or on their behalf.

(5) The Secretary of State may direct the [justices' chief executive for] each magistrates' court to which the direction is expressed to relate to transmit—

(a) to such person as may be specified in the direction; and

(b) at such times and in such form as he may direct;

such particulars as he may require with respect to proceedings of the court which relate to children.

(6) The Secretary of State shall in each year lay before Parliament a consolidated and classified abstract of the information transmitted to him under subsections (3) to (5).

(7) The Secretary of State may institute research designed to provide information on which requests for information under this section may be based.

(8) The Secretary of State shall keep under review the adequacy of the provision of child care training and for that purpose shall receive and consider any information from or representations made by—

(a) the Central Council for Education and Training in Social Work;

(b) such representatives of local authorities as appear to him to be appropriate; or

(c) such other persons or organisations as appear to him to be appropriate,

concerning the provision of such training.

(9) The enactments are—

(a) this Act;

(b) the Children and Young Persons Acts 1933 to 1969;

(c) section 116 of the Mental Health Act 1983 (so far as it relates to children looked after by local authorities);

(d) section 10 of the Mental Health (Scotland) Act 1984 (so far as it relates to children for whom local authorities have responsibility).

Date in force
14 October 1991: SI 1991/828.

Amendment
Sub-s (5): Access to Justice Act 1999, Sch 13, para 159, 160. Sub-s (1): in para (c) words "care home or independent hospital" in square brackets substituted by the Care Standards Act 2000, s 116, Sch 4, para 14(1), (19).

Definitions
For 'functions', 'local authority', 'child', 'residential care home', 'nursing home', 'mental nursing home', 'voluntary organisation' and 'independent hospital' see s 105(1); for 'care home' see s 23(10) as applied to the whole Act by s 105(1) and see note to s 53, ante; for 'child care training' see s 82(6).

Transfer of functions
Functions of the Secretary of State, so far as exercisable in relation to Wales, transferred to the National Assembly for Wales, by the National Assembly for Wales (Transfer of Functions) Order 1999, SI 1999/672, art 2, Sch 1.

84 Local authority failure to comply with statutory duty: default power of Secretary of State

(1) If the Secretary of State is satisfied that any local authority has failed, without reasonable excuse, to comply with any of the duties imposed on them by or under this Act he may make an order declaring that authority to be in default with respect to that duty.

(2) An order under subsection (1) shall give the Secretary of State's reasons for making it.

(3) An order under subsection (1) may contain such directions for the purpose of ensuring that the duty is complied with, within such period as may be specified in the order, as appears to the Secretary of State to be necessary.

(4) Any such direction shall, on the application of the Secretary of State, be enforceable by mandamus.

Date in force
14 October 1991: SI 1991/828.

Definition
For 'local authority', see s 105(1).

Reference
See para 13.56 ff.

Transfer of functions
Functions of the Secretary of State, so far as exercisable in relation to Wales, transferred to the National Assembly for Wales, by the National Assembly for Wales (Transfer of Functions) Order 1999, SI 1999/672, art 2, Sch 1.

PART XII
MISCELLANEOUS AND GENERAL

Notification of children accommodated in certain establishments

85 Children accommodated by health authorities and local education authorities

(1) Where a child is provided with accommodation by any [Health Authority, Special Health Authority,] [Primary Care Trust,] [National Health Service trust] or local education authority ('the accommodating authority')—

(a) for a consecutive period of at least three months; or
(b) with the intention, on the part of that authority, of accommodating him for such a period,

the accommodating authority shall notify the responsible authority.

(2) Where subsection (1) applies with respect to a child, the accommodating authority shall also notify the responsible authority when they cease to accommodate the child.

(3) In this section 'the responsible authority' means—

(a) the local authority appearing to the accommodating authority to be the authority within whose area the child was ordinarily resident immediately before being accommodated; or

(b) where it appears to the accommodating authority that a child was not ordinarily resident within the area of any local authority, the local authority within whose area the accommodation is situated.

(4) Where a local authority have been notified under this section, they shall—

(a) take such steps as are reasonably practicable to enable them to determine whether the child's welfare is adequately safeguarded and promoted while he is accommodated by the accommodating authority; and

(b) consider the extent to which (if at all) they should exercise any of their functions under this Act with respect to the child.

Date in force
14 October 1991: SI 1991/828.

Amendment
Sub-s (1): National Health Service and Community Care Act 1990, Sch 9, para 36(5); Health Authorities Act 1995, Sch 1, para 118,; SI 2000/90, Sch 1, para 24.

Definitions
For 'child', 'Health Authority', 'Special Health Authority', 'National Health Service Trust', 'local education authority', 'local authority' see 105(1); for 'the accommodating authority' see sub-s (1); for 'the responsible authority' see sub-s (3); for 'ordinarily resident' see s 105(6).

86 Children accommodated in residential care, nursing or mental nursing homes [Children accommodated in care homes or independent hospitals]

(1) Where a child is provided with accommodation in any *residential care home, nursing home or mental nursing home* [care home or independent hospital]—

(a) for a consecutive period of at least three months; or

(b) with the intention, on the part of the person taking the decision to accommodate him, of accommodating him for such period,

the person carrying on the home shall notify the local authority within whose area the home is carried on.

(2) Where subsection (1) applies with respect to a child, the person carrying on the home shall also notify that authority when he ceases to accommodate the child in the home.

(3) Where a local authority have been notified under this section, they shall—

(a) take such steps as are reasonably practicable to enable them to determine whether the child's welfare is adequately safeguarded and promoted while he is accommodated in the home; and

(b) consider the extent to which (if at all) they should exercise any of their functions under this Act with respect to the child.

(4) If the person carrying on any home fails, without reasonable excuse, to comply with this section he shall be guilty of an offence.

(5) A person authorised by a local authority may enter any *residential care home, nursing home or mental nursing home* [care home or independent hospital] within the authority's area for the purpose of establishing whether the requirements of this section have been complied with.

(6) Any person who intentionally obstructs another in the exercise of the power of entry shall be guilty of an offence.

(7) Any person exercising the power of entry shall, if so required, produce some duly authenticated document showing his authority to do so.

(8) Any person committing an offence under this section shall be liable on summary conviction to a fine not exceeding level 3 on the standard scale.

Date in force
14 October 1991: SI 1991/828.

Amendment
Section heading: words "Children accommodated in care homes or independent hospitals" in square brackets substituted by the Care Standards Act 2000, s 116, Sch 4, para 14(1), (20)(a).

Definitions
For 'child', 'residential care home', 'nursing home', 'mental nursing home', 'local authority', 'care home', 'independent hospital' see s 105(1).

References
For power to issue warrant to authorise a constable to assist in exercising the power under this section see s 102. For 'the standard scale' see the CJA 1982, s 37(2) (3) as amended; 'level 3' ie £1000.

Note
A number of children may be cared for away from home for fairly long periods and in circumstances where social services departments had, under the former legislation, no clear responsibilities for them. The powers and duties of local authorities to support families with children come from two main streams of law: health and welfare legislation and child care legislation. Health and Welfare legislation enables the provision of services to children as part of the local authority's responsibilities to particular groups of all ages, such as those who are mentally handicapped or physically disabled (see for example the National Health Service Act 1977, the National Assistance Act 1948 and the Chronically Sick and Disabled Persons Act 1970). Some children might have to stay in health establishments for considerable periods especially where they are handicapped or chronically ill. Others are placed in residential schools. Accordingly the Act provides that where a child has been in an NHS establishment a duty rests on the health authority to notify the appropriate social services department. This is to obviate concern that for a number of children contact with their families may diminish and the child's welfare suffer. Similar duties apply to care homes and independent hospitals. See s 85 for children accommodated by health authorities and local education authorities and s 87 for children accommodated in independent schools. See also ss 27 (co-operation between authorities) and 28 (consultation with local education authorities).

87 Welfare of children accommodated in boarding schools and colleges

(1) It shall be the duty of—

(a) the proprietor of any independent school which provides accommodation for any child; and

(b) any person who is not the proprietor of such a school but who is responsible for conducting it,

to safeguard and promote the child's welfare.

(2) Subsection (1) does not apply in relation to a school which is a children's home or a residential care home [(other than a small home)].

(3) Where accommodation is provided for a child by an independent school within the area of a local authority, the authority shall take such steps as are reasonably practicable to enable them to determine whether the child's welfare is adequately safeguarded and promoted while he is accommodated by the school.

(4) Where a local authority are of the opinion that there has been a failure to comply with subsection (1) in relation to a child provided with accommodation by a school within their area, they shall notify the Secretary of State.

(5) Any person authorised by a local authority may, for the purpose of enabling the authority to discharge their duty under this section, enter at any reasonable time any independent school within their area which provides accommodation for any child.

[(1) Where a school or college provides accommodation for any child, it shall be the duty of the relevant person to safeguard and promote the child's welfare.

(2) Subsection (1) does not apply in relation to a school or college which is a children's home or care home.

(3) Where accommodation is provided for a child by any school or college the appropriate authority shall take such steps as are reasonably practicable to enable them to determine whether the child's welfare is adequately safeguarded and promoted while he is accommodated by the school or college.

(4) Where the Commission are of the opinion that there has been a failure to comply with subsection (1) in relation to a child provided with accommodation by a school or college, they shall—

(a) in the case of a school other than an independent school or a special school, notify the local education authority for the area in which the school is situated;

(b) in the case of a special school which is maintained by a local education authority, notify that authority;

(c) in any other case, notify the Secretary of State.

(4A) Where the National Assembly for Wales are of the opinion that there has been a failure to comply with subsection (1) in relation to a child provided with accommodation by a school or college, they shall—

(a) in the case of a school other than an independent school or a special school, notify the local education authority for the area in which the school is situated;

(b) in the case of a special school which is maintained by a local education authority, notify that authority.

(5) Where accommodation is, or is to be, provided for a child by any school or college, a person authorised by the appropriate authority may, for the purpose of enabling that authority to discharge its duty under this section, enter at any time premises which are, or are to be, premises of the school or college.]

(6) Any person *entering an independent school in exercise of* [exercising] the power conferred by subsection (5) may carry out such inspection of premises, children and records as is prescribed by regulations made by the Secretary of State for the purposes of this section.

(7) Any person exercising that power shall, if asked to do so, produce some duly authenticated document showing his authority to do so.

(8) Any person authorised by the regulations to inspect records—

(a) shall be entitled at any reasonable time to have access to, and inspect and check the operation of, any computer and any associated apparatus or material which is or has been in use in connection with the records in question; and

(b) may require—

(i) the person by whom or on whose behalf the computer is or has been so used; or

(ii) any person having charge of, or otherwise concerned with the operation of, the computer, apparatus or material,

to afford him such assistance as he may reasonably require.

(9) Any person who intentionally obstructs another in the exercise of any power conferred by this section or the regulations shall be guilty of an offence and liable on summary conviction to a fine not exceeding level 3 on the standard scale.

(10) In this section 'proprietor' has the same meaning as in [the Education Act 1996].

[(10) In this section and sections 87A to 87D—
'the 1992 Act' means the Further and Higher Education Act 1992;
'appropriate authority' means—

(a) in relation to England, the National Care Standards Commission;

(b) in relation to Wales, the National Assembly for Wales;

'college' means an institution within the further education sector as defined in section 91 of the 1992 Act;
'the Commission' means the National Care Standards Commission;
'further education corporation' has the same meaning as in the 1992 Act;
'local education authority' and 'proprietor' have the same meanings as in the Education Act 1996'.

(11) In this section and sections 87A and 87D 'relevant person' means—

(a) in relation to an independent school, the proprietor of the school;

(b) in relation to any other school, or an institution designated under section 28 of the 1992 Act, the governing body of the school or institution;

(c) in relation to an institution conducted by a further education corporation, the corporation.

(12) Where a person other than the proprietor of an independent school is responsible for conducting the school, references in this section to the relevant person include references to the person so responsible.]

Date in force
14 October 1991: SI 1991/828.

Amendment
Section heading: substituted by the Care Standards Act 2000, s 116, Sch 4, para 14(1), (21). Sub-s (2): Registered Homes (Amendment) Act 1991, s 2(6). Sub-s (10): Education Act 1996, Sch 37, para 87. Sub-ss (1)–(5): substituted by the Care Standards Act 2000, s 105(1), (2).

Definitions
For 'proprietor' see sub-s (10); for 'child', 'independent school', 'school', 'local authority', 'care home', 'residential care home' see s 105(1); for 'the appropriate authority', 'the Commission', 'college', 'further education corporation' see sub-s (10); for 'relevant person' see sub-s (11); for 'local education authority' see sub-s (10) as applied to the whole Act by s 105(1).

[87A Suspension of duty under section 87(3)]

[(1) The Secretary of State may appoint a person to be an inspector for the purposes of this section if—

(a) that person already acts as an inspector for other purposes in relation to independent schools to which section 87(1) applies, and

(b) the Secretary of State is satisfied that the person is an appropriate person to determine whether the welfare of children provided with accommodation by such schools is adequately safeguarded and promoted while they are accommodated by them.

(2) Where—

(a) the proprietor of an independent school to which section 87(1) applies enters into an agreement in writing with a person appointed under subsection (1),

(b) the agreement provides for the person so appointed to have in relation to the school the function of determining whether section 87(1) is being complied with, and

(c) the local authority in whose area the school is situated receive from the person with whom the proprietor of the school has entered into the agreement notice in writing that the agreement has come into effect,

the authority's duty under section 87(3) in relation to the school shall be suspended.

(3) Where a local authority's duty under section 87(3) in relation to any school is suspended under this section, it shall cease to be so suspended if the authority receive—

(a) a notice under subsection (4) relating to the person with whom the proprietor of the school entered into the relevant agreement, or

(b) a notice under subsection (5) relating to that agreement.

(4) The Secretary of State shall terminate a person's appointment under subsection (1) if—

(a) that person so requests, or

(b) the Secretary of State ceases, in relation to that person, to be satisfied that he is such a person as is mentioned in paragraph (b) of that subsection,

and shall give notice of the termination of that person's appointment to every local authority.

(5) Where—

(a) a local authority's duty under section 87(3) in relation to any school is suspended under this section, and

(b) the relevant agreement ceases to have effect,

the person with whom the proprietor of the school entered into that agreement shall give to the authority notice in writing of the fact that it has ceased to have effect.

(6) In this section—

(a) 'proprietor' has the same meaning as in [the Education Act 1996], and

(b) references to the relevant agreement, in relation to the suspension of a local authority's duty under section 87(3) as regards any school, are to the agreement by virtue of which the authority's duty under that provision as regards that school is suspended.]

[(1) The Secretary of State may appoint a person to be an inspector for the purposes of this section if—

(a) that person already acts as an inspector for other purposes in relation to schools or colleges to which section 87(1) applies, and

(b) the Secretary of State is satisfied that the person is an appropriate person to determine whether the welfare of children provided with accommodation by such schools or colleges is adequately safeguarded and promoted while they are accommodated by them.

(2) Where—

(a) the relevant person enters into an agreement in writing with a person appointed under subsection (1),

(b) the agreement provides for the person so appointed to have in relation to the school or college the function of determining whether section 87(1) is being complied with, and

(c) the appropriate authority receive from the person mentioned in paragraph (b) ('the inspector') notice in writing that the agreement has come into effect,

the appropriate authority's duty under section 87(3) in relation to the school or college shall be suspended.

(3) Where the appropriate authority's duty under section 87(3) in relation to any school or college is suspended under this section, it shall cease to be so suspended if the appropriate authority receive—

(a) a notice under subsection (4) relating to the inspector, or

(b) a notice under subsection (5) relating to the relevant agreement.

(4) The Secretary of State shall terminate a person's appointment under subsection (1) if—

(a) that person so requests, or

(b) the Secretary of State ceases, in relation to that person, to be satisfied that he is such a person as is mentioned in paragraph (b) of that subsection,

and shall give notice of the termination of that person's appointment to the appropriate authority.

(5) Where—

(a) the appropriate authority's duty under section 87(3) in relation to any school or college is suspended under this section, and

(b) the relevant agreement ceases to have effect,

the inspector shall give to the appropriate authority notice in writing of the fact that it has ceased to have effect.

(6) In this section references to the relevant agreement, in relation to the suspension of the appropriate authority's duty under section 87(3) as regards any school or college, are to the agreement by virtue of which the appropriate authority's duty under that provision as regards that school or college is suspended.]

Date in force
To be appointed.

Amendment
Inserted by the Deregulation and Contracting Out Act 1994, s 38. Sub-s (6): Education Act 1996, Sch 37, para 88. Substituted by the Care Standards Act 2000, s 106(1).

Definitions
For 'independent school', 'local authority' see s 105(1); for 'proprietor', see sub-s (6); for 'relevant agreement' see sub-s (6).

Transfer of functions
Functions of the Secretary of State, so far as exercisable in relation to Wales, transferred to the National Assembly for Wales, by the National Assembly for Wales (Transfer of Functions) Order 1999, SI 1999/672, art 2, Sch 1.

[87B Duties of inspectors under section 87A]

[(1) The Secretary of State may impose on a person appointed under section 87A(1) ('an authorised inspector') such requirements relating to, or in connection with, the carrying out under substitution agreements of the function mentioned in section 87A(2)(b) as the Secretary of State thinks fit.

(2) Where, in the course of carrying out under a substitution agreement the function mentioned in section 87A(2)(b), it appears to an authorised inspector that there has been a failure to comply with section 87(1) in the case of a child provided with accommodation by the school [or college] to which the agreement relates, the inspector shall give notice of that fact *to the Secretary of State*

[(a) in the case of a school other than an independent school or a special school, to the local education authority for the area in which the school is situated;
(b) in the case of a special school which is maintained by a local education authority, to that authority;
(c) in any other case, to the Secretary of State].

(3) Where, in the course of carrying out under a substitution agreement the function mentioned in section 87A(2)(b), it appears to an authorised inspector that a child provided with accommodation by the school [or college] to which the agreement relates is suffering, or is likely to suffer, significant harm, the inspector shall—

(a) give notice of that fact to the local authority in whose area the school [or college] is situated, and
(b) where the inspector is required to make inspection reports to the Secretary of State, supply that local authority with a copy of the latest inspection report to have been made by the inspector to the Secretary of State in relation to the school [or college].

(4) In this section—

(a) 'proprietor' has the same meaning as in [the Education Act 1996], and
(b) references to substitution agreement are to an agreement between an authorised inspector and the proprietor of an independent school by virtue of which the local authority's duty in relation to the school under section 87(3) is suspended.

[(4) In this section 'substitution agreement' means an agreement by virtue of which the duty of the appropriate authority under section 87(3) in relation to a school or college is suspended.]]

Date in force
To be appointed.

Amendment
Inserted by the Deregulation and Contracting Out Act 1994, s 38. Sub-s (2): words "or college" in square brackets inserted by the Care Standards Act 2000, s 106(2)(a).

Definitions
For 'an authorised inspector' see sub-s (1); for 'child', 'school', 'local authority' see s 105(1); for 'substitution agreement' see sub-s (3).

Transfer of functions
Functions of the Secretary of State, so far as exercisable in relation to Wales, transferred to the National Assembly for Wales, by the National Assembly for Wales (Transfer of Functions) Order 1999, SI 1999/672, art 2, Sch 1.

[87C   Boarding schools: national minimum standards]

[(1) The Secretary of State may prepare and publish statements of national minimum standards for safeguarding and promoting the welfare of children for whom accommodation is provided in a school or college.

(2) The Secretary of State shall keep the standards set out in the statements under review and may publish amended statements whenever he considers it appropriate to do so.

(3) Before issuing a statement, or an amended statement which in the opinion of the Secretary of State effects a substantial change in the standards, the Secretary of State shall consult any persons he considers appropriate.

(4) The standards shall be taken into account—

(a) in the making by the appropriate authority of any determination under section 87(4) or (4A);

(b) in the making by a person appointed under section 87A(1) of any determination under section 87B(2); and

(c) in any proceedings under any other enactment in which it is alleged that the person has failed to comply with section 87(1).]

Date in force
In relation to Wales as from 1 July 2001, in relation to England as from a date to be appointed.

Amendment
Inserted by the Care Standards Act 2000, s107.

Definitions
For 'child', 'school' see s 105(1); for 'college', 'appropriate authority' see s 87A(10).

Transfer of functions
Functions of the Secretary of State, so far as exercisable in relation to Wales, transferred to the National Assembly for Wales, by the National Assembly for Wales (Transfer of Functions) Order 1999, SI 1999/672, art 2, Sch 1.

[87D   Annual fee for boarding school inspections]

[(1) Regulations under subsection (2) may be made in relation to any school or college in respect of which the appropriate authority is required to take steps under section 87(3).

(2) The Secretary of State may by regulations require the relevant person to pay the appropriate authority an annual fee of such amount, and within such time, as the regulations may specify.

(3) A fee payable by virtue of this section may, without prejudice to any other method of recovery, be recovered summarily as a civil debt.]

Date in force
In relation to Wales as from 1 July 2001, in relation to England as from a date to be appointed.

Amendment
Inserted by the Care Standards Act 2000, s108.

Definitions
For 'school' see s 105(1); for 'college' see s 87A(10).

Transfer of functions
Functions of the Secretary of State, so far as exercisable in relation to Wales, transferred to the National Assembly for Wales, by the National Assembly for Wales (Transfer of Functions) Order 1999, SI 1999/672, art 2, Sch 1.

Adoption

88 Amendments of adoption legislation

(1) The Adoption Act 1976 shall have effect subject to the amendments made by Part I of Schedule 10.
(2) The Adoption (Scotland) Act 1978 shall have effect subject to the amendments made by Part II of Schedule 10.

Paternity tests

89 *[Repealed by the Child Support, Pensions and Social Security Act 2000, s 85, Sch 9, Pt IX.]*

Criminal care and supervision orders

90 Care and supervision orders in criminal proceedings

(1) The power of a court to make an order under subsection (2) of section 1 of the Children and Young Persons Act 1969 (care proceedings in [youth courts]) where it is of the opinion that the condition mentioned in paragraph (f) of that subsection ('the offence condition') is satisfied is hereby abolished.

(2) The powers of the court to make care orders—

(a) under section 7(7)(a) of the Children and Young Persons Act 1969 (alteration in treatment of young offenders etc); and

(b) under section 15(1) of that Act, on discharging a supervision order made under section 7(7)(b) of that Act,

are hereby abolished.

(3) The powers given by that Act to include requirements in supervision orders shall have effect subject to amendments made by Schedule 12.

Date in force
14 October 1991: SI 1991/828.

Amendment
Sub-s (1): CJA, 1991, Sch 11, para 40.

Effect and duration of orders etc

91 Effect and duration of orders etc

(1) The making of a residence order with respect to a child who is the subject of a care order discharges the care order.

(2) The making of a care order with respect to a child who is the subject of any section 8 order discharges that order.

(3) The making of a care order with respect to a child who is the subject of a supervision order discharges that other order.

(4) The making of a care order with respect to a child who is a ward of court brings that wardship to an end.

(5) The making of a care order with respect to a child who is the subject of a school attendance order made under [section 437 of the Education Act 1996] discharges the school attendance order.

(6) Where an emergency protection order is made with respect to a child who is in care, the care order shall have effect subject to the emergency protection order.

(7) Any order made under section 4(1) or 5(1) shall continue in force until the child reaches the age of eighteen, unless it is brought to an end earlier.

(8) Any—

(a) agreement under section 4; or
(b) appointment under section 5(3) or (4),

shall continue in force until the child reaches the age of eighteen, unless it is brought to an end earlier.

(9) An order under Schedule 1 has effect as specified in that Schedule.

(10) A section 8 order shall, if it would otherwise still be in force, cease to have effect when the child reaches the age of sixteen, unless it is to have effect beyond that age by virtue of section 9(6).

(11) Where a section 8 order has effect with respect to a child who has reached the age of sixteen, it shall, if it would otherwise still be in force, cease to have effect when he reaches the age of eighteen.

(12) Any care order, other than an interim care order, shall continue in force until the child reaches the age of eighteen, unless it is brought to an end earlier.

(13) Any order made under any other provision of this Act in relation to a child shall, if it would otherwise still be in force, cease to have effect when he reaches the age of eighteen.

(14) On disposing of any application for an order under this Act, the court may (whether or not it makes any other order in response to the application) order that no application for an order under this Act of any specified kind may be made with respect to the child concerned by any person named in the order without leave of the court.

(15) Where an application ('the previous application') has been made for—

(a) the discharge of a care order;
(b) the discharge of a supervision order;
(c) the discharge of an education supervision order;
(d) the substitution of a supervision order for a care order; or
(e) a child assessment order,

no further application of a kind mentioned in paragraphs (a) to (e) may be made with respect to the child concerned, without leave of the court, unless the period between the disposal of the previous application and the making of the further application exceeds six months.

(16) Subsection (15) does not apply to applications made in relation to interim orders.

(17) Where—

(a) a person has made an application for an order under section 34;
(b) the application has been refused; and
(c) a period of less than six months has elapsed since the refusal,

that person may not make a further application for such an order with respect to the same child, unless he has obtained the leave of the court.

Date in force
14 October 1991: SI 1991/828.

Amendment
Sub-s (5) Education Act 1996, Sch 37, para 90.

Definitions
For 'residence order' see s 8(1); for 'child' see s 105(1); for care order' see s 31(11) and s 105(1); for 'a section 8 order' see s 8(2); for 'supervision order' see s 31(11); for 'emergency protection order' see s 44 as applied to the whole Act by s 105(1); for 'court' see s 92(7); for 'education supervision order' see s 36; for 'child assessment order' see s 43(2).

References
For the duration of supervision orders see also Sch 3, Pt II, para 6; for the discharge and variation of care and supervision orders see s 39; for interim orders see s 38.

Sub-s (2)
Where the court made a care order and made no order in respect of a pending application for a residence order, the application for a residence order was deemed to have been dismissed: Hounslow London Borough Council v A [1993] 1 FLR 702.

Sub-s (14)
For the application of this provision, see generally paras 5.154 ff.

Jurisdiction and procedure etc

92   Jurisdiction of courts

(1) The name 'domestic proceedings', given to certain proceedings in magistrates' courts, is hereby changed to 'family proceedings' and the names 'domestic court' and 'domestic court panel' are hereby changed to 'family proceedings court' and 'family panel', respectively.

(2) Proceedings under this Act shall be treated as family proceedings in relation to magistrates' courts.

(3) Subsection (2) is subject to the provisions of section 65(1) and (2) of the Magistrates' Courts Act 1980 (proceedings which may be treated as not being family proceedings), as amended by this Act.

(4) A magistrates' court shall not be competent to entertain any application, or make any order, involving the administration or application of—

(a)   any property belonging to or held in trust for a child; or
(b)   the income of any such property.

(5) The powers of a magistrates' court under section 63(2) of the Act of 1980 to suspend or rescind orders shall not apply in relation to any order made under this Act.

(6) Part I of Schedule 11 makes provision, including provision for the Lord Chancellor to make orders, with respect to the jurisdiction of courts and justices of the peace in relation to—

(a)   proceedings under this Act; and
(b)   proceedings under certain other enactments.

(7) For the purposes of this Act 'the court' means the High Court, a county court or a magistrates' court.

(8) Subsection (7) is subject to the provision made by or under Part I of Schedule 11 and to any express provision as to the jurisdiction of any court made by any other provision of this Act.

(9) The Lord Chancellor may by order make provision for the principal registry of the Family Division of the High Court to be treated as if it were a county court for such purposes of this Act, or of any provision made under this Act, as may be specified in the order.

(10) Any order under subsection (9) may make such provision as the Lord Chancellor thinks expedient for the purpose of applying (with or without modifications) provisions which apply in relation to the procedure in county courts to the principal registry when it acts as if it were a county court.

(11) Part II of Schedule 11 makes amendments consequential on this section.

Date in force
14 October 1991: SI 1991/828.

Reference
For the application of sub-s (2): *R v Oxfordshire County Council* [1992] Fam 150, [1992] 3 All ER 660.

93 Rules of court

(1) An authority having power to make rules of court may make such provision for giving effect to—

(a) this Act;

(b) the provisions of any statutory instrument made under this Act; or

(c) any amendment made by this Act in any other enactment,

as appears to that authority to be necessary or expedient.

(2) The rules may, in particular, make provision—

(a) with respect to the procedure to be followed in any relevant proceedings (including the manner in which any application is to be made or other proceedings commenced);

(b) as to the persons entitled to participate in any relevant proceedings, whether as parties to the proceedings or by being given the opportunity to make representations to the court;

(c) with respect to the documents and information to be furnished, and notices to be given, in connection with any relevant proceedings;

(d) applying (with or without modification) enactments which govern the procedure to be followed with respect to proceedings brought on a complaint made to a magistrates' court to relevant proceedings in such a court brought otherwise than on a complaint;

(e) with respect to preliminary hearings;

(f) for the service outside [England and Wales], in such circumstances and in such manner as may be prescribed, of any notice of proceedings in a magistrates' court;

(g) for the exercise by magistrates' courts, in such circumstances as may be prescribed, of such powers as may be prescribed (even though a party to the proceedings in question is [or resides] outside England and Wales);

(h) enabling the court, in such circumstances as may be prescribed, to proceed on any application even though the respondent has not been given notice of the proceedings;

(i) authorising a single justice to discharge the functions of a magistrates' court with respect to such relevant proceedings as may be prescribed;

(j) authorising a magistrates' court to order any of the parties to such relevant proceedings as may be prescribed, in such circumstances as may be prescribed, to pay the whole or part of the costs of all or any of the other parties.

(3) In subsection (2)—

'notice of proceedings' means a summons or such other notice of proceedings as is required; and 'given', in relation to a summons, means 'served';

'prescribed' means prescribed by the rules; and

'relevant proceedings' means any application made, or proceedings brought, under any of the provisions mentioned in paragraphs (*a*) to (*c*) of subsection (1) and any part of such proceedings.

(4) This section and any other power in this Act to make rules of court are not to be taken as in any way limiting any other power of the authority in question to make rules of court.

(5) When making any rules under this section an authority shall be subject to the same requirements as to consultation (if any) as apply when the authority makes rules under its general rule making power.

Date in force
14 October 1991: SI 1991/828.

Amendment
Sub-s (2): CLSA 1991, Sch 16, para 22.

Definitions
For 'notice of proceedings', 'prescribed' and 'relevant proceedings' see sub-s (3).

94 Appeals

(1) [Subject to any express provisions to the contrary made by or under this Act, an] appeal shall lie to the High Court against—

    (a)   the making by a magistrates' court of any order under this Act; or

    (b)   any refusal by a magistrates' court to make such an order.

(2) Where a magistrates' court has power, in relation to any proceedings under this Act, to decline jurisdiction because it considers that the case can more conveniently be dealt with by another court, no appeal shall lie against any exercise by that magistrates' court of that power.

(3) Subsection (1) does not apply in relation to an interim order for periodical payments made under Schedule 1.

(4) On an appeal under this section, the High Court may make such orders as may be necessary to give effect to its determination of the appeal.

(5) Where an order is made under subsection (4) the High Court may also make such incidental or consequential orders as appear to it to be just.

(6) Where an appeal from a magistrates' court relates to an order for the making of periodical payments, the High Court may order that its determination of the appeal shall have effect from such date as it thinks fit to specify in the order.

(7) The date so specified must not be earlier than the earliest date allowed in accordance with rules of court made for the purposes of this section.

(8) Where, on an appeal under this section in respect of an order requiring a person to make periodical payments, the High Court reduces the amount of those payments or discharges the order—

    (a)   it may order the person entitled to the payments to pay to the person making them such sum in respect of payments already made as the High Court thinks fit; and

    (b)   if any arrears are due under the order for periodical payments, it may remit payment of the whole, or part, of those arrears.

(9) Any order of the High Court made on an appeal under this section (other than one directing that an application be re-heard by a magistrates' court) shall, for the purposes—

    (a)   of the enforcement of the order; and

    (b)   of any power to vary, revive or discharge orders,

be treated as if it were an order of the magistrates' court from which the appeal was brought and not an order of the High Court.

(10) The Lord Chancellor may by order make provision as to the circumstances in which appeals may be made against decisions taken by courts on questions arising in connection with the transfer, or proposed transfer, of proceedings by virtue of any order under paragraph 2 of Schedule 11.

(11) Except to the extent provided for in any order made under subsection (10), no appeal may be made against any decision of a kind mentioned in that subsection.

Date in force
14 October 1991: SI 1991/828.

Amendment
Sub-s (1): CLSA 1990, Sch 16, para 23.

References
See generally chapter 13; Handbook of Best Practice in Children Act Cases (Children Act Advisory Committee, June 1997) in Clarke, Hall and Morrison at para 1 [2001].

Practice Directions
See *Practice Direction* [1992] 1 All ER 864 and in relation to magistrates' courts *Practice Direction (Children Act 1989 – Appeals)* [1992] 2 FLR 503.

There is no power for a magistrates' court to stay an order pending appeal but an application for a stay may be made to the High Court Re O (a minor) [1992] 4 All ER 905 and Re J (a minor) (Residence) [1993] 2 FCR 636, [1994] 1 FLR 369 but see para 13.24. On an appeal from a family proceedings court, the High Court may remit the matter for rehearing before any county court which is a care centre: Suffolk County Council v C [1999] 1 FCR 473n, [1999] 1 FLR 259n.

95 Attendance of child at hearing under Part IV or V

(1) In any proceedings in which a court is hearing an application for an order under Part IV or V, or is considering whether to make any such order, the court may order the child concerned to attend such stage or stages of the proceedings as may be specified in the order.

(2) The power conferred by subsection (1) shall be exercised in accordance with rules of court.

(3) Subsections (4) to (6) apply where—

(a) an order under subsection (1) has not been complied with; or

(b) the court has reasonable cause to believe that it will not be complied with.

(4) The court may make an order authorising a constable, or such person as may be specified in the order—

(a) to take charge of the child and to bring him to the court; and

(b) to enter and search any premises specified in the order if he has reasonable cause to believe that the child may be found on the premises.

(5) The court may order any person who is in a position to do so to bring the child to the court.

(6) Where the court has reason to believe that a person has information about the whereabouts of the child it may order him to disclose it to the court.

Date in force
14 October 1991: SI 1991/828.

Definitions
For 'court' see s 92(7); for 'child' see s 105(1).

References
See generally chapter 8. Part IV ie ss 31-42 and Sch 3 (care and supervision); Part V ie ss 43-52 (protection of children).

96 Evidence given by, or with respect to, children

(1) Subsection (2) applies where a child who is called as a witness in any civil proceedings does not, in the opinion of the court, understand the nature of an oath.

(2) The child's evidence may be heard by the court if, in its opinion—

(a) he understands that it is his duty to speak the truth; and

(b) he has sufficient understanding to justify his evidence being heard.

(3) The Lord Chancellor may by order make provision for the admissibility of evidence which would otherwise be inadmissible under any rule of law relating to hearsay.

(4) An order under subsection (3) may only be made with respect to—

(a) civil proceedings in general or such civil proceedings, or class of civil proceedings, as may be prescribed; and

(b) evidence in connection with the upbringing, maintenance or welfare of a child.

(5) An order under subsection (3)—

(a) may, in particular, provide for the admissibility of statements which are made orally or in a prescribed form or which are recorded by any prescribed method of recording;

(b) may make different provision for different purposes and in relation to different descriptions of court; and

(c) may make such amendments and repeals in any enactment relating to evidence (other than in this Act) as the Lord Chancellor considers necessary or expedient in consequence of the provision made by the order.

(6) Subsection (5)(b) is without prejudice to section 104(4).

(7) In this section—

['civil proceedings' means civil proceedings, before any tribunal, in relation to which the strict rules of evidence apply, whether as a matter of law or by agreement of the parties, and references to 'the court' shall be construed accordingly;]
'prescribed' means prescribed by an order under subsection (3).

Date in force
Sub-ss (1), (2): 14 October 1991: SI 1991/828. Sub-ss (3)-(7): 16 November 1989.

Amendment
Sub-s (7) Civil Evidence Act 1995, Sch 1, para 16.

Definitions
For 'child' see s 105(1); for 'court', 'civil proceedings' and 'prescribed' see sub-s (7).

Sub-s (3)
See the Children (Admissibility of Hearing Evidence) Order 1993 and para 11.04.

---

97   Privacy for children involved in certain proceedings

(1) Rules made under section 144 of the Magistrates' Courts Act 1980 may make provision for a magistrates' court to sit in private in proceedings in which any powers under this Act may be exercised by the court with respect to any child.

(2) No person shall publish any material which is intended, or likely, to identify—

(a) any child as being involved in any proceedings before [the High Court, a county court or] a magistrates' court in which any power under this Act may be exercised by the court with respect to that or any other child; or

(b) an address or school as being that of a child involved in any such proceedings.

(3) In any proceedings for an offence under this section it shall be a defence for the accused to prove that he did not know, and had no reason to suspect, that the published material was intended, or likely, to identify the child.

(4) The court or the [Lord Chancellor] may, if satisfied that the welfare of the child requires it, by order dispense with the requirements of subsection (2) to such extent as may be specified in the order.

(5) For the purposes of this section—
'publish' includes—

[(a) include a programme service (within the meaning of the Broadcasting Act 1990);] or

(b) cause to be published; and

'material' includes any picture or representation.

(6) Any person who contravenes this section shall be guilty of an offence and liable, on summary conviction, to a fine not exceeding level 4 on the standard scale.

(7) Subsection (1) is without prejudice to—

(a) the generality of the rule making power in section 144 of the Act of 1980; or

(b) any other power of a magistrates' court to sit in private.

(8) [Sections 69 (sittings of magistrates' courts for family proceedings) and 71 (newspaper reports of certain proceedings) of the Act of 1980] shall apply in relation to any proceedings [(before a magistrates' court)] to which this section applies subject to the provisions of this section.

Date in force
14 October 1991: SI 1991/828.

Amendments
Sub-ss (2), (8): Access to Justice Act 1999, Sch 14, para 18. Sub-s (4): SI 1992/709, art 3(2), Sch 2. Sub-s (5): Broadcasting Act 1990, Sch 20, para 53. Sub-s (8): CLSA 1990, Sch 16, para 24.

Definitions
For 'child' and 'school' see 105(1); for 'publish' and 'material' see sub-s (5).

References
See generally paras 4.50 ff. For 'the standard scale' see the CJA 1982 s 37(2)(3) as amended.

98 Self-incrimination

(1) In any proceedings in which a court is hearing an application for an order under Part IV or V, no person shall be excused from—

(a) giving evidence on any matter; or

(b) answering any question put to him in the course of his giving evidence,

on the ground that doing so might incriminate him or his spouse of an offence.

(2) A statement or admission made in such proceedings shall not be admissible in evidence against the person making it or his spouse in proceedings for an offence other than perjury.

Date in force
14 October 1991: SI 1991/828.

Definition
For 'court' see s 92(7).

References
'Part IV' ie ss 31-42 and Sch 3 (care and supervision); 'Part V' ie ss 43-52 (protection of children) for discussion on immunity from self-incrimination, see para 11.64 ff and see *Re M (disclosure. police investigation)* [2002] 1 FCR 655 where the court declined to order disclosure of a mother's admission of assault in care proceedings made subsequent to the closing of an inconclusive police investigation.

99 ... *[Repealed by the Access to Justice Act 1999, s 106, Sch 15, Pt 1].*

(1)–(4)   . . .

(5) . . .

Amendment
Repealed by the Access to Justice Act 1999, Sch 15.

Legal Aid
Now replaced by the Community Legal Service under the provisions of the Access to Justice Act 1999.

100 Restrictions on use of wardship jurisdiction

(1) . . .

(2) No court shall exercise the High Court's inherent jurisdiction with respect to children—

(a) so as to require a child to be placed in the care, or put under the supervision, of a local authority;

(b) so as to require a child to be accommodated by or on behalf of a local authority;

(c) so as to make a child who is the subject of a care order a ward of court; or

(d) for the purpose of conferring on any local authority power to determine any question which has arisen, or which may arise, in connection with any aspect of parental responsibility for a child.

(3) No application for any exercise of the court's inherent jurisdiction with respect to children may be made by a local authority unless the authority have obtained the leave of the court.

(4) The court may only grant leave if it is satisfied that—

(a) the result which the authority wish to achieve could not be achieved through the making of any order of a kind to which subsection (5) applies; and

(b) there is reasonable cause to believe that if the court's inherent jurisdiction is not exercised with respect to the child he is likely to suffer significant harm.

(5) This subsection applies to any order—

(a) made otherwise than in the exercise of the court's inherent jurisdiction; and

(b) which the local authority is entitled to apply for (assuming, in the case of any application which may only be made with leave, that leave is granted).

Date in force
14 October 1991: SI 1991/828.

Definitions
For 'local authority', 'child' see s 105(1); for 'care order' see s 31(11) and s 105(1); for 'parental responsibility' see s 3; for 'harm' see s 31(9) as applied to the whole Act by s 105(1) and as to whether harm is significant see s 31(10) as applied to the whole Act by s 105(1).

References
See generally paras 12.4 ff, wardship and 12.24 ff, inherent jurisdiction. For exclusion of applications under s 100(3) from the definition of 'family proceedings' under this Act see s 8(3).

---

101 Effect of orders as between England and Wales and Northern Ireland, the Channel Islands or the Isle of Man

(1) The Secretary of State may make regulations providing—

(a) for prescribed orders which—

(i)   are made by a court in Northern Ireland; and

(ii) appear to the Secretary of State to correspond in their effect to orders which may be made under any provision of this Act,

to have effect in prescribed circumstances, for prescribed purposes of this Act, as if they were orders of a prescribed kind made under this Act;

(b) for prescribed orders which—

(i)   are made by a court in England and Wales; and

(ii) appear to the Secretary of State to correspond in their effect to orders which may be made under any provision in force in Northern Ireland,

to have effect in prescribed circumstances, for prescribed purposes of the law of Northern Ireland, as if they were orders of a prescribed kind made in Northern Ireland.

(2) Regulations under subsection (1) may provide for the order concerned to cease to have effect for the purposes of the law of Northern Ireland, or (as the case may be) the law of England and Wales, if prescribed conditions are satisfied.

(3) The Secretary of State may make regulations providing for prescribed orders which—

(a) are made by a court in the Isle of Man or in any of the Channel Islands; and

(b) appear to the Secretary of State to correspond in their effect to orders which may be made under this Act,

to have effect in prescribed circumstances for prescribed purposes of this Act, as if they were orders of a prescribed kind made under this Act.

(4) Where a child who is in the care of a local authority is lawfully taken to live in Northern Ireland, the Isle of Man or any of the Channel Islands, the care order in question shall cease to have effect if the conditions prescribed in regulations made by the Secretary of State are satisfied.

(5) Any regulations made under this section may—

(a) make such consequential amendments (including repeals) in—

    (i) section 25 of the Children and Young Persons Act 1969 (transfers between England and Wales and Northern Ireland); or

    (ii) section 26 (transfers between England and Wales and Channel Islands or Isle of Man) of that Act,

as the Secretary of State considers necessary or expedient; and

(b) modify any provision of this Act, in its application (by virtue of the regulations) in relation to an order made otherwise than in England and Wales.

Date in force
14 October 1991: SI 1991/828.

Definitions
For 'court' see s 92(7); for 'prescribed' see s 105(1); for 'care order' see s 31(11) and s 105(1).

Regulations
See the Children (Prescribed Orders - Northern Ireland, Guernsey and Isle of Man) Regulations 1991, SI 1991/2032.

Search warrants

102 Power of constable to assist in exercise of certain powers to search for children or inspect premises

(1) Where, on an application made by any person for a warrant under this section, it appears to the court—

(a) that a person attempting to exercise powers under any enactment mentioned in subsection (6) has been prevented from doing so by being refused entry to the premises concerned or refused access to the child concerned; or

(b) that any such person is likely to be so prevented from exercising any such powers,

it may issue a warrant authorising any constable to assist that person in the exercise of those powers, using reasonable force if necessary.

(2) Every warrant issued under this section shall be addressed to, and executed by, a constable who shall be accompanied by the person applying for the warrant if—

(a) that person so desires; and

(b) the court by whom the warrant is issued does not direct otherwise.

(3) A court granting an application for a warrant under this section may direct that the constable concerned may, in executing the warrant, be accompanied by a registered medical practitioner, registered nurse or *registered health visitor* [registered midwife] if he so chooses.

(4) An application for a warrant under this section shall be made in the manner and form prescribed by rules of court.

(5) Where—

(a) an application for a warrant under this section relates to a particular child; and
(b) it is reasonably practicable to do so,

the application and any warrant granted on the application shall name the child; and where it does not name him it shall describe him as clearly as possible.

(6) The enactments are—

(a) sections 62, 64, 67, 76, [79U,] 80, 86 and 87;
(b) paragraph 8(1)(b) and (2)(b) of Schedule 3;
(c) section 33 of the Adoption Act 1976 (duty of local authority to secure that protected children are visited from time to time).

Date in force
14 October 1991: SI 1991/828.

Amendment
Sub-s (6): Regulation of Care (Scotland) Act 2001, Sch 4.

Definitions
For 'court' see s 92(7); for 'child', 'prescribed' see s 105(1).

Reference
For 'premises' see the note to s 72.

Procedure
Application may only be made to a magistrates' court: SI 1991/1395, arts 2(1)(m) and 6(2). With the leave of the justices' clerk, application may be made ex parte in which case the applicant must file an application for each child in Forms C1 and C19 prescribed in SI 1991/1395, Sch 1 either at the time the application is made or as directed by the justices' clerk: SI 1991/1395, r 4(4)(ii). An ex parte application may be heard before a single justice: s 93(2)(i) and SI 1991/1395, r 2(5)(a). Where the court or a single justice refuses to make an order or an ex parte application it may direct that the application be made inter partes: r 4(5).

Inter partes applications

The applicant must file with the justices' clerk the application and sufficient copies for one to be served on each respondent. The clerk will consider whether there should be a directions appointment to consider the matters specified in SI 1991/1395, r 14 (and see r 16 (attendance at directions appointment)). The clerk will then fix the date, time and place for a hearing or directions appointment (allowing sufficient time for the applicant to give the required notice to the respondent). The clerk will endorse the date so fixed on the copy applications which are returned to the applicant who thereupon serves a copy application on the person referred to in s 102(1) and any person preventing or likely to prevent such a person from exercising powers under enactments mentioned in sub-s (6) of that section at least one day before the day fixed for the hearing or directions appointment. The rules of service are provided for in SI 1991/1395, r 8, and service may be effected by first class post. The parties to the proceedings must file with the court and serve on the other parties written statements of the substance of the oral evidence which they intend to adduce at the directions appointment or hearing as provided for by SI 1991/1395, r 17.

General

103 Offences by bodies corporate

(1) This section applies where any offence under this Act is committed by a body corporate.

(2) If the offence is proved to have been committed with the consent or connivance of or to be attributable to any neglect on the part of any director, manager, secretary or other similar officer of the body corporate, or any person who was purporting to act in any such capacity he (as well as the body corporate) shall be guilty of the offence and shall be liable to be proceeded against and punished accordingly.

Date in force
14 October 1991: SI 1991/828.

104 Regulations and orders

(1) Any power of the Lord Chancellor or the Secretary of State under this Act to make an order, regulations, or rules, except an order under section 54(2), 56(4)(a), 57(3), 84 or 97(4) or paragraph 1(1) of Schedule 4, shall be exercisable by statutory instrument.

(2) Any such statutory instrument, except one made under section 17(4), 107 or 108(2), shall be subject to annulment in pursuance of a resolution of either House of Parliament.

(3) An order under section 17(4) shall not be made unless a draft of it has been laid before, and approved by a resolution of, each House of Parliament.

(4) Any statutory instrument made under this Act may—

(a) make different provision for different cases;
(b) provide for exemptions from any of its provisions; and
(c) contain such incidental, supplemental and transitional provisions as the person making it considers expedient.

Date in force
14 October 1991:SI 1991/828.

Transfer of functions
Functions of the Secretary of State, so far as exercisable in relation to Wales, transferred to the National Assembly for Wales, by the National Assembly for Wales (Transfer of Functions) Order 1999, SI 1999/672, art 2, Sch 1.

Regulations
See the Disabled Children (Direct Payments) (England) Regulations 2001, SI 2001/442, The Day Care and Child Minding (National Standards) (England)Regulations 2001, SI 2001/1828, Child Minding and Day Care (Registration and Annual Fees) Regulations 2001, SI 2001/1886 and the Disabled Children (Direct Payments) (Wales) Regulations 2001, SI 2001/2192.

105 Interpretation

(1) In this Act—

'adoption agency' means a body which may be referred to as an adoption agency by virtue of section 1 of the Adoption Act 1976;

['appropriate children's home' has the meaning given by section 23;]

'bank holiday' means a day which is a bank holiday under the Banking and Financial Dealings Act 1971;

['care home' has the same meaning as in the Care Standards Act 2000;]

'care order' has the meaning given by section 31(11) and also includes any order which by or under any enactment has the effect of, or is deemed to be, a care order for the purposes of this Act; and any reference to a child who is in the care of an authority is a reference to a child who is in their care by virtue of a care order;

'child' means, subject to paragraph 16 of Schedule 1, a person under the age of eighteen;

'child assessment order' has the meaning given by section 43(2);

'child minder' has the meaning given by section 71;

'child of the family', in relation to the parties to a marriage, means—

(a) a child of both of those parties;
(b) any other child, not being a child who is placed with those parties as foster parents by a local authority or voluntary organisation, who has been treated by both of those parties as a child of their family;

'children's home' has the same meaning as in section 63;

['children's home' has the meaning given by section 23;]

'community home' has the meaning given by section 53;

'contact order' has the meaning given by section 8(1);

'day care' [(except in Part XA)] has the same meaning as in section 18;

'disabled', in relation to a child, has the same meaning as in section 17(11); . . .

'domestic premises' has the meaning given by section 71(12);

[dwelling-house' includes—

(a) any building or part of a building which is occupied as a dwelling;

(b) any caravan, house-boat or structure which is occupied as a dwelling;

and any yard, garden, garage or outhouse belonging to it and occupied with it;]

'education supervision order' has the meaning given in section 36;

'emergency protection order' means an order under section 44;

'family assistance order' has the meaning given in section 16(2);

'family proceedings' has the meaning given by section 8(3);

'functions' includes powers and duties;

'guardian of a child' means a guardian (other than a guardian of the estate of a child) appointed in accordance with the provisions of section 5;

'harm' has the same meaning as in section 31(9) and the question of whether harm is significant shall be determined in accordance with section 31(10);

['Health Authority' means a Health Authority established under section 8 of the National Health Service Act 1977;]

'health service hospital' has the same meaning as in the National Health Service Act 1977;

'hospital' [(except in Schedule 9A)] has the same meaning as in the Mental Health Act 1983, except that it does not include a *special hospital within the meaning of that Act* [hospital at which high security psychiatric services within the meaning of that Act are provided];

'ill-treatment' has the same meaning as in section 31(9);

['income-based jobseeker's allowance' has the same meaning as in the Jobseekers Act 1995;]

['independent hospital' has the same meaning as in the Care Standards Act 2000;]

'independent school' has the same meaning as in [the Education Act 1996];

'local authority' means, in relation to England . . . the council of a county, a metropolitan district, a London Borough or the Common Council of the City of London[, in relation to Wales, the council of a county or a county borough] and, in relation to Scotland, a local authority within the meaning of section 1(2) of the Social Work (Scotland) Act 1968;

'local authority foster parent' has the same meaning as in section 23(3);

'local education authority' has the same meaning as in [the Education Act 1996];

'local housing authority' has the same meaning as in the Housing Act 1985;

'mental nursing home' has the same meaning as in the Registered Homes Act 1984;

'nursing home' has the same meaning as in the Act of 1984;

['officer of the Service' has the same meaning as in the Criminal Justice and Court Services Act 2000;]

'parental responsibility' has the meaning given in section 3;

'parental responsibility agreement' has the meaning given in section 4(1);

'prescribed' means prescribed by regulations made under this Act;

['private children's home' means a children's home in respect of which a person is registered under Part II of the Care Standards Act 2000 which is not a community home or a voluntary home;]

['Primary Care Trust' means a Primary Care Trust established under section 16A of the National Health Service Act 1977;]

'privately fostered child' and 'to foster a child privately' have the same meaning as in section 66;

'prohibited steps order' has the meaning given by section 8(1);

'protected child' has the same meaning as in Part III of the Adoption Act 1976;

'registered children's home' has the same meaning as in section 63;

'registered pupil' has the same meaning as in [the Education Act 1996];

'relative', in relation to a child, means a grandparent, brother, sister, uncle or aunt (whether of the full blood or half blood or by affinity) or step-parent;

'residence order' has the meaning given by section 8(1);

'residential care home' has the same meaning as in the Registered Homes Act 1984 [and 'small home' has the meaning given by section 1(4A) of that Act];

'responsible person', in relation to a child who is the subject of a supervision order, has the meaning given in paragraph 1 of Schedule 3;

'school' has the same meaning as in [the Education Act 1996] or, in relation to Scotland, in the Education (Scotland) Act 1980;

'service', in relation to any provision made under Part III, includes any facility;

'signed', in relation to any person, includes the making by that person of his mark;

'special educational needs' has the same meaning as in [the Education Act 1996];

['Special Health Authority' means a Special Health Authority established under section 11 of the National Health Service Act 1977;]

'specific issue order' has the meaning given by section 8(1);

'supervision order' has the meaning given by section 31(11);

'supervised child' and 'supervisor', in relation to a supervision order or an education supervision order, mean respectively the child who is (or is to be) under supervision and the person under whose supervision he is (or is to be) by virtue of the order;

'upbringing', in relation to any child, includes the care of the child but not his maintenance;

'voluntary home' has the meaning given by section 60;

'voluntary organisation' means a body (other than a public or local authority) whose activities are not carried on for profit.

(2) References in this Act to a child whose father and mother were, or (as the case may be) were not, married to each other at the time of his birth must be read with section 1 of the Family Law Reform Act 1987 (which extends the meaning of such references).

(3) References in this Act to—

(a) a person with whom a child lives, or is to live, as the result of a residence order; or

(b) a person in whose favour a residence order is in force,

shall be construed as references to the person named in the order as the person with whom the child is to live.

(4) References in this Act to a child who is looked after by a local authority have the same meaning as they have (by virtue of section 22) in Part III.

(5) References in this Act to accommodation provided by or on behalf of a local authority are references to accommodation so provided in the exercise of functions [of that or any other local authority which are social services functions within the meaning of] the Local Authority Social Services Act 1970.

[(5A) References in this Act to a child minder shall be construed—

(a) . . .

(b) in relation to England and Wales, in accordance with section 79A.]

[(5B) References in this Act to acting as a child minder and to a child minder shall be construed, in relation to Scotland, in accordance with section 2(17) of the Regulation of Care (Scotland) Act 2001 (asp 8).]

(6) In determining the 'ordinary residence' of a child for any purpose of this Act, there shall be disregarded any period in which he lives in any place—

(a) which is a school or other institution;

(b) in accordance with the requirements of a supervision order under this Act or an order under [section 63(1) of the Powers of Criminal Courts (Sentencing) Act 2000]; or

(c) while he is being provided with accommodation by or on behalf of a local authority.

(7) References in this Act to children who are in need shall be construed in accordance with section 17.

(8) Any notice or other document required under this Act to be served on any person may be served on him by being delivered personally to him, or being sent by post to him in a registered letter or by the recorded delivery service at his proper address.

(9) Any such notice or other document required to be served on a body corporate or a firm shall be duly served if it is served on the secretary or clerk of that body or a partner of that firm.

(10) For the purposes of this section, and of section 7 of the Interpretation Act 1978 in its application to this section, the proper address of a person—

(a) in the case of a secretary or clerk of a body corporate, shall be that of the registered or principal office of that body;

(b) in the case of a partner of a firm, shall be that of the principal office of the firm; and

(c) in any other case, shall be the last known address of the person to be served.

Date in force
14 October 1991: SI 1991/828.

Amendment
Sub-s (1): Registered Homes (Amendment) Act 1991, s 2(6), Local Government (Wales) Act 1994, Sch 10, para 13, Sch 18, Health Authorities Act 1995, Sch 1 ,para 118, Sch 3, Jobseekers Act 1995, Sch 2, para 19, Education Act 1996, Sch 37, para 19, SI 2000/90, Sch2, para 5, Care Standards Act 2001, Sch 4, paras 14, 23. Sub-s (5): Local Government Act 2000, Sch 5, para 22. Sub-s (6): Powers of Criminal Courts (Sentencing) Act 2000, Sch 9, para 129.

106 Financial provisions

(1) Any—

(a) grants made by the Secretary of State under this Act; and

(b) any other expenses incurred by the Secretary of State under this Act,

shall be payable out of money provided by Parliament.

(2) Any sums received by the Secretary of State under section 58, or by way of the repayment of any grant made under section 82(2) or (4) shall be paid into the Consolidated Fund.

Date in force
14 October 1991: SI 1991/828.

Transfer of functions
Functions of the Secretary of State, so far as exercisable in relation to Wales, transferred to the National Assembly for Wales, by the National Assembly for Wales (Transfer of Functions) Order 1999, SI 1999/672, art 2, Sch 1.

107 Application to Channel Islands

Her Majesty may by Order in Council direct that any of the provisions of this Act shall extend to any of the Channel Islands with such exceptions and modifications as may be specified in the Order.

Date in force
14 October 1991: SI 1991/828.

108 Short title, commencement, extent etc

(1) This Act may be cited as the Children Act 1989.

(2) Sections 89 and 96(3) to (7), and paragraph 35 of Schedule 12, shall come into force on the passing of this Act and paragraph 36 of Schedule 12 shall come into force at the end of the period of two months beginning with the day on which this Act is

passed but otherwise this Act shall come into force on such date as may be appointed by order made by the Lord Chancellor or the Secretary of State, or by both acting jointly.

(3) Different dates may be appointed for different provisions of this Act and in relation to different cases.

(4) The minor amendments set out in Schedule 12 shall have effect.

(5) The consequential amendments set out in Schedule 13 shall have effect.

(6) The transitional provisions and savings set out in Schedule 14 shall have effect.

(7) The repeals set out in Schedule 15 shall have effect.

(8) An order under subsection (2) may make such transitional provisions or savings as appear to the person making the order to be necessary or expedient in connection with the provisions brought into force by the order, including—

(a) provisions adding to or modifying the provisions of Schedule 14; and
(b) such adaptations —

    (i) of the provisions brought into force by the order; and
    (ii) of any provisions of this Act then in force,

as appear to him necessary or expedient in consequence of the partial operation of this Act.

(9) The Lord Chancellor may by order make such amendments or repeals, in such enactments as may be specified in the order, as appear to him to be necessary or expedient in consequence of any provision of this Act.

(10) This Act shall, in its application to the Isles of Scilly, have effect subject to such exceptions, adaptations and modifications as the Secretary of State may by order prescribe.

(11) The following provisions of this Act extend to Scotland—

. . .

section 25(8);
section 50(13);

. . .

. . .

section 88;
section 104 (so far as necessary);
section 105 (so far as necessary);
subsections (1) to (3), (8) and (9) and this subsection;
in Schedule 2, paragraph 24;
in Schedule 12, paragraphs 1, 7 to 10, 18, 27, 30(a) and 41 to 44;
in Schedule 13, paragraphs 18 to 23, 32, 46, 47, 50, 57, 62, 63, 68(a) and (b) and 71;
in Schedule 14, paragraphs 1, 33 and 34;
in Schedule 15, the entries relating to—

(a) the Custody of Children Act 1891;
(b) the Nurseries and Child Minders Regulation Act 1948;
(c) section 53(3) of the Children and Young Persons Act 1963;
(d) section 60 of the Health Services and Public Health Act 1968;
(e) the Social Work (Scotland) Act 1968;
(f) the Adoption (Scotland) Act 1978;
(g) the Child Care Act 1980;
(h) the Foster Children (Scotland) Act 1984;
(i) the Child Abduction and Custody Act 1985; and
(j) the Family Law Act 1986.

(12) The following provisions of this Act extend to Northern Ireland—
section 50;
section 101(1)(b), (2) and (5)(a)(i);
subsections (1) to (3), (8) and (9) and this subsection;
in Schedule 2, paragraph 24;
in Schedule 12, paragraphs 7 to 10, 18 and 27;

in Schedule 13, paragraphs 21, 22, 46, 47, 57, 62, 63, 68(c) to (e) and 69 to 71;
in Schedule 14, paragraphs . . . 28 to 30 and 38(a); and
in Schedule 15, the entries relating to the Guardianship of Minors Act 1971, the Children Act 1975, the Child Care Act 1980, and the Family Law Act 1986.

Dates in force
Sub-ss (1), (3), (5)-(12), sub-ss (2), (4), certain purposes: 14 October 1991: SI 1991/828. Sub-s (4), certain purposes: 16 January 1990: s 108(2). Sub-ss (2), (4), remaining purposes: 16 November 1989, s 108(2).

Amendment
Sub-s (12): CLSA 1990, Sch 16, para 25.

SCHEDULES

SCHEDULE 1
Financial Provision for Children

Section 15(1)

[Not reproduced]

SCHEDULE 2
Local Authority Support for Children and Families

Sections 17, 23, 29

PART I
PROVISION OF SERVICES FOR FAMILIES

Identification of children in need and provision of information

1 (1) Every local authority shall take reasonable steps to identify the extent to which there are children in need within their area.

(2) Every local authority shall—

(a) publish information—

    (i) about services provided by them under sections 17, 18, [20, 23B to 23D, 24A and 24B]; and

    (ii) where they consider it appropriate, about the provision by others (including, in particular, voluntary organisations) of services which the authority have power to provide under those sections; and

(b) take such steps as are reasonably practicable to ensure that those who might benefit from the services receive the information relevant to them.

[Children's services plans

1A (1) Every local authority shall, on or before 31st March 1997—

(a) review their provision of services under sections 17, 20, 21, 23 and 24; and

(b) having regard to that review and to their most recent review under section 19, prepare and publish a plan for the provision of services under Part III.

(2) Every local authority—

(a) shall, from time to time review the plan prepared by them under sub-paragraph (1)(b) (as modified or last substituted under this sub-paragraph), and

   (b) may, having regard to that review and to their most recent review under section 19, prepare and publish—

      (i)   modifications (or, as the case may be, further modifications) to the plan reviewed; or

      (ii) a plan in substitution for that plan.

(3) In carrying out any review under this paragraph and in preparing any plan or modifications to a plan, a local authority shall consult—

   (a) every [Health Authority and Primary Care Trust] the whole or any part of whose area lies within the area of the local authority;

   (b) every National Health Service trust which manages a hospital, establishment or facility (within the meaning of the National Health Service and Community Care Act 1990) in the authority's area;

   (c) if the local authority is not itself a local education authority, every local education authority the whole or any part of whose area lies within the area of the local authority;

   (d) any organisation which represents schools in the authority's area which are grant-maintained schools or grant-maintained special schools (within the meaning of the Education Act 1993);

   (e) the governing body of every such school in the authority's area which is not so represented;

   (f) such voluntary organisations as appear to the local authority—

      (i)   to represent the interests of persons who use or are likely to use services provided by the local authority under Part III; or

      (ii) to provide services in the area of the local authority which, were they to be provided by the local authority, might be categorised as services provided under that Part;

   (g) the chief constable of the police force for the area;

   (h) the probation committee for the area;

   (i) such other persons as appear to the local authority to be appropriate; and

   (j) such other persons as the Secretary of State may direct.

(4) Every local authority shall, within 28 days of receiving a written request from the Secretary of State, submit to him a copy of—

   (a) the plan prepared by them under sub-paragraph (1); or

   (b) where that plan has been modified or substituted, the plan as modified or last substituted.]

Maintenance of a register of disabled children

2 (1) Every local authority shall open and maintain a register of disabled children within their area.

(2) The register may be kept by means of a computer.

Note

The Children Act 1989 Guidance and Regulations, Volume 2, Family Support, Day Care and Educational Provision for Young Children (Dept of Health, 1991) at para 2.19 recommends that local authorities, local education authorities and health authorities should draw up a common register.

Assessment of children's needs

3 Where it appears to a local authority that a child within their area is in need, the authority may assess his needs for the purposes of this Act at the same time as any assessment of his needs is made under—

   (a) the Chronically Sick and Disabled Persons Act 1970;

   (b) [Part IV of the Education Act 1996];

(c) the Disabled Persons (Services, Consultation and Representation) Act 1986; or

(d) any other enactment.

Prevention of neglect and abuse

4 (1) Every local authority shall take reasonable steps, through the provision of services under Part III of this Act, to prevent children within their area suffering ill-treatment or neglect.

(2) Where a local authority believe that a child who is at any time within their area—

(a) is likely to suffer harm; but

(b) lives or proposes to live in the area of another local authority

they shall inform that other local authority.

(3) When informing that other local authority they shall specify—

(a) the harm that they believe he is likely to suffer; and

(b) (if they can) where the child lives or proposes to live.

Provision of accommodation in order to protect child

5 (1) Where—

(a) it appears to a local authority that a child who is living on particular premises is suffering, or is likely to suffer, ill treatment at the hands of another person who is living on those premises; and

(b) that other person proposes to move from the premises,

the authority may assist that other person to obtain alternative accommodation.

(2) Assistance given under this paragraph may be in cash.

(3) Subsections (7) to (9) of section 17 shall apply in relation to assistance given under this paragraph as they apply in relation to assistance given under that section.

Provision for disabled children

6 Every local authority shall provide services designed—

(a) to minimise the effect on disabled children within their area of their disabilities; and

(b) to give such children the opportunity to lead lives which are as normal as possible.

Provision to reduce need for care proceedings etc

7 Every local authority shall take reasonable steps designed—

(a) to reduce the need to bring—

(i) proceedings for care or supervision orders with respect to children within their area;

(ii) criminal proceedings against such children;

(iii) any family or other proceedings with respect to such children which might lead to them being placed in the authority's care; or

(iv) proceedings under the inherent jurisdiction of the High Court with respect to children;

(b) to encourage children within their area not to commit criminal offences; and

(c) to avoid the need for children within their area to be placed in secure accommodation.

Provision for children living with their families

8 Every local authority shall make such provision as they consider appropriate for the following services to be available with respect to children in need within their area while they are living with their families—

(a)　advice, guidance and counselling;

(b)　occupational, social, cultural, or recreational activities;

(c)　home help (which may include laundry facilities);

(d)　facilities for, or assistance with, travelling to and from home for the purpose of taking advantage of any other service provided under this Act or of any similar service;

(e)　assistance to enable the child concerned and his family to have a holiday.

Family centres

9　(1)　Every local authority shall provide such family centres as they consider appropriate in relation to children within their area.

(2)　'Family centre' means a centre at which any of the persons mentioned in sub-paragraph (3) may—

(a)　attend for occupational, social, cultural or recreational activities;

(b)　attend for advice, guidance or counselling; or

(c)　be provided with accommodation while he is receiving advice, guidance or counselling.

(3)　The persons are—

(a)　a child;

(b)　his parents;

(c)　any person who is not a parent of his but who has parental responsibility for him;

(d)　any other person who is looking after him.

Maintenance of the family home

10　Every local authority shall take such steps as are reasonably practicable, where any child within their area who is in need and whom they are not looking after is living apart from his family—

(a)　to enable him to live with his family; or

(b)　to promote contact between him and his family,

if, in their opinion, it is necessary to do so in order to safeguard or promote his welfare.

Duty to consider racial groups to which children in need belong

11　Every local authority shall, in making any arrangements—

(a)　for the provision of day care within their area; or

(b)　designed to encourage persons to act as local authority foster parents,

have regard to the different racial groups to which children within their area who are in need belong.

Date in force
14 October 1991: SI 1991/828.

Amendment
Para 1: in sub-para (2)(a)(i) words "20, 23B to 23D, 24A and 24B" in square brackets substituted by the Children (Leaving Care) Act 2000, s 7(1), (4).
Para 1A: inserted by SI 1996/785, art 2.
Para 1A: in sub-para (3)(a) words "Health Authority and Primary Care Trust" in square brackets substituted by SI 2000/90, art 3(1), Sch 1, para 24(1), (11).
Para 1A: in sub-para (3)(a) word "and" in italics repealed and subsequent word in square brackets substituted by the National Health SErvice REform and Health Care Professions Act 2002, s 2(5), Sch 2, Pt 2, para 52.
Para 3: in sub-para (b) words "Part IV of the Education Act 1996" in square brackets substituted by the Education Act 1996, s 582(1), Sch 37, para 92

Definitions

For 'local authority', 'child', 'voluntary organisation', 'service' see s 105(1); for 'child in need' and 'family' see s 17(10); for 'disabled' see s 17(11); for 'ill-treatment', 'harm', see s 31(9) as applied to the whole Act by s 105(1); for 'care order', 'supervision order' see s 31(11); for 'family proceedings' see s 8(3)(4)(a); for 'secure accommodation' see s 25(1); for 'family centre' see para (9); for 'parental responsibility' see s 3.

Reference

'Part III of this Act' ie ss 17-30 and Sch 2 (local authority support for children and families).

Transfer of functions

Functions of the Secretary of State, so far as exercisable in relation to Wales, transferred to the National Assembly for Wales, by the National Assembly for Wales (Transfer of Functions) Order 1999, SI 1999/672.

PART II
CHILDREN LOOKED AFTER BY LOCAL AUTHORITIES

Regulations as to placing of children with local authority foster parents

12 Regulations under section 23(2)(a) may, in particular, make provision—

(a) with regard to the welfare of children placed with local authority foster parents;

(b) as to the arrangements to be made by local authorities in connection with the health and education of such children;

(c) as to the records to be kept by local authorities;

(d) for securing that a child is not placed with a local authority foster parent unless that person is for the time being approved as a local authority foster parent by such local authority as may be prescribed;

(e) for securing that where possible the local authority foster parent with whom a child is to be placed is—

    (i) of the same religious persuasion as the child; or

    (ii) gives an undertaking that the child will be brought up in that religious persuasion;

(f) for securing that children placed with local authority foster parents, and the premises in which they are accommodated, will be supervised and inspected by a local authority and that the children will be removed from those premises if their welfare appears to require it;

(g) as to the circumstances in which local authorities may make arrangements for duties imposed on them by the regulations to be discharged, on their behalf.

Note

See the Foster Placement (Children) Regulations 1991, SI 1991/910 amended by SI 1995/2015, SI 1997/2308, SI 1999/2768 and SI 2001/2992 (England) and 3443 (Wales) revoked in so far as they apply to England and substituted by the Fostering Services Regulations 2002, SI 2002/57 amended by SI 2002/865, and the Arrangements for Placement of Children (General) Regulations 1999, SI 1991/890 amended by SI 1991/2033, SI 1993/3069, SI 1995/2015, SI 1997/649 and by SI 2002/546. For disqualification as a foster parent, see *Re S (Foster Placement (Children) Regulations 1991)* [2000] 1 FLR 648, FD.

Regulations as to arrangements under section 23(2)(f)

13 Regulations under section 23(2)(f) may, in particular, make provisions as to—

(a) the persons to be notified of any proposed arrangements;

(b) the opportunities such persons are to have to make representations in relation to the arrangements proposed;

(c) the persons to be notified of any proposed changes in arrangements;

(d) the records to be kept by local authorities;

(e) the supervision by local authorities of any arrangements made.

Note
See the Arrangements for Placement of Children (General) Regulations 1991, SI 1991/890 amended by SI 1991/2033, SI 1993/3069, SI 1995/2015, SI 1997/649 and by SI 2002/546.

Regulations as to conditions under which child in care is allowed to live with parent, etc

14 Regulations under section 23(5) may, in particular, impose requirements on a local authority as to—

(a) the making of any decision by a local authority to allow a child to live with any person falling within section 23(4) (including requirements as to those who must be consulted before the decision is made, and those who must be notified when it has been made);

(b) the supervision or medical examination of the child concerned;

(c) the removal of the child, in such circumstances as may be prescribed, from the care of the person with whom he has been allowed to live;

[(d) the records to be kept by local authorities.]

Date in force
14 October 1991: see SI 1991/828, art 3(2).

Amendment
Para 14: sub para (d) inserted by The Courts and Legal Services Act 1990, s 116, para 26.

Note
See the Placement of Children with Parents etc Regulations 1991, SI 1991/893 amended by SI 1995/2015 and SI 2002/546.

Promotion and maintenance of contact between child and family

15 (1) Where a child is being looked after by a local authority, the authority shall, unless it is not reasonably practicable or consistent with his welfare, endeavour to promote contact between the child and—

(a) his parents;

(b) any person who is not a parent of his but who has parental responsibility for him; and

(c) any relative, friend or other person connected with him.

(2) Where a child is being looked after by a local authority—

(a) the authority shall take such steps as are reasonably practicable to secure that—

(i) his parents; and

(ii) any person who is not a parent of his but who has parental responsibility for him,

are kept informed of where he is being accommodated; and

(b) every such person shall secure that the authority are kept informed of his or her address.

(3) Where a local authority ('the receiving authority') take over the provision of accommodation for a child from another local authority ('the transferring authority') under section 20(2)—

(a) the receiving authority shall (where reasonably practicable) inform—

(i) the child's parents; and

(ii) any person who is not a parent of his but who has parental responsibility for him;

(b) sub-paragraph (2)(a) shall apply to the transferring authority, as well as the receiving authority, until at least one such person has been informed of the change; and

(c) sub-paragraph (2)(b) shall not require any person to inform the receiving authority of his address until he has been so informed.

(4) Nothing in this paragraph requires a local authority to inform any person of the whereabouts of a child if—

(a) the child is in the care of the authority; and
(b) the authority has reasonable cause to believe that informing the person would prejudice the child's welfare.

(5) Any person who fails (without reasonable excuse) to comply with sub-paragraph (2)(b) shall be guilty of an offence and liable on summary conviction to a fine not exceeding level 2 on the standard scale.

(6) It shall be a defence in any proceedings under sub-paragraph (5) to prove that the defendant was residing at the same address as another person who was the child's parent or had parental responsibility for the child and had reasonable cause to believe that the other person had informed the appropriate authority that both of them were residing at that address.

Visits to or by children: expenses

16 (1) This paragraph applies where—

(a) a child is being looked after by a local authority; and
(b) the conditions mentioned in sub-paragraph (3) are satisfied.

(2) The authority may—

(a) make payments to—

(i) a parent of the child;
(ii) any person who is not a parent of his but who has parental responsibility for him; or
(iii) any relative, friend or other person connected with him,

in respect of travelling, subsistence or other expenses incurred by that person in visiting the child; or

(b) make payments to the child, or to any person on his behalf, in respect of travelling, subsistence or other expenses incurred by or on behalf of the child in his visiting—

(i) a parent of his;
(ii) any person who is not a parent of his but who has parental responsibility for him; or
(iii) any relative, friend or other person connected with him.

(3) The conditions are that—

(a) it appears to the authority that the visit in question could not otherwise be made without undue financial hardship; and
(b) the circumstances warrant the making of the payments.

Appointment of visitor for child who is not being visited

17 (1) Where it appears to a local authority in relation to any child that they are looking after that—

(a) communication between the child and—

(i) a parent of his, or
(ii) any person who is not a parent of his but who has parental responsibility for him,

has been infrequent; or

(b) he has not visited or been visited by (or lived with) any such person during the preceding twelve months,

and that it would be in the child's best interests for an independent person to be appointed to be his visitor for the purposes of this paragraph, they shall appoint such a visitor.

(2) A person so appointed shall—

(a) have the duty of visiting, advising and befriending the child; and

(b) be entitled to recover from the authority who appointed him any reasonable expenses incurred by him for the purposes of his functions under this paragraph.

(3) A person's appointment as a visitor in pursuance of this paragraph shall be determined if—

(a) he gives notice in writing to the authority who appointed him that he resigns the appointment; or

(b) the authority give him notice in writing that they have terminated it.

(4) The determination of such an appointment shall not prejudice any duty under this paragraph to make a further appointment.

(5) Where a local authority propose to appoint a visitor for a child under this paragraph, the appointment shall not be made if—

(a) the child objects to it; and

(b) the authority are satisfied that he has sufficient understanding to make an informed decision.

(6) Where a visitor has been appointed for a child under this paragraph, the local authority shall determine the appointment if—

(a) the child objects to its continuing; and

(b) the authority are satisfied that he has sufficient understanding to make an informed decision.

(7) The Secretary of State may make regulations as to the circumstances in which a person appointed as a visitor under this paragraph is to be regarded as independent of the local authority appointing him.

_____

Note

See the Definition of Independent Visitors (Children) Regulations 1991, SI 1991/892 amended by SI 2001/2237 (England).

_____

Power to guarantee apprenticeship deeds etc

18 (1) While a child is being looked after by a local authority, or is a person qualifying for advice and assistance, the authority may undertake any obligation by way of guarantee under any deed of apprenticeship or articles of clerkship which he enters into.

(2) Where a local authority have undertaken any such obligation under any deed or articles they may at any time (whether or not they are still looking after the person concerned) undertake the like obligation under any supplemental deed or articles.

Arrangements to assist children to live abroad

19 (1) A local authority may only arrange for, or assist in arranging for, any child in their care to live outside England and Wales with the approval of the court.

(2) A local authority may, with the approval of every person who has parental responsibility for the child arrange for, or assist in arranging for, any other child looked after by them to live outside England and Wales.

(3) The court shall not give its approval under sub-paragraph (1) unless it is satisfied that—

(a) living outside England and Wales would be in the child's best interests;

(b) suitable arrangements have been, or will be, made for his reception and welfare in the country in which he will live;

(c) the child has consented to living in that country; and

(d) every person who has parental responsibility for the child has consented to his living in that country.

(4) Where the court is satisfied that the child does not have sufficient understanding to give or withhold his consent, it may disregard sub-paragraph (3)(c) and give its approval if the child is to live in the country concerned with a parent, guardian, or other suitable person.

(5) Where a person whose consent is required by sub-paragraph (3)(d) fails to give his consent, the court may disregard that provision and give its approval if it is satisfied that that person—

(a) cannot be found;

(b) is incapable of consenting; or

(c) is withholding his consent unreasonably.

(6) Section 56 of the Adoption Act 1976 (which requires authority for the taking or sending abroad for adoption of a child who is a British subject) shall not apply in the case of any child who is to live outside England and Wales with the approval of the court given under this paragraph.

(7) Where a court decides to give its approval under this paragraph it may order that its decision is not to have effect during the appeal period.

(8) In sub-paragraph (7) 'the appeal period' means—

(a) where an appeal is made against the decision, the period between the making of the decision and the determination of the appeal; and

(b) otherwise, the period during which an appeal may be made against the decision.

[Preparation for ceasing to be looked after

19A It is the duty of the local authority looking after a child to advise, assist and befriend him with a view to promoting his welfare when they have ceased to look after him.

Date in force
14 October 1991: see SI 1991/828, art 3(2).

Amendment
Paras 19A–19C: inserted by the Children (Leaving Care) Act 2000 S1.

19B (1) A local authority shall have the following additional functions in relation to an eligible child whom they are looking after.

(2) In sub-paragraph (1) 'eligible child' means, subject to sub-paragraph (3), a child who—

(a) is aged sixteen or seventeen; and

(b) has been looked after by a local authority for a prescribed period, or periods amounting in all to a prescribed period, which began after he reached a prescribed age and ended after he reached the age of sixteen.

(3) The Secretary of State may prescribe—

(a) additional categories of eligible children; and

(b) categories of children who are not to be eligible children despite falling within sub-paragraph (2).

(4) For each eligible child, the local authority shall carry out an assessment of his needs with a view to determining what advice, assistance and support it would be appropriate for them to provide him under this Act—

(a) while they are still looking after him; and
(b) after they cease to look after him,

and shall then prepare a pathway plan for him.

(5) The local authority shall keep the pathway plan under regular review.

(6) Any such review may be carried out at the same time as a review of the child's case carried out by virtue of section 26.

(7) The Secretary of State may by regulations make provision as to assessments for the purposes of sub-paragraph (4).

(8) The regulations may in particular provide for the matters set out in section 23B(6).

Date in force
14 October 1991: see SI 1991/828, art 3(2).

Amendment
Paras 19A–19C: inserted by the Children (Leaving Care) Act 2000 S1.

Regulations
See the Children Leaving Care (Wales) Regulations 2001, SI 2001/2189 amended by SI 2002/546 and 1855 and the Children Leaving Care (England) Regulations 2001, SI 2001/2874 amended by SI 2002.546.

Personal advisers

19C A local authority shall arrange for each child whom they are looking after who is an eligible child for the purposes of paragraph 19B to have a personal adviser.]

Date in force
14 October 1991: see SI 1991/828, art 3(2).

Amendment
Paras 19A–19C: inserted by the Children (Leaving Care) Act 2000 S1.

Death of children being looked after by local authorities

20 (1) If a child who is being looked after by a local authority dies, the authority—

(a) shall notify the Secretary of State;
(b) shall, so far as is reasonably practicable, notify the child's parents and every person who is not a parent of his but who has parental responsibility for him;
(c) may, with the consent (so far as it is reasonably practicable to obtain it) of every person who has parental responsibility for the child, arrange for the child's body to be buried or cremated; and
(d) may, if the conditions mentioned in sub-paragraph (2) are satisfied, make payments to any person who has parental responsibility for the child, or any relative, friend or other person connected with the child, in respect of travelling, subsistence or other expenses incurred by that person in attending the child's funeral.

(2) The conditions are that—

(a) it appears to the authority that the person concerned could not otherwise attend the child's funeral without undue financial hardship; and
(b) that the circumstances warrant the making of the payments.

(3) Sub-paragraph (1) does not authorise cremation where it does not accord with the practice of the child's religious persuasion.

(4) Where a local authority have exercised their power under sub-paragraph (1)(c) with respect to a child who was under sixteen when he died, they may recover from any parent of the child any expenses incurred by them.

(5) Any sums so recoverable shall, without prejudice to any other method of recovery, be recoverable summarily as a civil debt.

(6) Nothing in this paragraph affects any enactment regulating or authorising the burial, cremation or anatomical examination of the body of a deceased person.

Date in force
14 October 1991: SI 1991/828.

Definitions
For 'a child who is looked after by a local authority' see s 22(1); for 'child', 'local authority', 'relative', 'child who is in the care of a local authority' see s 105(1); for 'local authority foster parent' see s 23(3); for 'parental responsibility' see s 3; for 'the receiving authority', 'the transferring authority' see para 15(3); for 'court' see s 92(7); for 'appeal period' see para 19(8).

References
For 'welfare of the child' see paras 2.2ff. For 'the standard scale' see the CJA 1982, s 37(2), (3) as amended.

Para 20(1)(c)
If the child dies any order in respect of him terminates. The local authority or other person who had parental responsibility under an order is not entitled to arrange for burial or cremation; the authority is given power to do so with the consent of the person having parental responsibility or in default. This would appear to be the effect of *R v Gwynedd County Council, ex p B* [1992] 3 All ER 317, [1991] 2 FLR 365, CA, a case under the CCA 1980, s 25.

PART III
CONTRIBUTIONS TOWARDS MAINTENANCE OF CHILDREN LOOKED AFTER BY LOCAL AUTHORITIES

Liability to contribute

21 (1) Where a local authority are looking after a child (other than in the cases mentioned in sub-paragraph (7)) they shall consider whether they should recover contributions towards the child's maintenance from any person liable to contribute ('a contributor').

(2) An authority may only recover contributions from a contributor if they consider it reasonable to do so.

(3) The persons liable to contribute are—

(a) where the child is under sixteen, each of his parents;
(b) where he has reached the age of sixteen, the child himself.

(4) A parent is not liable to contribute during any period when he is in receipt of income support[, working families' tax credit] [or disabled person's tax credit] under the [Part VII of the Social Security Contributions and Benefits Act 1992] [or of an income-based jobseeker's allowance].

(5) A person is not liable to contribute towards the maintenance of a child in the care of a local authority in respect of any period during which the child is allowed by the authority (under section 23(5)) to live with a parent of his.

(6) A contributor is not obliged to make any contribution towards a child's maintenance except as agreed or determined in accordance with this Part of this Schedule.

(7) The cases are where the child is looked after by a local authority under—

(a) section 21;
(b) an interim care order;
(c) [section 92 of the Powers of Criminal Courts (Sentencing) Act 2000].

Amendments
Para 21: in sub para (4) words "disabled person's tax credit" in square brackets substituted by virtue of the Tax Credit Act, S1(2), sch 1, paras 1(b), (6)(iii).

Para 21: in sub para (4) words "Part VII of the Social SEcurity Contribution and Benefits Act 1992" in square brackets substituted by the Social Security (Consequential Provisions) Act 1992, s 4, sch 2, para 108(C).

Para 21: in sub para (4) words "of any element " to "working tax credit" in square brackets inserted by the Tax Credits Act 2002, s 47, sch 3, paras 15, 20(b).

Para 21: in sub para (4) words "of an income-based jobseeker's allowance" in square brackets inserted by the Jobseekers Act 1995, s 41(4), sch 2, para 19(5).

Para 21: in sub para (4) words "working families' tax credit" in square brackets substituted by virtue of the Tax Credits Act 1999, s 1(2), sch 1, paras 1(a), 6(d)(iii).

Para 21: in sub para (4) words from "working families tax credit" to "tax credit under the" in italics repealed and subsequent words in square brackets substituted by the Tax Credits Act 2002, s 61.

Para 21: in sub para (7)(c) words "section 92 of the Powers of Criminal Courts (sentencing) Act 2000, s 165(1), sch 9, para 130.

Note

It should be noted that, unlike the provisions in Sch 1, para 4, ante, there is no reference in Sch 2 to the requirement for the court to have regard to the child's needs nor even of the the local authority's expenditure on behalf of the child, *see Re C (a minor) (Contribution Notice)* [1994] 1 FLR 111.

Agreed contributions

22 (1) Contributions towards a child's maintenance may only be recovered if the local authority have served a notice ('a contribution notice') on the contributor specifying—

(a)   the weekly sum which they consider that he should contribute; and

(b)   arrangements for payment.

(2) The contribution notice must be in writing and dated.

(3) Arrangements for payment shall, in particular, include—

(a)   the date on which liability to contribute begins (which must not be earlier than the date of the notice);

(b)   the date on which liability under the notice will end (if the child has not before that date ceased to be looked after by the authority); and

(c)   the date on which the first payment is to be made.

(4) The authority may specify in a contribution notice a weekly sum which is a standard contribution determined by them for all children looked after by them.

(5) The authority may not specify in a contribution notice a weekly sum greater than that which they consider—

(a)   they would normally be prepared to pay if they had placed a similar child with local authority foster parents; and

(b)   it is reasonably practicable for the contributor to pay (having regard to his means).

(6) An authority may at any time withdraw a contribution notice (without prejudice to their power to serve another).

(7) Where the authority and the contributor agree—

(a)   the sum which the contributor is to contribute; and

(b)   arrangements for payment,

(whether as specified in the contribution notice or otherwise) and the contributor notifies the authority in writing that he so agrees, the authority may recover summarily as a civil debt any contribution which is overdue and unpaid.

(8) A contributor may, by serving a notice in writing on the authority, withdraw his agreement in relation to any period of liability falling after the date of service of the notice.

(9) Sub-paragraph (7) is without prejudice to any other method of recovery.

Amendments
14 October 1991: SI 1991/828.

Note

Paragraph 22(4) is permissive only and not mandatory: *Re C (A minor) (Contribution Notice)* [1994] 1 FLR 111.

Contribution orders

23 (1) Where a contributor has been served with a contribution notice and has—

(a) failed to reach any agreement with the local authority as mentioned in paragraph 22(7) within the period of one month beginning with the day on which the contribution notice was served; or

(b) served a notice under paragraph 22(8) withdrawing his agreement,

the authority may apply to the court for an order under this paragraph.

(2) On such an application the court may make an order ('a contribution order') requiring the contributor to contribute a weekly sum towards the child's maintenance in accordance with arrangements for payment specified by the court.

(3) A contribution order—

(a) shall not specify a weekly sum greater than that specified in the contribution notice; and

(b) shall be made with due regard to the contributor's means.

(4) A contribution order shall not—

(a) take effect before the date specified in the contribution notice; or

(b) have effect while the contributor is not liable to contribute (by virtue of paragraph 21); or

(c) remain in force after the child has ceased to be looked after by the authority who obtained the order.

(5) An authority may not apply to the court under sub-paragraph (1) in relation to a contribution notice which they have withdrawn.

(6) Where—

(a) a contribution order is in force;

(b) the authority serve another contribution notice; and

(c) the contributor and the authority reach an agreement under paragraph 22(7) in respect of that other contribution notice,

the effect of the agreement shall be to discharge the order from the date on which it is agreed that the agreement shall take effect.

(7) Where an agreement is reached under sub-paragraph (6) the authority shall notify the court—

(a) of the agreement; and

(b) of the date on which it took effect.

(8) A contribution order may be varied or revoked on the application of the contributor or the authority.

(9) In proceedings for the variation of a contribution order, the authority shall specify—

(a) the weekly sum which, having regard to paragraph 22, they propose that the contributor should contribute under the order as varied; and

(b) the proposed arrangements for payment.

(10) Where a contribution order is varied, the order—

(a) shall not specify a weekly sum greater than that specified by the authority in the proceedings for variation; and

(b) shall be made with due regard to the contributor's means.

(11) An appeal shall lie in accordance with rules of court from any order made under this paragraph.

Court
FPC (CA 1989) R 1991, r 30.

Para 23(3)(b)
Due regard to means the liability is not prior to other items of reasonable expenditure: *Re C (a minor: contribution notice)* [1994] 1 FLR 111.

Enforcement of contribution orders etc

24 (1) A contribution order made by a magistrates' court shall be enforceable as a magistrates' court maintenance order (within the meaning of section 150(1) of the Magistrates' Courts Act 1980).

(2) Where a contributor has agreed, or has been ordered, to make contributions to a local authority, any other local authority within whose area the contributor is for the time being living may—

(a) at the request of the local authority who served the contributions notice; and
(b) subject to agreement as to any sum to be deducted in respect of services rendered,

collect from the contributor any contributions due on behalf of the authority who served the notice.

(3) In sub-paragraph (2) the reference to any other local authority includes a reference to—

(a) a local authority within the meaning of section 1(2) of the Social Work (Scotland) Act 1968; and
(b) a Health and Social Services Board established under Article 16 of the Health and Personal Social Services (Northern Ireland) Order 1972.

(4) The power to collect sums under sub-paragraph (2) includes the power to—

(a) receive and give a discharge for any contributions due; and
(b) (if necessary) enforce payment of any contributions,

even though those contributions may have fallen due at a time when the contributor was living elsewhere.

(5) Any contribution collected under sub-paragraph (2) shall be paid (subject to any agreed deduction) to the local authority who served the contribution notice.

(6) In any proceedings under this paragraph, a document which purports to be—

(a) a copy of an order made by a court under or by virtue of paragraph 23; and
(b) certified as a true copy by the [justices' chief executive for] the court,

shall be evidence of the order.

(7) In any proceedings under this paragraph, a certificate which—

(a) purports to be signed by the clerk or some other duly authorised officer of the local authority who obtained the contribution order; and
(b) states that any sum due to the authority under the order is overdue and unpaid,

shall be evidence that the sum is overdue and unpaid.

Date in force
14 October 1991: SI 1991/828.

Amendments
Para 24: in sub-para 6(b) words "justices' chief executive for" in square brackets substituted by the Access to Justice Act 1999, s 90(1), sch 13, paras 159, 162.

Regulations

25 The Secretary of State may make regulations—

(a) as to the considerations which a local authority must take into account in deciding—

    (i) whether it is reasonable to recover contributions; and

    (ii) what the arrangements for payment should be;

(b) as to the procedures they must follow in reaching agreements with—

    (i) contributors (under paragraphs 22 and 23); and

    (ii) any other local authority (under paragraph 23).

Date in force
14 October 1991: SI 1991/828.

Definitions
For 'local authority', 'child' see s 105(1); for 'a child who is looked after by a local authority' see s 22(1); for 'a contributor' see para 21(1); for 'a contribution notice' see para 22(1); for 'local authority foster parent' see s 23(3); for 'court' see s 92(7); for 'a contribution order' see para 23(2).

References
For 'charging for services' see Department of Health Guidance Volume 2, para 2.38. 'This Part of this Schedule' ie Pt III, paras 21-25 made under s 29(6). For interim care orders see s 38; for service of notices generally under the Act see s 105(8)-(10).

SCHEDULE 3
Supervision Orders

Sections 35, 36

PART I
GENERAL

Meaning of 'responsible person'

1 In this Schedule, 'the responsible person', in relation to a supervised child, means—

(a) any person who has parental responsibility for the child; and

(b) any other person with whom the child is living.

Power of supervisor to give directions to supervised child

2 (1) A supervision order may require the supervised child to comply with any directions given from time to time by the supervisor which require him to do all or any of the following things—

(a) to live at a place or places specified in the directions for a period or periods so specified;

(b) to present himself to a person or persons specified in the directions at a place or places and on a day or days so specified;

(c) to participate in activities specified in the directions on a day or days so specified.

(2) It shall be for the supervisor to decide whether, and to what extent, he exercises his power to give directions and to decide the form of any directions which he gives.

(3) Sub-paragraph (1) does not confer on a supervisor power to give directions in respect of any medical or psychiatric examination or treatment (which are matters dealt with in paragraphs 4 and 5).

Imposition of obligations on responsible person

3 (1) With the consent of any responsible person, a supervision order may include a requirement—

(a) that he take all reasonable steps to ensure that the supervised child complies with any direction given by the supervisor under paragraph 2;

(b) that he take all reasonable steps to ensure that the supervised child complies with any requirement included in the order under paragraph 4 or 5;

(c) that he comply with any directions given by the supervisor requiring him to attend at a place specified in the directions for the purpose of taking part in activities so specified.

(2) A direction given under sub-paragraph (1)(c) may specify the time at which the responsible person is to attend and whether or not the supervised child is required to attend with him.

(3) A supervision order may require any person who is a responsible person in relation to the supervised child to keep the supervisor informed of his address, if it differs from the child's.

Psychiatric and medical examinations

4 (1) A supervision order may require the supervised child—

(a) to submit to a medical or psychiatric examination; or

(b) to submit to any such examination from time to time as directed by the supervisor.

(2) Any such examination shall be required to be conducted—

(a) by, or under the direction of, such registered medical practitioner as may be specified in the order;

(b) at a place specified in the order and at which the supervised child is to attend as a non-resident patient; or

(c) at—

    (i) a health service hospital; or

    (ii) in the case of a psychiatric examination, a hospital *or mental nursing home* [, independent hospital or care home],

at which the child is, or is to attend as, a resident patient.

(3) A requirement of a kind mentioned in sub-paragraph (2)(c) shall not be included unless the court is satisfied, on the evidence of a registered medical practitioner, that—

(a) the child may be suffering from a physical or mental condition that requires, and may be susceptible to, treatment; and

(b) a period as a resident patient is necessary if the examination is to be carried out properly.

(4) No court shall include a requirement under this paragraph in a supervision order unless it is satisfied that—

(a) where the child has sufficient understanding to make an informed decision, he consents to its inclusion; and

(b) satisfactory arrangements have been, or can be, made for the examination.

Psychiatric and medical treatment

5 (1) Where a court which proposes to make or vary a supervision order is satisfied, on the evidence of a registered medical practitioner approved for the purposes of section 12 of the Mental Health Act 1983, that the mental condition of the supervised child—

(a) is such as requires, and may be susceptible to, treatment; but

(b) is not such as to warrant his detention in pursuance of a hospital order under Part III of that Act,

the court may include in the order a requirement that the supervised child shall, for a period specified in the order, submit to such treatment as is so specified.

(2) The treatment specified in accordance with sub-paragraph (1) must be—

(a) by, or under the direction of, such registered medical practitioner as may be specified in the order;

(b) as a non-resident patient at such a place as may be so specified; or

(c) as a resident patient in a hospital *or mental nursing home* [, independent hospital or care home].

(3) Where a court which proposes to make or vary a supervision order is satisfied, on the evidence of a registered medical practitioner, that the physical condition of the supervised child is such as requires, and may be susceptible to, treatment, the court may include in the order a requirement that the supervised child shall, for a period specified in the order, submit to such treatment as is so specified.

(4) The treatment specified in accordance with sub-paragraph (3) must be—

(a) by, or under the direction of, such registered medical practitioner as may be specified in the order;

(b) as a non-resident patient at such place as may be so specified; or

(c) as a resident patient in a health service hospital.

(5) No court shall include a requirement under this paragraph in a supervision order unless it is satisfied—

(a) where the child has sufficient understanding to make an informed decision, that he consents to its inclusion; and

(b) that satisfactory arrangements have been, or can be, made for the treatment.

(6) If a medical practitioner by whom or under whose direction a supervised person is being treated in pursuance of a requirement included in a supervision order by virtue of this paragraph is unwilling to continue to treat or direct the treatment of the supervised child or is of the opinion that—

(a) the treatment should be continued beyond the period specified in the order;

(b) the supervised child needs different treatment;

(c) he is not susceptible to treatment; or

(d) he does not require further treatment,

the practitioner shall make a report in writing to that effect to the supervisor.

(7) On receiving a report under this paragraph the supervisor shall refer it to the court, and on such a reference the court may make an order cancelling or varying the requirement.

Date in force
14 October 1991: SI 1991/828.

Definitions
For 'the responsible person' see para 1; for 'supervised child', 'child', 'supervisor' 'health service hospital', 'hospital', 'mental nursing home' see s 105(1); for 'parental responsibility' see s 3; for 'court' see s 92(7).

Note
Paragraphs 4 and 5 do not apply in relation to an interim supervision order s 38(9). For discussion of the imposition of requirements in a supervision order, see paras 8. 171ff.

Part II
Miscellaneous

Life of supervision order

6 (1) Subject to sub-paragraph (2) and section 91, a supervision order shall cease to have effect at the end of the period of one year beginning with the date on which it was made.

(2) A supervision order shall also cease to have effect if an event mentioned in section 25(1)(a) or (b) of the Child Abduction and Custody Act 1985 (termination of existing orders) occurs with respect to the child.

(3) Where the supervisor applies to the court to extend, or further extend, a supervision order the court may extend the order for such period as it may specify.

(4) A supervision order may not be extended so as to run beyond the end of the period of three years beginning with the date on which it was made.

Note

A supervision order may be made for a period of less than twelve months: *M v Warwickshire County Council* [1994] 2 FCR 121, [1994] 2 FLR 593. The threshold conditions of s 31(2) need not be satisfied on an application to extend a supervision order during the period of its currency; there is no jurisdiction to make an interim care order under s 31(5)(b) to replace the supervision order: *Re A (a minor) (Supervision Order: Extension)* [1995] 3 All ER 401, [1995] 2 FCR 114.

---

7 ... *(Repealed by the CLSA 1990, Sch 16, para 27, Sch 20.)*

Information to be given to supervisor etc

8 (1) A supervision order may require the supervised child—

(a) to keep the supervisor informed of any change in his address; and
(b) to allow the supervisor to visit him at the place where he is living.

(2) The responsible person in relation to any child with respect to whom a supervision order is made shall—

(a) if asked by the supervisor, inform him of the child's address (if it is known to him); and
(b) if he is living with the child, allow the supervisor reasonable contact with the child.

Selection of supervisor

9 (1) A supervision order shall not designate a local authority as the supervisor unless—

(a) the authority agree; or
(b) the supervised child lives or will live within their area.

(2) ...

(3) ...

(4) ...

(5) ...

Effect of supervision order on earlier orders

10 The making of a supervision order with respect to any child brings to an end any earlier care or supervision order which—

(a) was made with respect to that child; and
(b) would otherwise continue in force.

Local authority functions and expenditure

11 (1) The Secretary of State may make regulations with respect to the exercise by a local authority of their functions where a child has been placed under their supervision by a supervision order.

(2) Where a supervision order requires compliance with directions given by virtue of this section, any expenditure incurred by the supervisor for the purposes of the directions shall be defrayed by the local authority designated in the order.

Date in force
14 October 1991: SI 1991/828.

Definitions
For 'supervision order' see s 31(11); for 'supervisor', 'supervised child', 'local authority', 'functions' see s 105(1); for 'court' see s 92(7); for 'the responsible person' see para 1; for 'the appropriate authority' see para 9(3); for power to issue a warrant to authorise a constable to assist in exercising the power under para 8(1)(b), (2)(b) see s 102.

PART III
EDUCATION SUPERVISION ORDERS

Effect of orders

12 (1) Where an education supervision order is in force with respect to a child, it shall be the duty of the supervisor—

    (a) to advise, assist and befriend, and give directions to—

        (i) the supervised child; and
        (ii) his parents,

in such a way as will, in the opinion of the supervisor, secure that he is properly educated;

    (b) where any such directions given to—

        (i) the supervised child; or
        (ii) a parent of his,

have not been complied with, to consider what further steps to take in the exercise of the supervisor's powers under this Act.

(2) Before giving any directions under sub-paragraph (1) the supervisor shall, so far as is reasonably practicable, ascertain the wishes and feelings of—

    (a) the child; and
    (b) his parents,

including, in particular, their wishes as to the place at which the child should be educated.

(3) When settling the terms of any such directions, the supervisor shall give due consideration—

    (a) having regard to the child's age and understanding, to such wishes and feelings of his as the supervisor has been able to ascertain; and
    (b) to such wishes and feelings of the child's parents as he has been able to ascertain.

(4) Directions may be given under this paragraph at any time while the education supervision order is in force.

13 (1) Where an education supervision order is in force with respect to a child, the duties of the child's parents under [sections 7 and 444 of the Education Act 1996 (duties to secure education of children and] to secure regular attendance of registered pupils) shall be superseded by their duty to comply with any directions in force under the education supervision order.

(2) Where an education supervision order is made with respect to a child—

(a) any school attendance order—

    (i) made under [section 437 of the Education Act 1996] with respect to the child; and

    (ii) in force immediately before the making of the education supervision order,

shall cease to have effect; and

(b) while the education supervision order remains in force, the following provisions shall not apply with respect to the child—

    (i) [section 437] of that Act (school attendance orders);

    (ii) [section 9 of that Act] (pupils to be educated in accordance with wishes of their parents);

    (iii) [sections 411 and 423 of that Act] (parental preference and appeals against admission decisions);

(c) a supervision order made with respect to the child in criminal proceedings, while the education supervision order is in force, may not include an education requirement of the kind which could otherwise be included under [paragraph 7 of Schedule 6 to the Powers of Criminal Courts (Sentencing) Act 2000];

(d) any education requirement of a kind mentioned in paragraph (c), which was in force with respect to the child immediately before the making of the education supervision order, shall cease to have effect.

Effect where child also subject to supervision order

14 (1) This paragraph applies where an education supervision order and a supervision order, or order under [section 63(1) of the Powers of Criminal Courts (Sentencing) Act 2000], are in force at the same time with respect to the same child.

(2) Any failure to comply with a direction given by the supervisor under the education supervision order shall be disregarded if it would not have been reasonably practicable to comply with it without failing to comply with a direction given under the other order.

Duration of orders

15 (1) An education supervision order shall have effect for a period of one year, beginning with the date on which it is made.

(2) An education supervision order shall not expire if, before it would otherwise have expired, the court has (on the application of the authority in whose favour the order was made) extended the period during which it is in force.

(3) Such an application may not be made earlier than three months before the date on which the order would otherwise expire.

(4) The period during which an education supervision order is in force may be extended under sub-paragraph (2) on more than one occasion.

(5) No one extension may be for a period of more than three years.

(6) An education supervision order shall cease to have effect on—

(a) the child's ceasing to be of compulsory school age; or

(b) the making of a care order with respect to the child;

and sub-paragraphs (1) to (4) are subject to this sub-paragraph.

Information to be given to supervisor etc

16 (1) An education supervision order may require the child—

(a) to keep the supervisor informed of any change in his address; and

(b) to allow the supervisor to visit him at the place where he is living.

(2) A person who is the parent of a child with respect to whom an education supervision order has been made shall—

(a) if asked by the supervisor, inform him of the child's address (if it is known to him); and

(b) if he is living with the child, allow the supervisor reasonable contact with the child.

Discharge of orders

17 (1) The court may discharge any education supervision order on the application of—

(a) the child concerned;

(b) a parent of his; or

(c) the local education authority concerned.

(2) On discharging an education supervision order, the court may direct the local authority within whose area the child lives, or will live, to investigate the circumstances of the child.

Offences

18 (1) If a parent of a child with respect to whom an education supervision order is in force persistently fails to comply with a direction given under the order he shall be guilty of an offence.

(2) It shall be a defence for any person charged with such an offence to prove that—

(a) he took all reasonable steps to ensure that the direction was complied with;

(b) the direction was unreasonable; or

(c) he had complied with—

(i) a requirement included in a supervision order made with respect to the child; or

(ii) directions given under such a requirement,

and that it was not reasonably practicable to comply both with the direction and with the requirement or directions mentioned in this paragraph.

(3) A person guilty of an offence under this paragraph shall be liable on summary conviction to a fine not exceeding level 3 on the standard scale.

Persistent failure of child to comply with directions

19 (1) Where a child with respect to whom an education supervision order is in force persistently fails to comply with any direction given under the order, the local education authority concerned shall notify the appropriate local authority.

(2) Where a local authority have been notified under sub-paragraph (1) they shall investigate the circumstances of the child.

(3) In this paragraph 'the appropriate local authority' has the same meaning as in section 36.

Miscellaneous

20 The Secretary of State may by regulations make provision modifying, or displacing, the provisions of any enactment about education in relation to any child with respect to whom an education supervision order is in force to such extent as appears to the Secretary of State to be necessary or expedient in consequence of the provision made by this Act with respect to such orders.

Interpretation

21   In this Part of this Schedule 'parent' has the same meaning as in [the Education Act 1996].

Date in force
14 October 1991: SI 1991/828.

Amendments
Para 21: words "the Education Act 1996 in square brackets slubstituted by the Education Act 1996, s 582(1), sch 7, para 93(1), (3).

SCHEDULE 4
Management and Conduct of Community Homes

Section 53(6)

PART I
INSTRUMENTS OF MANAGEMENT

Instruments of management for controlled and assisted community homes

1   (1) The Secretary of State may by order make an instrument of management providing for the constitution of a body of managers for any . . . home which is designated as a controlled or assisted community home.

(2) Sub-paragraph (3) applies where two or more . . . homes are designated as controlled community homes or as assisted community homes.

(3) If—

(a)   those homes are, or are to be, provided by the same voluntary organisation; and
(b)   the same local authority is to be represented on the body of managers for those homes,

a single instrument of management may be made by the Secretary of State under this paragraph constituting one body of managers for those homes or for any two or more of them.

(4) The number of persons who, in accordance with an instrument of management, constitute the body of managers for a . . . home shall be such number (which must be a multiple of three) as may be specified in the instrument.

(5) The instrument shall provide that the local authority specified in the instrument shall appoint—

(a)   in the case of a . . . home which is designated as a controlled community home, two-thirds of the managers; and
(b)   in the case of a . . . home which is designated as an assisted community home, one-third of them.

(6) An instrument of management shall provide that the foundation managers shall be appointed, in such manner and by such persons as may be specified in the instrument—

(a)   so as to represent the interests of the voluntary organisation by which the home is, or is to be, provided; and
(b)   for the purpose of securing that—

(i)   so far as is practicable, the character of the home . . . will be preserved; and
(ii)   subject to paragraph 2(3), the terms of any trust deed relating to the home are observed.

(7) An instrument of management shall come into force on such date as it may specify.

(8) If an instrument of management is in force in relation to a . . . home the home shall be (and be known as) a controlled community home or an assisted community home, according to its designation.

(9) In this paragraph—

'foundation managers', in relation to a . . . home, means those of the managers of the home who are not appointed by a local authority in accordance with sub-paragraph (5); and

'designated' means designated in accordance with section 53.

2 (1) An instrument of management shall contain such provisions as the Secretary of State considers appropriate.

(2) Nothing in the instrument of management shall affect the purposes for which the premises comprising the home are held.

(3) Without prejudice to the generality of sub-paragraph (1), an instrument of management may contain provisions—

(a) specifying the nature and purpose of the home (or each of the homes) to which it relates;

(b) requiring a specified number or proportion of the places in that home (or those homes) to be made available to local authorities and to any other body specified in the instrument; and

(c) relating to the management of that home (or those homes) and the charging of fees with respect to—

(i) children placed there; or

(ii) places made available to any local authority or other body.

(4) Subject to sub-paragraphs (1) and (2), in the event of any inconsistency between the provisions of any trust deed and an instrument of management, the instrument of management shall prevail over the provisions of the trust deed in so far as they relate to the home concerned.

(5) After consultation with the voluntary organisation concerned and with the local authority specified in its instrument of management, the Secretary of State may by order vary or revoke any provisions of the instrument.

Date in force
14 October 1991: SI 1991/828.

Amendment
Para 1: CLSA 1990, ss 116(1), 125(7), Sch 16 para 28, Sch 20.

Definitions
For 'voluntary home' see s 60(3); for 'designated' and 'foundation managers' see para 1(9); for 'controlled community home' see s 53(4); for 'assisted community home' see s 53(5); for 'voluntary organisation', 'local authority', 'child' see s 105(1); for 'trust deed' see s 55(6).

Para 2(1) Instrument of management
Cannot alter the basic purposes for which premises comprising a voluntary home are held. When an organisation holds premises on trust for purposes inconsistent with use as a community home, it is for that organisation to secure appropriate modification of the trust deed. This cannot by virtue of para 2(2) be done by the instrument of management, and para (4) which deals with inconsistencies between the instrument of management and a trust deed is expressly made subject to para 2(2).

Para 2(4) Trust deed
The definition in s 55(6) is wide and is not confined to trust deeds properly so described. Para 2(5) Section 36(5) of the CCA 1980 formerly provided that the Secretary of State might vary or revoke any provisions of the instrument of management by a further instrument of management. Now any variation etc will be by order.

Transfer of functions
Functions of the Secretary of State, so far as exercisable in relation to Wales, transferred to the National Assembly for Wales, by the National Assembly for Wales (Transfer of Functions) Order 1999, SI 1999/672.

PART II
MANAGEMENT OF CONTROLLED AND ASSISTED COMMUNITY HOMES

3 (1) The management, equipment and maintenance of a controlled community home shall be the responsibility of the local authority specified in its instrument of management.

(2) The management, equipment and maintenance of an assisted community home shall be the responsibility of the voluntary organisation by which the home is provided.

(3) In this paragraph—

'home' means a controlled community home or (as the case may be) assisted community home; and

'the managers', in relation to a home, means the managers constituted by its instrument of management; and

'the responsible body', in relation to a home, means the local authority or (as the case may be) voluntary organisation responsible for its management, equipment and maintenance.

(4) The functions of a home's responsible body shall be exercised through the managers[, except in so far as, under section 53(3B), any of the accommodation is to be managed by another person.]

(5) Anything done, liability incurred or property acquired by a home's managers shall be done, incurred or acquired by them as agents of the responsible body[; and similarly, to the extent that a contract so provides, as respects anything done, liability incurred or property acquired by a person by whom, under section 53(3B), any of the accommodation is to be managed].

(6) In so far as any matter is reserved for the decision of a home's responsible body by—

(a) sub-paragraph (8);

(b) the instrument of management;

(c) the service by the body on the managers, or any of them, of a notice reserving any matter,

that matter shall be dealt with by the body and not by the managers.

(7) In dealing with any matter so reserved, the responsible body shall have regard to any representations made to the body by the managers.

(8) The employment of persons at a home shall be a matter reserved for the decision of the responsible body.

(9) Where the instrument of management of a controlled community home so provides, the responsible body may enter into arrangements with the voluntary organisation by which that home is provided whereby, in accordance with such terms as may be agreed between them and the voluntary organisation, persons who are not in the employment of the responsible body shall undertake duties at that home.

(10) Subject to sub-paragraph (11)—

(a) where the responsible body for an assisted community home proposes to engage any person to work at that home or to terminate without notice the employment of any person at that home, it shall consult the local authority specified in the instrument of management and, if that authority so direct, the responsible body shall not carry out its proposal without their consent; and

(b) that local authority may, after consultation with the responsible body, require that body to terminate the employment of any person at that home.

(11) Paragraphs (a) and (b) of sub-paragraph (10) shall not apply—

(a) in such cases or circumstances as may be specified by notice in writing given by the local authority to the responsible body; and

(b) in relation to the employment of any persons or class of persons specified in the home's instrument of management.

(12) The accounting year of the managers of a home shall be such as may be specified by the responsible body.

(13) Before such date in each accounting year as may be so specified, the managers of a home shall submit to the responsible body estimates, in such form as the body may require, of expenditure and receipts in respect of the next accounting year.

(14) Any expenses incurred by the managers of a home with the approval of the responsible body shall be defrayed by that body.

(15) The managers of a home shall keep—

(a) proper accounts with respect to the home; and
(b) proper records in relation to the accounts.

(16) Where an instrument of management relates to more than one home, one set of accounts and records may be kept in respect of all the homes to which it relates.

Date in force
14 October 1991: SI 1991/828.

Amendments
Para 3: in subparas (4), (5) words in square brackets inserted by the Criminal Justice and Public Order Act 1994, s 22(3).

Definitions
For 'controlled community home' see s 53(4); for 'local authority', 'voluntary organisation', 'functions' see s 105(1); for 'assisted community home' see s 53(5); for 'home', 'the managers', 'the responsible body' see para 3(3).

References
For service of notices under the Act generally see s 105(8)-(10).

Para 3(a): Employment
These arrangements would enable (if the instrument of management so provides) the employees of the voluntary organisation or, for example, members of religious orders, to undertake the care of children in a controlled community home.

PART III
REGULATIONS

4 (1) The Secretary of State may make regulations—

(a) as to the placing of children in community homes;
(b) as to the conduct of such homes; and
(c) for securing the welfare of children in such homes.

(2) The regulations may, in particular—

(a) prescribe standards to which the premises used for such homes are to conform;
(b) impose requirements as to the accommodation, staff and equipment to be provided in such homes, and as to the arrangements to be made for protecting the health of children in such homes;
(c) provide for the control and discipline of children in such homes;
(d) impose requirements as to the keeping of records and giving of notices in respect of children in such homes;
(e) impose requirements as to the facilities which are to be provided for giving religious instruction to children in such homes;
(f) authorise the Secretary of State to give and revoke directions requiring—

   (i) the local authority by whom a home is provided or who are specified in the instrument of management for a controlled community home, or
   (ii) the voluntary organisation by which an assisted community home is provided,

to accommodate in the home a child looked after by a local authority for whom no places are made available in that home or to take such action in relation to a child accommodated in the home as may be specified in the directions;

(g) provide for consultation with the Secretary of State as to applicants for appointment to the charge of a home;

(h) empower the Secretary of State to prohibit the appointment of any particular applicant except in the cases (if any) in which the regulations dispense with such consultation by reason that the person to be appointed possesses such qualifications as may be prescribed;

(i) require the approval of the Secretary of State for the provision and use of accommodation for the purpose of restricting the liberty of children in such homes and impose other requirements (in addition to those imposed by section 25) as to the placing of a child in accommodation provided for that purpose, including a requirement to obtain the permission of any local authority who are looking after the child;

(j) provide that, to such extent as may be provided for in the regulations, the Secretary of State may direct that any provision of regulations under this paragraph which is specified in the direction and makes any such provision as is referred to in paragraph (a) or (b) shall not apply in relation to a particular home or the premises used for it, and may provide for the variation or revocation of any such direction by the Secretary of State.

(3) Without prejudice to the power to make regulations under this paragraph conferring functions on—

(a) the local authority or voluntary organisation by which a community home is provided; or

(b) the managers of a controlled or assisted community home,

regulations under this paragraph may confer functions in relation to a controlled or assisted community home on the local authority named in the instrument of management for the home.

Date in force
14 October 1991: SI 1991/828.

Definitions
For 'child', 'local authority', 'voluntary organisation', see s 105(1). For 'community home' see s 53. For 'assisted community home' see s 53(5). For 'a child who is looked after by a local authority' see s 22(1). For 'controlled community home' see s 53(4).

Regulations
See the Arrangements for Placement of Children (General) Regulations 1991, SI 1991/890 amended by SI 1991/2033, SI 1993/3069, SI 1995/2015, SI 1997/649 and SI 2002/546, the Children (Secure Accommodation) Regulations 1991, SI 1991/1505 amended by SI 1992/2117, SI 1995/1398, SI 1996/692, SI 2000/694 and SI 2001/337 (England) and SI 2002/546.

SCHEDULE 5
Voluntary Homes and Voluntary Organisations

Section 60(4)

PART I
REGISTRATION OF VOLUNTARY HOMES

General

1 (1) An application for registration under this paragraph shall—

(a) be made by the persons intending to carry on the home to which the application relates; and

(b) be made in such manner, and be accompanied by such particulars, as the Secretary of State may prescribe.

(2) On an application duly made under sub-paragraph (1) the Secretary of State may—

(a) grant or refuse the application, as he thinks fit; or

(b) grant the application subject to such conditions as he considers appropriate.

(3) The Secretary of State may from time to time—

(a) vary any condition for the time being in force with respect to a voluntary home by virtue of this paragraph; or

(b) impose an additional condition,

either on the application of the person carrying on the home or without such an application.

(4) Where at any time it appears to the Secretary of State that the conduct of any voluntary home—

(a) is not [, or has not been,] in accordance with regulations made under paragraph 7; or

(b) is [, or has been,] otherwise unsatisfactory,

he may cancel the registration of the home and remove it from the register.

(5) Any person who, without reasonable excuse, carries on a voluntary home in contravention of—

(a) section 60; or

(b) a condition to which the registration of the home is for the time being subject by virtue of this Part,

shall be guilty of an offence.

(6) Any person guilty of such an offence shall be liable on summary conviction to a fine not exceeding—

(a) level 5 on the standard scale, if his offence is under sub-paragraph (5)(a); or

(b) level 4, if it is under sub-paragraph (5)(b).

(7) Where the Secretary of State registers a home under this paragraph, or cancels the registration of a home, he shall notify the local authority within whose area the home is situated.

Procedure

2 (1) Where—

(a) a person applies for registration of a voluntary home; and

(b) the Secretary of State proposes to grant his application,

the Secretary of State shall give him written notice of his proposal and of the conditions subject to which he proposes to grant the application.

(2) The Secretary of State need not give notice if he proposes to grant the application subject only to conditions which—

(a) the applicant specified in the application; or

(b) the Secretary of State and the applicant have subsequently agreed.

(3) Where the Secretary of State proposes to refuse such an application he shall give notice of his proposal to the applicant.

(4) The Secretary of State shall give any person carrying on a voluntary home notice of a proposal to—

(a) cancel the registration of the home;

(b) vary any condition for the time being in force with respect to the home by virtue of paragraph 1; or

(c) impose any additional condition.

(5) A notice under this paragraph shall give the Secretary of State's reasons for his proposal.

[(6) In relation to a home which has ceased to exist, the reference in sub-paragraph (4) to any person carrying on the home shall be taken to be a reference to each of the persons who carried it on.]

Right to make representations

3 (1) A notice under paragraph 2 shall state that within 14 days of service of the notice any person on whom it is served may (in writing) require the Secretary of State to give him an opportunity to make representations to the Secretary of State concerning the matter.

(2) Where a notice has been served under paragraph 2, the Secretary of State shall not determine the matter until either—

(a) any person on whom the notice was served has made representations to him concerning the matter; or

(b) the period during which any such person could have required the Secretary of State to give him an opportunity to make representations has elapsed without the Secretary of State being required to give such an opportunity; or

(c) the conditions specified in sub-paragraph (3) are satisfied.

(3) The conditions are that—

(a) a person on whom the notice was served has required the Secretary of State to give him an opportunity to make representations to the Secretary of State;

(b) the Secretary of State has allowed him a reasonable period to make his representations; and

(c) he has failed to make them within that period.

(4) The representations may be made, at the option of the person making them, either in writing or orally.

(5) If he informs the Secretary of State that he desires to make oral representations, the Secretary of State shall give him an opportunity of appearing before, and of being heard by, a person appointed by the Secretary of State.

Decision of Secretary of State

4 (1) If the Secretary of State decides to adopt the proposal, he shall serve notice in writing of his decision on any person on whom he was required to serve notice of his proposal.

(2) A notice under this paragraph shall be accompanied by a notice explaining the right of appeal conferred by paragraph 5.

(3) A decision of the Secretary of State, other than a decision to grant an application for registration subject only to such conditions as are mentioned in paragraph 2(2) or to refuse an application for registration, shall not take effect—

(a) if no appeal is brought, until the end of the period of 28 days referred to in paragraph 5(3); and

(b) if an appeal is brought, until it is determined or abandoned.

Appeals

5 (1) An appeal against a decision of the Secretary of State under Part VII shall lie to a Registered Homes Tribunal.

(2) An appeal shall be brought by notice in writing given to the Secretary of State.

(3) No appeal may be brought by a person more than 28 days after service on him of notice of the decision.

(4) On an appeal, the Tribunal may confirm the Secretary of State's decision or direct that it shall not have effect.

(5) A Tribunal shall also have power on an appeal to—

(a) vary any condition for the time being in force by virtue of Part VII with respect to the home to which the appeal relates;

(b) direct that any such condition shall cease to have effect; or

(c) direct that any such condition as it thinks fit shall have effect with respect to the home.

Notification of particulars with respect to voluntary homes

6 (1) It shall be the duty of the person in charge of any voluntary home established after the commencement of this Act to send to the Secretary of State within three months from the establishment of the home such particulars with respect to the home as the Secretary of State may prescribe.

(2) It shall be the duty of the person in charge of any voluntary home (whether established before or after the commencement of this Act) to send to the Secretary of State such particulars with respect to the home as may be prescribed.

(3) The particulars must be sent—

(a) in the case of a home established before the commencement of this Act, in every year, or

(b) in the case of a home established after the commencement of this Act, in every year subsequent to the year in which particulars are sent under sub-paragraph (1),

by such date as the Secretary of State may prescribe.

(4) Where the Secretary of State by regulations varies the particulars which are to be sent to him under sub-paragraph (1) or (2) by the person in charge of a voluntary home—

(a) that person shall send to the Secretary of State the prescribed particulars within three months from the date of the making of the regulations;

(b) where any such home was established before, but not more than three months before, the making of the regulations, compliance with paragraph (a) shall be sufficient compliance with the requirement of sub-paragraph (1) to send the prescribed particulars within three months from the establishment of the home;

(c) in the year in which the particulars are varied, compliance with paragraph (a) by the person in charge of any voluntary home shall be sufficient compliance with the requirement of sub-paragraph (2) to send the prescribed particulars before the prescribed date in that year.

(5) If the person in charge of a voluntary home fails without reasonable excuse, to comply with any of the requirements of this paragraph he shall be guilty of an offence.

(6) Any person guilty of such an offence shall be liable on summary conviction to a fine not exceeding level 2 on the standard scale.

Date in force
14 October 1991: SI 1991/828.

Definitions
For 'voluntary home' see s 60(3); for 'local authority' see s 105(1).

References
'This Part' ie Pt VII ss 59–62 and this schedule. For the standard scale' see the CJA 1982, s 37(2), (3) as amended; for service of notices generally under the Act see s 105(8)-(10).

Transfer of functions
Functions of the Secretary of State, so far as exercisable in relation to Wales, transferred to the National Assembly for Wales, by the National Assembly for Wales (Transfer of Functions) Order 1999, SI 1999/672.

PART II
REGULATIONS AS TO VOLUNTARY HOMES

Regulations as to conduct of voluntary homes

7 (1) The Secretary of State may make regulations—

(a) as to the placing of children in voluntary homes;

(b) as to the conduct of such homes; and

(c) for securing the welfare of children in such homes.

(2) The regulations may, in particular—

(a) prescribe standards to which the premises used for such homes are to conform;

(b) impose requirements as to the accommodation, staff and equipment to be provided in such homes, and as to the arrangements to be made for protecting the health of children in such homes;

(c) provide for the control and discipline of children in such homes;

(d) require the furnishing to the Secretary of State of information as to the facilities provided for—

    (i) the parents of children in the homes; and

    (ii) persons who are not parents of such children but who have parental responsibility for them; and

    (iii) other persons connected with such children,

to visit and communicate with the children;

(e) authorise the Secretary of State to limit the number of children who may be accommodated in any particular voluntary home;

(f) . . .

[(ff) require the approval of the Secretary of State for the provision and use of accommodation for the purpose of restricting the liberty of children in such homes and impose other requirements (in addition to those imposed by section 25) as to the placing of a child in accommodation provided for that purpose, including a requirement to obtain the permission of any local authority who are looking after the child;]

(g) impose requirements as to the keeping of the records and giving of notices with respect to children in such homes;

(h) impose requirements as to the facilities which are to be provided for giving religious instruction to children in such homes;

(i) require notice to be given to the Secretary of State of any change of the person carrying on or in charge of a voluntary home or of the premises used by such a home.

(3) The regulations may provide that a contravention of, or failure to comply with, any specified provision of the regulations without reasonable excuse shall be an offence against the regulations.

(4) Any person guilty of such an offence shall be liable to a fine not exceeding level 4 on the standard scale.

Note

See the Arrangements for Placement of Children (General) Regulations 1991, SI 1991/890 amended by SI 1991/2033, SI 1993/3069, SI 1995/2015, SI 1997/649 and SI 2002/546 and the Children (Secure Accommodation) Regulations 1991, SI 1991/1505 amended by SI 1992/2117, SI 1995/1398, SI 1996/692, SI 2000/694 and SI 2001/337 (England) and SI 2002/546.

Disqualification

8 The Secretary of State may by regulation make provision with respect to the disqualification of persons in relation to voluntary homes of a kind similar to that made in relation to children's homes by section 65.

Note

See the Disqualification for Caring for Children Regulations 1991, SI 1991/2094 amended by SI 1997/2308 and the Disqualificaiton for Caring for Children (England) Regulations 2002, SI 2002/635.

SCHEDULE 6
Registered Children's Homes [Private Children's Homes]

Section 63(11)

PART I
REGISTRATION

Application for registration

1 (1) An application for the registration of a children's home shall be made—

(a) by the person carrying on, or intending to carry on, the home; and
(b) to the local authority for the area in which the home is, or is to be, situated.

(2) The application shall be made in the prescribed manner and shall be accompanied by—

(a) such particulars as may be prescribed; and
(b) such reasonable fee as the local authority may determine.

(3) In this Schedule 'prescribed' means prescribed by regulations made by the Secretary of State.

(4) If a local authority are satisfied that a children's home with respect to which an application has been made in accordance with this Schedule complies or (as the case may be) will comply—

(a) with such requirements as may be prescribed, and
(b) with such other requirements (if any) as appear to them to be appropriate,

they shall grant the application, either unconditionally or subject to conditions imposed under paragraph 2.

(5) Before deciding whether or not to grant an application a local authority shall comply with any prescribed requirements.

(6) Regulations made for the purposes of sub-paragraph (5) may, in particular, make provision as to the inspection of the home in question.

(7) Where an application is granted, the authority shall notify the applicant that the home has been registered under this Act as from such date as may be specified in the notice.

(8) If the authority are not satisfied as mentioned in sub-paragraph (4), they shall refuse the application.

(9) For the purposes of this Act, an application which has not been granted or refused within the period of twelve months beginning with the date when it is served on the authority shall be deemed to have been refused by them, and the applicant shall be deemed to have been notified of their refusal at the end of that period.

(10) Where a school to which section 63(1) applies is registered it shall not cease to be a registered children's home by reason only of a subsequent change in the number of children for whom it provides accommodation.

Conditions imposed on registration

2 (1) A local authority may grant an application for registration subject to such conditions relating to the conduct of the home as they think fit.

(2) A local authority may from time to time—

(a) vary any condition for the time being in force with respect to a home by virtue of this paragraph; or
(b) impose an additional condition,

either on the application of the person carrying on the home or without such an application.

(3) If any condition imposed or varied under this paragraph is not complied with,

the person carrying on the home shall, if he has no reasonable excuse, be guilty of an offence and liable on summary conviction to a fine not exceeding level 4 on the standard scale.

Annual review of registration

3 (1) In this [Schedule] 'the responsible authority', in relation to a registered children's home means the local authority who registered it.

(2) The responsible authority for a registered children's home shall, at the end of the period of twelve months beginning with the date of registration, and annually thereafter, review its registration for the purpose of determining whether the registration should continue in force or be cancelled under paragraph 4(3).

(3) If on any such annual review the responsible authority are satisfied that the home is being [and has been] carried on in accordance with the relevant requirements they shall determine that, subject to sub-paragraph (4), the registration should continue in force.

(4) The responsible authority shall give to the person carrying on the home notice of their determination under sub-paragraph (3) and the notice shall require him to pay to the authority with respect to the review such reasonable fee as the authority may determine.

(5) It shall be a condition of the home's continued registration that the fee is so paid before the expiry of the period of twenty-eight days beginning with the date on which the notice is received by the person carrying on the home.

(6) In this Schedule 'the relevant requirements' means any requirements of Part VIII and of any regulations made under paragraph 10, and any conditions imposed under paragraph 2.

Cancellation of registration

4 (1) The person carrying on a registered children's home may at any time make an application, in such manner and including such particulars as may be prescribed, for the cancellation by the responsible authority for the registration of the home.

(2) If the authority are satisfied, in the case of a school registered by virtue of section 63(6), that it is no longer a school to which that provision applies, the authority shall give to the person carrying on the home notice that the registration of the home has been cancelled as from the date of the notice.

(3) If on any annual review under paragraph 3, or at any other time, it appears to the responsible authority that a registered home is being [, or has been,] carried on otherwise than in accordance with the relevant requirements, they may determine that the registration of the home should be cancelled.

(4) The responsible authority may at any time determine that the registration of a home should be cancelled on the ground—

(a) that the person carrying on the home has been convicted of an offence under this Part or any regulations made under paragraph 10; or

(b) that any other person has been convicted of such an offence in relation to the home.

[(5) In relation to a home which has ceased to exist, references in this paragraph and paragraph 5(4) to the person, or any person, carrying on the home include references to each of the persons who carried it on.]

Note
There is no power to cancel a registration where there are no premises in existence at which a registered children's home is being carried on: *Craig v Shropshire County Council* [2000] 2 FCR 628, DC.

Procedure

5 (1) Where—

(a) a person applies for the registration of a children's home; and
(b) the local authority propose to grant his application,

they shall give him written notice of their proposal and of the conditions (if any) subject to which they propose to grant his application.

(2) The authority need not give notice if they propose to grant the application subject only to conditions which—

(a) the applicant specified in the application; or
(b) the authority and the applicant have subsequently agreed.

(3) The authority shall give an applicant notice of a proposal to refuse his application.

(4) The authority shall give any person carrying on a registered children's home notice of a proposal—

(a) to cancel the registration;
(b) to vary any condition for the time being in force with respect to the home by virtue of Part VIII; or
(c) to impose any additional condition.

(5) A notice under this paragraph shall give the local authority's reasons for their proposal.

Right to make representations

6 (1) A notice under paragraph 5 shall state that within 14 days of service of the notice any person on whom it is served may in writing require the local authority to give him an opportunity to make representations to them concerning the matter.

(2) Where a notice has been served under paragraph 5, the local authority shall not determine the matter until—

(a) any person on whom the notice was served has made representations to them concerning the matter;
(b) the period during which any such person could have required the local authority to give him an opportunity to make representations has elapsed without their being required to give such an opportunity; or
(c) the conditions specified in sub-paragraph (3) below are satisfied.

(3) The conditions are—

(a) that a person on whom the notice was served has required the local authority to give him an opportunity to make representations to them concerning the matter;
(b) that the authority have allowed him a reasonable period to make his representations; and
(c) that he has failed to make them within that period.

(4) The representations may be made, at the option of the person making them, either in writing or orally.

(5) If he informs the local authority that he desires to make oral representations, the authority shall give him an opportunity of appearing before and of being heard by a committee or sub-committee of theirs.

Decision of local authority

7 (1) If the local authority decide to adopt a proposal of theirs to grant an application, they shall serve notice in writing of their decision on any person on whom they were required to serve notice of their proposal.

(2) A notice under this paragraph shall be accompanied by an explanation of the right of appeal conferred by paragraph 8.

(3) A decision of a local authority, other than a decision to grant an application for registration subject only to such conditions as are mentioned in paragraph 5(2) or to refuse an application for registration, shall not take effect—

(a) if no appeal is brought, until the end of the period of 28 days referred to in paragraph 8(3); and

(b) if an appeal is brought, until it is determined or abandoned.

Appeals

8 (1) An appeal against a decision of a local authority under Part VIII shall lie to a Registered Homes Tribunal.

(2) An appeal shall be brought by notice in writing given to the local authority.

(3) No appeal shall be brought by a person more than 28 days after service on him of notice of the decision.

(4) On an appeal the Tribunal may confirm the local authority's decision or direct that it shall not have effect.

(5) A Tribunal shall also have power on an appeal—

(a) to vary any condition in force with respect to the home to which the appeal relates by virtue of paragraph 2;

(b) to direct that any such condition shall cease to have effect; or

(c) to direct that any such condition as it thinks fit shall have effect with respect to the home.

(6) A local authority shall comply with any direction given by a Tribunal under this paragraph.

Prohibition on further applications

9 (1) Where an application for the registration of a home is refused, no further application may be made within the period of six months beginning with the date when the applicant is notified of the refusal.

(2) Sub-paragraph (1) shall have effect, where an appeal against the refusal of an application is determined or abandoned, as if the reference to the date when the applicant is notified of the refusal were a reference to the date on which the appeal is determined or abandoned.

(3) When the registration of a home is cancelled, no application for the registration of the home shall be made within the period of six months beginning with the date of cancellation.

(4) Sub-paragraph (3) shall have effect, where an appeal against the cancellation of the registration of a home is determined or abandoned, as if the reference to the date of cancellation were a reference to the date on which the appeal is determined or abandoned.

Date in force
14 October 1991: SI 1991/828.

Definitions
For 'children's home' see s 63(3) and s 23(10) as applied to the whole Act by s 105(1) and see note to s 53, ante; for 'child', 'local authority', 'school' see s 105(1); for 'prescribed' see para 1(3); for 'the responsible authority' see para 3(1); for 'the relevant requirements' see para 3(6); for 'registered children's home' see s 63(8).

References
For the standard scale' see the CJA 1982, s 37(2), (3) as amended. This Part' ie Pt VIII, ss 63-65, Schs 6 and 7 (registered (private) children's homes). For service of notices under the Act generally see s 105(8)-(10).

Transfer of functions
Functions of the Secretary of State, so far as exercisable in relation to Wales, transferred to the National Assembly for Wales, by the National Assembly for Wales (Transfer of Functions) Order 1999, SI 1999/672.

PART II
REGULATIONS

10 (1) The Secretary of State may make regulations—

(a) as to the placing of children in registered [private] children's homes;
(b) as to the conduct of such homes; and
(c) for securing the welfare of the children in such homes.

(2) The regulations may in particular—

(a) prescribe standards to which the premises used for such homes are to conform;
(b) impose requirements as to the accommodation, staff and equipment to be provided in such homes;
(c) impose requirements as to the arrangements to be made for protecting the health of children in such homes;
(d) provide for the control and discipline of children in such homes;
(e) require the furnishing to the responsible authority of information as to the facilities provided for—

(i) the parents of children in such homes;
(ii) persons who are not parents of such children but who have parental responsibility for them; and
(iii) other persons connected with such children, to visit and communicate with the children;

(f) impose requirements as to the keeping of records and giving of notices with respect to children in such homes;
(g) impose requirements as to the facilities which are to be provided for giving religious instruction to children in such homes;
(h) make provision as to the carrying out of annual reviews under paragraph 3;
(i) authorise the responsible authority to limit the number of children who may be accommodated in any particular registered home;
(j) . . .
[(jj) require the approval of the Secretary of State for the provision and use of accommodation for the purpose of restricting the liberty of children in such homes and impose other requirements (in addition to those imposed by section 25) as to the placing of a child in accommodation provided for that purpose, including a requirement to obtain the permission of any local authority who are looking after the child.]
(k) require notice to be given to the responsible authority of any change of the person carrying on or in charge of a registered home or of the premises used by such a home;
(l) make provision similar to that made by regulations under section 26.

(3) The regulations may provide that a contravention of or failure to comply with any specified provision of the regulations, without reasonable excuse, shall be an offence against the regulations.

(4) Any person guilty of an offence shall be liable on summary conviction to a fine not exceeding level 4 on the standard scale.

Date in force
14 October 1991: SI 1991/828.

Definitions
For child' see s 105(1); for 'registered children's home' see s 63(8); for 'the responsible authority' see para 3(1); for 'a child who is looked after by a local authority' see s 22(1).

Amendment
Para 10: in sub para (1)(a) word "private" in square brackets substituted by the Care Standards Act 2000, s 116, sch 4, para 14(1), (25)(b). Sub paras (1)(b), (c), (2)(a)-(k), (3), (4) repealed by the Care Standards Act, s 117(2), sch 6. Sub para (2) (jj) inserted by the Criminal Justice and Public Order Act 1994, ss 19(2)(b), 168(3), sch 11.

Reference
For 'the standard scale', see the CJA 1982, s 37(2), (3) as amended.

Regulations
See the Arrangements for Placement of Children (General) Regulations 1991, SI 1991/890 amended by SI 1991/2033, SI 1993/3069, SI 1995/2015, SI 1997/649 and SI 2002/546, the Representations Procedure (Children) Regulations 1991, SI 1991/894 amended by SI 1991/2033, SI 1993/3071, SI 2001/2874 (England) and SI 2002/546; the Review of Children's Cases Regulations 1991, SI 1991/895 amended by SI 1991/2033, SI 1993/3069, SI 1995/2015, SI 1997/649 and SI 2002/546; the Children (Secure Accommodation) Regulations 1991, SI 1991/1505 amended by SI 1992/2117, SI 1995/1398, SI 1996/692, SI 2000/694 and SI 2001/337 (England).

SCHEDULE 7
Foster Parents: Limits on Number of Foster Children

Section 63(12)

Interpretation

1 For the purposes of this Schedule, a person fosters a child if—

(a) he is a local authority foster parent in relation to the child;

(b) he is a foster parent with whom the child has been placed by a voluntary organisation; or

(c) he fosters the child privately.

The usual fostering limit

2 Subject to what follows, a person may not foster more than three children ('the usual fostering limit').

Siblings

3 A person may exceed the usual fostering limit if the children concerned are all siblings with respect to each other.

Exemption by local authority

4 (1) A person may exceed the usual fostering limit if he is exempted from it by the local authority within whose area he lives.

(2) In considering whether to exempt a person, a local authority shall have regard, in particular, to—

(a) the number of children whom the person proposes to foster;

(b) the arrangements which the person proposes for the care and accommodation of the fostered children;

(c) the intended and likely relationship between the person and the fostered children;

(d) the period of time for which he proposes to foster the children; and

(e) whether the welfare of the fostered children (and of any other children who are or will be living in the accommodation) will be safeguarded and promoted.

(3) Where a local authority exempt a person, they shall inform him by notice in writing—

(a) that he is so exempted;

(b) of the children, described by name, whom he may foster; and

(c) of any condition to which the exemption is subject.

(4) A local authority may at any time by notice in writing—

(a) vary or cancel an exemption; or

(b) impose, vary or cancel a condition to which the exemption is subject,

and, in considering whether to do so, they shall have regard in particular to the considerations mentioned in sub-paragraph (2).

(5) The Secretary of State may make regulations amplifying or modifying the provisions of this paragraph in order to provide for cases where children need to be placed with foster parents as a matter of urgency.

Effect of exceeding fostering limit

5 (1) A person shall cease to be treated as fostering and shall be treated[, for the purposes of this Act and the Care Standards Act 2000] as carrying on a children's home if—

(a) he exceeds the usual fostering limit; or

(b) where he is exempted under paragraph 4,—

    (i) he fosters any child not named in the exemption; and

    (ii) in so doing, he exceeds the usual fostering limit.

(2) Sub-paragraph (1) does not apply if the children concerned are all siblings in respect of each other.

Complaints etc

6 (1) Every local authority shall establish a procedure for considering any representations (including any complaint) made to them about the discharge of their functions under paragraph 4 by a person exempted or seeking to be exempted under that paragraph.

(2) In carrying out any consideration of representations under sub-paragraph (1), a local authority shall comply with any regulations made by the Secretary of State for the purposes of this paragraph.

Date in force
14 October 1991: SI 1991/828.

Definitions
For 'local authority foster parent' see s 23(3); for 'child', 'local authority', and 'voluntary organisation' see s 105(1); for 'to foster a child privately' see s 66(1)(b); for 'the usual fostering limit' see para 2.

References
For service of notices under the Act generally see s 105(8)-(10); for duty to register a children's home see s 63.

Para 4(5) Regulations
See Foster Placement (Children) Regulations 1991, SI 1991/910, revoked inso far as they apply to England and substituted by the Fostering Services Regulations 2002, SI 2002 57 amended by SI 2002/865.

Para 6
A private foster parent may appeal to the court against a refusal to make an exemption, or to vary or cancel such an exemption, or against a condition imposed in such an exemption (Sch 8, para 1(e)-(g). The right of appeal does not extend to those who would otherwise be a local authority foster parent or with whom a child would be placed by a voluntary organisation (Sch 8, para (8)).

Para 6(2) Regulations
See the Representations Procedure (Children) Regulations 1991, SI 1991/894 amended by SI 1991/2033, SI 1993/3071, SI 2001/2874 (England) and SI 2002/546.

Transfer of functions
Functions of the Secretary of State, so far as exercisable in relation to Wales, transferred to the National Assembly for Wales, by the National Assembly for Wales (Transfer of Functions) Order 1999, SI 1999/672.

SCHEDULE 8
Privately Fostered Children

Section 66(5)

Exemptions

1 A child is not a privately fostered child while he is being looked after by a local authority.

2 (1) A child is not a privately fostered child while he is in the care of any person—

(a) in premises in which any—

    (i) parent of his;

    (ii) person who is not a parent of his but who has parental responsibility for him; or

    (iii) person who is a relative of his and who has assumed responsibility for his care,

is for the time being living;

(b) in any children's home;

(c) in accommodation provided by or on behalf of any voluntary organisation;

(d) in any school in which he is receiving full-time education;

(e) in any health service hospital;

(f) in any residential care home [(other than a small home)], nursing home or mental nursing home;

[(f) in any care home or independent hospital;] or

(g) in any home or institution not specified in this paragraph but provided, equipped and maintained by the Secretary of State.

(2) Sub-paragraph (1)(b) [(1)(c)] to (g) does not apply where the person caring for the child is doing so in his personal capacity and not in the course of carrying out his duties in relation to the establishment mentioned in the paragraph in question.

3 A child is not a privately fostered child while he is in the care of any person in compliance with—

(a) an order under [section 63(1) of the Powers of Criminal Courts (Sentencing) Act 2000]; or

(b) a supervision requirement within the meaning of [Part II of the Children (Scotland) Act 1995].

4 A child is not a privately fostered child while he is liable to be detained, or subject to guardianship, under the Mental Health Act 1983.

5 A child is not a privately fostered child while—

(a) he is placed in the care of a person who proposes to adopt him under arrangements made by an adoption agency within the meaning of—

    (i) section 1 of the Adoption Act 1976;

    (ii) section 1 of the Adoption (Scotland) Act 1978; or

    (iii) Article 3 of the Adoption (Northern Ireland) Order 1987; or

(b) he is a protected child.

Power of local authority to impose requirements

6 (1) Where a person is fostering any child privately, or proposes to foster any child privately, the appropriate local authority may impose on him requirements as to—

(a) the number, age and sex of the children who may be privately fostered by him;
(b) the standard of the accommodation and equipment to be provided for them;
(c) the arrangements to be made with respect to their health and safety; and
(d) particular arrangements which must be made with respect to the provision of care for them,

and it shall be his duty to comply with any such requirement before the end of such period as the authority may specify unless, in the case of a proposal, the proposal is not carried out.

(2) A requirement may be limited to a particular child, or class of child.

(3) A requirement (other than one imposed under sub-paragraph (1)(a)) may be limited by the authority so as to apply only when the number of children fostered by the person exceeds a specified number.

(4) A requirement shall be imposed by notice in writing addressed to the person on whom it is imposed and informing him of—

(a) the reason for imposing the requirement;
(b) his right under paragraph 8 to appeal against it; and
(c) the time within which he may do so.

(5) A local authority may at any time vary any requirement, impose any additional requirement or remove any requirement.

(6) In this Schedule—

(a) 'the appropriate local authority' means—

(i) the local authority within whose area the child is being fostered; or
(ii) in the case of a proposal to foster a child, the local authority within whose area it is proposed that he will be fostered; and

(b) 'requirement', in relation to any person, means a requirement imposed on him under this paragraph.

Regulations requiring notification of fostering etc

7 (1) The Secretary of State may by regulations make provision as to—

(a) the circumstances in which notification is required to be given in connection with children who are, have been or are proposed to be fostered privately; and
(b) the manner and form in which such notification is to be given.

(2) The regulations may, in particular—

(a) require any person who is, or proposes to be, involved (whether or not directly) in arranging for a child to be fostered privately to notify the appropriate authority;
(b) require any person who is—

(i) a parent of a child; or
(ii) a person who is not a parent of his but who has parental responsibility for a child,

and who knows that it is proposed that the child should be fostered privately, to notify the appropriate authority;

(c) require any parent of a privately fostered child, or person who is not a parent of such a child but who has parental responsibility for him, to notify the appropriate authority of any change in his address;
(d) require any person who proposes to foster a child privately, to notify the appropriate authority of his proposal;
(e) require any person who is fostering a child privately, or proposes to do so, to notify the appropriate authority of—

    (i)   any offence of which he has been convicted;

    (ii)   any disqualification imposed on him under section 68; or

    (iii) any prohibition imposed on him under section 69;

  (f)   require any person who is fostering a child privately, to notify the appropriate authority of any change in his address;

  (g) require any person who is fostering a child privately to notify the appropriate authority in writing of any person who begins, or ceases, to be part of his household;

  (h) require any person who has been fostering a child privately, but has ceased to do so, to notify the appropriate authority (indicating, where the child has died, that that is the reason).

Appeals

8   (1) A person aggrieved by—

  (a)   a requirement imposed under paragraph 6;

  (b)   a refusal of consent under section 68;

  (c)   a prohibition imposed under section 69;

  (d)   a refusal to cancel such a prohibition;

  (e)   a refusal to make an exemption under paragraph 4 of Schedule 7;

  (f)   a condition imposed in such an exemption; or

  (g)   a variation or cancellation of such an exemption,

may appeal to the court.

(2) The appeal must be made within fourteen days from the date on which the person appealing is notified of the requirement, refusal, prohibition, condition, variation or cancellation.

(3) Where the appeal is against—

  (a)   a requirement imposed under paragraph 6;

  (b)   a condition of an exemption imposed under paragraph 4 of Schedule 7; or

  (c)   a variation or cancellation of such an exemption,

the requirement, condition, variation or cancellation shall not have effect while the appeal is pending.

(4) Where it allows an appeal against a requirement or prohibition, the court may, instead of cancelling the requirement or prohibition—

  (a)   vary the requirement, or allow more time for compliance with it; or

  (b)   if an absolute prohibition has been imposed, substitute for it a prohibition on using the premises after such time as the court may specify unless such specified requirements as the local authority had power to impose under paragraph 6 are complied with.

(5) Any requirement or prohibition specified or substituted by a court under this paragraph shall be deemed for the purposes of Part IX (other than this paragraph) to have been imposed by the local authority under paragraph 6 or (as the case may be) section 69.

(6) Where it allows an appeal against a refusal to make an exemption, a condition imposed in such an exemption or a variation or cancellation of such an exemption, the court may—

  (a)   make an exemption;

  (b)   impose a condition; or

  (c)   vary the exemption.

(7) Any exemption made or varied under sub-paragraph (6), or any condition imposed under that sub-paragraph, shall be deemed for the purposes of Schedule 7 (but not for the purposes of this paragraph) to have been made, varied or imposed under that Schedule.

(8) Nothing in sub-paragraph (1)(e) to (g) confers any right of appeal on—

(a) a person who is, or would be if exempted under Schedule 7, a local authority foster parent; or

(b) a person who is, or would be if so exempted, a person with whom a child is placed by a voluntary organisation.

Extension of Part IX to certain school children during holidays

9 (1) Where a child under sixteen who is a pupil at a school *which is not maintained by a local education authority* lives at the school during school holidays for a period of more than two weeks, Part IX shall apply in relation to the child as if—

(a) while living at the school, he were a privately fostered child; and

(b) paragraphs *2(1)(d)* [2(1)(c) and (d)] and 6 were omitted.

[But this sub-paragraph does not apply to a school which is an appropriate children's home.]

(2) Sub-paragraph (3) applies to any person who proposes to care for and accommodate one or more children at a school in circumstances in which some or all of them will be treated as private foster children by virtue of this paragraph.

(3) That person shall, not less than two weeks before the first of those children is treated as a private foster child by virtue of this paragraph during the holiday in question, give written notice of his proposal to the local authority within whose area the child is ordinarily resident ('the appropriate authority'), stating the estimated number of the children.

(4) A local authority may exempt any person from the duty of giving notice under sub-paragraph (3).

(5) Any such exemption may be granted for a special period or indefinitely and may be revoked at any time by notice in writing given to the person exempted.

(6) Where a child who is treated as a private foster child by virtue of this paragraph dies, the person caring for him at the school shall, not later than 48 hours after the death, give written notice of it—

(a) to the appropriate local authority; and

(b) where reasonably practicable, to each parent of the child and to every person who is not a parent of his but who has parental responsibility for him.

(7) Where a child who is treated as a foster child by virtue of this paragraph ceases for any other reason to be such a child, the person caring for him at the school shall give written notice of the fact to the appropriate local authority.

Prohibition of advertisements relating to fostering

10 No advertisement indicating that a person will undertake, or will arrange for, a child to be privately fostered shall be published, unless it states that person's name and address.

Avoidance of insurances on lives of privately fostered children

11 A person who fosters a child privately and for reward shall be deemed for the purposes of the Life Assurance Act 1774 to have no interest in the life of the child.

Date in force
14 October 1991: SI 1991/828.

Definitions
For 'child', 'local authority', 'relative', 'voluntary organisation', 'health service hospital', 'residential care home', 'nursing home', 'mental nursing home', 'protected child', 'local education authority', 'school' see s 105(1); for 'children's home' see s 63(3) as applied to the whole Act by s 105(1); for 'child who is looked after by a local authority' see s 22(1); for 'privately fostered child' see s 66(1)(a); for 'parental responsibility' see s 3; for 'court' see s 92(7); for 'requirement' see para 6(6)(b); for 'the appropriate authority' see para 6(6)(a); s 114; for 'ordinarily resident' see s 105(6).

References
For 'premises' see the note to s 72; for service of notices generally under the Act see s 105(8)-(10).

Premises
Common sense suggests this should be interpreted as household.

Para 6 May impose on him requirements
Responsibilities under this Act stand referred to the Social Services Committee. By the Local Government Act 1972, s 10(1), any functions of the authority can be delegated to a committee, sub-committee or officer. It is therefore a matter for the discretion of the committee whether it delegates powers under this section to officers. Arrangements to be made with respect to their health and safety will include medical arrangements to be made for protecting the health of the children and fire precautions.

Right of appeal
See Sch 8, para 8 for right of appeal. If there is an appeal a requirement shall not have effect pending appeal: Sch 8, para 8(3).

Notice in writing
May be given by post: s 105(8).

Para 7 Regulations
See the Children (Private Arrangements for Fostering) Regulations 1991, SI 1991/2050 amended by SI 1998/646. An obligation is placed on a parent or a person with parental responsibility to give notice where he knows it is proposed that the child be fostered privately.

Para 8 Person aggrieved
A person who has suffered a legal grievance or against whom a decision has been pronounced which has wrongfully deprived him of something, or wrongfully refused him something or wrongfully affected his title to something: *Re Baron, ex p The Debtor v Official Receiver* [1943] Ch 177 at 179; *R v London Quarter Sessions, ex p Westminster Corpn* [1951] 2 KB 508, [1951] 1 All ER 1032, 115 JP 350.

Within 14 days
Not including the day on which the notice is received.

Para 9
This continues similar provisions formerly contained in the Foster Children Act 1980, s 17 and is designed to apply, for example, provisions as to disqualification of individuals and inspection of premises to schools not maintained by a local education authority, which accommodate children during the school holidays.

Transfer of functions
Functions of the Secretary of State, so far as exercisable in relation to Wales, transferred to the National Assembly for Wales, by the National Assembly for Wales (Transfer of Functions) Order 1999, SI 1999/672.

SCHEDULE 9
Child Minding and Day Care for Young Children

Section 71(16)

[Repealed by the Care Standards Act 2000, s 79(5)]

[SCHEDULE 9A
Child Minding and Day Care for Young Children]

[Section 79B(9)]

[Exemption of certain schools

1 (1) Except in prescribed circumstances, Part XA does not apply to provision of day care within sub-paragraph (2) for any child looked after in—

(a) a maintained school;

(b)   a school assisted by a local education authority;

(c)   a school in respect of which payments are made by the Secretary of State or the Assembly under section 485 of the Education Act 1996;

(d)   an independent school.

(2)   The provision mentioned in sub-paragraph (1) is provision of day care made by—

(a)   the person carrying on the establishment in question as part of the establishment's activities; or

(b)   a person employed to work at that establishment and authorised to make that provision as part of the establishment's activities.

(3)   In sub-paragraph (1)—

'assisted' has the same meaning as in the Education Act 1996;

'maintained school' has the meaning given by section 20(7) of the School Standards and Framework Act 1998.

Amendment
Inserted by s 79, Sch 3 to the Care Standards Act 2000 as from 16 March 2001.

Definitions
For 'day care' see s 79A(6); for 'assisted', 'maintained school' see para 1(3); for 'appropriate children's home', 'care home' see s 23 as applied to the whole Act by s 105(1); for 'hospital' see para 2(1)(c); for 'premises' see s 79B(6); for 'year' see para 3(2).

Para 4 Regulations
See the Day Care and Child Minding (Disqualification) (England) Regulations 2001, SI 2001/1830.

Para 4(2)(g) Convicted of an offence
A conviction of an offence for which a person was discharged conditionally or absolutely is deemed not to be a conviction for any purpose other than the purposes of the proceedings in which the order is made and in any event must be disregarded for the purposes of any enactment or instrument which imposes any disqualification or disability upon convicted persons or authorises or requires the imposition of any such disqualification or disability: Powers of Criminal Courts (Sentencing) Act 2000, s 14.

Para 6 Regulations
See the Child Minding and Day Care (Disqualification) (England) Regulations 2001, SI 2001/1827.

Exemption for other establishments

2   (1)   Part XA does not apply to provision of day care within sub-paragraph (2) for any child looked after—

(a)   in an appropriate children's home;

(b)   in a care home;

(c)   as a patient in a hospital (within the meaning of the Care Standards Act 2000);

(d)   in a residential family centre.

(2)   The provision mentioned in sub-paragraph (1) is provision of day care made by—

(a)   the department, authority or other person carrying on the establishment in question as part of the establishment's activities; or

(b)   a person employed to work at that establishment and authorised to make that provision as part of the establishment's activities.

Amendment
Inserted by s 79, Sch 3 to the Care Standards Act 2000 as from 16 March 2001.

Definitions
For 'day care' see s 79A(6); for 'assisted', 'maintained school' see para 1(3); for 'appropriate children's home', 'care home' see s 23 as applied to the whole Act by s 105(1); for 'hospital' see para 2(1)(c); for 'premises' see s 79B(6); for 'year' see para 3(2).

Para 4 Regulations
See the Child Minding and Day Care (Disqualification) (England) Regulations 2001, SI 2001/1827.

Para 4(2)(g) Convicted of an offence
A conviction of an offence for which a person was discharged conditionally or absolutely is deemed not to be a conviction for any purpose other than the purposes of the proceedings in which the order is made and in any event must be disregarded for the purposes of any enactment or instrument which imposes any disqualification or disability upon convicted persons or authorises or requires the imposition of any such disqualification or disability: Powers of Criminal Courts (Sentencing) Act 2000, s 14.

Para 6 Regulations
See the Child Minding and Day Care (Disqualification) (England) Regulations 2001, SI 2001/1827.

Exemption for occasional facilities

3 (1) Where day care is provided on particular premises on less than six days in any year, that provision shall be disregarded for the purposes of Part XA if the person making it has notified the registration authority in writing before the first occasion on which the premises concerned are so used in that year.

(2) In sub-paragraph (1) 'year' means the year beginning with the day (after the commencement of paragraph 5 of Schedule 9) on which the day care in question was or is first provided on the premises concerned and any subsequent year.

Amendment
Inserted by s 79, Sch 3 to the Care Standards Act 2000 as from 16 March 2001.

Definitions
For 'day care' see s 79A(6); for 'assisted', 'maintained school' see para 1(3); for 'appropriate children's home', 'care home' see s 23 as applied to the whole Act by s 105(1); for 'hospital' see para 2(1)(c); for 'premises' see s 79B(6); for 'year' see para 3(2).

Para 4 Regulations
See the Child Minding and Day Care (Disqualification) (England) Regulations 2001, SI 2001/1827.

Para 4(2)(g) Convicted of an offence
A conviction of an offence for which a person was discharged conditionally or absolutely is deemed not to be a conviction for any purpose other than the purposes of the proceedings in which the order is made and in any event must be disregarded for the purposes of any enactment or instrument which imposes any disqualification or disability upon convicted persons or authorises or requires the imposition of any such disqualification or disability: Powers of Criminal Courts (Sentencing) Act 2000, s 14.

Para 6 Regulations
See the Child Minding and Day Care (Disqualification) (England) Regulations 2001, SI 2001/1827.

Disqualification for registration

4 (1) Regulations may provide for a person to be disqualified for registration for child minding or providing day care.

(2) The regulations may, in particular, provide for a person to be disqualified where—

(a) he is included in the list kept under section 1 of the Protection of Children Act 1999;

(b) he is included on the grounds mentioned in subsection (6ZA)(c) of section 218 of the Education Reform Act 1988 in the list kept for the purposes of regulations made under subsection (6) of that section;

(c) an order of a prescribed kind has been made at any time with respect to him;

(d) an order of a prescribed kind has been made at any time with respect to any child who has been in his care;

(e) a requirement of a prescribed kind has been imposed at any time with respect to such a child, under or by virtue of any enactment;

(f) he has at any time been refused registration under Part X or Part XA or any pre-scribed enactment or had any such registration cancelled;

(g) he has been convicted of any offence of a prescribed kind, or has been placed on probation or discharged absolutely or conditionally for any such offence;

(h) he has at any time been disqualified from fostering a child privately;

(j) a prohibition has been imposed on him at any time under section 69, section 10 of the Foster Children (Scotland) Act 1984 or any prescribed enactment;

(k) his rights and powers with respect to a child have at any time been vested in a prescribed authority under a prescribed enactment.

(3) Regulations may provide for a person who lives—

(a) in the same household as a person who is himself disqualified for registration for child minding or providing day care; or

(b) in a household at which any such person is employed,

to be disqualified for registration for child minding or providing day care.

(4) A person who is disqualified for registration for providing day care shall not pro-vide day care, or be concerned in the management of, or have any financial interest in, any provision of day care.

(5) No person shall employ, in connection with the provision of day care, a person who is disqualified for registration for providing day care.

(6) In this paragraph 'enactment' means any enactment having effect, at any time, in any part of the United Kingdom.

Amendment
Inserted by Sch 3 to the Care Standards Act 2000 as from 16 March 2001.

Definitions
For 'day care' see s 79A(6); for 'assisted', 'maintained school' see para 1(3); for 'appropriate chil-dren's home', 'care home' see s 23 as applied to the whole Act by s 105(1); for 'hospital' see para 2(1)(c); for 'premises' see s 79B(6); for 'year' see para 3(2).

Para 4 Regulations
See the Child Minding and Day Care (Disqualification) (England) Regulations 2001, SI 2001/1827.

Para 4(2)(g) Convicted of an offence
A conviction of an offence for which a person was discharged conditionally or absolutely is deemed not to be a conviction for any purpose other than the purposes of the proceedings in which the order is made and in any event must be disregarded for the purposes of any enactment or instrument which imposes any disqualification or disability upon convicted persons or autho-rises or requires the imposition of any such disqualification or disability: Powers of Criminal Courts (Sentencing) Act 2000, s 14.

Para 6 Regulations
See the Child Minding and Day Care (Disqualification) (England) Regulations 2001, SI 2001/1827.

---

5 (1) If any person—

(a) acts as a child minder at any time when he is disqualified for registration for child minding; or

(b) contravenes any of sub-paragraphs (3) to (5) of paragraph 4,

he shall be guilty of an offence.

(2) Where a person contravenes sub-paragraph (3) of paragraph 4, he shall not be guilty of an offence under this paragraph if he proves that he did not know, and had

no reasonable grounds for believing, that the person in question was living or employed in the household.

(3) Where a person contravenes sub-paragraph (5) of paragraph 4, he shall not be guilty of an offence under this paragraph if he proves that he did not know, and had no reasonable grounds for believing, that the person whom he was employing was disqualified.

(4) A person guilty of an offence under this paragraph shall be liable on summary conviction to imprisonment for a term not exceeding six months, or to a fine not exceeding level 5 on the standard scale, or to both.

Amendment
Inserted by Sch 3 to the Care Standards Act 2000 as from 16 March 2001.

Definitions
For 'day care' see s 79A(6); for 'assisted', 'maintained school' see para 1(3); for 'appropriate children's home', 'care home' see s 23 as applied to the whole Act by s 105(1); for 'hospital' see para 2(1)(c); for 'premises' see s 79B(6); for 'year' see para 3(2).

Para 4 Regulations
See the Child Minding and Day Care (Disqualification) (England) Regulations 2001, SI 2001/1827.

Para 4(2)(g) Convicted of an offence
A conviction of an offence for which a person was discharged conditionally or absolutely is deemed not to be a conviction for any purpose other than the purposes of the proceedings in which the order is made and in any event must be disregarded for the purposes of any enactment or instrument which imposes any disqualification or disability upon convicted persons or authorises or requires the imposition of any such disqualification or disability: Powers of Criminal Courts (Sentencing) Act 2000, s 14.

Para 6 Regulations
See the Child Minding and Day Care (Disqualification) (England) Regulations 2001, SI 2001/1827.

Certificates of registration

6 (1) If an application for registration is granted, the registration authority shall give the applicant a certificate of registration.

(2) A certificate of registration shall give prescribed information about prescribed matters.

(3) Where, due to a change of circumstances, any part of the certificate requires to be amended, the registration authority shall issue an amended certificate.

(4) Where the registration authority is satisfied that the certificate has been lost or destroyed, the authority shall issue a copy, on payment by the registered person of any prescribed fee.

(5) For the purposes of Part XA, a person is—

(a) registered for providing child minding (in England or in Wales); or
(b) registered for providing day care on any premises,

if a certificate of registration to that effect is in force in respect of him.

Amendment
Inserted by Sch 3 to the Care Standards Act 2000 as from 16 March 2001.

Definitions
For 'day care' see s 79A(6); for 'assisted', 'maintained school' see para 1(3); for 'appropriate children's home', 'care home' see s 23 as applied to the whole Act by s 105(1); for 'hospital' see para 2(1)(c); for 'premises' see s 79B(6); for 'year' see para 3(2).

Para 4 Regulations
See the Child Minding and Day Care (Disqualification) (England) Regulations 2001, SI 2001/1827.

Para 4(2)(g) Convicted of an offence
A conviction of an offence for which a person was discharged conditionally or absolutely is deemed not to be a conviction for any purpose other than the purposes of the proceedings in which the order is made and in any event must be disregarded for the purposes of any enactment or instrument which imposes any disqualification or disability upon convicted persons or authorises or requires the imposition of any such disqualification or disability: Powers of Criminal Courts (Sentencing) Act 2000, s 14.

Para 6 Regulations
See the Child Minding and Day Care (Disqualification) (England) Regulations 2001, SI 2001/1827.

Annual fees

7   Regulations may require registered persons to pay to the registration authority at prescribed times an annual fee of a prescribed amount.

Amendment
Inserted by Sch 3 to the Care Standards Act 2000 as from 16 March 2001.

Definitions
For 'day care' see s 79A(6); for 'assisted', 'maintained school' see para 1(3); for 'appropriate children's home', 'care home' see s 23 as applied to the whole Act by s 105(1); for 'hospital' see para 2(1)(c); for 'premises' see s 79B(6); for 'year' see para 3(2).

Para 4 Regulations
See the Child Minding and Day Care (Disqualification) (England) Regulations 2001, SI 2001/1827.

Para 4(2)(g) Convicted of an offence
A conviction of an offence for which a person was discharged conditionally or absolutely is deemed not to be a conviction for any purpose other than the purposes of the proceedings in which the order is made and in any event must be disregarded for the purposes of any enactment or instrument which imposes any disqualification or disability upon convicted persons or authorises or requires the imposition of any such disqualification or disability: Powers of Criminal Courts (Sentencing) Act 2000, s 14.

Para 6 Regulations
See the Child Minding and Day Care (Disqualification) (England) Regulations 2001, SI 2001/1827.

Cooperation between authorities

8   (1) Where it appears to the Chief Inspector that any local authority in England could, by taking any specified action, help in the exercise of any of his functions under Part XA, he may request the help of that authority specifying the action in question.

(2) Where it appears to the Assembly that any local authority in Wales could, by taking any specified action, help in the exercise of any of its functions under Part XA, the Assembly may request the help of that authority specifying the action in question.

(3) An authority whose help is so requested shall comply with the request if it is compatible with their own statutory or other duties and obligations and does not unduly prejudice the discharge of any of their functions.]

Amendment
Inserted by Sch 3 to the Care Standards Act 2000 as from 16 March 2001.

Definitions
For 'day care' see s 79A(6); for 'assisted', 'maintained school' see para 1(3); for 'appropriate children's home', 'care home' see s 23 as applied to the whole Act by s 105(1); for 'hospital' see para 2(1)(c); for 'premises' see s 79B(6); for 'year' see para 3(2).

Para 4 Regulations
See the Child Minding and Day Care (Disqualification) (England) Regulations 2001, SI 2001/1827.

Para 4(2)(g) Convicted of an offence
A conviction of an offence for which a person was discharged conditionally or absolutely is deemed not to be a conviction for any purpose other than the purposes of the proceedings in which the order is made and in any event must be disregarded for the purposes of any enactment or instrument which imposes any disqualification or disability upon convicted persons or authorises or requires the imposition of any such disqualification or disability: Powers of Criminal Courts (Sentencing) Act 2000, s 14.

Para 6 Regulations
See the Child Minding and Day Care (Disqualification) (England) Regulations 2001, SI 2001/1827.

SCHEDULE 10
Amendments of Adoption Legislation

Section 88

PART I
AMENDMENTS OF ADOPTION ACT 1976

1–28 ...
29 ...
30 ...
31 ...

PART II
AMENDMENTS OF ADOPTION (SCOTLAND) ACT 1978

...

SCHEDULE 11
Jurisdiction

Section 92

PART I
GENERAL

Commencement of proceedings

1 (1) The Lord Chancellor may by order specify proceedings under this Act or the Adoption Act 1976 which may only be commenced in—

  (a) a specified level of court;

  (b) a court which falls within a specified class of court; or

  (c) a particular court determined in accordance with, or specified in, the order.

(2) The Lord Chancellor may by order specify circumstances in which specified proceedings under this Act or the Adoption Act 1976 (which might otherwise be commenced elsewhere) may only be commenced in—

  (a) a specified level of court;

  (b) a court which falls within a specified class of court; or

  (c) a particular court determined in accordance with, or specified in, the order.

[(2A) Sub-paragraphs (1) and (2) shall also apply in relation to proceedings—

[(a) under section 55A of the Family Law Act 1986 (declarations of parentage); or]
(b) which are to be dealt with in accordance with an order made under section 45 [of the Child Support Act 1991] (jurisdiction of courts in certain proceedings under that Act).]

(3) The Lord Chancellor may by order make provision by virtue of which, where specified proceedings with respect to a child under—

(a) this Act;
(b) the Adoption Act 1976;
[(bb) section 20 (appeals) . . . of the Child Support Act 1991;] or
(c) the High Court's inherent jurisdiction with respect to children,

have been commenced in or transferred to any court (whether or not by virtue of an order under this Schedule), any other specified family proceedings which may affect, or are otherwise connected with, the child may, in specified circumstances, only be commenced in that court.

(4) A class of court specified in an order under this Schedule may be described by reference to a description of proceedings and may include different levels of court.

Transfer of proceedings

2 (1) The Lord Chancellor may by order provide that in specified circumstances the whole, or any specified part of, specified proceedings to which this paragraph applies shall be transferred to—

(a) a specified level of court;
(b) a court which falls within a specified class of court; or
(c) a particular court determined in accordance with, or specified in, the order.

(2) Any order under this paragraph may provide for the transfer to be made at any stage, or specified stage, of the proceedings and whether or not the proceedings, or any part of them, have already been transferred.

(3) The proceedings to which this paragraph applies are—

(a) any proceedings under this Act;
(b) any proceedings under the Adoption Act 1976;

[(ba) any proceedings under section 55A of the Family Law Act 1986;]
[(bb) [any proceedings under] section 20 (appeals) . . . of the Child Support Act 1991;]

(c) any other proceedings which—

(i) are family proceedings for the purposes of this Act, other than proceedings under the inherent jurisdiction of the High Court; and
(ii) may affect, or are otherwise connected with, the child concerned.

(4) Proceedings to which this paragraph applies by virtue of sub-paragraph (3)(*c*) may only be transferred in accordance with the provisions of an order made under this paragraph for the purpose of consolidating them with proceedings under—

(a) this Act;
(b) the Adoption Act 1976; or
(c) the High Court's inherent jurisdiction with respect to children.

(5) An order under this paragraph may make such provision as the Lord Chancellor thinks appropriate for excluding proceedings to which this paragraph applies from the operation of any enactment which would otherwise govern the transfer of those proceedings, or any part of them.

Hearings by single justice

3 (1) In such circumstances as the Lord Chancellor may by order specify—

(a) the jurisdiction of a magistrates' court to make an emergency protection order;

(b) any specified question with respect to the transfer of specified proceedings to or from a magistrates' court in accordance with the provisions of an order under paragraph 2,

may be exercised by a single justice.

(2) Any provision made under this paragraph shall be without prejudice to any other enactment or rule of law relating to the functions which may be performed by a single justice of the peace.

General

4 (1) For the purposes of this Schedule—

(a) the commencement of proceedings under this Act includes the making of any application under this Act in the course of proceedings (whether or not those proceedings are proceedings under this Act); and

(b) there are three levels of court, that is to say the High Court, any county court and any magistrates' court.

(2) In this Schedule 'specified' means specified by an order made under this Schedule.

(3) Any order under paragraph 1 may make provision as to the effect of commencing proceedings in contravention of any of the provisions of the order.

(4) An order under paragraph 2 may make provision as to the effect of a failure to comply with any of the provisions of the order.

(5) An order under this Schedule may—

(a) make such consequential, incidental or transitional provision as the Lord Chancellor considers expedient, including provision amending any other enactment so far as it concerns the jurisdiction of any court or justice of the peace;

(b) make provision for treating proceedings which are—

(i) in part proceedings of a kind mentioned in paragraph (*a*) or (*b*) of paragraph 2(3); and

(ii) in part proceedings of a kind mentioned in paragraph (*c*) of paragraph 2(3),

as consisting entirely of proceedings of one or other of those kinds, for the purposes of the application of any order made under paragraph 2.

Date in force
14 October 1991: SI 1991/828.

Amendments
Para 1: sub-para (2A) inserted by the Child Support Act 1991, s 45(3), (4).
Para 1: sub-para (2A)(a) substituted by the Child Support, Pensions and Social Security Act 2000, s 83(5), Sch 8, para 10(1), (2)(a).
Para 1: in sub-para (2A)(b) words "of the Child Support Act 1991" in square brackets substituted by the Child Support, Pensions and Social Security Act 2000, s 83(5), Sch 8, paras 10(1), (2)(b).
Para 1: sub-para (3)(bb) inserted by the Child Support Act 1991, s 45(3), (5).
Para 1: in sub-para (3)(bb) words omitted repealed by the Child Support, Pensions and Social Security Act 2000, s 85, Sch 9, Pt IX.
Para 2: sub-para (3)(ba) inserted by the Child Support, Pensions and Social Security Act 2000, s 83(5), Sch 8, para 10(1), (3)(a).
Para 2: sub-para (3)(bb) inserted by the Child Support Act 1991, s 45(3), (5).
Para 2: in sub-para (3)(bb) words "any proceedings under" in square brackets inserted by the Child Support, Pensions and Social Security Act 2000, s 83(5), Sch 8, para 10(1), (3)(b).
Para 2: in sub-para (3)(bb) words omitted repealed by the Child Support, Pensions and Social Security Act 2000, s 85, Sch 9, Pt IX.

Children Act 1989

References
See generally the Children (Allocation of Proceedings) Order 1991 and chapter 4 at paras 415ff.

PART II
CONSEQUENTIAL AMENDMENTS

[Not reproduced]

SCHEDULE 12
Minor Amendments

Section 108(4)

[Not reproduced]

SCHEDULE 13
Consequential Amendments

Section 108(5)

[Not reproduced]

SCHEDULE 14
Transitionals and Savings

Section 108(6)

Pending proceedings, etc

[Not reproduced]

Section 108(5)

SCHEDULE 15
Repeals

Section 108(7)

[Not reproduced]

Family Proceedings Rules 1991

(SI 1991/1247)

PRELIMINARY

1.1 Citation and commencement

These rules may be cited as the Family Proceedings Rules 1991 and shall come into force on 14th October 1991.

1.2 Interpretation

(1) In these rules, unless the context otherwise requires—

'the Act of 1973' means the Matrimonial Causes Act 1973;
'the Act of 1984' means the Matrimonial and Family Proceedings Act 1984;
'the Act of 1986' means the Family Law Act 1986;
'the Act of 1989' means the Children Act 1989;
['the Act of 1991' means the Child Support Act 1991;]

. . .

'business day' has the meaning assigned to it by rule 1.5(6);

. . .

'child' and 'child of the family' have, except in Part IV, the meanings respectively assigned to them by section 52(1) of the Act of 1973;

. . .

['Contracting State' means—

    (a)   one of the original parties to the Council Regulation, that is to say Belgium, Germany, Greece, Spain, France, Ireland, Italy, Luxembourg, the Netherlands, Austria, Portugal, Finland, Sweden and the United Kingdom, and

    (b)   a party which has subsequently adopted the Council Regulation;]

['the Council Regulation' means Council Regulation (EC) No 1347/2000 of 29th May 2000 on jurisdiction and the recognition and enforcement of judgments in matrimonial matters and in matters of parental responsibility for children of both spouses;]

'court' means a judge or the district judge;

. . .

. . .

'district judge', in relation to proceedings in the principal registry, a district registry or a county court, means the district judge or one of the district judges of that registry or county court, as the case may be;

'district registry'[, except in rule 4.22(2A),] means any district registry having a divorce county court within its district;

'divorce county court' means a county court so designated by the Lord Chancellor pursuant to section 33(1) of the Act of 1984;

. . .

'document exchange' means any document exchange for the time being approved by the Lord Chancellor;

'family proceedings' has the meaning assigned to it by section 32 of the Act of 1984;

. . .

. . .

'judge' does not include a district judge;

. . .

['officer of the service' has the same meaning as in the Criminal Justice and Court
Services Act 2000;]

. . .

. . .

'the President' means the President of the Family Division or, in the case of his
absence or incapacity through illness or otherwise or of a vacancy in the office
of President, the senior puisne judge of that Division;
'principal registry' means the Principal Registry of the Family Division;
'proper officer' means—
   (a)   in relation to the principal registry, the [family proceedings department
         manager], and
   (b)   in relation to any other court or registry, the [court manager],
or other officer of the court or registry acting on his behalf in accordance with
directions given by the Lord Chancellor;

. . .

. . .

'Royal Courts of Justice', in relation to matrimonial proceedings pending in a
divorce county court, means such place, being the Royal Courts of Justice or
elsewhere, as may be specified in directions given by the Lord Chancellor pursuant to section 42(2)(a) of the Act of 1984;
'senior district judge' means the senior district judge of the Family Division or, in
his absence from the principal registry, the senior of the district judges in attendance at the registry;

. . .

(3) Unless the context otherwise requires, a rule or Part referred to by number
means the rule or Part so numbered in these rules.

(4) In these rules a form referred to by number means the form so numbered in
Appendix 1 [or 1A] to these rules with such variation as the circumstances of the particular case may require.

(5) In these rules any reference to an Order and rule is—
(a)   if prefixed by the letters 'CCR', a reference to that Order and rule in the
      County Court Rules 1981, and
(b)   if prefixed by the letters 'RSC', a reference to that Order and rule in the Rules
      of the Supreme Court 1965.

[(5A) In these rules a reference to a Part or rule, if prefixed by the letters 'CPR', is a
reference to that Part or rule in the Civil Procedure Rules 1998.]

(6) References in these rules to a county court shall, in relation to matrimonial proceedings, be construed as references to a divorce county court.

(7) . . .

Date in force
14 October 1991.

Amendment

Para (1): definition 'the Act of 1991' inserted by SI 1993/295, r 3.

Para (1): definition 'Contracting State' inserted by SI 2001/821, r 8(a). Date in force: 1 April
2001: see SI 2001/821, r 1(b).

Para (1): definition 'the Council Regulation' inserted by SI 2001/821, r 8(a). Date in force: 1 April
2001: see SI 2001/821, r 1(b).

Para (1): in definition 'district registry' words ', except in rule 4.22(2A),' in square brackets
inserted by SI 1992/2067, r 3.

Para (1): definition 'officer of the service' inserted by SI 2001/821, r 8(b). Date in force: 1 April
2001: see SI 2001/821, r 1(b).

Para (1): in definition 'proper officer' in para (a) words 'family proceedings department manager' in square brackets substituted by SI 1997/1056, r 6.

Para (1): in definition 'proper officer' in para (b) words 'court manager' in square brackets substituted by SI 1997/1056, r 6.

Para (4): words 'or 1A' in square brackets inserted by SI 1999/3491, rr 2, 4(1). Date in force: 5 June 2000 (in relation to proceedings commenced by Form A or B on or after that date and, where the court considers it just and so directs, proceedings commenced before that date): see SI 1999/3491, r 1.

Para (5A): inserted by SI 1999/3491, rr 2, 4(2). Date in force: 5 June 2000 (in relation to proceedings commenced by Form A or B on or after that date and, where the court considers it just and so directs, proceedings commenced before that date): see SI 1999/3491, r 1.

Note
Only those definitions relevant to this work are printed here.

1.3   Application of other rules

(1) Subject to the provisions of these rules and of any enactment the County Court Rules 1981 and the Rules of the Supreme Court 1965 shall [continue to] apply, with the necessary modifications, to family proceedings in a county court and the High Court respectively.

(2) For the purposes of paragraph (1) any provision of these rules authorising or requiring anything to be done in family proceedings shall be treated as if it were, in the case of proceedings pending in a county court, a provision of the County Court Rules 1981 and, in the case of proceedings pending in the High Court, a provision of the Rules of the Supreme Court 1965.

Date in force
14 October 1991: SI 1991/828.

Amendment
Para (1): words 'continue to' in square brackets inserted by SI 1999/1012, rr 2, 3(2). Date in force: 26 April 1999: see SI 1999/1012, r 1.

1.4   County court proceedings in principal registry

(1) Subject to the provisions of these rules, matrimonial proceedings pending at any time in the principal registry which, if they had been begun in a divorce county court, would be pending at that time in such a court, shall be treated, for the purposes of these rules and of any provision of the County Court Rules 1981 and the County Courts Act 1984, as pending in a divorce county court and not in the High Court.

(2) Unless the context otherwise requires, any reference to a divorce county court in any provision of these rules which relates to the commencement or prosecution of proceedings in a divorce county court, or the transfer of proceedings to or from such a court, includes a reference to the principal registry.

1.5   Computation of time

(1) Any period of time fixed by these rules, or by any rules applied by these rules, or by any decree, judgment, order or direction for doing any act shall be reckoned in accordance with the following provisions of this rule.

(2) Where the act is required to be done not less than a specified period before a specified date, the period starts immediately after the date on which the act is done and ends immediately before the specified date.

(3) Where the act is required to be done within a specified period after or from a specified date, the period starts immediately after that date.

(4) Where, apart from this paragraph, the period in question, being a period of seven

days or less, would include a day which is not a business day, that day shall be excluded.

(5) Where the time so fixed for doing an act in the court office expires on a day on which the office is closed, and for that reason the act cannot be done on that day, the act shall be in time if done on the next day on which the office is open.

(6) In these rules 'business day' means any day other than—

(a) a Saturday, Sunday, Christmas Day or Good Friday; or
(b) a bank holiday under the Banking and Financial Dealings Act 1971, in England and Wales.

Part II
Matrimonial Causes

[Not reproduced]

Part III
Other Matrimonial etc Proceedings

[Not reproduced]

Part IV
Proceedings Under the Children Act 1989

4.1 Interpretation and application

(1) In this Part of these rules, unless a contrary intention appears—

a section or schedule referred to means the section or schedule so numbered in the Act of 1989;

'a section 8 order' has the meaning assigned to it by section 8(2);

'application' means an application made under or by virtue of the Act of 1989 or under these rules, and 'applicant' shall be construed accordingly;

'child', in relation to proceedings to which this Part applies—

(a) means, subject to sub-paragraph (b), a person under the age of 18 with respect to whom the proceedings are brought, and
(b) where the proceedings are under Schedule 1, also includes a person who has reached the age of 18;

['children and family reporter' means an officer of the service who has been asked to prepare a welfare report under section 7(1)(a);]

['children's guardian'—

(a) means an officer of the service appointed under section 41 for the child with respect to whom the proceedings are brought; but
(b) does not include such an officer appointed in relation to proceedings specified by Part IVA;]

'directions appointment' means a hearing for directions under rule 4.14(2);

'emergency protection order' means an order under section 44;

. . .

'leave' includes permission and approval;

'note' includes a record made by mechanical means;

'parental responsibility' has the meaning assigned to it by section 3;

'recovery order' means an order under section 50;

'specified proceedings' has the meaning assigned to it by section 41(6) and rule 4.2(2); and

'welfare officer' means a person who has been asked to prepare a welfare report under [section 7(1)(b)].

(2) Except where the contrary intention appears, the provisions of this Part apply to proceedings in the High Court and the county courts

(a) on an application for a section 8 order;

(b) on an application for a care order or a supervision order;

(c) on an application under section 4(1)(a), 4(3), 5(1), 6(7), 13(1), 16(6), 33(7), 34(2), 34(3), 34(4), 34(9), 36(1), 38(8)(b), 39(1), 39(2), 39(3), 39(4), 43(1), 43(12), 44, 45, 46(7), 48(9)[, 50(1) or 102(1)];

(d) under Schedule 1, except where financial relief is also sought by or on behalf of an adult,

(e) on an application under paragraph 19(1) of Schedule 2;

(f) on an application under paragraph 6(3), 15(2) or 17(1) of Schedule 3;

(g) on an application under paragraph 11(3) or 16(5) of Schedule 14; or

(h) under section 25.

Date in force
14 October 1991.

Amendment
Para (1): definition 'children and family reporter' inserted by SI 2001/821, r 15(a). Date in force: 1 April 2001: see SI 2001/821, r 1(b).

Para (1): definition 'children's guardian' inserted by SI 2001/821, r 15(a). Date in force: 1 April 2001: see SI 2001/821, r 1(b).

Para (1): definition 'guardian ad litem' (omitted) revoked by SI 2001/821, r 15(b). Date in force: 1 April 2001: see SI 2001/821, r 1(b).

Para (1): in definition 'welfare officer' words 'section 7(1)(b)' in square brackets substituted by SI 2001/821, r 15(c). Date in force: 1 April 2001: see SI 2001/821, r 1(b).

Para (2): in sub-para (c) words ', 50(1) or 102(1)' substituted by SI 1991/2113, r 5.

4.2 Matters prescribed for the purposes of the Act of 1989

(1) The parties to proceedings in which directions are given under section 38(6), and any person named in such a direction, form the prescribed class for the purposes of section 38(8) (application to vary directions made with interim care or interim supervision order).

(2) The following proceedings are specified for the purposes of section 41 in accordance with subsection (6)(i) thereof—

(a) proceedings under section 25;

(b) applications under section 33(7);

(c) proceedings under paragraph 19(1) of Schedule 2;

(d) applications under paragraph 6(3) of Schedule 3.

[(e) appeals against the determination of proceedings of a kind set out in sub-paragraphs (a) to (d)].

(3) The applicant for an order that has been made under section 43(1) and the persons referred to in section 43(11) may, in any circumstances, apply under section 43(12) for a child assessment order to be varied or discharged.

(4) The following persons form the prescribed class for the purposes of section 44(9) (application to vary directions)—

(a) the parties to the application for the order in respect of which it is sought to vary the directions;

(b) the [children's guardian];

(c) the local authority in whose area the child concerned is ordinarily resident;

(d) any person who is named in the directions.

Date in force
14 October 1991.

Amendment

Para (2): sub-para (e) inserted by SI 1991/2113, r 8.

Para (4): in sub-para (b) words 'children's guardian' in square brackets substituted by SI 2001/821, r 16(a). Date in force: 1 April 2001: see SI 2001/821, r 1(b).

4.3 Application for leave to commence proceedings

(1) Where the leave of the court is required to bring any proceedings to which this Part applies, the person seeking leave shall file—

(a) a written request for leave [in Form C2] setting out the reasons for the application; and

[(b) a draft of the application (being the documents referred to in rule 4.4(1A)) for the making of which leave is sought together with sufficient copies for one to be served on each respondent].

(2) On considering a request for leave filed under paragraph (1), the court shall—

(a) grant the request, whereupon the proper officer shall inform the person making the request of the decision, or

(b) direct that a date be fixed for the hearing of the request, whereupon the proper officer shall fix such a date and give such notice as the court directs to the person making the request and to such other persons as the court requires to be notified, of the date so fixed.

(3) Where leave is granted to bring proceedings to which this Part applies the application shall proceed in accordance with rule 4.4; but paragraph (1)(a) of that rule shall not apply.

(4) In the case of a request for leave to bring proceedings under Schedule 1, the draft application under paragraph (1) shall be accompanied by a statement setting out the financial details which the person seeking leave believes to be relevant to the request and containing a declaration that it is true to the maker's best knowledge and belief, together with sufficient copies for one to be served on each respondent.

Date in force

14 October 1991.

Amendment

Para (1): in sub-para (a) words 'in Form C2' inserted, and sub-para (b) substituted, by SI 1994/3155, r4.

4.4 Application

(1) Subject to paragraph (4), an applicant shall—

[(a) file the documents referred to in paragraph (1A) below (which documents shall together be called the 'application') together with sufficient copies for one to be served on each respondent, and]

(b) serve a copy of the application [together with Form C6 and such (if any) of Forms C7 and C10A as are given to him by the proper officer under paragraph (2)(b)] on each respondent such number of days prior to the date fixed under paragraph (2)(a) as is specified for that application in column (ii) of Appendix 3 to these rules.

[(1A) The documents to be filed under paragraph (1)(a) above are—

(a)

    (i) whichever is appropriate of Forms C1 to C4 or C51, and

    (ii) such of the supplemental Forms C10 or C11 to C20 as may be appropriate, or

(b)   where there is no appropriate form a statement in writing of the order sought, and where the application is made in respect of more than one child, all the children shall be included in one application.]

(2) On receipt of the documents filed under paragraph (1)(a) the proper officer shall—

(a)   fix the date for a hearing or a directions appointment, allowing sufficient time for the applicant to comply with paragraph (1)(b),

(b)   endorse the date so fixed upon [Form C6 and, where appropriate, Form C6A], and

[(c)   return forthwith to the applicant the copies of the application and Form C10A if filed with it, together with Form C6 and such of Forms C6A and C7 as are appropriate].

[(3) The applicant shall, at the same time as complying with paragraph (1)(b), serve Form C6A on the persons set out for the relevant class of proceedings in column (iv) of Appendix 3 to these rules.]

(4) An application for—

(a)   a [section 8 order],

(b)   an emergency protection order,

(c)   a warrant under section 48(9), . . .

(d)   a recovery order, [or

(e)   a warrant under section 102(1),]

may be made ex parte in which case the applicant shall—

(i)   file the application . . . in the appropriate form in Appendix 1 to these rules—

(a)   where the application is made by telephone, within 24 hours after the making of the application, or

(b)   in any other case, at the time when the application is made, and

(ii)   in the case of an application for a [section 8 order] or an emergency protection order, serve a copy of the application on each respondent within 48 hours after the making of the order.

(5) Where the court refuses to make an order on an ex parte application it may direct that the application be made inter partes

(6) In the case of proceedings under Schedule 1, the application under paragraph (1) shall be accompanied by a statement [in Form C10A] setting out the financial details which the applicant believes to be relevant to the application . . . together with sufficient copies for one to be served on each respondent.

Date in force
14 October 1991

Amendment
Para (1): sub-para (a) substituted, and in sub-para (b) words from 'together with' to 'paragraph (2)(b)' substituted, by SI 1994/3155, r 5.

Para (1A): inserted by SI 1994/3155, r 6.

Para (2): in sub-para (b) words 'Form C6 and, where appropriate, Form C6A' substituted, and sub-para (c) substituted, by SI 1994/3155, r 7.

Para (3): substituted by SI 1994/3155, r 8.

Para (4): words 'section 8 order' in both places where they occur substituted by SI 1992/2067, r 9; in sub-para (c) word omitted revoked and sub-para (e) and the word 'or' immediately preceding it inserted, by SI 1991/2113, r 9; in sub-para (i) words omitted revoked by SI 1994/3155, r 9.

Para (6): words 'in Form C10A' inserted and words omitted revoked, by SI 1994/3155, r 10.

Sections 8, 48(9), 102(1): Children Act 1989, ss 8, 48(9), 102(1).

4.5 Withdrawal of application

(1) An application may be withdrawn only with leave of the court.

(2) Subject to paragraph (3), a person seeking leave to withdraw an application shall file and serve on the parties a written request for leave setting out the reasons for the request.

(3) The request under paragraph (2) may be made orally to the court if the parties and either the [children's guardian] or the [welfare officer or children and family reporter] are present.

(4) Upon receipt of a written request under paragraph (2) the court shall—

(a) if—

    (i) the parties consent in writing,

    (ii) the [children's guardian] has had an opportunity to make representations, and

    (iii) the court thinks fit,

grant the request, in which case the proper officer shall notify the parties, the [children's guardian] and the [welfare officer or children and family reporter] of the granting of the request, or

(b) direct that a date be fixed for the hearing of the request in which case the proper officer shall give at least 7 days' notice to the parties, the [children's guardian] and the [welfare officer or children and family reporter], of the date fixed.

Date in force
14 October 1991

Amendment

Para (3): words 'children's guardian' in square brackets substituted by SI 2001/821, r 16(a). Date in force: 1 April 2001: see SI 2001/821, r 1(b).

Para (3): words 'welfare officer or children and family reporter' in square brackets substituted by SI 2001/821, r 16(b). Date in force: 1 April 2001: see SI 2001/821, r 1(b).

Para (4): in sub-para (a)(ii) words 'children's guardian' in square brackets substituted by SI 2001/821, r 16(a). Date in force: 1 April 2001: see SI 2001/821, r 1(b).

Para (4): in sub-para (a) words 'children's guardian' in square brackets substituted by SI 2001/821, r 16(a). Date in force: 1 April 2001: see SI 2001/821, r 1(b).

Para (4): in sub-para (a) words 'welfare officer or children and family reporter' in square brackets substituted by SI 2001/821, r 16(b). Date in force: 1 April 2001: see SI 2001/821, r 1(b).

Para (4): in sub-para (b) words 'children's guardian' in square brackets substituted by SI 2001/821, r 16(a). Date in force: 1 April 2001: see SI 2001/821, r 1(b).

Para (4): in sub-para (b) words 'welfare officer or children and family reporter' in square brackets substituted by SI 2001/821, r 16(b). Date in force: 1 April 2001: see SI 2001/821, r 1(b).

4.6 Transfer . . .

(1) Where an application is made, in accordance with the provisions of [the Allocation Order], to a county court for an order transferring proceedings from a magistrates' court following the refusal of the magistrates' court to order such a transfer, the applicant shall—

(a) file the application in Form [C2], together with a copy of the certificate issued by the magistrates' court, and

(b) serve a copy of the documents mentioned in sub-paragraph (a) personally on all parties to the proceedings which it is sought to have transferred,

within 2 days after receipt by the applicant of the certificate.

(2) Within 2 days after receipt of the documents served under paragraph (1)(b), any party other than the applicant may file written representations.

(3) The court shall, not before the fourth day after the filing of the application under paragraph (1), unless the parties consent to earlier consideration, consider the application and either—

(a) grant the application, whereupon the proper officer shall inform the parties of that decision, or

(b) direct that a date be fixed for the hearing of the application, whereupon the proper officer shall fix such a date and give not less than 1 day's notice to the parties of the date so fixed.

(4) Where proceedings are transferred from a magistrates' court to a county court in accordance with the provisions of [the Allocation Order], the county court shall consider whether to transfer those proceedings to the High Court in accordance with that Order and either—

(a) determine that such an order need not be made,

(b) make such an order,

(c) order that a date be fixed for the hearing of the question whether such an order should be made, whereupon the proper officer shall give such notice to the parties as the court directs of the date so fixed, or

(d) invite the parties to make written representations, within a specified period, as to whether such an order should be made; and upon receipt of the representations the court shall act in accordance with sub-paragraph (a), (b) or (c).

(5) The proper officer shall notify the parties of an order transferring the proceedings from a county court or from the High Court made in accordance with the provisions of [the Allocation Order].

[(6) Before ordering the transfer of proceedings from a county court to a magistrates' court in accordance with the Allocation Order, the county court shall notify the magistrates' court of its intention to make such an order and invite the views of the clerk to the justices on whether such an order should be made.

(7) An order transferring proceedings from a county court to a magistrates' court in accordance with the Allocation Order shall—

(a) be in form [C49], and

(b) be served by the court on the parties.

(8) In this rule 'the Allocation Order' means the Children (Allocation of Proceedings) Order 1991 or any Order replacing that Order.]

Date in force
14 October 1991

Amendment
Provision heading: words omitted revoked by SI 1991/2113, r 11.

Para (1): words 'the Allocation Order' substituted by SI 1991/2113, r 10; in sub-para (a) figure 'C2' substituted by SI 1994/3155, r 11.

Paras (4), (5): words 'the Allocation Order' substituted by SI 1991/2113, r 10.

Paras (6), (8): inserted by SI 1991/2113, r 12.

Para (7): inserted by SI 1991/2113, r 12; in sub-para (a) figure 'C49' substituted by SI 1994/3155, r 12.

4.7 Parties

(1) The respondents to proceedings to which this Part applies shall be those persons set out in the relevant entry in [column (iii)] of Appendix 3 to these rules.

(2) In proceedings to which this Part applies, a person may file a request [in Form C2] that he or another person—

(a) be joined as a party, or

(b) cease to be a party.

(3) On considering a request under paragraph (2) the court shall, subject to paragraph (4)—

(a) grant it without a hearing or representations, save that this shall be done only in the case of a request under paragraph (2)(a), whereupon the proper officer shall inform the parties and the person making the request of that decision, or

(b) order that a date be fixed for the consideration of the request, whereupon the proper officer shall give notice of the date so fixed, together with a copy of the request—

(i) in the case of a request under paragraph (2)(a), to the applicant, and

(ii) in the case of a request under paragraph (2)(b), to the parties, or

(c) invite the parties or any of them to make written representations, within a specified period, as to whether the request should be granted; and upon the expiry of the period the court shall act in accordance with sub-paragraph (a) or (b).

(4) Where a person with parental responsibility requests that he be joined under paragraph (2)(a), the court shall grant his request.

(5) In proceedings to which this Part applies the court may direct—

(a) that a person who would not otherwise be a respondent under these rules be joined as a party to the proceedings, or

(b) that a party to the proceedings cease to be a party.

Date in force
14 October 1991

Amendment
Para (1): words 'column (iii)' substituted by SI 1992/2067, r 7.
Para (2): words 'in Form C2' substituted by SI 1994/3155, r 13.

4.8   Service

(1)

(a) if the person to be served is not known by the person serving to be acting by solicitor—

(i) by delivering it to him personally, or

(ii) by delivering it at, or by sending it by first-class post to, his residence or his last known residence, or

(b) if the person to be served is known by the person serving to be acting by solicitor—

(i) by delivering the document at, or sending it by first-class post to, the solicitor's address for service,

(ii) where the solicitor's address for service includes a numbered box at a document exchange, by leaving the document at that document exchange or at a document exchange which transmits documents on every business day to that document exchange, or

(iii) by sending a legible copy of the document by facsimile transmission to the solicitor's office.

(2) In this rule 'first-class post' means first-class post which has been pre-paid or in respect of which pre-payment is not required.

(3) Where a child who is a party to proceedings to which this Part applies [is not prosecuting or defending them without a next friend or guardian ad litem under rule 9.2A and] is required by these rules or other rules of court to serve a document, service shall be effected by—

(a) the solicitor acting for the child, or
(b) where there is no such solicitor, [the children's guardian or] the guardian ad litem, or
(c) where there is neither such a solicitor [nor a children's guardian] nor a guardian ad litem, the court.

(4) Service of any document on a child [who is not prosecuting or defending the proceedings concerned without a next friend or guardian ad litem under rule 9.2A] shall, subject to any direction of the court, be effected by service on—

(a) the solicitor acting for the child, or
(b) where there is no such solicitor, [the children's guardian or] the guardian ad litem, or
(c) where there is neither such a solicitor [nor a children's guardian] nor a guardian ad litem, with leave of the court, the child.

(5) Where the court refuses leave under paragraph (4)(c) it shall give a direction under paragraph (8).

(6) A document shall, unless the contrary is proved, be deemed to have been served—

(a) in the case of service by first-class post, on the second business day after posting, and
(b) in the case of service in accordance with paragraph (1)(b)(ii), on the second business day after the day on which it is left at the document exchange.

(7) At or before the first directions appointment in, or hearing of, proceedings to which this Part applies the applicant shall file a statement [in Form C9] that service of—

(a) a copy of the application [and other documents referred to in rule 4.4(1)(b)] has been effected on each respondent, and
(b) notice of the proceedings has been effected under rule 4.4(3);

and the statement shall indicate—

    (i) the manner, date, time and place of service, or
    (ii) where service was effected by post, the date, time and place of posting.

[(8) In proceedings to which this Part applies, where these rules or other rules of court require a document to be served, the court may, without prejudice to any power under rule 4.14, direct that—

(a) the requirement shall not apply;
(b) the time specified by the rules for complying with the requirement shall be abridged to such extent as may be specified in the direction;
(c) service shall be effected in such manner as may be specified in the direction.]

Date in force
14 October 1991

Amendment
Para (3): words from 'is not prosecuting' to 'rule 9.2A and' in square brackets inserted by SI 1992/456, r 3.

Para (3): in sub-para (b) words 'the children's guardian or' in square brackets inserted by SI 2001/821, r 17(a)(i). Date in force: 1 April 2001: see SI 2001/821, r 1(b).

Para (3): in sub-para (c) words 'nor a children's guardian' in square brackets inserted by SI 2001/821, r 17(a)(ii). Date in force: 1 April 2001: see SI 2001/821, r 1(b).

Para (4): words from 'who is not prosecuting' to 'rule 9.2A' in square brackets inserted by SI 1992/456, r 4.

Para (4): in sub-para (b) words 'the children's guardian or' in square brackets substituted by SI 2001/821, r 17(b)(i). Date in force: 1 April 2001: see SI 2001/821, r 1(b).

Para (4): in sub-para (c) words 'nor a children's guardian' in square brackets inserted by SI 2001/821, r 17(b)(ii). Date in force: 1 April 2001: see SI 2001/821, r 1(b).

Para (7): words 'in Form C9' and 'and other documents referred to in rule 4.4(1)(b)', inserted by SI 1994/3155, r 14.

Para (8): substituted by SI 1992/2067, r 19.

4.9 Answer to application

(1) Within 14 days of service of an application for a section 8 order [or an application under Schedule 1], each respondent shall file, and serve on the parties, an [acknowledgment of] the application in Form [C7].

(2) . . .

(3) Following service of an application to which this Part applies, other than an application under rule 4.3 or for a section 8 order, a respondent may, subject to paragraph (4), file a written answer, which shall be served on the other parties.

(4) An answer under paragraph (3) shall, except in the case of an application under section 25, 31, 34, 38, 43, 44, 45, 46, 48 or 50, be filed, and served, not less than 2 days before the date fixed for the hearing of the application.

Date in force
14 October 1991

Amendment

Para (1): words 'or an application under Schedule 1' inserted, and words 'acknowledgment of' and 'C7' substituted, by SI 1994/3155, r 15(a).

Para (2): revoked by SI 1994/3155, r 15(b).

4.10 Appointment of [children's guardian]

(1) As soon as practicable after the commencement of specified proceedings, or the transfer of such proceedings to the court, the court shall appoint a [children's guardian], unless—

- (a) such an appointment has already been made by the court which made the transfer and is subsisting, or
- (b) the court considers that such an appointment is not necessary to safeguard the interests of the child.

(2) At any stage in specified proceedings a party may apply, without notice to the other parties unless the court directs otherwise, for the appointment of a [children's guardian].

(3) The court shall grant an application under paragraph (2) unless it considers such an appointment not to be necessary to safeguard the interests of the child, in which case it shall give its reasons; and a note of such reasons shall be taken by the proper officer.

(4) At any stage in specified proceedings the court may, of its own motion, appoint a [children's guardian].

[(4A) The court may, in specified proceedings, appoint more than one children's guardian in respect of the same child.]

(5) The proper officer shall, as soon as practicable, notify the parties and any [welfare officer or children and family reporter] of an appointment under this rule or, as the case may be, of a decision not to make such an appointment.

(6) Upon the appointment of a [children's guardian] the proper officer shall, as soon as practicable, notify him of the appointment and serve on him copies of the application and of documents filed under rule 4.17(1).

[(7) A children's guardian appointed by the court under this rule shall not—

(a)   be a member, officer or servant of a local authority which, or an authorised person (within the meaning of section 31(9)) who, is a party to the proceedings;

(b)   be, or have been, a member, officer or servant of a local authority or voluntary organisation (within the meaning of section 105(1)) who has been directly concerned in that capacity in arrangements relating to the care, accommodation or welfare of the child during the five years prior to the commencement of the proceedings; or

(c)   be a serving probation officer who has, in that capacity, been previously concerned with the child or his family.]

(8) When appointing a [children's guardian] the court shall consider the appointment of anyone who has previously acted as [children's guardian] of the same child.

(9) The appointment of a [children's guardian] under this rule shall continue for such time as is specified in the appointment or until terminated by the court.

(10) When terminating an appointment in accordance with paragraph (9), the court shall give its reasons in writing for so doing.

(11) Where the court appoints a [children's guardian] in accordance with this rule or refuses to make such an appointment, the court or the proper officer shall record the appointment or refusal in Form [C47].

Date in force
14 October 1991

Amendment

Provision heading: words 'children's guardian' in square brackets substituted by SI 2001/821, r 16(a). Date in force: 1 April 2001: see SI 2001/821, r 1(b).

Para (1): words 'children's guardian' in square brackets substituted by SI 2001/821, r 16(a). Date in force: 1 April 2001: see SI 2001/821, r 1(b).

Para (2): words 'children's guardian' in square brackets substituted by SI 2001/821, r 16(a). Date in force: 1 April 2001: see SI 2001/821, r 1(b).

Para (4): words 'children's guardian' in square brackets substituted by SI 2001/821, r 16(a). Date in force: 1 April 2001: see SI 2001/821, r 1(b).

Para (4A): inserted by SI 2001/821, r 18(a). Date in force: 1 April 2001: see SI 2001/821, r 1(b).

Para (5): words 'welfare officer or children and family reporter' in square brackets substituted by SI 2001/821, r 16(b). Date in force: 1 April 2001: see SI 2001/821, r 1(b).

Para (6): words 'children's guardian' in square brackets substituted by SI 2001/821, r 16(a). Date in force: 1 April 2001: see SI 2001/821, r 1(b).

Para (7): substituted by SI 2001/821, r 18(b). Date in force: 1 April 2001: see SI 2001/821, r 1(b).

Para (8): words 'children's guardian' in square brackets in both places they occur substituted by SI 2001/821, r 16(a).

Date in force: 1 April 2001: see SI 2001/821, r 1(b). Para (9): words 'children's guardian' in square brackets substituted by SI 2001/821, r 16(a). Date in force: 1 April 2001: see SI 2001/821, r 1(b).

Para (11): words 'children's guardian' in square brackets substituted by SI 2001/821, r 16(a). Date in force: 1 April 2001: see SI 2001/821, r 1(b).

Para (11): reference to 'C47' substituted by SI 1994/3155, r 16.

[4.11   Powers and duties of officers of the service]

[(1) In carrying out his duty under section 7(1)(a) or section 41(2), the officer of the service shall have regard to the principle set out in section 1(2) and the matters set out in section 1(3)(a) to (f) as if for the word 'court' in that section there were substituted the words 'officer of the service'.

(2) The officer of the service shall make such investigations as may be necessary for him to carry out his duties and shall, in particular—

   (a) contact or seek to interview such persons as he thinks appropriate or as the court directs;

   (b) obtain such professional assistance as is available to him which he thinks appropriate or which the court directs him to obtain.

(3) In addition to his duties, under other paragraphs of this rule, or rules 4.11A and 4.11B, the officer of the service shall provide to the court such other assistance as it may require.

(4) A party may question the officer of the service about oral or written advice tendered by him to the court.]

Date in force
14 October 1991

Amendment
Substituted by SI 2001/821, r 19. Date in force: 1 April 2001: see SI 2001/821, r 1(b).

[4.11A   Additional powers and duties of children's guardian]

[(1) The children's guardian shall—

   (a) appoint a solicitor to represent the child unless such a solicitor has already been appointed; and

   (b) give such advice to the child as is appropriate having regard to his understanding and, subject to rule 4.12(1)(a), instruct the solicitor representing the child on all matters relevant to the interests of the child including possibilities for appeal, arising in the course of proceedings.

(2) Where the children's guardian is an officer of the service authorised by the Service in the terms mentioned by and in accordance with section 15(1) of the Criminal Justice and Court Services Act 2000, paragraph (1)(a) shall not require him to appoint a solicitor for the child if he intends to have conduct of the proceedings on behalf of the child unless—

   (a) the child wishes to instruct a solicitor direct; and

   (b) the children's guardian or the court considers that he is of sufficient understanding to do so.

(3) Where it appears to the children's guardian that the child—

   (a) is instructing his solicitor direct; or

   (b) intends to conduct and is capable of conducting the proceedings on his own behalf,

he shall inform the court and from then he—

     (i)   shall perform all of his duties set out in rule 4.11 and this rule, other than those duties under paragraph (1)(a) of this rule, and such other duties as the court may direct;

    (ii) shall take such part in the proceedings as the court may direct; and

   (iii) may, with the leave of the court, have legal representation in the conduct of those duties.

(4) Unless excused by the court, the children's guardian shall attend all directions appointments in and hearings of the proceedings and shall advise the court on the following matters—

   (a) whether the child is of sufficient understanding for any purpose including the child's refusal to submit to a medical or psychiatric examination or other assessment that the court has the power to require, direct or order.

   (b) the wishes of the child in respect of any matter relevant to the proceedings including his attendance at court;

   (c) the appropriate forum for the proceedings;

   (d) the appropriate timing of the proceedings or any part of them;

   (e) the options available to it in respect of the child and the suitability of each such option including what order should be made in determining the application; and

(f)   any other matter concerning which the court seeks his advice or concerning which he considers that the court should be informed.

(5)   The advice given under paragraph (4) may, subject to any order of the court, by given orally or in writing; and if the advice be given orally, a note of it shall be taken by the court or the proper officer.

(6)   The children's guardian shall, where practicable, notify any person whose joinder as a party to those proceedings would be likely, in the opinion of the children's guardian, to safeguard the interests of the child of that person's right to apply to be joined under rule 4.7(2) and shall inform the court—

(a)   of any such notification given;

(b)   of anyone whom he attempted to notify under this paragraph but was unable to contact; and

(c)   of anyone whom he believes may wish to be joined to the proceedings.

(7)   The children's guardian shall, unless the court otherwise directs, not less than 14 days before the date fixed for the final hearing of the proceedings—

(a)   file a written report advising on the interests of the child; and

(b)   serve a copy of the filed report on the other parties.

(8)   The children's guardian shall serve and accept service of documents on behalf of the child in accordance with rule 4.8(3)(b) and (4)(b) and, where the child has not himself been served, and has sufficient understanding, advise the child of the contents of any document so served.

(9)   If the children's guardian inspects records of the kinds referred to in section 42, he shall bring to the attention of—

(a)   the court; and

(b)   unless the court otherwise directs, the other parties to the proceedings,

all records and documents which may, in his opinion, assist in the proper determination of the proceedings.

(10)   The children's guardian shall ensure that, in relation to a decision made by the court in the proceedings—

(a)   if he considers it appropriate to the age and understanding of the child, the child is notified of that decision; and

(b)   if the child is notified of the decision, it is explained to the child in a manner appropriate to his age and understanding.]

Date in force
14 October 1991

Amendment
Inserted by SI 2001/821, r 20.

[4.11B   Additional powers and duties of a children and family reporter]

[(1)   The children and family reporter shall—

(a)   notify the child of such contents of his report (if any) as he considers appropriate to the age and understanding of the child, including any reference to the child's own views on the application and the recommendation of the children and family reporter; and

(b)   if he does notify the child of any contents of his report, explain them to the child in a manner appropriate to his age and understanding.

(2)   Where the court has—

(a)   directed that a written report be made by a children and family reporter; and

    (b) notified the children and family reporter that his report is to be considered at a hearing,

the children and family reporter shall—

      (i)   file the report; and

      (ii) serve a copy on the other parties and on the children's guardian (if any),

by such time as the court may direct, and if no direction is given, not less than 14 days before that hearing.

(3) The court may direct that the children and family reporter attend any hearing at which his report is to be considered.

(4) The children and family reporter shall advise the court if he considers that the joinder of a person as a party to the proceedings would be likely to safeguard the interests of the child.

(5) The children and family reporter shall consider whether it is in the best interests of the child for the child to be made a party to the proceedings.

(6) If the children and family reporter considers the child should be made a party to the proceedings he shall notify the court of his opinion together with the reasons for that opinion.]

Date in force
14 October 1991

Amendment
Inserted by SI 2001/821, r 20.

4.12 Solicitor for child

(1) A solicitor appointed under section 41(3) or in accordance with [rule 4.11A (1)(a)] shall represent the child—

    (a) in accordance with instructions received from the [children's guardian] (unless the solicitor considers, having taken into account the views of the [children's guardian] and any direction of the court under [rule 4.11A(3)], that the child wishes to give instructions which conflict with those of the [children's guardian] and that he is able, having regard to his understanding, to give such instructions on his own behalf in which case he shall conduct the proceedings in accordance with instructions received from the child), or

    (b) where no [children's guardian] has been appointed for the child and the condition in section 41(4)(b) is satisfied, in accordance with instructions received from the child, or

    (c) in default of instructions under (a) or (b), in furtherance of the best interests of the child.

(2) A solicitor appointed under section 41(3) or in accordance with [rule 4.11A (1)(a)] shall serve and accept service of documents on behalf of the child in accordance with rule 4.8(3)(a) and (4)(a) and, where the child has not himself been served and has sufficient understanding, advise the child of the contents of any document so served.

(3) Where the child wishes an appointment of a solicitor under section 41(3) or in accordance with [rule 4.11A (1)(a)] to be terminated, he may apply to the court for an order terminating the appointment; and the solicitor and the [children's guardian] shall be given an opportunity to make representations.

(4) Where the [children's guardian] wishes an appointment of a solicitor under section 41(3) to be terminated, he may apply to the court for an order terminating the appointment; and the solicitor and, if he is of sufficient understanding, the child, shall be given an opportunity to make representations.

(5) When terminating an appointment in accordance with paragraph (3) or (4), the court shall give its reasons for so doing, a note of which shall be taken by the court or the proper officer.

(6) Where the court appoints a solicitor under section 41(3) or refuses to make such an appointment, the court or the proper officer shall record the appointment or refusal in Form [C48].

Date in force
14 October 1991

Amendment
Para (1): words 'rule 4.11A (1)(a)' in square brackets substituted by SI 2001/821, r 21(a).

Para (1): in sub-para (a) words 'children's guardian' in square brackets in each place they occur substituted by SI 2001/821, r 16(a).

Para (1): in sub-para (a) words 'rule 4.11A(3)' in square brackets substituted by SI 2001/821, r 21(b).

Para (1): in sub-para (b) words 'children's guardian' in square brackets substituted by SI 2001/821, r 16(a).

Para (2): words 'rule 4.11A (1)(a)' in square brackets substituted by SI 2001/821, r 21(a).

Para (3): words 'rule 4.11A (1)(a)' in square brackets substituted by SI 2001/821, r 21(a).

Para (3): words 'children's guardian' in square brackets substituted by SI 2001/821, r 16(a)

Para (4): words 'children's guardian' in square brackets substituted by SI 2001/821, r 16(a).

Para (6): figure 'C48' substituted by SI 1994/3155, r 17.

[4.13   Welfare officer]

[(1) Where the court has directed that a written report be made by a welfare officer [in accordance with section 7(1)(b)], the report shall be filed at or by such time as the court directs or, in the absence of such a direction, at least 14 days before a relevant hearing; and the proper officer shall, as soon as practicable, serve a copy of the report on the parties and any [children's guardian].

(2) In paragraph (1), a hearing is relevant if the proper officer has given the welfare officer notice that his report is to be considered at it

(3) After the filing of a report by a welfare officer, the court may direct that the welfare officer attend any hearing at which the report is to be considered; and

(a) except where such a direction is given at a hearing attended by the welfare officer, the proper officer shall inform the welfare officer of the direction; and

(b) at the hearing at which the report is considered any party may question the welfare officer about his report.

[(3A) The welfare officer shall consider whether it is in the best interests of the child for the child to be made a party to the proceedings.

(3B) If the welfare officer considers the child should be made a party to the proceedings he shall notify the court of his opinion together with the reasons for that opinion.]

(4) This rule is without prejudice to any power to give directions under rule 4.14.]

Date in force
14 October 1991

Amendment
Substituted by SI 1992/2067, r 12.

Para (1): words 'in accordance with section 7(1)(b)' in square brackets inserted by SI 2001/821, r 22(a).

Para (1): words 'children's guardian' in square brackets substituted by SI 2001/821, r 16(a).
Paras (3A), (3B): inserted by SI 2001/821, r 22(b).

4.14 Directions

(1) In this rule, 'party' includes the [children's guardian] and, where a request or a direction concerns a report under section 7, the [welfare officer or children and family reporter].

(2) In proceedings to which this Part applies the court may, subject to paragraph (3), give, vary or revoke directions for the conduct of the proceedings, including—

(a) the timetable for the proceedings;
(b) varying the time within which or by which an act is required, by these rules or by other rules or court, to be done;
(c) the attendance of the child;
[(d) the appointment of a children's guardian, a guardian ad litem, or of a solicitor under section 41(3);]
(e) the service of documents;
(f) the submission of evidence including experts' reports;
(g) the preparation of welfare reports under section 7;
(h) the transfer of the proceedings to another court;
(i) consolidation with other proceedings.

(3) Directions under paragraph (2) may be given, varied or revoked either—

(a) of the court's own motion having given the parties notice of its intention to do so, and an opportunity to attend and be heard or to make written representations,
(b) on the written request [in Form C2] of a party specifying the direction which is sought, filed and served on the other parties, or
(c) on the written request [in Form C2] of a party specifying the direction which is sought, to which the other parties consent and which they or their representatives have signed.

(4) In an urgent case the request under paragraph (3)(b) may, with the leave of the court, be made—

(a) orally, or
(b) without notice to the parties, or
(c) both as in sub-paragraph (a) and as in sub-paragraph (b).

(5) On receipt of a written request under paragraph (3)(b) the proper officer shall fix a date for the hearing of the request and give not less than 2 days' notice [in Form C6] to the parties of the date so fixed.

(6) On considering a request under paragraph (3)(c) the court shall either—

(a) grant the request, whereupon the proper officer shall inform the parties of the decision, or
(b) direct that a date be fixed for the hearing of the request, whereupon the proper officer shall fix such a date and give not less than 2 days' notice to the parties of the date so fixed.

(7) A party may apply for an order to be made under section 11(3) or, if he is entitled to apply for such an order, under section 38(1) in accordance with paragraph (3)(b) or (c).

(8) Where a court is considering making, of its own motion, a section 8 order, or an order under section 31, 34 or 38, the power to give directions under paragraph (2) shall apply.

(9) Directions of a court which are still in force immediately prior to the transfer of proceedings to which this Part applies to another court shall continue to apply following the transfer, subject to any changes of terminology which are required to apply

those directions to the court to which the proceedings are transferred, unless varied or discharged by directions under paragraph (2).

(10) The court or the proper officer shall take a note of the giving, variation or revocation of a direction under this rule and serve, as soon as practicable, a copy of the note on any party who was not present at the giving, variation or revocation.

Date in force
14 October 1991

Amendment

Para (1): words 'children's guardian' in square brackets substituted by SI 2001/821, r 16(a).

Para (1): words 'welfare officer or children and family reporter' in square brackets substituted by SI 2001/821, r 16(b).

Para (2): sub-para (d) substituted by SI 2001/821, r 23.

Para (3): words 'in Form C2' inserted by SI 1994/3155, r 18.

Para (5): words 'in Form C6' inserted by SI 1994/3155, r 19.

4.15 Timing of proceedings

(1) Where these rules or other rules of court provide a period of time within which or by which a certain act is to be performed in the course of proceedings to which this Part applies, that period may not be extended otherwise than by direction of the court under rule 4.14.

(2) At the—

(a) transfer to a court of proceedings to which this Part applies,

(b) postponement or adjournment of any hearing or directions appointment in the course of proceedings to which this Part applies, or

(c) conclusion of any such hearing or directions appointment other than one at which the proceedings are determined, or so soon thereafter as is practicable,

the court or the proper officer shall—

(i) fix a date upon which the proceedings shall come before the court again for such purposes as the court directs, which date shall, where paragraph (a) applies, be as soon as possible after the transfer, and

(ii) give notice to the parties, the [children's guardian] or the [welfare officer or children and family reporter] of the date so fixed.

Date in force
14 October 1991

Amendment

Para (2): in sub-para (ii) words 'children's guardian' in square brackets substituted by SI 2001/821, r 16(a).

Para (2): in sub-para (ii) words 'welfare officer or children and family reporter' in square brackets substituted by SI 2001/821, r 16(b).

4.16 Attendance at directions appointment and hearing

(1) Subject to paragraph (2), a party shall attend a directions appointment of which he has been given notice in accordance with rule 4.14(5) unless the court otherwise directs.

(2) Proceedings or any part of them shall take place in the absence of any party, including the child, if—

(a) the court considers it in the interests of the child, having regard to the matters to be discussed or the evidence likely to be given, and

(b)   the party is represented by a [children's guardian] or solicitor;

and when considering the interests of the child under sub-paragraph (a) the court shall give the [children's guardian], the solicitor for the child and, if he is of sufficient understanding, the child an opportunity to make representations.

(3) Subject to paragraph (4), where at the time and place appointed for a hearing or directions appointment the applicant appears but one or more of the respondents do not, the court may proceed with the hearing or appointment.

(4) The court shall not begin to hear an application in the absence of a respondent unless—

(a)   it is proved to the satisfaction of the court that he received reasonable notice of the date of the hearing; or

(b)   the court is satisfied that the circumstances of the case justify proceeding with the hearing.

(5) Where, at the time and place appointed for a hearing or directions appointment one or more of the respondents appear but the applicant does not, the court may refuse the application or, if sufficient evidence has previously been received, proceed in the absence of the applicant.

(6) Where at the time and place appointed for a hearing or directions appointment neither the applicant nor any respondent appears, the court may refuse the application.

(7) Unless the court otherwise directs, a hearing of, or directions appointment in, proceedings to which this Part applies shall be in chambers.

Date in force
14 October 1991

Amendment
Para (2): words 'children's guardian' in square brackets in both places they occur substituted by SI 2001/821, r 16(a).

4.17   Documentary evidence

(1) Subject to paragraphs (4) and (5), in proceedings to which this Part applies a party shall file and serve on the parties, any [welfare officer or children and family reporter] and any [children's guardian] of whose appointment he has been given notice under rule 4.10(5)—

(a)   written statements of the substance of the oral evidence which the party intends to adduce at a hearing of, or a directions appointment in, those proceedings, which shall—

(i)   be dated,

(ii)   be signed by the person making the statement, . . .

(iii) contain a declaration that the maker of the statement believes it to be true and understands that it may be placed before the court; and

[(iv) show in the top right hand corner of the first page—

(a)   the initials and surname of the person making the statement,

(b)   the number of the statement in relation to the maker,

(c)   the date on which the statement was made, and

(d)   the party on whose behalf it is filed; and]

(b)   copies of any documents, including experts' reports, upon which the party intends to rely at a hearing of, or a directions appointment in, those proceedings,

at or by such time as the court directs or, in the absence of a direction, before the hearing or appointment.

(2) A party may, subject to any direction of the court about the timing of statements under this rule, file and serve on the parties a statement which is supplementary to a statement served under paragraph (1).

(3) At a hearing or a directions appointment a party may not, without the leave of the court—

(a) adduce evidence, or
(b) seek to rely on a document,

in respect of which he has failed to comply with the requirements of paragraph (1).

(4) In proceedings for a section 8 order a party shall—

(a) neither file nor serve any document other than as required or authorised by these rules, and
(b) in completing a form prescribed by these rules, neither give information, nor make a statement, which is not required or authorised by that form,

without the leave of the court.

(5) In proceedings for a section 8 order no statement or copy may be filed under paragraph (1) until such time as the court directs.

Date in force
14 October 1991

Amendment
Para (1): words 'welfare officer or children and family reporter' in square brackets substituted by SI 2001/821, r 16(b).

Para (1): words 'children's guardian' in square brackets substituted by SI 2001/821, r 16(a).

Para (1): in sub-para (a)(ii) word omitted revoked by SI 1992/2067, r 20.

Para (1): sub-para (a)(iv) inserted by SI 1992/2067, r 20.

4.18 Expert evidence—examination of child

(1) No person may, without the leave of the court, cause the child to be medically or psychiatrically examined, or otherwise assessed, for the purpose of the preparation of expert evidence for use in the proceedings.

(2) An application for leave under paragraph (1) shall, unless the court otherwise directs, be served on all parties to the proceedings and on the [children's guardian].

(3) Where the leave of the court has not been given under paragraph (1), no evidence arising out of an examination or assessment to which that paragraph applies may be adduced without the leave of the court.

Date in force
14 October 1991

Amendment
Para (2): words 'children's guardian' in square brackets substituted by SI 2001/821, r 16(a).

4.19 Amendment

(1) Subject to rule 4.17(2), a document which has been filed or served in proceedings to which this Part applies, may not be amended without the leave of the court which shall, unless the court otherwise directs, be requested in writing.

(2) On considering a request for leave to amend a document the court shall either—

(a) grant the request, whereupon the proper officer shall inform the person making the request of that decision, or

(b) invite the parties or any of them to make representations, within a specified period, as to whether such an order should be made.

(3) A person amending a document shall file it and serve it on those persons on whom it was served prior to amendment; and the amendments shall be identified.

Date in force

14 October 1991

4.20 Oral evidence

The court or the proper officer shall keep a note of the substance of the oral evidence given at a hearing of, or directions appointment in, proceedings to which this Part applies.

Date in force

14 October 1991

4.21 Hearing

(1) The court may give directions as to the order of speeches and evidence at a hearing, or directions appointment, in the course of proceedings to which this Part applies.

(2) Subject to directions under paragraph (1), at a hearing of, or directions appointment in, proceedings to which this Part applies, the parties and the [children's guardian] shall adduce their evidence in the following order—

(a) the applicant,
(b) any party with parental responsibility for the child,
(c) other respondents,
(d) the [children's guardian],
(e) the child, if he is a party to the proceedings and there is no [children's guardian].

(3) After the final hearing of proceedings to which this Part applies, the court shall deliver its judgment as soon as is practicable.

[(4) When making an order or when refusing an application, the court shall—

(a) where it makes a finding of fact state such finding and complete Form C22; and
(b) state the reason's for the court's decision].

(5) An order made in proceedings to which this Part applies shall be recorded, by the court or the proper officer, either in the appropriate form in Appendix 1 to these rules or, where there is no such form, in writing.

(6) Subject to paragraph (7), a copy of an order made in accordance with paragraph (5) shall, as soon as practicable after it has been made, be served by the proper officer on the parties to the proceedings in which it was made [and] on any person with whom the child is living.

(7) Within 48 hours after the making ex parte of—

(a) a [section 8 order], or
(b) an order under section 44, 48(4), 48(9) or 50,

the applicant shall serve a copy of the order in the appropriate form in Appendix 1 to these Rules on—

(i) each party,
(ii) any person who has actual care of the child or who had such care immediately prior to the making of the order, and
(iii) in the case of an order referred to in sub-paragraph (b), the local authority in whose area the child lives or is found.

(8) At a hearing of or directions appointment in, an application which takes place outside the hours during which the court office is normally open, the court or the proper officer shall take a note of the substance of the proceedings.

Date in force
14 October 1991

Amendment
Para (2): words 'children's guardian' in square brackets substituted by SI 2001/821, r 16(a).

Para (2): in sub-para (d) words 'children's guardian' in square brackets substituted by SI 2001/821, r 16(a).

Para (2): in sub-para (e) words 'children's guardian' in square brackets substituted by SI 2001/821, r 16(a).

Para (4): substituted by SI 1994/3155, r 20.

Para (6): word 'and' inserted by SI 1992/456, r 14.

Para (7): words 'section 8 order' substituted by SI 1992/2067, r 10.

[4.21A   Attachment of penal notice to section 8 order]

[CCR Order 29, rule 1 (committal for breach of order or undertaking) shall apply to section 8 orders as if for paragraph (3) of that rule there were substituted the following:—

'(3) In the case of a section 8 order (within the meaning of section 8(2) of the Children Act 1989) enforceable by committal order under paragraph (1), the judge or the district judge may, on the application of the person entitled to enforce the order, direct that the proper officer issue a copy of the order, indorsed with or incorporating a notice as to the consequences of disobedience, for service in accordance with paragraph (2); and no copy of the order shall be issued with any such notice indorsed or incorporated save in accordance with such a direction.']

Date in force
14 October 1991

Amendment
Inserted by SI 1992/2067, r 13.

4.22   Appeals

(1) Where an appeal lies—

(a) to the High Court under section 94, or
(b) from any decision of a district judge to the judge of the court in which the decision was made,

it shall be made in accordance with the following provisions; and references to 'the court below' are references to the court from which, or person from whom, the appeal lies.

(2) The appellant shall file and serve on the parties to the proceedings in the court below, and on any [children's guardian],

(a) notice of the appeal in writing, setting out the grounds upon which he relies;
(b) a certified copy of the summons or application and of the order appealed against, and of any order staying its execution;
(c) a copy of any notes of the evidence;
(d) a copy of any reasons given for the decision.

[(2A) In relation to an appeal to the High Court under section 94, the documents required to be filed by paragraph (2) shall,—

(a) where the care centre listed in column (ii) of Schedule 2 to the Children (Allocation of Proceedings) Order 1991 against the entry in column (i) relating to the petty sessions area or London commission area in which the court below is situated—

(i) is the principal registry, or

(ii) has a district registry in the same place,

be filed in that registry, and

(b) in any other case, be filed in the district registry, being in the same place as a care centre within the meaning of article 2(c) of the said Order, which is nearest to the court below.]

(3) The notice of appeal shall be filed and served in accordance with paragraph (2)(a)—

(a) within 14 days after the determination against which the appeal is brought, or

(b) in the case of an appeal against an order under section 38(1), within 7 days after the making of the order, or

(c) with the leave of the court to which, or judge to whom, the appeal is to be brought, within such other time as that court or judge may direct.

(4) The documents mentioned in paragraph (2)(b) to (d) shall, subject to any direction of the court to which, or judge to whom, the appeal is to be brought, be filed and served as soon as practicable after the filing and service of the notice of appeal under paragraph (2)(a).

(5) Subject to paragraph (6), a respondent who wishes—

(a) to contend on the appeal that the decision of the court below should be varied, either in any event or in the event of the appeal being allowed in whole or in part, or

(b) to contend that the decision of the court below should be affirmed on grounds other than those relied upon by that court, or

(c) to contend by way of cross-appeal that the decision of the court below was wrong in whole or in part,

shall, within 14 days of receipt of notice of the appeal, file and serve on all other parties to the appeal a notice in writing, setting out the grounds upon which he relies.

(6) No notice under paragraph (5) may be filed or served in an appeal against an order under section 38.

(7) In the case of an appeal mentioned in paragraph (1)(a), an application to—

(a) withdraw the appeal,

(b) have the appeal dismissed with the consent of all the parties, or

(c) amend the grounds of appeal,

may be heard by a district judge.

(8) An appeal of the kind mentioned in paragraph (1)(a) shall, unless the President otherwise directs, be heard and determined by a single judge.

Date in force

14 October 1991

Amendment

Para (2): words 'children's guardian' in square brackets substituted by SI 2001/821, r 16(a).

Para (2A): inserted by SI 1992/2067, r 4.

4.23　Confidentiality of documents

(1) Notwithstanding any rule of court to the contrary, no document, other than a record of an order, held by the court and relating to proceedings to which this Part applies shall be disclosed, other than to—

(a) a party,

(b) the legal representative of a party,

(c)   the [children's guardian],

(d)   the Legal Aid Board, or

(e)   a [welfare officer or children and family reporter],

[(f)   an expert whose instruction by a party has been authorised by the court,]

without leave of the judge or district judge.

(2) Nothing in this rule shall prevent the notification by the court or the proper officer of a direction under section 37(1) to the authority concerned.

[(3) Nothing in this rule shall prevent the disclosure of a document prepared by an officer of the service for the purpose of—

(a)   enabling a person to perform functions required under section 62(3A) of the Justices of the Peace Act 1997;

(b)   assisting an officer of the service who is appointed by the court under any enactment to perform his functions.]

[(4) Nothing in this rule shall prevent the disclosure of any document relating to proceedings by an officer of the service to any other officer of the service unless that other officer is involved in the same proceedings but on behalf of a different party.]

Date in force
14 October 1991

Amendment

Para (1): in sub-para (c) words 'children's guardian' in square brackets substituted by SI 2001/821, r 16(a).

Para (1): in sub-para (e) words 'welfare officer or children and family reporter' in square brackets substituted by SI 2001/821, r 16(b).

Para (1): sub-para (f) inserted by SI 2001/821, r 24(a).

Para (3): inserted by SI 1997/1056, r 8.

Para (3): substituted by SI 2001/821, r 24(b). Date in force: 1 April 2001: see SI 2001/821, r 1(b).

Para (4): inserted by SI 2001/821, r 24(c). Date in force: 1 April 2001: see SI 2001/821, r 1(b).

4.24 Notification of consent

[(1)] Consent for the purposes of—

(a)   section 16(3), [or]

[(b)   section 38A(2)(b)(ii) or 44A(2)(b)(ii), or]

(c)   paragraph 19(3)(c) or (d) of Schedule 2,

shall be given either—

(i)   orally in court, or

(ii)   in writing to the court signed by the person giving his consent.

[(2) Any written consent given for the purposes of subsection (2) of section 38A or section 44A, shall include a statement that the person giving consent—

(a)   is able and willing to give to the child the care which it would be reasonable to expect a parent to give him; and

(b)   understands that the giving of consent could lead to the exclusion of the relevant person from the dwelling-house in which the child lives.]

Date in force
14 October 1991

Amendment

Para (1): numbered as such, in relation to proceedings commenced after 1 October 1997, by SI 1997/1893, rr 3(1), 9.

Para (1): in sub-para (a) word 'or' inserted by SI 1992/456, r 15.

Para (1): original sub-para (b) revoked by SI 1992/456, r 15.

Para (1): new sub-para (b) inserted, in relation to proceedings commenced after 1 October 1997, by SI 1997/1893, rr 3(2), 9.

Para (2): inserted, in relation to proceedings commenced after 1 October 1997, by SI 1997/1893, rr 3(2), 9.

[4.24A   Exclusion requirements: interim care orders and emergency protection orders]

[(1) This rule applies where the court includes an exclusion requirement in an interim care order or an emergency protection order.

(2) The applicant for an interim care order or emergency protection order shall—

(a) prepare a separate statement of the evidence in support of the application for an exclusion requirement;

(b) serve the statement personally on the relevant person with a copy of the order containing the exclusion requirement (and of any power of arrest which is attached to it);

(c) inform the relevant person of his right to apply to vary or discharge the exclusion requirement.

(3) Where a power of arrest is attached to an exclusion requirement in an interim care order or an emergency protection order, a copy of the order shall be delivered to the officer for the time being in charge of the police station for the area in which the dwelling-house in which the child lives is situated (or of such other station as the court may specify) together with a statement showing that the relevant person has been served with the order or informed of its terms (whether by being present when the order was made or by telephone or otherwise).

(4) Rules 3.9(5), 3.9A (except paragraphs (1) and (3)) and 3.10 shall apply, with the necessary modifications, for the service, variation, discharge and enforcement of any exclusion requirement to which a power of arrest is attached as they apply to an order made on an application under Part IV of the Family Law Act 1996.

(5) The relevant person shall serve the parties to the proceedings with any application which he makes for the variation or discharge of the exclusion requirement.

(6) Where an exclusion requirement ceases to have effect whether—

(a) as a result of the removal of a child under section 38A(10) or 44A(10),

(b) because of the discharge of the interim care order or emergency protection order, or

(c) otherwise,

the applicant shall inform—

(i)   the relevant person,

(ii)   the parties to the proceedings,

(iii) any officer to whom a copy of the order was delivered under paragraph (3), and

(iv) (where necessary) the court.

(7) Where the court includes an exclusion requirement in an interim care order or an emergency protection order of its own motion, paragraph (2) shall apply with the omission of any reference to the statement of the evidence.]

Date in force
14 October 1991

Amendment
Inserted, in relation to proceedings commenced after 1 October 1997, by SI 1997/1893, rr 4, 9.

4.25 Secure accommodation—evidence

In proceedings under section 25, the court shall, if practicable, arrange for copies of all written reports before it to be made available before the hearing to—

(a) the applicant;
(b) the parent or guardian of the child;
(c) any legal representative of the child;
(d) the [children's guardian]; and
(e) the child, unless the court otherwise directs;

and copies of such reports may, if the court considers it desirable, be shown to any person who is entitled to notice of the proceedings in accordance with these rules.

Date in force
14 October 1991

Amendment

In para (d) words 'children's guardian' in square brackets substituted by SI 2001/821, r 16(a).

4.26 Investigation under section 37

(1) This rule applies where a direction is given to an appropriate authority by the High Court or a county court under section 37(1).

(2) On giving a direction the court shall adjourn the proceedings and the court or the proper officer shall record the direction [in Form C40].

(3) A copy of the direction recorded under paragraph (2) shall, as soon as practicable after the direction is given, be served by the proper officer on the parties to the proceedings in which the direction is given and, where the appropriate authority is not a party, on that authority.

(4) When serving the copy of the direction on the appropriate authority the proper officer shall also serve copies of such of the documentary evidence which has been, or is to be, adduced in the proceedings as the court may direct.

(5) Where a local authority informs the court of any of the matters set out in section 37(3)(a) to (c) it shall do so in writing.

Date in force
14 October 1991

Amendment

Para (2): words 'in Form C40' substituted by SI 1994/3155, r 21.

4.27 Direction to local education authority to apply for education supervision order

(1) For the purposes of section 40(3) and (4) of the Education Act 1944 a direction by the High Court or a county court to a local education authority to apply for an education supervision order shall be given [in writing].

(2) Where, following such a direction, a local education authority informs the court that they have decided not to apply for an education supervision order, they shall do so in writing.

Date in force
14 October 1991

Amendment
Para (1): words 'in writing' in square brackets substituted by SI 1997/1893, r 15.

4.28 Transitional provision

Nothing in any provision of this Part of these rules shall affect any proceedings which are pending (within the meaning of paragraph 1 of Schedule 14 to the Act of 1989) immediately before these rules come into force.

[PART IVA
PROCEEDINGS UNDER SECTION 30 OF THE HUMAN FERTILISATION AND EMBRYOLOGY ACT 1990]

[Not reproduced]

PART V
WARDSHIP

[Not reproduced]

PART VI
CHILD ABDUCTION AND CUSTODY . . .

[Not reproduced]

PART VII
ENFORCEMENT OF ORDERS

[Not reproduced]

PART VIII
APPEALS

[Not reproduced]

PART IX
DISABILITY

9.1 Interpretation and application of Part IX

(1) In this Part—

'patient' means a person who, by reason of mental disorder within the meaning of the Mental Health Act 1983, is incapable of managing and administering his property and affairs;

'person under disability' means a person who is a minor or a patient;

'Part VII' means Part VII of the Mental Health Act 1983.

(2) So far as they relate to minors [who are the subject of applications], the provisions of this Part of these rules shall not apply to proceedings which are specified proceedings within the meaning of section 41(6) of the Children Act 1989 and, with respect to proceedings which are dealt with together with specified proceedings, this Part shall have effect subject to the said section 41 and Part IV of these rules.

[(3) Rule 9.2A shall apply only to proceedings under the Act of 1989 or the inherent jurisdiction of the High Court with respect to minors.]

Date in force
14 October 1991

Amendment

Para (2): words 'who are the subject of applications' inserted by SI 1991/2113, r 16.

Para (3): inserted by SI 1992/456, r 6.

9.2 Person under disability must sue by next friend etc

(1) [Except where rule 9.2A or any other rule otherwise provides, a person under disability may begin and prosecute any family proceedings only by his next friend and may defend any such proceedings only] by his guardian ad litem and, except as otherwise provided by this rule, it shall not be necessary for a guardian ad litem to be appointed by the court.

(2) No person's name shall be used in any proceedings as next friend of a person under disability unless he is the Official Solicitor or the documents mentioned in paragraph (7) have been filed.

(3) Where a person is authorised under Part VII to conduct legal proceedings in the name of a patient or on his behalf, that person shall, subject to [paragraph (2)], be entitled to be next friend or guardian ad litem of the patient in any family proceedings to which his authority extends.

(4) Where a person entitled to defend any family proceedings is a patient and there is no person authorised under Part VII to defend the proceedings in his name or on his behalf, then—

(a) the Official Solicitor shall, if he consents, be the patient's guardian ad litem, but at any stage of the proceedings an application may be made on not less than four days' notice to the Official Solicitor, for the appointment of some other person as guardian;

(b) in any other case, an application may be made on behalf of the patient for the appointment of a guardian ad litem;

and there shall be filed in support of any application under this paragraph the documents mentioned in paragraph (7).

(5) Where a petition, answer, originating application or originating summons has been served on a person whom there is reasonable ground for believing to be a person under disability and no notice of intention to defend has been given, or answer or affidavit in answer filed, on his behalf, the party at whose instance the document was served shall, before taking any further steps in the proceedings, apply to a district judge for directions as to whether a guardian ad litem should be appointed to act for that person in the cause, and on any such application the district judge may, if he considers it necessary in order to protect the interests of the person served, order that some proper person be appointed his guardian ad litem.

(6) [Except where a minor is prosecuting or defending proceedings under rule 9.2A, no] notice of intention to defend shall be given, or answer or affidavit in answer filed, by or on behalf of a person under disability unless the person giving the notice or filing the answer or affidavit—

(a) is the Official Solicitor or, in a case to which paragraph (4) applies, is the Official Solicitor or has been appointed by the court to be guardian ad litem; or

(b) in any other case, has filed the documents mentioned in paragraph (7).

(7) The documents referred to in paragraphs (2), (4) and (6) are—

(a) a written consent to act by the proposed next friend or guardian ad litem;

(b) where the person under disability is a patient and the proposed next friend or guardian ad litem is authorised under Part VII to conduct the proceedings in his name or on his behalf, an office copy, sealed with the seal of the Court of Protection, of the order or other authorisation made or given under Part VII; and

(c) except where the proposed next friend or guardian ad litem is authorised as mentioned in sub-paragraph (b), a certificate by the solicitor acting for the person under disability—

(i) that he knows or believes that the person to whom the certificate relates is a minor or patient, stating (in the case of a patient) the grounds of his knowledge or belief and, where the person under disability is a patient, that there is no person authorised as aforesaid, and

(ii) that the person named in the certificate as next friend or guardian ad litem has no interest in the cause or matter in question adverse to that of the person under disability and that he is a proper person to be next friend or guardian.

Date in force
14 October 1991

Amendment
Para (1): words from 'Except where rule' to 'such proceedings only' substituted by SI 1992/456, r 7.

Para (3): words 'paragraph (2)' substituted by SI 1991/2113, r 17.

Para (6): words 'Except where a minor is prosecuting or defending proceedings under rule 9.2A, no' substituted by SI 1992/456, r 8.

[9.2A Certain minors may sue without next friend etc]

[(1) Where a person entitled to begin, prosecute or defend any proceedings to which this rule applies, is a minor to whom this Part applies, he may, subject to paragraph (4), begin, prosecute or defend, as the case may be, such proceedings without a next friend or guardian ad litem—

(a) where he has obtained the leave of the court for that purpose; or

(b) where a solicitor—

(i) considers that the minor is able, having regard to his understanding, to give instructions in relation to the proceedings; and

(ii) has accepted instructions from the minor to act for him in the proceedings and, where the proceedings have begun, is so acting.

(2) A minor shall be entitled to apply for the leave of the court under paragraph (1)(a) without a next friend or guardian ad litem either—

(a) by filing a written request for leave setting out the reasons for the application, or

(b) by making an oral request for leave at any hearing in the proceedings.

(3) On considering a request for leave filed under paragraph (2)(a), the court shall either—

(a) grant the request, whereupon the proper officer shall communicate the decision to the minor and, where the leave relates to the prosecution or defence of existing proceedings, to the other parties to those proceedings, or

(b) direct that the request be heard *ex parte*, whereupon the proper officer shall fix a date for such a hearing and give to the minor making the request such notice of the date so fixed as the court may direct.

(4) Where a minor has a next friend or guardian ad litem in proceedings and the minor wishes to prosecute or defend the remaining stages of the proceedings without a next friend or guardian ad litem, the minor may apply to the court for leave for that purpose and for the removal of the next friend or guardian ad litem; and paragraph (2) shall apply to the application as if it were an application under paragraph (1)(a).

(5) On considering a request filed under paragraph (2) by virtue of paragraph (4), the court shall either—

(a) grant the request, whereupon the proper officer shall communicate the decision to the minor and next friend or guardian ad litem concerned and to all other parties to the proceedings, or

(b)   direct that the request be heard, whereupon the proper officer shall fix a date for such a hearing and give to the minor and next friend or guardian ad litem concerned such notice of the date so fixed as the court may direct;

provided that the court may act under sub-paragraph (a) only if it is satisfied that the next friend or guardian ad litem does not oppose the request.

(6)   Where the court is considering whether to

(a)   grant leave under paragraph (1)(a), or

(b)   grant leave under paragraph (4) and remove a next friend or guardian ad litem,

it shall grant the leave sought and, as the case may be, remove the next friend or guardian ad litem if it considers that the minor concerned has sufficient understanding to participate as a party in the proceedings concerned or proposed without a next friend or guardian ad litem.

[(6A)   In exercising its powers under paragraph (6) the court may order the next friend or guardian ad litem to take such part in the proceedings as the court may direct.]

(7)   Where a request for leave is granted at a hearing fixed under paragraph (3)(b) (in relation to the prosecution or defence of proceedings already begun) or (5)(b), the proper officer shall forthwith communicate the decision to the other parties to the proceedings.

(8)   The court may revoke any leave granted under paragraph (1)(a) where it considers that the child does not have sufficient understanding to participate as a party in the proceedings concerned without a next friend or guardian ad litem.

(9)   Without prejudice to any requirement of CCR Order 50, rule 5 or RSC Order 67, where a solicitor is acting for a minor in proceedings which the minor is prosecuting or defending without a next friend or guardian ad litem by virtue of paragraph (1)(b) and either of the conditions specified in paragraph (1)(b)(i) and (ii) cease to be fulfilled, he shall forthwith so inform the court.

(10)   Where—

(a)   the court revokes any leave under paragraph (8), or

(b)   either of the conditions specified in paragraph (1)(b)(i) and (ii) is no longer fulfilled,

the court may, if it considers it necessary in order to protect the interests of the minor concerned, order that some proper person be appointed his next friend or guardian ad litem.

(11)   Where a minor is of sufficient understanding to begin, prosecute or defend proceedings without a next friend or guardian ad litem—

(a)   he may nevertheless begin, prosecute or defend them by his next friend or guardian ad litem; and

(b)   where he is prosecuting or defending proceedings by his next friend or guardian ad litem, the respective powers and duties of the minor and next friend or guardian ad litem, except those conferred or imposed by this rule, shall not be affected by the minor's ability to dispense with a next friend or guardian ad litem under the provisions of this rule.]

Date in force

14 October 1991

Amendment

Inserted by SI 1992/456, r 9.

Para (6A): inserted by SI 1997/1893, r 19.

9.3 Service on person under disability

(1) Where a document to which rule 2.9 applies is required to be served on a person under disability . . . it shall be served—

  (a) in the case of a minor who is not also a patient, on his father or guardian or, if he has no father or guardian, on the person with whom he resides or in whose care he is;

  (b) in the case of a patient—

    (i) on the person (if any) who is authorised under Part VII to conduct in the name of the patient or on his behalf the proceedings in connection with which the document is to be served, or

    (ii) if there is no person so authorised, on the Official Solicitor if he has consented under rule 9.2(4) to be the guardian ad litem of the patient, or

    (iii) in any other case, on the person with whom the patient resides or in whose care he is:

Provided that the court may order that a document which has been, or is to be, served on the person under disability or on a person other than one mentioned in sub-paragraph (a) or (b) shall be deemed to be duly served on the person under disability.

(2) Where a document is served in accordance with paragraph (1) it shall be indorsed with a notice in Form M24; and after service has been effected the person at whose instance the document was served shall, unless the Official Solicitor is the guardian ad litem of the person under disability or the court otherwise directs, file an affidavit by the person on whom the document was served stating whether the contents of the document were, or its purport was, communicated to the person under disability and, if not, the reasons for not doing so.

Date in force
14 October 1991

Amendment
Para (1): words omitted revoked by SI 1992/2067, r 21.

9.4

. . .

9.5 Separate representation of children

[(1) Without prejudice to rules 2.57 and 9.2A, if in any family proceedings it appears to the court that it is in the best interest of any child to be made a party to the proceedings, the court may appoint—

  (a) an officer of the service;

  (b) (if he consents) the Official Solicitor; or

  (c) (if he consents) some other proper person,

to be the guardian ad litem of the child with authority to take part in the proceedings on the child's behalf.]

(2) An order under paragraph (1) may be made by the court of its own motion or on the application of a party to the proceedings or of the proposed guardian ad litem.

(3) The court may at any time direct that an application be made by a party for an order under paragraph (1) and may stay the proceedings until the application has been made.

(4) . . .

(5) Unless otherwise directed, a person appointed under this rule or rule 2.57 to be the guardian ad litem of a child in any family proceedings shall be treated as a party for the purpose of any provision of these rules requiring a document to be served on or notice to be given to a party to the proceedings.

[(6) Where the guardian ad litem appointed under this rule is an officer of the service, rules 4.11 and 4.11A shall apply to him as they apply to a children's guardian appointed under section 41 of the Children Act 1989.]

Date in force
14 October 1991

Amendment
Para (1): substituted by SI 2001/821, r 31(a).
Para (4): revoked by SI 2001/821, r 31(b).
Para (6): inserted by SI 2001/821, r 31(c).

PART X
PROCEDURE (GENERAL)

[Not reproduced]

APPENDIX 1
FORMS

[See Schedule 1 to the Family Proceedings Courts (Children Act 1989) Rules 1991

APPENDIX 2
CONTENTS OF PETITION (UNLESS OTHERWISE DIRECTED UNDER RULE 2.3)

[Not reproduced]

APPENDIX 3
NOTICES AND RESPONDENTS (RR, 4.4, 4.7)

Appendix 3

[(i)	(ii)	(iii)	(iv)
Provision under which proceedings brought	Minimum number of days prior to hearing or directions appointment for service under rule 4.4(1)(b)	Respondents	Persons to whom notice is to be given
All applications	See separate entries below	Subject to separate entries below:—	Subject to separate entries below:—
		every person whom the applicant believes to have parental responsibility for the child;	persons who are caring for the child at the time when the proceedings are commenced;
		where the child is the subject of a care order, every person whom the applicant believes to have had parental responsibility immediately prior to the making of the care order;	in the case of proceedings brought in respect of a child who is alleged to be staying in a refuge which is certificated under section 51(1) or (2), the person who is providing the refuge.

[(i)	(i)	(iii)	(iv)
		in the case of an application to extend, vary or discharge an order, the parties to the proceedings leading to the order which it is sought to have extended, varied or discharged; in the case of specified proceedings, the child.	
Section 4(1)(a), 4(3), 5(1), 6(7), 8, 13(1), 16(6), 33(7), Schedule 1, paragraph 19(1) of Schedule 2, or paragraph 11(3) or 16(5) of Schedule 14.	[14 days]	As for all applications above, and:	As for all applications above, and:
		in the case of proceedings under Schedule 1, those persons whom the applicant believes to be interested in or affected by the proceedings;	in the case of an application for a section 8 order, every person whom the applicant believes—
		in the case of an application under paragraph 11(3)(b) or 16(5) of Schedule 14, any person, other than the child, named in the order or directions which it is sought to discharge or vary.	(i) to be named in a court order with respect to the same child, which has not ceased to have effect,
			(ii) to be a party to pending proceedings in respect of the same child, or
			(iii) to be a person with whom the child has lived for at least 3 years prior to the application, unless, in a case to which (i) or (ii) applies, the applicant believes that the court order or pending proceedings are not relevant to the application;

672

[(i)	(i)	(iii)	(iv)
			in the case of an application under paragraph 19(1) of Schedule 2, the parties to the proceedings leading to the care order;
			in the case of an application under section 5(1), the father of the child if he does not have parental responsibility.
Section 36(1), 39(1), 39(2), 39(3), 39(4), 43(1), or Tparagraph 6(3), 15(2) or 17(1) of Schedule 3.	7 days	As for 'all applications' above and:	As for 'all applications' above and:
		in the case of an application under section 39(2) or (3), the supervisor;	in the case of an application for an order under section 43(1)—
			(i) every person whom the applicant believes to be a parent of the child,
		in the case of proceedings under paragraph 17(1) of Schedule 3, the local education authority concerned;	(ii) every person whom the applicant believes to be caring for the child,
		in the case of proceedings under section 36 or paragraph 15(2) or 17(1) of Schedule 3, the child.	(iii) every person in whose favour a contact order is in force with respect to the child, and
			(iv) every person who is allowed to have contact with the child by virtue of an order under section 34.
Section 31, 34(2), 34(3), 34(4), 34(9) or 38(8)(b).	3 days	As for 'all applications' above, and:	As for 'all applications' above, and:
		in the case of an application under section 34, the person whose contact with the child is the subject of the application.	in the case of an application under section 31—

673

[(i)	(i)	(iii)	(iv)
			(i) every person whom the applicant believes to be a party to pending relevant proceedings in respect of the same child, and
			(ii) every person whom the applicant believes to be a parent without parental responsibility for the child.
Section 43(12)	2 days	As for 'all applications' above.	Those of the persons referred to in section 43(11)(a) to (e) who were not party to the application for the order which it is sought to have varied or discharged.
Section 25, 44(1), 44(9)(b), 45(4), 45(8), 46(7), 48(9), 50(1) or 102(1)	1 day	As for 'all applications' above, and: in the case of an application under section 44(9)(b)— (i) the parties to the application for the order in respect of which it is sought to vary the directions; (ii) any person who was caring for the child prior to the making of the order, and (iii) any person whose contact with the child is affected by the direction which it is sought to have varied;	Except for applications under section 102(1), as for 'all applications' above, and: in the case of an application under section 44(1), every person whom the applicant believes to be a parent of the child; in the case of an application under section 44(9)(b)— (i) the local authority in whose area the child is living, and (ii) any person whom the applicant believes to be affected by the direction which it is sought to have varied;

[(i)	(i)	(iii)	(iv)
		in the case of an application under section 50, the person whom the applicant alleges to have effected or to have been or to be responsible for the taking or keeping of the child.	in the case of an application under section 102(1), the person referred to in section 102(1) and any person preventing or likely to prevent such a person from exercising powers under enactments mentioned in subsection (6) of that section.]
[section 30 of the Human Fertilisation and Embryology Act 1990]	[14 days]	[the birth parents (except where the applicants seek to dispense with their agreement under section 30(6) of the Human Fertilisation and Embryology Act 1990) and any other persons or body with parental responsibility for the child at the date of the application]	[any local authority or voluntary organisation that has at any time provided accommodation for the child]

Date in force
14 October 1991

Amendment
Substituted by SI 1992/2067, r 8, Sch 1.

Final entries in columns (i)–(iv) inserted by SI 1994/2165, r 6.

Family Proceedings Courts (Children Act 1989) Rules 1991

(SI 1991/1395)

PART I

INTRODUCTORY

1 Citation, commencement and interpretation

(1) These Rules may be cited as the Family Proceedings Courts (Children Act 1989) Rules 1991 and shall come into force on 14th October 1991.

(2) Unless a contrary intention appears—

a section or schedule referred to means the section or schedule in the Act of 1989,

'application' means an application made under or by virtue of the Act of 1989 or under these Rules, and 'applicant' shall be construed accordingly,

'business day' means any day other than—

    (a) a Saturday, Sunday, Christmas Day or Good Friday; or

    (b) a bank holiday, that is to say, a day which is, or is to be observed as, a bank holiday, or a holiday, under the Banking and Financial Dealings Act 1971, in England and Wales,

'child'

    (a) means, in relation to any relevant proceedings, subject to sub-paragraph (b), a person under the age of 18 with respect to whom the proceedings are brought, and

    (b) where paragraph 16(1) of Schedule 1 applies, also includes a person who has reached the age of 18;

['children and family reporter' means an officer of the service who has been asked to prepare a welfare report under section 7(1)(a)],

['children's guardian'—

    (a) means an officer of the service appointed under section 41 for the child with respect to whom the proceedings are brought; but

    (b) does not include such an officer appointed in relation to proceedings specified by rule 21A],

'contribution order' has the meaning assigned to it by paragraph 23(2) of Schedule 2,

'court' means a family proceedings court constituted in accordance with sections 66 and 67 of the Magistrates' Courts Act 1980 or, in respect of those proceedings prescribed in rule 2(5), a single justice who is a member of a family panel,

'directions appointment' means a hearing for directions under rule 14(2),

'emergency protection order' means an order under section 44,

'file' means deposit with the [justices['] chief executive],

'form' means a form in Schedule 1 to these Rules with such variation as the circumstances of the particular case may require,

. . .

['justices' chief executive' means a justices' chief executive appointed under section 40 of the Justices of the Peace Act 1997;]

'justices' clerk' has the meaning assigned to it by section 70 of the Justices of the Peace Act 1979 and includes any person who performs a justices' clerk's functions by virtue of rule 32,

'leave' includes approval,

'note' includes a record made by mechanical means,

['officer of the service' has the same meaning as in the Criminal Justice and Court
    Services Act 2000][,]
'parental responsibility' has the meaning assigned to it by section 3,
'parties' in relation to any relevant proceedings means the respondents specified for
    those proceedings in the third column of Schedule 2 to these Rules, and the
    applicant,
'recovery order' means an order under section 50,
'relevant proceedings' has the meaning assigned to it by section 93(3),
'section 8 order' has the meaning assigned to it by section 8(2),
'specified proceedings' has the meaning assigned to it by section 41(6) and rule
    2(2),
'the 1981 rules' means the Magistrates' Courts Rules 1981,
'the Act of 1989' means the Children Act 1989,
'welfare officer' means a person who has been asked to prepare a welfare report
    under [section 7(1)(b)].

Date in force
14 October 1991

Amendment
Para (2): definition 'children and family reporter' inserted by SI 2001/818, rr 2, 3(a)(i).

Para (2): definition 'children's guardian' inserted by SI 2001/818, rr 2, 3(a)(ii).

Para (2): in definition 'file' words 'justices' chief executive' in square brackets substituted by SI
2001/615, r 2(xx), Schedule, para 93.

Para (2): definition 'guardian ad litem' (omitted) revoked by SI 2001/818, rr 2, 3(b). Para (2): definition 'justices' chief executive' inserted by SI 2001/615, r 2(xx), Schedule, para 94.

Para (2): definition 'officer of the service' inserted by SI 2001/818, rr 2, 3(a)(iii).

Para (2): in definition 'welfare officer' words 'section 7(1)(b)' in square brackets substituted by
SI 2001/818, rr 2, 3(c).

---

2   Matters prescribed for the purposes of the Act of 1989

(1) The parties to proceedings in which directions are given under section 38(6),
and any person named in such a direction, form the prescribed class for the purposes
of section 38(8)(b) (application to vary directions made with interim care or interim
supervision order).

(2) The following proceedings [(in a family proceedings court)] are specified for the
purposes of section 41 in accordance with subsection (6)(i) thereof—

(a)   proceedings under section 25;
(b)   applications under section 33(7);
(c)   proceedings under paragraph 19(1) of Schedule 2;
(d)   applications under paragraph 6(3) of Schedule 3.

(3) The applicant for an order that has been made under section 43(1) and the persons referred to in section 43(11) may, in any circumstances, apply under section
43(12) for a child assessment order to be varied or discharged.

(4) The following persons form the prescribed class for the purposes of section
44(9)(b) (application to vary directions)—

(a)   the parties to the application for the order in respect of which it is sought to
      vary the directions;
(b)   the [children's guardian];
(c)   the local authority in whose area the child concerned is ordinarily resident;
(d)   any person who is named in the directions.

(5) The following proceedings are prescribed for the purposes of section 93(2)(i) as
being proceedings with respect to which a single justice may discharge the functions of
a family proceedings court, that is to say, proceedings—

(a) where an ex parte application is made, under sections 10, 44(1), 48(9), 50(1), 75(1) or 102(1),

(b) subject to rule 28, under sections 11(3) or 38(1),

(c) under sections 4(3)(b), 7, 14, 34(3)(b), 37, 41, 44(9)(b) and (11)(b)(iii), 48(4), 91(15) or (17), or paragraph 11(4) of Schedule 14,

(d) in accordance with any Order made by the Lord Chancellor under Part I of Schedule 11, and

(e) in accordance with rules 3 to 8, 10 to 19, 21, 22, or 27.

Date in force
14 October 1991

Amendment
Para (2): words '(in a family proceedings court)' in square brackets inserted by SI 1991/1991, r 26, Sch 2, para 8(1).

Para (4): in sub-para (b) words 'children's guardian' in square brackets substituted by SI 2001/818, rr 2, 4(a).

Part II
General

3 Application for leave to commence proceedings

(1) Where the leave of the court is required to bring any relevant proceedings, the person seeking leave shall file—

(a) a written request for leave [in Form C2] setting out the reasons for the application; and

[(b) a draft of the application (being the documents referred to in rule 4(1A)) for the making of which leave is sought together with sufficient copies for one to be served on each respondent.]

(2) On considering a request for leave filed under paragraph (1), the court shall—

(a) grant the request, whereupon the [justices['] chief executive] shall inform the person making the request of the decision, or

(b) direct that a date be fixed for a hearing of the request, whereupon the justices' clerk shall fix such a date and [the justices' chief executive shall] give such notice as the court directs to the person making the request and to such other persons as the court requires to be notified, of the date so fixed.

(3) Where leave is granted to bring any relevant proceedings, the application shall proceed in accordance with rule 4; but paragraph (1)(a) of that rule shall not apply.

Date in force
14 October 1991

Amendment
Para (1): in sub-para (a) words in square brackets inserted, and sub-para (b) substituted, by SI 1994/3156, r 4.

Para (2): in sub-para (a) words 'justices' chief executive' in square brackets substituted by SI 2001/615, r 2(xx), Schedule, para 93.

Para (2): in sub-para (b) words 'the justices' chief executive shall' in square brackets inserted by SI 2001/615, r 2(xx), Schedule, para 97.

4 Application

(1) Subject to paragraph (4), an applicant shall—

[(a) file the documents referred to in paragraph (1A) below (which documents shall together be called the 'application') together with sufficient copies for one to be served on each respondent, and]

(b) serve a copy of the application [together with Form C6 and such (if any) of Forms C7 and C10A as are given to him by the [justices['] chief executive] under paragraph 2(b)] on each respondent such minimum number of days prior to the date fixed under paragraph (2)(a) as is specified in relation to that application in column (ii) of Schedule 2 to these Rules.

[(1A) The documents to be filed under paragraph (1)(a) above are—

(a)

    (i)   whichever is appropriate of Forms C1 to C5 or C51, and

    (ii)   such of the supplemental Forms C10 or C11 to C20 as may be appropriate, or

(b) where there is no appropriate form a statement in writing of the order sought,

and where the application is made in respect of more than one child, all the children shall be included in one application.]

[(2) On receipt by the justices' chief executive of the documents filed under paragraph (1)(a)—

(a) the justices' clerk shall fix the date, time and place for a hearing or a directions appointment, allowing sufficient time for the applicant to comply with paragraph (1)(b), and

(b) the justices' chief executive shall—

    (i)   endorse the date, time and place so fixed upon Form C6, and where appropriate, Form C6A, and

    (ii)   return forthwith to the applicant the copies of the application and Form C10A if filed with it, together with Form C6, and such of Forms C6A and C7 as are appropriate.]

[(3) The applicant shall, at the same time as complying with paragraph (1)(b), serve Form C6A on the persons set out in relation to the relevant class of proceedings in column (iv) of Schedule 2 to these Rules.]

(4) An application for—

(a) [section 8 order],

(b) an emergency protection order,

(c) a warrant under section 48(9),

(d) a recovery order, or

(e) a warrant under section 102(1),

may, with leave of the justices' clerk, be made ex parte in which case the applicant shall—

    (i)   file with the [justices['] chief executive] or the court the application . . . in the appropriate form in Schedule 1 to these Rules at the time when the application is made or as directed by the justices' clerk, and

    (ii)   in the case of an application for a [section 8 order] or an emergency protection order, and also in the case of an application for an order under section 75(1) where the application is ex parte, serve a copy of the application on each respondent within 48 hours after the making of the order.

(5) Where the court refuses to make an order on an ex parte application it may direct that the application be made inter partes.

(6) In the case of proceedings under Schedule 1, the application under paragraph (1) shall be accompanied by a statement [in Form C10A] setting out the financial details which the applicant believes to be relevant to the application . . .together with sufficient copies for one to be served on each respondent.

Date in force
14 October 1991

Amendment
Para (1): sub-para (a) substituted by SI 1994/3156, r 5(a).

Para (1): in sub-para (b) words from 'together with Form C6' to 'under paragraph 2(b)' in square brackets substituted by SI 1994/3156, r 5(b).

Para (1): in sub-para (b) words 'justices' chief executive' in square brackets substituted by SI 2001/615, r 2(xx), Schedule, para 93.

Para (1A): inserted by SI 1994/3156, r 6.

Para (2): substituted by SI 2001/615, r 2(xx), Schedule, para 100.

Para (3): substituted by SI 1994/3156, r 8.

Para (4): words 'section 8 order' in square brackets in both places they occur substituted by SI 1992/2068, r 2, Schedule, para 1.

Para (4): in sub-para (i) words 'justices' chief executive' in square brackets substituted by SI 2001/615, r 2(xx), Schedule, para 93.

Para (4): in sub-para (i) words omitted revoked by SI 1994/3156, r 9.

Para (6): words in square brackets inserted, and words omitted revoked, by SI 1994/3156, r 10.

5 Withdrawal of application

(1) An application may be withdrawn only with leave of the court.

(2) Subject to paragraph (3), a person seeking leave to withdraw an application shall file and serve on the parties a written request for leave setting out the reasons for the request.

(3) The request under paragraph (2) may be made orally to the court if the parties and, if appointed, the [children's guardian] or the [welfare officer or children and family reporter] are present.

(4) Upon receipt of a written request under paragraph (2), the court shall—

(a) if—
    (i) the parties consent in writing,
    (ii) any [children's guardian] has had an opportunity to make representations, and
    (iii) the court thinks fit,

grant the request; in which case the [justices['] chief executive] shall notify the parties, the [children's guardian] and the [welfare officer or children and family reporter] of the granting of the request; or

(b) the justices' clerk shall fix a date for the hearing of the request and [the justices' chief executive shall] give at least 7 days' notice to the parties, the [children's guardian] and the [welfare officer or children and family reporter] of the date fixed.

Date in force
14 October 1991

Amendment
Para (3): words 'children's guardian' in square brackets substituted by SI 2001/818, rr 2, 4(a).

Para (3): words 'welfare officer or children and family reporter' in square brackets substituted by SI 2001/818, rr 2, 4(b).

Para (4): words 'children's guardian' in square brackets in each place they occur substituted by SI 2001/818, rr 2, 4(a).

Para (4): in sub-para (a) words 'justices' chief executive' in square brackets substituted by SI 2001/615, r 2(xx), Schedule, para 93.

Para (4): words 'welfare officer or children and family reporter' in square brackets in both places they occur substituted by SI 2001/818, rr 2, 4(b).

Para (4): in sub-para (b) words 'the justices' chief executive shall' in square brackets inserted by SI 2001/615, r 2(xx), Schedule, para 97.

6 Transfer of proceedings

(1) Where, in any relevant proceedings, the [justices['] chief executive] or the court receives a request in writing from a party that the proceedings be transferred to another family proceedings court or to a county court, the [justices['] chief executive] or court shall issue [an order or certificate] in the appropriate form in Schedule 1 to these Rules, granting or refusing the request in accordance with any Order made by the Lord Chancellor under Part I of Schedule 11.

(2) Where a request is granted under paragraph (1), the [justices['] chief executive] shall send a copy of the [order]—

    (a) to the parties,
    (b) to any [children's guardian], and
    (c) to the family proceedings court or to the county court to which the proceedings are to be transferred.

(3) Any consent given or refused by a justices' clerk in accordance with any Order made by the Lord Chancellor under Part I of Schedule 11 shall be recorded in writing by the justices' clerk at the time it is given or refused or as soon as practicable thereafter.

(4) Where a request to transfer proceedings to a county court is refused under paragraph (1), the person who made the request may apply in accordance with rule 4.6 of the Family Proceedings Rules 1991 for an order under any Order made by the Lord Chancellor under Part I of Schedule 11.

Date in force
14 October 1991

Amendment

Para (1): words 'justices' chief executive' in square brackets in both places they occur substituted by SI 2001/615, r 2(xx), Schedule, para 93.

Para (1): words 'an order or certificate' in square brackets substituted by SI 1994/3156, r 11.

Para (2): words 'justices' chief executive' in square brackets substituted by SI 2001/615, r 2(xx), Schedule, para 93.

Para (2): word 'order' in square brackets substituted by SI 1994/3156, r 11.

Para (2): in sub-para (b) words 'children's guardian' in square brackets substituted by SI 2001/818, rr 2, 4(a).

7 Parties

(1) The respondents to relevant proceedings shall be those persons set out in the relevant entry in column (iii) of Schedule 2 to these Rules.

(2) In any relevant proceedings a person may file a request [in Form C2] that he or another person—

    (a) be joined as a party, or
    (b) cease to be a party.

(3) On considering a request under paragraph (2) the court shall, subject to paragraph (4)—

    (a) grant it without a hearing or representations, save that this shall be done only in the case of a request under paragraph (2)(a), whereupon the [justices['] chief executive] shall inform the parties and the person making the request of that decision, or
    (b) order that a date be fixed for the consideration of the request, whereupon the

[justices['] chief executive] shall give notice of the date so fixed, together with a copy of the request—

 (i) in the case of a request under paragraph (2)(a), to the applicant, and

 (ii) in the case of a request under paragraph (2)(b), to the parties, or

(c) invite the parties or any of them to make written representations, within a specified period, as to whether the request should be granted; and upon the expiry of the period the court shall act in accordance with sub-paragraph (a) or (b).

(4) Where a person with parental responsibility requests that he be joined under paragraph (2)(a), the court shall grant his request.

(5) In any relevant proceedings the court may direct—

(a) that a person who would not otherwise be a respondent under these Rules be joined as a party to the proceedings, or

(b) that a party to the proceedings cease to be a party.

Date in force
14 October 1991

Amendment
Para (2): words in square brackets substituted by SI 1994/3156, r 12.

Para (3): in sub-para (a) words 'justices' chief executive' in square brackets substituted by SI 2001/615, r 2(xx), Schedule, para 93.

Para (3): in sub-para (b) words 'justices' chief executive' in square brackets substituted by SI 2001/615, r 2(xx), Schedule, para 93.

---

8 Service

(1) Where service of a document is required by these Rules (and not by a provision to which section 105(8) (service of notice or other document under the Act) applies) it may be effected—

(a) if the person to be served is not known by the person serving to be acting by solicitor—

 (i) by delivering it to him personally, or

 (ii) by delivering it at, or by sending it by first class post to, his residence or his last known residence, or

(b) if the person to be served is known by the person serving to be acting by solicitor—

 (i) by delivering the document at, or sending it by first-class post to, the solicitor's address for service,

 (ii) where the solicitor's address for service includes a numbered box at a document exchange, by leaving the document at that document exchange or at a document exchange which transmits documents on every business day to that document exchange, or

 (iii) by sending a legible copy of the document by facsimile transmission to the solicitor's office.

(2) In this rule, 'first-class post' means first-class post which has been pre-paid or in respect of which pre-payment is not required.

(3) Where a child who is a party to any relevant proceedings is required by these Rules to serve a document, service shall be effected by—

(a) the solicitor acting for the child,

(b) where there is no such solicitor, the [children's guardian], or

(c) where there is neither such a solicitor nor a [children's guardian], the [justices['] chief executive].

(4) Service of any document on a child shall, subject to any direction of the justices' clerk or the court, be effected by service on—

(a) the solicitor acting for the child,

(b) where there is no such solicitor, the [children's guardian], or

(c) where there is neither such a solicitor nor a [children's guardian], with leave of the justices' clerk or the court, the child.

(5) Where the justices' clerk or the court refuses leave under paragraph (4)(c), a direction shall be given under paragraph (8).

(6) A document shall, unless the contrary is proved, be deemed to have been served—

(a) in the case of service by first-class post, on the second business day after posting, and

(b) in the case of service in accordance with paragraph (1)(b)(ii), on the second business day after the day on which it is left at the document exchange.

(7) At or before the first directions appointment in, or hearing of, relevant proceedings, whichever occurs first, the applicant shall file a statement [in Form C9] that service of—

(a) a copy of the application [and other documents referred to in rule 4(1)(b)] has been effected on each respondent, and

(b) notice of the proceedings has been effected under rule 4(3);

and the statement shall indicate—

(i) the manner, date, time and place of service, or

(ii) where service was effected by post, the date, time and place of posting.

[(8) In any relevant proceedings, where these rules require a document to be served, the court or the justices' clerk may, without prejudice to any power under rule 14, direct that—

(a) the requirement shall not apply;

(b) the time specified by the rules for complying with the requirement shall be abridged to such extent as may be specified in the direction;

(c) service shall be effected in such manner as may be specified in the direction.]

Date in force
14 October 1991

Amendment
Para (3): words 'children's guardian' in square brackets in both places they occur substituted by SI 2001/818, rr 2, 4(a).

Para (3): in sub-para (c) words 'justices' chief executive' in square brackets substituted by SI 2001/615, r 2(xx), Schedule, para 93.

Para (4): words 'children's guardian' in square brackets in both places they occur substituted by SI 2001/818, rr 2, 4(a). Date in force: 1 April 2001: see SI 2001/818, r 1.

Para (7): words 'in Form C9' in square brackets inserted by SI 1994/3156, r 13.

Para (7): in sub-para (a) words 'and other documents referred to in rule 4(1)(b)' in square brackets inserted by SI 1994/3156, r 13.

Para (8): substituted by SI 1992/2068, r 2, Schedule, para 2.

[9 Acknowledgement of application]

[Within 14 days of service of an application for a section 8 order or an application under Schedule 1, each respondent shall file and serve on the parties an acknowledgement of the application in Form C7.]

Date in force
14 October 1991

Amendment

Substituted by SI 1994/3156, r 14.

---

10 Appointment of [children's guardian]

(1) As soon as practicable after the commencement of specified proceedings or the transfer of such proceedings to the court, the justices' clerk or the court shall appoint a [children's guardian] unless—

    (a) such an appointment has already been made by the court which made the transfer and is subsisting, or

    (b) the justices' clerk or the court considers that such an appointment is not necessary to safeguard the interests of the child.

(2) At any stage in specified proceedings a party may apply, without notice to the other parties unless the justices' clerk or the court otherwise directs, for the appointment of a [children's guardian].

(3) The justices' clerk or the court shall grant an application under paragraph (2) unless it is considered that such an appointment is not necessary to safeguard the interests of the child, in which case reasons shall be given; and a note of such reasons shall be taken by the justices' clerk.

(4) At any stage in specified proceedings the justices' clerk or the court may appoint a [children's guardian] even though no application is made for such an appointment.

[(4A) The justices' chief executive or the court may, in specified proceedings, appoint more than one children's guardian in respect of the same child.]

(5) The [justices['] chief executive] shall, as soon as practicable, notify the parties and any [welfare officer or children and family reporter] of an appointment under this rule or, as the case may be, of a decision not to make such an appointment.

(6) Upon the appointment of a [children's guardian] the [justices['] chief executive] shall, as soon as practicable, notify him of the appointment and serve on him copies of the application and of documents filed under rule 17(1).

[(7) A children's guardian appointed by the justices' chief executive or by the court under this rule shall not—

    (a) be a member, officer or servant of a local authority which, or an authorised person (within the meaning of section 31(9)) who, is a party to the proceedings;

    (b) be, or have been, a member, officer or servant of a local authority or voluntary organisation (within the meaning of section 105(1)) who has been directly concerned in that capacity in arrangements relating to the care, accommodation or welfare of the child during the five years prior to the commencement of the proceedings; or

    (c) be a serving probation officer who has, in that capacity, been previously concerned with the child or his family.]

(8) When appointing a [children's guardian], the justices' clerk or the court shall consider the appointment of anyone who has previously acted as [children's guardian] of the same child.

(9) The appointment of a [children's guardian] under this rule shall continue for such time as is specified in the appointment or until terminated by the court.

(10) When terminating an appointment in accordance with paragraph (9), the court shall give reasons in writing for so doing, a note of which shall be taken by the justices' clerk.

(11) Where the justices' clerk or the court appoints a [children's guardian] in accordance with this rule or refuses to make such an appointment, the justices' clerk shall record the appointment or refusal in the appropriate form in Schedule 1 to these Rules.

Date in force
14 October 1991

Amendment

Provision heading: words 'children's guardian' in square brackets substituted by SI 2001/818, rr 2, 4(a).

Para (1): words 'children's guardian' in square brackets substituted by SI 2001/818, rr 2, 4(a).

Para (2): words 'children's guardian' in square brackets substituted by SI 2001/818, rr 2, 4(a).

Para (4): words 'children's guardian' in square brackets substituted by SI 2001/818, rr 2, 4(a).

Para (4A): inserted by SI 2001/818, rr 2, 5(a).

Para (5): words 'justices' chief executive' in square brackets substituted by SI 2001/615, r 2(xx), Schedule, para 93.

Para (5): words 'welfare officer or children and family reporter' in square brackets substituted by SI 2001/818, rr 2, 4(b).

Para (6): words 'children's guardian' in square brackets substituted by SI 2001/818, rr 2, 4(a).

Para (6): words 'justices' chief executive' in square brackets substituted by SI 2001/615, r 2(xx), Schedule, para 93.

Para (7): substituted by SI 2001/818, rr 2, 5(b).

Para (8): words 'children's guardian' in square brackets in both places they occur substituted by SI 2001/818, rr 2, 4(a)..

Para (9): words 'children's guardian' in square brackets substituted by SI 2001/818, rr 2, 4(a).

Para (11): words 'children's guardian' in square brackets substituted by SI 2001/818, rr 2, 4(a).

[11   Powers and duties of officers of the service]

[(1) In carrying out his duty under section 7(1)(a) or section 41(2), the officer of the service shall have regard to the principle set out in section 1(2) and the matters set out in section 1(3)(a) to (f) as if for the word 'court' in that section there were substituted the words 'officer of the service'.

(2) The officer of the service shall make such investigations as may be necessary for him to carry out his duties and shall, in particular—

(a) contact or seek to interview such persons as he thinks appropriate or as the court directs;
(b) obtain such professional assistance as is available to him which he thinks appropriate or which the justices' clerk or the court directs him to obtain.

(3) In addition to his duties, under other paragraphs of this rule, or rules 11A or 11B, the officer of the service shall provide to the justices' chief executive, the justices' clerk and the court such other assistance as he or it may require.

(4) A party may question the officer of the service about oral or written advice tendered by him to the justices' chief executive, the justices' clerk or the court.]

Date in force
14 October 1991

Amendment

Substituted by SI 2001/818, rr 2, 6.

[11A   Additional powers and duties of children's guardian]

[(1) The children's guardian shall—

(a) appoint a solicitor to represent the child unless such a solicitor has already been appointed; and
(b) give such advice to the child as is appropriate having regard to his understanding and, subject to rule 12(1)(a), instruct the solicitor representing the

child on all matters relevant to the interests of the child including possibilities for appeal, arising in the course of proceedings.

(2) Where it appears to the children's guardian that the child—

(a) is instructing his solicitor direct; or

(b) intends to conduct and is capable of conducting the proceedings on his own behalf,

he shall inform the court through the justices' chief executive and from then he—

(i) shall perform all of his duties set out in rule 11 and this rule, other than those duties under paragraph (1)(a) of this rule, and such other duties as the justices' clerk or the court may direct;

(ii) shall take such part in the proceedings as the justices' clerk or the court may direct; and

(iii) may, with the leave of the justices' clerk or the court, have legal representation in the conduct of those duties.

(3) Unless excused by the justices' clerk or the court, the children's guardian shall attend all directions appointments in and hearings of the proceedings and shall advise the court on the following matters—

(a) whether the child is of sufficient understanding for any purpose including the child's refusal to submit to a medical or psychiatric examination or other assessment that the court has the power to require, direct or order;

(b) the wishes of the child in respect of any matter relevant to the proceedings including his attendance at court;

(c) the appropriate forum for the proceedings;

(d) the appropriate timing of the proceedings or any part of them;

(e) the options available to it in respect of the child and the suitability of each such option including what order should be made in determining the application; and

(f) any other matter concerning which the justices' chief executive, the justices' clerk or the court seeks his advice or concerning which he considers that the justices' chief executive, the justices' clerk or the court should be informed.

(4) The advice given under paragraph (3) may, subject to any order of the court, be given orally or in writing, and if the advice be given orally, a note of it shall be taken by the justices' clerk or the court.

(5) The children's guardian shall, where practicable, notify any person whose joinder as a party to those proceedings would be likely, in the opinion of the officer of the service, to safeguard the interests of the child of that person's right to apply to be joined under rule 7(2) and shall inform the justices' chief executive or the court—

(a) of any such notification given;

(b) of anyone whom he attempted to notify under this paragraph but was unable to contact; and

(c) of anyone whom he believes may wish to be joined to the proceedings.

(6) The children's guardian shall, unless the justices' clerk or the court otherwise directs, not less than 14 days before the date fixed for the final hearing of the proceedings—

(a) file a written report advising on the interests of the child;

(b) serve a copy of the filed report on the other parties.

(7) The children's guardian shall serve and accept service of documents on behalf of the child in accordance with rule 8(3)(b) and (4)(b) and, where the child has not himself been served, and has sufficient understanding, advise the child of the contents of any document so served.

(8) If the children's guardian inspects records of the kinds referred to in section 42, he shall bring to the attention of—

    (a) the court, through the justices' chief executive; and

    (b) unless the court or the justices' clerk otherwise directs, the other parties to the proceedings,

all records and documents which may, in his opinion, assist in the proper determination of the proceedings.

(9) The children's guardian shall ensure that, in relation to a decision made by the justices' clerk or the court in the proceedings—

    (a) if he considers it appropriate to the age and understanding of the child, the child is notified of that decision; and

    (b) if the child is notified of the decision, it is explained to the child in a manner appropriate to his age and understanding.]

Date in force

14 October 1991

Amendment

Inserted by SI 2001/818, rr 2, 7.

[11B   Additional powers and duties of a children and family reporter]

[(1) In addition to his duties under rule 11, the children and family reporter shall—

    (a) notify the child of such contents of his report (if any) as he considers appropriate to the age and understanding of the child, including any reference to the child's own views on the application and the recommendation of the children and family reporter; and

    (b) if he does notify the child of any contents of his report, explain them to the child in a manner appropriate to his age and understanding.

(2) Where the court has—

    (a) directed that a written report be made by a children and family reporter; and

    (b) notified the children and family reporter that his report is to be considered at a hearing,

the children and family reporter shall—

    (i)   file his report; and

    (ii)   serve a copy on the other parties and on the children's guardian (if any),

by such time as the court may direct and if no direction is given, not less than 14 days before that hearing.

(3) The court may direct that the children and family reporter attend any hearing at which his report is to be considered.

(4) The children and family reporter shall advise the court if he considers that the joinder of a person as a party to the proceedings would be likely to safeguard the interests of the child.

(5) The children and family reporter shall consider whether it is in the best interests of the child for the child to be made a party to the proceedings.

(6) If the children and family reporter considers the child should be made a party to the proceedings he shall notify the court of his opinion together with the reasons for that opinion.]

Date in force

14 October 1991

Amendment

Inserted by SI 2001/818, rr 2, 7.

12 Solicitor for child

(1) A solicitor appointed under section 41(3) or in accordance with [rule 11A(1)(a)] shall represent the child—

(a) in accordance with instructions received from the [children's guardian] (unless the solicitor considers, having taken into account the views of the [children's guardian] and any direction of the court under [rule 11A(2)], that the child wishes to give instructions which conflict with those of the [children's guardian] and that he is able, having regard to his understanding, to give such instructions on his own behalf in which case he shall conduct the proceedings in accordance with instructions received from the child), or

(b) where no [children's guardian] has been appointed for the child and the condition in section 41(4)(b) is satisfied, in accordance with instructions received from the child, or

(c) in default of instructions under (a) or (b), in furtherance of the best interests of the child.

(2) A solicitor appointed under section 41(3) or in accordance with [rule 11A(1)(a)] shall serve and accept service of documents on behalf of the child in accordance with rule 8(3)(a) and (4)(a) and, where the child has not himself been served and has sufficient understanding, advise the child of the contents of any document so served.

(3) Where the child wishes an appointment of a solicitor under section 41(3) or in accordance with [rule 11A(1)(a)] to be terminated, he may apply to the court for an order terminating the appointment; and the solicitor and the [children's guardian] shall be given an opportunity to make representations.

(4) Where the [children's guardian] wishes an appointment of a solicitor under section 41(3) to be terminated, he may apply to the court for an order terminating the appointment; and the solicitor and, if he is of sufficient understanding, the child, shall be given an opportunity to make representations.

(5) When terminating an appointment in accordance with paragraph (3) or (4), the court shall give reasons for so doing, a note of which shall be taken by the justices' clerk.

(6) Where the justices' clerk or the court appoints a solicitor under section 41(3) or refuses to make such an appointment, the justices' clerk shall record the appointment or refusal in the appropriate form in Schedule 1 to these Rules and [the justices' chief executive shall] serve a copy on the parties and, where he is appointed, on the solicitor.

Date in force
14 October 1991

Amendment
Para (1): words 'rule 11A(1)(a)' in square brackets substituted by SI 2001/818, rr 2, 8(a).

Para (1): words 'children's guardian' in square brackets in each place they occur substituted by SI 2001/818, rr 2, 4(a).

Para (1): in sub-para (a) words 'rule 11A(2)' in square brackets substituted by SI 2001/818, rr 2, 8(b).

Para (2): words 'rule 11A(1)(a)' in square brackets substituted by SI 2001/818, rr 2, 8(a).

Para (3): words 'rule 11A(1)(a)' in square brackets substituted by SI 2001/818, rr 2, 8(a).

Para (3): words 'children's guardian' in square brackets substituted by SI 2001/818, rr 2, 4(a).

Para (4): words 'children's guardian' in square brackets substituted by SI 2001/818, rr 2, 4(a).

Para (6): words 'the justices' chief executive shall' in square brackets inserted by SI 2001/615, r 2(xx), Schedule, para 97.

[13   Welfare officer]

[(1)   Where the court or a justices' clerk has directed that a written report be made by a welfare officer [in accordance with section 7(1)(b)], the report shall be filed at or by such time as the court or justices' clerk directs or, in the absence of such a direction, at least 14 days before a relevant hearing; and the [justices['] chief executive] shall, as soon as practicable, serve a copy of the report on the parties and any [children's guardian].

(2)   In paragraph (1), a hearing is relevant if the [justices['] chief executive] has given the welfare officer notice that his report is to be considered at it.

(3)   After the filing of a written report by a welfare officer, the court or the justices' clerk may direct that the welfare officer attend any hearing at which the report is to be considered; and

(a)   except where such a direction is given at a hearing attended by the welfare officer, the [justices['] chief executive] shall inform the welfare officer of the direction; and

(b)   at the hearing at which the report is considered any party may question the welfare officer about his report.

[(3A)   The welfare officer shall consider whether it is in the best interests of the child for the child to be made a party to the proceedings.

(3B)   If the welfare officer considers the child should be made a party to the proceedings he shall notify the court of his opinion together with the reasons for that opinion.]

(4)   This rule is without prejudice to the court's power to give directions under rule 14.]

Date in force
14 October 1991

Amendment
Substituted by SI 1992/2068, r 2, Schedule, para 3.

Para (1): words 'in accordance with section 7(1)(b)' in square brackets inserted by SI 2001/818, rr 2, 9(a).

Para (1): words 'justices' chief executive' in square brackets substituted by SI 2001/615, r 2(xx), Schedule, para 93.

Para (1): words 'children's guardian' in square brackets substituted by SI 2001/818, rr 2, 4(a).

Para (2): words 'justices' chief executive' in square brackets substituted by SI 2001/615, r 2(xx), Schedule, para 93.

Para (3): in sub-para (a) words 'justices' chief executive' in square brackets substituted by SI 2001/615, r 2(xx), Schedule, para 93.

Paras (3A), (3B): inserted by SI 2001/818, rr 2, 9(b).

---

14   Directions

(1)   In this rule, 'party' includes the [children's guardian] and, where a request or direction concerns a report under section 7, the [welfare officer or children and family reporter].

(2)   In any relevant proceedings the justices' clerk or the court may, subject to paragraph (5), give, vary or revoke directions for the conduct of the proceedings, including—

(a)   the timetable for the proceedings;
(b)   varying the time within which or by which an act is required, by these Rules, to be done;
(c)   the attendance of the child;

(d) the appointment of a [children's guardian] . . ., or of a solicitor under section 41(3);
(e) the service of documents;
(f) the submission of evidence including experts' reports;
(g) the preparation of welfare reports under section 7;
(h) the transfer of the proceedings to another court in accordance with any Order made by the Lord Chancellor under Part I of Schedule 11;
(i) consolidation with other proceedings;

and the justices' clerk shall, on receipt of an application [by the justices' chief executive], or where proceedings have been transferred to his court, consider whether such directions need to be given.

(3) Where the justices' clerk or a single justice who is holding a directions appointment considers, for whatever reason, that it is inappropriate to give a direction on a particular matter, he shall refer the matter to the court which may give any appropriate direction.

(4) Where a direction is given under paragraph (2)(h), [an order] shall be issued in the appropriate form in Schedule 1 to these Rules and the [justices['] chief executive] shall follow the procedure set out in rule 6(2).

(5) Directions under paragraph (2) may be given, varied or revoked either—

(a) of the justices' clerk or the court's own motion [the justices' chief executive] having given the parties notice of the intention to do so and an opportunity to attend and be heard or to make written representations,
(b) on the written request [in Form C2] of a party specifying the direction which is sought, filed and served on the other parties, or
(c) on the written request [in Form C2] of a party specifying the direction which is sought, to which the other parties consent and which they or their representatives have signed.

(6) In an urgent case, the request under paragraph (5)(b) may, with the leave of the justices' clerk or the court, be made—

(a) orally,
(b) without notice to the parties, or
(c) both as in sub-paragraph (a) and as in sub-paragraph (b).

(7) On receipt of a request [by the justices' chief executive] under paragraph (5)(b) the justices' clerk shall fix a date for the hearing of the request and [the justices' chief executive shall] give not less than 2 days' notice [in Form C6] to the parties of the date so fixed.

(8) On considering a request under paragraph (5)(c) the justices' clerk or the court shall either—

(a) grant the request, whereupon the [justices['] chief executive] shall inform the parties of the decision, or
(b) direct that a date be fixed for the hearing of the request, whereupon the justices clerk shall fix such a date and [the justices' chief executive shall] give not less than 2 days' notice to the parties of the date so fixed.

(9) Subject to rule 28, a party may request, in accordance with paragraph 5(b) or (c), that an order be made under section 11(3) or, if he is entitled to apply for such an order, under section 38(1), and paragraphs (6), (7) and (8) shall apply accordingly.

(10) Where, in any relevant proceedings, the court has power to make an order of its own motion, the power to give directions under paragraph (2) shall apply.

(11) Directions of the justices' clerk or a court which are still in force immediately prior to the transfer of relevant proceedings to another court shall continue to apply following the transfer, subject to any changes of terminology which are required to apply those directions to the court to which the proceedings are transferred, unless varied or discharged by directions under paragraph (2).

(12) The justices' clerk or the court shall [record] the giving, variation or revocation of a direction under this rule [in the appropriate form in Schedule 1 to these Rules] and [the justices' chief executive shall] serve, as soon as practicable, a copy of [the form] on any party who was not present at the giving, variation or revocation.

Date in force
14 October 1991

Amendment
Para (1): words 'children's guardian' in square brackets substituted by SI 2001/818, rr 2, 4(a).

Para (1): words 'welfare officer or children and family reporter' in square brackets substituted by SI 2001/818, rr 2, 4(b).

Para (2): in sub-para (d) words 'children's guardian' in square brackets substituted by SI 2001/818, rr 2, 4(a).

Para (2): in sub-para (d) words omitted revoked by SI 2001/818, rr 2, 10. Date in force: 1 April 2001: see SI 2001/818, r 1.

Para (2): words 'by the justices' chief executive' in square brackets inserted by SI 2001/615, r 2(xx), Schedule, para 99.

Para (4): words 'an order' in square brackets substituted by SI 1994/3156, r 15.

Para (4): words 'justices' chief executive' in square brackets substituted by SI 2001/615, r 2(xx), Schedule, para 93.

Para (5): in sub-para (a) words 'the justices' chief executive' in square brackets inserted by SI 2001/615, r 2(xx), Schedule, para 98.

Para (5): words 'in Form C2' in square brackets in both places they occur inserted by SI 1994/3156, rr 16, 17.

Para (7): words 'by the justices' chief executive' in square brackets inserted by SI 2001/615, r 2(xx), Schedule, para 99.

Para (7): words 'the justices' chief executive shall' in square brackets inserted by SI 2001/615, r 2(xx), Schedule, para 97.

Para (7): words 'in Form C6' in square brackets inserted by SI 1994/3156, rr 16, 17.

Para (8): in sub-para (a) words 'justices' chief executive' in square brackets substituted by SI 2001/615, r 2(xx), Schedule, para 93.

Para (8): in sub-para (b) words 'the justices' chief executive shall' in square brackets inserted by SI 2001/615, r 2(xx), Schedule, para 97.

Para (12): word 'record' in square brackets substituted by SI 1991/1991, r 26, Sch 2, para 8(2).

Para (12): words 'in the appropriate form in Schedule 1 to these Rules' in square brackets inserted by SI 1991/1991, r 26, Sch 2, para 8(2).

Para (12): words 'the justices' chief executive shall' in square brackets inserted by SI 2001/615, r 2(xx), Schedule, para 97.

Para (12): words 'the form' in square brackets substituted by SI 1991/1991, r 26, Sch 2, para 8(2).

15 Timing of proceedings

(1) Any period of time fixed by these Rules, or by any order or direction, for doing any act shall be reckoned in accordance with this rule.

(2) Where the period, being a period of 7 days or less, would include a day which is not a business day, that day shall be excluded.

(3) Where the time fixed for filing a document with the [justices['] chief executive] expires on a day on which the [office of the justices' chief executive] is closed, and for that reason the document cannot be filed on that day, the document shall be filed in time if it is filed on the next day on which the [office of the justices' chief executive] is open.

(4) Where these Rules provide a period of time within which or by which a certain act is to be performed in the course of relevant proceedings, that period may

not be extended otherwise than by a direction of the justices' clerk or the court under rule 14.

(5) At the—

(a)　transfer to a court of relevant proceedings,

(b)　postponement or adjournment of any hearing or directions appointment in the course of relevant proceedings, or

(c)　conclusion of any such hearing or directions appointment other than one at which the proceedings are determined, or so soon thereafter as is practicable,

[(i)　the justices' clerk shall fix a date upon which the proceedings shall come before him or the court again for such purposes as he or the court directs, which date shall, where paragraph (a) applies, be as soon as possible after the transfer, and

(ii)　the justices' chief executive shall give notice to the parties and to the guardian ad litem or the welfare officer of the date so fixed].

Date in force
14 October 1991

Amendment
Para (3): words 'justices' chief executive' in square brackets substituted by SI 2001/615, r 2(xx), Schedule, para 93.

Para (3): words 'office of the justices' chief executive' in square brackets in both places they occur substituted by SI 2001/615, r 2(xx), Schedule, para 95.

Para (5): sub-paras (i), (ii) substituted by SI 2001/615, r 2(xx), Schedule, para 96.

16　Attendance at directions appointment and hearing

(1) Subject to paragraph (2), a party shall attend a directions appointment of which he has been given notice in accordance with rule 14(5) unless the justices' clerk or the court otherwise directs.

(2) Relevant proceedings shall take place in the absence of any party including the child if—

(a)　the court considers it in the interests of the child, having regard to the matters to be discussed or the evidence likely to be given, and

(b)　the party is represented by a [children's guardian] or solicitor;

and when considering the interests of the child under sub-paragraph (a) the court shall give the [children's guardian], solicitor for the child and, if he is of sufficient understanding, the child, an opportunity to make representations.

(3) Subject to paragraph (4) below, where at the time and place appointed for a hearing or directions appointment the applicant appears but one or more of the respondents do not, the justices' clerk or the court may proceed with the hearing or appointment.

(4) The court shall not begin to hear an application in the absence of a respondent unless—

(a)　it is proved to the satisfaction of the court that he received reasonable notice of the date of the hearing; or

(b)　the court is satisfied that the circumstances of the case justify proceeding with the hearing.

(5) Where, at the time and place appointed for a hearing or directions appointment, one or more respondents appear but the applicant does not, the court may refuse the application or, if sufficient evidence has previously been received, proceed in the absence of the applicant.

(6) Where at the time and place appointed for a hearing or directions appointment neither the applicant nor any respondent appears, the court may refuse the application.

(7) If the court considers it expedient in the interests of the child, it shall hear any relevant proceedings in private when only the officers of the court, the parties, their legal representatives and such other persons as specified by the court may attend.

Date in force
14 October 1991

Amendment
Para (2): words 'children's guardian' in square brackets in both places they occur substituted by SI 2001/818, rr 2, 4(a).

---

17 Documentary Evidence

(1) Subject to paragraphs (4) and (5), in any relevant proceedings a party shall file and serve on the parties, any [welfare officer or children and family reporter] and any [children's guardian] of whose appointment he has been given notice under rule 10(5)—

(a) written statements of the substance of the oral evidence which the party intends to adduce at a hearing of, or a directions appointment in, those proceedings, which shall—

   (i)   be dated,
   (ii)   be signed by the person making the statement, ...
   (iii)   contain a declaration that the maker of the statement believes it to be true and understands that it may be placed before the court, and
   [(iv)   show in the top right hand corner of the first page—

      (a)   the initials and surname of the person making the statement,
      (b)   the number of the statement in relation to the maker,
      (c)   the date on which the statement was made, and
      (d)   the party on whose behalf it is filed; and]

(b) copies of any documents, including, subject to rule 18(3), experts' reports, upon which the party intends to rely, at a hearing of, or a directions appointment in, those proceedings,

at or by such time as the justices' clerk or the court directs or, in the absence of a direction, before the hearing or appointment.

(2) A party may, subject to any direction of the justices' clerk or the court about the timing of statements under this rule, file and serve on the parties a statement which is supplementary to a statement served under paragraph (1).

(3) At a hearing or directions appointment a party may not, without the leave of the justices' clerk, in the case of a directions appointment, or the court—

(a) adduce evidence, or
(b) seek to rely on a document,

in respect of which he has failed to comply with the requirements of paragraph (1).

(4) In proceedings for a section 8 order a party shall—

(a) neither file nor serve any document other than as required or authorised by these Rules, and
(b) in completing a form prescribed by these Rules, neither give information, nor make a statement, which is not required or authorised by that form,

without the leave of the justices' clerk or the court.

(5) In proceedings for a section 8 order, no statement or copy may be filed under paragraph (1) until such time as the justices' clerk or the court directs.

Date in force
14 October 1991

Amendment
Para (1): words 'welfare officer or children and family reporter' in square brackets substituted by SI 2001/818, rr 2, 4(b).
Para (1): words 'children's guardian' in square brackets substituted by SI 2001/818, rr 2, 4(a).
Para (1): in sub-para (a)(ii) word omitted revoked by SI 1992/2068, r 2, Schedule, para 4.
Para (1): sub-para (a)(iv) inserted by SI 1992/2068, r 2, Schedule, para 4.

18 Expert evidence – examination of child

(1) No person may, without the leave of the justices' clerk or the court, cause the child to be medically or psychiatrically examined, or otherwise assessed, for the purpose of the preparation of expert evidence for use in the proceedings.

(2) An application for leave under paragraph (1) shall, unless the justices' clerk or the court otherwise directs, be served on all the parties to the proceedings and on the [children's guardian].

(3) Where the leave of the justices' clerk or the court has not been given under paragraph (1), no evidence arising out of an examination or assessment to which that paragraph applies may be adduced without the leave of the court.

Date in force
14 October 1991

Amendment
Para (2): words 'children's guardian' in square brackets substituted by SI 2001/818, rr 2, 4(a).

19 Amendment

(1) Subject to rule 17(2), a document which has been filed or served in any relevant proceedings may not be amended without the leave of the justices' clerk or the court which shall, unless the justices' clerk or the court otherwise directs, be requested in writing.

(2) On considering a request for leave to amend a document the justices' clerk or the court shall either—

(a) grant the request, whereupon the [justices['] chief executive] shall inform the person making the request of that decision, or

(b) invite the parties or any of them to make representations, within a specified period, as to whether such an order should be made.

(3) A person amending a document shall file it with the [justices['] chief executive] and serve it on those persons on whom it was served prior to amendment; and the amendments shall be identified.

Date in force
14 October 1991

Amendment
Para (2): in sub-para (a) words 'justices' chief executive' in square brackets substituted by SI 2001/615, r 2(xx), Schedule, para 93.
Para (3): words 'justices' chief executive' in square brackets substituted by SI 2001/615, r 2(xx), Schedule, para 93.

20 Oral Evidence

The justices' clerk or the court shall keep a note of the substance of the oral evidence given at a hearing of, or directions appointment in, relevant proceedings.

Date in force
14 October 1991

Amendment

Para (2): in sub-para (a) words 'justices' chief executive' in square brackets substituted by SI 2001/615, r 2(xx), Schedule, para 93.

Para (3): words 'justices' chief executive' in square brackets substituted by SI 2001/615, r 2(xx), Schedule, para 93.

21 Hearing

(1) Before the hearing, the justice or justices who will be dealing with the case shall read any documents which have been filed under rule 17 in respect of the hearing.

(2) The justices' clerk at a directions appointment, or the court at a hearing or directions appointment, may give directions as to the order of speeches and evidence.

(3) Subject to directions under paragraph (2), at a hearing of, or directions appointment in, relevant proceedings, the parties and the [children's guardian] shall adduce their evidence in the following order—

(a) the applicant,
(b) any party with parental responsibility for the child,
(c) other respondents,
(d) the [children's guardian],
(e) the child if he is a party to the proceedings and there is no [children's guardian].

(4) After the final hearing of relevant proceedings, the court shall make its decision as soon as is practicable.

(5) Before the court makes an order or refuses an application or request, the justices' clerk shall record in writing—

(a) the names of the justice or justices constituting the court by which the decision is made, and
(b) in consultation with the justice or justices, the reasons for the court's decision and any findings of fact.

[(6) When making an order or when refusing an application, the court, or one of the justices constituting the court by which the decision is made shall

(a) where it makes a finding of fact state such finding and complete Form C22; and
(b) state the reasons for the court's decision.]

[(7) As soon as practicable after the court announces its decision—

(a) the justices' clerk shall make a record of any order made in the appropriate form in Schedule 1 to these Rules or, where there is no such form, in writing; and
(b) subject to paragraph (8), the justices' chief executive shall serve a copy of any order made on the parties to the proceedings and on any person with whom the child is living.]

(8) Within 48 hours after the making of an order under section 48(4) or the making, ex parte, of—

(a) [section 8 order], or
(b) an order under section 44, 48(9), 50, [or] 75(1) ... ,

the applicant shall serve a copy of the order in the appropriate form in Schedule 1 to these Rules on—

(i) each party,
(ii) any person who has actual care of the child, or who had such care immediately prior to the making of the order, and

(iii) in the case of an order referred to in sub-paragraph (b), the local authority in whose area the child lives or is found.

Date in force
14 October 1991

Amendment

Para (3): words 'children's guardian' in square brackets in each place they occur substituted by SI 2001/818, rr 2, 4(a).

Para (6): substituted by SI 1994/3156, r 18.

Para (7): substituted by SI 2001/615, r 2(xx), Schedule, para 101.

Para (8): in sub-para (a) words 'section 8 order' in square brackets substituted by SI 1992/2068, r 2, Schedule, paras 1, 5.

Para (8): in sub-para (b) word 'or' in square brackets inserted by SI 1992/2068, r 2, Schedule, paras 1, 5.

Para (8): in sub-para (b) words omitted revoked by SI 1992/2068, r 2, Schedule, paras 1, 5.

[PART IIA
PROCEEDINGS UNDER SECTION 30 OF THE HUMAN
FERTILISATION AND EMBRYOLOGY ACT 1990]

Date in force
14 October 1991

Amendment
Inserted by SI 1994 No 2166, r 4.

[21A   Interpretation]

[(1) In this Part of these Rules—

'the 1990 Act' means the Human Fertilisation and Embryology Act 1990;

'the birth father' means the father of the child, including a person who is treated as being the father of the child by section 28 of the 1990 Act where he is not the husband within the meaning of section 30 of the 1990 Act;

'the birth mother' means the woman who carried the child;

'the birth parents' means the birth mother and the birth father;

. . .

'the husband and wife' means the persons who may apply for a parental order where the conditions set out in section 30(1) of the 1990 Act are met;

'parental order' means an order under section 30 of the 1990 Act (parental orders in favour of gamete donors) providing for a child to be treated in law as a child of the parties to a marriage;

['parental order reporter' means an officer of the service appointed under section 41 of the Children Act 1989 in relation to proceedings specified by paragraph (2)].

(2) Applications under section 30 of the 1990 Act are specified proceedings for the purposes of section 41 of the Children Act 1989 in accordance with section 41(6)(i) of that Act.]

Date in force
14 October 1991

Amendment
Inserted by SI 1994/2166, r 4.

Para (1): definition 'the guardian ad litem' (omitted) revoked by SI 2001/818, rr 2, 11(a).

Para (1): definition 'parental order reporter' inserted by SI 2001/818, rr 2, 11(b).

[21B   Application of the remaining provisions of these Rules]

[Subject to the provisions of this Part, the remaining provisions of these Rules shall apply as appropriate with any necessary modifications to proceedings under this Part except that rules 7(1), 9, 10(1)(b), 10(11), [11A(1)], [11A(2)] and 12 shall not apply.]

Date in force
14 October 1991

Amendment
Inserted by SI 1994/2166, r 4.

Reference to '11A(1)' in square brackets substituted by SI 2001/818, rr 2, 12(a).

Reference to '11A(2)' in square brackets substituted by SI 2001/818, rr 2, 12(b).

[21C   Parties]

[The applicants shall be the husband and wife and the respondents shall be the persons set out in the relevant entry in column (iii) of Schedule 2.]

Date in force
14 October 1991

Amendment
Inserted by SI 1994/2166, r 4.

[21D   [Acknowledgement]]

[Within 14 days of the service of an application for a parental order, each respondent shall file and serve on all the other parties an [acknowledgement in Form C52].]

Date in force
14 October 1991

Amendment
Rule heading: substituted by SI 1994/3156, r 19(a). Inserted by SI 1994/2166, r 4. Words in square brackets substituted by SI 1994/3156, r 19(b).

[21E   Appointment and duties of the [parental order reporter]]

[(1) As soon as practicable after the application has been filed, the justices' clerk shall consider the appointment of a [parental order reporter] in accordance with section 41(1) of the Children Act 1989.

(2) . . .

(3) In addition to such of the matters set out in [rules 11 and 11A] as are appropriate, the [parental order reporter] shall—

   (i)   investigate the matters set out in section 30(1) to (7) of the 1990 Act;

  (ii)   so far as he considers necessary, investigate any matter contained in the application form or other matter which appears relevant to the making of a parental order;

 (iii)   advise the court on whether there is any reason under section 6 of the Adoption Act 1976, as applied with modifications by the Parental Orders (Human Fertilisation and Embryology) Regulations 1994, to refuse the parental order.]

Date in force
14 October 1991

Amendment
Provision heading: words 'parental order reporter' in square brackets substituted by SI 2001/818, rr 2, 13(a).

Inserted by SI 1994/2166, r 4.

Para (1): words 'parental order reporter' in square brackets substituted by SI 2001/818, rr 2, 13(a).

Para (2): revoked by SI 2001/818, rr 2, 13(b).

Para (3): words 'rules 11 and 11A' in square brackets substituted by SI 2001/818, rr 2, 13(c).

Para (3): words 'parental order reporter' in square brackets substituted by SI 2001/818, rr 2, 13(a).

[21F   Personal attendance of applicants]

[The court shall not make a parental order except upon the personal attendance before it of the applicants.]

Date in force
14 October 1991

Amendment
Inserted by SI 1994/2166, r 4.

[21G   Copies of orders]

[(1) Where a parental order is made by a court sitting in Wales in respect of a child who was born in Wales and the applicants so request before the order is drawn up, the [justices['] chief executive] shall obtain a translation into Welsh of the particulars set out in the order.

(2) Within 7 days after the making of a parental order, the [justices['] chief executive] shall send a copy of the order to the Registrar General.

(3) A copy of any parental order may be supplied to the Registrar General at his request.]

Date in force
14 October 1991

Amendment
Inserted by SI 1994/2166, r 4.

Para (1): words 'justices' chief executive' in square brackets substituted by SI 2001/615, r 2(xx), Schedule, para 93.

Para (2): words 'justices' chief executive' in square brackets substituted by SI 2001/615, r 2(xx), Schedule, para 93.

[21H   Amendment and revocation of orders]

[(1) Any application made under paragraph 4 of Schedule 1 to the Adoption Act 1976 as modified by the Parental Orders (Human Fertilisation and Embryology) Regulations 1994 for the amendment of a parental order or for the revocation of a direction to the Registrar General shall be made to a family proceedings court for the same petty sessions area as the family proceedings court which made the parental order, by delivering it to or sending it by post to the [justices' chief executive].

(2) Notice of the application shall be given by the [justices['] chief executive] to such persons (if any) as the court thinks fit.

(3) Where the application is granted, the [justices['] chief executive] shall send to the Registrar General a notice specifying the amendments or informing him of the revocation and shall give sufficient particulars of the order to enable the Registrar General to identify the case.]

Date in force
14 October 1991

Amendment
Inserted by SI 1994/2166, r 4.

Para (1): words 'justices' chief executive' in square brackets substituted by SI 2001/615, r 2(xx), Schedule, para 102.

Para (2): words 'justices' chief executive' in square brackets substituted by SI 2001/615, r 2(xx), Schedule, para 93.

Para (3): words 'justices' chief executive' in square brackets substituted by SI 2001/615, r 2(xx), Schedule, para 93.

[21I   Keeping of registers, custody, inspection and disclosure of documents and information]

[(1) Such part of the register kept in pursuance of rules made under the Magistrates' Courts Act 1980 as relates to proceedings for parental orders shall be kept in a separate book and the book shall not contain particulars of any other proceedings.

(2) The book kept in pursuance of paragraph (1) and all other documents relating to the proceedings for a parental order shall, while they are in the custody of the court, be kept in a place of special security.

(3) Any person who obtains information in the course of, or relating to proceedings for a parental order, shall treat that information as confidential and shall only disclose it if—

  (a) the disclosure is necessary for the proper exercise of his duties, or

  (b) the information is requested—

      (i) by a court or public authority (whether in Great Britain or not) having the power to determine proceedings for a parental order and related matters, for the purpose of the discharge of its duties in that behalf, or

     (ii) by a person who is authorised in writing by the Secretary of State to obtain the information for the purposes of research.]

Date in force
14 October 1991

Amendment
Inserted by SI 1994/2166, r 4.

[21J   Application for removal, return etc of child]

[(1) An application under sections 27(1), 29(1) or 29(2) of the Adoption Act 1976 as applied with modifications by the Parental Orders (Human Fertilisation and Embryology) Regulations 1994 shall be made by complaint to the family proceedings court in which the application under section 30 of the 1990 Act is pending.

(2) The respondents shall be all the parties to the proceedings under section 30 and such other person or body, not being the child, as the court thinks fit.

(3) The [justices['] chief executive] shall serve notice of the time fixed for the hearing,

together with a copy of the complaint on the guardian ad litem who may attend on the hearing of the application and be heard on the question of whether the application should be granted.

(4) The court may at any time give directions as to the conduct of the application under this rule.

(5) Where an application under this rule is determined, the [justices['] chief executive] shall serve notice of the determination on all the parties.

(6) A search warrant issued by a justice of the peace under section 29(4) of the Adoption Act 1976 (applied as above) (which relates to premises specified in an information to which an order made under the said section 29(1) relates, authorising a constable to search the said premises and if he finds the child to return the child to the person on whose application the said order was made) shall be in a warrant form as if issued under section 102 of the Children Act 1989 (warrant to search for or remove a child) or a form to the like effect.]

Date in force
14 October 1991

Amendment
Inserted by SI 1994/2166, r 4.

Para (3): words 'justices' chief executive' in square brackets substituted by SI 2001/615, r 2(xx), Schedule, para 93.

Para (5): words 'justices' chief executive' in square brackets substituted by SI 2001/615, r 2(xx), Schedule, para 93.

Part III
Miscellaneous

22 Costs

(1) In any relevant proceedings, the court may, at any time during the proceedings in that court, make an order that a party pay the whole or any part of the costs of any other party.

(2) A party against whom the court is considering making a costs order shall have an opportunity to make representations as to why the order should not be made.

[22A Power of court to limit cross-examination]

[The court may limit the issues on which an officer of the service may be cross-examined.]

Date in force
14 October 1991

Amendment
Inserted by SI 2001/818, rr 2, 14.

23 Confidentiality of documents

(1) No document, other than a record of an order, held by the court and relating to relevant proceedings shall be disclosed, other than to—

(a) a party,
(b) the legal representative of a party,
(c) the [children's guardian],
(d) the Legal Aid Board, or

    (e)   a [welfare officer or children and family reporter], [or

    (f)   an expert whose instruction by a party has been authorised by the court,]

without leave of the justices' clerk or the court.

(2) Nothing in this rule shall prevent the notification by the Court or the [justices['] chief executive] of a direction under section 37(1) to the authority concerned.

[(3) Nothing in this rule shall prevent the disclosure of a document prepared by an officer of the service for the purpose of—

    (a)   enabling a person to perform functions required under section 62(3A) of the Justices of the Peace Act 1997;

    (b)   assisting an officer of the service who is appointed by the court under any enactment to perform his functions.]

[(4) Nothing in this rule shall prevent the disclosure of any document relating to proceedings by an officer of the service to any other officer of the service unless that other officer is involved in the same proceedings but on behalf of a different party.]

Date in force
14 October 1991

Amendment
Para (1): in sub-para (c) words 'children's guardian' in square brackets substituted by SI 2001/818, rr 2, 4(a).

Para (1): in sub-para (e) words 'welfare officer or children and family reporter' in square brackets substituted by SI 2001/818, rr 2, 4(b).

Para (1): sub-para (f) and word 'or' immediately preceeding it inserted by SI 2001/818, rr 2, 15(a).

Para (2): words 'justices' chief executive' in square brackets substituted by SI 2001/615, r 2(xx), Schedule, para 93.

Para (3): inserted by SI 1997/1895, r 2.

Para (3): substituted by SI 2001/818, rr 2, 15(b).

Para (4): inserted by SI 2001/818, rr 2, 15(c).

24 Enforcement of residence order

Where a person in whose favour a residence order is in force wishes to enforce it he shall file a written statement describing the alleged breach of the arrangements settled by the order, whereupon the justices' clerk shall fix a date, time and place for a hearing of the proceedings and [the justices' chief executive shall] give notice, as soon as practicable, to the person wishing to enforce the residence order and to any person whom it is alleged is in breach of the arrangements settled by that order, of the date fixed.

Date in force
14 October 1991

Amendment
Words 'the justices' chief executive shall' in square brackets inserted by SI 2001/615, r 2(xx), Schedule, para 97.

25 Notification of consent

[(1)] Consent for the purposes of—

    (a)   section 16(3), [or]

    [(b)   section 38A(2)(b)(ii) or 44A(2)(b)(ii), or]

    (c)   paragraph 19(1) of Schedule 2,

shall be given either—

    (i)   orally in court, or

(ii) in writing to the [justices['] chief executive] or the court and signed by the person giving his consent.

[(2) Any written consent given for the purposes of subsection (2) of section 38A or section 44A, shall include a statement that the person giving consent—

(a) is able and willing to give to the child the care which it would be reasonable to expect a parent to give him; and

(b) understands that the giving of consent could lead to the exclusion of the relevant person from the dwelling-house in which the child lives.]

Date in force
14 October 1991

Amendment
Para (1): numbered as such, in relation to proceedings issued on or after 1 October 1997, by SI 1997/1895, rr 3(1), 8.

Para (1): in sub-para (a) word 'or' in square brackets inserted by SI 1992/2068, r 2, Schedule, para 6.

Para (1): original sub-para (b) revoked by SI 1992/2068, r 2.

Para (1): new sub-para (b) inserted, in relation to proceedings issued after 1 October 1997, by SI 1997/1895, rr 3(1), 8.

Para (1): in sub-para (ii) words 'justices' chief executive' in square brackets substituted by SI 2001/615, r 2(xx), Schedule, para 93.

Para (2): inserted, in relation to proceedings issued on or after 1 October 1997, by SI 1997/1895, rr 3(2), 8.

[25A Exclusion requirements: interim care orders and emergency protection orders]

[(1) This rule applies where the court includes an exclusion requirement in an interim care order or an emergency protection order.

(2) The applicant for an interim care order or emergency protection order shall

(a) prepare a separate statement of the evidence in support of the application for an exclusion requirement;

(b) serve the statement personally on the relevant person with a copy of the order containing the exclusion requirement (and of any power of arrest which is attached to it);

(c) inform the relevant person of his right to apply to vary or discharge the exclusion requirement.

(3) Where a power of arrest is attached to an exclusion requirement in an interim care order or an emergency protection order, a copy of the order shall be delivered to the officer for the time being in charge of the police station for the area in which the dwelling-house in which the child lives is situated (or of such other station as the court may specify) together with a statement that the relevant person has been served with the order or informed of its terms (whether by being present when the order was made or by telephone or otherwise).

(4) Rules 12A(3), 20 (except paragraphs (1) and (3)) and 21 of the Family Proceedings Courts (Matrimonial Proceedings etc) Rules 1991 shall apply, with the necessary modifications, for the service, variation, discharge and enforcement of any exclusion requirement to which a power of arrest is attached as they apply to an order made on an application under Part IV of the Family Law Act 1996.

(5) The relevant person shall serve the parties to the proceedings with any application which he makes for the Variation or discharge of the exclusion requirement.

(6) Where an exclusion requirement ceases to have effect whether—

(a) as a result of the removal of a child under section 38A(10) or 44A(10),

(b) because of the discharge of the interim care order or emergency protection order, or

(c) otherwise, the applicant shall inform—

    (i)   the relevant person,

    (ii) the parties to the proceedings,

    (iii) any officer to whom a copy of the order was delivered under paragraph (3), and

    (iv) (where necessary) the court.

(7) Where the court includes an exclusion requirement in an interim care order or an emergency protection order of its own motion, paragraph (2) shall apply with the omission of any reference to the statement of the evidence.]

Date in force

14 October 1991

Amendment

Inserted, in relation to proceedings issued on or after 1 October 1997, by SI 1997/1895, rr 4, 8.

26 Secure accommodation

In proceedings under section 25, the [justices' chief executive] shall, if practicable, arrange for copies of all written reports before the court to be made available before the hearing to—

    (a) the applicant,

    (b) the parent or guardian of the child,

    (c) any legal representative of the child,

    (d) the [children's guardian], and

    (e) the child, unless the [justices' chief executive] or the court otherwise directs;

and copies of such reports may, if the court considers it desirable, be shown to any person who is entitled to notice of the proceedings in accordance with these Rules.

Date in force

14 October 1991

Amendment

Words 'justices' chief executive' in square brackets in both places they occur substituted by SI 2001/615, r 2(xx), Schedule, para 93.

In para (d) words 'children's guardian' in square brackets substituted by SI 2001/818, rr 2, 4(a).

27 Investigation under section 37

(1) This rule applies where a direction is given to an appropriate authority by a family proceedings court under section 37(1).

(2) On giving a direction the court shall adjourn the proceedings and the justices' clerk or the court shall record the direction [in Form C40].

(3) A copy of the direction recorded under paragraph (2) shall, as soon as practicable after the direction is given, be served by the [justices['] chief executive] on the parties to the proceedings in which the direction is given and, where the appropriate authority is not a party, on that authority.

(4) When serving the copy of the direction on the appropriate authority the [justices['] chief executive] shall also serve copies of such of the documentary evidence which has been, or is to be, adduced in the proceedings as the court may direct.

(5) Where a local authority informs the court of any of the matters set out in section 37(3)(a) to (c) it shall do so in writing.

Date in force

14 October 1991

Amendment

Para (2): words in square brackets substituted by SI 1994/3156, r 20.

Para (3): words 'justices' chief executive' in square brackets substituted by SI 2001/615, r 2(xx), Schedule, para 93.

Para (4): words 'justices' chief executive' in square brackets substituted by SI 2001/615, r 2(xx), Schedule, para 93.

28 Limits on the power of a justices' clerk or a single justice to make an order under section 11(3) or section 38(1)

A justices' clerk or single justice shall not make an order under section 11(3) or section 38(1) unless—

(a) a written request for such an order has been made to which the other parties and any [children's guardian] consent and which they or their representatives have signed,

(b) a previous such order has been made in the same proceedings, and

(c) the terms of the order sought are the same as those of the last such order made.

Date in force
14 October 1991

Amendment

In para (a) words 'children's guardian' in square brackets substituted by SI 2001/818, rr 2, 4(a).

29 Appeals to a family proceedings court under section 77(6) and paragraph 8(1) of Schedule 8

(1) An appeal under section 77(6) or paragraph 8(1) of Schedule 8 shall be by application in accordance with rule 4.

(2) An appeal under section 77(6) shall be brought within 21 days from the date of the step to which the appeal relates.

Date in force
14 October 1991

Amendment

In para (a) words 'children's guardian' in square brackets substituted by SI 2001/818, rr 2, 4(a).

30 Contribution orders

(1) An application for a contribution order under paragraph 23(1) of Schedule 2 shall be accompanied by a copy of the contribution notice served in accordance with paragraph 22(1) of that Schedule and a copy of any notice served by the contributor under paragraph 22(8) of that Schedule.

(2) Where a local authority notifies the court of an agreement reached under paragraph 23(6) of Schedule 2, it shall do so in writing through the [justices['] chief executive].

(3) An application for the variation or revocation of a contribution order under paragraph 23(8) of Schedule 2 shall be accompanied by a copy of the contribution order which it is sought to vary or revoke.

Date in force
14 October 1991

Amendment

Para (2): words 'justices' chief executive' in square brackets substituted by SI 2001/615, r 2(xx), Schedule, para 93.

---

31 Direction to local education authority to apply for education supervision order

(1) For the purposes of section 40(3) and (4) of the Education Act 1944, a direction by a magistrates' court to a local education authority to apply for an education supervision order shall be given [in writing].

(2) Where, following such a direction, a local education authority informs the court that they have decided not to apply for an education supervision order, they shall do so in writing.

Date in force
14 October 1991

Amendment

Para (1): words 'in writing' in square brackets substituted by SI 1997/1895, r 5.

[31A Applications and orders under sections 33 and 34 of the Family Law Act 1986]

[(1) In this rule 'the 1986 Act' means the Family Law Act 1986.

(2) An application under section 33 of the 1986 Act shall be in Form C4 and an order made under that section shall be in Form C30.

(3) An application under section 34 of the 1986 Act shall be in Form C3 and an order made under that section shall be in Form C31.

(4) An application under section 33 or section 34 of the 1986 Act may be made ex parte in which case the applicant shall file the application—

(a) where the application is made by telephone, within 24 hours after the making of the application, or

(b) in any other case at the time when the application is made,

and shall serve a copy of the application on each respondent 48 hours after the making of the order.

(5) Where the court refuses to make an order on an ex parte application it may direct that the application be made inter partes.]

Date in force
14 October 1991

Amendment

Inserted by SI 1994/3156, r 22.

---

32 Delegation by justices' clerk

(1) In this rule, 'employed as a clerk in court' has the same meaning as in rule 2(1) of the Justices' Clerks (Qualifications of Assistants) Rules 1979.

(2) Anything authorised to be done by, to or before a justices' clerk under these Rules, or under paragraphs 13 to 15C of the Schedule to the Justices' Clerks Rules 1970 as amended by Schedule 3 to these Rules, may be done instead by, to or before a person employed as a clerk in court where that person is appointed by the magistrates' courts committee to assist him and where that person has been specifically authorised by the justices' clerk for that purpose.

(3) Any authorisation by the justices' clerk under paragraph (2) shall be recorded in writing at the time the authority is given or as soon as practicable thereafter.

Date in force
14 October 1991

Amendment
Inserted by SI 1994/3156, r 22.

33 Application of section 97 of the Magistrates' Courts Act 1980

Section 97 of the Magistrates' Courts Act 1980 shall apply to relevant proceedings in a family proceedings court as it applies to a hearing of a complaint under that section.

[33A Disclosure of addresses]

[(1) Nothing in these rules shall be construed as requiring any party to reveal the address of their private residence (or that of any child) except by order of the court.

(2) Where a party declines to reveal an address in reliance upon paragraph (1) he shall give notice of that address to the court in Form C8 and that address shall not be revealed to any person except by order of the court.]

Date in force
14 October 1991

Amendment
Inserted by SI 1994/3156, r 23.

[33B Setting aside on failure of service]

[Where an application has been sent to a respondent in accordance with rule 8(1) and, after an order has been made on the application, it appears to the court that the application did not come to the knowledge of the respondent in due time, the court may of its own motion set aside the order and may give such directions as it thinks fit for the rehearing of the application.]

Date in force
14 October 1991

Amendment
Inserted by SI 1997/1895, r 6.

34 Consequential and minor amendments, savings and transitionals

(1) Subject to paragraph (3) the consequential and minor amendments in Schedule 3 to these Rules shall have effect.

(2) Subject to paragraph (3), the provisions of the 1981 rules shall have effect subject to these Rules.

(3) Nothing in these Rules shall affect any proceedings which are pending (within the meaning of paragraph 1 of Schedule 14 to the Act of 1989) immediately before these Rules come into force.

Date in force
14 October 1991

Amendment
Inserted by SI 1997/1895, r 6.

[SCHEDULE 1
Forms]

[[C1	Application	for an order]
C2	Application	for an order or directions in existing family proceedings
	Application	to be joined as, or cease to be, a party in existing family proceedings
	Application	for leave to commence proceedings
C3	Application	for an order authorising search for, taking charge of, and delivery of a child
C4	Application	for an order for disclosure of a child's whereabouts
C5	Application	concerning the registration of a child-minder or a provider of day care
C6	Notice	of proceedings (Hearing) (Directions Appointment) (*Notice to parties*)
C6A	Notice	of proceedings (Hearing) (Directions Appointment) (*Notice to non-parties*)
C7		Acknowledgement
C8		Confidential Address
[C9	Statement	of Service]
C10	Supplement	for an application for financial provision for a child or for variation of financial provision for a child
C10A	Statement	of Means
[C11	Supplement	for an application for an Emergency Protection Order]
C12	Supplement	for an application for a Warrant to assist a person authorised by an Emergency Protection Order
C13	Supplement	for an application for a Care or Supervision Order
C14	Supplement	for an application for authority to refuse contact with a child in care
C15	Supplement	for an application for contact with a child in care
C16	Supplement	for an application for a Child Assessment Order
C17	Supplement	for an application for an Education Supervision Order
C17A	Supplement	for an application for an extension of an Education Supervision Order
C18	Supplement	for an application for a Recovery Order
C19	Supplement	for a Warrant of Assistance
C20	Supplement	for an application for an order to hold a child in Secure Accommodation
C21	Order or direction	Blank
C22	Record	of hearing
[C23	Order	Emergency Protection Order]
C24	Order	Variation of an Emergency Protection Order
		Extension of an Emergency Protection Order
		Discharge of an Emergency Protection Order
C25	Warrant	To assist a person authorised by an Emergency Protection Order
C26	Order	Authority to keep a child in Secure Accommodation
C27	Order	Authority to search for another child
C28	Warrant	To assist a person to gain access to a child or entry to premises
C29	Order	Recovery of a child
C30	Order	To disclose information about the whereabouts of a missing child
C31	Order	Authorising search for, taking charge of, and delivery of a child
C32	Order	Care Order
		Discharge of a Care Order
[C33	Order	Interim Care Order]
C34	Order	Contact with a child in care
		Authority to refuse contact with a child in care
C35	Order	Supervision Order
		Interim Supervision Order
C36	Order	Substitution of a Supervision Order for a Care Order
		Discharge of a Supervision Order

		Variation of a Supervision Order
		Extension of a Supervision Order
C37	Order	Education Supervision Order
C38	Order	Discharge of an Education Supervision Order
		Extension of an Education Supervision Order
C39	Order	Child Assessment Order
C40	Direction	To undertake an investigation
C41	Order	Cancellation of the registration of a child-minder or a provider of day care
		Removal, Variation or Imposition of a requirement on a child-minder or a provider of day care
C42	Order	Family Assistance Order
C43	Order	Residence Order
		Contact Order
		Specific Issue Order
		Prohibited Steps Order
C44	Order	Leave to change the surname by which a child is known
		Leave to remove a child from the United Kingdom
C45	Order	Parental Responsibility Order
		Termination of a Parental Responsibility Order
C46	Order	Appointment of a guardian
		Termination of the appointment of a guardian
C47	Order	Making or refusing the appointment of a [children's guardian]
		Termination of the appointment of a [children's guardian]
C48	Order	Appointment of a solicitor for a child
		Refusal of the appointment of a solicitor for a child
		Termination of the appointment of a solicitor for a child
C49	Order	Transfer of Proceedings to (the High Court) (a county court) (a family proceedings court)
C50	Certificate	Refusal to transfer proceedings
C51	Application	for a Parental Order
C52		Acknowledgment of an application for a Parental Order
C53	Order	Parental Order
C54	Notice	of Refusal of a Parental Order]

Amendment

Entries substituted by SI 1994/3156, r 24, Sch 1.

Entry for Form C1: substituted by SI 2001/818, rr 2, 16(a), Schedule.

Entry for Form C9: substituted by SI 2001/818, rr 2, 16(a), Schedule.

Entry for Form C11: substituted, in relation to proceedings issued on or after 1 October 1997, by SI 1997/1895, rr 7, 8, Schedule.

Entry for Form C23: substituted, in relation to proceedings issued on or after 1 October 1997, by SI 1997/1895, rr 7, 8, Schedule.

Entry for Form C33: substituted, in relation to proceedings issued on or after 1 October 1997, by SI 1997/1895, rr 7, 8, Schedule.

Form C47: words 'children's guardian' in square brackets in both places they occur substituted by SI 2001/818, rr 2, 4(a); Form C47 further amended by r 16(d) thereof.

SCHEDULE 2
Respondents and Notice

(i)	(ii)	(iii)	(iv)
Provision under which proceedings brought	Minimum number of days prior to hearing or directions appointment for service under rule 4(1)(b)	Respondents	Persons to whom notice is to be given

(i)	(ii)	(iii)	(iv)
All applications.	See separate entries below.	Subject to separate entries below;	Subject to separate entries below;
		every person whom the applicant believes to have parental responsibility for the child;	the local authority providing accommodation for the child;
		where the child is the subject of a care order, every person whom the applicant believes to have had parental responsibility immediately prior to the making of the care order;	persons who are caring for the child at the time when the proceedings are commenced;
		in the case of an application to extend, vary or discharge an order, the parties to the proceedings leading to the order which it is sought to have extended, varied or discharged;	in the case of proceedings brought in respect of a child who is alleged to be staying in a refuge which is certificated under section 51(1) or (2), the person who is providing the refuge.
		in the case of specified proceedings, the child.	
. . .	. . .	. . .	. . .
Section 4(1)(a), 4(3), 5(1), 6(7), [8], 13(1), 16(6), 33(7), 77(6), [Schedule 1], paragraph 19(1), 23(1) or 23(8) of Schedule 2, paragraph 8(1) of Schedule 8, or paragraph 11(3) or 16(5) of Schedule 14.	14 days	Except for proceedings under section 77(6), Schedule 2, or paragraph 8(1) of Schedule 8, as for 'all applications' above, and:	As for 'all applications' above, and:
		[in the case of proceedings under Schedule 1, those persons whom the applicant believes to be interested in or affected by the proceedings;]	in the case of an application under paragraph 19(1) of Schedule 2, the parties to the proceedings leading to the care order;
		in the case of an application under paragraph 11(3)(b) or 16(5) of Schedule 14, any person, other than the child, named in the order or directions which it is sought to discharge or vary;	in the case of an application under section 5(1), the father of the child if he does not have parental responsibility.

(i)	(ii)	(iii)	(iv)
		[in the case of proceedings] under section 77(6), the local authority against whose decision the appeal is made;	

in the case of an application under paragraph 23(1) of Schedule 2, the contributor;

in the case of an application under paragraph 23(8) of Schedule 2—

(i) if the applicant is the local authority, the contributor, and

(ii) if the applicant is the contributor, the local authority.

In the case of an application under paragraph 8(1) of Schedule 8, the local authority against whose decision the appeal is made.

[in the case of an application for a section 8 order, every person whom the applicant believes—

(i) to be named in a court order with respect to the same child, which has not ceased to have effect, (ii) to be a party to pending proceedings in respect of the same child, or (iii) to be a person with whom the child has lived for at least three years prior to the application,

unless, in a case to which (i) or (ii) applies, the applicant believes that the court order or pending proceedings are not relevant to the application.]

711

(i)	(ii)	(iii)	(iv)
Section 36(1), 39(1), 39(2), 39(3), 39(4), 43(1), or paragraph 6(3), 15(2) or 17(1) of Schedule 3.		As for 'all applications' above, and:	As for 'all applications' above, and:
		in the case of an application under section 39(2) or (3), the supervisor;	in the case of an application for an order under section 43(1)—
		in the case of proceedings under paragraph 17(1) of Schedule 3, the local education authority concerned;	(i) every person whom the applicant believes to be a parent of the child,
		in the case of proceedings under section 36 or paragraph 15(2) or 17(1) of Schedule 3, the child.	(ii) every person whom the applicant believes to be caring for the child,
			(iii) every person in whose favour a contact order is in force with respect to the child, and
			(iv) every person who is allowed to have contact with the child by virtue of an order under section 34.
Section 31, 34(2), 34(3), 34(4), 34(9) or 38(8)(b).	3 days	As for 'all applications' above, and:	As for 'all applications' above, and:
		in the case of an application under section 34, the person whose contact with the child is the subject of the application.	in the case of an application under section 31—
			(i) every person whom the applicant believes to be a party to pending relevant proceedings in respect of the same child, and
			(ii) every person whom the applicant believes to be a parent without parental responsibility for the child.

(i)	(ii)	(iii)	(iv)
Section 43(12).	2 days	As for 'all applications' above.	Those of the persons referred to in section 43(11)(a) to (e) who were not party to the application for the order which it is sought to have varied or discharged.
Section 25,44(1), 44(9)(b), 45(4), 45(8), 46(7), 48(9), 50(1), 75(1) or 102(1).	1 day	Except for applications under section 75(1) or 102(1), as for 'all applications' above, and: in the case of an application under section 44(9)(b) (i) the parties to the application for the order in respect of which it is sought to vary the directions; (ii) any person who was caring for the child prior to the making of the order; and (iii) any person whose contact with the child is affected by the direction which it is sought to have varied; in the case of an application under section 50, the person whom the applicant alleges to have effected or to have been or to be responsible for the taking or keeping of the child; in the case of an application under section 75(1), the registered person;	As for 'all applications' above, and: in the case of an application under section 44(1), every person whom the applicant believes to be a parent of the child; in the case of an application under section 44(9)(b)— (i) the local authority in whose area the child is living, and (ii) any person whom the applicant believes to be affected by the direction which it is sought to have varied.

(i)	(ii)	(iii)	(iv)
		in the case of an application under section 102(1), the person referred to in section 102(1) and any person preventing or likely to prevent such a person from exercising powers under enactments mentioned in subsection (6) of that section.	
[section 30 of the Human Fertilisation and Embryology Act 1990]	14 days	the birth parents (except where the applicants seek to dispense with their agreement under section 30(6) of the Human Fertilisation and Embryology Act 1990) and any other persons or body with parental responsibility for the child at the date of the application	any local authority or voluntary organisation that has at any time provided accommodation for the child]

Amendment

Entry omitted revoked, figure in square brackets and first, second and fourth words in square brackets inserted, and third words in square brackets substituted, by SI 1992/2068, r 2, Schedule, paras 8, 9; final words in square brackets inserted by SI 1994/2166, r 6.

SCHEDULE 3
Consequential and Minor Amendments

Rule 34(1)

[Not reproduced]

Parental Responsibility Agreement Regulations 1991

(SI 1991/1478)

1 Citation, commencement and interpretation

(1) These Regulations may be cited as the Parental Responsibility Agreement Regulations 1991 and shall come into force on 14th October 1991.

(2) In these Regulations, 'the Principal Registry' means the principal registry of the Family Division of the High Court.

2 Form of parental responsibility agreement

A parental responsibility agreement shall be made in the form set out in the Schedule to these Regulations.

3 Recording of parental responsibility agreement

(1) A parental responsibility agreement shall be recorded by the filing of the agreement, together with two copies, in the Principal Registry.

(2) Upon the filing of documents under paragraph (1), an officer of the Principal Registry shall seal the copies and send one to the child's mother and one to the child's father.

(3) The record of an agreement under paragraph (1) shall be made available, during office hours, for inspection by any person upon—

(a) written request to an officer of the Principal Registry, and

(b) payment of such fee as may be prescribed in an Order under section 41 of the Matrimonial and Family Proceedings Act 1984 (Fees in family proceedings)

[SCHEDULE
Form of Agreement]

_____

Date in force
14 October 1991.

Amendment
Substituted by SI 1994 No 3157, reg 2, Sch.

_____

[Regulation 2]

[Parental Responsibility Agreement	**Keep this form in a safe place**
Section 4(1)(b) Children Act 1989	_Date recorded at the principal Registry of the Family Division_
Read the notes on the other side before you make this agreement.	

[This is a Parental Responsibility Agreement regarding

the Child	*Name*
	Boy or Girl Date of birth Date of 18th birthday

Between

The Mother	*Name*
	Address

and

The Father	*Name*
	Address

We declare that   we are the mother and father of the above child and we agree that the father shall have parental responsibility for the child (in addition to the mother having parental responsibility).

Signed **(Mother)**	Signed **(Father)**
Date	Date

Certificate of witness

The following evidence of identity was produced by the person signing above:	The following evidence of identity was produced by the person signing above:
Signed in the presence of: *Name of witness*	Signed in the presence of: *Name of witness*
Address	*Address*
Signature of witness Signature of witness	
[A Justice of the Peace] [Justices' Clerk] [An Officer of the Court authorised by the judge to administer oaths]	[A Justice of the Peace] [Justices' Clerk] [An Officer of the Court authorised by the judge to administer oaths]

Notes about the Parental Responsibility Agreement

Read these notes before you make the agreement

About the Parental Responsibility Agreement

The making of this agreement will affect the legal position of the mother and the father. You should both seek legal advice before you make the Agreement. You can obtain the name and address of a solicitor from the Children Panel (020 7242 1222) or from

your local family proceeding court, or county court

a Citizens Advice Bureau

a Law centre

a Local library.

You may be eligible for public funding.

When you fill in the Agreement

Please use black ink (the Agreement will be copied). Put the name of one child only. If the father is to have parental responsibility for more than one child, fill in a separate form for each child. **Do not sign the Agreement.**

When you have filled in the Agreement

Take it to a local family proceedings court, or county court, or the Principal Registry of the Family Division (the address is below).

A justice of the Peace, a Justices' Clerk, or a court official who is authorised by the judge to administer oaths, will witness your signature and he or she will sign the certificate of the witness.

To the mother	When you make the declaration you will have to prove that you are the child's mother so take to the court the child's full birth certificate. You will also need evidence of you identity showing a photograph and signature (for example, a photocard, official pass or passport).
To the father	You will need evidence of your identity showing a photograph and signature (for example, a photocard, official pass or passport).

When the certificate has been signed and witnessed

Make 2 copies of the other side of this form. You do not need to copy these notes. Take, or send, this form and the copies to **The Principal Registry of the Family Division, First Avenue House, 42-49 High Holborn, London, WC1V 6NP.**

The Registry will record the Agreement and keep this form. The copies will be stamped and sent back to each parent at the address on the Agreement. The Agreement will not take effect until it has been received and recorded at the Principal Registry of the Family Division.

Ending the Agreement

Once a parental responsibility agreement has been made it can only end

by an order of the court made on the application of any person who has parental responsibility for the child

by an order of the court made on the application of the child with leave of the court

when the child reaches the age of 18.

Date in force
14 October 1991.

Amendment
Substituted by SI 1994/3157, reg 2, Sch.

Form further substituted by SI 2001/2262, reg 2, Schedule. Date in force: 1 September 2001: see SI 2001/2262, reg 1.

Children (Allocation of Proceedings) Order 1991

(SI 1991/1677)

1 Citation, commencement and interpretation

(1) This Order may be cited as the Children (Allocation of Proceedings) Order 1991 and shall come into force on 14th October 1991.

(2) In this Order, unless the context otherwise requires—
'child'—

    (a) means, subject to sub-paragraph (b), a person under the age of 18 with respect to whom proceedings are brought, and

    (b) where the proceedings are under Schedule 1, also includes a person who has reached the age of 18;

'London commission area' has the meaning assigned to it by section 2(1) of the Justices of the Peace Act 1979;

'petty sessions area' has the meaning assigned to it by section 4 of the Justices of the Peace Act 1979; and

'the Act' means the Children Act 1989, and a section, Part or Schedule referred to by number alone means the section, Part or Schedule so numbered in that Act.

Date in force

14 October 1991.

---

2 Classes of county court

For the purposes of this Order there shall be the following classes of county court:

    (a) divorce county courts, being those courts designated for the time being as divorce county courts by an order under section 33 of the Matrimonial and Family Proceedings Act 1984;

    (b) family hearing centres, being those courts set out in Schedule 1 to this Order;

    (c) care centres, being those courts set out in column (ii) of Schedule 2 to this Order.

Commencement of Proceedings

3 Proceedings to be commenced in magistrates' court

(1) Subject to paragraphs (2) and (3) and to article 4, proceedings under any of the following provisions shall be commenced in a magistrates' court:

    (a) section 25 (use of accommodation for restricting liberty);

    (b) section 31 (care and supervision orders);

    (c) section 33(7) (leave to change name of or remove from United Kingdom child in care);

    (d) section 34 (parental contact);

    (e) section 36 (education supervision orders);

    (f) section 43 (child assessment orders);

    (g) section 44 (emergency protection orders);

    (h) section 45 (duration of emergency protection orders etc);

    (i) section 46(7) (application for emergency protection order by police officer);

(j)   section 48 (powers to assist discovery of children etc);

(k)   section 50 (recovery orders);

(l)   section 75 (protection of children in an emergency);

(m)   section 77(6) (appeal against steps taken under section 77(1));

(n)   section 102 (powers of constable to assist etc);

(o)   paragraph 19 of Schedule 2 (approval of arrangements to assist child to live abroad);

(p)   paragraph 23 of Schedule 2 (contribution orders);

(q)   paragraph 8 of Schedule 8 (certain appeals);

(r)   section 21 of the Adoption Act 1976;

[(s)   . ..

(t)   section 20 of the Child Support Act 1991 (appeals) where the proceedings are to be dealt with in accordance with the Child Support Appeals (Jurisdiction of Courts) Order 1993;]

[(u)   section 30 of the Human Fertilisation and Embryology Act 1990 (parental orders in favour of gamete donors).]

(2) Notwithstanding paragraph (1) and subject to paragraph (3), proceedings of a kind set out in sub-paragraph (b), (e), (f), (g), (i) or (j) of paragraph (1), and which arise out of an investigation directed, by the High Court or a county court, under section 37(1), shall be commenced—

(a)   in the court which directs the investigation, where that court is the High Court or a care centre, or

(b)   in such care centre as the court which directs the investigation may order.

(3) Notwithstanding paragraphs (1) and (2), proceedings of a kind set out in sub-paragraph (a) to (k), (n) or (o) of paragraph (1) shall be [commenced in] a court in which are pending other proceedings, in respect of the same child, which are also of a kind set out in those sub-paragraphs.

Date in force

14 October 1991.

Amendment

Para (1): sub-para (s) (omitted) inserted by SI 1993/624, art 3.

Para (1): sub-para (s) revoked by SI 2001/775, arts 3, 4. Date in force: 1 April 2001 (in relation to proceedings beginning after that): see SI 2001/775, arts 1, 2.

Para (1): sub-para (t) inserted by SI 1993/624, art 3.

Para (1): sub-para (u) inserted by SI 1994/2164, art 3.

Para (3): words 'commenced in' in square brackets substituted by SI 1993/624, art 5.

---

4   Application to extend, vary or discharge order

(1) Subject to paragraphs (2) and (3), proceedings under the Act, or under the Adoption Act 1976—

(a)   to extend, vary or discharge an order, or

(b)   the determination of which may have the effect of varying or discharging an order,

shall be [commenced in] the court which made the order.

(2) Notwithstanding paragraph (1), an application for an order under section 8 which would have the effect of varying or discharging an order made, by a county court, in accordance with section 10(1)(b) shall be made to a divorce county court.

(3) Notwithstanding paragraph (1), an application to extend, vary or discharge an order made, by a county court, under section 38, or for an order which would have the effect of extending, varying or discharging such an order, shall be made to a care centre.

(4) A court may transfer proceedings [commenced] in accordance with paragraph (1) to any other court in accordance with the provisions of articles 5 to 13.

***

Date in force
14 October 1991.

Amendment

Paras (1), (4): words in square brackets substituted by SI 1993/624, arts 5, 6.

***

Transfer of Proceedings

5 Disapplication of enactments about transfer

Sections 38 and 39 of the Matrimonial and Family Proceedings Act 1984 shall not apply to proceedings under the Act or under the Adoption Act 1976.

6 Transfer from one magistrates' court to another

[(1)] A magistrates' court (the 'transferring court') shall transfer proceedings [to which this article applies] to another magistrates' court (the 'receiving court') where—

(a) having regard to the principle set out in section 1(2), the transferring court considers that the transfer is in the interests of the child—

   (i) because it is likely significantly to accelerate the determination of the proceedings,
   (ii) because it would be appropriate for those proceedings to be heard together with other family proceedings which are pending in the receiving court, or
   (iii) for some other reason, and

(b) the receiving court, by its justices' clerk (as defined by rule 1(2) of the Family Proceedings Courts (Children Act 1989) Rules 1991), consents to the transfer.

[(2) This article applies to proceedings—

(a) under the Act;
(b) under the Adoption Act 1976;
(c) of the kind mentioned in sub-paragraph [... (t) or (u)] of article 3(1) [and under section 55A of the Family Law Act 1986][;
(d) under section 11 of the Crime and Disorder Act 1998 (child safety orders)].]

***

Date in force
14 October 1991.

Amendment

Para (1): numbered as such, and words in square brackets substituted, by SI 1993/624, art 4(a), (b).

Para (2): inserted by SI 1993/624, art 4(c).

Para (2): in sub-para (c) words in square brackets ending with the words '(t), or (u)' substituted by SI 1994/2164, art 4.

Para (2): in sub-para (c) reference omitted revoked by SI 2001/775, arts 3, 5(a). Date in force: 1 April 2001 (in relation to proceedings beginning after that): see SI 2001/775, arts 1, 2.

Para (2): in sub-para (c) words 'and under section 55A of the Family Law Act 1986' in square brackets inserted by SI 2001/775, arts 3, 5(b). Date in force: 1 April 2001 (in relation to proceedings beginning after that): see SI 2001/775, arts 1, 2.

Para (2): sub-para (d) inserted by SI 1998/2166, art 2. Date in force: 30 September 1998: see SI 1998/2166, art 1.

***

7   Transfer from magistrates' court to county court by magistrates' court

(1) Subject to paragraphs (2), (3) and (4) and to articles 15 to 18, a magistrates' court may, upon application by a party or of its own motion, transfer to a county court proceedings of any of the kinds mentioned in article 3(1) [or proceedings under section 55A of the Family Law Act 1986] where it considers it in the interests of the child to do so having regard, first, to the principle set out in section 1(2) and, secondly, to the following questions:

(a)   whether the proceedings are exceptionally grave, important or complex, in particular—

   (i)   because of complicated or conflicting evidence about the risks involved to the child's physical or moral well-being or about other matters relating to the welfare of the child;

   (ii)   because of the number of parties;

   (iii)   because of a conflict with the law of another jurisdiction;

   (iv)   because of some novel and difficult point of law; or

   (v)   because of some question of general public interest;

(b)   whether it would be appropriate for those proceedings to be heard together with other family proceedings which are pending in another court; and

(c)   whether transfer is likely significantly to accelerate the determination of the proceedings, where—

   (i)   no other method of doing so, including transfer to another magistrates' court, is appropriate, and

   (ii)   delay would seriously prejudice the interests of the child who is the subject of the proceedings.

(2) Notwithstanding paragraph (1), proceedings of the kind mentioned in subparagraph (g) to (j), (l), (m), (p) or (q) of article 3(1) shall not be transferred from a magistrates' court.

(3) Notwithstanding paragraph (1), proceedings of the kind mentioned in subparagraph (a) or (n) of article 3(1) shall only be transferred from a magistrates' court to a county court in order to be heard together with other family proceedings which arise out of the same circumstances as gave rise to the proceedings to be transferred and which are pending in another court.

(4) Notwithstanding paragraphs (1) and (3), proceedings of the kind mentioned in article 3(1)(a) shall not be transferred from a magistrates' court which is not a family proceedings court within the meaning of section 92(1).

Date in force
14 October 1991.

Amendment

Para (1): words 'or proceedings under section 55A of the Family Law Act 1986' in square brackets inserted by SI 2001/775, arts 3, 6. Date in force: 1 April 2001 (in relation to proceedings beginning after that): see SI 2001/775, arts 1, 2.

---

8   Subject to articles 15 to 18, a magistrates' court may transfer to a county court proceedings under the Act or under the Adoption Act 1976, being proceedings to which article 7 does not apply, where, having regard to the principle set out in section 1(2), it considers that in the interests of the child the proceedings can be dealt with more appropriately in that county court.

Date in force
14 October 1991.

Amendment

Para (1): words 'or proceedings under section 55A of the Family Law Act 1986' in square brackets inserted by SI 2001/775, arts 3, 6. Date in force: 1 April 2001 (in relation to proceedings beginning after that): see SI 2001/775, arts 1, 2.

---

9 Transfer from magistrates' court following refusal of magistrates' court to transfer

(1) Where a magistrates' court refuses to transfer proceedings under article 7, a party to those proceedings may apply to the care centre listed in column (ii) of Schedule 2 to this Order against the entry in column (i) for the petty sessions area or London commission area in which the magistrates' court is situated for an order under paragraph (2).

(2) Upon hearing an application under paragraph (1) the court may transfer the proceedings to itself where, having regard to the principle set out in section 1(2) and the questions set out in article 7(1)(a) to (c), it considers it in the interests of the child to do so.

(3) Upon hearing an application under paragraph (1) the court may transfer the proceedings to the High Court where, having regard to the principle set out in section 1(2), it considers—

(a)   that the proceedings are appropriate for determination in the High Court, and
(b)   that such determination would be in the interests of the child.

[(4) This article shall apply (with the necessary modifications) to proceedings brought under Parts I and II as it applies where a magistrates' court refuses to transfer proceedings under article 7.]

Date in force
14 October 1991.

Amendment
Para (4): inserted by SI 1997/1897, art 2. Date in force: 1 October 1997: see SI 1997/1897, art 1.

---

10 Transfer from one county court to another

[(1)] Subject to articles 15 to 17, a county court (the 'transferring court') shall transfer proceedings [to which this article applies] to another county court (the 'receiving court') where—

(a)   the transferring court, having regard to the principle set out in section 1(2), considers the transfer to be in the interests of the child, and
(b)   the receiving court is—

(i)   of the same class or classes, within the meaning of article 2, as the transferring court, or
(ii)   to be presided over by a judge or district judge who is specified by directions under section 9 of the Courts and Legal Services Act 1990 for the same purposes as the judge or district judge presiding over the transferring court.

[(2) This article applies to proceedings—

(a)   under the Act;
(b)   under the Adoption Act 1976;
(c)   of the kind mentioned in sub-paragraph [… (t) or (u)] of article 3(1) [and under section 55A of the Family Law Act 1986].]

Date in force
14 October 1991.

Amendment
Para (1): numbered as such, and words in square brackets substituted, by SI 1993/624, art 4(a), (b).

Para (2): inserted by SI 1993/624, art 4(c).

Para (2): in sub-para (c) words in square brackets ending with the words '(t) or (u)' substituted by SI 1994/2164, art 4.

Para (2): in sub-para (c) reference omitted revoked by SI 2001/775, arts 3, 5(a). Date in force: 1 April 2001 (in relation to proceedings beginning after that): see SI 2001/775, arts 1, 2.

Para (2): in sub-para (c) words 'and under section 55A of the Family Law Act 1986' in square brackets inserted by SI 2001/775, arts 3, 5(b). Date in force: 1 April 2001 (in relation to proceedings beginning after that): see SI 2001/775, arts 1, 2.

---

11 Transfer from county court to magistrates' court by county court

[(1)] A county court may transfer to a magistrates' court before trial proceedings which were transferred under article 7(1) where the county court, having regard to the principle set out in section 1(2) and the interests of the child, considers that the criterion cited by the magistrates' court as the reason for transfer—

(a) in the case of the criterion in article 7(1)(a), does not apply,

(b) in the case of the criterion in article 7(1)(b), no longer applies, because the proceedings with which the transferred proceedings were to be heard have been determined,

(c) in the case of the criterion in article 7(1)(c), no longer applies.

[(2) Paragraph (1) shall apply (with the necessary modifications) to proceedings under Parts I and II brought in, or transferred to, a county court as it applies to proceedings transferred to a county court under article 7(1).]

Date in force
14 October 1991.

Amendment
Para (1): renumbered as such by SI 1997/1897, art 3. Date in force: 1 October 1997: see SI 1997/1897, art 1.

Para (2): inserted by SI 1997/1897, art 3. Date in force: 1 October 1997: see SI 1997/1897, art 1.

---

12 Transfer from county court to High Court by county court

[(1)] A county court may transfer proceedings [to which this article applies] to the High Court where, having regard to the principle set out in section 1(2), it considers—

(a) that the proceedings are appropriate for determination in the High Court, and

(b) that such determination would be in the interests of the child.

[(2) This article applies to proceedings—

(a) under the Act;

(b) under the Adoption Act 1976;

(c) of the kind mentioned in sub-paragraph [. . . (t) or (u)] of article 3(1) [and under section 55A of the Family Law Act 1986].]

Amendment
Para (1): numbered as such, and words in square brackets substituted, by SI 1993/624, art 4(a), (b).

Para (2): inserted by SI 1993/624, art 4(c).

Para (2): in sub-para (c) words in square brackets ending with the words '(t) or (u)' substituted by SI 1994/2164, art 4.

Para (2): in sub-para (c) reference omitted revoked by SI 2001/775, arts 3, 5(a). Date in force: 1 April 2001 (in relation to proceedings beginning after that): see SI 2001/775, arts 1, 2.

Para (2): in sub-para (c) words 'and under section 55A of the Family Law Act 1986' in square brackets inserted by SI 2001/775, arts 3, 5(b). Date in force: 1 April 2001 (in relation to proceedings beginning after that): see SI 2001/775, arts 1, 2.

13   Transfer from High Court to county court

[(1)] Subject to articles 15, 16 and 18, the High Court may transfer to a county court proceedings [to which this article applies] where, having regard to the principle set out in section 1(2), it considers that the proceedings are appropriate for determination in such a court and that such determination would be in the interests of the child.

[(2) This article applies to proceedings—

(a)   under the Act;

(b)   under the Adoption Act 1976;

(c)   of the kind mentioned in sub-paragraph [. . . (t) or (u)] of article 3(1) [and under section 55A of the Family Law Act 1986].]

Date in force
14 October 1991.

Amendment
Para (1): numbered as such, and words in square brackets substituted, by SI 1993/624, art 4(a), (b).

Para (2): inserted by SI 1993/624, art 4(c).

Para (2): in sub-para (c) words in square brackets ending with the words '(t) or (u)' substituted by SI 1994/2164, art 4.

Para (2): in sub-para (c) reference omitted revoked by SI 2001/775, arts 3, 5(a). Date in force: 1 April 2001 (in relation to proceedings beginning after that): see SI 2001/775, arts 1, 2.

Para (2): in sub-para (c) words 'and under section 55A of the Family Law Act 1986' in square brackets inserted by SI 2001/775, arts 3, 5(b). Date in force: 1 April 2001 (in relation to proceedings beginning after that): see SI 2001/775, arts 1, 2.

Allocation of Proceedings to Particular County Courts

14   Commencement

Subject to articles 18, 19 and 20 and to rule 2.40 of the Family Proceedings Rules 1991 (Application under Part I or II of the Children Act 1989 where matrimonial cause is pending), an application under the Act or under the Adoption Act 1976 which is to be [made to] a county court shall be commenced in a divorce county court.

Date in force
14 October 1991.

Amendment
Words in square brackets substituted by SI 1993/624, art 7.

15   Proceedings under Part I or II or Schedule 1

(1) Subject to paragraph (3), where an application under Part I or II or Schedule 1 is to be transferred from a magistrates' court to a county court, it shall be transferred to a divorce county court.

(2) Subject to paragraph (3), where an application under Part I or II or Schedule 1, other than an application for an order under section 8, is to be transferred from the High Court to a county court, it shall be transferred to a divorce county court.

(3) Where an application under Part I or II or Schedule 1, other than an application for an order under section 8, is to be transferred to a county court for the purpose of consolidation with other proceedings, it shall be transferred to the court in which those other proceedings are pending.

Date in force

14 October 1991.

16 Orders under section 8 of the Children Act 1989

(1) An application for an order under section 8 in a divorce county court, which is not also a family hearing centre, shall, if the court is notified that the application will be opposed, be transferred for trial to a family hearing centre.

(2) Subject to paragraph (3), where an application for an order under section 8 is to be transferred from the High Court to a county court it shall be transferred to a family hearing centre.

(3) Where an application for an order under section 8 is to be transferred ...county court for the purpose of consolidation with other proceedings, it may be transferred to the court in which those other proceedings are pending whether or not it is a family hearing centre; but paragraph (1) shall apply to the application following the transfer.

Date in force

14 October 1991.

17 Application for adoption or freeing for adoption

(1) Subject to article 22, proceedings in a divorce county court, which is not also a family hearing centre, under section 12 or 18 of the Adoption Act 1976 shall, if the court is notified that the proceedings will be opposed, be transferred for trial to a family hearing centre.

(2) Where proceedings under the Adoption Act 1976 are to be transferred from a magistrates' court to a county court, they shall be transferred to a divorce county court.

18 Applications under Part III, IV or V

(1) An application under Part III, IV or V, if it is to be [made to] a county court, shall be commenced in a care centre.

(2) An application under Part III, IV or V which is to be transferred from the High Court to a county court shall be transferred to a care centre.

(3) An application under Part III, IV or V which is to be transferred from a magistrates' court to a county court shall be transferred to the care centre listed against the entry in column (i) of Schedule 2 to this Order for the petty sessions area or London commission area in which the relevant magistrates' court is situated.

Date in force

14 October 1991.

Amendment

Para (1): words in square brackets substituted by SI 1993/624, art 7.

19 Principal Registry of the Family Division

The principal registry of the Family Division of the High Court shall be treated, for the purposes of this Order, as if it were a divorce county court, a family hearing centre and a care centre listed against every entry in column (i) of Schedule 2 to this Order (in addition to the entries against which it is actually listed).

Date in force

14 October 1991.

[20]   [Lambeth, Shoreditch and Woolwich County Courts]

Date in force
14 October 1991.

Amendment

Substituted by SI 1997/1897, art 4. Date in force: 1 October 1997: see SI 1997/1897, art 1.

[Notwithstanding articles 14, 16 and 17, an application for an order under section 4 or 8 or under the Adoption Act 1976 may be made to and tried in Lambeth, Shoreditch or Woolwich County Court.]

Date in force
14 October 1991.

Amendment

Substituted by SI 1997/1897, art 4. Date in force: 1 October 1997: see SI 1997/1897, art 1.

Miscellaneous

21   Contravention of provision of this Order

Where proceedings are commenced or transferred in contravention of a provision of this Order, the contravention shall not have the effect of making the proceedings invalid; and no appeal shall lie against the determination of proceedings on the basis of such contravention alone.

Date in force
14 October 1991

22   Transitional provision—proceedings under Adoption Act 1976

Proceedings under the Adoption Act 1976 which are commenced in a county court prior to the coming into force of this Order may, notwithstanding article 17(1), remain in that court for trial.

Date in force
14 October 1991.

SCHEDULE 1
Family Hearing Centres

Article 2

[Not reproduced]

SCHEDULE 2
Care Centres

Article 2

[Not reproduced]

Children (Allocation of Proceedings) (Appeals) Order 1991

(SI 1991/1801)

1 Citation, commencement and interpretation

(1) This Order may be cited as the Children (Allocation of Proceedings) (Appeals) Order 1991 and shall come into force on 14th October 1991.

(2) In this Order—

'district judge' includes an assistant district judge and a deputy district judge; and

'circuit judge' means any person who is capable of sitting as a judge for a county court district and who is allocated to hear appeals permitted by this Order in accordance with directions given under section 9 of the Courts and Legal Services Act 1990.

Date in force

14 October 1991.

2 Appeals

Where a district judge orders the transfer of proceedings to a magistrates' court in accordance with article 11 of the Children (Allocation of Proceedings) Order 1991 an appeal may be made against that decision—

(a) to a judge of the Family Division of the High Court, or

(b) except where the order was made by a district judge or deputy district judge of the principal registry of the Family Division, to a circuit judge.

Date in force

14 October 1991.

Practice Direction – Judicial Continuity [2002] 3 All ER 603, [2002] 2 FCR 667, [2002] 2 FLR 367, FD.

FAMILY DIVISION

Practice – Family Division – Cases proceeding in Royal Courts of Justice – Judicial continuity – Allocated judge – Case management conference – Children Act 1989, Pt IV.

1. This direction applies only to cases proceeding in the Family Division of the High Court at the Royal Courts of Justice in London.

   1.1   In order to achieve as much judicial continuity as possible in the hearing of cases and to avoid delay, the procedure described in this direction will apply as from 9 April 2002.

2. *Applications within Pt IV (care and supervision) of the Children Act 1989*

   2.1   Upon transfer to the High Court (or where applicable, commencement) the case will be allocated to a High Court judge (the allocated judge) and a date fixed for a case management conference. The clerk of the rules will notify the parties of the date for the case management conference and the name of the allocated judge as soon as practicable after receipt of the court file.

   2.2   Within 24 hours of transfer to the High Court (or commencement), the applicant must lodge with the clerk of the rules, a very brief (less than one page) summary of the case. This should be delivered to the office of the clerk of the rules or sent by fax (020 7947 7304).

   2.3   The case management conference and all further hearings (including directions hearings) will be conducted by the allocated judge, unless the case is released to another judge or when it is impracticable for the hearing to be before the allocated judge.

   2.4   As soon as practicable the clerk of the rules will send to the parties a copy of the standard directions (in the form attached to this direction) completed by a judge (usually the allocated judge), notifying the parties of the steps they are required to take in preparation for the case management conference.

   2.5   At the case management conference which is to be attended by all parties, the allocated judge will give directions, managing the case to a final hearing.

   2.6   It is of the essence of this procedure that counsel retained for the final hearing should attend the case management conference and any other directions hearings, except when all the directions have been agreed in advance. Counsel should therefore use their best endeavours to ensure attendance at these hearings. On occasions when one of these hearings coincides with a hearing in another case in which counsel is engaged, counsel should, whenever possible, seek release from the judge before whom they are appearing, so as to enable them to attend the directions hearing. This requirement applies equally to a solicitor who intends to appear as advocate at the final hearing.

   2.7   When a case is transferred to the High Court and an urgent hearing is required prior to the case management conference, the clerk of the rules should be requested to provide an immediate or early hearing date, if possible before the allocated judge. This may be obtained by telephone. Accordingly, other than to appoint a children's guardian (when required), it will not usually be necessary or appropriate for the transferring court to give any directions when transferring the case to the High Court.

   2.8   The final hearing will be before the allocated judge, unless it is impracticable so to arrange.

3. *Urgent Applications Court*

   3.1   Cases which have been allocated to a judge will not be taken by the Urgent Applications Court except to deal with an emergency. When the allocated judge is not in London, it will nevertheless usually be possible to communicate with the judge by telephone or by fax (or e-mail) in order to obtain directions or release of the case. A video conference may sometimes be appropriate.

4. *Applications within Pt II of the 1989 Act*
4.1 These cases (ie private law children cases) when commenced in or transferred to the High Court will not formally come within this direction except that judicial continuity will be observed whenever possible. The aim will be for the same judge to deal with the directions and other interlocutory hearings as well as the final hearing.

5. *Ancillary relief applications within matrimonial causes and applications for financial provision under the 1989 Act*
5.1 These applications when transferred to (or commenced in) the High Court will not formally come within this direction except that judicial continuity will be observed whenever possible, in particular in very complex cases and in cases where there are very substantial assets.
5.2 The above is subject to the requirement in r 2.61E of the Family Proceedings Rules 1991, SI 1991/1247, in relation to the judge before whom any financial dispute resolution (FDR) hearing takes place.
5.3 In cases which are suitable for adjudication in the High Court by a High Court judge and in which it would be appropriate for the first appointment to be listed before a judge, for example because of the likelihood of substantial dispute about the extent of financial disclosure or the desirability of using the first appointment as an FDR, it may be appropriate for the applications for transfer to be made at an early stage of the proceedings, before the date initially given for the first appointment.

6. The standard directions form attached to this direction may be amended from time to time as experience requires.

22 March 2002   DAME ELIZABETH BUTLER-SLOSS
                                                                President

Index

All references are to paragraph number

731